CHAMBERS

W	O	R	D	S

for crosswords and wordgames

CHAMBERS

WORDS

for crosswords and wordgames

Introduced by Frank Muir

ISBN 0 550 19001 5

Set in the Netherlands by Eltrac-Infonet nv Amsterdam
Printed in Great Britain by T & A Constable Ltd Edinburgh

Introduction

There are a few rather odd people like, for example, well, me, who happily read dictionaries as other people read cookery books, or road maps, or long novels about people with names like Giles and Ariadne. We dictionary-fanciers enjoy everything about the definitions; the helpful guide to pronunciation, e.g. '**resound** (re-zownd')'; the delicate humour, e.g. '**middle-aged** — between youth and old age, variously reckoned to suit the reckoner'; the wild poetry of the origins, e.g. '**hang** (O.E. *hangian*, pa.t. *hangode*, pa.p. *hangod* (intrans.) and *hōn,* pa.t. *heng,* pa.p. *hangen* (trans.), and O.N. *hanga* and *hengja;* cf. Du. and Ger. *hangen.*)'

Great stuff!

But there are times when people, even dictionary-fanciers, simply want to know whether a particular word exists, not how to pronounce it, what it means or where it came from. How many times, bent low over the Scrabble ® board or breathing heavily over the clue to 19 Down, have we uttered the despairing cry, 'Is there such a word?'

At last we wordgame players have the right tool to hand. A new kind of dictionary which tells us exactly what we want to know and nothing more.

The entries are culled from the latest edition of *Chambers Twentieth Century Dictionary* and neatly arranged according to the length of the word and its place in the alphabet.

From now on, when the familiar argument arises as to whether there is such a word as 'ogdoad' or 'muu-muu' or 'fragwump' or 'canisterisation', there will no longer be any danger of us becoming overheated and braining a guest with a shovel, or throttling a loved one: we will simply reach for our *Chambers Words* and, in a flash, the truth will be laid before us ('ogdoad' — yes, it is a real word; 'muu-muu' — yes: 'fragwump' — no, there is no such word: 'canisterisation' — unhappily, yes).

My word!

Frank Muir

How to use this book

Nearly 115,000 entries from *Chambers Twentieth Century Dictionary* have been arranged by computer for the benefit of all who play, in fun or in earnest, with words — crossword puzzlers, players of Scrabble ® and Lexicon ®, and wordpuzzle enthusiasts in general.

The words are given in order of length (from 2 to 45 letters), and then alphabetically within each wordlength section, so that all the five-letter words, for example, are found together in alphabetical order. Hyphenated compounds such as **battering-ram** are listed according to the total number of letters.

Included in the book are irregularly formed plurals (*e.g.* **geese, loaves** and .**minima**), such verb forms as **got, wove** and **caught,** and alternative spellings of words such as **fantasy/ phantasy** and **bauxite/beauxite.**

For quick and easy reference, each page is clearly marked with the initial letter and length of the words it contains.

Various devices may be used to extend the already wide scope of the book :

 adding as appropriate '-s', '-ing', '-d', '-ed', or sometimes '-ly' may be all that is needed to produce the right word of the right length ;

 changing such words as **authorise** to **authorize,** or **realisation** to **realization** (a matter of choice anyway) may solve a particular problem ;

 using transatlantic forms such as **esthetic** (aesthetic) and **color** (colour) might sometimes be the answer when all else fails !

Chambers Words is not intended as a replacement for the Dictionary, but its wide vocabulary coverage and clear layout commend it as a shortcut to inspiration.

A	BO	EL	H	K	N	OR	SH	W
	BY	EM				OS	SI	
AB		EN	HA	KA	NA	OU	SO	WA
AD	C	EO	HE	KY	NE	OW		WE
AE	CA	ER	HI		NO	OX	T	WO
AH	CH	ES	HO	L	NU	OY	TA	
AM	CO	EX		LA			TE	X
AN			I	LI	O	P	TI	XI
AR	D	F	ID	LO	OB	PA	TO	
AS	DA	FA	IF		OD	PI		Y
AT	DO	FY	IN	M	OE		U	YE
AX			IO	MA	OF	R	UG	YO
AY	E	G	IS	ME	OH	RA	UN	YU
	EA	GO	IT	MI	OK	RE	UP	
B	EE	GU		MO	ON		UR	Z
BA	EF		J	MU	OO	S	US	ZO
BE	EH		JO	MY	OP	SA	UT	

A	ARK	BIG	CEE	DAM	DUX	ESS	FLY	GET
	ARM	BIN	CHA	DAN	DYE	ETA	FOB	GEY
ABA	ART	BIS	CHE	DAP	DZO	ETH	FOE	GHI
ABB	ARY	BIT	CHI	DAW		EUK	FOG	GIB
ABC	ASH	BIZ	CID	DAY	E	EVE	FOH	GID
ABY	ASK	BOA	CIG	DEB		EWE	FON	GIE
ACE	ASP	BOB	CIT	DEE	EAN	EWK	FOP	GIG
ACT	ASS	BOD	CLY	DEN	EAR	EWT	FOR	GIN
ADD	ATE	BOG	COB	DEW	EAT	EXS	FOU	GIO
ADO	AUF	BOH	COD	DEY	EAU	EYE	FOX	GIP
AFT	AUK	BOK	COG	DIB	EBB		FOY	GIZ
AGA	AVA	BOO	COL	DID	ÉCU	F	FRO	GJU
AGE	AVE	BOP	CON	DIE	EDH		FRY	GNU
AGO	AWE	BOR	COO	DIG	EEL	FAB	FUB	GOA
AHA	AWL	BOT	COP	DIM	EEN	FAD	FUD	GOB
AIA	AWN	BOW	COR	DIN	E'ER	FAG	FUG	GOD
AID	AXE	BOX	COS	DIP	EFT	FAH	FUM	GOE
AIL	AYE	BOY	COT	DIS	EGG	FAN	FUN	GOG
AIM		BRA	COW	DIT	EGO	FAP	FUR	GOO
AIN	B	BUB	COX	DIV	EIK	FAR		GOT
AIR	BAA	BUD	COY	DOD	EKE	FAT	G	GOY
AIT	BAD	BUG	COZ	DOE	E-LA	FAW	GAB	GUE
ALA	BAG	BUM	CRU	DOG	ELD	FAY	GAD	GUM
ALB	BAH	BUN	CRY	DOH	ELF	FED	GAE	GUN
ALE	BAM	BUR	CUB	DOM	ELK	FEE	GAG	GUP
ALL	BAN	BUS	CUD	DON	ELL	FÉE	GAL	GUR
ALP	BAP	BUT	CUE	DOO	ELM	FEN	GAM	GUT
ALT	BAR	BUY	CUM	DOP	ELT	FEU	GAN	GUY
AMP	BAT	BYE	CUP	DOR	EME	FEW	GAP	GYM
ANA	BAY		CUR	DOT	EMU	FEY	GAR	GYP
AND	BED	C	CUT	DOW	END	FEZ	GAS	
ANE	BEE	CAB	CWM	DRY	ENE	FIB	GAT	H
ANN	BEG	CAD		DSO	ENS	FID	GAU	HAD
ANT	BEL	CAM	D	DUB	EON	FIE	GAY	HAE
AN'T	BEN	CAN	DAB	DUD	ERA	FIG	GED	HAG
ANY	BET	CAP	DAD	DUE	ERE	FIN	GEE	HAH
APE	BEY	CAR	DAG	DUG	ERF	FIR	GEL	HAM
APT	BEZ	CAT	DAH	DUN	ERG	FIT	GEM	HAN
ARC	BIB	CAW	DAK	DUO	ERK	FIX	GEN	HAP
ARE	BID	CAY	DAL	DUP	ERR	FIZ	GEO	HAS
					ERS	FLU		

H

HAT HAW HAY HEL HEM HEN HEP HER HET HEW HEX HEY HIC HID HIE HIM HIN HIP HIS HIT HOA HOB HOD HOE HOG HOO HOP HOT HOW HOX HOY HUB HUE HUG HUM HUN HUP HUT HYP

I

ICE ICH ICY IDE IDO ILK ILL IMP IND INK INN ION IOS IOU IRE IRK ISH ISM ITA ITS IVY

J

JAB JAG JAH JAK JAM JAP JAR JAT JAW JAY JEE JET JEW JIB JIG JIZ JOB JOE JOG JOT JOW JOY JUD JUG JUT

K

KAE KAI KAM KAT KAW KAY KEA KEB KED KEF KEG KEN KEP KET KEX KEY KID KIN KIP KIT KOA KOB KON KOP KOS KOW K'RI KRU KYE

L

LAB LAC LAD LAG LAH LAM LAP LAR LAT LAW LAX LAY LEA LED LEE LEG LEI LEM LEN LEO LEP LET LEU LEV LEW LEY LIB LID LIE LIG LIN LIP LIS LOB LO'E LOG LOO LOP LOR LOS LOT LOW LOX LOY LUD LUG LUM LUR LUX LUZ LYE LYM

M

MAB MAC MAD MAE MAG MAK MAN MAP MAR MAS MAT MAW MAX MAY MCK MEN MES MET MEU MEW MHO MID MIL MIM MIR MIS MIX MNA MOA MOB MOD MOE MOG MOL MOO MOP MOR MOT MOU MOW MUD MUG MUM MUN MUX MYA

N

NAB NAE NAG NAM NAP NAS NAY NEB NÉE NEF NEK NEO NEP NET NEW NIB NID NIL NIM NIP NIS NIT NIX NOB NOD NOG NOH NON NOR NOT NOW NOY NUB NUN NUR NUT NYS

O

OAF OAK OAR OAT OBI OCA OCH ODD ODE O'ER OES OFF OFT OHM OHO OIL OKE OLD ONE OOF OOM OON OOP OPE OPT ORB ORC ORD ORE ÖRE ORT OUK OUP OUR OUT OVA OWE OWL OWN OYE

P

PAD PAH PAL PAM PAN PAP PAR PAT PAW PAX PAY PEA PEC PED PEE PEG PEN PEP PER PET PEW PHI PHO PIA PIE PIG PIN PIP PIT PIX PLY POA POD POH POI POM 'PON POP POS POT POW POX POZ PRO PRY PSI PUB PUD PUG PUH PUN PUP PUR PUS PUT PUY PYE PYX

Q

QUA QUO'

R

RAD RAF RAG RAH RAJ RAM RAN RAP RAS RAT RAW RAX RAY RED REE REH REM REP RET REV REX RHO RIA RIB RID RIG RIM RIN RIP RIT RIZ ROB ROC ROD ROE ROK ROM ROT ROW RUB RUC RUD RUE RUG RUM RUN RUT RYE

S

SAB SAC SAD SAE SAG SAI SAL SAM SAN SAP SAR SAT SAW SAX SAY SEA SEC SEE SEG SEL SEN SET SEW SEX SEY SEZ SHE SHY SIB SIC SIN SIP SIR SIS SIT SIX SKI SKY SLY SOB SOC SOD SOG SOH SOL SON SOP SOS SOT SOU SOW SOX SOY SPA SPY SRI STY SUB SUD SUE SUI SUM SUN SUP SYE

T

TAB TAE TAG TAI TAJ TAK TAM TAN TAP TAR TAT TAU T'AV TAW TAX TEA TEC 'TEC TED TEE TEF TEG TEL TEN TEW THE THO THY TIB TIC TID TIE TIG TIL TIN TIP 'TIS TIT TIW TOD TOE TOG TOM TON TOO TOP TOR TOT TOW TOY TRY TUB TUG TUI TUM TUN TUP TUT TWA TWI TWO TYE TYR

U

UDO UDS UGH ULE UPO URE URN USE UVA

V

VAC VAE VAN VAS VAT VAU VEE VET VEX VIA VIE VIM VLY VOE VOL VOR VOW VOX VUG VUM

W

WAD WAE WAG WAN WAP WAR WAS WAT WAW WAX WAY

'WAY	WEY	WOE	WOX	YAK	YES	YIP	**Z**	ZEN
WEB	WHO	WOG	WRY	YAM	YET	YOB		ZHO
WED	WHY	WON	WUD	YAP	YEW	YOD	ZAX	ZIP
WEE	WIG	WOO	WYE	YAW	YEX	YON	ZEA	ZOA
WEM	WIN	WOP		YEA	YGO	YOU	ZED	ZOO
WEN	WIS	WOT	**Y**	YEN	YID	YOW	ZEE	ZUZ
WET	WIT	WOW	YAH	YEP	YIN	YUG	ZEL	

A	AKIN	ARGO	BACH	BEAT	BITT	BORT
	ALAE	ARIA	BACK	BEAU	BIXA	BOSH
ABBA	ALAR	ARID	BADE	BECK	BLAB	BOSK
ABBÉ	ALAS	ARIL	BAEL	BEDE	BLAE	BOS'N
ABED	ALBE	ARMY	BAFF	BEEF	BLAH	BOSS
ABET	ALEE	AROW	BAFT	BEEN	BLAT	BOTH
ABIB	ALFA	ARRY	BAIL	BEER	BLAY	BOTT
ABLE	ALGA	ARSE	BAIT	BEET	BLEB	BOUK
ABLY	ALIT	ARTY	BAKE	BEIN	BLED	BOUN
ABUT	ALLY	ARUM	BALD	BELL	BLEE	BOUT
ABYE	ALMA	ARYL	BALE	BELT	BLET	BOWL
ACER	ALME	ASAR	BALK	BEMA	BLEW	BOWR
ACHE	ALMS	ASCI	BALL	BEND	BLEY	BOYG
ACHY	ALOD	ASHY	BALM	BENE	BLIN	BRAD
ACID	ALOE	ASTI	BALT	BENJ	BLIP	BRAE
ACME	ALOW	ATAP	BALU	BENT	BLOB	BRAG
ACNE	ALSO	ATOC	BANC	BERE	BLOC	BRAN
ACRE	ALTO	ATOK	BAND	BERG	BLOT	BRAT
ACTA	ALUM	ATOM	BANE	BERM	BLOW	BRAW
ADAM	AMAH	ATOP	BANG	BEST	BLUB	BRAY
ADAR	AMBO	AULA	BANK	BETA	BLUE	BRED
ADIT	AMEN	AULD	BANT	BETE	BLUR	BREE
ADRY	AMID	AUNT	BAPU	BETH	BOAR	BREN
ADZE	AMIR	AURA	BARB	BEVY	BOAT	BRER
AEON	AMOK	AUTO	BARD	BHEL	BOCK	BREW
AERY	AMYL	AVAL	BARE	BIAS	BODE	BRIE
AESC	ANAL	AVER	BARK	BICE	BODY	BRIG
AFAR	ANAS	AVES	BARM	BIDE	BOER	BRIM
AFFY	ANCE	AVID	BARN	BIEN	BOGY	BRIO
AFRO	ANEW	AVOW	BASE	BIER	BOIL	BRIT
AGAR	ANIL	AWAY	BASH	BIFF	BOKO	BROD
AGED	ANKH	AWED	BASK	BIGA	BOLD	BROG
AGEE	ANNA	AWNY	BASS	BIGG	BOLE	BROO
AGHA	ANOA	AWRY	BAST	BIKE	BOLL	BROW
AGIN	ANON	AXES	BATE	BILE	BOLT	BRUM
AGIO	ANTA	AXIL	BATH	BILK	BOMA	BRUT
AGOG	ANTE	AXIS	BATS	BILL	BOMB	BUAT
AGON	ANUS	AXLE	BATT	BIND	BOND	BUBO
AGUE	APAY	AXON	BAUD	BINE	BONE	BUCK
AHEM	APEX	AYAH	BAUK	BING	BONY	BUFF
AHOY	APOD	AZYM	BAUR	BINK	BOOB	BUFO
AIN'T	APSE		BAWD	BINT	BOOH	BUHL
AINU	ARAB	**B**	BAWL	BIRD	BOOK	BULB
AIRT	ARAK		BAWN	BIRK	BOOM	BULK
AIRY	ARAR	BAAL	BAWR	BIRL	BOON	BULL
AITU	ARBA	BAAS	BEAD	BIRR	BOOR	BUMF
AJAR	ARCH	BABA	BEAK	BISE	BOOT	BUMP
AJAX	AREA	BABE	BEAM	BISK	BORA	BUNA
AJEE	ARED	BABI	BEAN	BITE	BORE	BUND
AKEE	ARET	BABU	BEAR	BITO	BORN	BUNG
		BABY				

BUNK	CAVE	CLOU	COZE	DARK	DINE	DOZE
BUNT	CAVY	CLOW	COZY	DARN	DING	DOZY
BUOY	CAWK	CLOY	CRAB	DART	DINK	DRAB
BURD	CEAS	CLUB	CRAG	DASH	DINT	DRAG
BURG	CEDE	CLUE	CRAM	DATA	DIRE	DRAM
BURL	CEDI	COAL	CRAN	DATE	DIRK	DRAP
BURN	CEIL	COAT	CRAP	DAUB	DIRL	DRAT
BURP	CELL	COAX	CRAW	DAUD	DIRT	DRAW
BURR	CELT	COCA	CRAX	DAUR	DISC	DRAY
BURS	CENT	COCK	CREE	DAUT	DISH	DREE
BURY	CERE	COCO	CREW	DAVY	DISK	DREW
BUSH	CERT	CODA	CRIB	DAWD	DISS	DREY
BUSK	CESS	CODE	CROP	DAWK	DITA	DRIB
BUSS	CHAD	COED	CROW	DAWN	DITE	DRIP
BUST	CHAI	COFF	CRUD	DAWT	DITT	DROP
BUSY	CHAL	COFT	CRUX	DAZE	DIVA	DROW
BUTT	CHAM	COHO	CUBE	D-DAY	DIVE	DRUB
BUZZ	CHAP	COIF	CUFF	DEAD	DIVI	DRUG
BYKE	CHAR	COIL	CUIF	DEAF	DIXY	DRUM
BYRE	CHAT	COIN	CUIT	DEAL	DOAB	DRUZ
	CHAW	COIR	CULL	DEAN	DOAT	DUAD
C	CHAY	COKE	CULM	DEAR	DOCK	DUAL
CABA	CHEF	COLA	CULT	DEBT	DODO	DUAN
CADE	CHEW	COLD	CUNT	DECK	DOER	DUAR
CADI	CHEZ	COLE	CURB	DEED	DOES	DUCE
CAFÉ	CHIC	COLL	CURD	DEEM	DOFF	DUCK
CAFF	CHID	COLT	CURE	DEEP	DOGE	DUCT
CAGE	CHIK	COMA	CURÉ	DEER	DOGY	DUDE
CAGY	CHIN	COMB	CURL	DEEV	DOIT	DUEL
CAIN	CHIP	COME	CURN	DEFT	DOLE	DUET
CAKE	CHIT	COMP	CURR	DEFY	DOLL	DUFF
CAKY	CHIV	CONE	CURT	DEID	DOLT	DUKE
CALF	CHOP	CONK	CUSH	DEIL	DOME	DULE
CALK	CHOU	CONN	CUSK	DELE	DOMY	DULL
CALL	CHOW	CONY	CUSP	DELF	DOÑA	DULY
CALM	CHUB	COOF	CUSS	DELL	DONE	DUMA
CALP	CHUG	COOK	CUTE	DEME	DON'T	DUMB
CALX	CHUM	COOL	CYAN	DEMO	DOOB	DUMP
CAMA	CHUT	COOM	CYMA	DEMY	DOOK	DUNE
CAME	CIAO	COON	CYME	DENE	DOOL	DUNG
CAMP	CILL	COOP	CYST	DENT	DOOM	DUNK
CANE	CIRE	CO-OP	CYTE	DENY	DOOR	DUNT
CANG	CIRL	COOT	CZAR	DERE	DOPE	DUPE
CANN	CIST	COPE		DERM	DOPY	DURA
CANT	CITE	COPT	**D**	DERN	DORA	DURE
CAN'T	CITS	COPY	DACE	DERV	DORP	DURN
CANY	CITY	CORD	DADA	DESK	DORR	DURO
CAPA	CIVE	CORE	DADO	DEVA	DORT	DUSH
CAPE	CLAD	CORF	DAFF	DEWY	DORY	DUSK
CAPS	CLAG	CORK	DAFT	DHAK	DOSE	DUST
CARD	CLAM	CORM	DAGO	DHAL	DOSS	DUTY
CARE	CLAN	CORN	DAIL	DHOW	DOST	DYAD
CARK	CLAP	COSE	DAIS	DIAL	DOTE	DYED
CARL	CLAT	COSH	DALE	DIAN	DOTH	DYER
CARP	CLAW	COSS	DALI	DICE	DOTY	DYKE
CARR	CLAY	COST	DALT	DICK	DOUC	DYNE
CART	CLEF	COSY	DAME	DICT	DOUP	
CASE	CLEG	COTE	DAMN	DIDO	DOUR	**E**
CASH	CLEM	COTH	DAMP	DIEB	DOUT	EACH
CASK	CLEW	COTT	DANE	DIED	DOVE	EARD
CAST	CLIO	COUP	DANG	DIET	DOWD	EARL
CATE	CLIP	COVE	DANK	DIGS	DOWF	EARN
CAUK	CLOD	COWL	DANT	DIKA	DOWL	EASE
CAUL	CLOG	COWP	DARE	DIKE	DOWN	EAST
CAUM	CLOP	COXA	DARG	DILL	DOWS	EASY
CAUP	CLOT	COXY	DARI	DIME	DOXY	EATH

EBON	EXAM	FÊTE	FONT	GALA	GIRT	GRID
ECHE	EXES	FEUD	FOOD	GALE	GIST	GRIG
ECHO	EXIT	FIAT	FOOL	GALL	GITE	GRIM
ECRU	EXON	FICO	FOOT	GAMB	GIVE	GRIN
EDAM	EYAS	FIEF	FORD	GAME	GIZZ	GRIP
EDDA	EYED	FIFE	FORE	GAMP	GLAD	GRIS
EDDO	EYES	FIGO	FORK	GAMY	GLAM	GRIT
EDDY	EYNE	FIKY	FORM	GANG	GLED	GROG
EDEN	EYOT	FILE	FORT	GANT	GLEE	GROT
EDGE	EYRA	FILL	FOSS	GAOL	GLEG	GROW
EDGY	EYRE	FILM	FOUD	GAPE	GLEN	GRUB
EDIT	EYRY	FIND	FOUL	GAPO	GLEY	GRUE
EERY		FINE	FOUR	GARB	GLIA	GRUM
EGAD	**F**	FINK	FOWL	GARE	GLIB	GUAN
EGAL		FINN	FOXY	GART	GLIM	GUAR
EGER	FACE	FINO	FOZY	GASH	GLIT	GUDE
EGGY	FACT	FIRE	FRAB	GASP	GLOW	GUFF
EGIS	FADE	FIRK	FRAE	GAST	GLUE	GUID
EILD	FADO	FIRM	FRAP	GATE	GLUM	GULA
EINE	FADY	FIRN	FRAU	GAUD	GLUT	GULE
EKKA	FAIK	FISC	FRAY	GAUL	G-MAN	GULF
ÉLAN	FAIL	FISH	FREE	GAUM	GNAR	GULL
ELMY	FAIN	FISK	FRET	GAUN	GNAT	GULP
ELSE	FAIR	FIST	FRIG	GAUP	GNAW	GULY
ELUL	FAIX	FITT	FRIS	GAUR	GOAD	GUMP
EMEU	FAKE	FITZ	FRIT	GAVE	GOAF	GUNK
EMIR	FA-LA	FIVE	FRIZ	GAWD	GOAL	GÜNZ
EMIT	FALL	FIZZ	FROG	GAWK	GOAT	GURL
EMMA	FALX	FLAG	FROM	GAWP	GO-BY	GURU
EMMY	FAME	FLAK	FROW	GAZE	GOBY	GUSH
EMYS	FAND	FLAM	FUCI	GAZY	GOEL	GUST
ENEW	FANE	FLAN	FUCK	GEAL	GOER	GYAL
ENOW	FANG	FLAP	FUEL	GEAN	GOFF	GYBE
ENVY	FANK	FLAT	FUFF	GEAR	GOGO	GYMP
EOAN	FARD	FLAW	FULL	GEAT	GOLD	GYRE
EOKA	FARE	FLAX	FUME	GECK	GOLF	GYTE
EORL	FARL	FLAY	FUMY	GEEZ	GOLP	GYVE
ÉPÉE	FARM	FLEA	FUND	GEIT	GONE	
EPHA	FARO	FLED	FUNG	GELD	GONG	**H**
EPIC	FART	FLEE	FUNK	GELT	GOOD	
EPOS	FASH	FLEG	FURL	GENA	GOOF	HAAF
ERGO	FAST	FLEW	FURR	GENE	GOOK	HAAR
ERIC	FATE	FLEX	FURY	GENS	GOOL	HACK
ERNE	FAUN	FLEY	FUSC	GENT	GOON	HADE
EROS	FAWN	FLIP	FUSE	GERM	GOOP	HADJ
ERSE	FAZE	FLIT	FUSS	GEST	GOOR	HAEM
ERST	FEAL	FLIX	FUST	GEUM	GORE	HAET
ESNE	FEAR	FLOE	FUZE	GHAT	GORM	HAFF
ESPY	FEAT	FLOG	FUZZ	GHEE	GORY	HAFT
ESSE	FECK	FLOP	FYKE	GIBE	GOSH	HAGG
ESTH	FEED	FLOW	FYRD	GIED	GOTH	HA-HA
ETCH	FEEL	FLOX		GIEN	GOUK	HAIK
ETEN	FEER	FLUB	**G**	GIFT	GOUT	HAIL
ETHE	FEES	FLUE		GILA	GOWD	HAIN
ETNA	FEHM	FLUX	GABY	GILD	GOWF	HAIR
ETON	FEIS	FOAL	GADE	GILL	GOWK	HA'IT
ETUI	FELL	FOAM	GADI	GILT	GOWL	HAJJ
EUGE	FELT	FOCI	GAED	GIMP	GOWN	HAKA
EUOI	FEME	FOES	GAEL	GING	GRAB	HAKE
EURO	FEND	FOGY	GAFF	GINK	GRAF	HALE
EVEN	FENT	FÖHN	GAGA	GINN	GRAM	HALF
EVER	FEOD	FOIL	GAGE	GIRD	GRAT	HALL
EVET	FERE	FOIN	GAID	GIRL	GRAY	HALM
EVIL	FERM	FOLD	GAIN	GIRN	GREE	HALO
EVOE	FERN	FOLK	GAIR	GIRO	GREW	HALT
EWER	FESS	FOND	GAIT	GIRR	GREY	HAME
			GAJO			HAND

HANG	HILL	HUNK	JANN	**K**	KIRK	LARD
HANK	HILT	HUNT	JAPE		KIRN	LARE
HARD	HIND	HURL	JARK	KADE	KISS	LARK
HARE	HING	HURT	JARL	KADI	KIST	LASE
HARK	HINT	HUSH	JASP	KAGO	KITE	LASH
HARL	HIPT	HUSK	JASY	KAID	KITH	LASS
HARM	HIRE	HUSO	JATO	KAIF	KIWI	LAST
HARN	HISH	HWYL	JAUP	KAIL	KNAG	LATE
HARO	HISN	HYKE	JAVA	KAIM	KNAP	LATH
HARP	HISS	HYLE	JAZY	KAIN	KNAR	LAUD
HART	HIST	HYMN	JAZZ	KAKA	KNEE	LAVA
HASH	HIVE	HYPE	JEAN	KAKI	KNEW	LAVE
HASK	HIZZ	HYPO	JEEL	KALE	KNIT	LAWK
HASP	HOAR		JEEP	KALI	KNOB	LAWN
HAST	HOAX	**I**	JEER	KAMA	KNOP	LAZE
HATE	HOBO		JEFF	KAME	KNOT	LAZY
HATH	HOCK	IAMB	JEHU	KAMI	KNOW	LEAD
HAUD	HOED	IBEX	JELL	KANA	KNUB	LEAF
HAUL	HOER	IBIS	JENA	KANG	KNUR	LEAK
HAUT	HOIK	ICED	JERK	KANS	KNUT	LEAL
HAVE	HOLD	ICER	JESS	KANT	KOFF	LEAM
HAWK	HOLE	ICON	JEST	KAON	KOHL	LEAN
HAWM	HOLI	IDEA	JESU	KART	KOLA	LEAP
HAZE	HOLM	IDES	JETÉ	KAVA	KOLO	LEAR
HAZY	HOLP	IDLE	JIBE	KAYF	KOND	LEAT
HEAD	HOLS	IDLY	JIFF	KAYO	KONK	LEEK
HEAL	HOLT	IDOL	JILL	KECK	KOOK	LEER
HEAP	HOLY	IDYL	JILT	KEEK	KORA	LEES
HEAR	HOME	IGAD	JIMP	KEEL	KOSS	LEET
HEAT	HOMO	IKON	JINK	KEEN	KOTO	LEFT
HEBE	HOMY	ILEX	JINN	KEEP	KRIS	LEHR
HECH	HONE	ILIA	JINX	KEIR	KROO	LEIR
HECK	HONG	ILKA	JIVE	KELL	KUDU	LEME
HEED	HONK	ILLY	JOBE	KELP	KURD	LEND
HEEL	HOOD	IMAM	JOCK	KELT	KYAT	LENG
HEFT	HOOF	IMPI	JOCO	KEMB	KYLE	LENO
HE-HE	HOOK	INBY	JOEY	KEMP	KYTE	LENS
HEIR	HOOP	INCA	JOHN	KENT		LENT
HELD	HOOT	INCH	JOIN	KEPI	**L**	LERE
HELE	HOPE	INFO	JOKE	KEPT		LESS
HELL	HORN	INIA	JOLE	KERB	LACE	LEST
HELM	HOSE	INKY	JOLL	KERF	LACK	LETT
HELP	HOSS	INLY	JOLT	KERN	LACY	LEVA
HEME	HOST	INRO	JOMO	KETA	LADE	LEVE
HEMP	HOTE	INTO	JOOK	KEYS	LADY	LEVY
HEND	HOUR	IOTA	JOSH	KHAN	LAER	LEWD
HENT	HOUT	IRID	JOSS	KHAT	LAIC	LIAS
HERB	HOVA	IRIS	JOTA	KHOR	LAID	LICE
HERD	HOVE	IRON	JOUK	KHUD	LAIK	LICH
HERE	HOWE	ISIS	JOVE	KIBE	LAIN	LICK
HERL	HOWK	ISLE	JOWL	KICK	LAIR	LIDO
HERM	HOWL	ISMY	JUBA	KIER	LAKE	LIED
HERN	HUCK	I-SPY	JUBE	KILL	LAKH	LIEF
HERO	HUED	ITCH	JUDO	KILN	LAKY	LIEN
HERR	HUER	ITEM	JUDY	KILO	LAMA	LIER
HERS	HUFF	IVY'D	JU-JU	KILP	LAMB	LIEU
HERY	HUGE	IWIS	JUKE	KILT	LAME	LIFE
HESP	HUGY	IYNX	JULY	KINA	LAMÉ	LIFT
HEST	HUIA		JUMP	KIND	LAMP	LIKE
HEWN	HULA	**J**	JUNE	KINE	LANA	LILL
HICK	HULE		JUNK	KING	LAND	LILT
HIDE	HULK	JACK	JUNO	KINK	LANE	LILY
HIED	HULL	JADE	JURY	KINO	LANG	LIMA
HI-FI	HUMA	JAIL	JUST	KIPE	LANK	LIMB
HIGH	HUMP	JAIN	JUTE	KIPP	LANT	LIME
HIKE	HUNG	JAKE	JYNX	KIRI	LANX	LIMN
		JAMB			LAPP	
		JANE				

LIMP	LOWN	MASU	MIRA	MULL	NICE	ODDS
LIMY	LUCE	MATE	MIRE	MUMP	NICK	ODIC
LIND	LUCK	MATÉ	MIRK	MUON	NIDE	ODIN
LINE	LUDO	MATH	MIRV	MURE	NIDI	ODSO
LING	LUES	MATT	MIRY	MURK	NIEF	ODYL
LINK	LUFF	MATY	MISE	MURL	NIFE	OGAM
LINN	LUGE	MAUD	MISS	MUSA	NIFF	OGEE
LINO	LUIT	MAUL	MIST	MUSE	NIGH	OGLE
LINT	LUKE	MAUN	MITE	MUSH	NIKE	OGPU
LION	LULL	MAWK	MITT	MUSK	NILL	OGRE
LIRA	LULU	MAWR	MITY	MUSS	NINE	OILY
LIRE	LUMP	MAYA	MIXT	MUST	NIPA	OINT
LIRK	LUNE	MAZE	MIXY	MUTE	NIRL	OKAY
LISP	LUNG	MAZY	MOAN	MUTT	NISI	OKRA
LIST	LUNT	MEAD	MOAT	MYAL	NIXY	OLEA
LITE	LURE	MEAL	MOCK	MYNA	NOCK	OLEO
LITH	LURK	MEAN	MODE	MYTH	NODE	OLID
LIVE	LUSK	MEAT	MODI		NODI	OLIO
LOAD	LUST	MEDE	MODS	**N**	NOEL	OLLA
LOAF	LUTE	MEED	MOHO		NOES	OLPE
LOAM	LYAM	MEEK	MOHR	NAAM	NOIL	OMBÚ
LOAN	LYME	MEET	MOIL	NABK	NOLL	OMEN
LOBE	LYNX	MEIN	MOIT	NABS	NOME	OMER
LOBI	LYON	MELD	MOKE	NAGA	NONE	OMIT
LOCH	LYRA	MELL	MOLE	NAIA	NON-U	ONCE
LOCK	LYRE	MELT	MOLL	NAÏF	NOOK	ONER
LOCO	LYSE	MEMO	MOLY	NAIK	NOON	ONLY
LODE	LYTE	MEND	MOME	NAIL	NOOP	ONTO
LOFT		MENE	MONA	NAIN	NOPE	ONUS
LOGO	**M**	MENG	MONG	NAIR	NORM	ONYX
LOID		MENT	MONK	NAJA	NORN	OONS
LOIN	MA'AM	MENU	MONO	NALA	NOSE	OONT
LOKI	MACE	MERE	MONY	NAME	NOSH	OOZE
LOLL	MACK	MERI	MOOD	NANA	NOSY	OOZY
LOMA	MADE	MERK	MOOI	NAOS	NOTE	OPAH
LONE	MAGE	MESA	MOOL	NAPE	NOT-I	OPAL
LONG	MAGG	MESE	MOON	NARD	NOTT	OPEN
LOOF	MAGI	MESH	MOOP	NARE	NOUN	OPUS
LOOK	MAGS	MESS	MOOR	NARK	NOUP	ORAL
LOOM	MAID	METE	MOOT	NARY	NOUS	ORBY
LOON	MAIK	MEWL	MOPE	NATO	NOUT	ORCA
LOOP	MAIL	MEWS	MOPY	NAVE	NOVA	ORFE
LOOR	MAIM	MICA	MORA	NAVY	NOWL	ORGY
LOOS	MAIN	MICE	MORN	NAZE	NOWN	ORLE
LOOT	MAKE	MICK	MORO	NAZI	NOWT	ORRA
LOPE	MALE	MICO	MORT	NEAL	NOWY	ORYX
LORD	MALI	MIDI	MOSS	NEAP	NUDE	OTIC
LORE	MALL	MIEN	MOST	NEAR	NULL	OTTO
LORN	MALM	MIFF	MOTE	NEAT	NUMB	OUCH
LORY	MALT	MIKE	MOTH	NECK	NURL	OULK
LOSE	MAMA	MILD	MOUE	NEED	NURR	OUPH
LOSH	MANA	MILE	MOUP	NEEM	NUTS	OURN
LOSS	MANE	MILK	MOVE	NEEP	NYAS	OURS
LOSS	MANX	MILL	MOVY	NE'ER		OUST
LOST	MANY	MILT	MOWA	NEIF	**O**	OUZO
LOTA	MARA	MIME	MOWN	NEON		OVAL
LOTE	MARC	MINA	MOXA	NESH	OAKY	OVEN
LOTH	MARE	MIND	MOYL	NESS	OARY	OVER
LOTO	MARK	MINE	MOZE	NEST	OAST	OVUM
LOUD	MARL	MING	MUCH	NETE	OATH	OWED
LOUN	MARM	MINI	MUCK	NETT	OATS	OWER
LOUP	MARS	MINK	MUFF	NEUK	OBEY	OWLY
LOUR	MART	MINO	MUID	NEUM	OBIA	OWRE
LOUT	MASH	MINT	MUIL	NÉVÉ	OBIT	OXEN
LOVE	MASK	MINX	MUIR	NEWS	OBOE	OXER
LOWE	MASS	MINY	MULE	NEWT	OBOL	OYER
	MAST			NEXT	ODAL	

OYES	PELE	PLIM	PROA	RADE	RENY	RORY
OYEZ	PELF	PLOD	PRO'D	RAFF	REPP	ROSA
P	PELL	PLOP	PROD	RAFT	REPS	ROSE
	PELT	PLOT	PROF	RAGA	REST	ROSÉ
PACA	PEND	PLOY	PROG	RAGE	RETE	ROSY
PACE	PENK	PLUG	PROM	RAGG	RHEA	ROTA
PACK	PENT	PLUM	PROO	RAGI	RHUS	ROTE
PACO	PEON	PLUS	PROP	RAHU	RIAL	ROTL
PACT	PEPO	PNYX	PROW	RAID	RICE	ROUÉ
PAGE	PERI	POCK	PRUH	RAIK	RICH	ROUP
PAID	PERK	POEM	PUCE	RAIL	RICK	ROUT
PAIK	PERM	POET	PUCK	RAIT	RICY	ROUX
PAIL	PERN	POKE	PUER	RAJA	RIDE	ROVE
PAIN	PERT	POKY	PUFF	RAKE	RIEM	ROWT
PAIR	PERU	POLE	PUGH	RAKI	RIFE	RUBE
PAIS	PESO	POLK	PUIR	RÂLE	RIFF	RUBY
PALE	PEST	POLL	PUJA	RAMA	RIFT	RUCK
PALI	PHEW	POLO	PUKE	RAMI	RILE	RUDD
PALL	PHIZ	POLT	PULE	RAMP	RILL	RUDE
PALM	PHOH	POME	PULK	RANA	RIMA	RUED
PALP	PHON	POMP	PULL	RAND	RIME	RUFF
PALY	PHOT	POND	PULP	RANG	RIMY	RUIN
PAND	PHUT	PONE	PULU	RANI	RIND	RUKH
PANE	PICA	PONG	PULY	RANK	RING	RULE
PANG	PICE	PONS	PUMA	RANT	RINK	RULY
PANT	PICK	PONY	PUMP	RAPE	RIOT	RUMP
PAPA	PICT	POOD	PUNA	RAPT	RIPE	RUND
PAPE	PIED	POOF	PUNK	RARE	RIPP	RUNE
PARA	PIER	POOH	PUNT	RASE	RIPT	RUNG
PARÁ	PIET	POOK	PUNY	RASH	RISE	RUNT
PARD	PIKA	POOL	PUPA	RASP	RISK	RUSA
PARE	PIKE	POON	PURE	RATA	RISP	RUSE
PARK	PILA	POOP	PURL	RATE	RISS	RUSÉ
PARR	PILE	POOR	PURR	RATH	RITE	RUSH
PART	PILI	POOT	PUSH	RATS	RITT	RUSK
PASH	PILL	POPE	PUSS	RAUN	RIVA	RUSS
PASS	PIMP	PORE	PUTT	RAVE	RIVE	RUST
PAST	PIÑA	PORK	PYAT	RAWN	RIVO	RUTA
PATE	PINE	PORN	PYET	RAZE	ROAD	RUTH
PATÉ	PING	PORT	PYNE	RAZZ	ROAM	RYAL
PATH	PINK	PORY	PYOT	READ	ROAN	RYFE
PAUA	PINT	POSE	PYRE	REAK	ROAR	RYKE
PAUL	PINY	POSÉ	PYRO	REAL	ROBE	RYND
PAVE	PION	POSH	**Q**	REAM	ROCH	RYOT
PAVO	PIOY	POSS		REAN	ROCK	RYPE
PAWA	PIPE	POST	QUAD	REAP	RODE	RYVE
PAWK	PIPI	POSY	QUAG	REAR	ROED	
PAWL	PIPY	POTE	QUAT	RECK	ROIL	**S**
PAWN	PIRL	POTT	QUAY	REDD	ROIN	
PEAG	PIRN	POUF	QUEP	REDE	ROKE	SABA
PEAK	PISÉ	POUK	QUEY	RE-DO	ROKY	SACK
PEAL	PISH	POUR	QUID	REED	RÔLE	SAFE
PEAN	PISS	POUT	QUIN	REEF	ROLL	SAGA
PEAR	PITA	POWN	QUIP	REEK	ROME	SAGE
PEAT	PITH	POZZ	QUIT	REEL	ROMP	SAGO
PEBA	PITY	PRAD	QUIZ	REEN	RONE	SAIC
PECH	PIUM	PRAM	QUOD	REFT	ROOD	SAID
PECK	PIXY	PRAT	QUOP	REIF	ROOF	SAIL
PEEK	PIZE	PRAU	**R**	REIK	ROOK	SAIM
PEEL	PLAN	PRAY		REIN	ROOM	SAIN
PEEN	PLAP	PREE	RABI	REIS	ROON	SAIR
PEEP	PLAT	PREP	RACA	REKE	ROOP	SAKE
PEER	PLAY	PREX	RACE	RELY	ROOT	SAKI
PEGH	PLEA	PREY	RACH	REND	ROPE	SALE
PEKE	PLEB	PRIG	RACK	RENT	ROPY	SALK
PELA	PLED	PRIM	RACY		RORT	SALP
						SALT

SAME	SETA	SKAT	SNOT	SPUD	SYNE	TEHR
SAMP	SETT	SKAW	SNOW	SPUE	SYPE	TEIL
SAND	SEWN	SKEO	SNUB	SPUN		TELA
SANE	SEXT	SKEP	SNUG	SPUR	T	TELL
SANG	SEXY	SKER	SOAK	STAB		TELT
SANK	SHAD	SKEW	SOAP	STAG	TAAL	TEMS
SANS	SHAG	SKI'D	SOAR	STAP	TABU	TEND
SARD	SHAH	SKID	SOCK	STAR	TACE	TENE
SARI	SHAM	SKIM	SODA	STAY	TACH	TENT
SARK	SHAN	SKIN	SOFA	STEM	TACK	TERM
SASH	SHAW	SKIO	SOFI	STEN	TACT	TERN
SASS	SHAY	SKIP	SOFT	STEP	TAEL	TEST
SATE	SHEA	SKIT	SO-HO	STET	TA'EN	TETE
SATI	SHED	SKRY	SOIL	STEW	TAHA	TEXT
SAUL	SHET	SKUA	SOJA	STEY	TAHR	THAE
SAUT	SHEW	SKUG	SOKE	STIE	TAIL	THAI
SAVE	SHIM	SKYE	SOLA	STIR	TAIT	THAN
SAWN	SHIN	SKYR	SOLD	STOA	TAKE	THAR
SAXE	SHIP	SLAB	SOLE	STOB	TAKY	THAT
SCAB	SHIR	SLAE	SOLI	STOP	TALC	THAW
SCAD	SHIT	SLAG	SOLO	STOT	TALE	THEA
SCAN	SHIV	SLAM	SOMA	STOW	TALK	THEE
SCAR	SHOD	SLAP	SOME	STUB	TALL	THEM
SCAT	SHOE	SLAT	SONE	STUD	TAME	THEN
SCAW	SHOG	SLAV	SONG	STUM	TAMP	THEW
SCOG	SHOO	SLAW	SOOK	STUN	TANA	THEY
SCOT	SHOP	SLAY	SOOM	STYE	TANE	THIG
SCOW	SHOT	SLED	SOON	STYX	TANG	THIN
SCRY	SHOW	SLEE	SOOP	SUCH	TANH	THIR
SCUD	SHRI	SLEW	SOOT	SUCK	TANK	THIS
SCUG	SHUL	SLEY	SOPH	SUDD	TAPA	THON
SCUM	SHUN	SLID	SORA	SUDS	TAPE	THOR
SCUP	SHUT	SLIM	SORB	SUED	TAPU	THOU
SCUR	SIAL	SLIP	SORD	SUET	TARA	THRO
SCUT	SICK	SLIT	SORE	SUFI	TARE	THUD
SCYE	SIDA	SLOB	SORI	SUIT	TARN	THUG
SEAL	SIDE	SLOE	SORN	SULK	TARO	THUS
SEAM	SIEN	SLOG	SORT	SUMO	TART	TICE
SEAN	SIFT	SLOP	SO-SO	SUMP	TASH	TICK
SEAR	SIGH	SLOT	SOSS	SUNG	TASK	TIDE
SEAT	SIGN	SLOW	SOUK	SUNK	TASS	TIDY
SECT	SIKA	SLUB	SOUL	SUNN	TATA	TIED
SEED	SIKE	SLUE	SOUM	SURA	TATE	TIER
SEEK	SIKH	SLUG	SOUP	SURD	TATH	TIFF
SEEL	SILD	SLUM	SOUR	SURE	TATT	TIFT
SEEM	SILE	SLUR	SOUS	SURF	TATU	TIGE
SEEP	SILK	SLUT	SOWF	SWAB	TAUT	TIKA
SEER	SILL	SMEE	SOWL	SWAD	TAWS	TIKE
SEGO	SILO	SMEW	SOWM	SWAG	TAWT	TIKI
SEIL	SILT	SMIR	SOWN	SWAM	TAXA	TILE
SELD	SIMA	SMIT	SOWP	SWAN	TAXI	TILL
SELF	SIMP	SMOG	SOYA	SWAP	T-BAR	TILT
SELL	SINE	SMUG	SPAE	SWAT	TEAD	TIME
SEME	SING	SMUR	SPAN	SWAY	TEAK	TIND
SEMI	SINH	SMUT	SPAR	SWEE	TEAL	TINE
SEND	SINK	SNAB	SPAT	SWIG	TEAM	TING
SENT	SIPE	SNAG	SPAY	SWIM	TEAN	TINK
SEPS	SIRE	SNAP	SPEC	SWIZ	TEAR	TINT
SEPT	SIRI	SNAR	SPED	SWOB	TEAT	TINY
SERB	SISS	SNED	SPET	SWOP	TEDY	TIPT
SERE	SIST	SNIB	SPEW	SWOT	TEED	TIRE
SERF	SITE	SNIG	SPIN	SWUM	TEEL	TIRL
SERK	SITH	SNIP	SPIT	SYBO	TEEM	TIRO
SERR	SIUM	SNOB	SPIV	SYCE	TEEN	TIRR
SESE	SIVA	SNOD	SPOT	SYKE	TEER	TITE
SESS	SIZE	SNOG	SPRY	SYND	TEFF	TITI
					TEGG	

TOAD	TROW	UPAS	VIED	WASH	WILY	YAWL
TO-BE	TROY	UPBY	VIEW	WASP	WIND	YAWN
TOBY	TRUE	UPGO	VILD	WAST	WINE	YAWS
TOCO	TRUG	UPON	VILE	WATE	WING	YAWY
TO-DO	TSAR	UPSY	VILL	WATS	WINK	YBET
TODY	TSHI	URAL	VINA	WATT	WINO	YEAD
TOED	TUAN	URAO	VINE	WAUL	WINY	YEAH
TOFF	TUBA	URDÉ	VINT	WAUR	WIPE	YEAN
TOFT	TUBE	URDU	VINY	WAVE	WIRE	YEAR
TOGA	TUCK	URDY	VIOL	WAVY	WIRY	YEDE
TOHO	TUFA	UREA	VIRL	WAWE	WISE	YEED
TOIL	TUFF	URGE	VISA	WAWL	WISH	YEGG
TOKO	TUFT	URIC	VISÉ	WAXY	WISP	YELD
TOLA	TULE	URIM	VISE	WEAK	WIST	YELK
TOLD	TUMP	URSA	VITA	WEAL	WITE	YELL
TOLE	TUNA	URUS	VITE	WEAN	WITH	YELP
TOLL	TUND	URVA	VIVA	WEAR	WIVE	YELT
TOLT	TUNE	USED	VIVE	WEED	WOAD	YERD
TOLU	TUNY	USER	VIVO	WEEK	WOLD	YERK
TOMB	TUPI	UTAS	VIZY	WEEL	WOLF	YESK
TOME	TURD	UTIS	VLEI	WEEM	WOMB	YEST
TONE	TURF	UVEA	VOAR	WEEN	WONT	YETI
TONG	TURK		VOID	WEEP	WON'T	YETT
TONY	TURM	V	VOLA	WEET	WOOD	YEUK
TOOK	TURN	VADE	VOLE	WEFT	WOOF	YEVE
TOOL	TUSH	VAGI	VOLT	WEID	WOOL	YGOE
TOOM	TUSK	VAIL	VOTE	WEIL	WOOT	YILL
TOON	TUTS	VAIN	VRIL	WEIR	WORD	YIRD
TOOT	TUTU	VAIR	VULN	WEKA	WORE	YIRK
TOPE	TUZZ	VALE		WELD	WORK	YITE
TOPI	TWAE	VALI	W	WELK	WORM	YLEM
TORC	TWAL	VAMP	WAAC	WELL	WORN	YLKE
TORE	TWAS	VANE	WAAF	WELT	WORT	YODE
TORI	TWAT	VANG	WADD	WEMB	WOST	YOGA
TORN	TWAY	VANT	WADE	WEND	WOTS	YOGH
TORR	TWEE	VARA	WADI	WENT	WOVE	YOGI
TORT	TWIG	VARE	WADY	WEPT	WOWF	YO-HO
TORY	TWIN	VARY	WAFD	WERE	WRAP	YOKE
TOSE	TWIT	VASA	WAFF	WERT	WREN	YOLK
TOSH	TYKE	VASE	WAFT	WEST	WRIT	YOND
TOSS	TYMP	VAST	WAGE	WHAP	WULL	YONI
TOST	TYND	V-DAY	WAIF	WHAT	WURM	YONT
TOTE	TYNE	VEAL	WAIL	WHEN	WYND	YOOP
TOUK	TYPE	VEDA	WAIN	WHET	WYTE	YORE
TOUR	TYPO	VEER	WAIT	WHEW		YORK
TOUT	TYRE	VEGA	WAKE	WHEY	X	YOUK
TOWN	TZAR	VEHM	WALD	WHID	XEMA	YOUR
TOWT		VEIL	WALE	WHIG	XOSA	YOWE
TOWY	U	VEIN	WALI	WHIM	X-RAY	YOWL
TOZE	UDAL	VELA	WALK	WHIN	XYST	YO-YO
TRAD	UGLI	VELD	WALL	WHIP		YUAN
TRAM	UGLY	VELL	WALY	WHIR	Y	YUCA
TRAP	ULEX	VENA	WAME	WHIT	YACK	YUCK
TRAY	ULNA	VEND	WAND	WHIZ	YAFF	YUFT
TREE	UMBO	VENT	WANE	WHOA	YALD	YUGA
TREK	UMPH	VERA	WANG	WHOM	YAMA	YUKE
TRET	UNAU	VERB	WANT	WHOP	YANG	YUKY
TREY	UNBE	VERS	WARD	WHOW	YANK	YULE
TRIG	UNCE	VERT	WARE	WICK	YAPP	YUNX
TRIM	UNCI	VERY	WARK	WIDE	YARD	YURT
TRIN	UNCO	VEST	WARM	WIEL	YARE	YWIS
TRIO	UNDÉ	VETO	WARN	WIFE	YARN	
TRIP	UNDO	VIAL	WARP	WILD	YARR	Z
TROD	UNIO	VIBE	WART	WILE	YATE	ZACK
TRON	UNIT	VICE	WARY	WILL	YAUD	ZANY
TROT	UNTO	VIDE	WASE	WILT	YAUP	ZARF

ZATI	ZEIN	ZETA	ZINC	ZOEA	ZOOM	ZUPA
'ZBUD	ZEND	ZEUS	ZION	ZOIC	ZOON	ZURF
ZEAL	ZERO	ZILA	ZOBO	ZONA	ZULU	ZYME
ZEBU	ZEST	ZIMB	ZOBU	ZONE	ZUÑI	

A	ACUTE	AGING	ALINE	AMMON	APAYD	ARISH
	ADAGE	AGIST	ALIVE	AMNIA	APEAK	ARLES
ABACA	ADAPT	AGLEE	ALKYD	AMONG	APEEK	ARMED
ABACI	ADAYS	AGLET	ALKYL	AMORT	APERT	ARMET
ABACK	ADDAX	AGLEY	ALLAH	AMOUR	APERY	ARMIL
ABAFT	ADDER	AGLOW	ALLAY	AMOVE	APHID	ARNUT
ABASE	ADDIO	AGOGE	ALL-BE	AMPEX	APHIS	AROAD
ABASH	ADDLE	AGONE	ALLEY	AMPLE	APIAN	AROBA
ABASK	ADD-TO	AGONY	ALLIS	AMPLY	APISH	AROID
ABATE	ADEEM	AGOOD	ALLOD	AMPUL	APISM	AROMA
ABAYA	ADENI	AGORA	ALLOT	AMUCK	APODE	AROSE
ABBEY	ADEPT	AGREE	ALLOW	AMUSE	APOOP	ARRAH-
ABBOT	ADIEU	AGRIN	ALLOY	ANANA	APORT	ARRAS
ABCEE	ADIOS	AGUED	ALL-TO	ANCON	APPAL	ARRAY
ABEAM	AD-LIB	AGUTI	ALL-UP	ANEAR	APPAY	ARRÊT
ABEAR	AD-MAN	AHEAD	ALLYL	ANELE	APPLE	ARRIS
ABELE	ADMIT	AHEAP	ALMAH	ANEND	APPLY	ARROW
ABHOR	ADMIX	AHIGH	ALMEH	ANENT	APPRO	ARSES
ABIDE	ADOBE	AHIND	ALMUG	ANGEL	APPUI	ARSIS
ABIES	ADOPT	AHINT	ALOED	ANGER	APPUY	ARSON
ABLET	ADORE	AHOLD	ALOFT	ANGLE	APRIL	ARTEL
ABLOW	ADORN	AHULL	ALOHA	ANGRY	APRON	ARVAL
ABODE	ADOWN	AIDED	ALONE	ANGST	APSIS	ARYAN
A'BODY	ADULT	AIDER	ALONG	ANIGH	APSOS	ASCUS
ABOIL	ADUNC	AIERY	ALOOF	ANILE	APTLY	ASDIC
ABOMB	ADUST	AIRER	ALOUD	ANIMA	ARABA	ASHEN
ABORD	ADYTA	AISLE	ALPHA	ANIMÉ	ARABY	ASHET
ABORT	AEGIS	AITCH	ALTAR	ANIME	ARBOR	ASIAN
ABOUT	AERIE	AJWAN	ALTER	ANION	ARCUS	ASIDE
ABOVE	AESIR	AKENE	ALTOS	ANISE	ARDEA	ASKER
ABRIM	AFALD	ALACK	ALULA	ANKER	ARDEB	ASKEW
ABRIN	AFFIX	ALAND	ALURE	ANKLE	ARD-RI	ASPEN
ABRUS	AFIRE	ALANG	ALWAY	ANKUS	AREAD	ASPER
ABSEY	AFOOT	ALARM	AMAIN	ANNAL	AREAL	ASPIC
ABSIT	AFORE	ALARY	AMASS	ANNAT	ARECA	ASSAI
ABUNA	AFOUL	ALATE	AMATE	ANNEX	AREDD	ASSAY
ABUNE	AFRIC	ALBAN	AMAZE	ANNOY	AREDE	ASSES
ABUSE	AFRIT	ALBEE	AMBAN	ANNUL	AREFY	ASSET
ABUZZ	AFTER	ALBUM	AMBER	ANODE	ARENA	ASSOT
ABYSM	AGAIN	ALDER	AMBIT	ANOMY	ARÊTE	ASTER
ABYSS	AGAMA	ALEFT	AMBLE	ANONA	ARETT	ASTIR
ACARI	AGAMI	ALEPH	AMBOS	ANTAE	ARGAN	ASWAY
ACCOY	AGAPE	ALERT	AMBRY	ANTAR	ARGIL	ASWIM
ACERB	AGATE	ALGAE	AMEER	ANTIC	ARGOL	ATAXY
ACINI	AGAVE	ALGID	AMEND	ANTRE	ARGON	ATILT
ACKEE	AGAZE	ALGIN	AMENE	ANURA	ARGOT	ATIMY
ACOCK	AGENT	ALGOL	AMENT	ANVIL	ARGUE	ATLAS
ACOLD	AGGER	ALGUM	AMICE	ANZAC	ARGUS	ATMAN
ACORN	AGGRI	ALIAS	AMIDE	ANZUS	ARIAN	ATOKE
ACRED	AGGRO	ALIBI	AMINE	AORTA	ARIEL	ATOLL
ACRID	AGGRY	ALIEN	AMISS	APACE	ARIES	ATOMY
ACTON	AGILA	ALIGN	AMITY	APAID	ARIOT	ATONE
ACTOR	AGILE	ALIKE	AMMAN	APART	ARISE	ATONY

ATRIA	**B**	BATTA	BESOM	BLIMP	BORER	BREVE
ATRIP		BATTS	BESOT	BLIMY	BORIC	BRIAR
ATTAP	BABEE	BATTY	BETEL	BLIND	BORNE	BRIBE
ATTAR	BABEL	BAULK	BETID	BLINK	BORNÉ	BRICK
ATTIC	BABOO	BAVIN	BÉTON	BLISS	BORON	BRIDE
AUDIT	BABUL	BAWDY	BETTY	BLITE	BOSCH	BRIEF
AUGER	BACCA	BAYLE	BEVEL	BLITZ	BOSKY	BRIER
AUGHT	BACCO	BAYOU	BEVER	BLOAT	BOSOM	BRILL
AUGUR	BACCY	BAZAR	BEVUE	BLOCK	BOSON	BRINE
AULIC	BACON	BEACH	BEWET	BLOKE	BOSSY	BRING
AUMIL	BADDY	BEADY	BEWIG	BLOND	BOSUN	BRINK
AUNTY	BADGE	BE-ALL	BEZEL	BLOOD	BOTCH	BRINY
AURAE	BADLY	BEAMY	BHANG	BLOOM	BOTHY	BRISK
AURAL	BAFFY	BEANO	BIBBY	BLORE	BOUGH	BRIZE
AURAS	BAGEL	BEARD	BIBLE	BLOWN	BOULE	BROAD
AURIC	BAGGY	BEAST	BIDDY	BLOWY	BOULT	BROCH
AUXIN	BAHAI	BEAUT	BIDED	BLUDE	BOUND	BROCK
AVAIL	BAHA'I	BEAUX	BIDET	BLUEY	BOURD	BROGH
AVALE	BA'ING	BEBOP	BIELD	BLUFF	BOURG	BROIL
AVAST	BAIRN	BEDAD	BIFID	BLUID	BOURN	BROKE
AVENA	BAIZE	BEDEL	BIGAE	BLUNK	BOUSE	BRONX
AVENS	BAJAN	BEDEW	BIGHA	BLUNT	BOUSY	BROOD
AVERT	BAJRA	BEDIM	BIGHT	BLURB	BOWAT	BROOK
AVIAN	BAJRI	BEDYE	BIGOT	BLURT	BOWED	BROOL
AVINE	BAKED	BEECH	BIJOU	BLUSH	BOWEL	BROOM
AVISE	BAKEN	BEEFS	BILBO	BOARD	BOWER	BROSE
AVISO	BAKER	BEEFY	BILGE	BOART	BOWET	BROTH
AVIZE	BALAS	BEERY	BILGY	BOAST	BOWIE	BROWN
AVOID	BALER	BEFIT	BILLY	BOBAC	BOWNE	BRUIN
AVYZE	BALKY	BEFOG	BINGE	BOBAK	BOWSE	BRUIT
AWAIT	BALLY	BEGAD	BINGO	BOBBY	BOXEN	BRÛLÉ
AWAKE	BALMY	BEGAN	BIOTA	BOCHE	BOXER	BRUME
AWARD	BALOO	BEGAR	BIPED	BODGE	BOYAR	BRUNT
AWARE	BALSA	BEGAT	BIPOD	BODHI	BOYAU	BRUSH
AWARN	BANAL	BEGEM	BIRCH	BODLE	BRACE	BRUTE
AWASH	BANAT	BEGET	BIRLE	BOGEY	BRACH	BUAZE
AWAVE	BANCO	BEGIN	BIRSE	BOGGY	BRACK	BUBBY
AWAYS	BANDH	BEGOT	BIRSY	BOGIE	BRACT	BUCHU
A-WEEK	BANDY	BEGUM	BIRTH	BOGLE	BRAID	BUCKO
AWEEL	BANJO	BEGUN	BISON	BOGUS	BRAIL	BUCKU
AWETO	BANNS	BEIGE	BITCH	BOHEA	BRAIN	BUDDY
AWFUL	BANTU	BEING	BITER	BOLAS	BRAKE	BUDGE
A-WING	BARBE	BEKAH	BITTY	BOLUS	BRAKY	BUFFA
AWMRY	BARDY	BELAY	BIVVY	BOMBE	BRAME	BUFFE
AWNED	BARGE	BELCH	BLACK	BONCE	BRAND	BUFFI
AWNER	BARIC	BELEE	BLADE	BONED	BRANK	BUFFO
AWOKE	BARKY	BELGA	BLAIN	BONER	BRASH	BUGGY
AWORK	BARMY	BELIE	BLAME	BONGO	BRASS	BUGLE
AXIAL	BARON	BELLE	BLAND	BONNE	BRAST	BUILD
AXILE	BARYE	BELLY	BLANK	BONNY	BRAVA	BUILT
AXIOM	BASAL	BELOW	BLARE	BONUS	BRAVE	BUIST
AXOID	BASAN	BEMAD	BLASÉ	BONZE	BRAVI	BULGE
AYELP	BASED	BEMUD	BLASH	BOOBY	BRAVO	BULGY
AYONT	BASES	BENCH	BLAST	BOODY	BRAWL	BULKY
AYRIE	BASIC	BENDY	BLATE	BOOKY	BRAWN	BULLA
AZOIC	BASIL	BENET	BLAUD	BOONG	BRAWS	BULLY
AZOTE	BASIN	BENTY	BLAZE	BOOSE	BRAXY	BULSE
AZOTH	BASIS	BEPAT	BLEAK	BOOST	BRAZE	BUMBO
AZTEC	BASSE	BERAY	BLEAR	BOOTH	BREAD	BUMPH
AZURE	BASSO	BERET	BLEAT	BOOTS	BREAK	BUMPY
AZURN	BASTE	BERRY	BLEED	BOOTY	BREAM	BUNCH
AZURY	BASTO	BERTH	BLEEP	BOOZE	BREED	BUNCO
AZYGY	BATCH	BERYL	BLEND	'BOOZY	BREEM	BUNIA
AZYME	BATHE	BESEE	BLENT	BORAX	BREER	BUNKO
	BATIK	BESET	BLESS	BOREE	BREME	BUNNY
	BATON	BESIT	BLEST	BOREL	BRENT	BUNTY

BUNYA	CAMAS	CHACO	CHOIR	CLINE	COMPO	CRAIG
BURAN	CAMEL	CHAFE	CHOKE	CLING	COMPT	CRAKE
BURGH	CAMEO	CHAFF	CHOKY	CLINK	COMUS	CRAME
BURIN	CAMIS	CHAFT	CHOLI	CLIPE	CONCH	CRAMP
BURKA	CAMUS	CHAIN	CHORD	CLIPT	CONEY	CRANE
BURKE	CANAL	CHAIR	CHORE	CLOAK	CONGA	CRANK
BURLY	CANDY	CHALK	CHOSE	CLOAM	CONGÉ	CRAPE
BURNT	CANEH	CHAMP	CHOUT	CLOCK	CONGO	CRAPS
BURRO	CANIS	CHANK	CHOUX	CLOFF	CONIA	CRAPY
BURRY	CANNA	CHANT	CHUBB	CLONE	CONIC	CRARE
BURSA	CANNY	CHAOS	CHUCK	CLOOP	CONKY	CRASH
BURSE	CANOE	CHAPE	CHUFA	CLOOT	CONTÉ	CRASS
BURSH	CAÑON	CHAPS	CHUFF	CLOSE	CONTO	CRATE
BURST	CANON	CHARA	CHUMP	CLOTE	COOED	CRAVE
BUSBY	CANST	CHARD	CHUNK	CLOTH	COOEE	CRAWL
BUSES	CANTO	CHARE	CHURL	CLOUD	COOEY	CRAZE
BUSHY	CANTY	CHARK	CHURN	CLOUR	COOKY	CRAZY
BUSSU	CAPER	CHARM	CHURR	CLOUT	COOLY	CREAK
BUTCH	CAPLE	CHARR	CHUTE	CLOVE	COOMB	CREAM
BUTEA	CAPON	CHART	CHYLE	CLOWN	COOMY	CREDO
BUTTE	CAPOT	CHARY	CHYME	CLUBS	CO-OPT	CREED
BUTTY	CAPUL	CHASE	CIBOL	CLUCK	COPAL	CREEK
BUTYL	CAPUT	CHASM	CIDER	CLUMP	COPER	CREEL
BUXOM	CARAT	CHAVE	CIGAR	CLUNG	COPRA	CREEP
BUYER	CARET	CHAYA	CIMAR	CLUNK	COPSE	CREME
BUZZY	CAREX	CHEAP	CIMEX	CLYPE	COPSY	CRENA
BWANA	CARGO	CHEAT	CINCH	CNIDA	CORAL	CRÊPE
BWAZI	CARIB	CHECK	CIPPI	COACH	CORED	CREPT
BY-END	CARNY	CHEEK	CIRCA	COACT	CORER	CRESS
BYLAW	CAROB	CHEEP	CIRCS	COALY	CORGI	CREST
BYWAY	CAROL	CHEER	CIRRI	COAPT	CORKY	CREWE
C	CAROM	CHEKA	CISCO	COARB	CORNO	CRICK
	CARRY	CHELA	CISSY	COAST	CORNU	CRIED
CABAL	CARSE	CHERT	CITAL	COATI	CORNY	CRIER
CABAS	CARTA	CHESS	CIVET	COBBY	CORPS	CRIES
CABBY	CARTE	CHEST	CIVIC	COBIA	CORSE	CRIME
CABER	CARVE	CHEVY	CIVIL	COBLE	CORSO	CRIMP
CABIN	CARVY	CHIAN	CIVVY	COBOL	COSEC	CRINE
CABLE	CASCO	CHIAO	CLACK	COBRA	COSTA	CRISP
CABOB	CASTE	CHICA	CLAES	COCCI	COTTA	CRITH
CABOC	CATCH	CHICH	CLAIM	COCCO	COUCH	CROAK
CABRE	CATER	CHICK	CLAMP	COCKY	COUDÉ	CROCK
CACAO	CATES	CHIDE	CLANG	COCOA	COUGH	CROFT
CACHE	CATTY	CHIEF	CLANK	CODEX	COULD	CROMB
CACTI	CAULD	CHIEL	CLARE	CODON	COUNT	CROME
CADDY	CAULK	CHILD	CLARY	COGIE	COUPÉ	CRONE
CADET	CAUSE	CHILE	CLASH	COGUE	COUPE	CRONK
CADGE	CAVEL	CHILI	CLASP	COHOE	COURB	CRONY
CADGY	CAVIE	CHILL	CLASS	COHOG	COURT	CROOK
CADRE	CAVIL	CHIMB	CLAUT	COIGN	COUTH	CROON
CAECA	CAXON	CHIME	CLAVE	COKES	COVED	CRORE
CAESE	CEASE	CHINA	CLEAN	COLEY	COVEN	CROSS
CAGED	CEBUS	CHINE	CLEAR	COLIC	COVER	CROST
CAGEY	CEDAR	CHINK	CLEAT	COLIN	COVET	CROUP
CAGOT	CEDIS	CHINO	CLECK	COLLY	COVEY	CROUT
CAIRD	CELLA	CHIPS	CLEEK	COLON	COVIN	CROWD
CAIRN	CELLO	CHIRK	CLEEP	COLZA	COWAN	CROWN
CALID	CENSE	CHIRL	CLEFT	COMAL	COWED	CROZE
CALIF	CENTO	CHIRM	CLEPE	COMBE	COWER	CRUCK
CALIX	CEORL	CHIRP	CLERK	COMBO	COWRY	CRUDE
CALLA	CERES	CHIRR	CLEVE	COMBY	COXAL	CRUDY
CALMY	CERGE	CHIRT	CLICK	COMER	COYLY	CRUEL
CALPA	CERIA	CHIVE	CLIFF	COMET	COYPU	CRUET
CALVE	CESSE	CHIVY	CLIFT	COMFY	COZEN	CRUMB
CALYX	CETYL	CHOCK	CLIMB	COMIC	CRACK	CRUMP
CAMAN	CHACK	CHODE	CLIME	COMMA	CRAFT	CRUOR

CRUSE	DAGGA	DEMON	DOCHT	DOZER	DUNCH	ELATE
CRUSH	DAGON	DEMOS	DODDY	DRACO	DUNGY	ELBOW
CRUST	DAILY	DEMUR	DODGE	DRAFF	DUNNY	ELCHI
CRUSY	DAIRY	DENEB	DODGY	DRAFT	DUNSH	ELDER
CRUVE	DAISY	DENIM	DODOS	DRAIL	DUOMO	ELDIN
CRWTH	DAKER	DENSE	DOEST	DRAIN	DUPER	ELECT
CRYPT	DALAI	DEPOT	DOETH	DRAKE	DUPLE	ELEGY
CTENE	DALLE	DEPTH	DOGGO	DRAMA	DUPLY	ELEMI
CUBAN	DALLY	DERAY	DOGGY	DRANK	DUPPY	ELFIN
CUBBY	DAMAN	DERBY	DOGIE	DRANT	DUROY	ELIAD
CUBEB	DAMAR	DERMA	DOGMA	DRAPE	DURRA	ELIAN
CUBIC	DAMPY	DETER	DOILT	DRAWL	DURST	ELIDE
CUBIT	DANCE	DEUCE	DOILY	DRAWN	DURUM	ÉLITE
CUDDY	DANDY	DEVEL	DOING	DREAD	DUSKY	ELMEN
CUFFO	DARED	DEVIL	DOLCE	DREAM	DUSTY	ELOGE
CUFIC	DARES	DEWAN	DOLIA	DREAR	DUTCH	ELOGY
CUISH	DARGA	DHOBI	DOLLY	DREGS	DUVET	ELOIN
CULCH	DARIC	DHOLE	DOMAL	DRESS	DWALE	ELOPE
CULET	DARKY	DHOTI	DOMED	DREST	DWALM	ELOPS
CULEX	DARZI	DIACT	DONAH	DRIED	DWARF	ELSIN
CULLY	DATAL	DIANA	DONAT	DRIER	DWAUM	ELUDE
CUMIN	DATER	DIARY	DONEE	DRIFT	DWELL	ELUTE
CUPEL	DATUM	DICER	DONET	DRILL	DWELT	ELVAN
CUPID	DAUBY	DICEY	DONGA	DRILY	DWINE	ELVER
CUPPA	DAULT	DICHT	DONNA	DRINK	DYING	ELVES
CURAT	DAUNT	DICKY	DONOR	DRIVE		EMBAR
CURCH	DAVIS	DICTA	DONUT	DROIL	**E**	EMBAY
CURDY	DAVIT	DIDST	DOOMS	DROIT		EMBED
CURER	DAZED	DIGHT	DOORN	DRÔLE	EAGER	EMBER
CURIA	DEALT	DIGIT	DOPER	DROLL	EAGLE	EMBOG
CURIE	DEARN	DIKER	DOPEY	DROME	EAGRE	EMBOW
CURIO	DEARY	DILDO	DORAD	DRONE	EARED	EMBOX
CURLY	DEATH	DILLI	DORAS	DRONY	EARLY	EMBUS
CURNY	DEAVE	DILLY	DORIC	DROOK	EARTH	EMCEE
CURRY	DEBAR	DIMLY	DORIS	DROOL	EASEL	EMEER
CURSE	DEBBY	DINAR	DORMY	DROOP	EASLE	EMEND
CURST	DEBEL	DINER	DORSE	DROSS	EATEN	EMERY
CURVE	DEBIT	DINGE	DORTS	DROUK	EATER	EMMER
CURVY	DEBUG	DINGO	DORTY	DROVE	EATHE	EMMET
CUSEC	DÉBUT	DINGY	DOSEH	DROWN	EAVES	EMMEW
CUSHY	DEBYE	DINIC	DOTAL	DRUID	EBLIS	EMOTE
CUTCH	DECAD	DINKY	DOTER	DRUNK	E-BOAT	EMOVE
CUTEY	DECAL	DIODE	DOTTY	DRUPE	EBONY	EMPTY
CUTIE	DECAY	DIOTA	DOUAR	DRUSE	ÉCLAT	EMURE
CUT-IN	DECCA	DIPPY	DOUAY	DRUSY	EDDIC	ENACT
CUTIN	DÉCOR	DIRGE	DOUBT	DRUXY	EDEMA	ENARM
CUTIS	DECOY	DIRTY	DOUCE	DRUZE	EDGED	ENATE
CUTTO	DECRY	DISHY	DOUGH	DRYAD	EDICT	ENDED
CUTTY	DEDAL	DISME	DOUMA	DRYER	EDIFY	END-ON
CUVÉE	DEEDY	DITAL	DOURA	DRYLY	EDILE	ENDOW
CYCAD	DEFER	DITCH	DOUSE	DSOBO	EDUCE	ENDUE
CYCLE	DEGUM	DITTO	DOVER	DSOMO	EDUCT	ENEMA
CYCLO	DE-ICE	DITTY	DOWAR	DUCAL	EERIE	ENEMY
CYDER	DEIFY	DIVAN	DOWDY	DUCAT	EGEST	ENIAC
CYLIX	DEIGN	DIVER	DOWED	DUCHY	EGGAR	ENJOY
CYMAR	DEISM	DIVES	DOWEL	DUCKS	EGGER	ENMEW
CYMRY	DEIST	DIVOT	DOWER	DUCKY	EGRET	ENNUI
CYNIC	DEITY	DIVVY	DOWIE	DUDDY	EGYPT	ENROL
CYTON	DEKKO	DIWAN	DOWLE	DUETT	EIDER	ENSKY
CZECH	DELAY	DIXIE	DOWNA	DULIA	EIGHT	ENSUE
D	DELFT	DIZEN	DOWNY	DULLY	EIGNE	ENTER
	DELPH	DIZZY	DOWRY	DULSE	EIKON	ENTIA
DACHA	DELTA	DJINN	DOWSE	DUMKA	EISEL	ENTRY
DADDY	DELVE	D-MARK	DOYEN	DUMMY	EJECT	ENURE
DADOS	DEMIT	DO-ALL	DOZED	DUMPY	E-LA-MI	ENVOI
DAFFY	DEMOB	DOBBY	DOZEN	DUNCE	ELAND	ENVOY
					ELAPS	

EOLIC	EXIST	FELIS	FIVES	FLYER	FRILL	GALUT
EOSIN	EXODE	FELLY	FIXED	FLYPE	FRISK	GAMBA
EPACT	EXPEL	FELON	FIXER	FLYSH	FRIST	GAMIC
EPHAH	EXTOL	FEMUR	FIZZY	FLYTE	FRITH	GAMIN
EPHOD	EXTRA	FENCE	FJORD	FOAMY	FRIZZ	GAMMA
EPHOR	EXUDE	FENDY	FLAFF	FOCAL	FROCK	GAMMY
EPOCH	EXULT	FENKS	FLAIL	FOCUS	FROND	GAMUT
EPODE	EYETI	FENNY	FLAIR	FOEHN	FRONT	GANCH
EPOPT	EYING	FEOFF	FLAKE	FOGEY	FRORE	GANJA
EPOXY	EYRIE	FERAL	FLAKY	FOGGY	FRORN	GAPER
EQUAL	EYTIE	FERLY	FLAME	FOGLE	FRORY	GAPPY
EQUIP		FERMI	FLAMM	FOIST	FROST	GARBE
EQUUS	**F**	FERNY	FLAMY	FOLIA	FROTH	GARNI
ERASE	FA'ARD	FERRY	FLANK	FOLIC	FROWN	GARTH
ERATO	FABLE	FESSE	FLARE	FOLIO	FROWY	GASES
ERECT	FACED	FETAL	FLARY	FOLLY	FROZE	GASPY
ERGOT	FACER	FETCH	FLASH	FOMES	FRUIT	GASSY
ERICA	FACET	FETID	FLASK	FONLY	FRUMP	GATED
ERICK	FACIA	FETOR	FLAWN	FOOTS	FRUSH	GAUCY
ERNIE	FADDY	FETUS	FLAWY	FOOTY	FRUST	GAUDY
ERODE	FADGE	FETWA	FLAXY	FORAY	FRYER	GAUGE
EROSE	FAERY	FEUAR	FLEAM	FORBY	FRY-UP	GAULT
ERRED	FAGOT	FEVER	FLECK	FORCE	FUBBY	GAUMY
ERROR	FAGUS	FEZES	FLEER	FORDO	FUBSY	GAUNT
ERUCT	FAINT	F-HOLE	FLEET	FOREL	FUCUS	GAUSS
ERUPT	FAIRY	FIARS	FLEMÉ	FORGE	FUDGE	GAUZE
ERVEN	FAITH	FIBER	FLESH	FORGO	FUERO	GAUZY
ESCOT	FAKER	FIBRE	FLICK	FORKY	FUFFY	GAVEL
ESILE	FAKES	FICHU	FLIER	FORME	FUGAL	GAWCY
ESKER	FAKIR	FIDGE	FLIES	FORTE	FUGGY	GAWKY
ESSAY	FALSE	FIELD	FLIMP	FORTH	FUGIE	GAWSY
ESTER	FAMED	FIEND	FLING	FORTY	FUGLE	GAYAL
ESTOC	FANAL	FIERE	FLINT	FORUM	FUGUE	GAYER
ESTOP	FANCY	FIERY	FLIRT	FOSSA	FULLY	GAZAL
ETHAL	FANGO	FIFER	FLISK	FOSSE	FUMET	GAZEL
ETHER	FANNY	FIFTH	FLITE	FOUAT	FUNGI	GAZER
ETHIC	FANON	FIFTY	FLITT	FOUET	FUNKY	GAZON
ETHOS	FANTI	FIGHT	FLOAT	FOULÉ	FUNNY	G-CLEF
ETHYL	FARCE	FILAR	FLOCK	FOUND	FURAL	GEBUR
ETTIN	FARCI	FILCH	FLONG	FOUNT	FURAN	GECKO
ETTLE	FARCY	FILED	FLOOD	FOUTH	FUROR	GEESE
ÉTUDE	FARLE	FILER	FLOOR	FOVEA	FURRY	GEIST
ETWEE	FARSE	FILET	FLORA	FOWTH	FURTH	GELID
EURUS	FASCI	FILLY	FLORY	FOXED	FURZE	GEMEL
EUSOL	FASTI	FILMY	FLOSH	FOYER	FURZY	GEMMA
EVADE	FATAL	FILTH	FLOSS	FRACK	FUSEE	GEMMY
EVENS	FATED	FINAL	FLOTA	FRACT	FUSIL	GEMOT
EVENT	FATLY	FINCH	FLOTE	FRAIL	FUSSY	GENAL
EVERT	FATTY	FINER	FLOUR	FRAIM	FUSTY	GENET
EVERY	FAUGH	FINES	FLOUT	FRAME	FUZEE	GENIC
EVHOE	FAULT	FINIS	FLOWN	FRANC	FUZZY	GENIE
EVICT	FAUNA	FINKS	FLUEY	FRANK	FYTTE	GENII
EVITE	FAURD	FINNY	FLUFF	FRASS		GENOA
EVOKE	FAUVE	FIORD	FLUID	FRAUD	**G**	GENRE
EWEST	FAVUS	FIRED	FLUKE	FREAK		GENRO
EWHOW	F-CLEF	FIRER	FLUKY	FREED	GABBY	GENTS
EXACT	FEARE	FIRRY	FLUME	FREER	GABLE	GENTY
EXALT	FEAST	FIRST	FLUMP	FREET	GADGE	GENUS
EXCEL	FECAL	FIRTH	FLUNG	FREIT	GADSO	GEODE
EXEAT	FECES	FISHY	FLUNK	FREMD	GADUS	GEOID
EXEEM	FECHT	FISTY	FLUOR	FREON	GAFFE	GERAH
EXEME	FECIT	FITCH	FLURR	FRESH	GAILY	GERBE
EXERT	FEEZE	FITLY	FLUSH	FRIAR	GALAH	GERNE
EXIES	FEHME	FITTE	FLUTE	FRIED	GALEA	GERRY
EXILE	FEIGN	FIT-UP	FLUTY	FRIER	GALLY	GESSO
EXINE	FEINT	FIVER	FLY-BY	FRIES	GALOP	GESTE

GET-UP	GLYPH	GREEN	GUMMY	HASTE	HILAR	HOUGH
GHAST	GNARL	GREES	GUNNY	HASTY	HILCH	HOUND
GHAUT	GNARR	GREET	GUPPY	HATCH	HILLO	HOURI
GHAZI	GNASH	GREGO	GURGE	HATER	HILLY	HOUSE
GHOST	GNAWN	GREIN	GURLY	HAUGH	HILUM	HOVEL
GHOUL	GNOME	GRESE	GURRY	HAULD	HINDI	HOVEN
GHYLL	GOATY	GREVE	GUSHY	HAULM	HINDU	HOVER
GIANT	GOBAR	GRICE	GUSLA	HAULT	HINGE	HOWBE
GIBEL	GODET	GRIDE	GUSLE	HAUNT	HINNY	HOWDY
GIBER	GODLY	GRIEF	GUSLI	HAUSE	HIPPO	HOWFF
GIBUS	GODSO	GRIFF	GUSTO	HAVEN	HIPPY	HOWRE
GIDDY	GOETY	GRIKE	GUTSY	HAVER	HIRED	HOWSO
GIGOT	GOFER	GRILL	GUTTA	HAVES	HIRER	HUBBY
GIGUE	GOING	GRIME	GUTTY	HAVOC	HITCH	HUFFY
GILET	GOLDY	GRIMY	GUYOT	HAWSE	HITHE	HULKY
GILPY	GOLEM	GRIND	GYPSY	HAYLE	HIVER	HULLO
GILTS	GOLGI	GRIPE	GYRAL	HAZEL	HIVES	HULLY
GIMME	GOLLY	GRISE	GYRON	HAZER	HOARD	HUMAN
GIPSY	GOLPE	GRIST	GYRUS	HEADY	HOARY	HUMIC
GIRON	GOMBO	GRISY	H-BOMB	HEALD	HOAST	HUMID
GIRTH	GONAD	GRITH		HEAPY	HOBBY	HUMPH
GIVEN	GONER	GRITS	**H**	HEARD	HOBOB	HUMPY
GIVER	GOODY	GRIZE	HABIT	HEART	HOCUS	HUMUS
GLACE	GOOEY	GROAN	HABLE	HEATH	HODGE	HUNCH
GLADE	GO-OFF	GROAT	HADES	HEAVE	HODJA	HUNKS
GLADY	GOOFY	GROIN	HADJI	HEAVY	HOGAN	HUNKY
GLAIK	GOOPY	GROMA	HADST	HECHT	HOGEN	HURDS
GLAIR	GOOSE	GROOM	HAICK	HEDGE	HO-HUM	HURLY
GLAND	GOPAK	GROPE	HAIKH	HEDGY	HOICK	HURRA
GLANS	GORAL	GROSS	HAIKU	HEEZE	HOISE	HURRY
GLARE	GORGE	GROUF	HAILY	HEFTY	HOIST	HURST
GLARY	GORSE	GROUP	HAIRY	HEIGH	HOKKU	HUSKY
GLASS	GORSY	GROUT	HAITH	HEIST	HOKUM	HUSSY
GLAUM	GOUDA	GROVE	HAJJI	HEJRA	HOLEY	HUTCH
GLAUR	GOUGE	GROWL	HAKAM	HELIX	HOLLA	HUTIA
GLAUX	GOURA	GROWN	HAKIM	HELLO	HOLLO	HUZZA
GLAZE	GOURD	GRUEL	HALAL	HELOT	HOLLY	HUZZY
GLEAM	GOUTY	GRUFF	HALES	HELVE	HOMER	HYDRA
GLEAN	GOWAN	GRUME	HALFA	HEMAL	HOMEY	HYDRO
GLEBE	GOYIM	GRUNT	HALLO	HE-MAN	HOMIA	HYENA
GLEBY	GRAAL	GRYDE	HALMA	HEMPY	HONEY	HYLEG
GLEDE	GRACE	GRYKE	HALOD	HENCE	HOOCH	HYLIC
GLEED	GRADE	GRYPE	HALOS	HENGE	HOOEY	HYMEN
GLEEK	GRAFF	G-SUIT	HALSE	HENNA	HOO-HA	HYOID
GLEET	GRAFT	GUACO	HALVA	HENNY	HOOKA	HYPED
GLENT	GRAIL	GUANA	HALVE	HENRY	HOOKY	HYPHA
GLIAL	GRAIN	GUANO	HAMAL	HEPAR	HOOLY	HYRAX
GLIDE	GRAIP	GUARD	HAMMY	HERBY	HOO-OO	HYSON
GLIFF	GRAMA	GUAVA	HANAP	HERMA	HOOSH	HYTHE
GLIFT	GRAME	GUELF	HANCE	HERON	HOOVE	
GLIKE	GRAND	GUESS	HANCH	HERRY	HOPPY	**I**
GLINT	GRANT	GUEST	HANDY	HERSE	HORAL	IAMBI
GLISK	GRAPE	GUEUX	HANKY	HERTZ	HORDE	IBLIS
GLOAT	GRAPH	GUIDE	HANSE	HERYE	HORME	ICHOR
GLOBE	GRAPY	GUILD	HAOMA	HEUCH	HORNY	ICING
GLOBY	GRASP	GUILE	HAPLY	HEUGH	HORSE	ICKER
GLOOM	GRASS	GUILT	HAPPY	HEWED	HORST	ICTIC
GLORY	GRATE	GUIMP	HARAM	HEWER	HORSY	ICTUS
GLOSS	GRAVE	GUISE	HARDS	HEWGH	HOSED	IDANT
GLOUT	GRAVY	GULAR	HARDY	HEXAD	HOSEN	IDEAL
GLOVE	GRAZE	GULCH	HAREM	HIANT	HOSTA	IDIOM
GLOZE	GREAT	GULES	HARIM	HIEMS	HOTCH	IDIOT
GLUED	GREBE	GULFY	HARNS	HIGHT	HOTEL	IDIST
GLUER	GRECE	GULLY	HARPY	HIJRA	HOTEN	IDLER
GLUEY	GREED	GUMBO	HARRY	HIKER	HOTLY	IDOLA
GLUME	GREEK	GUMMA	HARSH		HOUFF	IDYLL

IGAPÓ	INUST	JEWRY	KARST	KOALA	LAMMY	LEGER
IGLOO	INVAR	JIBER	KASBA	KOBAN	LANCE	LEGGE
IHRAM	INWIT	JIFFY	KAUGH	KOINE	LANCH	LEGGY
ILEAC	IODIC	JIGOT	KAURI	KOKRA	LANDE	LEMAN
ILEUM	IONIC	JIHAD	KAYAK	KOKUM	LANKY	LEMMA
ILEUS	IRADE	JIMMY	KAYLE	KOOKY	LAPEL	LEMNA
ILIAC	IRAQI	JIMPY	KAYOE	KOPJE	LAPIS	LEMON
ILIAD	IRATE	JINGO	KAZOO	KOPPA	LAPJE	LEMUR
ILIAN	IRISH	JINNI	KEBAB	KORAN	LAPSE	LENTO
ILIUM	IRONY	JINNS	KEBOB	KOTOW	LARCH	LEPER
ILLTH	ISIAC	JOCKO	KECKS	KOTYS	LARDY	LEPID
IMAGE	ISLAM	JODEL	KEDGE	KRAAL	LARES	LEPRA
IMAGO	ISLET	JOINT	KEDGY	KRAIT	LARGE	LEPTA
IMAUM	ISSEI	JOIST	KEECH	KRANG	LARGO	LERNA
IMBAR	ISSUE	JOKER	KEEVE	KRANS	LARKY	LERNE
IMBED	ISTLE	JOKOL	KEFIR	KRANZ	LARUM	LETCH
IMBUE	ITCHY	JOLLY	KELPY	KRAUT	LARUS	LETHE
IMMEW	IVIED	JONAH	KELTY	KRENG	LARVA	LET-UP
IMMIT	IVORY	JONTY	KEMBO	KRILL	LASER	LEUCH
IMMIX	IXTLE	JORAM	KEMPT	KRONA	LASSO	LEUGH
IMPEL	IYYAR	JORUM	KENDO	KRONE	LASSU	LEVEE
IMPLY	IZARD	JOTUN	KENNO	KUDOS	LATCH	LEVEL
IMPOT	IZZET	JOUGS	KENTE	KUDZU	LATED	LEVER
IMSHI		JOULE	KERNE	KUFIC	LATEN	LEVIN
IMSHY	**J**	JOUST	KETCH	KUKRI	LATER	LEVIS
INANE		JOWAR	KEVEL	KULAK	LATEX	LEWIS
INAPT	JABOT	JOYED	KEYED	KULAN	LATHE	LIANA
INARM	JADED	JUDAS	KHADI	KUO-YÜ	LATHI	LIANE
INBYE	JAFFA	JUDGE	KHAKI	KUTCH	LATHY	LIARD
INCOG	JÄGER	JUGAL	KHAYA	KVASS	LATIN	LIBEL
INCUR	JAGGY	JUICE	KHEDA	KWELA	LAUCH	LIBER
INCUS	JAGIR	JUICY	KHMER	KYANG	LAUGH	LIBRA
INCUT	JAINA	JULEP	KHOJA	KYDST	LAUND	LICHT
INDEX	JAKES	JUMBO	KIANG	KYLEY	LAURA	LICIT
INDIC	JALAP	JUMBY	KIDDY	KYLIE	LAVAS	LIEGE
INDOL	JAMBE	JUMPY	KIDEL	KYLIN	LAVER	LIEVE
INDRA	JAMBU	JUNCO	KIDGE	KYLIX	LAVRA	LIFER
INDRI	JAMES	JUNTA	KIEVE	KYLOE	LAWKS	LIGAN
INDUE	JAMMY	JUNTO	KILEY	KYRIE	LAWNY	LIGER
INEPT	JANTY	JUPON	KILTY	KYTHE	LAXLY	LIGGE
INERM	JANUS	JURAL	KIMBO		LAYBY	LIGHT
INERT	JAPAN	JURAT	KINKY	**L**	LAYER	LIGNE
INFER	JARTA	JUROR	KIOSK		LAY-UP	LIKEN
INFIX	JARUL	JUTTY	KISAN	LABDA	LAZAR	LIKER
INFRA	JASEY		KITHE	LABEL	LEACH	LIKIN
INGAN	JASPE	**K**	KITTY	LABIA	LEADY	LILAC
INGLE	JAUNT		KLANG	LABIS	LEAFY	LIMAX
INGOT	JAVAN	KAABA	KLOOF	LABRA	LEAKY	LIMBO
INION	JAVEL	KAAMA	KNACK	LACED	LEANT	LIMEN
INJUN	JAWAN	KABAB	KNARL	LACET	LEANY	LIMES
INKER	JAWED	KABOB	KNAVE	LACEY	LEAPT	LIMEY
INKLE	JAZZY	KACHA	KNEAD	LADED	LEARE	LIMIT
IN-LAW	JEELY	KAFIR	KNEED	LADEN	LEARN	LIMMA
INLAY	JEHAD	KAIAK	KNEEL	LADIN	LEASE	LINAC
INLET	JELLO	KALIF	KNELL	LADLE	LEASH	LINCH
INNER	JELLY	KALPA	KNELT	LAGAN	LEAST	LINED
IN-OFF	JEMMY	KAMIS	KNIFE	LAGER	LEAVE	LINEN
INORB	JENNY	KAMME	KNIVE	LAHAR	LEAVY	LINER
INPUT	JERID	KANDY	KNOCK	LAIGH	LEAZE	LINGA
INSET	JERKY	KANEH	KNOLL	LAIKA	LEDGE	LINGO
INTER	JERRY	KANZU	KNOSP	LAIRD	LEDGY	LINGY
INTIL	JESSE	KAPOK	KNOUT	LAIRY	LEDUM	LININ
INTRO	JESUS	KAPPA	KNOWE	LAITH	LEEAR	LINNY
INULA	JETON	KAREN	KNOWN	LAITY	LEECH	LIPID
INURE	JETTY	KARMA	KNURL	LAKER	LEERY	LIPPY
INURN	JEUNE	KAROO	KNURR	LAKIN	LEGAL	LIRAS
	JEWEL	KARRI		LAMIA		

LISLE	LOWSE	MALAR	MAYST	MILER	MOPED	MULGA
LITHE	LOYAL	MALAX	MAZER	MILKY	MOPPY	MULSH
LITRE	LOZEN	MALAY	MAZUT	MILOR	MOPSY	MUMMY
LIVED	LUBRA	MALIC	MEALY	MIMER	MOP-UP	MUMPS
LIVEN	LUCES	MALTA	MEANE	MIMIC	MOPUS	MUNCH
LIVER	LUCID	MALTY	MEANS	MIMUS	MORAL	MUNDA
LIVES	LUCKY	MALVA	MEANT	MINAR	MORAT	MUNGO
LIVID	LUCRE	MAMBA	MEANY	MINCE	MORAY	MUNRO
LIVOR	LUFFA	MAMBO	MEASE	MINER	MOREL	MURAL
LIVRE	LUING	MAMMA	MEATY	MINGY	MORES	MUREX
LLAMA	LUMEN	MAMMY	MEBOS	MINIE	MORIA	MURKY
LLANO	LUMME	MANED	MECCA	MINIM	MORNE	MURLY
LOACH	LUMMY	MANEH	MEDAL	MINOR	MORNE	MURRA
LOAMY	LUMPY	MANES	MEDIA	MINTY	MORON	MURRE
LOATH	LUNAR	MANGE	MEDIC	MINUS	MORRA	MURRY
LOAVE	LUNCH	MANGO	MEDOC	MIRKY	MORSE	MURVA
LOBAR	LUNGE	MANGY	MEINT	MIRLY	MORUS	MUSCA
LOBBY	LUNGI	MANIA	MEINY	MIRTH	MOSES	MUSCI
LOBED	LUPIN	MANIC	MEITH	MIRZA	MOSEY	MUSED
LOBUS	LUPUS	MANIS	MELEE	MISDO	MOSSY	MUSER
LOCAL	LURCH	MANLY	MELIA	MISER	MOTED	MUSET
LOCUM	LURGI	MANNA	MELIC	MISGO	MOTEL	MUSHA
LOCUS	LURID	MANOR	MELON	MISSY	MOTEN	MUSHY
LODGE	LURRY	MANSE	MENGE	MISTY	MOTET	MUSIC
LOESS	LUSHY	MANTA	MENSA	MITRE	MOTEY	MUSIT
LOFTY	LUSTY	MANTO	MENSE	MITTY	MOTHY	MUSKY
LOGAN	LUTER	MANTY	MERCY	MIXED	MOTIF	MUSSE
LOGIA	LUXES	MANUL	MEREL	MIXEN	MOTOR	MUSSY
LOGIC	LYART	MANUS	MERGE	MIXER	MOTTE	MUSTY
LOGIE	LYCEE	MAORI	MERIL	MIX-IN	MOTTO	MUTCH
LOGOS	LYING	MAPLE	MERIT	MIX-UP	MOTTY	MUTED
LOLLY	LYMPH	MAQUI	MERLE	MIZEN	MOUCH	MUTON
LOLOG	LYNCH	MARAH	MERRY	MNEME	MOULD	MUZAK
LONER	LYRIC	MARCH	MESEL	MOBBY	MOULS	MUZZY
LONGA	LYSIN	MARDY	MESHY	MOBLE	MOULT	MVULE
LONGE	LYSIS	MARGE	MESIC	MOCHA	MOUND	MYALL
LOOBY	LYSOL	MARIA	MESNE	MODAL	MOUNT	MYNAH
LOOFA	LYTHE	MARID	MESON	MODEL	MOURN	MYOID
LOONY	LYTTA	MARLS	MESSY	MODII	MOUSE	MYOMA
LOOPY		MARLY	MESTO	MODUS	MOUST	MYOPE
LOORD	**M**	MARRY	METAL	MOGGY	MOUSY	MYRRH
LOOSE		MARSH	METED	MOGUL	MOUTH	
LORAL	MACAW	MASAI	METER	MOHUR	MOVED	**N**
LORAN	MACER	MASER	METHS	MOIRA	MOVER	
LOREL	MACLE	MASHY	METIC	MOIRE	MOVIE	NAAFI
LORIC	MACON	MASON	METIF	MOIST	MOWED	NABOB
LORIS	MADAM	MASSA	METIS	MOLAL	MOWER	NACHE
LORRY	MADGE	MASSE	METOL	MOLAR	MOWRA	NACRE
LOSEL	MADID	MASSY	METRE	MOLLA	MPRET	NADIR
LOSER	MADLY	MASTY	METRO	MOLLY	M-ROOF	NAEVE
LOTAH	MAFIA	MATCH	MEUSE	MOLTO	MUCIC	NAEVI
LOTOS	MAGGS	MATER	MEYNT	MOMUS	MUCID	NAIAD
LOTTO	MAGIC	MATEY	MHORR	MONAD	MUCIN	NAIAS
LOTUS	MAGMA	MATHS	MIAOW	MONAL	MUCKY	NAIVE
LOUGH	MAGOG	MATIN	MIASM	MONAS	MUCOR	NAKED
LOUIS	MAGOT	MATLO	MIAUL	MONER	MUCRO	NAKER
LOUND	MAGUS	MATTE	MICHE	MONEY	MUCUS	NALLA
LOURE	MAHDI	MATZA	MICKY	MONTE	MUDDY	NAMED
LOURY	MAHUA	MATZO	MIDAS	MONTH	MUDIR	NAMER
LOUSE	MAHWA	MAUND	MIDDY	MOOCH	MUFTI	NANCE
LOUSY	MAILE	MAUVE	MIDGE	MOODY	MUGGY	NANCY
LOVER	MAINS	MAVIS	MIDST	MOOLS	MUIST	NANDI
LOWER	MAISE	MAXIM	MIFFY	MOOLY	MUJIK	NANDU
LOWLY	MAIZE	MAYAN	MIFTY	MOONY	MULCH	NANNA
LOWND	MAJOR	MAYBE	MIGHT	MOORY	MULCT	NANNY
LOWNE	MAKAR	MAYOR	MILCH	MOOSE	MULEY	NANTZ
	MAKER					NAPOO

NAPPE	NINON	NUCHA	OOMPH	OVULE	PARGE	PENCE
NAPPY	NINTH	NUDGE	OORIE	OWCHE	PARIS	PENES
NARAS	NIOBE	NUGAE	OPERA	OWING	PARKA	PENIS
NARES	NIPPY	NULLA	OPINE	OWLER	PARKI	PENNA
NARKY	NIRLY	NURSE	OPIUM	OWLET	PARKY	PENNE
NARRE	NISAN	NUTTY	OPTIC	OWNER	PARLE	PENNY
NASAL	NISEI	NYLON	ORACH	OWRIE	PARLY	PEONY
NASIK	NISSE	NYMPH	ORACY	OWSEN	PAROL	PEPPY
NASTY	NISUS	**O**	ORANG	OX-BOT	PARRY	PERAI
NATAL	NITID		ORANT	OX-BOW	PARSE	PERCA
NATCH	NITON	OAKEN	ORATE	OXEYE	PARSI	PERCH
NATES	NITRE	OAKUM	ORBED	OXIDE	PARTY	PERDU
NATTY	NITRY	OARED	ORBIT	OXLIP	PASCH	PERDY
NAUNT	NITTY	OASES	ORCIN	OXTER	PASEO	PERIL
NAVAL	NIVAL	OASIS	ORDER	OZONE	PASHA	PERKY
NAVEL	NIXIE	OATEN	OREAD		PASHM	PERRY
NAVEW	NIZAM	OAVES	ORGAN	**P**	PASPY	PERSE
NAVVY	NOBBY	OBANG	ORGIA		PASTA	PESKY
NAWAB	NOBLE	OBEAH	ORGIC	PACED	PASTE	PETAL
NAYAR	NOBLY	OBELI	ORGUE	PACER	PASTY	PETER
NAZIR	NODAL	OBESE	ORIBI	PADDY	PATCH	PETIT
NEATH	NODDY	OBOLI	ORIEL	PADLE	PATED	PETRE
NEBEK	NODUS	OCCUR	ORION	PADMA	PATEN	PETRI
NEBEL	NOHOW	OCEAN	ORIYA	PADRE	PATER	PETTY
NEDDY	NOILS	OCHRE	ORLOP	PAEAN	PATIO	PEWIT
NEEDS	NOINT	OCHRY	ORMER	PAEON	PATLY	PEYSE
NEEDY	NOISE	OCREA	ORNIS	PAGAN	PATTE	PHAGE
NEESE	NOISY	OCTAD	ORPIN	PAGLE	PATTÉ	PHARE
NEEZE	NOMAD	OCTAL	ORRIS	PAGOD	PATTY	PHASE
NEGRO	NO-MAN	OCTET	ORTHO	PAGRI	PAUSE	PHEER
NEGUS	NOMIC	ODDLY	ORVAL	PAINT	PAVAN	PHENE
NEIGH	NOMOS	ODEON	ORYZA	PAISA	PAVED	PHEON
NEIST	NONCE	ODEUM	OSAGE	PAKKA	PAVEN	PHESE
NEIVE	NONES	ODISM	OSCAN	PALAS	PAVER	PHIAL
NELIS	NONET	ODIST	OSCAR	PALAY	PAVID	PHLOX
NELLY	NONNY	ODIUM	OSHAC	PALEA	PAVIN	PHOCA
NEMPT	NOOKY	ODOUR	OSIER	PALET	PAVIS	PHONE
NEPER	NO-ONE	ODYLE	OSMIC	PALKI	PAWAW	PHONY
NERKA	NOOSE	O'ERBY	OSSIA	PALLA	PAWKY	PHOTO
NERVE	NOPAL	OFFAL	OSTIA	PALLY	PAYED	PHYLA
NERVY	NORIA	OFFER	OTARY	PALMY	PAYEE	PHYLE
NESKI	NORMA	OFTEN	OTHER	PALPI	PAYER	· PIANO
NETTY	NORNA	OGEED	OTTAR	PALSY	P-CELT	PICEA
NEUME	NORSE	OGHAM	OTTER	PAMPA	PEACE	PICOT
NEVEL	NORTH	OGIVE	OUBIT	PANAX	PEACH	· PICRA
NEVER	NOSED	OGLER	OUGHT	PANDA	PEAKY	PICUL
NEWEL	NOSER	OGMIC	OUIJA	PANDY	PEARL	PICUS
NEWLY	NOSEY	OHMIC	OUNCE	PANED	PEART	PI-DOG
NEWSY	NOTAL	OHONE	OUNDY	PANEL	PEASE	PIECE
NEXUS	NOTCH	OKAPI	OUPHE	PANGA	PEATY	PIEL'D
NGAIO	NOTED	OLDEN	OURIE	PANIC	PEAVY	PIEND
NICHE	NOTER	OLEIC	OUSEL	PANNE	PEAZE	PIERT
NICOL	NOTUM	OLEIN	OUTBY	PANSY	PECAN	PIETÀ
NIDAL	NOTUS	OLENT	OUTDO	PANTO	PECHT	PIETY
NIDOR	NOULD	OLIVE	OUTED	PANTS	PEDAL	PIEZO
NIDUS	NOUNS	OLLAV	OUTER	PAOLI	PEEOY	PIGGY
NIECE	NOVAE	OMBRE	OUTGO	PAOLO	PEERY	PIGHT
NIEVE	NOVEL	OMEGA	OUTRÉ	PAPAL	PEGGY	PIGMY
NIFFY	NOVUM	OMLAH	OUZEL	PAPAW	PEGHT	PI-JAW
NIFTY	NOWAY	OMRAH	OVARY	PAPER	PEISE	PIKED
NIGER	NOWED	ONCER	OVATE	PAPPY	PEIZE	PIKER
NIGHT	NOWEL	ON-DIT	OVERT	PARCA	PEKAN	PIKUL
NIHIL	NOXAL	ONENE	OVINE	PARCH	PEKOE	PILAU
NILOT	NOYAU	ONION	OVIST	PARDI	PELMA	PILAW
NIMBI	NUBBY	ONSET	OVOID	PARDY	PELTA	PILCH
NINNY	NUBIA	OOBIT	OVOLO	PARER	PENAL	PILEA

PILEI	PLUMY	PRAHU	PUDOR	QUELL	RANGE	REGUR
PILER	PLUNK	PRANG	PUDSY	QUEME	RANGY	REICH
PILOT	PLUSH	PRANK	PUFFY	QUERN	RANKE	REIFY
PILOW	PLUTO	PRASE	PUGGY	QUERY	RAPER	REIGN
PILUM	POACH	PRATE	PUGIL	QUEST	RAPHE	REINS
PILUS	POAKA	PRATY	PUKER	QUEUE	RAPID	REIRD
PINCH	POCKY	PRAWN	PUKKA	QUEYN	RASPY	REIST
PINEY	PODAL	PREDY	PULER	QUICH	RASSE	REIVE
PINKY	PODDY	PREEN	PULEX	QUICK	RATAN	REJIG
PINNA	PODEX	PRENT	PULKA	QUIET	RATCH	RELAX
PINNY	PODGE	PRESS	PULMO	QUIFF	RATED	RELAY
PIÑON	PODGY	PREST	PULPY	QUI-HI	RATEL	RELET
PINTA	PODIA	PREXY	PULSE	QUILL	RATER	RELIC
PINTO	POESY	PRIAL	PUMIE	QUILT	RATHE	REMEX
PIN-UP	POGGE	PRICE	PUNCE	QUINA	RATIO	REMIT
PIONY	POIND	PRICK	PUNCH	QUINE	RATTY	RENAL
PIOUS	POINT	PRIDE	PUNIC	QUINT	RAVEL	RENAY
PIOYE	POISE	PRIED	PUNKA	QUIPO	RAVEN	RENEW
PIPAL	POKAL	PRIEF	PUNTO	QUIPU	RAVER	RENEY
PIPED	POKED	PRIER	PUNTY	QUIRE	RAVIN	RENGA
PIPER	POKER	PRIES	PUPAE	QUIRK	RAWLY	RENIG
PIPIT	POLAR	PRIMA	PUPAL	QUIRT	RAYAH	RENTE
PIPPY	POLEY	PRIME	PUPIL	QUIST	RAYED	REPAY
PIPUL	POLIO	PRIMO	PUPPY	QUITE	RAYON	REPEL
PIQUE	POLKA	PRIMP	PURÉE	QUITS	RAZED	REPLY
PIRAI	POLLY	PRIMY	PURGE	QUOIF	RAZEE	REPOT
PISKY	POLYP	PRINK	PURIM	QUOIN	RAZOR	RESET
PISTE	POMAK	PRINT	PURIN	QUOIT	REACH	RESIN
PITCH	POMMY	PRIOR	PURPY	QUOTA	REACT	RESIT
PITHY	PONCE	PRISE	PURSE	QUOTE	READY	RESTY
PITON	PONGO	PRISM	PURSY	QUOTH	REALM	RETCH
PITTA	PONTY	PRIVY	PUSSY	QURÂN	REAMY	RETIE
PIVOT	POOCH	PRIZE	PUTID	QUYTE	REARM	RETRY
PIXIE	POOJA	PROBE	PUTTI		REAST	REUSE
PIZZA	POORT	PROEM	PUTTO	**R**	REATA	REVEL
P-KELT	POPPA	PROKE	PUTTY	RABAT	REATE	REVET
PLACE	POPPY	PROLE	PUT-UP	RABBI	REAVE	REVIE
PLACK	POPSY	PRONE	PUZEL	RABIC	REBEC	REVUE
PLAGE	PORAL	PRONG	PYGAL	RABID	REBEL	RHEUM
PLAID	PORCH	PROOF	PYGMY	RACER	REBID	RHINE
PLAIN	PORER	PRORE	PYLON	RACHE	REBUS	RHINO
PLAIT	PORGY	PROSE	PYOID	RADAR	REBUT	RHOMB
PLANE	PORKY	PROSY	PYRAL	RADII	RECAP	RHONE
PLANK	PORTA	PROUD	PYRUS	RADIO	RECCE	RHUMB
PLANT	PORTE	PROVE	PYXIS	RADIX	RECTA	RHYME
PLASH	PORTY	PROWL		RADON	RECTI	RHYTA
PLASM	POSER	PROXY	**Q**	RAGED	RECTO	RIANT
PLATE	POSIT	PRUCE	Q-BOAT	RAGER	RECUR	RIATA
PLATY	POSSE	PRUDE	Q-CELT	RAGGY	REDAN	RIBES
PLAYA	POTCH	PRUNE	Q-KELT	RAINY	REDDY	RICEY
PLAZA	POTIN	PRUNT	QORAN	RAIRD	REDIA	RICHT
PLEAD	POTTO	PRYER	QUACK	RAISE	RE-DID	RIDER
PLEAT	POTTY	PRYSE	QUAFF	RAJAH	REDIP	RIDGE
PLEBS	POUCH	PSALM	QUAIL	RAKEE	REDLY	RIDGY
PLEON	POUKE	PSHAW	QUAKE	RAKER	REECH	RIFLE
PLESH	POULE	PSOAS	QUAKY	RALLY	REEDY	RIGEL
PLICA	POULP	PSORA	QUALM	RALPH	REEKY	RIGHT
PLIED	POULT	PSYCH	QUANT	RAMAL	REEST	RIGID
PLIER	POUND	PUBES	QUARK	RAMEE	REEVE	RIGIL
PLIES	POUPE	PUBIC	QUART	RAMIE	REFEL	RIGOL
PLONK	POUPT	PUBIS	QUASH	RAMMY	REFER	RIGOR
PLUCK	POWAN	PUCKA	QUASI	RAMUS	REFIT	RILLE
PLUFF	POWER	PUDDY	QUAYD	RANCE	REGAL	RIMAE
PLUMB	POWIN	PUDGE	QUEAN	RANCH	REGAR	RIMED
PLUME	POWNY	PUDGY	QUEEN	RANDY	RÉGIE	RIMER
PLUMP	PRAAM	PUDIC	QUEER	RANEE	REGMA	RINDY

RINSE	ROUTH	SAILY	SAVEY	SCRAG	SERAI	SHEET
RIPEN	ROVER	SAINT	SAVIN	SCRAM	SERGE	SHEIK
RIPER	ROWAN	SAIST	SAVOY	SCRAN	SERIC	SHELF
RISEN	ROWDY	SAITH	SAVVY	SCRAP	SERIF	SHELL
RISER	ROWEL	SAIVA	SAWED	SCRAT	SERIN	SHEMA
RISHI	ROWEN	SAJOU	SAWER	SCRAW	SERON	SHEND
RISKY	ROWER	SAKAI	SAWNY	SCRAY	SEROW	SHENT
RISUS	ROWME	SAKER	SAXON	SCREE	SERRA	SHE'OL
RITZY	ROWTH	SAKIA	SAYER	SCREW	SERRE	SHERD
RIVAL	ROYAL	SAKTA	SAYID	SCRIM	SERRY	SHEVA
RIVED	ROYNE	SAKTI	SAYNE	SCRIP	SERUM	SHEWN
RIVEL	ROYST	SALAD	SAYON	SCROG	SERVE	SHIAH
RIVEN	ROZET	SALAL	SAY-SO	SCROW	SERVO	SHIED
RIVER	ROZIT	SALEP	SAYST	SCRUB	SESEY	SHIEL
RIVET	RUBIA	SALIC	SCAFF	SCRUM	SESSA	SHIER
ROACH	RUBIN	SALIX	SCAIL	SCUBA	SETAE	SHIFT
ROARY	RUBLE	SALLY	SCALA	SCUDI	SETON	SHILL
ROAST	RUBUS	SALMI	SCALD	SCUDO	SET-TO	SHILY
ROATE	RUCHE	SALMO	SCALE	SCUFF	SET-UP	SHINE
ROBIN	RUDAS	SALON	SCALL	SCUFT	SEVEN	SHINY
ROBLE	RUDDY	SALOP	SCALP	SCULL	SEVER	SHIRE
ROBOT	RUFFE	SALSE	SCALY	SCULP	SEWED	SHIRK
ROCKY	RUGBY	SALTY	SCAMP	SCURF	SEWEL	SHIRR
RODEO	RUGGY	SALUE	SCANT	SCUSE	SEWEN	SHIRT
ROGER	RUING	SALVE	SCAPA	SCUTA	SEWER	SHITE
ROGUE	RULER	SALVO	SCAPE	SCUTE	SEWIN	SHIVE
ROGUY	RUMAL	SAMBA	SCAPI	SDAYN	SEXED	SHOAL
ROILY	RUMAN	SAMBO	SCARE	SDEIN	'SFOOT	SHOAT
ROIST	RUMBA	SAMEL	SCARF	SEAME	SHACK	SHOCK
ROKER	RUMBO	SAMEN	SCARP	SEAMY	SHADE	SHOED
ROMAL	RUMEN	SAMMY	SCART	SEBAT	SHADY	SHOER
ROMAN	RUMEX	SAMPI	SCARY	SEBUM	SHAFT	SHOES
ROMEO	RUMLY	SANDY	SCATT	SECCO	SHAKE	SHOJI
ROMIC	RUMMY	SANKO	SCAUD	SEDAN	SHAKO	SHOLA
RONDE	RUNCH	SANSA	SCAUP	SEDGE	SHAKY	SHONA
RONDO	RUNED	SAPAN	SCAUR	SEDGY	SHALE	SHONE
RONEO	RUNIC	SAPID	SCEAT	SEDUM	SHALL	SHOOK
ROOFY	RUNNY	SAPOR	SCENA	SEEDY	SHALM	SHOOL
ROOKY	RUN-ON	SAPPY	SCEND	SEELY	SHALT	SHOON
ROOMY	RUNTY	SAREE	SCENE	SEEPY	SHALY	SHOOT
ROOPY	RUPEE	SARGE	SCENT	SEGNO	SHAMA	SHORE
ROOSA	RUPIA	SARGO	SCHMO	SEGOL	SHAME	SHORN
ROOSE	RURAL	SARKY	SCHUL	SEINE	SHAND	SHORT
ROOST	RUSHY	SAROS	SCHWA	SEISE	SHANK	SHOTE
ROOTY	RUSMA	SARSA	SCION	SEISM	SHAN'T	SHOTT
ROPED	RUSTY	SARUS	SCLIM	SEITY	SHAPE	SHOUT
ROPER	RUTIN	SARZA	SCOFF	SEIZE	SHAPS	SHOVE
ROQUE	RUTTY	SASIN	SCOLD	SEKOS	SHARD	SHOWN
RORAL	RYBAT	SASSE	SCONE	SELAH	SHARE	SHOWY
RORIC	RYPER	SATAN	SCOOG	SELLE	SHARK	SHRED
RORID		SATED	SCOOP	SELVA	SHARN	SHREW
RORIE	**S**	SATEM	SCOOT	SEMEE	SHARP	SHROW
RORTY		SATIN	SCOPA	SEMEN	SHASH	SHRUB
ROSED	SABAL	SATYR	SCOPE	SEMIE	SHAVE	SHRUG
ROSET	SABER	SAUBA	SCOPS	SEMIS	SHAWL	SHUCK
ROSIN	SABIN	SAUCE	SCORE	SENNA	SHAWM	SHUNT
ROSIT	SABLE	SAUCH	SCORN	SEÑOR	SHAYA	SHUSH
ROTCH	SABOT	SAUCY	SCOTS	SENSE	SHCHI	SHYER
ROTOR	SABRA	SAUGH	SCOUG	SENVY	SHEAF	SHYLY
ROUGE	SABRE	SAULT	SCOUP	SENZA	SHEAL	SIBYL
ROUGH	SACRA	SAUNA	SCOUR	SEPAD	SHEAR	SICAN
ROUND	SADHU	SAUNT	SCOUT	SEPAL	SHEBA	SICEL
ROUPY	SADLY	SAURY	SCOWL	SEPIA	SHEEL	SIDED
ROUSE	SAGUM	SAUTE	SCOWP	SEPOY	SHEEN	SIDER
ROUST	SAHIB	SAVED	SCRAB	SEPTA	SHEEP	SIDLE
ROUTE	SAICK	SAVER	SCRAE	SERAC	SHEER	SIEGE
	SAIGA					

S5

SIEVE	SKOAL	SMARM	SODDY	SPADO	SPOIL	STEAM
SIGHT	SKOFF	SMART	SODIC	SPAER	SPOKE	STEAN
SIGIL	SKRAN	SMASH	SODOM	SPAHI	SPOOF	STEED
SIGLA	SKULK	SMEAR	SOFTA	SPAIN	SPOOK	STEEK
SIGMA	SKULL	SMELL	SOFTY	SPAKE	SPOOL	STEEL
SIKEL	SKUNK	SMELT	SOGER	SPALD	SPOOM	STEEM
SILEN	SKYEY	SMILE	SOGGY	SPALE	SPOON	STEEN
SILER	SKYRE	SMIRK	SOILY	SPALL	SPOOR	STEEP
SILEX	SKYTE	SMIRR	SOKEN	SPALT	SPORE	STEER
SILKY	SLACK	SMITE	SOKOL	SPANE	SPORT	STEIL
SILLY	SLADE	SMITH	SOLAH	SPANG	SPOSH	STEIN
SILOD	SLAID	SMOCK	SOLAN	SPANK	SPOUT	STELA
SILTY	SLAIN	SMOKE	SOLAR	SPARE	SPRAT	STELE
SILVA	SLAKE	SMOKO	SOLDE	SPARK	SPRAY	STELL
SIMAR	SLANE	SMOKY	SOLDI	SPART	SPREE	STEME
SINCE	SLANG	SMOLT	SOLDO	SPASM	SPRIG	STEND
SINEW	SLANT	SMOOR	SOLEN	SPATE	SPRIT	STENT
SINGE	SLASH	SMOOT	SOLER	SPAUL	SPROD	STEPT
SINIC	SLATE	SMORE	SOL-FA	SPAWL	SPRUE	STERE
SINKY	SLATY	SMOTE	SOLID	SPAWN	SPRUG	STERN
SINUS	SLAVE	SMOUS	SOLON	SPAYD	SPULE	STEWY
SIOUX	SLEEK	SMOUT	SOLUM	SPEAK	SPUME	STICH
SIREN	SLEEP	SMOWT	SOLUS	SPEAN	SPUMY	STICK
SIRIH	SLEET	SNACK	SOLVE	SPEAR	SPUNK	STIED
SIROC	SLEPT	SNAFU	SONAR	SPEAT	SPURN	STIES
SIRUP	SLICE	SNAIL	SONCE	SPECK	SPURT	STIFF
SISAL	SLICK	SNAKE	SONDE	SPECS	SPUTA	STILB
SISSY	SLIDE	SNAKY	SONIC	SPEED	SPYAL	STILE
SITAR	'SLIFE	SNARE	SONNY	SPEEL	SQUAB	STILL
SITHE	SLILY	SNARK	SONSE	SPEER	SQUAD	STILT
SITKA	SLIME	SNARL	SONSY	SPEIR	SQUAT	STIME
SITTA	SLIMY	SNARY	SOOLE	SPELD	SQUAW	STIMY
SIVAN	SLING	SNASH	SOOTE	SPELL	SQUIB	STING
SIXER	SLINK	SNATH	SOOTH	SPELT	SQUID	STINK
SIXTE	SLIPE	SNEAD	SOOTY	SPEND	SQUIT	STINT
SIXTH	SLIPT	SNEAK	SOPHA	SPENT	STACK	STIPA
SIXTY	SLISH	SNEAP	SOPHI	SPEOS	STADE	STIPE
SIZAR	SLIVE	SNECK	SOPHY	SPERM	STAFF	STIRK
SIZED	SLOAN	SNEER	SOPOR	SPEWY	STAGE	STIRP
SIZEL	SLOID	SNELL	SOPPY	SPIAL	STAGY	STIVE
SIZER	SLOOM	SNICK	SOPRA	SPICA	STAID	STIVY
SKAIL	SLOOP	SNIDE	SORAL	SPICE	STAIG	STOAI
SKALD	SLOOT	SNIFF	SORDA	SPICK	STAIN	STOAT
SKART	SLOPE	SNIFT	SORDO	SPICY	STAIR	STOEP
SKATE	SLOPS	SNIPE	SOREE	SPIED	STAKE	STOIC
SKEAN	SLOPY	SNIPS	SOREX	SPIEL	STAL'D	STOIT
SKEET	SLOSH	SNIPY	SORGO	SPIES	STALE	STOKE
SKEIN	SLOTH	SNIRT	SORRA	SPIFF	STALK	STOLA
SKELM	SLOVE	SNOEK	SORRY	SPIKE	STALL	STOLE
SKELP	SLOYD	SNOKE	SORUS	SPIKY	STAMP	STOMA
SKENE	SLUBB	SNOOD	SOTHO	SPILE	STAND	STOMP
SKIED	SLUED	SNOOK	SOUGH	SPILL	STANE	STONE
SKIER	SLUIT	SNOOL	SOUND	SPILT	STANG	STONK
SKIEY	SLUMP	SNOOP	SOUPY	SPINA	STANK	STONY
SKIFF	SLUNG	SNOOT	SOUSE	SPINE	STARE	STOOD
SKILL	SLUNK	SNORE	SOUTH	SPINK	STARK	STOOK
SKIMP	SLURB	SNORT	SOWAR	SPINY	STARN	STOOL
SKINK	SLUSH	SNOUT	SOWED	SPIRE	STARR	STOOP
SKINT	SLYER	SNOWK	SOWER	SPIRT	START	STOOR
SKIRL	SLYLY	SNOWY	SOWFF	SPIRY	STASH	STOPE
SKIRR	SLYPE	SNUFF	SOWLE	SPITE	STATE	STORE
SKIRT	SMACK	SNUSH	SOWND	SPITZ	STAVE	STORK
SKITE	SMAIK	SOAPY	SOWTH	SPLAT	STAYS	STORM
SKIVE	SMALL	SOBER	SOYLE	SPLAY	STEAD	STORY
SKIVY	SMALM	SOCKS	SPACE	SPLIT	STEAK	STOUN
SKLIM	SMALT	SOCLE	SPADE	SPODE	STEAL	STOUP

STOUR	SUPER	SYKER	TASTY	TERNE	THROW	TOMMY
STOUT	SURAH	SYLPH	TATAR	TERRA	THRUM	TONAL
STOVE	SURAL	SYLVA	TATER	TERRY	THUJA	TONDO
STOWN	SURAT	SYMAR	TATIE	TERSE	THULE	TONED
STRAD	SURFY	SYNOD	TATOU	TERTS	THUMB	TONEY
STRAE	SURGE	SYREN	TATOW	TESLA	THUMP	TONGA
STRAG	SURGY	SYRUP	TATTS	TESTA	THUYA	TONGS
STRAK	SURLY	SYTHE	TATTY	TESTE	THYME	TONIC
STRAP	SURRA	SYVER	TAUBE	TESTY	THYMY	TONNE
STRAW	SURYA		TAULD	TETRA	TIARA	TON-UP
STRAY	SUTOR	T	TAUNT	TEUCH	TIBET	TONUS
STREW	SUTRA		TAVER	TEUGH	TIBIA	TOOTH
STRIA	SWACK	TABBY	TAWER	TEWEL	TICAL	TOOTS
STRID	SWAGE	TABES	TAWIE	TEWIT	TICCA	TOPAZ
STRIG	SWAIN	TABID	TAWNY	TEXAS	TIDAL	TOPEE
STRIP	SWALE	TABLA	TAWSE	THACK	TIDDY	TOPEK
STROP	SWALY	TABLE	TAXED	THAGI	TIE-UP	TOPER
STROW	SWAMI	TABOO	TAXER	THAIM	TIGER	TOPHI
STROY	SWAMP	TABOR	TAXIS	THANA	TIGHT	TOPIC
STRUM	SWANG	TACET	TAXON	THANE	TIGON	TOQUE
STRUT	SWANK	TACHE	TAXOR	THANK	TILDE	TORAH
STUDY	SWAPT	TACIT	TAXUS	THAWY	TILED	TORAN
STUFF	SWARD	TACKY	TAYRA	THECA	TILER	TORCH
STULL	SWARE	TAFFY	TAZZA	THEEK	TILIA	TORIC
STULM	SWARF	TAFIA	TAZZE	THEFT	TILTH	TORII
STUMP	SWARM	TAIGA	T-CART	THEGN	TIMBO	TORSE
STUNG	SWART	TAINO	TEACH	THEIC	TIMED	TORSK
STUNK	SWASH	TAINT	TEADE	THEIR	TIMER	TORSO
STUNT	SWATH	TAIRA	TEA-HO	THEMA	TIMID	TORUS
STUPA	SWATS	TAISH	TEARY	THEME	TIMON	TOSHY
STUPE	SWAYL	TAKEN	TEASE	THEOW	TINCT	TOSSY
STURE	SWEAL	TAKER	TECHY	THERE	TINEA	TOTAL
STURT	SWEAR	TAKIN	TEDDY	THERM	TINED	TOTEM
STYED	SWEAT	TALAR	TEEND	THESE	TINGE	TOTTY
STYES	SWEDE	TALES	TEENE	THETA	TINNY	TOUCH
STYLE	SWEEL	TALLY	TEENY	THETE	TINTY	TOUGH
STYLO	SWEEP	TALMA	TEETH	THEWS	TIPPY	TOUSE
STYME	SWEER	TALON	TEHEE	THEWY	TIPSY	TOUSY
STYRE	SWEET	TALPA	TEIAN	THICK	TIP-UP	TOUZE
SUAVE	SWEIR	TALUK	TEIND	THIEF	TIRED	TOWEL
SUBAH	SWELL	TALUS	TELAE	THIGH	TIROS	TOWER
SUBER	SWELT	TAMAL	TELEX	THILK	'TISN'T	TOWNY
SUCCI	SWEPT	TAMER	TELIC	THILL	TISRI	TOWSE
SUCRE	SWIFT	TAMIL	TELL'D	THINE	TITAN	TOWSY
SUDAN	SWILL	TAMIN	TELLY	THING	TITER	TOWZE
SUDOR	SWINE	TAMIS	TEMPE	THINK	TITHE	TOXIC
SUDRA	SWING	TAMMY	TEMPI	THIRD	TITLE	TOXIN
SUEDE	SWINK	TANGO	TEMPO	THIRL	TITRE	TOYER
SUETY	SWIPE	TANKA	TEMPT	THOFT	TITTY	TOZIE
SUFIC	SWIRE	TANNA	TEMSE	THOLE	TITUP	TRACE
SUFIS	SWIRL	TANSY	TENCH	THOLI	TIZZY	TRACK
SUGAR	SWISH	TAPEN	TENET	THONG	TOADY	TRACT
SUING	SWISS	TAPER	TENIA	THORN	TOAST	TRADE
SUINT	SWITH	TAPET	TENNE	THORP	TOAZE	TRAGI
SUITE	SWOLN	TAPIR	TENON	THOSE	TOBIT	TRAID
SULCI	SWOON	TAPIS	TENOR	THOTH	TODAY	TRAIK
SULKY	SWOOP	TAPPA	TENSE	THOU'D	TODDY	T-RAIL
SULLY	SWOPT	TARDY	TENTH	THOUS	TOFFY	TRAIL
SUMAC	SWORD	TARGE	TENTY	THOWL	TOGAD	TRAIN
SUMMA	SWORE	TAROK	TENUE	THRAE	TOGED	TRAIT
SUMPH	SWORN	TAROT	TEPEE	THRAW	TOGUE	TRAMP
SUNNA	SWOUN	TARRY	TEPID	THREE	TOING	TRANT
SUNNI	SWUNG	TARSI	TERAI	THREW	TOISE	TRAPE
SUNNY	SYBOE	TARTY	TERAS	THRID	TOKAY	TRASH
SUN-UP	SYBOW	TASAR	TERCE	THROB	TOKEN	TRAWL
SUOMI	SYCEE	TASSE	TEREK	THROE	TOMAN	TREAD

TREAT	TUMPY	ULMIN	UNSOD	VAILS	VILLI	**W**
TRECK	TUNED	ULMUS	UNTAX	VAIRE	VINAL	
TREEN	TUNER	ULNAE	UNTIE	VAIRY	VINCA	WACKE
TREMA	TUNIC	ULNAR	UNTIL	VAKIL	VINER	WACKY
TREND	TUNNY	ULTRA	UNTIN	VALES	VINEW	WADDY
TRESS	TUPIK	ULYIE	UNWED	VALET	VINYL	WADER
TREWS	TUQUE	ULZIE	UNWET	VALID	VIOLA	WAEFU'
TRIAL	TURBO	UMBEL	UNWIT	VALSE	VIPER	WAFER
TRIAS	TURCO	UMBER	UNWON	VALUE	VIRAL	WAGER
TRIBE	TURFY	UMBRA	UNZIP	VALVE	VIREO	WAGES
TRICE	TURKI	UMBRE	UP-BOW	VANED	VIRGA	WAGON
TRICK	TURPS	UMIAK	UPBYE	VAPID	VIRGE	WAHOO
TRIED	TUSKY	UMPTY	UP-END	VAPOR	VIRGO	WAIST
TRIER	TUTOR	UNAPT	UPJET	VARAN	VIRID	WAIVE
TRIES	TUTTI	UNARM	UPLAY	VARDY	VIRTU	WAKED
TRIKE	TUTTY	UNBAG	UPLED	VAREC	VIRUS	WAKEN
TRILL	TWAIN	UNBAR	UPPED	VARIX	VISIE	WAKER
TRINE	TWANG	UNBED	UPPER	VARUS	VISIT	WALER
TRIOR	TWANK	UNBID	UPRUN	VARVE	VISNE	WALLA
TRIPE	TWEAK	UNCAP	UPSEE	VASAL	VISON	WALLY
TRIST	TWEED	UNCLE	UPSET	VASTY	VISOR	WALTY
TRITE	TWEEL	UNCUS	UPSEY	VATIC	VISTA	WALTZ
TROAT	'TWEEN	UNCUT	UPTAK	VAULT	VISTO	WAMED
TROCK	TWEER	UNDAM	UPTIE	VAUNT	VITAL	WAMUS
TROIC	TWEET	UNDÉÉ	URALI	V-BOMB	VITEX	WANED
TROKE	'TWERE	UNDER	URARI	VEALY	VITIS	WANLE
TROLL	TWERP	UNDID	URATE	VEDDA	VITTA	WANLY
TROMP	TWICE	UNDUE	URBAN	VEDIC	VITUS	WANTY
TRONA	TWIER	UNDUG	URDEE	VEENA	VIVAT	WANZE
TRONC	'TWILL	UNETH	UREAL	VEERY	VIVDA	WARRE
TRONE	TWILL	UNFED	UREDO	VEGAN	VIVER	WARST
TROOP	TWILT	UNFIT	URENA	VEHME	VIVES	WARTY
TROPE	TWINE	UNFIX	URENT	VEILY	VIVID	WASHY
TROTH	TWINK	UNGET	URGER	VELAR	VIXEN	WASPY
TROUT	TWINY	UNGOD	URIAL	VELDT	VIZIR	WASTE
TROVE	TWIRE	UNGOT	URINE	VELUM	VIZOR	WATCH
TRUCE	TWIRL	UNGUM	URITE	VENAE	VLACH	WATER
TRUCK	TWIST	UNHAT	URMAN	VENAL	V-NECK	WAUFF
TRULL	TWITE	UNIAT	URNAL	VENGE	VOCAL	WAUGH
TRULY	'TWIXT	UNIFY	URNED	VENOM	VOCES	WAVED
TRUMP	TWOER	UNION	URSON	VENUE	VODKA	WAVER
TRUNK	TWO-UP	UNITE	URSUS	VENUS	VOGIE	WAVEY
TRUSS	TWYER	UNITY	URUBU	VERGE	VOGUE	WAXEN
TRUST	TYCHE	UNKED	USAGE	VERSE	VOICE	WAXER
TRUTH	TYING	UNKET	USEN'T	VERSO	VOILE	WAZIR
TRYER	TYLER	UNKID	USHER	VERST	VOLAE	WEALD
TRY-ON	TYNDE	UNLAW	USNEA	VERTU	VOLAR	WEAMB
TRYST	TYNED	UNLAY	USUAL	VERVE	VOLET	WEARY
TSUGA	TYPAL	UNLED	USURE	VESPA	VOLTA	WEAVE
TUART	TYPHA	UNLET	USURP	VESTA	VOLTE	WEBBY
TUATH	TYPIC	UNLID	USURY	VETCH	VOLVA	WEBER
TUBAE	TYPTO	UNLIT	UTERI	VEXED	VOLVE	WECHT
TUBAL	TYRAN	UNMAN	U-TRAP	VEXER	VOMER	WEDGE
TUBAR	TYRED	UNMEW	UTTER	VEZIR	VOMIT	WEEDY
TUBBY	**U**	UNPAY	U-TUBE	VIAND	VOTER	WEEPY
TUBED		UNPEG	U-TURN	VIBES	VOUCH	WEETE
TUBER	U-BOAT	UNPEN	UVEAL	VIBEX	VOUGE	WEFTE
TUDOR	U-BOLT	UNPIN	UVULA	VICAR	VOULU	WEIGH
TUFFE	UDDER	UNRED	UZBEG	VICHY	VOWED	WEIRD
TUFTY	UGRIC	UNRID	UZBEK	VIDEO	VOWEL	WEISE
TUISM	UH-HUH	UNRIG	**V**	VIEWY	VRAIC	WEIZE
TULIP	UHLAN	UNRIP		VIFDA	VROUW	WELCH
TULLE	UHURU	UNSAY	VACUA	VIGIA	V-SIGN	WELKT
TUMID	UKASE	UNSET	VAGAL	VIGIL	VUGGY	WELLY
TUMMY	ULCER	UNSEW	VAGUE	VILDE	VULVA	WELSH
TUMOR	ULEMA	UNSEX	VAGUS	VILLA	VYING	WENCH

WENNY	WHORE	WODGE	WREST	YAKUT	YOICK	ZIMBI
WERSH	WHORL	WOFUL	WRICK	YAMEN	YOJAN	ZINCO
WHACK	WHORT	WOKEN	WRING	YAPOK	YOKEL	ZINCY
WHALE	WHOSE	WOLOF	WRIST	YAPON	YOKUL	ZINKE
WHANG	WHOSO	WOMAN	WRITE	YARFA	YOLKY	ZINKY
WHARE	WICKY	WOMBY	WROKE	YARTA	YORKS	ZIPPY
WHARF	WIDDY	WOMEN	WRONG	YARTO	YOUNG	ZIZEL
WHAUP	WIDEN	WONGA	WROTE	YAULD	YOURN	ZLOTY
WHAUR	WIDOW	WONKY	WROTH	YAWEY	YOURS	ZOCCO
WHEAT	WIDTH	WOODY	WRUNG	YAWNY	YOURT	ZOEAE
WHEEL	WIELD	WOOED	WRYLY	YBORE	YOUTH	ZOEAL
WHEEN	WIGAN	WOOER		YCLAD	YRAPT	ZOISM
WHELK	WIGHT	WOOFY	**X**	YCLED	YRENT	ZOIST
WHELM	WILLY	WOOLD	X-BODY	YCOND	YRIVD	ZOMBI
WHELP	WINCE	WOOTZ	XEBEC	YDRAD	YSAME	ZONAE
WHERE	WINCH	WOOZY	XENON	YDRED	YTOST	ZONAL
WHICH	WINDS	WORDY	XERES	YEARD	YUCCA	ZONDA
WHIFF	WINDY	WORLD	XERIC	YEARN	YUCKY	ZONED
WHIFT	WINEY	WORMY	XEROX	YEAST	YULAN	ZOOEA
WHILE	WINGE	WORRY	XHOSA	YERBA	YUPON	ZOOID
WHILK	WINGY	WORSE	X-RAYS	YESTY		ZOOKS
WHINE	WINNA	WORST	XYLEM ,	YEVEN	**Z**	ZOPPO
WHINY	WINZE	WORTH	XYLIC	YEWEN	ZABRA	ZORIL
WHIPT	WIPER	WOULD	XYLOL	YEZDI	ZAMBO	ZORRO
WHIRL	WIRED	WOUND	XYLYL	YFERE	ZAMIA	ZOWIE
WHIRR	WIRER	WOVEN	XYRIS	YIELD	ZANJA	ZUPAN
WHISH	WISPY	WOXEN		YINCE	ZANTE	ZYGAL
WHISK	WITAN	WRACK	**Y**	YIPPY	ZANZE	ZYGON
WHISS	WITCH	WRAPT	YACCA	YLIKE	ZEBEC	ZYMIC
WHIST	WITHE	WRAST	YACHT	Y-MOTH	ZEBRA	
WHITE	WITHY	WRATE	YAGER	YOBBO	ZEBUB	
WHITY	WITTY	WRATH	YAHOO	YODEL	ZERDA	
WHIZZ	WIVES	WRAWL	YAHVE	YODLE	ZHOMO	
WHOLE	WIZEN	WREAK	YAHWE	YOGIC	ZIBET	
WHOOP	WODEN	WRECK	YAKKA	YOGIN	ZIGAN	

A	ABORAL	ACCEND	ACKNOW	ADHERE	ADVERB
	ABOUND	ACCENT	ACMITE	ADIEUS	ADVERT
ABACUS	ABRADE	ACCEPT	ACORUS	ADIEUX	ADVICE
ABASED	ABRAID	ACCESS	ACQUIT	ADIPIC	ADVISE
ABATED	ABROAD	ACCITE	ACRAWL	ADJOIN	ADYTUM
ABATIS	ABROMA	ACCLOY	ACROSS	ADJURE	AEDILE
ABATOR	ABRUPT	ACCOIL	ACTING	ADJUST	AEFALD
ABBACY	ABSENT	ACCORD	ACTION	AD-MASS	AENEID
ABBESS	ABSORB	ACCOST	ACTIVE	ADMIRE	AEOLIC
ABDUCE	ABSURD	ACCRUE	ACTUAL	ADNATE	AERATE
ABDUCT	ABULIA	ACCUSE	ACUITY	ADONAI	AERIAL
ABEIGH	ABURST	ACEDIA	ACUMEN	ADONIA	AEROBE
ABIDED	ABUSER	ACETAL	ADAGIO	ADONIC	AETHER
ABJECT	ABVOLT	ACETIC	ADAMAL	ADONIS	AFAWLD
ABJURE	ACACIA	ACETYL	ADAMIC	ADOORS	AFFAIR
ABLAUT	ACAJOU	ACHAGE	ADDEEM	ADORER	AFFECT
ABLAZE	ACANTH	ACHENE	ADDEND	ADREAD	AFFEER
ABLINS	ACARID	ACHING	ADDICT	ADRIFT	AFFIED
ABLOOM	ACARUS	ACHKAN	ADDLED	ADROIT	AFFINE
ABLUSH	ACATER	ACIDIC	ADDOOM	ADSORB	AFFIRM
ABOARD	ACATES	ACINUS	ADDUCE	ADVENE	AFFLUX
ABOLLA	ACCEDE	ACK-ACK	ADDUCT	ADVENT	AFFORD

AFFRAP	ALBANY	AMBLER	ANONYM	ARCANA	ASCIAN
AFFRAY	ALBATA	AMBUSH	ANORAK	ARCANE	ASEITY
AFFRET	ALBEDO	AMELIA	ANOURA	ARCHED	ASGARD
AFGHAN	ALBEIT	AMENDS	ANOXIA	ARCHER	ASHAKE
AFIELD	ALBERT	AMENTA	ANOXIC	ARCHIE	ASHAME
AFLAME	ALBINO	AMERCE	ANSATE	ARCHIL	ASH-BIN
AFLOAT	ALBION	AMIDST	ANSWER	ARCHLY	ASH-CAN
AFRAID	ALBITE	AMNION	ANT-COW	ARCHON	ASHERY
AFREET	ALBUGO	AMOEBA	ANTHEM	ARCING	ASHINE
AFRESH	ALCAIC	AMOMUM	ANTHER	ARCTIC	ASH-KEY
AFRONT	ALCOVE	AMORAL	ANTIAR	ARDENT	ASHLAR
AFTERS	ALDERN	AMORCE	ANTING	ARDOUR	ASHLER
AGADAH	ALDINE	AMORET	ANTLER	AREACH	ASHORE
AGAMIC	ALDOSE	AMOUNT	ANTLIA	AREOLA	ASH-PAN
AGAMID	ALECTO	AMPERE	ANTRUM	AREOLE	ASH-PIT
AGAPAE	ALEGAR	AMRITA	ANUBIS	ARGALA	ASHRAM
AGARIC	ALERCE	AMTMAN	ANURIA	ARGALI	ASKANT
AGAZED	A-LEVEL	AMULET	ANYHOW	ARGAND	ASKARI
AGEING	ALEVIN	AMUSER	ANYWAY	ARGENT	ASLAKE
AGENCY	ALEXIA	AMYLUM	AONIAN	ARGHAN	ASLANT
AGENDA	ALEXIN	AMYTAL	AORIST	ARGIVE	ASLEEP
AGHAST	ALGATE	ANABAS	AORTAL	ARGOSY	ASLOPE
AGLAIA	ALGOID	ANADEM	AORTIC	ARGUER	ASMEAR
AGNAIL	ALHAGI	ANANAS	AOUDAD	ARGUFY	ASPECT
AGNAME	ALIDAD	ANARAK	APACHE	ARGUTE	ASPICK
AGNATE	ALIGHT	ANARCH	APATHY	ARIDLY	ASPIRE
AGNISE	ALIPED ·	ANATTA	APEDOM	ARIGHT	ASPORT
AGOGIC	ALISMA	ANATTO	APEPSY	ARILLI	ASPOUT
AGOING	ALKALI	ANBURY	APERÇU	ARIOSO	ASQUAT
AGONIC	ALL-DAY	ANCHOR	A-PER-SE	ARISEN	ASSAIL
AGOUTA	ALLEGE	ANCILE	APEXES	ARISTA	ASSART
AGOUTI	ALLELE	ANCOME	APHIDS	ARKITE	ASSENT
AGREED	ALLEYS	ANCONA	APHONY	ARKOSE	ASSERT
AGRISE	ALLHID	ANCORA	APHTHA	ARMADA	ASSESS
AGRIZE	ALLICE	ANDEAN	APIARY	ARMFUL	ASSETS
AGRYZE	ALLIED	ANDINE	APICAL	ARMLET	ASSIGN
AGUISE	ALLIES	ANEATH	APICES	ARMORY	ASSIST
AGUISH	ALL-OUT	ANEMIA	APIECE	ARMOUR	ASSIZE
AGUIZE	ALL-RED	ANEMIC	APLOMB	ARMPIT	ASSOIL
AHIMSA	ALLUDE	ANERLY	APNOEA	ARNAUT	ASSORT
AIDANT	ALLURE	ANETIC	APODAL	ARNICA	ASSOTT
AIDFUL	ALMAIN	ANGARY	APOGEE	AROINT	ASSUME
AIDING	ALMANY	ANGICO	APOLLO	AROLLA	ASSURE
AIGLET	ALMERY	ANGINA	APORIA	AROUND	ASTARE
AIKIDO	ALMOND	ANGLED	APOZEM	AROUSE	ASTART
AILING	ALMOST	ANGLER	APPAID	AROYNT	ASTELY
AIR-ARM	ALNAGE	ANGOLA	APPAYD	ARPENT	ASTERN
AIR-BED	ALOGIA	ANGORA	APPEAL	ARRACK	ASTERT
AIR-BUS	ALPACA	ANGUIS	APPEAR	ARRANT	ASTHMA
AIR-CAR	ALPEEN	ANICUT	APPEND	ARREAR	ASTOOP
AIR-GAP	ALPINE	ANIGHT	APPORT	ARRECT	ASTRAL
AIR-GAS	ALPINI	ANIMAL	APPOSE	ARREST	ASTRAY
AIR-GUN	ALPINO	ANIMUS	APTOTE	ARRIDE	ASTREX
AIRILY	ALSIKE	ANKLED	AQUILA	ARRIET	ASTRUT
AIRING	ALTAIR	ANKLET	ARABIC	ARRISH	ASTUTE
AIRMAN	ALTERN	ANKOLE	ARABIN	ARRIVE	ASWARM
AIR-SAC	ALUDEL	ANLACE	ARABIS	ARROBA	ASWING
AIR-SEA	ALUMNA	ANLAGE	ARABLE	ARROWY	ASWIRL
AIRWAY	ALUMNI	ANNEAL	ARAISE	ARROYO	ASWOON
AISLED	ALVINE	ANNEXE	ARALIA	ARSHIN	ASYLUM
AIZOON	ALWAYS	ANNUAL	ARANEA	ARSINE	ATABAL
AJOWAN	AMADOU	ANNULI	ARAYSE	ARTERY	ATABEG
AKIMBO	AMATOL	ANODAL	ARBOUR	ARTFUL	ATABEK
ALALIA	AMAZON	ANODIC	ARBUTE	ARTIST	ATAMAN
ALARUM	AMBAGE	ANOINT	ARCADE	ASCEND	ATAXIA
ALATED	AMBERY	ANOMIE	ARCADY	ASCENT	ATAXIC

ATHENA	AVOCET	BALATA	BARYTA	BEDRAL	BEMOAN
ATHENE	AVOSET	BALBOA	BASALT	BEDROP	BEMOCK
ATHING	AVOUCH	BALDLY	BASELY	BED-SIT	BEMOIL
AT-HOME	AVOURE	BALEEN	BASHAW	BEDUCK	BEMUSE
ATHROB	AVOWAL	BALKER	BASHER	BEDUIN	BENAME
ATOCIA	AVOWED	BALLAD	BASING	BEDUNG	BENDED
ATOKAL	AVOWRY	BALLAN	BASKET	BEDUST	BENDER
ATOMIC	AVULSE	BALLAT	BASNET	BEDYED	BENGAL
ATONAL	AWAKED	BALLED	BASQUE	BEEGAH	BENIGN
ATONER	AWAKEN	BALLET	BASSET	BEENAH	BENNET
ATONIC	AWATCH	BALLOT	BASUTO	BEETLE	BEN-NUT
ATRIAL	AWEARY	BALSAM	BASUTU	BEEVES	BEN-OIL
ATRIUM	A-WEIGH	BALTIC	BATATA	BEFALL	BENUMB
ATROPA	AWHAPE	BAMBOO	BATEAU	BEFANA	BENZAL
ATTACH	AWHEEL	BANANA	BATHER	BEFELL	BENZIL
ATTACK	AWHERE	BANATE	BATHOS	BEFLUM	BENZOL
ATTAIN	AWHILE	BANDAR	BATING	BEFOAM	BENZYL
ATTEND	AWMOUS	BANDED	BATMAN	BEFOOL	BEPELT
ATTENT	AWMRIE	BANDIT	BATTED	BEFORE	BEPITY
ATTEST	AWNING	BANDOG	BATTEN	BEFOUL	BEPUFF
ATTIRE	AWOKEN	BANGED	BATTER	BEGGAR	BERATE
ATTORN	AWRACK	BANGER	BATTLE	BEGGED	BERBER
ATTRAP	AWRONG	BANGLE	BATTUE	BEGIFT	BEREAN
ATTUNE	AWSOME	BANG-UP	BAUBLE	BEGILD	BEREFT
ATWAIN	AXILLA	BANIAN	BAWBEE	BEGIRD	BERLIN
ATWEEL	AYE-AYE	BANISH	BAWBLE	BEGIRT	BERRET
ATWEEN	AZALEA	BANKER	BAWDRY	BEGNAW	BERTHA
ATWIXT	AZIONE	BANKET	BAWLER	BEGONE	BERTHE
AUBADE	AZODYE	BANNAT	BAWLEY	BEGUIN	BESEEM
AUBURN	AZONAL	BANNER	BAXTER	BEGUNK	BESEEN
AUCUBA	AZONIC	BANTAM	BAYARD	BEHALF	BESIDE
AUDILE	AZOTIC	BANTER	BAY-RUM	BEHAVE	BESIGH
AUGEAN	AZRAEL	BANYAN	BAZAAR	BEHEAD	BESING
AUGITE		BANZAI	BEACHY	BEHELD	BESMUT
AUGURY	**B**	BAOBAB	BEACON	BEHEST	BESORT
AUGUST	BAAING	BARBED	BEADED	BEHIND	BESPAT
AUKLET	BAALIM	BARBEL	BEADLE	BEHOLD	BESPED
AUMAIL	BABBLE	BARBER	BEAGLE	BEHOOF	BESPIT
AUMBRY	BABBLY	BARBET	BEAKED	BEHOTE	BESPOT
AUNTER	BABISM	BARDED	BEAKER	BEHOVE	BESTAR
AUNTIE	BABIST	BARDIC	BEAMER	BEHOWL	BESTIR
AURATE	BABLAH	BAREGE	BEARER	BEJADE	BESTOW
AUREUS	BABOON	BARELY	BEATEN	BEJANT	BESTUD
AURIFY	BACKED	BARFLY	BEATER	BEKISS	BESUNG
AURIGA	BACKET	BARFUL	BEAT-UP	BELACE	BETAKE
AURIST	BADDIE	BARGEE	BEAUTY	BELAMY	BETEEM
AURORA	BADGER	BARISH	BEAVER	BELATE	BETHEL
AUROUS	BADMAN	BARITE	BEBUNG	BELAUD	BETIDE
AUSSIE	BAETYL	BARIUM	BECALL	BELDAM	BETIME
AUSTER	BAFFLE	BARKEN	BECALM	BELFRY	BETOIL
AUSTIN	BAGFUL	BARKER	BECAME	BELGIC	BETONY
AUTEUR	BAGGED	BARLEY	BECKET	BELIAL	BETOOK
AUTHOR	BAGGIT	BARMAN	BECKON	BELIED	BETOSS
AUTISM	BAGMAN	BARNEY	BECOME	BELIEF	BETRAY
AUTUMN	BAGNIO	BAROCK	BECURL	BELIKE	BETRIM
AVAILE	BAGUIO	BARONY	BEDASH	BELIVE	BETROD
AVATAR	BAGWIG	BARQUE	BEDAUB	BELLOW	BETTED
AVAUNT	BAILEE	BARRAT	BEDAZE	BELONG	BETTER
AVENGE	BAILER	BARRED	BEDBUG	BELOVE	BETTOR
AVENUE	BAILEY	BARREL	BEDDED	BELTED	BETULA
AVERSE	BAILIE	BARREN	BEDDER	BELUGA	BEULAH
AVESTA	BAIRAM	BARRET	BEDECK	BEMAUL	BEURRE
AVIARY	BAJREE	BARROW	BEDELL	BEMBEX	BEWAIL
AVIATE	BAKERY	BARTER	BED-KEY	BEMEAN	BEWARE
AVIDLY	BAKING	BARTON	BEDLAM	BEMETE	BEWEEP
AVITAL	BALAAM	BARYON	BEDPAN	BEMIRE	BEWEPT

BEWRAY	BIZONE	BOHUNK	BOTTLE	BRETON	BUGOUT
BEYOND	BLADED	BOILED	BOTTOM	BREVET	BUKSHI
BEZANT	BLAGUE	BOILER	BOUCLÉ	BREWER	BULBAR
BEZOAR	BLAMED	BOLDEN	BOUFFE	BREWIS	BULBED
BEZZLE	BLANCH	BOLDLY	BOUGHT	BRIARD	BULBIL
BHARAL	BLANKY	BOLERO	BOUGIE	BRIBER	BULBUL
BHARAT	BLASHY	BOLIDE	BOULLE	BRICKY	BULGAR
BHISTI	BLAZER	BOLLED	BOUNCE	BRIDAL	BULGER
BIASED	BLAZES	BOLLEN	BOUNCY	BRIDGE	BULIMY
BIAXAL	BLAZON	BOLSHY	BOUNTY	BRIDIE	BULKER
BIBBER	BLEACH	BOLTER	BOURNE	BRIDLE	BULLER
BICEPS	BLEAKY	BOMBAX	BOURSE	BRIERY	BULLET
BICKER	BLEARY	BOMBAY	BOUTON	BRIGHT	BUMALO
BIDDEN	BLENCH	BOMBER	BOVATE	BRIGUE	BUM-BEE
BIDDER	BLENDE	BOMBYX	BOVINE	BRIONY	BUMBLE
BIDENT	BLENNY	BONBON	BOW-BOY	BRISKY	BUMKIN
BIDING	BLIGHT	BONDED	BOWERY	BRITON	BUMMED
BIELDY	BLIMEY	BONDER	BOWFIN	BROACH	BUMMER
BIFFIN	BLINKS	BONDUC	BOW-LEG	BROCHÉ	BUMMLE
BIFOLD	BLITHE	BONING	BOWLER	BROGAN	BUMPER
BIFORM	BLONDE	BONITO	BOWMAN	BROGUE	BUNCHY
BIGAMY	BLOODY	BONNET	BOW-OAR	BROKEN	BUNDLE
BIG-BUD	BLOOMY	BONNIE	BOWPOT	BROKER	BUNGLE
BIGGER	BLOTCH	BONSAI	BOW-SAW	BROLLY	BUNION
BIGGIN	BLOTTO	BONXIE	BOWSER	BROMIC	BUNKER
BIGWIG	BLOTTY	BONZER	BOWWOW	BRONCO	BUNKUM
BIJOUX	BLOUSE	BOODLE	BOWYER	BRONZE	BUNNIA
BIKINI	BLOWED	BOOHOO	BOX-BED	BRONZY	BUNSEN
BILIAN	BLOWER	BOOKIE	BOXCAR	BROOCH	BUNTED
BILKER	BLOWZE	BOOMER	BOX-DAY	BROODY	BUNTER
BILLED	BLOWZY	BOOTED	BOXFUL	BROOMY	BUNYIP
BILLET	BLUDGE	BOOTEE	BOXING	BROOSE	BURBLE
BILLIE	BLUDIE	BOÖTES	BOYAUX	BROUGH	BURBOT
BILLON	BLUGGY	BOOZED	BOYISH	BROWNY	BURDEN
BILLOW	BLUIDY	BOOZER	BRACER	BROWSE	BURDIE
BILLY-O	BLUING	BOPEEP	BRAHMA	BROWST	BUREAU
BIMANA	BLUISH	BORAGE	BRAHMI	BRUISE	BURELL
BINARY	BLUNGE	BORANE	BRAIDE	BRUMAL	BURGEE
BINATE	BOATER	BORATE	BRAINY	BRUMBY	BURGLE
BINDER	BOBBED	BORDAR	BRAIRD	BRUNCH	BURGOO
BINGLE	BOBBIN	BORDEL	BRAISE	BRUNET	BURHEL
BIOGEN	BOBBLE	BORDER	BRAIZE	BRUSHY	BURIAL
BIOPSY	BOBCAT	BOREAL	BRANCH	BRUTAL	BURIED
BIOTIC	BOB-FLY	BOREAS	BRANDY	BRUTUS	BURITI
BIOTIN	BOBWIG	BOREEN	BRANKS	BRYONY	BURKHA
BIRDIE	BOCAGE	BORIDE	BRANKY	BUBBLE	BURLAP
BIREME	BODACH	BORING	BRANLE	BUBBLY·	BURLER
BIRKEN	BODDLE	BORREL	BRANNY	BUCCAL	BURMAN
BIRKIE	BODEGA	BORROW	BRASHY	BUCKER	BURNED
BIRLER	BODGER	BORSCH	BRASSY	BUCKET	BURNER
BIRSLE	BODGIE	BORZOI	BRAVOS	BUCKIE	BURNET
BISECT	BODICE	BOSBOK	BRAWLY	BUCKLE	BURREL
BISHOP	BODIED	BOSCHE	BRAWNY	BUCKRA	BURROW
BISMAR	BODIES	BOSHTA	BRAZEN	BUDDED	BURSAE
BISQUE	BODILY	BOSKER	BRAZIL	BUDDHA	BURSAL
BISSON	BODING	BOSKET	BREACH	BUDDLE	BURSAR
BISTER	BODKIN	BOSSED	BREAST	BUDGER	BURSCH
BISTRE	BODRAG	BOSTON	BREATH	BUDGET	BURSEA
BISTRO	BOFFIN	BOTANY	BREECH	BUDGIE	BURTON
BITCHY	BOFORS	BOTCHY	BREEKS	BUFFER	BUS-BAR
BITING	BOGEYS	BOTFLY	BREESE	BUFFET	BUSBOY
BITTED	BOGGLE	BOTHAN	BREEZE	BUGGED	BUSHED
BITTEN	BOGIES	BOTHER	BREEZY	BUGGER	BUSHEL
BITTER	BOGOAK	BOTHIE	BREGMA	BUGLER	BUSIED
BITTIE	BOGONG	BOTONÉ	BREHON	BUGLET	BUSILY
BIVIUM	BOG-ORE	BO-TREE	BRENNE	BUGONG	BUSKED

BUSKER	CAGING	CANTAB	CASSIA	CERCUS	CHEVEN
BUSKET	CAHOOT	CANTAR	CASSIS	CEREAL	CHEVIN
BUSKIN	CAIMAC	CANTER	CASTED	CEREUS	CHEWET
BUSMAN	CAIMAN	CANTHI	CASTER	CERIPH	CHIASM
BUSTED	CAIQUE	CANTLE	CASTLE	CERISE	CHIAUS
BUSTEE	CAJOLE	CANTON	CASTOR	CERITE	CHIBOL
BUSTER	CAKING	CANTOR	CASUAL	CERIUM	CHICHA
BUSTLE	CALAMI	CANTOS	CATALO	CERMET	CHI-CHI
BUST-UP	CALASH	CANTUS	CATCHY	CEROON	CHICLE
BUTANE	CALCAR	CANUCK	CATENA	CERRIS	CHIDED
BUT-END	CALCED	CANVAS	CAT-GUT	CERTES	CHIDER
BUTENE	CALCES	CANYON	CATION	CERUSE	CHIELD
BUTLER	CALCIC	CAPITA	CATKIN	CERVIX	CHIGOE
BUTTED	CALEFY	CAPLIN	CAT-LAP	CESTUI	CHIGRE
BUTTER	CALICO	CAPOTE	CATNAP	CESTUS	CHIKOR
BUTTLE	CALIGO	CAPPED	CATNEP	CESURA	CHILLI
BUTTON	CALIPH	CAPRIC	CATNIP	CESURE	CHILLY
BUYING	CALKER	CAPSID	CATSUP	CETANE	CHIMER
BUZZER	CALKIN	CAPTOR	CATTLE	CHA-CHA	CHINAR
BY-BLOW	CALLER	CARACK	CAUCUS	CHACMA	CHINCH
BYELAW	CALLET	CARACT	CAUDAL	CHAFER	CHINKS
BY-FORM	CALLID	CARAFE	CAUDEX	CHAFFY	CHINKY
BYGONE	CALLOW	CARANX	CAUDLE	CHAGAN	CHINTZ
BY-LANE	CALL-UP	CARAPA	CAUGHT	CHAISE	CHIPPY
BYLINE	CALLUS	CARBON	CAUKER	CHALAN	CHI-RHO
BY-NAME	CALMED	CARBOY	CAULES	CHALET	CHIRPY
BYPASS	CALMLY	CARDER	CAULIS	CHALKY	CHISEL
BY-PAST	CALPAC	CAREEN	CAUSAL •	CHANCE	CHITAL
BYPATH	CALQUE	CAREER	CAUSER	CHANCY	CHITIN
BY-PLAY	CALVER	CARESS	CAUSEY	CHANGE	CHITON
BY-PLOT	CALVES	CARFAX	CAUTEL	CHAPEL	CHITTY
BYRLAW	CALXES	CARFOX	CAUTER	CHAPPY	CHIVVY
BYRNIE	CAMASH	CARIBE	CAVASS	CHARAS	CHOICE
BYROAD	CAMASS	CARICA	CAVEAT	CHARED	CHOKER
BYROOM	CAMBER	CARIES	CAVERN	CHARGE	CHOLER
BYSSAL	CAMEOS	CARINA	CAVIAR	CHARIS	CHOLIC
BYSSUS	CAMERA	CARLEY	CAVING	CHARON	CHOOSE
BY-TIME	CAMESE	CARLOT	CAVITY	CHARRY	CHOOSY
BYWORD	CAMION	CARMAN	CAVORT	CHARTA	CHOPIN
BY-WORK	CAMISE	CARNAL	CAWING	CHASER	CHOPPY
BYZANT	CAMLET	CARNET	CAWKER	CHASMY	CHORAL
C	CAMPER	CARNEY	CAXTON	CHASSE	CHOREA
	CAMPLE	CARPAL	CAYMAN	CHASSÉ	CHOREE
CABALA	CAMPUS	CARPEL	CAYUSE	CHASTE	CHORIA
CABANA	CAMSHO	CARPER	CECILS	CHATON	CHORIC
CABIRI	CANADA	CARPET	CECITY	CHATTA	CHORUS
CABMAN	CANAPÉ	CARPUS	CEDARN	CHATTY	CHOSEN
CABRIE	CANARD	CARRAT	CEDULA	CHAUNT	CHOUGH
CABRIT	CANARY	CARRON	CELERY	CHECKY	CHOUSE
CACHET	CANCAN	CARROT	CELIAC	CHEEKY	CHOWRY
CACHOU	CANCEL	CARTEL	CELLAR	CHEERO	CHRISM
CACKLE	CANCER	CARTER	CELLED	CHEERS	CHRIST
CACOON	CANDID	CARTON	CELTIC	CHEERY	CHROMA
CACTUS	CANDIE	CARVED	CEMBRA	CHEESE	CHROME
CADDIE	CANDLE	CARVEL	CEMENT	CHEESY	CHROMO
CADDIS	CANFUL	CARVEN	CENSER	CHEMIC	CHUBBY
CADENT	CANGUE	CARVER	CENSOR	CHEMMY	CHUFFY
CADGER	CANINE	CASBAH	CENSUS	CHENAR	CHUKAR
CADUAC	CANING	CASEIN	CENTAL	CHEQUE	CHUKKA
CAECAL	CANKER	CASERN	CENTER	CHEQUY	CHUKOR
CAECUM	CANNED	CASHAW	CENTOS	CHERRY	CHUMMY
CAESAR	CANNEL	CASHEW	CENTRE	CHERTY	CHUNKY
CAFARD	CANNER	CASING	CENTRY	CHERUB	CHURCH
CAFFRE	CANNON	CASINO	CENTUM	CHERUP	CHYPRE
CAFILA	CANNOT	CASKET	CERATE	CHESIL	CICADA
CAFTAN	CANOPY	CASQUE	CERCAL	CHESTY	CICALA

C6

CICELY	CLODDY	COGGER	CON-MAN	COSIER	CRAYER
CICERO	CLODLY	COGGIE	CONNED	COSILY	CRAYON
CICUTA	CLOGGY	COGGLE	CONNER	COSINE	CRAZED
CIDERY	CLONIC	COGGLY	CONOID	COSMIC	CREACH
CIERGE	CLONUS	COGNAC	CONSUL	COSMOS	CREAGH
CILICE	CLOOTS	CO-HEIR	CONTRA	COSSET	CREAKY
CILIUM	CLOQUÉ	COHERE	CONVEX	COSTAL	CREAMY
CIMIER	CLOSED	COHORN	CONVEY	COSTER	CREANT
CINDER	CLOSER	COHORT	CONVOY	COSTLY	CREASE
CINEMA	CLOSET	COHUNE	COOING	COSTUS	CREASY
CINEOL	CLOTHE	COIGNE	COOKER	COTEAU	CREATE
CINQUE	CLOTHO	COINER	COOKIE	COTISE	CRÊCHE
CIPHER	CLOTHS	COJOIN	COOLER	COTTAR	CREDAL
CIPPUS	CLOTTY	COLDLY	COOLIE	COTTED	CREDIT
CIRCAR	CLOUDY	COLLAR	COOLLY	COTTER	CREEKY
CIRCLE	CLOUGH	COLLET	COOLTH	COTTON	CREEPY
CIRCUS	CLOVEN	COLLIE	COONTY	COTTUS	CREESE
CIRQUE	CLOVER	COLLOP	COOPER	COTWAL	CREESH
CIRRUS	CLOYED	COLMAR	COOSER	COTYLE	CREMOR
CISTED	CLUMPS	COLONY	COPECK	COUCAL	CRENEL
CISTIC	CLUMPY	COLOUR	COPIED	COUGAR	CREOLE
CISTUS	CLUMSY	COLTER	COPIER	COULÉE	CREPON
CITESS	CLUNCH	COLUGO	COPING	COUNTY	CRESOL
CITHER	CLUPEA	COLUMN	COPITA	COUPED	CRESSY
CITOLE	CLUSIA	COLURE	COPPED	COUPEE	CRETAN
CITRIC	CLUTCH	COMARB	COPPER	COUPER	CRETIC
CITRIN	CNICUS	COMART	COPPIN	COUPLE	CRETIN
CITRON	CNIDAE	COMATE	COPPLE	COUPON	CREWEL
CITRUS	COACHY	COMBAT	COPTIC	COURSE	CRIANT
CIVICS	COAITA	COMBED	COPULA	COUSIN	CRIBLÉ
CIVISM	COARSE	COMBER	COQUET	COUTER	CRICKY
CLAGGY	COATEE	COMEDO	CORBAN	COUTIL	CRIKEY
CLAMMY	COAXEN	COMEDY	CORBEL	COVERT	CRIMPY
CLAQUE	COBALT	COMELY	CORBIE	COVING	CRINAL
CLARET	COBBER	COMFIT	CORDED	COVYNE	CRINGE
CLARTY	COBBLE	COMING	CORDON	COWAGE	CRIPES
CLASSY	COBNUT	COMITY	CORIUM	COWARD	CRISES
CLATCH	COBRIC	COMMIE	CORKED	COWBOY	CRISIS
CLAUSE	COBURG	COMMIS	CORKER	COWISH	CRISPY
CLAVER	COBWEB	COMMIT	CORKIR	COWLED	CRISTA
CLAVES	COCCID	COMMIX	CORMUS	COW-PEA	CRITIC
CLAVIE	COCCUS	COMMON	CORNEA	COWPOX	CROAKY
CLAVIS	COCCYX	COMMOT	CORNED	COWRIE	CROCHE
CLAWED	COCHIN	COMOSE	CORNEL	COYISH	CROCOS
CLAYED	COCKED	COMOUS	CORNER	COYOTE	CRONET
CLAYEY	COCKER	COMPEL	CORNET	COZIER	CROPPY
CLEAVE	COCKET	COMPLY	CORNUA	CRABBY	CROTAL
CLECHÉ	COCKLE	COMPOT	CORNUS	CRADLE	CROTCH
CLENCH	COCKSY	COMSAT	CORODY	CRAFTY	CROTON
CLERGY	COCK-UP	CONCHA	CORONA	CRAGGY	CROUCH
CLERIC	COCOON	CONCHY	COROZO	CRAMBO	CROUPE
CLEUCH	CODDED	CONCUR	CORPSE	CRAMPY	CROUPY
CLEUGH	CODDLE	CONDER	CORPUS	CRANCH	CROUSE
CLEVER	CODGER	CONDOM	CORRAL	CRANIA	CROÛTE
CLEVIS	CODIFY	CONDOR	CORRIE	CRANKY	CROWED
CLICHÉ	CODIST	CONFAB	CORSET	CRANNY	CRUCES
CLIENT	CODLIN	CONFER	CORTES	CRANTS	CRUDDY
CLIFFY	COELOM	CONFIT	CORTEX	CRASES	CRUELS
CLIFTY	COERCE	CONFIX	CORVEE	CRASIS	CRUISE
CLIMAX	COEVAL	CONGEE	CORVES	CRATCH	CRUIVE
CLINCH	COFFEE	CONGER	CORVET	CRATER	CRUMBY
CLINGY	COFFER	CONGOU	CORVUS	CRATUR	CRUMEN
CLINIC	COFFIN	CONIMA	CORYMB	CRAVAT	CRUMMY
CLIQUE	COFFLE	CONINE	CORYZA	CRAVEN	CRUMPY
CLOACA	COGENT	CONJEE	COSECH	CRAVER	CRUNCH
CLOCHE	COGGED	CONKER	COSHER	CRAWLY	CRURAL

CRUSET	CURSER	DAGOES	DEALER	DEHORT	DETAIL
CRUSIE	CURSOR	DAHLIA	DEANER	DE-ICER	DETAIN
CRUSTA	CURSUS	DAIDLE	DEARIE	DEIFIC	DETECT
CRUSTY	CURTAL	DAIKER	DEARLY	DEJECT	DETENT
CRUTCH	CURTLY	DAIMEN	DEARTH	DELATE	DETEST
CRUXES	CURTSY	DAIMIO	DEASIL	DELETE	DETORT
CRYING	CURULE	DAIMIO	DEATHY	DELIAN	DETOUR
CRYPTO	CURVED	DAKOIT	DEBARK	DELICE	DEUCED
CUBAGE	CURVET	DALILA	DEBASE	DELICT	DEUTON
CUBBED	CUSCUS	DALLOP	DEBATE	DELUDE	DEVALL
CUBICA	CUSHAT	DAMAGE	DEBILE	DELUGE	DEVEST
CUBISM	CUSPED	DAMASK	DEBOSH	DELVER	DEVICE
CUBIST	CUSPID	DAMMAR	DEBRIS	DELVES	DEVISE
CUBOID	CUSSED	DAMMED	DEBTED	DEMAIN	DEVOID
CUCKOO	CUSSER	DAMNED	DEBTEE	DEMAND	DEVOIR
CUDDIE	CUSTOM	DAMPEN	DEBTOR	DEMARK	DEVOTE
CUDDLE	CUSTOS	DAMPER	DEBUNK	DEMEAN	DEVOUR
CUDGEL	CUTCHA	DAMPLY	DECADE	DEMENT	DEVOUT
CUEIST	CUTLER	DAMSEL	DECAMP	DEMIES	DEVVEL
CUERPO	CUTLET	DAMSON	DECANE	DEMISE	DEWALI
CUESTA	CUT-OFF	DANCER	DECANI	DEMISS	DEWANI
CUFFIN	CUT-OUT	DANDER	DECANT	DEMOTE	DEW-BOW
CUFFLE	CUTTER	DANDLE	DECARB	DEMURE	DEWITT
CUISSE	CUTTLE	DANGER	DECEIT	DENARY	DEWLAP
CUITER	CUTTOE	DANGLE	DECENT	DENGUE	DEXTER
CULDEE	CYANIC	DANIEL	DECERN	DENIAL	DHARMA
CULLER	CYANIN	DANISH	DECIDE	DENIED	DHARNA
CULLET	CYBELE	DANITE	DÉCIME	DENIER	DHOOLY
CULLIS	CYCLER	DANTON	DECKED	DENNET	DHURRA
CULMEN	CYCLIC	DAPHNE	DECKER	DENOTE	DIACID
CULTCH	CYCLUS	DAPPER	DECKLE	DENTAL	DIADEM
CULTER	CYESIS	DAPPLE	DECOCT	DENTEL	DIAMYL
CULTIC	CYGNET	DARGLE	DECODE	DENTEX	DIAPER
CULTUS	CYMBAL	DARING	DECOKE	DENTIL	DIARCH
CULVER	CYMOID	DARKEN	DECREE	DENUDE	DIATOM
CUMBER	CYMOSE	DARKEY	DECTRA	DEODAR	DIAXON
CUMMER	CYMOUS	DARKLE	DECURY	DEPART	DIBBED
CUMMIN	CYMRIC	DARKLY	DEDANS	DEPEND	DIBBER
CUMULI	CYNIPS	DARNEL	DEDUCE	DEPICT	DIBBLE
CUNEAL	CYPHER	DARNER	DEDUCT	DEPLOY	DICAST
CUNNER	CYPRID	DARTER	DEE-JAY	DEPONE	DICING
CUPFUL	CYPRIS	DARTLE	DEEMED	DEPORT	DICKER
CUPMAN	CYPRUS	DARTRE	DEEPEN	DEPOSE	DICKEY
CUPOLA	CYSTIC	DASHER	DEEPIE	DEPUTE	DICTUM
CUPPED	CYSTID	DASSIE	DEEPLY	DEPUTY	DIDDLE
CUPPER	CYTASE	DATARY	DEFACE	DERAIL	DIEDRE
CUPRIC	CYTODE	DATIVE	DEFAME	DERATE	DIESEL
CUP-TIE	CYTOID	DATURA	DEFEAT	DERHAM	DIESIS
CUPULE		DAUBER	DEFECT	DERIDE	DIETER
CURACY	**D**	DAUNER	DEFEND	DERIVE	DIFFER
CURARA		DAUTIE	DEFIED	DERMAL	DIGAMY
CURARE	DABBED	DAWDLE	DEFIER	DERMIC	DIGEST
CURARI	DABBER	DAWISH	DEFILE	DERMIS	DIGGED
CURATE	DABBLE	DAWNER	DEFINE	DERNLY	DIGGER
CURDLE	DACITE	DAWTIE	DEFLEX	DERRIS	DIGLOT
CURFEW	DACKER	DAY-BED	DEFORM	DESALT	DIKAST
CURIET	DACOIT	DAY-BOY	DEFOUL	DESCRY	DIK-DIK
CURIOS	DACTYL	DAY-FLY	DEFRAY	DESERT	DIKTAT
CURIUM	DADDLE	DAY-OLD	DEFTLY	DESIGN	DILATE
CURLED	DADOES	DAZZLE	DEFUSE	DESIRE	DILDOE
CURLER	DAEDAL	DEACON	DEFUZE	DESIST	DILUTE
CURLEW	DAEMON	DEADEN	DÉGAGÉ	DESMAN	DIMBLE
CURNEY	DAFTIE	DEADER	DEGRAS	DESMID	DIMITY
CURPEL	DAFTLY	DEADLY	DEGREE	DESORB	DIMMED
CURSAL	DAGGER	DEAFEN	DEGUST	DESPOT	DIMMER
CURSED	DAGGLE	DEAFLY	DEHORN	DETACH	DIMPLE
	DAGOBA				

DIMPLY	DOCILE	DORSAL	DROMON	DUTIED	EGERIA
DINDLE	DOCKEN	DORSEL	DROMOS	DUYKER	EGESTA
DINFUL	DOCKER	DORSER	DRONGO	DYADIC	EGG-BOX
DINGED	DOCKET	DORSUM	DROPSY	DYBBUK	EGG-CAS
DINGER	DOCTOR	DORTER	DROSKY	DYEING	EGGCUP
DINGES	DODDED	DOSAGE	DROSSY	DYNAMO	EGGERY
DINGEY	DODDER	DOSI-DO	DROUTH	DYNAST	EGGLER
DINGHY	DODGEM	DOSSAL	DROVER	DYSURY	EGGNOG
DINGLE	DODGER	DOSSEL	DROWSE	DYVOUR	EGOISM
DINGUS	DODKIN	DOSSER	DROWSY	DZEREN	EGOIST
DINKUM	DODMAN	DOSSIL	DRUDGE		EGOITY
DINNED	DODOES	DOTAGE	DRUMLY	E	EGRESS
DINNER	DOFFER	DOTANT	DRUPEL		EIDENT
DINNLE	DOG-APE	DOTARD	DRY-FLY	EADISH	EIDOLA
DIODON	DOGATE	DOTING	DRYING	EAGLET	EIGHTH
DIPLEX	DOG-BEE	DOTISH	DRYISH	EARBOB	EIGHTY
DIPLOE	DOG-EAR	DOTTED	DRY-ROT	EAR-CAP	EIRACK
DIPLON	DOG-END	DOTTLE	DUALIN	EARING	EISELL
DIP-NET	DOG-FOX	DOUBLE	DUBBED	EARLAP	EITHER
DIPNOI	DOGGED	DOUBLY	DUBBIN	EARNER	EJECTA
DIPODY	DOGGER	DOUCET	DUCKER	EARTHY	ELAEIS
DIPOLE	DOG-HEP	DOUCHE	DUDDER	EARWAX	ELANCE
DIPPED	DOG-HIP	DOUGHT	DUDEEN	EARWIG	ELANET
DIPPER	DOG-LEG	DOUGHY	DUDISH	EASILY	ELAPSE
DIPSAS	DOILED	DOUSER	DUDISM	EASSEL	ELATER
DIRDUM	DOITED	DOUTER	DUEFUL	EASSIL	E-LAYER
DIRECT	DOITIT	DOWLAS	DUELLO	EASTER	ELCHEE
DIRHAM	DOLENT	DOWNED	DUENNA	EATAGE	ELDEST
DIRHEM	DOLIUM	DOWSER	DUETTO	EATCHE	ELDING
DIRIGE	DOLLAR	DOWSET	DUFFEL	EATHLY	ELENCH
DIRNDL	DOLLOP	DOYLEY	DUFFER	EATING	ELEVEN
DISARM	DOLMAN	DOZING	DUFFLE	ECARTÉ	ELEVON
DISBAR	DOLMEN	DRABBY	DUGONG	ECBOLE	ELFISH
DISBUD	DOLOUR	DRABLY	DUGOUT	ECHOED	ELICIT
DISCUS	DOMAIN	DRACHM	DUIKER	ECHOER	ELIXIR
DISHED	DOMETT	DRAFFY	DUKERY	ECHOES	ELLOPS
DISMAL	DOMINO	DRAFTS	DULCET	ECHOIC	ELODEA
DISMAN	DONARY	DRAGEE	DUMBLY	ÉCLAIR	ELOHIM
DISMAY	DONATE	DRAGON	DUMDUM	ECLOSE	ELOIGN
DISOWN	DONJON	DRAPED	DUMOSE	ECTOPY	ELOPER
DISPEL	DONKEY	DRAPER	DUMOUS	ECTYPE	ELSHIN
DISTAL	DONNAT	DRAPET	DUMPLE	ÉCURIE	ELTCHI
DISTIL	DONNED	DRAPPY	DUN-COW	ECZEMA	ELUANT
DISUSE	DONNEE	DRAUNT	DUNDER	EDDAIC	ELUATE
DITHER	DONNOT	DRAWEE	DUNITE	EDDIED	ELUTOR
DITONE	DONSIE	DRAWER	DUNKER	EDDISH	ELVISH
DITTAY	DONZEL	DRAZEL	DUNLIN	EDDOES	ELYTRA
DITTED	DOOCOT	DREAMT	DUNLOP	EDENIC	EMBAIL
DITTIT	DOODAD	DREAMY	DUNNED	EDGING	EMBALE
DITTOS	DOODAH	DREARY	DUPERY	EDIBLE	EMBALL
DIVALI	DOODLE	DREDGE	DUPLET	EDITOR	EMBALM
DIVERS	DOOKET	DREGGY	DUPLEX	EEL-SET	EMBANK
DIVERT	DOOLIE	DREICH	DURANT	EERILY	EMBARK
DIVEST	DOOMED	DRENCH	DURBAR	EFFACE	EMBASE
DIVIDE	DOPING	DRESSY	DURDUM	EFFECT	EMBLEM
DIVINE	DOPPER	DRIEST	DURESS	EFFEIR	EMBLIC
DIVING	DOPPIE	DRIFTY	DURGAN	EFFERE	EMBODY
DIWALI	DORADO	DRIVEL	DURHAM	EFFETE	EMBOIL
DIZAIN	DOR-BUG	DRIVEN	DURIAN	EFFIGY	EMBOLY
DJINNI	DORCAS	DRIVER	DURING	EFFLUX	EMBOSS
DOABLE	DOR-FLY	DROGER	DURION	EFFORT	EMBRUE
DOATER	DORIAN	DROGUE	DURRIE	EFFUSE	EMBRYO
DOBBIE	DORISE	DROICH	DUSKEN	EFTEST	EMBUSY
DOBBIN	DORISM	DROLLY	DUSKLY	EGALLY	EMERGE
DOCENT	DORMER	DROMIC	DUSTER	EGENCE	EMESIS
DOCETE	DORMIE	DROMOI	DUST-UP	EGENCY	EMETIC

EMETIN
EMEUTE
EMIGRE
EMMESH
EMPALE
EMPERY
EMPIRE
EMPLOY
EMPUSA
EMPUSE
EMULGE
EMUNGE
EMYDES
ENABLE
ENAMEL
ENARCH
ENCAGE
ENCALM
ENCAMP
ENCASE
ENCASH
ENCAVE
ENCODE
ENCORE
ENCYST
END-ALL
ENDART
ENDEAR
ENDING
ENDIVE
ENDOSS
ENDURE
ENERGY
ENERVE
ENFACE
ENFIRE
ENFOLD
ENFREE
ENGAGE
ENGAOL
ENGILD
ENGINE
ENGIRD
ENGIRT
ENGLUT
ENGORE
ENGRAM
ENGULF
ENHALO
ENIGMA
ENISLE
ENJAMB
ENJOIN
ENLACE
ENLARD
ENLEVE
ENLINK
ENLIST
ENLOCK
ENMESH
ENMITY
ENMOVE
ENNEAD
ENNUYE
ENODAL
ENOSIS

ENOUGH
ENRACE
ENRAGE
ENRANK
ENRAPT
ENRICH
ENRING
ENROBE
ENROLL
ENROOT
ENSATE
ENSEAL
ENSEAM
ENSEAR
ENSIGN
ENSILE
ENSOUL
ENSUED
ENSURE
ENTAIL
ENTAME
ENTERA
ENTICE
ENTIRE
ENTITY
ENTOIL
ENTOMB
ENTRAP
ENTREE
ENVIER
ENWALL
ENWIND
ENWOMB
ENWRAP
ENZONE
ENZYME
EOCENE
EOLIAN
EOLITH
EONISM
EOTHEN
EOZOIC
EOZOON
EPARCH
EPAULE
EPEIRA
EPHEBE
EPHEBI
EPICAL
EPIGON
EPIZOA
EPOCHA
EPODIC
EPONYM
EPOPEE
EPULIS
EQUATE
EQUINE
EQUIPE
EQUITY
ERASED
ERASER
ERBIUM
EREBUS
EREMIC
ERENOW

ERGATE
ERG-TEN
ERIACH
ERINYS
ERMINE
ERODED
EROTIC
ERRAND
ERRANT
ERRATA
ERRING
ERSATZ
ERYNGO
ESCAPE
ESCARP
ESCHAR
ESCHEW
ESCORT
ESCROL
ESCROW
ESCUDO
ESKIMO
ESLOIN
ESNECY
ESPIAL
ESPIED
ESPRIT
ESSENE
ESSIVE
ESSOIN
ESTATE
ESTEEM
ESTRAY
ETALON
ETCHER
ETERNE
ETHANE
ETHENE
ETHICS
ETHINE
ETHIOP
ETHNIC
ETNEAN
ETRIER
ETYMIC
ETYMON
ETYPIC
EUCAIN
EUCHRE
EULOGY
EUNUCH
EUPHON
EUREKA
EUTAXY
EVEJAR
EVENLY
EVILLY
EVINCE
EVOLUE
EVOLVE
EVULSE
EXAMEN
EXARCH
EXCAMB
EXCEED
EXCEPT

EXCESS
EXCIDE
EXCISE
EXCITE
EXCUSE
EXEDRA
EXEMPT
EXEQUY
EXEUNT
EXHALE
EXHORT
EXHUME
EXILIC
EXITED
EXODIC
EXODUS
EXOGEN
EXOMIS
EXOPOD
EXOTIC
EXPAND
EXPECT
EXPEND
EXPERT
EXPIRE
EXPIRY
EXPORT
EXPOSE
EXPOSÉ
EXPUGN
EXSECT
EXSERT
EXTANT
EXTASY
EXTEND
EXTENT
EXTERN
EXTINE
EXTIRP
EXTORT
EYALET
EYEFUL
EYEING
EYELET
EYELID
EYE-PIT
EYETIE
EYLIAD

F

FAÇADE
FABIAN
FABLED
FABLER
FABRIC
FACETE
FACIAL
FACIES
FACILE
FACING
FACTOR
FACTUM
FACULA
FADDLE
FADE-IN
FADING

FAECAL
FAECES
FAERIE
FAG-END
FAGGED
FAGGOT
FAIBLE
FAIKES
FAILED
FAILLE
FAINLY
FAINTS
FAINTY
FAIRLY
FAITOR
FALCES
FALCON
FALLAL
FALLEN
FALL-IN
FALLOW
FALSER
FALSIE
FALTER
FAMILY
FAMINE
FAMISH
FAMOUS
FANDED
FANDOM
FANGED
FANGLE
FANION
FAN-JET
FANKLE
FANNED
FANNEL
FANNER
FANTAD
FANTAN
FANTEE
FANTOD
FANTOM
FAQUIR
FARAND
FARCIN
FARDEL
FARINA
FARMER
FAR-OFF
FAR-OUT
FARROW
FASCES
FASCIA
FASCIO
FASTEN
FASTER
FASTLY
FAT-HEN
FATHER
FATHOM
FATTED
FATTEN
FATTER
FAUCAL
FAUCES

FAUCET
FAULTY
FAUNAE
FAUNAL
FAUTOR
FAVISM
FAVOSE
FAVOUR
FAVOUS
FAWNER
FEAGUE
FEALTY
FEARED
FEATLY
FECIAL
FECKLY
FECULA
FECUND
FEDORA
FEEBLE
FEEBLY
FEEDER
FEEING
FEELER
FEERIE
FEGARY
FEHMIC
FEINTS
FELINE
FELLAH
FELLER
FELLOE
FELLOW
FELONY
FELTER
FEMALE
FEMORA
FENCED
FENCER
FENDER
FENIAN
FENMAN
FENNEC
FENNEL
FEODAL
FERIAL
FERINE
FERITY
FERREL
FERRET
FERRIC
FERRIS
FERULA
FERULE
FERVID
FESCUE
FESTAL
FESTER
FETIAL
FETICH
FETISH
FETTER
FETTLE
FEUDAL
FEUTRE
FEWMET

					G
FEWTER	FITCHE	FLOURY	FORMAL	FRISKY	
FEZZED	FITCHY	FLOUSE	FORMAT	FRIVOL	GABBER
FEZZES	FITFUL	FLOUSH	FORMED	FRIZZY	GABBLE
FIACRE	FIT-OUT	FLOWED	FORMER	FROGGY	GABBRO
FIANCÉ	FITTED	FLOWER	FORMIC	FROING	GABION
FIASCO	FITTER	FLUATE	FORMOL	FROISE	GABLED
FIBBED	FIXATE	FLUENT	FORNIX	FROLIC	GABLET
FIBBER	FIXING	FLUFFY	FORPET	FRONDE	GADDED
FIBRED	FIXITY	FLURRY	FORPIT	FROREN	GADDER
FIBRIL	FIXIVE	FLUSHY	FORRAD	FRORNE	GADFLY
FIBRIN	FIXURE	FLUTER	FORRIT	FROSTY	GADGET
FIBULA	FIZGIG	FLYING	FORSAY	FROTHY	GADHEL
FICKLE	FIZZED	FLY-MAN	FORTHY	FROWST	GADOID
FICTOR	FIZZEN	FO'C'SLE	FORWHY	FROWSY	GAELIC
FIDDLE	FIZZER	FODDER	FOSSED	FROWZY	GAFFER
FIDGET	FIZZLE	FOEMAN	FOSSIL	FROZEN	GAGGED
FIERCE	FLABBY	FOEMEN‑	FOSSOR	FRUGAL	GAGGER
FIESTA	FLACON	FOETAL	FOSTER	FRUITY	GAGGLE
FIFISH	FLAGGY	FOETID	FOTHER	FRUMPY	GAIETY
FIGGED	FLAGON	FOETOR	FOUGHT	FRUSTA	GAINER
FIGURE	FLAMBÉ	FOETUS	FOULLY	FRUTEX	GAINLY
FIKERY	FLAMED	FOGASH	FOURTH	FRYING	GAITED
FIKISH	FLAMEN	FOG-BOW	FOUSSA	FUCKED	GAITER
FILFOT	FLANCH	FOG-DOG	FOUTER	FUCOID	GALAGO
FILIAL	FLANGE	FOGGED	FOUTRA	FUDDLE	GALANT
FILING	FLASER	FOGGER	FOUTRE	FUGATO	GALAXY
FILLER	FLASHY	FOGMAN	FOVEAE	FÜHRER	GALENA
FILLET	FLATLY	FOGRAM	FOVEAL	FULFIL	GALIOT
FILLIP	FLATUS	FOIBLE	FOWLER	FULGID	GALLEY
FILMIC	FLAUNE	FOILED	FOX-BAT	FULGOR	GALLIC
FILOSE	FLAUNT	FOISON	FOXING	FULHAM	GALLIO
FILTER	FLAVIN	FOLDER	FRACAS	FULLAM	GALLON
FILTHY	FLAWED	FOLIAR	FRAGOR	FULLAN	GALLOP
FIMBLE	FLAXEN	FOLIUM	FRAISE	FULLER	GALLOW
FINALE	FLAYED	FOLKSY	FRAMER	FULMAR	GALLUS
FINDER	FLAYER	FOLLOW	FRANZY	FULVID	GALOOT
FINEER	FLÈCHE	FOMENT	FRAPPÉ	FUMADO	GALORE
FINELY	FLEDGE	FONDED	FRATCH	FUMAGE	GALOSH
FINERY	FLEDGY	FONDLE	FRATER	FUMBLE	GALUTH
FINGAN	FLEECE	FONDLY	FRATRY	FUMOUS	GAMASH
FINGER	FLEECH	FONDUE	FRAZIL	FUNDED	GAMBET
FINIAL	FLEECY	FONTAL	FREAKY	FUNDUS	GAMBIR
FINING	FLEMIT	FOOTED	FREELY	FUNEST	GAMBIT
FINISH	FLENCH	FOOTER	FREEST	FUNGAL	GAMBLE
FINITE	FLENSE	FOOTLE	FREETY	FUNGUS	GAMBOL
FINJAN	FLESHY	FOOTRA	FREEZE	FUNKIA	GAMELY
FINNAC	FLETCH	FOOZLE	FREITY	FUNNEL	GAMETE
FINNAN	FLEURY	FORÇAT	FREMIT	FURCAL	GAMINE
FINNED	FLEWED	FORAGE	FRENCH	FURFUR	GAMING
FINNER	FLEXOR	FORANE	FRENNE	FUROLE	GAMMER
FINNIC	FLIGHT	FORBAD	FRENUM	FURORE	GAMMON
FIN-RAY	FLIMSY	FORBID	FRENZY	FURRED	GANDER
FINSKO	FLINCH	FORCED	FRESCO	FURROW	GANESA
FIORIN	FLINTY	FORCER	FRETTY	FUSIAN	GANGAL
FIPPLE	FLISKY	FORDID	FRIARY	FUSILE	GANGER
FIRING	FLITCH	FOREGO	FRICHT	FUSION	GANGLY
FIRKIN	FLOATY	FOREST	FRIDAY	FUSSER	GANGUE
FIRLOT	FLOCCI	FORFEX	FRIDGE	FUSTET	GANNET
FIRMAN	FLOOSY	FORGER	FRIEND	FUSTIC	GANOID
FIRMLY	FLOOZY	FORGET	FRIEZE	FUSTOC	GANOIN
FISCAL	FLOPPY	FORGOT	FRIGHT	FUTILE	GANTRY
FISGIG	FLORAL	FORHOO	FRIGID	FUTURE	GAOLER
FISHER	FLORET	FORHOW	FRIJOL	FUZZLE	GAPING
FISHES	FLORID	FORINT	FRILLY	FYLFOT	GARÇON
FISSLE	FLORIN	FORKED	FRINGE		GARAGE
FISTIC	FLOSSY	FORKER	FRISKA		

GARAND	GEMMEN	GIPSEN	GODDEN	GRAKLE	GRU-GRU
GARBLE	GEMONY	GIRDED	GODOWN	GRAMME	GRUMLY
GARDEN	GENDER	GIRDER	GODSON	GRANGE	GRUMPH
GARGET	GENERA	GIRDLE	GODWIT	GRANNY	GRUMPY
GARGLE	GENEVA	GIRKIN	GOFFER	GRANTH	GRUTCH
GARIAL	GENIAL	GIRLIE	GOGGLE	GRAPPA	GRYFON
GARISH	GENIUS	GIRNEL	GOGGLY	GRASSY	GUANIN
GARJAN	GENTES	GIRNIE	GOGLET	GRATED	GUDDLE
GARLIC	GENTLE	GIUSTO	GOIDEL	GRATER	GUEBER
GARNER	GENTOO	GIVING	GOITRE	GRATIS	GUEBRE
GARNET	GENTRY	GIZZEN	GO-KART	GRAVED	GUELPH
GARRAN	GEODIC	GLACIS	GOLDEN	GRAVEL	GUENON
GARRED	GEOMYS	GLADLY	GOLFER	GRAVEN	GUFFAW
GARRET	GEORGE	GLAIRY	GOLIAS	GRAVER	GUGGLE
GARRON	GERBIL	GLAIVE	GOLLAN	GRAVES	GUIDER
GARROT	GERENT	GLANCE	GOLLAR	GRAVID	GUIDON
GARTER	GERMAN	GLASSY	GOLLOP	GRAZER	GUILED
GARUDA	GERMEN	GLAURY	GOLOSH	GREASE	GUILER
GARVIE	GERMIN	GLAZEN	GOMBRO	GREASY	GUILTY
GAS-BAG	GERUND	GLAZER	GOMUTI	GREATS	GUINEA
GASCON	GESTIC	GLEAMY	GOMUTO	GREAVE	GUISER
GASHLY	GETTER	GLEDGE	GOODLY	GREECE	GUITAR
GASIFY	GEWGAW	GLEETY	GOOGLE	GREEDY	GULDEN
GAS-JAR	GEYSER	GLEYED	GOOGLY	GREENY	GULLAH
GAS-JET	GHARRI	GLIBLY	GOOGOL	GREESE	GULLER
GASKET	GHARRY	GLIDER	GOONEY	GREYLY	GULLET
GASKIN	GHAZAL	GLIRES	GOOROO	GRICES	GULLEY
GAS-LIT	GHAZEL	GLITCH	GOOSES	GRIECE	GUMMED
GAS-MAK	GHEBER	GLOBAL	GOOSEY	GRIEVE	GUNITE
GASMAN	GHEBRE	GLOBED	GOPHER	GRIFFE	GUNMAN
GASPER	GHETTO	GLOOMY	GOPURA	GRI-GRI	GUNNEL
GASSED	GHOSTY	GLORIA	GORAMY	GRILLE	GUNNER
GAS-TAP	GHUBAR	GLOSSY	GORGED	GRILSE	GUNSEL
GAS-TAR	GIAOUR	GLOVED	GORGET	GRIMLY	GUNSHY
GÂTEAU	GIBBER	GLOVER	GORGIO	GRINGO	GUNTER
GATHER	GIBBET	GLOWER	GORGON	GRIPER	GUNYAH
GATING	GIBBON	GLUING	GORILY	GRIPPE	GURAMI
GAUCHE	GIB-CAT	GLUISH	GORING	GRIPPY	GURGLE
GAUCHO	GIBLET	GLUMLY	GOSHEN	GRIQUA	GURJUN
GAUCIE	GIFTED	GLUMPS	GOSLET	GRISLY	GURKHA
GAUFER	GIGGIT	GLUMPY	GO-SLOW	GRISON	GURLET
GAUFRE	GIGGLE	GLUTEN	GOSPEL	GRITTY	GURNET
GAUGER	GIGGLY	GLYCIN	GOSSAN	GRIVET	GURRAH
GAUNCH	GIGLET	GLYCOL	GOSSIP	GROATS	GUSHER
GAUPUS	GIGLOT	GNAMMA	GOTHIC	GROCER	GUSLAR
GAVAGE	GIGMAN	GNARLY	GOTTEN	GROGGY	GUSSET
GAVIAL	GIGOLO	GNAWED	GOURDE	GROMET	GUTTAE
GAWPUS	GILCUP	GNAWER	GOURDS	GROOLY	GUTTED
GAYEST	GILDED	GNEISS	GOURDY	GROOVE	GUTTER
GAY-YOU	GILDEN	GNETUM	GOUSTY	GROOVY	GUTTLE
GAZEBO	GILDER	GNOMAE	GOVERN	GROPER	GUZZLE
GAZOON	GILLET	GNOMIC	GOWANY	GROSER	GYLDEN
GEARED	GILLIE	GNOMON	GOWF-BA'	GROSET	GYMNAL
GEASON	GILPEY	GNOSIS	GOWFER	GROTTO	GYMNIC
GEE-GEE	GIMBAL	GOALIE	GOWNED	GROTTY	GYPPED
GEEZER	GIMLET	GOANNA	GOWPEN	GROUCH	GYPSUM
GEISHA	GIMMAL	GOATEE	GOYISH	GROUND	GYRANT
GELDED	GIMMER	GOBANG	GOZZAN	GROUSE	GYRATE
GELDER	GINGAL	GOBBET	GRABEN	GROUTY	GYROSE
GELLED	GINGER	GOBBLE	GRACED	GROVEL	GYROUS
GEMARA	GINGKO	GOBLET	GRADIN	GROWER	
GEMINI	GINGLE	GOBLIN	GRADUS	GROWLY	**H**
GEMINY	GINKGO	GOBONY	GRÄFIN	GROWTH	HABOOB
GEMMAE	GINNED	GO-CART	GRAINE	GROYNE	HACHIS
GEMMAN	GINNER	GODDAM	GRAINY	GRUBBY	HACKEE
GEMMED	GIORGI	GODDED	GRAITH	GRUDGE	HACKLE

HACKLY	HARASS	HECATE	HIDING	HONOUR	HUMIAN
HADDIE	HARDEN	HECKLE	HIEING	HOODED	HUMIFY
HADITH	HARDLY	HECTIC	HIEMAL	HOODOO	HUMISM
HADRON	HARD-UP	HECTOR	HIGGLE	HOOFED	HUMIST
HAEMAL	HARELD	HEDDLE	HIGHER	HOOKAH	HUMITE
HAEMIN	HARISH	HEDERA	HIGHLY	HOOKED	HUMLIE
HAFFET	HARKEN	HEDGER	HIGHTH	HOOKER	HUMMED
HAFFIT	HARLOT	HEEHAW	HIGH-UP	HOOKEY	HUMMEL
HAGBUT	HARMAN	HEELED	HIJACK	HOOK-UP	HUMMER
HAGDEN	HARMEL	HEELER	HIJRAH	HOOPER	HUMMUM
HAGDON	HARMIN	HEEZIE	HILARY	HOOP-LA	HUMOUR
HAGGED	HARPER	HEGIRA	HILLED	HOOPOE	HUMOUS
HAGGIS	HARROW	HEIFER	HINDER	HOOTCH	HUMPED
HAGGLE	HARTAL	HEIGHT	HINDOO	HOOTER	HUNGER
HAGLET	HASLET	HELIAC	HINGED	HOOVEN	HUNGRY
HAIDUK	HASSAR	HELIUM	HIPPED	HOOVES	HUNKER
HAIKAI	HASTEN	HELLER	HIPPIC	HOPDOG	HUNNIC
HAINCH	HAT-BOX	HELMED	HIPPUS	HOP-FLY	HUNTER
HAINED	HATFUL	HELMET	HIRING	HOP-OFF	HURDEN
HAIQUE	HAT-PEG	HELPED	HIRPLE	HOPPED	HURDLE
HAIR-DO	HAT-PIN	HELPER	HIRSEL	HOPPER	HURLER
HAIRST	HATRED	HEMMED	HIRSLE	HOPPLE	HURLEY
HALFEN	HATTED	HEMPEN	HISPID	HORARY	HURRAH
HALIDE	HATTER	HEN-BIT	HISTIE	HORKEY	HURRAY
HALITE	HAUGHT	HENNER	HITCHY	HORMIC	HURTER
HALLAL	HAULER	HEN-PEN	HITHER	HORNED	HURTLE
HALLAN	HAULST	HEN-RUN	HITTER	HORNER	HUSHED
HALLOA	HAUNCH	HEP-CAT	HOARSE	HORNET	HUSHER
HALLOO	HAÜYNE	HEPTAD	HOAXER	HORNIE	HUSKED
HALLOW	HAVANA	HERALD	HOBBLE	HORRID	HUSKER
HALLUX	HAVE-ON	HERBAL	HOBDAY	HORROR	HUSSAR
HALOED	HAVING	HERBAR	HOBNOB	HOSIER	HUSSIF
HALOES	HAW-HAW	HERDEN	HOBOES	HOSTEL	HUSTLE
HALOID	HAWKED	HERDIC	HOCKER	HOSTRY	HUTTED
HALSED	HAWKER	HEREAT	HOCKEY	HOT-AIR	HUZOOR
HALSER	HAWKEY	HEREIN	HODDEN	HOTBED	HUZZA'D
HALTER	HAWKIE	HEREOF	HODDLE	HOTPOT	HYADES
HALVAH	HAWKIT	HEREON	HODMAN	HOTTER	HYAENA
HALVER	HAWSER	HERERO	HOEING	HOUDAH	HYBRID
HALVES	HAYBOX	HERESY	HOGGED	HOUDAN	HYBRIS
HAMATE	HAYING	HERETO	HOGGER	HOURLY	HYDRIA
HAMBLE	HAYMOW	HERIOT	HOGGET	HOUSEL	HYDRIC
HAMITE	HAYSEL	HERMES	HOGGIN	HOWDAH	HYDYNE
HAMLET	HAZARD	HERMIT	HOG-PEN	HOWDIE	HYETAL
HAMMAL	HAZILY	HERNIA	HOG-RAT	HOWKER	HYKSOS
HAMMAM	HAZING	HEROES	HOICKS	HOWLED	HYLISM
HAMMER	HEADED	HEROIC	HOIDEN	HOWLER	HYLIST
HAMOSE	HEADER	HEROIN	HOISED	HOWLET	HYMNAL
HAMPER	HEAD-ON	HEROON	HOLDEN	HOYDEN	HYMNED
HANDED	HEALER	HERPES	HOLDER	HUBBUB	HYMNIC
HANDER	HEALTH	HERREN	HOLD-UP	HUB-CAP	HYPATE
HAND-IN	HEARER	HERSED	HOLILY	HUBRIS	HYPHAE
HANDLE	HEARSE	HESPER	HOLING	HUCKLE	HYPHAL
HANGAR	HEARSY	HESVAN	HOLISM	HUDDEN	HYPHEN
HANGED	HEARTH	HETMAN	HOLIST	HUDDLE	HYPNIC
HANGER	HEARTY	HEWING	HOLLER	HUDDUP	HYPNOS
HANG-UP	HEATED	HEXACT	HOLLOA	HUGELY	HYPNUM
HANJAR	HEATER	HEXANE	HOLLOW	HUGGED	HYSSOP
HANKER	HEATHY	HEXENE	HOLPEN	HUMANE	
HANKIE	HEAUME	HEXOSE	HOMAGE	HUMBLE	I
HANSEL	HEAVED	HEYDAY	HOMELY	HUMBLY	
HANSOM	HEAVEN	HIATUS	HOMILY	HUMBUG	IAMBIC
HANTLE	HEAVER	HICCUP	HOMING	HUMEAN	IAMBUS
HAPPED	HEBONA	HIDAGE	HOMINY	HUMECT	IASTIC
HAPPEN	HEBREW	HIDDEN	HONEST	HUMERI	IATRIC
HAPTIC	HEBRID	HIDDER	HONIED	HUMHUM	IBERIS
					IBEXES

IBICES	INBENT	INHUME	INWORN	JAMBOK	JIRBLE
ICE-AXE	INBORN	INISLE	INWOVE	JAMBUL	JITNEY
ICEBOX	INBRED	INJECT	INWRAP	JAMMED	JITTER
ICE-CAP	INCAGE	IN-JOKE	INYALA	JAMPAN	JOBBED
ICEMAN	IN-CALF	INJURE	IODATE	JAMPOT	JOBBER
ICE-PAN	INCASE	INJURY	IODIDE	JANGLE	JOB-LOT
ICE-RUN	INCAVE	INK-BAG	IODINE	JANGLY	JOCKEY
ICICLE	INCAVO	INKPOT	IODISE	JANIAN	JOCOSE
ICONIC	INCEDE	INK-SAC	IODISM	JANKER	JOCUND
IDAEAN	INCEPT	INLACE	IOLITE	JANTEE	JOGGED
IDEAED	INCEST	INLAID	IONIAN	JARFUL	JOGGER
IDEATE	INCHED	INLAND	IONISE	JARGON	JOGGLE
IDIOCY	INCISE	IN-LAWS	IONISM	JAROOL	JOHNNY
IDOIST	INCITE	INLIER	IONIST	JARRAH	JOINER
IDOLON	INCLIP	INLOCK	IONIUM	JARRED	JOLTER
IDOLUM	INCOME	INMATE	IPECAC	JARVEY	JORDAN
IGNARO	INCONY	INMOST	IRANIC	JASHAR	JOSEPH
IGNITE	INCUBI	INNATE	IREFUL	JASHER	JOSHER
IGNOMY	INCULT	INNING	IRENIC	JASPER	JOSKIN
IGNORE	INCUSE	INROAD	IRIDAL	JASPIS	JOSSER
IGUANA	INDABA	INRUSH	IRIDES	JATAKA	JOSTLE
ILEXES	INDART	INSANE	IRISED	JAUNCE	JOTTED
ILICES	INDEED	INSEAM	IRISES	JAUNSE	JOTTER
ILL-GOT	INDENE	INSECT	IRITIC	JAUNTY	JÖTUNN
ILLIAD	INDENT	INSERT	IRITIS	JAWARI	JOUNCE
ILLIPE	INDIAN	INSHIP	IRONER	JAWBOX	JOVIAL
ILL-OFF	INDICT	INSIDE	IRONIC	JAWING	JOWARI
ILLUDE	INDIGN	INSIST	IRRUPT	JEAMES	JOWLER
ILLUME	INDIGO	INSOLE	ISABEL	JEERER	JOYFUL
ILLUPI	INDITE	INSOUL	ISATIN	JEJUNE	JOYOUS
ILL-USE	INDIUM	INSPAN	ISATIS	JEMIMA	JUBATE
IMAGOS	INDOLE	INSTAL	ISLAND	JENNET	JUBBAH
IMBARK	INDOOR	INSTAR	ISOBAR	JERBOA	JUDAIC
IMBASE	INDRIS	INSTEP	ISODIA	JEREED	JUDDER
IMBIBE	INDUCE	INSTIL	ISOHEL	JERKER	JUDEAN
IMBODY	INDUCT	INSULA	ISOMER	JERKIN	JUDICA
IMBOSK	INDULT	INSULT	ISOPOD	JERQUE	JUGATE
IMBOSS	INDUNA	INSURE	ISSUER	JERSEY	JUGFUL
IMBREX	INFALL	INTACT	ITALIC	JESSED	JUGGED
IMBRUE	INFAME	INTAKE	ITSELF	JESSIE	JUGGLE
IMMANE	INFAMY	INTEND	IVY-TOD	JESTEE	JUG-JUG
IMMASK	INFANT	INTENT	IZZARD	JESTER	JUJUBE
IMMESH	INFARE	INTERN		JESUIT	JULIAN
IMMUNE	INFECT	INTIME	**J**	JETSAM	JUMART
IMMURE	INFEFT	INTINE		JETSON	JUMBAL
IMPACT	INFELT	INTOED	JABBER	JETTON	JUMBIE
IMPAIR	INFERE	INTONE	JABBLE	JEWESS	JUMBLE
IMPALA	INFEST	INTOWN	JABERS	JEWISH	JUMBLY
IMPALE	INFIRM	IN-TRAY	JABIRU	JEZAIL	JUMPED
IMPARK	INFLOW	INTUIT	JAÇANA	JIBBAH	JUMPER
IMPARL	INFLUX	INTUSE	JACENT	JIBBED	JUNCUS
IMPART	IN-FOAL	INULIN	JACKAL	JIBBER	JUNGLE
IMPAVE	INFOLD	INVADE	JACKET	JIGGED	JUNGLI
IMPAWN	INFORM	INVENT	JACQUE	JIGGER	JUNGLY
IMPEDE	INFULA	INVERT	JADERY	JIGGLE	JUNIOR
IMPEND	INFUSE	INVEST	JADISH	JIGJIG	JUNKER
IMPISH	INGATE	INVIS'D	JAEGER	JIG-JOG	JUNKET
IMPLEX	INGEST	INVITE	JAGGED	JIGSAW	JUNKIE
IMPONE	INGINE	INVOKE	JAGGER	JILLET	JUPATI
IMPORT	INGOES	INWALL	JAGHIR	JIMINY	JURANT
IMPOSE	INGRAM	INWARD	JAGUAR	JIMJAM	JURIST
IMPOST	INGRUM	INWICK	JAHVEH	JIMPLY	JUSTLE
IMPUGN	INGULF	INWIND	JAILER	JINGAL	JUTTED
IMPURE	INHALE	INWITH	JAILOR	JINGLE	JYMOLD
IMPUTE	INHERE	IN-WORD	JALOPY	JINGLY	
INARCH	INHOOP	INWORK	JAMBEE	JINNEE	
			JAMBER		

K-L6

K

KABALA
KABAYA
KABUKI
KABYLE
KAFFER
KAFFIR
KAFILA
KAFTAN
KAIKAI
KAISER
KAKAPO
KALIAN
KALIUM
KALMIA
KALONG
KALPAK
KALPIS
KAMALA
KAMEES
KAMELA
KAMILA
KAMSIN
KANAKA
KANTAR
KANTEN
KANUCK
KAOLIN
KAPUTT
KARAIT
KARAKA
KARATE
KARITE
KAROSS
KARROO
KASBAH
KATION
KAVASS
KEBBIE
KEBLAH
KECKLE
KECKSY
KEDDAH
KEDGER
KEEKER
KEELED
KEELER
KEELIE
KEENER
KEENLY
KEEPER
KEFFEL
KEKSYE
KELPIE
KELSON
KELTER
KELTIC
KELTIE
KELVIN
KEMPER
KEMPLE
KENNED
KENNEL
KENNER
KENNET

KEPHIR
KEPPIT
KERMES
KERMIS
KERNEL
KERSEY
KETONE
KETTLE
KEUPER
KEY-PIN
KEY-WAY
KGOTLA
KHALAT
KHALIF
KHANUM
KHARIF
KHILAT
KHODJA
KIA-ORA
KIAUGH
KIBBLE
KIBLAH
KIBOSH
KICKER
KICK-UP
KIDDED
KIDDER
KIDDLE
KIDFOX
KIDNAP
KIDNEY
KIE-KIE
KIERIE
KIKUYU
KILERG
KILLAS
KILLER
KILLUT
KILTER
KILTIE
KIMMER
KIMONO
KINCOB
KINDLE
KINDLY
KINEMA
KINGLE
KINGLY
KINKLE
KINONE
KIPPER
KIRBEH
KIRKIN'
KIRSCH
KIRTLE
KISLEU
KISLEV
KISMET
KISSER
KISS-ME
KIT-BAG
KIT-CAR
KITCAT
KITSCH
KITTEN

KITTLE
KITTLY
KITTUL
KLAXON
KLEPHT
KNACKY
KNAGGY
KNAWEL
KNICKS
KNIGHT
KNITCH
KNIVES
KNOBBY
KNOTTY
KNOWER
KNUBBY
KOBANG
KOBOLD
KOMODO
KONFYT
KOODOO
KOOKIE
KOOLAH
KOPECK
KOPPIE
KORKIR
KOSHER
KOSMOS
KOTWAL
KOULAN
KOWHAI
KOWTOW
KRAKEN
KRANTZ
KREESE
KRISES
KRONEN
KRONER
KRONOR
KRONOS
K'THIBH
KU-KLUX
KULTUR
KUMARA
KUMARI
KUMISS
KÜMMEL
KUNKAR
KUNKUR
KURGAN
KURVEY
KUTCHA

L

LAAGER
LABIAL
LABILE
LABIUM
LABLAB
LABOUR
LABRET
LABRUM
LABRUS
LABRYS
LAC-DYE
LACHES

LACING
LACKER
LACKEY
LACMUS
LACTIC
LACUNA
LADDER
LADDIE
LA-DI-DA
LADIES
LADIFY
LADING
LADINO
LADYFY
LAGENA
LAGEND
LAGGED
LAGGEN
LAGGER
LAGGIN
LAGOON
LAGUNE
LAICAL
LAIDLY
LAISSE
LAKISH
LALANG
LALLAN
LAMBDA
LAMBIE
LAMELY
LAMENT
LAMINA
LAMISH
LAMMAS
LAMMER
LAMMIE
LAMPAD
LAMPAS
LANATE
LANCER
LANCES
LANCET
LANDAU
LANDED
LANDER
LANGUR
LANKLY
LANNER
LANUGO
LAPDOG
LAPFUL
LAPITH
LAPPED
LAPPER
LAPPET
LAPPIE
LAPSED
LAPUTA
LARDER
LARDON
LARIAT
LARKER
LAROID
LARRUP
LARVAE

LARVAL
LARYNX
LASCAR
LASHER
LASH-UP
LASKET
LASSIE
LASSOS
LASTER
LASTLY
LATEEN
LATELY
LATENT
LATEST
LATHEE
LATHEN
LATHER
LATIAN
LATISH
LATRIA
LATRON
LATTEN
LATTER
LAUDER
LAUGHY
LAUNCE
LAUNCH
LAUREL
LAURIC
LAURUS
LAURYL
LAVABO
LAVAGE
LAVEER
LAVISH
LAVOLT
LAW-DAY
LAWFUL
LAWING
LAWMAN
LAWYER
LAXISM
LAXIST
LAXITY
LAY-BYE
LAY-BYS
LAY-DAY
LAYING
LAYMAN
LAY-OFF
LAY-OUT
LAZILY
LAZULI
LEACHY
LEADED
LEADEN
LEADER
LEAD-IN
LEAFED
LEAGUE
LEALTY
LEANED
LEANLY
LEAN-TO
LEAPED
LEAPER

LEA-RIG
LEARNT
LEASER
LEASOW
LEAVED
LEAVEN
LEAVES
LEBBEK
LECHER
LECTOR
LEDDEN
LEDGER
LEERIE
'LEETLE
LEEWAY
LEGACY
LEGATE
LEGATO
LEG-BYE
LEGEND
LEGGED
LEGGER
LEGION
LEGIST
LEGLAN
LEGLEN
LEGLET
LEGLIN
LEGMAN
LEGUME
LEIGER
LEIPOA
LEMANS
LEMONY
LENDER
LENGER
LENGTH
LENIFY
LENITY
LENSES
LENTEN
LENTIL
LENTOR
LENVOY
LEONID
LEPPED
LEPTON
LESION
LESSEE
LESSEN
LESSER
LESSON
LESSOR
LET-A-BE
LETHAL
LETHEE
LET-OFF
LETTED
LETTER
LETTIC
LEUCIN
LEVANT
LEVIED
LEVITE
LEVITY
LEWDLY

LIABLE	LIPOID	LOLIGO	LUMHAT	MAGNUM	MANTIS
LIAISE	LIPOMA	LOLIUM	LUMINA	MAGPIE	MANTLE
LIBANT	LIPPED	LOLLER	LUMINE	MAGUEY	MANTRA
LIBATE	LIPPEN	LOLLOP	LUMPEN	MAGYAR	MANTUA
LIBIDO	LIPPIE	LOMENT	LUMPER	MAHMAL	MANUAL
LIBKEN	LIQUID	LONELY	LUNACY	MAHOUN	MANUKA
LIBYAN	LIQUOR	LONGAN	LUNARY	MAHOUT	MANURE
LICHEE	LISBON	LONGER	LUNATE	MAHSIR	MAOISM
LICHEN	LISPER	LONGLY	LUNGED	MAIDAN	MAOIST
LICKER	LISSES	LONG-ON	LUNGIE	MAIDEN	MAORIS
LICTOR	LISSOM	LOOFAH	LUNULA	MAIGRE	MAPPED
LIDDED	LISTED	LOOKER	LUNULE	MAILED	MAPPER
LIEBIG	LISTEL	LOOK-IN	LUNYIE	MAILER	MAQUIS
LIEDER	LISTEN	LOONIE	LUPINE	MAIMED	MARACA
LIEFER	LISTER	LOOPED	LUPPEN	MAINLY	MARAUD
LIEGER	LITANY	LOOPER	LURDAN	MAINOR	MARBLE
LIENAL	LITCHI	LOOSEN	LURDEN	MAJLIS	MARBLY
LIERNE	LITHER	LOOTEN	LURKER	MAKE-DO	MARCEL
LIEVER	LITHIA	LOOVES	LUSHER	MAKE-UP	MARGAY
LIFTER	LITHIC	LOPPED	LUSHLY	MAKING	MARGIN
LIGATE	LITMUS	LOPPER	LUSIAD	MALADY	MARIAN
LIGGEN	LITTEN	LOQUAT	LUSTER	MALAGA	MARINA
LIGGER	LITTER	LORATE	LUSTRA	MALATE	MARINE
LIGHTS	LITTLE	LORCHA	LUSTRE	MALEIC	MARISH
LIGNIN	LITUUS	LORDLY	LUTEIN	MALGRE	MARIST
LIGNUM	LIVELY	LORICA	LUTING	MALIBU	MARKED
LIGULA	LIVERY	LORING	LUTIST	MALICE	MARKER
LIGULE	LIVING	LORIOT	LUTTEN	MALIGN	MARKET
LIGURE	LIZARD	LOSING	LUXATE	MALKIN	MARLED
LIKELY	LLANOS	LOTION	LUXURY	MALLEE	MARLIN
LIKING	LOADED	LOTTED	LUZERN	MALLET	MARMOT
LILIED	LOADEN	LOUDEN	LUZULA	MALLOW	MAROON
LILIUM	LOADER	LOUDLY	LYCEUM	MALMAG	MARQUE
LIMBED	LOAFER	LOUNGE	LYCHEE	MALTHA	MARRAM
LIMBER	LOATHE	LOUPEN	LYCOSA	MAMMAE	MARRED
LIMBUS	LOATHY	LOUPIT	LYDIAN	MAMMAL	MARROW
LIMING	LOAVES	LOUSES	LYNXES	MAMMEE	MARRUM
LIMMER	LOBATE	LOUVER	LYRATE	MAMMER	MARSHY
LIMNER	LOBBED	LOUVRE	LYRISM	MAMMET	MARTEL
LIMOUS	LOBING	LOVAGE	LYRIST	MAMMON	MARTEN
LIMPET	LOBOSE	LOVELY	LYSINE	MANAGE	MARTIN
LIMPID	LOBULE	LOVING		MANATI	MARTYR
LINAGE	LOBULI	LOWBOY	**M**	MANCHE	MARVEL
LINDEN	LOCALE	LOWERY	MACHAN	MANCHU	MASCLE
LINEAL	LOCATE	LOWEST	MACKLE	MANCUS	MASCON
LINEAR	LOCHAN	LOWING	MACLED	MAN-DAY	MASCOT
LINE-UP	LOCHIA	LOWRIE	MACOYA	MANDIR	MASHER
LINGAM	LOCKER	LOWSIT	MACRON	MANDOM	MASHIE
LINGEL	LOCKET	LOZELL	MACULA	MANÈGE	MASJID
LINGER	LOCK-UP	LUBBER	MACULE	MANFUL	MASKED
LINGLE	LOCOED	LUBRIC	MADAME	MANGAL	MASKER
LINGOT	LOCULI	LUCENT	MADCAP	MANGEL	MASLIN
LINGUA	LOCUST	LUCERN	MADDEN	MANGER	MASORA
LINHAY	LODGER	LUCINA	MADDER	MANGEY	MASQUE
LINING	LOFTER	LUCKEN	MADEFY	MANGLE	MASSIF
LINK-UP	LOGGAT	LUCKIE	MADMAN	MANIAC	MASTED
LINNET	LOGGED	LUCUMA	MADRAS	MANILA	MASTER
LINSEY	LOGGER	LUCUMO	MAENAD	MANIOC	MASTIC
LINTEL	LOGGIA	LUETIC	MAFFIA	MANITO	MASULA
LINTER	LOGGIE	LUGGED	MAGGOT	MANNED	MATICO
LINTIE	LOG-HUT	LUGGER	MAGIAN	MANNER	MATINS
LIONEL	LOGION	LUGGIE	MAGILP	MANQUÉ	MATLOW
LIONET	LOG-JAM	LUGING	MAGISM	MANRED	MATRIC
LIONLY	LOGLOG	LUITEN	MAGMAS	MANTEL	MATRIX
LIPASE	LOG-MAN	LUMBAR	MAGNES	MANTIC	MATRON
LIPIDE	LOITER	LUMBER	MAGNET	MANTID	MATTED

MATTER	MELTED	MID-GUT	MISSAL	MONIED	MOUSMÉ
MATURE	MELTON	MID-LEG	MISSAY	MONIES	MOUSSE
MATZAH	MEMBER	MID-OFF	MISSEE	MONISM	MOUTAN
MATZOH	MEMNON	MIDRIB	MISSEL	MONIST	MOUTER
MATZOT	MEMOIR	MID-SEA	MISSES	MONKEY	MOUTHY
MAUGRE	MEMORY	MID-SKY	MISSET	MONODY	MOVIES
MAUMET	MENACE	MIDWAY	MISSIS	MONOSY	MOVING
MAUNDY	MÉNAGE	MIGHTY	MISSUS	MONTEM	MOWING
MAUNNA	MENDER	MIHRAB	MISTER	MONTRE	MUCATE
MAUSER	MENGED	MIKADO	MISTLE	MOOLAH	MUCHEL
MAUVIN	MENHIR	MIKRON	MISUSE	MOONED	MUCHLY
MAWKIN	MENIAL	MILADI	MITHRA	MOONER	MUCKER
MAWMET	MENINX	MILADY	MITRAL	MOORVA	MUCKLE
MAWPUS	MENSAL	MILAGE	MITTEN	MOOTER	MUCLUC
MAXIMA	MENSES	MILDEN	MIURUS	MOPISH	MUCOID
MAXIXE	MENSUR	MILDEW	MIZZEN	MOPOKE	MUCOUS
MAY-BUG	MENTAL	MILDLY	MIZZLE	MOPPED	MUD-CAT
MAYDAY	MENTOR	MILIEU	MIZZLY	MOPPER	MUDDLE
MAY-DEW	MENTUM	MILKEN	MNEMIC	MOPPET	MUD-PIE
MAYEST	MERCAT	MILKER	MNEMON	MORALE	MUFFIN
MAYFLY	MERCER	MILLED	MOATED	MORASS	MUFFLE
MAYHAP	MERELL	MILLER	MOBBED	MORBID	MUFLON
MAYHEM	MERELY	MILLET	MOBBIE	MORBUS	MUG-EWE
MAYING	MERGER	MILORD	MOBBLE	MOREEN	MUGFUL
MAZARD	MERINO	MILSEY	MOBCAP	MORGAY	MUGGER
MAZILY	MERISM	MILTER	MOBILE	MORGEN	MUKLUK
MAZOUT	MERLIN	MILVUS	MOB-LAW	MORGUE	MULISH
MEADOW	MERLON	MIMBAR	MOBLED	MORION	MULLAH
MEAGRE	MERMAN	MIMOSA	MOCKER	MORISH	MULLED
MEALER	MEROME	MINBAR	MOCK-UP	MORISK	MULLER
MEALIE	MEROPS	MINCED	MOCOCK	MORKIN	MULLET
MEANIE	MESAIL	MINCER	MOCUCK	MORMON	MULLEY
MEANLY	MESCAL	MINDED	MODENA	MORNAY	MULTUM
MEASLE	MESIAL	MINDEL	MODERN	MORNED	MUMBLE
MEASLY	MESIAN	MINDER	MODEST	MOROSE	MUMMED
MEATAL	MESSAN	MINGED	MODIFY	MORPHO	MUMMER
MEATUS	MESSRS	MINGLE	MODISH	MORRIS	MUMMIA
MEAZEL	MESS-UP	MINIFY	MODIST	MORROW	MUMPER
MEDDLE	MESTEE	MINIMA	MODIUS	MORSAL	MUNDIC
MEDIAL	METAGE	MINING	MODULE	MORSEL	MUNICH
MEDIAN	METEOR	MINION	MODULI	MORTAL	MUNIFY
MEDICK	METHOD	MINISH	MODULO	MORTAR	MUNITE
MEDICO	METHYL	MINIUM	MOGGAN	MORULA	MUNSHI
MEDISE	MÉTIER	MINNIE	MOHAIR	MOSAIC	MUNTIN
MEDISM	METMAN	MINNOW	MOHAWK	MOSLEM	MUONIC
MEDIUM	METOPE	MINOAN	MOHOCK	MOSQUE	MURAGE
MEDIUS	METRED	MINTER	MOIDER	MOSTLY	MURDER
MEDLAR	METRIC	MINUET	MOIETY	MOTETT	MURENA
MEDLEY	METTLE	MINUTE	MOILER	MOTHED	MURINE
MEDUSA	MEWSES	MIOSIS	MOIRAI	MOTHER	MURKEN
MEEKEN	MEZAIL	MIRAGE	MOLECH	MOTILE	MURLAN
MEEKLY	MEZUZA	MIRITI	MOLEST	MOTION	MURLIN
MEERED	MIASMA	MIRROR	MOLINE	MOTIVE	MURMUR
MEETLY	MIASMS	MISAIM	MOLLAH	MOTLEY	MURPHY
MEGASS	MICATE	MISCUE	MOLLIE	MOTMOT	MURRAM
MEGILP	MICHER	MISDID	MOLOCH	MOTORY	MURRAY
MEGOHM	MICKEY	MISÈRE	MOMENT	MOTTLE	MURREY
MEGRIM	MICKLE	MISERY	MOMMET	MOTTO'D	MURRHA
MEILIS	MICMAC	MISFIT	MONACT	MOTUCA	MUSANG
MEINEY	MICRON	MISHAP	MONAUL	MOUJIK	MUSCAE
MEINIE	MID-AGE	MISHIT	MONDAY	MOULDY	MUSCAT
MEJLIS	MID-AIR	MISHMI	MONERA	MOULIN	MUSCID
MELANO	MIDDAY	MISHNA	MONGER	MOUNTY	MUSCLE
MELLAY	MIDDEN	MISKEN	MONGOL	MOUSER	MUSEUM
MELLOW	MIDDLE	MISLAY	MONGST	MOUSIE	MUSHER
MELODY	MIDGET	MISLED	MONIAL	MOUSLE	MUSING

MUSIVE	NANKIN	NERVED	NIRLIE	NOZZLE	OBVERT
MUSKED	NAPALM	NERVER	NIRLIT	NUANCE	OCCAMY
MUSKEG	NAPERY	NESHKI	NISSEN	NUBBLE	OCCULT
MUSKET	NAPKIN	NESIOT	NITRIC	NUBBLY	OCCUPY
MUSKLE	NAPPED	NESTLE	NITRYL	NUBILE	OCELLI
MUSK-OX	NAPPER	NESTOR	NITWIT	NUCHAL	OCELOT
MUSLIM	NAPRON	NETFUL	NIVOSE	NUCLEI	OCHERY
MUSLIN	NARDOO	NETHER	NIX-NIE	NUCULE	OCHONE
MUSMON	NARIAL	NETTED	NO-BALL	NUDELY	OCHREA
MUSROL	NARINE	NETTLE	NOBBLE	NUDISM	OCHREY
MUSSEL	NARKED	NEURAL	NOBBUT	NUDIST	O'CLOCK
MUSTEE	NARRAS	NEURON	NOBODY	NUDITY	OCREAE
MUSTER	NARROW	NEUTER	NOCAKE	NUGGET	OCTANE
MUTANT	NASARD	NEWELL	NOCENT	NULLAH	OCTANS
MUTATE	NASION	NEWISH	NOCHEL	NUMBED	OCTANT
MUTELY	NASTIC	NEW-OLD	NOCKET	NUMBER	OCTAVE
MUTINE	NASUTE	NEW-SAD	NOCTUA	NUMNAH	OCTAVO
MUTINY	NATANT	NEWTON	NODDED	NUNCIO	OCTETT
MUTISM	NATION	NEXTLY	NODDER	NUNCLE	OCTROI
MUTTER	NATIVE	NIACIN	NODDLE	NUPHAR	OCTUOR
MUTTON	NATRON	NIBBED	NODOSE	NURHAG	OCULAR
MUTUAL	NATTER	NIBBLE	NODOUS	NURSER	ODDISH
MUTUCA	NATURE	NICELY	NODULE	NURSLE	ODDITY
MUTULE	NAUGHT	NICENE	NOESIS	NUTANT	ODD-JOB
MUTUUM	NAUSEA	NICETY	NOETIC	NUTATE	ODD-MAN
MUU-MUU	NAUTCH	NICHED	NOGGIN	NUTLET	ODDS-ON
MUZHIK	NAUTIC	NICHER	NOMADE	NUTMEG	ODIOUS
MUZZLE	NAY-SAY	NICKAR	NOMISM	NUT-OIL	OECIST
MYELIN	NAZIFY	NICKEL	NONAGE	NUTRIA	OEDEMA
MYELON	NAZISM	NICKER	NONANE	NUTTED	O'ERLAY
MYGALE	NEANIC	NICKUM	NONARY	NUTTER	OESTAL
MYOGEN	NEAPED	NIDGET	NON-COM	NUZZER	ŒUVRE
MYOPIA	NEAR-BY	NIDIFY	NON-CON	NUZZLE	OFFCUT
MYOPIC	NEARER	NIDING	NON-EGO	NYANZA	OFF-DAY
MYOSIN	NEARLY	NID-NOD	NOODLE	NYMPHO	OFFEND
MYOSIS	NEATEN	NIELLI	NORDIC		OFFICE
MYOTIC	NEATLY	NIELLO	NORITE	**O**	OFFING
MYRIAD	NEBBED	NIFFER	NORLAN'	OAFISH	OFFISH
MYRICA	NEBBUK	NIGGER	NORMAL	OAK-NUT	OFF-KEY
MYRTLE	NEBECK	NIGGLE	NORMAN	OARAGE	OFFPUT
MYRTUS	NEB-NEB	NIGGLY	NORROY	OAR-LAP	OFFSET
MYSELF	NEBRIS	NIGHLY	NORWAY	OBDURE	OGAMIC
MYSTIC	NEBULA	NIGHTS	NOSEAN	OBECHE	OGDOAD
MYTHIC	NEBULE	NIGHTY	NO-SIDE	OBEISM	OGIVAL
MYTHOS	NEBULY	NIGNOG	NOSING	OBELUS	OGLING
MYTHUS	NECKED	NILGAI	NOSTOC	OBERON	OGRESS
MYXOMA	NECTAR	NILGAU	NOSTOS	OBEYER	OGRISH
N	NEED-BE	NILLED	NOTARY	OBIISM	OIDIUM
	NEEDER	NILOTE	NOTICE	OBI-MAN	OIKIST
NABBED	NEEDLE	NIMBED	NOTIFY	OBITAL	OILCAN
NABBER	NEEDLY	NIMBLE	NOTION	OBJECT	OILERY
NACKET	NEFAST	NIMBLY	NOTOUR	OBJURE	OIL-GAS
NAEVUS	NEGATE	NIMBUS	NOT-OUT	OBLAST	OILILY
NAGANA	NEKTON	NIMMED	NOUGAT	OBLATE	OILLET
NAGARI	NELIES	NIMMER	NOUGHT	OBLIGE	OILMAN
NAGGED	NELSON	NIM-OIL	NOUNAL	OBLONG	OIL-NUT
NAGGER	NEMEAN	NIMROD	NOUSLE	OBOIST	OIL-RIG
NAIADS	NEPHEW	NINCOM	NOVENA	OBOLUS	OKAPIS
NAIANT	NEREID	NINCUM	NOVIAL	OBSESS	OLDEST
NAILED	NERINE	NINETY	NOVICE	OBSIGN	OLD-HAT
NAILER	NERITA	NIPPED	NOVITY	OBTAIN	OLDISH
NALLAH	NERITE	NIPPER	NOWAYS	OBTECT	OLEATE
NAMELY	NERIUM	NIPPLE	NOWELL	OBTEND	OLEFIN
NAMING	NERNST	NIPPON	NOWISE	OBTEST	OLENUS
NANDOO	NEROLI	NIPTER	NOYADE	OBTUND	O-LEVEL
NANISM	NERVAL	NIRLED	NOYOUS	OBTUSE	OLFACT

OLIVER	ORDEAL	OUTJET	PAIDLE	PARADE	PATTED
OLIVET	ORDURE	OUTJUT	PAID-UP	PARAGE	PATTÉE
OLLAMH	OREIDE	OUTLAW	PAIGLE	PARAMO	PATTEN
OMASAL	OREXIS	OUTLAY	PAINED	PARANÁ	PATTER
OMASUM	ORGANA	OUTLER	PAINIM	PARANG	PATTLE
OMELET	ORGASM	OUTLET	PAINTY	PARAPH	PAUNCH
OMENED	ORGEAT	OUTLIE	PAIRED	PARCAE	PAUPER
OMENTA	ORGIES	OUTMAN	PAKEHA	PARCEL	PAUSAL
OMNIFY	ORGONE	OUTPUT	PAKHTO	PARDAL	PAUSER
OMNIUM	ORIENT	OUTRED	PAKHTU	PARDED	PAVAGE
ONAGER	ORIFEX	OUTRUN	PALACE	PARDIE	PAVANE
ONAGRA	ORIGAN	OUTSET	PALAMA	PARDON	PAVING
ONCOME	ORIGIN	OUTSIT	PALATE	PARENT	PAVIOR
ONCOST	ORIOLE	OUTSUM	PALEAE	PARGET	PAVISE
ONDINE	ORISON	OUTTEL	PALELY	PARIAH	PAVONE
ONDING	ORMAZD	OUTTOP	PALING	PARIAL	PAWNEE
ONE-MAN	ORMOLU	OUTVIE	PALISH	PARIAN	PAWNER
ONE-WAY	ORMUZD	OUTWIN	PALKEE	PARING	PAWPAW
ONFALL	ORNATE	OUTWIT	PALLAE	PARITY	PAXWAX
ONIONY	ORNERY	OVALLY	PALLAH	PARKEE	PAY-BOX
ONIRIC	OROIDE	OVATOR	PALLAS	PARKER	PAY-DAY
ONRUSH	ORPHAN	OVERBY	PALLED	PARKIN	PAYING
ONSIDE	ORPHIC	OVERDO	PALLET	PARKLY	PAYNIM
ONWARD	ORPINE	OVERGO	PALLIA	PARLAY	PAY-OFF
ONYCHA	ORRERY	OVERLY	PALLID	PARLEY	PAYOLA
OOCYTE	OSCINE	OVIBOS	PALLOR	PARODY	PEACHY
OODLES	OSCULE	OVISAC	PALMAE	PAROLE	PEACOD
OOGAMY	OSIERY	OVULAR	PALMAR	PARPEN	PEA-HEN
OOGENY	OSIRIS	OWELTY	PALMED	PARRAL	PEAKED
OOIDAL	OSMATE	OWERBY	PALMER	PARREL	PEANUT
OOLITE	OSMIUM	OWL-CAR	PALOLO	PARROT	PEA-POD
OOLOGY	OSMOSE	OWLERY	PALPAL	PARSEC	PEARLY
OOLONG	OSMOUS	OWLISH	PALPUS	PARSEE	PEASON
OOMIAK	OSPREY	OXALIC	PALTER	PARSER	PEAVEY
OORIAL	OSSEIN	OXALIS	PALTRY	PARSON	PEBBLE
OOZILY	OSSIAN	OX-BIRD	PAMPAS	PARTAN	PEBBLY
OPALED	OSSIFY	OX-EYED	PAMPER	PARTED	PECKER
OPAQUE	OSTEAL	OXFORD	PANADA	PARTER	PECORA
OPENER	OSTENT	OXGANG	PANAMA	PARTLY	PECTEN
OPENLY	OSTIAK	OXGATE	PANARY	PARURE	PECTIC
OPHISM	OSTIAL	OXHEAD	PANDAR	PARVIS	PECTIN
OPHITE	OSTIUM	OXLAND	PANDER	PASCAL	PEDANT
OPIATE	OSTLER	OXSLIP	PANDIT	PASEAR	PEDATE
OPPOSE	OSTMEN	OX-TAIL	PANFUL	PASHIM	PEDDER
OPPUGN	OSTREA	OXYGEN	PANGEN	PASHTO	PEDDLE
OPTANT	OSTYAK	OXYMEL	PANGFU'	PASHTU	PEDLAR
OPTICS	OTALGY	OYSTER	PANICK	PASSED	PEELED
OPTIMA	OTIOSE	OZAENA	PANISC	PASSER	PEELER
OPTIME	OTITIS		PANISK	PASSIM	PEENGE
OPTION	OTTAVA	P	PANTER	PASSUS	PEEPER
OPULUS	OULONG		PANTON	PASTEL	PEEPUL
ORACHE	OURALI	PACHAK	PANTRY	PASTER	PEERIE
ORACLE	OURARI	PACIFY	PANTUM	PASTIL	PEEVER
ORALLY	OUREBI	PACKER	PANZER	PASTOR	PEEWEE
ORANGE	OUROOT	PACKET	PAPACY	PASTRY	PEEWIT
ORATOR	OUSTER	PADANG	PAPAIN	PATCHY	PEG-BOX
ORBITA	OUTAGE	PADAUK	PAPAYA	PATENT	PEGGED
ORBITY	OUT-ASK	PADDED	PAPERY	PATERA	PEG-LEG
ORCEIN	OUTBAR	PADDER	PAPISH	PATHAN	PEG-TOP
ORCHAT	OUTBID	PADDLE	PAPISM	PATHIC	PELAGE
ORCHEL	OUTBYE	PAD-NAG	PAPIST	PATHOS	PELHAM
ORCHID	OUTCRY	PADOUK	PAPPUS	PATINA	PELITE
ORCHIL	OUTFIT	PADUAN	PAPUAN	PAT-LID	PELLET
ORCHIS	OUTFLY	PAELLA	PAPULA	PATOIS	PELMET
ORCINE	OUTGAS	PAEONY	PAPULE	PATROL	PELOID
ORDAIN	OUTING	PAGING	PAPYRI	PATRON	PELORY
		PAGODA			

PELOTA
PELTER
PELTRY
PELVES
PELVIC
PELVIS
PENCIL
PENFUL
PEN-GUN
PENIAL
PENMAN
PENNAE
PENNAL
PENNED
PENNER
PEN-NIB
PENNON
PENPAL
PENSIL
PENSUM
PENTAD
PENULT
PENURY
PEOPLE
PEPFUL
PEPLOS
PEPLUM
PEPPER
PEPSIN
PEPTIC
PERDIE
PERDUE
PEREIA
PERFAY
PERIOD
PERISH
PERKIN
PERMIT
PERONE
PERRON
PERSIC
PERSON
PERSUE
PERTLY
PERUKE
PERUSE
PESADE
PESETA
PESEWA
PESHWA
PESTER
PESTLE
PETARA
PETARD
PETARY
PETHER
PETITE
PETREL
PETROL
PETTED
PETTER
PETTLE
PEWTER
PEYOTE
PEZIZA
PHAEIC

PHALLI
PHAROS
PHASED
PHASIC
PHASIS
PHASMA
PHATIC
PHEERE
PHEEZE
PHENIC
PHENOL
PHENYL
PHIZOG
PHLEGM
PHLEUM
PHLOEM
PHOBIA
PHOBIC
PHOCAE
PHOEBE
PHOLAS
PHONAL
PHONEY
PHONIC
PHONON
PHOTIC
PHOTON
PHRASE
PHRASY
PHYLUM
PHYSIC
PIAFFE
PIAZZA
PICENE
PICINE
PICKED
PICKER
PICKET
PICKLE
PICK-UP
PICNIC
PICOTE
PICRIC
PIDDLE
PIDGIN
PIECEN
PIECER
PIE-DOG
PIEING
PIEMAN
PIERCE
PIERID
PIERIS
PIFFLE
PIG-BED
PIGEON
PIGGED
PIGGIE
PIGGIN
PIGLET
PIG-MAN
PIG-NUT
PIG-RAT
PIGSNY
PIGSTY
PILAFF

PILEUM
PILE-UP
PILEUS
PILFER
PILLAR
PILLAU
PILLOW
PILOSE
PILOUS
PILULA
PILULE
PIMENT
PIMPLE
PIMPLY
PINCER
PINDER
PINEAL
PINERY
PINETA
PINGER
PINGLE
PINION
PINKED
PINKIE
PIN-LEG
PIN-MAN
PINNAE
PINNED
PINNER
PINNET
PINNIE
PINOLE
PINTLE
PINXIT
PIOLET
PIONED
PIONER
PIONEY
PIOTED
PIPAGE
PIPING
PIPKIN
PIPPED
PIPPIN
PIQUET
PIRACY
PIRATE
PIRAYA
PIRNIE
PIRNIT
PISCES
PISSED
PISTIL
PISTOL
PISTON
PITAKA
PITARA
PITCHY
PITHOS
PITIED
PITIER
PITMAN
PITPAT
PIT-SAW
PITTED
PITTEN

PITTER
PIZZLE
PLACED
PLACER
PLACET
PLACID
PLACIT
PLAGAL
PLAGUE
PLAGUY
PLAICE
PLAINT
PLANAR
PLANCH
PLANER
PLANET
PLANTA
PLAQUE
PLASHY
PLASMA
PLATAN
PLATED
PLATEN
PLATER
PLAYER
PLEACH
PLEASE
PLEBBY
PLEDGE
PLEIAD
PLENTY
PLENUM
PLEUCH
PLEUGH
PLEURA
PLEXOR
PLEXUS
PLIANT
PLICAE
PLIERS
PLIGHT
PLINTH
PLISSE
PLOTTY
PLOUGH
PLOVER
PLUCKY
PLUFFY
PLUG-IN
PLUMED
PLUMMY
PLUMPY
PLUNGE
PLURAL
PLUSHY
PLUTUS
PLYING
PNEUMA
POACHY
POCHAY
POCKED
POCKET
PODDED
PODIAL
PODITE
PODIUM

PODLEY
PODSOL
PODUNK
PODURA
PODZOL
POETIC
POETRY
POFFLE
POGROM
POINTE
POISER
POISON
POKING
POLACK
POLAND
POLDER
POLE-AX
POLICE
POLICY
POLING
POLISH
POLITE
POLITY
POLLAN
POLLED
POLLEN
POLLER
POLLEX
POLLUX
POLONY
POLYPE
POLYPI
POLYPS
POMACE
POMADE
POMATO
POMELO
POMMEL
POMONA
POMPEY
POMPOM
POMPON
POMROY
PONCHO
PONDER
PONENT
PONGEE
PONGID
PONTAL
PONTES
PONTIC
PONTIE
PONTIL
PONTON
POODLE
POOJAH
POOKIT
POONAC
POOPED
POORLY
POOTER
POPERY
POP-EYE
POP-GUN
POPIAN
POPISH

POPJOY
POPLAR
POPLIN
POPPED
POPPER
POPPET
POPPLE
POPPLY
PORGIE
PORISM
PORKER
POROSE
POROUS
PORTAL
PORTAS
PORTER
PORTLY
POSADA
POSEUR
POSHLY
POSING
POSNET
POSSET
POSSUM
POSTAL
POSTER
POSTIL
POTAGE
POT-ALE
POTASH
POTASS
POTATO
POT-BOY
POTCHE
POTEEN
POTENT
POTFUL
POT-GUN
POT-HAT
POTHER
POTION
POT-LID
POTMAN
POTTED
POTTER
POTTLE
POUCHY
POUFED
POUFFE
POUKIT
POULPE
POUNCE
POURER
POURIE
POUTER
POWDER
POWNEY
POWNIE
POWTER
POWWAW
POWWOW
PRAISE
PRANCE
PRANCK
PRANKY
PRATER

PRATIE	PUDDEN	PURPLE	QUELEA	RAGTAG	RARITY
PRAWLE	PUDDLE	PURPLY	QUENCH	RAGULY	RASCAL
PRAXIS	PUDDLY	PURSER	QUERPO	RAIDER	RASHER
PRAYED	PUDENT	PURSUE	QUETCH	RAILER	RASHLY
PRAYER	PUDSEY	PURVEY	QUEUED	RAILLY	RASPER
PREACH	PUEBLO	PUSHED	QUICHE	RAISER	RASTER
PRÉCIS	PUFFED	PUSHER	QUIDAM	RAISIN	RASURE
PREEVE	PUFFER	PUSHTO	QUI-HYE	RAITED	RATHER
PREFAB	PUFFIN	PUSHTU	QUINCE	RAIYAT	RATIFY
PREFER	PUG-DOG	PUSSEL	QUINIC	RAJPUT	RATINE
PREFIX	PUISNE	PUTEAL	QUINIE	RAKERY	RATING
PRELIM	PUISNY	PUTELI	QUINOA	RAKING	RATION
PREPAY	PULING	PUTLOG	QUINOL	RAKISH	RATITE
PRESES	PULKHA	PUT-OFF	QUINSY	RALLUS	RATLIN
PRESTO	PULLER	PUTOIS	QUINTA	RAMATE	RATOON
PRETTY	PULLET	PUT-PUT	QUINZE	RAMBLE	RAT-PIT
PRICED	PULLEY	PUTRID	QUIRKY	RAMCAT	RATTAN
PRICEY	PULL-IN	PUTSCH	QUITCH	RAMEAL	RAT-TAT
PRIEFE	PULL-ON	PUTTED	QUITED	RAMEAN	RATTED
PRIEST	PULL-UP	PUTTEE	QUIVER	RAMIFY	RATTEN
PRIEVE	PULPER	PUTTEN	QUOIST	RAMISM	RATTER
PRIMAL	PULPIT	PUTTER	QUORUM	RAMIST	RATTLE
PRIMER	PULQUE	PUTTIE	QUOTER	RAM-JET	RATTON
PRIMLY	PULSAR	PUTURE	QUOTES	RAMMED	RAUCID
PRIMUS	PULSED	PUZZEL	QUOTHA	RAMMER	RAUCLE
PRINCE	PULTAN	PUZZLE	QUOTUM	RAMOSE	RAUGHT
PRIORY	PULTON	PYCNIC		RAMOUS	RAVAGE
PRISMY	PULTUN	PYCNON	**R**	RAMPER	RAVINE
PRISON	PULVER	PYE-DOG	RABATO	RAMROD	RAVING
PRISSY	PULVIL	PYEING	RABBET	RAMSON	RAVISH
PRIVET	PULWAR	PYEMIA	RABBIN	RAMULI	RAWING
PRIZED	PUMELO	PYGARG	RABBIT	RANCEL	RAWISH
PRIZER	PUMICE	PYKNIC	RABBLE	RANCHO	RAZURE
PROFIT	PUMMEL	PYLONS	RABIES	RANCID	RAZZIA
PROGNE	PUMPED	PYONER	RACEME	RANDAN	RAZZLE
PROING	PUMPER	PYRENE	RACE-UP	RANDEM	READER
PROKER	PUNCTA	PYRITE	RACHIS	RANDIE	REALLY
PROLEG	PUNCTO	PYROLA	RACIAL	RANDOM	RE-ALLY
PROLIX	PUNDIT	PYROPE	RACILY	RANGER	REALTY
PROMPT	PUNICA	PYTHIA	RACING	RANINE	REAMER
PRONTO	PUNIER	PYTHIC	RACISM	RANKED	REAPER
PROOFS	PUNILY	PYTHON	RACIST	RANKER	REARER
PROPEL	PUNISH		RACKER	RANKLE	REARLY
PROPER	PUNKAH	**Q**	RACKET	RANKLY	REASON
PROPYL	PUNNED	QUAERE	RACOON	RANNEL	REASTY
PROSER	PUNNER	QUAGGA	RADDLE	RANNLE	REAVER
PROSIT	PUNNET	QUAGGY	RADIAL	RANSEL	REBACK
PROTEA	PUNTEE	QUAHOG	RADIAN	RANSOM	REBATE
PROTON	PUNTER	QUAICH	RADISH	RANTER	REBATO
PROVED	PUPATE	QUAIGH	RADIUM	RANTLE	REBECK
PROVEN	PUPPED	QUAINT	RADIUS	RANULA	REBIND
PROVER	PUPPET	QUAKER	RADOME	RANZEL	REBITE
PRUINA	PURANA	QUALMY	RADULA	RAPHIA	REBOIL
PRUNER	PURDAH	QUANTA	RAETIA	RAPHIS	REBORE
PRYING	PURELY	QUARRY	RAFALE	RAPIER	REBORN
PSEUDO	PURFLE	QUARTE	RAFFIA	RAPINE	REBUFF
PSORIC	PURFLY	QUARTO	RAFFLE	RAPING	REBUKE
PSYCHE	PURGER	QUARTZ	RAFTER	RAPIST	REBURY
PTERIA	PURIFY	QUASAR	RAG-BAG	RAPPED	RECALL
PTERIN	PURINE	QUATCH	RAGGED	RAPPEE	RECANT
PTERIS	PURISM	QUAVER	RAGGEE	RAPPEL	RECAST
PTISAN	PURIST	QUEACH	RAGGLE	RAPPER	RECEDE
PTOSIS	PURITY	QUEASY	RAGING	RAPTOR	RECENT
PTYXIS	PURLER	QUEAZY	RAGLAN	RAREFY	RECEPT
PUBLIC	PURLIN	QUEEST	RAGMAN	RARELY	RECESS
PUCKER	PURPIE	QUELCH	RAGOUT	RARING	RECIPE

RECITE	REGEST	REPEAL	REVERE	RIGOUR	ROOTED
RECKAN	REGGAE	REPEAT	REVERS	RIG-OUT	ROOTER
RECKED	RÉGIME	REPENT	REVERT	RILLET	ROOTLE
RECKON	REGINA	REPINE	REVERY	RIMMED	ROPERY
RECOIL	REGION	REPLAY	REVEST	RIMOSE	ROPILY
RECORD	REGIUS	REPLUM	REVIED	RIMOUS	ROPING
RECOUP	REGIVE	REPONE	REVIEW	RINDED	ROQUET
RECTAL	REGLET	REPORT	REVILE	RINGED	RORTER
RECTOR	REGNAL	REPOSE	REVISE	RINGER	ROSACE
RECTUM	REGRET	REPOST	REVIVE	RINSER	ROSARY
RECTUS	REGULA	REPPED	REVOKE	RIOTER	ROSCID
RECURE	REHASH	REPUGN	REVOLT	RIOTRY	ROSEAL
RECUSE	REHEAR	REPULP	REVVED	RIPECK	ROSERY
REDACT	REHEAT	REPURE	REWARD	RIPELY	ROSIER
RED-BOX	REHEEL	REPUTE	REWIND	RIPPED	ROSILY
RED-BUD	REITER	REQUIT	REWIRE	RIPPER	ROSETY
RED-CAP	REIVER	RERAIL	REWORD	RIPPLE	ROSINY
REDDEN	REJECT	REREAD	REWORK	RIPPLY	ROSSER
REDDER	REJOIN	RESALE	RHESUS	RIPPON	ROSTER
REDDLE	RELAID	RESCUE	RHETOR	RIP-RAP	ROSTRA
RED-DOG	RELATE	RESEAT	RHEUMY	RIP-SAW	ROSULA
REDEEM	RELENT	RÉSEAU	RHEXIS	RISING	ROTARY
REDEYE	RELICT	RESECT	RHINAL	RISKER	ROTATE
RED-GUM	RELIDE	RESEDA	RHIZIC	RISQUÉ	ROTCHE
RED-HAT	RELIED	RESELL	RHODES	RITTER	ROT-GUT
RED-HOT	RELIEF	RESENT	RHODIC	RITUAL	ROTHER
REDIAE	RELIER	RESHIP	RHOMBI	RIVAGE	ROTOLO
RED-MAN	RELINE	RESIDE	RHUMBA	RIVERY	ROTTAN
RE-DONE	RELISH	RESIGN	RHYMED	RIZARD	ROTTED
REDOWA	RELIVE	RESILE	RHYMER	RIZZAR	ROTTEN
REDRAW	RELOAD	RESIST	RHYTHM	RIZZER	ROTTER
REDTOP	RELUCT	RESITE	RHYTON	RIZZOR	ROTULA
REDUCE	RELUME	RESOLD	RIALTO	ROAMER	ROTUND
REDUIT	REMADE	RESORB	RIANCY	ROARER	ROUBLE
REDWUD	REMAIN	RESORT	RIBALD	ROARIE	ROUCOU
REEBOK	REMAKE	RESTEM	RIBAND	ROBALO	ROUGHY
RE-ECHO	REMAND	RESTER	RIBBED	ROBBED	ROUMAN
REECHY	REMARK	RESULT	RIBBON	ROBBER	ROUNCE
REEDED	REMBLE	RÉSUMÉ	RIBIBE	ROBING	ROUNCY
REEDEN	REMEAD	RESUME	RIBOSE	ROBUST	ROUPIT
REEDER	REMEDE	RETAIL	RICCIA	ROCHET	ROUSER
RE-EDIT	REMEDY	RETAIN	RICHEN	ROCKER	ROUTER
REEFER	REMEID	RETAKE	RICHES	ROCKET	ROVING
REEKIE	REMIND	RETAMA	RICHLY	ROCOCO	ROW-DOW
REELER	REMISE	RETARD	RICKER	RODENT	ROZZER
REESTY	REMISS	RETELL	RICKLE	RODING	RUBATO
REEVED	REMORA	RETENE	RICKLY	RODMAN	RUBBED
REFACE	REMOTE	RETIAL	RIC-RAC	ROLAND	RUBBER
REFECT	REMOVE	RETINA	RICTAL	ROLLED	RUBBET
REFILL	REMUDA	RETIRE	RICTUS	ROLLER	RUBBIT
REFINE	RENAME	RETOLD	RIDDED	ROLL-ON	RUBBLE
REFLET	RENDER	RETOOK	RIDDEN	ROLL-UP	RUBBLY
REFLEX	RENEGE	RETORT	RIDDLE	ROMAGE	RUBEFY
REFLOW	RENIED	RETOUR	RIDENT	ROMAIC	RUBIED
REFLUX	RENNET	RETREE	RIDGED	ROMANY	RUBIFY
REFOOT	RENOWN	RETRIM	RIDGEL	ROMISH	RUBINE
REFORM	RENTAL	RETROD	RIDGIL	ROMPER	RUBRIC
REFUEL	RENTER	RETTED	RIDING	RONDEL	RUCKLE
REFUGE	RENVOI	RETUND	RIFELY	RONDOS	RUCKUS
REFUND	RENVOY	RETURF	RIFFLE	RONYON	RUDDER
REFUSE-	REOPEN	RETURN	RIFLER	ROOFED	RUDDLE
REFUTE	REPAID	RETUSE	RIGGED	ROOFER	RUDELY
REGAIN	REPAIR	REURGE	RIGGER	ROOKIE	RUDISH
REGALE	REPAND	REVAMP	RIGHTO	ROOMED	RUEFUL
REGARD	REPASS	REVEAL	RIGLIN	ROOMER	RUEING
REGENT	REPAST	REVERB	RIGOLL	ROOPIT	RUELLE

RUFFED	SAFELY	SANELY	SBIRRO	SCRAWM	SEA-MAW
RUFFIN	SAFETY	SANGAR	'SBLOOD	SCRAYE	SEAMER
RUFFLE	SAGELY	SANIES	SCABBY	SCREAK	SEA-MEW
RUFOUS	SAGENE	SANIFY	SCAITH	SCREAM	SEANAD
RUGGED	SAGGAR	SANITY	SCALAE	SCREED	SÉANCE
RUGGER	SAGGED	SANJAK	SCALAR	SCREEN	SEA-OWL
RUGOSE	SAGGER	SANNUP	SCALED	SCREWY	SEA-PAY
RUGOUS	SAGOIN	SANPAN	SCALER	SCRIBE	SEA-PEN
RUINED	SAGUIN	SANTAL	SCAMEL	SCRIED	SEA-PIE
RUINER	SAHIBA	SANTIR	SCAMPI	SCRIKE	SEA-PIG
RULING	SAIDST	SANTON	SCAMPO	SCRIMP	SEA-RAT
RUMBLE	SAILED	SANTUR	SCANTY	SCRINE	SEARCE
RUM-BUD	SAILER	SAPEGO	SCAPUS	SCRIPT	SEARCH
RUMINA	SAILOR	SAPELE	SCARAB	SCRIVE	SEARED
RUMKIN	SAIQUE	SAPFUL	SCARCE	SCROBE	SEASON
RUMMER	SAITHE	SAPIUM	SCARER	SCROLL	SEATED
RUMOUR	SAKIEH	SAPOTA	SCARRE	SCROOP	SEAWAY
RUMPER	SAKKOS	SAPPAN	SCARRY	SCRUFF	SEBATE
RUMPLE	SALAAM	SAPPED	SCARTH	SCRUMP	SECANT
RUMPUS	SALADE	SAPPER	SCARUS	SCRUNT	SECEDE
RUNDLE	SALAME	SAPPHO	SCATCH	SCRUTO	SECERN
RUNKLE	SALAMI	SAP-ROT	SCATHE	SCRUZE	SECESH
RUNLET	SALARY	SARDEL	SCATTY	SCRYER	SECKEL
RUNNEL	SALEWD	SARGUS	SCAURY	SCRYNE	SECOND
RUNNER	SALIAN	SARONG	SCAZON	SCUFFY	SECRET
RUNNET	SALIFY	SARSEN	SCEATT	SCULPT	SECTOR
RUN-OFF	SALINA	SARTOR	SCENIC	SCUMMY	SECUND
RUNRIG	SALINE	SASINE	SCERNE	SCURFY	SECURE
RUNTED	SALIVA	SATARA	SCHELM	SCURRY	SEDATE
RUNWAY	SALLAL	SATEEN	SCHEMA	SCURVY	SEDENT
RUSCUS	SALLEE	SATHAN	SCHEME	SCUTAL	SEDGED
RUSHEN	SALLET	SATINY	SCHISM	SCUTCH	SEDILE
RUSHER	SALLOW	SATIRE	SCHIST	SCUTUM	SEDUCE
RUSINE	SALMON	SATIVE	SCHLEP	SCYLLA	SEEDED
RUSSEL	SALOON	SATORI	SCHMOE	SCYPHI	SEEDER
RUSSET	SALOOP	SATRAP	SCHOOL	SCYTHE	SEEING
RUSSIA	SALTED	SATURN	SCHORL	SDAINE	SEEKER
RUSTED	SALTER	SATYRA	SCHOUT	'SDEATH	SEEMER
RUSTIC	SALTLY	SAUCER	SCHUIT	SEA-AIR	SEEMLY
RUSTLE	SALTUS	SAUGER	SCHUSS	SEA-APE	SEESAW
RUSTRE	SALUED	SAULGE	SCHUYT	SEA-BAT	SEETHE
RUTILE	SALUKI	SAULIE	SCIENT	SEABEE	SEGGAR
RUTTED	SALUTE	SAUREL	SCILLA	SEA-BOY	SEGHOL
RUTTER	SALVED	SAURIA	SCIROC	SEA-BUN	SEICHE
RYPECK	SALVER	SAVAGE	SCLAFF	SEA-CAP	SEINER
	SALVIA	SAVANT	SCLATE	SEA-CAT	SEISED
S	SALVOR	SAVATE	SCLERA	SEA-COB	SEISIN
	SAMARA	SAVINE	SCLERE	SEA-COW	SEIZER
SABBAT	SAMBAR	SAVING	SCOGAN	SEA-DOG	SEIZIN
SABEAN	SAMBUR	SAVORY	SCOLEX	SEA-EAR	SEJANT
SABIAN	SAMELY	SAVOUR	SCONCE	SEA-EEL	SELDOM
SABINE	SAMIAN	SAVVEY	SCOPAE	SEA-EGG	SELECT
SACCOS	SAMIEL	SAWDER	SCORCH	SEA-FAN	SELENE
SACHEM	SAMIOT	SAW-FLY	SCORER	SEA-FIR	SELJUK
SACHET	SAMITE	SAWING	SCORIA	SEA-FOG	SELLER
SACQUE	SAMLET	SAWNEY	SCORSE	SEA-FOX	SELVES
SACRAL	SAMOED ,	SAWPIT	SCOTCH	SEA-GOD	SEMBLE
SACRED	SAMPAN	SAW-SET	SCOTER	SEA-HOG	SEMEIA
SACRUM	SAMPLE	SAWYER	SCOTIA	SEA-ICE	SEMITE
SADDEN	SAMSHU	SAXAUL	SCOTIC	SEA-LAW	SEMMIT
SADDER	SAMSON	SAXONY	SCOTTY	SEALCH	SEMPLE
SADDHU	SANCHO	SAYEST	SCOUSE	SEALED	SEMPRE
SADDLE	SANDAL	SAYING	SCOUTH	SEALER	SEMSEM
SADISM	SANDED	SAYYID	SCOWTH	SEALGH.	SENARY
SADIST	SANDER	SAZHEN	SCRAPE	SEAMAN	SENATE
SAETER	SANDHI	SBIRRI	SCRAWL	SEA-MAT	SENDAL
SAFARI					

SENDED	SHADED	SHINNY	SIMIAL	SKI-BOB	SLUDGE
SENDER	SHADOW	SHINTO	SIMIAN	SKIING	SLUDGY
SEND-UP	SHADUF	SHINTY	SIMILE	SKILLY	SLUICE
SENECA	SHAGGY	SHIPPO	SIMKIN	SKIMPY	SLUICY
SENEGA	SHAIRN	SHIRRA	SIMMER	SKINNY	SLUMMY
SENHOR	SHAIVA	SHIRTY	'SIMMON	SKIVER	SLUMPY
SENILE	SHAKEN	SHIVER	SIMNEL	SKIVIE	SLURRY
SENIOR	SHAKER	SHOALY	SIMONY	SKIVVY	SLUSHY
SENNET	SHAKTA	SHODDY	SIMOOM	SKLATE	SLYEST
SENNIT	SHAKTI	SHODER	SIMOON	SKOLIA	SLYISH
SEÑORA	SHALLI	SHOGUN	SIMORG	SKREEN	SMALMY
SENSED	SHALOT	SHOPPY	SIMPAI	SKRIMP	SMALTO
SENSOR	SHAMAN	SHORER	SIMPER	SKRUMP	SMARMY
SENSUM	SHAMED	SHOUGH	SIMPLE	SKRYER	SMARTY
SENTRY	SHAMER	SHOULD	SIMPLY	SKURRY	SMATCH
SEPHEN	SHAMMY	SHOVEL	SIMURG	SKYISH	SMEARY
SEPIUM	SHAMOY	SHOVER	SINDON	SKYMAN	SMEATH
SEPSIS	SHANDY	SHOWED	SINEWY	SKYWAY	SMEECH
SEPTAL	SHANNY	SHOWER	SINFUL	SLABBY	SMEETH
SEPTET	SHANTY	SHRANK	SINGED	SLAGGY	SMEGMA
SEPTIC	SHAPED	SHREWD	SINGER	SLALOM	SMELLY
SEPTUM	SHAPEN	SHRIEK	SINGLE	SLANGY	SMIDDY
SEQUEL	SHAPER	SHRIFT	SINGLY	SLAP-UP	SMILAX
SEQUIN	SHARER	SHRIKE	SINKER	SLATED	SMILER
SERAIL	SHARNY	SHRILL	SINNED	SLATER	SMILET
SERANG	SHAVED	SHRIMP	SINNER	SLAVER	SMIRCH
SERAPE	SHAVEN	SHRINE	SINNET	SLAVEY	SMIRKY
SERAPH	SHAVER	SHRINK	SINTER	SLAVIC	SMIRRY
SERBAL	SHAVIE	SHRIVE	SIOUAN	SLAYER	SMITER
SERDAB	SHEAFY	SHROFF	SIPHON	SLEAVE	SMITHY
SEREIN	SHEARS	SHROUD	SIPPED	SLEAZY	SMOKED
SERENE	'SHEART	SHROVE	SIPPER	SLEDED	SMOKER
SERIAL	SHE-ASS	SHRUNK	SIPPET	SLEDGE	SMOOCH
SERIES	SHEATH	SHUCKS	SIPPLE	SLEECH	SMOOTH
SERIPH	SHEAVE	SHUT-IN	SIRCAR	SLEEKY	SMOUCH
SERMON	SHEBAT	SHYEST	SIRDAR	SLEEPY	SMOUSE
SEROON	SHEENY	SHYING	SIRENE	SLEETY	SMOYLE
SEROSA	SHEEPY	SHYISH	SIRIAN	SLEEVE	SMUDGE
SEROUS	SHEERS	SIALIC	SIRIUS	SLEEZY	SMUDGY
SERRAE	SHEETY	SICCAN	SIRKAR	SLEIGH	SMUGLY
SERRAN	SHEIKH	SICCAR	SIRRAH	SLEUTH	SMURRY
SERRAS	SHEILA	SICKEN	SIRREE	SLEWED	SMUTCH
SERVAL	SHEKEL	SICKER	SISKIN	SLICER	SMUTTY
SERVER	SHELFY	SICKLE	SISSOO	SLIDED	SNAGGY
SESAME	SHELLY	SICKLY	SISTER	SLIDER	SNAILS
SESELI	SHELTA	SIDE-ON	SISTRA	SLIGHT	SNAILY
SESTET	SHELTY	SIDING	SITHEN	SLIMLY	SNAPPY
SET-OFF	SHELVE	SIEGER	SITHES	SLIMSY	SNARER
SETOSE	SHELVY	SIENNA	SITTAR	SLINKY	SNARLY
SET-OUT	SHE-OAK	SIERRA	SITTER	SLIP-ON	SNASTE
SETTEE	SHERIF	SIESTA	SITULA	SLIPPY	SNATCH
SETTER	SHERPA	SIFFLE	SIWASH	SLIP-UP	SNATHE
SETTLE	SHERRY	SIFTER	SIX-DAY	SLIVED	SNAZZY
SET-TOS	SHEUCH	SIGNAL	SIX-GUN	SLIVEN	SNEAKY
SEVERE	SHEUGH	SIGNER	SIZING	SLIVER	SNEATH
SEVERY	SHEWEL	SIGNET	SIZZLE	SLOBBY	SNEERY
SEVRES	SHIELD	SIGNOR	SKAITH	SLOGAN	SNEESH
SEWAGE	SHIEST	SILAGE	SKARTH	SLOKEN	SNEEZE
SEWING	SHIFTY	SILENE	SKATER	SLOOMY	SNEEZY
SEXFID	SHIITE	SILENT	SKEELY	SLOPPY	SNELLY
SEXPOT	SHIKAR	SILICA	SKEIGH	SLOSHY	SNIFFY
SEXTAN	SHIKSA	SILKEN	SKELLY	SLOUCH	SNIFTY
SEXTET	SHIMMY	SILLER	SKERRY	SLOUGH	SNIPER
SEXTON	SHINDY	SILOED	SKETCH	SLOVAK	SNIPPY
SEXUAL	SHINED	SILVAN	SKEWED	SLOVEN	SNITCH
SHABBY	SHINER	SILVER	SKEWER	SLOWLY	SNIVEL

SNOBBY	SOPITE	SPEWER	SPURRY	STEARE	STRACK
SNOOKS	SOPPED	SPHENE	SPUTUM	STEELD	STRAFE
SNOOTY	SORAGE	SPHERE	SPYING	STEELY	STRAFF
SNOOZE	SORBET	SPHERY	SQUAIL	STEEPY	STRAIK
SNORER	SORBIC	SPHINX	SQUALL	STEERY	STRAIN
SNORTY	SORDES	SPICED	SQUAMA	STEEVE	STRAIT
SNOTTY	SORDID	SPICER	SQUAME	STELAE	STRAKE
SNOUTY	SORDOR	SPIDER	SQUARE	STELAR	STRAMP
SNUBBY	SORELY	SPIFFY	SQUASH	STEMMA	STRAND
SNUDGE	SORGHO	SPIGOT	SQUAWK	STEMME	STRASS
SNUFFY	SORNER	SPIKED	SQUEAK	STENCH	STRATA
SNUGLY	SORREL	SPILTH	SQUEAL	STEP-IN	STRATH
SOAKED	SORROW	SPINAL	SQUIER	STEPPE	STRAWY
SOAKEN	SORTER	SPINED	SQUIFF	STEP-UP	STREAK
SOAKER	SORTES	SPINEL	SQUILL	STEREO	STREAM
SOBBED	SORTIE	SPINET	SQUINT	STERIC	STREEK
SOBEIT	SOTHIC	SPINNY	SQUINY	STEROL	STREEL
SOBOLE	SOTTED	SPIRAL	SQUIRE	STEVEN	STREET
SOCAGE	SOUARI	SPIRED	SQUIRM	STEWED	STRESS
SOCCER	SOUDAN	SPIRIC	SQUIRR	STEWER	STREWN
SOCIAL	SOUGHT	SPIRIT	SQUIRT	STICKY	STRIAE
SOCKER	SOULED	SPITAL	SQUISH	STIEVE	STRICH
SOCKET	SOUPER	SPLASH	STABLE	STIFLE	STRICT
SOCMAN	SOUPLE	SPLEEN	STABLY	STIGMA	STRIDE
SODAIC	SOURCE	SPLENT	STACTE	STIGME	STRIFE
SODDEN	SOURLY	SPLICE	STADDA	STILET	STRIFT
SODGER	SOUSED	SPLINE	STADIA	STILLY	STRIGA
SODIUM	SOUSES	SPLINT	STAGED	STILTY	STRIKE
SOEVER	SOUTAR	SPLORE	STAGER	STIMIE	STRINE
SOFFIT	SOUTER	SPOFFY	STAGEY	STINGO	STRING
SOFISM	SOVIET	SPOILT	STAITH	STINGY	STRIPE
SOFTEN	SOVRAN	SPOKEN	STALAG	STINTY	STRIPY
SOFTLY	SOWANS	SPONGE	STALKO	STIPEL	STRIVE
SOGGED	SOW-BUG	SPONGY	STALKY	STIPES	STROAM
SOIGNÉ	SOWENS	SPOOKY	STAMEN	STIRPS	STROBE
SOILED	SOWING	SPOONY	STANCE	STITCH	STRODE
SOIRÉE	SOWTER	SPORTS	STANCH	STITHY	STROKE
SOLACE	SOZZLE	SPORTY	STANCK	STIVED	STROLL
SOLAND	SOZZLY	SPOSHY	STANZA	STIVER	STROMA
SOLANO	SPACED	SPOT-ON	STANZE	STOCKY	STROMB
SOLDAN	SPACER	SPOTTY	STANZO	STODGE	STRONG
SOLDER	SPADIX	SPOUSE	STAPES	STODGY	STROUD
SOLELY	SPAHEE	SPOUTY	STAPLE	STOKER	STROUP
SOLEMN	SPARER	SPRACK	STARCH	STOKES	STROUT
SOLEUS	SPARGE	SPRAID	STARER	STOLED	STROVE
SOL-FA'D	SPARKE	SPRAIN	STARRY	STOLEN	STROWN
SOLIDI	SPARRY	SPRANG	STARVE	STOLID	STRUCK
SOLITO	SPARSE	SPRAWL	STASIS	STOLON	STRUMA
SOLIVE	SPARTA	SPREAD	STATAL	STONED	STRUNG
SOLLAR	SPARTH	SPRENT	STATED	STONEN	STRUNT
SOLLER	SPATHE	SPRING	STATER	STONER	STUBBY
SO-LONG	SPAULD	SPRINT	STATIC	STOOGE	STUCCO
SOLUTE	SPAVIN	SPRITE	STATOR	STOOPE	STUDIO
SOLVER	SPAYAD	SPROUT	STATUA	STOP-GO	STUFFY
SOMBRE	SPEARY	SPRUCE	STATUE	STORAX	STUGGY
SOMITE	SPECIE	SPRUIT	STATUS	STORER	STUMER
SOMNUS	SPECKY	SPRUNG	STAVED	STOREY	STUMPY
SONANT	SPEECH	SPRUSH	STAVES	STORGE	STUPID
SONATA	SPEEDO	SPRYER	STAWED	STORMY	STUPOR
SONERI	SPEEDY	SPRYLY	STAYER	STOUND	STURDY
SONNET	SPEISS	SPUDDY	STAY-IN	STOURY	STYING
SONSIE	SPENCE	SPULYE	STEADY	STOUTH	STYLAR
SONTAG	SPERRE	SPUNGE	STEALE	STOVER	STYLET
SOOTHE	SPERSE	SPUNKY	STEALT	STOWER	STYLUS
SOPHIA	SPERST	SPURGE	STEAMY	STOWND	STYMIE
SOPHIC	SPETCH	SPURNE	STEANE	STOWRE	STYRAX

SUABLE
SUBACT
SUBBED
SUBDUE
SUBFEU
SUBLET
SUBMAN
SUBMIT
SUBORN
SUBTIL
SUBTLE
SUBTLY
SUBURB
SUBWAY
SUCCUS
SUCKED
SUCKEN
SUCKER
SUCKET
SUCK-IN
SUCKLE
SUDARY
SUDATE
SUDDEN
SUDDER
SUETTY
SUFFER
SUFFIX
SUFISM
SUGARY
SUIDAE
SUITED
SUITOR
SUIVEZ
SULCAL
SULCUS
SULLEN
SULPHA
SULTAN
SULTRY
SUMACH
SUMMAR
SUMMAT
SUMMED
SUMMER
SUMMIT
SUMMON
SUMPIT
SUNBOW
SUNDAE
SUNDAY
SUNDER
SUN-DEW
SUN-DOG
SUNDRA
SUNDRI
SUNDRY
SUNGAR
SUN-GOD
SUN-HAT
SUNKEN
SUNKET
SUNKIE
SUNLIT
SUNNED
SUN-RAY

SUNSET
SUNTAN
SUOMIC
SUPAWN
SUPERB
SUPINE
SUPPED
SUPPER
SUPPLE
SURBED
SURBET
SURELY
SURETE
SURETY
SURFER
SURREY
SURTAX
SURVEY
SUSLIK
SUTILE
SUTLER
SUTTEE
SUTTLE
SUTURE
SVARGA
SVELTE
SWADDY
SWAMPY
SWANKY
SWANNY
SWARAJ
SWARDY
SWARGA
SWARTH
SWARTY
SWARVE
SWASHY
SWATHE
SWATHY
SWAYED
SWAYER
SWEATY
SWEENY
SWEEPY
SWEERT
SWEETY
SWEIRT
SWERGA
SWERVE
SWEVEN
SWIMMY
SWINGE
SWIPER
SWIPES
SWIPEY
SWIRLY
SWISHY
SWITCH
SWIVEL
SWOUND
SYLVAN
SYLVIA
SYMBOL
SYNDET
SYNDIC

SYNTAN
SYNTAX
SYPHON
SYRIAC
SYRIAN
SYRINX
SYRTES
SYRTIS
SYRUPY
SYSTEM
SYZYGY

T

TABARD
TABBED
TABEFY
TABLED
TABLET
TABOUR
TABRET
TABULA
TACKED
TACKER
TACKET
TACKLE
TACTIC
TAENIA
TAGDAY
TAGEND
TAGGED
TAGGER
TAGRAG
TAGUAN
TAHSIL
TAIGLE
TAILED
TAILOR
TAIL-UP
TAILYE
TAISCH
TAIVER
TAKAHE
TAKE-IN
TAKING
TALBOT
TALCKY
TALCUM
TALENT
TALION
TALKER
TALKIE
TALLAT
TALLOT
TALLOW
TALMUD
TALWEG
TAMALE
TAMANU
TAMARA
TAMBER
TAMELY
TAMINE
TAMING
TAMISE
TAMMUZ

TAMPER
TAMPON
TAM-TAM
TAN-BED
TANDEM
TANGED
TANGIE
TANGLE
TANGLY
TANGUN
TANIST
TANKED
TANKER
TANKIA
TANNAH
TANNED
TANNER
TANNIC
TANNIN
TANNOY
TAN-PIT
TANREC
TANTRA
TAN-VAT
TAOISM
TAOIST
TAPETA
TAPETI
TAPIST
TAPPED
TAPPER
TAPPET
TAPPIT
TARAND
TAR-BOX
TARCEL
TARGET
TARGUM
TARIFF
TARMAC
TARNAL
TARPAN
TARPON
TARRAS
TARRED
TARROW
TARSAL
TARSEL
TARSIA
TARSUS
TARTAN
TARTAR
TARTLY
TARZAN
TASKER
TASLET
TASSEL
TASSET
TASSIE
TASTED
TASTER
TATLER
TATTER
TATTIE
TATTLE
TATTOO

TAUGHT
TAUPIE
TAURIC
TAURUS
TAUTEN
TAUTIT
TAUTOG
TAVERN
TAVERT
TAWDRY
TAWERY
TAWING
TAWPIE
TAWTIE
TAXIED
TAXING
TCHICK
T-CLOTH
T-CROSS
TEA-BAG
TEA-CUP
TEAGLE
TEAGUE
TEAMED
TEAMER
TEA-POT
TEAPOY
TEARER
TEASEL
TEASER
TEA-SET
TEATED
TEA-URN
TEAZEL
TEAZLE
TEBBAD
TEBETH
TECKEL
TEDDED
TEDDER
TEDIUM
TEEING
TEENTY
TEEPEE
TEE-TEE
TEETER
TEGMEN
TEGULA
TELARY
TELEDU
TELEGA
TELESM
TELLAR
TELLER
TELLUS
TELSON
TELUGU
TEMPER
TEMPLE
TENACE
TENAIL
TENANT
TENDED
TENDER
TENDON
TENDRE

TEN-GUY
TENIAE
TENNER
TENNIS
TENREC
TENSON
TENSOR
TENTED
TENTER
TENTIE
TENUES
·TENUIS
TENURE
TENUTO
TENZON
TEPEFY
TERAPH
TERATA
TERBIC
TERCEL
TERCET
TERCIO
TEREDO
TEREFA
TERETE
TERGAL
TERGUM
TERMER
TERMES
TERMLY
TERMOR
TERNAL
TERRET
TERRIT
TERROR
TERTIA
TESTEE
TESTER
TESTES
TESTIS
TESTON
TETANY
TETCHY
TETHER
TETHYS
TETRAD
TETTER
TETTIX
TEUTON
TEWART
TEWHIT
THAIRM
THALER
THALIA
THANAH
THANNA
THATCH
THAWER
THEAVE
THEBAN
THEBES
THECAE
THECAL
THECLA
THEINE
THEIRS

THEISM
THEIST
THEMIS
THENAR
THENCE
THEORY
THESES
THESIS
THETCH
THETIC
THEWED
THEWES
THIBET
THIBLE
THICKY
THIEVE
THINGY
THINLY
THIRST
THIRTY
THIVEL
THOLOI
THOLOS
THOLUS
THORAH
THORAX
THORNY
THORON
THORPE
THOUGH
THOWEL
THRALL
THRANG
THRASH
THRAVE
THRAWN
THREAD
THREAP
THREAT
THREEP
THRENE
THRESH
THRICE
THRIFT
THRILL
THRIPS
THRIVE
THROAT
THRONE
THRONG
THROVE
THROWN
THRUSH
THRUST
THULIA
THUMBY
THWACK
THWART
THYINE
THYMOL
THYMUS
THYRSE
THYRSI
TIARA'D
TIB-CAT
TIBERT

TIBIAL
TICKED
TICKEN
TICKER
TICKET
TICKEY
TICKLE
TICKLY
TICTAC
TIDBIT
TIDDLE
TIDDLY
TIDIED
TIDILY
TIE-PIN
TIERCE
TIE-ROD
TIE-WIG
TIFFIN
TIGERY
TIGHTS
TILERY
TILING
TILLER
TIL-OIL
TILTED
TILTER
TIMBAL
TIMBER
TIMBRE
TIMELY
TIMING
TIMIST
TIMOUS
TINCAL
TIN-CAN
TINDAL
TINDED
TINDER
TINFUL
TINGLE
TINGLY
TINIER
TINKER
TINKLE
TINKLY
TINMAN
TINNED
TINNER
TINNIE
TINPOT
TINSEL
TINSEY
TINTER
TIP-CAT
TIP-OFF
TIPPED
TIPPER
TIPPET
TIPPLE
TIPTOE
TIPTOP
TIPULA
TIRADE
TIRING
TIROES

TIRRIT
TISANE
TISICK
TISSUE
TITBIT
TITELY
TITFER
TITHED
TITHER
TITIAN
TITLED
TITLER
TITOKI
TI-TREE
TITTER
TITTLE
TITTUP
TITULE
TITUPY
TMESIS
TOCHER
TOCSIN
TODDLE
TOECAP
TOEING
TO-FALL
TOFFEE
TOFORE
TOGAED
TOGATE
TOGGLE
TOILED
TOILER
TOILET
TOKEN'D
TOLEDO
TOLING
TOLLER
TOL-LOL
TOLSEL
TOLSEY
TOLTER
TOLUIC
TOLUOL
TOLZEY
TOMATO
TOMBAC
TOMBAK
TOMBIC
TOMBOC
TOMBOY
TOM-CAT
TOMIAL
TOMIUM
TOMPON
TOMTIT
TOM-TOM
TO-NAME
TONANT
TONEME
TONGUE
TONISH
TONITE
TONNAG
TONSIL
TONSOR

TOOART
TOORIE
TOOTER
TOOTHY
TOOTLE
TOO-TOO
TOP-HAT
TOPHET
TOPHUS
TOPMAN
TOPPED
TOPPER
TOPPLE
TORANA
TO-REND
TO-RENT
TORERO
TORIFY
TOROID
TORPID
TORPOR
TORQUE
TORRET
TORRID
TORSEL
TORULA
TORYFY
TOSHER
TOSSED
TOSSEN
TOSSER
TOSS-UP
TO-TEAR
TOTHER
TOTTER
TOTTIE
TOUCAN
TOUCHE
TOUCHY
TOUPEE
TOUPET
TOURER
TOUSER
TOUSLE
TOUTER
TOUTIE
TOUZLE
TOWAGE
TOWARD
TOWERY
TOWHEE
TOWING
TOWMON
TOWNEE
TOW-NET
TOWNLY
TOWSER
TOXOID
TOYING
TOYISH
TOYMAN
T-PLATE
TRACER
TRADED
TRADER
TRAGIC

TRAGUS
TRANCE
TRANSE
TRAPAN
TRAPES
TRAPPY
TRASHY
TRAUMA
TRAVEL
TRAVIS
TRAYNE
TREATY
TREBLE
TREBLY
TREK-OX
TREMIE
TREMOR
TRENCH
TRENDY
TREPAN
TREPID
TRESSY
TREVIS
TRIACT
TRIAGE
TRIBAL
TRICAR
TRICKY
TRICOT
TRIFID
TRIFLE
TRIGLY
TRIGON
TRILBY
TRILLO
TRIMLY
TRINAL
TRIODE
TRIPLE
TRIPLY
TRIPOD
TRIPOS
TRISUL
TRITON
TRIUNE
TRIVET
TRIVIA
TROCAR
TROCHE
TROELY
TROGGS
TROGON
TROIKA
TROJAN
TROLLY
TROMPE
TROPHI
TROPHY
TROPIC
TROPPO
TROUGH
TROUPE
TROUSE
TROUTY
TROVER
TROWEL

TROYAN
TRUANT
TRUDGE
TRUISM
TRUSTY
TRUTHY
TRYGON
TRYING
TRY-OUT
TSAMBA
TSETSE
T-SHIRT
TSOTSI
TSWANA
TUAREG
TUBAGE
TUBBER
TUBFUL
TUBING
TUBULE
TUCHUN
TUCKER
TUCKET
TUCK-IN
TUFFET
TUFTED
TUFTER
TUGGED
TUGGER
TUILLE
TULBAN
TULIPA
TULWAR
TUMBLE
TUMEFY
TUMOUR
TUMPHY
TUM-TUM
TUMULI
TUMULT
TUNDRA
TUNDUN
TUNGUS
TUNING
TUNKER
TUNNEL
TUPAIA
TUPELO
TUPIAN
TURBAN
TURBID
TURBIT
TURBOT
TURDUS
TUREEN
TURFED
TURFEN
TURGID
TURGOR
TURION
TURKEY
TURKIC
TURKIS
TURNED
TURNER
TURNIP

TURN-UP	ULOSIS	UNEYED	UNLEAD	UNSOLD	UPGAZE
TURRET	ULSTER	UNFACT	UNLEAL	UNSOUL	UPGREW
TURTLE	ULTIMO	UNFAIR	UNLESS	UNSOWN	UPGROW
TURVES	ULTION	UNFEED	UNLICH	UNSPAR	UPGUSH
TUSCAN	UMBERY	UNFELT	UNLIKE	UNSPED	UPHAND
TUSKAR	UMBLES	UNFINE	UNLIME	UNSPUN	UPHANG
TUSKED	UMBRAL	UNFIRM	UNLINE	UNSTEP	UPHAUD
TUSKER	UMBREL	UNFOLD	UNLINK	UNSTOP	UPHEAP
TUSSAH	UMBRIL	UNFOOL	UNLIVE	UNSTOW	UPHELD
TUSSEH	UMLAUT	UNFORM	UNLOAD	UNSUIT	UPHILD
TUSSER	UMPIRE	UNFREE	UNLOCK	UNSUNG	UPHILL
TUSSLE	UNABLE	UNFURL	UNLORD	UNSURE	UPHOLD
TUTMAN	UNAWED	UNGAIN	UNLOST	UNTACK	UPHURL
TUTRIX	UNBARE	UNGEAR	UNLOVE	UNTAME	UPKEEP
TUTSAN	UNBARK	UNGILD	UNMADE	UNTEAM	UPKNIT
TUT-TUT	UNBEAR	UNGILT	UNMAKE	UNTENT	UPLAND
TU-WHOO	UNBELT	UNGIRD	UNMASK	UNTHAW	UPLEAD
TUXEDO	UNBEND	UNGIRT	UNMEEK	UNTIDY	UPLEAN
TUYERE	UNBENT	UNGLAD	UNMEET	UNTIED	UPLEAP
TWAITE	UNBIAS	UNGLUE	UNMIRY	UNTILE	UPLIFT
TWANGY	UNBIND	UNGOWN	UNMOOR	UNTOLD	UP-LINE
TWEENY	UNBITT	UNGUAL	UNMOWN	UNTOMB	UPLOCK
TWELVE	UNBOLT	UNGUES	UNNAIL	UNTORN	UPLOOK
TWENTY	UNBONE	UNGUIS	UNNEST	UNTRIM	UPMAKE
TWICER	UNBOOT	UNGULA	UNOWED	UNTROD	UPMOST
TWIGGY	UNBORN	UNGYVE	UNPACK	UNTRUE	UPPING
TWIGHT	UNBRED	UNHAIR	UNPAID	UNTUCK	UPPISH
TWILIT	UNBURY	UNHAND	UNPENT	UNTUNE	UPPITY
TWILLY	UNBUSY	UNHANG	UNPICK	UNTURF	UPREAR
TWINED	UNCAGE	UNHASP	UNPLUG	UNTURN	UPREST
TWINER	UNCAPE	UNHEAD	UNPOPE	UNUSED	UPRISE
TWINGE	UNCART	UNHEAL	UNPRAY	UNVEIL	UPRIST
TWIRLY	UNCASE	UNHELE	UNPROP	UNWARE	UPROAR
TWISTY	UNCATE	UNHELM	UNRAKE	UNWARY	UPROLL
TWITCH	UNCIAL	UNHEWN	UNREAD	UNWEAL	UPROOT
TWO-BIT	UNCINI	UNHIVE	UNREAL	UNWELL	UPROSE
TWO-PLY	UNCLAD	UNHOLY	UNREEL	UNWEPT	UPRUSH
TWO-WAY	UNCLEW	UNHOOD	UNREIN	UNWILL	UPSEND
TWYERE	UNCLOG	UNHOOK	UNRENT	UNWIND	UPSHOT
TYBURN	UNCOCK	UNHOOP	UNREST	UNWIRE	UPSIDE
TYCOON	UNCOIL	UNHUNG	UNRIPE	UNWISE	UPSTAY
TYLOTE	UNCOLT	UNHURT	UNROBE	UNWISH	UPSWAY
TYMBAL	UNCOPE	UNHUSK	UNROLL	UNWIST	UPTAKE
TYMPAN	UNCORD	UNIATE	UNROOF	UNWIVE	UPTEAR
TYPHON	UNCORK	UNICEF	UNROOT	UNWONT	UP-TILL
TYPHUS	UNCOWL	UNIFIC	UNROPE	UNWORK	UPTILT
TYPIFY	UNCURL	UNIPED	UNRUDE	UNWORN	UPTORN
TYPING	UNDATE	UNIPOD	UNRULE	UNWRAP	UPTOWN
TYPIST	UNDEAF	UNIQUE	UNRULY	UNYOKE	UPTURN
TYRANT	UNDEAR	UNISEX	UNSAFE	UPBEAR	UPWAFT
TYRIAN	UNDECK	UNISON	UNSAID	UPBEAT	UPWARD
TYRING	UNDERN	UNITAL	UNSEAL	UPBIND	UPWELL
TYROES	UNDIES	UNITED	UNSEAM	UPBLOW	UPWIND
	UNDINE	UNITER	UNSEAT	UPBOIL	URACIL
U	UNDOCK	UNJUST	UNSEEL	UPBRAY	URAEUS
	UNDOER	UNKENT	UNSEEN	UPCAST	URALIC
UBERTY	UNDONE	UNKEPT	UNSELF	UPCOIL	URANIA
UBIETY	UNDRAW	UNKIND	UNSENT	UPCOME	URANIC
UGLILY	UNDULY	UNKING	UNSEWN	UPCURL	URANIN
UGRIAN	UNDYED	UNKISS	UNSHED	UPDATE	URANUS
UGSOME	UNEASE	UNKNIT	UNSHIP	UPDRAG	URANYL
ULICON	UNEASY	UNKNOT	UNSHOD	UPDRAW	URBANE
ULIKON	UNEATH	UNLACE	UNSHOE	UPFILL	URCHIN
ULITIS	UNEDGE	UNLADE	UNSHOT	UPFLOW	UREMIA
ULLAGE	UNESCO	UNLAID	UNSHUT	UPFURL	UREMIC
ULLING	UNEVEN	UNLASH	UNSOFT	UPGANG	URESIS
ULNARE					

URETER
URETIC
URGENT
URGING
URINAL
URNFUL
UROPOD
UROSIS
URSINE
URTICA
USABLE
USAGER
USANCE
USED-UP
USEFUL
USTION
USURER
USWARD
UTERUS
UTGARD
UTMOST
UTOPIA
UVULAR

V

VACANT
VACATE
VACKED
VACUUM
VAGARY
VAGILE
VAGINA
VAGROM
VAINLY
VAISYA
VAKASS
VAKEEL
VALETA
VALGUS
VALISE
VALLAR
VALLEY
VALLUM
VALOUR
VALUED
VALUER
VALUTA
VALVAL
VALVAR
VALVED
VAMOSE
VAMPER
VANDAL
VANISH
VANITY
VANNED
VANNER
VAPOUR
VARECH
VARIED
VARIER
VARLET
VARSAL
VARUNA
VARVED
VARVEL

VASSAL
VASTLY
VATFUL
VAUDOO
VAULTY
VAUNCE
VAWARD
VEADAR
VECTOR
VEDISM
VEDIST
VEGETE
VEHMIC
VEILED
VEINED
VELATE
VELETA
VELLON
VELLUM
VELOCE
VELOUR
VELURE
VELVET
VENDEE
VENDER
VENDIS
VENDOR
VENDUE
VENEER
VENERY
VENGER
VENIAL
VENICE
VENIRE
VENITE
VENNEL
VENOSE
VENOUS
VENSON
VENTED
VENTER
VENTIL
VENULE
VERBAL
VERDET
VERDIT
VERDOY
VERGER
VERIER
VERIFY
VERILY
VERISM
VERIST
VERITY
VERMES
VERMIL
VERMIN
VERMIS
VERNAL
VERREL
VERREY
VERSAL
VERSED
VERSER
VERSET
VERSIN

VERSUS
VERTEX
VERTUE
VERVEL
VERVET
VESICA
VESPER
VESSEL
VESTAL
VESTAS
VESTED
VESTRY
VETCHY
VETOES
VETTED
VEXING
VIABLE
VIATOR
VIBIST
VIBRIO
VICARY
VICTIM
VICTOR
VICUÑA
VIDAME
VIDUAL
VIELLE
VIEWER
VIEWLY
VIGOUR
VIHARA
VIKING
VILDLY
VILELY
VILIFY
VILLAN
VILLAR
VILLUS
VIMANA
VINERY
VINOUS
VINTRY
VIOLER
VIOLET
VIOLIN
VIPERA
VIRAGO
VIRENT
VIRGER
VIRGIN
VIRILE
VIROSE
VIROUS
VIRTUE
VISAED
VISAGE
VISCID
VISCIN
VISCUM
VISCUS
VISÉED
VISHNU
VISIER
VISILE
VISION
VISITE

VISIVE
VISTA'D
VISTAL
VISUAL
VITALS
VITRIC
VITTAE
VIVACE
VIVARY
VIVELY
VIVERS
VIVIFY
VIVRES
VIZARD
VIZIER
VIZZIE
VOCULE
VOGUEY
VOICED
VOICER
VOIDED
VOIDEE
VOIDER
VOLAGE
VOLANS
VOLANT
VOLARY
VOLERY
VOLLEY
VOLOST
VOLUME
VOLUTE
VOLVOX
VOMICA
VOMITO
VOODOO
VORAGO
VORANT
VORPAL
VORTEX
VOTARY
VOTEEN
VOTIVE
VOUDOU
VOULGE
VOWESS
VOYAGE
VOYEUR
VULCAN
VULGAR
VULGUS
VULNED
VULPES
VULVAL
VULVAR

W

WABAIN
WABBLE
WABOOM
WADDED
WADDIE
WADDLE
WADING
WADMAL
WADMOL

WADSET
WAEFUL
WAFERY
WAFFLE
WAFTED
WAFTER
WAGGED
WAGGLE
WAGGLY
WAGGON
WAHABI
WAHINE
WAILER
WAITER
WAIVER
WAKIKI
WAKING
WALISE
WALKER
WALK-ON
WALLAH
WALLED
WALLER
WALLET
WALLOP
WALLOW
WALNUT
WALRUS
WAMBLE
WAMBLY
WAMMUS
WAMPEE
WAMPUM
WAMPUS
WANDER
WANDLE
WANGAN
WANGLE
WANGUN
WANION
WANKLE
WANNED
WANNEL
WANTED
WANTER
WANTON
WAPITI
WAPPER
WARBLE
WAR-CRY
WARDEN
WARDER
WARDOG
WAR-GOD
WARILY
WARMAN
WARMED
WARMER
WARMLY
WARMTH
WARM-UP
WARNER
WARPED
WARPER
WARRAY

WARRED
WARREN
WARREY
WARSLE
WARTED
WASHED
WASHEN
WASHER
WASH-IN
WASH-UP
WASTEL
WASTER
WASTRY
WATERY
WATTLE
WAUCHT
WAUGHT
WAURST
WAVERY
WAVING
WAX-END
WAXING
WAX-RED
WAYLAY
WAY-OUT
WEAKEN
WEAKLY
WEALTH
WEANEL
WEAPON
WEARER
WEASEL
WEAVED
WEAVER
WEAZEN
WEBBED
WEDDED
WEDGED
WEEDED
WEEDER
WEEKLY
WEEPER
WEEPIE
WEETEN
WEEVER
WEEVIL
WEIGHT
WELDER
WELDOR
WELKIN
WELTER
WENDED
WENDIC
WESTER
WETHER
WETTED
WHACKY
WHALER
WHALLY
WHARES
WHARVE
WHATEN
WHATNA
WHATSO
WHEELY
WHEEZE

WHEEZY	WIMBLE	WOMAN'D	WUNNER	YELPER	ZENITH
WHELKY	WIMPLE	WOMBAT	WURLEY	YEOMAN	ZEPHYR
WHENAS	WINCER	WOMERA	WUTHER	YEOMEN	ZEREBA
WHENCE	WINCEY	WONDER	WUZZLE	YES-MAN	ZERIBA
WHERRY	WINDAC	WONING	WYVERN	YESTER	ZEUGMA
WHEUGH	WINDAS	WONTED		YEZIDI	ZIGZAG
WHEYEY	WINDED	WOOBUT	**X**	YIPPEE	ZILLAH
WHIFFY	WINDER	WOODED	XENIAL	Y-LEVEL	ZINCED
WHILES	WINDLE	WOODEN	XENIUM	YNAMBU	ZINCKY
WHILLY	WINDOW	WOODIE	XHOSAN	YODLER	ZINGEL
WHILOM	WIND-UP	WOODSY	XOANON	YOGISM	ZINKED
WHILST	WINGED	WOOFED	XYLENE	YOICKS	ZINNIA
WHIMMY	WINGER	WOOFER	XYLOID	YOJANA	ZIPPER
WHIMSY	WINGUN	WOOING	XYLOMA	YOKING	ZIRCON
WHINER	WINKER	WOOLLY	XYLOSE	YOLKED	ZITHER
WHINGE	WINKLE	WOOSEL	XYSTER	YONDER	ZLOTYS
WHINNY	WINNER	WORDED	XYSTOS	YONKER	ZODIAC
WHIPPY	WINNOW	WORKED	XYSTUS	YORKER	ZOETIC
WHIRRY	WINSEY	WORKER		YORUBA	ZOMBIE
WHISHT	WINTER	WORK-IN	**Y**	YOUTHY	ZONARY
WHISKY	WINTLE	WORMED	YABBER	YOWLEY	ZONATE
WHITEN	WINTRY	WORMER	YACKER	YPIGHT	ZONING
WHITES	WIPING	WORRAL	YAFFLE	YPLAST	ZONOID
WHOLLY	WIRILY	WORREL	YAGGER	YSHEND	ZONULA
WHY-NOT	WIRING	WORRIT	YAHVEH	Y-TRACK	ZONULE
WICKED	WISARD	WORSEN	YAHWEH	YTTRIA	ZOOEAL
WICKEN	WISDOM	WORSER	YAKKER	YTTRIC	ZOONAL
WICKER	WISELY	WORTHY	Y-ALLOY	YUCKER	ZOONIC
WICKET	WISHER	WORTLE	YAMMER	YWRAKE	ZOOZOO
WIDELY	WISKET	WOUBIT	YANKEE	YWROKE	ZORINO
WIELDY	WISTLY	WOUNDY	YANKER		ZOSTER
WIFELY	WITHAL	WOU-WOU	YANKIE	**Z**	ZOUAVE
WIGEON	WITHER	WOWSER	YAOURT	ZABETA	ZOUNDS
WIGGED	WITHIN	WOW-WOW	YAPOCK	ZABIAN	ZUFOLO
WIGGLE	WITTED	WRAITH	YAPPER	ZAFFER	ZUNIAN
WIGGLY	WITTOL	WRASSE	YARELY	ZAFFRE	ZYGOMA
WIGWAG	WIVERN	WRATHY	YARPHA	ZANDER	ZYGOSE
WIGWAM	WIZARD	WRAXLE	YARROW	ZARAPE	ZYGOTE
WILDER	WIZIER	WREATH	YATTER	ZAREBA	ZYMASE
WILFUL	WOADED	WRENCH	YAUPON	ZARNEC	ZYMITE
WILILY	WOBBLE	WRETCH	YBLENT	ZEALOT	ZYMOID
WILLER	WOBBLY	WRIGHT	YBRENT	ZEBECK	ZYMOME
WILLET	WOEFUL	WRITER	YCLEPT	ZELANT	ZYTHUM
WILLEY	WOGGLE	WRITHE	YEARLY	ZELOSO	
WILLOW	WOLFER	WROATH	YEASTY	ZENANA	
WILTON	WOLVES	WROKEN	YELLOW	ZENDIK	

A	ABBASID	ABOUGHT	ABSENCE	ABYSSAL
	ABDOMEN	ABOULIA	ABSINTH	ACADEME
AARONIC	ABETTED	ABRAXAS	ABSOLVE	ACADEMY
ABACTOR	ABETTOR	ABREAST	ABSTAIN	ACADIAN
ABADDON	ABIDDEN	ABRIDGE	ABTHANE	ACALEPH
ABALONE	ABIDING	ABROACH	ABUSION	ACANTHA
ABANDON	ABIGAIL	ABROOKE	ABUSIVE	ACAPNIA
ABASHED	ABILITY	ABSCESS	ABUTTAL	ACARIAN
ABATTIS	ABJOINT	ABSCIND	ABUTTED	ACARIDA
ABATURE	ABJURER	ABSCISS	ABUTTER	ACARINA
ABAXIAL	ABOLISH	ABSCOND	ABYSMAL	ACARINE

ACAROID
ACATOUR
ACCEDER
ACCIDIE
ACCINGE
ACCLAIM
ACCOAST
ACCOMPT
ACCOUNT
ACCOURT
ACCRETE
ACCRUAL
ACCURSE
ACCUSAL
ACCUSED
ACCUSER
ACERBIC
ACEROSE
ACEROUS
ACETATE
ACETIFY
ACETONE
ACETOSE
ACETOUS
ACHAEAN
ACHAIAN
ACHATES
ACHERON
ACHIEVE
ACIDIFY
ACIDITY
ACIFORM
ACK-EMMA
ACLINIC
ACOLYTE
ACOLYTH
ACONITE
ACORNED
ACOUCHY
ACQUEST
ACQUIRE
ACREAGE
ACRIDIN
ACROBAT
ACROGEN
ACRONYM
ACROTER
ACRYLIC
ACTAEON
ACTINAL
ACTINIA
ACTINIC
ACTINON
ACTRESS
ACTUARY
ACTUATE
ACUSHLA
ACUTELY
ACYCLIC
ADAGIOS
ADAMANT
ADAMITE
ADAPTED
ADAPTER
ADAPTOR
ADAXIAL

ADDENDA
ADDRESS
ADDUCER
ADENINE
ADENOID
ADENOMA
ADERMIN
ADHARMA
ADHERER
ADHIBIT
ADIPOSE
ADJOINT
ADJOURN
ADJUDGE
ADJUNCT
ADMIRAL
ADMIRER
ADONISE
ADOPTED
ADPRESS
ADRENAL
ADULATE
ADVANCE
ADVERSE
ADVISED
ADVISER
ADVISOR
AECIDIA
AEFAULD
A-EFFECT
AEOLIAN
AEONIAN
AERATOR
AEROBIC
AEROBUS
AEROSOL
AETNEAN
AFFABLE
AFFABLY
AFFAIRE
AFFINED
AFFLICT
AFFORCE
AFFRONT
AFFYING
AFRICAN
AFTMOST
AGAINST
AGAMOID
AGAMOUS
AGELESS
AGELONG
AGGRATE
AGGRESS
AGILELY
AGILITY
AGISTER
AGISTOR
AGITATE
AGITATO
AGNAMED
AGNATIC
AGNOMEN
AGOGICS
AGONISE
AGONIST

AGRAFFE
AGRAPHA
AGRAVIC
AGRISED
AGROUND
AGUE-FIT
AHEIGHT
AHRIMAN
AHUNGRY
AIBLINS
AIDANCE
AIDLESS
AILANTO
AILERON
AILETTE
AILMENT
AIMLESS
AIR-BASE
AIR-BATH
AIR-BELL
AIR-CELL
AIR-CREW
AIR-DROP
AIRHOLE
AIR-LANE
AIRLESS
AIR-LIFT
AIR-LOCK
AIR-MAIL
AIR-MISS
AIRPORT
AIR-PUMP
AIR-RAID
AIR-RAIL
AIRSHIP
AIR-SICK
AIR-STOP
AIR-TRAP
AIRWARD
AJUTAGE
AKVAVIT
ALAMEDA
ALAMODE
ALAMORT
ALANNAH
ALARMED
ALBINOS
ALBUMEN
ALBUMIN
ALCHEMY
ALCHYMY
ALCIDES
ALCOHOL
ALCORAN
ALE-BUSH
ALE-COST
ALE-HOOF
ALEMBIC
ALENGTH
ALEPINE
ALE-POLE
ALERION
ALERTLY
ALEWIFE
ALFALFA
ALGATES

ALGEBRA
ALGESIA
ALGESIS
ALGINIC
ALIASES
ALICANT
ALIDADE
ALIENED
ALIENEE
ALIENOR
ALIMENT
ALIMONY
ALIQUOT
ALIZARI
ALKALIS
ALKANET
ALKORAN
ALLAYER
ALLEGED
ALLEGRO
ALLERGY
ALLEYED
ALL-GOOD
ALL-HAIL
ALLHEAL
ALLONGE
ALL-OVER
ALLOWED
ALL-SEED
ALL-SEER
ALL-STAR
ALL-TIME
ALLUVIA
ALL-WORK
ALLYING
ALLY-TAW
ALLY-TOR
ALMAINE
ALMANAC
ALMIRAH
ALMONER
ALMONRY
ALMS-FEE
ALMS-MAN
ALNAGER
ALODIAL
ALODIUM
ALOETIC
ALOOFLY
ALPHORN
ALREADY
ALRIGHT
ALSATIA
ALSO-RAN
ALTERNE
ALTHAEA
ALTHING
ALTHORN
ALUMINA
ALUMISH
ALUMIUM
ALUMNAE
ALUMNUS
ALUNITE
ALVEARY
ALVEOLE

ALVEOLI
ALYSSUM
AMALGAM
AMANITA
AMARANT
AMATEUR
AMATIVE
AMATORY
AMAZING
AMBAGES
AMBASSY
AMBATCH
AMBERED
AMBIENT
AMBITTY
AMBLING
AMBONES
AMBROID
AMBS-ACE
AMENAGE
AMENDER
AMENITY
AMENTAL
AMENTIA
AMENTUM
AMERIND
AMES-ACE
AMHARIC
AMIABLE
AMIABLY
AMILDAR
AMMETER
AMMONAL
AMMONIA
AMNESIA
AMNESIC
AMNESTY
AMOEBAE
AMOEBIC
AMONGST
AMORINI
AMORINO
AMORISM
AMORIST
AMOROSA
AMOROSO
AMOROUS
AMPASSY
AMPHORA
AMPLIFY
AMPOULE
AMPULLA
AMPUTEE
AMTRACK
AMUSING
AMUSIVE
AMYGDAL
AMYLASE
AMYLENE
AMYLOID
ANAEMIA
ANAEMIC
ANAGOGE
ANAGOGY
ANAGRAM
ANALOGY

ANALYSE	ANTHOID	APRAXIA	AROUSAL	ASTARTE
ANALYST	ANTHONY	APRICOT	AROUSER	ASTATIC
ANANIAS	ANTHRAX	APROPOS	ARRAIGN	ASTATKI
ANAPEST	ANTIGEN	APSIDAL	ARRANGE	ASTEISM
ANARCHY	ANTILOG	APSIDES	ARRASED	ASTERIA
ANATASE	ANTIQUE	APTERAL	ARREEDE	ASTERID
ANATOMY	ANTLIAE	APTERIA	ARRIAGE	ASTOUND
ANCHOVY	ANT-LION	APTERYX	ARRIERO	ASTRAND
ANCIENT	ANTONYM	APTNESS	ARRIVAL	ASTRICT
ANCONES	ANUROUS	APTOTIC	ARRYISH	ASTRIDE
ANCRESS	ANXIETY	AQUAFER	ARSENAL	ASTROID
ANDANTE	ANXIOUS	AQUARIA	ARSENIC	ASTYLAR
ANDIRON	ANYBODY	AQUATIC	ARSHEEN	ASUDDEN
ANELACE	ANYTIME	AQUAVIT	ARSHINE	ASUNDER
ANEMONE	ANYWAYS	AQUEOUS	ARTICLE	ASYLUMS
ANEROID	ANYWHEN	AQUIFER	ARTISAN	ATABRIN
ANEURIN	ANYWISE	AQUILON	ARTISTE	ATACTIC
ANGELIC	APAGOGE	ARABIAN	ARTLESS	ATAGHAN
ANGELUS	APANAGE	ARABISM	ARTSMAN	ATALAYA
ANGERLY	APATITE	ARABIST	ART-SONG	ATAMANS
ANGEVIN	APEHOOD	ARACEAE	ASCARID	ATARAXY
ANGINAL	APEPSIA	ARACHIS	ASCARIS	ATAVISM
ANGIOMA	APETALY	ARAMAIC	ASCESIS	ATEBRIN
ANGLIAN	APHAGIA	ARANEAE	ASCETIC	ATELIER
ANGLICE	APHASIA	ARANEID	ASCIDIA	ATHANOR
ANGLIFY	APHASIC	ARAROBA	ASCITES	ATHEISE
ANGLING	APHELIA	ARBITER	ASCONCE	ATHEISM
ANGLIST	APHELIC	ARBLAST	ASCRIBE	ATHEIST
ANGRILY	APHESIS	ARBORET	ASEPSIS	ATHEOUS
ANGUINE	APHETIC	ARBUTUS	ASEPTIC	ATHIRST
ANGUISH	APHIDES	ARCADED	ASEXUAL	ATHLETA
ANGULAR	APHONIA	ARCANUM	ASHAMED	ATHLETE
ANILINE	APHONIC	ARCHAIC	ASH-HEAP	ATHRILL
ANILITY	APHOTIC	ARCHERY	ASH-HOLE	ATHWART
ANIMATE	APHTHAE	ARCHEUS	ASHIVER	ATINGLE
ANIMISM	APHYLLY	ARCH-FOE	ASHRAMA	ATLASES
ANIMIST	APICIAN	ARCHIVE	ASH-TRAY	ATOKOUS
ANIONIC	APIEZON	ARCHLET	ASIANIC	ATOMISE
ANISEED	APISHLY	ARCHWAY	ASIATIC	ATOMISM
ANNATES	APLASIA	ARCKING	ASININE	ATOMIST
ANNATTA	APOCOPE	ARC-LAMP	ASKANCE	ATRESIA
ANNATTO	APODOUS	ARCTOID	ASKESIS	ATROPHY
ANNELID	APOGAMY	ARCUATE	ASKLENT	ATROPIA
ANNICUT	APOGEAL	ARDENCY	ASMODAY	ATROPIN
ANNUITY	APOGEAN	ARD-RIGH	ASOCIAL	ATROPOS
ANNULAR	APOLOGY	ARDUOUS	ASPASIA	ATTACHÉ
ANNULET	APOPLEX	AREOLAE	ASPERGE	ATTAINT
ANNULUS	APOSTIL	AREOLAR	ASPERSE	ATTEMPT
ANODISE	APOSTLE	ARGYRIA	ASPHALT	ATTRACT
ANODYNE	APOTHEM	ARICIAN	ASPHYXY	ATTRIST
ANOESIS	APPARAT	ARIDITY	ASPIRIN	ATTRITE
ANOETIC	APPAREL	ARIETTA	ASPRAWL	ATTUENT
ANOMALY	APPEACH	ARIETTE	ASPREAD	ATTUITE
ANONYMA	APPEASE	ARILLUS	ASPROUT	AUBERGE
ANOREXY	APPLAUD	ARIMASP	ASQUINT	AUCTION
ANOSMIA	APPLIED	ARIPPLE	ASSAGAI	AUDIBLE
ANOTHER	APPOINT	ARMBAND	ASSAULT	AUDIBLY
ANSATED	APPOSER	ARMHOLE	ASSAYER	AUDIENT
ANTACID	APPRESS	ARMIGER	ASSEGAI	AUDITOR
ANTARES	APPRISE	ARMILLA	ASSEVER	AUFGABE
ANT-BEAR	APPRIZE	ARMLESS	ASSIEGE	AUGITIC
ANT-BIRD	APPROOF	ARMOIRE	ASSIZER	AUGMENT
ANTEFIX	APPROVE	ARMORIC	ASSUAGE	AUGURAL
ANT-EGGS	APPUIED	ARMOURY	ASSUMED	AUGURER
ANTENNA	APPULSE	ARNAOUT	ASSURED	AUGUSTE
ANT-HILL	APPUYED	ARNOTTO	ASSURER	AURALLY

AURATED
AUREATE
AUREITY
AURELIA
AUREOLA
AUREOLE
AURICLE
AUROCHS
AURORAL
AUSPICE
AUSTERE
AUSTRAL
AUSTRIC
AUTARKY
AUTOBUS
AUTOCAR
AUTOCUE
AUTOMAT
AUTONYM
AUTOPSY
AUTOVAC
AUXESIS
AUXETIC
AVARICE
AVENGER
AVERAGE
AVERNUS
AVERRED
AVERTED
AVESTAN
AVESTIC
AVIATOR
AVICULA
AVIDITY
AVIETTE
AVIFORM
AVIONIC
AVOCADO
AVOUTRY
AWAKING
AWELESS
AWESOME
AWFULLY
AWKWARD
AWNLESS
AXIALLY
AXILLAE
AXILLAR
AXINITE
AXLE-BOX
AXOLOTL
AZILIAN
AZIMUTH
AZOTISE
AZOTOUS
AZUREAN
AZURINE
AZURITE
AZYGOUS
AZYMITE
AZYMOUS

B

BAALISM
BAALITE
BAASKAP

BABASSU
BABBITT
BABBLER
BABIISM
BABOOSH
BABUCHE
BABUDOM
BABUISM
BABYISH
BABY-SIT
BACCARA
BACCARE
BACCATE
BACCHIC
BACCHII
BACCHUS
BACILLI
BACKARE
BACK-END
BACKING
BACKLOG
BACKSAW
BACKSET
BACKSEY
BADDISH
BADIOUS
BADMASH
BADNESS
BAFFLER
BAGASSE
BAGFULS
BAGGAGE
BAGGILY
BAGGING
BAGPIPE
BAHADUR
BAHAISM
BAHAIST
BAHAITE
BAILIFF
BAILLIE
BAIRNLY
BAITING
BALADIN
BALANCE
BALANUS
BALCONY
BALDING
BALDISH
BALDRIC
BALDWIN
BALEFUL
BALISTA
BALKING
BALLADE
BALLANT
BALLAST
BALLING
BALLIUM
BALLOON
BALNEAL
BALONEY
BALSAMY
BAMBINO
BANDAGE
BANDANA

BAND-BOX
BANDEAU
BANDIED
BANDITS
BANDORE
BANDROL
BAND-SAW
BANEFUL
BANGING
BANGLED
BANKSIA
BANNOCK
BANQUET
BANSHEE
BANTENG
BANTING
BAPTISE
BAPTISM
BAPTIST
BARACAN
BARBARY
BARBATE
BAR-BELL
BARBOLA
BARBULE
BARGAIN
BARGEST
BARILLA
BAR-IRON
BARK-BED
BARMAID
BARMKIN
BARNABY
BAROCCO
BARONET
BAROQUE
BARRACE
BARRACK
BARRAGE
BARRICO
BARRIER
BARRING
BAR-ROOM
BARWOOD
BARYTES
BARYTIC
BARYTON
BASBLEU
BASCULE
BASEMAN
BASENJI
BASHFUL
BASHLYK
BASIDIA
BASILAR
BASINET
BASOCHE
BA'SPIEL
BASQUED
BASS-BAR
BASSOON
BASTARD
BASTING
BASTION
BATABLE
BATEAUX

BATHMIC
BATHTUB
BATISTE
BATSMAN
BATTELS
BATTERY
BATTING
BATTUTA
BAUCHLE
BAUDRIC
BAUHAUS
BAUSOND
BAUXITE
BAWCOCK
BAWDKIN
BAWLING
BAY-LEAF
BAY-LINE
BAYONET
BAY-SALT
BAY-TINE
BAZOOKA
BEACHED
BEADING
BEAGLER
BEAMILY
BEAMING
BEAMISH
BEAN-BAG
BEAR-CAT
BEARDED
BEARING
BEARISH
BEASTIE
BEASTLY
BEATIFY
BEATING
BEATNIK
BEAUFET
BEAUFIN
BEAUISH
BEAVERY
BEBEERU
BECAUSE
BECHARM
BECLOUD
BEDAWIN
BEDAZED
BEDDING
BEDERAL
BEDEVIL
BEDFAST
BEDIGHT
BEDIZEN
BEDOUIN
BEDPOST
BEDRIDD
BEDRITE
BEDROCK
BEDROOM
BEDROPT
BEDSIDE
BEDSORE
BEDTICK
BEDTIME
BEDWARD

BEDWARF
BEDWORK
BEECHEN
BEEF-HAM
BEEF-TEA
BEE-GLUE
BEEHIVE
BEE-KITE
BEELINE
BEE-MOTH
BEE-SKEP
BEESOME
BEESWAX
BEET-FLY
BEFFANA
BEGGARY
BEGGING
BEGHARD
BEGINNE
BEGLOOM
BEGONIA
BEGORED
BEGORRA
BEGRIME
BEGUILE
BEGUINE
BEHAVED
BEHIGHT
BEHOOVE
BEINKED
BEJEWEL
BEKNAVE
BEKNOWN
BELATED
BELCHER
BELDAME
BELGARD
BELGIAN
BELIEVE
BELL-BOY
BELLHOP
BELLIED
BELLMAN
BELLONA
BELLOWS
BELOVED
BELTANE
BELTING
BELYING
BEMAZED
BEMEDAL
BEMIRED
BEMOUTH
BENAMED
BENCHER
BENDING
BENDLET
BENEATH
BENEFIC
BENEFIT
BENELUX
BENEMPT
BENGALI
BENIGHT
BENISON
BENTHIC

BENTHOS	BIASSED	BLADDER	BLUSTER	BOREDOM
BENZENE	BIAXIAL	BLANDLY	BOARDER	BORNITE
BENZINE	BIBCOCK	BLANKET	BOARISH	BOROUGH
BENZOIC	BIBELOT	BLANKLY	BOASTER	BORRELL
BENZOIN	BIBLIST	BLARNEY	BOAT-FLY	BORSTAL
BENZOLE	BICYCLE	BLASTED	BOATING	BORTSCH
BENZOYL	BIDDING	BLASTER	BOATMAN	BOSCAGE
BEPAINT	BIFILAR	BLATANT	BOBADIL	BOSHTER
BEPEARL	BIFOCAL	BLATHER	BOBBERY	BOSOMED
BEPROSE	BIGENER	BLATTER	BOBBING	BOSTRYX
BEQUEST	BIGGEST	BLAUBOK	BOBBISH	BOTANIC
BEREAVE	BIGGISH	BLAWORT	BOBSLED	BOTARGO
BERGYLT	BIGHEAD	BLEAKLY	BOBTAIL	BOTCHER
BERLINE	BIGHORN	BLEARED	BODEFUL	BOTHOLE
BERMUDA	BIGNESS	BLEEDER	BODIKIN	BOTTEGA
BERRIED	BIGOTED	BLEEPER	BODYING	BOTTINE
BERRIES	BIGOTRY	BLEMISH	BOGBEAN	BOTTLED
BERSERK	BIG-TIME	BLENDED	BOGGARD	BOTTONY
BESAINT	BILBOES	BLENDER	BOGGLER	BOUDOIR
BESEECH	BILIARY	BLESBOK	BOG-IRON	BOUILLI
BESHAME	BILIMBI	BLESSED	BOGLAND	BOULDER
BESHINE	BILIOUS	BLETHER	BOG-MOSS	BOULTER
BESHONE	BILLIES	BLETTED	BOGYISM	BOUNCER
BESHREW	BILLING	BLEWART	BOGYMAN	BOUNDED
BESIDES	BILLION	BLEWITS	BOILERY	BOUNDEN
BESIEGE	BILLMAN	BLIGHTY	BOILING	BOUNDER
BESLAVE	BILLOWY	BLINDED	BOLETUS	BOUQUET
BESMEAR	BILOBAR	BLINDER	BOLIVAR	BOURBON
BESPAKE	BILOBED	BLINDLY	BOLLARD	BOURDER
BESPEAK	BILTONG	BLINKED	BOLOGNA	BOURDON
BESPEED	BIMANAL	BLINKER	BOLONEY	BOURKHA
BESPICE	BINDERY	BLISTER	BOLSHIE	BOURLAW
BESPOKE	BINDING	BLITHER	BOLSTER	BOURRÉE
BESPORT	BINOCLE	BLOATED	BOLTING	BOUSING
BESPOUT	BIOGENY	BLOATER	BOMBARD	BOUTADE
BESTAIN	BIOLOGY	BLOCKED	BOMBAST	BOWBENT
BESTEAD	BIONICS	BLOODED	BONANZA	BOW-HAND
BESTIAL	BIOPHOR	BLOOMER	BONASUS	BOWLDER
BESTICK	BIOTITE	BLOSSOM	BONDAGE	BOWLINE
BESTILL	BIPEDAL	BLOTCHY	BONDING	BOWLING
BESTORM	BIPLANE	BLOTTED	BONDMAN	BOWSHOT
BESTREW	BIRCHEN	BLOTTER	BONE-ASH	BOX-CALF
BESTRID	BIRD-DOG	BLOUBOK	BONE-BED	BOX-COAT
BESTUCK	BIRDING	BLOUSON	BONE-DRY	BOXFULS
BETAKEN	BIRETTA	BLOWFLY	BONE-OIL	BOXHAUL
BETEEME	BIRLING	BLOWGUN	BONESET	BOX-IRON
BETHINK	BIRLINN	BLOWING	BONFIRE	BOX-KITE
BETHUMB	BISCUIT	BLOW-OUT	BONKERS	BOXROOM
BETHUMP	BISMUTH	BLOWZED	BONNILY	BOXSEAT
BETIDED	BISTORT	BLUBBER	BOOBOOK	BOX-TREE
BETIMES	BISTRED	BLUCHER	BOOK-END	BOXWOOD
BETITLE	BITONAL	BLUDGER	BOOKFUL	BOYCOTT
BETOKEN	BIT-PART	BLUECAP	BOOKISH	BOYHOOD
BETREAD	BITTERN	BLUE-EYE	BOOKLET	BOZZETO
BETROTH	BITTERS	BLUEING	BOOKMAN	BRABBLE
BETTING	BITTING	BLUEROT	BOOKSIE	BRACCIA
BETWEEN	BITTOCK	BLUETTE	BOOLEAN	BRACCIO
BETWIXT	BITUMED	BLUFFER	BOOMING	BRACHET
BEWHORE	BITUMEN	BLUFFLY	BOORISH	BRACING
BEWITCH	BIVALVE	BLUNDER	BOOSTER	BRACKEN
BEZIQUE	BIVIOUS	BLUNGER	BOOTLEG	BRACKET
BEZ-TINE	BIVOUAC	BLUNKER	BOOZILY	BRADAWL
BHARATI	BIZARRE	BLUNTLY	BOOZING	BRAGGED
BHEESTY	BLABBED	BLURRED	BORACIC	BRAHMAN
BHISTEE	BLABBER	BLUSHER	BORAZON	BRAHMIN
BIASING	BLACKEN	BLUSHET	BORDURE	BRAIDED

BRAILLE
BRAINED
BRAMBLE
BRAMBLY
BRANCHY
BRANDED
BRANDER
BRANGLE
BRAN-NEW
BRAN-PIE
BRANSLE
BRANTLE
BRAN-TUB
BRASERO
BRASIER
BRASSET
BRASSIE
BRATTLE
BRAVADO
BRAVELY
BRAVERY
BRAVOES
BRAVURA
BRAWLER
BRAWNED
BRAZIER
BREADTH
BREAKER
BREAK-UP
BREATHE
BREATHY
BRECCIA
BRECHAM
BREEDER
BREVIER
BREVITY
BREWAGE
BREWERY
BREWING
BRIARED
BRIBERY
BRICKEN
BRICKLE
BRICOLE
BRIDLER
BRIDOON
BRIEFLY
BRIERED
BRIGADE
BRIGAND
BRIMFUL
BRIMING
BRIMMED
BRIMMER
BRINDED
BRINDLE
BRINGER
BRINISH
BRINJAL
BRIOCHE
BRISKEN
BRISKET
BRISKLY
BRISTLE
BRISTLY
BRISTOL

BRISURE
BRITISH
BRITSKA
BRITTLE
BRITZKA
BROADEN
BROADLY
BROCADE
BROCAGE
BROCARD
BROCHAN
BROCKED
BROCKET
BROCKIT
BRODKIN
BROIDER
BROILER
BROKAGE
BROKERY
BROMATE
BROMIDE
BROMINE
BROMMER
BRONCHI
BRONCHO
BRONZED
BRONZEN
BROODER
BROTHEL
BROTHER
BROUGHT
BROWNIE
BRUCINE
BRUCITE
BRUCKLE
BRUHAHA
BRUISER
BRULZIE
BRUMMER
BRUMOUS
BRUSHER
BRUSQUE
BRUTIFY
BRUTISH
BRUXISM
BRYOZOA
BRYTHON
BUBALIS
BUBINGA
BUBONIC
BUBUKLE
BUCCINA
BUCKEEN
BUCKEYE
BUCKING
BUCKISH
BUCKLER
BUCKRAM
BUCK-SAW
BUCOLIC
BUDDING
BUDGERO
BUDLESS
BUDMASH
BUFFALO
BUFFOON

BUGABOO
BUGBANE
BUGBEAR
BUGEYED
BUGGERY
BUGGING
BUGLOSS
BUGWORD
BUGWORT
BUILDER
BUILDUP
BUILTIN
BUILT-UP
BUIRDLY
BUKSHEE
BULBOUS
BULGING
BULIMIA
BULIMUS
BULLACE
BULLARY
BULLATE
BULLBAT
BULLDOG
BULLIED
BULLION
BULLISH
BULLOCK
BULL-PEN
BULL-PUP
BULRUSH
BULWARK
BUMBAZE
BUM-BOAT
BUMMALO
BUMMING
BUMMOCK
BUMPKIN
BUNCHED
BUNDOOK
BUNGLER
BUNRAKU
BUNTING
BUOYAGE
BUOYANT
BUPHAGA
BURDASH
BURDOCK
BUREAUS
BUREAUX
BURETTE
BURGAGE
BURGEON
BURGESS
BURGHAL
BURGHER
BURGLAR
BURMESE
BURNING
BURNISH
BURNOUS
BUR-REED
BURRELL
BURRHEL
BURSARY
BURSERA

BURSTED
BURSTEN
BURSTER
BURST-UP
BURTHEN
BURWEED
BURYING
BUS-FARE
BUSGIRL
BUSH-CAT
BUSHIDO
BUSHMAN
BUSH-TIT
BUSTARD
BUSTLER
BUSYING
BUTCHER
BUTLERY
BUTMENT
BUTT-END
BUTTERY
BUTTOCK
BUTTONY
BUTYRIC
BUYABLE
BUZZARD
BUZZING
BUZZ-SAW
BUZZ-WIG
BY-AND-BY
BYCOKET
BYGOING
BYGONES
BY-PLACE
BYREMAN
BYRLADY
BYRONIC
BYSSINE
BYSSOID
BY-THING
BYWONER

C

CABARET
CABBAGE
CABBAGY
CABBALA
CABEIRI
CABINET
CABIRIC
CABLING
CABOOSE
CAB-RANK
CAB-TOUT
CACHEXY
CACIQUE
CACKLER
CACODYL
CACOLET
CACUMEN
CADAVER
CADDICE
CADDISH
CADENCE
CADENCY
CADENZA

CADMEAN
CADMIUM
CADRANS
CADUCEL
CAERULE
CAESIUM
CAESTUS
CAESURA
CAFFILA
CAIN-HEN
CAINITE
CAIRENE
CAISSON
CAITIFF
CAITIVE
CAJEPUT
CAJOLER
CAJUPUT
CALAMUS
CALANDO
CALANUS
CALCIFY
CALCINE
CALCITE
CALCIUM
CALCULI
CALDERA
CALDRON
CALENDS
CALIBAN
CALIBER
CALIBRE
CALICHE
CALIPEE
CALIVER
CALLANT
CALL-BOX
CALL-BOY
CALLING
CALLOUS
CALLUNA
CALMANT
CALMUCK
CALOMEL
CALORIC
CALORIE
CALOTTE
CALOYER
CALPACK
CALTRAP
CALTROP
CALUMBA
CALUMET
CALUMNY
CALVARY
CALYCES
CALYCLE
CALYPSO
CALYXES
CAMAIEU
CAMBIAL
CAMBISM
CAMBIST
CAMBIUM
CAMBOGE
CAMBREL

CAMBRIC
CAMELOT
CAMELRY
CAMERAL
CAMHINE
CAMORRA
CAMPANA
CAMP-BED
CAMPHOR
CAMPION
CAM-WOOD
CANAKIN
CANASTA
CANDELA
CANDENT
CANDIED
CANDIES
CANDOCK
CANDOUR
CANELLA
CANIDAE
CANIKIN
CANKERY
CANNACH
CANNERY
CANNILY
CANNING
CANNULA
CANONIC
CANONRY
CANOPIC
CANOPUS
CANTATA
CANTATE
CANTEEN
CANTHUS
CANTICO
CANTING
CANTION
CANTLET
CANTRED
CANTREF
CANTRIP
CANVASS
CANZONE
CANZONI
CAPABLE
CAP-À-PIE
CAP-CASE
CAPELIN
CAPELLA
CAPERER
CAPITAL
CAPITAN
CAPITOL
CAPORAL
CAPPING
CAPRATE
CAPRICE
CAPRIFY
CAPRINE
CAPROIC
CAPSIAN
CAPSIZE
CAPSTAN
CAPSULE

CAPTAIN
CAPTION
CAPTIVE
CAPTURE
CAPUCHE
CARABUS
CARACAL
CARACOL
CARACUL
CARAMEL
CARANNA
CARAUNA
CARAVAN
CARAVEL
CARAWAY
CARBIDE
CARBINE
CARCAKE
CARCASE
CARCASS
CARDECU
CARDIAC
CARDOON
CARDUUS
CAREFUL
CARGOES
CARIAMA
CARIBOU
CARIOCA
CARIOLE
CARIOUS
CARITAS
CARKING
CARLINE
CARLISH
CARLISM
CARLIST
CARLOCK
CARMINE
CARNAGE
CARNOSE
CAROCHE
CAROLUS
CAROMEL
CAROTID
CAROTIN
CAROUSE
CARPING
CARPORT
CARRACK
CARRACT
CARRECT
CARRICK
CARRIED
CARRIER
CARRION
CARROTY
CARRY-ON
CARTAGE
CARTOON
CARTWAY
CARVING
CASCADE
CASCARA
CASE-LAW
CASEMAN

CASEOUS
CASERNE
CASHIER
CASSAVA
CASSINO
CASSOCK
CASSONE
CASTILE
CASTING
CASTLED
CASTOCK
CAST-OFF
CASTORY
CASTRAL
CASUALS
CASUIST
CATAIAN
CATALAN
CATALPA
CATAPAN
CATARRH
CATASTA
CATAWBA
CATAYAN
CATBIRD
CATBOAT
CATCALL
CATCHER
CATCHUP
CATECHU
CATERAN
CATERER
CAT-EYED
CATFISH
CATHARI
CATHEAD
CATHODE
CAT-HOLE
CATHOOD
CAT-LIKE
CATLING
CATMINT
CAT'S-EAR
CAT'S-EYE
CATSKIN
CAT'S-PAW
CATSUIT
CATTABU
CATTALO
CATTERY
CATTISH
CAT-WALK
CAUDATE
CAULINE
CAULKER
CAULOME
CAUSTIC
CAUTERY
CAUTION
CAVALLY
CAVALRY
CAVEMAN
CAVETTO
CAVIARE
CAYENNE
CAYMANS

CAZIQUE
CEASING
CEBIDAE
CEDARED
CEDILLA
CEDRATE
CEDRELA
CEDRINE
CEILIDH
CEILING
CELADON
CELESTA
CELESTE
CELLIST
CELLULE
CELSIUS
CEMBALO
CENACLE
CENSUAL
CENSURE
CENTAGE
CENTAUR
CENTAVO
CENTIME
CENTNER
CENTRAL
CENTRED
CENTRIC
CENTRUM
CENTURY
CEPHEID
CEPHEUS
CERAMET
CERAMIC
CERASIN
CEREOUS
CERRIAL
CERTAIN
CERTIFY
CERUMEN
CERVINE
CESSION
CESTODE
CESTOID
CETACEA
CETESES
CHABLIS
CHABOUK
CHAFFER
CHAGRIN
CHAINED
CHALAZA
CHALDEE
CHALDER
CHALICE
CHALLAN
CHALLIS
CHALONE
CHAMADE
CHAMBER
CHAMBRE
CHAMFER
CHAMISO
CHAMLET
CHAMOIS
CHAMPAC

CHAMPAK
CHANCEL
CHANCRE
CHANGER
CHANNEL
CHANOYU
CHANSON
CHANTER
CHANTEY
CHANTIE
CHANTOR
CHANTRY
CHAOTIC
CHAPATI
CHAPEAU
CHAPLET
CHAPMAN
CHAPPED
CHAPPIE
CHAPTER
CHARADE
CHARGER
CHARILY
CHARING
CHARIOT
CHARISM
CHARITY
CHARLEY
CHARLIE
CHARMED
CHARMER
CHARNEL
CHARPIE
CHARPOY
CHARQUI
CHARRED
CHARTER
CHASMED
CHASSIS
CHASTEN
CHÂTEAU
CHATTED
CHATTEL
CHATTER
CHAUNCE
CHAUNGE
CHAUVIN
CHEAPEN
CHEAPLY
CHEATER
CHECHIA
CHECKER
CHECK-UP
CHEDDAR
CHEEPER
CHEERER
CHEERIO
CHEERLY
CHEESED
CHEETAH
CHEKIST
CHELATE
CHELSEA
CHEMISE
CHEMISM
CHEMIST

CHEQUER	CHOROID	CLAMPER	CLOTURE	COFFRET
CHERISH	CHORTLE	CLANGER	CLOUDED	COGENCE
CHEROOT	CHOWDER	CLAPNET	CLOUTED	COGENCY
CHERUBS	CHRISOM	CLAPPED	CLOVERY	COGGING
CHERVIL	CHRISTY	CLAPPER	CLOYING	COGNATE
CHESSEL	CHROMIC	CLARIFY	CLUBBED	COGNISE
CHESTED	CHRONIC	CLARION	CLUB-LAW	COHABIT
CHEVIOT	CHUBBED	CLARITY	CLUBMAN	COHERER
CHEVRON	CHUCKIE	CLARKIA	CLUMBER	COHIBIT
CHEWINK	CHUCKLE	CLASPER	CLUNIAC	COINAGE
CHIANTI	CHUDDAH	CLASSED	CLUPEID	COINING
CHIASMA	CHUDDAR	CLASSIC	CLUSTER	COITION
CHIBOUK	CHUFFED	CLASSIS	CLUTTER	COLDISH
CHICAGO	CHUKKER	CLASTIC	CLYPEAL	COLIBRI
CHICANE	CHUNNEL	CLATTER	CLYPEUS	COLICKY
CHICKEN	CHUNNER	CLAUCHT	CLYSTER	COLITIS
CHICORY	CHUNTER	CLAUGHT	COACHEE	COLLAGE
CHIDDEN	CHUPATI	CLAVATE	COACHER	COLLARD
CHIDING	CHURCHY	CLAVIER	COAGENT	COLLATE
CHIEFER	CHURRUS	CLAYISH	COAL-BED	COLLECT
CHIEFLY	CHUTNEY	CLAY-PIT	COAL-BOX	COLLEEN
CHIEFRY	CHYMIFY	CLEANER	COAL-GAS	COLLEGE
CHIFFON	CHYMOUS	CLEANLY	COALISE	COLLIDE
CHIGGER	CIBORIA	CLEANSE	COALITE	COLLIED
CHIGNON	CICHLID	CLEAN-UP	COALMAN	COLLIER
CHIKARA	CIDARIS	CLEARER	COAL-OIL	COLLING
CHIKHOR	CILIARY	CLEARLY	COAL-PIT	COLLINS
CHILDED	CILIATA	CLEAVED	COAL-TAR	COLLOID
CHILDLY	CILIATE	CLEAVER	COAL-TIT	COLLUDE
CHILIAD	CILICID	CLEEKED	COARSEN	COLOBUS
CHILLED	CIMELIA	CLEEKIT	COASTAL	COLONEL
CHILLUM	CINDERY	CLEMENT	COASTER	COLOURY
CHIMERA	CINEOLE	CLERISY	COATING	COLTISH
CHIMERE	CINEREA	CLERKLY	COAXIAL	COLUBER
CHIMNEY	CIPOLIN	CLERUCH	COBBLER	COLUMBA
CHINDIT	CIRCAEA	CLICKER	COB-LOAF	COLUMEL
CHINESE	CIRCEAN	CLICKET	COB-PIPE	COMBINE
CHINOOK	CIRCLED	CLIFFED	COB-SWAN	COMB-OUT
CHINTZY	CIRCLER	CLIFTED	COB-WALL	COMBUST
CHINWAG	CIRCLET	CLIMATE	COCAGNE	COME-OFF
CHIP-HAT	CIRCUIT	CLIMBED	COCAINE	COMETIC
CHIPPED	CIRCUSY	CLIMBER	COCCOID	COMFORT
CHIPPER	CIRRATE	CLINKER	COCHLEA	COMFREY
CHIRPER	CIRROSE	CLIPPED	COCKADE	COMICAL
CHIRRUP	CIRROUS	CLIPPER	COCKEYE	COMIQUE
CHISLEV	CISSOID	CLIPPIE	COCKLED	COMITAL
CHITTER	CISTERN	CLITTER	COCKNEY	COMITIA
CHLAMYS	CITABLE	CLIVERS	COCKPIT	COMMAND
CHLORAL	CITADEL	CLOACAE	COCKSHY	COMMEND
CHLORIC	CITHARA	CLOACAL	COCONUT	COMMENT
CHOBDAR	CITHERN	CLOBBER	COCOTTE	COMMÈRE
CHOCTAW	CITIZEN	CLOCKER	COCTILE	COMMODE
CHOLERA	CITRATE	CLODDED	COCTION	COMMONS
CHOLINE	CITRINE	CLOGGED	CODDING	COMMOVE
CHOLTRY	CITTERN	CLOGGER	CODEINE	COMMUNE
CHONDRE	CIVILLY	CLOISON	CODFISH	COMMUTE
CHONDRI	CIVVIES	CLOOTIE	CODICES	COMPACT
CHOOSER	CLABBER	CLOSELY	CODICIL	COMPAGE
CHOOSEY	CLACHAN	CLOSE-UP	CODILLA	COMPANY
CHOPINE	CLACKER	CLOSING	CODILLE	COMPARE
CHOPPER	CLADODE	CLOSURE	CODLING	COMPART
CHORALE	CLAIMER	CLOTBUR	COEHORN	COMPASS
CHOREUS	CLAMANT	CLOTHED	COELIAC	COMPEAR
CHORINE	CLAMBER	CLOTHES	COELOME	COMPEER
CHORION	CLAMMED	CLOTTED	COEQUAL	COMPEND
CHORIST	CLAMOUR	CLOTTER	COEXIST	COMPERE

COMPETE	CONNECT	CO-RIVAL	COTTISE	CRAMESY
COMPILE	CONNING	CORKAGE	COTTOID	CRAMMED
COMPLEX	CONNIVE	CORKING	COTTONY	CRAMMER
COMPLIN	CONNOTE	CORK-LEG	COT-TOWN	CRAMPET
COMPLOT	CONQUER	CORK-MAT	COTYLAE	CRAMPIT
COMPONE	CONSENT	CORK-OAK	COTYLES	CRAMPON
COMPONY	CONSIGN	CORNAGE	COUCHEE	CRANAGE
COMPORT	CONSIST	CORN-BIN	COUEISM	CRANIAL
COMPOSE	CONSOLE	CORN-COB	COUEIST	CRANIUM
COMPOST	CONSOLS	CORNEAL	COUGHER	CRANKLE
COMPOTE	CONSORT	CORNETT	CCUGUAR	CRANNOG
COMPTER	CONSTER	CORN-FED	COULOIR	CRASSLY
COMPUTE	CONSULT	CORNFLY	COULOMB	CRAUNCH
COMRADE	CONSUME	CORNICE	COULTER	CRAVING
COMTIAN	CONTACT	CORNISH	COUNCIL	CRAWLER
COMTISM	CONTAIN	CORNIST	COUNSEL	CRAZILY
COMTIST	CONTECK	CORN-LAW	COUNTED	CREANCE
CONACRE	CONTEMN	CORN-PIT	COUNTER	CREATIC
CONATUS	CONTEND	CORN-RIG	COUNTRY	CREATOR
CONCAVE	CONTENT	CORNUAL	COUPLER	CREDENT
CONCEAL	CONTEST	CORNUTE	COUPLET	CREEDAL
CONCEDE	CONTEXT	CORNUTO	COUPURE	CREEPER
CONCEIT	CONTORT	CORN-VAN	COURAGE	CREEPIE
CONCENT	CONTOUR	COROLLA	COURANT	CREESHY
CONCEPT	CONTROL	CORONAE	COURIER	CREMATE
CONCERN	CONTUND	CORONAL	COURLAN	CREMONA
CONCERT	CONTUSE	CORONAS	COURSER	CRENATE
CONCISE	CONVENE	CORONER	COURTLY	CRESSET
CONCOCT	CONVENT	CORONET	COUTHIE	CRESTED
CONCORD	CONVERT	CORONIS	COUTURE	CRETISM
CONCUPY	CONVICT	CORPORA	COUVADE	CREVICE
CONCUSS	CONVOKE	CORRECT	COVELET	CREWELS
CONDEMN	COOKERY	CORRODE	COVERED	CRIBBED
CONDIGN	COOLANT	CORRODY	COVER-UP	CRIBBLE
CONDOLE	COOLISH	CORRUPT	COVETED	CRICKET
CONDONE	COON-CAN	CORSAGE	COWBANE	CRICKEY
CONDUCE	COONTIE	CORSAIR	COWBELL	CRICOID
CONDUCT	COOPERY	CORSIVE	COWBIRD	CRIMINE
CONDUIT	COPAIBA	CORSLET	COW-CALF	CRIMINI
CONDYLE	COPAIVA	CORSNED	COWFISH	CRIMPER
CONFECT	COPEPOD	CORTÈGE	COWGIRL	CRIMPLE
CONFESS	CO-PILOT	CORTILE	COWHAGE	CRIMSON
CONFEST	COPIOUS	CORVINE	COWHAND	CRINATE
CONFIDE	COPPERY	CORYDON	COWHEEL	CRINGER
CONFINE	COPPICE	CORYLUS	COWHERD	CRINGLE
CONFIRM	COPULAR	CORYPHA	COWHIDE	CRINITE
CONFLUX	COPY-CAT	CORYPHE	COWITCH	CRINKLE
CONFORM	COPYING	COSHERY	COWLICK	CRINKLY
CONFUSE	COPYISM	COSMISM	COWLING	CRINOID
CONFUTE	COPYIST	COSMIST	COWPOKE	CRINOSE
CON-GAME	COQUITO	COSSACK	COWSHED	CRIPPLE
CONGEAL	CORACLE	COSTARD	COWSLIP	CRISPER
CONGERY	CORALLA	COSTATE	COW-TREE	CRISPIN
CONGEST	CORANTO	COSTEAN	COW-WEED	CRISPLY
CONGREE	CORBEAU	COSTIVE	COXCOMB	CRITTER
CONGRUE	CORBEIL	COSTREL	COYNESS	CRITTUR
CONICAL	CORCASS	COSTUME	COZENER	CROAKER
CONIDIA	CORDAGE	COTEAUX	CRABBED	CROCHET
CONIFER	CORDATE	COTERIE	CRAB-NUT	CROCKET
CONIINE	CORDIAL	COT-FOLK	CRAB-OIL	CROESUS
CONJECT	CORDING	COTHURN	CRACKED	CROFTER
CONJOIN	CORDITE	CO-TIDAL	CRACKER	CROMACK
CONJURE	CÓRDOBA	COTINGA	CRACKLE	CROODLE
CONJURY	CORELLA	COTLAND	CRACKLY	CROOKED
CONKERS	CORINTH	COTTAGE	CRACOWE	CROONER
CONNATE	CORIOUS	COTTIER	CRAGGED	CROP-EAR

CROPFUL
CROPPED
CROPPER
CROQUET
CROSIER
CROSSED
CROSSLY
CROTTLE
CROUPON
CROUTON
CROWBAR
CROWDED
CROWDER
CROWDIE
CROWNED
CROWNER
CROWNET
CROW-TOE
CROZIER
CRUCIAL
CRUCIAN
CRUCIFY
CRUDDLE
CRUDELY
CRUDITY
CRUELLS
CRUELLY
CRUELTY
CRUISER
CRUISIE
CRULLER
CRUMBLE
CRUMBLY
CRUMPET
CRUMPLE
CRUNCHY
CRUNKLE
CRUPPER
CRUSADE
CRUSADO
CRUSHED
CRUSHER
CRUSIAN
CRUSTAE
CRUSTAL
CRY-BABY
CRYOGEN
CRYPTAL
CRYPTIC
CRYPTON
CRYSTAL
CSÁRDÁS
C-SPRING
CTENOID
CUBBING
CUBBISH
CUBHOOD
CUBICAL
CUBICLE
CUBITAL
CUBITUS
CUBLESS
CUCKOLD
CUDBEAR
CUDWEED
CUIRASS

CUISINE
CUISSER
CUITTLE
CULICES
CULLIED
CULLING
CULLION
CULPRIT
CULTISM
CULTIST
CULTURE
CULVERT
CUMARIN
CUMBENT
CUMQUAT
CUMSHAW
CUMULUS
CUNEATE
CUNETTE
CUNNING
CUPFULS
CUPGALL
CUPHEAD
CUP-MARK
CUP-MOSS
CUPOLAD
CUPOLAR
CUPPING
CUPRITE
CUPROUS
CUPULAR
CURAÇAO
CURAÇOA
CURABLE
CURATOR
CURCUMA
CURE-ALL
CURETTE
CURIOUS
CURLING
CURRACH
CURRAGH
CURRANT
CURRENT
CURRIED
CURRIER
CURRISH
CURSING
CURSIVE
CURSORY
CURTAIL
CURTAIN
CURTANA
CURTATE
CURTAXE
CURTSEY
CURVATE
CURVING
CURVITY
CUSHION
CUSPATE
CUSTARD
CUSTOCK
CUSTODE
CUSTODY
CUSTREL

CUTAWAY
CUTBACK
CUTICLE
CUTIKIN
CUTLASS
CUTLERY
CUTTING
CUTWORM
CUVETTE
CYANATE
CYANIDE
CYANINE
CYANISE
CYANITE
CYATHEA
CYATHUS
CYCLIST
CYCLOID
CYCLONE
CYCLOPS
CYLICES
CYMBALO
CYNICAL
CYPERUS
CYPRESS
CYPRIAN
CYPRINE
CYPRIOT
CYSTOID
CYTISUS
CZARDAS
CZARDOM
CZARINA
CZARISM
CZARIST
CZECHIC

D

DABBING
DABBLER
DABSTER
DACOITY
DADAISM
DADAIST
DADDOCK
DAEDALE
DAFFING
DAGWOOD
DAISIED
DAKOITI
DALILAH
DALLIED
DALLIER
DAMBROD
DAMMING
DAMNIFY
DAMNING
DAMOSEL
DAMOZEL
DAMPISH
DANCING
DANDIFY
DANDILY
DANELAW
DANGLER
DANKISH

DANTEAN
DANTIST
DAPPLED
DAPSONE
DARBIES
DAREFUL
DARIOLE
DARKISH
DARLING
DARNING
DARRAIN
DARRAYN
DARSHAN
DART-SAC
DASHING
DASH-POT
DASTARD
DASYPOD
DASYPUS
DASYURE
DATABLE
DATARIA
DATIVAL
DAUBERY
DAUBING
DAUNDER
DAUNTON
DAUPHIN
DAWCOCK
DAWDLER
DAWNING
DAWNMAN
DAY-BOOK
DAY-COAL
DAY-GIRL
DAY-LILY
DAYLONG
DAYMARK
DAY-PEEP
DAYSMAN
DAYSTAR
DAYTIME
DAY-WORK
DAZEDLY
DAZZLER
DEAD-END
DEAD-EYE
DEAD-MEN
DEADPAN
DEAD-PAY
DEAD-SET
DEAF-AID
DEALING
DEANERY
DEARNLY
DEASIUL
DEASOIL
DEATHLY
DÉBÂCLE
DEBASED
DEBATER
DEBAUCH
DEBOUCH
DEBRETT
DEBRIEF
DECADAL

DECAGON
DECANAL
DECAPOD
DECAYED
DECEASE
DECEIVE
DECENCY
DECIARE
DECIBEL
DECIDED
DECIDER
DECIDUA
DECIMAL
DECKING
DECKLED
DECLAIM
DECLARE
DECLASS
DECLINE
DECOLOR
DECORUM
DECREED
DECREET
DECRIAL
DECRIED
DECRIER
DECROWN
DECUMAN
DECUPLE
DECURIA
DEDIMUS
DEEDFUL
DEEDILY
DEEP-FET
DEEP-SEA
DEERLET
DEFAULT
DEFENCE
DEFIANT
DEFICIT
DEFILER
DEFLATE
DEFLECT
DEFORCE
DEFRAUD
DEFROST
DEFUNCT
DEFYING
DEGAUSS
DEGRADE
DEHISCE
DEICIDE
DEICTIC
DEIFIED
DEISEAL
DEISTIC
DEJECTA
DEJEUNE
DELAINE
DELAPSE
DELATOR
DELAYED
DELAYER
DELEBLE
DELENDA
DELIBLE

DELIGHT
DELILAH
DELIMIT
DELIVER
DELOUSE
DELPHIC
DELPHIN
DELTAIC
DELTOID
DELUDED
DELUDER
DEMENTI
DEMERGE
DEMERIT
DEMERSE
DEMESNE
DEMIGOD
DEMIREP
DEMODED
DEMONIC
DEMONRY
DEMOTIC
DEMOUNT
DENDRON
DENIZEN
DENSITY
DENTARY
DENTATE
DENTINE
DENTIST
DENTOID
DENTURE
DENYING
DEODAND
DEODATE
DEPAINT
DEPLETE
DEPLORE
DEPLUME
DEPOSAL
DEPOSIT
DEPRAVE
DEPRESS
DEPRIVE
DERAIGN
DERANGE
DERIDER
DERNFUL
DERRICK
DERVISH
DESCANT
DESCEND
DESCENT
DESERVE
DESIRER
DESMINE
DESMOID
DESPAIR
DESPISE
DESPITE
DESPOIL
DESPOND
DESSERT
DESTINE
DESTINY
DESTROY

DÉTENTE
DETERGE
DETINUE
DETRACT
DETRAIN
DETRUDE
DEUTZIA
DEVALUE
DEVELOP
DEVIATE
DEVILET
DEVILRY
DEVIOUS
DEVISAL
DEVISEE
DEVISER
DEVISOR
DEVLING
DEVOLVE
DEVOTED
DEVOTEE
DEWANNY
DEW-CLAW
DEWDROP
DEW-FALL
DEWLAPT
DEW-POND
DEW-WORM
DEXTRAL
DEXTRAN
DEXTRIN
DHURRIE
DIABASE
DIABOLO
DIADROM
DIAGRAM
DIALECT
DIALIST
DIALLED
DIALLER
DIALYSE
DIAMOND
DIANDRY
DIAPASE
DIARCHY
DIARIAL
DIARIAN
DIARISE
DIARIST
DIASONE
DIBASIC
DIBBING
DIBBLER
DIBUTYL
DICE-BOX
DICHORD
DICKENS
DICTATE
DICTION
DIDDLER
DIE-AWAY
DIEDRAL
DIE-HARD
DIETARY
DIETHYL
DIETINE

DIETIST
DIE-WORK
DIFFORM
DIFFUSE
DIGAMMA
DIGGING
DIGINIA
DIGITAL
DIGLYPH
DIGNIFY
DIGNITY
DIGONAL
DIGRAPH
DIGRESS
DIKA-OIL
DILATED
DILATER
DILATOR
DILEMMA
DILLING
DILUENT
DILUTEE
DILUTER
DILUTOR
DIMERIC
DIMETER
DIMMING
DIMMISH
DIMNESS
DIMPLED
DINE-OUT
DINETTE
DINGOES
DINKY-DI
DINMONT
DINNING
DIOCESE
DIOECIA
DIONAEA
DIOPTER
DIOPTRE
DIORAMA
DIORISM
DIORITE
DIOXIDE
DIPHONE
DIPLOID
DIPLOMA
DIPNOAN
DIPOLAR
DIPPING
DIP-PIPE
DIPTERA
DIP-TRAP
DIPTYCH
DIREFUL
DIRT-BED
DIRTIED
DIRTILY
DIRT-PIE
DISABLE
DISALLY
DISAVOW
DISBAND
DISBARK
DISCAGE

DISCANT
DISCARD
DISCASE
DISCEPT
DISCERN
DISCERP
DISCIDE
DISCOID
DISCORD
DISCUSS
DISDAIN
DISEASE
DISEDGE
DISFAME
DISFORM
DISGEST
DISGOWN
DISGUST
DISHELM
DISHFUL
DISHING
DISHOME
DISHORN
DISJECT
DISJOIN
DISJUNE
DISLEAF
DISLIKE
DISLIMB
DISLIMN
DISLINK
DISLOAD
DISMASK
DISMAST
DISMISS
DISNEST
DISOBEY
DISPACE
DISPARK
DISPART
DISPEND
DISPLAY
DISPONE
DISPORT
DISPOSE
DISPOST
DISPUTE
DISRANK
DISRATE
DISROBE
DISROOT
DISRUPT
DISSEAT
DISSECT
DISSENT
DISTAFF
DISTAIN
DISTANT
DISTEND
DISTENT
DISTICH
DISTILL
DISTORT
DISTUNE
DISTURB
DISTYLE

DISYOKE
DITCHER
DITTANY
DIURNAL
DIVERGE
DIVERSE
DIVIDER
DIVINER
DIVISOR
DIVORCE
DIVULGE
DIZZARD
DIZZILY
DJIBBAH
D-NOTICE
DOATING
DOBHASH
DOCETAE
DOCETIC
DOCKAGE
DOCKING
DOCKISE
DOCQUET
DODDARD
DODDERY
DODGEMS
DODGERY
DOESKIN
DOGBANE
DOG-BELT
DOGBOLT
DOGCART
DOG-CRAB
DOGDAYS
DOGEATE
DOGFISH
DOGGERY
DOGGESS
DOGGING
DOGGISH
DOGGONE
DOGGREL
DOG-HEAD
DOG-HOLE
DOG-ROSE
DOG'S-EAR
DOGSHIP
DOG-SICK
DOGSKIN
DOGSTAR
DOG-TICK
DOGTOWN
DOGTROT
DOGVANE
DOGWOOD
DOITKIN
DOLEFUL
DOLLDOM
DOLLIED
DOLLIER
DOLLISH
DOLPHIN
DOLTISH
DOMATIA
DOMICAL
DOMINIE

DONATOR	DRASTIC	DRY-DOCK	DWELLED	ECTASIS
DONKEYS	DRAUGHT	DRY-EYED	DWELLER	ECTHYMA
DONNÉES	DRAW-BAR	DRY-FIST	DWINDLE	ECTOPIA
DONNING	DRAW-BOY	DRY-FOOT	DYARCHY	ECTOPIC
DONNISH	DRAWING	DRYNESS	DYESTER	ECTOZOA
DONNISM	DRAWLER	DRY-SALT	DYE-WOOD	ECTYPAL
DONSHIP	DRAW-NET	DRY-SHOD	DYE-WORK	ÉCUELLE
DOOMFUL	DRAYAGE	DRY-WASH	DYINGLY	EDACITY
DOOMING	DRAYMAN	DUALISM	DYNAMIC	EDAPHIC
DOOR-MAN	DREADER	DUALIST	DYNASTY	EDDYING
DOORMAT	DREADLY	DUALITY	DYSLOGY	EDENTAL
DOORWAY	DREAMED	DUARCHY	DYSODIL	EDICTAL
DOPPING	DREAMER	DUBBING	DYSPNEA	EDIFICE
DOPPLER	DREDGER	DUBIETY	DYSURIA	EDIFIED
DORHAWK	DRESDEN	DUBIOUS	DYSURIC	EDIFIER
DORKING	DRESSED	DUCALLY	DYVOURY	EDITION
DORLACH	DRESSER	DUCDAME		EDUCATE
DORMANT	DREVILL	DUCHESS	E	EDUCTOR
DORMICE	DRIBBER	DUCK-ANT		EEL-FARE
DORNICK	DRIBBLE	DUCKING	EAGERLY	EELPOUT
DORTOUR	DRIBLET	DUCTILE	EANLING	EELWORM
DOS-À-DOS	DRIFTER	DUDDERY	EARACHE	EFFABLE
DOSSIER	DRINKER	DUDGEON	EAR-BONE	EFFENDI
DOTTING	DRIP-DRY	DUELLED	EARDROP	EFFORCE
DOTTLED	DRIPPED	DUELLER	EARDRUM	EFFULGE
DOTTREL	DRIP-TIP	DUKEDOM	EARHOLE	EGALITY
DOUBLER	DRIVE-IN	DULCIFY	EARLDOM	EGG-BIRD
DOUBLET	DRIVING	DULCITE	EARLESS	EGG-CELL
DOUBLE-U	DRIZZLE	DULCOSE	EARLIER	EGG-COSY
DOUBTED	DRIZZLY	DULLARD	EARLOCK	EGG-FLIP
DOUBTER	DROGHER	DULLISH	EARMARK	EGGHEAD
DOUCELY	DROGUET	DULNESS	EARNEST	EGGMASS
DOUCEUR	DROICHY	DULOSIS	EARPICK	EGG-PLUM
DOUCINE	DROMOND	DULOTIC	EARPLUG	EGOTISE
DOUGHTY	DRONISH	DUMAIST	EARRING	EGOTISM
DOULEIA	DROOKIT	DUM-PALM	EARSHOT	EGOTIST
DOURINE	DROPFLY	DUMPISH	EARTHEN	EIDETIC
DOVECOT	DROPLET	DUN-BIRD	EARTHLY	EIDOLON
DOVEKIE	DROP-NET	DUNCERY	EASEFUL	EILDING
DOVELET	DROP-OUT	DUNCIAD	EASTERN	EIRENIC
DOWABLE	DROPPED	DUN-FISH	EASTING	EJECTOR
DOWAGER	DROPPER	DUNGEON	EASTLIN	ELASTIC
DOWDILY	DROPPLE	DUNKIRK	EASY-OSY	ELASTIN
DOWNA-DO	DROSERA	DUNNAGE	EATABLE	ELATION
DOWN-BED	DROSHKY	DUNNING	EBBLESS	ELDERLY
DOWNBOW	DROUGHT	DUNNISH	EBB-TIDE	ELEATIC
DOYENNE	DROUKIT	DUNNOCK	EBONISE	ELECTOR
DOZENTH	DROUTHY	DUODENA	EBONIST	ELECTRO
DRABBER	DROWNED	DUPABLE	EBONITE	ELEGANT
DRABBET	DROWNER	DURABLE	EBRIATE	ELEGIAC
DRABBLE	DRUBBED	DURABLY	EBRIETY	ELEGISE
DRABLER	DRUCKEN	DURAMEN	EBRIOSE	ELEGIST
DRACHMA	DRUDGER	DURANCE	ECBOLIC	ELEMENT
DRAFTEE	DRUDGED	DUREFUL	ECDYSIS	ELENCHI
DRAFTER	DRUGGED	DURESSE	ECHELON	ELEVATE
DRAFT-OX	DRUGGER	DURMAST	ECHIDNA	ELEVENS
DRAG-BAR	DRUGGET	DUSKILY	ECHINUS	ELF-BOLT
DRAGGED	DRUIDIC	DUSKISH	ECHOING	ELFHOOD
DRAGGLE	DRUMBLE	DUST-BIN	ECHOISE	ELFLAND
DRAG-MAN	DRUMLIN	DUSTMAN	ECHOISM	ELF-SHOT
DRAG-NET	DRUMMED	DUST-PAN	ECHOIST	ELISION
DRAGOON	DRUMMER	DUTEOUS	ECLIPSE	ELITISM
DRAINER	DRUNKEN	DUTIFUL	ECLOGUE	ELITIST
DRAPERY	DRUSIAN	DUUMVIR	ECOLOGY	ELLAGIC
DRAPIER	DRYADES	DVORNIK	ECONOMY	ELLIPSE
DRAPPIE	DRYBEAT	DWARFED	ÉCORCHÉ	ELLWAND
	DRY-CELL		ECSTASY	

ELOGIST	EMPTIER	ENHANCE	EPHUIST	EROTISM
ELOGIUM	EMPTIES	ENJOYER	EPICARP	ERRABLE
ELOHIST	EMPTION	ENLARGE	EPICEDE	ERRATIC
ELUSION	EMPYEMA	ENLIGHT	EPICENE	ERRATUM
ELUSIVE	EMULATE	ENLIVEN	EPICISM	ERRHINE
ELUSORY	EMULOUS	ENNOBLE	EPICIST	ERUDITE
ELUTION	EMULSIN	ENOMOTY	EPICURE	ESCALOP
ELUVIAL	EMULSOR	ENOUNCE	EPIDOTE	ESCAPEE
ELUVIUM	ENACTOR	ENPRINT	EPIGEAL	ESCHEAT
ELYSIAN	ENAMOUR	ENQUIRE	EPIGEAN	ESCOLAR
ELYSIUM	ENARMED	ENQUIRY	EPIGENE	ESCRIBE
ELYTRAL	ENATION	ENRAGED	EPIGONE	ESCROLL
ELYTRON	ENCHAFE	ENRANGE	EPIGONI	ESCUAGE
ELYTRUM	ENCHAIN	ENRIVEN	EPIGONS	ESLOYNE
ELZEVIR	ENCHANT	ENROUGH	EPIGRAM	ESOTERY
EMANANT	ENCHARM	ENROUND	EPIGYNY	ESPARTO
EMANATE	ENCHASE	ENSHELL	EPILATE	ESPOUSE
EMBARGO	ENCHEER	ENSLAVE	EPISODE	ESPYING
EMBASED	ENCLASP	ENSNARE	EPISTLE	ESQUIRE
EMBASSY	ENCLAVE	ENSNARL	EPITAPH	ESSAYED
EMBATHE	ENCLOSE	ENSTAMP	EPITHEM	ESSAYER
EMBLAZE	ENCLOUD	ENSTEEP	EPITHET	ESSENCE
EMBLEMA	ENCOMIA	ENSTYLE	EPITOME	ESSOYNE
EMBLOOM	ENCRATY	ENSUING	EPIZOAN	ESTOILE
EMBOGUE	ENCRUST	ENSWEEP	EPIZOIC	ESTOVER
EMBOLIC	ENDARCH	ENTASIS	EPIZOON	ESTRADE
EMBOLUS	ENDEMIC	ENTAYLE	EPOCHAL	ESTREAT
EMBOSOM	ENDERON	ENTENTE	EPOXIDE	ESTREPE
EMBOUND	ENDIRON	ENTERAL	EPSILON	ESTRICH
EMBOWED	ENDLANG	ENTERER	EPURATE	ESTUARY
EMBOWEL	ENDLESS	ENTERIC	EQUABLE	ETACISM
EMBOWER	ENDLONG	ENTERON	EQUABLY	ETAERIO
EMBRACE	ENDMOST	ENTHRAL	EQUALLY	ETCHING
EMBRAID	ENDOGEN	ENTHUSE	EQUATOR	ETERNAL
EMBRAVE	ENDORSE	ENTICER	EQUERRY	ETESIAN
EMBROIL	ENDOWER	ENTITLE	EQUIDAE	ETHANOL
EMBROWN	ENDOZOA	ENTOMIC	EQUINAL	ETHERIC
EMBRUTE	END-SHIP	ENTOPIC	EQUINIA	ETHICAL
EMBRYON	ENDURER	ENTOTIC	EQUINOX	ETHIOPS
EMBRYOS	ENDWAYS	ENTOZOA	ERASION	ETHMOID
EMERALD	ENDWISE	ENTRAIL	ERASURE	ETIOLIN
EMERITI	ENEMATA	ENTRAIN	ERECTED	ETONIAN
EMERODS	ENERGIC	ENTRANT	ERECTER	ETRURIA
EMERSED	ENERGID	ENTREAT	ERECTLY	EUCAINE
EMETINE	ENFELON	ENTROPY	ERECTOR	EUCLASE
EMICANT	ENFEOFF	ENTRUST	ERELONG	EUCRITE
EMICATE	ENFILED	ENTWINE	EREMITE	EUGENIA
EMINENT	ENFLESH	ENTWIST	EREPSIN	EUGENIC
EMIRATE	ENFORCE	ENVAULT	EREWHON	EUGLENA
EMITTED	ENFRAME	ENVELOP	ERGATES	EUPEPSY
EMOTION	ENGAGED	ENVENOM	ERG-NINE	EUPHONY
EMOTIVE	ENGAGER	ENVIOUS	ERGODIC	EUPHORY
EMPANEL	ENGINER	ENVIRON	ERICOID	EURATOM
EMPATHY	ENGLISH	ENVYING	ERINITE	EURIPUS
EMPERCE	ENGLOBE	ENWHEEL	ERINYES	EUSTASY
EMPEROR	ENGLOOM	EPACRID	ERISTIC	EUSTYLE
EMPIGHT	ENGORGE	EPACRIS	ERL-KING	EUTERPE
EMPIRIC	ENGRACE	EPAGOGE	ERMELIN	EUTEXIA
EMPLACE	ENGRAFF	EPARCHY	ERMINED	EUTROPY
EMPLANE	ENGRAFT	EPAULET	ERODENT	EVACUEE
EMPLUME	ENGRAIL	EPAXIAL	ERODIUM	EVANGEL
EMPORIA	ENGRAIN	EPEIRID	EROSION	EVANISH
EMPOWER	ENGRASP	EPERGNE	EROSIVE	EVASION
EMPRESS	ENGRAVE	EPHEBIC	EROTEMA	EVASIVE
EMPRISE	ENGROSS	EPHEBUS	EROTEME	EVENING
EMPTIED	ENGUARD	EPHEDRA	EROTICA	EVICTOR

EVIDENT	EXTINCT	FALL-GUY	FAUNIST	FIBBERY
EVIRATE	EXTRACT	FALLING	FAUVISM	FIBBING
EVITATE	EXTREAT	FALL-OUT	FAUVIST	FIBROID
EVOCATE	EXTREME	FALSELY	FAWNING	FIBROIN
EVOLUTE	EXTRUDE	FALSIES	FAYENCE	FIBROMA
EWE-LAMB	EXUDATE	FALSIFY	FEARFUL	FIBROSE
EWE-MILK	EXUVIAE	FALSISH	FEASTER	FIBROUS
EWE-NECK	EXUVIAL	FALSITY	FEATHER	FIBSTER
EXACTER	EYEBALL	FAMULUS	FEATOUS	FIBULAR
EXACTLY	EYE-BATH	FANATIC	FEATURE	FICTILE
EXACTOR	EYE-BEAM	FANCIED	FEBRILE	FICTION
EXALTED	EYEBROW	FANCIER	FEDARIE	FICTIVE
EXAMINE	EYE-DROP	FANFARE	FEDAYEE	FIDDLER
EXAMPLE	EYE-FLAP	FANGLED	FEDERAL	FIDDLEY
EXARATE	EYE-HOLE	FANNELL	FEEDING	FIDGETY
EXCERPT	EYELASH	FANNING	FEE-FARM	FIDIBUS
EXCITED	EYELESS	FANTAIL	FEELING	FIELDED
EXCITER	EYELIAD	FANTASM	FEIGNED	FIELDER
EXCITON	EYE-SHOT	FANTAST	FÉLIBRE	FIERILY
EXCITOR	EYESORE	FANTASY	FELIDAE	FIFTEEN
EXCLAIM	EYE-SPOT	FANTEEG	FELINAE	FIFTHLY
EXCLAVE	EYE-WASH	FARADAY	FELONRY	FIFTIES
EXCLUDE	EYE-WINK	FARADIC	FELSITE	FIGGERY
EXCRETA		FARAWAY	FELSPAR	FIGGING
EXCRETE	**F**	FARCEUR	FELTING	FIGHTER
EXCUDIT		FARCIED	FELUCCA	FIG-LEAF
EXCURSE	FABERGÉ	FARCIFY	FELWORT	FIGMENT
EXCUSAL	FABLIAU	FARCING	FEMINAL	FIG-TREE
EXECUTE	FABLING	FARDAGE	FEMITER	FIGURAL
EXEDRAE	FABULAR	FARDING	FEMORAL	FIGURED
EXEGETE	FACETED	FARMERY	FENCING	FIGWORT
EXEMPLA	FACONNÉ	FARMING	FEN-FIRE	FILABEG
EXERGUE	FACTION	FARMOST	FENITAR	FILACER
EXHAUST	FACTIVE	FARNESS	FENLAND	FILARIA
EXHEDRA	FACTORY	FARRAGO	FENNISH	FILASSE
EXHIBIT	FACTUAL	FARRAND	FEODARY	FILAZER
EXHUMER	FACTURE	FARRANT	FEOFFEE	FILBERT
EXIGENT	FACULAE	FARRIER	FEOFFER	FILCHER
EXILITY	FACULTY	FARRUCA	FEOFFOR	FILEMOT
EXOCARP	FADDISH	FARTHEL	FERMATA	FILIATE
EXODIST	FADDISM	FARTHER	FERMENT	FILIBEG
EXOGAMY	FADDIST	FASCIAL	FERMIUM	FILICES
EXOMION	FADEDLY	FASCINE	FERNERY	FILLING
EXORDIA	FADE-OUT	FASCISM	FERN-OWL	FILMDOM
EXPANSE	FAGGERY	FASCIST	FERRATE	FILMISH
EXPENSE	FAGGING	FASHERY	FERRETY	FIMBRIA
EXPIATE	FAGOTTO	FASHION	FERRIED	FINABLE
EXPIRED	FAHLERZ	FAST-DAY	FERRITE	FINAGLE
EXPLAIN	FAHLORE	FASTENS	FERROUS	FINALLY
EXPLANT	FAIENCE	FASTING	FERRUGO	FINANCE
EXPLODE	FAILING	FASTISH	FERRULE	FINBACK
EXPLOIT	FAILURE	FATALLY	FERTILE	FINCHED
EXPLORE	FAINTED	FATEFUL	FERVENT	FINDING
EXPOSAL	FAINTLY	FAT-FACE	FERVOUR	FINEISH
EXPOSED	FAIR-DAY	FAT-HEAD	FESTIVE	FINESSE
EXPOSER	FAIRILY	FATIGUE	FESTOON	FINICAL
EXPOUND	FAIRING	FATIMID	FETICHE	FINICKY
EXPRESS	FAIRISH	FATLING	FETLOCK	FINIKIN
EXPULSE	FAIRWAY	FAT-LUTE	FETTLER	FINLESS
EXPUNCT	FAITOUR	FATNESS	FEUDARY	FINNACK
EXPUNGE	FALANGE	FATTEST	FEUDING	FINNISH
EXPURGE	FALBALA	FATTING	FEUDIST	FINNOCK
EXSCIND	FALCADE	FATTISH	FEU-DUTY	FINNSKO
EXTATIC	FALCATE	FATUITY	FEVERED	FIN-TOED
EXTENSE	FALCULA	FATUOUS	FEWNESS	FIR-CONE
EXTERNE	FALDAGE	FAUCIAL	FIANCÉE	FIRE-ARM
	FALLACY			

FIRE-BAR	FLATTED	FLUTINA	FORAMEN	FOULDER
FIREBOX	FLATTEN	FLUTING	FORAYER	FOUMART
FIREBUG	FLATTER	FLUTIST	FORBADE	FOUNDER
FIREDOG	FLAUGHT	FLUTTER	FORBEAR	FOUNDRY
FIREFLY	FLAUNTY	FLUVIAL	FORBODE	FOUR-ALE
FIREMAN	FLAVIAN	FLUXION	FORBORE	FOURGON
FIRE-NEW	FLAVINE	FLUXIVE	FORCEPS	FOUR-OAR
FIREPAN	FLAVOUR	FLYABLE	FORDONE	FOURSES
FIREPOT	FLAYING	FLYAWAY	FOREARM	FOVEATE
FIRRING	FLEA-PIT	FLY-BANE	FORECAR	FOVEOLA
FIRSTLY	FLECKED	FLY-BELT	FOREDAY	FOVEOLE
FIR-TREE	FLECKER	FLY-BLOW	FORE-END	FOWLING
FIR-WOOD	FLEDGED	FLY-BOAT	FOREIGN	FOX-EVIL
FISH-DAY	FLEECED	FLY-BOOK	FORELAY	FOXHOLE
FISHERY	FLEECER	FLY-FLAP	FORELEG	FOX-HUNT
FISH-EYE	FLEEING	FLY-HALF	FORELIE	FOXSHIP
FISH-FAG	FLEERER	FLY-KICK	FOREMAN	FOX-TAIL
FISHGIG	FLEETLY	FLYLEAF	FOREMEN	FOX-TRAP
FISH-GOD	FLEMING	FLYOVER	FORERAN	FOXTROT
FISHIFY	FLEMISH	FLY-SLOW	FORERUN	FRABBIT
FISHING	FLESHED	FLYTING	FORESAW	FRACTED
FISHNET	FLESHER	FLY-TRAP	FORESAY	FRAENUM
FISH-OIL	FLESHLY	FOAMING	FORESEE	FRAGILE
FISHWAY	FLETTON	FOCUSED	FORETOP	FRAILLY
FISSILE	FLEURET	FOCUSES	FOREVER	FRAILTY
FISSION	FLEURON	FOG-BANK	FORFAIR	FRAKTUR
FISSIVE	FLEXILE	FOG-BELL	FORFEIT	FRAME-UP
FISSURE	FLEXION	FOGGAGE	FORFEND	FRAMING
FISTFUL	FLEXURE	FOGGILY	FORGAVE	FRAMPAL
FIST-LAW	FLICKER	FOG-HORN	FORGERY	FRANION
FISTULA	FLIGHTY	FOGLESS	FORGING	FRANKLY
FITCHÉE	FLINDER	FOGYDOM	FORGIVE	FRANTIC
FITCHET	FLIP–DOG	FOGYISH	FORGONE	FRAPPÉE
FITCHEW	FLIPPER	FOGYISM	FORHENT	FRATCHY
FITLIER	FLITTED	FOILING	FORLANA	FRATERY
FITMENT	FLITTER	FOISTER	FORLEND	FRAUGHT
FITNESS	FLIVVER	FOLDING	FORLENT	FRAYING
FITTING	FLOATER	FOLIAGE	FORLORN	FRAZZLE
FIVEBAR	FLOCCUS	FOLIATE	FORMANT	FRECKLE
FIVEPIN	FLOGGED	FOLIOLE	FORMATE	FRECKLY
FIXABLE	FLOODED	FOLIOSE	FORMING	FREE-ARM
FIXEDLY	FLOORED	FOLK-ART	FORMULA	FREEDOM
FIXTURE	FLOORER	FOLK-WAY	FORNENT	FREEING
FIZZING	FLOOSIE	FOMITES	FORPINE	FREEMAN
FLACCID	FLOOZIE	FONDANT	FORSAKE	FREEMEN
FLACKER	FLORÉAL	FONDLER	FORSLOE	FREESIA
FLACKET	FLOREAT	FONTLET	FORSLOW	FREEWAY
FLAFFER	FLORIST	FOODFUL	FORSOOK	FREEZER
FLAG-DAY	FLORUIT	FOOLERY	FORTIES	FREIGHT
FLAGGED	FLOTAGE	FOOLING	FORTIFY	FRENCHY
FLAMFEW	FLOTANT	FOOLISH	FORTLET	FRESHEN
FLAMING	FLOTSAM	FOOTAGE	FORTRAN	FRESHER
FLÂNEUR	FLOUNCE	FOOT-BAR	FORTUNE	FRESHET
FLANGED	FLOWAGE	FOOTBOY	FORWARD	FRESHLY
FLANKER	FLOWERY	FOOTING	FORWARN	FRETFUL
FLANNEL	FLOWING	FOOT-JAW	FORWENT	FRETSAW
FLANNEN	FLUENCY	FOOTMAN	FORWORN	FRETTED
FLAPPED	FLUIDAL	FOOTMEN	FORZATO	FRIABLE
FLAPPER	FLUIDIC	FOOTPAD	FOSSICK	FRIARLY
FLARE-UP	FLUMMOX	FOOT-ROT	FOSSULA	FRIBBLE
FLARING	FLUNKEY	FOOTWAY	FOSSWAY	FRIESIC
FLASHER	FLUORIC	FOOZLER	FOUDRIE	FRIEZED
FLASKET	FLUSHED	FOPLING	FOUETTÉ	FRIGATE
FLAT-CAP	FLUSHER	FOPPERY	FOUGADE	FRIGGER
FLATLET	FLUSTER	FOPPISH	FOUGHTY	FRIJOLE
	FLUSTRA	FORAGER	FOULARD	FRINGED

FRIPPER
FRISIAN
FRISKER
FRISKET
FRISSON
FRITTED
FRITTER
FRIZZED
FRIZZLE
FRIZZLY
FROCKED
FROGBIT
FROGGED
FROGLET
FROGMAN
FRONDED
FRONTAL
FRONTED
FRONTON
FROSTED
FROUGHY
FROUNCE
FROWARD
FROWSTY
FRUCTED
FRUMPLE
FRUSTUM
FUBBERY
FUCHSIA
FUCKING
FUCUSED
FUCUSES
FUDDLED
FUDDLER
FUELLED
FUELLER
FUGALLY
FUGUIST
FULCRUM
FULGENT
FULGOUR
FULLAGE
FULLEST
FULL-FED
FULL-HOT
FULLISH
FULL-OUT
FULMINE
FULNESS
FULSOME
FULVOUS
FUMARIA
FUMARIC
FUMBLER
FUMETTE
FUNERAL
FUNFAIR
FUNGOID
FUNGOUS
FUNICLE
FUNNIES
FUNNILY
FUNNING
FURBISH
FURCATE
FURCULA

FURFAIR
FURIOSO
FURIOUS
FURLANA
FURLONG
FURMETY
FURMITY
FURNACE
FURNISH
FURRIER
FURRING
FURROWY
FUR-SEAL
FURTHER
FURTIVE
FUSAROL
FUSCOUS
FUSE-BOX
FUSE-OIL
FUSHION
FUSIBLE
FUSSILY
FUSS-POT
FUSTIAN
FUTCHEL
FUTHARK
FUTHORC
FUTHORK
FUTTOCK
FUZZILY

G

GABBARD
GABBART
GABBLER
GABELLE
GABNASH
GADDING
GADIDAE
GADLING
GADROON
GADSMAN
GADWALL
GAEKWAR
GAFFING
G-AGENTS
GAGGING
GAHNITE
GAIKWAR
GAINFUL
GAINSAY
GALANGA
GALANTY
GALATEA
GALEATE
GALENIC
GALILEE
GALIPOT
GALLANT
GALLATE
GALLEON
GALLERY
GALL-FLY
GALLICE
GALLING
GALLIOT

GALLISE
GALLIUM
GALL-NUT
GALLOON
GALLOWS
GALOCHE
GALOPIN
GALUMPH
GAMBADO
GAMBIER
GAMBIST
GAMBLER
GAMBOGE
GAMBREL
GAME-BAG
GAMELAN
GAMETAL
GAMETIC
GAMMOCK
GAMPISH
GANGBYE
GANGING
GANGLIA
GANGREL
GANTLET
GARBAGE
GARBLER
GARBOIL
GARDANT
GARFISH
GARLAND
GARMENT
GARNISH
GAROTTE
GARPIKE
GARVOCK
GAS-BUOY
GAS-COAL
GAS-COKE
GASEITY
GASEOUS
GAS-FIRE
GASHFUL
GASKINS
GAS-LAMP
GAS-LIME
GAS-MAIN
GAS-MASK
GASPING
GAS-PIPE
GAS-RING
GASSING
GAS-TANK
GAS-TRAP
GASTRIC
GAS-WELL
GATEMAN
GATEWAY
GAUDERY
GAUDILY
GAUGING
GAULISH
GAULTER
GAUNTLY
GAUNTRY
GAVOTTE

GAYNESS
GAYSOME
GAZEFUL
GAZELLE
GAZETTE
GEAR-BOX
GEEBUNG
GEHENNA
GELATIN
GELDING
GELIDLY
GELLING
GEMINID
GEMMATE
GEMMERY
GEMMING
GEMMULE
GEMSBOK
GENAPPE
GENERAL
GENERIC
GENESES
GENESIS
GENETIC
GENETTE
GENEVAN
GENIPAP
GENISTA
GENITAL
GENITOR
GENIZAH
GENOESE
GENTEEL
GENTIAN
GENTILE
GENUINE
GEODESY
GEOGENY
GEOGONY
GEOIDAL
GEOLOGY
GEORDIE
GEORGIC
GERBERA
GERMAIN
GERMANE
GESTALT
GESTANT
GESTAPO
GESTATE
GESTURE
GETAWAY
GETTING
GHARIAL
GHASTLY
GHERKIN
GHILLIE
GHOSTLY
GIANTLY
GIANTRY
GIBBOSE
GIBBOUS
GIBLETS
GIDDILY
GIGGLER
GILBERT

GILDING
GILTCUP
GIMMICK
GIN-FIZZ
GINGALL
GINGHAM
GINGILI
GINNERY
GINNING
GINSENG
GINSHOP
GIRAFFE
GIRASOL
GIRDING
GIRDLED
GIRDLER
GIRLISH
GITTERN
GIZZARD
GLACIAL
GLACIER
GLADDED
GLADDEN
GLADDON
GLADIUS
GLAIKIT
GLAIRIN
GLAMOUR
GLAREAL
GLARING
GLASSEN
GLAUCUS
GLAZIER
GLAZING
GLEANER
GLEBOUS
GLEEFUL
GLEEMAN
GLENOID
GLIADIN
GLIDDER
GLIDING
GLIMMER
GLIMPSE
GLISTEN
GLISTER
GLITTER
GLOBATE
GLOBOID
GLOBOSE
GLOBOUS
GLOBULE
GLORIED
GLORIFY
GLOSSER
GLOSSIC
GLOTTAL
GLOTTIC
GLOTTIS
GLOWING
GLOZING
GLUCINA
GLUCOSE
GLUE-POT
GLUTEAL
GLUTEUS

GLUTTED
GLUTTON
GLYCINE
GLYCOSE
GLYPHIC
GLYPTAL
GLYPTIC
GNARLED
GNARRED
GNATHIC
GNOCCHI
GNOMISH
GNOSTIC
GO-AHEAD
GOATEED
GOAT-FIG
GOAT-GOD
GOATISH
GOBBLER
GOBELIN
GOBURRA
GODDAMN
GODDESS
GODETIA
GODHEAD
GODHOOD
GODLESS
GODLIKE
GODLILY
GODLING
GODROON
GODSEND
GODSHIP
GODWARD
GOGGLED
GOGGLER
GOITRED
GOLD-BUG
GOLDERY
GOLDEYE
GOLDISH
GOLF-BAG
GOLFING
GOLIARD
GOLIATH
GOLLAND
GOMBEEN
GOMERAL
GOMERIL
GONADIC
GONDOLA
GONIDIA
GOODBYE
GOOD-DAY
GOOD-DEN
GOOD-E'EN
GOODISH
GOODMAN
GOOD-NOW
GOODSON
GOORKHA
GOOSERY
GORCOCK
GORCROW
GORDIAN
GORDIUS

GORILLA
GORMAND
GORSEDD
GORSOON
GOSHAWK
GOSLING
GOSSIPY
GOSSOON
GÖTHITE
GOUACHE
GOULASH
GOURAMI
GOURMET
GOUTFLY
GOWLAND
GOWNBOY
GOWNMAN
GRAB-BAG
GRABBED
GRABBER
GRABBLE
GRACILE
GRACKLE
GRADATE
GRADDAN
GRADELY
GRADINE
GRADINO
GRADUAL
GRAFTER
GRAINED
GRAINER
GRALLAE
GRAMARY
GRAMMAR
GRAMPUS
GRANARY
GRANDAD
GRANDAM
GRANDEE
GRANDLY
GRANDMA
GRANDPA
GRANFER
GRANITE
GRANNAM
GRANNIE
GRANTEE
GRANTER
GRANTOR
GRANULE
GRAPERY
GRAPHIC
GRAPHIS
GRAPNEL
GRAPPLE
GRASPER
GRASSER
GRASSUM
GRATIFY
GRATING
GRAVELY
GRAVING
GRAVITY
GRAVURE
GRAYFLY

GRAZIER
GRAZING
GREASER
GREATEN
GREATER
GREATLY
GREAVES
GRECIAN
GRECISE
GRECISM
GRECQUE
GREENLY
GREENTH
GREETED
GREGALE
GREGORY
GREISEN
GREMIAL
GREMLIN
GRENADE
GRESHAM
GREYHEN
GREYISH
GREYLAG
GRIBBLE
GRIDDLE
GRIECED
GRIEVER
GRIFFIN
GRIFFON
GRILLED
GRIMACE
GRIMILY
GRINDER
GRINNED
GRIPING
GRIPPED
GRIPPER
GRIPPLE
GRISKIN
GRISTLE
GRISTLY
GRIZZLE
GRIZZLY
GROBIAN
GROCERY
GROGRAM
GROINED
GROLIER
GROMMET
GROSERT
GROSSLY
GROTIAN
GROUCHY
GROUPER
GROUSER
GROWING
GROWLER
GROWN-UP
GRUBBED
GRUBBER
GRUBBLE
GRUFFLY
GRUMBLE
GRUMBLY
GRUMMET

GRUMOSE
GRUMOUS
GRUNTER
GRUNTLE
GRUTTEN
GRUYÈRE
GRYPHON
GRYSBOK
GRYSELY
G-STRING
GUANACO
GUANINE
GUARANA
GUARANÍ
GUARDED
GUARISH
GUAYULE
GUDE-MAN
GUDGEON
GUELFIC
GUERDON
GUEREZA
GUESSER
GUESTEN
GUICHET
GUIDAGE
GUIDING
GUIGNOL
GUILDER
GUILDRY
GUIPURE
GUISARD
GULLERY
GULLEYS
GULLIED
GULLIES
GULLISH
GUMBOIL
GUMBOOT
GUMMATA
GUMMING
GUMMITE
GUMMOUS
GUMSHOE
GUM-TREE
GUNBOAT
GUNFIRE
GUNNAGE
GUNNERA
GUNNERY
GUNNING
GUNPORT
GUNROOM
GUNSHOT
GUNWALE
GUNZIAN
GURNARD
GUSHING
GUSTFUL
GUTCHER
GUTTATE
GUTTING
GUY-ROPE
GWINIAD
GWYNAID
GYMNAST

GYRALLY
GYROCAR
GYRONNY
GYTRASH

H

HABITAT
HABITUÉ
HACHURE
HACKBUT
HACKERY
HACKING
HACKLER
HACKLET
HACKLOG
HACKNEY
HACKSAW
HADDOCK
HADROME
HAEMONY
HAFFLIN
HAFNIUM
HAGBOLT
HAGDOWN
HAGFISH
HAGGADA
HAGGARD
HAGGISH
HAGGLER
HAG-RIDE
HAG-SEED
HAG-WEED
HAINING
HAIRCUT
HAIR-EEL
HAIR-NET
HAIR-OIL
HAIRPIN
HALACHA
HALAKAH
HALAVAH
HALBERD
HALBERT
HALCYON
HALF-APE
HALF-CAP
HALFLIN
HALF-ONE
HALF-PAY
HALFWAY
HALF-WIT
HALIBUT
HALIDOM
HALIMOT
HALITUS
HALLALI
HALLIAN
HALLING
HALLION
HALLWAY
HALLYON
HALOGEN
HALTING
HALVERS
HALYARD
HAMBURG

H7

HAMITIC
HAMMOCK
HAMSTER
HAMULAR
HAMULUS
HANAPER
HANDBAG
HAND-CAR
HANDFUL
HAND-GUN
HANDILY
HANDJAR
HANDLED
HANDLER
HAND-OFF
HANDOUT
HANDSAW
HANDSEL
HAND-SET
HANGDOG
HANGING
HANGMAN
HANGOUT
HANSARD
HANUMAN
HA'PENCE
HA'PENNY
HAPLESS
HAPLOID
HAP'ORTH
HAPPILY
HAPPING
HAPTICS
HARBOUR
HARD-GOT
HARD-HIT
HARDILY
HARDISH
HARDOKE
HARD-PAN
HARD-RUN
HARD-SET
HARD-WON
HARE-LIP
HARICOT
HARIJAN
HARLING
HARMALA
HARMFUL
HARMINE
HARMONY
HARMOST
HARNESS
HARN-PAN
HARPIST
HARPOON
HARRIED
HARRIER
HARSHEN
HARSHLY
HARSLET
HARVEST
HAS-BEEN
HASHISH
HASSOCK
HASTATE

HASTILY
HATABLE
HAT-BAND
HATCHEL
HATCHER
HATCHET
HATEFUL
HATFULS
HATLESS
HAT-RACK
HATTING
HATTOCK
HAUBERK
HAUGHTY
HAULAGE
HAULIER
HAUNTED
HAUNTER
HAUTBOY
HAUTEUR
HAVENED
HAVE-NOT
HAVEOUR
HAVEREL
HAVIOUR
HAWBUCK
HAWKBIT
HAWKING
HAWKISH
HAYBAND
HAYBOTE
HAYCOCK
HAYFORK
HAYLOFT
HAYRICK
HAYSEED
HAYWARD
HAYWIRE
HAZELLY
HEADILY
HEADING
HEADMAN
HEADRIG
HEADWAY
HEALING
HEALTHY
HEARING
HEARKEN
HEARSAY
HEARTED
HEARTEN
HEARTLY
HEATHEN
HEATHER
HEAVIER
HEAVILY
HEAVING
HEBENON
HEBRAIC
HECKLER
HECTARE
HEDERAL
HEDGING
HEDONIC
HEEDFUL
HEELING

HEEL-TAP
HEIGH-HO
HEINOUS
HEIRDOM
HEIRESS
HEISTER
HELCOID
HELIBUS
HELICAL
HELICES
HELIMAN
HELIXES
HELL-CAT
HELLENE
HELLIER
HELLION
HELLISH
HELLISM
HELLOVA
HELLUVA
HELOTRY
HELPFUL
HELPING
HEMIONE
HEMLOCK
HEMMING
HENBANE
HEN-COOP
HENNAED
HENNERY
HENOTIC
HENPECK
HEN-TOED
HEN-WIFE
HEPARIN
HEPATIC
HEPSTER
HEPTANE
HERBAGE
HERBARY
HERBIST
HERBLET
HERBOSE
HERBOUS
HERB-TEA
HERDBOY
HERDESS
HERDMAN
HERETIC
HÉRISSÉ
HERITOR
HERLING
HERNIAL
HEROINE
HEROISM
HERONRY
HERRING
HERSALL
HERSELF
HERSHIP
HESHVAN
HESSIAN
HETAERA
HETAIRA
HETMANS
HEUREKA

HEURISM
HEXADIC
HEXAGON
HEXAPLA
HEXAPOD
HEXARCH
HEYDUCK
HEY-PASS
HICATEE
HICCUPY
HICKORY
HIDALGA
HIDALGO
HIDEOUS
HIDEOUT
HIDLING
HIDLINS
HIELAND
HIGGLER
HIGHBOY
HIGHERS
HIGHEST
HIGH-FED
HIGH-HAT
HIGHISH
HIGH-LOW
HIGHMAN
HIGHMEN
HIGH-SET
HIGH-TOP
HIGHWAY
HIJINKS
HILDING
HILLMEN
HILLOCK
HILLTOP
HIMSELF
HIND-GUT
HIND-LEG
HINGING
HIP-BATH
HIP-BELT
HIP-BONE
HIP-GOUT
HIP-KNOB
HIP-LOCK
HIPPING
HIPPISH
HIP-ROOF
HIP-SHOT
HIPSTER
HIRABLE
HIRCINE
HIRLING
HIRSTIE
HIRSUTE
HIRUDIN
HISSING
HISTOID
HISTORY
HISTRIO
HITCHER
HITTING
HITTITE
HIVE-BEE
HOARDER

HOARILY
HOARSEN
HOATZIN
HOB-A-NOB
HOBBIAN
HOBBISH
HOBBISM
HOBBIST
HOBBLER
HOBNAIL
HOBODOM
HOBOISM
HOCK-DAY
HOCUSED
HOE-CAKE
HOEDOWN
HOGBACK
HOG-DEER
HOG-FISH
HOGGING
HOGGISH
HOGHOOD
HOG-MANE
HOG-NOSE
HOG-PLUM
HOGSKIN
HOGWARD
HOGWASH
HOGWEED
HOLD-ALL
HOLDING
HOLIBUT
HOLIDAY
HOLLAHO
HOLLAND
HOLMIUM
HOLM-OAK
HOLSTER
HOLY-ALE
HOLYDAM
HOMAGER
HOMBURG
HOMELYN
HOMERIC
HOMERID
HOMINID
HOMMOCK
HOMONYM
HONESTY
HONEYED
HONITON
HOODLUM
HOODMAN
HOOF-ROT
HOOGERY
HOOK-PIN
HOOLOCK
HOOP-ASH
HOOSGOW
HOPBIND
HOPBINE
HOPEFUL
HOP-FLEA
HOP-HEAD
HOPLITE
HOP-OAST

HOPPING
HOP-POLE
HOPSACK
HOP-TREE
HOP-VINE
HOPYARD
HORDEIN
HORDEUM
HORDOCK
HORIZON
HORMONE
HORNBUG
HORNFUL
HORNING
HORNISH
HORNIST
HORNITO
HORNLET
HORN-MAD
HORN-NUT
HORRENT
HORRIFY
HORSING
HOSANNA
HOSEMAN
HOSE-NET
HOSIERY
HOSPICE
HOSTAGE
HOSTESS
HOSTILE
HOSTLER
HOTFOOT
HOTHEAD
HOTNESS
HOTSPUR
HOTTISH
HOT-TROD
HOUSING
HOWBEIT
HOWDY-DO
HOWEVER
HOWLING
HUANACO
HUDDLED
HUELESS
HUFF-CAP
HUFFILY
HUFFISH
HUGEOUS
HUGGING
HUITAIN
HULKING
HULSEAN
HUMANLY
HUMBLES
HUMBUZZ
HUMDRUM
HUMERAL
HUMERUS
HUMIDLY
HUMIDOR
HUMMAUM
HUMMING
HUMMOCK
HUMOGEN

HUMORAL
HUNDRED
HUNGARY
HUNKERS
HUNNISH
HUNTING
HUNT'S-UP
HURDIES
HURDLER
HURL-BAT
HURLING
HURRIED
HURTFUL
HUSBAND
HUSHABY
HUSKILY
HUSKING
HUSSITE
HUSTLER
HUSWIFE
HUTMENT
HUTTING
HUZZAED
HYACINE
HYALINE
HYALITE
HYALOID
HYDATID
HYDRANT
HYDRATE
HYDRIDE
HYDROID
HYDROUS
HYGEIAN
HYGIENE
HYLOIST
HYMENAL
HYMNARY
HYMNING
HYMNIST
HYMNODY
HYPERON
HYPNOID
HYPNONE
HYPOGEA
HYPURAL

I

IAMBIST
IBERIAN
ICARIAN
ICE-BELT
ICEBERG
ICE-BIRD
ICE-BOAT
ICE-COLD
ICE-FALL
ICE-FERN
ICE-FLOE
ICE-FOOT
ICE-FREE
ICE-HILL
ICELAND
ICEPACK
ICE-RINK
ICE-SHOW

ICE-SPAR
ICE-WORM
ICHABOD
ICHTHIC
ICHTHYS
ICINESS
ICTERIC
ICTERUS
ICTUSES
IDALIAN
IDEALLY
IDENTIC
IDIOTCY
IDIOTIC
IDLESSE
IDOLISE
IDOLISM
IDOLIST
IDYLLIC
IGARAPÉ
IGNEOUS
IGNITER
IGNOBLE
IGNOBLY
IGNORER
IGUVINE
IKEBANA
ILEITIS
ILKADAY
ILLAPSE
ILL-BRED
ILLEGAL
ILL-FAME
ILLICIT
ILLNESS
ILL-TURN
ILL-USED
ILL-WILL
IMAGERY
IMAGINE
IMAGISM
IMAGIST
IMAMATE
IMBATHE
IMBIBER
IMBOSOM
IMBOWER
IMBROWN
IMBRUTE
IMBURSE
IMITANT
IMITATE
IMMENSE
IMMERGE
IMMERSE
IMMORAL
IMPAINT
IMPANEL
IMPASSE
IMPASTE
IMPASTO
IMPAVID
IMPEACH
IMPEARL
IMPERIL
IMPETUS

IMPIETY
IMPINGE
IMPIOUS
IMPLANT
IMPLATE
IMPLEAD
IMPLETE
IMPLIED
IMPLODE
IMPLORE
IMPOSER
IMPOUND
IMPREGN
IMPRESA
IMPRESE
IMPRESS
IMPREST
IMPRINT
IMPROVE
IMPULSE
IMPUTER
IN-AND-IN
INANITY
INAPTLY
INBEING
INBOARD
INBREAK
INBREED
INBRING
INBURST
INCENSE
INCHASE
INCHPIN
INCISED
INCISOR
INCITER
INCLASP
INCLINE
INCLOSE
INCLUDE
INCONIE
INCRUST
INCUBUS
INCUDES
INCURVE
INDEXER
INDEXES
INDICAN
INDICES
INDITER
INDOORS
INDORSE
INDRAFT
INDRAWN
INDUCER
INDULGE
INDUSIA
INDWELL
INDWELT
INEARTH
INEPTLY
INERTIA
INERTLY
INEXACT
INFANCY
INFANTA

INFANTE
INFARCT
INFAUST
INFERNO
INFIDEL
INFIELD
INFLAME
INFLATE
INFLECT
INFLICT
INFORCE
INFRACT
INFULAE
INGENER
INGÉNUE
INGESTA
INGLOBE
INGOING
INGOWES
INGRAIN
INGRATE
INGRESS
IN-GROUP
INGROWN
INHABIT
INHALER
INHAUST
INHERCE
INHERIT
INHIBIT
INHUMAN
INITIAL
INJELLY
INJOINT
INJURER
INK-FEED
INK-HORN
INKLING
IN-KNEED
INKWELL
INLAYER
INNARDS
INNERVE
INNINGS
INNYARD
INPHASE
INQUEST
INQUIET
INQUIRE
INQUIRY
INSANIE
INSCULP
INSECTA
INSECTY
INSHELL
INSHORE
INSIDER
INSIGHT
INSINEW
INSIPID
INSNARE
INSOFAR
INSOOTH
INSPECT
INSPIRE
INSTALL

INSTANT	ISOBASE	JANEITE	JOCULAR	KALMUCK
INSTATE	ISOBATH	JANGLER	JOGGING	KAMERAD
INSTEAD	ISOCHOR	JANITOR	JOGGLED	KAMICHI
INSTILL	ISODOMA	JANIZAR	JOG-TROT	KAMPONG
INSULAR	ISODONT	JANKERS	JOHNIAN	KANNADA
INSULIN	ISOETES	JANNOCK	JOHNNIE	KANTIAN
INSULSE	ISOGAMY	JANUARY	JOINDER	KANTISM
INSURER	ISOGENY	JAPONIC	JOINERY	KANTIST
INSWING	ISOGRAM	JAP-SILK	JOINING	KARAITE
INTEGER	ISOHYET	JARFULS	JOINTED	KARAKUL
INTENSE	ISOKONT	JARGOON	JOINTER	KARENNI
INTERIM	ISOLATE	JARKMAN	JOINTLY	KARLING
INTERNE	ISOMERE	JARRING	JOLLILY	KARTELL
IN-THING	ISONOMY	JASMINE	JOLLITY	KARTING
INTONER	ISOPODA	JASPERY	JONQUIL	KASHMIR
INTRANT	ISOTONE	JAUNTEE	JOOKERY	KATHODE
INTROIT	ISOTOPE	JAUNTIE	JOTTING	KATYDID
INTRUDE	ISOTOPY	JAVELIN	JOUKERY	KEBBOCK
INTWINE	ISOTRON	JAVELLE	JOURNAL	KEBBUCK
INTWIST	ISOTYPE	JAWBONE	JOURNEY	KEELAGE
INULASE	ISRAELI	JAW-FALL	JOYANCE	KEELING
INVADER	ISSUANT	JAW-FOOT	JOYCEAN	KEELMAN
INVALID	ISTHMUS	JAWHOLE	JOYLESS	KEELSON
INVEIGH	ITACISM	JAYWALK	JOY-RIDE	KEEPING
INVENIT	ITALIAN	JAZZILY	JUBILEE	KEITLOA
INVERSE	ITALIOT	JEALOUS	JUDAEAN	KELLAUT
INVEXED	ITEMISE	JEDDART	JUDAISE	KEMPING
INVIOUS	ITERANT	JEERING	JUDAISM	KENNICK
INVITER	ITERATE	JEHOVAH	JUDAIST	KENNING
INVOICE	IVORIED	JEJUNUM	JUGFULS	KENOSIS
INVOLVE	IVORIST	JELLIED	JUGGING	KENOTIC
INWARDS	IVY-BUSH	JELLIFY	JUGGINS	KENTISH
INWEAVE		JEMADAR	JUGGLER	KERAMIC
INWOVEN	**J**	JEMIDAR	JUGLANS	KERATIN
IODURET		JENKINS	JUGULAR	KERMESS
IPOMOEA	JACAMAR	JEOFAIL	JU-JITSU	KERNISH
IRACUND	JACCHUS	JEOPARD	JUKE-BOX	KERNITE
IRANIAN	JACINTH	JERICHO	JUMELLE	KEROGEN
IRATELY	JACKASS	JERKING	JUMPING	KERYGMA
IRENICS	JACKDAW	JERQUER	JUMP-JET	KESTREL
IRICISM	JACKMAN	JERSIAN	JUMP-OFF	KETCHUP
IRIDEAE	JACKPOT	JESSAMY	JUNCATE	KEY-COLD
IRIDEAL	JACK-TAR	JESSANT	JUNIPER	KEY-DESK
IRIDIAL	JACOBIN	JESTFUL	JUNKMAN	KEYHOLE
IRIDIAN	JACOBUS	JESTING	JUPITER	KEYLESS
IRIDISE	JACONET	JETHART	JURALLY	KEYNOTE
IRIDIUM	JADEDLY	JEWELRY	JURY-BOX	KEY-RING
IRISATE	JADEITE	JEWFISH	JURYMAN	KEY-SEAT
IRISHER	J'ADOUBE	JEW'S-EAR	JURYMEN	KHADDAR
IRISHRY	JAGGERY	JEZEBEL	JUSSIVE	KHALIFA
IRKSOME	JAGGING	JIBBING	JUSTICE	KHAMSIN
IRONING	JAGHIRE	JIB-BOOM	JUSTIFY	KHANATE
IRONIST	JAINISM	JIB-DOOR	JUTTING	KHEDIVA
IRON-ORE	JALAPIC	JIGAJIG	JUVENAL	KHEDIVE
IRON-PAN	JALAPIN	JIGAJOG		KHOTBAH
ISATINE	JALOPPY	JIGGING	**K**	KHOTBEH
ISCHIAL	JALOUSE	JIGGISH		KHUTBAH
ISCHIUM	JAMADAR	JIM-CROW	KACHCHA	KIBBUTZ
ISEGRIM	JAMAICA	JINGLER	KACHERI	KIBITKA
ISHMAEL	JAMBEAU	JINGLET	KADDISH	KICK-OFF
ISIACAL	JAMBEUX	JINJILI	KAIL-PAT	KIDDIER
ISLAMIC	JAMBIER	JITTERS	KAIL-POT	KIDDIES
ISLEMAN	JAMBONE	JITTERY	KAINITE	KIDDING
ISMAILI	JAMBOOL	JOANNES	KAJAWAH	KIDLING
ISMATIC	JAMDANI	JOBBERY	KAKODYL	KIDSKIN
ISOBARE	JAMMING	JOBBING	KALENDS	KIKUMON
	JAMPANI		KALLIMA	

KILL-COW
KILLDEE
KILLICK
KILLING
KILLJOY
KILLOCK
KILN-DRY
KILOBAR
KIMBOED
KINCHIN
KINDLER
KINDRED
KINESIS
KINETIC
KINGCUP
KINGDOM
KINGLET
KINGPIN
KING-ROD
KINLESS
KINSHIP
KINSMAN
KIPPAGE
KIP-SHOP
KIPSKIN
KIRIMON
KIRKING
KIRKTON
KIRMESS
KIRTLED
KIT-BOAT
KITCHEN
KITHARA
KITLING
KITTENY
KLAVIER
KLINKER
KLIPDAS
KNACKER
KNAPPED
KNAPPER
KNAPPLE
KNARRED
KNAVERY
KNAVISH
KNEADER
KNEE-CAP
KNEELED
KNEELER
KNEE-PAN
KNESSET
KNEVELL
KNICKER
KNITTED
KNITTER
KNITTLE
KNOBBED
KNOBBER
KNOBBLE
KNOBBLY
KNOCKER
KNOCK-ON
KNOCK-UP
KNOTTED
KNOTTER
KNOW-ALL

KNOWHOW
KNOWING
KNUBBLE
KNUBBLY
KNUCKLE
KNURLED
KOFTGAR
KOLKHOZ
KOMMERS
KORANIC
KOTYTTO
KOUMISS
KREMLIN
KRILIUM
KRISHNA
KROO-BOY
KROOMAN
KRYPSIS
KRYPTON
KUCHCHA
KUH-HORN
KUMQUAT
KURBASH
KURDISH
KURHAUS
KURSAAL
KYANISE
KYANITE

L

LABARUM
LABELLA
LABIATE
LABROID
LABROSE
LACE-MAN
LACERTA
LACE-UPS
LACINIA
LACK-ALL
LACKING
LAC-LAKE
LACONIC
LACQUER
LACQUEY
LACTASE
LACTATE
LACTEAL
LACTOSE
LACTUCA
LACUNAE
LACUNAL
LACUNAR
LADANUM
LADDERY
LADRONE
LADYBUG
LADYCOW
LADYFLY
LADYISH
LADYISM
LADYKIN
LAETARE
LAGGARD
LAGGING
LAGTING

LAICISE
LAIRAGE
LAITHFU'
LAKELET
LAKSHMI
LALLING
LAMAISM
LAMAIST
LAMB-ALE
LAMBAST
LAMBENT
LAMBERT
LAMBKIN
LAMBOYS
LAMELLA
LAMETER
LAMIGER
LAMINAE
LAMINAR
LAMITER
LAMMING
LAMPERN
LAMP-FLY
LAMPING
LAMPION
LAMPOON
LAMPREY
LANDING
LAND-LAW
LANDLER
LANDMAN
LAND-RAT
LANDTAG
LAND-TAX
LANGAHA
LANGREL
LANGUED
LANGUET
LANGUID
LANGUOR
LANIARD
LANIARY
LANOLIN
LANTANA
LANTERN
LANYARD
LAOTIAN
LAPILLI
LAPPING
LAPPISH
LAPUTAN
LAPWING
LAPWORK
LARCENY
LARCHEN
LARDOON
LARGELY
LARGESS
LARGISH
LARIDAE
LARKISH
LARMIER
LARVATE
LASAGNA
LASAGNE
LASHING

LASHKAR
LASSOCK
LASSOED
LASSOES
LASTAGE
LASTING
LATAKIA
LATCHET
LATENCE
LATENCY
LATERAL
LATERAN
LATHERY
LATHING
LATINER
LATITAT
LATRINE
LATTICE
LATVIAN
LAUGHER
LAUNDER
LAUNDRY
LAUWINE
LAVOLTA
LAW-BOOK
LAW-CALF
LAWLAND
LAWLESS
LAW-LIST
LAW-LORD
LAWSUIT
LAXATOR
LAXNESS
LAYAWAY
LAYBACK
LAYERED
LAYETTE
LAYLOCK
LAZARET
LAZY-BED
LEADING
LEAFAGE
LEAF-BUD
LEAFING
LEAFLET
LEAGUER
LEAKAGE
LEANING
LEAP-DAY
LEAPING
LEARNED
LEARNER
LEASING
LEASOWE
LEATHER
LEAVING
LECHERY
LECTERN
LECTION
LECTURE
LEECHEE
LEE-GAGE
LEE-LANE
LEERING
LEFTISM
LEFTIST

LEFT-OFF
LEGALLY
LEGATEE
LEGATOR
LEG-BAIL
LEGGING
LEGGISM
LEGHORN
LEGIBLE
LEGIBLY
LEG-IRON
LEGITIM
LEG-PULL
LEG-REST
LEG-SHOW
LEGUMIN
LEIDGER
LEISTER
LEISURE
LEMMATA
LEMMING
LEMNIAN
LEMURES
LEMURIA
LENDING
LENGEST
LENGTHY
LENIENT
LENTIGO
LENTISK
LENTOID
LENTOUS
LEONINE
LEOPARD
LEOTARD
LEPROSE
LEPROSY
LEPROUS
LEPTOME
LERNEAN
LESBIAN
LET-DOWN
LETHEAN
LETHIED
LETTING
LETTISH
LETTUCE
LEUCHEN
LEUCINE
LEUCITE
LEUCOMA
LEUGHEN
LEVATOR
LEVERET
LEVITIC
LEVYING
LEWDSBY
LEXICAL
LEXICON
LIAISON
LIASSIC
LIBBARD
LIBERAL
LIBERTY
LIBRARY
LIBRATE

LIBRIUM
LICENCE
LICH-OWL
LICHTLY
LICHWAY
LICITLY
LICKING
LIDLESS
LIE-ABED
LIEFEST
LIEVEST
LIFEFUL
LIFT-OFF
LIGHTED
LIGHTEN
LIGHTER
LIGHTLY
LIGNIFY
LIGNITE
LIGROIN
LIGULAR
LIKABLE
LIMACEL
LIMACES
LIMACON
LIMBATE
LIMBOUS
LIMINAL
LIMITED
LIMITER
LIMITES
LIMNAEA
LIMNING
LIMOSIS
LIMPING
LIMULUS
LINCHET
LINCTUS
LINDANE
LINEAGE
LINEATE
LINEMAN
LINE-OUT
LINGUAL
LINGULA
LINKAGE
LINKBOY
LINKMAN
LINNEAN
LINOCUT
LINSANG
LINSEED
LIONCEL
LIONESS
LIONISE
LIONISM
LIP-DEEP
LIPLESS
LIPPING
LIP-READ
LIQUATE
LIQUEFY
LIQUEUR
LISPING
LISPUND
LISSOME

LISTETH
LISTFUL
LITERAL
LITHATE
LITHELY
LITHITE
LITHIUM
LITHOID
LITOTES
LITTERY
LITTLIN
LITURGY
LIVABLE
LIVE-BOX
LIVE-OAK
LIVERED
LLANERO
LOADING
LOAFING
LOANING
LOATHED
LOATHER
LOATHLY
LOBELET
LOBELIA
LOBIPED
LOBSTER
LOBULAR
LOBULUS
LOBWORM
LOCALLY
LOCHIAL
LOCKAGE
LOCKFUL
LOCKIAN
LOCKIST
LOCK-JAW
LOCKMAN
LOCK-OUT
LOCKRAM
LOCRIAN
LOCULAR
LOCULUS
LOCUSTA
LODGING
LOFTILY
LOGANIA
LOG-BOOK
LOGGING
LOG-HEAD
LOGICAL
LOGLINE
LOG-REEL
LOG-ROLL
LOG-SHIP
LOGWOOD
LOLLARD
LOMBARD
LOMENTA
LONDONY
LONG-AGO
LONGBOW
LONGEST
LONGING
LONGISH
LONG-LEG

LONG-OFF
LONG-OIL
LONG-PIG
LOOBILY
LOOFFUL
LOOKING
LOOKOUT
LOOK-SEE
LOONING
LOOPING
LOOSELY
LOPPING
LORDING
LORDKIN
LORETTE
LORGNON
LORICAE
LORIMER
LORINER
LORRELL
LOSABLE
LOTTERY
LOTTING
LOUDISH
LOUNDER
LOUNGER
LOURING
LOUSILY
LOUTISH
LOVABLE
LOVE-DAY
LOVERED
LOVERLY
LOW-BELL
LOW-BORN
LOW-BRED
LOW-BROW
LOWDOWN
LOW-GEAR
LOWLAND
LOW-LIFE
LOWLILY
LOWNESS
LOW-PAID
LOXYGEN
LOYALLY
LOYALTY
LOZENGE
LOZENGY
LUBBARD
LUBFISH
LUCARNE
LUCENCY
LUCERNE
LUCIDLY
LUCIFER
LUCIGEN
LUCKILY
LUDDISM
LUDDITE
LUDSHIP
LUFFING
LUGEING
LUGGAGE
LUGGING
LUGSAIL

LUGWORM
LULLABY
LUMBAGO
LUMBANG
LUM-HEAD
LUMINAL
LUMPILY
LUMPING
LUMPISH
LUMPKIN
LUNATED
LUNATIC
LUNCHER
LUNETTE
LUNGING
LUNULAR
LUPULIN
LURCHER
LURDANE
LURIDLY
LURKING
LUSIADS
LUSKISH
LUSTFUL
LUSTICK
LUSTILY
LUSTRAL
LUSTRES
LUSTRUM
LUTEOUS
LUTHIER
LYCAENA
LYCEUMS
LYCHNIC
LYCHNIS
LYCOPOD
LYDDITE
LYING-IN
LYINGLY
LYMNAEA
LYMPHAD
LYNCEAN
LYNCHET
LYOMERI
LYOPHIL
LYRATED
LYRA-WAY
LYRICAL
LYTHRUM

M

MACABRE
MACADAM
MACAQUE
MACCHIE
MACE-ALE
MACHAIR
MACHETE
MACHINE
MACRAMÉ
MACRAMI
MACRURA
MACULAE
MAD-BRED
MADDEST
MADDING

MADEIRA
MADLING
MADNESS
MADONNA
MADOQUA
MADRASA
MADRONA
MADRONO
MADWORT
MAESTRO
MAFFICK
MAFFLED
MAFFLIN
MAGENTA
MAGGOTY
MAGICAL
MAGMATA
MAGNATE
MAGNETO
MAGNIFY
MAGSMAN
MAHATMA
MAHDISM
MAHDIST
MAH-JONG
MAHONIA
MAHOUND
MAHSEER
MAIDISH
MAIDISM
MAILBAG
MAILBOX
MAIL-CAR
MAIL-GIG
MAILING
MAILLOT
MAILMAN
MAIL-VAN
MAIMING
MAINOUR
MAINTOP
MAISTER
MAJESTY
MAJORAT
MALACIA
MALAISE
MALARIA
MALARKY
MALAYAN
MALEFIC
MALICHO
MALINES
MALISON
MALLARD
MALLEUS
MALMSEY
MALONIC
MALTASE
MALTESE
MALTING
MALTMAN
MALTOSE
MAMELON
MAMILLA
MAMMARY
MAMMATE

MAMMOCK
MAMMOTH
MANACLE
MANAGER
MANAKIN
MANATEE
MAN-BODY
MANCHET
MANCHOO
MAN-COOK
MANDALA
MANDATE
MAN-DAYS
MANDIOC
MANDIRA
MANDOLA
MANDORA
MANDREL
MANDRIL
MANGLER
MANGOES
MANGOLD
MANHOLE
MANHOOD
MAN-HOUR
MANIHOC
MANIHOT
MANIKIN
MANILLA
MANILLE
MANIPLE
MANITOU
MANJACK
MANKIND
MANLIKE
MAN-MADE
MANNING
MANNISH
MANNITE
MANNOSE
MANRENT
MANSARD
MANSION
MANTEAU
MANTEEL
MANTLET
MANTRAM
MANTRAP
MANTUAN
MANUMIT
MANURER
MAN-WEEK
MANXMAN
MAN-YEAR
MAPPERY
MAPPING
MAPPIST
MAPWISE
MARABOU
MARANTA
MARATHA
MARATHI
MARBLED
MARBLER
MARCATO
MÄRCHEN

MARCHER
MARCHES
MARCONI
MAREMMA
MARGENT
MARGOSA
MARIMBA
MARINER
MARITAL
MARKHOR
MARKING
MARKMAN
MARLINE
MARLING
MARLPIT
MARMOSE
MARPLOT
MARQUEE
MARQUIS
MARRELS
MARRIED
MARRIER
MARRING
MARROWY
MARSALA
MARSHAL
MARTEXT
MARTIAL
MARTIAN
MARTINI
MARTLET
MARXIAN
MARXISM
MARXIST
MARYBUD
MASCARA
MASCLED
MASCULY
MASHING
MASHLAM
MASHLIM
MASHLIN
MASHLUM
MASH-TUB
MASH-TUN
MASH-VAT
MAS-JOHN
MASONIC
MASONRY
MASORAH
MASQUER
MASSAGE
MASSEUR
MASSIVE
MASSORA
MASTABA
MASTERY
MAST-FED
MASTFUL
MASTICH
MASTIFF
MASTOID
MATADOR
MATCHER
MATELOT
MATINAL

MATRASS
MATRICE
MATROSS
MATTERY
MATTING
MATTINS
MATTOCK
MATTOID
MATWEED
MATZOTH
MAUDLIN
MAULGRE
MAUNDER
MAURIST
MAUTHER
MAWKISH
MAWSEED
MAWTHER
MAWWORM
MAXILLA
MAXIMAL
MAXIMUM
MAXWELL
MAY-DUKE
MAYFAIR
MAY-GAME
MAY-LADY
MAY-LILY
MAY-LORD
MAY-MORN
MAYORAL
MAYPOLE
MAY-TIME
MAYWEED
MAZDEAN
MAZEFUL
MAZURKA
MAZZARD
MEACOCK
MEADOWY
MEAL-ARK
MEAL-MAN
MEANDER
MEANING
MEASLED
MEASLES
MEASURE
MEAT-FLY
MEAT-MAN
MEAT-PIE
MEAT-TEA
MEAT-TUB
MECHLIN
MECONIC
MECONIN
MEDALET
MEDDLER
MEDIACY
MEDIANT
MEDIATE
MEDICAL
MEDULLA
MEDUSAE
MEDUSAN
MEERCAT
MEERKAT

MEETING
MEGAERA
MEGAFOG
MEGARON
MEGASSE
MEGATON
MEIOSIS
MEIOTIC
MEISSEN
MELANGE
MELANIC
MELANIN
MELILOT
MELISMA
MELLITE
MELLOWY
MELODIC
MELTING
MELTITH
MEMBRAL
MEMENTO
MENDING
MENFOLK
MENISCI
MEN-SIZE
MENSUAL
MENTHOL
MENTION
MERCERY
MERCHET
MERCIFY
MERCURY
MERFOLK
MERINOS
MERLING
MERMAID
MERRILY
MERSION
MESEEMS
MESELED
MESHING
MES-JOHN
MESONIC
MESOZOA
MESSAGE
MESSIAH
MESSIAS
MESSILY
MESS-TIN
MESTIZA
MESTIZO
METALLY
METAMER
METAYER
METAZOA
METCAST
METHANE
METHINK
METHODY
METISSE
METONIC
METONYM
METOPIC
METOPON
METRIST
METTLED

MEXICAN
MEZUZAH
MIASMAL
MIASMAS
MIASMIC
MICELLA
MICELLE
MICHING
MICROBE
MICROHM
MICTION
MIDDEST
MIDGARD
MID-HOUR
MIDLAND
MID-LENT
MIDMOST
MIDNOON
MIDRASH
MIDRIFF
MIDSHIP
MID-WEEK
MIDWEST
MIDWIFE
MID-YEAR
MIGHTST
MIGRANT
MIGRATE
MILDEWY
MILEAGE
MILFOIL
MILIARY
MILITIA
MILK-BAR
MILK-COW
MILKILY
MILKING
MILK-LEG
MILKMAN
MILK-RUN
MILKSOP
MILLDAM
MILL-EYE
MILLIME
MILLING
MILLION
MILREIS
MILTOWN
MILVINE
MIMESIS
MIMETIC
MIMICAL
MIMICRY
MIMMICK
MIM-MOU'D
MIMULUS
MINARET
MINCING
MINDFUL
MINERAL
MINERVA
MINETTE
MINEVER
MINGLER
MINIATE
MINI-BUS

MINI-CAB	MISSEND	MOLLIFY	MORGLAY	MUDPACK
MINI-CAR	MISSENT	MOLLUSC	MORICHE	MUDSCOW
MINIKIN	MISSILE	MOLLUSK	MORINGA	MUDWORT
MINIMAL	MISSING	MOLOSSI	MORISCO	MUEDDIN
MINIMUM	MISSION	MOMENTA	MORLING	MUEZZIN
MINIMUS	MISSISH	MONACID	MORMANS	MUFFLED
MINI-SUB	MISSIVE	MONADIC	MORMAOR	MUFFLER
MINIVER	MISSTEP	MONARCH	MORMOPS	MUGFULS
MINIVET	MISSUIT	MONAXON	MORNING	MUGGINS
MINNICK	MISTA'EN	MONERON	MOROCCO	MUGGISH
MINNOCK	MISTAKE	MONEYED	MORONIC	MUG-LAMB
MINORCA	MISTELL	MONEYER	MORPHEW	MUGWORT
MINSTER	MISTERM	MONGERY	MORPHIA	MUGWUMP
MINTAGE	MISTERY	MONGREL	MORPHIC	MUKHTAR
MINT-MAN	MISTFUL	MONIKER	MORRHUA	MULATTA
MINUEND	MISTICO	MONILIA	MORRICE	MULATTO
MINUTIA	MISTILY	MONITOR	MORRION	MULCTED
MIOCENE	MISTIME	MONKERY	MORSURE	MULLEIN
MIRABLE	MISTING	MONKISH	MORTAGE	MULLION
MIRACLE	MISTOLD	MONOCLE	MORTICE	MULLOCK
MIRADOR	MISTOOK	MONOCOT	MORTIFY	MULTURE
MIRBANE	MISTRAL	MONODIC	MORTISE	MUMBLER
MIRIFIC	MISTUNE	MONODON	MORULAR	MUMESON
MISBORN	MISWEEN	MONOFIL	MORWONG	MUMMERY
MISCALL	MISWEND	MONOMER	MOSAISM	MUMMIED
MISCAST	MISWENT	MONOSIS	MOSELLE	MUMMIFY
MISCOPY	MISWORD	MONSOON	MOSHAVA	MUMMING
MISDATE	MISYOKE	MONSTER	MOSS-HAG	MUMMOCK
MISDEAL	MITHRAS	MONTAGE	MOTH-EAT	MUMPISH
MISDEED	MITOSIS	MONTANE	MOTHERY	MUNCHER
MISDEEM	MITOTIC	MONTANT	MOTTLED	MUNDANE
MISDIET	MITZVAH	MONTERO	MOTTOED	MUNDIFY
MISDOER	MIXEDLY	MONTHLY	MOTTOES	MUNNION
MISDONE	MIXED-UP	MONTURE	MOUCHER	MUNTING
MISDRAW	MIXTION	MOOCHER	MOUFLON	MUNTJAC
MISEASE	MIXTURE	MOODILY	MOUILLÉ	MUNTJAK
MISERLY	MIZMAZE	MOOKTAR	MOULDER	MUONIUM
MISFALL	MJÖLNIR	MOON-BOW	MOULTEN	MURAENA
MISFARE	MOABITE	MOON-EYE	MOUNTED	MUREXES
MISFELL	MOANFUL	MOON-GOD	MOUNTER	MURGEON
MISFIRE	MOBBING	MOONISH	MOUNTIE	MURIATE
MISFORM	MOBBISH	MOONLIT	MOURNER	MURICES
MISGAVE	MOBSMAN	MOONSET	MOUSERY	MURIDAE
MISGIVE	MOBSTER	MOORAGE	MOUSING	MURKILY
MISGONE	MOCKADO	MOORERY	MOUTHED	MURKISH
MISHEAR	MOCKAGE	MOORESS	MOUTHER	MURLAIN
MISHMEE	MOCKERY	MOORHEN	MOVABLE	MURRAIN
MISHNAH	MOCKING	MOOR-ILL	MOVABLY	MURRINE
MISHNIC	MODALLY	MOORING	MOWBURN	MURTHER
MISJOIN	MODESTY	MOORISH	MOZARAB	MUSALES
MISKNOW	MODICUM	MOOR-LOG	MOZETTA	MUSCLED
MISLAID	MODIOLA	MOORMAN	MUCIGEN	MUSCOID
MISLEAD	MODISTE	MOOR-PAN	MUD-BATH	MUSCOSE
MISLIKE	MODULAR	MOOTING	MUD-BOAT	MUSCOVY
MISLIVE	MODULUS	MOOTMAN	MUD-CONE	MUSEFUL
MISLUCK	MOELLON	MOPPING	MUDDIED	MUSETTE
MISMADE	MOFETTE	MORAINE	MUDDILY	MUSHILY
MISMAKE	MOHEGAN	MORALLY	MUD-FISH	MUSICAL
MISMATE	MOHICAN	MORASSY	MUD-FLAP	MUSIMON
MISNAME	MOIDORE	MORCEAU	MUD-FLAT	MUSK-BAG
MISPLAY	MOINEAU	MORDANT	MUD-HOLE	MUSK-CAT
MISRATE	MOISTEN	MORDENT	MUD-HOOK	MUSK-COD
MISREAD	MOISTLY	MOREISH	MUDIRIA	MUSKILY
MISRULE	MOLASSE	MORELLO	MUDLARK	MUSK-POD
MISSAID	MOLE-RAT	MORENDO	MUD-LAVA	MUSK-RAT
MISSEEM	MOLIMEN	MORESCO	MUD-LUMP	MUSK-SAC

MUSTANG
MUSTARD
MUSTELA
MUTABLE
MUTABLY
MUTAGEN
MUTANDA
MUTTONY
MUZZILY
MUZZLER
MYALGIA
MYALGIC
MYALISM
MYCELIA
MYCETES
MYCOSIS
MYCOTIC
MYELOID
MYIASIS
MYLODON
MYNHEER
MYOGRAM
MYOLOGY
MYRBANE
MYRINGA
MYRRHIC
MYRRHOL
MYSTERY
MYSTIFY
MYTHISE
MYTHISM
MYTHIST
MYTILUS

N

NAARTJE
NABBING
NACELLE
NACRITE
NACROUS
NAEBODY
NAEVOID
NAGGING
NAGMAAL
NAHUATL
NAIADES
NAIL-BED
NAILERY
NAILING
NAIL-ROD
NAINSEL
NAÏVELY
NAÏVETÉ
NAÏVETY
NAKEDLY
NAMABLE
NAME-DAY
NAME-SON
NANDINE
NANKEEN
NAPHTHA
NAPLESS
NAPPING
NARGILE
NARGILY
NARRATE

NARTHEX
NARTJIE
NARWHAL
NASALIS
NASALLY
NASCENT
NASHGAB
NASTILY
NATHEMO
NATRIUM
NATTERY
NATTILY
NATURAL
NATURED
NAUGHTY
NAUPLII
NAUTICS
NAUTILI
NAVARCH
NAVARHO
NAVVIED
NAYWARD
NAYWORD
NAZIISM
NEAREST
NEBBISH
NEBULAE
NEBULAR
NECKING
NECKLET
NECKTIE
NECROSE
NECTARY
NEEDFUL
NEEDILY
NEEDLER
NE'ERDAY
NEGLECT
NÉGLIGÉ
NEGRESS
NEGRITO
NEGROES
NEGROID
NEITHER
NELUMBO
NEMESIA
NEMESIS
NEMORAL
NEOGAEA
NEOGENE
NEOLITH
NEOLOGY
NEONATE
NEOTENY
NEOZOIC
NEPHRIC
NEPOTIC
NEPTUNE
NERITIC
NERONIC
NERVATE
NERVINE
NERVOUS
NERVULE
NERVURE
NEST-EGG

NETBALL
NET-CORD
NET-FISH
NET-PLAY
NETSUKE
NETTING
NETWORK
NEURINE
NEUROMA
NEURONE
NEUSTON
NEUTRAL
NEUTRON
NEWBORN
NEWCOME
NEWGATE
NEW-LAID
NEW-MADE
NEW-MOWN
NEWNESS
NEWSBOY
NEWSMAN
NIBBLER
NIBLICK
NICAEAN
NICEISH
NICKADE
NICTATE
NIGELLA
NIGGARD
NIGGERY
NIGGLER
NIGHTED
NIGHTIE
NIGHTLY
NIGRIFY
NIKSNIE
NILOTIC
NIMIETY
NIMIOUS
NINEPIN
NINTHLY
NIOBEAN
NIOBIUM
NIPPING
NIRVANA
NITHING
NITRATE
NITRIAN
NITRIDE
NITRIFY
NITRILE
NITRITE
NITROUS
NIVEOUS
NOACHIC
NOBBILY
NOBBLER
NOCTUID
NOCTULE
NOCTURN
NOCUOUS
NODATED
NODDING
NODICAL
NODULAR

NODULED
NOETIAN
NO-FINES
NOGGING
NOISILY
NOISOME
NOMADIC
NOMARCH
NOMBRIL
NOMINAL
NOMINEE
NONAGED
NONAGON
NONETTE
NONETTO
NON-HERO
NONPLUS
NON-SKID
NON-SLIP
NON-STOP
NONSUCH
NONSUIT
NON-TERM
NON-USER
NOOLOGY
NOONDAY
NOONING
NOR'-EAST
NORFOLK
NORIMON
NORLAND
NORTHER
NORWARD
NOR'-WEST
NOSEBAG
NOSEGAY
NOSE-LED
NOSE-RAG
NOSTRIL
NOSTRUM
NOTABLE
NOTABLY
NOTAEUM
NOTANDA
NOTCHED
NOTCHEL
NOTEDLY
NOTELET
NOTHING
NOTITIA
NO-TRUMP
NOUMENA
NOURICE
NOURISH
NOURSLE
NOUSELL
NOVALIA
NOVELLA
NOVELLE
NOVELTY
NOWHERE
NOXIOUS
NOYANCE
NOYSOME
NUCLEAL
NUCLEAR

NUCLEIN
NUCLEON
NUCLEUS
NUCLIDE
NULLIFY
NULLING
NULLITY
NUMBING
NUMBLES
NUMERAL
NUMERIC
NUMMARY
NUNATAK
NUN-BUOY
NUNDINE
NUNHOOD
NUNNERY
NUNNISH
NUNSHIP
NUPTIAL
NURAGHE
NURAGHI
NURSERY
NURTURE
NUT-CASE
NUT-GALL
NUT-HOOK
NUT-MEAL
NUT-PINE
NUTTING
NUT-TREE
NYLGHAU
NYMPHAE
NYMPHAL
NYMPHET
NYMPHIC
NYMPHLY

O

OAK-FERN
OAK-GALL
OAKLING
OAK-LUMP
OAK-MAST
OAK-TREE
OAK-WOOD
OAR-FISH
OARLESS
OAR-LOCK
OARSMAN
OARWEED
OATCAKE
OATMEAL
OBCONIC
OBELION
OBELISE
OBELISK
OBESITY
OBITUAL
OBLIGEE
OBLIGOR
OBLIQUE
OBLOQUY
OBOLARY
OBOVATE
OBOVOID

OBSCENE
OBSCURE
OBSEQUY
OBSERVE
OBTRUDE
OBVERSE
OBVIATE
OBVIOUS
OCARINA
OCCIPUT
OCCLUDE
OCEANIC
OCEANID
OCELLAR
OCELLUS
OCELOID
OCHROID
OCHROUS
OCREATE
OCTADIC
OCTAGON
OCTAPLA
OCTAVAL
OCTETTE
OCTOBER
OCTOFID
OCTOPOD
OCTOPUS
OCTUPLE
OCULATE
OCULIST
ODALISK
ODALLER
ODDBALL
ODD-EVEN
ODD-LIKE
ODDMENT
ODDNESS
ODDSMAN
OD-FORCE
ODONATA
ODONTIC
ODORANT
ODORATE
ODOROUS
ODOURED
OD'S-BOBS
OD'S-LIFE
ODYLISM
ODYSSEY
ODZOOKS
OEDIPUS
OENOMEL
O'ERCOME
O'ERGANG
OERSTED
O'ERWORD
OESTRUM
OESTRUS
ŒUVRES
OFFBEAT
OFF-COME
OFFENCE
OFFENSE
OFFERED
OFFERER

OFFHAND
OFFICER
OFFLOAD
OFFPEAK
OFFSCUM
OFFSIDE
OFFTAKE
OFFWARD
OFTIMES
OGHAMIC
OGREISH
OGYGIAN
OIL-BATH
OIL-BELT
OIL-BIRD
OIL-CAKE
OIL-MILL
OIL-PALM
OIL-SEED
OIL-SILK
OILSKIN
OIL-WELL
OLDNESS
OLDSTER
OLD-TIME
OLEFINE
OLIGIST
OLITORY
OLIVARY
OLIVINE
OLYCOOK
OLYKOEK
OLYMPIA
OLYMPIC
OLYMPUS
OMENTAL
OMENTUM
OMICRON
OMINOUS
OMITTED
OMITTER
OMMATEA
OMNEITY
OMNIANA
OMNIBUS
OMNIETY
OMNIFIC
ONANISM
ONDATRA
ONE-EYED
ONEFOLD
ONEIRIC
ONEROUS
ONESELF
ONESTEP
ONGOING
ONISCUS
ONSHORE
ONSTEAD
ONWARDS
ONYCHIA
ONYMOUS
OODLINS
OOFTISH
OOGONIA
OOLAKAN

OOLITIC
OOMIACK
OOPHYTE
OOSPORE
OPACITY
OPACOUS
OPALINE
OPEN-AIR
OPEN-END
OPENING
OPERAND
OPERANT
OPERATE
OPEROSE
OPHIDIA
OPHITIC
OPHIURA
OPIATED
OPINION
OPORICE
OPOSSUM
OPPIDAN
OPPOSER
OPPRESS
OPSONIC
OPSONIN
OPTICAL
OPTIMAL
OPTIMUM
OPULENT
OPUNTIA
OPUSCLE
ORARIAN
ORARION
ORARIUM
ORATION
ORATORY
ORATRIX
ORBITAL
ORCHARD
ORCINOL
ORDERER
ORDERLY
ORDINAL
ORDINAR
ORDINEE
OREADES
ORECTIC
OREGANO
OREWEED
ORGANIC
ORGANON
ORGANUM
ORGANZA
ORGIAST
ORIENCY
ORIFICE
ORIGAMI
ORIGANE
ORLEANS
OROLOGY
OROPESA
OROTUND
ORPHEAN
ORPHEUS
ORPHISM

ORPHREY
ORTHIAN
ORTHROS
ORTOLAN
ORVIETO
OSCHEAL
OSCINES
OSCULAR
OSCULUM
OSIERED
OSMANLI
OSMIATE
OSMIOUS
OSMOSIS
OSMOTIC
OSMUNDA
OSSELET
OSSEOUS
OSSETER
OSSICLE
OSSIFIC
OSSUARY
OSTEOID
OSTIARY
OSTIATE
OSTIOLE
OSTRACA
OSTRAKA
OSTRICH
OTALGIA
OTARIES
OTARINE
OTOCYST
OTOLITH
OTOLOGY
OTTOMAN
OUABAIN
OULAKAN
OURSELF
OUSTITI
OUTBACK
OUTBRAG
OUTBRED
OUTBURN
OUTCAST
OUTCOME
OUTCROP
OUTDARE
OUTDATE
OUTDOOR
OUTDURE
OUTEDGE
OUTFACE
OUTFALL
OUTFLOW
OUTFOOT
OUTGATE
OUTGIVE
OUTGOER
OUTGONE
OUTGROW
OUTGUSH
OUTHAUL
OUTHIRE
OUTJEST
OUTLAND

OUTLASH
OUTLAST
OUTLEAP
OUTLIER
OUTLINE
OUTLIVE
OUTLOOK
OUTMODE
OUTMOST
OUTMOVE
OUTNAME
OUTNESS
OUT-OVER
OUT-OWRE
OUTPACE
OUTPART
OUTPEEP
OUTPEER
OUTPLAY
OUTPORT
OUTPOST
OUTPOUR
OUTPRAY
OUTRAGE
OUTRANK
OUTRIDE
OUTROAR
OUTROOP
OUTROOT
OUTROPE
OUTRUSH
OUTSAIL
OUTSELL
OUTSHOT
OUTSIDE
OUTSIZE
OUTSOAR
OUTSOLE
OUTSPAN
OUTSTAY
OUTSTEP
OUTTAKE
OUTTALK
OUT-TRAY
OUTVOTE
OUTWALK
OUTWALL
OUTWARD
OUTWEAR
OUTWEED
OUTWEEP
OUTWELL
OUTWENT
OUTWICK
OUTWIND
OUTWING
OUTWITH
OUTWORK
OUTWORN
OVARIAN
OVATION
OVEN-TIT
OVERACT
OVER-AGE
OVERALL
OVERARM

OVERAWE	PACTION	PANEITY	PARLOUR	PATULIN
OVERBID	PADDING	PANFULS	PARLOUS	PAUCITY
OVERBUY	PADDLER	PANGAMY	PARODIC	PAUGHTY
OVERDUE	PADDOCK	PANGENE	PARONYM	PAULIAN
OVERDYE	PADELLA	PANGING	PAROTID	PAULINE
OVEREAT	PADLOCK	PANICKY	PAROTIS	PAUNCHY
OVEREYE	PADRONE	PANICLE	PARPANE	PAUSING
OVERFAR	PADRONI	PANICUM	PARPEND	PAVIOUR
OVERFED	PAD-TREE	PANJABI	PARPENT	PAWKILY
OVERFLY	PADYISM	PANNAGE	PARQUET	PAXIUBA
OVERGET	PAENULA	PANNICK	PARRIED	PAYABLE
OVERJOY	PAEONIC	PANNIER	PARROTY	PAY-BILL
OVERLAP	PAGEANT	PANNING	PARSING	PAY-DESK
OVERLAY	PAGINAL	PANNOSE	PARSISM	PAY-DIRT
OVERLIE	PAHLAVI	PANOCHA	PARSLEY	PAY-LIST
OVERMAN	PAILFUL	PANOPLY	PARSNEP	PAY-LOAD
OVERNET	PAILLON	PANSIED	PARSNIP	PAYMENT
OVERPAY	PAINFUL	PAN-SLAV	PARTAKE	PAY-ROLL
OVERPLY	PAINTED	PANTHER	PARTIAL	PAYSAGE
OVERRAN	PAINTER	PANTIES	PARTING	P-CELTIC
OVERRED	PAIRIAL	PANTILE	PARTITA	PEACHER
OVERRUN	PAIRING	PANTINE	PARTITE	PEA-COAT
OVERSEA	PAIR-OAR	PANTING	PARTLET	PEACOCK
OVERSEE	PAISLEY	PANTLER	PARTNER	PEA-CRAB
OVERSET	PAJAMAS	PANTOUM	PARTOOK	PEA-FOWL
OVERSEW	PAKFONG	PAPABLE	PARVENU	PEA-IRON
OVERSOW	PAKTONG	PAPALLY	PARVISE	PEAKING
OVERTAX	PALADIN	PAPAVER	PASCHAL	PEARLED
OVERTLY	PALAMAE	PAP-BOAT	PASQUIL	PEARLER
OVERTOP	PALATAL	PAPHIAN	PASQUIN	PEARLIN
OVICIDE	PALAVER	PAPILIO	PASSADE	PEARTLY
OVIDIAN	PALETOT	PAPILLA	PASSADO	PEASANT
OVIDUCT	PALETTE	PAP-MEAT	PASSAGE	PEASCOD
OVIFORM	PALFREY	PAPOOSE	PASSANT	PEA-SOUP
OVOIDAL	PALILIA	PAPPOSE	PASSING	PEATARY
OVULATE	PALLIAL	PAPPOUS	PASSION	PEAT-BED
OWENIAN	PALLING	PAPRIKA	PASSIVE	PEAT-BOG
OWENISM	PALLIUM	PAPULAE	PASSKEY	PEATERY
OWENIST	PALLONE	PAPULAR	PASSMAN	PEAT-HAG
OWENITE	PALMARY	PAPULES	PASSOUT	PEATMAN
OWL-EYED	PALMATE	PAPYRUS	PASTERN	PEBBLED
OWL-MOTH	PALM-CAT	PARABLE	PASTIME	PEBRINE
OXALATE	PALMFUL	PARACME	PASTURE	PECCANT
OX-FENCE	PALMIET	PARADOS	PATAGIA	PECCARY
OXIDASE	PALMIST	PARADOX	PATAMAR	PECKING
OXIDATE	PALM-OIL	PARAFLE	PATARIN	PECKISH
OXIDISE	PALMYRA	PARAGON	PATBALL	PECTISE
OXONIAN	PALPATE	PARAPET	PATCHED	PECTOSE
OXONIUM	PALSIED	PARA-RED	PATCHER	PEDDLER
OXY-ACID	PALUDAL	PARASOL	PATCH-UP	PEDESIS
OXY-SALT	PALUDIC	PARAZOA	PATELLA	PEDETIC
OXYTONE	PAMPEAN	PARBOIL	PATENCY	PEDICAB
OZONISE	PAMPERO	PARCHED	PATERAE	PEDICEL
	PANACEA	PARDINE	PATHWAY	PEDICLE
P	PANACHE	PARDNER	PATIBLE	PEDLARY
	PANAGIA	PAREIRA	PATIENT	PEDRAIL
PABULAR	PANCAKE	PARELLA	PATINED	PEDRERO
PABULUM	PANCHEN	PARELLE	PATNESS	PEEKABO
PACABLE	PANDEAN	PARERGA	PATONCE	PEELING
PACE-EGG	PANDECT	PARESIS	PATRIAL	PEELITE
PACHISI	PANDION	PARETIC	PATRICK	PEEP-TOE
PACIFIC	PANDOOR	PARFAIT	PATRICO	PEERAGE
PACKAGE	PANDORA	PARGANA	PATRIOT	PEERESS
PACK-ICE	PANDORE	PARITOR	PATROON	PEEVISH
PACKING	PANDOUR	PARKISH	PATTERN	PEGASUS
PACKMAN	PANDURA	PARKWAY	PATTING	PEGGING
PACKWAY				

PEHLEVI	PEREION	PHARYNX	PIG-FISH	PINNULE
PEISHWA	PERFECT	PHASMID	PIGGERY	PINOCLE
PELAGIC	PERFIDY	PHEAZAR	PIGGIES	PINTADO
PELICAN	PERFORM	PHELLEM	PIGGING	PINTAIL
PELISSE	PERFUME	PHENATE	PIGGISH	PINT-POT
PELITIC	PERFUMY	PHILTER	PIG-HERD	PIN-TUCK
PELLACH	PERFUSE	PHILTRE	PIGHTLE	PINXTER
PELLACK	PERGOLA	PHLEGMY	PIG-IRON	PIONEER
PELLOCK	PERHAPS	PHOBISM	PIG-JUMP	PIONIES
PELOPID	PERIAPT	PHOBIST	PIG-LEAD	PIONING
PELORIA	PERIDOT	PHOEBUS	PIG-LILY	PIOUSLY
PELORIC	PERIGEE	PHOENIX	PIGLING	PIPEFUL
PELORUS	PERIOST	PHONATE	PIGMEAN	PIPE-KEY
PELTAST	PERIQUE	PHONEME	PIGMENT	PIPERIC
PELTATE	PERIWIG	PHONICS	PIGSKIN	PIPETTE
PELTING	PERJINK	PHOTICS	PIGSNEY	PIPLESS
PEMICAN	PERJURE	PHOTISM	PIGSNIE	PIPPING
PENALLY	PERJURY	PHRASAL	PIGTAIL	PIQUANT
PENALTY	PERKILY	PHRASER	PIGWASH	PIRAGUA
PENANCE	PERLITE	PHRATRY	PIGWEED	PIRANHA
PENATES	PERMIAN	PHRENIC	PIKELET	PIRATIC
PEN-CASE	PERMUTE	PHYSICS	PIKEMAN	PISCARY
PENDANT	PERPEND	PIAFFER	PILCHER	PISCINA
PENDENT	PERPENT	PIANINO	PILCORN	PISCINE
PENDING	PERPLEX	PIANISM	PILCROW	PISMIRE
PENEIAN	PERRIER	PIANIST	PILEATE	PISS-POT
PENFOLD	PERSEID	PIANOLA	PILFERY	PISTOLE
PENGUIN	PERSEUS	PIARIST	PILGRIM	PITAPAT
PEN-NAME	PERSIAN	PIASTRE	PILI-NUT	PITARAH
PENNANT	PERSICO	PIBROCH	PILLAGE	PIT-BROW
PENNATE	PERSISM	PICADOR	PILL-BOX	PITCHED
PENNIED	PERSIST	PICAMAR	PILL-BUG	PITCHER
PENNIES	PERSONA	PICCOLO	PILLION	PIT-COAL
PENNILL	PERTAIN	PICEOUS	PILLORY	PITEOUS
PENNINE	PERTURB	PICKAXE	PILLOWY	PITFALL
PENNING	PERTUSE	PICKEER	PILSNER	PITHEAD
PENSILE	PERUSAL	PICKERY	PILULAR	PITHFUL
PENSION	PERUSER	PICKING	PIMENTO	PITH-HAT
PENSIVE	PERVADE	PICKLED	PI-MESON	PITHILY
PENTACT	PERVERT	PICKLER	PIMPING	PITIFUL
PENTANE	PESANTE	PICKMAW	PIMPLED	PIT-MIRK
PENTENE	PESHITO	PICOTEE	PINBALL	PIT-PONY
PENTHIA	PESKILY	PICQUET	PINCASE	PIT-PROP
PENTICE	PESSARY	PICRATE	PINCHED	PITTING
PENTISE	PESTFUL	PICRITE	PINCHER	PITTISM
PENTODE	PETASUS	PICTISH	PINDARI	PITTITE
PENTOSE	PETIOLE	PICTURE	PIN-DUST	PITUITA
PEONAGE	PETRARY	PIDDLER	PINETUM	PITUITE
PEONISM	PETRIFY	PIDDOCK	PIN-EYED	PITYING
PEPPERY	PETRINE	PIDGEON	PIN-FIRE	PIVOTAL
PEPTICS	PETROUS	PIEBALD	PINFISH	PIVOTED
PEPTIDE	PETTILY	PIEDISH	PINFOLD	PIVOTER
PEPTISE	PETTING	PIE-EYED	PINGLER	PIXYLED
PEPTONE	PETTISH	PIERAGE	PINGUID	P-KELTIC
PERAEON	PETUNIA	PIERCED	PINGUIN	PLACARD
PERCALE	PEW-RENT	PIERCER	PINHEAD	PLACATE
PERCASE	PFENNIG	PIERIAN	PINHOLE	PLACEBO
PERCEPT	PHACOID	PIERROT	PINK-EYE	PLACITA
PERCHED	PHAEISM	PIE-SHOP	PINKING	PLACKET
PERCHER	PHAETON	PIETISM	PINKISH	PLACOID
PERCINE	PHALANX	PIETIST	PINNACE	PLAFOND
PERCOCT	PHALLIC	PIFFERO	PINNATE	PLAGIUM
PERCOID	PHALLIN	PIFFLER	PINNING	PLAIDED
PERCUSS	PHALLUS	PIGBOAT	PINNOCK	PLAINLY
PERDURE	PHANTOM	PIG-DEER	PINNOED	PLAITED
PEREGAL	PHARAOH	PIG-EYED	PINNULA	PLAITER

PLANISH	PLOSIVE	POLLENT	PORTMAN	PRANCER
PLANNED	PLOTFUL	POLLMAN	PORTOUS	PRANCKE
PLANNER	PLOTTED	POLLOCK	PORTRAY	PRANKLE
PLANTAR	PLOTTER	POLL-TAX	POSAUNE	PRATING
PLANTER	PLOTTIE	POLLUTE	POSEUSE	PRATTLE
PLANULA	PLOUTER	POLOIST	POSITED	PRAVITY
PLANURY	PLOVERY	POLONIA	POSITON	PRAWLIN
PLANXTY	PLOWTER	POLONIE	POSSESS	PRAYING
PLASHET	PLUCKED	POLYACT	POSTAGE	PREACHY
PLASMIC	PLUCKER	POLYGON	POST-BAG	PREBEND
PLASMIN	PLUGGED	POLYMER	POST-BOX	PRECAST
PLASTER	PLUGGER	POLYNIA	POST-DAY	PRECEDE
PLASTIC	PLUG-HAT	POLYNYA	POSTEEN	PRECEPT
PLASTID	PLUMAGE	POLYPES	POSTERN	PRECISE
PLATANE	PLUMATE	POLYPOD	POSTFIX	PREDATE
PLATEAU	PLUMBER	POLYPUS	POSTING	PREDIAL
PLATINA	PLUMBIC	POLYZOA	POSTMAN	PREDICT
PLATING	PLUMCOT	POMATUM	POSTURE	PREDOOM
PLATOON	PLUMERY	POMEROY	POST-WAR	PRE-EMPT
PLATTED	PLUMIST	POMFRET	POTABLE	PREFACE
PLATTER	PLUMMET	POMMELE	POTAMIC	PREFECT
PLAUDIT	PLUMOSE	POMPANO	POTASSA	PREFORM
PLAY-ACT	PLUMOUS	POMPELO	POT-BANK	PREHEND
PLAY-BOX	PLUMPEN	POMPIER	POTCHER	PREJINK
PLAYBOY	PLUMPER	POMPION	POTENCE	PRELACY
PLAY-DAY	PLUMPIE	POMPOON	POTENCE	PRELATE
PLAYFUL	PLUMPLY	POMPOUS	POTENCY	PRELATY
PLAYLET	PLUMULA	PONCEAU	POTFULS	PRELECT
PLAY-OFF	PLUMULE	PONCHOS	POT-HEAD	PRELIMS
PLAYPEN	PLUNDER	PONDAGE	POTHEEN	PRELUDE
PLAY-WAY	PLUNGER	PONIARD	POT-HERB	PREMIER
PLEADED	PLUNKER	PONTAGE	POTHERY	PREMISE
PLEADER	PLUSAGE	PONTIFF	POTHOLE	PREMISS
PLEASED	PLUTEAL	PONTIFY	POTHOOK	PREMIUM
PLEASER	PLUTEUS	PONTILE	POTICHE	PREMOVE
PLEBIFY	PLUVIAL	PONTOON	POT-LUCK	PRENZIE
PLECTRA	PLYWOOD	POOH-BAH	POTOROO	PREORAL
PLECTRE	POACHER	POON-OIL	POT-SHOP	PREPAID
PLEDGEE	POCHARD	POOR-BOX	POT-SHOT	PREPARE
PLEDGER	POCKARD	POORISH	POT-SICK	PREPUCE
PLEDGET	POCKPIT	POOR-LAW	POTTAGE	PRERUPT
PLEDGOR	PODAGRA	POPADUM	POTTERY	PRESAGE
PLEIADE	PODALIC	POPCORN	POTTING	PRESENT
PLEIADS	PODDING	POPEDOM	POUCHED	PRESIDE
PLENARY	PODESTA	POPERIN	POULARD	PRESSER
PLENIPO	POE-BIRD	POP-EYED	POULTER	PRESUME
PLENISH	POETESS	POPPIED	POULTRY	PRETEND
PLENIST	POETISE	POPPING	POUNCED	PRETEXT
PLEOPOD	PO-FACED	POP-SHOP	POUNCET	PRETZEL
PLEROMA	POINDER	POP-SONG	POUNDAL	PREVAIL
PLEROME	POINTED	POPULAR	POUNDER	PREVENE
PLESSOR	POINTEL	POPWEED	POURING	PREVENT
PLEURAE	POINTER	PORCINE	POUTHER	PREVIEW
PLEURAL	POITREL	PORIFER	POUTING	PREVISE
PLEURON	POKEFUL	PORK-PIE	POVERTY	PREYFUL
PLEXURE	POLACCA	POROSIS	POWDERY	PRIAPIC
PLIABLE	POLACRE	PORRECT	POWERED	PRIAPUS
PLIABLY	POLARIS	PORRIGO	POY-BIRD	PRIBBLE
PLIANCY	POLE-AXE	PORTAGE	PRABBLE	PRICKER
PLICATE	POLECAT	PORTATE	PRACTIC	PRICKET
PLISKIE	POLEMIC	PORTEND	PRAESES	PRICKLE
PLODDED	POLENTA	PORTENT	PRAETOR	PRICKLY
PLODDER	POLITIC	PORTESS	PRAIRIE	PRIDIAN
PLONKER	POLLACK	PORTHOS	PRAISER	PRIGGER
PLOPPED	POLLARD	PORTICO	PRÂKRIT	PRIMACY
PLOSION	POLL-AXE	PORTION	PRALINE	PRIMAGE

PRIMARY
PRIMATE
PRIMELY
PRIMERO
PRIMINE
PRIMING
PRIMMED
PRIMSIE
PRIMULA
PRINCOX
PRINTER
PRISAGE
PRITHEE
PRIVACY
PRIVADO
PRIVATE
PRIVILY
PRIVITY
PROBALL
PROBANG
PROBATE
PROBITY
PROBLEM
PROCEED
PROCESS
PROCTAL
PROCTOR
PROCURE
PROCYON
PRODDED
PRODIGY
PRODUCE
PRODUCT
PROFACE
PROFANE
PROFESS
PROFFER
PROFILE
PROFUSE
PROGENY
PROGRAM
PROJECT
PROLATE
PROLONG
PROMISE
PROMMER
PROMOTE
PRONAOI
PRONAOS
PRONATE
PRONELY
PRONEUR
PRONGED
PRONOTA
PRONOUN
PROOTIC
PROPAGE
PROPALE
PROPANE
PROPEND
PROPENE
PROPHET
PROPINE
PROP-JET
PROPONE
PROPOSE

PROPPED
PROPYLA
PROSAIC
PROSILY
PROSING
PROSODY
PROSPER
PROTEAN
PROTECT
PROTÉGÉ
PROTEID
PROTEIN
PROTEND
PROTEST
PROTEUS
PROTHYL
PROTIST
PROTIUM
PROTYLE
PROUDLY
PROVAND
PROVANT
PROVEND
PROVERB
PROVIDE
PROVINE
PROVISO
PROVOKE
PROVOST
PROWESS
PROWEST
PROWLER
PROXIMO
PRUDENT
PRUDERY
PRUDISH
PRUNING
PRUNTED
PRURIGO
PRUSSIC
PRYTHEE
PSALTER
PSYCHIC
PTARMIC
PTERION
PTEROIC
PTERYLA
PTYALIN
PUBERAL
PUBERTY
PUBISES
PUBLISH
PUCCOON
PUCELLE
PUCKERY
PUCKISH
PUDDING
PUDDLER
PUDDOCK
PUDENCY
PUDENDA
PUERILE
PUFF-BOX
PUFFERY
PUFFILY
PUFFING

PUGGERY
PUGGING
PUGGISH
PUGGREE
PUG-MILL
PUG-MOTH
PUG-NOSE
PUGWASH
PULDRON
PULLMAN
PULPIFY
PULPOUS
PULSATE
PULTOON
PULTURE
PULVINI
PUMP-GUN
PUMPION
PUMPKIN
PUNCHER
PUNCH-UP
PUNCTUM
PUNGENT
PUNIEST
PUNJABI
PUNNING
PUNSTER
PUNT-GUN
PUPPING
PUPUNHA
PURANIC
PURBECK
PURFLED
PURGING
PURITAN
PURLIEU
PURLINE
PURLING
PURLOIN
PURPORT
PURPOSE
PURPURA
PURPURE
PURRING
PURSUAL
PURSUER
PURSUIT
PURVIEW
PUSHFUL
PUSHING
PUSH-OFF
PUSH-PIN
PUSHTOO
PUSTULE
PUTAMEN
PUTCHUK
PUTLOCK
PUTREFY
PUTTIED
PUTTIER
PUTTING
PUTTOCK
PUZZLER
PYAEMIA
PYAEMIC
PYCNITE

PYEBALD
PYGMEAN
PYGMOID
PYJAMA'D
PYJAMAS
PYLORIC
PYLORUS
PYRALID
PYRALIS
PYRAMID
PYRETIC
PYREXIA
PYRITES
PYRITIC
PYROPUS
PYROSIS
PYRRHIC
PYTHIAN
PYTHIUM
PYXIDIA

Q

Q-CELTIC
Q-KELTIC
QUACKLE
QUADRAT
QUADRIC
QUAFFER
QUAHAUG
QUAKING
QUALIFY
QUALITY
QUAMASH
QUANNET
QUANTIC
QUANTUM
QUARREL
QUARTAN
QUARTER
QUARTET
QUARTIC
QUARTZY
QUASHEE
QUASSIA
QUAVERY
QUAYAGE
QUEACHY
QUECHUA
QUEECHY
QUEENLY
QUEERLY
QUELLER
QUERCUS
QUERIED
QUERIST
QUESTER
QUESTOR
QUETSCH
QUETZAL
QUEUING
QUEYNIE
QUIBBLE
QUIBLIN
QUICHUA
QUICKEN
QUICKIE

QUICKLY
QUIDDIT
QUIDDLE
QUIESCE
QUIETEN
QUIETER
QUIETLY
QUIETUS
QUILLED
QUILLET
QUILLON
QUILTED
QUILTER
QUINARY
QUINATE
QUINCHE
QUININE
QUINNAT
QUINONE
QUINTAL
QUINTAN
QUINTET
QUINTIC
QUITING
QUITTAL
QUITTED
QUITTER
QUITTOR
QUIZZED
QUIZZER
QUIZZES
QUODLIN
QUOITER
QUONDAM

R

RABANNA
RABATTE
RABBITY
RABBLER
RABBONI
RABIDLY
RACCOON
RACEMED
RACEMIC
RACEWAY
RACHIAL
RACKETT
RACKETY
RACKING
RACLOIR
RACQUET
RADDLED
RADIALE
RADIANT
RADIATA
RADIATE
RADICAL
RADICEL
RADICES
RADICLE
RADULAR
RAETIAN
RAFFISH
RAFFLER
RAFTMAN

RAG-BABY	RAREBIT	REBUILD	REFINER	REMOVAL
RAGBOLT	RASORES	REBUKER	REFLATE	REMOVED
RAG-BOOK	RASPING	REBUSES	REFLECT	REMOVER
RAG-BUSH	RASTRUM	RECEIPT	REFOUND	RENAGUE
RAG-DOLL	RATABLE	RECEIVE	REFRACT	RENAYED
RAG-DUST	RATABLY	RECENCY	REFRAIN	RENEGER
RAGEFUL	RATAFIA	RECENSE	REFRAME	RENEGUE
RAG-FAIR	RAT-A-TAT	RECHATE	REFRESH	RENEWAL
RAGGEDY	RATCHET	RECHEAT	REFUGEE	RENEWER
RAGGERY	RAT-FLEA	RECITAL	REFUSAL	RENT-DAY
RAGGING	RATHEST	RECITER	REFUSER	RENTIER
RAGMENT	RAT-HOLE	RECLAIM	REFUTAL	RENYING
RAGTIME	RATITAE	RÉCLAME	REFUTER	REPAINT
RAGULED	RAT-TAIL	RECLINE	REGALIA	REPAPER
RAGWEED	RATTEEN	RECLOSE	REGALLY	REPINER
RAGWORK	RATTERY	RECLUSE	REGATTA	REPIQUE
RAGWORM	RATTING	RECOUNT	REGENCE	REPLACE
RAGWORT	RATTISH	RECOVER	REGENCY	REPLANT
RAILBUS	RATTLER	RECROSS	REGIMEN	REPLETE
RAIL-CAR	RATTLIN	RECRUIT	REGINAL	REPLEVY
RAILING	RAT-TRAP	RECTIFY	REGMATA	REPLICA
RAILMAN	RAUCOUS	RECTION	REGNANT	REPLIED
RAILWAY	RAVAGER	RECTORY	REGORGE	REPLIER
RAIMENT	RAVELIN	RECTRIX	REGRANT	REPOSAL
RAINBOW	RAVINED	RECURVE	REGRATE	REPOSED
RAISING	RAVIOLI	RECYCLE	REGREDE	REPOSIT
RAITING	RAWBONE	RED-BOOK	REGREET	REPRESS
RAJPOOT	RAWHEAD	REDCOAT	REGRESS	REPRIME
RAKE-OFF	RAWHIDE	RED-COWL	REGRIND	REPRINT
RAKSHAS	RAWNESS	RED-DEER	REGROUP	REPRISE
RALLIED	RAYLESS	REDDEST	REGULAE	REPROOF
RALLIER	REACHED	REDDING	REGULAR	REPROVE
RALLINE	REACHER	REDDISH	REGULUS	REPTILE
RAMADAN	REACTOR	RED-HAND	REHOUSE	REPULSE
RAMAKIN	READIER	RED-HEAD	REIN-ARM	REPUTED
RAMBLER	READILY	RED-HEAT	REINTER	REQUEST
RAMEKIN	READING	REDNESS	REISSUE	REQUIEM
RAMENTA	READMIT	REDOUBT	REJOICE	REQUIRE
RAMEOUS	READOPT	REDOUND	REJOURN	REQUITE
RAMIIES	READ-OUT	REDPOLL	RELAPSE	REREDOS
RAMMING	REAGENT	REDRAFT	RELATED	RESCALE
RAMMISH	REALGAR	REDRESS	RELATER	RESCIND
RAMPAGE	REALIGN	REDRIVE	RELATOR	RESCUED
RAMPANT	REALISE	RED-ROOT	RELAYED	RESCUER
RAMPART	REALISM	REDSEAR	RELEASE	RESEIZE
RAMPICK	REALIST	RED-SEED	RELIANT	RESERVE
RAMPIKE	REALITY	REDSKIN	RELIEVE	RESHAPE
RAMPION	REALLOT	RED-TAPE	RELIEVO	RESIANT
RAMPIRE	RE-ALTER	REDUCED	RELIGHT	RESIDUA
RAMSTAM	REALTIE	REDUCER	RELIQUE	RESIDUÆ
RAMULAR	REALTOR	REDWOOD	RELIVER	RESINER
RAMULUS	RE-AMEND	REED-BED	RELLISH	RESOLVE
RANCHER	REAMING	RE-EDIFY	RELYING	RESOUND
RANCOUR	RE-ANNEX	REEDING	REMAINS	RESPEAK
RANIDAE	REAPPLY	REEFING	REMANET	RESPECT
RANKINE	REAR-DOS	REEKING	REMANIÉ	RESPELL
RANSACK	REARISE	RE-ELECT	REMARRY	RESPIRE
RAPE-OIL	REAUMUR	REELING	REMBLAI	RESPITE
RAPHIDE	REAWAKE	RE-ENACT	REMERCY	RESPOND
RAPIDLY	REBATER	RE-ENDOW	REMERGE	RESTART
RAPLOCH	REBECCA	RE-ENTER	REMIGES	RESTATE
RAPPING	REBIRTH	RE-ENTRY	REMNANT	RESTDAY
RAPPIST	REBLOOM	RE-ERECT	REMODEL	RESTFUL
RAPPITE	REBOANT	RE-EXIST	REMORSE	RESTING
RAPPORT	REBOUND	REFEREE	REMOULD	RESTIVE
RAPTURE	REBRACE	REFINED	REMOUNT	RESTOCK

RESTORE	RHIZOID	RIPPLER	ROODMAS	ROYALET
RESURGE	RHIZOME	RIPPLET	ROOFING	ROYALLY
RETABLE	RHODIAN	RIPTIDE	ROOINEK	ROYALTY
RETAKEN	RHODIUM	RISIBLE	ROOKERY	ROYNISH
RETAKER	RHODORA	RISKFUL	ROOKISH	ROYSTER
RETHINK	RHODOUS	RISKILY	ROOMFUL	ROZELLE
RETIARY	RHOMBIC	RISOTTO	ROOMILY	RUB-A-DUB
RETICLE	RHOMBOI	RISSIAN	ROOSTER	RUBBERY
RETINAE	RHOMBOS	RISSOLE	ROOTAGE	RUBBING
RETINAL	RHOMBUS	RIVALRY	ROOT-CAP	RUBBISH
RETINOL	RHUBARB	RIVERED	ROOTING	RUBDOWN
RETINUE	RHYMIST	RIVERET	ROOTLET	RUBELLA
RETIRAL	RHYTINA	RIVETED	ROPABLE	RUBEOLA
RETIRED	RIBBAND	RIVETER	ROPER-IN	RUBICON
RETOUCH	RIBBING	RIVIERA	ROPEWAY	RUBIOUS
RETRACE	RIBBONE	RIVIÈRE	RORQUAL	RUBYING
RETRACT	RIBBONY	RIVULET	ROSAKER	RUBY-RED
RETRATE	RIBIBLE	RIZZART	ROSALIA	RUCHING
RETREAD	RIBLESS	ROAD-BED	ROSCIAN	RUCTION
RETREAT	RIBLIKE	ROAD-END	ROSCIUS	RUDDIED
RETRIAL	RIBSTON	ROAD-HOG	ROSEATE	RUDDIER
RETRIED	RIBWORK	ROADING	ROSE-BAY	RUDDILY
RETSINA	RIBWORT	ROADMAN	ROSE-BUD	RUDDOCK
RETTERY	RICHTER	ROADWAY	ROSE-BUG	RUDERAL
RETTING	RICINUS	ROARING	ROSE-CUT	RUDESBY
REUNION	RICKETS	ROASTER	ROSE-HIP	RUELLIA
REUNITE	RICKETY	ROBBERY	ROSELLA	RUFFIAN
REUTTER	RICKSHA	ROBBING	ROSELLE	RUFFLED
REVALUE	RIDABLE	ROBINIA	ROSEOLA	RUFFLER
REVELRY	RIDDING	ROCK-COD	ROSE-RED	RUGGING
REVENGE	RIDDLER	ROCKERY	ROSETTA	RUG-GOWN
REVENUE	RIDERED	ROCKIER	ROSETTE	RUINATE
REVERER	RIDGING	ROCKILY	ROSETTY	RUINING
REVERIE	RIDOTTO	ROCKING	ROSINED	RUINOUS
REVERSE	RIFFLER	ROCKLAY	ROSOLIO	RULABLE
REVERSI	RIFLING	ROCK-OIL	ROSTRAL	RULLION
REVERSO	RIGGALD	ROCK-TAR	ROSTRUM	RULLOCK
REVILER	RIGGING	ROCQUET	ROTATOR	RUMBLER
REVISAL	RIGGISH	RODLESS	ROTCHIE	RUMMAGE
REVISER	RIGHTEN	RODLIKE	ROTIFER	RUMMILY
REVISIT	RIGHTER	RODSMAN	ROTTING	RUMMISH
REVISOR	RIGHTLY	RODSTER	ROTUNDA	RUMP-END
REVIVAL	RIGHT-OH	ROEBUCK	ROUGHEN	RUMP-FED
REVIVER	RIGIDLY	ROE-DEER	ROUGHER	RUM-SHOP
REVIVOR	RIGLING	ROGUERY	ROUGHIE	RUNAWAY
REVOLVE	RIGSDAG	ROGUING	ROUGHLY	RUNDALE
REVVING	RIGVEDA	ROGUISH	ROULADE	RUNDLED
REVVYING	RILIEVO	ROINISH	ROULEAU	RUNDLET
REWRITE	RIMLESS	ROISTER	ROUMING	RUN-DOWN
REWROTE	RIMMING	ROKELAY	ROUNDED	RUNNING
REYNARD	RING-BIT	ROLLICK	ROUNDEL	RUNNION
REYNOLD	RINGENT	ROLLING	ROUNDER	RUNTISH
RHABDOM	RINGING	ROLLOCK	ROUNDLE	RUPTURE
RHABDUS	RINGLET	ROLL-OUT	ROUNDLY	RURALLY
RHACHIS	RINGMAN	ROLL-TOP	ROUND-UP	RUSALKA
RHAETIA	RING-TAW	ROMAIKA	ROUSANT	RUSSETY
RHAETIC	RINSING	ROMANCE	ROUSING	RUSSIAN
RHAMNUS	RIOTING	ROMANES	ROUSTER	RUSSIFY
RHAPHIS	RIOTISE	ROMANIC	ROUTHIE	RUSTILY
RHATANY	RIOTOUS	ROMANSH	ROUTINE	RUSTING
RHEMISH	RIP-CORD	ROMAUNT	ROUTING	RUSTLER
RHEMIST	RIPIENI	ROMMANY	ROUTOUS	RUSTRED
RHENISH	RIPIENO	ROMPISH	ROWBOAT	RUTHENE
RHENIUM	RIPOSTE	RONDEAU	ROWDILY	RUTHFUL
RHEUMED	RIPPIER	RONDINO	ROWLOCK	RUT-TIME
RHIZINE	RIPPING	RÖNTGEN	ROW-PORT	RUTTING

RUTTISH
RYE-CORN
RYE-PECK
RYE-ROLL
RYE-WOLF

S

SABAEAN
SABAISM
SABAOTH
SABATON
SABBATH
SABELLA
SABURRA
SACCULE
SACCULI
SACELLA
SACKAGE
SACKBUT
SACKFUL
SACKING
SACLESS
SACRING
SACRIST
SADDISH
SADDLER
SAD-EYED
SAD-IRON
SADNESS
SAFFIAN
SAFFRON
SAGAMAN
SAGATHY
SAGE-TEA
SAGGARD
SAGGING
SAGITTA
SAGOUIN
SAGUARO
SAHIBAH
SAIDEST
SAILING
SAIMIRI
SAINTED
SAINTLY
SAIVISM
SAKERET
SAKIYEH
SAKSAUL
SAKTISM
SALABLE
SALABLY
SALAMON
SALBAND
SALFERN
SALICET
SALICIN
SALIENT
SALIGOT
SALIQUE
SALIVAL
SALLIED
SALLOWY
SALPIAN
SALPINX
SALSAFY

SALSIFY
SALSOLA
SALTANT
SALTATE
SALT-BOX
SALT-CAT
SALTERN
SALT-FAT
SALTIER
SALTING
SALTIRE
SALTISH
SALT-PAN
SALT-PIT
SALUTER
SALVAGE
SALVING
SALVOES
SAMBUCA
SAMIOTE
SAMISEN
SAMNITE
SAMOVAR
SAMOYED
SAMPIRE
SAMPLER
SAMSHOO
SAMURAI
SANCTUM
SANCTUS
SANDBAG
SAND-BAR
SAND-BED
SAND-BOX
SAND-BOY
SAND-EEL
SANDERS
SAND-FLY
SAND-HOG
SANDING
SANDMAN
SAND-PIT
SANGRIA
SANICLE
SANKHYA
SANTOUR
SAOUARI
SAPAJOU
SAPHEAD
SAPIENT
SAPLESS
SAPLING
SAPONIN
SAPPHIC
SAPPING
SAPPLES
SAPROBE
SAPSAGO
SAP-WOOD
SARACEN
SARAFAN
SARANGI
SARAPIC
SARAPIS
SARCASM
SARCODE

SARCOID
SARCOMA
SARCOUS
SARDINE
SARDIUS
SARKFUL
SARKING
SARMENT
SARSDEN
SARSNET
SASSABY
SATANAS
SATANIC
SATCHEL
SATIATE
SATIETY
SATINET
SATIRIC
SATISFY
SATRAPY
SATSUMA
SATYRAL
SATYRIC
SAUCIER
SAUCILY
SAUNTER
SAURIAN
SAUROID
SAUSAGE
SAVABLE
SAVANNA
SAVE-ALL
SAVELOY
SAVIOUR
SAVOURY
SAW-BILL
SAWDUST
SAW-EDGE
SAW-EGED
SAW-FISH
SAW-GATE
SAW-KERF
SAWMILL
SAWN-OFF
SAW-WORT
SAXHORN
SAXONIC
SAYABLE
SCABBED
SCABBLE
SCABIES
SCABRID
SCAFFIE
SCAGLIA
SCALADE
SCALADO
SCALDER
SCALDIC
SCALENE
SCALING
SCALLED
SCALLOP
SCALPEL
SCALPER
SCAMBLE
SCAMPER

SCANDAL
SCANDIC
SCANDIX
SCANNED
SCANNER
SCANTLE
SCANTLY
SCAPPLE
SCAPULA
SCARFED
SCARIFY
SCARLET
SCARPED
SCARPER
SCARRED
SCARVES
SCATOLE
SCATTER
SCAUPER
SCAVAGE
SCENARY
SCENERY
SCENTED
SCEPSIS
SCEPTIC
SCEPTRE
SCEPTRY
SCHAPPE
SCHEMER
SCHERZO
SCHISMA
SCHLICH
SCHLOCK
SCHLOSS
SCHMELZ
SCHMOCK
SCHMOES
SCHMUCK
SCHNAPS
SCHNOOK
SCHOLAR
SCHOLIA
SCHOOLE
SCIAENA
SCIARID
SCIATIC
SCIENCE
SCIOLTO
SCIRPUS
SCISSEL
SCISSIL
SCISSOR
SCIURUS
SCLERAL
SCOFFER
SCOGGIN
SCOLDER
SCOLLOP
SCOMBER
SCOOPED
SCOOPER
SCOOTER
SCOPATE
SCOPULA
SCORIAC
SCORIAE

SCORIFY
SCORING
SCORNER
SCORPER
SCORPIO
SCOTCHY
SCOTIAN
SCOTICE
SCOTIFY
SCOTISM
SCOTIST
SCOTOMA
SCOTOMY
SCOURER
SCOURGE
SCOURIE
SCOURSE
SCOUTER
SCOWDER
SCOWRIE
SCRAGGY
SCRAICH
SCRAIGH
SCRANCH
SCRANNY
SCRAPER
SCRAPPY
SCRATCH
SCRAUCH
SCRAUGH
SCRAWLY
SCRAWNY
SCREECH
SCREEVE
SCREICH
SCREIGH
SCREWED
SCREWER
SCRIBAL
SCRIBER
SCRIECH
SCRIEVE
SCRIMPY
SCRITCH
SCROGGY
SCROOGE
SCROTUM
SCROUGE
SCROYLE
SCRUBBY
SCRUFFY
SCRUMMY
SCRUMPY
SCRUNCH
SCRUNTY
SCRUPLE
SCRYING
SCUDDED
SCUDDER
SCUDDLE
SCUDLER
SCUFFLE
SCULLER
SCULPIN
SCUMBER
SCUMBLE

SCUMMED	SEA-MILE	SEGMENT	SERVIAN	SHEARED
SCUMMER	SEA-MOSS	SEINING	SERVICE	SHEARER
SCUNNER	SEAM-SET	SEISMAL	SERVILE	SHEATHE
SCUPPER	SEA-PASS	SEISMIC	SERVING	SHEATHY
SCURRIL	SEA-PATH	SEIZING	SERVITE	SHEAVED
SCUTAGE	SEA-PIKE	SEIZURE	SESSILE	SHEAVES
SCUTATE	SEA-PINK	SELENIC	SESSION	SHEBANG
SCUTTER	SEAPORT	SELF-END	SESTETT	SHE-BEAR
SCUTTLE	SEA-REED	SELF-FED	SESTINA	SHEBEEN
SCYBALA	SEARING	SELFISH	SESTINE	SHEDDER
SCYPHUS	SEA-RISK	SELFISM	SETBACK	SHEERLY
SCYTALE	SEA-ROAD	SELFIST	SET-DOWN	SHEETED
SCYTHED	SEA-ROOM	SELL-OUT	SETNESS	SHELLAC
SCYTHER	SEA-SALT	SELTZER	SETTING	SHELLED
SDEIGNE	SEA-SAND	SELVAGE	SETTLED	SHELLER
SEA-BANK	SEASICK	SEMATIC	SETTLER	SHELTER
SEA-BASS	SEASIDE	SEMEION	SETUALE	SHELTIE
SEA-BEAN	SEA-SLUG	SEMILOG	SETWALL	SHELVES
SEA-BEAR	SEA-STAR	SEMINAL	SEVENTH	SHEMITE
SEA-BEAT	SEA-TANG	SEMINAR	SEVENTY	SHERBET
SEA-BEET	SEA-TERM	SEMIPED	SEVERAL	SHEREEF
SEA-BIRD	SEATING	SEMITIC	SEX-CELL	SHERIAT
SEA-BLUE	SEA-TOST	SENATOR	SEXFOIL	SHERIFF
SEA-BOAT	SEA-TURN	SENDING	SEXLESS	SHERRIS
SEA-BORN	SEA-VIEW	SEND-OFF	SEXTANS	SHICKER
SEA-CALF	SEA-WALL	SENECAN	SEXTANT	SHICKSA
SEA-CARD	SEAWARD	SENECIO	SEXTETT	SHIDDER
SEA-COAL	SEAWARE	SENHORA	SEXTILE	SHIFTED
SEA-COCK	SEA-WAVE	SENSILE	SEXTUOR	SHIFTER
SEA-COOK	SEAWEED	SENSING	SHABBLE	SHIKARI
SEA-CROW	SEA-WIFE	SENSISM	SHACKLE	SHILPIT
SEA-DACE	SEA-WIND	SENSIST	SHADILY	SHINDIG
SEA-DOVE	SEA-WING	SENSORY	SHADING	SHINESS
SEA-DUCK	SEA-WOLF	SENSUAL	SHADOOF	SHINGLE
SEA-DUST	SEA-WORM	SENUSSI	SHADOWY	SHINGLY
SEA-FIRE	SEAWORN	SEPIOST	SHAFTED	SHINING
SEA-FISH	SEBACIC	SEPPUKU	SHAFTER	SHIP-BOY
SEA-FOAM	SEBIFIC	SEPTATE	SHAGGED	SHIPFUL
SEA-FOLK	SEBUNDY	SEPTETT	SHAITAN	SHIPLAP
SEA-FOOD	SECEDER	SEPTIME	SHAKILY	SHIPMAN
SEA-FOWL	SECLUDE	SEPTUOR	SHAKING	SHIPMEN
SEA-FRET	SECONDE	SEQUELA	SHALLON	SHIPPED
SEA-GATE	SECONDO	SEQUENT	SHALLOP	SHIPPEN
SEA-GIRT	SECRECY	SEQUOIA	SHALLOT	SHIPPER
SEA-GOWN	SECRETA	SERAPHS	SHALLOW	SHIPPON
SEA-GULL	SECRETE	SERAPIC	SHAMBLE	SHIPWAY
SEA-HAAR	SECTARY	SERAPIS	SHAMMED	SHIRKER
SEA-HARE	SECTILE	SERBIAN	SHAMMER	SHIRRED
SEA-HAWK	SECTION	SERFAGE	SHAMPOO	SHITTAH
SEA-KALE	SECULAR	SERFDOM	SHANDRY	SHITTIM
SEA-KING	SECULUM	SERFISH	SHANKED	SHIVERY
SEA-LANE	SECURER	SERIATE	SHAPELY	SHMOOSE
SEALANT	SEDILIA	SERICIN	SHAPING	SHOCKED
SEA-LARK	SEDUCER	SERICON	SHARDED	SHOCKER
SEA-LEGS	SEEABLE	SERIEMA	SHARING	SHOEING
SEALERY	SEED-BED	SERINGA	SHARKER	SHOE-PEG
SEA-LIKE	SEED-BOX	SERIOUS	SHARPEN	SHOE-TIE
SEA-LILY	SEEDILY	SERKALI	SHARPER	SHOGGED
SEA-LINE	SEEDING	SEROSAE	SHARPLY	SHOOTER
SEALING	SEED-LAC	SERPENT	SHASTER	SHOP-BOY
SEALION	SEED-LIP	SERPIGO	SHASTRA	SHOPFUL
SEA-LOCH	SEED-OIL	SERPULA	SHATTER	SHOPMAN
SEA-LORD	SEEMING	SERRATE	SHAVIAN	SHOPPED
SEAL-WAX	SEEPAGE	SERRIED	SHAVING	SHOPPER
SEA-MAID	SEETHED	SERVANT	SHAWNEE	SHORING
SEA-MARK	SEETHER	SERVERY	SHEA-NUT	SHORTEN

SHORTLY	SIGNIFY	SIVAISM	SKYSAIL	SLOVENE
SHOTGUN	SIGNIOR	SIVAITE	SKY-SIGN	SLOWING
SHOTTED	SIGNORA	SIXAINE	SKYWARD	SLOWISH
SHOTTEN	SIGNORE	SIXFOLD	SLABBED	SLUBBED
SHOTTLE	SIGNORY	SIX-FOOT	SLABBER	SLUBBER
SHOUTER	SIKHISM	SIXTEEN	SLACKER	SLUMBER
SHOWBIZ	SILENCE	SIXTHLY	SLACKLY	SLUMBRY
SHOW-BOX	SILENUS	SIXTIES	SLADANG	SLUMMER
SHOWERY	SILICIC	SIXTINE	SLAINTE	SLURRED
SHOWILY	SILICLE	SIZABLE	SLAMMED	SLYNESS
SHOWING	SILICON	SIZZLER	SLANDER	SMACKER
SHOWMAN	SILIQUA	SJAMBOK	SLANTED	SMARAGD
SHOW-OFF	SILIQUE	SKALDIC	SLANTLY	SMARTEN
SHREDDY	SILK-HAT	SKATING	SLAPPED	SMARTLY
SHRIEVE	SILKILY	SKATOLE	SLAPPER	SMASHER
SHRIGHT	SILK-MAN	SKEETER	SLASHED	SMASH-UP
SHRILLY	SILLERY	SKEGGER	SLASHER	SMATTER
SHRINAL	SILLILY	SKELDER	SLATHER	SMEDDUM
SHRITCH	SILLOCK	SKELLUM	SLATING	SMELLER
SHRIVED	SILURUS	SKELTER	SLATTED	SMELTER
SHRIVEL	SILVERN	SKEPFUL	SLATTER	SMICKER
SHRIVEN	SILVERY	SKEPSIS	SLAVDOM	SMICKET
SHRIVER	SIMARRE	SKEPTIC	SLAVERY	SMICKLY
SHROUDY	SIMILAR	SKETCHY	SLAVIFY	SMILING
SHRUBBY	SIMILOR	SKEW-PUT	SLAVISH	SMOKE-HO
SHUCKER	SIMIOUS	SKIABLE	SLEAVED	SMOKILY
SHUDDER	SIMITAR	SKI-BOBS	SLEDDED	SMOKING
SHUFFLE	SIMPKIN	SKID-LID	SLEDGER	SMOLDER
SHUNNED	SIMPLER	SKIDPAN	SLEECHY	SMOOTHE
SHUNTER	SIMPLEX	SKIFFLE	SLEEKEN	SMOTHER
SHUT-OUT	SIMULAR	SKILFUL	SLEEKER	SMOUSER
SHUTTER	SIMURGH	SKI-LIFT	SLEEKIT	SMUDGER
SHUTTLE	SINAEAN	SKILLED	SLEEKLY	SMUGGLE
SHY-COCK	SINCERE	SKILLET	SLEEPER	SMUTTED
SHYLOCK	SINEWED	SKIMMED	SLEEPRY	SMYTRIE
SHYNESS	SINGING	SKIMMER	SLEEVED	SNABBLE
SHYSTER	SINGLET	SKIMMIA	SLEIDED	SNAFFLE
SIALOID	SINGULT	SKINFUL	SLEIGHT	SNAGGED
SIAMANG	SINHALA	SKINKER	SLENDER	SNAKILY
SIAMESE	SINKAGE	SKINNED	SLICING	SNAKISH
SIBLING	SINKING	SKINNER	SLICKEN	SNAPPED
SIBSHIP	SINLESS	SKIPPED	SLICKER	SNAPPER
SICCITY	SINNING	SKIPPER	SLICKLY	SNARING
SICK-BAY	SINOPIA	SKIPPET	SLIDDEN	SNARLED
SICK-BED	SINOPIS	SKIRRET	SLIDDER	SNARLER
SICKISH	SINSYNE	SKIRTED	SLIDING	SNATCHY
SICKLED	SINTERY	SKIRTER	SLIMILY	SNEAKER
SICK-MAN	SINUATE	SKITTER	SLIMMED	SNEAK-UP
SICLIKE	SINUOSE	SKITTLE	SLIMMER	SNEERER
SIDE-BOX	SINUOUS	SKIVING	SLINGER	SNEEZER
SIDE-CAR	SIPOREX	SKOLION	SLINKER	SNICKER
SIDERAL	SIPPING	SKREIGH	SLIPPED	SNICK-UP
SIDEWAY	SIRENIA	SKRIECH	SLIPPER	SNIFFER
SIEMENS	SIRENIC	SKRIEGH	SLIPWAY	SNIFFLE
SIENESE	SIRGANG	SKUDLER	SLITHER	SNIFTER
SIERRAN	SIRLOIN	SKULKER	SLITTER	SNIGGER
SIFTING	SIRNAME	SKULPIN	SLOBBER	SNIGGLE
SIGHFUL	SIROCCO	SKUMMER	SLOCKEN	SNIPING
SIGHING	SISTINE	SKUTTLE	SLOE-GIN	SNIPPED
SIGHTED	SISTRUM	SKY-BLUE	SLOGGER	SNIPPER
SIGHTER	SITDOWN	SKY-BORN	SLOPING	SNIPPET
SIGHTLY	SITFAST	SKY-BRED	SLOPPED	SNIRTLE
SIGMATE	SITHENS	SKY-CLAD	SLOSHED	SNODDED
SIGMOID	SITTINE	SKY-HIGH	SLOT-CAR	SNODDIT
SIGNARY	SITTING	SKYLARK	SLOUCHY	SNOODED
SIGNEUR	SITUATE	SKYLINE	SLOUGHY	SNOOKER

SNOOPER	SOMITAL	SOZZLED	SPICULA	SPRAYER
SNOOZER	SOMITIC	SPACIAL	SPICULE	SPRAYEY
SNOOZLE	SOMNIAL	SPACING	SPIDERY	SPREAGH
SNORING	SONANCE	SPADOES	SPIELER	SPREAZE
SNORKEL	SONANCY	SPAEMAN	SPIGNEL	SPREEZE
SNORTER	SONDAGE	SPAIRGE	SPIKILY	SPRIGGY
SNOTTER	SONDELI	SPANCEL	SPILING	SPRIGHT
SNOUTED	SONGFUL	SPANGLE	SPILITE	SPRINGE
SNOW-BOX	SONG-HIT	SPANGLY	SPILLED	SPRINGY
SNOWCAP	SONGMAN	SPANIEL	SPILLER	SPRYEST
SNOW-FED	SONLESS	SPANISH	SPINACH	SPULYIE
SNOW-FLY	SONNITE	SPANKER	SPINAGE	SPULZIE
SNOW-ICE	SONSHIP	SPANNED	SPINATE	SPUMOUS
SNOWILY	SONTIES	SPANNER	SPINDLE	SPUNKIE
SNOWISH	SOOTHER	SPAN-NEW	SPIN-DRY	SPUN-OUT
SNOWMAN	SOOTHLY	SPARELY	SPINNER	SPURIAE
SNUBBED	SOOTILY	SPARGER	SPINNET	SPURNER
SNUBBER	SOPHISM	SPARING	SPINNEY	SPURRED
SNUFFER	SOPHIST	SPARKLE	SPINODE	SPURRER
SNUFFLE	SOPPILY	SPAROID	SPIN-OFF	SPURREY
SNUGGED	SOPPING	SPARRED	SPINOSE	SPURTLE
SNUGGLE	SOPRANI	SPARRER	SPINOUS	SPURWAY
SNUZZLE	SOPRANO	SPARROW	SPINULE	SPUTNIK
SOAKAGE	SORBENT	SPARTAN	SPIRAEA	SPUTTER
SOAKING	SORBIAN	SPARTHE	SPIRANT	SPYHOLE
SO-AND-SO	SORBISH	SPASMIC	SPIREME	SQUABBY
SOAPBOX	SORCERY	SPASTIC	SPIRITY	SQUACCO
SOAPILY	SORDINE	SPATHED	SPIRTLE	SQUALID
SOARING	SORDINI	SPATHIC	SPIT-BOX	SQUALLY
SOBBING	SORDINO	SPATIAL	SPITTED	SQUALOR
SOBERLY	SOREDIA	SPATTEE	SPITTEN	SQUAMAE
SOBOLES	SOREHON	SPATTER	SPITTER	SQUARED
SOCCAGE	SORGHUM	SPATULA	SPITTLE	SQUARER
SOCIATE	SORITES	SPATULE	SPLASHY	SQUASHY
SOCIETY	SORNING	SPA-WELL	SPLATCH	SQUATTY
SOCKEYE	SOROBAN	SPAWNER	SPLEENY	SQUAWKY
SODOMOY	SOROCHE	SPEAKER	SPLENIC	SQUEAKY
SOFA-BED	SORORAL	SPEARED	SPLODGE	SQUEEZE
SOFTISH	SOROSIS	SPECIAL	SPLODGY	SQUEEZY
SOGGILY	SORRIER	SPECIES	SPLOTCH	SQUELCH
SOGGING	SORRILY	SPECIFY	SPLURGE	SQUIFFY
SOIGNÉE	SORTING	SPECKLE	SPLURGY	SQUINCH
SOILING	SOSSING	SPECTRA	SPODIUM	SQUINNY
SOILURE	SOTADIC	SPECTRE	SPOILED	SQUISHY
SOJOURN	SOTTING	SPECULA	SPOILER	SQUITCH
SOKEMAN	SOTTISH	SPEEDED	SPONDEE	SRADDHA
SOLANUM	SOUBISE	SPEEDER	SPONDYL	STABBED
SOLDADO	SOUFFLE	SPEED-UP	SPONGER	STABBER
SOLDIER	SOUFFLÉ	SPEELER	SPONGIN	STABILE
SOL-FAED	SOULDAN	SPELDER	SPONSAL	STABLER
SOLIDLY	SOULFUL	SPELDIN	SPONSON	STACKET
SOLIDUM	SOUMING	SPELEAN	SPONSOR	STADDLE
SOLIDUS	SOUNDER	SPELLED	SPOOFER	STADIUM
SOLIPED	SOUNDLY	SPELLER	SPOOLER	STAGERY
SOLOIST	SOUPÇON	SPELTER	SPOONEY	STAGGER
SOLOMON	SOURING	SPENCER	SPOORER	STAGGLE
SOLPUGA	SOURISH	SPENDER	SPORRAN	STAGILY
SOLUBLE	SOUROCK	SPERSED	SPORTER	STAGING
SOLVATE	SOUR-SOP	SPERTHE	SPORULE	STAIDLY
SOLVENT	SOUSING	SPHENIC	SPOTTED	STAINED
SOMATIC	SOUSLIK	SPHERAL	SPOTTER	STAINER
SOMEDAY	SOUTANE	SPHERED	SPOUSAL	STAIRED
SOMEHOW	SOUTHER	SPHERIC	SPOUTER	STAITHE
SOMEONE	SOWARRY	SPICATE	SPRAINT	STALELY
SOMEWAY	SOW-SKIN	SPICERY	SPRAWLY	STALKED
SOMEWHY	SOY-BEAN	SPICILY	SPRAYED	STALKER

STALLED	STELENE	STOICAL	STUCCO'D	SUBTACK
STAMINA	STELLAR	STOITER	STUCCOS	SUBTEND
STAMMEL	STELLED	STOMACH	STUCK-UP	SUBTILE
STAMMER	STEMBOK	STOMATA	STUDDED	SUBVERT
STAMNOS	STEMMED	STONERN	STUDDEN	SUBZONE
STAMPER	STEMPEL	STONILY	STUDDLE	SUCCADE
STAND-BY	STEMPLE	STONKER	STUDENT	SUCCEED
STANDEN	STEMSON	STOODEN	STUDIED	SUCCESS
STANDER	STENCHY	STOOKER	STUDIER	SUCCORY
STAND-IN	STENCIL	STOOPED	STUFFED	SUCCOSE
STAND-TO	STENGAH	STOOPER	STUFFER	SUCCOUR
STAND-UP	STENTOR	STOP-GAP	STUMBLE	SUCCOUS
STANIEL	STEPNEY	STOPING	STUMBLY	SUCCUBA
STANNEL	STEPPED	STOP-OFF	STUMMED	SUCCUBI
STANNIC	STEPPER	STOPPED	STUMMEL	SUCCUMB
STANYEL	STEPSON	STOPPER	STUMPER	SUCCUSS
STAPLER	STERILE	STOPPLE	STUNNED	SUCKING
STAPPLE	STERLET	STORAGE	STUNNER	SUCKLER
STARCHY	STERNAL	STORIED	STUNTED	SUCROSE
STARDOM	STERNED	STOTTER	STUPEFY	SUCTION
STARING	STERNLY	STOUTEN	STUPENT	SUDAMEN
STARKEN	STERNUM	STOUTLY	STURNUS	SUEABLE*
STARKLY	STEROID	STOVIES	STUTTER	SUFFETE
STAR-LED	STETSON	STOVING	STYGIAN	SUFFICE
STARLET	STETTED	STOWAGE	STYLATE	SUFFUSE
STARLIT	STEWARD	STOWING	STYLISE	SUFIISM
STAR-MAN	STEW-CAN	STRAINT	STYLISH	SUGARED
STAR-MAP	STEWING	STRANGE	STYLIST	SUGGEST
STARNIE	STEWPAN	STRATUM	STYLITE	SUICIDE
STARRED	STEWPOT	STRATUS	STYLOID	SUITING
STARTER	STHENIC	STRAWED	STYPTIC	SULCATE
STARTLE	STIBBLE	STRAWEN	STYRENE	SULKILY
STARTLY	STIBIAL	STRAYED	SUASION	SULLAGE
START-UP	STIBINE	STRAYER	SUASIVE	SULLIED
STARVED	STIBIUM	STREAKY	SUASORY	SULPHUR
STASIMA	STICHIC	STREAMY	SUAVELY	SULTANA
STATANT	STICHOI	STREETY	SUAVITY	SUMATRA
STATELY	STICHOS	STRETCH	SUBACID	SUMLESS
STATICE	STICKED	STRETTA	SUBADAR	SUMMAND
STATICS	STICKER	STRETTO	SUBARID	SUMMARY
STATION	STICKIT	STREWED	SUBATOM	SUMMING
STATISM	STICKLE	STREWER	SUBBING	SUMMIST
STATIST	STICKUP	'STREWTH	SUBDEAN	SUMMONS
STATIVE	STIDDIE	STRIATE	SUBDUAL	SUMPTER
STATUED	STIFFEN	STRIDOR	SUBDUCE	SUNBATH
STATURE	STIFFLY	STRIGAE	SUBDUCT	SUN-BEAM
STATUTE	STIFLED	STRIGES	SUBDUED	SUN-BEAR
STAUNCH	STIFLER	STRIGIL	SUBDUER	SUN-BEAT
STAYING	STILLER	STRIKER	SUBEDAR	SUN-BIRD
STEADED	STILTED	STRINGY	SUBEDIT	SUNBURN
STEALED	STILTER	STRIPED	SUBERIC	SUN-CLAD
STEALER	STILTON	STRIPES	SUBERIN	SUN-CULT
STEALTH	STIMULI	STRIVEN	SUBFUSC	SUNDARI
STEAMED	STINGED	STRIVER	SUBFUSK	SUN-DAWN
STEAMER	STINGER	STROBIC	SUBHEAD	SUNDIAL
STEARIC	STINKER	STRODLE	SUBJECT	SUN-DISK
STEARIN	STINTED	STROKER	SUBJOIN	SUNDOWN
STEEKIT	STINTER	STROPHE	SUBLATE	SUN-FISH
STEELED	STIPEND	STROPPY	SUBLIME	SUN-LAMP
STEEPEN	STIPPLE	STROWED	SUBMISS	SUNLESS
STEEPER	STIPULE	STROWER	SUBPLOT	SUNLIKE
STEEPLE	STIRPES	STRUDEL	SUBSIDE	SUN-MYTH
STEEPLY	STIRRED	STRUMAE	SUBSIDY	SUNNILY
STEEP-TO	STIRRER	STUBBED	SUBSIST	SUNNING
STEEP-UP	STIRRUP	STUBBLE	SUBSOIL	SUNNITE
STEERER	STODGER	STUBBLY	SUBSUME	SUNRISE

SUNSPOT	SWEERED	**T**	TALLY-HO	TARTANA
SUNWARD	SWEETEN		TALONED	TARTANE
SUNWISE	SWEETIE	TABANID	TAMABLE	TARTARE
SUOMISH	SWEETLY	TABANUS	TAMARIN	TARTARY
SUPPAWN	SWELLED	TABARET	TAMASHA	TARTINE
SUPPING	SWELLER	TABASCO	TAMBOUR	TARTISH
SUPPORT	SWELTED	TABBIED	TAMILIC	TARTLET
SUPPOSE	SWELTER	TABLEAU	TAMMANY	TARTUFE
SUPREME	SWELTRY	TABLING	TAMPICO	TARWEED
SUPREMO	SWERVER	TABLOID	TAMPING	TASKING
SURANCE	SWIFTER	TABOOED	TAMPION	TASSELL
SURBASE	SWIFTLY	TABORER	TAMULIC	TASTILY
SURBATE	SWILLER	TABORIN	TANADAR	TASTING
SURCOAT	SWIMMER	TABULAE	TANAGER	TATARIC
SURDITY	SWINDGE	TACHISM	TANAGRA	TATTERY
SURFACE	SWINDLE	TACHIST	TAN-BARK	TATTILY
SURFEIT	SWINERY	TACHYON	TANGELO	TATTING
SURFING	SWINGER	TACITLY	TANGENT	TATTLER
SURFMAN	SWINGLE	TACKETY	TANGHIN	TAUNTER
SURGENT	SWINISH	TACKING	TANGLED	TAURINE
SURGEON	SWINKED	TACKLED	TANGLER	TAXABLE
SURGERY	SWIPPLE	TACKLER	TANGOED	TAXABLY
SURGING	SWISHER	TACTFUL	TANGRAM	TAX-CART
SURINAM	SWITCHY	TACTICS	TANKAGE	TAX-FREE
SURLILY	SWITHER	TACTILE	TANKARD	TAXI-CAB
SURLOIN	SWITZER	TACTION	TANK-CAR	TAXYING
SURMISE	SWIZZLE	TACTISM	TANKFUL	TEA-CAKE
SURNAME	SWOBBED	TACTUAL	TANLING	TEACHER
SURPASS	SWOBBER	TADPOLE	TANNAGE	TEACHIE
SURPLUS	SWOLLEN	TAEDIUM	TANNATE	TEACH-IN
SURREAL	SWOONED	TAENIAE	TANNERY	TEA-COSY
SURTOUT	SWOPPED	TAFFETA	TANNING	TEA-DISH
SURVIEW	SWOPPER	TAFFETY	TAN-OOZE	TEA-GOWN
SURVIVE	SWORDER	TAGALOG	TAN-RIDE	TEA-LEAD
SUSPECT	SWOTTER	TAGETES	TANTARA	TEA-LEAF
SUSPEND	SYBOTIC	TAGGERS	TANTIVY	TEAMING
SUSPIRE	SYCOSIS	TAGGING	TANTONY	TEAR-BAG
SUSTAIN	SYENITE	TAGTAIL	TANTRIC	TEARFUL
SUTLERY	SYLLABI	TAILARD	TANTRUM	TEAR-GAS
SUTURAL	SYLPHID	TAIL-END	TANYARD	TEARING
SUTURED	SYLVIAN	TAIL-FLY	TAOSTIC	TEA-ROOM
SWABBED	SYLVINE	TAILING	TAP-BOLT	TEA-ROSE
SWABBER	SYLVITE	TAILLIE	TAPERED	TEAR-PIT
SWADDLE	SYMBION	TAILZIE	TAPERER	TEA-SHOP
SWAGGED	SYMPTOM	TAINTED	TAPETAL	TEASING
SWAGGER	SYNAPSE	T'AIP'ING	TAPETUM	TEA-TIME
SWAGMAN	SYNAPTE	TAIVERT	TAPIOCA	TEA-TRAY
SWAHILI	SYNAXIS	TAKAHEA	TAP-LASH	TEA-TREE
SWALING	SYNCOPE	TAKE-OFF	TAPPICE	TECHNIC
SWALLET	SYNERGY	TALARIA	TAPPING	TECTRIX
SWALLOW	SYNESIS	TALAYOT	TAPROOM	TEDDING
SWANKER	SYNGAMY	TALCOSE	TAPROOT	TEDESCA
SWANKEY	SYNODAL	TALCOUS	TAPSMAN	TEDESCO
SWAPPED	SYNODIC	TALEFUL	TAPSTER	TEDIOUS
SWAPPER	SYNONYM	TALIPAT	TARBUSH	TEEMFUL
SWARDED	SYNOVIA	TALIPES	TARDILY	TEEMING
SWARMER	SYNTONY	TALIPOT	TARDIVE	TEENAGE
SWARTHY	SYRIASM	TALKING	TAR-HEEL	TEGMINA
SWASHER	SYRINGA	TALLAGE	TARNISH	TEGULAE
SWATTER	SYRINGE	TALLBOY	TARRIED	TEGULAR
SWAYING	SYRPHID	TALLENT	TARRIER	TEKTITE
SWEARER	SYRPHUS	TALLIED	TARRING	TELAMON
SWEATED	SYSTOLE	TALLIES	TARROCK	TELEOST
SWEATER	SYSTYLE	TALLITH	TARSIER	TELERGY
SWEDISH	SYZGIAL	TALL-OIL	TARSIUS	TELLING
SWEEPER	SZEKLER	TALLOWY	TAR-SPOT	TELPHER

TELSTAR	TESTRIL	THONDER	TILTING	TOLUENE
TEMENOS	TESTUDO	THORITE	TIMBALE	TOMBOLA
TEMPERA	TETANIC	THORIUM	TIMBREL	TOMBOLO
TEMPEST	TETANUS	THORNED	TIME-GUN	TOMFOOL
TEMPLAR	TETRACT	THOUGHT	TIME-LAG	TOMPION
TEMPLED	TETRODE	THREADY	TIMEOUS	TOM-TROT
TEMPLET	TEXTILE	THREAVE	TIMIDLY	TONE-ARM
TEMPTER	TEXT-MAN	THRENOS	TIMOTHY	TONEMIC
TENABLE	TEXTUAL	THRETTY	TIMPANI	TONGUED
TENANCY	TEXTURE	THRIFTY	TIMPANO	TONIGHT
TENDENZ	THALAMI	THRILLY	TINAMOU	TONNAGE
TENDRIL	THALIAN	THRIVED	TINCHEL	TONNEAU
TENDRON	THALLIC	THRIVEN	TINDERY	TONNISH
TENFOLD	THALLUS	THRIVER	TINFOIL	TONSURE
TEN-FOOT	THALWEG	THROATY	TINFULS	TONTINE
TENIATE	THAMMUZ	THRONED	TINGING	TOOLING
TENIOID	THANAGE	THROUGH	TINGLER	TOOTHED
TENONER	THANKEE	THROWER	TINIEST	TOPARCH
TENPINS	THANKER	THROW-IN	TINKLER	TOP-BOOT
TENSELY	THANNAH	THRUMMY	TINNING	TOP-COAT
TENSILE	THATCHT	THRUTCH	TIN-TACK	TOPFULL
TENSION	THAWING	THRUWAY	TINTING	TOP-HOLE
TENSITY	THEATRE	THUGGEE	TINTYPE	TOPIARY
TENSIVE	THEBAIC	THULITE	TINWARE	TOPICAL
TENT-BED	THEBAID	THULIUM	TIP-CART	TOP-KNOT
TENTFUL	THECATE	THUMBED	TIPPING	TOPLESS
TENTHLY	THEMATA	THUMMIM	TIPPLER	TOP-LINE
TENTIGO	THEORBO	THUMPER	TIPSIFY	TOPMAST
TENTING	THEOREM	THUNDER	TIPSILY	TOPMOST
TENT-PEG	THEORIC	THURIFY	TIPSTER	TOPPING
TENT-PIN	THERAPY	THWAITE	TIPTOED	TOPSAIL
TENUITY	THEREAT	THYLOSE	TIRASSE	TOPSIDE
TENUOUS	THEREBY	THYMINE	TITANIA	TOPSMAN
TEQUILA	THEREIN	THYROID	TITANIC	TOP-SOIL
TERBIUM	THEREOF	THYRSUS	TITHING	TORCHER
TEREBRA	THEREON	THYSELF	TITLARK	TORCHON
TEREFAH	THERETO	TIARAED	TITLING	TORGOCH
TERGITE	THERIAC	TIBETAN	TITMICE	TORMENT
TERM-DAY	THERMAE	TICKING	TITOISM	TORMINA
TERMINI	THERMAL	TICKLER	TITOIST	TORNADE
TERMITE	THERMIC	TIDDLER	TITRATE	TORNADO
TERNARY	THERMOS	TIDDLEY	TITTUPY	TORPEDO
TERNATE	THEROID	TIDE-RIP	TITULAR	TORPEFY
TERNION	THETHER	TIDE-WAY	TOADIED	TORQUED
TERPENE	THEURGY	TIDINGS	TOASTED	TORREFY
TERRACE	THIAMIN	TIDYING	TOASTER	TORRENT
TERRAIN	THIASUS	TIE-BEAM	TOBACCO	TORSADE
TERREEN	THICKEN	TIELESS	TO-BRAKE	TORSION
TERRENE	THICKET	TIERCEL	TO-BREAK	TORSIVE
TERRIER	THICKLY	TIE-TACK	TOBY-JUG	TORTILE
TERRIFY	THICKUN	TIFFANY	TOCCATA	TORTIVE
TERRINE	THIEVES	TIFFING	TODDLER	TORTRIX
TERSELY	THIGGER	TIGERLY	TOECLIP	TORTURE
TERSION	THIGGIT	TIGHTEN	TOE-HOLD	TORULIN
TERTIAL	THILLER	TIGHTLY	TOENAIL	TORULUS
TERTIAN	THIMBLE	TIGRESS	TOFFISH	TORYISM
TESSERA	THINKER	TIGRINE	TOGATED	TOSSILY
TESTACY	THINNED	TIGRISH	TOGGERY	TOSSING
TESTATE	THINNER	TIGROID	TOHEROA	TOSSPOT
TEST-BED	THIRDLY	TILBURY	TOILFUL	TOTALLY
TESTERN	THIRSTY	TILE-HAT	TOILING	TOTANUS
TEST-FLY	THISTLE	TILE-RED	TOISECH	TOTEMIC
TESTIFY	THISTLY	TILLAGE	TOLLAGE	TOTIENT
TESTILY	THITHER	TILLING	TOLL-BAR	TO-TORNE
TESTING	THOMISM	TILLITE	TOLLING	TOTTERY
TESTOON	THOMIST	TIL-SEED	TOLLMAN	TOTTING

TOUCHED
TOUCHER
TOUGHEN
TOUGHLY
TOURACO
TOURING
TOURISM
TOURIST
TOURNEY
TOUSING
TOUSTIE
TOWARDS
TOWERED
TOW-HEAD
TOW-IRON
TOWLINE
TOWMOND
TOWMONT
TOWN-END
TOWNISH
TO-WORNE
TOWPATH
TOW-ROPE
TOXICAL
TOYSHOP
TOYSOME
TRACERY
TRACHEA
TRACING
TRACKED
TRACKER
TRACTOR
TRACTUS
TRADE-IN
TRADING
TRADUCE
TRAFFIC
TRAGEDY
TRAGULE
TRAIKIT
TRAILER
TRAINED
TRAINEE
TRAINER
TRAIPSE
TRAITOR
TRAJECT
TRAM-CAR
TRAMMEL
TRAMPER
TRAMPLE
TRAMWAY
TRANCED
TRANCHE
TRANECT
TRANGAM
TRANGLE
TRANKUM
TRANSIT
TRANSOM
TRANTER
TRAP-CUT
TRAPEZE
TRAPPED
TRAPPER
TRAVAIL

TRAVOIS
TRAWLER
TRAYBIT
TRAYFUL
TREACLE
TREACLY
TREADER
TREADLE
TREAGUE
TREASON
TREATER
TREDDLE
TREETOP
TREFOIL
TREHALA
TREILLE
TREKKED
TREKKER
TRELLIS
TREMBLE
TREMBLY
TREMOLO
TRENAIL
TRENISE
TRENTAL
TREPANG
TRESSED
TRESSEL
TRESTLE
TREVISS
TREYBIT
TRIABLE
TRIACID
TRIADIC
TRIARCH
TRIATIC
TRIAXON
TRIBADE
TRIBADY
TRIBBLE
TRIBLET
TRIBUNE
TRIBUTE
TRICEPS
TRICKER
TRICKLE
TRICKLY
TRICKSY
TRICORN
TRIDENT
TRIDUAN
TRIDUUM
TRIFLER
TRIFOLY
TRIFORM
TRIGAMY
TRIGGER
TRIGLOT
TRIGRAM
TRILITH
TRILLED
TRILOBE
TRILOGY
TRIMMED
TRIMMER
TRINARY

TRINDLE
TRINGLE
TRINITY
TRINKET
TRINKUM
TRIOLET
TRIONES
TRIONYM
TRIPERY
TRIPLET
TRIPLEX
TRIPODY
TRIPOLI
TRIPPED
TRIPPER
TRIPPET
TRIPPLE
TRIPSIS
TRIREME
TRISECT
TRISEME
TRISHAW
TRISMUS
TRISULA
TRITELY
TRITIUM
TRITOMA
TRITONE
TRIUMPH
TRIVIAL
TRIVIUM
TRIZONE
TROCHAL
TROCHEE
TROCHUS
TRODDEN
TROELIE
TROLLER
TROLLEY
TROLLOP
TROMMEL
TROOLIE
TROOPER
TROPHIC
TROPISM
TROPIST
TROTTED
TROTTER
TROUBLE
TROUNCE
TROUPER
TROUTER
TRUANCY
TRUCAGE
TRUCIAL
TRUCKER
TRUCKLE
TRUDGEN
TRUDGER
TRUEMAN
TRUFFLE
TRULLAN
TRUMEAU
TRUMPET
TRUNCAL
TRUNDLE

TRUNKED
TRUSSED
TRUSSER
TRUSTEE
TRUSTER
TRYPSIN
TRYPTIC
TRYSAIL
TRYSTER
TSABIAN
TSARDOM
TSARISM
TSARIST
T-SHAPED
TSIGANE
T-SQUARE
TSUNAMI
TUATARA
TUATERA
TUBBING
TUBBISH
TUBEFUL
TUBFAST
TUBFISH
TUBULAR
TUCK-BOX
TUCK-OUT
TUESDAY
TUFTING
TUG-BOAT
TUGGING
TUILYIE
TUILZIE
TUITION
TULCHAN
TULLIAN
TUMBLER
TUMBREL
TUMBRIL
TUMIDLY
TUMULAR
TUMULUS
TUNABLE
TUNABLY
TUN-DISH
TUNEFUL
TUNG-OIL
TUNICIN
TUNNAGE
TUNNING
TURACIN
TURBARY
TURBINE
TURBITH
TURDINE
TURFING
TURFITE
TURGENT
TURKESS
TURKIES
TURKISH
TURMOIL
TURNDUN
TURNERY
TURNING
TURNKEY

TURN-OUT
TURPETH
TURTLER
TUSHERY
TUSSOCK
TUSSORE
TUTANIA
TUTELAR
TUTENAG
TUTRESS
TUTWORK
TWADDLE
TWADDLY
TWAFALD
TWANGLE
TWANKAY
TWASOME
TWATTLE
TWEEDLE
TWEETER
TWELFTH
TWIBILL
TWIDDLE
TWIDDLY
TWIFOLD
TWIGGEN
TWIGGER
TWILLED
TWINING
TWINKLE
TWINNED
TWIN-SET
TWINTER
TWIRLER
TWISCAR
TWISTED
TWISTER
TWITCHY
TWITTED
TWITTEN
TWITTER
TWO-EYED
TWOFOLD
TWO-FOOT
TWO-FOUR
TWO-HAND
TWO-INCH
TWO-LINE
TWONESS
TWO-PAIR
TWO-PART
TWOSOME
TWO-STEP
TWO-TIME
TWO-TONE
TWYFOLD
TYCHISM
TYLOPOD
TYLOSES
TYLOSIS
TYMPANA
TYMPANO
TYMPANY
TYNWALD
TYPE-BAR
TYPHOID

TYPHOON	UNCHILD	UNHORSE	UNREEVE	UNTENTY
TYPHOUS	UNCINUS	UNHOUSE	UNRIGHT	UNTHINK
TYPICAL	UNCIVIL	UNHUMAN	UNRIMED	UNTILED
TYRANNE	UNCLASP	UNICITY	UNRISEN	UNTIRED
TYRANNY	UNCLEAN	UNICORN	UNRIVEN	UNTONED
TYRONES	UNCLEAR	UNIDEAD	UNRIVET	UNTRACE
TZIGANY	UNCLIPT	UNIDEAL	UNROOST	UNTREAD
	UNCLOAK	UNIFIED	UNROUGH	UNTRIED
U	UNCLOSE	UNIFIER	UNROUND	UNTRULY
	UNCLOUD	UNIFORM	UNROYAL	UNTRUSS
UBEROUS	UNCOUTH	UNITARY	UNRUFFE	UNTRUST
UDALLER	UNCOVER	UNITING	UNRULED	UNTRUTH
UDDERED	UNCROSS	UNITION	UNSAINT	UNTUNED
UFOLOGY	UNCROWN	UNITIVE	UNSATED	UNTWINE
UKELELE	UNCTION	UNJADED	UNSAVED	UNTWIST
UKULELE	UNCURED	UNJOINT	UNSCALE	UNTYING
ULCERED	UNCURSE	UNKEMPT	UNSCREW	UNURGED
ULICHON	UNDATED	UNKNOWN	UNSENSE	UNUSUAL
ULNARIA	UNDEIFY	UNLADEN	UNSEWED	UNVEXED
ULULANT	UNDERDO	UNLATCH	UNSEXED	UNVISOR
ULULATE	UNDERGO	UNLEARN	UNSHALE	UNVITAL
UMBERED	UNDIGHT	UNLEASH	UNSHAPE	UNVOCAL
UMBONAL	UNDOING	UNLIMED	UNSHELL	UNVOICE
UMBONES	UNDRESS	UNLINED	UNSHENT	UNWAKED
UMBRAGE	UNDRIED	UNLOOSE	UNSHEWN	UNWARES
UMBRERE	UNDRUNK	UNLOVED	UNSHORN	UNWATER
UMBRIAN	UNDYING	UNLUCKY	UNSHOUT	UNWAYED
UMBROSE	UNEARED	UNMANLY	UNSHOWN	UNWEARY
UMBROUS	UNEARTH	UNMARRY	UNSIGHT	UNWEAVE
UMPTEEN	UNEATEN	UNMATED	UNSINEW	UNWHIPT
UMWHILE	UNEQUAL	UNMEANT	UNSIZED	UNWIPED
UNACTED	UNFADED	UNMETED	UNSLAIN	UNWITCH
UNAIDED	UNFAITH	UNMIXED	UNSLING	UNWITTY
UNAIMED	UNFAMED	UNMORAL	UNSLUNG	UNWIVED
UNAIRED	UNFEUED	UNMOULD	UNSMART	UNWOMAN
UNAKING	UNFILED	UNMOUNT	UNSMOTE	UNWOOED
UNALIST	UNFIRED	UNMOVED	UNSNARL	UNWORTH
UNALIVE	UNFITLY	UNNAMED	UNSOLID	UNWOUND
UNAPTLY	UNFIXED	UNNEATH	UNSONSY	UNWOVEN
UNARMED	UNFLESH	UNNERVE	UNSOOTE	UNWRITE
UNASKED	UNFLUSH	UNNOBLE	UNSOUND	UNWRUNG
UNAWARE	UNFOUND	UNNOTED	UNSPEAK	UNYOKED
UNBAKED	UNFROCK	UNOFTEN	UNSPELL	UNZONED
UNBATED	UNFUMED	UNOILED	UNSPENT	UP-ALONG
UNBEGET	UNFUNNY	UNORDER	UNSPIED	UPBLOWN
UNBEGOT	UNGAZED	UNOWNED	UNSPILT	UPBOUND
UNBEGUN	UNGIRTH	UNPAGED	UNSPOKE	UPBRAID
UNBEING	UNGLOVE	UNPAINT	UNSTACK	UPBRAST
UNBLENT	UNGODLY	UNPANEL	UNSTAID	UPBREAK
UNBLESS	UNGORED	UNPAPER	UNSTATE	UPBRING
UNBLEST	UNGROWN	UNPARED	UNSTEEL	UPBUILD
UNBLIND	UNGUARD	UNPAVED	UNSTICK	UPBURST
UNBLOCK	UNGUENT	UNPERCH	UNSTOCK	UPCATCH
UNBLOWN	UNGYVED	UNPINKT	UNSTRAP	UPCHEER
UNBOSOM	UNHANDY	UNPLACE	UNSTRIP	UPCLIMB
UNBOUND	UNHAPPY	UNPLAIT	UNSTUCK	UPCLOSE
UNBOWED	UNHARDY	UNPLUMB	UNSUNNY	UPCOAST
UNBRACE	UNHASTY	UNPLUME	UNSURED	UPDRAWN
UNBROKE	UNHEARD	UNPURSE	UNSWEAR	UPFLUNG
UNBUILD	UNHEART	UNQUEEN	UNSWEET	UPGOING
UNBUILT	UNHEEDY	UNQUIET	UNSWEPT	UPGRADE
UNBURNT	UNHINGE	UNQUOTE	UNSWORN	UPGROWN
UNCANNY	UNHIRED	UNRAKED	UNTAKEN	UPHEAVE
UNCHAIN	UNHITCH	UNRAVEL	UNTAMED	UPHOARD
UNCHARM	UNHOARD	UNREADY	UNTAXED	UPHOIST
UNCHECK	UNHOPED	UNREAVE	UNTEACH	UPLYING

UP-PILED	USURPED	VARIOLA	VERMIAN	VINTAGE
UPRAISE	USURPER	VARIOLE	VERMINY	VINTNER
UPRIGHT	UTENSIL	VARIOUS	VERNANT	VIOLATE
UPRISAL	UTERINE	VARMENT	VERNIER	VIOLENT
UPRISEN	UTILISE	VARMINT	VERRUCA	VIOLIST
UPRIVER	UTILITY	VARNISH	VERRUGA	VIOLONE
UPROUSE	UTOPIAN	VARSITY	VERSANT	VIRELAY
UPSHOOT	UTOPISM	VARYING	VERSIFY	VIRETOT
UPSIDES	UTOPIST	VASCULA	VERSINE	VIRGATE
UPSILON	UTRICLE	VASSAIL	VERSING	VIRGULE
UPSPAKE	UTTERER	VASTITY	VERSION	VIROSIS
UPSPEAK	UTTERLY	VATICAN	VERSUTE	VIRTUAL
UPSPEAR	UVA-URSI	VAUDOIS	VERTIGO	VISAGED
UPSPOKE	UVEITIS	VAUDOUX	VERVAIN	VIS-À-VIS
UPSTAGE	UXORIAL	VAULTED	VESICAE	VISCERA
UPSTAND		VAULTER	VESICAL	VISCOSE
UPSTARE	**V**	VAUNTED	VESICLE	VISCOUS
UPSTART		VAUNTER	VESPINE	VISIBLE
UPSTOOD	VACANCE	VEDANTA	VESPOID	VISIBLY
UPSURGE	VACANCY	VEDDOID	VESSAIL	VISITEE
UPSWARM	VACATUR	VEDETTE	VESTIGE	VISITOR
UPSWEEP	VACCINE	VEERING	VESTING	VISNOMY
UPSWELL	VACKING	VEGANIC	VESTRAL	VISORED
UPSWEPT	VACUATE	VEGETAL	VESTURE	VISTAED
UPSWING	VACUIST	VEHICLE	VETERAN	VITALLY
UPTHROW	VACUITY	VEILING	VETIVER	VITAMIN
UPTIGHT	VACUOLE	VEINING	VETTING	VITELLI
UP-TRAIN	VACUOUS	VEINOUS	VETTURA	VITIATE
UPTRAIN	V-AGENTS	VELAMEN	VEXEDLY	VITRAGE
UPTREND	VAGINAE	VELARIA	VEXILLA	VITRAIL
UPWARDS	VAGINAL	VELARIC	VIADUCT	VITRAIN
UPWHIRL	VAGINAS	VELATED	VIALFUL	VITRAUX
UPWOUND	VAGRANT	VELIGER	VIALLED	VITREUM
URACHUS	VAGUELY	VELOURS	VIBICES	VITRICS
URAEMIA	VAISHYA	VELOUTÉ	VIBRANT	VITRIFY
URAEMIC	VAIVODE	VELVETY	VIBRATE	VITRINA
URALIAN	VALANCE	VENALLY	VIBRATO	VITRINE
URALITE	VALENCE	VENATIC	VICEROY	VITRIOL
URANIAN	VALENCY	VENDACE	VICINAL	VITTATE
URANIDE	VALIANT	VENDAGE	VICIOUS	VITULAR
URANISM	VALIDLY	VENDEAN	VICTORY	VIVARIA
URANITE	VALLARY	VENDISS	VICTRIX	VIVENCY
URANIUM	VALONIA	VENEFIC	VICTUAL	VIVERRA
URANOUS	VALUATE	VENERER	VIDENDA	VIVIDLY
UREDINE	VALVATE	VENISON	VIDETTE	VIVIFIC
URETHAN	VALVULA	VENOMED	VIDICON	VIXENLY
URETHRA	VALVULE	VENTAGE	VIDIMUS	VIZORED
URGENCE	VAMOOSE	VENTANA	VIDUAGE	V-NECKED
URGENCY	VAMPING	VENTIGE	VIDUITY	VOCABLE
URICASE	VAMPIRE	VENTING	VIDUOUS	VOCALIC
URINANT	VAMPISH	VENTOSE	VIEWING	VOCALLY
URINARY	VANADIC	VENTÔSE	VILAYET	VOCULAR
URINATE	VANDYKE	VENT-PEG	VILIACO	VOGUISH
URINOUS	VANESSA	VENTRAL	VILLAGE	VOICING
URODELA	VANILLA	VENTURE	VILLAIN	VOIDING
URODELE	VANNING	VENTURI	VILLANY	VOITURE
UROLOGY	VANTAGE	VERANDA	VILLEIN	VOIVODE
UROMERE	VANWARD	VERBENA	VILLOSE	VOLABLE
UROSOME	VAPIDLY	VERBOSE	VILLOUS	VOLANTE
USELESS	VAPOURY	VERDANT	VINALIA	VOLAPÜK
U-SHAPED	VAQUERO	VERDICT	VINASSE	VOLATIC
USUALLY	VARANUS	VERDURE	VINCULA	VOLCANO
USUCAPT	VAREUSE	VERGLAS	VINEGAR	VOLPINO
USURESS	VARIANT	VERIEST	VINE-ROD	VOLTAGE
USURING	VARIATE	VERISMO	VINEWED	VOLTAIC
USUROUS	VARICES	VERMEIL	VINGT-UN	VOLUBLE
	VARIETY			

VOLUBLY
VOLUMED
VOLUSPA
VOLUTED
VOLUTIN
VOMITED
VOSGEAN
VOSGIAN
VOUCHEE
VOUCHER
VOWELLY
VOYAGER
V-SHAPED
VULGATE
VULPINE
VULTURE
VULTURN
VULVATE
VYINGLY

W

WABBLER
WABSTER
WADDING
WADDLER
WADMAAL
WADMOLL
WADSETT
WAENESS
WAESOME
WAFTAGE
WAFTING
WAFTURE
WAGERER
WAGGERY
WAGGING
WAGGISH
WAGONER
WAGTAIL
WAHABEE
WAILFUL
WAILING
WAINAGE
WAISTED
WAISTER
WAITING
WAIVODE
WAKEFUL
WAKEMAN
WAKENED
WAKENER
WALKING
WALK-OUT
WALKWAY
WALLABA
WALLABY
WALL-EYE
WALLING
WALLOON
WALL-RUE
WALTZER
WAMEFUL
WAMPISH
WANGLER
WANHOPE
WANIGAN

WANNESS
WANNION
WANNISH
WANTAGE
WANTING
WANTWIT
WAPPEND
WARATAH
WARBLER
WARDIAN
WARDING
WARDROP
WAR-DRUM
WARFARE
WARHEAD
WARISON
WARLIKE
WARLING
WARLOCK
WARLORD
WARMING
WARNING
WARPATH
WARPING
WARRANT
WARRING
WARRIOR
WARSHIP
WAR-SONG
WARTHOG
WARTIME
WAR-WOLF
WAR-WORN
WASHING
WASH-OUT
WASHPOT
WASH-TUB
WASPISH
WASSAIL
WASTAGE
WASTERY
WASTING
WASTREL
WATCHER
WATCHET
WATERED
WATERER
WATTAGE
WATTEAU
WATTLED
WAULING
WAVELET
WAVERER
WAVESON
WAWLING
WAX-BILL
WAX-DOLL
WAX-MOTH
WAX-PALM
WAX-TREE
WAX-WING
WAXWORK
WAY-BILL
WAYFARE
WAYGONE
WAYLESS

WAYMARK
WAYMENT
WAY-POST
WAYSIDE
WAYWARD
WAYWORN
WEALDEN
WEALTHY
WEARIED
WEARILY
WEARING
WEARISH
WEASAND
WEATHER
WEAVING
WEAZAND
WEBBING
WEB-FOOT
WEBSTER
WEB-TOED
WEBWORM
WEDDING
WEDGING
WEDLOCK
WEEDERY
WEEDING
WEEKDAY
WEEK-END
WEEPING
WEETING
WEEVILY
WEFTAGE
WEIGHED
WEIGHER
WEIGH-IN
WEIGHTY
WEIRDIE
WEIRDLY
WELAWAY
WELCHER
WELCOME
WELDING
WELFARE
WELL-FED
WELLING
WELL-OFF
WELL-SET
WELL-WON
WELSHER
WENCHER
WENDISH
WENLOCK
WENNISH
WERGILD
WERWOLF
WESTERN
WESTING
WESTLIN
WETBACK
WET-DOCK
WETNESS
WET-SHOD
WETTING
WETTISH
WHACKED
WHACKER

WHAISLE
WHAIZLE
WHALERY
WHALING
WHAMPLE
WHANGAM
WHANGEE
WHARVES
WHATE'ER
WHATNOT
WHATTEN
WHEATEN
WHEEDLE
WHEELED
WHEELER
WHEENGE
WHEEPLE
WHEESHT
WHEESON
WHEEZLE
WHELKED
WHEMMLE
WHENE'ER
WHEREAS
WHEREAT
WHEREBY
WHERE'ER
WHEREIN
WHEREOF
WHEREON
WHERESO
WHERETO
WHERRET
WHETHER
WHETTED
WHETTER
WHEYISH
WHEY-TUB
WHICKER
WHIDDER
WHIFFER
WHIFFET
WHIFFLE
WHIMPER
WHIMPLE
WHIMSEY
WHINGER
WHINING
WHIPCAT
WHIPPED
WHIPPER
WHIPPET
WHIP-SAW
WHIP-TOP
WHIRLER
WHIRRED
WHIRRET
WHIRTLE
WHISKER
WHISKET
WHISKEY
WHISPER
WHISTER
WHISTLE
WHITELY
WHITHER

WHITING
WHITISH
WHITLOW
WHITRET
WHITSUN
WHITTAW
WHITTLE
WHIZZED
WHIZZER
WHOEVER
WHOMBLE
WHOMMLE
WHOOBUB
WHOOPEE
WHOOPER
WHOPPER
WHORISH
WHORLED
WHUMMLE
WHYEVER
WIDE-GAB
WIDENER
WIDGEON
WIDOWER
WIELDER
WIGGERY
WIGGING
WIGGLER
WIGHTLY
WIGLESS
WILD-ASS
WILD-CAT
WILD-DOG
WILDING
WILDISH
WILD-OAT
WILEFUL
WILLEST
WILLIES
WILLING
WILLOWY
WIMBREL
WINCING
WINDAGE
WIND-BAG
WIND-EGG
WIND-GUN
WINDILY
WINDING
WINDOCK
WINDORE
WINDROW
WINDSOR
WINE-BAG
WINE-FAT
WINE-SAP
WINE-VAT
WING-LED
WINGLET
WINKING
WINNING
WINNOCK
WINSOME
WINTERY
WIRE-MAN
WIRE-WAY

		X		
WISHFUL	WORK-DAY		YOUNGLY	ZINCODE
WISHING	WORKFUL		YOUNGTH	ZINCOID
WISTFUL	WORKING	XANTHIC	YOUNKER	ZINCOUS
WISTITI	WORKMAN	XANTHIN	YOUTHLY	ZINGANA
WITCHEN	WORK-OUT	XENOPUS	YOWLING	ZINGANE
WITHERS	WORK-SHY	XENURUS	YPLIGHT	ZINGANI
WITHOUT	WORLDED	XERAFIN	YPSILON	ZINGANO
WITLESS	WORLDLY	XERARCH	YSLAKED	ZINGARA
WITLING	WORMIAN	XERASIA	YTTRIUM	ZINGARE
WITLOOF	WORN-OUT	XEROSIS	YU-STONE	ZINGARI
WITNESS	WORRIED	XEROTES	YWROKEN	ZINGARO
WITTILY	WORRIER	XEROTIC		ZINKIFY
WITTING	WORSHIP	XIPHIAS	**Z**	ZINKING
WITWALL	WORSTED	XIPHOID		ZIONISM
WIZENED	WOSBIRD	XYLENOL	ZABTIEH	ZIONIST
WOBBLER	WOTTEST	XYLOGEN	ZADKIEL	ZIPHIUS
WOESOME	WOTTETH	XYLONIC	ZAKUSKA	ZITHERN
WOEWORN	WOTTING	XYLOPIA	ZAKUSKI	ZIZANIA
WOFULLY	WOULD-BE		ZAMARRA	ZOARIUM
WOIWODE	WOUNDER	**Y**	ZAMARRO	ZOCCOLO
WOLF-DOG	WOURALI		ZAMOUSE	ZOEFORM
WOLFIAN	WRANGLE	YACHTER	ZANELLA	ZOILEAN
WOLFING	WRAPPED	YAHVIST	ZANJERO	ZOILISM
WOLFISH	WRAPPER	YAHWIST	ZANTIOT	ZOILIST
WOLFKIN	WREAKED	YAKHDAN	ZANYISM	ZOISITE
WOLFRAM	WREAKER	YANKING	ZAPTIAH	ZOLAISM
WOLVISH	WREATHE	YAPSTER	ZAPTIEH	ZONATED
WOMANLY	WREATHS	YARDAGE	ZAREEBA	ZONULAR
WONDRED	WREATHY	YARDANG	ZARNICH	ZONULET
WOOD-ASH	WRECKER	YARD-ARM	ZEALANT	ZONURUS
WOODCUT	WREN-TIT	YARDMAN	ZEALFUL	ZOOECIA
WOODMAN	WRESTER	YASHMAK	ZEALOUS	ZOOGAMY
WOOD-OIL	WRESTLE	YATAGAN	ZEBRASS	ZOOGENY
WOOD-OWL	WRIGGLE	YAWNING	ZEBRINE	ZOOGONY
WOOD-TAR	WRINGED	YCLEAP'D	ZEBROID	ZOOLITE
WOOD-TIN	WRINGER	YCLEEPE	ZEBRULA	ZOOLITH
WOOD-WAX	WRINKLE	YCLEPED	ZEBRULE	ZOONITE
WOOLDED	WRINKLY	YEADING	ZEDOARY	ZOONOMY
WOOLDER	WRITE-UP	YEALDON	ZEMSTVO	ZOOPERY
WOOLFAT	WRITHEN	YEGGMAN	ZEOLITE	ZOOTAXY
WOOLLED	WRITING	YELLING	ZESTFUL	ZOOTOMY
WOOLLEN	WRITTEN	YELLOCH	ZETETIC	ZOOTYPE
WOOLMAN	WRIZLED	YELLOWY	ZEUXIAN	ZORGITE
WOOL-OIL	WRONGER	YELPING	ZEUXITE	ZORILLE
WOOLSEY	WRONGLY	YESTERN	ZEZIDEE	ZORILLO
WOOMERA	WROUGHT	YEW-TREE	ZIFFIUS	ZOSTERA
WOORALI	WRYBILL	YEZIDEE	ZIGANKA	ZUFFOLO
WOORARA	WRYNECK	YIBBLES	ZIMOCCA	ZYGAENA
WOOSELL	WRYNESS	YIDDISH	ZINCALA	ZYGOSIS
WORDILY	WURLIES	YIELDER	ZINCALI	ZYGOTIC
WORDING	WÜRMIAN	YOGHURT	ZINCALO	ZYMOGEN
WORDISH	WYCH-ELM	YOLK-SAC	ZINCIFY	ZYMOSIS
WORK-BAG		YORKISH	ZINCING	ZYMOTIC
WORK-BOX		YORKIST	ZINCITE	ZYMURGY
		YORUBAN	ZINCKED	

A **8**

A	AARDWOLF	ABATABLE	ABBATIAL	ABDICANT
	AASVOGEL	ABATTOIR	ABDERIAN	ABDICATE
AARDVARK	ABAMPERE	ABBASIDE	ABDERITE	ABDUCENT

ABDUCTOR	ACCREDIT	ADHESION	AFFLATUS	AIRWARDS
ABERDEEN	ACCURACY	ADHESIVE	AFFLUENT	AIRWOMAN
ABERRANT	ACCURATE	ADIANTUM	AFFOREST	ALACRITY
ABERRATE	ACCURSED	ADJACENT	AFFRAYED	ALARMING
ABETMENT	ACCUSTOM	ADJURING	AFFRIGHT	ALARMIST
ABETTING	ACERBATE	ADJUSTER	AFFRONTÉ	ALASTRIM
ABEYANCE	ACERBITY	ADJUSTOR	AFFUSION	ALBACORE
ABEYANCY	ACERVATE	ADJUTAGE	AFTEREYE	ALBICORE
ABHORRED	ACESCENT	ADJUTANT	AGALLOCH	ALBINESS
ABHORRER	ACHENIAL	ADJUVANT	AGAMIDAE	ALBINISM
ABIDANCE	ACHENIUM	ADMITTED	AGANIPPE	ALBITISE
ABJECTLY	ACHERNAR	ADMONISH	AGAR-AGAR	ALBURNUM
ABLATION	ACICULAR	ADNATION	AGEDNESS	ALCAHEST
ABLATIVE	ACID-HEAD	ADOPTION	AGENTIAL	ALCATRAS
ABLUTION	ACIDOSIS	ADOPTIVE	AGGRIEVE	ALCHEMIC
ABNEGATE	ACIERAGE	ADORABLE	AGIOTAGE	ALDEHYDE
ABNORMAL	ACIERATE	ADORABLY	AGITATED	ALDER-FLY
ABOIDEAU	ACKNOWNE	ADROITLY	AGITATOR	ALDERMAN
ABOITEAU	ACOEMETI	ADSCRIPT	AGITPROP	ALDERMEN
ABOMASUM	ACONITIC	ADULARIA	AGLIMMER	ALDERNEY
ABOMASUS	ACONITUM	ADULATOR	AGLITTER	ALEATORY
ABORIGEN	ACORN-CUP	ADULTERY	AGNATION	ALEBENCH
ABORIGIN	ACOSMISM	ADUNCATE	AGNOSTIC	ALE-BERRY
ABORTION	ACOSMIST	ADUNCITY	AGONISED	ALE-HOUSE
ABORTIVE	ACOUSTIC	ADUNCOUS	AGRAPHIA	ALEMAINE
ABRADANT	ACQUAINT	ADVANCED	AGRAPHIC	ALE-STAKE
ABRAM-MAN	ACQUIRED	ADVISING	AGRAPHON	ALEURONE
ABRASION	ACRIDINE	ADVISORY	AGRARIAN	ALEWIVES
ABRASIVE	ACRIDITY	ADVOCAAT	AGRÉMENS	ALFRESCO
ABRICOCK	ACRIMONY	ADVOCACY	AGRÉMENT	ALGAROBA
ABRIDGER	ACROLEIN	ADVOCATE	AGRESTIC	ALGERIAN
ABROGATE	ACROLITH	ADVOUTRY	AGRIMONY	ALGERINE
ABRUPTLY	ACROMIAL	ADVOWSON	AGROLOGY	ALGIDITY
ABSCISSA	ACROMION	ADYNAMIA	AGRONOMY	ALGINATE
ABSCISSE	ACROSTIC	ADYNAMIC	AGUACATE	ALGOLOGY
ABSENTEE	ACROTISM	AECIDIUM	AGUE-CAKE	ALGONKIN
ABSENTLY	ACTINIAN	AEGIRINE	AGUISHLY	ALGORISM
ABSINTHE	ACTINIDE	AEGIRITE	AIGRETTE	ALGUACIL
ABSOLUTE	ACTINISM	AEGLOGUE	AIGUILLE	ALGUAZIL
ABSOLVER	ACTINIUM	AEGROTAT	AIR-BENDS	ALHAMBRA
ABSONANT	ACTINOID	AERATION	AIRBORNE	ALIENAGE
ABSORBED	ACTIVATE	AERIALLY	AIR-BRAKE	ALIENATE
ABSORBER	ACTIVELY	AERIFORM	AIR-BRICK	ALIENISM
ABSTERGE	ACTIVISM	AEROBOMB	AIR-BRUSH	ALIENIST
ABSTRACT	ACTIVIST	AERODART	AIR-BUILT	ALIGHTED
ABSTRICT	ACTIVITY	AERODYNE	AIR-COVER	ALIQUANT
ABSTRUSE	ACTUALLY	AEROFOIL	AIRCRAFT	ALIZARIN
ABSURDLY	ACTUATOR	AEROGRAM	AIR-DRAIN	ALKAHEST
ABUNDANT	ACULEATE	AEROLITE	AIR-DRAWN	ALKALIES
ABUTILON	ADAMICAL	AEROLITH	AIRDROME	ALKALIFY
ABUTMENT	ADAMITIC	AEROLOGY	AIREDALE	ALKALINE
ABUTTING	ADAPTION	AERONAUT	AIRFIELD	ALKALISE
ACADEMIC	ADAPTIVE	AERONOMY	AIR-FORCE	ALKALOID
ACALEPHA	ADDENDUM	AEROSTAT	AIRGRAPH	ALLAYING
ACALEPHE	ADDICTED	AESCULIN	AIR-HOUSE	ALL-CLEAR
ACANTHIN	ADDITION	AESCULUS	AIRINESS	ALLEGORY
ACANTHUS	ADDITIVE	AESTHETE	AIRLINER	ALLELUIA
ACARIDAN	ADDORSED	AESTIVAL	AIRPLANE	ALLERGEN
ACARPOUS	ADDUCENT	AFFECTED	AIR-PLANT	ALLERGIC
ACCENTOR	ADDUCTOR	AFFECTER	AIR-POWER	ALLERION
ACCEPTER	ADENITIS	AFFEERED	AIRSCREW	ALLEY-TAW
ACCEPTOR	ADENOIDS	AFFERENT	AIRSHAFT	ALLEY-TOR
ACCIDENT	ADEQUACY	AFFIANCE	AIR-SPACE	ALLEYWAY
ACCOLADE	ADEQUATE	AFFINITY	AIRSTRIP	ALL-FIRED
ACCORDER	ADESPOTA	AFFIRMER	AIRTIGHT	ALL-FIVES
ACCOUTRE	ADHERENT	AFFLATED	AIR-TO-AIR	ALL-FOURS

ALL-GIVER	AMICABLY	ANGEKKOK	ANTLERED	APRILIAN
ALLIANCE	AMIDMOST	ANGELICA	ANTLIATE	APRILISH
ALLIGATE	AMISSING	ANGLICAN	ANTRORSE	APRON-MAN
ALL-NIGHT	AMITOSIS	ANGSTROM	ANTS-EGGS	APTERIUM
ALLOCATE	AMITOTIC	ANGUILLA	ANYTHING	APTEROUS
ALLODIAL	AMMONIAC	ANGUIPED	ANYWHERE	APTITUDE
ALLODIUM	AMMONITE	ANICONIC	AORTITIS	APYRETIC
ALLOGAMY	AMMONIUM	ANIMALLY	APAGOGIC	APYREXIA
ALLOPATH	AMNESIAC	ANIMATED	APANAGED	AQUACADE
ALLOTTED	AMNIOTIC	ANIMATOR	APERIENT	AQUALUNG
ALL-RISKS	AMOEBOID	ANISETTE	APERITIF	AQUANAUT
ALL-ROUND	AMORETTI	ANKERITE	APERTURE	AQUARIAN
ALLSPICE	AMORETTO	ANKYLOSE	APHASIAC	AQUARIST
ALLURING	AMORTISE	ANNALISE	APHELIAN	AQUARIUM
ALLUSION	AMPERAGE	ANNALIST	APHELION	AQUARIUS
ALLUSIVE	AMPHIBIA	ANNEALER	APHETISE	AQUATINT
ALLUVIAL	AMPHICAR	ANNELIDA	APHICIDE	AQUEDUCT
ALLUVION	AMPHIPOD	ANNEXION	APHIDIAN	AQUILINE
ALLUVIUM	AMPHORAE	ANNEXURE	APHONOUS	ARACEOUS
ALMAGEST	AMPHORIC	ANNOTATE	APHORISE	ARACHNID
ALMIGHTY	AMPULLAE	ANNOUNCE	APHORISM	ARAMAEAN
ALMS-DEED	AMPUTATE	ANNUALLY	APHORIST	ARAMAISM
ALMS-DISH	AMULETIC	ANNULATA	APHTHOUS	ARANEIDA
ALMS-FOLK	AMUSABLE	ANNULATE	APIARIAN	ARANEOUS
ALOGICAL	AMUSEDLY	ANNULLED	APIARIST	ARANIDAE
ALOPECIA	AMUSETTE	ANNULOSE	APICALLY	ARAPAIMA
ALPHABET	AMYGDALA	ANOPLURA	APLASTIC	ARAPUNGA
ALPINISM	AMYGDALE	ANOREXIA	APLUSTRE	ARBALEST
ALPINIST	AMYGDULE	ANORTHIC	APOCYNUM	ARBALIST
ALSATIAN	ANABASIS	ANOUROUS	APODOSIS	ARBITRAL
ALTARAGE	ANABATIC	ANSERINE	APOGAEIC	ARBOREAL
ALTERANT	ANABLEPS	ANSWERER	APOGRAPH	ARBORETA
ALTERITY	ANABOLIC	ANT-EATER	APOLLINE	ARBORIST
ALTERNAT	ANACONDA	ANTEDATE	APOLLYON	ARBOROUS
ALTHOUGH	ANAEROBE	ANTEFIXA	APOLOGIA	ARBOURED
ALTITUDE	ANAGLYPH	ANTELOPE	APOLOGUE	ARCADIAN
ALTRICES	ANAGOGIC	ANTENATI	APOMIXIS	ARCADING
ALTRUISM	ANALCIME	ANTENNAE	APOPHYGE	ARCANIST
ALTRUIST	ANALCITE	ANTENNAL	APOPLEXY	ARCHAEAN
ALUMINUM	ANALECTA	ANTENNAS	APOSITIA	ARCHAEUS
ALUM-ROOT	ANALECTS	ANTEPAST	APOSPORY	ARCHAISE
ALVEATED	ANALOGIC	ANTE-POST	APOSTASY	ARCHAISM
ALVEOLAR	ANALOGON	ANTERIOR	APOSTATE	ARCHAIST
ALVEOLUS	ANALOGUE	ANTEROOM	APOTHEGM	ARCHDUKE
AMADAVAT	ANALYSER	ANTHELIA	APPALLED	ARCHIVAL
AMANDINE	ANALYSES	ANTHELIX	APPANAGE	ARCHLUTE
AMARACUS	ANALYSIS	ANTHEMIA	APPARENT	ARCHNESS
AMARANTH	ANALYTIC	ANTHESIS	APPEARER	ARCH-POET
AMAZEDLY	ANAPAEST	ANTHOZOA	APPENDIX	ARCHWISE
AMBERITE	ANAPHASE	ANTIBODY	APPETENT	ARC-LIGHT
AMBEROID	ANAPHORA	ANTICIZE	APPETISE	ARCTURUS
AMBEROUS	ANARCHAL	ANTICOUS	APPETITE	ARDENTLY
AMBIANCE	ANARCHIC	ANTIDOTE	APPLAUSE	ARECA-NUT
AMBIENCE	ANASARCA	ANTI-HERO	APPLE-PIE	ARENARIA
AMBITION	ANATHEMA	ANTILOGY	APPLIQUE	AREOLATE
AMBIVERT	ANATOMIC	ANTILOPE	APPLYING	ARGEMONE
AMBROSIA	ANCESTOR	ANTIMASK	APPOSITE	ARGESTES
AMBULANT	ANCESTRY	ANTIMONY	APPRAISE	ARGONAUT
AMBULATE	ANCHORET	ANTINODE	APPRIZER	ARGUABLE
AMELCORN	ANDESINE	ANTINOMY	APPROACH	ARGUABLY
AMENABLE	ANDESITE	ANTIPHON	APPROVAL	ARGUMENT
AMENABLY	ANDROGEN	ANTIPODE	APPROVER	ARGUTELY
AMERICAN	ANECDOTE	ANTIPOLE	APPUYING	ARIANISE
AMETHYST	ANECHOIC	ANTIPOPE	APRÈS-SKI	ARIANISM
AMIANTUS	ANEURISM	ANTITHET	APRICATE	ARIDNESS
AMICABLE	ANEURYSM	ANTITYPE	APRICOCK	ARILLARY

ARILLATE	ASPIRANT	ATTESTER	AVOWABLE	BAGUETTE
ARILLODE	ASPIRATE	ATTESTOR	AVOWEDLY	BAILABLE
ARISTATE	ASPIRING	ATTICISE	AVULSION	BAIL-BALL
ARK-SHELL	ASSASSIN	ATTICISM	AWANTING	BAIL-BOND
ARMAGNAC	ASSAYING	ATTIRING	AWEARIED	BAIL-DOCK
ARMAMENT	ASSEMBLE	ATTITUDE	AWEATHER	BAILMENT
ARMATURE	ASSEMBLÉ	ATTORNEY	AXESTONE	BAILSMAN
ARMCHAIR	ASSEMBLY	ATYPICAL	AXILLARY	BAITFISH
ARMENIAN	ASSENTER	AUDACITY	AXIOLOGY	BAJOCIAN
ARMENOID	ASSENTOR	AUDIENCE	AXLE-TREE	BAKELITE
ARM-IN-ARM	ASSERTER	AUDITION	AYENBITE	BAKEMEAT
ARMINIAN	ASSERTOR	AUDITORY		BALADINE
ARMORIAL	ASSESSOR	AUGER-BIT	**B**	BALANCED
ARMORIST	ASSIENTO	AUGUSTAN		BALANCER
ARMOURED	ASSIGNAT	AUGUSTLY	BABBITRY	BALCONET
ARMOURER	ASSIGNEE	AULARIAN	BABBLING	BALD-COOT
ARMOZEEN	ASSIGNOR	AURELIAN	BABEEISM	BALD-HEAD
ARMOZINE	ASSISTED	AUREOLED	BABELDOM	BALDNESS
AROMATIC	ASSONANT	AURICLED	BABELISH	BALDPATE
ARPEGGIO	ASSONATE	AURICULA	BABELISM	BALDRICK
ARQUEBUS	ASSORTED	AURIFORM	BABOUCHE	BALE-DOCK
ARRASENE	ASSOTTED	AUROREAN	BABUSHKA	BALE-FIRE
ARRAUGHT	ASSUMING	AUSONIAN	BABY-FARM	BALINESE
ARRESTEE	ASSYRIAN	AUSTRIAN	BABYHOOD	BALKLINE
ARRESTER	ASTATINE	AUTACOID	BABY-TALK	BALLADRY
ARRESTOR	ASTERIAS	AUTARCHY	BACCARAT	BALL-COCK
ARROGANT	ASTERISM	AUTARKIC	BACCHANT	BALL-GAME
ARROGATE	ASTEROID	AUTISTIC	BACCHIAC	BALLISTA
ARSENATE	ASTHENIA	AUTOBAHN	BACCHIAN	BALLONET
ARSENIDE	ASTHENIC	AUTOCADE	BACCHIUS	BALLOTED
ARSENITE	ASTOMOUS	AUTOCARP	BACHELOR	BALL-ROOM
ARSONIST	ASTONISH	AUTOCRAT	BACILLAR	BALLYHOO
ARSONITE	ASTRAGAL	AUTO-DA-FÉ	BACILLUS	BALLYRAG
ARTEFACT	ASTRINGE	AUTODYNE	BACKACHE	BALMORAL
ARTERIAL	ASTUCITY	AUTOGAMY	BACKBAND	BALNEARY
ARTESIAN	ASTUTELY	AUTOGENY	BACKBITE	BALSAMIC
ARTFULLY	ASYSTOLE	AUTOGIRO	BACKBOND	BALUSTER
ARTICLED	ATALANTA	AUTOGYRO	BACKBONE	BANALITY
ARTIFACT	ATARAXIA	AUTOHARP	BACKCHAT	BANAUSIC
ARTIFICE	ATARAXIC	AUTOLOGY	BACK-DOOR	BANDANNA
ARTISTIC	ATHANASY	AUTOLYSE	BACKDROP	BANDEAUX
ARTISTRY	ATHELING	AUTOMATA	BACKFALL	BANDELET
ARVICOLA	ATHENIAN	AUTOMATE	BACKFIRE	BANDEROL
ARYANISE	ATHERINA	AUTONOMY	BACK-HAIR	BAND-FISH
ASBESTIC	ATHERINE	AUTOPSIA	BACKHAND	BANDITRY
ASBESTOS	ATHEROMA	AUTOPTIC	BACKLASH	BANDITTI
ASCENDER	ATHETISE	AUTOSOME	BACK-LILL	BANDSMAN
ASCIDIAN	ATHETOID	AUTOTOMY	BACKMOST	BANDSTER
ASCIDIUM	ATHLETIC	AUTOTYPE	BACKROOM	BANDYING
ASCORBIC	ATLANTES	AUTUMNAL	BACKROPE	BANDYMAN
ASEPTATE	ATLANTIC	AUTUNITE	BACKSIDE	BANGSTER
ASHAMING	ATLANTIS	AUXILIAR	BACKVELD	BANG-TAIL
ASH-LEACH	ATMOLOGY	AVADAVAT	BACKWARD	BANISTER
ASH-PLANT	ATMOLYSE	AVAILING	BACKWASH	BANJOIST
ASH-STAND	ATOMICAL	AVENGING	BACKWORD	BANK-BILL
ASHY-GREY	ATOMISER	AVENTAIL	BACKYARD	BANK-BOOK
ASMODEUS	ATREMBLE	AVERMENT	BACONIAN	BANK-HIGH
ASPARTIC	ATROCITY	AVERRING	BACTERIA	BANK-NOTE
ASPERATE	ATROPINE	AVERSELY	BACTERIC	BANK-RATE
ASPERGER	ATROPISM	AVERSION	BACTRIAN	BANKROLL
ASPERGES	ATROPOUS	AVERSIVE	BACULINE	BANKRUPT
ASPERITY	ATTACHED	AVIARIST	BACULITE	BANKSMAN
ASPEROUS	ATTEMPER	AVIATION	BADGERLY	BANNERED
ASPHODEL	ATTENDER	AVIATRIX	BADINAGE	BANNERET
ASPHYXIA	ATTERCOP	AVIFAUNA	BAFFLING	BANNEROL
ASPIDIUM	ATTESTED	AVIONICS	BAGPIPER	BANTERER
			BAGPIPES	

BANTHINE	BASS-TUBA	BEDSTEAD	BENJAMIN	BHEESTIE
BANTLING	BASS-VIOL	BEDSTRAW	BENTWOOD	BIANNUAL
BANXRING	BASSWOOD	BED-TABLE	BENUMBED	BIASSING
BAPHOMET	BASTARDY	BEDWARDS	BENZOATE	BIATHLON
BARATHEA	BASTILLE	BEE-BREAD	BEPEPPER	BIBATION
BARBADOS	BATAVIAN	BEECH-OIL	BEPESTER	BIBLICAL
BARBARIC	BATCHING	BEE-EATER	BEPLUMED	BIBULOUS
BARBATED	BATELESS	BEEFCAKE	BEPOMMEL	BICK-IRON
BARBECUE	BATELEUR	BEEF-WOOD	BEPOWDER	BICONVEX
BARBERRY	BATEMENT	BEEHOUSE	BEPRAISE	BICUSPID
BARBETTE	BATHETIC	BEER-PUMP	BEQUEATH	BIDDABLE
BARBICAN	BATHMISM	BEESWING	BERBERIS	BIDENTAL
BARBITAL	BATHORSE	BEETLING	BERCEUSE	BIENNIAL
BARDLING	BATHROBE	BEETROOT	BEREAVED	BIFACIAL
BARDSHIP	BATHROOM	BEFALLEN	BEREAVEN	BIFOCALS
BAREBACK	BATOLOGY	BEFITTED	BERGAMOT	BIGAMIST
BAREBONE	BATTALIA	BEFLOWER	BERGFALL	BIGAMOUS
BAREFOOT	BATTELER	BEFRIEND	BERGHAAN	BIGNONIA
BAREGINE	BATTLE-AX	BEFRINGE	BERGMEHL	BIJWONER
BARENESS	BATWOMAN	BEFUDDLE	BERIBERI	BILABIAL
BARGAIST	BAUBLING	BEGETTER	BERMUDAS	BILANDER
BARGEMAN	BAUDEKIN	BEGGARLY	BERRYING	BILBERRY
BARGHEST	BAUDRICK	BEGINNER	BERYLLIA	BILE-DUCT
BAR-GRAPH	BAUDRONS	BEGIRDED	BESCRAWL	BILLBOOK
BARITONE	BAWD-BORN	BEGORRAH	BESCREEN	BILLETED
BARKLESS	BAYADÈRE	BEGOTTEN	BESEEMLY	BILLFOLD
BARNACLE	BAYBERRY	BEGRUDGE	BESETTER	BILLHEAD
BARNDOOR	BDELLIUM	BEGUILER	BESHADOW	BILLHOOK
BARNYARD	BEAD-ROLL	BEHAPPEN	BESIEGER	BILLIARD
BAROMETZ	BEADSMAN	BEHEADAL	BESLAVER	BILLOWED
BARONAGE	BEAGLING	BEHEMOTH	BESMIRCH	BILLYBOY
BARONESS	BEAM-ENDS	BEHOLDEN	BESMUTCH	BILLY-CAN
BARONIAL	BEAMLESS	BEHOLDER	BESOGNIO	BIMANOUS
BAROUCHE	BEAN-KING	BEHOVELY	BESOTTED	BIMBASHI
BARRACAN	BEANPOLE	BEINNESS	BESOUGHT	BINAURAL
BARRANCA	BEARABLE	BEJESUIT	BESOULED	BINDWEED
BARRANCO	BEARABLY	BELABOUR	BESPOKEN	BINNACLE
BARRATOR	BEARBINE	BELAYING	BESPREAD	BINOMIAL
BARRATRY	BEAR'S-EAR	BELFRIED	BESPRENT	BIOBLAST
BARTERER	BEARSKIN	BELIEVER	BESSEMER	BIOCIDAL
BARTISAN	BEARWARD	BELITTLE	BESTIARY	BIOGRAPH
BARTIZAN	BEATIFIC	BELLBIND	BESTOWAL	BIOMETRY
BARTLEMY	BEAUFORT	BELL-BIRD	BESTOWER	BIOMORPH
BARYTONE	BEAU-PERE	BELL-BUOY	BESTREAK	BIONOMIC
BASALTIC	BEAUTIFY	BELLCOTE	BESTREWN	BIOPHORE
BASANITE	BEAUXITE	BELLETER	BESTRIDE	BIOPLASM
BASEBALL	BEAVERED	BELLOWER	BESTRODE	BIOPLAST
BASE-BORN	BECALMED	BELLPULL	BESTROWN	BIOSCOPE
BASELARD	BECHAMEL	BELLPUSH	BETACISM	BIPAROUS
BASELESS	BECHANCE	BELL-ROPE	BETATRON	BIRDBATH
BASE-LINE	BECK-IRON	BELLTENT	BETEL-NUT	BIRD-BOLT
BASEMENT	BECOMING	BELLWORT	BETHESDA	BIRDCAGE
BASENESS	BEDABBLE	BELLYFUL	BETHRALL	BIRDCALL
BASHLESS	BEDAGGLE	BELLY-GOD	BETHWACK	BIRD-EYED
BASICITY	BEDARKEN	BELLYING	BETRAYAL	BIRD-LICE
BASIDIAL	BEDAZZLE	BELOVING	BETRAYER	BIRD-LIME
BASIDIUM	BEDCOVER	BEMOANER	BETTERED	BIRDSEED
BASILIAN	BEDEAFEN	BEMUDDLE	BEVATRON	BIRD'S-EYE
BASILICA	BEDEGUAR	BEMUFFLE	BEVELLED	BIRTHDAY
BASILISK	BEDESMAN	BENDWISE	BEVELLER	BIRTHDOM
BASINFUL	BEDIMMED	BENEDICK	BEVERAGE	BISCACHA
BASKETRY	BEDMAKER	BENEDICT	BEWAILED	BISCAYAN
BASQUINE	BED-PLATE	BENEFACT	BEWETTED	BISECTOR
BASS-DRUM	BEDRENCH	BENEFICE	BEWIGGED	BISERIAL
BASS-HORN	BEDRIGHT	BENIGNLY	BEWILDER	BISEXUAL
BASSINET	BED-STAFF	BENITIER	BEZONIAN	BISTABLE

BISTOURY	BLOTCHED	BONEHEAD	BOUGHPOT	BREEDING
BITTACLE	BLOTTING	BONE-IDLE	BOUGHTEN	BREGMATA
BITTERLY	BLOWBALL	BONE-LACE	BOUILLON	BRELOQUE
BIVALENT	BLOWHOLE	BONELESS	BOULTING	BRETESSE
BI-WEEKLY	BLOWLAMP	BONE-MEAL	BOUNCING	BRETHREN
BIXACEAE	BLOWPIPE	BONE-MILL	BOUNDARY	BRETTICE
BIZCACHA	BLUDGEON	BONGRACE	BOUNDING	BREVETED
BLABBING	BLUEBACK	BONHOMIE	BOUNTREE	BREVIARY
BLACKBOY	BLUEBELL	BONIBELL	BOURGEON	BREVIATE
BLACKCAP	BLUEBIRD	BONIFACE	BOURTREE	BREWSTER
BLACK-CAT	BLUE-BUCK	BONINESS	BOUTIQUE	BREZONEK
BLACK-FOX	BLUE-CHIP	BONNETED	BOUTONNÉ	BRIAREAN
BLACKING	BLUECOAT	BONSPIEL	BOUZOUKI	BRICKBAT
BLACKISH	BLUE-EYED	BONTEBOK	BOWELLED	BRICKING
BLACKLEG	BLUE-FISH	BOOBYISH	BOWSPRIT	BRICK-NOG
BLACK-NEB	BLUEGOWN	BOOBYISM	BOX-CLOTH	BRICK-RED
BLACKOUT	BLUE-GREY	BOOKCASE	BOX-LOBBY	BRICK-TEA
BLACKTOP	BLUENESS	BOOK-CLUB	BOX-PLEAT	BRIDE-ALE
BLADDERY	BLUENOSE	BOOK-DEBT	BOX-WAGON	BRIDE-BED
BLAH-BLAH	BLUEWEED	BOOKED-UP	BOYISHLY	BRIDEMAN
BLAMABLE	BLUEWING	BOOKLAND	BRACCATE	BRIDGING
BLAMABLY	BLUNTISH	BOOKLESS	BRACELET	BRIEF-BAG
BLAMEFUL	BLURRING	BOOKLICE	BRACHIAL	BRIEFING
BLANDISH	BLURTING	BOOKLORE	BRACKISH	BRIGHTEN
BLANKETY	BLUSHFUL	BOOKMARK	BRACTEAL	BRIGHTLY
BLASTEMA	BLUSHING	BOOK-MATE	BRACTLET	BRIGUING
BLASTING	BLUSTERY	BOOK-OATH	BRADSHAW	BRIM-FULL
BLAST-OFF	BOARDING	BOOK-POST	BRAGGART	BRIMIDIC
BLASTOID	BOARFISH	BOOKSHOP	BRAGGING	BRIMLESS
BLASTULA	BOASTFUL	BOOKWORM	BRAIDING	BRIMMING
BLAZONER	BOASTING	BOOM-IRON	BRAIDISM	BRINDLED
BLAZONRY	BOATBILL	BOOSTAND	BRAIN-FAG	BRINE-PAN
BLEACHER	BOAT-DECK	BOOT-HOOK	BRAINISH	BRINE-PIT
BLEATING	BOAT-HOOK	BOOTHOSE	BRAINPAN	BRINGING
BLEEDING	BOAT-LOAD	BOOTIKIN	BRAKE-VAN	BRINKMAN
BLENDING	BOAT-RACE	BOOT-JACK	BRANCARD	BRISKISH
BLENHEIM	BOAT-SONG	BOOTLACE	BRANCHED	BRISLING
BLESSING	BOAT-TAIL	BOOTLAST	BRANCHER	BRISTLED
BLETTING	BOBBINET	BOOTLESS	BRANCHIA	BRITCHES
BLIGHTER	BOBOLINK	BOOTLICK	BRANDIED	BRITZSKA
BLIMBING	BOBSTAYS	BOOTTREE	BRANDISE	BROACHER
BLINDAGE	BOBWHEEL	BORACHIO	BRANDISH	BROADISH
BLIND-GUT	BOB-WHITE	BORACITE	BRANDNEW	BROADWAY
BLINDING	BODEMENT	BORDEAUX	BRAN-MASH	BROCADED
BLINKARD	BODILESS	BORDELLO	BRASSARD	BROCATEL
BLINKING	BODY-LINE	BORDERED	BRASSART	BROCCOLI
BLISSFUL	BOEOTIAN	BORDERER	BRASSICA	BROCHURE
BLISTERY	BOGEYISM	BORECOLE	BRASSILY	BROCKRAM
BLITHELY	BOGEYMAN	BOREHOLE	BRATCHET	BRODEKIN
BLIZZARD	BOG-LATIN	BORNHOLM	BRATLING	BROIDERY
BLOATING	BOHEMIAN	BORROWED	BRATTICE	BROKENLY
BLOCKADE	BOLDNESS	BORROWER	BRATTISH	BROMELIA
BLOCKAGE	BOLL-WORM	BORSTALL	BRAVADOS	BRONCHIA
BLOCKING	BOLT-HEAD	BOSCHBOK	BRAWLING	BRONCHUS
BLOCKISH	BOLTHOLE	BOSS-EYED	BRAZENLY	BRONZIFY
BLOCK-TIN	BOLT-ROPE	BOSTANGI	BRAZENRY	BRONZING
BLONCKET	BOMB-SITE	BOTANISE	BREADNUT	BRONZITE
BLOOD-HOT	BOMBYCID	BOTANIST	BREAKAGE	BROOKITE
BLOODILY	BONA-ROBA	BOTCHERY	BREAKING	BROOKLET
BLOOD-RED	BONASSUS	BOTCHING	BREAK-JAW	BROUGHAM
BLOOD-TAX	BONDAGER	BOTHYMAN	BREAK-VOW	BROUHAHA
BLOOD-WIT	BONDMAID	BOTRYOID	BREASTED	BROWBEAT
BLOOMERS	BONDSMAN	BOTRYOSE	BREATHED	BROWLESS
BLOOMERY	BONE-ACHE	BOTTOMED	BREATHER	BROWNIAN
BLOOMING	BONE-CAVE	BOTULISM	BREECHED	BROWNING
BLOSSOMY	BONE-DUST	BOUFFANT	BREECHES	BROWNISH

BROWNISM
BROWNIST
BROWSING
BROW-TINE
BRUILZIE
BRUISING
BRUMAIRE
BRUNELLA
BRUNETTE
BRUSHING
BRUSH-OFF
BRUSSELS
BRUTALLY
BRYOLOGY
BUBALINE
BUCCINUM
BUCELLAS
BUCKAROO
BUCKBEAN
BUCKCART
BUCKHORN
BUCKLING
BUCKSHOT
BUCKSKIN
BUCK-WASH
BUDDHISM
BUDDHIST
BUDDLEIA
BUDGEREE
BUDGEROW
BUDGETED
BUD-SCALE
BUFF-COAT
BUFFERED
BUGHOUSE
BUILDING
BULGARIC
BULKHEAD
BULL-BEEF
BULL-CALF
BULLDOZE
BULLETIN
BULLFROG
BULLHEAD
BULL-HOOF
BULL-RING
BULL'S-EYE
BULLYING
BULLYISM
BULLYOFF
BULLYRAG
BULRUSHY
BUM-CLOCK
BUMMAREE
BUNCHING
BUNCOMBE
BUN-FIGHT
BUNGALOW
BUNG-HOLE
BUNGLING
BUNG-VENT
BUNKERED
BUNNY-HUG
BUNODONT
BUNTLINE
BUOYANCE

BUOYANCY
BUPLEVER
BURBLING
BURGANET
BURGLARY
BURGONET
BURGRAVE
BURGUNDY
BURINIST
BURLETTA
BURNOUSE
BURNSIAN
BURNSIDE
BURNSITE
BURNT-EAR
BURSCHEN
BURSITIS
BUSHBABY
BUSH-BUCK
BUSH-ROPE
BUSHVELD
BUSINESS
BUSKINED
BUSYBODY
BUSYNESS
BUTCHERY
BUTCHING
BUTTRESS
BUTYLENE
BUTYRATE
BUZZ-BOMB
BY-CORNER
BYLANDER
BY-MOTIVE
BYRLAKIN
BYRONISM
BY-SPEECH
BY-STREET

C

CAATINGA
CABALISM
CABALIST
CABALLED
CABALLER
CABIN-BOY
CABIRIAN
CABLEWAY
CABOCEER
CABOCHED
CABOCHON
CABOODLE
CABOSHED
CABOTAGE
CABRIOLE
CAB-STAND
CACAFOGO
CACHALOT
CACHE-POT
CACHEXIA
CACHOLOT
CACHUCHA
CACODOXY
CACOLOGY
CACOMIXL
CACTUSES

CADASTRE
CADDY-CAR
CADENCED
CADUCEAN
CADUCEUS
CADUCITY
CADUCOUS
CAECILIA
CAESIOUS
CAESURAL
CAFFEINE
CAFFEISM
CAGEBIRD
CAGELING
CAGINESS
CAGYNESS
CAILLACH
CAIMACAM
CAJOLERY
CAKEWALK
CALABASH
CALADIUM
CALAMARY
CALAMINE
CALAMINT
CALAMITE
CALAMITY
CALCEATE
CALCIFIC
CALCSPAR
CALC-TUFF
CALCULAR
CALCULUS
CALENDAR
CALENDER
CALENDRY
CALFLESS
CALF-LICK
CALF-LOVE
CALFSKIN
CALF-TIME
CALIBRED
CALICOES
CALIDITY
CALIPASH
CALIPERS
CALIPPIC
CALISAYA
CALIXTIN
CALL-BIRD
CALL-GIRL
CALLIOPE
CALLIPER
CALL-LOAN
CALL-NOTE
CALMNESS
CALORIST
CALOTYPE
CALTHROP
CALVADOS
CALVERED
CALYCINE
CALYCLED
CALYCOID
CALYCULE

CALYPTRA
CAMBRIAN
CAMELEER
CAMELEON
CAMELINE
CAMELISH
CAMELLIA
CAMELOID
CAMISADE
CAMISADO
CAMISARD
CAMISOLE
CAMOMILE
CAMPAGNA
CAMPAIGN
CAMP-FIRE
CAMPHANE
CAMPHENE
CAMPHIRE
CAMPODEA
CAMP-SHOT
CAMSHAFT
CAMSHOCH
CAMSTANE
CAMSTONE
CAMWHEEL
CANADIAN
CANAIGRE
CANAILLE
CANALISE
CANARESE
CANASTER
CANCELLI
CANCROID
CANDIDLY
CANE-MILL
CANEPHOR
CANICULA
CANINITY
CANISTER
CANITIES
CANKERED
CANNABIC
CANNABIN
CANNABIS
CANNIBAL
CANNIKIN
CANNONRY
CANOEING
CANOEIST
CANONESS
CANONISE
CANONIST
CANOODLE
CANOPIED
CANOROUS
CANSTICK
CANTHARI
CANTICLE
CANTICOY
CANTICUM
CANTONAL
CANTONED
CANTORIS
CANT-RAIL
CANZONET

CAPACITY
CAPELINE
CAPELLET
CAPER-TEA
CAPITANO
CAPITATE
CAPITULA
CAPONIER
CAPONISE
CAP-PAPER
CAPPARIS
CAPRIFIG
CAPRIOLE
CAPROATE
CAPRYLIC
CAPSICIN
CAPSICUM
CAPSULAR
CAPTIOUS
CAPUCHIN
CAPYBARA
CARABINE
CARACARA
CARACOLE
CARAPACE
CARAP-OIL
CARBOLIC
CARBONIC
CARBONYL
CARBOXYL
CARBURET
CARCAJOU
CARCANET
CARDAMOM
CARD-CASE
CARDECUE
CARDIGAN
CARDINAL
CARDIOID
CARDITIS
CARD-VOTE
CARELESS
CAREWORN
CARGEESE
CARGOOSE
CARIACOU
CARIBBEE
CARILLON
CARINATE
CARJACOU
CARL-HEMP
CARNALLY
CARNAUBA
CARNEOUS
CARNIFEX
CARNIVAL
CAROLINA
CAROLINE
CAROLLED
CAROLLER
CAROTENE
CAROUSAL
CAROUSEL
CAROUSER
CARPETED
CARRAWAY

CARRIAGE	CAUDATED	CETYWALL	CHERUBIM	CHORDATE
CARRIOLE	CAUDEXES	CHACONNE	CHERUBIN	CHOREGIC
CARRITCH	CAUDICES	CHAFFERY	CHESSMAN	CHOREGUS
CARRY-ALL	CAUDICLE	CHAFFING	CHESTFUL	CHORIAMB
CARRYING	CAUDILLO	CHAFFRON	CHESTNUT	CHORIOID
CARTLOAD	CAULDRON	CHAINLET	CHEVALET	CHORISIS
CARTOUCH	CAULICLE	CHAINSAW	CHEVEREL	CHORUSED
CART-ROAD	CAULKING	CHAIR-BED	CHEVERIL	CHOULTRY
CARUCAGE	CAUSALLY	CHAIRMAN	CHEVERON	CHOW-CHOW
CARUCATE	CAUSERIE	CHALDAIC	CHEVILLE	CHOW-MEIN
CARUNCLE	CAUSEWAY	CHALDEAN	CHEVRONY	CHOY-ROOT
CARYATIC	CAUSEYED	CHALDRON	CHIASMUS	CHRISMAL
CARYATID	CAUTIOUS	CHALICED	CHIASTIC	CHRISTEN
CARYOCAR	CAVALIER	CHALKPIT	CHICANER	CHRISTIE
CASANOVA	CAVATINA	CHALONIC	CHICCORY	CHRISTLY
CASCABEL	CAVE-BEAR	CHAMISAL	CHICK-PEA	CHRISTOM
CASEBOOK	CAVERNED	CHAMPART	CHIEFDOM	CHROMATE
CASEMATE	CAVESSON	CHAMPION	CHIEFERY	CHROMIJE
CASEMENT	CAVICORN	CHANCERY	CHIEFESS	CHROMIUM
CASE-SHOT	CAVILLED	CHANDLER	CHIEFEST	CHTHONIC
CASE-WORK	CAVILLER	CHANTAGE	CHILDBED	CHUCKIES
CASE-WORM	CAVITIED	CHAPATTI	CHILDING	CHUGGING
CASH-BOOK	CAYENNED	CHAPBOOK	CHILDISH	CHUMMAGE
CASHMERE	CECROPIA	CHAPELRY	CHILDREN	CHUPATTI
CASSETTE	CEDAR-NUT	CHAPERON	CHILIASM	CHURCHLY
CASTANEA	CELERIAC	CHAPITER	CHILIAST	CHURINGA
CASTAWAY	CELERITY	CHAPLAIN	CHILLILY	CHURLISH
CAST-IRON	CELIBACY	CHAPLESS	CHILLING	CHURNING
CASTRATE	CELIBATE	CHAPTREL	CHIMAERA	CHURN-OWL
CASTRATI	CELLARER	CHARCOAL	CHIMERIC	CHUTZPAH
CASTRATO	CELLARET	CHARISMA	CHINAMAN	CHYLURIA
CASUALLY	CELLULAR	CHARITES	CHINAMPA	CHYMICAL
CASUALTY	CEMETERY	CHARLOCK	CHIN-CHIN	CIBATION
CATACOMB	CENOBITE	CHARMFUL	CHINKARA	CIBORIUM
CATALASE	CENOTAPH	CHARMING	CHIPMUCK	CICATRIX
CATALYSE	CENOZOIC	CHARNECO	CHIPMUNK	CICERONE
CATALYST	CENTAURY	CHARRING	CHIPPING	CICERONI
CATAMITE	CENTERED	CHARTISM	CHIP-SHOT	CICHLOID
CATAPULT	CENTESIS	CHASSEUR	CHIRAGRA	CICINNUS
CATARACT	CENTIARE	CHASTELY	CHIRPILY	CICISBEI
CATATONY	CENTOIST	CHASTISE	CHIRPING	CICISBEO
CATCHFLY	CENTRING	CHASTITY	CHIRRUPY	CICLATON
CATCHING	CENTRODE	CHASUBLE	CHITCHAT	CIDER-AND
CATCH-PIT	CENTROID	CHÂTEAUX	CHIVALRY	CIDER-CUP
CATECHOL	CENTUPLE	CHATTING	CHLOASMA	CIDERKIN
CATEGORY	CEPHALIC	CHAUFFER	CHLORATE	CILIATED
CATENARY	CERAMIST	CHAUNTER	CHLORIDE	CIMINITE
CATENATE	CERASTES	CHAUNTRY	CHLORINE	CIMOLITE
CATERESS	CERATOID	CHAUSSES	CHLORITE	CINCHONA
CATERING	CERBERUS	CHAWDRON	CHLOROUS	CINCTURE
CATHAIAN	CERCARIA	CHAY-ROOT	CHOICELY	CINÉASTE
CATHAYAN	CEREBRAL	CHEATERY	CHOIRBOY	CINERAMA
CATHEDRA	CEREBRIC	CHECHAKO	CHOIRMAN	CINERARY
CATHETER	CEREBRUM	CHECK-KEY	CHOKIDAR	CINEREAL
CATHETUS	CEREMENT	CHEECHEE	CHOLERIC	CINGULUM
CATHEXIS	CEREMONY	CHEERFUL	CHOLIAMB	CINNABAR
CATHISMA	CERNUOUS	CHEERILY	CHONDRAL	CINNAMIC
CATHODAL	CERULEAN	CHEEWINK	CHONDRIN	CINNAMON
CATHODIC	CERULEIN	CHELIFER	CHONDRUS	CINQUAIN
CATHOLIC	CERUSITE	CHELLEAN	CHOP-CHOP	CIRCAEAN
CATILINE	CERVICAL	CHELONIA	CHOPPING	CIRCLING
CATONIAN	CESAREAN	CHEMICAL	CHOP-SUEY	CIRCUITY
CAT'S-FOOT	CESSPOOL	CHEMURGY	CHORAGIC	CIRCULAR
CAT'S-MEAT	CETACEAN	CHENILLE	CHORAGUS	CIRCUSSY
CAT'S-TAIL	CETERACH	CHEROKEE	CHORALLY	CISELEUR
CAT-STICK	CETOLOGY	CHERUBIC	CHORDATA	CISELURE

CISTVAEN	CLERKESS	CLYPEATE	COGENTLY	COMMONEY
CITATION	CLERKISH	CNIDARIA	COGITATE	COMMONLY
CITATORY	CLERUCHY	COACH-BOX	COGNOMEN	COMMUNAL
CITRANGE	CLEVEITE	COACHDOG	COGNOSCE	COMMUTER
CITREOUS	CLEVERLY	COACHING	COGNOVIT	COMPAGES
CIVILIAN	CLICKING	COACHMAN	COG-WHEEL	COMPESCE
CIVILISE	CLIENTAL	COACHWAY	COHERENT	COMPILER
CIVILIST	CLIMATAL	COACTION	COHESION	COMPITAL
CIVILITY	CLIMATIC	COACTIVE	COHESIVE	COMPLAIN
CLACK-BOX	CLIMBING	COAGENCY	COIFFEUR	COMPLEAT
CLADDING	CLINAMEN	COAGULUM	COIFFURE	COMPLECT
CLAIMANT	CLINCHER	COALBALL	COINCIDE	COMPLETE
CLAMANCY	CLINICAL	COAL-DUST	COINHERE	COMPLICE
CLAMBAKE	CLINIQUE	COALESCE	COISTREL	COMPLIED
CLAMMILY	CLINKING	COAL-FACE	COISTRIL	COMPLIER
CLAMMING	CLIP-CLOP	COALFISH	COKERNUT	COMPLINE
CLANGING	CLIP-HOOK	COAL-FLAP	COLANDER	COMPOSED
CLANGOUR	CLIPPING	COAL-HOLE	COLATION	COMPOSER
CLANKING	CLIQUISH	COAL-MINE	COLATURE	COMPOUND
CLANNISH	CLIQUISM	COALPORT	COLDNESS	COMPRESS
CLANSHIP	CLITELLA	COAMINGS	COLE-SEED	COMPRINT
CLANSMAN	CLITHRAL	COARSELY	COLE-SLAW	COMPRISE
CLAPDISH	CLITORIS	COARSISH	COLE-WORT	COMPULSE
CLAPPING	CLOAK-BAG	COASTING	COLIFORM	COMPUTER
CLAPSILL	CLODDING	COAT-CARD	COLISEUM	COMSOMOL
CLAPTRAP	CLODDISH	COATLESS	COLLAGEN	CONARIAL
CLAQUEUR	CLODPATE	COATRACK	COLLAPSE	CONARIUM
CLARENCE	CLODPOLE	COBALTIC	COLLARED	CONATION
CLARINET	CLODPOLL	COBBLERY	COLLATOR	CONATIVE
CLARSACH	CLOISTER	COBBLING	COLLEGER	CONCAUSE
CLASHING	CLOP-CLOP	COBWEBBY	COLLIERY	CONCEDER
CLASPING	CLOSETED	COCA-COLA	COLLOGUE	CONCEITY
CLASSIFY	CLOTEBUR	COCAIGNE	COLLOQUE	CONCEIVE
CLASSMAN	CLOTHIER	COCCIDAE	COLLOQUY	CONCERTO
CLASS-WAR	CLOTHING	COCCULUS	COLLUDER	CONCETTI
CLAUDIAN	CLOTPOLL	COCCYGES	COLONIAL	CONCETTO
CLAUSTRA	CLOTTING	COCHLEAR	COLONISE	CONCHATE
CLAUSULA	CLOUDAGE	COCKATOO	COLONIST	CONCHOID
CLAVATED	CLOUDILY	COCKAYNE	COLOPHON	CONCLAVE
CLAVECIN	CLOUDING	COCKBIRD	COLOSSAL	CONCLUDE
CLAVICLE	CLOUDLET	COCK-BOAT	COLOSSUS	CONCOLOR
CLAVIGER	CLOVERED	COCK-CROW	COLOTOMY	CONCRETE
CLAWBACK	CLOWNERY	COCKEREL	COLOURED	CONDENSE
CLAWLESS	CLOWNING	COCKEYED	COLTWOOD	CONDYLAR
CLAY-BANK	CLOWNISH	COCKLOFT	COLUMBAN	CONFEREE
CLAY-COLD	CLOYLESS	COCKSHOT	COLUMBIC	CONFERVA
CLAY-MARL	CLOYMENT	COCKSHUT	COLUMNAL	CONFETTI
CLAY-MILL	CLOYSOME	COCKSPUR	COLUMNAR	CONFIDER
CLAYMORE	CLUBABLE	COCKSURE	COLUMNED	CONFINED
CLAY-PIPE	CLUBBING	COCKTAIL	COMATOSE	CONFINER
CLEANING	CLUBBISH	COCOA-FAT	COMBATED	CONFLATE
CLEANSER	CLUBBISM	COCOANUT	COMBINED	CONFLICT
CLEARAGE	CLUBBIST	COCO-PALM	COMBINGS	CONFOUND
CLEAR-CUT	CLUB-FACE	COCOPLUM	COMBLESS	CONFRERE
CLEARING	CLUB-FOOT	COCO-TREE	COMB-WISE	CONFRONT
CLEARWAY	CLUB-HAUL	COCO-WOOD	COME-BACK	CONFUSED
CLEAVAGE	CLUB-HEAD	CODIFIED	COMEDDLE	CONGENER
CLEAVERS	CLUB-LINE	CODIFIER	COMEDIAN	CONGIARY
CLEAVING	CLUB-MOSS	COD-PIECE	COMEDOWN	CONGLOBE
CLECKING	CLUBROOM	COELOMIC	COMETARY	CONGOESE
CLEMATIS	CLUB-RUSH	COENOBIA	COMETHER	CONGREET
CLEMENCE	CLUELESS	COENZYME	COMMANDO	CONGRESS
CLEMENCY	CLUMSILY	COERCION	COMMENCE	CONGREVE
CLERICAL	CLUPEOID	COERCIVE	COMMERCE	CONIDIAL
CLERIHEW	CLUSTERY	COEXTEND	COMMERGE	CONIDIUM
CLERKDOM	CLY-FAKER	COFFERED	COMMONER	CONIFORM

CONJOINT
CONJUGAL
CONJUNCT
CONJURER
CONJUROR
CONNIVER
CONOIDAL
CONOIDIC
CONQUEST
CONSERVE
CONSIDER
CONSOLER
CONSOMMÉ
CONSPIRE
CONSTANT
CONSTATE
CONSTRUE
CONSULAR
CONSUMER
CONSUMPT
CONTANGO
CONTEMPT
CONTINUA
CONTINUE
CONTINUO
CONTLINE
CONTORNO
CONTRACT
CONTRAIL
CONTRARY
CONTRAST
CONTRATE
CONTRIST
CONTRITE
CONTRIVE
CONURBAN
CONURBIA
CONVENER
CONVERGE
CONVERSE
CONVEXED
CONVEXLY
CONVEYAL
CONVEYER
CONVEYOR
CONVINCE
CONVOLVE
CONVULSE
CONY-WOOL
COOINGLY
COOK-BOOK
COOKMAID
COOKROOM
COOKSHOP
COOLABAH
COOLNESS
COON-SONG
CO-OPTION
COOTIKIN
COPEPODA
COPPERAS
COPULATE
COPYBOOK
COPYHOLD
COQUETRY
COQUETTE

COQUILLA
CORACOID
CORALLUM
CORAMINE
CORANACH
CORDINER
CORDOVAN
CORDUROY
CORDWAIN
CORD-WOOD
CO-REGENT
CORELESS
CORK-HEEL
CORK-SOLE
CORK-TREE
CORKWING
CORKWOOD
CORNACRE
CORN-BABY
CORN-BALL
CORN-BEEF
CORN-CAKE
CORN-CURE
CORNEOUS
CORNERED
CORNETCY
CORN-FLAG
CORNHUSK
CORNICED
CORNICHE
CORNICLE
CORNIFIC
CORN-KIST
CORNLAND
CORN-LOFT
CORNMILL
CORN-MOTH
CORNPIPE
CORN-PONE
CORN-RENT
CORN-SNOW
CORNUTED
CORNWORM
COROCORE
COROCORO
CORONACH
CORONARY
CORONATE
CORONIUM
CORONOID
CORPORAL
CORPORAS
CORRIDOR
CORSELET
CORSETED
CORTICAL
CORTICES
CORUNDUM
CORVETTE
CORVIDAE
CORVINAE
CORYBANT
CORYPHEE
COSECANT
COSHERER
COSMESIS

COSMETIC
COSMICAL
COSSETED
COSTATED
COST-FREE
COSTMARY
COST-PLUS
COSTUMED
COSTUMER
COTELINE
CO-TENANT
COT-HOUSE
COTHURNI
COTILLON
COT-QUEAN
COTSWOLD
COTTABUS
COTTAGED
COTTAGER
COTYLOID
COUCHANT
COUCHING
COUGHING
COULISSE
COUMARIC
COUMARIN
COUNTESS
COUNT-OUT
COUPLING
COURANTE
COURSING
COURT-DAY
COURTESY
COURTIER
COURTING
COURTLET
COUSCOUS
COUSINLY
COUSINRY
COUTILLE
COVALENT
COVENANT
COVENTRY
COVERAGE
COVERALL
COVERING
COVERLET
COVERLID
COVERTLY
COVETING
COVETISE
COVETOUS
COVINOUS
COWARDLY
COWARDRY
COWBERRY
COWGRASS
COWHOUSE
COW-LEECH
COW-PILOT
COW-PLANT
COW-WHEAT
COXALGIA
COXINESS
COXSWAIN
COYISHLY

COYSTREL
COYSTRIL
COZENAGE
CRABLIKE
CRAB-TREE
CRABWISE
CRAB-WOOD
CRAB-YAWS
CRACKERS
CRACKJAW
CRACKNEL
CRACKPOT
CRADLING
CRAFTILY
CRAGFAST
CRAGSMAN
CRAM-FULL
CRAMMING
CRAMOISY
CRANE-FLY
CRANIATA
CRANKILY
CRANNIED
CRASHPAD
CRATCHES
CRAVENLY
CRAWFISH
CRAWLING
CRAYFISH
CREAKILY
CREAMERY
CREAM-NUT
CREASOTE
CREATINE
CREATION
CREATIVE
CREATRIX
CREATURE
CREDENCE
CREDENDA
CREDIBLE
CREDIBLY
CREDITOR
CREEPING
CREMATOR
CREMORNE
CRENATED
CREODONT
CREOLIAN
CREOSOTE
CREPANCE
CREPITUS
CRESCENT
CRESCIVE
CRETONNE
CREUTZER
CREVASSE
CRIBBAGE
CRIBBING
CRIBBLED
CRIBELLA
CRIBRATE
CRIBROSE
CRIBWORK
CRICETUS
CRIMEFUL

CRIMINAL
CRINATED
CRINGING
CRISPATE
CRISTATE
CRITERIA
CRITICAL
CRITIQUE
CROAKILY
CROAKING
CROCEATE
CROCEOUS
CROCKERY
CROCOITE
CROFTING
CROMLECH
CROMORNA
CROMORNE
CROONING
CROPFULS
CROPPING
CROPSICK
CROSSBAR
CROSSBOW
CROSS-BUN
CROSSCUT
CROSSING
CROSSISH
CROSSLET
CROSS-PLY
CROSS-RIB
CROSS-ROW
CROSS-TIE
CROSSWAY
CROTALUM
CROTALUS
CROTCHED
CROTCHET
CROUPADE
CROUPIER
CROUPOUS
CROUSELY
CROWBILL
CROWFOOT
CROWN-CAP
CROWNING
CROWNLET
CROWN-SAW
CRUCIATE
CRUCIBLE
CRUCIFER
CRUCIFIX
CRUMENAL
CRUMHORN
CRUMMACK
CRUMMOCK
CRUMPLED
CRUSADER
CRUSH-HAT
CRUSHING
CRUSTATE
CRUSTILY
CRUTCHED
CRUZEIRO
CRYOGENY
CRYOLITE

CRYOSTAT
CRYOTRON
CUBATURE
CUB-DRAWN
CUBIFORM
CUBOIDAL
CUCKOLDY
CUCUMBER
CUCURBIT
CUITIKIN
CUL-DE-SAC
CULICINE
CULINARY
CULLYING
CULLYISM
CULOTTES
CULPABLE
CULPABLY
CULTIVAR
CULTRATE
CULTURAL
CULTURED
CULVERIN
CUMBERED
CUMBERER
CUMBROUS
CUM-SAVVY
CUMULATE
CUMULOSE
CUNABULA
CUNEATIC
CUPBOARD
CUP-CORAL
CUPELLED
CUPIDITY
CUPOLAED
CUPREOUS
CUPULATE
CURARINE
CURARISE
CURASSOW
CURATIVE
CURATORY
CURATRIX
CURBABLE
CURBLESS
CURB-ROOF
CURBSIDE
CURCULIO
CURELESS
CURLICUE
CURRANTY
CURRENCY
CURRICLE
CURRYING
CURSEDLY
CURSITOR
CURSORES
CURTAL-AX
CURTNESS
CURVATED
CURVETED
CURVITAL
CUSHIONY
CUSPARIA
CUSPIDAL

CUSPIDOR
CUSS-WORD
CUSTOMED
CUSTOMER
CUTCHERY
CUTHBERT
CUT-HROAT
CUTINISE
CUT-PRICE
CUT-PURSE
CUTWATER
CYANOGEN
CYANOSIS
CYANOTIC
CYANURET
CYATHIUM
CYCLAMEN
CYCLE-CAR
CYCLICAL
CYCLONIC
CYCLOPES
CYCLOPIC
CYCLOSIS
CYLINDER
CYMATIUM
CYNANCHE
CYNICISM
CYNOSURE
CYPRINUS
CYPRIOTE
CYRENAIC
CYRILLIC
CYSTITIS
CYTISINE
CYTOLOGY
CYTOSINE
CZAREVNA
CZARITZA

D

DABBLING
DABCHICK
DACTYLAR
DACTYLIC
DACTYLIS
DAEMONIC
DAFFODIL
DAFTNESS
DAHABIEH
DAIDLING
DAINTILY
DAIQUIRI
DAIRYING
DAIRYMAN
DALESMAN
DALLYING
DALMAHOY
DALMATIC
DAMASKIN
DAMASSIN
DAMBOARD
DAMNABLE
DAMNABLY
DAMPNESS
DANCETTE
DANCETTÉ

DANCETTY
DANDRIFF
DANDRUFF
DANDY-HEN
DANDYISH
DANDYISM
DANEGELD
DANE-HOLE
DANGLING
DANKNESS
DANSEUSE
DARBYITE
DARING-DO
DARINGLY
DARKLING
DARKMANS
DARKNESS
DARK-ROOM
DARKSOME
DARRAIGN
DARRAINE
DART-MOTH
DARTROUS
DASTARDY
DASYURUS
DATELESS
DATE-LINE
DATE-PALM
DATE-PLUM
DATE-TREE
DATOLITE
DATURINE
DAUGHTER
DAVY-LAMP
DAY-BREAK
DAYDREAM
DAY-LEVEL
DAYLIGHT
DAY-SIGHT
DAY-TO-DAY
DAY-WOMAN
DAZZLING
DEACONRY
DEAD-BEAT
DEAD-BOLT
DEAD-BORN
DEAD-CART
DEAD-DEAL
DEADENER
DEAD-FALL
DEAD-FIRE
DEAD-HAND
DEAD-HEAD
DEAD-HEAT
DEAD-LIFT
DEADLINE
DEADLOCK
DEAD-MEAT
DEADNESS
DEAD-PULL
DEAD-ROPE
DEAD-SHOT
DEAD-WALL
DEAD-WIND
DEAD-WOOD
DEAD-WORK

DEAF-MUTE
DEAFNESS
DEALBATE
DEALFISH
DEANSHIP
DEARLING
DEARNESS
DEARNFUL
DEATH-BED
DEATH-CAP
DEATH-CUP
DEATHFUL
DEATH-RAY
DEBARRED
DEBASING
DEBELLED
DEBILITY
DEBONAIR
DÉBOUCHÉ
DÉBUTANT
DECADENT
DECAGRAM
DECANTER
DECAPODA
DECEASED
DECEDENT
DECEIVER
DECEMBER
DECEMVIR
DECENTLY
DECIGRAM
DECIMATE
DECIPHER
DECISION
DECISIVE
DECISORY
DECK-GAME
DECK-HAND
DECK-LOAD
DECLARED
DECLARER
DÉCLASSÉ
DECLINAL
DECLUTCH
DECOLOUR
DECORATE
DECOROUS
DECREASE
DECREPIT
DECRETAL
DECRYING
DECURION
DEDALIAN
DEDICANT
DEDICATE
DEEDLESS
DEEMSTER
DEEP-DYED
DEEP-FELT
DEEP-LAID
DEEPMOST
DEEPNESS
DEEP-READ
DEER-HAIR
DEER-HORN
DEER-LICK

DEER-NECK
DEER-PARK
DEERSKIN
DEFAMING
DEFECATE
DEFECTOR
DEFENCED
DEFENDED
DEFENDER
DEFERENT
DEFERRED
DEFERRER
DEFIANCE
DEFILADE
DEFINITE
DEFLEXED
DEFLOWER
DEFLUENT
DEFOREST
DEFORMED
DEFORMER
DEFRAYAL
DEFRAYED
DEFTNESS
DEGRADED
DEGREASE
DEHORTER
DEIFICAL
DEIFYING
DEISHEAL
DEJECTED
DELATION
DELAYING
DELEGACY
DELEGATE
DELETION
DELETIVE
DELETORY
DELIBATE
DELICACY
DELICATE
DELIRIUM
DELIVERY
DELPHIAN
DELUBRUM
DELUSION
DELUSIVE
DELUSORY
DEMAGOGY
DEMANDER
DEMENTED
DEMENTIA
DEMERARA
DEMERSAL
DEMERSED
DEMIJOHN
DEMI-LUNE
DEMISSLY
DEMIURGE
DEMI-VOLT
DEMI-WOLF
DEMOBBED
DEMOCRAT
DEMOLISH
DEMOLOGY
DEMONESS

DEMONIAC	DETAINEE	DIASTASE	DIOECISM	DISINTER
DEMONIAN	DETAINER	DIASTEMA	DIOGENIC	DISINURE
DEMONISE	DETECTOR	DIASTOLE	DIONYSIA	DISJOINT
DEMONISM	DETERRED	DIASTYLE	DIOPSIDE	DISJUNCT
DEMONIST	DETHRONE	DIATOMIC	DIOPTASE	DISLEAVE
DEMOTION	DETONATE	DIATONIC	DIOPTRIC	DISLODGE
DEMPSTER	DETOXIFY	DIATRIBE	DIORAMIC	DISLOIGN
DEMURELY	DETRITAL	DICACITY	DIORITIC	DISLOYAL
DEMURRED	DETRITUS	DICE-COAL	DIOSCURI	DISMALLY
DEMURRER	DEUCE-ACE	DICENTRA	DIPCHICK	DISMODED
DEMYSHIP	DEUCEDLY	DICE-PLAY	DIPHENYL	DISMOUNT
DENARIUS	DEUTERON	DICHASIA	DIPLOGEN	DISORBED
DENATURE	DEVIATOR	DICHROIC	DIPLOIDY	DISORDER
DENDRITE	DEVILDOM	DICROTIC	DIPLOMAT	DISPATCH
DENDROID	DEVILESS	DICTATOR	DIPLOPIA	DISPEACE
DENEBOLA	DEVILING	DICYCLIC	DIPNOOUS	DISPENSE
DENE-HOLE	DEVILISH	DIDACTIC	DIPSACUS	DISPERSE
DENIABLE	DEVILISM	DIDACTYL	DIP-SLOPE	DISPIRIT
DENOTATE	DEVILKIN	DIDAPPER	DIP-STICK	DISPLACE
DENOUNCE	DEVILLED	DIDRACHM	DIPTERAL	DISPLANT
DENTARIA	DEVILTRY	DIDYMIUM	DIPTERAN	DISPLODE
DENTELLE	DEVONIAN	DIDYMOUS	DIPTEROS	DISPLUME
DENTICLE	DEVOTION	DIEGESIS	DIRECTLY	DISPONEE
DEPARTER	DEVOURER	DIELYTRA	DIRECTOR	DISPONER
DEPICTER	DEVOUTLY	DIERESES	DIRIGENT	DISPONGE
DEPICTOR	DEW-BERRY	DIERESIS	DIRIGISM	DISPOSAL
DEPILATE	DEWINESS	DIE-STOCK	DIRIMENT	DISPOSED
DEPONENT	DEWPOINT	DIETETIC	DIRT-ROAD	DISPOSER
DEPRAVED	DEXTRINE	DIFFRACT	DIRTYING	DISPREAD
DEPRIVAL	DEXTROSE	DIFFUSED	DISABUSE	DISPRIZE
DEPURANT	DEXTROUS	DIFFUSER	DISADORN	DISPROOF
DEPURATE	DEY-WOMAN	DIGAMIST	DISAGREE	DISPROVE
DEPUTISE	DIABASIC	DIGAMOUS	DISALLOW	DISPUNGE
DÉRACINÉ	DIABETES	DIGESTER	DISANNEX	DISPUTER
DERAILER	DIABETIC	DIGGABLE	DISANNUL	DISQUIET
DERANGED	DIABLERY	DIGGINGS	DISARRAY	DISSEISE
DERATING	DIABOLIC	DIGITATE	DISASTER	DISSEIZE
DERATION	DIACONAL	DIGITISE	DISBENCH	DISSERVE
DER-DOING	DIACTINE	DIGO-BLUE	DISBOSOM	DISSEVER
DERELICT	DIADEMED	DIGYNIAN	DISBOWEL	DISSIGHT
DERISION	DIADOCHI	DIGYNOUS	DISBURSE	DISSOLVE
DERISIVE	DIAGLYPH	DIHEDRAL	DISCANDY	DISSUADE
DERISORY	DIAGNOSE	DIHEDRON	DISCINCT	DISTALLY
DERIVATE	DIAGONAL	DIHYBRID	DISCIPLE	DISTANCE
DERMATIC	DIAGRAPH	DILATANT	DISCLAIM	DISTASTE
DEROGATE	DIALLAGE	DILATION	DISCLOSE	DISTHENE
DESCRIBE	DIALLING	DILATIVE	DISCOUNT	DISTICHS
DESCRIED	DIALOGIC	DILATORY	DISCOVER	DISTINCT
DESERTER	DIALOGUE	DILIGENT	DISCREET	DISTRACT
DESERVED	DIALYSER	DILLY-BAG	DISCRETE	DISTRAIN
DESIGNER	DIALYSES	DILUTION	DISCROWN	DISTRESS
DESILVER	DIALYSIS	DILUVIAL	DISEASED	DISTRICT
DESINENT	DIALYTIC	DILUVIAN	DISENDOW	DISTRUST
DESIROUS	DIAMANTÉ	DILUVION	DISENROL	DISUNION
DESK-WORK	DIAMETER	DILUVIUM	DISFLESH	DISUNITE
DESOLATE	DIANDRIA	DIMERISM	DISFROCK	DISUNITY
DESPATCH	DIANODAL	DIMEROUS	DISGAVEL	DISUSAGE
DESPISAL	DIANTHUS	DIMETHYL	DISGORGE	DISVALUE
DESPISER	DIAPASON	DIMETRIC	DISGRACE	DISVOUCH
DESPOTAT	DIAPENTE	DIMINISH	DISGRADE	DITCH-DOG
DESPOTIC	DIAPHONE	DINARCHY	DISGUISE	DITHECAL
DESTRIER	DIARCHAL	DING-DONG	DISHABIT	DITHEISM
DESTRUCT	DIARCHIC	DINKY-DIE	DISHERIT	DITHEIST
DESYATIN	DIARRHEA	DINORNIS	DISHEVEL	DITOKOUS
DETACHED	DIASPORA	DINOSAUR	DISHORSE	DITTY-BAG
DETAILED	DIASPORE	DIOCESAN	DISHOUSE	DITTY-BOX

DIURESIS
DIURETIC
DIVAGATE
DIVALENT
DIVAN-BED
DIVE-BOMB
DIVERSLY
DIVIDEND
DIVIDING
DIVIDIVI
DIVIDUAL
DIVINELY
DIVINIFY
DIVINISE
DIVINITY
DIVISION
DIVISIVE
DIVORCEE
DIVORCER
DIZZYING
DJELLABA
DOBCHICK
DOBERMAN
DOCETISM
DOCETIST
DOCHMIAC
DOCHMIUS
DOCILITY
DOCIMASY
DOCK-DUES
DOCKETED
DOCKLAND
DOCKYARD
DOCTORAL
DOCTORLY
DOCTRESS
DOCTRINE
DOCUMENT
DODDERED
DODDERER
DODONIAN
DOGBERRY
DOG-CHEAP
DOG-DAISY
DOG-EARED
DOGESHIP
DOG-FACED
DOG-FIGHT
DOGGEDLY
DOGGEREL
DOGGONED
DOG-GRASS
DOG-HOUSE
DOG-LATIN
DOG-LEECH
DOG-LOUSE
DOGMATIC
DO-GOODER
DOG'SBANE
DOG'S-BODY
DOG-SLEEP
DOG'S-MEAT
DOG'S-NOSE
DOG-TIRED
DOGTOOTH
DOG-TRICK

DOG-WATCH
DOG-WEARY
DOG-WHEAT
DOG-WHELK
DOLDRUMS
DOLERITE
DOLESOME
DOLICHOS
DOLLARED
DOLLHOOD
DOLLY-MOP
DOLLY-TUB
DOLOMITE
DOLOROSO
DOLOROUS
DOMAINAL
DOMANIAL
DOMATIUM
DOMESTIC
DOMICILE
DOMINANT
DOMINATE
DOMINEER
DOMINION
DOMINOES
DONATARY
DONATION
DONATISM
DONATIST
DONATIVE
DONATORY
DO-NAUGHT
DO-NOUGHT
DOOM-PALM
DOOMSDAY
DOOMSMAN
DOOMSTER
DOOR-BELL
DOOR-CASE
DOOR-KNOB
DOOR-NAIL
DOORPOST
DOOR-SILL
DOORSTEP
DOOR-YARD
DORICISM
DORIDOID
DORMANCY
DORMIENT
DORMOUSE
DORSALLY
DOSOLOGY
DOTATION
DOTTEREL
DOUBLING
DOUBLOON
DOUBTFUL
DOUBTING
DOUGH-BOY
DOUGHNUT
DOUM-PALM
DOURNESS
DOUZEPER
DOVECOTE
DOVE-EYED

DOVELIKE
DOVETAIL
DOWDYISH
DOWDYISM
DOWEL-PIN
DOWEL-ROD
DOWFNESS
DOWNBEAT
DOWNCAST
DOWNCOME
DOWNFALL
DOWN-HAUL
DOWNHILL
DOWNLAND
DOWN-LINE
DOWNMOST
DOWNPOUR
DOWNRUSH
DOWNTOWN
DOWNTROD
DOWNTURN
DOWNWARD
DOXOLOGY
DOZINESS
DRABBISH
DRABBLER
DRABETTE
DRABNESS
DRACAENA
DRACHMAE
DRACHMAI
DRACHMAS
DRACONIC
DRAFFISH
DRAFT-BAR
DRAGGING
DRAG-HUNT
DRAG-LINE
DRAGOMAN
DRAGÓNET
DRAGONNÉ
DRAG-SHOT
DRAGSMAN
DRAGSTER
DRAINAGE
DRAMATIC
DRAMMACH
DRAMMOCK
DRAM-SHOP
DRAUGHTY
DRAWABLE
DRAWBACK
DRAW-GEAR
DRAW-TUBE
DRAW-WELL
DREADFUL
DREAMERY
DREAMFUL
DREAMILY
DREAMING
DREARILY
DREARING
DRENCHER
DRESSAGE
DRESSING
DRESS-TIE

DRIBBLER
DRIBBLET
DRICKSIE
DRIFTAGE
DRIFT-ICE
DRIFT-NET
DRIFT-WAY
DRILLING
DRINKING
DRIPPING
DRIVEWAY
DROLLERY
DROLLING
DROLLISH
DROMICAL
DROOKING
DROP-GOAL
DROP-HEAD
DROP-KICK
DROPPING
DROP-RIPE
DROP-SHOT
DROPSIED
DROPWISE
DROP-WORT
DROUGHTY
DROUKING
DROWNING
DROWSILY
DRUBBING
DRUDGERY
DRUDGISM
DRUGGING
DRUGGIST
DRUIDESS
DRUIDISM
DRUMFIRE
DRUMFISH
DRUMHEAD
DRUMMING
DRUMMOCK
DRUNKARD
DRUPELET
DRY-BIBLE
DRY-CLEAN
DRY-GOODS
DRY-NURSE
DRY-PLATE
DRY-POINT
DRY-STANE
DRY-STONE
DRY-STOVE
DUBITATE
DUCATOON
DUCHESSE
DUCKBILL
DUCK-HAWK
DUCKLING
DUCK-POND
DUCK-SHOT
DUCK-TAIL
DUCKWEED
DUCTLESS
DUELLING
DUELLIST
DUELSOME

DUETTINO
DUETTIST
DUKELING
DUKESHIP
DUKHOBOR
DULCIANA
DULCIMER
DULCINEA
DULCITOL
DULE-TREE
DULL-EYED
DULLNESS
DUMB-BELL
DUMB-CANE
DUMBNESS
DUMB-SHOW
DUMFOUND
DUMMERER
DUMOSITY
DUMPLING
DUNCEDOM
DUN-DIVER
DUNGAREE
DUNG-CART
DUNG-FORK
DUNGHEAP
DUNGHILL
DUNGMERE
DUODENAL
DUODENUM
DUOLOGUE
DURATION
DURUKULI
DUSKNESS
DUST-BALL
DUST-BOWL
DUST-CART
DUST-COAT
DUST-HOLE
DUSTLESS
DUST-SHOT
DUTCHMAN
DUTCHMEN
DUTIABLE
DUTY-FREE
DUTY-PAID
DUUMVIRI
DUUMVIRS
DWARFISH
DWELLING
DYE-HOUSE
DYESTUFF
DYE-WORKS
DYHYDRIC
DYNAMICS
DYNAMISM
DYNAMIST
DYNAMITE
DYNASTIC
DYSCHROA
DYSGENIC
DYSLEXIA
DYSLEXIC
DYSMELIA
DYSMELIC
DYSODILE

DYSODYLE
DYSPATHY
DYSPEPSY
DYSPHAGY
DYSPNEAL
DYSPNEIC
DYSPNOEA
DYTISCID
DYTISCUS

E
EAGLE-OWL
EAGLE-RAY
EARLIEST
EARMUFFS
EARNINGS
EARPHONE
EAR-SHELL
EARTH-BAG
EARTH-FED
EARTH-HOG
EARTHNUT
EARTH-PEA
EARTHWAX
EARWIGGY
EASEMENT
EASINESS
EASTERLY
EASTLAND
EASTLING
EASTLINS
EASTMOST
EASTWARD
EBENEZER
EBIONISE
EBIONISM
EBIONITE
EBRIATED
EBURNEAN
ECAUDATE
ECCLESIA
ECCRISIS
ECCRITIC
ECHINATE
ECHINOID
ECHINOPS
ECHOGRAM
ECHOLESS
ECLAMPSY
ECLECTIC
ECLIPTIC
ECLOGITE
ECLOSION
ECOLOGIC
ECONOMIC
ECOSTATE
ECSTASIS
ECSTATIC
ECTODERM
ECTOGENY
ECTOSARC
ECTOZOAN
ECTOZOIC
ECTOZOON
ECTROPIC
ECUMENIC

EDACIOUS
EDENTATA
EDENTATE
EDGEBONE
EDGELESS
EDGEWAYS
EDGEWISE
EDGINESS
EDIFYING
EDITRESS
EDUCABLE
EDUCATOR
EDUCIBLE
EDUCTION
EEL-GRASS
EEL-SPEAR
EEL-WRACK
EERINESS
EFFECTER
EFFECTOR
EFFERENT
EFFICACY
EFFIERCE
EFFIGIES
EFFLUENT
EFFLUVIA
EFFULGED
EFFUSION
EFFUSIVE
EFTSOONS
EGESTION
EGESTIVE
EGG-APPLE
EGG-BOUND
EGG-DANCE
EGG-FRUIT
EGG-GLASS
EGG-PLANT
EGG-PURSE
EGGSHELL
EGG-SLICE
EGG-SPOON
EGG-TIMER
EGG-TOOTH
EGG-WHISK
EGLATERE
EGOISTIC
EGOMANIA
EIGHT-DAY
EIGHTEEN
EIGHTHLY
EIGHTIES
EIGHT-OAR
EJECTION
EJECTIVE
EKISTICS
EKLOGITE
ELAPHINE
ELATEDLY
ELATERIN
ELDER-GUN
ELDORADO
ELDRITCH
ELECTION
ELECTIVE
ELECTRIC

ELECTRON
ELECTRUM
ELEGANCE
ELEGANCY
ELEGIAST
ELENCHUS
ELENCTIC
ELEPHANT
ELEVATED
ELEVATOR
ELEVENTH
ELF-ARROW
ELF-CHILD
ELFLOCKS
ELF-SHOOT
ELIGIBLE
ELIGIBLY
ELKHOUND
ELLIPSES
ELLIPSIS
ELLIPTIC
ELONGATE
ELOQUENT
ELSEWISE
ELUDIBLE
ELVANITE
EMACIATE
EMBALMER
EMBANKER
EMBARKED
EMBARRED
EMBATTLE
EMBEZZLE
EMBITTER
EMBLAZON
EMBODIED
EMBOLDEN
EMBOLISM
EMBORDER
EMBOSSED
EMBOSSER
EMBRACED
EMBRACER
EMBRASOR
EMBRYONS
EMBUSSED
EMENDALS
EMENDATE
EMERGENT
EMERITUS
EMERSION
EMERY-BAG
EMETICAL
EMICTION
EMICTORY
EMIGRANT
EMIGRATE
EMINENCE
EMINENCY
EMISSARY
EMISSILE
EMISSION
EMISSIVE
EMITTING
EMMANUEL
EMMARBLE

EMMENTAL
EMPACKET
EMPATHIC
EMPATRON
EMPEOPLE
EMPERISE
EMPERISH
EMPHASES
EMPHASIS
EMPHATIC
EMPIERCE
EMPLOYED
EMPLOYEE
EMPLOYER
EMPOISON
EMPORIUM
EMPTYING
EMPTYSIS
EMPURPLE
EMPYESIS
EMPYREAL
EMPYREAN
EMULATOR
EMULGENT
EMULSIFY
EMULSION
EMULSIVE
EMULSOID
ENACTING
ENACTION
ENACTIVE
ENACTURE
ENALLAGE
ENARCHED
ENAUNTER
ENCAENIA
ENCARPUS
ENCEINTE
ENCHARGE
ENCHASED
ENCHORIC
ENCIPHER
ENCIRCLE
ENCLISIS
ENCLITIC
ENCLOSER
ENCLOTHE
ENCOLOUR
ENCOLURE
ENCOMION
ENCOMIUM
ENCRADLE
ENCRINAL
ENCRINIC
ENCROACH
ENCUMBER
ENCYCLIC
ENCYSTED
ENDAMAGE
ENDANGER
ENDEARED
ENDEIXIS
ENDEMIAL
ENDEMISM
ENDERMIC
ENDOCARP

ENDODERM
ENDODYNE
ENDOGAMY
ENDOGENY
ENDORSED
ENDORSEE
ENDORSER
ENDOSARC
ENDOZOIC
ENDOZOON
END-PAPER
ENERGISE
ENERVATE
ENFEEBLE
ENFESTED
ENFETTER
ENFIERCE
ENFILADE
ENFLOWER
ENFOREST
ENFREEZE
ENFROSEN
ENGAGING
ENGENDER
ENGINEER
ENGINERY
ENGIRDLE
ENGORGED
ENGOULED
ENGRAMMA
ENGRAVED
ENGRAVEN
ENGRAVER
ENGRIEVE
ENGROOVE
ENHEARSE
ENHUNGER
ENHYDROS
ENJOINER
ENKERNEL
ENKINDLE
ENLARGED
ENLUMINE
ENMOSSED
ENNEADIC
ENNEAGON
ENORMITY
ENORMOUS
ENQUIRER
ENRAUNGE
ENRAVISH
ENRIDGED
ENROLLED
ENROLLER
ENSAMPLE
ENSCONCE
ENSEMBLE
ENSHEATH
ENSHIELD
ENSHRINE
ENSHROUD
ENSIFORM
ENSIGNCY
ENSILAGE
ENSLAVED
ENSLAVER

ENSPHERE	EPINASTY	ESCALLOP	EULOGIUM	EXCHANGE
ENSWATHE	EPINOSIC	ESCAPADE	EUMERISM	EXCISION
ENTAILER	EPIPHANY	ESCAPADO	EUONYMIN	EXCITANT
ENTANGLE	EPIPHYTE	ESCAPISM	EUONYMUS	EXCITING
ENTELLUS	EPIPLOIC	ESCAPIST	EUPATRID	EXCLUDED
ENTENDER	EPIPLOON	ESCARGOT	EUPEPSIA	EXCUBANT
ENTERATE	EPIPOLIC	ESCAROLE	EUPEPTIC	EXCURSUS
ENTERING	EPISCOPE	ESCHALOT	EUPHONIA	EXCUSIVE
ENTHALPY	EPISCOPY	ESCULENT	EUPHONIC	EXECRATE
ENTHRALL	EPISEMON	ESOTERIC	EUPHORIA	EXECUTER
ENTHRONE	EPISODAL	ESPALIER	EUPHORIC	EXECUTOR
ENTICING	EPISODIC	ESPECIAL	EUPHRASY	EXECUTRY
ENTIRELY	EPISPERM	ESPIÈGLE	EUPHUISE	EXEGESIS
ENTIRETY	EPISPORE	ESPOUSAL	EUPHUISM	EXEGETIC
ENTODERM	EPISTLER	ESPOUSER	EURASIAN	EXEMPLAR
ENTOPTIC	EPISTYLE	ESPRESSO	EUROMART	EXEMPLUM
ENTOZOAL	EPITASIS	ESQUIMAU	EUROPEAN	EXEQUIAL
ENTOZOIC	EPITHEMA	ESSAYING	EUROPIUM	EXEQUIES
ENTOZOON	EPITOMIC	ESSAYISH	EURYTHMY	EXERCISE
ENTRACTE	EPITONIC	ESSAYIST	EUSEBIAN	EXERGUAL
ENTRAILS	EPITRITE	ESSENISM	EUSTATIC	EXERTION
ENTRANCE	EPOPOEIA	ESSOINER	EUTAXITE	EXERTIVE
ENTREATY	EPSOMITE	ESSONITE	EUTECTIC	EXHALANT
ENTREMES	EPULOTIC	ESTACADE	EUTHERIA	EXHEDRAE
ENTRENCH	EPYLLION	ESTANCIA	EUTROPHY	EXHORTER
ENTREPOT	EPYORNIS	ESTEEMED	EUTROPIC	EXHUMATE
ENTRESOL	EQUALISE	ESTERIFY	EUXENITE	EXIGENCE
ENURESIS	EQUALITY	ESTIMATE	EVACUANT	EXIGENCY
ENURETIC	EQUALLED	ESTONIAN	EVACUATE	EXIGIBLE
ENVASSAL	EQUATION	ESTOPPED	EVALUATE	EXIGUITY
ENVEIGLE	EQUINITY	ESTOPPEL	EVANESCE	EXIGUOUS
ENVELOPE	EQUIPAGE	ESTRANGE	EVANGELY	EXIMIOUS
ENVIABLE	EQUIPPED	ESTRIDGE	EVASIBLE	EXISTENT
ENVIABLY	EQUITANT	ESURIENT	EVECTION	EX-LIBRIS
ENVIRONS	EQUIVOKE	ETERNISE	EVEN-DOWN	EXOGAMIC
ENVISAGE	ERADIATE	ETERNITY	EVENFALL	EXOPHAGY
ENVISION	ERASABLE	ETHERCAP	EVENNESS	EXORABLE
ENWALLOW	ERASTIAN	ETHEREAL	EVENSONG	EXORCISE
ENZOOTIC	ERECTILE	ETHERIAL	EVENTFUL	EXORCISM
EOHIPPUS	ERECTION	ETHERION	EVENTIDE	EXORCIST
EOLIENNE	ERECTIVE	ETHERISE	EVENTUAL	EXORDIAL
EOLIPILE	EREMITAL	ETHERISM	EVERMORE	EXORDIUM
EOLITHIC	EREMITIC	ETHERIST	EVERSION	EXOSMOSE
EPAGOGIC	ERETHISM	ETHICISE	EVERYDAY	EXOSPORE
EPANODOS	EREWHILE	ETHICISM	EVERYMAN	EXOTERIC
EPHEMERA	ERGATOID	ETHICIST	EVERYONE	EXPECTED
EPHESIAN	ERGOGRAM	ETHIOPIC	EVERYWAY	EXPECTER
EPIBLAST	ERGOTISE	ETHNARCH	EVICTION	EXPEDITE
EPICALLY	ERGOTISM	ETHNICAL	EVIDENCE	EXPELLED
EPICALYX	ERIGERON	ETHOLOGY	EVIL-DOER	EXPERTLY
EPICOTYL	EROGENIC	ETHYLENE	EVILNESS	EXPIABLE
EPICYCLE	EROTESIS	ETIOLATE	EVINCIVE	EXPIATOR
EPIDEMIC	EROTETIC	ETRURIAN	EVITABLE	EXPIRANT
EPIDOTIC	EROTICAL	ETRUSCAN	EVOLVENT	EXPIRING
EPIDURAL	ERRANTLY	ETTERCAP	EVULGATE	EXPLICIT
EPIFOCAL	ERRANTRY	ETYPICAL	EVULSION	EXPLODED
EPIGAEAL	ERRINGLY	EUCALYPT	EWIGKEIT	EXPLODER
EPIGAEAN	ERRORIST	EUCRITIC	EXACTING	EXPLORER
EPIGAMIC	ERUCTATE	EUCYCLIC	EXACTION	EXPONENT
EPIGEOUS	ERUPTION	EUGENICS	EXAMINEE	EXPORTER
EPIGONES	ERUPTIVE	EUGENISM	EXAMINER	EXPOSURE
EPIGRAPH	ERYSIMUM	EUGENIST	EXAMPLAR	EXSERTED
EPILATOR	ERYTHEMA	EUGUBINE	EXANTHEM	EXTENDED
EPILEPSY	ESCALADE	EULACHON	EXCAVATE	EXTENDER
EPILOGIC	ESCALADO	EULOGISE	EXCELLED	EXTENSOR
EPILOGUE	ESCALATE	EULOGIST	EXCEPTOR	EXTERIOR

EXTERNAL
EXTERNAT
EXTOLLED
EXTRADOS
EXTREMER
EXTRORSE
EXULTANT
EXUVIATE
EYE-GLASS
EYE-PIECE
EYE-RHYME
EYE-SALVE
EYESIGHT
EYE-TOOTH
EYE-WATER

F

FABLIAUX
FABULISE
FABULIST
FABULOUS
FABURDEN
FACE-ACHE
FACE-CARD
FACELESS
FACE-LIFT
FACETIAE
FACIALLY
FACILELY
FACILITY
FACTIOUS
FACTOTUM
FADE-AWAY
FADELESS
FAGACEAE
FAGOTING
FAHLBAND
FAIL-DIKE
FAIL-SAFE
FAINÉANT
FAINNESS
FAINTING
FAINTISH
FAIRLEAD
FAIRNESS
FAIRYDOM
FAIRYISM
FAITHFUL
FAKEMENT
FAKIRISM
FALCATED
FALCHION
FALCONER
FALCONET
FALCONRY
FALDERAL
FALDETTA
FALLIBLE
FALLIBLY
FALL-TRAP
FALSETTO
FALTBOAT
FAMELESS
FAMILIAL
FAMILIAR
FAMILISM

FAMILIST
FAMOUSLY
FANARIOT
FANCIFUL
FANCYING
FANDANGO
FANFARON
FANGLESS
FANLIGHT
FANTASIA
FANTIGUE
FARADISE
FARADISM
FARCEUSE
FARCICAL
FARCY-BUD
FAREWELL
FAR-FLUNG
FAR-FORTH
FARINGEE
FARINOSE
FARMHAND
FARM-TOUN
FARMYARD
FAROUCHE
FARRIERY
FAR-SPENT
FARTHEST
FARTHING
FASCICLE
FASCIOLA
FASCIOLE
FASCISMO
FASCISTA
FASCISTI
FASCISTS
FASHIOUS
FASTENER
FASTNESS
FASTUOUS
FATALISM
FATALIST
FATALITY
FAT-FACED
FATHERLY
FATIGATE
FATIGUED
FATTENER
FATTRELS
FAUBOURG
FAULCHIN
FAULTFUL
FAULTILY
FAUTEUIL
FAUVETTE
FAVONIAN
FAVOURED
FAVOURER
FAYALITE
FEARLESS
FEARSOME
FEASIBLE
FEASIBLY
FEAST-DAY
FEASTFUL
FEASTING

FEAST-WON
FEATEOUS
FEATHERY
FEATUOUS
FEATURED
FEBRIFIC
FEBRUARY
FECKLESS
FECULENT
FEDAYEEN
FEDELINI
FEDERACY
FEDERARY
FEDERATE
FEED-BACK
FEED-HEAD
FEED-PIPE
FEED-PUMP
FEE-GRIEF
FEIGNING
FELDGRAU
FELDSHER
FELDSPAR
FELICITY
FELINITY
FELLABLE
FELLAHIN
FELLATIO
FELLNESS
FELLOWLY
FELSITIC
FELSTONE
FEMALITY
FEMERALL
FEMETARY
FEMININE
FEMINISE
FEMINISM
FEMINIST
FEMINITY
FEN-BERRY
FENCIBLE
FENESTRA
FERACITY
FERETORY
FERINGHI
FERN-ALLY
FERN-SEED
FERNSHAW
FEROCITY
FERREOUS
FERRETED
FERRETER
FERRIAGE
FERRITIC
FERRYING
FERRYMAN
FERVENCY
FERVIDLY
FESTALLY
FESTIVAL
FETCHING
FETICIDE
FETTLING
FEUDALLY
FEVERFEW

FEVERISH
FEVEROUS
FEWTRILS
FIBRILLA
FIBROSIS
FIBROTIC
FIDDIOUS
FIDDLING
FIDELITY
FIDGETED
FIDUCIAL
FIELD-DEW
FIELDING
FIENDISH
FIERCELY
FIFTIETH
FIFTYISH
FIGHTING
FIGULINE
FIGURANT
FIGURATE
FIGURINE
FIGURIST
FILAGREE
FILAMENT
FILANDER
FILARIAL
FILATORY
FILATURE
FILCHING
FILE-FISH
FILIALLY
FILIFORM
FILIGREE
FILIOQUE
FILIPINA
FILIPINO
FILLETED
FILLIBEG
FILLIPED
FILMABLE
FILM-GOER
FILMLAND
FILTHILY
FILTRATE
FINALISE
FINALISM
FINALIST
FINALITY
FINE-DRAW
FINELESS
FINENESS
FINE-SPUN
FINESSER
FINGERED
FINISHED
FINISHER
FINITELY
FINITUDE
FINNESKO
FIN-WHALE
FIPPENCE
FIRE-BACK
FIRE-BALL
FIRE-BIRD
FIRE-BOTE

FIREBRAT
FIRE-CLAY
FIREDAMP
FIRE-EDGE
FIRE-EYED
FIRE-FLAG
FIRE-HOOK
FIRE-HOSE
FIRELESS
FIRE-LOCK
FIRE-MARK
FIRE-OPAL
FIRE-PLUG
FIRE-RISK
FIRESHIP
FIRESIDE
FIRE-STEP
FIRE-TUBE
FIRE-WALK
FIREWEED
FIREWOOD
FIREWORK
FIREWORM
FIRMLESS
FIRMNESS
FIRST-AID
FIRST-DAY
FISHABLE
FISHBALL
FISH-BONE
FISHCAKE
FISH-DIVE
FISH-GLUE
FISH-GUTS
FISH-HAWK
FISH-HOOK
FISH-MEAL
FISHPOND
FISH-SKIN
FISH-STEW
FISH-TAIL
FISH-WEIR
FISHWIFE
FISSIPED
FISSURED
FISTIANA
FISTICAL
FISTULAR
FITFULLY
FITLIEST
FIVEFOLD
FIVEPINS
FIXATION
FIXATIVE
FIXATURE
FLAGELLA
FLAGGING
FLAGPOLE
FLAGRANT
FLAGSHIP
FLAG-WORM
FLAMBEAU
FLAMBEED
FLAMELET
FLAMENCO
FLAMINGO

FLAMMULE
FLANCHED
FLÂNERIE
FLAPJACK
FLAPPING
FLASH-GUN
FLASHILY
FLASHING
FLAT-BOAT
FLAT-FISH
FLAT-FOOT
FLAT-HEAD
FLAT-IRON
FLATLING
FLATLONG
FLATNESS
FLAT-RACE
FLATTERY
FLATTING
FLATTISH
FLATUOUS
FLATWAYS
FLATWISE
FLAT-WORM
FLAUNTER
FLAUTIST
FLAWLESS
FLAX-BUSH
FLAX-COMB
FLAX-LILY
FLAX-MILL
FLAX-SEED
FLEA-BANE
FLEA-BITE
FLEASOME
FLEERING
FLEETING
FLESH-FLY
FLESH-POT
FLETCHER
FLEXIBLE
FLEXIBLY
FLEXUOSE
FLEXUOUS
FLEXURAL
FLICHTER
FLIGHTED
FLIM-FLAM
FLIMSILY
FLINCHER
FLINGING
FLINTIFY
FLINTILY
FLIP-FLAP
FLIP-FLOP
FLIPPANT
FLIPPING
FLIP-SIDE
FLIRTING
FLIRTISH
FLITTERN
FLITTING
FLIX-WEED
FLOATAGE
FLOATANT
FLOATING

FLOCCOSE
FLOCCULE
FLOCCULI
FLOCK-BED
FLOGGING
FLOODING
FLOODLIT
FLOODWAY
FLOORING
FLOPPILY
FLORALLY
FLORENCE
FLORIDLY
FLORIGEN
FLOSCULE
FLOTILLA
FLOUNDER
FLOURISH
FLOWERED
FLOWERER
FLOWERET
FLUELLIN
FLUENTLY
FLUEWORK
FLUIDICS
FLUIDIFY
FLUIDISE
FLUIDITY
FLUMMERY
FLUORIDE
FLUORINE
FLUORITE
FLURRIED
FLUSH-BOX
FLUSHING
FLUSTERY
FLY-BLOWN
FLY-MAKER
FLY-PAPER
FLYUNDER
FLY-WHEEL
FOALFOOT
FOAMLESS
FOCALISE
FOCUSING
FODDERER
FOEDARIE
FOG-BOUND
FOG-SMOKE
FOLDBOAT
FOLDEROL
FOLIAGED
FOLIATED
FOLK-FREE
FOLKLAND
FOLKLORE
FOLKMOOT
FOLK-ROCK
FOLK-SONG
FOLK-TALE
FOLK-TUNE
FOLLICLE
FOLLOWER
FOLLOW-ON
FOMENTER
FONDLING

FONDNESS
FONTANEL
FONTANGE
FOOD-CARD
FOODLESS
FOOL-BORN
FOOLSCAP
FOOTBALL
FOOT-BATH
FOOTFALL
FOOT-GEAR
FOOTHILL
FOOTHOLD
FOOTLING
FOOTMARK
FOOT-MUFF
FOOTNOTE
FOOT-PACE
FOOT-PAGE
FOOTPATH
FOOT-POST
FOOT-PUMP
FOOT-RACE
FOOT-REST
FOOT-ROPE
FOOTRULE
FOOTSLOG
FOOTSORE
FOOTSTEP
FOOTWEAR
FOOTWORK
FOOTWORN
FOOZLING
FORAMINA
FORBORNE
FORCEDLY
FORCEFUL
FORCIBLE
FORCIBLY
FORCIPES
FORDABLE
FORDOING
FOREBEAR
FOREBITT
FOREBODE
FOREBODY
FORECAST
FOREDATE
FOREDECK
FOREDOOM
FORE-EDGE
FOREFEEL
FOREFEET
FOREFELT
FOREFOOT
FOREGOER
FOREGONE
FOREHAND
FOREHEAD
FOREHENT
FOREKING
FOREKNOW
FORELAND
FORELEND
FORELENT
FORELIFT

FORELOCK
FOREMAST
FOREMEAN
FORENAME
FORENOON
FORENSIC
FOREPART
FOREPEAK
FOREPLAN
FORE-RANK
FOREREAD
FORESAID
FORESAIL
FORESEEN
FORESHEW
FORESHIP
FORESHOW
FORESIDE
FORESKIN
FORESLOW
FORESTAL
FORESTAY
FORESTED
FORESTER
FORESTRY
FORETELL
FORETOLD
FOREWARD
FOREWARN
FOREWENT
FOREWIND
FOREWORD
FORFAIRN
FORGEMAN
FORGIVEN
FORGOING
FORHAILE
FORHOOIE
FORINSEC
FORKEDLY
FORKHEAD
FORK-LIFT
FORK-TAIL
FORMALIN
FORMALLY
FORMERLY
FORMIATE
FORMLESS
FORMULAE
FORMULAR
FORMWORK
FORNENST
FORRADER
FORSAKEN
FORSLACK
FORSOOTH
FORSPEAK
FORSPEND
FORSPENT
FORSWATT
FORSWEAR
FORSWINK
FORSWORE
FORSWORN
FORSWUNK
FORTHINK

FORTIETH
FORTRESS
FORTUITY
FORTUNED
FORTYISH
FORWARDS
FORWASTE
FORWEARY
FORZANDO
FOSSETTE
FOSSEWAY
FOSTERER
FOSTRESS
FOUGASSE
FOUGHTEN
FOUL-FISH
FOULMART
FOULNESS
FOUL-PLAY
FOUNDING
FOUNTAIN
FOUNTFUL
FOUR-BALL
FOUR-EYES
FOURFOLD
FOUR-FOOT
FOUR-LEAF
FOUR-PART
FOURSOME
FOURTEEN
FOURTHLY
FOWL-PEST
FOXBERRY
FOX-BRUSH
FOX-EARTH
FOXGLOVE
FOX-GRAPE
FOXHOUND
FOXINESS
FOX-SHARK
FOZINESS
FRABJOUS
FRACTION
FRACTURE
FRAGARIA
FRAGMENT
FRAGRANT
FRAILISH
FRAME-SAW
FRAMPLER
FRAMPOLD
FRANCIUM
FRANK-FEE
FRANKISH
FRANKLIN
FRAUDFUL
FRÄULEIN
FRAXINUS
FREAKFUL
FREAKISH
FREAK-OUT
FRECKLED
FREEBORN
FREE-CITY
FREE-COST
FREEDMAN

FREEDMEN
FREE-FALL
FREE-HAND
FREEHOLD
FREENESS
FREE-REED
FREE-SHOT
FREE-SOIL
FREE-WILL
FREEZE-UP
FREEZING
FREMITUS
FRENETIC
FRENZIED
FREQUENT
FRESCADE
FRESCOED
FRESCOER
FRESCOES
FRESHISH
FRESHMAN
FRESHNER
FRESH-NEW
FRESH-RUN
FRETTING
FRETWORK
FREUDIAN
FRIBBLER
FRICTION
FRIENDED
FRIENDLY
FRIESIAN
FRIESISH
FRIGGING
FRIGHTEN
FRIGIDLY
FRIJOLES
FRILLIES
FRILLING
FRIMAIRE
FRIPPERY
FRISKFUL
FRISKILY
FRISKING
FRITTING
FROCKING
FROGFISH
FROGGERY
FROGLING
FROG-SPIT
FRONDAGE
FRONDENT
FRONDEUR
FRONDOSE
FRONTAGE
FRONTIER
FRONTLET
FRONTOON
FROSTILY
FROSTING
FROTHERY
FROTH-FLY
FROTHILY
FROTTAGE
FROTTEUR
FROU-FROU

FROWARDS
FROWNING
FROWSTER
FRUCTIFY
FRUCTOSE
FRUGALLY
FRUITAGE
FRUIT-BAT
FRUIT-BUD
FRUITERY
FRUIT-FLY
FRUITFUL
FRUITING
FRUITION
FRUITIVE
FRUMENTY
FRUMPISH
FRUSTULE
FRUTICES
FUCHSINE
FUCHSITE
FUCOIDAL
FUDDLING
FUEL-CELL
FUELLING
FUGACITY
FUGHETTA
FUGITIVE
FUGLEMAN
FULCRATE
FULGENCY
FULGURAL
FULL-AGED
FULL-COCK
FULL-EYED
FULL-FACE
FULLNESS
FULL-PAGE
FULL-PELT
FULL-SAIL
FULL-TILT
FULL-TIME
FULMINIC
FUMAROLE
FUMATORY
FUMIGANT
FUMIGATE
FUMITORY
FUMOSITY
FUNCTION
FUNDABLE
FUNDLESS
FUNEBRAL
FUNERARY
FUNEREAL
FUNGUSES
FUNKHOLE
FUNTUMIA
FURACITY
FURBELOW
FURCATED
FURCRAEA
FURCULAR
FURFURAL
FURFURAN
FURFUROL

FURIBUND
FURLOUGH
FURMENTY
FURRIERY
FURTHEST
FURUNCLE
FUSAROLE
FUSELAGE
FUSIFORM
FUSILEER
FUSILIER
FUSS-BALL
FUTILELY
FUTILITY
FUTURISM
FUTURIST
FUTURITY
FUZZ-BALL

G

GABBLING
GABBROIC
GABBROID
GABELLER
GABIONED
GABLE-END
GADABOUT
GADGETRY
GADHELIC
GADZOOKS
GAGGLING
GAG-TOOTH
GAILLARD
GAINABLE
GAININGS
GAINLESS
GAINSAID
GAIRFOWL
GALACTIC
GALANGAL
GALAPAGO
GALBANUM
GALEATED
GALENISM
GALENIST
GALENITE
GALENOID
GALILEAN
GALL-DUCT
GALLEASS
GALLIARD
GALLIASS
GALLICAN
GALLIPOT
GALLIVAT
GALL-LESS
GALLOPER
GALLOWAY
GALLUSES
GALL-WASP
GALOWSES
GALVANIC
GAMBESON
GAMBOGIC
GAMBROON
GAME-BIRD

GAME-COCK
GAMENESS
GAMESOME
GAMESTER
GAMMONER
GANGLIAR
GANGLING
GANGLION
GANGRENE
GANGSMAN
GANGSTER
GANISTER
GANOIDEI
GANTLINE
GANTLOPE
GANYMEDE
GAOLBIRD
GAPESEED
GAPEWORM
GAPINGLY
GARAMOND
GARBLING
GARBOARD
GARCINIA
GARDENER
GARDENIA
GARDYLOO
GAREFLOW
GARGANEY
GARGOYLE
GARISHLY
GARLICKY
GAROTTED
GAROTTER
GARRETED
GARRISON
GARROTTE
GASALIER
GASELIER
GAS-FIELD
GAS-FIRED
GAS-GLOBE
GAS-LIGHT
GAS-METER
GAS-MOTOR
GASOGENE
GASOLENE
GASOLINE
GAS-PLANT
GAS-POKER
GAS-SHELL
GAS-STOVE
GAS-TIGHT
GASTRAEA
GASTRULA
GAS-WATER
GAS-WORKS
GATE-FINE
GATELESS
GATE-POST
GATE-VEIN
GATHERER
GAUDY-DAY
GAULLISM
GAULLIST
GAUMLESS

GAUNTLET
GAUNTREE
GAUSSIAN
GAVELMAN
GAVELOCK
GAZEMENT
GAZETTED
GAZOGENE
GEAR-CASE
GECKONES
GEFUFFLE
GELASTIC
GELATINE
GELATION
GELIDITY
GEMATRIA
GEMINATE
GEMINOUS
GEMMA-CUP
GEMMEOUS
GEMSTONE
GENDARME
GENERALE
GENERANT
GENERATE
GENEROUS
GENESIAC
GENETICS
GENETRIX
GENEVESE
GENIALLY
GENITALS
GENITIVE
GENITRIX
GENITURE
GENIUSES
GENOCIDE
GENOTYPE
GENOVESE
GENTILIC
GENTRICE
GEOCARPY
GEODESIC
GEODETIC
GEOGNOST
GEOGNOSY
GEOGONIC
GEOLATRY
GEOLOGIC
GEOMANCY
GEOMETER
GEOMETRY
GEOMYOID
GEOPHAGY
GEOPHYTE
GEOPONIC
GEORGIAN
GEOTAXIS
GERANIOL
GERANIUM
GERBILLE
GERIATRY
GERMAINE
GERMANIC
GERM-CELL
GERMINAL

GERONTIC
GEROPIGA
GESNERIA
GESTURAL
GHANAIAN
GHASTFUL
GHOULISH
GIANTESS
GIANTISM
GIBINGLY
GIFF-GAFF
GIFT-BOOK
GIGANTIC
GIGGLING
GIG-LAMPS
GILLAROO
GILLYVOR
GILT-HEAD
GILT-TAIL
GIMCRACK
GIMMICKY
GINGELLY
GINGERLY
GINGIVAL
GINGLYMI
GINHOUSE
GIN-SLING
GIRASOLE
GIRLHOOD
GIRONDIN
GIRTLINE
GIVEAWAY
GLABELLA
GLABROUS
GLACIATE
GLACISES
GLADDING
GLADIATE
GLADIOLE
GLADIOLI
GLADNESS
GLADSOME
GLANCING
GLANDERS
GLANDULE
GLAREOUS
GLASSFUL
GLASSILY
GLASSINE
GLASSITE
GLASSMAN
GLAUCOMA
GLAUCOUS
GLEAMING
GLEANING
GLEESOME
GLIBBERY
GLIBNESS
GLIDDERY
GLIFFING
GLIMMERY
GLISSADE
GLOAMING
GLOBALLY
GLOBATED
GLOBULAR

GLOBULET
GLOBULIN
GLOOMFUL
GLOOMILY
GLOOMING
GLORIOLE
GLORIOSA
GLORIOUS
GLORYING
GLORY-PEA
GLOSSARY
GLOSSILY
GLOSSINA
GLOWLAMP
GLOWWORM
GLOXINIA
GLUCINUM
GLUCONIC
GLUMELLA
GLUMNESS
GLUMPISH
GLUTAEAL
GLUTAEUS
GLUTAMIC
GLUTTING
GLUTTONY
GLYCERIN
GLYCEROL
GLYCERYL
GLYCOGEN
GLYPTICS
GNATHITE
GNATLING
GNEISSIC
GNETALES
GNOMONIC
GOADSMAN
GOADSTER
GOAL-KICK
GOAL-LINE
GOAL-POST
GOAT-FISH
GOATHERD
GOATLING
GOAT-MOTH
GOATSKIN
GOAT'S-RUE
GOATWEED
GOBELINS
GOBIIDAE
GOD-AWFUL
GODCHILD
GOD-GIVEN
GOD-SMITH
GODSPEED
GODWARDS
GO-GETTER
GOGGLING
GOIDELIC
GOINGS-ON
GOITROUS
GOLCONDA
GOLD-DUST
GOLD-ENDS
GOLDENLY
GOLDFISH

GOLD-FOIL
GOLD-LACE
GOLD-LEAF
GOLDLESS
GOLD-MINE
GOLD-RUSH
GOLD-SIZE
GOLD-WASP
GOLD-WIRE
GOLF-BALL
GOLF-CLUB
GOLGOTHA
GOLIARDY
GOLLIWOG
GOLLYWOG
GONADIAL
GONENESS
GONFALON
GONFANON
GONGSTER
GONIDIAL
GONIDIUM
GOOD-DAME
GOOD-EVEN
GOOD-LACK
GOODLIER
GOODNESS
GOODSIRE
GOODWIFE
GOODWILL
GOODYEAR
GOOFBALL
GOOSE-CAP
GOOSE-EGG
GOR-BELLY
GORBLIMY
GORGEOUS
GORGONIA
GOSPODAR
GOSSAMER
GOSSIPRY
GOSSYPOL
GOURMAND
GOUTWEED
GOUTWORT
GOVERING
GOVERNOR
GOWNSMAN
GRAAFIAN
GRABBING
GRACEFUL
GRACIOSO
GRACIOUS
GRADATIM
GRADIENT
GRADUAND
GRADUATE
GRAECISE
GRAECISM
GRAFFITI
GRAFFITO
GRAFTING
GRAINAGE
GRAINING
GRAITHLY
GRALLOCH

GRAMARYE
GRAM-ATOM
GRAMERCY
GRANDDAD
GRANDEUR
GRANDSON
GRANITIC
GRANULAR
GRAPHEME
GRAPHICS
GRAPHITE
GRAPHIUM
GRASPING
GRASSING
GRASS-OIL
GRATEFUL
GRATTOIR
GRATUITY
GRAVAMEN
GRAVELLY
GRAVITON
GRAYLING
GREASILY
GREEDILY
GREEGREE
GREEKDOM
GREEKISH
GREEN-BAG
GREENERY
GREENFLY
GREENING
GREENISH
GREENLET
GREESING
GREETING
GREFFIER
GRESSING
GREY-COAT
GREY-EYED
GREY-FISH
GREYNESS
GRIDELIN
GRIDIRON
GRIEFFUL
GRIEVOUS
GRILLADE
GRILLAGE
GRILLING
GRIMNESS
GRIMOIRE
GRINDERY
GRINDING
GRINNING
GRIPPING
GRIPSACK
GRISELDA
GRISEOUS
GRISETTE
GRISGRIS
GRIZZLED
GRIZZLER
GROANFUL
GROANING
GRO-CHILY
GROGGERY
GROG-SHOP

GROINING
GROMWELL
GROO-GROO
GROSBEAK
GROSCHEN
GROSSART
GROUNDED
GROUNDEN
GROUNDER
GROUPING
GROUPIST
GROUTING
GROWLERY
GROWLING
GRUBBING
GRUDGING
GRUESOME
GRUFFISH
GRUMBLER
GRUMNESS
GRUMPHIE
GRUMPILY
GRUNTING
GUACHARO
GUAIACUM
GUARANTY
GUARDAGE
GUARDANT
GUARDIAN
GUDE-DAME
GUDESIRE
GUERILLA
GUERNSEY
GUESSING
GUICOWAR
GUIDABLE
GUIDANCE
GUILEFUL
GUILTILY
GUJARATH
GUJARATI
GULFWEED
GULLABLE
GULLIBLE
GULOSITY
GUMMOSIS
GUMPHION
GUMPTION
GUNFIGHT
GUNFLINT
GUNLAYER
GUNMAKER
GUNMETAL
GUNSMITH
GUNSTICK
GUNSTOCK
GUNSTONE
GURDWARA
GURGOYLE
GURMUKHI
GUSTABLE
GUTTATED
GUTTURAL
GYMKHANA
GYMNASIA
GYMNASIC

GYNANDRY
GYPSEOUS
GYPSYDOM
GYPSYISM
GYRATION
GYRATORY
GYRODYNE
GYROIDAL
GYROSTAT

H

HABANERA
HABITANS
HABITANT
HABITUAL
HABITUDE
HACIENDA
HACKBOLT
HACK-WORK
HAD-I-WIST
HAEMATIC
HAEMATIN
HAGBERRY
HAGGADAH
HAGGADIC
HAG-TAPER
HAILSHOT
HAIR-BALL
HAIRBELL
HAIRLESS
HAIRLINE
HAIR-SEAL
HAIR-TAIL
HAIR-WAVE
HAIR-WORK
HAIR-WORM
HALACHAH
HALACHIC
HALATION
HALENESS
HALF-BACK
HALF-BEAK
HALF-BLUE
HALF-BOOT
HALF-BRED
HALF-CALF
HALF-COCK
HALF-DONE
HALF-DOOR
HALF-FACE
HALF-LIFE
HALFLING
HALF-LOAF
HALF-MAST
HALF-MOON
HALF-NOTE
HALFPACE
HALF-PIKE
HALF-PINT
HALF-TERM
HALF-TEXT
HALF-TIDE
HALF-TIME
HALF-TINT
HALF-TONE
HALF-YEAR

HALICORE
HALIMOTE
HALIOTIS
HALITOUS
HALLALOO
HALL-DOOR
HALLIARD
HALLMARK
HALL-MOOT
HALLUCES
HALTERES
HAMARTIA
HAMBURGH
HAMEWITH
HAMPSTER
HAMULATE
HAND-BALL
HAND-BELL
HANDBILL
HANDBOOK
HAND-CART
HANDCLAP
HANDCUFF
HANDFAST
HANDFULS
HANDGRIP
HANDHOLD
HAND-HORN
HANDICAP
HANDLESS
HAND-LINE
HANDLING
HAND-LIST
HAND-LOOM
HAND-MADE
HANDMAID
HAND-MILL
HAND-PICK
HANDPLAY
HAND-POST
HANDRAIL
HAND-SEWN
HANDSOME
HANDWORK
HANDYMAN
HANEPOOT
HANGABLE
HANGBIRD
HANGER-ON
HANGFIRE
HANGNAIL
HANGNEST
HANGOVER
HAPLOIDY
HAPTERON
HAQUETON
HARA-KIRI
HARANGUE
HARASSED
HARASSER
HARD-A-LEE
HARD-BAKE
HARDBEAM
HARDCORE
HARDENED
HARDENER

HARDFACE
HARD-FERN
HARDHACK
HARD-HEAD
HARD-LINE
HARDNESS
HARDSHIP
HARDTACK
HARDWARE
HARDWOOD
HAREBELL
HARE-FOOT
HARE'S-EAR
HARIGALS
HARI-KARI
HARK-BACK
HARLEIAN
HARLOTRY
HARMALIN
HARMLESS
HARMONIC
HARMOSTY
HARPINGS
HARP-SEAL
HARRIDAN
HARRUMPH
HARRYING
HARTBEES
HARUSPEX
HAS-BEENS
HASHEESH
HASSOCKY
HASTATED
HASTENER
HASTINGS
HAT-BRUSH
HATCHERY
HATCHETY
HATCHING
HATCHWAY
HATEABLE
HATELESS
HATERENT
HATGUARD
HAT-PLANT
HATSTAND
HATTERIA
HAT-TRICK
HAUNTING
HAURIANT
HAURIENT
HAUSFRAU
HAVELOCK
HAVE-NOTS
HAVILDAR
HAVOCKED
HAWAIIAN
HAWFINCH
HAWK-BELL
HAWK-EYED
HAWK-MOTH
HAWKWEED
HAWTHORN
HAY-DE-GUY
HAYFIELD
HAYMAKER

HAYSTACK
HAZARDRY
HAZELNUT
HAZINESS
HEADACHE
HEADACHY
HEAD-BOOM
HEADFAST
HEADGEAR
HEADLAMP
HEADLAND
HEADLESS
HEADLINE
HEADLONG
HEADMARK
HEADMOST
HEADNOTE
HEADRACE
HEADRAIL
HEADREST
HEADRING
HEADROOM
HEADROPE
HEADSHIP
HEADSMAN
HEAD-TIRE
HEADWORD
HEADWORK
HEALABLE
HEALSOME
HEARTILY
HEARTLET
HEARTPEA
HEART-ROT
HEATHERY
HEATH-HEN
HEATSPOT
HEAVENLY
HEAVIEST
HEBDOMAD
HEBETANT
HEBETATE
HEBETUDE
HEBRAISE
HEBRAIST
HECATOMB
HECTICAL
HECTORER
HECTORLY
HEDGEHOG
HEDGE-HOP
HEDGEPIG
HEDGEROW
HEDONICS
HEDONISM
HEDONIST
HEEDLESS
HEEL-BALL
HEGELIAN
HEGEMONY
HEICH-HOW
HEIGHTEN
HEIRLESS
HEIRLOOM
HEIRSHIP

HELIACAL
HELICOID
HELIODOR
HELIOSIS
HELIOZOA
HELIPORT
HELLADIC
HELL-BENT
HELL-BORN
HELL-BRED
HELLENIC
HELL-FIRE
HELL-GATE
HELL-HOLE
HELLICAT
HELLISHY
HELL-KITE
HELLWARD
HELMETED
HELMINTH
HELMLESS
HELMSMAN
HELOTAGE
HELOTISM
HELPLESS
HELPMATE
HELPMEET
HELVETIC
HEMATITE
HEMIOLIA
HEMIOLIC
HEMIONUS
HEMIOPIA
HEMIOPIC
HEMP-BUSH
HEMP-PALM
HEMP-SEED
HENCHMAN
HENCHMEN
HEN-COURT
HENEQUEN
HENEQUIN
HENFLESH
HEN-HOUSE
HEN-HUSSY
HEN-PADLE
HEN-PARTY
HEN-ROOST
HEPATICA
HEPATISE
HEPATITE
HEPTAGON
HEPTARCH
HERACLID
HERALDIC
HERALDRY
HERBAGED
HERBARIA
HERB-BEER
HERBELET
HERBLESS
HERD-BOOK
HERDSMAN
HERDWICK
HEREAWAY
HEREDITY

H8

HEREFORD	HIGHTAIL	HOLISTIC	HORNBEAK	HUMANITY
HEREFROM	HIGH-TEST	HOLLAHOA	HORNBEAM	HUMANOID
HERENESS	HIJACKER	HOLLANDS	HORNBILL	HUMBLING
HEREROES	HILARITY	HOLLIDAM	HORNBOOK	HUMIDIFY
HEREUNTO	HILLFOLK	HOLLOWLY	HORNFELS	HUMIDITY
HEREUPON	HILL-FORT	HOLLY-OAK	HORNGELD	HUMILITY
HEREWITH	HILLOCKY	HOLOGRAM	HORNLESS	HUMMOCKY
HERISSON	HILLSIDE	HOLOPTIC	HORNPIPE	HUMORESK
HERITAGE	HIMALAYA	HOLOSTEI	HORN-POUT	HUMORIST
HERITRIX	HIMATION	HOLOZOIC	HORN-RIMS	HUMOROUS
HERMETIC	HIMSEEMS	HOLYDAME	HORNTAIL	HUMOURED
HERNSHAW	HINDERER	HOLY-ROOD	HORNWORK	HUMPBACK
HEROICAL	HIND-FOOT	HOMALOID	HORNWORM	HUMSTRUM
HEROICLY	HIND-HEAD	HOME-BORN	HORNWORT	HUNG-BEEF
HERONSEW	HINDMOST	HOME-BRED	HOROLOGE	HUNGERLY
HEROSHIP	HINDUISE	HOME-FARM	HOROLOGY	HUNG-OVER
HERPETIC	HINDUISM	HOME-FELT	HORRIBLE	HUNGRILY
HERSEEMS	HINDWARD	HOME-FIRE	HORRIBLY	HUNTRESS
HERTZIAN	HIND-WING	HOMELAND	HORRIDLY	HUNTSMAN
HESITANT	HIP-FLASK	HOMELESS	HORRIFIC	HUON-PINE
HESITATE	HIP-JOINT	HOME-LIFE	HORSE-BOY	HURCHEON
HESPERID	HIPPURIC	HOMELIKE	HORSECAR	HURDLING
HESPERIS	HIPPURIS	HOMELILY	HORSEFLY	HURONIAN
HESPERUS	HIPSTERS	HOME-MADE	HORSEMAN	HURRYING
HETAIRAI	HIREABLE	HOMEOSIS	HORSEWAY	HURTLESS
HETAIRIA	HIRELING	HOMESICK	HOSEPIPE	HUSH-BOAT
HEURETIC	HIRRIENT	HOMESPUN	HOSE-REEL	HUSH-HUSH
HEXAGLOT	HISPANIC	HOME-TOWN	HOSPITAL	HUSTINGS
HEXAGRAM	HISTIOID	HOMEWARD	HOSPITIA	HUZZAING
HEXAPLAR	HISTOGEN	HOMEWORK	HOSPODAR	HYACINTH
HEXAPODA	HISTORIC	HOMICIDE	HOSTELER	HYBLAEAN
HEXAPODY	HISTRION	HOMILIST	HOSTELRY	HYDATOID
HEXYLENE	HITCHILY	HOMINOID	HOT-BRAIN	HYDRANTH
HEY-GO-MAD	HITHERTO	HOMODONT	HOTCHPOT	HYDROGEN
HIATUSES	HIVELESS	HOMODYNE	HOTELIER	HYDROMEL
HIBERNAL	HIVELIKE	HOMOGAMY	HOTHOUSE	HYDROMYS
HIBISCUS	HIVE-NEST	HOMOLOGY	HOT-PRESS	HYDROPIC
HICCATEE	HIVEWARD	HOMONYMY	HOT-SHORT	HYDROPSY
HICCUPED	HOACTZIN	HOMOTONY	HOUR-HAND	HYDROSKI
HICKWALL	HOAR-HEAD	HOMOTYPE	HOUSE-DOG	HYDROXYL
HIDALGAS	HOARSELY	HOMOTYPY	HOUSE-FLY	HYDROZOA
HIDALGOS	HOASTMAN	HOMUNCLE	HOUSEFUL	HYGIENIC
HIDDENLY	HOBBLING	HONESTLY	HOUSEMAN	HYLICISM
HIDEAWAY	HOBBYISM	HONEY-ANT	HOUSE-TOP	HYLICIST
HIDLINGS	HOBBYIST	HONEY-BAG	HOUSLING	HYLOBATE
HIDROSIS	HOBDAYED	HONEY-BEE	HOUT-TOUT	HYMENEAL
HIDROTIC	HOBNOBBY	HONEY-DEW	HOVELLER	HYMENEAN
HIDY-HOLE	HOCK-CART	HONEYING	HOVERBED	HYMENIAL
HIELAMAN	HOCK-TIDE	HONEYPOT	HOVERBUS	HYMENIUM
HIERARCH	HOCUSING	HONORARY	HOVERCAR	HYOSCINE
HIERATIC	HOCUSSED	HONOURED	HOVER-FLY	HYPALGIA
HIERURGY	HOG-FRAME	HONOURER	HOW-D'YE-DO	HYPERION
HIGGLING	HOGGEREL	HOODLESS	HOWITZER	HYPHENIC
HIGHBALL	HOGMANAY	HOODWINK	HUB-BRAKE	HYPNOSIS
HIGH-BORN	HOG-MANED	HOOFLESS	HUBBUBOO	HYPNOTIC
HIGH-BRED	HOG-REEVE	HOOFMARK	HUCKSTER	HYPOBOLE
HIGHBROW	HOG'S-BACK	HOOK-WORM	HUGENESS	HYPOCIST
HIGHER-UP	HOG-SCORE	HOOLIGAN	HUGUENOT	HYPODERM
HIGH-GEAR	HOGSHEAD	HOOSEGOW	HUISSIER	HYPOGAEA
HIGHJACK	HOISTING	HOOT-TOOT	HULA-HOOP	HYPOGEAL
HIGHLAND	HOISTMAN	HOPELESS	HULA-HULA	HYPOGEAN
HIGH-LONE	HOISTWAY	HOPINGLY	HULL-DOWN	HYPOGENE
HIGHMOST	HOKY-POKY	HOPPED-UP	HUMANELY	HYPOGEUM
HIGHNESS	HOLD-BACK	HORATIAN	HUMANISE	HYPOGYNY
HIGH-RISE	HOLD-FAST	HORMONAL	HUMANISM	HYPOTHEC
HIGHROAD	HOLINESS	HORMONIC	HUMANIST	HYSTERIA

HYSTERIC

I

IAMBUSES
IANTHINE
IATRICAL
ICE-APRON
ICEBLINK
ICE-BOUND
ICECRAFT
ICECREAM
ICE-FIELD
ICE-FRONT
ICE-HOUSE
ICE-LEDGE
ICE-PLANT
ICE-SHEET
ICE-STONE
ICE-WATER
ICE-YACHT
ICHOROUS
ICTERINE
IDEALESS
IDEALISE
IDEALISM
IDEALIST
IDEALITY
IDEATION
IDEATIVE
IDENTIFY
IDENTITY
IDEOGRAM
IDEOLOGY
IDIOLECT
IDIOTISH
IDIOTISM
IDLEHOOD
IDLENESS
IDOCRASE
IDOLATER
IDOLATRY
IDOLISER
IDYLLIAN
IDYLLIST
IGNATIAN
IGNITION
IGNITRON
IGNOMINY
IGNORANT
ILLATION
ILLATIVE
ILL-BEING
ILL-BLOOD
ILL-DEEDY
ILL-FACED
ILL-FATED
ILL-FAURD
ILLINIUM
ILLISION
ILL-SPENT
ILL-TIMED
ILL-TREAT
ILLUMINE
ILL-USAGE
ILLUSION
ILLUSIVE

ILLUSORY
ILMENITE
IMAGINAL
IMAGINER
IMAGINES
IMBECILE
IMBITTER
IMBORDER
IMBRICES
IMITABLE
IMITANCY
IMITATOR
IMMANELY
IMMANENT
IMMANITY
IMMANTLE
IMMANUEL
IMMATURE
IMMERSED
IMMINENT
IMMINGLE
IMMITTED
IMMOBILE
IMMODEST
IMMOLATE
IMMOMENT
IMMORTAL
IMMUNISE
IMMUNITY
IMPANATE
IMPANNEL
IMPARITY
IMPARTER
IMPASTOD
IMPELLED
IMPELLER
IMPERIAL
IMPERIUM
IMPETIGO
IMPISHLY
IMPLEACH
IMPLEDGE
IMPLICIT
IMPLORER
IMPLUNGE
IMPLUVIA
IMPLYING
IMPOCKET
IMPOLDER
IMPOLICY
IMPOLITE
IMPONENT
IMPORTER
IMPOSING
IMPOSTER
IMPOSTOR
IMPOTENT
IMPRESSE
IMPRIMIS
IMPRISON
IMPROPER
IMPROVER
IMPUDENT
IMPUGNER
IMPUNITY
IMPURELY

IMPURITY
IMPURPLE
INACTION
INACTIVE
IN-AND-OUT
INARABLE
INASMUCH
INAURATE
INCENSER
INCENSOR
INCENTRE
INCEPTOR
INCHMEAL
INCHOATE
INCH-TAPE
INCH-WORM
INCIDENT
INCISION
INCISIVE
INCISURE
INCITANT
INCIVISM
INCLINED
INCLUDED
INCOMING
INCORPSE
INCREASE
INCREATE
INCUBATE
INCUBOUS
INCURRED
INCURVED
INDAGATE
INDEBTED
INDECENT
INDENTED
INDENTER
INDIAMAN
INDICANT
INDICATE
INDICTEE
INDIGENE
INDIGENT
INDIGEST
INDIRECT
INDOCILE
INDOLENT
INDRENCH
INDUCTOR
INDULGER
INDULINE
INDURATE
INDUSIAL
INDUSIUM
INDUSTRY
INDUVIAE
INDUVIAL
INEDIBLE
INEDITED
INEQUITY
INERRANT
INERTIAL
INESSIVE
INEXPERT
INFAMISE
INFAMOUS

INFANTRY
INFECTOR
INFECUND
INFEFTED
INFERIOR
INFERNAL
INFERRED
INFICETE
INFILTER
INFINITE
INFINITY
INFIRMLY
INFLAMED
INFLAMER
INFLATED
INFLATOR
INFLATUS
INFLEXED
INFLUENT
INFORMAL
INFORMED
INFORMER
INFRA-RED
INFRINGE
INFUSION
INFUSIVE
INFUSORY
INGENIUM
INGROOVE
INGROWTH
INGUINAL
INHALANT
INHEARSE
INHERENT
INHESION
INHOLDER
INHUMANE
INHUMATE
INIMICAL
INIQUITY
INITIATE
INJECTOR
INJURANT
INKINESS
INKSTAND
INKSTONE
INLANDER
INLAYING
INNATELY
INNATIVE
INNOCENT
INNOVATE
INNUENDO
INOCULUM
INORNATE
INOSITOL
INQUIRER
INSANELY
INSANITY
INSCIENT
INSCRIBE
INSCROLL
INSCULPT
INSECURE
INSENSOR
INSERTED

INSHRINE
INSIGNIA
INSOLATE
INSOLENT
INSOMUCH
INSOMNIA
INSPHERE
INSPIRED
INSPIRER
INSPIRIT
INSTABLE
INSTANCE
INSTANCY
INSTINCT
INSTRUCT
INSUCKEN
INSULANT
INSULATE
INSULTER
INSURANT
INSWATHE
INTAGLIO
INTARSIA
INTARSIO
INTEGRAL
INTELSAT
INTENDED
INTENDER
INTENTLY
INTERACT
INTERCOM
INTEREST
INTERIOR
INTERMIT
INTERMIX
INTERNAL
INTERNEE
INTERPOL
INTERRED
INTERREX
INTERSEX
INTERTIE
INTERVAL
INTERWAR
INTIMACY
INTIMATE
INTIMISM
INTIMIST
INTIMITY
INTITULE
INTONATE
INTONING
INTORTED
INTRADOS
INTREPID
INTRIGUE
INTRINCE
INTROMIT
INTRORSE
INTRUDER
INTUBATE
INTUITED
INUNDANT
INUNDATE
INURBANE
INUSTION

INVASION
INVASIVE
INVEAGLE
INVECKED
INVECTED
INVEIGLE
INVERTED
INVERTER
INVERTOR
INVESTOR
INVIABLE
INVITING
INVOCATE
INVOLUTE
INWARDLY
IODOFORM
IODYRITE
IONICISE
IOTACISM
IREFULLY
IRENICAL
IRENICON
IRISATED
IRISCOPE
IRISHISM
IRISHMAN
IRONBARK
IRON-CLAD
IRON-CLAY
IRON-GRAY
IRON-GREY
IRONICAL
IRON-MAIL
IRON-MINE
IRON-MOLE
IRON-SAND
IRON-SICK
IRONSIDE
IRONWARE
IRONWOOD
IRONWORK
IRRIGATE
IRRISION
IRRISORY
IRRITANT
IRRITATE
ISABELLA
ISAGOGIC
ISCHEMIA
ISCHEMIC
ISCHURIA
ISENGRIM
ISLAMISE
ISLAMISM
ISLAMITE
ISLANDER
ISLESMAN
ISOBARIC
ISOBRONT
ISOCHASM
ISOCHEIM
ISOCHORE
ISOCRYME
ISODICON
ISODOMON
ISODOMUM

ISOGAMIC
ISOGLOSS
ISOGONAL
ISOGONIC
ISOLABLE
ISOLATOR
ISOMERIC
ISOMETRY
ISOMORPH
ISOPLETH
ISOPRENE
ISOPTERA
ISOSPORY
ISOSTASY
ISOTHERE
ISOTHERM
ISOTONIC
ISOTOPIC
ISOTROPY
ISSUABLE
ISSUANCE
ISTHMIAN
ITALIOTE
ITCH-MITE
ITCHWEED
ITERANCE
IVORY-NUT

J

JABBERER
JACKAROO
JACKBOOT
JACKEROO
JACKETED
JACK-FOOL
JACK-HIGH
JACK-PINE
JACK-TREE
JACOBEAN
JACOBITE
JACQUARD
JACULATE
JAGGEDLY
JAILBIRD
JALOUSIE
JAMAICAN
JAMBEAUX
JAMBOLAN
JAMBOREE
JAMESIAN
JAMPANEE
JANGLING
JANIFORM
JANITRIX
JANIZARY
JANUFORM
JAPANESE
JAPANESY
JAPANNED
JAPANNER
JAPHETIC
JAPONICA
JARARACA
JARARAKA
JAUNDICE
JAUNTILY

JAUNTING
JAVANESE
JAW-TOOTH
JEALOUSE
JEALOUSY
JEBUSITE
JEHOVIST
JEJUNELY
JELUTONG
JEOPARDY
JEREMIAD
JEROBOAM
JERQUING
JERRICAN
JERRYCAN
JESTBOOK
JESUITIC
JESUITRY
JET-BLACK
JET-DRIVE
JET-PLANE
JETTISON
JEWELLED
JEWELLER
JEWISHLY
JEW'S-HARP
JIBBINGS
JIB-CRANE
JIBINGLY
JICKAJOG
JIGGERED
JIMCRACK
JIMPNESS
JINGBANG
JINGLING
JINGOISH
JINGOISM
JIRKINET
JIU-JITSU
JOBATION
JOCOROUS
JOCOSELY
JOCOSITY
JOCUNDLY
JODHPURS
JOGGLING
JOHANNES
JOIN-HAND
JOINT-FIR
JOINT-OIL
JOINTURE
JOKESOME
JOKINGLY
JOLTHEAD
JONATHAN
JONGLEUR
JORDELOO
JOSTLING
JOVIALLY
JOWING-IN
JOYFULLY
JOYOUSLY
JOY-STICK
JOY-WHEEL
JUBILANT
JUBILATE

JUDAICAL
JUDAISER
JUDGMENT
JUDICIAL
JUGGLERY
JUGGLING
JUGOSLAV
JUGULATE
JULIENNE
JUMBOISE
JUMPED-UP
JUMP-SEAT
JUNCTION
JUNCTURE
JUNKETED
JUNK-RING
JUNKSHOP
JUNONIAN
JURASSIC
JURATORY
JURISTIC
JURYMAST
JUSTICER
JUSTNESS
JUVENILE

K

KABELJOU
KACHAHRI
KAFFIYEH
KAIL-RUNT
KAILYARD
KAIMAKAM
KAKA-BEAK
KAKA-BILL
KAKEMONO
KALA-AZAR
KALAMDAN
KALENDAR
KALEVALA
KALINITE
KALIYUGA
KALOTYPE
KALUMPIT
KALYPTRA
KAMADEVA
KAMIKAZE
KANARESE
KANGAROO
KANTIKOY
KAOLIANG
KATAKANA
KAURI-GUM
KECKLING
KEDGEREE
KEELHAUL
KEENNESS
KEEPSAKE
KEEPSAKY
KEESHOND
KEFFIYEH
KEFUFFLE
KENSPECK
KEPHALIC
KERB-SIDE
KERCHIEF

KERNELLY
KEROSENE
KEROSINE
KEYBOARD
KEYBUGLE
KEY-FRUIT
KEY-PLATE
KEYSTONE
KHALIFAH
KHALIFAT
KHEDIVAL
KHILAFAT
KHUSKHUS
KIBITZER
KICKABLE
KICKBACK
KICKSHAW
KID-GLOVE
KILLADAR
KILLCROP
KILLOGIE
KILN-HOLE
KILODYNE
KILOGRAM
KILOVOLT
KILOWATT
KINAKINA
KINDLESS
KINDLILY
KINDLING
KINDNESS
KINESICS
KINETICS
KING-BIRD
KING-BOLT
KING-CRAB
KING-CROW
KINGFISH
KINGHOOD
KINGLESS
KINGLIKE
KINGLING
KINGPOST
KINGSHIP
KING-SIZE
KINGSMAN
KINGWOOD
KINKAJOU
KINK-HOST
KINSFOLK
KIPPERER
KIRK-TOWN
KIRKWARD
KIRKYARD
KIRN-BABY
KIRN-MILK
KISS-CURL
KISTVAEN
KITE-MARK
KLEPHTIC
KLONDIKE
KLONDYKE
KLYSTRON
KNACKERY
KNACKISH
KNAPPING

KNAPSACK	LACINIAE	LAND-RAIL	LAVATORY	LEGERITY
KNAPSCAL	LACKADAY	LAND-ROLL	LAVEMENT	LEG-GUARD
KNAPWEED	LACKLAND	LAND-SHIP	LAVENDER	LEGIONED
KNEE-DEEP	LACK-LOVE	LANDSKIP	LAVEROCK	LEISURED
KNEE-HIGH	LACONIAN	LANDSLIP	LAVISHLY	LEKYTHOS
KNEE-JERK	LACONISM	LANDSMÅL	LAW-AGENT	LEMONADE
KNEE-STOP	LACRIMAL	LANDSMAN	LAW-COURT	LEMON-DAB
KNICKERS	LACROSSE	LANDWARD	LAWFULLY	LEMURIAN
KNIFE-BOX	LACRYMAL	LANDWEHR	LAWGIVER	LEMURINE
KNIFE-BOY	LACTEOUS	LANDWIND	LAW-MAKER	LEMUROID
KNIGHTLY	LACTIFIC	LANGLAUF	LAWYERLY	LENGTHEN
KNITTING	LACUNARS	LANGRAGE	LAXATIVE	LENIENCE
KNITWEAR	LACUNARY	LANGSHAN	LAYABOUT	LENIENCY
KNOCKING	LACUNATE	LANGSPEL	LAYERING	LENINISM
KNOCKOUT	LACUNOSE	LANGUAGE	LAY-SHAFT	LENINIST
KNOT-HOLE	LADDERED	LANGUISH	LAY-STALL	LENINITE
KNOTLESS	LADIFIED	LANKNESS	LAZARIST	LENITIVE
KNOTTING	LADINITY	LANNARET	LAZINESS	LENTANDO
KNOTWORK	LADLEFUL	LANOLINE	LAZULITE	LENTICEL
KNOWABLE	LADYBIRD	LANTHORN	LAZURITE	LENTICLE
KNURLING	LADY-FERN	LANTSKIP	LAZY-JACK	LENT-LILY
KOFTGARI	LADYFIED	LAP-BOARD	LEACHING	LEPIDOTE
KOFTWORK	LADY-HELP	LAPELLED	LEACH-TUB	LEPORINE
KOHLRABI	LADYHOOD	LAPIDARY	LEADENLY	LERNAEAN
KOK-SAGYZ	LADYLIKE	LAPIDATE	LEADLESS	LET-ALONE
KOLARIAN	LADY-LOVE	LAPIDIFY	LEAD-LINE	LETHARGY
KOLINSKY	LADYSHIP	LAPPETED	LEADSMAN	LETTERED
KOMISSAR	LAGTHING	LAPSABLE	LEAF-BASE	LETTERER
KOMITAJI	LAH-DI-DAH	LAPSTONE	LEAF-CURL	LETTLAND
KOMSOMOL	LALLYGAG	LAPUTIAN	LEAF-FALL	LEUCITIC
KORFBALL	LAMANTIN	LARBOARD	LEAFLESS	LEUCOJUM
KOTTABOS	LAMASERY	LARCENER	LEAF-LIKE	LEVANTER
KOURBASH	LAMBASTE	LARDERER	LEAF-ROLL	LEVELLED
KOUSKOUS	LAMBDOID	LARGESSE	LEAF-SCAR	LEVELLER
KRAMERIA	LAMBENCY	LARKSPUR	LEANNESS	LEVERAGE
KREASOTE	LAMBLIKE	LARRIKIN	LEAP-FROG	LEVIABLE
KREATINE	LAMBLING	LARVATED	LEAP-YEAR	LEVIGATE
KREOSOTE	LAMBSKIN	LARYNGAL	LEARNING	LEVIRATE
KREUTZER	LAMELLAE	LARYNGES	LEASABLE	LEVITATE
KROMESKY	LAMELLAR	LARYNXES	LEASE-ROD	LEVULOSE
KRUMHORN	LAMENESS	LASSLORN	LEATHERN	LEWDNESS
KUROSHIO	LAMENTED	LASSOING	LEATHERY	LEWDSTER
KURVEYOR	LAMINARY	LATCHKEY	LEAVINGS	LEWISIAN
KYLLOSIS	LAMINATE	LATENESS	LECANORA	LEWISITE
KYPHOSIS	LAMMIGER	LATENTLY	LECITHIN	LEWISSON
KYPHOTIC	LAMPASSE	LATERITE	LECTRESS	LIBATION
KYRIELLE	LAMP-HOLE	LATEWAKE	LECTURER	LIBATORY
	LAMP-HOUR	LATHYRUS	LECYTHIS	LIBECCIO
L	LAMPPOST	LATINISE	LECYTHUS	LIBELLED
	LAMPREYS	LATINISM	LEE-BOARD	LIBELLER
LABDANUM	LANCEGAY	LATINIST	LEECHDOM	LIBERATE
LABELLED	LANCELET	LATINITY	LEFT-BANK	LIBRETTI
LABELLUM	LANCETED	LATITANT	LEFT-HAND	LIBRETTO
LABIALLY	LAND-ARMY	LATITUDE	LEFT-OVER	LICENSED
LABIATAE	LAND-CRAB	LATTERLY	LEFTWARD	LICENSEE
LABOURED	LANDDROS	LAUDABLE	LEFT-WING	LICENSER
LABOURER	LANDFALL	LAUDABLY	LEGALISE	LICHANOS
LABRADOR	LAND-FISH	LAUDANUM	LEGALISM	LICHENED
LABRIDAE	LANDGIRL	LAUGHFUL	LEGALIST	LICHENIN
LABURNUM	LAND-HERD	LAUGHING	LEGALITY	LICHGATE
LACEBARK	LANDLADY	LAUGHTER	LEGATARY	LICHWAKE
LACE-BOOT	LANDLESS	LAUNCHER	LEGATINE	LICKER-IN
LACE-LEAF	LAND-LINE	LAUREATE	LEGATION	LICORICE
LACERANT	LANDLORD	LAVAFORM	LEG-BREAK	LIEGEDOM
LACERATE	LANDMARK	LAVA-LAVA	LEGENDRY	LIEGEMAN
LACE-WING	LAND-MINE	LAVATION	LEGERING	LIENTERY
LACHESIS				

LIFEBELT
LIFEBOAT
LIFEBUOY
LIFEHOLD
LIFELESS
LIFELIKE
LIFELINE
LIFELONG
LIFE-PEER
LIFE-RENT
LIFE-SIZE
LIFESOME
LIFETIME
LIFE-WORK
LIFTABLE
LIFT-PUMP
LIGAMENT
LIGATION
LIGATURE
LIGHTFUL
LIGHTING
LIGHTISH
LIGNEOUS
LIGNITIC
LIGULATE
LIKEABLE
LIKENESS
LIKEWAKE
LIKEWALK
LIKEWISE
LILLIPUT
LIMACEAE
LIMATION
LIMA-WOOD
LIMBLESS
LIMBMEAL
LIMEKILN
LIMERICK
LIME-TREE
LIME-TWIG
LIMEWASH
LIME-WOOD
LIMINESS
LIMITARY
LIMITING
LIMNAEID
LIMNETIC
LIMONITE
LIMOUSIN
LIMPIDLY
LINCHPIN
LINCTURE
LINDWORM
LINEALLY
LINEARLY
LINEATED
LINE-FISH
LINESMAN
LINGERER
LINGERIE
LINGSTER
LINGUIST
LINGULAR
LINIMENT
LINKSTER
LINKWORK

LINNAEAN
LINOLEIC
LINOLEUM
LINOTYPE
LINSTOCK
LINTSEED
LION-LIKE
LIPARITE
LIPOGRAM
LIPOMATA
LIPSALVE
LIPSTICK
LIQUABLE
LIQUESCE
LIQUIDLY
LIQUORED
LIRIPIPE
LIRIPOOP
LISPOUND
LISTENER
LISTLESS
LITERACY
LITERARY
LITERATE
LITERATI
LITERATO
LITEROSE
LITHARGE
LITHERLY
LITIGANT
LITIGATE
LITTERED
LITTLE-GO
LITTLING
LITTORAL
LITURGIC
LIVEABLE
LIVE-AXLE
LIVE-BAIT
LIVE-BORN
LIVELILY
LIVELONG
LIVE-RAIL
LIVERIED
LIVERISH
LIVER-ROT
LIVE-WELL
LIVE-WIRE
LIVIDITY
LIXIVIAL
LIXIVIUM
LOAD-LINE
LOADSTAR
LOAF-CAKE
LOANABLE
LOAN-WORD
LOATHFUL
LOATHING
LOBATION
LOBBYING
LOBBYIST
LOBE-FOOT
LOBELINE
LOBLOLLY
LOBOTOMY
LOBULATE

LOCALISE
LOCALISM
LOCALITY
LOCATION
LOCATIVE
LOCKFAST
LOCK-GATE
LOCKSMAN
LOCKSTEP
LOCOFOCO
LOCOMOTE
LOCO-WEED
LOCULATE
LOCUSTAE
LOCUTION
LOCUTORY
LODESMAN
LODESTAR
LODGMENT
LODICULA
LODICULE
LOGBOARD
LOG-CABIN
LOG-CANOE
LOG-GLASS
LOG-HOUSE
LOGICIAN
LOGICISE
LOGISTIC
LOG-JUICE
LOGOGRAM
LOGOTYPE
LOG-SLATE
LOITERER
LOLLARDY
LOLLIPOP
LOLLYGAG
LOMENTUM
LONDONER
LONENESS
LONESOME
LONGBOAT
LONGERON
LONG-FIRM
LONG-HAIR
LONGHAND
LONG-HEAD
LONGHORN
LONG-LEGS
LONGNESS
LONG-NINE
LONGSHIP
LONG-SLIP
LONGSOME
LONG-SPUN
LONG-STOP
LONG-TAIL
LONG-TERM
LONG-TOGS
LONGUEUR
LONGWALL
LONG-WAVE
LONGWAYS
LONGWISE
LOOKER-IN
LOOKER-ON

LOOPHOLE
LOOP-LINE
LOOSE-BOX
LOOSENER
LOO-TABLE
LOP-EARED
LOPGRASS
LOP-SIDED
LORDLESS
LORDLING
LORDOSIS
LORDOTIC
LORDSHIP
LORICATE
LORIKEET
LORRY-HOP
LOSINGLY
LOTHARIO
LOUDNESS
LOUIS-D'OR
LOUNGING
LOVEBIRD
LOVE-DRUG
LOVE-FEAT
LOVE-GAME
LOVE-KNOT
LOVELACE
LOVELESS
LOVELILY
LOVELOCK
LOVELORN
LOVE-NEST
LOVE-SEAT
LOVESICK
LOVESOME
LOVE-SONG
LOVINGLY
LOWERING
LOW-LIVED
LOW-SLUNG
LOW-WATER
LOYALIST
LOZENGED
LUBBERLY
LUBRICAL
LUCIDITY
LUCKLESS
LUCKY-BAG
LUCKY-DIP
LUCULENT
LUCULLAN
LUCULLIC
LUG-CHAIR
LUKEWARM
LUMBERER
LUMBERLY
LUMINANT
LUMINARY
LUMINIST
LUMINOUS
LUMPFISH
LUMPY-JAW
LUNARIAN
LUNARIST
LUNATION
LUNCHEON

LUNG-BOOK
LUNGEING
LUNG-FISH
LUNGWORT
LUNULATE
LUPERCAL
LUPULINE
LUSCIOUS
LUSHNESS
LUSTIQUE
LUSTLESS
LUSTRATE
LUSTRINE
LUSTRING
LUSTROUS
LUTANIST
LUTECIUM
LUTENIST
LUTEOLIN
LUTETIAN
LUTETIUM
LUTHERAN
LUXATION
LUXMETER
LUXURIST
LYCHGATE
LYKE-WAKE
LYMPHOMA
LYNCH-LAW
LYNX-EYED
LYOPHILE
LYOPHOBE
LYRA-VIOL
LYRA-WISE
LYRE-BIRD
LYRICISM
LYSERGIC
LYSOZYME

M

MACAHUBA
MACARISE
MACARISM
MACARONI
MACAROON
MACERATE
MACKEREL
MACKINAW
MACRURAL
MACULATE
MACULOSE
MAD-APPLE
MADBRAIN
MADHOUSE
MADRASAH
MADRIGAL
MAECENAS
MAENADIC
MAEONIAN
MAESTOSO
MAFFLING
MAGAZINE
MAGDALEN
MAGESHIP
MAGICIAN
MAGISTER

MAGMATIC
MAGNESIA
MAGNETIC
MAGNETON
MAGNIFIC
MAGNOLIA
MAGOT-PIE
MAHADEVA
MAHARAJA
MAHARANI
MAHDIISM
MAHDIIST
MAH-JONGG
MAHOGANY
MAHRATTA
MAIDENLY
MAIDHOOD
MAIDLESS
MAID-PALE
MAIEUTIC
MAILABLE
MAIL-BOAT
MAIL-CART
MAIL-CLAD
MAIL-DRAG
MAINBOOM
MAIN-DECK
MAIN-DOOR
MAINLAND
MAINLINE
MAINMAST
MAINSAIL
MAINSTAY
MAINTAIN
MAINYARD
MAJESTIC
MAJOLICA
MAJORITY
MAKEBATE
MAKELESS
MAKIMONO
MALAGASH
MALAGASY
MALAMUTE
MALANDER
MALAPERT
MALARIAL
MALARIAN
MALARKEY
MALAXAGE
MALAXATE
MALEDICT
MALE-FERN
MALEFICE
MALEMUTE
MALGRADO
MALIGNER
MALIGNLY
MALINGER
MALLEATE
MALLECHO
MALODOUR
MALSTICK
MALT-DUST
MALT-KILN
MALT-MILL

MALTREAT
MALTSTER
MALTWORM
MALVASIA
MALVESIE
MAMELUCO
MAMELUKE
MAMILLAE
MAMILLAR
MAMMALIA
MAMMETRY
MAMMIFER
MAMMILLA
MANAGING
MANCANDO
MAN-CHILD
MANCIPLE
MANDAEAN
MANDAMUS
MANDARIN
MANDATOR
MANDIBLE
MANDINGO
MANDIOCA
MANDOLIN
MANDORLA
MANDRAKE
MANDRILL
MAN-EATER
MANELESS
MANFULLY
MANGABEY
MANGANIC
MANGANIN
MANGONEL
MANGROVE
MAN-HOURS
MANIACAL
MANICHEE
MANICURE
MANIFEST
MANIFOLD
MANIFORM
MANNA-ASH
MANNA-DEW
MANNERED
MANNERLY
MANNIKIN
MANNITOL
MAN-OF-WAR
MANORIAL
MANPOWER
MAN-SIZED
MANSUETE
MANSWORN
MANTÉLET
MANTILLA
MANTISSA
MANTLING
MANUALLY
MANUBRIA
MANURIAL
MANURING
MANY-EYED
MANY-ROOT
MAPSTICK

MAQUETTE
MARABOUT
MARASMIC
MARASMUS
MARATHON
MARATTIA
MARAUDER
MARAVEDI
MARBLING
MARCELLA
MARCHESA
MARCHESE
MARCHMAN
MARGARIC
MARGARIN
MARGINAL
MARGINED
MARGRAVE
MARIGOLD
MARIGRAM
MARINADE
MARINATE
MARINISM
MARINIST
MARITAGE
MARITIME
MARJORAM
MARKEDLY
MARKETED
MARKETER
MARKSMAN
MARMOSET
MAROCAIN
MARONIAN
MARONITE
MAROONER
MAROQUIN
MARQUESS
MARQUISE
MARRIAGE
MARRYING
MARSH-GAS
MARSHMAN
MARSILEA
MARSILIA
MARSPORT
MARTAGON
MARTELLO
MARTENOT
MARTINET
MARZIPAN
MASCARON
MASHLOCH
MASOOLAH
MASORETE
MASORETH
MASSACRE
MASS-BELL
MASS-BOOK
MASSETER
MASSEUSE
MASSICOT
MASS-JOHN
MASSOOLA
MASSORAH
MASTERLY

MASTHEAD
MASTICOT
MASTITIS
MASTLESS
MASTODON
MASURIUM
MATACHIN
MATADORE
MATAMATA
MATCHBOX
MATELESS
MATELOTE
MATERIAL
MATÉRIEL
MATERNAL
MATFELON
MATGRASS
MATHESIS
MATHURIN
MATRICES
MATRIXES
MATRONAL
MATRONLY
MATTRESS
MATURATE
MATURELY
MATURITY
MATUTINE
MAUMETRY
MAUVEINE
MAVERICK
MAWBOUND
MAWMETRY
MAXILLAE
MAXIMISE
MAXIMIST
MAY-APPLE
MAY-BLOOM
MAYOLOGY
MAYORESS
MAY-QUEEN
MAZARINE
MAZDAISM
MAZDEISM
MAZEMENT
MAZINESS
MEAGRELY
MEAL-POKE
MEAL-TIDE
MEAL-TIME
MEAL-TREE
MEAL-WORM
MEALY-BUG
MEAN-BORN
MEANNESS
MEANTIME
MEAN-TONE
MEASURED
MEASURER
MEATLESS
MEAT-SAFE
MEATUSES
MECHANIC
MECONATE
MECONIUM
MEDALLED

MEDALLIC
MEDDLING
MEDIALLY
MEDIATOR
MEDICATE
MEDICEAN
MEDICINE
MEDIEVAL
MEDIOCRE
MEDITATE
MEDJIDIE
MEDULLAR
MEDUSOID
MEEKNESS
MEETNESS
MEGALITH
MEGAPODE
MEGAWATT
MEIONITE
MELAMINE
MELANISM
MELANITE
MELANOUS
MELILITE
MELINITE
MELLITIC
MELLOWLY
MELODEON
MELODICS
MELODISE
MELODIST
MEMBERED
MEMBRANE
MEMORIAL
MEMORIAM
MEMORISE
MEMPHIAN
MEMPHITE
MEM-SAHIB
MENACING
MENARCHE
MENEVIAN
MENFOLKS
MENHADEN
MENINGES
MENISCUS
MENOLOGY
MENOPOME
MENSEFUL
MENSTRUA
MENSURAL
MENSUREN
MENTALLY
MEPHISTO
MEPHITIC
MEPHITIS
MERCATOR
MERCHANT
MERCHILD
MERCIFUL
MERCURIC
MERESMAN
MERICARP
MERIDIAN
MERIMAKE
MERINGUE

MERISTEM	MIDWIVED	MIRLITON	MISUSAGE	MONAURAL
MERISTIC	MIDWIVES	MIRRORED	MISWRITE	MONAXIAL
MEROGONY	MIGHTEST	MIRTHFUL	MITHRAEA	MONAZITE
MEROSOME	MIGHTFUL	MISALLOT	MITHRAIC	MONETARY
MERRYMAN	MIGHTILY	MISAPPLY	MITIGANT	MONETISE
MERSALYL	MIGRAINE	MISARRAY	MITIGATE	MONEY-BAG
MERULIUS	MIGRATOR	MISBEGOT	MITTENED	MONEY-BOX
MERYCISM	MILCH-COW	MISBIRTH	MITTIMUS	MONGCORN
MESARAIC	MILDNESS	MISCARRY	MITZVOTH	MONGOLIC
MESCALIN	MILESIAN	MISCEGEN	MIXY-MAXY	MONGOOSE
MESDAMES	MILITANT	MISCHIEF	MIZZLING	MONICKER
MESEEMED	MILITARY	MISCIBLE	MJÖLLNIR	MONISTIC
MESHWORK	MILITATE	MISCOUNT	McNAGHTEN	MONITION
MESIALLY	MILKLESS	MISCREED	MOBILISE	MONITIVE
MESMERIC	MILKLIKE	MISDEALT	MOBILITY	MONITORY
MESOCARP	MILK-LOAF	MISDIGHT	MOBOCRAT	MONK-FISH
MESODERM	MILKMAID	MISDOING	MOCASSIN	MON-KHMER
MESOLITE	MILK-TREE	MISDOUBT	MOCCASIN	MONKHOOD
MESOTRON	MILK-WALK	MISDREAD	MOCKABLE	MONK-SEAL
MESOZOIC	MILK-WARM	MISENTRY	MOCUDDUM	MONOACID
MESQUITE	MILK-WEED	MISERERE	MODALISM	MONOCRAT
MESSIDOR	MILKWOOD	MISFAITH	MODALIST	MONODIST
MESS-JOHN	MILKWORT	MISFEIGN	MODALITY	MONODONT
MESSMATE	MILLEPED	MISGIVEN	MODELLED	MONOECIA
MESS-ROOM	MILL-GIRL	MISGRAFF	MODELLER	MONOGAMY
MESSUAGE	MILL-HAND	MISGRAFT	MODERATE	MONOGENY
MESTIZAS	MILLIARD	MISGUIDE	MODERATO	MONOGLOT
MESTIZOS	MILLIARE	MISHMASH	MODERNLY	MONOGONY
METABOLA	MILLIARY	MISHNAIC	MODESTLY	MONOGRAM
METAIRIE	MILLIBAR	MISJUDGE	MODIFIED	MONOGYNY
METALLED	MILLIÈME	MISLIGHT	MODIFIER	MONOHULL
METALLIC	MILLINER	MISMARRY	MODIOLAR	MONOLITH
METAMERE	MILLIPED	MISMATCH	MODIOLUS	MONOLOGY
METAPHOR	MILLPOND	MISMATED	MODISHLY	MONOMIAL
METAYAGE	MILLRACE	MISMETRE	MODIWORT	MONOPODE
METAZOAN	MILL-TAIL	MISNOMER	MODULATE	MONOPOLY
METAZOIC	MILL-WORK	MISOGAMY	MOFUSSIL	MONORAIL
METAZOON	MILTONIC	MISOGYNY	MOHARRAM	MONOTINT
METEORIC	MIMESTER	MISOLOGY	MOISTIFY	MONOTONE
METEWAND	MIMETITE	MISORDER	MOISTURE	MONOTONY
METEYARD	MIMICKED	MISPLACE	MOKADDAM	MONOTYPE
METHANOL	MIMICKER	MISPLEAD	MOLALITY	MONOXIDE
METHINKS	MINACITY	MISPOINT	MOLARITY	MONSIEUR
METHODIC	MINATORY	MISPRINT	MOLASSES	MONTARIA
METHYLIC	MINCE-PIE	MISPRISE	MOLDWARP	MONTEITH
METHYSIS	MIND-CURE	MISPRIZE	MOLECAST	MONTICLE
METONYMY	MINDLESS	MISPROUD	MOLECULE	MONUMENT
METOPISM	MINGLING	MISQUOTE	MOLE-EYED	MOODY-MAD
METOPRYL	MINIMENT	MISSHAPE	MOLE-HILL	MOONBEAM
METRICAL	MINIMISE	MISSHOOD	MOLESKIN	MOONCALF
MEZEREON	MINIMISM	MISSPEAK	MOLESTER	MOON-FACE
MEZUZAHS	MINIMIST	MISSPELL	MOLINISM	MOON-FISH
MEZUZOTH	MINI-SKIS	MISSPELT	MOLINIST	MOONLESS
MIASMATA	MINISTER	MISSPEND	MOLLUSCA	MOONRISE
MIASMOUS	MINISTRY	MISSPENT	MOLOSSUS	MOONSAIL
MICELLAR	MINORESS	MISSTATE	MOLTENLY	MOONSEED
MICROBAR	MINORITE	MISTAKEN	MOLYBDIC	MOONSHEE
MICROBIC	MINORITY	MISTEACH	MOMENTLY	MOONSHOT
MICRODOT	MINOTAUR	MISTHINK	MOMENTUM	MOON-TYPE
MICROLUX	MINSTREL	MISTIMED	MONACHAL	MOONWORT
MICRURGY	MINT-MARK	MISTITLE	MONACHUS	MOOR-BAND
MID-BRAIN	MINUTELY	MISTREAT	MONADISM	MOORCOCK
MIDDLING	MINUTIAE	MISTRESS	MONANDRY	MOORFOWL
MIDNIGHT	MIRE-DRUM	MISTRIAL	MONARCHO	MOORLAND
MIDSHIPS	MIRINESS	MISTRUST	MONARCHY	MOOR-POUT
MIDWIFED	MIRKSOME	MISTRYST	MONASTIC	MOOTABLE

MOOT-HALL
MOOT-HILL
MOPEHAWK
MOPINGLY
MOPISHLY
MOPSTICK
MOQUETTE
MORACEAE
MORAINIC
MORALISE
MORALISM
MORALIST
MORALITY
MORALLER
MORATORY
MORAVIAN
MORBIDLY
MORBIFIC
MORBILLI
MORCEAUX
MORDANCY
MOREOVER
MORE-PORK
MORESQUE
MORIBUND
MORNINGS
MOROSELY
MOROSITY
MORPHEAN
MORPHEME
MORPHEUS
MORPHINE
MORTALLY
MORTBELL
MORT-HEAD
MORTIFIC
MORTLING
MORTMAIN
MORT-SAFE
MORTUARY
MOSLEMIN
MOSLINGS
MOSQUITO
MOSS-BACK
MOSS-CROP
MOSS-FLOW
MOSS-HAGG
MOSSLAND
MOSS-ROSE
MOSTWHAT
MOTE-HILL
MOTH-BALL
MOTHERLY
MOTILITY
MOTIONAL
MOTIVATE
MOTIVITY
MOTORAIL
MOTOR-BUS
MOTOR-CAR
MOTORIAL
MOTORISE
MOTORIST
MOTORIUM
MOTOR-JET
MOTORMAN

MOTORWAY
MOTTLING
MOUFFLON
MOULDING
MOULINET
MOULTING
MOUNSEER
MOUNTAIN
MOUNTANT
MOUNTING
MOURNFUL
MOURNIAL
MOURNING
MOUSE-DUN
MOUSE-EAR
MOUSEKIN
MOUSEMEE
MOUSSAKA
MOUTERER
MOUTHFUL
MOVABLES
MOVEABLE
MOVEABLY
MOVELESS
MOVEMENT
MOVINGLY
MOWBURNT
MUCHNESS
MUCILAGE
MUCK-HEAP
MUCKLUCK
MUCK-RAKE
MUCK-WORM
MUCOSITY
MUCULENT
MUD-CLERK
MUDDYING
MUD-GUARD
MUDIRIEH
MUD-PUPPY
MUDSTONE
MUG-HOUSE
MUG-SHEEP
MUHARRAM
MUHARREM
MUIR-POOT
MUIR-POUT
MULBERRY
MULCIBER
MULE-DEER
MULETEER
MULISHLY
MULTEITY
MULTIFID
MULTIFIL
MULTIPED
MULTIPLE
MULTIPLY
MULTURER
MUMBLING
MUMMYING
MUNGCORN
MUNGOOSE
MUNIMENT
MUNITION
MUQADDAM

MURDERER
MURIATED
MURIATIC
MURICATE
MURIFORM
MURMURER
MURPHIES
MURRELET
MURRHINE
MUSACEAE
MUSCADEL
MUSCADIN
MUSCATEL
MUSCIDAE
MUSCLING
MUSCULAR
MUSHROOM
MUSICALE
MUSIC-BOX
MUSICIAN
MUSICKER
MUSIC-PEN
MUSINGLY
MUSK-BALL
MUSK-CAVY
MUSK-DEER
MUSK-DUCK
MUSKETRY
MUSK-PEAR
MUSK-PLUM
MUSK-ROSE
MUSLINED
MUSLINET
MUSQUASH
MUSTACHE
MUSULMAN
MUTANDUM
MUTATION
MUTATIVE
MUTATORY
MUTCHKIN
MUTENESS
MUTICOUS
MUTILATE
MUTINEER
MUTINIED
MUTINOUS
MUTTERER
MUTUALLY
MYCELIAL
MYCELIUM
MYCETOMA
MYCOLOGY
MYELITIS
MYLODONT
MYLONITE
MYOBLAST
MYOGENIC
MYOGRAPH
MYOMANCY
MYOSITIC
MYOSITIS
MYOSOTIS
MYRIADTH
MYRIAPOD
MYRIOPOD

MYRISTIC
MYRMIDON
MYRRHINE
MYSTICAL
MYSTIQUE
MYTHICAL
MYTILOID
MYXEDEMA
MYXOMATA

N

NACARATI
NACREOUS
NAETHING
NAIL-BOMB
NAIL-FILE
NAIL-HEAD
NAIL-HOLE
NAINSELL
NAINSOOK
NAISSANT
NAMEABLE
NAME-DROP
NAMELESS
NAME-PART
NAMESAKE
NANCY-BOY
NANOGRAM
NAPERIAN
NAPHTHOL
NAPIFORM
NAPOLEON
NARCISSI
NARCOSES
NARCOSIS
NARCOTIC
NARGHILE
NARGILEH
NARICORN
NARRATOR
NARROWLY
NASALISE
NASALITY
NASCENCE
NASCENCY
NATALITY
NATATION
NATATORY
NATHLESS
NATIFORM
NATIONAL
NATIVELY
NATIVISM
NATIVIST
NATIVITY
NATTERED
NATURING
NATURISM
NATURIST
NAUMACHY
NAUPLIUS
NAUSEANT
NAUSEATE
NAUSEOUS
NAUTICAL
NAUTILUS

NAVALISM
NAVARCHY
NAVICERT
NAVICULA
NAVIGATE
NAVVYING
NAVY-BLUE
NAVY-LIST
NAVY-YARD
NAYTHLES
NAZAREAN
NAZARENE
NAZARITE
NAZIRITE
NEAPTIDE
NEAR-BEER
NEARCTIC
NEAR-GAUN
NEAR-HAND
NEARNESS
NEAR-SILK
NEAT-HERD
NEATNESS
NEBULISE
NEBULIUM
NEBULOUS
NECKATEE
NECK-BAND
NECK-BEEF
NECK-BONE
NECK-GEAR
NECKLACE
NECKLINE
NECKWEAR
NECKWEED
NECROPSY
NECROSIS
NECROTIC
NECTARED
NEED-FIRE
NEEDLESS
NEEDMENT
NEGATION
NEGATIVE
NEGATORY
NEGATRON
NEGLIGEE
NEGRILLO
NEGRITOS
NEGROISM
NEMATODA
NEMATODE
NEMATOID
NEMERTEA
NEMOROUS
NENUPHAR
NEOGAEAN
NEO-LATIN
NEOLOGIC
NEOMYCIN
NEONATAL
NEOPAGAN
NEOPHYTE
NEOPLASM
NEOPRENE
NEOTENIC

NEOTERIC	NIHILIST	NORTHERN	NUMINOUS	OCEANAUT
NEPENTHE	NIHILITY	NORTHING	NUMMULAR	OCEANIAN
NEPHRITE	NIMBUSED	NORTHMAN	NUMSKULL	OCELLATE
NEPHROID	NIMBUSES	NOSE-BAND	NUNCHEON	OCHEROUS
NEPIONIC	NINE-EYES	NOSE-DIVE	NUNDINAL	OCHIDORE
NEPOTISM	NINEFOLD	NOSE-HERB	NURSLING	OCHOTONA
NEPOTIST	NINE-FOOT	NOSE-LEAF	NURTURAL	OCHREATE
NERITINA	NINE-HOLE	NOSELESS	NURTURER	OCHREOUS
NERONIAN	NINE-INCH	NOSELITE	NUTARIAN	OCTANTAL
NERVE-END	NINE-MILE	NOSE-RING	NUTATION	OCTAPODY
NERVELET	NINEPINS	NOSINESS	NUT-BROWN	OCTAROON
NERVULAR	NINETEEN	NOSOLOGY	NUT-GRASS	OCTONARY
NESCIENT	NINETIES	NOTANDUM	NUTHATCH	OCTOPODA
NESHNESS	NISBERRY	NOTARIAL	NUT-HOUSE	OCTOROON
NESTLING	NIT-GRASS	NOTATION	NUTRIENT	OCTUPLET
NETHINIM	NITROGEN	NOT-BEING	NUTSHELL	OCULARLY
NEURITIC	NITROXYL	NOTCHING	NYMPHAEA	OCULATED
NEURITIS	NOACHIAN	NOTEBOOK	NYMPHEAN	ODALIQUE
NEUROSES	NOBELIUM	NOTECASE	NYMPHISH	ODIOUSLY
NEUROSIS	NOBILITY	NOTELESS		ODOGRAPH
NEUROTIC	NOBLEMAN	NOTIFIED	**O**	ODOMETER
NEUTRINO	NOBLEMEN	NOTIONAL	OAK-APPLE	ODONTIST
NEVER-WAS	NOBLESSE	NOTOGAEA	OAK-EGGER	ODONTOID
NEW-BLOWN	NOCENTLY	NOTORNIS	OAT-GRASS	ODONTOMA
NEWCOMER	NOCTILIO	NOT-PATED	OATHABLE	ODYSSEAN
NEWELLED	NOCTUARY	NO-TRUMPS	OBDURACY	OEDIPEAN
NEW-FOUND	NOCTURNE	NOUMENAL	OBDURATE	ŒILLADE
NEW-MODEL	NODALISE	NOUMENON	OBEAHISM	OENOLOGY
NEW-RISEN	NODALITY	NOVATIAN	OBEDIENT	OENOPHIL
NEWSCAST	NODATION	NOVATION	OBEISANT	OERLIKON
NEWSHAWK	NODOSITY	NOVELDOM	OBITUARY	OESTROUS
NEWSPEAK	NODULOSE	NOVELISE	OBI-WOMAN	OFF-AND-ON
NEWSREEL	NODULOUS	NOVELISH	OBJECTOR	OFF-BREAK
NEWSROOM	NOHOWISH	NOVELISM	OBLATION	OFF-DRIVE
NEWTONIC	NOISEFUL	NOVELIST	OBLIGANT	OFFENDER
NEXT-DOOR	NOISETTE	NOVELLAE	OBLIGATE	OFFERING
NEXTNESS	NOLITION	NOVEMBER	OBLIGING	OFFICIAL
NIBBLING	NOMADISE	NOVENARY	OBLIQUID	OFFPRINT
NIBELUNG	NOMADISM	NOVERCAL	OBLIVION	OFF-SHAKE
NICENESS	NOMARCHY	NOVERINT	OBSCURER	OFFSHOOT
NICKELIC	NOMINATE	NOWADAYS	OBSERVER	OFFSHORE
NICKNAME	NOMISTIC	NOWT-HERD	OBSIDIAN	OFF-SORTS
NICKYTAM	NOMOGENY	NUBECULA	OBSOLETE	OFF-STAGE
NICOTIAN	NOMOGRAM	NUBIFORM	OBSTACLE	OFFWARDS
NICOTINE	NOMOLOGY	NUBILITY	OBSTRUCT	OFF-WHITE
NIDATION	NON-CLAIM	NUBILOUS	OBTAINER	OHMMETER
NIDERING	NON-ELECT	NUCELLAR	OBTECTED	OILCLOTH
NIDOROUS	NON-ENTRY	NUCELLUS	OBTEMPER	OIL-FIELD
NIELLIST	NONESUCH	NUCLEARY	OBTRUDER	OIL-FIRED
NIELLOED	NON-EVENT	NUCLEASE	OBTURATE	OIL-GLAND
NIEVEFUL	NON-JUROR	NUCLEATE	OBTUSELY	OILINESS
NIFFNAFF	NON-METAL	NUCLEIDE	OBTUSITY	OIL-PRESS
NIFLHEIM	NON-MORAL	NUCLEOLE	OBVOLUTE	OIL-SHALE
NIGER-OIL	NON-PARTY	NUCLEOLI	OCCAMISM	OILSTONE
NIGGLING	NON-QUOTA	NUDATION	OCCAMIST	OINTMENT
NIGH-HAND	NON-RIGID	NUDENESS	OCCASION	OITICICA
NIGHNESS	NONSENSE	NUDICAUL	OCCIDENT	OLD-TIMER
NIGHTCAP	NON-STICK	NUDITIES	OCCLUSAL	OLD-WORLD
NIGHT-DOG	NON-UNION	NUGATORY	OCCLUSOR	OLEACEAE
NIGHT-FLY	NONUPLET	NUISANCE	OCCULTED	OLEANDER
NIGHT-FOE	NON-WHITE	NULLNESS	OCCULTLY	OLEASTER
NIGHT-HAG	NOOMETRY	NUMBERER	OCCUPANT	OLEFIANT
NIGHTJAR	NOONTIDE	NUMERACY	OCCUPATE	OLIBANUM
NIGHT-MAN	NORMALCY	NUMERARY	OCCUPIED	OLIGARCH
NIGHT-OWL	NORMALLY	NUMERATE	OCCUPIER	OLIPHANT
NIHILISM	NORSEMAN	NUMEROUS	OCCURRED	OLIVE-OIL

OLIVETAN	OPSONIUM	OSIER-BED	OUTSIZED	OVERGANG
OLYMPIAD	OPTATIVE	OSNABURG	OUTSKIRT	OVERGIVE
OLYMPIAN	OPTICIAN	OSSARIUM	OUTSLEEP	OVERGROW
OLYMPICS	OPTIMATE	OSSIANIC	OUTSMART	OVERHAIR
OMADHAUN	OPTIMISE	OSSIFIED	OUTSPEAK	OVERHALE
OMELETTE	OPTIMISM	OSTEITIS	OUTSPENT	OVERHAND
OMISSION	OPTIMIST	OSTINATO	OUTSPORT	OVERHANG
OMISSIVE	OPTIONAL	OSTRACOD	OUTSTAND	OVERHAUL
OMITTING	OPTOLOGY	OSTRACON	OUTSTARE	OVERHEAD
OMMATEUM	OPULENCE	OSTRAKON	OUTSTRIP	OVERHEAR
OMNIFORM	OPUSCULA	OSTREGER	OUTSWEAR	OVERHEAT
OMOHYOID	OPUSCULE	OTIOSITY	OUTSWELL	OVERHENT
OMOPHAGY	ORACULAR	OTOSCOPE	OUTSWING	OVERHOLD
OMOPLATE	ORAGIOUS	OTTAMITE	OUTTAKEN	OVERHUNG
OMPHALIC	ORANGERY	OTTAVINO	OUTVALUE	OVERJUMP
OMPHALOS	ORANGISM	OTTOMITE	OUTVENOM	OVERKEEP
ONCE-OVER	ORATORIO	OUISTITI	OUTVOICE	OVERKILL
ONCIDIUM	ORATRESS	OULACHON	OUTVOTER	OVERKIND
ONCOLOGY	ORBILIUS	OUROLOGY	OUTWARDS	OVERKING
ONCOMING	ORCADIAN	OUTBOARD	OUTWATCH	OVERKNEE
ONE-HORSE	ORCHELLA	OUTBOUND	OUTWEARY	OVERLADE
ONE-PIECE	ORCHILLA	OUTBRAVE	OUTWEIGH	OVERLAID
ONE-SIDED	ORCHITIC	OUTBREAK	OUTWORTH	OVERLAIN
ONE-TO-ONE	ORCHITIS	OUTBURST	OUTWREST	OVERLAND
ONE-TRACK	ORDAINER	OUTCASTE	OVARIOLE	OVERLARD
ONLOOKER	ORDALIAN	OUTCLASS	OVARIOUS	OVERLEAF
ONSETTER	ORDALIUM	OUTDANCE	OVARITIS	OVERLEAP
ONTOGENY	ORDERING	OUTDATED	OVEN-BIRD	OVERLIER
ONTOLOGY	ORDINAND	OUTDOORS	OVENWARE	OVERLIVE
ONWARDLY	ORDINANT	OUTDRIVE	OVENWOOD	OVERLOAD
ONYCHITE	ORDINARY	OUTDWELL	OVERARCH	OVERLONG
OOGAMOUS	ORDINATE	OUTFIELD	OVERBEAR	OVERLOOK
OOGONIAL	ORDNANCE	OUTFIGHT	OVERBEAT	OVERLORD
OOGONIUM	ORDUROUS	OUTFLANK	OVERBLOW	OVERMAST
OOLOGIST	OREOLOGY	OUTFLASH	OVERBOIL	OVERMUCH
OOPHORON	ORE-STARE	OUTFLING	OVERBOLD	OVERNAME
OOSPHERE	ORGANDIE	OUTFLUSH	OVERBROW	OVERNEAT
OOZINESS	ORGANISE	OUTFROWN	OVERBULK	OVERNICE
OPALISED	ORGANISM	OUTGLARE	OVERBURN	OVERPART
OPAQUELY	ORGANIST	OUTGOING	OVERBUSY	OVERPAST
OPENABLE	ORGANITY	OUTGUARD	OVERCALL	OVERPEER
OPEN-CAST	ORGASTIC	OUT-HEROD	OVERCAST	OVERPLAY
OPEN-EYED	ORGULOUS	OUTHOUSE	OVERCLAD	OVERPLUS
OPENNESS	ORICHALC	OUTLAWRY	OVERCLOY	OVERPOST
OPEN-PLAN	ORIELLED	OUTLEARN	OVERCOAT	OVERRACK
OPERABLE	ORIENTAL	OUTLYING	OVERCOME	OVERRAKE
OPERA-HAT	ORIENTED	OUTMARCH	OVER-COOL	OVERRANK
OPERATIC	ORIGANUM	OUTMATCH	OVERCROP	OVERRASH
OPERATOR	ORIGINAL	OUTMODED	OVERCROW	OVERRATE
OPERCULA	ORILLION	OUTNIGHT	OVERDOER	OVERREAD
OPERETTA	ORNAMENT	OUTPOINT	OVERDONE	OVERRIDE
OPHIDIAN	ORNATELY	OUTPOWER	OVERDOSE	OVERRIPE
OPHITISM	ORNITHIC	OUTPRIZE	OVERDRAW	OVERRUFF
OPHIURAN	OROGENIC	OUTRANCE	OVERDUST	OVERRULE
OPHIURID	ORPIMENT	OUTREACH	OVERFALL	OVERSAIL
OPIFICER	ORSEILLE	OUTREIGN	OVERFEED	OVERSEAS
OPINABLE	ORSELLIC	OUTREMER	OVERFILL	OVERSEEN
OPINICUS	ORTHICON	OUTRIDER	OVERFINE	OVERSEER
OPIUM-DEN	ORTHODOX	OUTRIGHT	OVERFIRE	OVERSELL
OPOPANAX	ORTHOEPY	OUTRIVAL	OVERFISH	OVERSHOE
OPPILATE	ORVIETAN	OUTROPER	OVERFLOW	OVERSHOT
OPPONENT	OSCININE	OUTSCOLD	OVERFOLD	OVERSIDE
OPPOSING	OSCITANT	OUTSCORN	OVERFOND	OVERSIZE
OPPOSITE	OSCITATE	OUTSHINE	OVERFREE	OVERSKIP
OPPUGNER	OSCULANT	OUTSIDER	OVERFULL	OVERSLIP
OPSIMATH	OSCULATE	OUTSIGHT	OVERGALL	OVERSMAN

OVERSOUL
OVERSPIN
OVERSTAY
OVERSTEP
OVERSWAY
OVERSWIM
OVERTAKE
OVERTALK
OVERTASK
OVERTEEM
OVERTIME
OVERTOIL
OVERTONE
OVERTRIP
OVERTURE
OVERTURN
OVERVEIL
OVERVIEW
OVERWASH
OVERWEAR
OVERWEEN
OVERWIND
OVERWING
OVERWISE
OVERWORD
OVERWORE
OVERWORK
OVERWORN
OVERYEAR
OVIDUCAL
OVIPOSIT
OWERLOUP
OWL-GLASS
OWL-LIGHT
OWL-TRAIN
OWRECOME
OWREWORD
OXBRIDGE
OXIDISER
OXIMETER
OX-PECKER
OX-TONGUE
OX-WARBLE
OXYMORON
OXYTOCIN
OZONISER

P
PABOUCHE
PABULOUS
PACATION
PACHALIC
PACIFIER
PACIFISM
PACIFIST
PACKAGED
PACKFONG
PACK-LOAD
PACK-MULE
PAD-CLOTH
PADDLING
PADERERO
PADISHAH
PADUASOY
PAGANISE
PAGANISH

PAGANISM
PAGANIZE
PAGEHOOD
PAGINATE
PAINLESS
PAINT-BOX
PAINTING
PAINTURE
PAIRWISE
PAITRICK
PALAMATE
PALAMINO
PALATIAL
PALATINE
PALEBUCK
PALE-DEAD
PALE-EYED
PALE-FACE
PALENESS
PALESTRA
PALEWISE
PALIFORM
PALINODE
PALINODY
PALISADE
PALISADO
PALLADIC
PALLETED
PALLIATE
PALLIDLY
PALL-MALL
PALMATED
PALMERIN
PALMETTE
PALMETTO
PALMIPED
PALMITIC
PALMITIN
PALM-PLAY
PALM-TREE
PALM-WINE
PALOMINO
PALPABLE
PALPABLY
PALSTAFF
PALSTAVE
PALTERER
PALTRILY
PALUDINE
PALUDISM
PALUDOSE
PALUDOUS
PAMPERER
PAMPHLET
PANCHEON
PANCHION
PANCREAS
PANDANUS
PANDEMIC
PANDERLY
PANDOWDY
PANEGYRY
PANELLED
PANGAMIC
PANGFULL
PANGLESS

PANGOLIN
PANHAGIA
PANICKED
PANICLED
PANIONIC
PANISLAM
PANMIXIA
PANNICLE
PANNIKEL
PANNIKIN
PANORAMA
PAN-PIPES
PANSOPHY
PANTABLE
PANTALON
PANTHEON
PANTILED
PANTOFLE
PAPALISE
PAPALISM
PAPALIST
PAPER-BOY
PAPER-DAY
PAPERING
PAPILLAE
PAPILLAR
PAPILLON
PAPISHER
PAPISTIC
PAPISTRY
PAPPADOM
PAP-SPOON
PAPULOSE
PAPULOUS
PARABEMA
PARABOLA
PARABOLE
PARADIGM
PARADISE
PARADOXY
PARAFFIN
PARAFFLE
PARAFOIL
PARAGOGE
PARAGRAM
PARAGUAY
PARAKEET
PARALLAX
PARALLEL
PARALOGY
PARALYSE
PARAMENT
PARAMESE
PARAMOUR
PARANETE
PARANOEA
PARANOIA
PARANOIC
PARANOID
PARAQUAT
PARASANG
PARASITE
PARAVAIL
PARAVANE
PARAVANT
PARBREAK

PARCENER
PARCLOSE
PARDALIS
PARDONER
PARENTAL
PAREOEAN
PARERGON
PARGETED
PARGETER
PARHELIA
PARHELIC
PARIETAL
PARISHEN
PARISIAN
PARKLAND
PARKLIKE
PARKWARD
PARLANCE
PARLANDO
PARMESAN
PAROCHIN
PARODIED
PARODIST
PAROEMIA
PARONYMY
PAROQUET
PAROUSIA
PAROXYSM
PARPOINT
PARRITCH
PARROTED
PARROTER
PARROTRY
PARRYING
PARSI-ISM
PARSONIC
PARTAKEN
PARTAKER
PARTERRE
PARTHIAN
PARTIBLE
PARTICLE
PARTISAN
PARTITUR
PARTIZAN
PART-SONG
PART-TIME
PARTYISM
PARTY-MAN
PASCH-EGG
PASHALIK
PASHMINA
PASPALUM
PASSABLE
PASSABLY
PASS-BOOK
PASSER-BY
PASSERES
PASSIBLE
PASSIBLY
PASSLESS
PASSMENT
PASSOVER
PASSPORT
PASSWORD
PASTANCE

PASTE-EEL
PASTICCI
PASTICHE
PASTILLE
PASTORAL
PASTORLY
PASTURAL
PATAGIAL
PATAGIUM
PATARINE
PATCH-BOX
PATCHERY
PATCHILY
PATCHING
PATELLAE
PATELLAR
PATENTEE
PATENTLY
PATENTOR
PATERERO
PATERNAL
PATHETIC
PATHLESS
PATHOGEN
PATIENCE
PATRONAL
PATTENED
PATTERER
PATULOUS
PAULDRON
PAUL'S-MAN
PAUSEFUL
PAVEMENT
PAVILION
PAVONIAN
PAVONINE
PAWNSHOP
PAX-BOARD
PAX-BREDE
PAYNIMRY
PAY-SHEET
PEABERRY
PEACEFUL
PEA-CHICK
PEACOCKY
PEA-GREEN
PEAK-LOAD
PEA-PLANT
PEAR-DROP
PEA-RIFLE
PEARL-ASH
PEARL-EYE
PEARLIES
PEARLING
PEARLITE
PEARMAIN
PEAR-PUSH
PEAR-TREE
PEASE-COD
PEA-SOUPY
PEA-STONE
PEA-STRAW
PEAT-BANK
PEAT-HAGG
PEAT-HOLE
PEAT-MOOR

PEAT-MOSS	PENNEECK	PERRADII	PHISNOMY	PIER-HEAD
PEAT-REEK	PENNONED	PERRUQUE	PHLEGMON	PIERIDAE
PEATSHIP	PENNORTH	PERSEITY	PHOCAENA	PIERIDES
PEBBLING	PENNY-DOG	PERSICOT	PHOCIDAE	PIFFLING
PECAN-NUT	PENNY-FEE	PERSONAL	PHOEBEAN	PIGEONRY
PECCABLE	PENNY-PIG	PERSPIRE	PHOLADES	PIG-FACED
PECCANCY	PENOLOGY	PERSUADE	PHONEMIC	PIG'S-WASH
PECTINAL	PENONCEL	PERTHITE	PHONETIC	PIG-WOMAN
PECTINES	PENSTOCK	PERTNESS	PHORMINX	PIKADELL
PECTORAL	PENTACLE	PERTUSED	PHORMIUM	PIKE-HEAD
PECULATE	PENTADIC	PERUVIAN	PHOSGENE	PILASTER
PECULIAR	PENTAGON	PERVERSE	PHOSPHOR	PILCHARD
PECULIUM	PENTARCH	PERVIATE	PHOTO-FIT	PILEATED
PEDAGOGY	PENTELIC	PERVIOUS	PHOTOGEN	PILEWORK
PEDALIER	PENTOSAN	PESHITTA	PHOTOPIA	PILE-WORM
PEDALLED	PENTROOF	PESHITTO	PHOTOPIC	PILEWORT
PEDALLER	PENUMBRA	PESTERER	PHOTOPSY	PILFERER
PEDANTIC	PEN-WIPER	PETALINE	PHRASING	PILHORSE
PEDANTRY	PENWOMAN	PETALISM	PHREATIC	PILIFORM
PEDATELY	PEPERINO	PETALLED	PHRYGIAN	PILLAGER
PEDDLING	PEPPERER	PETALODY	PHTHALIC	PILLOWED
PEDERERO	PEPYSIAN	PETALOID	PHTHALIN	PILL-WORM
PEDESTAL	PERACUTE	PÉTANQUE	PHTHISIC	PILLWORT
PEDICLED	PERCEIVE	PETCHARY	PHTHISIS	PILOSITY
PEDICURE	PERCHING	PETECHIA	PHYLARCH	PILOTAGE
PEDIGREE	PERCIDAE	PETER-MAN	PHYLETIC	PILOT-JET
PEDIMENT	PERCOLIN	PETIOLAR	PHYLLARY	PILSENER
PEDIPALP	PERDENDO	PETIOLED	PHYLLITE	PILTDOWN
PEDOLOGY	PERFECTI	PETITION	PHYLLODE	PINACOID
PEDUNCLE	PERFECTO	PETITORY	PHYLLODY	PINAFORE
PEEKABOO	PERFORCE	PETRIFIC	PHYLLOID	PINAKOID
PEEP-HOLE	PERFUMED	PETROLIC	PHYLLOME	PINASTER
PEEP-O'-DAY	PERFUMER	PETRONEL	PHYSALIA	PINCE-NEZ
PEEP-SHOW	PERIAGUA	PETROSAL	PHYSALIS	PINCHGUT
PEERLESS	PERIANTH	PETTEDLY	PHYSETER	PINCH-HIT
PEESWEEP	PERIBLEM	PETTIFOG	PHYSICAL	PINCHING
PEETWEET	PERICARP	PETULANT	PHYSICKY	PINDAREE
PEGASEAN	PERICOPE	PETUNTSE	PHYSIQUE	PINDARIC
PEGBOARD	PERIDERM	PETUNTZE	PHYTOSIS	PINE-CONE
PEIGNOIR	PERIDIAL	PEW-CHAIR	PIACULAR	PINE-TREE
PEISHWAH	PERIDIUM	PEWTERER	PIANETTE	PINE-WOOD
PEJORATE	PERIDOTE	PEZIZOID	PIANISTE	PINE-WOOL
PEKINESE	PERIGEAL	PFENNING	PIASSABA	PINGLING
PELAGIAN	PERIGEAN	PHAETHON	PIASSAVA	PING-PONG
PELASGIC	PERIGONE	PHALANGE	PIAZZIAN	PINGUEFY
PELERINE	PERIGYNY	PHALLISM	PICARIAE	PINK-EYED
PELLAGRA	PERILLED	PHALLOID	PICARIAN	PINKNESS
PELLICLE	PERILOUS	PHANTASM	PICAROON	PINKROOT
PELL-MELL	PERINEAL	PHANTASY	PICAYUNE	PINKSTER
PELLUCID	PERINEUM	PHANTOMY	PICHURIM	PIN-MAKER
PELMATIC	PERIODIC	PHARISEE	PICKBACK	PIN-MONEY
PELOLOGY	PERIOTIC	PHARMACY	PICKEREL	PINNACLE
PELORISM	PERIPETY	PHEASANT	PICKETED	PINNATED
PEMBROKE	PERIPLUS	PHELLOID	PICKETER	PINNIPED
PEMMICAN	PERISARC	PHENGITE	PICKLOCK	PINOCHLE
PENALISE	PERISHED	PHENOGAM	PICK-ME-UP	PINPOINT
PENCHANT	PERISHER	PHENOLIC	PICNICKY	PINPRICK
PENCRAFT	PERJURED	PHENYLIC	PICOTITE	PINSCHER
PENDEMIA	PERJURER	PHIALLED	PICTURAL	PINTABLE
PENDENCY	PERLITIC	PHILABEG	PIDDLING	PINTADOS
PENDICLE	PERMEATE	PHILAMOT	PIECENER	PIN-WHEEL
PENDULAR	PERNANCY	PHILIBEG	PIECRUST	PIOU-PIOU
PENDULUM	PERONEAL	PHILOMEL	PIEDMONT	PIPE-CASE
PENITENT	PERONEUS	PHILOMOT	PIEDNESS	PIPECLAY
PENKNIFE	PERORATE	PHIMOSIS	PIE-PLANT	PIPE-FISH
PENNEECH	PEROXIDE	PHINNOCK	PIERCING	PIPELESS

PIPELIKE	PLANTAGO	PLOTTING	POLLIWOG	POPINJAY
PIPELINE	PLANTAIN	PLOUGHER	POLLSTER	POPISHLY
PIPE-RACK	PLANTING	PLUCKILY	POLLUTED	POPLITIC
PIPERINE	PLANTLET	PLUGGING	POLLUTER	POP-MUSIC
PIPE-STEM	PLANT-POT	PLUG-UGLY	POLLYWIG	POPPADUM
PIPE-TREE	PLANTULE	PLUMAGED	POLLYWOG	POPPY-OIL
PIPEWINE	PLANULAR	PLUMBAGO	POLONIAN	POPULACE
PIPEWORK	PLANURIA	PLUMBATE	POLONISE	POPULATE
PIPEWORT	PLASHING	PLUMB-BOB	POLONISM	POPULISM
PIQUANCY	PLASTERY	PLUMBERY	POLONIUM	POPULIST
PIRARUCU	PLASTICS	PLUMBING	POLTFOOT	POPULOUS
PIRLICUE	PLASTRAL	PLUMBISM	POLTROON	POP-VISIT
PIRRAURU	PLASTRON	PLUMBITE	POLYACID	PORIFERA
PISCATOR	PLATANNA	PLUMBOUS	POLYARCH	PORINESS
PISCINAE	PLATANUS	PLUM-CAKE	POLYAXON	PORISTIC
PISHOGUE	PLATBAND	PLUM-DUFF	POLYGALA	PORK-CHOP
PISIFORM	PLATEASM	PLUMELET	POLYGAMY	PORKLING
PISOLITE	PLATEAUX	PLUMIPED	POLYGENY	POROGAMY
PISS-A-BED	PLATEFUL	PLUMPISH	POLYGLOT	POROSITY
PISTOLET	PLATELET	PLUM-TREE	POLYGONY	PORPHYRA
PITA-FLAX	PLATEMAN	PLUMULAE	POLYGYNY	PORPHYRY
PITA-HEMP	PLATFORM	PLUMULAR	POLYMATH	PORPOISE
PITCHING	PLATINIC	PLUNGING	POLYMERY	PORRIDGE
PITHBALL	PLATINUM	PLURALLY	POLYMNIA	PORTABLE
PITHLESS	PLATONIC	PLURISIE	POLYONYM	PORTAGUE
PITHLIKE	PLATTING	PLUSSAGE	POLYPARY	PORTANCE
PITH-TREE	PLATYPUS	PLUTONIC	POLYPHON	PORTEOUS
PITIABLE	PLATYSMA	PLUVIOSE	POLYPIDE	PORTERLY
PITIABLY	PLAUDITE	PLUVIOUS	POLYPINE	PORTESSE
PITILESS	PLAUSIVE	PLYMOUTH	POLYPITE	PORT-FIRE
PITTANCE	PLAYABLE	POACHING	POLYPODY	PORTHOLE
PITTYPAT	PLAYBACK	PO'CHAISE	POLYPOID	PORTHORS
PIT-VIPER	PLAY-BILL	POCHETTE	POLYPOUS	PORTIÈRE
PITYROID	PLAYBOOK	POCKETED	POLYSEME	PORTIGUE
PIVOTING	PLAY-DEBT	POCKMARK	POLYSEMY	PORTLAND
PIVOT-MAN	PLAYGIRL	PODAGRAL	POLYSOMY	PORTLAST
PIXY-RING	PLAY-GOER	PODAGRIC	POLYZOAN	PORTOISE
PIZZERIA	PLAY-MARE	PODARGUS	POLYZOIC	PORTOLAN
PLACABLE	PLAYMATE	PODIATRY	POLYZOON	PORTRAIT
PLACABLY	PLAYROOM	PODOGONA	POMANDER	PORTRESS
PLACEMAN	PLAYSOME	POEMATIC	POMMETTY	PORTUGEE
PLACEMEN	PLAYTIME	POETICAL	POMOLOGY	PORTWINE
PLACENTA	PLEADING	POETSHIP	POMPEIAN	PORTWINY
PLACIDLY	PLEASANT	POIGNANT	POMWATER	POSEIDON
PLACITUM	PLEASING	POINDING	PONCEAUX	POSHNESS
PLAGIARY	PLEASURE	POINTING	PONDERAL	POSHTEEN
PLAGUILY	PLEBEIAN	POISONER	PONDERER	POSINGLY
PLAIDING	PLECTRON	POKERISH	POND-LIFE	POSITING
PLAIDMAN	PLECTRUM	POLABIAN	POND-LILY	POSITION
PLAINANT	PLEIADES	POLANDER	POND-WEED	POSITIVE
PLAINESS	PLEIN-AIR	POLARISE	PONTIFEX	POSITRON
PLAINFUL	PLENARTY	POLARITY	PONTIFIC	POSOLOGY
PLAINING	PLEONASM	POLAROID	PONY-SKIN	POSSIBLE
PLAINISH	PLEONAST	POLEMISE	PONY-TAIL	POSSIBLY
PLAISTER	PLETHORA	POLEMIST	POOH-POOH	POSTCARD
PLAITING	PLEURISY	POLISHED	POON-WOOD	POSTCODE
PLANCHED	PLEXUSES	POLISHER	POOR-JOHN	POSTDATE
PLANCHET	PLIANTLY	POLITELY	POORNESS	POST-FREE
PLANETIC	PLICATED	POLITICK	POOR-RATE	POST-HORN
PLANGENT	PLIGHTED	POLITICO	POOR'S-BOX	POSTICHE
PLANK-BED	PLIGHTER	POLITICS	POORTITH	POSTLUDE
PLANKING	PLIMSOLL	POLKA-DOT	POORWILL	POSTMARK
PLANKTON	PLIOCENE	POLLICES	POPEHOOD	POST-MILL
PLANLESS	PLODDING	POLLINIA	POPELING	POST-NATI
PLANNING	PLOPPING	POLLINIC	POPESHIP	POST-OBIT
PLANTAGE	PLOTLESS	POLLIWIG	POP-GROUP	POST-PAID

POSTPONE
POST-ROAD
POST-TIME
POST-TOWN
POSTURAL
POSTURER
POTASHES
POTASSIC
POTATION
POTATOES
POT-BELLY
POT-BOUND
POTENTLY
POTHOUSE
POTICARY
POTLATCH
POT-METAL
POT-PLANT
POT-ROAST
POTSHERD
POT-STICK
POT-STILL
POTSTONE
POTTERER
POUCHFUL
POULAINE
POULDRON
POULTICE
POUNALUA
POUNDAGE
POUND-DAY
POUND-NET
POWDERED
POWERFUL
POWSOWDY
PRACTICE
PRACTISE
PRACTIVE
PRAEDIAL
PRAEFECT
PRAIRIAL
PRAIRIED
PRAISING
PRANCING
PRANDIAL
PRANKFUL
PRANKING
PRANKISH
PRATFALL
PRATIQUE
PRATTLER
PREACHER
PREAMBLE
PRECEESE
PRECEPIT
PRECINCT
PRECIOUS
PRECLUDE
PRECURSE
PREDATOR
PREDELLA
PRE-ELECT
PRE-EXIST
PREGNANT
PREHNITE
PREHUMAN

PREJUDGE
PRELATIC
PRELUDIO
PREMIÈRE
PREMISED
PREMISES
PREMOLAR
PREMORSE
PRENASAL
PRENATAL
PRENTICE
PREORDER
PREPARED
PREPARER
PREPENSE
PREPRINT
PRESAGER
PRESBYTE
PRESCIND
PRESENCE
PRESERVE
PRESIDIO
PRESS-BED
PRESS-BOX
PRESSFAT
PRESSFUL
PRESSING
PRESSION
PRESSMAN
PRESSURE
PRESTIGE
PRESUMER
PRETENCE
PRETTIFY
PRETTILY
PREVIOUS
PRIAPEAN
PRIAPISM
PRICKING
PRIDEFUL
PRIE-DIEU
PRIESTLY
PRIGGERY
PRIGGING
PRIGGISH
PRIGGISM
PRIMALLY
PRIMATAL
PRIMATES
PRIMATIC
PRIMEVAL
PRIMMING
PRIMNESS
PRIMROSE
PRIMROSY
PRINCELY
PRINCESS
PRINCOCK
PRINTING
PRIORATE
PRIORESS
PRIORITY
PRISMOID
PRISONER
PRISTINE
PRIZABLE

PRIZE-MAN
PROBABLE
PROBABLY
PROCAINE
PROCINCT
PROCLAIM
PROCLIVE
PROCURER
PRODDING
PRODIGAL
PRODITOR
PRODROME
PRODROMI
PRODUCER
PROEMIAL
PROFANER
PROFILER
PROFITER
PROFOUND
PROFUSER
PROGERIA
PROGGINS
PROGRESS
PROHIBIT
PROLAMIN
PROLAPSE
PROLIFIC
PROLIXLY
PROLOGUE
PROLONGE
PROMETAL
PROMISEE
PROMISER
PROMISOR
PROMOTER
PROMOTOR
PROMPTED
PROMPTER
PROMPTLY
PROMULGE
PRONATOR
PRONG-HOE
PRONOTAL
PRONOTUM
PROOFING
PROPENSE
PROPERLY
PROPERTY
PROPHASE
PROPHECY
PROPHESY
PROPHYLL
PROPOLIS
PROPOSAL
PROPOSER
PROPOUND
PROPPING
PROP-ROOT
PROPYLIC
PROPYLON
PROROGUE
PROSAISM
PROSAIST
PROSEMAN
PROSODIC
PROSPECT

PROSTATE
PROSTYLE
PROTASIS
PROTATIC
PROTEASE
PROTÉGÉE
PROTENSE
PROTHYLE
PROTISTA
PROTOCOL
PROTONIC
PROTOZOA
PROTRACT
PROTRUDE
PROUDISH
PROVABLE
PROVABLY
PROVEDOR
PROVIANT
PROVIDED
PROVIDER
PROVIDOR
PROVINCE
PROVISOR
PROVOKER
PROWLING
PROXIMAL
PRUDENCE
PRUINOSE
PRUNELLA
PRUNELLO
PRURIENT
PRURITIC
PRURITUS
PRUSSIAN
PRUSSIFY
PRYINGLY
PSALMIST
PSALMODY
PSALTERY
PSAMMITE
PSELLISM
PSEPHISM
PSEPHITE
PSILOSIS
PSILOTIC
PSILOTUM
PSYCHICS
PSYCHISM
PSYCHIST
PSYCHOID
PTEROPOD
PTERYGIA
PTERYLAE
PTILOSIS
PTOMAINE
PTYALISE
PTYALISM
PUB-CRAWL
PUBLICAN
PUBLICLY
PUCCINIA
PUCELAGE
PUCKFIST
PUDDINGY
PUDDLING

PUDENDAL
PUDENDUM
PUDIBUND
PUDICITY
PUFFBALL
PUFF-BIRD
PUFF-PUFF
PUG-FACED
PUGGAREE
PUGILISM
PUGILIST
PUG-NOSED
PUISSANT
PULINGLY
PULL-BACK
PULLOVER
PULMONES
PULMONIC
PULPITED
PULPITER
PULPITRY
PULPITUM
PULPMILL
PULPWOOD
PULSATOR
PULSIDGE
PULSIFIC
PULSOJET
PULVILIO
PULVILLE
PULVILLI
PULVINAR
PULVINUS
PULZA-OIL
PUMICATE
PUMP-HEAD
PUMP-HOOD
PUMP-ROOM
PUMP-WELL
PUNALUAN
PUNCHEON
PUNCTATE
PUNCTUAL
PUNCTULE
PUNCTURE
PUNDITRY
PUNDONOR
PUNGENCE
PUNGENCY
PUNINESS
PUNISHER
PUNITION
PUNITIVE
PUNITORY
PUNJABEE
PUNT-POLE
PUNTSMAN
PUPA-CASE
PUPARIAL
PUPARIUM
PUPATION
PUPILAGE
PUPILARY
PUPILATE
PUPPETRY
PUPPY-DOG

PUPPYDOM
PUPPY-FAT
PUPPYISH
PUPPYISM
PURBLIND
PURCHASE
PURE-BRED
PURENESS
PURFLING
PURIFIED
PURIFIER
PURISTIC
PURLICUE
PURPLISH
PURPOSED
PURPURIC
PURPURIN
PURSEFUL
PURSE-NET
PURSLAIN
PURSLANE
PURSUANT
PURSUING
PURULENT
PURVEYOR
PUSEYISM
PUSEYITE
PUSH-BALL
PUSH-BIKE
PUSH-CART
PUSH-OVER
PUSH-PULL
PUSS-MOTH
PUSSY-CAT
PUSTULAR
PUTATIVE
PUTCHOCK
PUTRIDLY
PUTTER-ON
PUTTYING
PUZZLING
PYELITIC
PYELITIS
PYENGADU
PYGIDIAL
PYGIDIUM
PYGMAEAN
PYJAMAED
PYOGENIC
PYONINGS
PYRENEAN
PYRENOID
PYRIDINE
PYRIFORM
PYRITISE
PYRITOUS
PYROSOMA
PYROSOME
PYROXENE
PYROXYLE
PYRRHOUS
PYTHONIC
PYXIDIUM

Q

QUACKERY
QUADRANS
QUADRANT
QUADRATE
QUADRIGA
QUADROON
QUAESTOR
QUAGMIRE
QUAGMIRY
QUAILING
QUAINTLY
QUAKERLY
QUALMING
QUALMISH
QUANDANG
QUANDARY
QUANDONG
QUANTIFY
QUANTISE
QUANTITY
QUANTONG
QUARRIED
QUARRIER
QUARTERN
QUARTETT
QUARTIER
QUARTILE
QUART-POT
QUASHINE
QUATORZE
QUATRAIN
QUAVERER
QUAYSIDE
QUEASILY
QUECHUAN
QUEEN-BEE
QUEENDOM
QUEENING
QUEENITE
QUEENLET
QUEERISH
QUEERITY
QUENCHER
QUENELLE
QUERYING
QUESTANT
QUESTING
QUESTION
QUEUEING
QUIBBLER
QUICHUAN
QUICKSET
QUIDDANY
QUIDDITY
QUIDDLER
QUIDNUNC
QUIETING
QUIETISM
QUIETIST
QUIETIVE
QUIETUDE
QUILLING
QUILLMAN
QUILL-NIB

QUILL-PEN
QUILTING
QUINCUNX
QUINTAIN
QUINTETT
QUIPPISH
QUIRINAL
QUIRINUS
QUIRITES
QUIRKISH
QUISLING
QUIT-RENT
QUITTING
QUIVERED
QUIXOTIC
QUIXOTRY
QUIZZERY
QUIZZIFY
QUIZZING
QUOTABLE
QUOTABLY
QUOTIENT

R

RABBETED
RABBINIC
RABBITER
RABBITRY
RABBLING
RABIDITY
RACAHOUT
RACE-BALL
RACE-CARD
RACE-GOER
RACEMISE
RACEMISM
RACEMOSE
RACE-PATH
RACHILLA
RACHITIC
RACHITIS
RACINESS
RACKETED
RACKETER
RACKETRY
RACK-RAIL
RACK-RENT
RACKWORK
RACOVIAN
RADIALIA
RADIALLY
RADIANCE
RADIANCY
RADIATED
RADIATOR
RADICANT
RADICULE
RADULATE
RAFTERED
RAFT-PORT
RAFT-ROPE
RAFTSMAN
RAGGEDLY
RAGINGLY
RAG-MONEY
RAGNARÖK

RAG-PAPER
RAGSTONE
RAGTIMER
RAGWHEEL
RAGWOMAN
RAILHEAD
RAILLERY
RAILLESS
RAILROAD
RAIN-BAND
RAIN-BIRD
RAINBOWY
RAINCOAT
RAINDROP
RAINFALL
RAINLESS
RAINTREE
RAIN-WASH
RAISABLE
RAISONNE
RAJASHIP
RAKEHELL
RAKISHLY
RAKSHASA
RALLIDAE
RALLYING
RAMADHAN
RAMAYANA
RAMBLING
RAMENTUM
RAMEQUIN
RAMIFIED
RAMPANCY
RAMPAUGE
RAMPSMAN
RAM'S-HORN
RAMULOSE
RAMULOUS
RANARIAN
RANARIUM
RANCHERO
RANCHING
RANCHMAN
RANDOMLY
RANIFORM
RANKNESS
RANNELLE
RANSOMER
RAPACITY
RAPE-CAKE
RAPE-SEED
RAPHANIA
RAPHANUS
RAPHIDES
RAPIDITY
RAPPAREE
RAPTORES
RAPTURED
RAREFIED
RARENESS
RASCALLY
RASHNESS
RASORIAL
RATAPLAN
RATEABLE
RATEABLY

RAT-GUARD
RATHRIPE
RATIFIED
RATIFIER
RATIONAL
RATOONER
RATPROOF
RAT-RHYME
RATSBANE
RAT'S-TAIL
RATTLINE
RATTLING
RAVELLED
RAVENOUS
RAVINGLY
RAVISHER
RAWBONED
RAZMATAZ
REABSORB
REACHING
REACTANT
REACTION
REACTIVE
READABLE
READABLY
READIEST
READJUST
READVISE
REAEDIFY
REAFFIRM
REAGENCY
REALISER
REALNESS
REANSWER
REAPPEAR
REAR-ARCH
REAR-LAMP
REARMICE
REARMOST
REAR-RANK
REARREST
REARWARD
REASCEND
REASCENT
REASONED
REASONER
REASSERT
REASSESS
REASSIGN
REASSUME
REASSURE
REATTAIN
REAWAKEN
REBELDOM
REBELLED
REBELLER
REBELLOW
REBUTTAL
REBUTTED
REBUTTER
RECANTER
RECAPTOR
RECEDING
RECEIVAL
RECEIVED
RECEIVER

RECENTLY
RECENTRE
RECEPTOR
RECESSED
RECHARGE
RECISION
RECKLESS
RECKLING
RECKONER
RECLINED
RECLINER
RECLOTHE
RÉCOLLET
RECOMMIT
RECONVEY
RECORDER
RECOURSE
RECOVERY
RECREANT
RECREATE
RECTALLY
RECTITIC
RECTITIS
RECTORAL
RECTRESS
RECURRED
RECURVED
RECUSANT
REDACTOR
REDARGUE
RED-BELLY
RED-BRICK
REDCROSS
REDDENDA
REDDENDO
REDEEMER
REDELESS
REDEPLOY
REDIRECT
REDISTIL
REDIVIDE
RED-LIGHT
REDOLENT
REDOUBLE
RED-SHANK
REDSHARE
REDSHIRE
RED-SHIRT
REDSHORT
RED-START
REDUCING
RED-WATER
REED-BAND
REED-BIRD
REEDLING
REED-MACE
REED-PIPE
REED-RAND
REED-ROND
REED-STOP
REED-WREN
REEF-BAND
REEF-KNOT
RE-EMBARK
RE-EMBODY
RE-EMERGE

RE-ENGAGE
RE-ENLIST
RE-EXPAND
RE-EXPORT
REFELLED
REFERENT
REFERRAL
REFERRED
REFIGURE
REFINERY
REFINING
REFLEXED
REFLEXLY
REFLUENT
REFORMED
REFORMER
REFRINGE
REFUNDER
REFUSION
REGAINER
REGALIAN
REGALISM
REGALIST
REGALITY
REGARDER
REGELATE
REGICIDE
REGIMENT
REGIONAL
REGISTER
REGISTRY
REGOLITH
REGRATER
REGRATOR
REGROWTH
REGULATE
REGULINE
REGULISE
REHANDLE
REHEARSE
REHEATER
REHOBOAM
RE-IGNITE
REILLUME
REIMPOSE
REINDEER
REINETTE
REINFORM
REINFUND
REINFUSE
REIN-HAND
REINLESS
REINSERT
REINSMAN
REINSURE
REINVEST
REJECTER
REJECTOR
REJIGGER
REJOICER
REKINDLE
RELAPSED
RELAPSER
RELATION
RELATIVE
RELAXANT

RELAXING
RELEASEE
RELEASER
RELEASOR
RELEGATE
RELEVANT
RELIABLE
RELIABLY
RELIANCE
RELIEVER
RELIGION
RELUCENT
RELUMINE
REMANENT
REMARKED
REMARKER
REMARQUÉ
REMEDIAL
REMEDIAT
REMEDIED
REMEMBER
REMIGATE
REMINDER
REMISSLY
REMITTAL
REMITTED
REMITTEE
REMITTER
REMOTELY
REMOTION
REMURMUR
RENAYING
RENDERER
RENEGADE
RENEGADO
RENEGATE
RENEGUER
RENEWING
RENFORCE
RENIFORM
RENITENT
RENOUNCE
RENOVATE
RENOWNED
RENOWNER
RENTABLE
RENT-FREE
RENT-ROLL
RENUMBER
RENVERSE
RENVERST
REOCCUPY
REORDAIN
REORIENT
REPAIRER
REPARTEE
REPAYING
REPEALER
REPEATED
REPEATER
REPELLED
REPELLER
REPENTER
REPEOPLE
REPERUSE
REPETEND

REPINING
REPLACER
REPLEVIN
REPLYING
REPORTER
REPOSURE
REPOUSSÉ
REPRIEFE
REPRIEVE
REPRISAL
REPROACH
REPROVAL
REPROVER
REPTILIA
REPUBLIC
REPUTING
REQUIRED
REQUIRER
REQUITAL
REQUITED
REQUITER
RERE-ARCH
REREMICE
REREVISE
REREWARD
RESALGAR
RESALUTE
RESCRIPT
RESCUING
RESEARCH
RESEMBLE
RESENTER
RESERVED
RESETTER
RESETTLE
RESIANCE
RESIDENT
RESIDUAL
RESIDUUM
RESIGNED
RESIGNER
RESINATA
RESINATE
RESINIFY
RESINISE
RESINOUS
RESISTOR
RESOLUTE
RESOLVED
RESOLVER
RESONANT
RESONATE
RESORCIN
RESORTER
RESOURCE
RESPLEND
RESPONSE
RESTCURE
RESTHOME
RESTLESS
RESTORER
RESTRAIN
RESTRICT
RESTROOM
RESUPINE
RESURVEY

RETAILER
RETAINER
RETAKING
RETARDED
RETARDER
RETELLER
RETICENT
RETICULE
RETIFORM
RETINITE
RETINULA
RETIRACY
RETIRING
RETORTED
RETORTER
RETRAITT
RETRENCH
RETRIEVE
RETROACT
RETRORSE
RETRYING
REVANCHE
REVEALER
REVEILLE
REVELLED
REVELLER
REVENANT
REVENGER
REVENUED
REVEREND
REVERENT
REVERIST
REVERSAL
REVERSED
REVERSER
REVERSIS
REVERTED
REVESTRY
REVETTED
REVIEWAL
REVIEWER
REVILING
REVISION
REVISORY
REVIVIFY
REVIVING
REVOLTED
REVOLTER
REVOLUTE
REVOLVER
REWARDER
RHABDOID
RHAETIAN
RHAPHIDE
RHAPSODE
RHAPSODY
RHEMATIC
RHEOCORD
RHEOLOGY
RHEOSTAT
RHEOTOME
RHETORIC
RH-FACTOR
RHINITIS
RHINODON
RHIZOPOD

R-S**8**

RHIZOPUS	RINGSIDE	ROENTGEN	ROSOGLIO	RUMINANT
RHODANIC	RINGSTER	ROESTONE	ROSTRATE	RUMINATE
RHODESIA	RING-TAIL	ROGATION	ROSULATE	RUMMAGER
RHODITES	RING-TIME	ROGATORY	ROSY-DROP	RUMONSCH
RHOMBOID	RING-WALK	ROISTING	ROTARIAN	RUMOROUS
RHONCHAL	RING-WALL	ROLL-CALL	ROTATION	RUMOURER
RHONCHUS	RINGWISE	ROLY-POLY	ROTATIVE	RUMP-BONE
RHOPALIC	RINGWORK	ROMANCER	ROTATORY	RUMPLESS
RHUBARBY	RINGWORM	ROMANISE	ROTENONE	RUMP-POST
RHYOLITE	RINSINGS	ROMANISH	ROT-GRASS	RUM-PUNCH
RHYTHMAL	RIPARIAL	ROMANISM	ROTIFERA	RUM-SHRUB
RHYTHMED	RIPARIAN	ROMANIST	ROT-STONE	RUNABOUT
RHYTHMIC	RIPENESS	ROMANSCH	ROTTENLY	RUNAGATE
RHYTHMUS	RIPPLING	ROMANTIC	ROTUNDLY	RUNCIBLE
RHYTISMA	RISALDAR	ROME-SCOT	ROTURIER	RUNNABLE
RIBALDRY	RISOLUTO	ROMEWARD	ROUGHAGE	RUNNER-UP
RIBAUDRY	RISPINGS	RONCADOR	ROUGH-DRY	RURALISE
RIBBONRY	RITENUTO	RONDACHE	ROUGH-HEW	RURALISM
RIB-GRASS	RITORNEL	RONDAVEL	ROUGHISH	RURALIST
RIBOSOME	RITUALLY	RONDEAUX	ROULEAUX	RURALITY
RIB-ROAST	RIVALESS	ROOD-BEAM	ROULETTE	RUSH-LIKE
RIBSTONE	RIVALISE	ROOD-LOFT	ROUND-ARM	RUSH-RING
RICE-BEER	RIVALITY	ROOD-TREE	ROUNDING	RUSSNIAK
RICE-BIRD	RIVALLED	ROOFLESS	ROUNDISH	RUSTICAL
RICE-GLUE	RIVELLED	ROOF-LIKE	ROUNDLET	RUSTLESS
RICE-MILK	RIVERAIN	ROOF-TREE	ROUND-TOP	RUSTLING
RICERCAR	RIVER-BED	ROOM-MATE	ROUNDURE	RUTABAGA
RICE-SOUP	RIVER-GOD	ROOMSOME	ROUT-CAKE	RUTACEAE
RICHESSE	RIVER-HOG	ROOT-BEER	ROUT-SEAT	RUTHLESS
RICH-LEFT	RIVERINE	ROOT-CROP	ROVE-OVER	RUTILANT
RICHNESS	RIVERMAN	ROOTEDLY	ROVINGLY	RYE-BREAD
RICKETTY	RIVER-RAT	ROOT-FAST	ROW-BARGE	RYE-FLOUR
RICK-RACK	RIVERWAY	ROOT-HAIR	ROWDEDOW	RYE-GRASS
RICKSHAW	RIVETING	ROOTHOLD	ROWDYDOW	RYE-STRAW
RICKYARD	RIVETTED	ROOT-KNOT	ROWDYISH	RYOTWARI
RICOCHET	ROAD-BOOK	ROOTLESS	ROWDYISM	
RIDDANCE	ROADSIDE	ROPEABLE	ROWELLED	**S**
RIDDLING	ROADSMAN	ROPE-RIPE	ROWNDELL	SABBATIC
RIDEABLE	ROADSTER	ROPE'S-END	ROYALISE	SABOTAGE
RIDGEWAY	ROASTING	ROPE-WALK	ROYALISM	SABOTEUR
RIDGLING	ROBORANT	ROPEWORK	ROYALIST	SABOTIER
RIDICULE	ROBURITE	ROPE-YARN	ROYSTING	SABRE-CUT
RIESLING	ROBUSTLY	ROPINESS	RUBBISHY	SABULOUS
RIFENESS	ROCAILLE	ROSACEAE	RUBELLAN	SABURRAL
RIFF-RAFF	ROCCELLA	ROSARIAN	RUBICUND	SACCATEA
RIFLEMAN	ROCHELLE	ROSARIUM	RUBIDIUM	SACCULAR
RIFLE-PIT	ROCK-ALUM	ROSE-BOWL	RUBRICAL	SACCULES
RIGADOON	ROCKAWAY	ROSE-BUSH	RUBSTONE	SACCULUS
RIGHTFUL	ROCK-BIRD	ROSE-COMB	RUBY-TAIL	SACELLUM
RIGHTING	ROCK-CAKE	ROSE-DROP	RUCKSACK	SACK-COAT
RIGHTIST	ROCK-COOK	ROSE-FISH	RUDDIEST	SACKFULS
RIGIDITY	ROCK-CORK	ROSE-HUED	RUDDYING	SACKLESS
RIGORISM	ROCK-DOVE	ROSE-KNOT	RUDENESS	SACK-RACE
RIGORIST	ROCKETER	ROSE-LEAF	RUDIMENT	SACK-TREE
RIGOROUS	ROCKETRY	ROSELESS	RUEFULLY	SACREDLY
RILLMARK	ROCK-FALL	ROSELIKE	RUFFLING	SACRISTY
RIM-BRAKE	ROCK-FISH	ROSEMARY	RUGGEDLY	SADDLERY
RINDLESS	ROCK-HEWN	ROSE-PINK	RUGOSELY	SADDUCEE
RING-BARK	ROCK-LARK	ROSE-RASH	RUGOSITY	SAD-FACED
RING-BOLT	ROCKLING	ROSE-ROOT	RUGULOSE	SADISTIC
RINGBONE	ROCK-ROSE	ROSE-TREE	RUINABLE	SAECULUM
RING-DIAL	ROCK-SALT	ROSETTED	RULELESS	SAFENESS
RING-DOVE	ROCKWEED	ROSEWOOD	RUMANIAN	SAFFRONY
RING-DYKE	ROCK-WOOD	ROSINATE	RUMANSCH	SAFRANIN
RINGLESS	ROCK-WORK	ROSINESS	RUMBELOW	SAGACITY
RING-ROAD	RODENTIA	ROSIN-OIL	RUMBLING	SAGAMORE

SAGE-COCK	SAMPLERY	SARCODES	SAXICOLA	SCHIEDAM
SAGENESS	SAMPLING	SARCODIC	SAXONDOM	SCHILLER
SAGENITE	SANATIVE	SARDELLE	SAXONISE	SCHIMMEL
SAGINATE	SANATORY	SARDONIC	SAXONISM	SCHIZAEA
SAGITTAL	SANCTIFY	SARDONYX	SAXONIST	SCHIZOID
SAGO-PALM	SANCTION	SARGASSO	SAXONITE	SCHLÄGER
SAIBLING	SANCTITY	SARK-TAIL	SAYONARA	SCHMALTZ
SAIKLESS	SANDARAC	SARMATIA	SAY-PIECE	SCHMOOZE
SAILABLE	SAND-BANK	SARMATIC	SCABBARD	SCHNAPPS
SAIL-BOAT	SAND-BATH	SARMENTA	SCABIOSA	SCHOLION
SAIL-FISH	SAND-DART	SARRASIN	SCABIOUS	SCHOLIUM
SAILLESS	SAND-DUNE	SARRAZIN	SCABROUS	SCHOOLED
SAIL-LOFT	SAND-FLAG	SARSENET	SCAFFOLD	SCHOONER
SAILORLY	SAND-FLEA	SARTRIAN	SCALABLE	SCIATICA
SAIL-ROOM	SAND-HEAP	SASARARA	SCALARIA	SCIENCED
SAIL-YARD	SAND-HILL	SASH-DOOR	SCALAWAG	SCILICET
SAINFOIN	SAND-HOLE	SASH-TOOL	SCALDING	SCIMITAR
SAINTDOM	SANDIVER	SASSANID	SCALDINI	SCINCOID
SAINTESS	SAND-LARK	SASSOLIN	SCALDINO	SCIOLISM
SAINTISH	SANDLING	SASTRUGA	SCALLION	SCIOLIST
SAINTISM	SAND-MOLE	SATANISM	SCALPRUM	SCIOLOUS
SALACITY	SAND-PEEP	SATANIST	SCALY-LEG	SCIROCCO
SALADING	SAND-PIPE	SATANITY	SCAMBLER	SCIRRHUS
SALARIAT	SAND-PUMP	SATELESS	SCAMMONY	SCISSILE
SALARIED	SANDSHOE	SATELLES	SCAMPING	SCISSION
SALEABLE	SAND-STAR	SATHANAS	SCAMPISH	SCISSORS
SALEABLY	SAND-TRAP	SATIABLE	SCANDENT	SCISSURE
SALE-ROOM	SAND-WASP	SATINETT	SCANDIAN	SCIURINE
SALESIAN	SANDWICH	SATIRISE	SCANDIUM	SCIUROID
SALESMAN	SAND-WORM	SATIRIST	SCANNING	SCLEREID
SALES-TAX	SANDWORT	SATRAPAL	SCANSION	SCLEREMA
SALEWORK	SANDYISH	SATRAPIC	SCANTILY	SCLERITE
SALICETA	SANENESS	SATURANT	SCANTITY	SCLEROMA
SALIENCE	SANGAREE	SATURATE	SCAPHOID	SCLEROSE
SALIENCY	SANGLIER	SATURDAY	SCAPULAR	SCLEROUS
SALIFIED	SANGRAAL	SATURNIA	SCARABEE	SCOFFING
SALINITY	SANGRADO	SATURNIC	SCARCELY	SCOINSON
SALIVARY	SANGRAIL	SATYRESS	SCARCITY	SCOLDING
SALIVATE	SANGREAL	SATYRISK	SCARFING	SCOLECES
SALLYING	SANGUIFY	SAUBA-ANT	SCARFISH	SCOLECID
SALLYMAN	SANGUINE	SAUCE-BOX	SCARF-PIN	SCOLOPAX
SALMONET	SANIDINE	SAUCEMAN	SCARIDAE	SCOLYTUS
SALMONID	SANITARY	SAUCEPAN	SCARIOUS	SCOMFISH
SALOPIAN	SANITATE	SAUCIEST	SCARLESS	SCONTION
SALTANDO	SANSCRIT	SAUCISSE	SCARMOGE	SCOOPFUL
SALT-BUSH	SANSERIF	SAURURAE	SCARPING	SCOOPING
SALT-CAKE	SANSKRIT	SAUTERNE	SCARRING	SCOOP-NET
SALT-COTE	SANTALIN	SAVAGELY	SCATHING	SCOPELUS
SALT-FOOT	SANTALUM	SAVAGERY	SCATTERY	SCORCHED
SALT-JUNK	SANTONIN	SAVANNAH	SCAVAGER	SCORCHER
SALTLESS	SAPALINE	SAVEGARD	SCAVENGE	SCORDATO
SALT-LICK	SAP-GREEN	SAVINGLY	SCEATTAS	SCORIOUS
SALT-MINE	SAPIDITY	SAVOROUS	SCELERAT	SCORNFUL
SALTNESS	SAPIENCE	SAVOURED	SCENARIO	SCORNING
SALT-WORK	SAPINDUS	SAVOURLY	SCENE-MAN	SCORPION
SALT-WORT	SAPI-UTAN	SAVOYARD	SCENICAL	SCOT-FREE
SALUTARY	SAPONIFY	SAW-BLADE	SCENT-BAG	SCOTICAN
SALVABLE	SAPONITE	SAW-BONES	SCENT-BOX	SCOTLAND
SALVIFIC	SAPOROUS	SAWDUSTY	SCENTFUL	SCOTOPIA
SALVINIA	SAPPHIRE	SAW-FRAME	SCENTING	SCOTOPIC
SAMARIUM	SAPPHISM	SAW-HORSE	SCEPTRAL	SCOTSMAN
SAMAVEDA	SAPROPEL	SAW-SHARK	SCEPTRED	SCOTTICE
SAMENESS	SAPUCAIA	SAW-TONES	SCHEDULE	SCOTTIFY
SAMNITIS	SARABAND	SAW-TOOTH	SCHELLUM	SCOTTISH
SAMOYEDE	SARATOGA	SAXATILE	SCHEMATA	SCOURGER
SAMPHIRE	SARCENET	SAXICAVA	SCHEMING	SCOURING

SCOUTHER
SCOUTING
SCOUT-LAW
SCOWLING
SCOWTHER
SCRABBLE
SCRAG-END
SCRAGGED
SCRAGGLY
SCRAMBLE
SCRANNEL
SCRAPING
SCRAP-MAN
SCRAPPED
SCRATCHY
SCRATTLE
SCRAWLER
SCREAMER
SCREECHY
SCREENER
SCREEVER
SCREWING
SCREWTOP
SCRIBBLE
SCRIBBLY
SCRIBING
SCRIBISM
SCRIGGLE
SCRIGGLY
SCRIMPED
SCRIMPLY
SCRIMURE
SCROFULA
SCROGGIE
SCROLLED
SCROUGER
SCROUNGE
SCROWDGE
SCRUBBED
SCRUBBER
SCRUNCHY
SCRUPLER
SCRUTINY
SCUDDING
SCUFFLER
SCULLERY
SCULLING
SCULLION
SCULPSIT
SCULPTOR
SCUMFISH
SCUMMING
SCUPPAUG
SCURRIER
SCURRILE
SCURVILY
SCUTCHER
SCUTELLA
SCUTIGER
SCUTTLER
SCYBALUM
SCYTHIAN
SEA-ACORN
SEA-ADDER
SEA-BEACH
SEA-BEAST

SEABERRY
SEA-BLITE
SEABOARD
SEABORNE
SEA-BREAM
SEA-BRIEF
SEA-CHART
SEA-CHEST
SEA-CLIFF
SEA-COAST
SEACRAFT
SEACUNNY
SEA-DEVIL
SEADROME
SEA-EAGLE
SEAFARER
SEAFIGHT
SEA-FLOOR
SEA-FRONT
SEA-FROTH
SEA-GOING
SEA-GRAPE
SEA-GRASS
SEA-GREEN
SEA-HEATH
SEA-HOLLY
SEA-HORSE
SEA-HOUND
SEA-JELLY
SEA-LEMON
SEA-LEVEL
SEA-LOACH
SEAL-PIPE
SEAL-RING
SEALSKIN
SEA-LUNGS
SEALYHAM
SEAMANLY
SEA-MARGE
SEAMLESS
SEA-MOUNT
SEA-MOUSE
SEAM-RENT
SEAMSTER
SEA-NYMPH
SEA-ONION
SEA-ORACH
SEA-OTTER
SEA-PERCH
SEA-PIECE
SEAPLANE
SEA-POWER
SEA-PURSE
SEAQUAKE
SEARCHER
SEARNESS
SEA-ROBIN
SEA-ROVER
SEASCAPE
SEA-SCOUT
SEASHELL
SEASHORE
SEA-SHRUB
SEA-SNAIL
SEA-SNAKE
SEA-SNIPE

SEASONAL
SEASONED
SEASONER
SEA-STICK
SEA-STOCK
SEA-STORM
SEAS-TOST
SEA-SWINE
SEAT-BELT
SEATLESS
SEAT-RENT
SEA-TROUT
SEAWARDS
SEA-WATER
SEA-WOMAN
SEA-WRACK
SEBESTEN
SECATEUR
SECESHER
SECLUDED
SECODONT
SECONDER
SECONDLY
SECRETIN
SECRETLY
SECTATOR
SECTORAL
SECURELY
SECURITY
SEDATELY
SEDATION
SEDATIVE
SEDERUNT
SEDIMENT
SEDITION
SEDUCING
SEDUCTOR
SEDULITY
SEDULOUS
SEECATCH
SEEDCAKE
SEED-COAT
SEED-CORN
SEED-FISH
SEED-LEAF
SEEDLESS
SEED-LIKE
SEEDLING
SEED-LOBE
SEEDNESS
SEED-PLOT
SEED-SHOP
SEEDSMAN
SEED-TIME
SEEDY-TOE
SEEMLESS
SEEMLIER
SEETHING
SEGOLATE
SEGREANT
SEIDLITZ
SEIGNEUR
SEIGNIOR
SEIGNORY
SEINE-NET
SEISMISM

SEIZABLE
SELADANG
SELCOUTH
SELDSEEN
SELECTED
SELECTOR
SELENATE
SELENIDE
SELENITE
SELENIUM
SELEUCID
SELF-BORN
SELF-HEAL
SELF-HELP
SELFHOOD
SELF-LEFT
SELFLESS
SELF-LIFE
SELF-LIKE
SELF-LOST
SELF-LOVE
SELF-MADE
SELFNESS
SELF-PITY
SELF-SOWN
SELF-WILL
SELICTAR
SELLABLE
SELVEDGE
SEMANTIC
SEMANTRA
SEMBLANT
SEMESTER
SEMI-AXIS
SEMIBULL
SEMICOMA
SEMI-DOME
SEMILUNE
SEMI-MUTE
SEMINARY
SEMINATE
SEMINOLE
SEMI-NUDE
SEMI-OPAL
SEMIOTIC
SEMI-RING
SEMITISE
SEMITISM
SEMITIST
SEMITONE
SEMOLINA
SEMPLICE
SEMPSTER
SEMUNCIA
SENARIUS
SENGREEN
SENILITY
SENNIGHT
SENONIAN
SEÑORITA
SENOUSSI
SENSEFUL
SENSIBLE
SENSIBLY
SENSUISM
SENSUIST

SENSUOUS
SENTENCE
SENTIENT
SENTINEL
SENTRY-GO
SEPALODY
SEPALOID
SEPALOUS
SEPARATE
SEPIMENT
SEPTARIA
SEPTETTE
SEPT-FOIL
SEPTIMAL
SEPTLEVA
SEPTUPLE
SEQUELAE
SEQUENCE
SERAFILE
SERAGOLI
SERAPEUM
SERAPHIC
SERAPHIM
SERAPHIN
SERENADE
SERENATA
SERENELY
SERENESS
SERENITY
SERFHOOD
SERFSHIP
SERGEANT
SERIALLY
SERIATIM
SERICITE
SERJEANT
SERMONER
SERMONET
SERMONIC
SEROLOGY
SEROSITY
SEROTINE
SERPULAE
SERRANID
SERRANUS
SERRATED
SERRATUS
SERVIENT
SERVITOR
SESAMOID
SESSPOOL
SESTERCE
SESTETTE
SESTETTO
SETSCREW
SETTER-ON
SETTER-UP
SETTLING
SEVEN-DAY
SEVERELY
SEVERITY
SEWELLEL
SEWERAGE
SEWER-GAS
SEWERING
SEWER-RAT

SEXINESS
SEXTETTE
SEXTOLET
SEXTUPLE
SEXUALLY
SFORZATO
SHABBILY
SHABRACK
SHADBUSH
SHADDOCK
SHADOWER
SHAFIITE
SHAFTING
SHAG-BARK
SHAGGILY
SHAGREEN
SHAGROON
SHAIVISM
SHAKABLE
SHAKE-BAG
SHAKE-RAG
SHAKTISM
SHALE-OIL
SHALLOON
SHAMANIC
SHAMEFUL
SHAMIANA
SHAMISEN
SHAMMING
SHAMPOO'D
SHAMROCK
SHANDEAN
SHANGHAI
SHANTUNG
SHAPABLE
SHAREMAN
SHARE-OUT
SHARKING
SHARK-OIL
SHARP-CUT
SHARPING
SHARPISH
SHARP-SET
SHATTERY
SHAUCHLE
SHAUCHLY
SHAWLING
SHEADING
SHEALING
SHEAR-HOG
SHEARING
SHEAR-LEG
SHEARMAN
SHEATHED
SHEA-TREE
SHEDDING
SHE-DEVIL
SHEELING
SHEEP-DIP
SHEEPDOG
SHEEPISH
SHEEP-KED
SHEEP-PEN
SHEEP-POX
SHEEP-ROT
SHEEP-RUN

SHEETING
SHEET-TIN
SHEILING
SHEKINAH
SHELDUCK
SHELFFUL
SHELL-EGG
SHELLFUL
SHELL-ICE
SHELLING
SHELL-LAC
SHELTERY
SHELVING
SHEPHERD
SHERATON
SHETLAND
SHIELDER
SHIELING
SHIFTING
SHIFT-KEY
SHIKAREE
SHILLING
SHIMMERY
SHIN-BONE
SHINGLED
SHINGLER
SHINGLES
SHIPLESS
SHIP-LOAD
SHIPMATE
SHIPMENT
SHIPPING
SHIP-TIRE
SHIP-WORM
SHIPYARD
SHIREMAN
SHIRRING
SHIRTING
SHIRT-PIN
SHIVAREE
SHOALING
SHOCK-DOG
SHOCKING
SHODDILY
SHOE-BILL
SHOEHORN
SHOE-LACE
SHOELESS
SHOE-NAIL
SHOE-ROSE
SHOE-SHOP
SHOE-TREE
SHOGGING
SHOGUNAL
SHOOTING
SHOP-BELL
SHOP-DOOR
SHOP-GIRL
SHOPPING
SHOP-SIGN
SHOPWORN
SHORE-DUE
SHOREMAN
SHORTAGE
SHORT-CUT
SHORTISH

SHORT-LEG
SHORT-OIL
SHORT-RIB
SHOT-CLOG
SHOT-FREE
SHOT-HOLE
SHOTTING
SHOULDER
SHOULDST
SHOUTHER
SHOUTING
SHOW-BILL
SHOW-BOAT
SHOW-CARD
SHOW-CASE
SHOW-DOWN
SHOWGIRL
SHOWROOM
SHOW-YARD
SHRADDHA
SHRAPNEL
SHREDDED
SHREDDER
SHRED-PIE
SHREWDLY
SHREWISH
SHREW-RUN
SHRIEKER
SHRIEVAL
SHRIEVED
SHRIMPER
SHRINKER
SHRIVING
SHROUDED
SHRUGGED
SHRUNKEN
SHUCKING
SHUDDERY
SHUFFLER
SHUNLESS
SHUNNING
SHUNTING
SHUT-DOWN
SHUTTING
SIBILANT
SIBILATE
SIBILOUS
SICANIAN
SICELIAN
SICELIOT
SICILIAN
SICKENER
SICKERLY
SICK-FLAG
SICKLIED
SICKLILY
SICK-LIST
SICKNESS
SICULIAN
SIDEARMS
SIDE-BAND
SIDE-COMB
SIDE-DISH
SIDE-DOOR
SIDE-DRUM
SIDE-FACE

SIDE-KICK
SIDELINE
SIDELING
SIDE-LOCK
SIDELONG
SIDE-NOTE
SIDE-PATH
SIDE-POST
SIDEREAL
SIDERITE
SIDE-ROAD
SIDE-SHOW
SIDE-SLIP
SIDESMAN
SIDE-STEP
SIDE-VIEW
SIDEWALK
SIDEWARD
SIDEWAYS
SIDE-WIND
SIDEWISE
SIEGE-GUN
SIENNESE
SIGISBEO
SIGMATIC
SIGNALLY
SIGNETED
SIGNIEUR
SIGNLESS
SIGNORIA
SIGNPOST
SIKELIAN
SIKELIOT
SILENCED
SILENCER
SILENTLY
SILICANE
SILICATE
SILICIDE
SILICIFY
SILICIUM
SILICONE
SILICULA
SILICULE
SILK-TAIL
SILKWORM
SILLABUB
SILLADAR
SILLY-HOW
SILPHIUM
SILURIAN
SILURIST
SILUROID
SILVATIC
SILVERLY
SIMARUBA
SIMILISE
SIMONIAC
SIMONIST
SIMPERER
SIMPLIFY
SIMPLING
SIMPLISM
SIMPLIST
SIMULANT
SIMULATE

SINAITIC
SINAPISM
SINCIPUT
SINDINGS
SIN-EATER
SINECURE
SINFONIA
SINGABLE
SINGEING
SINGLING
SINGSONG
SINGULAR
SINICISE
SINICISM
SINISTER
SINK-HOLE
SINOLOGY
SINOPHIL
SINOPITE
SINUATED
SINUITIS
SINUSOID
SIPHONAL
SIPHONET
SIPHONIC
SIRENIAN
SIRIASIS
SIRVENTE
SISERARY
SISTERLY
SITHENCE
SITOLOGY
SITTER-IN
SITUATED
SITZ-BATH
SIXPENCE
SIXPENNY
SIX-SCORE
SIXTIETH
SIZEABLE
SIZINESS
SIZZLING
SKEAN-DHU
SKELETAL
SKELETON
SKELLOCH
SKELPING
SKENE-DHU
SKETCHER
SKEW-BACK
SKEWBALD
SKIAGRAM
SKIATRON
SKILLESS
SKILLING
SKIM-MILK
SKIMMING
SKIMPILY
SKIMPING
SKIN-DEEP
SKIN-GAME
SKINHEAD
SKINKING
SKINLESS
SKINNING
SKIN-WOOL

SKIPJACK
SKIPPING
SKIRLING
SKIRMISH
SKIRTING
SKI-SLOPE
SKITTISH
SKITTLES
SKUA-GULL
SKULKING
SKULL-CAP
SKYLIGHT
SKY-PILOT
SKYSCAPE
SKYWARDS
SLABBERY
SLACK-JAW
SLAG-WOOL
SLAISTER
SLAMMING
SLANGILY
SLANGING
SLANGISH
SLANTING
SLAP-BANG
SLAP-DASH
SLAPJACK
SLAPPING
SLASHING
SLATE-AXE
SLATTERN
SLATTERY
SLAVE-ANT
SLAVERER
SLAVONIA
SLAVONIC
SLEDDING
SLEDGING
SLEEKING
SLEEPERY
SLEEPILY
SLEEPING
SLICKING
SLIDDERY
SLIGHTLY
SLIME-PIT
SLIMMEST
SLIMMING
SLIMMISH
SLIMNESS
SLIP-DOCK
SLIPFORM
SLIP-KNOT
SLIP-OVER
SLIPPERY
SLIPPING
SLIPRAIL
SLIPSHOD
SLIP-SHOE
SLIPSLOP
SLITHERY
SLITTING
SLIVOVIC
SLOBBERY
SLOBLAND
SLOEBUSH

SLOETREE
SLOGORNE
SLOP-BOWL
SLOP-PAIL
SLOPPILY
SLOPPING
SLOP-SHOP
SLOPWORK
SLOTHFUL
SLOUCHER
SLOUGHED
SLOVENLY
SLOVENRY
SLOWBACK
SLOW-DOWN
SLOW-FOOT
SLOWNESS
SLOWPOKE
SLOW-WORM
SLUBBING
SLUG-A-BED
SLUGFEST
SLUGGARD
SLUGGISH
SLUGHORN
SLUMBERY
SLUMMING
SLURRING
SLUTTERY
SLUTTISH
SLYBOOTS
SMACKING
SMALLAGE
SMALL-ALE
SMALL-ARM
SMALLISH
SMALLPOX
SMALMILY
SMALTITE
SMARMILY
SMASH-HIT
SMASHING
SMEAR-DAB
SMEARILY
SMELLING
SMELTERY
SMELTING
SMILEFUL
SMITHERS
SMITHERY
SMOCKING
SMOKABLE
SMOKE-BOX
SMOKE-DRY
SMOOCHER
SMOOTHEN
SMOOTHER
SMOOTHIE
SMOOTHLY
SMÖRBRÖD
SMORZATO
SMOTHERY
SMOULDER
SMOULDRY
SMUDGILY
SMUGGLED

SMUGGLER
SMUGNESS
SMUTTILY
SNACK-BAR
SNAILERY
SNAKE-EEL
SNAKE-FLY
SNAKE-OIL
SNAKE-PIT
SNAP-BRIM
SNAP-LINK
SNAPPILY
SNAPPING
SNAPPISH
SNAPSHOT
SNARLING
SNATCHER
SNEAK-CUP
SNEAKILY
SNEAKING
SNEAKISH
SNEAKSBY
SNEAPING
SNEERING
SNEESHAN
SNEESHIN
SNEEZING
SNIFFILY
SNIFFING
SNIFFLER
SNIGGLER
SNIPPETY
SNIPPING
SNIP-SNAP
SNITCHER
SNIVELLY
SNOBBERY
SNOBBISH
SNOBBISM
SNOBLING
SNOOTFUL
SNORTING
SNOTTERY
SNOTTILY
SNOWBALL
SNOW-BIRD
SNOW-BOOT
SNOW-CAPT
SNOW-COLD
SNOWDROP
SNOW-EYES
SNOWFALL
SNOW-FLEA
SNOWLESS
SNOWLIKE
SNOWLINE
SNOW-SHOE
SNUBBING
SNUBBISH
SNUFFBOX
SNUFFERS
SNUFFING
SNUFFLER
SNUGGERY
SNUGGING
SNUGNESS

SOAKAWAY
SOAP-BALL
SOAP-BARK
SOAP-DISH
SOAPLESS
SOAP-ROOT
SOAP-SUDS
SOAP-TEST
SOAP-TREE
SOAPWORK
SOAPWORT
SOBERISE
SOBRANJE
SOBRANYE
SOBRIETY
SOB-STORY
SOB-STUFF
SO-CALLED
SOCIABLE
SOCIABLY
SOCIALLY
SOCIETAL
SOCINIAN
SOCKETED
SOCRATIC
SODA-LAKE
SODA-LIME
SODALITE
SODALITY
SODAMIDE
SODOMITE
SOFFIONI
SOFTBALL
SOFT-BOIL
SOFTENER
SOFT-HEAD
SOFTLING
SOFTNESS
SOFT-SHOE
SOFT-SLOW
SOFT-SOAP
SOFTWARE
SOFTWOOD
SOILLESS
SOIL-PIPE
SOLANDER
SOLANINE
SOLARISE
SOLARISM
SOLARIST
SOLARIUM
SOLATION
SOLATIUM
SOLDERER
SOLDIERY
SOLECISE
SOLECISM
SOLECIST
SOLEMNLY
SOLENESS
SOLENOID
SOL-FAING
SOL-FAISM
SOL-FAIST
SOLFEGGI
SOLIDARE

SOLIDARY
SOLIDATE
SOLIDIFY
SOLIDISH
SOLIDISM
SOLIDIST
SOLIDITY
SOLITARY
SOLITUDE
SOLLERET
SOLSTICE
SOLUTION
SOLUTIVE
SOLVABLE
SOLVENCY
SOMATISM
SOMATIST
SOMBRELY
SOMBRERO
SOMBROUS
SOMEBODY
SOMEDEAL
SOMEDELE
SOMEGATE
SOMERSET
SOMETIME
SOMEWAYS
SOMEWHAT
SOMEWHEN
SOMEWISE
SOMNIFIC
SONATINA
SONGBIRD
SONGBOOK
SONGLESS
SONGLIKE
SONGSTER
SON-IN-LAW
SONNETRY
SONOBUOY
SONORITY
SONOROUS
SOOTHFUL
SOOTHING
SOOTHSAY
SOOTLESS
SOPHERIC
SOPHERIM
SOPHICAL
SOPOROSE
SOPOROUS
SORBONNE
SORCERER
SORDIDLY
SOREDIAL
SOREDIUM
SORE-HAWK
SORE-HEAD
SORENESS
SORICINE
SORICOID
SORORATE
SORORIAL
SORORISE
SORORITY
SORRIEST

SORROWED
SORROWER
SORRYISH
SORTABLE
SORTANCE
SORTMENT
SOTADEAN
SOTERIAL
SOUCHONG
SOUL-BELL
SOULLESS
SOUL-SCAT
SOUL-SCOT
SOUL-SHOT
SOUL-SICK
SOUND-BAR
SOUND-BOX
SOUNDING
SOUPED-UP
SOUR-COLD
SOURDINE
SOUR-EYED
SOURNESS
SOURPUSS
SOUSE-TUB
SOUTACHE
SOUTERLY
SOUTHERN
SOUTHING
SOUTHPAW
SOUTHRON
SOUTHSAY
SOUVENIR
SOVIETIC
SOVRANTY
SOWARREE
SOW-BREAD
SOW-DRUNK
SOYA-BEAN
SOY-FLOUR
SPACE-BAR
SPACEMAN
SPACIOUS
SPADEFUL
SPADEMAN
SPADICES
SPADILLE
SPADILLO
SPADONES
SPADROON
SPAEWIFE
SPAGERIC
SPAGIRIC
SPAGYRIC
SPALPEEN
SPANDREL
SPANDRIL
SPANGLED
SPANGLER
SPANGLET
SPANIARD
SPANKING
SPANLESS
SPAN-LONG
SPANNING
SPAN-ROOF

SPARABLE
SPAR-COIL
SPAR-HAWK
SPARIDAE
SPARK-GAP
SPARKISH
SPARKLER
SPARKLET
SPARLING
SPARRING
SPARSELY
SPARSITY
SPATHOSE
SPATULAR
SPAVINED
SPAWNING
SPEAKING
SPEARMAN
SPECIATE
SPECIFIC
SPECIMEN
SPECIOUS
SPECKLED
SPECTRAL
SPECTRUM
SPECULAR
SPECULUM
SPEED-COP
SPEEDFUL
SPEEDILY
SPEEDING
SPEEDWAY
SPEISADE
SPEKBOOM
SPELAEAN
SPELDING
SPELDRIN
SPELIKIN
SPELLFUL
SPELLING
SPENDALL
SPENDING
SPERGULA
SPERLING
SPERMARY
SPERM-OIL
SPHAGNUM
SPHENOID
SPHERICS
SPHEROID
SPHERULE
SPHINGID
SPHYGMIC
SPHYGMUS
SPICATED
SPICCATO
SPICE-BOX
SPICKNEL
SPICULAR
SPICULUM
SPIFFING
SPIGELIA
SPIKELET
SPIKE-OIL
SPILIKIN
SPILITIC

SPILLAGE
SPILLWAY
SPINETTE
SPINIFEX
SPINNERY
SPINNEYS
SPINNIES
SPINNING
SPINSTER
SPINTEXT
SPIRACLE
SPIRALLY
SPIRATED
SPIRIFER
SPIRILLA
SPIRITED
SPIRITUS
SPITCHER
SPIT-CURL
SPITEFUL
SPIT-FIRE
SPITTING
SPITTOON
SPIVVERY
SPLASHER
SPLATTER
SPLENDID
SPLENIAL
SPLENIUM
SPLENIUS
SPLINTER
SPLIT-NEW
SPLITTED
SPLITTER
SPLOTCHY
SPLUTTER
SPOFFISH
SPOILAGE
SPOILFUL
SPOLIATE
SPONDAIC
SPONGILY
SPONGOID
SPONSING
SPONSION
SPONTOON
SPOOFERY
SPOOKERY
SPOOKILY
SPOOKISH
SPOOMING
SPOON-FED
SPOONFUL
SPOONILY
SPORADIC
SPOROZOA
SPORTFUL
SPORTILY
SPORTING
SPORTIVE
SPORULAR
SPOTLESS
SPOTTILY
SPOTTING
SPOUSAGE
SPRACKLE

SPRAGGED
SPRANGLE
SPRATTLE
SPRAWLER
SPRAY-GUN
SPREADER
SPREATHE
SPREETHE
SPRIGGED
SPRINGAL
SPRINGER
SPRINGLE
SPRINKLE
SPRINTER
SPRITELY
SPROCKET
SPROUTED
SPRUCELY
SPRYNESS
SPUILZIE
SPUN-YARN
SPUR-GALL
SPUR-GEAR
SPURIOUS
SPURLESS
SPURLING
SPURNING
SPUR-RIAL
SPURRIER
SPURRING
SPUR-RYAL
SPUTTERY
SPYGLASS
SPY-MONEY
SQUABASH
SQUABBLE
SQUAB-PIE
SQUADRON
SQUAILER
SQUALLER
SQUAMATA
SQUAMATE
SQUAMOSE
SQUAMOUS
SQUAMULA
SQUAMULE
SQUANDER
SQUARELY
SQUARING
SQUARISH
SQUARSON
SQUASHER
SQUATTED
SQUATTER
SQUATTLE
SQUAWKER
SQUAWMAN
SQUEAKER
SQUEALER
SQUEEGEE
SQUEEZER
SQUELCHY
SQUIFFER
SQUIGGLE
SQUIGGLY
SQUILGEE

SQUINTER
SQUIRAGE
SQUIREEN
SQUIRELY
SQUIRESS
SQUIRREL
SQUIRTER
STABBING
STABLING
STABLISH
STACCATO
STACKING
STAFFAGE
STAGE-BOX
STAGGARD
STAG-HEAD
STAGHORN
STAG-HUNT
STAGNANT
STAGNATE
STAHLIAN
STAHLISM
STAINING
STAIR-ROD
STAIRWAY
STAKE-NET
STALAGMA
STALKING
STALLAGE
STALL-FED
STALLING
STALLION
STALLMAN
STALWART
STAMENED
STAMINAL
STAMPEDE
STAMPEDO
STAMPING
STANCHEL
STANCHER
STANCHLY
STANDARD
STANDING
STANDISH
STAND-OFF
STANHOPE
STANNARY
STANNATE
STANNITE
STANNOUS
STANZAIC
STAPELIA
STAPHYLE
STARAGEN
STARCHED
STARCHER
STAR-DUST
STARFISH
STARGAZE
STARLESS
STARLIKE
STARLING
STAR-NOSE
STAROSTA
STAROSTY

S8

STAR-PAV'D
STAR-READ
STARRILY
STARRING
STARTFUL
STARTING
STARTISH
STARTLED
STARTLER
STAR-TRAP
STAR-TURN
STARVING
STARWORT
STASIMON
STATABLE
STATEDLY
STATICAL
STATUARY
STATURED
STAY-BOLT
STAY-DOWN
STAY-LACE
STAYLESS
STAYSAIL
STAY-TAPE
STEADIED
STEADIER
STEADILY
STEADING
STEALING
STEALTHY
STEAM-CAR
STEAMILY
STEAMING
STEAM-TUG
STEARATE
STEARINE
STEATITE
STEATOMA
STEELBOW
STEELING
STEEL-PEN
STEENBOK
STEENING
STEEPE-UP
STEEPISH
STEEPLED
STEERAGE
STEERING
STEEVELY
STEEVING
STELLATE
STELLIFY
STELLION
STEMBUCK
STEM-FORM
STEMLESS
STEMMATA
STEMMING
STENLOCK
STENOSED
STENOSIS
STENTOUR
STEPDAME
STEPHANE
STEPPING

STEPWISE
STEREOME
STERIGMA
STERLING
STERNAGE
STERNESS
STERNITE
STERNSON
STERNWAY
STETTING
STEWPOND
STIBBLER
STIBNITE
STICCADO
STICCATO
STICKFUL
STICKILY
STICKING
STICKJAW
STICK-LAC
STICKLER
STIEVELY
STIFF-BIT
STIFFISH
STIFLING
STIGMATA
STILBITE
STILETTO
STILLAGE
STILLING
STILLION
STILTING
STILTISH
STIMULUS
STINGILY
STINGING
STING-RAY
STINKARD
STINKING
STINK-POT
STINTING
STIPITES
STIPPLED
STIPPLER
STIPULAR
STIPULED
STIRLESS
STIRRING
STITCHED
STITCHER
STIVED-UP
STOCCADO
STOCCATA
STOCKADE
STOCK-CAR
STOCKILY
STOCKING
STOCKISH
STOCKIST
STOCKMAN
STOCK-POT
STODGILY
STOICISM
STOLIDLY
STOMACHY
STOMATAL

STOMATIC
STONE-BOW
STONE-FLY
STONE-OIL
STONE-PIT
STONE-RAG
STONE-RAW
STOOPING
STOP-COCK
STOPLESS
STOP-OVER
STOPPAGE
STOPPING
STORABLE
STOREYED
STORMFUL
STORMILY
STORMING
STORYING
STOUTISH
STOVAINE
STOWAWAY
STOWDOWN
STOWLINS
STRABISM
STRADDLE
STRADIOT
STRAGGLY
STRAICHT
STRAIGHT
STRAINED
STRAINER
STRAITEN
STRAITLY
STRAMASH
STRAMMEL
STRANDED
STRANGER
STRANGLE
STRAP-OIL
STRAPPED
STRAPPER
STRATEGY
STRATIFY
STRATOSE
STRATOUS
STRAUCHT
STRAUGHT
STRAVAIG
STRAW-HAT
STRAYING
STREAKED
STREAMER
STREETED
STRELITZ
STRELTZI
STRENGTH
STREPENT
STREPHON
STREPYAN
STRESSED
STRETCHY
STREWAGE
STREWING
STRIATED
STRIATUM

STRICKEN
STRICKLE
STRICTLY
STRIDDEN
STRIDDLE
STRIDENT
STRIGATE
STRIGINE
STRIGOPS
STRIGOSE
STRIKING
STRINGED
STRINGER
STRINKLE
STRIPING
STRIPPED
STRIPPER
STRIVING
STROBILA
STROBILE
STROBILI
STRODDLE
STROKING
STROLLER
STROMATA
STROMBUS
STRONGER
STRONGLY
STRONTIA
STROPHIC
STROPPED
STROWING
STRUGGLE
STRUMMED
STRUMMEL
STRUMOSE
STRUMOUS
STRUMPET
STRUTHIO
STRUTTED
STRUTTER
STUBBING
STUBBLED
STUBBORN
STUB-NAIL
STUCCOED
STUCCOER
STUD-BOLT
STUD-BOOK
STUDDING
STUD-FARM
STUDIOUS
STUDWORK
STUDYING
STUFFILY
STUFFING
STULTIFY
STUMBLER
STUMMING
STUMPILY
STUNDISM
STUNDIST
STUNKARD
STUNNING
STUNSAIL
STUNTMAN

STUPIDLY
STUPRATE
STURDIED
STURDILY
STURGEON
STURNINE
STURNOID
SUASIBLE
SUBACRID
SUBACUTE
SUBAGENT
SUBAHDAR
SUBBASAL
SUBCLASS
SUBCOSTA
SUBDUPLE
SUBEQUAL
SUBERATE
SUBERECT
SUBERISE
SUBEROSE
SUBEROUS
SUBGENUS
SUBGROUP
SUBHUMAN
SUBIMAGO
SUBLEASE
SUBLIMED
SUBLUNAR
SUBMERGE
SUBMERSE
SUBORDER
SUBORNER
SUBOVATE
SUBPOENA
SUBPRIOR
SUBSERVE
SUBSHRUB
SUBSIZAR
SUBSOLAR
SUBSONIC
SUBSTAGE
SUBSTYLE
SUBTENSE
SUBTILLY
SUBTITLE
SUBTLETY
SUBTLIST
SUBTONIC
SUBTOPIA
SUBTRACT
SUBTRIBE
SUBTRIST
SUBTRUDE
SUBUCULA
SUBULATE
SUBURBAN
SUBURBIA
SUBVERSE
SUBZONAL
SUCCINCT
SUCCINIC
SUCCINUM
SUCCUBAE
SUCCUBAS

SUCCUBUS
SUCHLIKE
SUCHNESS
SUCHWISE
SUCKENER
SUCKERED
SUCKLERS
SUCKLING
SUCTORIA
SUCURUJÚ
SUDAMINA
SUDANESE
SUDARIUM
SUDATION
SUDATORY
SUDDENLY
SUDDENTY
SUDOROUS
SUFFERER
SUFFRAGE
SUFISTIC
SUGAR-GUM
SUGARING
SUICIDAL
SUITABLE
SUITABLY
SUIT-CASE
SUITRESS
SUKIYAKI
SULCATED
SULLENLY
SULLYING
SULPHATE
SULPHIDE
SULPHITE
SULPHONE
SULPHURY
SULTANIC
SULTRILY
SUMMERLY
SUMMITRY
SUMMONER
SUMPHISH
SUMPITAN
SUN-BAKED
SUNBATHE
SUNBEAMY
SUN-BLIND
SUN-BLINK
SUNBURNT
SUNBURST
SUN-CRACK
SUN-CURED
SUNDÈRED
SUNDERER
SUN-DRIED
SUNDRIES
SUN-DROPS
SUNLIGHT
SUNN-HEMP
SUN-PRINT
SUNPROOF
SUNSHADE
SUNSHINE
SUNSHINY
SUNSTONE

SUNWARDS
SUPERADD
SUPERATE
SUPERBLY
SUPER-EGO
SUPERHET
SUPERIOR
SUPERMAN
SUPERNAL
SUPERTAX
SUPINATE
SUPINELY
SUPPEAGO
SUPPLANT
SUPPLIAL
SUPPLIED
SUPPLIER
SUPPOSAL
SUPPOSED
SUPPOSER
SUPPOSES
SUPPRESS
SURBASED
SURBATED
SURCEASE
SURCULUS
SURE-FIRE
SURENESS
SURFACED
SURFACER
SURF-BIRD
SURF-BOAT
SURF-DUCK
SURF-FISH
SURGEFUL
SURGICAL
SURICATE
SURMISAL
SURMISER
SURMOUNT
SURPLICE
SURPRISE
SURQUEDY
SURREBUT
SURROUND
SURROYAL
SURUCUCU
SURVEYAL
SURVEYOR
SURVIVAL
SURVIVOR
SUSPENSE
SUSURRUS
SUTORIAL
SUTORIAN
SUVERSED
SUZERAIN
SVASTIKA
SWABBERS
SWABBING
SWADDLER
SWADESHI
SWAGSHOP
SWAGSMAN
SWAINING
SWAINISH

SWANHERD
SWANKING
SWANLIKE
SWAN-MARK
SWAN-NECK
SWANNERY
SWAN-SHOT
SWAN-SKIN
SWAN-SONG
SWAPPING
SWARMING
SWASHING
SWASTIKA
SWAY-BACK
SWAYLING
SWEALING
SWEARING
SWEATING
SWEEPING
SWEEP-NET
SWEEP-SAW
SWEET-BAY
SWEETING
SWEETISH
SWEET-OIL
SWEETPEA
SWEET-SOP
SWELCHIE
SWELLDOM
SWELLING
SWELLISH
SWELL-MOB
SWERVING
SWIFTLET
SWILLING
SWILL-TUB
SWIMMING
SWIMSUIT
SWINDLER
SWINE-POX
SWINE-STY
SWINGING
SWINGISM
SWISHING
SWISSING
SWITCHEL
SWOBBERS
SWOBBING
SWOONING
SWOPPING
SWORD-ARM
SWORD-CUT
SWORD-LAW
SWORDMAN
SWOTTING
SYBARITE
SYBOTISM
SYCAMINE
SYCAMORE
SYCOMORE
SYCONIUM
SYENITIC
SYLLABIC
SYLLABLE
SYLLABUB
SYLLABUS

SYLPHIDE
SYLPHINE
SYLPHISH
SYLVATIC
SYLVIINE
SYMBIONT
SYMBOLIC
SYMMETRY
SYMPATHY
SYMPHILE
SYMPHILE
SYMPHILY
SYMPHONY
SYMPHYLA
SYMPLOCE
SYMPOSIA
SYNANTHY
SYNAPHEA
SYNAPSIS
SYNAPTIC
SYNARCHY
SYNASTRY
SYNCLINE
SYNCOPAL
SYNCOPIC
SYNDESIS
SYNDETIC
SYNDICAL
SYNDINGS
SYNDROME
SYNECHIA
SYNEDRIA
SYNERGIC
SYNERGID
SYNGAMIC
SYNGRAPH
SYNONYMY
SYNOPSES
SYNOPSIS
SYNOPTIC
SYNOVIAL
SYNTAGMA
SYNTEXIS
SYNTONIC
SYNTONIN
SYPHILIS
SYRIARCH
SYRINGES
SYRINXES
SYSSITIA
SYSTEMED
SYSTEMIC
SYSTOLIC
SYZYGIES

T

TABASHIR
TABBINET
TABBY-CAT
TABBYING
TABERDAR
TABLEAUX
TABLE-CUT
TABLEFUL
TABLE-MAT
TABLE-TOP

TABOGGAN
TABOOING
TABORITE
TABOURET
TABOURIN
TABULATE
TACAHOUT
TAC-AU-TAC
TACHISME
TACHISTE
TACITURN
TACKED-ON
TACKLING
TACKSMAN
TACTICAL
TACTLESS
TAENIATE
TAENIOID
TAFFEREL
TAFFETAS
TAFFRAIL
TAGHAIRM
TAGLIONI
TAIL-BOOM
TAIL-COAT
TAIL-GATE
TAILLESS
TAIL-PIPE
TAIL-RACE
TAIL-ROPE
TAIL-SPIN
TAINTURE
TAKE-DOWN
TAKE-OVER
TAKINGLY
TALAPOIN
TALENTED
TALESMAN
TALISMAN
TALKABLE
TALK-BACK
TALLIATE
TALLNESS
TALLYING
TALLYMAN
TALMUDIC
TALPIDAE
TALUKDAR
TAMANDUA
TAMANOIR
TAMARACK
TAMARIND
TAMARISK
TAMBOURA
TAMEABLE
TAMELESS
TAMENESS
TAMILIAN
TAMPERER
TANAISTE
TAN-BALLS
TANGENCY
TANGIBLE
TANGIBLY
TANGLING
TANGOIST

TANISTRY	TAX-PAYER	TENACITY	TETRADIC	THIN-SOWN
TANNABLE	T-BANDAGE	TENAILLE	TETRAGON	THIN-SPUN
TANTALIC	TEA-BOARD	TENANTRY	TETRAPLA	THIO-ACID
TANTALUM	TEA-BREAD	TENDANCE	TETRAPOD	THIO-SALT
TANTALUS	TEA-BREAK	TENDENCE	TETRARCH	THIRDING
TANTRISM	TEA-CADDY	TENDENCY	TETRAXON	THIRLAGE
TANTRIST	TEA-CHEST	TENDERER	TETRONAL	THIRSTER
TAPACOLO	TEACHING	TENDERLY	TEUCRIAN	THIRTEEN
TAPACULO	TEA-CLOTH	TENEBRAE	TEUTONIC	THISNESS
TAPADERA	TEA-FIGHT	TENEBRIO	TEXT-BOOK	THLIPSIS
TAPADERO	TEA-HOUSE	TENEMENT	TEXT-HAND	THOLE-PIN
TAPELESS	TEAM-MATE	TENENDUM	TEXTUARY	THORACIC
TAPE-LINE	TEAMSTER	TENESMUS	TEXTURAL	THORNSET
TAPERING	TEAMWISE	TENIASIS	TEXTURED	THOROUGH
TAPER-ROD	TEAM-WORK	TENON-SAW	THALAMIC	THOUSAND
TAPESTRY	TEA-PARTY	TENORIST	THALAMUS	THOWLESS
TAPE-TIED	TEA-PLANT	TENORITE	THALLINE	THRALDOM
TAPEWORM	TEARAWAY	TENOROON	THALLIUM	THRAPPLE
TAP-HOUSE	TEAR-DROP	TENOTOMY	THALLOID	THRASHER
TAP-WATER	TEAR-DUCT	TENPENCE	THALLOUS	THRAWARD
TARA-FERN	TEARLESS	TENPENNY	THANADAR	THRAWART
TARANTAS	TEASELED	TEN-POUND	THANEDOM	THREADEN
TARBOOSH	TEASELER	TEN-SCORE	THANKFUL	THREADER
TARBOUSH	TEASPOON	TENSIBLE	THANKING	THREAPIT
TAR-BRUSH	TEA-TABLE	TENTACLE	THATCHED	THREATEN
TARGETED	TEA-TOWEL	TENT-POLE	THATCHER	THREE-MAN
TARGUMIC	TEBILISE	TENT-ROPE	THATNESS	THREEPIT
TARLATAN	TECTONIC	TENTWISE	THAWLESS	THREE-PLY
TARPEIAN	TEDESCHE	TENT-WORK	THEACEAE	THREE-WAY
TARRAGON	TEDESCHI	TENUIOUS	THEARCHY	THRENODE
TARRYING	TEDISOME	TENURIAL	THEATINE	THRENODY
TARSIOID	TEEMLESS	TEOCALLI	THEATRAL	THRESHEL
TARSIPES	TEENAGER	TEPHRITE	THEATRIC	THRESHER
TARTANED	TEE-SHIRT	TEPIDITY	THEBAINE	THRIDACE
TARTARIC	TEETHING	TERAPHIM	THEISTIC	THRILLER
TARTARIE	TEETOTAL	TERATOID	THEMATIC	THRIPSES
TARTARLY	TEETOTUM	TERATOMA	THEOCRAT	THRISSEL
TARTARUS	TEGUEXIN	TERCELET	THEODICY	THRISTLE
TARTNESS	TEGUILLA	TEREBENE	THEOGONY	THRIVING
TARTRATE	TEGUMENT	TERMINAL	THEOLOGY	THROATED
TARTUFFE	TELECAST	TERMINER	THEORISE	THROBBED
TAR-WATER	TELECINE	TERMINUS	THEORIST	THROMBIN
TARWHINE	TELEFILM	TERMLESS	THEOSOPH	THROMBUS
TASKWORK	TELEGONY	TERM-TIME	THEREFOR	THRONGED
TASSELLY	TELEGRAM	TERRACED	THEREOUT	THROPPLE
TASTABLE	TELEMARK	TERRAPIN	THERIACA	THROSTLE
TASTE-BUD	TELEPATH	TERRAZZO	THERMION	THROTTLE
TASTEFUL	TELERGIC	TERRELLA	THERMITE	THROWING
TATARIAN	TELESEME	TERRIBLE	THESPIAN	THROW-OUT
TATTERED	TELESTIC	TERRIBLY	THETICAL	THRUM-CAP
TATTLING	TELETHON	TERRIFIC	THEURGIC	THRUMMED
TATTOOED	TELETRON	TERTIARY	THEWLESS	THRUMMER
TAU-CROSS	TELEVIEW	TERU-TERO	THIAMINE	THRUSTER
TAUNTING	TELEVISE	TERZETTA	THICKETY	THUGGERY
TAU-STAFF	TELLABLE	TESSELLA	THICKISH	THUGGISM
TAUTNESS	TELL-TALE	TESSERAE	THICKSET	THUMB-POT
TAUTOMER	TELLURAL	TESSERAL	THIEVERY	THUMPING
TAUTONYM	TELLURIC	TESTABLE	THIEVING	THUNDERY
TAVERNER	TEMERITY	TESTAMUR	THIEVISH	THURIBLE
TAWDRILY	TEMEROUS	TESTATOR	THIGGING	THURIFER
TAXACEAE	TEMPERED	TESTATUM	THINGAMY	THURSDAY
TAXATION	TEMPERER	TESTICLE	THINKING	THUSNESS
TAXATIVE	TEMPLATE	TESTRILL	THINNESS	THUSWISE
TAXIARCH	TEMPORAL	TEST-TUBE	THINNEST	THWACKER
TAXODIUM	TEMPTING	TETANISE	THINNING	THWARTED
TAXONOMY	TEMULENT	TETCHILY	THINNISH	THWARTER

THWARTLY	TIRELING	TONALITY	TOXAEMIC	TRECENTO
THYLOSES	TIRESOME	TONE-DEAF	TOXICANT	TREDILLE
THYLOSIS	TIRONIAN	TONELESS	TOXICITY	TREE-CALF
THYREOID	TIRRIVEE	TONGUING	TOYISHLY	TREE-FERN
THYROXIN	TIRRIVIE	TONICITY	TOYWOMAN	TREE-FROG
THYRSOID	TITANATE	TONISHLY	TRABEATE	TREELESS
TICKLING	TITANESS	TONSURED	TRACHEAE	TREE-LILY
TICKLISH	TITANIAN	TONTINER	TRACHEAL	TREE-MOSS
TICK-SHOP	TITANISM	TOOL-SHED	TRACHEID	TREENAIL
TICK-TACK	TITANITE	TOOTHFUL	TRACHOMA	TREESHIP
TICK-TICK	TITANIUM	TOPARCHY	TRACHYTE	TREKKING
TICK-TOCK	TITANOUS	TOPAZINE	TRACKAGE	TREMATIC
TIDE-GATE	TITHABLE	TOPDRESS	TRACKING	TREMBLER
TIDELESS	TITHE-PIG	TOP-HEAVY	TRACKMAN	TREMELLA
TIDE-LOCK	TITIVATE	TOP-LEVEL	TRACKWAY	TRENCHER
TIDE-MARK	TITMOUSE	TOP-LINER	TRACTATE	TREPHINE
TIDE-MILL	TITTERER	TOPLOFTY	TRACTION	TRESPASS
TIDE-RACE	TITUBANT	TOP-NOTCH	TRACTIVE	TRESSURE
TIDESMAN	TITUBATE	TOPOLOGY	TRACTRIX	TREVALLY
TIDE-WAVE	TITYRE-TU	TOPONYMY	TRADEFUL	TREWSMAN
TIDINESS	TOAD-FISH	TOP-PROUD	TRADITOR	TREY-TINE
TIDIVATE	TOAD-FLAX	TOP-SHELL	TRADUCER	TRIADIST
TIGER-CAT	TOAD-RUSH	TOP-STONE	TRAGICAL	TRIAL-DAY
TIGER-EYE	TOAD-SPIT	TORCHÈRE	TRAGOPAN	TRIALISM
TIGERISH	TOADYING	TORCULAR	TRAIL-NET	TRIALIST
TIGERISM	TOADYISH	TOREADOR	TRAINING	TRIALITY
TIGER-NUT	TOADYISM	TOREUTIC	TRAIN-OIL	TRIANGLE
TIGHTISH	TOASTING	TORMINAL	TRAM-LINE	TRIAPSAL
TIGHTWAD	TOBOGGAN	TORNADIC	TRAMPLER	TRIARCHY
TILEFISH	TOBOGGIN	TORN-DOWN	TRAM-ROAD	TRIASSIC
TILLABLE	TO-BROKEN	TOROIDAL	TRAM-STOP	TRIAXIAL
TILT-BOAT	TO-BRUISE	TORPIDLY	TRANQUIL	TRIBALLY
TILT-YARD	TOCOLOGY	TORQUATE	TRANSACT	TRIBASIC
TIMARIOT	TODDLING	TORTILLA	TRANSECT	TRIBRACH
TIMBERED	TODDY-CAT	TORTIOUS	TRANSEPT	TRIBUNAL
TIME-BALL	TOE-PIECE	TORTOISE	TRANSFER	TRIBUTER
TIME-BILL	TOGETHER	TORTUOUS	TRANSFIX	TRICHINA
TIME-BOMB	TOILETED	TORTURER	TRANSHIP	TRICHITE
TIME-FUZE	TOILETRY	TORULOSE	TRANSIRE	TRICHOID
TIMELESS	TOILETTE	TOTALISE	TRANSMEW	TRICHOME
TIME-WORK	TOILINET	TOTALITY	TRANSMIT	TRICHORD
TIME-WORN	TOILLESS	TOTALLED	TRANSUDE	TRICKERY
TIME-ZONE	TOILSOME	TOTEMISM	TRANSUME	TRICKILY
TIMIDITY	TOIL-WORN	TOTEMIST	TRAP-BALL	TRICKING
TIMONEER	TOKOLOGY	TOTITIVE	TRAP-DOOR	TRICKISH
TIMONISE	TOLBOOTH	TOTTERED	TRAPEZIA	TRICKLET
TIMONISM	TOLERANT	TOTTERER	TRAP-FALL	TRICOLOR
TIMONIST	TOLERATE	TOUCANET	TRAPPEAN	TRICORNE
TIMOROUS	TOLLABLE	TOUCH-BOX	TRAPPING	TRIC-TRAC
TIMOUSLY	TOLL-BAIT	TOUCHILY	TRAPPIST	TRICYCLE
TINCTURE	TOLL-CALL	TOUCHING	TRAP-ROCK	TRIDACNA
TINEIDAE	TOLLDISH	TOUGHISH	TRASH-CAN	TRIETHYL
TINGLISH	TOLL-FREE	TOURNURE	TRASHERY	TRIFLING
TINKLING	TOLLGATE	TOVARISH	TRASHILY	TRIFOCAL
TINNITUS	TOMAHAWK	TOWARDLY	TRAUCHLE	TRIFORIA
TIN-PLATE	TOMALLEY	TOWELLED	TRAVERSE	TRIGLYPH
TINSELLY	TOMATOES	TOWERING	TRAVESTY	TRIGNESS
TINSELRY	TOMBLESS	TOWNHALL	TRAWLING	TRIGONAL
TINSMITH	TOMENTUM	TOWNLAND	TRAWL-NET	TRIGONIC
TINSTONE	TOMMY-BAR	TOWNLING	TREACHER	TRIGRAPH
TIN-TERNE	TOMMY-GUN	TOWNSHIP	TREADING	TRIGYNIA
TINTLESS	TOMMY-ROT	TOWNSKIP	TREADLER	TRILEMMA
TINT-TOOL	TOM-NODDY	TOWNSMAN	TREASURE	TRILLING
TIPSTAFF	TOMOGRAM	TOWN-TALK	TREASURY	TRILLION
TIPSY-KEY	TOMORROW	TOW-PLANE	TREATING	TRILLIUM
TIRELESS	TONALITE	TOXAEMIA	TREATISE	TRILOBED

TRIMARAN	TRUCKAGE	TURBANED	TYPECAST	UNBARRED
TRIMERIC	TRUCKING	TURBIDLY	TYPE-FACE	UNBATHED
TRIMETER	TRUDGING	TURBINAL	TYPE-HIGH	UNBEATEN
TRIMMING	TRUE-BLUE	TURBINED	TYPHOEAN	UNBEDDED
TRIMNESS	TRUE-BORN	TURBINES	TYPHOEUS	UNBELIEF
TRIMURTI	TRUE-BRED	TURBO-JET	TYPHONIC	UNBELTED
TRIODION	TRUE-LOVE	TURCOMAN	TYPIFIED	UNBENDED
TRIOXIDE	TRUENESS	TURF-CLAD	TYPIFIER	UNBENIGN
TRIPEDAL	TRUFFLED	TURGIDLY	TYPOLOGY	UNBEREFT
TRIPEMAN	TRUISTIC	TURKOMAN	TYRANNIC	UNBESEEM
TRIPHONE	TRUMEAUX	TURLOUGH	TYRANNIS	UNBIASED
TRIP-HOOK	TRUMPERY	TURMERIC	TYRELESS	UNBIDDEN
TRIPLANE	TRUNCATE	TURNBACK	TYROLEAN	UNBISHOP
TRIPLING	TRUNKFUL	TURNCOAT	TYROLESE	UNBITTED
TRIPLOID	TRUNKING	TURNCOCK	TYROSINE	UNBLAMED
TRIPODAL	TRUNNION	TURN-DOWN	TYRRHENE	UNBLOODY
TRIPPANT	TRUQUAGE	TURNOVER	TYRTAEAN	UNBLOWED
TRIPPERY	TRUQUEUR	TURNPIKE		UNBODIED
TRIPPING	TRUSSING	TURNSKIN	**U**	UNBODING
TRIPPLER	TRUSTFUL	TURNSOLE		UNBOLTED
TRIPTANE	TRUSTIER	TURNSPIT	UDDERFUL	UNBONNET
TRIPTOTE	TRUSTILY	TURRETED	UDOMETER	UNBOOKED
TRIPTYCH	TRUSTING	TURTLING	UGLINESS	UNBOUGHT
TRIP-WIRE	TRUTHFUL	TUSKLESS	UINTAITE	UNBRACED
TRISEMIC	TRY-HOUSE	TUSSOCKY	ULCERATE	UNBREECH
TRISKELE	TRYINGLY	TUTELAGE	ULCEROUS	UNBRIDLE
TRISOMIC	TSAREVNA	TUTELARY	ULMACEAE	UNBROKEN
TRISTFUL	TSARITSA	TUTORAGE	ULOTHRIX	UNBUCKLE
TRISTICH	TUBE-FOOT	TUTORESS	ULSTERED	UNBUDDED
TRITICAL	TUBELESS	TUTORIAL	ULTERIOR	UNBURDEN
TRITICUM	TUBERCLE	TUTORING	ULTIMACY	UNBURIED
TRITONIA	TUBEROSE	TUTORISE	ULTIMATA	UNBURNED
TRIUMVIR	TUBEROUS	TUTORISM	ULTIMATE	UNBURROW
TRIUNITY	TUBE-WELL	TWADDLER	ULTONIAN	UNBUTTON
TRIVALVE	TUBE-WORM	TWANGING	ULTRAISM	UNCALLED
TRIZONAL	TUBICOLE	TWATTLER	ULTRAIST	UNCANDID
TROCHAIC	TUBIFORM	TWEEZERS	ULTRA-RED	UNCARING
TROCHISK	TUBULATE	TWELVEMO	UMBLE-PIE	UNCAUGHT
TROCHLEA	TUBULOUS	TWICHILD	UMBONATE	UNCAUSED
TROCHOID	TUCKAHOE	TWIDDLER	UMBRATED	UNCHANCY
TROILITE	TUCK-MILL	TWIGSOME	UMBRATIC	UNCHARGE
TROLLING	TUCK-SHOP	TWILIGHT	UMBRELLA	UNCHASTE
TROLLOPY	TUCOTUCO	TWIN-AXIS	UMBRETTE	UNCHEWED
TROMBONE	TUCUTUCO	TWIN-BORN	UMBRIERE	UNCHOSEN
TROOPIAL	TUG-OF-WAR	TWINKLER	UMPIRAGE	UNCHURCH
TROPARIA	TULIPANT	TWINLING	UMPTIETH	UNCIFORM
TROPHESY	TUMBLING	TWINNING	UMQUHILE	UNCINATE
TROPHIED	TUMEFIED	TWINSHIP	UNABATED	UNCIPHER
TROPICAL	TUMIDITY	TWISTING	UNACHING	UNCLENCH
TROSSERS	TUMOROUS	TWITCHER	UNACTIVE	UNCLOSED
TROT-COZY	TUMP-LINE	TWITTERY	UNADORED	UNCLOTHE
TROTHFUL	TUNBELLY	TWITTING	UNAFRAID	UNCLOUDY
TROTTING	TUNEABLE	TWO-EDGED	UNALLIED	UNCLUTCH
TROTTOIR	TUNELESS	TWO-FACED	UNAMUSED	UNCOINED
TROUBLED	TUNGSTEN	TWO-HORSE	UNANCHOR	UNCOMBED
TROUBLER	TUNGSTIC	TWOPENCE	UNANELED	UNCOMELY
TROUNCER	TUNG-TREE	TWO-PIECE	UNARGUED	UNCOMMON
TROUPIAL	TUNGUSES	TWO-SCORE	UNARISEN	UNCOOKED
TROUSERS	TUNGUSIC	TWO-SIDED	UNARTFUL	UNCOSTLY
TROUTFUL	TUNICATA	TWO-TIMER	UNATONED	UNCOUPLE
TROUTING	TUNICATE	TYCHONIC	UNAVOWED	UNCOWLED
TROUTLET	TUNICKED	TYLOPODA	UNAWARES	UNCOYNED
TROUT-ROD	TUNICKLE	TYMPANAL	UNBACKED	UNCREATE
TROUVERE	TUPPENCE	TYMPANIC	UNBAITED	UNCTUOUS
TRUANTRY	TUPPENNY	TYMPANUM	UNBANDED	UNCULLED
TRUCHMAN	TURANIAN	TYPE-BODY	UNBARBED	UNCURBED

UNCURLED	UNFABLED	UNHEALED	UNLOVELY	UNPURGED
UNDAMMED	UNFADING	UNHEALTH	UNLOVING	UNRACKED
UNDAMNED	UNFAIRLY	UNHEARSE	UNMAILED	UNRAISED
UNDAMPED	UNFALLEN	UNHEATED	UNMAIMED	UNREALLY
UNDASHED	UNFANNED	UNHEDGED	UNMAKING	UNREAPED
UNDAZZLE	UNFASTEN	UNHEEDED	UNMANNED	UNREASON
UNDECENT	UNFAULTY	UNHELMED	UNMANTLE	UNRECKED
UNDECKED	UNFEARED	UNHELPED	UNMARKED	UNREINED
UNDEEDED	UNFELLED	UNHEPPEN	UNMARRED	UNREPAID
UNDEFIED	UNFENCED	UNHEROIC	UNMASKED	UNREPAIR
UNDERACT	UNFETTER	UNHIDDEN	UNMASKER	UNRHYMED
UNDER-AGE	UNFEUDAL	UNHINGED	UNMEETLY	UNRIBBED
UNDERARM	UNFILIAL	UNHOLILY	UNMELTED	UNRIDDEN
UNDERBID	UNFILLED	UNHOLPEN	UNMILKED	UNRIDDLE
UNDER-BOY	UNFILMED	UNHOMELY	UNMILLED	UNRIFLED
UNDERBUY	UNFISHED	UNHONEST	UNMINDED	UNRIGGED
UNDERCUT	UNFITTED	UNHOODED	UNMISSED	UNRINGED
UNDERDID	UNFIXITY	UNHOUSED	UNMOANED	UNRIPPED
UNDERDOG	UNFLAWED	UNHUNTED	UNMODISH	UNROOFED
UNDERFED	UNFOLDED	UNIAXIAL	UN-MOSAIC	UNROOTED
UNDERFUR	UNFOLDER	UNICOLOR	UNMOVING	UNROTTED
UNDER-JAW	UNFOOTED	UNICYCLE	UNMUFFLE	UNROTTEN
UNDERLAP	UNFORBID	UNIFILAR	UNMUZZLE	UNROUGED
UNDERLAY	UNFORCED	UNIFYING	UNNATIVE	UNRUBBED
UNDERLET	UNFORGED	UNILOBAR	UNNERVED	UNRUFFLE
UNDERLIE	UNFORGOT	UNILOBED	UNNETHES	UNSADDLE
UNDERLIP	UNFORMAL	UNIMBUED	UNNETTED	UNSAFELY
UNDERMAN	UNFORMED	UNINURED	UNOBEYED	UNSAFETY
UNDERPAY	UNFOUGHT	UNIONISM	UNOPENED	UNSAILED
UNDERPIN	UNFRAMED	UNIONIST	UNPACKED	UNSAINED
UNDERRUN	UNFREEZE	UNIPOLAR	UNPACKER	UNSALTED
UNDERSAY	UNFRIEND	UNIQUELY	UNPAINED	UNSAPPED
UNDERSEA	UNFROZEN	UNISONAL	UNPAIRED	UNSASHED
UNDERSET	UNFUNDED	UNITEDLY	UNPANGED	UNSATING
UNDERSKY	UNFURRED	UNIVALVE	UNPANNEL	UNSCALED
UNDERTOW	UNGAINLY	UNIVERSE	UNPATHED	UNSEALED
UNDERWIT	UNGALLED	UNIVOCAL	UNPEELED	UNSEAMED
UNDESERT	UNGAUGED	UNJOYFUL	UNPEERED	UNSEASON
UNDEVOUT	UNGENIAL	UNJOYOUS	UNPENNED	UNSEATED
UNDIMMED	UNGENTLE	UNJUSTLY	UNPEOPLE	UNSECRET
UNDINTED	UNGENTLY	UNKENNED	UNPERSON	UNSEEDED
UNDIPPED	UNGIFTED	UNKENNEL	UNPICKED	UNSEEING
UNDIVINE	UNGILDED	UNKINDLY	UNPINKED	UNSEEMLY
UNDOCKED	UNGIRDED	UNKINGLY	UNPINNED	UNSEIZED
UNDOOMED	UNGIVING	UNKISSED	UNPITIED	UNSELDOM
UNDOUBLE	UNGLAZED	UNKNIGHT	UNPLACED	UNSENSED
UNDRAPED	UNGLOVED	UNLADING	UNPLIANT	UNSETTLE
UNDREAMT	UNGORGED	UNLAWFUL	UNPOETIC	UNSEXUAL
UNDRIVEN	UNGOTTEN	UNLEARNT	UNPOISED	UNSHADED
UNDROSSY	UNGOWNED	UNLEASED	UNPOISON	UNSHADOW
UNDUBBED	UNGRACED	UNLICKED	UNPOLISH	UNSHAKED
UNDULANT	UNGRADED	UNLIDDED	UNPOLITE	UNSHAKEN
UNDULATE	UNGROUND	UNLIKELY	UNPOLLED	UNSHAMED
UNDULLED	UNGUIDED	UNLINEAL	UNPOSTED	UNSHAPED
UNDULOSE	UNGUILTY	UNLINKED	UNPRAISE	UNSHAPEN
UNDULOUS	UNGULATA	UNLISTED	UNPREACH	UNSHARED
UNEARNED	UNGULATE	UNLIVELY	UNPRETTY	UNSHAVED
UNEASILY	UNGUMMED	UNLIVING	UNPRICED	UNSHAVEN
UNEATHES	UNHACKED	UNLOADED	UNPRIEST	UNSHROUD
UNEDITED	UNHAILED	UNLOADER	UNPRISON	UNSICKER
UNELATED	UNHAIRED	UNLOCKED	UNPRIZED	UNSIFTED
UNENDING	UNHALLOW	UNLOOKED	UNPROPER	UNSIGNED
UNENVIED	UNHALSED	UNLOOSEN	UNPROVED	UNSLAKED
UNERRING	UNHANGED	UNLOPPED	UNPROVEN	UNSLUICE
UNESPIED	UNHARMED	UNLORDED	UNPRUNED	UNSMOOTH
UNEVENLY	UNHATTED	UNLORDLY	UNPULLED	UNSOAPED

UNSOCIAL
UNSOCKET
UNSODDEN
UNSOILED
UNSOLDER
UNSOLEMN
UNSOLVED
UNSORTED
UNSOUGHT
UNSOULED
UNSOURED
UNSPARED
UNSPHERE
UNSPOILT
UNSPOKEN
UNSPRUNG
UNSTABLE
UNSTARCH
UNSTATED
UNSTAYED
UNSTEADY
UNSTITCH
UNSTRING
UNSTRUCK
UNSTRUNG
UNSTUFFY
UNSUCKED
UNSUED-TO
UNSUITED
UNSUMMED
UNSUNNED
UNSWATHE
UNSWAYED
UNTACKLE
UNTANGLE
UNTANNED
UNTAPPED
UNTARRED
UNTASTED
UNTAUGHT
UNTEMPER
UNTENANT
UNTENDED
UNTENDER
UNTENTED
UNTESTED
UNTETHER
UNTHATCH
UNTHAWED
UNTHREAD
UNTHRIFT
UNTHRONE
UNTIDILY
UNTILLED
UNTIMELY
UNTINGED
UNTINNED
UNTIRING
UNTITLED
UNTOMBED
UNTOWARD
UNTRACED
UNTRADED
UNTRUISM
UNTRUSTY
UNTUCKED

UNTURBID
UNTURNED
UNUSEFUL
UNVALUED
UNVARIED
UNVEILED
UNVEILER
UNVENTED
UNVERSED
UNVIEWED
UNVIRTUE
UNVIZARD
UNVOICED
UNVULGAR
UNWALLED
UNWANTED
UNWARDED
UNWARELY
UNWARILY
UNWARMED
UNWARNED
UNWARPED
UNWASHED
UNWASTED
UNWATERY
UNWEANED
UNWEAPON
UNWEBBED
UNWEDDED
UNWEEDED
UNWEENED
UNWETTED
UNWIELDY
UNWIFELY
UNWIGGED
UNWILFUL
UNWILLED
UNWINGED
UNWISDOM
UNWISELY
UNWONTED
UNWOODED
UNWORDED
UNWORKED
UNWORMED
UNWORTHY
UNYEANED
UPADAISY
UP-ANCHOR
UPANISAD
UPAS-TREE
UPCAUGHT
UPCURVED
UPFOLLOW
UPGATHER
UPGROWTH
UPHEAVAL
UPHOLDER
UPLANDER
UPLIFTED
UPLIFTER
UPLOCKED
UPMAKING
UPPISHLY
UPRAISED
UPREARED

UPRISING
UPROOTAL
UPROOTER
UPSETTER
UPSPRANG
UPSPRING
UPSPRUNG
UPSTAIRS
UPSTREAM
UPSTROKE
UPTHRUST
UPTILTED
UPTURNED
UPWARDLY
URALITIC
URANITIC
URBANELY
URBANISE
URBANITY
URCEOLUS
UREDINES
URETERAL
URETERIC
URETHANE
URETHRAL
URGENTLY
URINATOR
UROCHORD
URODELAN
UROSCOPY
UROSTEGE
UROSTYLE
URSULINE
URTICANT
URTICATE
USEFULLY
USHERESS
USHERING
USTILAGO
USUFRUCT
USURIOUS
USURPING
UTERITIS
UTILISER
UTOPIAST
UTTEREST
UTTERING
UVULARLY
UVULITIS
UXORIOUS

V

VACANTLY
VACATION
VACCINAL
VACCINIA
VACUOLAR
VAGABOND
VAGARIES
VAGARISH
VAGILITY
VAGINANT
VAGINATE
VAGINULA
VAGINULE
VAGRANCY

VAINESSE
VAINNESS
VALANCED
VALERIAN
VALETING
VALHALLA
VALIANCE
VALIANCY
VALIDATE
VALIDITY
VALKYRIE
VALLONIA
VALORISE
VALOROUS
VALUABLE
VALUABLY
VALUATOR
VALVELET
VALVULAR
VAMBRACE
VAMPLATE
VANADATE
VANADIUM
VANDALIC
VANDYKED
VANELESS
VANGUARD
VANILLIN
VANISHER
VANQUISH
VAPIDITY
VAPORISE
VAPOROUS
VAPOURED
VAPOURER
VAPULATE
VARACTOR
VARGUEÑO
VARIABLE
VARIABLY
VARIANCE
VARICOSE
VARIEDLY
VARIETAL
VARIFORM
VARIOLAR
VARIORUM
VARLETRY
VARLETTO
VARTABED
VASCULAR
VASCULUM
VASIFORM
VASSALRY
VASTNESS
VATICIDE
VAULTAGE
VAULTING
VAUNCING
VAUNTAGE
VAUNTERY
VAUNTFUL
VAUNTING
VAVASORY
VAVASOUR
VEDANTIC

VEE-JOINT
VEGETANT
VEGETATE
VEGETIVE
VEHEMENT
VEHMIQUE
VEILLESS
VELAMINA
VELARISE
VELARIUM
VELATURA
VELLEITY
VELLOZIA
VELOCITY
VELSKOEN
VELVERET
VELVETED
VENALITY
VENATION
VENDETTA
VENDEUSE
VENDIBLE
VENDIBLY
VENEERER
VENERATE
VENEREAL
VENEREAN
VENETIAN
VENGEFUL
VENIALLY
VENOMOUS
VENOSITY
VENTAILE
VENTAYLE
VENT-HOLE
VENT-PIPE
VENT-PLUG
VENTURER
VENUSIAN
VENUTIAN
VERACITY
VERANDA'D
VERANDAH
VERATRIN
VERATRUM
VERBALLY
VERBATIM
VERBIAGE
VERBLESS
VERDANCY
VERDERER
VERDITER
VERDURED
VERECUND
VERGENCY
VERIFIED
VERIFIER
VERISTIC
VERITIES
VERJUICE
VERMINED
VERMOUTH
VERNALLY
VERNICLE
VERONICA
VERQUERE

VERQUIRE
VERRUCAE
VERRUGAS
VERSELET
VERSE-MAN
VERSICLE
VERTEBRA
VERTICAL
VERTICES
VERTICIL
VERTUOUS
VESICANT
VESICATE
VESICULA
VESPERAL
VESPIARY
VESPIDAE
VESTIARY
VESTMENT
VESTURAL
VESTURED
VESTURER
VESUVIAN
VEXATION
VEXATORY
VEXILLUM
VEXINGLY
VIAMETER
VIATICUM
VIBRANCY
VIBRATOR
VIBRISSA
VIBURNUM
VICARAGE
VICARATE
VICARESS
VICARIAL
VICE-DEAN
VICE-KING
VICENARY
VICHYITE
VICINAGE
VICINITY
VICTORIA
VICTRESS
VIDENDUM
VIENNESE
VIEWABLE
VIEWLESS
VIGILANT
VIGNERON
VIGNETTE
VIGOROUS
VILDNESS
VILENESS
VILIFIED
VILIFIER
VILIPEND
VILLADOM
VILLAGER
VILLAGIO
VILLAINY
VILLATIC
VILLIAGO
VINCIBLE
VINCULUM

VINE-CLAD
VINE-GALL
VINEGARY
VINE-LEAF
VINE-PROP
VINEYARD
VINOLENT
VINOLOGY
VINOSITY
VINTAGER
VIOLABLE
VIOLABLY
VIOLATOR
VIOLENCE
VIPERINE
VIPERISH
VIPEROUS
VIREMENT
VIRGINAL
VIRGINIA
VIRGINLY
VIRICIDE
VIRIDIAN
VIRIDITE
VIRIDITY
VIRILISM
VIRILITY
VIROLOGY
VIRTUOSA
VIRTUOSE
VIRTUOSI
VIRTUOSO
VIRTUOUS
VIRULENT
VISCACHA
VISCERAL
VISCOUNT
VISIGOTH
VISIONAL
VISIONED
VISIONER
VISITANT
VISITING
VISNOMIE
VISUALLY
VITACEAE
VITALISE
VITALISM
VITALIST
VITALITY
VITATIVE
VITELLIN
VITELLUS
VITIABLE
VITIATOR
VITICIDE
VITILIGO
VITREOUS
VITULINE
VIVACITY
VIVARIUM
VIVIDITY
VIVIFIER
VIVIPARY
VIVISECT
VIXENISH

VIZARDED
VIZCACHA
VIZIRATE
VIZIRIAL
VOCALION
VOCALISE
VOCALISM
VOCALIST
VOCALITY
VOCATION
VOCATIVE
VOICE-BOX
VOICEFUL
VOIDABLE
VOIDANCE
VOIDNESS
VOLATILE
VOLCANIC
VOLITANT
VOLITATE
VOLITION
VOLITIVE
VOLLEYED
VOLPLANE
VOLSCIAN
VOLSUNGS
VOLTAISM
VOLUMIST
VOLUTION
VOLUTOID
VOLVULUS
VOMERINE
VOMITING
VOMITIVE
VOMITORY
VORACITY
VORTEXES
VORTICAL
VORTICES
VOTARESS
VOTARIST
VOTELESS
VOUSSOIR
VOWELISE
VOWELLED
VOYAGEUR
VRAICKER
VULCANIC
VULGARLY
VULSELLA
VULVITIS

W

WABBLING
WADDLING
WAESUCKS
WAGE-FUND
WAGE-WORK
WAGGONER
WAGMOIRE
WAGONAGE
WAGON-BED
WAGON-BOX
WAGONFUL
WAGON-LIT
WAHABISM

WAHABITE
WAINSCOT
WAIT-A-BIT
WAITLIST
WAITRESS
WAKELESS
WAKENING
WAKERIFE
WALDHORN
WALHALLA
WALKABLE
WALK-AWAY
WALKER-ON
WALK-MILL
WALK-OVER
WALKYRIE
WALLAROO
WALL-EYED
WALLFISH
WALL-GAME
WALL-KNOT
WALL-LESS
WALL-MOSS
WALL-NEWT
WALLOPER
WALLOWED
WALLOWER
WALLSEND
WALL-TREE
WALLWORT
WALTZING
WAMBLING
WANDERED
WANDERER
WANDEROO
WANGLING
WANTHILL
WANTONLY
WANWORDY
WANWORTH
WARBLING
WAR-DANCE
WARD-CORN
WARDENRY
WARD-MOTE
WARDRESS
WARDROBE
WARD-ROOM
WARDSHIP
WARELESS
WARFARER
WARHABLE
WAR-HORSE
WARIMENT
WARINESS
WARMED-UP
WARMNESS
WARPROOF
WARRAGAL
WARRANTY
WARRENER
WARRIGAL
WARRISON
WARTLESS
WARTWEED
WARTWORT

WAR-WEARY
WAR-WHOOP
WASHABLE
WASH-AWAY
WASH-BALL
WASH-BOWL
WASH-DIRT
WASHED-UP
WASTEFUL
WATCH-BOX
WATCH-DOG
WATCHFUL
WATCH-KEY
WATCHMAN
WATCH-OUT
WATERAGE
WATER-BAG
WATER-BED
WATER-BOA
WATER-BOX
WATER-BUG
WATER-BUS
WATER-COW
WATER-DOG
WATER-FLY
WATER-GAP
WATER-GAS
WATER-GOD
WATER-HEN
WATER-ICE
WATERING
WATERISH
WATER-JET
WATERLOG
WATERLOO
WATER-LOT
WATERMAN
WATER-POT
WATER-POX
WATER-RAM
WATER-RAT
WATER-TAP
WATERWAY
WATER-YAM
WATT-HOUR
WATTLING
WAUKRIFE
WAVEBAND
WAVEFORM
WAVELESS
WAVELIKE
WAVERING
WAVEROUS
WAVINESS
WAX-CLOTH
WAXINESS
WAX-LIGHT
WAX-PAPER
WAY-BOARD
WAYBREAD
WAYFARER
WAY-GOING
WAYGOOSE
WAYLAYER
WAY-LEAVE
WAY-MAKER

WAY-TRAIN
WAYWISER
WEAKENER
WEAK-EYED
WEAKLING
WEAKNESS
WEALSMAN
WEANLING
WEAPONED
WEAPONRY
WEARABLE
WEARIFUL
WEAR-IRON
WEASELLY
WEAZENED
WEDGWOOD
WEEDLESS
WEETLESS
WEEVILED
WEEVILLY
WEIGHAGE
WEIGHING
WEIGH-OUT
WELCOMER
WELDABLE
WELDLESS
WELDMENT
WELLADAY
WELLAWAY
WELL-BOAT
WELL-BORN
WELL-BRED
WELL-CURB
WELL-DECK
WELL-DOER
WELL-HEAD
WELL-HOLE
WELL-HUNG
WELL-KNIT
WELL-NIGH
WELL-READ
WELL-ROOM
WELL-SEEN
WELLSIAN
WELL-TO-DO
WELL-WISH
WELL-WORN
WELSHMAN
WEREGILD
WEREWOLF
WESLEYAN
WESTERLY
WESTMOST
WESTWARD
WET-NURSE
WHACKING
WHALE-MAN
WHALE-OIL
WHARFAGE
WHARFING
WHARF-RAT
WHATEVER
WHAT-LIKE
WHATNESS
WHEAT-EAR
WHEATEAR

WHEAT-EEL
WHEAT-FLY
WHEEDLER
WHEEL-CUT
WHEELING
WHEELMAN
WHEEZILY
WHEEZING
WHENEVER
WHEREFOR
WHEREOUT
WHEREVER
WHERRIES
WHETTING
WHEY-FACE
WHIFFING
WHIFFLER
WHIGGERY
WHIGGISH
WHIGGISM
WHIGSHIP
WHILE-ERE
WHIMBREL
WHIMSILY
WHIM-WHAM
WHINCHAT
WHINIARD
WHINNIED
WHINYARD
WHIPCORD
WHIP-HAND
WHIPJACK
WHIPLASH
WHIPPING
WHIPSTER
WHIP-TAIL
WHIPWORM
WHIRL-BAT
WHIRLING
WHIRRING
WHISKERY
WHISKING
WHISPERY
WHISTLER
WHITE-ALE
WHITE-ANT
WHITE-ARM
WHITEBOY
WHITECAP
WHITE-HOT
WHITE-LEG
WHITENER
WHITE-OUT
WHITE-POT
WHITE-WAX
WHITLING
WHITTRET
WHITWEEK
WHIZZING
WHIZZ-KID
WHOA-HO-HO
WHO-DUN-IT
WHOLE-HOG
WHOMEVER
WHOPPING
WHOREDOM

WHORESON
WHORL-BAT
WHOSEVER
WICKEDLY
WICKERED
WIDENESS
WIDE-OPEN
WIDOW-MAN
WIFEHOOD
WIFELESS
WIFE-LIKE
WIG-BLOCK
WIG-MAKER
WILD-BOAR
WILD-BORN
WILD-DUCK
WILDERED
WILDFIRE
WILD-FOWL
WILD-LAND
WILDNESS
WILD-WOOD
WILFULLY
WILINESS
WILLOWED
WILLYARD
WILLYART
WINCH-MAN
WINDBURN
WIND-CONE
WINDFALL
WIND-GALL
WINDLASS
WINDLESS
WINDMILL
WINDOWED
WINDPIPE
WIND-RODE
WINDROSE
WIND-SAIL
WIND-SIDE
WIND-SOCK
WINDWARD
WINE-CASK
WINE-PALM
WINE-SKIN
WING-CASE
WINGEDLY
WINGLESS
WING-SHOT
WINNOWED
WINNOWER
WINTERED
WINTERLY
WIRE-DRAW
WIRE-HAIR
WIRE-HEEL
WIRELESS
WIRE-LINE
WIRE-ROPE
WIREWORK
WIRE-WORM
WIREWOVE
WIRINESS
WIRRICOW
WISEACRE

WISE-LIKE
WISELING
WISENESS
WISH-BONE
WISH-WASH
WISTARIA
WISTERIA
WITCH-ELM
WITCHERY
WITCHING
WITELESS
WITHDRAW
WITHDREW
WITHERED
WITHHELD
WITHHOLD
WITHWIND
WITTOLLY
WIVEHOOD
WIZARDLY
WIZARDRY
WOBBLING
WOBEGONE
WODENISM
WOEFULLY
WOLFFIAN
WOLF-FISH
WOLFLING
WOLF-NOTE
WOLF-PACK
WOLF-SKIN
WOMANISE
WOMANISH
WONDERED
WONDERER
WONDROUS
WONTLESS
WOOD-ACID
WOODBIND
WOODBINE
WOOD-BORN
WOOD-CHAT
WOOD-COAL
WOODCOCK
WOODENLY
WOOD-EVIL
WOOD-HOLE
WOOD-IBIS
WOODLAND
WOOD-LARK
WOODLESS
WOOD-LICE
WOOD-MITE
WOODNESS
WOOD-NOTE
WOOD-OPAL
WOOD-PILE
WOOD-PULP
WOOD-ROOF
WOODRUFF
WOOD-RUSH
WOOD-SAGE
WOODSHED
WOOD-SKIN
WOODSMAN
WOOD-TICK

WOODWALE
WOODWARD
WOOD-WASP
WOOD-WIND
WOOD-WOOL
WOODWORK
WOOD-WORM
WOOD-WREN
WOOL-BALL
WOOL-CARD
WOOL-CLIP
WOOL-COMB
WOOLDING
WOOL-DYED
WOOLFELL
WOOLLIES
WOOLMILL
WOOL-PACK
WOOLSACK
WOOLWARD
WOOLWORK
WORDBOOK
WORDLESS
WORDLORE
WORKABLE
WORKADAY
WORKFOLK
WORKGIRL
WORK-MATE
WORKROOM
WORKSHOP
WORKSOME
WORKY-DAY
WORLD-OLD
WORM-CAST
WORM-GEAR
WORM-HOLE
WORM-SEED
WORMWOOD
WORRICOW
WORRYCOW
WORRYING
WORTHFUL
WORTHIES
WORTHILY
WOUNDILY
WOUNDING
WRACKFUL
WRANGLER
WRAPPAGE
WRAPPING
WRATHFUL
WRATHILY
WRAXLING
WREAKFUL
WREATHED
WREATHEN
WREATHER
WRECKAGE
WRECKFUL
WRECKING
WRESTLER
WREST-PIN
WRETCHED
WRIGGLER
WRINGING

WRINKLED
WRISTLET
WRIST-PIN
WRITABLE
WRITE-OFF
WRITHING
WRITHLED
WRONGFUL
WRONGOUS
WURTZITE
WYE-LEVEL

X

XANTHATE
XANTHEIN
XANTHENE
XANTHIAN
XANTHINE
XANTHIUM
XANTHOMA
XANTHOUS
XANTHURA
XANTIPPE
XENOGAMY
XENOLITH
XENOPHYA
XENOTIME
XENURINE
XERANSIS
XERANTIC
XERAPHIM
XYLOCARP

XYLOIDIN
XYLOLOGY
XYLONITE

Y

YACHTING
YARDLAND
YARDWAND
YATAGHAN
YEANLING
YEAR-BOOK
YEARLING
YEARLONG
YEARNING
YELDRING
YELDROCK
YEOMANLY
YEOMANRY
YESTREEN
YGDRASIL
YGLAUNST
YIELDING
YODELLER
YOGHOURT
YOKELISH
YOKE-MATE
YOKE-TOED
YOLDRING
YONGTHLY
YOUNGISH
YOURSELF
YOUTHFUL

YPSILOID
YTTRIOUS
YUGOSLAV
YULETIDE

Z

ZABAIONE
ZALOPHUS
ZAMBOMBA
ZAMINDAR
ZAMPOGNA
ZANTIOTE
ZANTIPPE
ZARATITE
ZARZUELA
ZASTRUGA
ZEALLESS
ZEALOTRY
ZEBRINNY
ZECCHINE
ZECCHINO
ZELANIAN
ZEMINDAR
ZENITHAL
ZENTIPPE
ZEOLITIC
ZEPPELIN
ZERUMBET
ZIBELINE
ZIGEUNER
ZIGGURAT
ZIGZAGGY

ZIKKURAT
ZINCKIFY
ZINCKING
ZINGIBER
ZIONWARD
ZIRCONIA
ZIRCONIC
ZIZYPHUS
ZOANTHUS
ZODIACAL
ZOETROPE
ZOIATRIA
ZOMBIISM
ZOMBORUK
ZONATION
ZONELESS
ZOOBLAST
ZOOCHORE
ZOOCHORY
ZOOCYTIA
ZOOECIUM
ZOOGENIC
ZOOGLOEA
ZOOGRAFT
ZOOLATER
ZOOLATRY
ZOOLITIC
ZOOMANCY
ZOOMETRY
ZOOMORPH
ZOONITIC
ZOONOMIA

ZOONOMIC
ZOONOSES
ZOONOSIS
ZOOPATHY
ZOOPERAL
ZOOPHAGA
ZOOPHILE
ZOOPHILY
ZOOPHYTA
ZOOPHYTE
ZOOSCOPY
ZOOSPERM
ZOOSPORE
ZOOTHOME
ZOOTOMIC
ZOOTOXIN
ZOOTROPE
ZOOTYPIC
ZOPILOTE
ZUCCHINI
ZUCHETTA
ZUCHETTO
ZUGZWANG
ZWIEBACK
ZYGAENID
ZYGODONT
ZYLONITE
ZYMOLOGY

A

AARONICAL
ABACTINAL
ABANDONED
ABANDONEE
ABASEMENT
ABASHLESS
ABASHMENT
ABATEMENT
ABBOTSHIP
ABDICABLE
ABDOMINAL
ABDUCTION
ABERRANCE
ABERRANCY
ABHORRENT
ABHORRING
ABIDINGLY
ABJECTION
ABLATIVAL
ABNEGATOR
ABNORMITY
ABNORMOUS
ABODEMENT

ABOLITION
ABOMINATE
ABORIGINE
ABOUNDING
ABOUT-FACE
ABOUT-SHIP
ABOUT-TURN
ABROGATOR
ABRUPTION
ABSCISSAE
ABSCISSAS
ABSCISSES
ABSCONDER
ABSEILING
ABSORBENT
ABSORBING
ABSTAINER
ABSTINENT
ABSURDITY
ABUNDANCE
ABUNDANCY
ABUSIVELY
ABYSMALLY
ACADEMIST
ACALEPHAN

ACANTHINE
ACANTHOID
ACANTHOUS
ACARIASIS
ACARICIDE
ACARIDEAN
ACARIDIAN
ACAROLOGY
ACCEDENCE
ACCENSION
ACCENTUAL
ACCEPTANT
ACCEPTIVE
ACCESSARY
ACCESSION
ACCESSORY
ACCIDENCE
ACCLIMATE
ACCLIVITY
ACCLIVOUS
ACCOMPANY
ACCORDANT
ACCORDING
ACCORDION
ACCOUTRED

ACCRETION
ACCRETIVE
ACCUSABLE
ACERACEAE
ACESCENCE
ACESCENCY
ACETABULA
ACETAMIDE
ACETYLENE
ACHAENIUM
ACHEULEAN
ACHEULIAN
ACHILLEAN
ACICULATE
ACIDIFIED
ACIDULATE
ACIDULOUS
ACINIFORM
ACOCK-BILL
ACOLUTHIC
ACONITINE
ACOUSTICS
ACQUITTAL
ACQUITTED
ACROBATIC

ACROPETAL
ACROPHONY
ACROPOLIS
ACROSPIRE
ACROTERIA
ACTINOZOA
ACTIVATOR
ACTUALISE
ACTUALIST
ACTUALITY
ACTUARIAL
ACTUATION
ACULEATED
ACUMINATE
ACUTENESS
ADAMITISM
ADANSONIA
ADAPTABLE
ADDERWORT
ADDICTION
ADDLEMENT
ADDRESSED
ADDRESSEE
ADDRESSER
ADDRESSOR
ADDUCIBLE
ADDUCTION
ADDUCTIVE
ADEMPTION
ADENOIDAL
ADENOMATA
ADHERENCE
ADIABATIC
ADIAPHORA
ADIPOCERE
ADIPOSITY
ADJACENCY
ADJECTIVE
ADJOINING
ADJOURNAL
ADJUNCTLY
ADJUTANCY
ADJUVANCY
ADMEASURE
ADMINICLE
ADMIRABLE
ADMIRABLY
ADMIRALTY
ADMISSION
ADMISSIVE
ADMITTING
ADMIXTURE
ADMONITOR
ADNASCENT
ADOPTIOUS
ADORATION
ADORINGLY
ADORNMENT
ADPRESSED
ADRENALIN
ADSORBATE
ADSORBENT
ADULATION
ADULATORY
ADULTERER
ADULTHOOD

ADUMBRATE
ADUNCATED
ADVANTAGE
ADVECTION
ADVENTIST
ADVENTIVE
ADVENTURE
ADVERBIAL
ADVERSARY
ADVERSELY
ADVERSITY
ADVERTENT
ADVERTISE
ADVICEFUL
ADVISABLE
ADVISABLY
ADVISEDLY
ADVOCATOR
ADVOUTRER
AEOLIPILE
AEOLIPYLE
AEPYORNIS
AERIALITY
AEROBIONT
AERODROME
AEROGRAPH
AEROLITIC
AEROMANCY
AEROMETER
AEROMETRY
AEROMOTOR
AEROPHYTE
AEROPLANE
AEROSPACE
AEROTAXIS
AEROTRAIN
AESTHESIA
AESTHESIS
AESTHETIC
AESTIVATE
AETIOLOGY
AFFECTING
AFFECTION
AFFECTIVE
AFFIANCED
AFFIDAVIT
AFFILIATE
AFFIRMANT
AFFLATION
AFFLICTED
AFFLUENCE
AFFLUXION
AFFRICATE
AFFRONTED
AFFRONTÉE
AFOREHAND
AFORESAID
AFORETIME
AFRICANER
AFRIKAANS
AFRIKANER
AFRO-ASIAN
AFTERCARE
AFTER-CLAP
AFTER-CROP
AFTER-DAMP

AFTERGAME
AFTERGLOW
AFTERINGS
AFTER-LIFE
AFTERMATH
AFTERMOST
AFTERNOON
AFTERTIME
AFTERWARD
AFTERWORD
AGALACTIA
AGAMEMNON
AGAPEMONE
AGGRAVATE
AGGREGATE
AGGRESSOR
AGGRIEVED
AGISTMENT
AGITATION
AGITATIVE
AGNATICAL
AGONISING
AGONISTES
AGONISTIC
AGREEABLE
AGREEABLY
AGREEMENT
AGRIOLOGY
AGROLOGIC
AGRONOMIC
AGUE-PROOF
AHUNGERED
AILANTHUS
AIMLESSLY
AIR-BRIDGE
AIR-BUBBLE
AIR-CAVITY
AIR-COOLED
AIR-ENGINE
AIR-JACKET
AIR-MINDED
AIR-POCKET
AIR-SPLINT
AIR-STRIKE
AIRWORTHY
AIRY-FAIRY
AITCHBONE
AIZOACEAE
AKOLUTHOS
ALABAMINE
ALABASTER
ALACK-A-DAY
ALARM-BELL
ALARMEDLY
ALBATROSS
ALBERTITE
ALBESCENT
ALBESPINE
ALBESPYNE
ALBINOISM
ALBINOTIC
ALBUM-LEAF
ALBURNOUS
ALCHEMIST
ALCOHOLIC
ALCYONIUM

ALDEBARAN
ALE-CONNER
ALE-DRAPER
ALEMANNIC
ALEMBROTH
ALERTNESS
ALEURITES
ALEWASHED
ALGARROBA
ALGARROBO
ALGEBRAIC
ALGONKIAN
ALGONQUIN
ALGORITHM
ALICYCLIC
ALIENABLE
ALIENATOR
ALIGNMENT
ALIMENTAL
ALINEMENT
ALIPHATIC
ALIZARINE
ALLANTOIC
ALLANTOID
ALLANTOIS
ALLAYMENT
ALLEGEDLY
ALLEGIANT
ALLEGORIC
ALLELUIAH
ALLEMANDE
ALLENARLY
ALL-ENDING
ALLEVIATE
ALL-FATHER
ALLICHOLY
ALLIGATOR
ALLOCARPY
ALLOGRAPH
ALLOMORPH
ALLOPATHY
ALLOPHONE
ALLOPLASM
ALLOTMENT
ALLOTROPE
ALLOTROPY
ALLOTTING
ALLOWABLE
ALLOWABLY
ALLOWANCE
ALLOWEDLY
ALL-RULING
ALL-SEEING
ALMANDINE
ALMOND-OIL
ALMS-DRINK
ALMS-HOUSE
ALMS-WOMAN
ALOESWOOD
ALONENESS
ALONGSIDE
ALOOFNESS
ALPARGATA
ALPENHORN
ALTAR-TOMB
ALTARWISE

ALTERABLE
ALTERCATE
ALTERNANT
ALTERNATE
ALTIMETER
ALTISSIMO
ALTRICIAL
ALUMINATE
ALUMINISE
ALUMINIUM
ALUMINOUS
ALUM-SHALE
ALUM-SLATE
ALUM-STONE
ALVEOLATE
AMARANTUS
AMARYLLID
AMARYLLIS
AMASSABLE
AMASSMENT
AMATORIAL
AMATORIAN
AMAUROSIS
AMAUROTIC
AMAZEMENT
AMAZINGLY
AMAZON-ANT
AMAZONIAN
AMBAGIOUS
AMBASSAGE
AMBER-FISH
AMBERGRIS
AMBIGUITY
AMBIGUOUS
AMBITIOUS
AMBLYOPIA
AMBROSIAL
AMBROSIAN
AMBULACRA
AMBULANCE
AMBULATOR
AMBUSCADE
AMBUSCADO
AMENDABLE
AMENDMENT
AMERICIUM
AMETABOLA
AMIANTHUS
AMIDSHIPS
AMINO-ACID
AMISSIBLE
AMOEBAEAN
AMORALISM
AMORALIST
AMORNINGS
AMOROSITY
AMOROUSLY
AMORPHISM
AMORPHOUS
AMOURETTE
AMPERSAND
AMPERZAND
AMPHIBIAN
AMPHIBOLE
AMPHIBOLY
AMPHIGORY

AMPHIOXUS
AMPHIPODA
AMPHOLYTE
AMPLENESS
AMPLIFIED
AMPLIFIER
AMPLITUDE
AMPLOSOME
AMPUTATOR
AMUSEMENT
AMUSINGLY
AMYGDALIN
AMYGDALUS
AMYLOIDAL
ANABIOSIS
ANABIOTIC
ANABOLISM
ANABRANCH
ANACHARIS
ANACRUSES
ANACRUSIS
ANAEROBIC
ANALECTIC
ANALEPTIC
ANALGESIA
ANALGESIC
ANALOGISE
ANALOGIST
ANALOGOUS
ANAMNESIS
ANAPLASTY
ANAPTYXIS
ANARCHIAL
ANARCHISE
ANARCHISM
ANARCHIST
ANASTASIS
ANASTATIC
ANATHEMAS
ANATOMISE
ANATOMIST
ANCESTRAL
ANCHORAGE
ANCHORESS
ANCHOR-ICE
ANCHORITE
ANCHORMAN
ANCHYLOSE
ANCIENTLY
ANCIENTRY
ANCILLARY
ANDANTINO
ANDESITIC
ANDROGYNY
ANDROMEDA
ANECDOTAL
ANEMOGRAM
ANEMOLOGY
ANGEL-CAKE
ANGEL-FISH
ANGEL-FOOD
ANGELHOOD
ANGELICAL
ANGERLESS
ANGIOGRAM
ANGIOMATA

ANGLESITE
ANGLEWISE
ANGLE-WORM
ANGLICISE
ANGLICISM
ANGLICIST
ANGLISTIC
ANGLOPHIL
ANGOSTURA
ANGRINESS
ANGUIFORM
ANGUIPEDE
ANGUISHED
ANGULATED
ANHYDRIDE
ANHYDRITE
ANHYDROUS
ANICONISM
ANICONIST
ANIMALISE
ANIMALISM
ANIMALIST
ANIMALITY
ANIMATING
ANIMATION
ANIMATISM
ANIMISTIC
ANIMOSITY
ANKLE-BOOT
ANKLE-JACK
ANKYLOSED
ANKYLOSIS
ANNEALING
ANNEXMENT
ANNOTATOR
ANNOUNCER
ANNOYANCE
ANNUITANT
ANNULATED
ANNULLING
ANNULMENT
ANOMALOUS
ANONACEAE
ANONYMITY
ANONYMOUS
ANOPHELES
ANORTHITE
ANSCHLUSS
ANTARCTIC
ANTEFIXAL
ANTEFIXES
ANTELUCAN
ANTENATAL
ANTENNARY
ANTENNULE
ANTHELION
ANTHEMION
ANTHOCARP
ANTHOCYAN
ANTHOLOGY
ANTHRACIC
ANTHROPIC
ANTHURIUM
ANTICHLOR
ANTICIVIC
ANTICLINE

ANTIDOTAL
ANTIHELIX
ANTIKNOCK
ANTIMONIC
ANTINODAL
ANTINOMIC
ANTI-NOVEL
ANTIPAPAL
ANTIPASTO
ANTIPATHY
ANTIPHONY
ANTIPODAL
ANTIPODES
ANTIQUARY
ANTIQUATE
ANTIQUELY
ANTIQUITY
ANTISCIAN
ANTISPAST
ANTITOXIC
ANTITOXIN
ANTITRADE
ANTITYPAL
ANTITYPIC
ANTIVIRAL
ANTRYCIDE
ANT-THRUSH
ANXIOUSLY
APARTHEID
APARTMENT
APARTNESS
APATHETIC
APERIODIC
APERITIVE
APERTNESS
APETALOUS
APHERESIS
APHIDICAL
APHORISER
APHYLLOUS
APICULATE
APISHNESS
APIVOROUS
APLANATIC
APOCOPATE
APOCRYPHA
APODICTIC
APOGAMOUS
APOLOGISE
APOLOGIST
APOPHYSES
APOPHYSIS
APOSTATIC
APOSTILLE
APOSTOLIC
APOTHECIA
APPALLING
APPANAGED
APPARATUS
APPARENCY
APPARITOR
APPEALING
APPELLANT
APPELLATE
APPENDAGE
APPENDANT

APPERTAIN
APPETENCE
APPETENCY
APPETIBLE
APPETISER
APPLAUDER
APPLE-CART
APPLE-JACK
APPLE-JOHN
APPLE-TREE
APPLE-WIFE
APPLIABLE
APPLIANCE
APPLICANT
APPLICATE
APPOINTED
APPORTION
APPRAISAL
APPRAISER
APPREHEND
APPRIZING
APPROBATE
APRIL-FISH
APRIL-FOOL
APRIORISM
APRIORIST
APRIORITY
APSIDIOLE
AQUABATIC
AQUABOARD
AQUADROME
AQUAPLANE
AQUA-REGIA
AQUARELLE
AQUARIIST
AQUARIUMS
AQUATINTA
AQUA-VITAE
AQUILEGIA
ARABESQUE
ARABINOSE
ARACHNIDA
ARACHNOID
ARAGONITE
ARAUCARIA
ARBITRAGE
ARBITRARY
ARBITRATE
ARBITRESS
ARBLASTER
ARBOREOUS
ARBORETUM
ARCHAISER
ARCHANGEL
ARCH-DRUID
ARCHDUCAL
ARCHDUCHY
ARCH-ENEMY
ARCHERESS
ARCHETYPE
ARCH-FELON
ARCH-FIEND
ARCHIBALD
ARCHILOWE
ARCHIMAGE
ARCHITECT

ARCHIVIST
ARCHIVOLT
ARCHOLOGY
ARCHONATE
ARCHONTIC
ARCTIIDAE
ARCTOGAEA
ARCUATION
ARDUOUSLY
AREA-SNEAK
ARENATION
AREOLATED
AREOMETER
AREOPAGUS
AREOSTYLE
ARETINIAN
ARGENTINE
ARGENTINO
ARGENTITE
ARGILLITE
ARGUS-EYED
ARGY-BARGY
ARILLATED
ARISTARCH
ARISTIDES
ARLE-PENNY
ARMADILLO
ARMIGERAL
ARMILLARY
ARMISTICE
ARMORICAN
AROMATISE
ARQUEBUSE
ARRACACHA
ARRAIGNER
ARRAYMENT
ARREARAGE
ARRESTIVE
ARRIVANCE
ARRIVANCY
ARRIVISME
ARRIVISTE
ARROGANCE
ARROGANCY
ARROW-HEAD
ARROW-ROOT
ARROW-SHOT
ARSENIATE
ARSENICAL
ARSENIOUS
ARSY-VERSY
ARTEMISIA
ARTERIOLE
ARTERITIS
ARTHRITIC
ARTHRITIS
ARTHROPOD
ARTHROSIS
ARTHURIAN
ARTICHOKE
ARTICULAR
ARTIFICER
ARTILLERY
ARTLESSLY
ARYBALLOS
ARYTENOID

ASAFETIDA
ASBESTINE
ASBESTOUS
ASCARIDAE
ASCENDANT
ASCENDENT
ASCENDING
ASCENSION
ASCENSIVE
ASCERTAIN
ASCETICAL
ASCITICAL
ASCLEPIAD
ASCLEPIAS
ASCLEPIOS
ASCLEPIUS
ASCOSPORE
ASEPALOUS
ASEXUALLY
ASHAMEDLY
ASH-BUCKET
ASHEN-GREY
ASHLARING
ASHLERING
ASHTAROTH
ASHTORETH
ASININITY
ASMOULDER
ASPARAGUS
ASPEN-LIKE
ASPERGILL
ASPERSION
ASPERSIVE
ASPERSOIR
ASPERSORY
ASPHALTIC
ASPHALTUM
ASPIDIOID
ASPIRATOR
ASPLENIUM
ASSAILANT
ASSAULTER
ASSAYABLE
ASSEMBLER
ASSENTIVE
ASSERTION
ASSERTIVE
ASSERTORY
ASSIDUITY
ASSIDUOUS
ASSISTANT
ASSOCIATE
ASSOILZIE
ASSONANCE
ASSUAGING
ASSUASIVE
ASSUETUDE
ASSUMABLE
ASSUMABLY
ASSUMEDLY
ASSUMPSIT
ASSURABLE
ASSURANCE
ASSUREDLY
ASSURGENT
ASTHMATIC

ASTICHOUS
ASTOUNDED
ASTRADDLE
ASTRAKHAN
ASTRANTIA
ASTRODOME
ASTROFELL
ASTROLABE
ASTROLOGY
ASTRONAUT
ASTRONOMY
ASTROPHEL
ASTUCIOUS
ASYMMETRY
ASYMPTOTE
ASYNDETIC
ASYNDETON
ASYNERGIA
ATACAMITE
ATARACTIC
ATAVISTIC
ATHEISTIC
ATHEMATIC
ATHENAEUM
ATHEOLOGY
ATHETESIS
ATHETOSIS
ATHLETICS
ATLANTEAN
ATMOLYSIS
ATMOMETER
ATOMICITY
ATOMISTIC
ATONALISM
ATONALITY
ATONEMENT
ATONICITY
ATONINGLY
ATROCIOUS
ATROPHIED
ATTAINDER
ATTEMPTER
ATTENDANT
ATTENTION
ATTENTIVE
ATTENUANT
ATTENUATE
ATTOLLENT
ATTRACTOR
ATTRAHENT
ATTRIBUTE
ATTRITION
ATTUITION
ATTUITIVE
AUBERGINE
AUBRIETIA
AUCTORIAL
AUDACIOUS
AUDIOLOGY
AUDIOPHIL
AUDIPHONE
AUDITRESS
AUGER-HOLE
AUGER-WORM
AUGMENTED
AUGMENTER

AUGMENTOR
AUGURSHIP
AUGUSTINE
AULD-WARLD
AUNT-SALLY
AURICULAR
AURORALLY
AUSGLEICH
AUSPICATE
AUSTENITE
AUSTERELY
AUSTERITY
AUTARCHIC
AUTARKIST
AUTHENTIC
AUTHORESS
AUTHORIAL
AUTHORING
AUTHORISE
AUTHORISH
AUTHORISM
AUTHORITY
AUTOCLAVE
AUTOCRACY
AUTOCROSS
AUTOCYCLE
AUTOFLARE
AUTOGAMIC
AUTOGRAFT
AUTOGRAPH
AUTOLATRY
AUTOLYCUS
AUTOLYSIS
AUTOLYTIC
AUTOMATIC
AUTOMATON
AUTONOMIC
AUTOPHAGY
AUTOPHOBY
AUTOPHONY
AUTOPILOT
AUTOPOINT
AUTOS-DA-FÉ
AUTOSOMAL
AUTOTELIC
AUTOTROPH
AUXILIARY
AUXOMETER
AVAILABLE
AVAILABLY
AVALANCHE
AVENGEFUL
AVENTAILE
AVERROISM
AVERROIST
AVERTEDLY
AVERTIBLE
AVISANDUM
AVISEMENT
AVIZANDUM
AVIZEFULL
AVOCATION
AVOCHMENT
AVOIDABLE
AVOIDANCE
AVOUTERER

AVUNCULAR
AWAKENING
AWARENESS
AWESOMELY
AWESTRIKE
AWE-STRUCK
AWFULNESS
AWKWARDLY
AXIOMATIC
AXLE-GUARD
AXMINSTER
AYLESBURY
AZEOTROPE
AZIMUTHAL

B

BABACOOTE
BABBITISM
BABIRUSSA
BABOONERY
BABOONISH
BACCHANAL
BACCHANTE
BACCIFORM
BACHARACH
BACILLARY
BACKBITER
BACK-BLOCK
BACK-BOARD
BACKCHAIN
BACK-CLOTH
BACKCROSS
BACKFISCH
BACK-GREEN
BACK-PEDAL
BACKPIECE
BACKPLATE
BACKSHISH
BACKSIGHT
BACK-SLANG
BACKSLIDE
BACKSPAUL
BACKSPEER
BACKSPEIR
BACKSTAGE
BACKSTALL
BACKSTAYS
BACKSWORD
BACKTRACK
BACKWARDS
BACKWATER
BACKWOODS
BACTERIAL
BACTERIAN
BACTERISE
BACTERIUM
BACTEROID
BACULITES
BADGER-DOG
BADMINTON
BAGATELLE
BAGPIPING
BAIGNOIRE
BAILIWICK
BAINMARIE
BAIRNLIKE

BAIRN-TEAM
BAIRN-TIME
BAISEMAIN
BAKEBOARD
BAKEHOUSE
BAKESTONE
BAKHSHISH
BAKSHEESH
BALAAM-BOX
BALAAMITE
BALACLAVA
BALALAIKA
BALCONIED
BALDACHIN
BALDAQUIN
BALD-EAGLE
BALD-FACED
BALDI-COOT
BALDMONEY
BALDPATED
BALECTION
BALEFULLY
BALKANISE
BALKINGLY
BALLADEER
BALLADIST
BALLASTED
BALL-DRESS
BALLERINA
BALLERINE
BALLISTIC
BALLOT-BOX
BALLOTING
BALL-POINT
BALL-PROOF
BALMINESS
BALSAMINA
BALTIMORE
BALTOSLAV
BALZARINE
BAMBOOZLE
BANAUSIAN
BANDALORE
BAND-BRAKE
BANDELIER
BANDEROLE
BANDICOOT
BANDOBAST
BANDOLEER
BANDOLERO
BANDOLIER
BANDOLINE
BANDSTAND
BAND-STONE
BANDWAGON
BAND-WHEEL
BANDY-BALL
BANEBERRY
BANEFULLY
BANGSRING
BANJULELE
BANK-AGENT
BANK-PAPER
BANK-STOCK
BANQUETED
BANQUETER

BANQUETTE
BANTERING
BANTUSTAN
BAPTISMAL
BAPTISTRY
BARAGOUIN
BARATHRUM
BARBADIAN
BARBADOES
BARBARIAN
BARBARISE
BARBARISM
BARBARITY
BARBAROUS
BARBASTEL
BARBITONE
BARCAROLE
BARDCRAFT
BAREFACED
BARGAINER
BARGE-POLE
BARK-BOUND
BARKEEPER
BAR-MAGNET
BARMBRACK
BARM-CLOTH
BARMECIDE
BARNABITE
BARNACLED
BARNSTORM
BAROGRAPH
BAROMETER
BAROMETRY
BARONETCY
BAROSCOPE
BARRACKER
BARRACOON
BARRACUDA
BARRELAGE
BARRELFUL
BARRELLED
BARRET-CAP
BARRICADE
BARRICADO
BARRISTER
BARROW-BOY
BARTENDER
BARTLEMEW
BASECOURT
BASEPLATE
BASHAWISM
BASHFULLY
BASICALLY
BASIFIXED
BASIFUGAL
BASILICAL
BASILICAN
BASILICON
BASINFULS
BASIN-WIDE
BASIPETAL
BASKETFUL
BAS-RELIEF
BASTARDLY
BASTINADE
BASTINADO

BASTIONED
BATH-BRICK
BATHHOUSE
BATHOLITE
BATHOLITH
BATHONIAN
BATHYBIUS
BATHYLITE
BATHYLITH
BATRACHIA
BATTALION
BATTENING
BATTLE-AXE
BATTLE-CRY
BATTOLOGY
BAVARDAGE
BAWDINESS
BAY-ANTLER
BAYONETED
BEACHHEAD
BEAD-HOUSE
BEADLEDOM
BEAD-PROOF
BEAMINESS
BEAMINGLY
BEANFEAST
BEANSTALK
BEAR-BERRY
BEARDLESS
BEARNAISE
BEAR'S-FOOT
BEASTHOOD
BEASTINGS
BEASTLIKE
BEATITUDE
BEAU-IDEAL
BEAUTEOUS
BEAUTIFUL
BEAVER-RAT
BEBEERINE
BECCAFICO
BEDAZZLED
BED-CLOSET
BEDELSHIP
BEDFELLOW
BEDIMMING
BEDIZENED
BED-JACKET
BEDLAMISM
BEDLAMITE
BEDRAGGLE
BEDRIDDEN
BEDROPPED
BED-SITTER
BEDSPREAD
BEECH-FERN
BEECH-MAST
BEEF-BROTH
BEEFEATER
BEE-FLOWER
BEEFSTEAK
BEEKEEPER
BEELZEBUB
BEEMASTER
BEE-ORCHIS
BEER-HOUSE

BEERINESS
BEER-MONEY
BEESTINGS
BEFALLING
BEFITTING
BEFORTUNE
BEGETTING
BEGGARDOM
BEGGAR-MAN
BEGGINGLY
BEGINNING
BEGLERBEG
BEGUINAGE
BEHAVIOUR
BEHEADING
BEHOLDING
BEHOVEFUL
BEINGLESS
BEINGNESS
BELAMOURE
BELEAGUER
BELEMNITE
BELIEVING
BELLATRIX
BELL-GLASS
BELLIBONE
BELLICOSE
BELL-METAL
BELL-PUNCH
BELL-TOWER
BELLYACHE
BELLY-BAND
BELLY-FLOP
BELOMANCY
BELVEDERE
BEMOANING
BEMONSTER
BENCH-HOLE
BENCH-MARK
BENDINGLY
BENEDIGHT
BENEFICED
BENEFITED
BENGALINE
BENIGHTED
BENIGHTEN
BENIGHTER
BENIGNANT
BENIGNITY
BENT-GRASS
BENZIDINE
BENZOLINE
BEPATCHED
BEPLASTER
BERBERINE
BERG-ADDER
BERGAMASK
BERGANDER
BERG-CEDAR
BERGOMASK
BERKELIUM
BERNADINE
BERSERKER
BERYLLIUM
BESAINTED
BESCATTER

BESEECHED
BESEECHER
BESEEMING
BESETMENT
BESETTING
BESIEGING
BESITTING
BESLOBBER
BESLUBBER
BESMUTTED
BESOM-HEAD
BESOTTING
BESPANGLE
BESPATTER
BESPECKLE
BESPOTTED
BESTEADED
BESTREWED
BETHANKIT
BETHOUGHT
BETHUMBED
BETRODDEN
BETROTHAL
BETROTHED
BETTERING
BETUMBLED
BEVEL-GEAR
BEVELLING
BEVELMENT
BEWAILING
BEZ-ANTLER
BEZOARDIC
BIBACIOUS
BIBLICISM
BIBLICIST
BICAMERAL
BICIPITAL
BICONCAVE
BICYCLIST
BIDENTATE
BIESTINGS
BIFARIOUS
BIFOLIATE
BIFURCATE
BIGENERIC
BIG-HEADED
BILABIATE
BILATERAL
BILGE-KEEL
BILGE-PUMP
BILHARZIA
BILIMBING
BILINGUAL
BILIOUSLY
BILIRUBIN
BILITERAL
BILLABONG
BILLBOARD
BILLETING
BILLIARDS
BILLIONTH
BILLOWING
BILLYCOCK
BILLY-GOAT
BILOBULAR
BILOCULAR

BIMONTHLY
BINERVATE
BINOCULAR
BINOMINAL
BINTURONG
BIOGENOUS
BIOGRAPHY
BIOLOGIST
BIOMETRIC
BIONOMICS
BIOSPHERE
BIPARTITE
BIPINNATE
BIPYRAMID
BIRD-ALANE
BIRD-ALONE
BIRD-LOUSE
BIRD'S-FOOT
BIRD'S-NEST
BIRD-TABLE
BIRLIEMAN
BIRTHMARK
BIRTHRATE
BIRTHWORT
BISECTION
BISERRATE
BISHOPDOM
BISHOPESS
BISHOPRIC
BISMILLAH
BISULCATE
BITTERISH
BITTER-PIT
BIVALENCE
BIVALENCY
BIVARIANT
BIVARIATE
BLACKBALL
BLACKBAND
BLACKBIRD
BLACKBUCK
BLACKCOCK
BLACKFEET
BLACKFISH
BLACKFOOT
BLACKGAME
BLACKHEAD
BLACKJACK
BLACKLEAD
BLACKLIST
BLACKMAIL
BLACKNESS
BLACK-WASH
BLADDERED
BLADE-BONE
BLAEBERRY
BLAMELESS
BLANDNESS
BLANKNESS
BLASPHEME
BLASPHEMY
BLAST-HOLE
BLASTMENT
BLAST-PIPE
BLASTULAR
BLATANTLY

BLEACHERY	BOGGINESS	BOWSTRING	BREVETING
BLEACHING	BOG-SPAVIN	BOWSTRUNG	BREVETTED
BLEAKNESS	BOLD-FACED	BOW-WINDOW	BREW-HOUSE
BLEAR-EYED	BOLECTION	BOX-GIRDER	BRIC-À-BRAC
BLESSEDLY	BOLIVIANO	BOXING-DAY	BRICK-CLAY
BLIGHTING	BOLLETRIE	BOXKEEPER	BRICK-DUST
BLIND-COAL	BOLOGNESE	BOX-NUMBER	BRICKKILN
BLINDFISH	BOLOMETER	BOXOFFICE	BRICKWALL
BLINDFOLD	BOLSHEVIK	BOXWALLAH	BRICKWORK
BLINDLESS	BOLSTERED	BOYFRIEND	BRICKYARD
BLINDNESS	BOMBARDON	BRACHYURA	BRIDECAKE
BLIND-SIDE	BOMBASINE	BRACTEATE	BRIDEMAID
BLINDWORM	BOMBASTIC	BRACTEOLE	BRIDESMAN
BLISSLESS	BOMBAZINE	BRACTLESS	BRIDEWELL
BLOCK-BOOK	BOMB-HAPPY	BRAHMANIC	BRIEFCASE
BLOCK-COAL	BOMBILATE	BRAHMINEE	BRIEFLESS
BLOCKHEAD	BOMBINATE	BRAHMINIC	BRIER-ROOT
BLOCKSHIP	BOMB-KETCH	BRAINCASE	BRIER-WOOD
BLOND-LACE	BOMBPROOF	BRAINLESS	BRIGADIER
BLOOD-BATH	BOMBSHELL	BRAINSICK	BRIGANDRY
BLOOD-BIRD	BOND-PAPER	BRAINWASH	BRILLIANT
BLOOD-DUST	BONDSLAVE	BRAINWAVE	BRIMSTONE
BLOOD-FEUD	BONDSTONE	BRAKELESS	BRIMSTONY
BLOOD-HEAT	BONDWOMAN	BRAKE-SHOE	BRINJARRY
BLOODLESS	BONE-BLACK	BRAKES-MAN	BRIQUETTE
BLOODLUST	BONE-EARTH	BRAMBLING	BRISKNESS
BLOOD-RAIN	BONHOMMIE	BRANCHERY	BRISTLING
BLOODROOT	BONING-ROD	BRANCHIAE	BRITANNIA
BLOODSHED	BONNIBELL	BRANCHIAL	BRITANNIC
BLOODSHOT	BONNINESS	BRANCHING	BRITICISE
BLOOD-TEST	BOOBY-TRAP	BRANCHLET	BRITICISM
BLOOD-WITE	BOOKED-OUT	BRANDERED	BRITISHER
BLOODWOOD	BOOKLOUSE	BRAND-IRON	BRITONESS
BLOOD-WORM	BOOKMAKER	BRANDLING	BRITSCHKA
BLOOMLESS	BOOKPLATE	BRANDRETH	BROAD-BEAN
BLOTCHING	BOOKSHELF	BRANGLING	BROAD-BRIM
BLOWVALVE	BOOKSTAND	BRASS-BAND	BROADCAST
BLUBBERED	BOOKSTALL	BRASSERIE	BROAD-LEAF
BLUEBERRY	BOOK-TALLY	BRASSIÈRE	BROADLOOM
BLUE-BLACK	BOOK-TOKEN	BRATTLING	BROADNESS
BLUEGRASS	BOOK-TRADE	BRAVADOES	BROADSIDE
BLUE-GREEN	BOOMERANG	BRAZELESS	BROADWAYS
BLUEPRINT	BOOM-SLANG	BRAZILIAN	BROADWISE
BLUESTONE	BOONDOCKS	BRAZIL-NUT	BROIDERER
BLUFFNESS	BOORISHLY	BREAD-CORN	BROKERAGE
BLUNDERER	BOOTBLACK	BREADLINE	BROMELIAD
BLUNTNESS	BOOTMAKER	BREADROOM	BROMOFORM
BLUSHLESS	BORROWING	BREADROOT	BRONCHIAL
BLUSH-ROSE	BOSCHVELD	BREAD-TREE	BRONZE-AGE
BLUTWURST	BOSKINESS	BREAKABLE	BROOKLIME
BOANERGES	BOSSANOVA	BREAKAWAY	BROOKWEED
BOARD-FOOT	BOTANICAL	BREAKBACK	BROOM-CORN
BOARHOUND	BOTTLE-GAS	BREAKBONE	BROOMRAPE
BOAR-SPEAR	BOTTLE-IMP	BREAKDOWN	BROTHERLY
BOASTLESS	BOULEVARD	BREAKFAST	BROW-BOUND
BOATHOUSE	BOUNDLESS	BREAKNECK	BROWNNESS
BOATSWAIN	BOUNTEOUS	BREAK-WIND	BRUMMAGEM
BOAT-TRAIN	BOUNTIFUL	BREASTPIN	BRUNONIAN
BOBBIN-NET	BOURASQUE	BREATHFUL	BRUSHWOOD
BOBBYSOCK	BOURGEOIS	BREATHILY	BRUSHWORK
BOB-CHERRY	BOUTONNÉE	BREATHING	BRUSQUELY
BOBSLEIGH	BOW-BACKED	BREECHING	BRUTALISE
BOBTAILED	BOWELLING	BREED-BATE	BRUTALITY
BODY-CURER	BOWER-BIRD	BREGMATIC	BRUTENESS
BODYGUARD	BOW-LEGGED	BRETASCHE	BRUTIFIED
BOG-BUTTER	BOWLER-HAT	BRETWALDA	BRUTISHLY

BRYOPHYTA
BRYOPHYTE
BRYTHONIC
BUBBLE-CAR
BUBBLE-GUM
BUCCANEER
BUCCANIER
BUCENTAUR
BUCKBOARD
BUCKETFUL
BUCKETING
BUCKHOUND
BUCKSHISH
BUCK'S-HORN
BUCKTHORN
BUCKTOOTH
BUCK-WAGON
BUCKWHEAT
BUCOLICAL
BUDGETING
BUFFALOES
BUFFETING
BUFF-STICK
BUFF-WHEEL
BUGHUNTER
BUGLE-BAND
BUGLE-CALL
BUGLE-HORN
BUHRSTONE
BULGARIAN
BULGINESS
BULKINESS
BULL-BOARD
BULL-DANCE
BULLDOZER
BULLETRIE
BULLFIGHT
BULLFINCH
BULLISHLY
BULL-TROUT
BULLWHACK
BULLYBEEF
BULLYROOK
BULLY-TREE
BUM-BAYLIE
BUMBLE-BEE
BUMBLEDOM
BUMMALOTI
BUMPINESS
BUMPOLOGY
BUMPTIOUS
BUNDOBUST
BUNGALOID
BUPRESTIS
BURD-ALANE
BURDENOUS
BURLESQUE
BURLINESS
BURNISHER
BURNT-CORK
BURRSTONE
BURSARIAL
BURSASHIP
BURSIFORM
BUSHCRAFT
BUSHELLER

BUSHELMAN
BUSH-FRUIT
BUSHINESS
BUSH-METAL
BUSHWHACK
BUTADIENE
BUTCHERLY
BUTLERAGE
BUTTER-BOX
BUTTERBUR
BUTTERCUP
BUTTER-FAT
BUTTERFLY
BUTTERINE
BUTTERNUT
BUTTER-PAT
BUTT-SHAFT
BUTTY-GANG
BUXOMNESS
BUZZINGLY
BY-ORDINAR
BY-PASSAGE
BY-PRODUCT
BYREWOMAN
BYRLAW-MAN
BYSTANDER
BYTOWNITE
BYZANTINE

C
CABALLERO
CABALLINE
CABALLING
CABBALISM
CABBALIST
CABIN-CREW
CABLEGRAM
CABLE-LAID
CABRIOLET
CAB-RUNNER
CACAFUEGO
CACHAEMIA
CACHAEMIC
CACHECTIC
CACHOLONG
CACODEMON
CACOETHES
CACOPHONY
CACTACEAE
CACTIFORM
CACUMINAL
CADASTRAL
CADAVERIC
CADDIE-CAR
CADDIS-FLY
CADETSHIP
CAECILIAN
CAEN-STONE
CAERULEAN
CAESAREAN
CAESARIAN
CAESARISM
CAESARIST
CAFETERIA
CAILLEACH
CAILLIACH

CAINOZOIC
CAIRNGORM
CALABOOSE
CALAMANCO
CALANDRIA
CALAVANCE
CALCANEAL
CALCANEAN
CALCANEUM
CALCARATE
CALCARINE
CALCEATED
CALCEDONY
CALCICOLE
CALCIFUGE
CALCULARY
CALCULATE
CALCULOSE
CALCULOUS
CALDARIUM
CALENDRER
CALENDULA
CALENTURE
CALF-BOUND
CALFDOZER
CALF'S-FOOT
CALIATOUR
CALIBERED
CALIBRATE
CALIOLOGY
CALIPHATE
CALIXTINE
CALLED-FOR
CALLIDITY
CALLIGRAM
CALLIPERS
CALLIPPIC
CALL-MONEY
CALLOSITY
CALLOUSLY
CALMATIVE
CALMSTANE
CALORIFIC
CALVINISM
CALVINIST
CALVITIES
CALYCINAL
CAMANACHD
CAMARILLA
CAMASS-RAT
CAMBIFORM
CAMBISTRY
CAMELBACK
CAMEMBERT
CAMERAMAN
CAMERATED
CAMORRISM
CAMORRIST
CAMOUFLET
CAMPANERO
CAMPANILE
CAMPANILI
CAMPANIST
CAMPANULA
CAMP-CHAIR
CAMPEADOR

CAMP-FEVER
CAMPHORIC
CAMP-STOOL
CAMSHEUGH
CAMSTAIRY
CAMSTEARY
CANAL-BOAT
CANAL-CELL
CANAL-RAYS
CANCELEER
CANCELIER
CANCELLED
CANCERATE
CANCEROUS
CANDIDACY
CANDIDATE
CANDLE-END
CANDLEMAS
CANDLE-NUT
CANDYTUFT
CANE-BRAKE
CANE-CHAIR
CANE-FRUIT
CANEPHORA
CANEPHORE
CANESCENT
CANE-SUGAR
CANE-TRASH
CANICULAR
CANKEROUS
CANNELURE
CANNINESS
CANNONADE
CANNONEER
CANNONIER
CANNULATE
CANONICAL
CANOPYING
CANTABANK
CANTABILE
CANTALOUP
CANT-BOARD
CANTHARID
CANTHARIS
CANTHARUS
CANTILENA
CANTINESS
CANTORIAL
CANVASSER
CAPACIOUS
CAPACITOR
CAPARISON
CAPELLINE
CAPER-BUSH
CAPILLARY
CAPITALLY
CAPITELLA
CAPITULAR
CAPITULUM
CAPONIERE
CAPOTAINE
CAPRICCIO
CAPRICORN
CAPRIFOLE
CAPRIFORM
CAPRYLATE

CAPSULARY	CARTILAGE	CATCHWORD	CENTERING
CAPSULATE	CARTOGRAM	CATECHISE	CENTIGRAM
CAPTAINCY	CARTOLOGY	CATECHISM	CENTIPEDE
CAPTAINRY	CARTOUCHE	CATECHIST	CENTONATE
CAPTIVATE	CARTRIDGE	CATERWAUL	CENTONIST
CAPTIVITY	CART'S-TAIL	CAT-HAMMED	CENTRALLY
CARABIDAE	CARTULARY	CATHARISE	CENTRE-BIT
CARAMBOLA	CARTWHEEL	CATHARISM	CENTRICAL
CARAMBOLE	CARVACROL	CATHARIST	CENTUMVIR
CARANGOID	CARYATIDS	CATHARSIS	CENTURIAL
CARAP-NUTS	CARYOPSIS	CATHARTIC	CENTURION
CARAP-WOOD	CASEATION	CATHECTIC	CEPHALATE
CARAVANCE	CASE-KNIFE	CATHEDRAL	CEPHALOUS
CARAVANED	CASEMAKER	CATOPTRIC	CERACEOUS
CARBAMIDE	CASEMATED	CAT-RIGGED	CERASTIUM
CARBONADO	CASHIERER	CAT-SILVER	CERATITIS
CARBONARI	CASSANDRA	CATTLEMAN	CERATODUS
CARBONATE	CASSAREEP	CAT-WITTED	CERBERIAN
CARBONISE	CASSARIPE	CAUCASIAN	CERCARIAN
CARBUNCLE	CASSATION	CAULD-RIFE	CEREALIST
CARBURATE	CASSEROLE	CAULIFORM	CEREBRATE
CARBURISE	CASSIMERE	CAULINARY	CERE-CLOTH
CARCINOMA	CASSOCKED	CAUMSTANE	CEROGRAPH
CARDAMINE	CASSONADE	CAUSALITY	CEROMANCY
CARDBOARD	CASSOULET	CAUSATION	CERTAINLY
CARDIACAL	CASSOWARY	CAUSATIVE	CERTAINTY
CARDIALGY	CASTALIAN	CAUSELESS	CERTIFIED
CARD-INDEX	CASTANETS	CAUTELOUS	CERTIFIER
CARD-TABLE	CASTELLAN	CAUTERISE	CERTITUDE
CAREENAGE	CASTE-MARK	CAUTERISM	CERULEOUS
CAREERISM	CASTIGATE	CAUTIONER	CERUSSITE
CAREERIST	CASTILIAN	CAUTIONRY	CESAREVNA
CAREFULLY	CASTOREUM	CAVALCADE	CESPITOSE
CARESSING	CASTOR-OIL	CAVALIERO	CESSATION
CARETAKER	CASTRATED	CAVE-EARTH	CETACEOUS
CARFUFFLE	CAST-STEEL	CAVENDISH	CEVADILLA
CARIBBEAN	CASUALISE	CAVERNOUS	CEVITAMIC
CARLYLEAN	CASUALISM	CAVILLING	CEYLANITE
CARLYLESE	CASUARINA	CEANOTHUS	CEYLONESE
CARLYLISM	CASUISTIC	CEASE-FIRE	CEYLONITE
CARMELITE	CASUISTRY	CEASELESS	CHABAZITE
CARNAHUBA	CATACLASM	CEBADILLA	CHA-CHA-CHA
CARNALISE	CATACLYSM	CEDAR-BIRD	CHAETODON
CARNALISM	CATAFALCO	CEE-SPRING	CHAETOPOD
CARNALIST	CATALEPSY	CEILINGED	CHAFFERER
CARNALITY	CATALEXIS	CELANDINE	CHAFFINCH
CARNATION	CATALOGUE	CELEBRANT	CHAFFLESS
CARNELIAN	CATALYSER	CELEBRATE	CHAGRINED
CARNIVORA	CATALYSIS	CELEBRITY	CHAIN-BOLT
CARNIVORE	CATALYTIC	CELESTIAL	CHAIN-GANG
CARNOSITY	CATAMARAN	CELESTINE	CHAIN-GEAR
CARNOTITE	CATAMENIA	CELLARAGE	CHAINLESS
CAROLLING	CATAMOUNT	CELLARIST	CHAIN-MAIL
CARPENTER	CAT-AND-DOG	CELLARMAN	CHAIN-PIER
CARPENTRY	CATAPHYLL	CELLAROUS	CHAIN-PUMP
CARPET-BAG	CATAPLASM	CELLULOID	CHAIN-RULE
CARPETING	CATAPLEXY	CELLULOSE	CHAIN-SHOT
CARPET-ROD	CATARHINE	CELSITUDE	CHAINWORK
CARPINGLY	CATARRHAL	CELTICISM	CHAIR-DAYS
CARRAGEEN	CATATONIA	CEMBALIST	CHAIRLIFT
CARRONADE	CATATONIC	CEMENTITE	CHALDAEAN
CARRYTALE	CATCHABLE	CENSORIAL	CHALDAISM
CARTELISE	CATCHMENT	CENSORIAN	CHALLENGE
CARTESIAN	CATCHPOLE	CENTAURUS	CHALUMEAU
CART-HORSE	CATCHPOLL	CENTENARY	CHALYBEAN
CART-HOUSE	CATCHWEED	CENTENIER	CHALYBITE

CHAMBERED
CHAMBERER
CHAMELEON
CHAMFERED
CHAMFRAIN
CHAMOMILE
CHAMPAGNE
CHAMPAIGN
CHAMPERTY
CHAMPLEVÉ
CHANCEFUL
CHANCROID
CHANCROUS
CHANDLERY
CHANGEFUL
CHANTEUSE
CHANTILLY
CHANTRESS
CHAPARRAL
CHAPELESS
CHAPERONE
CHAPLETED
CHAPRASSI
CHARABANC
CHAR-À-BANC
CHARACEAE
CHARACTER
CHARGEFUL
CHARGE-MAN
CHARINESS
CHARIVARI
CHARLATAN
CHARLOTTE
CHARMEUSE
CHARMLESS
CHAROLAIS
CHARTERED
CHARTERER
CHARTLESS
CHARTREUX
CHARTROOM
CHARWOMAN
CHARYBDIS
CHASE-PORT
CHASSEPOT
CHASTENED
CHASTENER
CHÂTELAIN
CHATOYANT
CHATTERER
CHAUFFEUR
CHAUSSURE
CHAVENDER
CHAW-BACON
CHEAPENER
CHEAPNESS
CHECHACHO
CHECHAQUO
CHECKERED
CHECKLIST
CHECKMATE
CHECK-REIN
CHECKROOM
CHECK-TILL
CHEECHAKO
CHEEK-BONE

CHEERLESS
CHEESE-VAT
CHELASHIP
CHELICERA
CHELONIAN
CHEMICKED
CHEMISTRY
CHEMITYPE
CHEMITYPY
CHEMOSTAT
CHEMURGIC
CHEONG-SAM
CHEQUERED
CHERALITE
CHERIMOYA
CHERNOZEM
CHERRY-BOB
CHERRY-PIE
CHERRY-PIT
CHERUBIMS
CHEST-NOTE
CHEST-TONE
CHEVALIER
CHEVELURE
CHEVRETTE
CHEVRONED
CHIBOUQUE
CHICANERY
CHICANING
CHICKADEE
CHICKAREE
CHICKLING
CHICKWEED
CHIEFLESS
CHIEFLING
CHIEFSHIP
CHIEFTAIN
CHIHUAHUA
CHILBLAIN
CHILDHOOD
CHILDLESS
CHILDLIKE
CHILDNESS
CHILD-WIFE
CHILIAGON
CHILIARCH
CHILLNESS
CHILOPODA
CHINAROOT
CHINA-TOWN
CHINA-WARE
CHINCAPIN
CHINCOUGH
CHINKAPIN
CHINOVNIK
CHIPBOARD
CHIPOLATA
CHIRAGRIC
CHIRIMOYA
CHIROLOGY
CHIRONOMY
CHIROPODY
CHISELLED
CHITINOUS
CHIVALRIC
CHLAMYDES

CHLORELLA
CHLORITIC
CHLOROSIS
CHLOROTIC
CHOCK-FULL
CHOCOLATE
CHOICEFUL
CHOKEBORE
CHOKEDAMP
CHOKE-FULL
CHOKE-PEAR
CHOLAEMIA
CHOLAEMIC
CHOLECYST
CHOLELITH
CHOLERAIC
CHONDRIFY
CHONDRITE
CHONDROID
CHONDRULE
CHOP-HOUSE
CHOP-LOGIC
CHORISTER
CHORIZONT
CHOROLOGY
CHORUSING
CHOWKIDAR
CHRISTIAN
CHRISTMAS
CHROMATIC
CHROMATIN
CHROMIDIA
CHRONICAL
CHRONICLE
CHRYSALID
CHRYSALIS
CHTHONIAN
CHUBB-LOCK
CHUB-FACED
CHUCK-FULL
CHUCKLING
CHUPRASSY
CHURCH-ALE
CHURCHING
CHURCHISM
CHURCHMAN
CHURCHWAY
CHURN-MILK
CHURR-WORM
CHYMISTRY
CICATRICE
CICATRISE
CICERONIC
CICHLIDAE
CICHORIUM
CICINDELA
CICLATOUN
CIGARETTE
CIGAR-TREE
CILICIOUS
CILIOLATE
CIMICIDAE
CIMMERIAN
CINCHONIC
CINCINNUS
CINCTURED

CINEMATIC
CINERARIA
CINERATOR
CINEREOUS
CINGALESE
CIPHERING
CIPHER-KEY
CIPOLLINO
CIRCADIAN
CIRCINATE
CIRCUITRY
CIRCULATE
CIRRHOPOD
CIRRHOSIS
CIRRIFORM
CIRRIPEDE
CISALPINE
CISPADANE
CISTACEAE
CITHARIST
CITIGRADE
CITIZENRY
CIVILISED
CIVILISER
CLACKDISH
CLAIMABLE
CLAMOROUS
CLAMOURER
CLAM-SHELL
CLANKLESS
CLAPBOARD
CLAPBREAD
CLARENDON
CLARET-CUP
CLARET-JUG
CLARIFIED
CLARIFIER
CLARIONET
CLASSABLE
CLASS-BOOK
CLASSIBLE
CLASSICAL
CLASSIFIC
CLASSLESS
CLASSMATE
CLASSROOM
CLATHRATE
CLATTERER
CLAUSTRAL
CLAUSTRUM
CLAUSULAE
CLAUSULAR
CLAVATION
CLAVICORN
CLAVICULA
CLAVIFORM
CLAVULATE
CLAY-EATER
CLAY-SLATE
CLEANNESS
CLEANSING
CLEARANCE
CLEARCOLE
CLEAR-EYED
CLEARNESS
CLEAR-SKIN

CLEARWING
CLEAVABLE
CLEITHRAL
CLEMENTLY
CLEPSYDRA
CLERECOLE
CLERGYMAN
CLERICALS
CLERICATE
CLERICITY
CLERKLESS
CLERK-LIKE
CLERKLING
CLERKSHIP
CLERUCHIA
CLEVERISH
CLEW-LINES
CLIENTAGE
CLIENTÈLE
CLIFFHANG
CLIMACTIC
CLIMATISE
CLIMATURE
CLIMBABLE
CLIMB-DOWN
CLINICIAN
CLINOAXIS
CLINQUANT
CLIP-JOINT
CLITELLAR
CLITELLUM
CLOACALIN
CLOACINAL
CLOAKROOM
CLOCK-GOLF
CLOCKWISE
CLOCKWORK
CLODPATED
CLOGDANCE
CLOISONNÉ
CLOISTRAL
CLOSENESS
CLOSETING
CLOTH-HALL
CLOTH-YARD
CLOUDLAND
CLOUDLESS
CLOUTERLY
CLOUT-NAIL
CLOUT-SHOE
CLOVE-HOOK
CLOVE-PINK
CLOVE-TREE
CLOWNSHIP
CLUBBABLE
CLUBHOUSE
CLUBWOMAN
CLUPEIDAE
CLUSTERED
CLY-FAKING
COACH-HIRE
COACH-HORN
COACH-ROAD
COACHWHIP
COACHWORK
COADJUTOR

COADUNATE
COAGULANT
COAGULATE
COAL-BLACK
COAL-BRASS
COALFIELD
COAL-HOUSE
COALITION
COAL-MINER
COAL-MOUSE
COAL-OWNER
COAL-PLANT
COAL-PLATE
COARCTATE
COASTLINE
COASTWARD
COASTWISE
COAT-DRESS
COAT-FROCK
COATSTAND
COAT-STYLE
COAXIALLY
COAXINGLY
COBALTITE
COBDENISM
COBDENITE
COBRIFORM
COCAINISE
COCAINISM
COCAINIST
COCCIDIUM
COCCOLITE
COCCOLITH
COCCYGEAL
COCCYGIAN
COCHINEAL
COCHLEATE
COCK-A-HOOP
COCKAIGNE
COCKATEEL
COCKATIEL
COCK-BROTH
COCKFIGHT
COCKHORSE
COCKLAIRD
COCKLE-BUR
COCKLE-HAT
COCKMATCH
COCKNEYFY
COCK-PADLE
COCKROACH
COCK-ROBIN
COCKSCOMB
COCKSFOOT
COCKSHOOT
COCKSWAIN
COCKYOLLY
COCOA-NIBS
COCOA-WOOD
COCO-DE-MER
COCOONERY
COCUS-WOOD
CODFISHER
CODIFYING
COELOMATA
COELOMATE

COELOSTAT
COEMPTION
COENOBITE
COENOBIUM
COENOSARC
COEQUALLY
COERCIBLE
COERCIBLY
COETERNAL
COFFEE-BUG
COFFEE-CUP
COFFEE-POT
COFFER-DAM
COFFINITE
COGITABLE
COGNATION
COGNISANT
COGNITION
COGNITIVE
COHEIRESS
COHERENCE
COHERENCY
COHERITOR
COHESIBLE
COIFFEUSE
COINTREAU
COLCANNON
COLCHICUM
COLCOTHAR
COLD-DRAWN
COLD-FRAME
COLD-HOUSE
COLD-SHORT
COLE-GARTH
COLLATION
COLLATIVE
COLLEAGUE
COLLECTED
COLLECTOR
COLLEGIAL
COLLEGIAN
COLLEGIUM
COLLIGATE
COLLIMATE
COLLINEAR
COLLISION
COLLOCATE
COLLODION
COLLOIDAL
COLLOQUIA
COLLOTYPE
COLLUSION
COLLUVIES
COLLYRIUM
COLOCASIA
COLOCYNTH
COLONELCY
COLONNADE
COLOPHONY
COLORIFIC
COLOSSEUM
COLOSTOMY
COLOSTRIC
COLOSTRUM
COLOURFUL
COLOURING

COLOURIST
COLOURMAN
COLTSFOOT
COLUBRIAD
COLUBRINE
COLUMBARY
COLUMBATE
COLUMBIAN
COLUMBINE
COLUMBITE
COLUMBIUM
COLUMELLA
COLUMNIST
COMBATANT
COMBATING
COMBATIVE
COMBINATE
COMBINING
COMBRETUM
COME-AND-GO
COME-O'-WILL
COMFITURE
COMFORTER
COMICALLY
COMINFORM
COMINGS-IN
COMINTERN
COMITADJI
COMITATUS
COMMANDER
COMMELINA
COMMENDAM
COMMENSAL
COMMENTER
COMMENTOR
COMMINATE
COMMINGLE
COMMINUTE
COMMISSAR
COMMITTAL
COMMITTED
COMMITTEE
COMMODITY
COMMODORE
COMMONAGE
COMMORANT
COMMOTION
COMMUNARD
COMMUNING
COMMUNION
COMMUNISE
COMMUNISM
COMMUNIST
COMMUNITY
COMMUTATE
COMMUTUAL
COMPACTED
COMPACTLY
COMPANIED
COMPANION
COMPELLED
COMPENDIA
COMPETENT
COMPLAINT
COMPLETED
COMPLEXLY

COMPLEXUS
COMPLIANT
COMPLYING
COMPONENT
COMPOSITE
COMPOSURE
COMPRADOR
COMPRISAL
COMPTABLE
COMPTIBLE
COMPTROLL
COMPUTANT
COMPUTIST
COMRADELY
CONCAVELY
CONCAVITY
CONCEITED
CONCENTER
CONCENTRE
CONCERNED
CONCERTED
CONCERTOS
CONCHITIS
CONCIERGE
CONCILIAR
CONCISELY
CONCISION
CONCLUDED
CONCOCTER
CONCOCTOR
CONCORDAT
CONCOURSE
CONCREATE
CONCUBINE
CONCURRED
CONCYCLIC
CONDEMNED
CONDENSER
CONDIDDLE
CONDIGNLY
CONDIMENT
CONDITION
CONDOLENT
CONDUCIVE
CONDUCTOR
CONDYLOID
CONDYLOMA
CONFERRED
CONFERRER
CONFESSED
CONFESSOR
CONFESTLY
CONFIDANT
CONFIDENT
CONFIDING
CONFIGURE
CONFINING
CONFIRMED
CONFIRMEE
CONFIRMER
CONFIRMOR
CONFITEOR
CONFITURE
CONFLUENT
CONFORMER
CONFRÉRIE

CONFRONTÉ
CONFUCIAN
CONFUSION
CONGENIAL
CONGER-EEL
CONGERIES
CONGESTED
CONGOLESE
CONGRUENT
CONGRUITY
CONGRUOUS
CONICALLY
CONIFERAE
CONJOINED
CONJUGATE
CONJURING
CONNATION
CONNATURE
CONNECTED
CONNECTER
CONNECTOR
CONNEXION
CONNEXIVE
CONNIVENT
CONNOTATE
CONNOTIVE
CONNUBIAL
CONQUEROR
CONSCIENT
CONSCIOUS
CONSCRIBE
CONSCRIPT
CONSENSUS
CONSERVER
CONSIGNED
CONSIGNEE
CONSIGNER
CONSIGNOR
CONSOLATE
CONSONANT
CONSONOUS
CONSORTED
CONSORTER
CONSORTIA
CONSPIRER
CONSTABLE
CONSTANCY
CONSTRAIN
CONSTRICT
CONSTRUCT
CONSTRUER
CONSULAGE
CONSULATE
CONSULTEE
CONSULTER
CONSULTOR
CONSUMING
CONTACTOR
CONTADINA
CONTADINE
CONTADINI
CONTADINO
CONTAGION
CONTAGIUM
CONTAINER
CONTANGOS

CONTEMNED
CONTEMNER
CONTEMPER
CONTENDER
CONTENTED
CONTESTED
CONTICENT
CONTINENT
CONTINUAL
CONTINUED
CONTINUER
CONTINUUM
CONTORTED
CONTRALTI
CONTRALTO
CONTRIVER
CONTUMACY
CONTUMELY
CONTUSION
CONTUSIVE
CONUNDRUM
CONVECTOR
CONVERTER
CONVERTOR
CONVEXITY
CONVIVIAL
CONVOCATE
CONVOLUTE
CONY-CATCH
COOKHOUSE
COOL-HOUSE
COOPERAGE
CO-OPERANT
CO-OPERATE
COOPERING
COPACETIC
COPARTNER
COPATAINE
COPATRIOT
COPES-MATE
COPE-STONE
COPING-SAW
COPIOUSLY
CO-POLYMER
CO-PORTION
COPPERING
COPPERISH
CO-PRESENT
COPROLITE
COPROLOGY
COPSE-WOOD
COPYRIGHT
COQUETTED
CORAL-FISH
CORALLIAN
CORALLINE
CORALLITE
CORALLOID
CORAL-REEF
CORAL-ROCK
CORAL-ROOT
CORAL-TREE
CORAL-WORT
CORBEILLE
CORBELLED
CORBICULA

CORCHORUS
CORDAITES
CORDELIER
CORD-GRASS
CORDIALLY
CORDIFORM
CORDOTOMY
CORDYLINE
COREGONUS
CORF-HOUSE
CORIANDER
CO-RIVALRY
CORK-BORER
CORKINESS
CORK-SCREW
CORMORANT
CORNACEAE
CORN-BORER
CORN-BRAKE
CORNBRASH
CORN-BREAD
CORNCRAKE
CORNELIAN
CORNEMUSE
CORNER-BOY
CORNER-MAN
CORNETIST
CORNFIELD
CORNFLOUR
CORNIFORM
CORNOPEAN
CORN-SALAD
CORN-SHUCK
CORNSTALK
CORNSTONE
COROLLARY
COROLLINE
CORONATED
CORONETED
CORPORATE
CORPOREAL
CORPORIFY
CORPOSANT
CORPULENT
CORPUSCLE
CORRASION
CORRECTLY
CORRECTOR
CORRELATE
CORRIGENT
CORRODENT
CORROSION
CORROSIVE
CORRUGATE
CORRUPTER
CORRUPTLY
CORSETIER
CORSETING
CORSLETED
CORTICATE
CORTICOID
CORTISONE
CORUSCANT
CORUSCATE
CORYBANTS
CORYDALIS

CORYMBOSE
CORYPHAEI
CORYPHENE
COSEISMAL
COSEISMIC
COSHERING
COSMOCRAT
COSMOGENY
COSMOGONY
COSMOLOGY
COSMONAUT
COSMORAMA
COSMOTRON
CO-SPHERED
COSSETING
COSTIVELY
COSTUMIER
COTANGENT
CO-TENANCY
COTHURNUS
COTICULAR
COTILLION
COTROPHIN
COTTERPIN
COTTONADE
COTTON-GIN
COTYLEDON
COUCHETTE
COUGH-DROP
COUNCILOR
COUNTABLE
COUNT-DOWN
COUNTLESS
COUNTSHIP
COURBARIL
COURGETTE
COURT-CARD
COURTEOUS
COURTESAN
COURTEZAN
COURT-FOOL
COURT-HAND
COURT-LEET
COURTLIKE
COURTLING
COURT-ROLL
COURTSHIP
COURTYARD
COUTURIER
COVALENCY
COVELLITE
COVERTURE
COVETABLE
COVIN-TREE
COWARDICE
COWDIE-GUM
COWFEEDER
COWL-STAFF
COXCOMBIC
COXCOMBRY
CRAB-APPLE
CRABBEDLY
CRAB-EATER
CRAB-FACED
CRAB-LOUSE
CRAB'S-EYES

CRAB-SIDLE
CRAB-STICK
CRACK-HEMP
CRACKLING
CRACK-ROPE
CRACKSMAN
CRACOVIAN
CRAFTLESS
CRAFTSMAN
CRAMMABLE
CRAMP-BARK
CRAMP-BONE
CRAMP-FISH
CRAMP-IRON
CRAMP-RING
CRANBERRY
CRANKCASE
CRANKNESS
CRANREUCH
CRAPULENT
CRAPULOUS
CRASH-DIVE
CRASH-LAND
CRASSNESS
CRATAEGUS
CRATEROUS
CRAZINESS
CREAM-CAKE
CREAM-LAID
CREAM-WOVE
CREATABLE
CREATRESS
CREATURAL
CREDENDUM
CREDULITY
CREDULOUS
CREEPERED
CREEP-HOLE
CREMASTER
CREMATION
CREMATORY
CREMOCARP
CRENATION
CRENATURE
CRENELLED
CRENULATE
CREOLISED
CREPITANT
CREPITATE
CREPOLINE
CRESCENDO
CRESTLESS
CRETINISM
CRETINOID
CRETINOUS
CREWELIST
CRIBELLAR
CRIBELLUM
CRICKETER
CRIMELESS
CRIMINATE
CRIMINOUS
CRINOIDAL
CRINOIDEA
CRINOLINE
CRIPPLING

CRISPATED
CRISPNESS
CRITERION
CRITICISE
CRITICISM
CROCHETED
CROCODILE
CROISSANT
CRO-MAGNON
CROOKBACK
CROOKEDLY
CROPBOUND
CROP-EARED
CROQUETTE
CROSIERED
CROSSBAND
CROSSBEAM
CROSSBILL
CROSSBITE
CROSSBRED
CROSSETTE
CROSS-EYED
CROSSFALL
CROSSFIRE
CROSSFISH
CROSS-HEAD
CROSSJACK
CROSSNESS
CROSSOVER
CROSSROAD
CROSS-RUFF
CROSS-SILL
CROSS-TALK
CROSS-TREE
CROSS-WIND
CROSSWISE
CROSSWORD
CROSSWORT
CROTALINE
CROTALISM
CROTCHETY
CROUSTADE
CROW-BERRY
CROW-FOOTS
CROWN-BARK
CROWN-GALL
CROWN-HEAD
CROWN-LAND
CROWNLESS
CROWN-POST
CROWN-WORK
CROW-QUILL
CROW'S-BILL
CROW'S-FOOT
CROW'S-NEST
CROWSTEPS
CRUCIFIED
CRUCIFIER
CRUCIFORM
CRUDENESS
CRUELNESS
CRUMB-TRAY
CRUMPLING
CRUSH-ROOM
CRUSTACEA
CRUSTATED

CRUSTLESS
CRYOGENIC
CRYOMETER
CRYOSCOPE
CRYOSCOPY
CRYPTADIA
CRYPTICAL
CRYPTOGAM
CRYPTONYM
CTENIFORM
CTESIPHON
CUBBY-HOLE
CUBICALLY
CUCKOLDLY
CUCKOLDOM
CUCKOLDRY
CUCKOO-BUD
CUCKOO-FLY
CUCULLATE
CUDDEEHIH
CUDGELLED
CUDGELLER
CUISINIER
CUL-DE-FOUR
CULICIDAE
CULLENDER
CULLIONLY
CULMINANT
CULMINATE
CULPATORY
CULTIVATE
CULTORIST
CULTRATED
CULTURIST
CULVER-KEY
CUMBRANCE
CUMULATED
CUNCTATOR
CUNEIFORM
CUNNINGLY
CUPBEARER
CUPELLING
CUP-LICHEN
CUPOLATED
CUPRESSUS
CURBSTONE
CURCUMINE
CURDINESS
CURETTAGE
CURFUFFLE
CURIALISM
CURIALIST
CURIOSITY
CURIOUSLY
CURLINESS
CURL-PAPER
CURRENTLY
CURRISHLY
CURRY-COMB
CURRY-LEAF
CURSIVELY
CURSORIAL
CURSORILY
CURSTNESS
CURTATION
CURTILAGE

CURVATION
CURVATIVE
CURVATURE
CURVESOME
CURVETING
CURVETTED
CURVIFORM
CUSHIONED
CUSHIONET
CUSPIDATE
CUSPIDORE
CUSTODIAL
CUSTODIAN
CUSTODIER
CUSTOMARY
CUSTUMARY
CUTANEOUS
CUTCHERRY
CUTICULAR
CUT-LEAVED
CUT-THROAT
CUTTY-SARK
CYANAMIDE
CYANIDING
CYANOTYPE
CYCLAMATE
CYCLOIDAL
CYCLOPEAN
CYCLOPIAN
CYCLOPSES
CYCLORAMA
CYCLOTRON
CYLINDRIC
CYMAGRAPH
CYMBALIST
CYMBIFORM
CYMOGRAPH
CYMOPHANE
CYNEGETIC
CYNICALLY
CYNIPIDAE
CYNOSURUS
CYPRINOID
CYSTIDEAN
CYSTIFORM
CYSTOCARP
CYSTOCELE
CYSTOIDEA
CYSTOLITH
CYSTOTOMY
CYTHEREAN
CYTOLYSIS
CYTOPLASM
CYTOTOXIC
CYTOTOXIN
CZAREVICH

D

DACHSHUND
DACOITAGE
DACTYLIST
DAEDALIAN
DAE-NETTLE
DAHABEEAH
DAHABIYAH
DAHABIYEH

DAIRY-FARM
DAIRYMAID
DALLIANCE
DALMATIAN
DALRADIAN
DALTONIAN
DALTONISM
DAMASCENE
DAMASKEEN
DAMASQUIN
DAMNATION
DAMNATORY
DAMOCLEAN
DAMP-PROOF
DANCE-BAND
DANCE-HALL
DANCETTEE
DANCE-TUNE
DANDELION
DANDIACAL
DANDIFIED
DANDIPRAT
DANDY-CART
DANDY-COCK
DANDYFUNK
DANDYPRAT
DANDY-ROLL
DANGEROUS
DANNEBROG
DANTESQUE
DAPPLE-BAY
DARE-DEVIL
DARK-HOUSE
DARKLINGS
DARRAIGNE
DART-BOARD
DARTINGLY
DARWINIAN
DARWINISM
DASHBOARD
DASHINGLY
DASH-WHEEL
DASTARDLY
DATE-SHELL
DATE-SUGAR
DATUM-LINE
DAUNTLESS
DAVENPORT
DAVY-JONES
DAY-LABOUR
DAY-NETTLE
DAY-SCHOOL
DAYSPRING
DEACONESS
DEAD-ALIVE
DEADENING
DEAD-HOUSE
DEAD-LEVEL
DEAD-MARCH
DEAD-POINT
DEAD-WATER
DEAFENING
DEATH-BELL
DEATH-BLOW
DEATH-DAMP

DEATH-FIRE
DEATHLESS
DEATHLIKE
DEATH-MASK
DEATH-RATE
DEATH-ROLL
DEATHSMAN
DEATH-SONG
DEATH-TRAP
DEATHWARD
DEBARMENT
DEBARRASS
DEBARRING
DEBATABLE
DEBAUCHED
DEBAUCHEE
DEBAUCHER
DEBELLING
DEBENTURE
DEBRUISED
DEBUTANTE
DECACHORD
DECADENCE
DECADENCY
DECAGONAL
DECAGYNIA
DECALCIFY
DECALITRE
DECALOGUE
DECAMERON
DECAMETRE
DECANDRIA
DECANTATE
DECAPODAL
DECAPODAN
DECASTERE
DECASTICH
DECASTYLE
DECATHLON
DECAUDATE
DECEITFUL
DECEMVIRI
DECEMVIRS
DECENNARY
DECENNIAL
DECENNIUM
DECEPTION
DECEPTIVE
DECEPTORY
DECESSION
DECIDABLE
DECIDEDLY
DECIDUATE
DECIDUOUS
DECILITRE
DECILLION
DECIMALLY
DECIMATOR
DECIMETRE
DECISTERE
DECK-CARGO
DECK-CHAIR
DECK-HOUSE
DECLAIMER
DECLARANT
DECLASSEE

DECLINANT
DECLINATE
DECLIVITY
DECLIVOUS
DECOCTION
DECOCTIVE
DECOCTURE
DECOHERER
DECOLLATE
DÉCOLLETÉ
DECOMPLEX
DECOMPOSE
DECONGEST
DECONTROL
DECORATED
DECORATOR
DECOY-DUCK
DECREEING
DECREMENT
DECRETIST
DECRETIVE
DECRETORY
DECUBITUS
DECUMBENT
DECURRENT
DECURSION
DECURSIVE
DECUSSATE
DEDICATEE
DEDICATOR
DEDUCIBLE
DEDUCTION
DEDUCTIVE
DEEP-DRAWN
DEEP-TONED
DEER-BERRY
DEER-FENCE
DEER-HOUND
DEER-MOUSE
DEFAECATE
DEFALCATE
DEFAULTER
DEFEATISM
DEFEATIST
DEFEATURE
DEFECTION
DEFECTIVE
DEFENDANT
DEFENSIVE
DEFERENCE
DEFERMENT
DEFERRING
DEFIANTLY
DEFICIENT
DEFINABLE
DEFINABLY
DEFLATION
DEFLECTED
DEFLECTOR
DEFLEXION
DEFLEXURE
DEFLORATE
DEFLUXION
DEFOLIANT
DEFOLIATE
DEFORMITY

DEFRAYING
DEFROSTER
DEGARNISH
DEGRADING
DEGUSTATE
DEHISCENT
DEHYDRATE
DEID-THRAW
DEINORNIS
DEINOSAUR
DEIPAROUS
DEISTICAL
DEJECTION
DEJECTORY
DEKABRIST
DELAPSION
DELFTWARE
DELICIOUS
DELIGHTED
DELINEATE
DELIQUIUM
DELIRIOUS
DELIVERER
DELIVERLY
DELPHINUS
DELTA-WING
DELUDABLE
DELUNDUNG
DEMAGOGIC
DEMAGOGUE
DEMANDANT
DEMARCATE
DEMEANOUR
DEMENTATE
DEMERSION
DEMI-DEIFY
DEMI-DEVIL
DEMI-GORGE
DEMI-LANCE
DEMI-MONDE
DEMIPIQUE
DEMISABLE
DEMISSION
DEMISSIVE
DEMIURGIC
DEMIURGUS
DEMOBBING
DEMOCRACY
DEMULCENT
DEMULSIFY
DEMURRAGE
DEMURRING
DENDRITIC
DENIGRATE
DENITRATE
DENITRIFY
DENOTABLE
DENOUNCER
DENSENESS
DENTALIUM
DENTATION
DENTIFORM
DENTISTRY
DENTITION
DENYINGLY
DEODORANT

DEODORISE
DEOXIDATE
DEOXIDISE
DEPARTING
DEPARTURE
DEPASTURE
DEPENDANT
DEPENDENT
DEPENDING
DEPICTION
DEPICTIVE
DEPICTURE
DEPLETION
DEPLETIVE
DEPLETORY
DEPOSABLE
DEPOSITOR
DEPRAVITY
DEPRECATE
DEPREDATE
DEPREHEND
DEPRESSED
DEPRESSOR
DEPTH-BOMB
DEPTHLESS
DEPURATOR
DERIVABLE
DERIVABLY
DERMATOID
DERRING-DO
DERRINGER
DESALTING
DESCENDED
DESCRIBER
DESCRYING
DESECRATE
DESERTION
DESERVING
DESICCANT
DESICCATE
DESIGNATE
DESIGNFUL
DESIGNING
DESINENCE
DESIPIENT
DESIRABLE
DESIRABLY
DESMODIUM
DESOLATER
DESOLATOR
DESPERADO
DESPERATE
DESPOILER
DESPOTATE
DESPOTISM
DESPUMATE
DESTEMPER
DESTINATE
DESTITUTE
DESTROYED
DESTROYER
DESUETUDE
DESULPHUR
DESULTORY
DETECTION
DETECTIVE

DETENTION
DETERGENT
DETERMENT
DETERMINE
DETERRENT
DETERRING
DETERSION
DETERSIVE
DETHRONER
DETONATOR
DETORSION
DETORTION
DETRACTOR
DETRIMENT
DETRITION
DETRUSION
DEUTERIUM
DEVALUATE
DEVASTATE
DEVELOPED
DEVELOPER
DEVIATION
DEVICEFUL
DEVIL-CRAB
DEVIL-FISH
DEVILLING
DEVILMENT
DEVIL'S-BIT
DEVILSHIP
DEVIOUSLY
DEVISABLE
DEVITRIFY
DEVONPORT
DEVOTEDLY
DEVOURING
DEWLAPPED
DEXTERITY
DEXTEROUS
DEXTRALLY
DEXTRORSE
DHARMSALA
DIABLERIE
DIABOLISE
DIABOLOGY
DIACHYLON
DIACHYLUM
DIACODION
DIACODIUM
DIACONATE
DIACRITIC
DIACTINAL
DIACTINIC
DIAERESES
DIAERESIS
DIAGNOSES
DIAGNOSIS
DIALECTAL
DIALECTIC
DIALLAGIC
DIALOGISE
DIALOGIST
DIALOGITE
DIAL-PLATE
DIAMETRAL
DIAMÉTRIC
DIAMONDED

DIANDROUS
DIANETICS
DIANOETIC
DIAPERING
DIAPHRAGM
DIAPHYSIS
DIAPYESIS
DIAPYETIC
DIARRHEAL
DIARRHOEA
DIASTATIC
DIASTATIS
DIASTOLIC
DIATHERMY
DIATHESIS
DIATHETIC
DIATOMITE
DIATROPIC
DIAZEUXIS
DIB-STONES
DICACIOUS
DICASTERY
DICHASIAL
DICHASIUM
DICHOGAMY
DICHOTOMY
DICHROISM
DICHROITE
DICHROMAT
DICHROMIC
DICKSONIA
DICKY-BIRD
DICLINISM
DICLINOUS
DICOTYLAE
DICROTISM
DICROTOUS
DICTATION
DICTATORY
DICTATRIX
DICTATURE
DICTYOGEN
DIDACTICS
DIDELPHIA
DIDELPHIC
DIDELPHYS
DIDRACHMA
DIDYNAMIA
DIESELISE
DIE-SINKER
DIETARIAN
DIET-BREAD
DIET-DRINK
DIETETICS
DIETICIAN
DIETITIAN
DIFFERENT
DIFFICULT
DIFFIDENT
DIFFLUENT
DIFFUSELY
DIFFUSION
DIFFUSIVE
DIGASTRIC
DIGESTION
DIGESTIVE

DIGITALIN
DIGITALIS
DIGITATED
DIGNIFIED
DIGNITARY
DIKA-BREAD
DILATABLE
DILATANCY
DILATATOR
DILIGENCE
DILL-WATER
DIMENSION
DIMIDIATE
DIMISSORY
DIMORPHIC
DIMYARIAN
DINANTIAN
DINGINESS
DINING-CAR
DINNER-SET
DINOCERAS
DIOECIOUS
DIONYSIAC
DIONYSIAN
DIOPTRATE
DIOPTRICS
DIORISTIC
DIOSCOREA
DIP-CIRCLE
DIPHTHONG
DIPHYSITE
DIPLOMACY
DIPLOMATE
DIPLOZOON
DIP-SECTOR
DIPTERIST
DIPTEROUS
DIRECTION
DIRECTIVE
DIRECTORY
DIRECTRIX
DIREFULLY
DIRIGIBLE
DIRIGISME
DIRT-CHEAP
DIRTINESS
DIRT-TRACK
DISACCORD
DISAFFECT
DISAFFIRM
DISANCHOR
DISANOINT
DISAPPEAR
DISARMING
DISATTIRE
DISATTUNE
DISAVOUCH
DISAVOWAL
DISBELIEF
DISBODIED
DISBRANCH
DISBURDEN
DISBURSAL
DISCALCED
DISCANDIE
DISCERNER

DISCHARGE
DISCHURCH
DISCOIDAL
DISCOLOUR
DISCOMFIT
DISCOMMON
DISCOURSE
DISCOVERT
DISCOVERY
DISCREDIT
DISCUMBER
DISCURSUS
DISDAINED
DISEMBARK
DISEMBODY
DISEMPLOY
DISENABLE
DISENGAGE
DISENTAIL
DISENTOMB
DISESTEEM
DISFAVOUR
DISFIGURE
DISFOREST
DISGODDED
DISGRACER
DISGUISED
DISGUISER
DISHALLOW
DISH-CLOTH
DISH-CLOUT
DISH-COVER
DISH-FACED
DISHONEST
DISHONOUR
DISHUMOUR
DISH-WATER
DISILLUDE
DISIMMURE
DISINFECT
DISINFEST
DISINHUME
DISINVEST
DISJASKIT
DISLOCATE
DISLUSTRE
DISMALITY
DISMANTLE
DISMAYFUL
DISMEMBER
DISMISSAL
DISOBLIGE
DISORIENT
DISPARAGE
DISPARATE
DISPARITY
DISPAUPER
DISPELLED
DISPENSED
DISPENSER
DISPEOPLE
DISPERSAL
DISPERSER
DISPLAYED
DISPLAYER
DISPLEASE

DISPONDEE
DISPOSING
DISPOSURE
DISPRAISE
DISPRISON
DISPROFIT
DISPROVAL
DISPROVED
DISPROVEN
DISPURVEY
DISPUTANT
DISREGARD
DISRELISH
DISREPAIR
DISREPUTE
DISSECTED
DISSECTOR
DISSEISIN
DISSEISOR
DISSEIZIN
DISSEIZOR
DISSEMBLE
DISSEMBLY
DISSENTER
DISSIDENT
DISSIMILE
DISSIPATE
DISSOCIAL
DISSOLUTE
DISSONANT
DISSUADER
DISSUNDER
DISTANTLY
DISTEMPER
DISTHRONE
DISTILLED
DISTILLER
DISTINGUÉ
DISTORTED
DISTRAINT
DISTURBED
DISTURBER
DITHECOUS
DITHELETE
DITHELISM
DITHYRAMB
DITROCHEE
DITTANDER
DITTOLOGY
DIURNALLY
DIUTURNAL
DIVELLENT
DIVERGENT
DIVERGING
DIVERSELY
DIVERSIFY
DIVERSION
DIVERSITY
DIVERTING
DIVERTIVE
DIVIDABLE
DIVIDEDLY
DIVIDUOUS
DIVINATOR
DIVISIBLE
DIVISIBLY

DIVORCIVE
DIVULGATE
DIVULSION
DIVULSIVE
DIXIELAND
DIZYGOTIC
DIZZINESS
DOBERMANN
DOCK-CRESS
DOCKETING
DOCTORAND
DOCTORATE
DOCTORESS
DOCTORIAL
DOCTRINAL
DODDERING
DODDIPOLL
DODDYPOLL
DODECAGON
DODONAEAN
DOGARESSA
DOG-COLLAR
DOG-EAT-DOG
DOGGERMAN
DOGGINESS
DOGGISHLY
DOG-KENNEL
DOG-LEGGED
DOG-LETTER
DOGMATICS
DOGMATISE
DOGMATISM
DOGMATIST
DOGMATORY
DO-GOODERY
DO-GOODISM
DOG-SALMON
DOGSHORES
DOG'S-TOOTH
DOG-VIOLET
DOLEFULLY
DOLERITIC
DOLLINESS
DOLLY-SHOP
DOLOMITIC
DOLORIFIC
DOLPHINET
DOLTISHLY
DOMDANIEL
DOMICILED
DOMINANCE
DOMINANCY
DOMINATOR
DOMINICAL
DOMINICAN
DONKEY-MAN
DO-NOTHING
DOODLEBUG
DOOR-CHEEK
DOORNBOOM
DOOR-PLATE
DOOR-STEAD
DOOR-STONE
DOPE-FIEND
DOR-BEETLE
DORIDIDAE

DORMITION
DORMITIVE
DORMITORY
DORSIFLEX
DOSE-METER
DOSIMETER
DOSIOLOGY
DOSS-HOUSE
DOTTIPOLL
DOUBLE-AXE
DOUBLE-BAR
DOUBLE-YOU
DOUBTABLE
DOUBTLESS
DOUCENESS
DOUCEPERE
DOUGHTILY
DOUKHOBOR
DOUZEPERS
DOVE-HOUSE
DOVE'S-FOOT
DOWDINESS
DOWERLESS
DOWN-GOING
DOWNGRADE
DOWN-GYVED
DOWNINESS
DOWN-LYING
DOWN-QUILT
DOWNRIGHT
DOWNSTAGE
DOWNSTAIR
DOWN-THROW
DOWN-TRAIN
DOWNWARDS
DRABBLING
DRACONIAN
DRACONISM
DRACONTIC
DRAFTSMAN
DRAG-CHAIN
DRAG-HOUND
DRAGOMANS
DRAGONESS
DRAGONFLY
DRAGONISE
DRAGONISH
DRAGONISM
DRAINABLE
DRAINPIPE
DRAIN-TILE
DRAIN-TRAP
DRAMATICS
DRAMATISE
DRAMATIST
DRAMATURG
DRAPERIED
DRAPERIES
DRATCHELL
DRAUGHTER
DRAUGHT-OX
DRAVIDIAN
DRAWN-WORK
DRAW-PLATE
DRAW-SHEET
DRAY-HORSE

DREADLESS
DREAMBOAT
DREAMHOLE
DREAMLAND
DREAMLESS
DREDGE-BOX
DREPANIUM
DRESS-COAT
DRESS-SUIT
DRIFT-BOLT
DRIFT-LAND
DRIFTLESS
DRIFT-SAIL
DRIFT-WEED
DRIFTWOOD
DRINKABLE
DRINK-HAIL
DRIP-STONE
DRIVELLED
DRIVELLER
DROLLNESS
DROMEDARE
DROMEDARY
DRONE-PIPE
DRONISHLY
DROP-DRILL
DROP-PRESS
DROP-SCENE
DROP-SCONE
DROPSICAL
DROP-STONE
DROVE-ROAD
DRUG-FIEND
DRUGSTORE
DRUIDICAL
DRUM-MAJOR
DRUMSTICK
DRUNKENLY
DRYASDUST
DRY-FISTED
DRYSALTER
DRY-WALLER
DUALISTIC
DUBIOSITY
DUBIOUSLY
DUBITABLE
DUBITANCY
DUCK-BOARD
DUCK'S-FOOT
DUCK'S-MEAT
DUCTILITY
DUFFERDOM
DUFFERISM
DULCAMARA
DULCIFIED
DULCITONE
DULCITUDE
DULOCRACY
DUMBFOUND
DUMB-PIANO
DUMMINESS
DUMPINESS
DUMPISHLY
DUNDREARY
DUNGEONER
DUNSTABLE

DUODECIMO
DUODENARY
DUPLICAND
DUPLICATE
DUPLICITY
DURALUMIN
DUSKINESS
DUSKISHLY
DUST-BRAND
DUST-BRUSH
DUST-COVER
DUST-DEVIL
DUSTINESS
DUSTPROOF
DUSTSHEET
DUST-STORM
DUSTY-FOOT
DUTEOUSLY
DUTIFULLY
DUUMVIRAL
DYER'S-WEED
DYER'S-WELD
DYINGNESS
DYNAMICAL
DYNAMITER
DYSCHROIA
DYSCRASIA
DYSENTERY
DYSGENICS
DYSLECTIC
DYSPEPSIA
DYSPEPTIC
DYSPHAGIA
DYSPHAGIC
DYSPHONIA
DYSPHORIA
DYSPNOEAL
DYSPNOEIC
DYSTECTIC
DYSTHESIA
DYSTHETIC
DYSTHYMIA
DYSTHYMIC
DYSTROPHY
DZIGGETAI

E

EAGERNESS
EAGLE-EYED
EAGLE-HAWK
EAGLEWOOD
EALDORMAN
EAR-COCKLE
EARLINESS
EARNESTLY
EARTH-BATH
EARTHBORN
EARTHBRED
EARTHFALL
EARTHFAST
EARTHFLAX
EARTHLING
EARTH-STAR
EARTHWARD
EARTHWOLF
EARTHWORK

EARTHWORM
EASTENDER
EASTER-EGG
EASTERNER
EASTLINGS
EASTWARDS
EASY-CHAIR
EASY-GOING
EAVESDRIP
EAVESDROP
EBENACEAE
EBIONITIC
EBRILLADE
EBRIOSITY
EBULLIENT
EBURNEOUS
ECARDINES
ECCENTRIC
ECCLESIAL
ECDYSIAST
ECHIDNINE
ECHINATED
ECHOLALIA
ECLAMPSIA
ECLAMPTIC
ECLECTICS
ECOLOGIST
ECONOMICS
ECONOMISE
ECONOMIST
ECOSSAISE
ECOSYSTEM
ÉCRITOIRE
ECSTASIED
ECSTASISE
ECTOBLAST
ECTOGENIC
ECTOMORPH
ECTOPHYTE
ECTOPLASM
ECTROPION
ECTROPIUM
ECUMENISM
EDELWEISS
EDEMATOSE
EDEMATOUS
EDIBILITY
EDICTALLY
EDIFICIAL
EDITORIAL
EDUCATION
EDUCATIVE
EDUCEMENT
EDWARDIAN
EEL-BASKET
EFFECTIVE
EFFECTUAL
EFFICIENT
EFFLUENCE
EFFLUVIAL
EFFLUVIUM
EFFLUXION
EFFULGENT
EFFULGING
EGG-BEATER
EGG-POWDER

EGLANTINE
EGOMANIAC
EGOTHEISM
EGOTISTIC
EGREGIOUS
EGRESSION
EIDERDOWN
EIDER-DUCK
EIDOGRAPH
EIGENTONE
EIGHT-FOIL
EIGHTFOLD
EIGHT-FOOT
EIGHT-HOUR
EIGHTIETH
EIGHTSMAN
EIGHTSOME
EIRENICON
EJACULATE
EJECTMENT
ELABORATE
ELAEAGNUS
ELAEOLITE
ELASTANCE
ELASTOMER
ELATERITE
ELATERIUM
ELBOW-ROOM
ELDERSHIP
ELECTORAL
ELECTRESS
ELECTRIFY
ELECTRISE
ELECTRODE
ELECTUARY
ELEGANTLY
ELEGIACAL
ELEMENTAL
ELEUTHERI
ELEVATION
ELEVATORY
ELEVENSES
ELIMINANT
ELIMINATE
ELLIPSOID
ELOCUTION
ELOHISTIC
ELOINMENT
ELONGATED
ELOPEMENT
ELOQUENCE
ELSEWHERE
ELUCIDATE
ELUSIVELY
ELUTRIATE
EMACIATED
EMANATION
EMANATIST
EMANATIVE
EMANATORY
EMBALLING
EMBALMING
EMBARGOED
EMBARGOES
EMBARKING
EMBARRASS

EMBARRING
EMBASSADE
EMBASSAGE
EMBATTLED
EMBAYMENT
EMBEDMENT
EMBELLISH
EMBER-DAYS
EMBER-WEEK
EMBEZZLER
EMBLEMATA
EMBLEMISE
EMBLOSSOM
EMBODYING
EMBOSCATA
EMBRACEOR
EMBRACERY
EMBRACING
EMBRACIVE
EMBRANGLE
EMBRASURE
EMBRAZURE
EMBREATHE
EMBROCATE
EMBROGLIO
EMBROIDER
EMBRYONAL
EMBRYONIC
EMBRYO-SAC
EMBRYOTIC
EMBUSSING
EMENDABLE
EMENDATOR
EMERGENCE
EMERGENCY
EMICATION
EMINENTLY
EMMENTHAL
EMMETROPE
EMOLLIATE
EMOLLIENT
EMOLUMENT
EMOTIONAL
EMPAESTIC
EMPANOPLY
EMPATHISE
EMPENNAGE
EMPHASISE
EMPHLYSIS
EMPHYSEMA
EMPIRICAL
EMPLASTER
EMPLASTIC
EMPLECTON
EMPLECTUM
EMPTINESS
EMPTIONAL
EMPYREUMA
EMULATION
EMULATIVE
EMULGENCE
EMULOUSLY
EMUNCTORY
ENACTMENT
ENAMELLED
ENAMELLER

ENAMORADO
ENAMOURED
ENCANTHIS
ENCAUSTIC
ENCHANTED
ENCHANTER
ENCHEASON
ENCHORIAL
ENCLOSURE
ENCOLPION
ENCOLPIUM
ENCOMIAST
ENCOMPASS
ENCOUNTER
ENCOURAGE
ENCRATISM
ENCRATITE
ENCRIMSON
ENCRINITE
ENCURTAIN
ENDEARING
ENDEAVOUR
ENDECAGON
ENDEICTIC
ENDEMICAL
ENDENIZEN
ENDLESSLY
ENDOBLAST
ENDOCRINE
ENDOGAMIC
ENDOGENIC
ENDOLYMPH
ENDOMIXIS
ENDOMORPH
ENDOPHAGY
ENDOPHYTE
ENDOPLASM
ENDOSCOPE
ENDOSCOPY
ENDOSMOSE
ENDOSPERM
ENDOSPORE
ENDOSTEAL
ENDOSTEUM
ENDOWMENT
END-READER
ENDUNGEON
ENDURABLE
ENDURABLY
ENDURANCE
ENERGETIC
ENERGUMEN
ENFREEDOM
ENGARLAND
ENGENDURE
ENGINE-MAN
ENGISCOPE
ENGLANDER
ENGLIFIED
ENGLISHER
ENGLISHRY
ENGOUMENT
ENGRAINED
ENGRAINER
ENGRAVERY
ENGRAVING

ENGROSSER
ENGYSCOPE
ENHANCIVE
ENHEARTEN
ENHYDRITE
ENHYDROUS
ENIGMATIC
ENJOYABLE
ENJOYABLY
ENJOYMENT
ENKINDLED
ENLIGHTEN
ENLIVENER
ENRANCKLE
ENRAPTURE
ENROLLING
ENROLMENT
ENSHEATHE
ENSHELTER
ENSORCELL
ENSTATITE
ENTELECHY
ENTERABLE
ENTERITIS
ENTERTAIN
ENTERTAKE
ENTHYMEME
ENTOBLAST
ENTOPHYTE
ENTOPTICS
ENTOURAGE
ENTRAMMEL
ENTRAPPER
ENTRECHAT
ENTRECÔTE
ENTREMETS
ENTROPION
ENTROPIUM
ENUCLEATE
ENUMERATE
ENUNCIATE
ENVELOPED
ENVERMEIL
ENVIOUSLY
ENVOYSHIP
ENWREATHE
ENZYMATIC
EPAENETIC
EPAINETIC
EPARCHATE
EPAULETTE
EPEDAPHIC
EPEIRIDAE
EPEOLATRY
EPHEDRINE
EPHEMERAL
EPHEMERID
EPHEMERIS
EPHEMERON
EPHIALTES
EPHORALTY
EPICEDIAL
EPICEDIAN
EPICEDIUM
EPICENTRE
EPICLESIS

EPICUREAN
EPICURISE
EPICURISM
EPICYCLIC
EPIDERMAL
EPIDERMIC
EPIDERMIS
EPIDOSITE
EPIGAEOUS
EPIGRAPHY
EPIGYNOUS
EPILATION
EPILEPTIC
EPILOBIUM
EPILOGISE
EPINASTIC
EPINICIAN
EPINICION
EPINIKIAN
EPINIKION
EPIPHRAGM
EPIPHYSES
EPIPHYSIS
EPIPHYTAL
EPIPHYTIC
EPIPOLISM
EPIRRHEMA
EPISCOPAL
EPISODIAL
EPISTAXIS
EPISTOLER
EPISTOLET
EPISTOLIC
EPITAPHER
EPITAPHIC
EPITHESIS
EPITHETIC
EPITHETON
EPITOMISE
EPITOMIST
EPIZEUXIS
EPIZOOTIC
EPONYMOUS
EPULATION
EPURATION
EQUALISER
EQUALLING
EQUALNESS
EQUIPMENT
EQUIPOISE
EQUIPPING
EQUISETIC
EQUISETUM
EQUITABLE
EQUITABLY
EQUIVALVE
EQUIVOCAL
EQUIVOQUE
ERADICATE
ERASEMENT
ERECTNESS
EREMITISM
ERETHITIC
ERGATANER
ERGOGRAPH
ERGOMETER

ERICACEAE
ERIOMETER
ERISTICAL
EROGENOUS
EROSTRATE
EROTICISM
ERRAND-BOY
ERRATICAL
ERRONEOUS
ERSTWHILE
ERUCIFORM
ERUDITELY
ERUDITION
ERVALENTA
ERYTHRINA
ERYTHRISM
ERYTHRITE
ESCALATOR
ESCAPABLE
ESCHEATOR
ESCLANDRE
ESCOPETTE
ESCORTAGE
ESEMPLASY
ESOPHAGUS
ESOTERISM
ESPERANCE
ESPERANTO
ESPIONAGE
ESPLANADE
ESQUIMAUX
ESSAYETTE
ESSENTIAL
ESTABLISH
ESTAFETTE
ESTAMINET
ESTATE-CAR
ESTHONIAN
ESTIMABLE
ESTIMABLY
ESTIMATOR
ESTOPPAGE
ESTOPPING
ESTRANGED
ESTRANGER
ESTRAPADE
ESTUARIAL
ESTUARIAN
ESTUARINE
ESURIENCE
ESURIENCY
ÉTAT-MAJOR
ETERNALLY
ETHEREOUS
ETHERICAL
ETHICALLY
ETHIOPIAN
ETHMOIDAL
ETHNARCHY
ETHNICISM
ETHNOLOGY
ETHOLOGIC
ETIQUETTE
ETYMOLOGY
EUCALYPTI
EUCHARIST

EUCHLORIC
EUCHOLOGY
EUCLIDEAN
EUDIALYTE
EUMELANIN
EUMENIDES
EUMYCETES
EUNUCHISM
EUNUCHOID
EUPHEMISE
EUPHEMISM
EUPHONISE
EUPHONIUM
EUPHORBIA
EURAQUILO
EURHYTHMY
EUSKARIAN
EUTAXITIC
EUTECTOID
EUTERPEAN
EUTHANASY
EUTHENICS
EUTROPHIC
EUTROPOUS
EUTYCHIAN
EVACUATOR
EVAGATION
EVAGINATE
EVANGELIC
EVANITION
EVAPORATE
EVASIVELY
EVENTUATE
EVERGLADE
EVERGREEN
EVERYBODY
EVERYWHEN
EVIDENTLY
EVINCIBLE
EVINCIBLY
EVITATION
EVITERNAL
EVOCATION
EVOCATIVE
EVOCATORY
EVOLUTION
EVOLUTIVE
EVOLVABLE
EWE-CHEESE
EWE-NECKED
EXACTMENT
EXACTNESS
EXACTRESS
EXAMINANT
EXAMINATE
EXAMINING
EXANIMATE
EXANTHEMA
EXARATION
EXARCHATE
EXARCHIST
EXCALIBUR
EXCAMBION
EXCAMBIUM
EXCAVATOR
EXCEEDING

EXCELLENT
EXCELLING
EXCELSIOR
EXCENTRIC
EXCEPTANT
EXCEPTING
EXCEPTION
EXCEPTIVE
EXCERPTOR
EXCESSIVE
EXCHANGER
EXCHEQUER
EXCIPIENT
EXCISABLE
EXCISEMAN
EXCITABLE
EXCITANCY
EXCLOSURE
EXCLUSION
EXCLUSIVE
EXCLUSORY
EXCORIATE
EXCREMENT
EXCRETION
EXCRETIVE
EXCRETORY
EXCULPATE
EXCURRENT
EXCURSION
EXCURSIVE
EXCUSABLE
EXCUSABLY
EXECRABLE
EXECRABLY
EXECUTANT
EXECUTION
EXECUTIVE
EXECUTORY
EXECUTRIX
EXEGETICS
EXEGETIST
EXEMPLARY
EXEMPLIFY
EXEMPTION
EXEQUATUR
EXFOLIATE
EXHALABLE
EXHAUSTED
EXHAUSTER
EXHIBITER
EXHIBITOR
EXILEMENT
EXISTENCE
EX-LIBRISM
EX-LIBRIST
EXODERMAL
EXODERMIS
EXOGAMOUS
EXOGENOUS
EXONERATE
EXOPODITE
EXORATION
EXORCISER
EXOSMOSIS
EXOSMOTIC
EXOSPHERE

EXOSPORAL
EXOSTOSIS
EXOTICISM
EXPANSILE
EXPANSION
EXPANSIVE
EXPATIATE
EXPECTANT
EXPECTING
EXPEDIENT
EXPELLANT
EXPELLENT
EXPELLING
EXPENSIVE
EXPERTISE
EXPIATION
EXPIATORY
EXPIRABLE
EXPISCATE
EXPLAINER
EXPLETIVE
EXPLETORY
EXPLICATE
EXPLOITER
EXPLORING
EXPLOSION
EXPLOSIVE
EXPONIBLE
EXPOSITOR
EXPOSTURE
EXPOUNDER
EXPRESSLY
EXPULSION
EXPULSIVE
EXPURGATE
EXQUISITE
EXSECTION
EXSERTILE
EXSERTION
EX-SERVICE
EXSICCANT
EXSICCATE
EXSUCCOUS
EXTEMPORE
EXTENDANT
EXTENSILE
EXTENSION
EXTENSITY
EXTENSIVE
EXTENUATE
EXTERMINE
EXTIRPATE
EXTOLLING
EXTOLMENT
EXTORSIVE
EXTORTION
EXTORTIVE
EXTRACTOR
EXTRADITE
EXTRAVERT
EXTREMELY
EXTREMEST
EXTREMISM
EXTREMIST
EXTREMITY
EXTRICATE

EXTRINSIC
EXTROVERT
EXTRUSION
EXTRUSIVE
EXTRUSORY
EXUBERANT
EXUBERATE
EXUDATION
EXULTANCE
EXULTANCY
EYE-BRIGHT
EYE-GLANCE
EYE-OPENER
EYESHADOW
EYE-SPLICE
EYE-STRING

F

FABACEOUS
FABIANISM
FABRICANT
FABRICATE
FACE-CLOTH
FACE-GUARD
FACETIOUS
FACSIMILE
FACTIONAL
FACTITIVE
FACTORAGE
FACTORIAL
FACTORISE
FACTOTUMS
FACUNDITY
FADDINESS
FAGACEOUS
FAGGOTING
FAGOTTIST
FAINEANCE
FAINEANCY
FAINTNESS
FAIR-FACED
FAIRYHOOD
FAIRYLAND
FAIRYLIKE
FAIRY-RING
FAIRY-TALE
FAITH-CURE
FAITHLESS
FALANGISM
FALCATION
FALCIFORM
FALCONINE
FALCULATE
FALDSTOOL
FALERNIAN
FALLALERY
FALLOPIAN
FALSE-CARD
FALSEHOOD
FALSENESS
FALSIFIED
FALSIFIER
FALTERING
FANATICAL
FANCILESS
FANCY-FREE

FANCY-SICK
FANCY-WORK
FANDANGLE
FANFARADE
FANFARONA
FAN-SHAPED
FANTASIED
FANTASISE
FANTASQUE
FANTASTIC
FANTASTRY
FARANDINE
FARANDOLE
FARDEL-BAG
FARMERESS
FARMHOUSE
FARMPLACE
FARMSTEAD
FAR-SEEING
FAR-SOUGHT
FASCIATED
FASCICLED
FASCICULE
FASCICULI
FASCINATE
FASHIONER
FASTEN-E'EN
FASTENING
FASTIGIUM
FATEFULLY
FAT-HEADED
FATIDICAL
FATIGABLE
FATIGUING
FATISCENT
FAT-TAILED
FATTENING
FATTINESS
FATUITOUS
FAT-WITTED
FAULCHION
FAULTLESS
FAUNISTIC
FAVEOLATE
FAVOURITE
FAWNINGLY
FEARFULLY
FEAST-RITE
FEATHERED
FEATURELY
FEBRICITY
FEBRICULA
FEBRICULE
FEBRIFUGE
FEBRILITY
FECULENCE
FECULENCY
FECUNDATE
FECUNDITY
FEDERARIE
FEED-WATER
FEE-FAW-FUM
FEELINGLY
FEIGNEDLY
FEISEANNA
FELDSPATH

FÉLIBRIGE
FELLOW-MAN
FELONIOUS
FEMINEITY
FENCELESS
FENESTRAL
FENIANISM
FEN-SUCKED
FENUGREEK
FEOFFMENT
FERACIOUS
FERALISED
FERINGHEE
FERMENTED
FERNTICLE
FEROCIOUS
FERRETING
FERROTYPE
FERRY-BOAT
FERTILELY
FERTILISE
FERTILITY
FERVENTLY
FERVIDITY
FERVOROUS
FESSE-WISE
FESTILOGY
FESTINATE
FESTIVELY
FESTIVITY
FESTIVOUS
FESTOLOGY
FETICHISM
FETICHIST
FETICIDAL
FETIDNESS
FETISHISM
FETISHIST
FETLOCKED
FEUDALISE
FEUDALISM
FEUDALIST
FEUDALITY
FEUDATORY
FEVER-HEAT
FIBONACCI
FIBRELESS
FIBRIFORM
FIBRILLAE
FIBRILLAR
FIBRINOUS
FIBROLINE
FIBROLITE
FIBROMATA
FICTIONAL
FIDDLE-BOW
FIDGETING
FIDUCIARY
FIELDFARE
FIELDSMAN
FIELDWARD
FIELDWORK
FIEND-LIKE
FIERINESS
FIFE-MAJOR
FIFTEENER

FIFTEENTH
FIG-PECKER
FIGURABLE
FIGURANTE
FILACEOUS
FILIATION
FILICALES
FILIGRAIN
FILIGRANE
FILIGREED
FILLETING
FILL-HORSE
FILLIPEEN
FILLIPING
FILLISTER
FILMINESS
FILOPLUME
FILOSELLE
FILTER-BED
FILTER-TIP
FILTRABLE
FIMBRIATE
FINANCIAL
FINANCIER
FIND-FAULT
FINE-DRAWN
FINESSING
FIN-FOOTED
FINGER-END
FINGERING
FINGERTIP
FINICALLY
FINICKING
FINING-POT
FINISHING
FINLANDER
FIORITURA
FIORITURE
FIRE-ALARM
FIRE-ARROW
FIRE-BLAST
FIREBRAND
FIRE-BREAK
FIRE-BRICK
FIRECREST
FIRE-DRAKE
FIRE-DRILL
FIRE-EATER
FIREFLOAT
FIRE-GRATE
FIREGUARD
FIRE-HOUSE
FIRE-IRONS
FIRELIGHT
FIREPLACE
FIRE-POWER
FIREPROOF
FIRE-ROBED
FIRE-STICK
FIRESTONE
FIRE-WATER
FIRMAMENT
FIRST-BORN
FIRST-FOOT
FIRST-HAND
FIRSTLING

FIRST-RATE
FIRST-TIME
FISH-CREEL
FISHERMAN
FISH-GARTH
FISH-GUANO
FISHINESS
FISH-JOINT
FISH-LOUSE
FISH-PLATE
FISH-SAUCE
FISH-SCRAP
FISH-SLICE
FISH-SPEAR
FISHWOMAN
FISHYBACK
FISSILITY
FISSIPEDE
FISTICUFF
FISTULOSE
FISTULOUS
FITTINGLY
FIVE-A-SIDE
FIVEPENCE
FIVEPENNY
FIXEDNESS
FLABELLUM
FLACCIDLY
FLAGELLUM
FLAGEOLET
FLAGITATE
FLAGRANCE
FLAGRANCY
FLAGSTAFF
FLAGSTICK
FLAGSTONE
FLAKINESS
FLAMBEAUX
FLAME-LEAF
FLAMELESS
FLAMINGLY
FLAMINGOS
FLAMMABLE
FLANNELLY
FLAP-EARED
FLARE-PATH
FLARINGLY
FLASH-BACK
FLASH-BULB
FLATLINGS
FLATTERER
FLATULENT
FLAUGHTER
FLAUNTING
FLAVOROUS
FLAX-WENCH
FLAY-FLINT
FLECKLESS
FLEDGLING
FLEECHING
FLEET-FOOT
FLEETNESS
FLESHHOOD
FLESH-HOOK
FLESHINGS
FLESHLESS

FLESHLING
FLESH-MEAT
FLESHMENT
FLESH-TINT
FLESH-WORM
FLIGHTILY
FLINTLOCK
FLIPPANCY
FLIRT-GILL
FLOATABLE
FLOCCULAR
FLOCCULUS
FLOODGATE
FLOODMARK
FLOODTIDE
FLOOR-HEAD
FLOPHOUSE
FLOREATED
FLORIATED
FLORIDEAE
FLORIDEAN
FLORIDITY
FLORIFORM
FLORISTIC
FLORISTRY
FLOSCULAR
FLOTATION
FLOUNCING
FLOURISHY
FLOWERAGE
FLOWER-BED
FLOWER-BUD
FLOWERING
FLOWERPOT
FLOWINGLY
FLOWMETER
FLUCTUANT
FLUCTUATE
FLUGELMAN
FLUIDNESS
FLUKEWORM
FLUORESCE
FLUOROSIS
FLUORSPAR
FLURRYING
FLUSHNESS
FLUSTRATE
FLUTE-À-BEC
FLUTE-BIRD
FLUVIATIC
FLUXIONAL
FLY-BITTEN
FLY-FISHER
FLY-WEIGHT
FOAMINGLY
FOCIMETER
FODDERING
FOEDERATI
FOETICIDE
FOGGINESS
FOGRAMITE
FOGRAMITY
FOG-SIGNAL
FOININGLY
FOLIATION
FOLIATURE

FOLIOLATE
FOLIOLOSE
FOLKCRAFT
FOLK-DANCE
FOLKETING
FOLK-MUSIC
FOLK-RIGHT
FOLK-WEAVE
FOLLOWING
FOMALHAUT
FONT-STONE
FOODSTUFF
FOOL-HAPPY
FOOLHARDY
FOOLISHLY
FOOLPROOF
FOOT-BOARD
FOOT-CLOTH
FOOTFAULT
FOOTLIGHT
FOOT-LOOSE
FOOTPLATE
FOOT-POUND
FOOTPRINT
FOOT-STALK
FOOT-STALL*
FOOTSTOOL
FOPPISHLY
FORAGE-CAP
FORASMUCH
FORBIDDAL
FORBIDDEN
FORCE-LAND
FORCELESS
FORCEMEAT
FORCEPSES
FORCE-PUMP
FOREANENT
FOREBODER
FOREBRACE
FOREBRAIN
FORECABIN
FORECADDY
FORE-CITED
FORECLOSE
FORECOURT
FOREFRONT
FOREGLEAM
FOREGOING
FORE-HORSE
FOREIGNER
FOREJUDGE
FOREKNOWN
FORENAMED
FORENIGHT
FOREPOINT
FOREREACH
FORESHEWN
FORESHORE
FORESHOWN
FORESIGHT
FORESKIRT
FORESLACK
FORESPEAK
FORESPEND
FORESTAGE

FORESTAIR
FORESTALL
FOREST-FLY
FORESTINE
FOREST-OAK
FORETASTE
FORETEACH
FORETEETH
FORETHINK
FORETOKEN
FORETOOTH
FOREWEIGH
FOREWHEEL
FOREWOMAN
FOREWOMEN
FORFEITER
FORFICULA
FORGATHER
FORGETFUL
FORGETIVE
FORGETTER
FORGIVING
FORGOTTEN
FORJASKIT
FORJESKIT
FORK-CHUCK
FORKINESS
FORKY-TAIL
FORLORNLY
FORMALISE
FORMALISM
FORMALIST
FORMALITY
FORMATION
FORMATIVE
FORMICANT
FORMICARY
FORMICATE
FORMULARY
FORMULATE
FORMULISE
FORNICATE
FORSAKING
FORSYTHIA
FORTALICE
FORTHCOME
FORTHWITH
FORTIFIED
FORTIFIER
FORTILAGE
FORTITUDE
FORTNIGHT
FORTUNATE
FORTUNIZE
FORTY-FIVE
FORWANDER
FORWARDER
FORWARDLY
FOSSICKER
FOSSILISE
FOSSORIAL
FOSSULATE
FOSTERAGE
FOSTER-SON
FOUL-BROOD
FOUNDLING

FOUNDRESS
FOUR-BY-TWO
FOURCROYA
FOUR-FLUSH
FOUR-HORSE
FOUR-HOURS
FOURPENCE
FOURPENNY
FOURSCORE
FOUR-WHEEL
FOX-HUNTER
FRACTIOUS
FRAGILITY
FRAGRANCE
FRAGRANCY
FRAILNESS
FRAMEWORK
FRANCHISE
FRANCOLIN
FRANGIBLE
FRANGLAIS
FRANKENIA
FRANKNESS
FRATCHETY
FRATCHING
FRATERNAL
FRAUDSTER
FRECKLING
FREE-AGENT
FREE-BENCH
FREE-BOARD
FREEBOOTY
FREE-DIVER
FREE-LANCE
FREE-LIVER
FREEMASON
FREE-RANGE
FREE-RIDER
FREESTONE
FREE-TRADE
FREE-WHEEL
FREEWOMAN
FREEWOMEN
FREEZABLE
FREIGHTER
FRENCHIFY
FRENZICAL
FREQUENCE
FREQUENCY
FRESCOING
FRESCOIST
FRESHNESS
FRETFULLY
FRIARBIRD
FRIBBLING
FRIBBLISH
FRICASSEE
FRICATIVE
FRIEDCAKE
FRIENDING
FRIGATOON
FRIGHTFUL
FRIGIDITY
FRIPPERER
FRITHBORH
FRITHGILD

FRITTERER
FRIVOLITY
FRIVOLOUS
FROCK-COAT
FROCKLESS
FROG-EATER
FROGMARCH
FROGMOUTH
FROLICKED
FRONTLESS
FRONT-PAGE
FRONT-RANK
FRONTWARD
FRONTWAYS
FRONTWISE
FROSTBITE
FROSTLESS
FROST-NAIL
FROSTWORK
FROTH-FOMY
FROTHLESS
FROWARDLY
FRUCTIDOR
FRUCTUARY
FRUCTUATE
FRUCTUOUS
FRUGALIST
FRUGALITY
FRUIT-CAKE
FRUITERER
FRUITLESS
FRUIT-TREE
FRUSTRATE
FRUTICOSE
FRYING-PAN
FUDDLE-CAP
FUGACIOUS
FULFILLED
FULFILLER
FULGENTLY
FULGOROUS
FULGURANT
FULGURATE
FULGURITE
FULGUROUS
FULL-BLOOD
FULL-BLOWN
FULL-BOUND
FULL-DRESS
FULL-FACED
FULL-GROWN
FULL-ORBED
FULL-SCALE
FULL-SPEED
FULL-SPLIT
FULL-TIMER
FULMINANT
FULMINATE
FULMINOUS
FULSOMELY
FUMIGATOR
FUNDAMENT
FUNEBRIAL
FUNGIBLES
FUNGICIDE
FUNGIFORM

FUNGOIDAL
FUNGOSITY
FUNICULAR
FUNICULUS
FUNKINESS
FUNNELLED
FUNNEL-NET
FUNNINESS
FURACIOUS
FURBISHER
FURCATION
FURFUROUS
FURIOSITY
FURIOUSLY
FURNISHED
FURNISHER
FURNITURE
FURTHERER
FURTIVELY
FUSILLADE
FUSIONISM
FUSIONIST
FUSSINESS
FUSTIGATE
FUSTILUGS
FUSTINESS
FUZZINESS

G

GABARDINE
GABERDINE
GABIONADE
GABIONAGE
GADROONED
GAELICISE
GAELICISM
GAELTACHT
GAINFULLY
GAINSAYER
GALACTOSE
GALA-DRESS
GALANTINE
GALDRAGON
GALENGALE
GALENICAL
GALINGALE
GALIONGEE
GALLANTLY
GALLANTRY
GALLERIED
GALLICISE
GALLICISM
GALLICROW
GALLINAZO
GALLINGLY
GALLINULE
GALLISISE
GALLIVANT
GALLIWASP
GALL-MIDGE
GALLOONED
GALLOPADE
GALLOPHIL
GALLOPING
GALLOWSES
GALL-STONE

GALLY-CROW	GAUCHERIE	GEOSPHERE	GLARINGLY
GALRAVAGE	GAUDEAMUS	GEOSTATIC	GLASS-CRAB
GALVANISE	GAUDINESS	GEOTACTIC	GLASS-GALL
GALVANISM	GAUGEABLE	GEOTROPIC	GLASS-LIKE
GALVANIST	GAULEITER	GERFALCON	GLASS-ROPE
GALWEGIAN	GAUNTNESS	GERIATRIC	GLASS-SOAP
GAMA-GRASS	GAUZE-TREE	GERMANDER	GLASSWARE
GAMBOGIAN	GAUZINESS	GERMANISE	GLASSWORK
GAMBOLLED	GAVELKIND	GERMANISH	GLASSWORT
GAMINERIE	GAWKIHOOD	GERMANISM	GLENGARRY
GAMMADION	GAWKINESS	GERMANIST	GLENLIVET
GAMMATION	GAZE-HOUND	GERMANIUM	GLENOIDAL
GAMMONING	GAZETTEER	GERMICIDE	GLIDINGLY
GANDERISM	GAZETTING	GERMINANT	GLISSANDO
GANGBOARD	GEAR-LEVER	GERMINATE	GLOBE-FISH
GANGLIATE	GEAR-RATIO	GERM-LAYER	GLOBOSITY
GANGLIONS	GEAR-SHIFT	GERM-PLASM	GLOBULITE
GANGPLANK	GEAR-STICK	GERUNDIAL	GLOBULOUS
GANNISTER	GEAR-WHEEL	GERUNDIVE	GLOMERATE
GAOL-FEVER	GEE-STRING	GESTATION	GLOMERULE
GARDENING	GELIDNESS	GESTATORY	GLORIFIED
GARDEROBE	GELIGNITE	GET-AT-ABLE	GLORY-HOLE
GARGARISE	GELSEMINE	GETTERING	GLOSSATOR
GARGARISM	GELSEMIUM	GEYSERITE	GLOSSITIS
GARIBALDI	GEMEL-RING	GHASTNESS	GLOWINGLY
GARLANDRY	GEMMATION	GHIBELINE	GLUCINIUM
GARMENTED	GEMMATIVE	GHOST-LIKE	GLUCOSIDE
GARNISHEE	GEMMOLOGY	GHOST-MOTH	GLUEYNESS
GARNISHER	GENEALOGY	GHOST-WORD	GLUTAMATE
GARNISHRY	GENERABLE	GIANTHOOD	GLUTINOUS
GARNITURE	GENERALIA	GIANT-RUDE	GLYCERIDE
GAROTTING	GENERALLY	GIANTSHIP	GLYCERINE
GARRETEER	GENERATOR	GIBBERISH	GLYCOCOLL
GARROTTED	GENERICAL	GIBBOSITY	GLYPTODON
GARROTTER	GENESITIC	GIBBOUSLY	GMELINITE
GARRULITY	GENETICAL	GIBEONITE	GNATHONIC
GARRULOUS	GENIALISE	GIDDINESS	GNEISSOID
GAS-BOTTLE	GENIALITY	GIER-EAGLE	GNEISSOSE
GAS-BURNER	GENITALIA	GIGANTEAN	GNETACEAE
GAS-CARBON	GENITIVAL	GIGANTISM	GNOMONICS
GASCONADE	GENOCIDAL	GIGMANITY	GOAT'S-HAIR
GASCONISM	GENOTYPIC	GILLFLIRT	GO-BETWEEN
GAS-COOKER	GENTEELLY	GILL-HOUSE	GOD-A-MERCY
GAS-ENGINE	GENTILISE	GILRAVAGE	GODDAMNED
GAS-ESCAPE	GENTILISH	GILT-EDGED	GODFATHER
GAS-FILLED	GENTILISM	GIMMALLED	GOD-GIFTED
GAS-FITTER	GENTILITY	GIMMICKRY	GODLESSLY
GAS-HEATER	GENTLEMAN	GINGERADE	GODLINESS
GAS-HELMET	GENTLEMEN	GINGEROUS	GODMOTHER
GAS-HOLDER	GENUFLECT	GINGLYMUS	GODPARENT
GAS-LIQUOR	GENUINELY	GIN-PALACE	GOFFERING
GAS-MANTLE	GEOCARPIC	GIRAFFINE	GOGGLE-BOX
GASOMETER	GEODESIST	GIRANDOLE	GOING-AWAY
GASOMETRY	GEOGNOSIS	GIRLISHLY	GOINGS-OUT
GASPEREAU	GEOGRAPHY	GIRONDIST	GOLD-BRICK
GASPINESS	GEOLOGISE	GIRTHLINE	GOLD-CLOTH
GASPINGLY	GEOLOGIST	GIVENNESS	GOLDCREST
GAS-RETORT	GEOMANCER	GLABELLAR	GOLDEN-EYE
GASTRAEUM	GEOMANTIC	GLADIATOR	GOLDEN-ROD
GASTRITIS	GEOMETRIC	GLADIOLUS	GOLD-FEVER
GASTROPOD	GEOMETRID	GLADSTONE	GOLDFIELD
GATECRASH	GEOMYIDAE	GLAIREOUS	GOLDFINCH
GATE-HOUSE	GEOPHILIC	GLAMORISE	GOLDFINNY
GATE-MONEY	GEOPHYTIC	GLAMOROUS	GOLD-LACED
GATE-TOWER	GEOPONICS	GLANDERED	GOLDMINER
GATHERING	GEORGETTE	GLANDULAR	GOLD-PLATE

GOLD-SINNY
GOLDSMITH
GOLDSPINK
GOLDSTICK
GOLF-LINKS
GOLIARDIC
GOLOMYNKA
GOMPHOSIS
GONDOLIER
GONGORISM
GONG-STICK
GONIATITE
GONOPHORE
GOOD-CHEAP
GOOD-FACED
GOODINESS
GOODLIEST
GOOD-NIGHT
GOOD-SPEED
GOODYEARS
GOOSANDER
GOOSE-CLUB
GOOSE-FISH
GOOSEFOOT
GOOSE-GIRL
GOOSE-HERD
GOOSE-NECK
GOOSE-STEP
GOOSE-WING
GORE-BLOOD
GORGONIAN
GORGONISE
GORILLINE
GOSLARITE
GOSPELISE
GOSPELLER
GOSSAMERY
GOSSIPING
GOSSYPINE
GOSSYPIUM
GOTHAMIST
GOTHAMITE
GOTHICISE
GOTHICISM
GOURD-WORM
GOUSTROUS
GOUTINESS
GOVERNALL
GOVERNESS
GOVERNING
GOWDSPINK
GOWPENFUL
GRACELESS
GRACILITY
GRADATION
GRADGRIND
GRADUALLY
GRADUATED
GRADUATOR
GRAMINEAE
GRAMMATIC
GRANDAUNT
GRANDIOSE
GRANDNESS
GRANDPAPA
GRANDSIRE

GRANITISE
GRANITITE
GRANITOID
GRANTABLE
GRANULARY
GRANULATE
GRANULITE
GRANULOSE
GRANULOUS
GRAPELESS
GRAPESEED
GRAPESHOT
GRAPETREE
GRAPEVINE
GRAPHEMIC
GRAPHICAL
GRAPHITIC
GRASPABLE
GRASPLESS
GRASSLAND
GRASS-MOTH
GRASS-PLOT
GRASS-TREE
GRATICULE
GRATIFIED
GRATIFIER
GRATINGLY
GRATITUDE
GRATULANT
GRATULATE
GRAVELESS
GRAVELLED
GRAVEL-PIT
GRAVENESS
GRAVEYARD
GRAVIDITY
GRAVITATE
GRAVY-BOAT
GRAYWACKE
GREASE-GUN
GREAT-AUNT
GREATCOAT
GREEKLESS
GREEKLING
GREENBACK
GREEN-BONE
GREEN-EYED
GREENGAGE
GREENHAND
GREENHORN
GREENNESS
GREENROOM
GREEN-SAND
GREENWEED
GREENWICH
GREENWOOD
GREGARIAN
GREGARINA
GREGARINE
GREGORIAN
GRENADIER
GRENADINE
GREWHOUND
GREYBEARD
GREY-GOOSE
GREYHOUND .

GREYWACKE
GRIEFLESS
GRIEF-SHOT
GRIEVANCE
GRILL-ROOM
GRIMALKIN
GRIMINESS
GRIPINGLY
GRISAILLE
GRIS-AMBER
GRIST-MILL
GRITSTONE
GROOMSMAN
GROPINGLY
GROSGRAIN
GROSSNESS
GROSSULAR
GROTESQUE
GROUCHILY
GROUNDAGE
GROUND-ASH
GROUND-HOG
GROUNDING
GROUND-IVY
GROUNDMAN
GROUND-NUT
GROUND-OAK
GROUNDSEL
GROVELLED
GROVELLER
GRUB-STAKE
GRUDGEFUL
GRUELLING
GRUFFNESS
GRUMBLING
GRUNDYISM
GRUPPETTO
GUANAZOLO
GUARANIES
GUARANTEE
GUARANTOR
GUARDABLE
GUARD-BOOK
GUARD-CELL
GUARDEDLY
GUARDLESS
GUARD-RING
GUARD-ROOM
GUARD-SHIP
GUARDSMAN
GUERRILLA
GUESSABLE
GUESSWORK
GUEST-ROOM
GUESTWISE
GUIDE-BOOK
GUIDELESS
GUIDELINE
GUIDE-POST
GUIDE-RAIL
GUIDE-ROPE
GUIDESHIP
GUILDHALL
GUILELESS
GUILLEMOT
GUILLOCHE

GUILTLESS
GUINEA-HEN
GUINEA-PIG
GUITARIST
GUJERATHI
GULLY-HOLE
GUMMATOUS
GUMMINESS
GUMMOSITY
GUMPTIOUS
GUNCOTTON
GUNPOWDER
GUNRUNNER
GUSHINGLY
GUSTATION
GUSTATIVE
GUSTATORY
GUSTINESS
GUTSINESS
GUTTATION
GUTTER-MAN
GYMNASIAL
GYMNASIEN
GYMNASIUM
GYMNASTIC
GYMNOSOPH
GYNAECEUM
GYNOECIUM
GYNOPHORE
GYPSYWORT
GYRFALCON
GYROMANCY
GYROPLANE
GYROSCOPE
GYROVAGUE

H

HAANEPOOT
HABERDINE
HABERGEON
HABILABLE
HABITABLE
HABITABLY
HABITUATE
HACKAMORE
HACKBERRY
HACKNEYED
HACQUETON
HAECCEITY
HAEMATITE
HAEMATOID
HAEMATOMA
HAEMOSTAT
HAGGADIST
HAGGARDLY
HAGGISHLY
HAGIARCHY
HAGIOLOGY
HAG-RIDDEN
HAILSTONE
HAILSTORM
HAIR-BRUSH
HAIR-CLOTH
HAIR-GRASS
HAIRINESS
HAIR-PIECE

HAIR-SHIRT	HANDSPIKE	HAVERSACK	HEDGE-BORN
HAIR-SPACE	HANDSTAFF	HAVERSINE	HEDGE-BOTE
HAIRST-RIG	HANDSTAND	HAVOCKING	HEDYPHANE
HAIR-WAVER	HANDSTURN	HAWK-NOSED	HEEDFULLY
HALF-BAKED	HANDYWORK	HAWKSBILL	HEEDINESS
HALF-BLOOD	HANKERING	HAWSEHOLE	HEEL-PIECE
HALF-BOARD	HANSEATIC	HAWSEPIPE	HEGEMONIC
HALF-BOUND	HANSELLED	HAYMAKING	HEINOUSLY
HALF-BREED	HANSOM-CAB	HAZARDIZE	HEIR-AT-LAW
HALF-CASTE	HAPHAZARD	HAZARDOUS	HELICALLY
HALF-CHEEK	HAPLESSLY	HEAD-CHAIR	HELICIDAE
HALF-CLOSE	HAPLOLOGY	HEAD-CLOTH	HELIDROME
HALF-CROWN	HAPPENING	HEAD-DRESS	HELIOLOGY
HALF-DOZEN	HAPPINESS	HEADFRAME	HELIOSTAT
HALF-FACED	HARANGUED	HEADINESS	HELIOTYPE
HALF-HARDY	HARANGUER	HEADLIGHT	HELIOZOAN
HALF-HITCH	HARASSING	HEADLINER	HELIOZOIC
HALF-LIGHT	HARBINGER	HEADPHONE	HELIPILOT
HALF-PENCE	HARBOURER	HEAD-PIECE	HELISCOOP
HALF-PENNY	HARDBOARD	HEADREACH	HELL-BLACK
HALF-PLATE	HARD-CURED	HEADSHAKE	HELL-BROTH
HALF-POUND	HARD-DRAWN	HEADSTALL	HELLEBORE
HALF-PRICE	HARDGRASS	HEADSTICK	HELLENISE
HALF-ROUND	HARDIHEAD	HEADSTOCK	HELLENIST
HALF-ROYAL	HARDIHOOD	HEADSTONE	HELL-HATED
HALF-SHELL	HARDIMENT	HEADWATER	HELL-HOUND
HALF-SHIFT	HARDINESS	HEALINGLY	HELLISHLY
HALF-SWORD	HARD-LINER	HEALTHFUL	HELLWARDS
HALF-TIMER	HARD-METAL	HEALTHILY	HELVETIAN
HALF-TITLE	HARD-PASTE	HEAPSTEAD	HELVETIUM
HALF-TRACK	HARD-RULED	HEARKENER	HEMIHEDRY
HALF-TRUTH	HARDSHELL	HEARTACHE	HEMIOPSIA
HALIEUTIC	HARE'S-FOOT	HEART-BEAT	HEMIPTERA
HALITOSIS	HARE-STANE	HEART-BOND	HEMISTICH
HALLOWE'EN	HARIGALDS	HEARTBURN	HEMITROPE
HALLOWMAS	HARIOLATE	HEART-DEAR	HEM-STITCH
HALLSTAND	HARLEQUIN	HEART-FREE	HENDIADYS
HALLSTATT	HARMALINE	HEARTH-RUG	HEN-DRIVER
HALOPHILE	HARMATTAN	HEARTH-TAX	HEN-PADDLE
HALOPHILY	HARM-DOING	HEARTIKIN	HEN-PAIDLE
HALOPHYTE	HARMFULLY	HEARTLAND	HEN-WITTED
HALORAGIS	HARMONICA	HEARTLESS	HEPATICAE
HALOTHANE	HARMONISE	HEARTLING	HEPATICAL
HALTINGLY	HARMONIST	HEARTSEED	HEPATITIS
HAMADRYAD	HARMONITE	HEART-SICK	HEPTAGLOT
HAMAMELIS	HARMONIUM	HEARTSOME	HEPTAPODY
HAMBURGER	HARMOTOME	HEART-SORE	HEPTARCHY
HAMFATTER	HARPOONER	HEARTWOOD	HERACEOUS
HAM-FISTED	HARP-SHELL	HEATH-BIRD	HERACLEAN
HAM-HANDED	HARQUEBUS	HEATH-COCK	HERBALIST
HAMMERING	HARROVIAN	HEATHENRY	HERBARIAN
HAMMERKOP	HARROWING	HEATH-FOWL	HERBARIUM
HAMMERMAN	HARSHNESS	HEAVINESS	HERB-GRACE
HAMMER-TOE	HARTSHORN	HEAVISIDE	HERBICIDE
HAMSTRING	HARUSPICY	HEBRAICAL	HERBIVORA
HAMSTRUNG	HARVESTER	HEBRAISER	HERBIVORE
HANDCRAFT	HASTINESS	HEBREWESS	HERBORIST
HAND-GLASS	HATCHMENT	HEBREWISM	HERB-PARIS
HANDINESS	HATEFULLY	HEBRIDEAN	HERB-PETER
HANDIWORK	HAUGHTILY	HEBRIDIAN	HERCOGAMY
HANDLEBAR	HAUSE-BANE	HECOGENIN	HERCULEAN
HAND-ORGAN	HAUSE-LOCK	HECTOGRAM	HERCYNIAN
HAND-PAPER	HAUSTELLA	HECTORISM	HERCYNITE
HAND-PRESS	HAUSTORIA	HEDDLE-EYE	HERDGROOM
HAND-SCREW	HAVE-AT-HIM	HEDERATED	HEREABOUT
HANDSHAKE	HAVERINGS	HEDGEBILL	HEREAFTER

HERETICAL
HEREUNDER
HERITABLE
HERITABLY
HERITRESS
HERKOGAMY
HERMANDAD
HERMETICS
HERMITAGE
HERMITESS
HERNIATED
HERONSHAW
HERPESTES
HERPETOID
HERRIMENT
HERRINGER
HERRYMENT
HERSEEMED
HESITANCY
HESITATOR
HESPERIAN
HESSONITE
HESTERNAL
HESYCHASM
HESYCHAST
HETAIRISM
HETAIRIST
HETERODOX
HETERONYM
HETEROPOD
HETEROSIS
HETMANATE
HEURISTIC
HEXACHORD
HEXAGONAL
HEXAGYNIA
HEXAMETER
HEXANDRIA
HEXAPLOID
HEXASTICH
HEXASTYLE
HEXATEUCH
HEY-PRESTO
HIBERNATE
HIBERNIAN
HIBERNISE
HICCUPING
HIDDENITE
HIDEBOUND
HIDEOSITY
HIDEOUSLY
HIERACIUM
HIERARCHY
HIERATICA
HIEROCRAT
HIERODULE
HIEROGRAM
HIEROLOGY
HIGH-BLEST
HIGH-BLOWN
HIGH-CHAIR
HIGH-CLASS
HIGH-DRIED
HIGH-FLIER
HIGH-FLOWN
HIGH-FLYER

HIGH-GRADE
HIGH-GROWN
HIGHLANDS
HIGH-LEVEL
HIGHLIGHT
HIGH-PLACE
HIGH-PROOF
HIGH-SPEED
HIGH-TAPER
HIGH-TONED
HIGH-VICED
HILARIOUS
HILL-BILLY
HILLINESS
HIMALAYAN
HIMSEEMED
HIMYARITE
HINDBERRY
HIND-BRAIN
HINDER-END
HINDRANCE
HINDSIGHT
HIND-WHEEL
HINTINGLY
HIP-GIRDLE
HIPPARION
HIPPIATRY
HIP-POCKET
HIPPOCRAS
HIPPODAME
HIPPURITE
HIRCOSITY
HIRUDINEA
HIRUNDINE
HISPIDITY
HISSINGLY
HISTAMINE
HISTIDINE
HISTOGENY
HISTOGRAM
HISTOLOGY
HISTORIAN
HISTORIFY
HIT-AND-RUN
HITCH-HIKE
HITLERISM
HITLERIST
HITLERITE
HIT-OR-MISS
HIT-PARADE
HIVE-HONEY
HIVEWARDS
HOAR-FROST
HOARHOUND
HOARINESS
HOAR-STONE
HOB-AND-NOB
HOBBESIAN
HOBBINOLL
HOBBYLESS
HOBGOBLIN
HOBJOBBER
HOBNAILED
HOCUSSING
HODIERNAL
HODMANDOD

HODOGRAPH
HODOMETER
HOGGISHLY
HOG-RINGER
HOLARCTIC
HOLDERBAT
HOLING-AXE
HOLLANDER
HOLLY-FERN
HOLLYHOCK
HOLLYWOOD
HOLOCAUST
HOLOGRAPH
HOLOPHOTE
HOLSTERED
HOLY-CRUEL
HOLYSTONE
HOMEBOUND
HOME-COMER
HOMECRAFT
HOME-CROFT
HOME-GROWN
HOME-GUARD
HOMEOMERY
HOMEOPATH
HOMERIDAE
HOME-RULER
HOMESTALL
HOMESTEAD
HOME-TRUTH
HOMEWARDS
HOMICIDAL
HOMILETIC
HOMINIDAE
HOMOEOSIS
HOMOGAMIC
HOMOGENCY
HOMOGRAFT
HOMOGRAPH
HOMOLOGUE
HOMOMORPH
HOMONYMIC
HOMOPHONE
HOMOPHONY
HOMOPLASY
HOMOPTERA
HOMOTAXIC
HOMOTAXIS
HOMOTONIC
HOMOTYPAL
HOMOTYPIC
HOMOUSIAN
HOMUNCULE
HONE-STONE
HONEY-BEAR
HONEY-BIRD
HONEY-BLOB
HONEY-CART
HONEYCOMB
HONEYLESS
HONEYMOON
HONKY-TONK
HONORIFIC
HOOD-MOULD
HOOF-BOUND
HOOFPRINT

HOOK-NOSED
HOOPED-POT
HOOP-SNAKE
HOOTNANNY
HOPE-CHEST
HOPEFULLY
HOP-GARDEN
HOPLOLOGY
HOP-PICKER
HOP-POCKET
HOPSCOTCH
HORDEOLUM
HOREHOUND
HORNINESS
HORN-MAKER
HORNSTONE
HORNWRACK
HORNYHEAD
HOROLOGER
HOROLOGIC
HOROMETRY
HOROSCOPE
HOROSCOPY
HORRIFIED
HORSEBACK
HORSE-FOOT
HORSEHAIR
HORSEHIDE
HORSELESS
HORSEMEAT
HORSE-MINT
HORSEPLAY
HORSE-POND
HORSESHOE
HORSETAIL
HORSEWHIP
HORSINESS
HORTATION
HORTATIVE
HORTATORY
HOSPITAGE
HOSPITALE
HOSPITIUM
HOSTELLER
HOSTILELY
HOSTILITY
HOSTLESSE
HOT-AND-HOT
HOTHEADED
HOTTENTOT
HOUND-FISH
HOUR-ANGLE
HOUR-GLASS
HOUR-PLATE
HOUSEBOAT
HOUSE-BOTE
HOUSE-CARL
HOUSECOAT
HOUSE-DUTY
HOUSE-FLAG
HOUSEFULS
HOUSEHOLD
HOUSE-LEEK
HOUSELESS
HOUSE-LINE
HOUSELLED

HOUSEMAID
HOUSE-MATE
HOUSE-ROOM
HOUSEWIFE
HOUSEWORK
HOUYHNHNM
HOVEL-POST
HOWSOEVER
HOYDENISH
HOYDENISM
HUBRISTIC
HUCKABACK
HUCKSTERY
HUFFINESS
HUFFISHLY
HUGEOUSLY
HUMANKIND
HUMANLIKE
HUMANNESS
HUMBLE-BEE
HUMBLE-PIE
HUMBLESSE
HUMBUGGED
HUMBUGGER
HUMDINGER
HUMECTANT
HUMECTATE
HUMECTIVE
HUMIDNESS
HUMILIANT
HUMILIATE
HUMMELLER
HUMMOCKED
HUNCHBACK
HUNDREDER
HUNDREDOR
HUNDREDTH
HUNGARIAN
HUNGERFUL
HUNKY-DORY
HUNTERIAN
HURRICANE
HURRICANO
HURRIEDLY
HURTFULLY
HUSBANDLY
HUSBANDRY
HUSKINESS
HUT-CIRCLE
HUTTONIAN
HYAENIDAE
HYALONEMA
HYBRIDISE
HYBRIDISM
HYBRIDITY
HYBRIDOUS
HYDATHODE
HYDRAEMIA
HYDRANGEA
HYDRATION
HYDRAULIC
HYDRAZINE
HYDRIODIC
HYDROCELE
HYDROFOIL
HYDROLOGY

HYDROLYSE
HYDROLYTE
HYDROPTIC
HYDROPULT
HYDROSOMA
HYDROSOME
HYDROSTAT
HYDROVANE
HYDROXIDE
HYDROZOAN
HYDROZOON
HYETOLOGY
HYGIENICS
HYGIENIST
HYGRODEIK
HYGROPHIL
HYGROSTAT
HYLOBATES
HYLOPHYTE
HYLOZOISM
HYLOZOIST
HYMNOLOGY
HYPALLAGE
HYPERBOLA
HYPERBOLE
HYPERGAMY
HYPERICUM
HYPEROPIA
HYPHENATE
HYPHENISE
HYPHENISM
HYPINOSIS
HYPNOGENY
HYPNOIDAL
HYPNOLOGY
HYPNOTISE
HYPNOTISM
HYPNOTIST
HYPNOTOID
HYPOBLAST
HYPOCAUST
HYPOCOTYL
HYPOCRISY
HYPOCRITE
HYPODERMA
HYPOGAEAL
HYPOGAEAN
HYPOGAEUM
HYPOGEOUS
HYPOMANIA
HYPOMANIC
HYPONASTY
HYPOSTYLE
HYPOTAXIS
HYSON-SKIN
HYSTERICS
HYSTEROID

I

IATROGENY
ICE-ACTION
ICE-ANCHOR
ICE-BUCKET
ICE-HOCKEY
ICELANDER
ICELANDIC

ICHNEUMON
ICHNOLOGY
ICHTHYOID
ICONOLOGY
ICTERICAL
ICTERIDAE
IDEALISER
IDEALLESS
IDEALOGUE
IDENTICAL
IDENTIKIT
IDEOGRAPH
IDEOLOGIC
IDEOLOGUE
IDIOGRAPH
IDIOMATIC
IDIOPATHY
IDIOPLASM
IDIOTICAL
IDIOTICON
IDLE-WHEEL
IDLE-WORMS
IGNESCENT
IGNITABLE
IGNITIBLE
IGNORABLE
IGNORAMUS
IGNORANCE
IGUANIDAE
IGUANODON
ILL-BODING
ILLEGALLY
ILLEGIBLE
ILLEGIBLY
ILL-GOTTEN
ILL-HAIRED
ILL-HEADED
ILLIBERAL
ILLICITLY
ILLIMITED
ILL-JUDGED
ILL-MANNED
ILLOGICAL
ILL-OMENED
ILLUMINER
ILL-WISHER
IMAGEABLE
IMAGELESS
IMAGINARY
IMAGINING
IMAGINIST
IMBALANCE
IMBRANGLE
IMBRICATE
IMBROGLIO
IMITATION
IMITATIVE
IMMANACLE
IMMANENCE
IMMANENCY
IMMATURED
IMMEDIACY
IMMEDIATE
IMMENSELY
IMMENSITY
IMMERSION

IMMIGRANT
IMMIGRATE
IMMINENCE
IMMINENCY
IMMISSION
IMMITTING
IMMODESTY
IMMOLATOR
IMMORALLY
IMMOVABLE
IMMOVABLY
IMMUTABLE
IMMUTABLY
IMPACABLE
IMPACTION
IMPARTIAL
IMPASSION
IMPASSIVE
IMPASTOED
IMPATIENS
IMPATIENT
IMPAVIDLY
IMPEACHER
IMPECCANT
IMPEDANCE
IMPELLENT
IMPELLING
IMPENDENT
IMPENDING
IMPERATOR
IMPERFECT
IMPERIOUS
IMPETICOS
IMPETRATE
IMPETUOUS
IMPETUSES
IMPINGENT
IMPINGING
IMPLEADER
IMPLEMENT
IMPLETION
IMPLEXION
IMPLICATE
IMPLIEDLY
IMPLODENT
IMPLOSION
IMPLOSIVE
IMPLUVIUM
IMPOLITIC
IMPORTANT
IMPORTUNE
IMPOSABLE
IMPOSTUME
IMPOSTURE
IMPOTENCE
IMPOTENCY
IMPOUNDER
IMPRECATE
IMPRECISE
IMPRESARI
IMPROBITY
IMPROMPTU
IMPROVING
IMPROVISE
IMPRUDENT
IMPUDENCE,

IMPULSION
IMPULSIVE
IMPULSORY
IMPUTABLE
IMPUTABLY
INABILITY
INAIDABLE
INAMORATA
INAMORATO
INANIMATE
INANITION
INAPTNESS
INAUDIBLE
INAUDIBLY
INAUGURAL
IN-BETWEEN
INBREATHE
INBROUGHT
INBURNING
INCAPABLE
INCAPABLY
INCARNATE
INCAUTION
INCENTIVE
INCEPTION
INCEPTIVE
INCESSANT
INCIDENCE
INCIPIENT
INCLEMENT
INCLINING
INCLOSURE
INCLUSION
INCLUSIVE
INCOGNITA
INCOGNITO
INCOMMODE
INCONDITE
INCORRECT
INCORRUPT
INCREASER
INCREMATE
INCREMENT
INCUBATOR
INCUBUSES
INCULCATE
INCULPATE
INCUMBENT
INCUNABLE
INCURABLE
INCURABLY
INCURIOUS
INCURRENT
INCURRING
INCURSION
INCURSIVE
INCURVATE
INCURVITY
INDAGATOR
INDECENCY
INDECORUM
INDELIBLE
INDELIBLY
INDEMNIFY
INDEMNITY
INDENTION

INDENTURE
INDEXICAL
INDEXLESS
INDIANISE
INDIANIST
INDICATOR
INDICTION
INDIGENCE
INDIGENCY
INDIGNANT
INDIGNIFY
INDIGNITY
INDIGOTIN
INDIRUBIN
INDISPOSE
INDOCIBLE
INDOLENCE
INDOLENCY
INDRAUGHT
INDUBIOUS
INDUCIBLE
INDUCTILE
INDUCTION
INDUCTIVE
INDULGENT
INDUSIATE
INDUVIATE
INDWELLER
INEBRIANT
INEBRIATE
INEBRIETY
INEFFABLE
INEFFABLY
INELASTIC
INELEGANT
INEPTNESS
INEQUABLE
INERRABLE
INERRABLY
INERRANCY
INERTNESS
INERUDITE
INEXACTLY
INFANTILE
INFANTINE
INFATUATE
INFECTION
INFECTIVE
INFERABLE
INFERENCE
INFERRING
INFERTILE
INFIELDER
INFILLING
INFIRMARY
INFIRMITY
INFLATION
INFLATIVE
INFLEXION
INFLEXURE
INFLOWING
INFLUENCE
INFLUENZA
INFLUXION
INFORMANT
INFORTUNE

INFRACTED
INFRACTOR
INFURIATE
INFUSCATE
INFUSIBLE
INFUSORIA
INGENIOUS
INGENUITY
INGENUOUS
INGESTION
INGESTIVE
INGLENOOK
INGLE-SIDE
INGLUVIAL
INGLUVIES
INGRAINED
INGROWING
INHABITOR
INHALATOR
INHARMONY
INHERENCE
INHERENCY
INHERITOR
INHIBITOR
INHUMANLY
INITIALLY
INITIATOR
INJECTION
INJURIOUS
INJUSTICE
INK-BOTTLE
INK-ERASER
INK-HOLDER
INNERMOST
INNERVATE
INNHOLDER
INNKEEPER
INNOCENCE
INNOCENCY
INNOCUITY
INNOCUOUS
INNOVATOR
INNOXIOUS
INNUENDOS
INOCULATE
INODOROUS
INOPINATE
INORGANIC
IN-PATIENT
INPOURING
INQUILINE
INQUINATE
INQUIRING
INSATIATE
INSATIETY
INSCIENCE
INSCRIBER
INSECTILE
INSECTION
INSECT-NET
INSELBERG
INSENSATE
INSENSORY
INSERTION
IN-SERVICE
INSHALLAH

INSHEATHE
INSHELTER
INSIDE-CAR
INSIDIOUS
INSINCERE
INSINUATE
INSIPIDLY
INSIPIENT
INSISTENT
INSISTURE
INSOLENCE
INSOLUBLE
INSOLUBLY
INSOLVENT
INSOMNIAC
INSPANNED
INSPECTOR
INSPHEARE
INSTALLED
INSTANTER
INSTANTLY
INSTIGATE
INSTILLED
INSTITUTE
INSULANCE
INSULARLY
INSULATOR
INSULSITY
INSULTANT
INSULTING
INSURABLE
INSURANCE
INSURGENT
INSWINGER
INTEGRAND
INTEGRANT
INTEGRATE
INTEGRITY
INTELLECT
INTENABLE
INTENDANT
INTENIBLE
INTENSATE
INTENSELY
INTENSIFY
INTENSION
INTENSITY
INTENSIVE
INTENTION
INTENTIVE
INTER-ARTS
INTERBRED
INTERCEDE
INTERCEPT
INTERCITY
INTERCROP
INTERDASH
INTERDEAL
INTERDICT
INTERDINE
INTERFACE
INTERFERE
INTERFLOW
INTERFOLD
INTERFUSE
INTERGROW

INTERJECT
INTERJOIN
INTERKNIT
INTERLACE
INTERLARD
INTERLEAF
INTERLINE
INTERLINK
INTERLOCK
INTERLOPE
INTERLUDE
INTERMENT
INTERMURE
INTERNODE
INTERPAGE
INTERPLAY
INTERPONE
INTERPOSE
INTERPRET
INTERRING
INTERRUPT
INTERSECT
INTERSERT
INTERVALE
INTERVEIN
INTERVENE
INTERVIEW
INTERWIND
INTERWORK
INTERZONE
INTESTACY
INTESTATE
INTESTINE
INTONATOR
INTORSION
INTORTION
INTRICACY
INTRICATE
INTRIGANT
INTRIGUER
INTRINSIC
INTRODUCE
INTROITUS
INTROJECT
INTROVERT
INTRUSION
INTRUSIVE
INTUITION
INTUITIVE
INTUMESCE
INUMBRATE
INUNCTION
INUREMENT
INUSITATE
INUTILITY
INVALIDLY
INVARIANT
INVECTIVE
INVEIGLER
INVENTION
INVENTIVE
INVENTORY
INVERNESS
INVERSELY
INVERSION
INVERSIVE

INVERTASE
INVIDIOUS
INVIOLATE
INVISIBLE
INVISIBLY
INVOLUCEL
INVOLUCRE
INVOLUTED
INWORKING
INWREATHE
INWROUGHT
IODOPHILE
IRASCIBLE
IRASCIBLY
IRIDACEAE
IRISATION
IRKSOMELY
IRON-BOUND
IRON-CASED
IRON-MINER
IRON-MOULD
IRON-SIDED
IRONSIDES
IRONSMITH
IRONSTONE
IROQUOIAN
IRRADIANT
IRRADIATE
IRREALITY
IRREGULAR
IRRELATED
IRRIGABLE
IRRIGATOR
IRRIGUOUS
IRRITABLE
IRRITABLY
IRRITANCY
IRRUPTION
IRRUPTIVE
IRVINGISM
IRVINGITE
ISAGOGICS
ISALLOBAR
ISCHAEMIA
ISCHAEMIC
ISCHIADIC
ISCHIATIC
ISENERGIC
ISIDORIAN
ISINGLASS
ISLAMITIC
ISMAILIAN
ISMAILISM
ISMATICAL
ISOBATHIC
ISOCHORIC
ISOCHRONE
ISOCLINAL
ISOCLINIC
ISOCRYMAL
ISOCYCLIC
ISODOMOUS
ISODONTAL
ISOGAMETE
ISOGAMOUS
ISOGENOUS

ISOHYETAL
ISOKONTAE
ISOKONTAN
ISOLATION
ISOLATIVE
ISOMERISE
ISOMERISM
ISOMEROUS
ISOMETRIC
ISONIAZID
ISO-OCTANE
ISOPODOUS
ISOPOLITY
ISOSCELES
ISOSTATIC
ISOTHERAL
ISOTROPIC
ISRAELITE
ISSUELESS
ITALICISE
ITALICISM
ITCHINESS
ITERATION
ITERATIVE
ITINERACY
ITINERANT
ITINERARY
ITINERATE
IVORY-GATE
IVORY-PALM
IVORY-TREE
IVY-LEAVED

J

JABBERING
JABORANDI
JACARANDA
JACK-A-LENT
JACKALLED
JACK-BLOCK
JACK-FRUIT
JACK-KNIFE
JACK-PLANE
JACK-SAUCE
JACK-SLAVE
JACKSMITH
JACK-SNIPE
JACK-STAFF
JACK-STAYS
JACK-STRAW
JACOBINIC
JACOBITIC
JACQUERIE
JACTATION
JACULATOR
JAGANNATH
JAGHIRDAR
JAILERESS
JAIL-FEVER
JALOUSIED
JAMBOLANA
JANISSARY
JANITRESS
JANSENISM
JANSENIST
JAPANESES

JAPANNING
JARGONEER
JARGONIST
JARRINGLY
JASPERISE
JASPEROUS
JASPIDEAN
JAUNDICED
JAWBATION
JAW-FALLEN
JAYWALKER
JAZZINESS
JEALOUSLY
JEANNETTE
JEBUSITIC
JEERINGLY
JELLIFORM
JELLYFISH
JEMMINESS
JENNETING
JENNY-WREN
JEOPARDER
JEQUIRITY
JERFALCON
JERKINESS
JERRY-SHOP
JERUSALEM
JESSAMINE
JESSERANT
JESTINGLY
JESUITISM
JET-DRIVEN
JET-STREAM
JETTATURA
JETTINESS
JEWEL-CASE
JEWELLERY
JEWELLING
JEWEL-WEED
JEW'S-PITCH
JEW'S-STONE
JEW'S-TRUMP
JIGAMAREE
JIGGUMBOB
JILLFLIRT
JINGO-RING
JITTERBUG
JOBERNOWL
JOB-MASTER
JOCKEYISM
JOCKSTRAP
JOCKTELEG
JOCULARLY
JOCULATOR
JOCUNDITY
JOHANNEAN
JOHANNINE
JOHN-APPLE
JOHNNY-RAW
JOINT-HEIR
JOINTLESS
JOINTNESS
JOINTRESS
JOINT-WORM
JOKESMITH
JOLLIMENT

JOLLINESS
JOLLYBOAT
JOLLYHEAD
JOLTINGLY
JORDANIAN
JOSS-BLOCK
JOSS-HOUSE
JOSS-STICK
JOURNEYED
JOURNEYER
JOVIALITY
JOYLESSLY
JOY-RIDING
JUBILANCE
JUDAISTIC
JUDAS-HOLE
JUDAS-KISS
JUDAS-TREE
JUDGE-MADE
JUDGEMENT
JUDGESHIP
JUDICABLE
JUDICATOR
JUDICIARY
JUDICIOUS
JUICELESS
JUICINESS
JUKE-JOINT
JUMPINESS
JUNCACEAE
JUNE-BERRY
JUNIORITY
JUNIPERUS
JUNKERDOM
JUNKERISM
JUNKETING
JUNOESQUE
JURIDICAL
JURYWOMAN
JURYWOMEN
JUSTICIAR
JUSTIFIED
JUSTIFIER
JUTTINGLY
JUT-WINDOW
JUVENILIA
JUXTAPOSE

K

KABELJOUW
KAILYAIRD
KAINOZOIC
KAISERDOM-
KAISERISM
KALAMKARI
KALLITYPE
KALSOMINE
KAOLINISE
KAOLINITE
KARABINER
KATABASIS
KATABATIC
KATABOLIC
KATHAKALI
KATHARSIS
KAURI-PINE

KEELIVINE
KEELYVINE
KELTICISM
KENNELLED
KENNEL-MAN
KENT-BUGLE
KENTLEDGE
KEPLERIAN
KERATITIS
KERBSTONE
KERMESITE
KETTLEFUL
KEYNESIAN
KHALIFATE
KHEDIVATE
KHEDIVIAL
KIBBUTZIM
KICKSHAWS
KICK-START
KIDNAPPED
KIDNAPPER
KIDNEY-ORE
KIESERITE
KILDERKIN
KILN-DRIED
KILOCYCLE
KILOGAUSS
KILOHERTZ
KILOLITRE
KILOMETRE
KINEMATIC
KINETICAL
KING-APPLE
KING-COBRA
KINGCRAFT
KINGDOMED
KING-MAKER
KING'S-EVIL
KING'S-HOOD
KING-SIZED
KINK-COUGH
KINK-HOAST
KINSFOLKS
KINSWOMAN
KINTLEDGE
KIRKYAIRD
KITCHENER
KITTENISH
KITTIWAKE
KLENDUSIC
KLEPHTISM
KLINOSTAT
KNAPSCULL
KNAPSKULL
KNAVESHIP
KNAVISHLY
KNEE-CORDS
KNEE-DRILL
KNEE-HOLLY
KNEE-JOINT
KNEE-SWELL
KNICKERED
KNIFE-EDGE
KNIFELESS
KNIFE-REST
KNIGHTAGE

KNIPHOFIA
KNOB-STICK
KNOCKDOWN
KNOCKER-UP
KNOCK-KNEE
KNOTGRASS
KNOWINGLY
KNOWLEDGE
KOMINFORM
KOMINTERN
KONIMETER
KONISCOPE
KOSMONAUT
KRAKOWIAK
KRUMMHORN
KRYOMETER
KSHATRIYA
KURRAJONG
KYMOGRAPH

L

LABDACISM
LABELLING
LABELLOID
LABIALISE
LABIALISM
LABORIOUS
LABOURISM
LABOURIST
LABYRINTH
LACCOLITE
LACCOLITH
LACE-FRAME
LACE-PAPER
LACERABLE
LACERATED
LACERTIAN
LACERTINE
LACHRYMAL
LACINIATE
LACK-BEARD
LACK-BRAIN
LACK-LATIN
LACK-LINEN
LACONICAL
LACQUERER
LACRIMARY
LACRIMOSE
LACRYMARY
LACRYMOSE
LACTATION
LACUNARIA
LADLEFULS
LADY'S-MAID
LADY-SMOCK
LAEVULOSE
LAGGINGLY
LAGNIAPPE
LAGRIMOSO
LAIRDSHIP
LAKE-BASIN
LALLATION
LAMASERAI
LAMBENTLY
LAMBITIVE
LAMB'S-WOOL

LAMELLATE
LAMELLOID
LAMELLOSE
LAMENTING
LAMINABLE
LAMINARIA
LAMINATED
LAMPADARY
LAMPADIST
LAMP-BLACK
LAMP-GLASS
LAMPLIGHT
LAMPOONER
LAMPSHADE
LAMP-SHELL
LANCE-JACK
LANCEOLAR
LANCE-WOOD
LANCIFORM
LANCINATE
LAND-AGENT
LANDAMMAN
LANDAULET
LANDDAMNE
LANDDROST
LAND-FLOOD
LAND-FORCE
LANDGRAVE
LANDLOPER
LANDOWNER
LAND-PILOT
LAND-PLANE
LAND-REEVE
LANDSCAPE
LAND-SCRIP
LAND-SHARK
LANDSLIDE
LANDSMAAL
LANDSTING
LANDSTURM
LAND-VALUE
LANDWARDS
LAND-YACHT
LANGOBARD
LANGOUSTE
LANGRIDGE
LANGSPIEL
LANGUAGED
LANGUETTE
LANGUIDLY
LANKINESS
LANTERLOO
LANTHANUM
LAODICEAN
LAPIDEOUS
LAPIDIFIC
LAPLANDER
LAP-ROLLER
LAPSTREAK
LARCENIST
LARCENOUS
LARDALITE
LARGACTIL
LARGENESS
LARGHETTO
LARGITION

LARKINESS
LARK'S-HEEL
LARUM-BELL
LARVICIDE
LARVIFORM
LARVIKITE
LARYNGEAL
LASERWORT
LASSITUDE
LASTINGLY
LATERALLY
LATESCENT
LATHYRISM
LATICLAVE
LATIFONDI
LATITANCY
LATRATION
LATROCINY
LATTER-DAY
LATTER-WIT
LAUDATION
LAUDATIVE
LAUDATORY
LAUGHABLE
LAUGHABLY
LAUGHSOME
LAUNDERER
LAUNDRESS
LAURACEAE
LAURELLED
LAVALIÉRE
LAWGIVING
LAWLESSLY
LAWMONGER
LAWNMOWER
LAWN-PARTY
LAW-WRITER
LAYER-CAKE
LAY-FIGURE
LAZARETTO
LAZAR-LIKE
LAZY-BONES
LAZY-TONGS
LAZZARONE
LAZZARONI
LEAD-PAINT
LEAF-GREEN
LEAFINESS
LEAF-METAL
LEAF-MOULD
LEAF-NOSED
LEAF-STALK
LEAF-TRACE
LEAKINESS
LEAN-FACED
LEARNABLE
LEARNEDLY
LEASE-BAND
LEASEHOLD
LEASE-LEND
LEASTWAYS
LEASTWISE
LEAVENING
LEAVENOUS
LECHEROUS
LECTORATE

LEERINGLY
LEFEGUARD
LEFTWARDS
LEGENDARY
LEGENDIST
LEGER-LINE
LEGGINESS
LEGIONARY
LEGISLATE
LEG-PULLER
LEICESTER
LEISURELY
LEITMOTIF
LEITMOTIV
LEMNACEAE
LEMON-SOLE
LEMON-WEED
LEND-LEASE
LENGTHFUL
LENGTHILY
LENIENTLY
LENTIFORM
LEPROSERY
LEPROSITY
LEPTOSOME
LESSONING
LETHALITY
LETHARGIC
LETTER-BOX
LETTER-GAE
LETTERING
LEUCAEMIA
LEUCISCUS
LEUCO-BASE
LEUCOCYTE
LEUCOTOME
LEUCOTOMY
LEUKAEMIA
LEVANTINE
LEVEL-COIL
LEVELLING
LEVIATHAN
LEVIGABLE
LEVITICAL
LEVITICUS
LEXICALLY
LIABILITY
LIBECCHIO
LIBELLANT
LIBELLING
LIBELLOUS
LIBERALLY
LIBERATOR
LIBERTINE
LIBIDINAL
LIBRARIAN
LIBRATION
LIBRATORY
LIBRICITY
LICENSURE
LICHENISM
LICHENIST
LICHENOUS
LICKERISH
LICKPENNY
LIEGELESS

LIEGE-LORD
LIENTERIC
LIFE-BLOOD
LIFE-CYCLE
LIFE-FORCE
LIFE-SAVER
LIFE-SIZED
LIFE-TABLE
LIFE-WEARY
LIGHT-BALL
LIGHT-DUES
LIGHT-FOOT
LIGHTLESS
LIGHT-MILL
LIGHTNESS
LIGHTNING
LIGHTSHIP
LIGHTSOME
LIGHT-YEAR
LIGNALOES
LIGNIFIED
LIGUORIAN
LILIACEAE
LILY-WHITE
LIMACEOUS
LIME-HOUND
LIME-JUICE
LIMELIGHT
LIMESTONE
LIME-WATER
LIMITABLE
LIMITEDLY
LIMITLESS
LIMNOLOGY
LIMONITIC
LIMOUSINE
LIMPIDITY
LIMPINGLY
LINCTUSES
LINEALITY
LINEAMENT
LINEARITY
LINEATION
LINE-FENCE
LINE-GROVE
LINEN-FOLD
LINEOLATE
LINE-STORM
LINGERING
LINGUALLY
LINGULATE
LINOLENIC
LINTELLED
LINTSTOCK
LINTWHITE
LIONCELLE
LION-HEART
LIOPHILIC
LIPPENING
LIPPITUDE
LIPPIZANA
LIP-READER
LIQUATION
LIQUEFIED
LIQUEFIER
LIQUIDATE

LIQUIDISE
LIQUIDITY
LIQUIFIED
LIQUORICE
LIQUORISH
LISPINGLY
LISTERIAN
LISTERISE
LISTERISM
LITERALLY
LITERATIM
LITERATOR
LITERATUS
LITHENESS
LITHESOME
LITHIASIS
LITHISTID
LITHOCYST
LITHOIDAL
LITHOLOGY
LITHOPONE
LITHOTOME
LITHOTOMY
LITIGABLE
LITIGIOUS
LITTER-BIN
LITTER-BUG
LITTLEANE
LITURGICS
LITURGIST
LIVE-BIRTH
LIVER-WING
LIVERWORT
LIVERYMAN
LIVESTOCK
LIVIDNESS
LIVRAISON
LIXIVIATE
LIXIVIOUS
LOADSTONE
LOAF-BREAD
LOAFERISH
LOAF-SUGAR
LOAN-SHARK
LOATHSOME
LOBSCOUSE
LOBULATED
LOCALISER
LOCELLATE
LOCK-CHAIN
LOCKHOUSE
LOCKSMITH
LOCOMOTOR
LOCO-PLANT
LOCUPLETE
LODESTONE
LODGE-GATE
LODGEMENT
LODGE-POLE
LODICULAE
LOFTINESS
LOGAOEDIC
LOGARITHM
LOGICALLY
LOGISTICS
LOGOGRIPH

LOGOMACHY
LOGOTHETE
LOG-ROLLER
LOIN-CLOTH
LOITERING
LOLLARDRY
LOLLINGLY
LOLL-SHROB
LOMBARDIC
LONDONESE
LONDONIAN
LONDONISE
LONDONISH
LONDONISM
LONGAEVAL
LONG-CLOTH
LONG-COATS
LONG-DRAWN
LONG-EARED
LONGEVITY
LONGEVOUS
LONG-FACED
LONG-FIELD
LONG-HOUSE
LONGICORN
LONGINGLY
LONGITUDE
LONG-LIVED
LONGOBARD
LONG-RANGE
LONGSHORE
LONG-SIXES
LOOK-ROUND
LOOP-LIGHT
LOOSE-LEAF
LOOSENESS
LOPHODONT
LOQUACITY
LORGNETTE
LOTOPHAGI
LOTUS-LAND
LOURINGLY
LOUSEWORT
LOUSINESS
LOUTISHLY
LOVE-APPLE
LOVE-ARROW
LOVE-CHARM
LOVE-CHILD
LOVE-FEAST
LOVE-JUICE
LOVELIGHT
LOVE-MAKER
LOVE-MATCH
LOVERLESS
LOVE-SHAFT
LOVE-STORY
LOVE-TOKEN
LOVING-CUP
LOW-DOWNER
LOWER-CASE
LOWER-DECK
LOWERMOST
LOWLANDER
LOWLIHEAD
LOWLINESS

LOW-LOADER
LOW-MINDED
LOW-NECKED
LOWRIE-TOD
LOXODROME
LUBRICANT
LUBRICATE
LUBRICOUS
LUCIDNESS
LUCIFERIN
LUCKIE-DAD
LUCKINESS
LUCK-PENNY
LUCRATIVE
LUCTATION
LUCUBRATE
LUCULLEAN
LUCULLIAN
LUDICROUS
LUMBERING
LUMBERMAN
LUMBER-PIE
LUMBRICAL
LUMBRICUS
LUMINAIRE
LUMINANCE
LUMPINESS
LUMPISHLY
LUMP-SUGAR
LUNCH-HOUR
LUNCH-TIME
LUNG-GROWN
LUNISOLAR
LUNULATED
LUPULINIC
LURIDNESS
LUSH-HOUSE
LUSTFULLY
LUSTIHEAD
LUSTIHOOD
LUSTINESS
LUTEOLOUS
LUTESCENT
LUTHERISM
LUTHERIST
LUXURIANT
LUXURIATE
LUXURIOUS
LYAM-HOUND
LYCOSIDAE
LYME-GRASS
LYME-HOUND
LYMPHATIC
LYOMEROUS
LYOPHOBIC
LYSIGENIC
LYSIMETER

M

MACARONIC
MACARONIS
MACAW-PALM
MACAW-TREE
MACCABEAN
MACEDOINE
MACERATOR

MACHINATE
MACHINERY
MACHINIST
MACHMETER
MACINTOSH
MACROAXIS
MACROBIAN
MACROCOPY
MACROCOSM
MACROCYTE
MACRODOME
MACROLOGY
MACRUROUS
MACTATION
MADAROSIS
MADDENING
MADDINGLY
MAD-DOCTOR
MADELEINE
MADRASSAH
MADREPORE
MAELSTROM
MAEONIDES
MAFFICKER
MAGDALENE
MAGGOT-PIE
MAGIANISM
MAGICALLY
MAGISTERY
MAGISTRAL
MAGNALIUM
MAGNESIAN
MAGNESITE
MAGNESIUM
MAGNETICS
MAGNETISE
MAGNETISM
MAGNETIST
MAGNETITE
MAGNETRON
MAGNIFICO
MAGNIFIED
MAGNIFIER
MAGNITUDE
MAGYARISE
MAGYARISM
MAHARAJAH
MAHARANEE
MAHLSTICK
MAHOMETAN
MAID-CHILD
MAIDENISH
MAIEUTICS
MAIL-COACH
MAIL-ORDER
MAIL-PLANE
MAIL-TRAIN
MAINBRACE
MAINLINER
MAINPRISE
MAINSHEET
MAISTRING
MAJOR-DOMO
MAJORETTE
MAJORSHIP
MAJUSCULE

MAKE-PEACE
MAKE-READY
MAKESHIFT
MALACHITE
MALADROIT
MALARIOUS
MALAXATOR
MALAYALAM
MALAYSIAN
MALEBOLGE
MALENGINE
MALFORMED
MALICIOUS
MALIGNANT
MALIGNITY
MALINGERY
MALLEABLE
MALLEE-HEN
MALLEMUCK
MALLENDER
MALLEOLAR
MALLEOLUS
MALPIGHIA
MALTALENT
MALT-FLOOR
MALT-HORSE
MALT-HOUSE
MALVACEAE
MALVOISIE
MAMILLARY
MAMILLATE
MAMMALIAN
MAMMALOGY
MAMMIFORM
MAMMONISH
MAMMONISM
MAMMONIST
MAMMONITE
MAN-AT-ARMS
MANCHUKUO
MANCHURIA
MANCIPATE
MANCUNIAN
MANDARINE
MANDATARY
MANDATORY
MANDIOCCA
MANDOLINE
MANDUCATE
MANE-SHEET
MANGANATE
MANGANESE
MANGANITE
MANGANOUS
MANGINESS
MANGOSTAN
MANGOUSTE
MANHANDLE
MANHATTAN
MANICHEAN
MANIFESTO
MANIPLIES
MANIPULAR
MANLINESS
MAN-MINDED
MANNEQUIN

MANNERISM
MANNERIST
MANOEUVRE
MANOMETER
MAN-ORCHIS
MANOR-SEAT
MANSIONRY
MAN-SLAYER
MANTICORA
MANTICORE
MANUBRIAL
MANUBRIUM
MANURANCE
MANXWOMAN
MANYPLIES
MANY-SIDED
MANZANITA
MAPPEMOND
MAQUISARD
MARANATHA
MARASMIUS
MARCASITE
MARCELLED
MARCH-DIKE
MARCH-DYKE
MARCHPANE
MARESCHAL
MARE'S-NEST
MARE'S-TAIL
MARGARINE
MARGARITE
MARGINATE
MARIALITE
MARIGRAPH
MARIHUANA
MARIJUANA
MARISCHAL
MARITALLY
MARKET-DAY
MARKETING
MARKET-MAN
MARK-WHITE
MARLSTONE
MARMALADE
MARMARISE
MARMOREAL
MAROONING
MARQUETRY
MARROWFAT
MARROWISH
MARROW-MEN
MARROWSKY
MARSHALCY
MARSHLAND
MARSHWORT
MARSUPIAL
MARSUPIUM
MARTELLED
MARTIALLY
MARTINMAS
MARTYRDOM
MARTYRISE
MARVELLED
MASCULINE
MASHALLAH
MASOCHISM

MASOCHIST
MASONRIED
MASORETIC
MASSAGIST
MASSINESS
MASSIVELY
MASSORETE
MASSYMORE
MASTERATE
MASTERDOM
MASTERFUL
MASTERING
MASTER-KEY
MASTHOUSE
MASTICATE
MASTOIDAL
MATCHABLE
MATCHLESS
MATCHLOCK
MATCHWOOD
MATELASSÉ
MATERNITY
MATHURINE
MATRIARCH
MATRICIDE
MATRICULA
MATRILINY
MATRIMONY
MATRONAGE
MATRONISE
MATTAMORE
MATTERFUL
MATURABLE
MATUTINAL
MAULSTICK
MAUNDERER
MAURITIUS
MAUSOLEAN
MAUSOLEUM
MAWKISHLY
MAXILLARY
MAXILLULA
MAXIMALLY
MAY-BEETLE
MAYFLOWER
MAYORALTY
MAYORSHIP
MEADOW-RUE
MEALINESS
MEANDERED
MEANDRIAN
MEANDROUS
MEANINGLY
MEANWHILE
MEASURING
MEAT-EATER
MEATINESS
MECHANICS
MECHANISE
MECHANISM
MECHANIST
MECOPTERA
MEDAEWART
MEDALLING
MEDALLION
MEDALLIST

MEDIAEVAL
MEDIATELY
MEDIATION
MEDIATISE
MEDIATIVE
MEDIATORY
MEDIATRIX
MEDICABLE
MEDICALLY
MEDICATED
MEDICINAL
MEDITATED
MEDRESSEH
MEDULLARY
MEDULLATE
MEGACYCLE
MEGADEATH
MEGAFARAD
MEGAPHONE
MEGASCOPE
MEGASPORE
MEKOMETER
MELAMPODE
MELANOSIS
MELANOTIC
MELANURIC
MELAPHYRE
MELASTOMA
MELIACEAE
MELIBOEAN
MELIORATE
MELIORISM
MELIORIST
MELIORITY
MELOCOTON
MELODIOUS
MELODRAMA
MELODRAME
MELOMANIA
MELOMANIC
MELPOMENE
MELTINGLY
MELT-WATER
MEMNONIAN
MEMOIRISM
MEMOIRIST
MEMORABLE
MEMORABLY
MEMORANDA
MEMORITER
MEMPHITIC
MENADIONE
MENAGERIE
MENDACITY
MENDELIAN
MENDELISM
MENDICANT
MENDICITY
MENINGEAL
MENIPPEAN
MENISCOID
MENNONITE
MENOMINEE
MENOPAUSE
MENSELESS
MENSHEVIK

MENSTRUAL
MENSTRUUM
MENTALISM
MENTALIST
MENTALITY
MENTATION
MENTICIDE
MENTORIAL
MEPACRINE
MEPHITISM
MERCAPTAN
MERCENARY
MERCERISE
MERCIABLE
MERCILESS
MERCURIAL
MERCUROUS
MERCY-SEAT
MERESTONE
MERESWINE
MERGANSER
MERMAIDEN
MEROISTIC
MEROPIDAE
MEROPIDAN
MERPEOPLE
MERRIMENT
MERRINESS
MERRYMAKE
MESCALISM
MESENTERY
MESMERISE
MESMERISM
MESMERIST
MESOBLAST
MESOGLOEA
MESOMORPH
MESOPHYLL
MESOPHYTE
MESSENGER
MESSIANIC
MESSIEURS
MESSINESS
METABASIS
METABATIC
METABOLIC
METALLINE
METALLING
METALLISE
METALLIST
METALLOID
METAL-WORK
METAMERIC
METAPHASE
METAPLASM
METEORIST
METEORITE
METEOROID
METEOROUS
METESTICK
METHADONE
METHEGLIN
METHODISE
METHODISM
METHODIST
METHOUGHT

METHYLATE
METHYLENE
METHYSTIC
METONYMIC
METRICATE
METRICIAN
METRICISE
METRICIST
METRIFIER
METRONOME
MEZZANINE
MEZZOTINT
MIASMATIC
MICACEOUS
MICA-SLATE
MICROBIAL
MICROBIAN
MICROCARD
MICROCOSM
MICROCYTE
MICROFILM
MICROGRAM
MICROLITE
MICROLITH
MICROLOGY
MICROPSIA
MICROPYLE
MICROSOME
MICROTOME
MICROTOMY
MICROTONE
MICROWATT
MICROWAVE
MICROWIRE
MICTURATE
MIDDLE-AGE
MIDDLEMAN
MID-HEAVEN
MIDINETTE
MIDRASHIM
MID-SEASON
MIDSTREAM
MIDSUMMER
MID-WICKET
MIDWIFERY
MIDWIFING
MID-WINTER
MIDWIVING
MIGRATION
MIGRATORY
MILESTONE
MILITANCY
MILITARIA
MILKEN-WAY
MILK-FEVER
MILK-FLOAT
MILK-GLAND
MILK-HOUSE
MILKINESS
MILK-MOLAR
MILK-PUNCH
MILKSHAKE
MILK-SUGAR
MILK-TOOTH
MILK-VETCH
MILK-WHITE

MILL-BOARD
MILLENARY
MILLENNIA
MILLEPEDE
MILLEPORE
MILLERIAN
MILLERITE
MILL-HORSE
MILLINERY
MILLIONTH
MILLIPEDE
MILLOCRAT
MILL-OWNER
MILLSTONE
MILL-TOOTH
MILLWHEEL
MILTONIAN
MILTONISM
MIMETICAL
MIMICKING
MINACIOUS
MINCEMEAT
MINCINGLY
MIND-CURER
MINDELIAN
MINDFULLY
MINE-FIELD
MINE-LAYER
MINE-OWNER
MINIATION
MINIATURE
MINI-SKIRT
MINKSTONE
MINORSHIP
MINT-JULEP
MINT-SAUCE
MINUSCULE
MINUTE-GUN
MINUTEMAN
MINUTIOSE
MIRABILIA
MIRABILIS
MIRE-SNIPE
MIRIFICAL
MIRLIGOES
MIRRORING
MIRTHLESS
MISADVISE
MISALLEGE
MISALLIED
MISASSIGN
MISAUNTER
MISAVISED
MISBECOME
MISBEHAVE
MISBELIEF
MISBESEEM
MISBESTOW
MISCEGENE
MISCEGINE
MISCHANCE
MISCHANCY
MISCHARGE
MISCOLOUR
MISCREANT
MISCREATE

MISCREDIT
MISDEEMED
MISDEMEAN
MISDESERT
MISDIRECT
MISEMPLOY
MISERABLE
MISERABLY
MISESTEEM
MISFALLEN
MISFARING
MISFEASOR
MISGIVING
MISGOTTEN
MISGOVERN
MISGROWTH
MISGUGGLE
MISGUIDED
MISHANDLE
MISHANTER
MISHAPPEN
MISINFORM
MISINTEND
MISLEADER
MISLEARED
MISLIPPEN
MISMANAGE
MISOCLERE
MISONEISM
MISONEIST
MISPICKEL
MISPLEASE
MISPRAISE
MISPRISED
MISRECKON
MISREGARD
MISRELATE
MISREPORT
MISSAYING
MISSHAPED
MISSHAPEN
MISSINGLY
MISSIONER
MISTAKING
MISTAUGHT
MISTEMPER
MISTIGRIS
MISTINESS
MISTLETOE
MITHRAEUM
MITHRAISM
MITHRAIST
MITIGABLE
MITIGATOR
MITRAILLE
MITRIFORM
MIXEDNESS
MIZZONITE
MNEMONIST
MNEMOSYNE
MOANFULLY
MOBOCRACY
MOCKER-NUT
MOCKINGLY
MODELLING
MODERATOR

MODERNISE
MODERNISM
MODERNIST
MODERNITY
MODIFYING
MODILLION
MODULATOR
MOISTNESS
MOLECULAR
MOLE-SPADE
MOLESTFUL
MOLLIFIED
MOLLIFIER
MOLLUSCAN
MOLLYMAWK
MOLOCHISE
MOLOSSIAN
MOLYBDATE
MOMENTANY
MOMENTARY
MOMENTOUS
MONACHISM
MONACHIST
MONACTINE
MONADICAL
MONANDRIA
MONARCHAL
MONARCHIC
MONASTERY
MONASTRAL
MONATOMIC
MONAXONIC
MONDAYISH
MONECIOUS
MONERGISM
MONEY-BILL
MONEYLESS
MONEY-WISE
MONEYWORT
MONGERING
MONGOLIAN
MONGOLISE
MONGOLISM
MONGOLOID
MONGOOSES
MONGRELLY
MONIPLIES
MONITRESS
MONKEY-BAG
MONKEYISH
MONKEYISM
MONKEY-JAR
MONKEY-NUT
MONKEY-POT
MONKEY-RUN
MONKSHOOD
MONOBASIC
MONOCEROS
MONOCHORD
MONOCLINE
MONOCOQUE
MONOCRACY
MONOCULAR
MONODICAL
MONODRAMA
MONOECISM

MONOGAMIC
MONOGRAPH
MONOGYNIA
MONOLATER
MONOLATRY
MONOLOGIC
MONOLOGUE
MONOMACHY
MONOMANIA
MONOMETER
MONOPHAGY
MONOPHASE
MONOPLANE
MONOPTOTE
MONORCHID
MONORHINE
MONORHYME
MONOSTICH
MONOSTYLE
MONOTONIC
MONOTREME
MONOTROCH
MONOTROPA
MONOTYPIC
MONOXYLON
MONROEISM
MONSIGNOR
MONSOONAL
MONSTROUS
MONTANISM
MONTANIST
MONTHLING
MONTICULE
MONYPLIES
MONZONITE
MOODINESS
MOON-BLIND
MOON-FACED
MOON-GLADE
MOON-KNIFE
MOONLIGHT
MOON-LOVED
MOONRAKER
MOONSCAPE
MOONSHINE
MOONSHINY
MOONSTONE
MOOSEYARD
MOOTCOURT
MOOTHOUSE
MOP-HEADED
MORACEOUS
MORALISER
MORATORIA
MORBIDITY
MORDACITY
MORDANTLY
MORMANISE
MORMANISM
MORMONISM
MORMONITE
MORPHEMIC
MORPHETIC
MORPHOSIS
MORPHOTIC
MORTALISE

MORTALITY
MORTCLOTH
MORTGAGEE
MORTGAGER
MORTGAGOR
MORTICIAN
MORTIFIED
MORTIFIER
MORT-STONE
MOSAICISM
MOSAICIST
MOSCHATEL
MOSLEMISM
MOSS-AGATE
MOSS-GROWN
MOSSINESS
MOSS-PLANT
MOTETTIST
MOTH-EATEN
MOTHERING
MOTHER-LYE
MOTHER-WIT
MOTIONIST
MOTION-MAN
MOTOCROSS
MOTOR-BOAT
MOTORCADE
MOTOR-SHIP
MOUDIWART
MOUDIWORT
MOULDABLE
MOULD-LOFT
MOULDWARP
MOUND-BIRD
MOUSE-DEER
MOUSE-HOLE
MOUSE-HUNT
MOUSE-TAIL
MOUSE-TRAP
MOUSTACHE
MOUTHABLE
MOUTHFULS
MOUTHLESS
MOUTH-MADE
MOVEABLES
MOWDIWART
MOWDIWORT
MOZARABIC
MUCKENDER
MUCKINESS
MUCK-RAKER
MUCK-SWEAT
MUCORALES
MUCRONATE
MUDDINESS
MUD-MINNOW
MUFFETTEE
MUFFIN-CAP
MUFFINEER
MUFFIN-MAN
MUGEARITE
MUG-HUNTER
MULLIONED
MULTIFOIL
MULTIFORM
MULTIPARA

MULTIPEDE
MULTIPLET
MULTIPLEX
MULTITUDE
MULTIWALL
MUM-BUDGET
MUMCHANCE
MUMMIFIED
MUMMIFORM
MUMMY-CASE
MUMPISHLY
MUMPSIMUS
MUNDANELY
MUNDANITY
MUNDUNGUS
MUNICHISM
MUNICIPAL
MURDERESS
MURDEROUS
MURICATED
MURKINESS
MURMURING
MURMUROUS
MURRAINED
MURTHERER
MUSACEOUS
MUSCADINE
MUSCLE-MAN
MUSCOLOGY
MUSCOVADO
MUSCOVIAN
MUSCOVITE
MUSCULOUS
MUSEFULLY
MUSHINESS
MUSICALLY
MUSIC-CASE
MUSIC-DEMY
MUSIC-HALL
MUSICKING
MUSIC-RACK
MUSIC-ROLL
MUSIC-ROOM
MUSKETEER
MUSKETOON
MUSK-GLAND
MUSKINESS
MUSK-MELON
MUSK-PLANT
MUSK-POUCH
MUSK-SHEEP
MUSK-SHREW
MUSSELLED
MUSSINESS
MUSSITATE
MUSSULMAN
MUSSULMEN
MUSTACHIO
MUSTELINE
MUTAGENIC
MUTILATED
MUTILATOR
MUTINYING
MUTOSCOPE
MUTTERING
MUTTON-HAM

MUTUALISE
MUTUALISM
MUTUALITY
MUZZINESS
MUZZLE-BAG
MYCENAEAN
MYCETOZOA
MYCOLOGIC
MYCOPHAGY
MYCORHIZA
MYDRIASIS
MYDRIATIC
MYLOHYOID
MYLONITIC
MYOGRAPHY
MYOLOGIST
MYOMANTIC
MYRIAPODA
MYRIORAMA
MYRISTICA
MYRMECOID
MYROBALAN
MYRTACEAE
MYRTLEWAX
MYSTAGOGY
MYSTERIES
MYSTICISM
MYSTIFIED
MYSTIFIER
MYTHICISE
MYTHICISM
MYTHICIST
MYTHOLOGY
MYTHOPOET
MYXOEDEMA

N

NABATAEAN
NACHTMAAL
NAIL-BRUSH
NAKEDNESS
NAME-CHILD
NAME-PLATE
NANNY-GOAT
NAPIERIAN
NAPPINESS
NARCISSUS
NARCOTINE
NARCOTISE
NARCOTISM
NARCOTIST
NARGHILLY
NARRATION
NARRATIVE
NARRATORY
NARROWING
NASEBERRY
NASTINESS
NATHELESS
NATHEMORE
NATROLITE
NATTINESS
NATURALLY
NATURE-GOD
NAUGHTILY
NAUMACHIA

NAUPLIOID
NAVELWORT
NAVICULAR
NAVIGABLE
NAVIGATOR
NAZARITIC
NEAR-WHITE
NEAT-HOUSE
NEAT-STALL
NEBULISER
NECESSARY
NECESSITY
NECK-CLOTH
NECK-PIECE
NECKVERSE
NECROLOGY
NECROTISE
NECTAREAL
NECTAREAN
NECTARIAL
NECTARINE
NECTAROUS
NEEDFULLY
NEEDINESS
NEEDLEFUL
NEEDLE-GUN
NEEDLE-TIN
NEEDY-HOOD
NEESBERRY
NEFANDOUS
NEFARIOUS
NEGLECTER
NEGLIGENT
NEGOTIATE
NEGRILLOS
NEGRITUDE
NEGRO-CORN
NEGROHEAD
NEGROIDAL
NEGROPHIL
NEIGHBOUR
NELUMBIUM
NEMERTEAN
NEMERTIAN
NEMERTINE
NEMOPHILA
NEOCOMIAN
NEODYMIUM
NEO-GOTHIC
NEOLITHIC
NEOLOGIAN
NEOLOGISE
NEOLOGISM
NEOLOGIST
NEONOMIAN
NEOPHOBIA
NEOPHYTIC
NEOPILINA
NEOTEINIA
NEOTEINIC
NEOTERISE
NEOTERISM
NEOTERIST
NEPENTHES
NEPHALISM
NEPHALIST

NEPHELINE
NEPHELITE
NEPHOLOGY
NEPHRALGY
NEPHRITIC
NEPHRITIS
NEPHROSIS
NEPTUNIAN
NEPTUNIST
NEPTUNIUM
NERITIDAE
NERVATION
NERVATURE
NERVE-CELL
NERVELESS
NERVINESS
NERVOUSLY
NESCIENCE
NESTORIAN
NETHELESS
NET-PLAYER
NET-VEINED
NET-WINGED
NEURALGIA
NEURALGIC
NEURATION
NEURILITY
NEUROGLIA
NEUROLOGY
NEUROPATH
NEUTRALLY
NEUTRETTO
NEVERMORE
NEW-CREATE
NEW-FALLEN
NEWFANGLE
NEWMARKET
NEWSAGENT
NEWS-FLASH
NEWSHOUND
NEWSINESS
NEWSPAPER
NEWSPRINT
NEWS-SHEET
NEWS-STAND
NEWS-VALUE
NEWTONIAN
NICCOLITE
NICKELINE
NICKELISE
NICKELLED
NICKELOUS
NICKIE-BEN
NICKNACKY
NICKSTICK
NICOMPOOP
NICOTIANA
NICOTINIC
NICTATION
NICTITATE
NIDDERING
NIDERLING
NIELLATED
NIELLOING
NIFFNAFFY
NIFTINESS

NIGGARDLY
NIGGERDOM
NIGGERISH
NIGGERISM
NIGHT-BELL
NIGHT-BIRD
NIGHT-CART
NIGHT-CLUB
NIGHT-CROW
NIGHTFALL
NIGHTFIRE
NIGHT-FOWL
NIGHT-GEAR
NIGHTGOWN
NIGHT-HAWK
NIGHTLESS
NIGHT-LINE
NIGHTLONG
NIGHTMARE
NIGHTMARY
NIGHT-RAIL
NIGHT-REST
NIGHT-ROBE
NIGHT-RULE
NIGHT-SIDE
NIGHT-SOIL
NIGHT-TIDE
NIGHT-TIME
NIGHT-WALK
NIGHTWARD
NIGHTWORK
NIGRICANT
NIGRITIAN
NIGRITUDE
NIGROSINE
NILOMETER
NINE-HOLES
NINEPENCE
NINEPENNY
NINE-SCORE
NINETIETH
NIP-CHEESE
NIPPERKIN
NIPPINGLY
NIPPONESE
NITHSDALE
NITRATINE
NITRATION
NITRIDING
NITRIFIED
NITRO-SILK
NITWITTED
NO-ACCOUNT
NOBBINESS
NOBILIARY
NOBLENESS
NOCTILUCA
NOCTUIDAE
NOCTURNAL
NOCUOUSLY
NODULATED
NOISELESS
NOISINESS
NOISOMELY
NO-MEANING
NOMINABLE

NOMINALLY
NOMINATOR
NOMOCRACY
NOMOGRAPH
NOMOTHETE
NON-ACCESS
NONCE-WORD
NONENTITY
NONILLION
NON-JURING
NON-LINEAR
NON-MEMBER
NONPAREIL
NON-PERSON
NON-SMOKER
NON-USAGER
NOODLEDOM
NOOSPHERE
NOR'-EASTER
NORMALISE
NORMALITY
NORMATIVE
NORTH-EAST
NORTHERLY
NORTHLAND
NORTHMOST
NORTHWARD
NORTH-WEST
NORWEGIAN
NOR'-WESTER
NOSE-BLEED
NOSE-FLUTE
NOSE-PIECE
NOSTALGIA
NOSTALGIC
NOSTOLOGY
NOTABILIA
NOTEDNESS
NOTEPAPER
NOT-HEADED
NOTIFYING
NOTIONIST
NOTOCHORD
NOTODONTA
NOTOGAEAN
NOTOGAEIC
NOTONECTA
NOTORIETY
NOTORIOUS
NOTOTREMA
NOTRE-DAME
NO-TRUMPER
NOURISHER
NOURITURE
NOVELETTE
NOVELTIES
NOVENNIAL
NOVICIATE
NOVITIATE
NOWHITHER
NOXIOUSLY
NUBECULAE
NUCLEATED
NUCLEOLAR
NUCLEOLUS
NUISANCER

NULLIFIED
NULLIFIER
NULLIPARA
NUMBLE-PIE
NUMERABLE
NUMERABLY
NUMERALLY
NUMERATOR
NUMERICAL
NUMMULARY
NUMMULINE
NUMMULITE
NUNATAKKR
NUNCUPATE
NUNNATION
NUN'S-FLESH
NURSELIKE
NURSELING
NURSEMAID
NURSE-TEND
NUT-BUTTER
NUTJOBBER
NUTMEGGED
NUTPECKER
NUTRIMENT
NUTRITION
NUTTINESS
NUT-WEEVIL
NUT-WRENCH
NYCTALOPS
NYMPHAEUM
NYMPHALID
NYMPHICAL
NYMPH-LIKE
NYSTAGMIC
NYSTAGMUS

O

OAKENSHAW
OAR-FOOTED
OASTHOUSE
OBBLIGATO
OBCONICAL
OBCORDATE
OBEDIENCE
OBEISANCE
OBELISCAL
OBESENESS
OBFUSCATE
OBJECTIFY
OBJECTION
OBJECTIVE
OBJURGATE
OBLIQUELY
OBLIQUITY
OBLIVIOUS
OBNOXIOUS
OBOVATELY
OBREPTION
OBSCENELY
OBSCENITY
OBSCURANT
OBSCURELY
OBSCURITY
OBSECRATE
OBSEQUENT

OBSEQUIAL
OBSEQUIES
OBSERVANT
OBSERVING
OBSESSION
OBSESSIVE
OBSIGNATE
OBSOLESCE
OBSTETRIC
OBSTINACY
OBSTINATE
OBSTRUENT
OBTENTION
OBTRUDING
OBTRUSION
OBTRUSIVE
OBTUNDENT
OBTURATOR
OBUMBRATE
OBVENTION
OBVERSELY
OBVERSION
OBVIATION
OBVIOUSLY
OBVOLUTED
OBVOLVENT
OCCIPITAL
OCCLUDENT
OCCLUSION
OCCLUSIVE
OCCULTISM
OCCULTIST
OCCUPANCE
OCCUPANCY
OCCUPYING
OCCURRENT
OCCURRING
OCEANIDES
OCELLATED
OCHLOCRAT
OCTACHORD
OCTAGONAL
OCTAHEDRA
OCTAMETER
OCTANDRIA
OCTAPLOID
OCTAPODIC
OCTASTICH
OCTASTYLE
OCTENNIAL
OCTILLION
OCTOBRIST
OCTOGYNIA
OCTOPLOID
OCTOPODES
OCTOPUSES
OCTOSTYLE
OCTRACEAN
ODALISQUE
ODDFELLOW
ODD-JOBBER
ODD-JOBMAN
ODD-MAN-OUT
ODONTALGY
ODOROUSLY
ODOURLESS

OECUMENIC
OENANTHIC
OENOMANCY
OENOMANIA
OENOMETER
OENOPHILE
OENOPHILY
OENOTHERA
OESTROGEN
OFF-CHANCE
OFF-COLOUR
OFFENSIVE
OFFERABLE
OFFERTORY
OFFHANDED
OFFICE-BOY
OFFICIANT
OFFICIATE
OFFICINAL
OFFICIOUS
OFFPUTTER
OFFSADDLE
OFFSEASON
OFFSPRING
OFF-STREET
OFTENNESS
OIL-BEETLE
OIL-BURNER
OIL-COLOUR
OIL-ENGINE
OIL-TANKER
OLEACEOUS
OLECRANAL
OLECRANON
OLENELLUS
OLEOGRAPH
OLEORESIN
OLEPHILIC
OLFACTION
OLFACTIVE
OLFACTORY
OLIGARCHY
OLIGOCENE
OLIGOPOLY
OLIVENITE
OLIVERIAN
OLIVE-YARD
OMBROPHIL
OMBUDSMAN
OMINOUSLY
OMISSIBLE
OMITTANCE
OMMATIDIA
OMNIBUSES
OMOPHAGIA
OMOPHAGIC
OMPHACITE
OMPHALOID
ONANISTIC
ONCOMETER
ONE-HANDED
ONE-LEGGED
ONEROUSLY
ONION-EYED
ONION-SKIN
ONIROLOGY

ON-LICENCE
ONLOOKING
ONOMASTIC
ONSETTING
ONSLAUGHT
ON-THE-SPOT
ONTOGENIC
ONTOLIGIC
ONYCHITIS
OOGENESIS
OOGENETIC
OPAL-GLASS
OPEN-ARMED
OPEN-CHAIN
OPEN-ENDED
OPEN-FIELD
OPEN-STEEK
OPERATING
OPERATION
OPERATIVE
OPERCULAR
OPERCULUM
OPEROSELY
OPEROSITY
OPHIOLOGY
OPHIUCHUS
OPHIURIDA
OPHIUROID
OPINIONED
OPOBALSAM
OPODELDOC
OPPONENCY
OPPORTUNE
OPPOSABLE
OPPRESSOR
OPPUGNANT
OPSIMATHY
OPSOMANIA
OPTICALLY
OPTIMATES
OPTOMETER
OPTOMETRY
OPTOPHONE
OPULENTLY
OPUSCULUM
ORACULOUS
ORANGEADE
ORANGEISM
ORANGEMAN
ORANGE-TIP
ORANG-UTAN
ORATORIAL
ORATORIAN
ORATORIES
ORBICULAR
ORCHESTIC
ORCHESTRA
ORCHIDEAE
ORCHIDIST
ORDER-BOOK
ORDERLESS
ORDINANCE
ORE-RAUGHT
ORE-RESTED
ORGANELLE
ORGANICAL

ORGANISED
ORGANISER
ORGAN-PIPE
ORGANZINE
ORGIASTIC
ORGILLOUS
ORIENTATE
ORIFICIAL
ORIFLAMME
ORIGENISM
ORIGENIST
ORIGINATE
ORIOLIDAE
ORLEANISM
ORLEANIST
ORNITHOID
OROBANCHE
OROGRAPHY
OROLOGIST
OROROTUND
ORPHANAGE
ORPHANISM
ORPHARION
ORPINGTON
ORRIS-ROOT
ORTANIQUE
ORTHOAXIS
ORTHODOXY
ORTHOEPIC
ORTHOPEDY
ORTHOPTIC
ORTHOTONE
OSCILLATE
OSCITANCY
OSMETERIA
OSMOMETER
OSSICULAR
OSSIFRAGA
OSSIFRAGE
OSSIFYING
OSTENSIVE
OSTENSORY
OSTEODERM
OSTEOGENY
OSTEOLOGY
OSTEOPATH
OSTEOTOME
OSTEOTOMY
OSTIOLATE
OSTLERESS
OSTRACION
OSTRACISE
OSTRACISM
OSTRACODA
OSTROGOTH
OTHERNESS
OTHERWISE
OTOLOGIST
OTORRHOEA
OTTRELITE
OUBLIETTE
OUDENARDE
OUGHTNESS
OUROSCOPY
OURSELVES
OUT-AND-OUT

OUTBACKER
OUTBOUNDS
OUTCRAFTY
OUTERMOST
OUTERWEAR
OUTFITTER
OUTGIVING
OUTGROWTH
OUTHAULER
OUTLANDER
OUTLAUNCH
OUTLINEAR
OUTLUSTRE
OUTMANTLE
OUTNUMBER
OUT-OF-DATE
OUT-OF-WORK
OUTPARISH
OUT-PORTER
OUTPOURER
OUTREDDEN
OUTRELIEF
OUTRIGGER
OUTROOPER
OUTRUNNER
OUT-SENTRY
OUTSPOKEN
OUTSPREAD
OUTSPRING
OUTSTRAIN
OUTSTRIKE
OUTTONGUE
OUTTRAVEL
OUTWARDLY
OUTWITTED
OUZEL-COCK
OVEN-READY
OVERALLED
OVERBLOWN
OVERBOARD
OVERBOUND
OVERBUILD
OVERCARRY
OVERCATCH
OVERCHECK
OVERCLOUD
OVERCOUNT
OVERCOVER
OVERCROWD
OVERDATED
OVERDIGHT
OVERDRAFT
OVERDRESS
OVERDRIVE
OVEREXERT
OVERFLOWN
OVERFLUSH
OVERGLAZE
OVERGLOOM
OVERGOING
OVERGORGE
OVERGRAIN
OVERGRASS
OVERGREAT
OVERGREEN
OVERGROWN

OVERHAILE
OVERHAPPY
OVERHASTE
OVERHASTY
OVERISSUE
OVERLADEN
OVERLUSTY
OVERLYING
OVERMATCH
OVERMERRY
OVERMOUNT
OVERNIGHT
OVERPAINT
OVERPERCH
OVERPITCH
OVERPOISE
OVERPOWER
OVERPRESS
OVERPRINT
OVERPRIZE
OVERPROOF
OVERPROUD
OVERREACH
OVERRIPEN
OVERROAST
OVERRULER
OVERSCORE
OVERSEXED
OVERSHADE
OVERSHINE
OVERSHOOT
OVERSIGHT
OVERSIZED
OVERSKIRT
OVERSLEEP
OVERSPEND
OVERSPENT
OVERSPILL
OVERSTAIN
OVERSTAND
OVERSTARE
OVERSTATE
OVERSTEER
OVERSTINK
OVERSTOCK
OVERSTREW
OVERSTUDY
OVERSTUNK
OVERSWEAR
OVERSWELL
OVERTAKEN
OVERTHROW
OVERTIMER
OVERTOWER
OVERTRADE
OVERTRAIN
OVERTRICK
OVERTRUMP
OVERTRUST
OVERVALUE
OVERWATCH
OVERWEARY
OVERWEIGH
OVERWHELM
OVERWOUND
OVERWREST

OVERWRITE
OVIBOVINE
OVIDUCTAL
OVIFEROUS
OVIGEROUS
OVIPARITY
OVIPAROUS
OVULATION
OWLE-GLASS
OWL-PARROT
OWNERLESS
OWNERSHIP
OXFORDIAN
OXIDATION
OXYGENATE
OXYGENISE
OXYGENOUS
OXY-HALIDE
OXY-IODIDE
OYSTER-BED
OZOCERITE
OZOKERITE
OZONATION

P

PACEMAKER
PACHYDERM
PACIFICAL
PACK-CINCH
PACK-CLOTH
PACK-DRILL
PACK-HORSE
PACKSHEET
PACKSTAFF
PACK-TRAIN
PACK-TWINE
PACTIONAL
PADDLE-BOX
PADDY-BIRD
PADEMELON
PAD-SADDLE
PADYMELON
PAEDERAST
PAEDEUTIC
PAEDIATRY
PAGEANTRY
PAGE-PROOF
PAIDEUTIC
PAILLASSE
PAILLETTE
PAINFULLY
PAINTABLE
PAINTRESS
PAIR-HORSE
PAIR-ROYAL
PAKISTANI
PALACE-CAR
PALAESTRA
PALAFITTE
PALAMPORE
PALANKEEN
PALANQUIN
PALATABLE
PALATABLY
PALAVERER
PALEMPORE

PALFREYED
PALILLOGY
PALLADIAN
PALLADIUM
PALLADOUS
PALLIASSE
PALLIDITY
PALMARIAN
PALMATELY
PALMATION
PALM-CIVET
PALM-HONEY
PALMHOUSE
PALMIPEDE
PALMISTRY
PALMITATE
PALM-SUGAR
PALPATION
PALPEBRAL
PALPITANT
PALPITATE
PALSGRAVE
PALUDINAL
PALUDRINE
PALUSTRAL
PANCHAYAT
PANCRATIC
PANDATION
PANDEMIAN
PANDERESS
PANDERISM
PANDEROUS
PANDURATE
PANEGOISM
PANEGYRIC
PANELLING
PAN-GERMAN
PANHANDLE
PANIC-BOLT
PANICKING
PANLOGISM
PANNIERED
PANNIKELL
PANOISTIC
PANOPLIED
PANORAMIC
PANSEXUAL
PAN-SLAVIC
PANSOPHIC
PANSPERMY
PANTAGAMY
PANTALEON
PANTALETS
PANTALOON
PANTHEISM
PANTHEIST
PANTHENOL
PANTILING
PANTINGLY
PANTOFFLE
PANTOMIME
PANTOUFLE
PANTRYMAN
PAPERBACK
PAPER-CASE
PAPER-CLIP

PAPER-COAL
PAPER-FILE
PAPER-GIRL
PAPER-MILL
PAPER-PULP
PAPER-REED
PAPETERIE
PAPILLARY
PAPILLATE
PAPILLOMA
PAPILLOSE
PAPILLOTE
PAPILLOUS
PAPILLULE
PARABASIS
PARABOLAS
PARABOLIC
PARACHUTE
PARACLETE
PARACUSIS
PARADISAL
PARADISIC
PARADOXAL
PARADOXER
PARAFFINE
PARAFFINY
PARAGOGIC
PARAGRAPH
PARALALIA
PARALEXIA
PARALOGIA
PARALYSER
PARALYSIS
PARALYTIC
PARAMATTA
PARAMECIA
PARAMEDIC
PARAMETER
PARAMORPH
PARAMOUNT
PARANOEIC
PARANOIAC
PARANYMPH
PARAPETED
PARAPODIA
PARAQUITO
PARASCEVE
PARASITIC
PARATAXIS
PARATONIC
PARAVAUNT
PARBUCKLE
PARCELLED
PARCENARY
PARCHEDLY
PARCHMENT
PARDONING
PAREGORIC
PARENESIS
PARENTAGE
PARFLECHE
PARGASITE
PARGETING
PARGE-WORK
PARHELION
PARHYPATE

PARISCHAN
PARKLANDS
PARKWARDS
PARLEYVOO
PARNASSUS
PAROCHIAL
PAROCHINE
PARODICAL
PARODYING
PAROEMIAC
PAROEMIAL
PAROTITIS
PARQUETED
PARQUETRY
PARRAKEET
PARRHESIA
PARRICIDE
PARROQUET
PARROT-CRY
PARROT-JAW
PARSEEISM
PARSIMONY
PARSONAGE
PARSONISH
PARTAKING
PARTHENON
PARTIALLY
PARTITION
PARTITIVE
PARTITURA
PART-OWNER
PARTRIDGE
PART-TIMER
PARTY-CALL
PARTY-JURY
PARTY-LINE
PARTY-WALL
PASQUILER
PASSAMENT
PASS-CHECK
PASSEMENT
PASSENGER
PASSEPIED
PASSERS-BY
PASSIONAL
PASSIONED
PASSIVELY
PASSIVITY
PASTICCIO
PASTINESS
PASTORALE
PASTORATE
PASTURAGE
PATCHABLE
PATCHOCKE
PATCHOULI
PATCHOULY
PATCHWORK
PATELLATE
PATERCOVE
PATERNITY
PATHOGENY
PATHOLOGY
PATIENTLY
PATINATED
PATRIARCH

PATRICIAN
PATRICIDE
PATRIMONY
PATRIOTIC
PATRISTIC
PATROLLED
PATROLLER
PATROLMAN
PATROLOGY
PATRONAGE
PATRONESS
PATRONISE
PAULICIAN
PAULINIAN
PAULINISM
PAULINIST
PAULOWNIA
PAUPERESS
PAUPERISE
PAUPERISM
PAUSELESS
PAUSINGLY
PAWKINESS
PAY-GRAVEL
PAYMASTER
PAY-OFFICE
PAY-PACKET
PAYSAGIST
PEACEABLE
PEACEABLY
PEACELESS
PEACE-PIPE
PEACETIME
PEACH-BLOW
PEACH-PALM
PEACH-TREE
PEACH-WOOD
PEA-JACKET
PEARL-EDGE
PEARL-EYED
PEARL-GRAY
PEARL-GREY
PEARLITIC
PEARL-SAGO
PEARL-SPAR
PEARL-WORT
PEASANTRY
PEASE-MEAL
PEASE-SOUP
PEASEWEEP
PEA-SOUPER
PEAT-CREEL
PEAT-SMOKE
PEAT-SPADE
PEAT-STACK
PECAN-TREE
PECCANTLY
PECTINATE
PECTINEAL
PECTOLITE
PECULATOR
PECUNIARY
PECUNIOUS
PEDAGOGIC
PEDAGOGUE
PEDAL-BONE

PEDALLING
PEDANTISE
PEDANTISM
PEDATIFID
PEDICULAR
PEDICULUS
PEDIGREED
PEDIPALPI
PEDOMETER
PEEL-HOUSE
PEEL-TOWER
PEEP-SIGHT
PEEVISHLY
PEGMATITE
PEIRASTIC
PEKINGESE
PELASGIAN
PELLAGRIN
PELLITORY
PELORISED
PELTINGLY
PELVIFORM
PEMPHIGUS
PEN-AND-INK
PENCILLED
PENCILLER
PENCIL-ORE
PENDENTLY
PENDICLER
PENDRAGON
PEN-DRIVER
PENDULATE
PENDULINE
PENDULOUS
PENEPLAIN
PENEPLANE
PENETRANT
PENETRATE
PENFRIEND
PENGUINRY
PENHOLDER
PENINSULA
PENISTONE
PENITENCE
PENITENCY
PENNALISM
PENNATULA
PENNIFORM
PENNILESS
PENNINITE
PENNONCEL
PENNY-BANK
PENNYLAND
PENNY-POST
PENNY-RENT
PENNY-WISE
PENNYWORT
PENSILITY
PENSIONER
PENSIVELY
PENTAGRAM
PENTALPHA
PENTAMERY
PENTANGLE
PENTAPODY
PENTARCHY

PENTECOST
PENTHOUSE
PENTOSANE
PENTYLENE
PENULTIMA
PENUMBRAL
PENURIOUS
PEPPER-BOX
PEPPERING
PEPPER-POT
PEPTICITY
PEPTONISE
PERAEOPOD
PERCALINE
PERCEIVER
PERCENTAL
PERCHANCE
PERCHERON
PERCIFORM
PERCOLATE
PERCUSSED
PERCUSSOR
PERDITION
PEREGRINE
PEREIOPOD
PERENNATE
PERENNIAL
PERFECTER
PERFECTLY
PERFECTOR
PERFERVID
PERFERVOR
PERFORANS
PERFORANT
PERFORATE
PERFORMER
PERFUMERY
PERFUSION
PERFUSIVE
PERGUNNAH
PERIAKTOS
PERIBOLOS
PERIBOLUS
PERICLASE
PERICLEAN
PERICLINE
PERICRANY
PERICYCLE
PERIDOTIC
PERIDROME
PERILLING
PERILYMPH
PERIMETER
PERIMETRY
PERIMORPH
PERINAEAL
PERINAEUM
PERINATAL
PERIODATE
PERIPATUS
PERIPETIA
PERIPHERY
PERIPLAST
PERIPROCT
PERISCIAN
PERISCOPE

PERISHING
PERISPERM
PERISTOME
PERISTYLE
PERJUROUS
PERKINESS
PERMANENT
PERMEABLE
PERMEABLY
PERMEANCE
PERMITTED
PERMITTER
PERMUTATE
PERNETTYA
PERPETUAL
PERRADIAL
PERRADIUS
PERSECUTE
PERSEVERE
PERSICISE
PERSIENNE
PERSIMMON
PERSONAGE
PERSONATE
PERSONIFY
PERSONISE
PERSONNEL
PERSUADER
PERTHITIC
PERTINENT
PERTURBED
PERTURBER
PERTUSATE
PERTUSION
PERTUSSAL
PERTUSSIS
PERVASION
PERVASIVE
PERVERTER
PERVICACY
PESSIMISM
PESSIMIST
PESTEROUS
PESTHOUSE
PESTICIDE
PESTILENT
PESTOLOGY
PETAURINE
PETAURIST
PETECHIAE
PETECHIAL
PETER-BOAT
PETERSHAM
PETHIDINE
PETIOLATE
PETIOLULE
PETRIFIED
PETRINISM
PETROLAGE
PETROLEUM
PETROLLED
PETROLOGY
PETTICOAT
PETTINESS
PETTISHLY
PETTITOES

PETULANCE
PETULANCY
PEW-FELLOW
PEW-HOLDER
PEW-OPENER
PHACOIDAL
PHACOLITE
PHACOLITH
PHAENOGAM
PHAGEDENA
PHAGOCYTE
PHALANGAL
PHALANGER
PHALANGES
PHALANGID
PHALANXES
PHALAROPE
PHANARIOT
PHANTASIM
PHANTASMA
PHANTASMS
PHARAONIC
PHARISAIC
PHARYNGAL
PHARYNGES
PHARYNXES
PHASELESS
PHASMIDAE
PHELLOGEN
PHELONION
PHENACITE
PHENAKISM
PHENAKITE
PHENGITES
PHENICIAN
PHENOLATE
PHENOLOGY
PHENOMENA
PHENOTYPE
PHEROMONE
PHIALLING
PHILANDER
PHILATELY
PHILHORSE
PHILIPPIC
PHILISTER
PHILLABEG
PHILLIBEG
PHILLYREA
PHILOGYNY
PHILOLOGY
PHILOMATH
PHILOMELA
PHILOMENE
PHLEBITIS
PHONATION
PHONATORY
PHONEMICS
PHONETICS
PHONETISM
PHONETIST
PHONINESS
PHONMETER
PHONOGRAM
PHONOLITE
PHONOLOGY

PHONOPORE
PHONOTYPE
PHONOTYPY
PHOSPHATE
PHOSPHENE
PHOSPHIDE
PHOSPHINE
PHOSPHITE
PHOSSY-JAW
PHOTOCELL
PHOTOCOPY
PHOTOGENE
PHOTOGENY
PHOTOPHIL
PHOTOPSIA
PHOTOTYPE
PHOTOTYPY
PHRASEMAN
PHRENESIS
PHRENETIC
PHRENITIC
PHRENITIS
PHTHALATE
PHTHALEIN
PHYCOCYAN
PHYCOLOGY
PHYLARCHY
PHYLLOPOD
PHYLOGENY
PHYSICIAN
PHYSICISM
PHYSICIST
PHYSICKED
PHYSIC-NUT
PHYTOGENY
PHYTOLOGY
PHYTOTOMY
PHYTOTRON
PIACEVOLE
PIANISTIC
PIANO-WIRE
PICCADILL
PICKABACK
PICKAPACK
PICKEERER
PICKETING
PICK-PURSE
PICK-THANK
PICK-TOOTH
PICNICKED
PICNICKER
PICTARNIE
PICTOGRAM
PICTORIAL
PIECELESS
PIECEMEAL
PIECE-WORK
PIEPOWDER
PIER-GLASS
PIERRETTE
PIER-TABLE
PIETISTIC
PIFFERARI
PIFFERARO
PIGEON-PEA
PIGGISHLY

PIGGYBACK
PIGGY-BANK
PIGHEADED
PIGMENTAL
PIGNERATE
PIGNORATE
PIGSCONCE
PIKE-PERCH
PIKESTAFF
PILFERAGE
PILFERING
PILGRIMER
PILLAR-BOX
PILLARIST
PILLICOCK
PILLORIED
PILLORISE
PILLOW-CUP
PILOT-BOAT
PILOT-FISH
PILOT-FLAG
PILOT-JACK
PILOTLESS
PIMPERNEL
PIÑA-CLOTH
PINAFORED
PINCHBECK
PINCHCOCK
PINCHFIST
PINDARISE
PINDARISM
PINDARIST
PINEAPPLE
PINE-FINCH
PINE-HOUSE
PINKERTON
PINKINESS
PIN-MAKING
PINNACLED
PINNATELY
PINNIPEDE
PINNULATE
PINSTRIPE
PINTAILED
PINT-STOUP
PIPE-DREAM
PIPE-LAYER
PIPE-LIGHT
PIPE-MAJOR
PIPE-ORGAN
PIPESTONE
PIPE-TRACK
PIPSQUEAK
PIQUANTLY
PIRATICAL
PIROUETTE
PISCATORY
PISCATRIX
PISCIFORM
PISOLITIC
PISTACHIO
PISTAREEN
PISTOLEER
PISTOLLED
PISTON-ROD
PITCH-DARK

PITCHFORK
PITCHPINE
PITCHPIPE
PITCH-TREE
PITEOUSLY
PITHECOID
PITHINESS
PITIFULLY
PIT-SAWYER
PITUITARY
PITUITRIN
PITYINGLY
PIVOTALLY
PIXILATED
PIXY-STOOL
PIZZICATO
PLACATION
PLACATORY
PLACE-KICK
PLACELESS
PLACEMENT
PLACE-NAME
PLACENTAE
PLACENTAL
PLACIDITY
PLACITORY
PLACKLESS
PLACODERM
PLAGUEPIT
PLAID-NEUK
PLAIN-COOK
PLAIN-DARN
PLAINSMAN
PLAINSONG
PLAINTIFF
PLAINTIVE
PLAINWORK
PLANARIAN
PLANATION
PLANETARY
PLANETOID
PLANE-TREE
PLANGENCY
PLANISHER
PLANORBIS
PLANTABLE
PLANTLESS
PLANT-LICE
PLANT-LIKE
PLANTLING
PLANT-LORE
PLANULOID
PLAQUETTE
PLASMATIC
PLASMODIA
PLASTERED
PLASTERER
PLATE-MARK
PLATE-RACK
PLATE-RAIL
PLATE-ROOM
PLATE-SHIP
PLATINISE
PLATINOID
PLATINOUS
PLATITUDE

PLATONISE
PLATONISM
PLATONIST
PLAUSIBLE
PLAUSIBLY
PLAUSTRAL
PLAY-ACTOR
PLAYED-OUT
PLAYFULLY
PLAY-GOING
PLAYHOUSE
PLAY-SPELL
PLAYTHING
PLAY-WORLD
PLEADABLE
PLEASANCE
PLEASEMAN
PLEASURER
PLEIOCENE
PLEIOMERY
PLENARILY
PLENILUNE
PLENITUDE
PLENTEOUS
PLENTIFUL
PLEONASTE
PLETHORIC
PLEURITIC
PLEURITIS
PLICATELY
PLICATION
PLICATURE
PLIGHTFUL
PLOT-PROOF
PLOUGHBOY
PLOUGHING
PLOUGHMAN
PLOUGHMEN
PLUMBEOUS
PLUMBLESS
PLUMB-LINE
PLUMB-RULE
PLUMDAMAS
PLUME-BIRD
PLUMELESS
PLUME-MOTH
PLUMPNESS
PLUM-STONE
PLUMULATE
PLUMULOSE
PLUNDERER
PLURALISE
PLURALISM
PLURALIST
PLURALITY
PLURIPARA
PLUS-FOURS
PLUTOCRAT
PLUTOLOGY
PLUTONIAN
PLUTONISM
PLUTONIST
PLUTONIUM
PLUTONOMY
PNEUMATIC
PNEUMONIA

PNEUMONIC
POCKETFUL
POCKETING
POCKMANKY
PODAGROUS
PODGINESS
POENOLOGY
POETASTER
POETASTRY
POETICISE
POETICISM
POETICULE
POETRESSE
POGO-STICK
POIGNANCY
POINCIANA
POINT-DUTY
POINTEDLY
POINTILLE
POINT-LACE
POINTLESS
POINTSMAN
POISON-GAS
POISON-IVY
POISON-NUT
POISON-OAK
POISONOUS
POKEBERRY
POKER-FACE
POKERWEED
POKER-WORK
POLARISED
POLARISER
POLE-CLIPT
POLEMARCH
POLEMICAL
POLE-VAULT
POLIANITE
POLICE-DOG
POLICEMAN
POLITBURO
POLITICAL
POLITICLY
POLITIQUE
POLLEN-SAC
POLLINATE
POLLINIUM
POLL-MONEY
POLLUTANT
POLLUTION
POLONAISE
POLVERINE
POLYAMIDE
POLYANDRY
POLYARCHY
POLYAXIAL
POLYBASIC
POLYESTER
POLYGAMIA
POLYGAMIC
POLYGENIC
POLYGLOTT
POLYGONAL
POLYGONUM
POLYGRAPH
POLYGYNIA

POLYMASTY
POLYMATHY
POLYMERIC
POLYMORPH
POLYONYMY
POLYPHAGY
POLYPHASE
POLYPHONE
POLYPHONY
POLYPIDOM
POLYPLOID
POLYPORUS
POLYPOSIS
POLYSTYLE
POLYTERUS
POLYTHENE
POLYTONAL
POLYTYPIC
POLYVINYL
POLYWATER
POLYZOARY
POLYZONAL
POLYZOOID
POMACE-FLY
POMACEOUS
POME-WATER
POMMELLED
POMOERIUM
POMPADOUR
POMPHOLYX
POMPOSITY
POMPOUSLY
PONDERATE
PONDEROUS
POND-SNAIL
PONTIANAC
PONTIANAK
PONTIFICE
PONTLEVIS
PONTONEER
PONTONIER
PONTOONER
POODLE-DOG
POORHOUSE
POOR'S-ROLL
POOTERISM
POPLITEAL
POPPERING
POPPYCOCK
POPPY-HEAD
POPPY-SEED
POP-RECORD
POP-SINGER
POPULARLY
PORBEAGLE
PORCELAIN
PORCUPINE
PORIFERAL
PORIFERAN
POROGAMIC
POROMERIC
POROSCOPE
POROSCOPY
PORPHYRIA
PORPHYRIO
PORPORATE

PORRENGER
PORRINGER
PORTATILE
PORTATIVE
PORTERAGE
PORTERESS
PORTFOLIO
PORTHOUSE
PORTICOED
PORTICOES
PORTIONED
PORTIONER
PORTOLANO
PORTRAYAL
PORTRAYER
PORTREEVE
PORTUGUESE
PORTULACA
PORWIGGLE
POSSESSED
POSSESSOR
POSTCRIPT
POST-ENTRY
POSTERIOR
POSTERITY
POST-HASTE
POST-HORSE
POSTHOUSE
POSTICOUS
POSTILION
POSTILLER
POST-NASAL
POST-NATAL
POSTPONER
POSTULANT
POSTULATE
POSTURIST
POST-WOMAN
POTASSIUM
POTATO-PIT
POTATO-ROT
POT-BARLEY
POT-BOILER
POTENTATE
POTENTIAL
POT-HANGER
POTHECARY
POTHOLING
POT-HUNTER
POT-LIQUOR
POTOMETER
POT-POURRI
POTTERING
POTTINGAR
POTTINGER
POTTLE-POT
POT-VALOUR
POT-WALLER
POUCHFULS
POUJADISM
POUJADIST
POULTERER
POULT-FOOT
POUNCE-BOX
POUND-CAKE
POURBOIRE

POURPOINT
POUSOWDIE
POUSSETTE
POUTINGLY
POWDER-BOX
POWELLISE
POWELLISM
POWELLITE
POWER-DIVE
POWERLESS
POWER-LOOM
POZZOLANA
PRACTICAL
PRACTISED
PRACTISER
PRAECOCES
PRAENOMEN
PRAGMATIC
PRAISEFUL
PRAKRITIC
PRANKSOME
PRANKSTER
PRATINGLY
PRAYERFUL
PRAYER-RUG
PRAYINGLY
PREACHIFY
PREACHILY
PREACHING
PRE-ADAMIC
PREBENDAL
PRECANCEL
PRECATIVE
PRECATORY
PRECEDENT
PRECEDING
PRECENTOR
PRECEPTOR
PRECIEUSE
PRECIPICE
PRECISELY
PRECISIAN
PRECISION
PRECISIVE
PRECOCIAL
PRECOCITY
PRECONISE
PRECURRER
PRECURSOR
PREDATION
PREDATIVE
PREDATORY
PREDEFINE
PREDESIGN
PREDEVOTE
PREDICANT
PREDICATE
PREDICTOR
PREDIGEST
PREDIKANT
PREDILECT
PRE-EMPLOY
PRE-EMPTOR
PRE-ENGAGE
PRE-EXILIC
PREFACIAL

PREFATORY	PRETERITE	PROCURESS	PROPODEON
PREFERRED	PRETERMIT	PRODITORY	PROPODEUM
PREFERRER	PRETTYISH	PRODROMAL	PROPONENT
PREFIGURE	PRETTYISM	PRODROMIC	PROPRIETY
PREFIXION	PREVALENT	PRODROMUS	PROPTOSIS
PREGNABLE	PREVENTER	PROEMBRYO	PROPYLAEA
PREGNANCE	PREVERNAL	PROENZYME	PROPYLENE
PREGNANCY	PREVISION	PROFANELY	PROPYLITE
PREHALLUX	PRICELESS	PROFANITY	PRORECTOR
PREHENSOR	PRICE-LIST	PROFESSED	PROROGATE
PREJUDICE	PRICKLING	PROFESSOR	PROSAICAL
PRELATESS	PRICK-SONG	PROFFERED	PROSCRIBE
PRELATIAL	PRICK-SPUR	PROFFERER	PROSCRIPT
PRELATION	PRIDELESS	PROFILIST	PROSECTOR
PRELATISE	PRIESTESS	PROFITEER	PROSECUTE
PRELATISH	PRIEST-RID	PROFITING	PROSELYTE
PRELATISM	PRIMAEVAL	PROFLUENT	PROSE-POEM
PRELATIST	PRIMALITY	PROFUSELY	PROSEUCHA
PRELATURE	PRIMARILY	PROFUSION	PROSEUCHE
PRELECTOR	PRIMATIAL	PROGESTIN	PROSINESS
PRELUDIAL	PRIMENESS	PROGNOSES	PROSODIAL
PRELUSION	PRIMIPARA	PROGNOSIS	PROSODIAN
PRELUSIVE	PRIMITIAE	PROGRAMME	PROSODIST
PRELUSORY	PRIMITIAL	PROJECTOR	PROSTATIC
PREMATURE	PRIMITIAS	PROLAMINE	PROSTRATE
PREMONISH	PRIMITIVE	PROLAPSUS	PROTANDRY
PREMOSAIC	PRIMROSED	PROLATELY	PROTECTED
PREMOTION	PRIMULINE	PROLATION	PROTECTOR
PRENOTION	PRINCEDOM	PROLATIVE	PROTEINIC
PRENUBILE	PRINCEKIN	PROLEPSES	PROTESTER
PREOCCUPY	PRINCELET	PROLEPSIS	PROTESTOR
PREOPTION	PRINCESSE	PROLEPTIC	PROTHALLI
PREORALLY	PRINCIPAL	PROLETARY	PROTHESIS
PREORDAIN	PRINCIPIA	PROLICIDE	PROTHETIC
PREPACKED	PRINCIPLE	PROLIXITY	PROTHORAX
PREPOLLEX	PRINTABLE	PROLOGISE	PROTISTIC
PREPOTENT	PRINTLESS	PROLONGER	PROTOGINE
PREPUTIAL	PRINT-SHOP	PROLUSION	PROTOGYNY
PREROSION	PRIORSHIP	PROLUSORY	PROTONEMA
PRESBYOPE	PRISMATIC	PROMACHOS	PROTOTYPE
PRESBYOPY	PRISONOUS	PROMENADE	PROTOXIDE
PRESBYTER	PRISON-VAN	PROMINENT	PROTOZOAN
PRESCIENT	PRIVATEER	PROMISING	PROTOZOIC
PRESCIOUS	PRIVATELY	PROMISSOR	PROTOZOON
PRESCRIBE	PRIVATION	PROMOTION	PROUDNESS
PRESCRIPT	PRIVATIVE	PROMOTIVE	PROUD-PIED
PRESCUTUM	PRIVILEGE	PROMPTING	PROUSTIAN
PRESELECT	PRIZE-CREW	PROMPTURE	PROUSTITE
PRESENTEE	PRIZE-LIST	PROMUSCIS	PROVEABLY
PRESENTER	PRIZE-RING	PRONATION	PROVEDORE
PRESENTLY	PROBATION	PRONENESS	PROVENÇAL
PRESERVER	PROBATIVE	PRONGBUCK	PROVENDER
PRESHRINK	PROBATORY	PRONGHORN	PROVIDENT
PRESIDENT	PROBOSCIS	PRONOUNCE	PROVISION
PRESIDIAL	PROCACITY	PROOEMION	PROVISORY
PRESIDIUM	PROCEDURE	PROOEMIUM	PROVOCANT
PRESS-BOOK	PROCEEDER	PROOFLESS	PROVOKING
PRESS-GANG	PROCERITY	PROOF-MARK	PROVOSTRY
PRESS-MARK	PROCESSED	PROOF-READ	PROWESSED
PRESS-ROOM	PROCIDENT	PROOF-TEXT	PROXIMATE
PRESS-STUD	PROCLITIC	PROPAGATE	PROXIMITY
PRESS-WORK	PROCONSUL	PROPELLED	PROZYMITE
PRESUMING	PROCREANT	PROPELLER	PRUDENTLY
PRETENDED	PROCREATE	PROPERDIN	PRUDHOMME
PRETENDER	PROCTITIS	PROPHETIC	PRUDISHLY
PRETERIST	PROCURACY	PROPIONIC	PRUNELLOS

PRURIENCE
PRURIENCY
PRUSSIATE
PRYTANEUM
PSALM-BOOK
PSALMODIC
PSALM-TUNE
PSALTRESS
PSAMMITIC
PSEUDAXIS
PSEUDONYM
PSEUDOPOD
PSITTACUS
PSORIASIS
PSORIATIC
PSYCHICAL
PSYCHOGAS
PSYCHOSES
PSYCHOSIS
PSYCHOTIC
PTARMIGAN
PTERIDIUM
PTEROPODA
PTEROSAUR
PTERYGIAL
PTERYGIUM
PTERYGOID
PTOLEMAIC
PUBESCENT
PUBLICISE
PUBLICIST
PUBLICITY
PUBLISHER
PUCK-HAIRY
PUDDENING
PUDENDOUS
PUDGINESS
PUERILITY
PUERPERAL
PUFF-ADDER
PUFFINESS
PUFFINGLY
PUFF-PASTE
PUG-ENGINE
PUGNACITY
PUISSANCE
PUISSAUNT
PULICIDAE
PULLULATE
PULMONARY
PULMONATA
PULMONATE
PULPBOARD
PULPINESS
PULPITEER
PULPSTONE
PULSATILE
PULSATION
PULSATIVE
PULSATORY
PULSELESS
PULSE-RATE
PULSE-WAVE
PULVERINE
PULVERING
PULVERISE

PULVEROUS
PULVILLAR
PULVILLED
PULVILLIO
PULVILLUS
PULVINATE
PULVINULE
PUMICEOUS
PUMMELLED
PUMP-WATER
PUNCH-BALL
PUNCHBOWL
PUNCH-CARD
PUNCH-PROP
PUNCTATOR
PUNCTILIO
PUNCTUATE
PUNCTURED
PUNGENTLY
PUNISHING
PUNJAUBEE
PUPILLAGE
PUPILLARY
PUPILLATE
PUPPETEER
PUPPYHOOD
PURCHASER
PURDONIUM
PURE-BLOOD
PURGATION
PURGATIVE
PURGATORY
PURIFYING
PURITANIC
PURLOINER
PURPOSELY
PURPOSIVE
PURPUREAL
PURRINGLY
PURSUABLE
PURSUANCE
PURULENCE
PURULENCY
PUSH-CHAIR
PUSH-CYCLE
PUSHFULLY
PUSHINGLY
PUSSYFOOT
PUSTULATE
PUSTULOUS
PUTREFIED
PUTRIDITY
PUTTER-OUT
PUZZLEDOM
PUZZLE-PEG
PUZZOLANA
PYCNIDIUM
PYGOSTYLE
PYORRHOEA
PYRACANTH
PYRALIDAE
PYRAMIDAL
PYRAMIDES
PYRAMIDIC
PYRAMIDON
PYRENAEAN

PYRENEITE
PYRETHRUM
PYRIDOXIN
PYRITICAL
PYROGENIC
PYROLATER
PYROLATRY
PYROLYSIS
PYROMANCY
PYROMANIA
PYROMETER
PYROMETRY
PYROPHONE
PYROSCOPE
PYROXENIC
PYROXYLIC
PYROXYLIN
PYRRHONIC
PYTHONESS

Q

QUADRATIC
QUADRATUS
QUADRIFID
QUADRIGAE
QUADRILLE
QUADRUMAN
QUADRUPED
QUADRUPLE
QUADRUPLY
QUAERITUR
QUAESITUM
QUAIL-CALL
QUAIL-PIPE
QUAKERDOM
QUAKERESS
QUAKERISH
QUAKERISM
QUAKINESS
QUAKINGLY
QUALIFIED
QUALIFIER
QUALITIED
QUALMLESS
QUANTICAL
QUARENDEN
QUARENDER
QUARRYING
QUARRYMAN
QUARRY-SAP
QUARTERED
QUARTERLY
QUARTETTE
QUARTETTO
QUARTZITE
QUARTZOSE
QUASIMODO
QUAVERING
QUEBRACHO
QUEENHOOD
QUEENLESS
QUEEN-LIKE
QUEEN-POST
QUEEN'S-ARM
QUEENSHIP
QUEERNESS

QUENCHING
QUERCETUM
QUERIMONY
QUERULOUS
QUESTRIST
QUIBBLING
QUICK-BEAM
QUICK-BORN
QUICKENER
QUICK-EYED
QUICK-FIRE
QUICKLIME
QUICKNESS
QUICKSAND
QUICKSTEP
QUIESCENT
QUIETNESS
QUIETSOME
QUILLWORT
QUINOLINE
QUINQUINA
QUINTETTE
QUINTETTO
QUINTROON
QUINTUPLE
QUIRISTER
QUIT-CLAIM
QUITTANCE
QUIVERFUL
QUIVERISH
QUIXOTISM
QUIZZICAL
QUOTATION
QUOTATIVE
QUOTIDIAN
QUOTITION

R

RABATMENT
RABATTING
RABBETING
RABBINATE
RABBINISM
RABBINIST
RABBINITE
RABIDNESS
RACCAHOUT
RACE-GOING
RACEHORSE
RACETRACK
RACHIDIAL
RACHIDIAN
RACIALISM
RACIALIST
RACIATION
RACING-BIT
RACKETEER
RACKETING
RACK-PUNCH
RACONTEUR
RADDLEMAN
RADIALISE
RADIALITY
RADIAL-PLY
RADIANTLY
RADIATELY

RADIATION
RADIATIVE
RADICALLY
RADICATED
RADICULAR
RADIOGRAM
RADIOLOGY
RAFFINATE
RAFFINOSE
RAFFISHLY
RAFFLESIA
RAFTERING
RAGPICKER
RAILBORNE
RAIL-FENCE
RAILINGLY
RAIL-MOTOR
RAIN-BOUND
RAINBOWED
RAINCHECK
RAIN-CLOUD
RAIN-GAUGE
RAININESS
RAIN-MAKER
RAIN-PRINT
RAINPROOF
RAIN-STONE
RAINSTORM
RAINTIGHT
RAINWATER
RAJAHSHIP
RAKEHELLY
RAKESHAME
RAMBUNTAN
RAMFEEZLE
RAMIFYING
RAMILLIES
RAMPANTLY
RAMPICKED
RANCHERIA
RANCIDITY
RANCOROUS
RANGINESS
RANK-RIDER
RANSACKER
RANSHAKLE
RANTERISM
RANTINGLY
RANTIPOLE
RANUNCULI
RANZELMAN
RAPACIOUS
RAPIDNESS
RAPTORIAL
RAPTURISE
RAPTURIST
RAPTUROUS
RARE-EARTH
RAREE-SHOW
RAREFYING
RASCAILLE
RASCALDOM
RASCALISM
RASCALITY
RASKOLNIK
RASPATORY

RASPBERRY
RASP-HOUSE
RASPINGLY
RATEPAYER
RATHEREST
RATHERIPE
RATHERISH
RATIFYING
RATIONALE
RAT-POISON
RATTENING
RATTLEBAG
RAUCOUSLY
RAUWOLFIA
RAVELLING
RAVELMENT
RAVEN-BONE
RAVEN-DUCK
RAVISHING
RAY-FUNGUS
RAZORABLE
RAZOR-BACK
RAZOR-BILL
RAZOR-CLAM
RAZOR-EDGE
RAZOR-FISH
REACHABLE
REACHLESS
REACQUIRE
REACTANCE
READDRESS
READINESS
READVANCE
READY-MADE
REALISING
REALISTIC
REALMLESS
REANIMATE
REAPPAREL
REAPPOINT
REAR-DORSE
REARGUARD
REARHORSE
REAR-LIGHT
REARMOUSE
REARRANGE
REASONING
REASSURER
REBAPTISE
REBAPTISM
REBEL-LIKE
REBELLING
REBELLION
REBLOSSOM
REBOATION
REBUKABLE
REBUKEFUL
REBUTTING
RECALESCE
RECALMENT
RECAPTION
RECAPTURE
RECENSION
RECEPTION
RECEPTIVE
RECESSION

RECESSIVE
RECHABITE
RECHAUFFÉ
RECHERCHÉ
RECIPIENT
RECKONING
RECLINATE
RECLINING
RECLUSELY
RECLUSION
RECLUSIVE
RECLUSORY
RECOGNISE
RECOINAGE
RECOLLECT
RECOMBINE
RECOMFORT
RECOMMEND
RECOMPACT
RECOMPOSE
RECONCILE
RECONDITE
RECONFIRM
RECONQUER
RECONVERT
RECORDING
RECOVEREE
RECOVERER
RECOVEROR
RECREANCE
RECREANCY
RECREMENT
RECRUITAL
RECRUITER
RECTANGLE
RECTIFIED
RECTIFIER
RECTITUDE
RECTORATE
RECTORESS
RECTORIAL
RECTRICES
RECUMBENT
RECURRENT
RECURRING
RECURSION
RECURSIVE
RECUSANCE
REDACTION
REDBREAST
RED-CARPET
REDDENDUM
REDDING-UP
REDDLEMAN
REDECRAFT
REDEEMING
REDELIVER
REDESCEND
REDEVELOP
RED-HAIRED
RED-HANDED
RED-HEADED
RED-HEELED
REDINGOTE
REDIVIVUS
RED-LEGGED

RED-LETTER
RED-LOOKED
REDOLENCE
REDOLENCY
REDOUBTED
RED-PLAGUE
RED-POLLED
REDRESSER
REDSTREAK
RED-TAPISM
RED-TAPIST
REDUCIBLE
REDUCTANT
REDUCTION
REDUCTIVE
REDUNDANT
REED-GRASS
RE-EDIFIER
REEDINESS
REED-KNIFE
REED-ORGAN
RE-EDUCATE
REEF-POINT
RE-ELEVATE
REELINGLY
RE-ENFORCE
RE-ENTRANT
RE-EXAMINE
REFASHION
REFECTION
REFECTORY
REFELLING
REFERABLE
REFERENCE
REFERENDA
REFERRING
REFINEDLY
REFITMENT
REFITTING
REFLATION
REFLECTED
REFLECTER
REFLECTOR
REFLEXION
REFLEXIVE
REFLOWING
REFLUENCE
REFORMADE
REFORMADO
REFORMISM
REFORMIST
REFORTIFY
REFOUNDER
REFRACTED
REFRACTOR
REFRESHEN
REFRESHER
REFULGENT
REFURBISH
REFURNISH
REFUSABLE
REFUTABLE
REFUTABLY
REGARDANT
REGARDFUL
REGARDING

REGICIDAL
REGIMINAL
REGIONARY
REGISTRAR
REGRATING
REGRETFUL
REGRETTED
REGUERDON
REGULARLY
REGULATOR
REHEARING
REHEARSAL
REHEARSER
REHOUSING
REICHSRAT
REICHSTAG
REIMBURSE
REINFORCE
REINHABIT
REINSPECT
REINSPIRE
REINSTALL
REINSTATE
REINSURER
REINVOLVE
REITERANT
REITERATE
REJECTION
REJOICING
REJOINDER
RELAPSING
RELATIVAL
RELAY-RACE
RELEGABLE
RELENTING
RELEVANCE
RELEVANCY
RELIEVING
RELIGIOSE
RELIGIOUS
RELIQUARY
RELIQUIAE
RELUCTANT
RELUCTATE
REMAINDER
REMANENCE
REMANENCY
REMARQUED
REMEASURE
REMEDIATE
REMEDYING
REMERCIED
REMIGRATE
REMINDFUL
REMINISCE
REMISSION
REMISSIVE
REMISSORY
REMITMENT
REMITTENT
REMITTING
REMONTANT
REMOVABLE
REMOVABLY
RENASCENT
RENCONTRE

RENDERING
RENDITION
RENEWABLE
RENFIERST
RENITENCY
RENNET-BAG
RENOUNCER
RENOVATOR
RENTALLER
RENVERSED
REPAIR-MAN
REPARABLE
REPARABLY
REPASSAGE
REPASTURE
REPAYABLE
REPAYMENT
REPEATING
REPECHAGE
REPELLANT
REPELLENT
REPELLING
REPENTANT
REPERCUSS
REPERTORY
REPERUSAL
REPLENISH
REPLETION
REPLICATE
REPORTAGE
REPORTING
REPOSEDLY
REPOSEFUL
REPOSITOR
REPOSSESS
REPOTTING
REPREHEND
REPRESENT
REPRESSOR
REPRIEVAL
REPRIMAND
REPROBACY
REPROBATE
REPRODUCE
REPROVING
REPTATION
REPTILIAN
REPUBLISH
REPUDIATE
REPUGNANT
REPULSION
REPULSIVE
REPUTABLE
REPUTABLY
REPUTEDLY
REQUESTER
REQUICKEN
REQUIRING
REQUISITE
REREBRACE
REREDORSE
REREDOSSE
REREMOUSE
RESCUABLE
RESECTION
RESEMBLER

RESENTFUL
RESENTIVE
RESERPINE
RESERVIST
RESERVOIR
RESHUFFLE
RESIDENCE
RESIDENCY
RESIDUARY
RESIDUOUS
RESILIENT
RESINOSIS
RESISTANT
RESISTENT
RESISTIVE
RESOLUBLE
RESOLVENT
RESONANCE
RESONATOR
RESORBENT
RESPECTER
RESPONDER
RESSALDAR
RESTARTER
RESTFULLY
RESTHOUSE
RESTIFORM
RESTITUTE
RESTIVELY
RESTRAINT
RESTRINGE
RESULTANT
RESULTFUL
RESULTING
RESUMABLE
RESURGENT
RESURRECT
RETAINING
RETALIATE
RETARDANT
RETENTION
RETENTIVE
RETEXTURE
RETIARIUS
RETICENCE
RETICENCY
RETICULAR
RETICULUM
RETINITIS
RETINULAE
RETINULAR
RETIREDLY
RETORSION
RETORTION
RETORTIVE
RETOUCHER
RETRACTED
RETRACTOR
RETREADED
RETRIBUTE
RETRIEVAL
RETRIEVER
RETROCEDE
RETRODDEN
RETROFLEX
RETROUSSÉ

RETROVERT
REVALENTA
REVEALING
REVELATOR
REVELLING
REVEL-ROUT
REVENGING
REVENGIVE
REVERABLE
REVERENCE
REVERSELY
REVERSING
REVERSION
REVERTIVE
REVETMENT
REVETTING
REVICTUAL
REVISABLE
REVIVABLE
REVIVABLY
REVOCABLE
REVOCABLY
REVOLTING
REVOLVING
REVULSION
REVULSIVE
REWARDFUL
REWARDING
REWRITTEN
RHACHITIS
RHAMPHOID
RHAPHIDES
RHAPONTIC
RHAPSODIC
RHEOCHORD
RHEOLOGIC
RHEOMETER
RHEOTAXIS
RHEOTROPE
RHETORISE
RHEUMATIC
RHEUMATIZ
RHINEODON
RHINEWINE
RHINOLITH
RHINOLOGY
RHIPIDATE
RHIPIDION
RHIPIDIUM
RHIZOCARP
RHIZOCAUL
RHIZOIDAL
RHIZOPODA
RHODAMINE
RHODANATE
RHODANISE
RHODESIAN
RHODOLITE
RHODONITE
RHODOPSIN
RHOEADINE
RHONCHIAL
RHOPALISM
RHOTACISE
RHOTACISM
RHUMB-LINE

RHYMELESS
RHYMESTER
RHYME-WORD
RHYNCHOTA
RHYOLITIC
RHYTHMISE
RHYTHMIST
RIBATTUTA
RIBAUDRED
RIBBONISM
RIBBON-MAN
RIB-PLOUGH
RICARDIAN
RICEFIELD
RICE-FLOUR
RICEGRAIN
RICEGRASS
RICE-PAPER
RICERCARE
RICERCATA
RICE-WATER
RICHARDIA
RICINULEI
RICKETILY
RICKSTAND
RICKSTICK
RIDDLINGS
RIDERLESS
RIDGEBACK
RIDGEBONE
RIDGE-POLE
RIDGE-ROPE
RIDGE-TILE
RIDICULER
RIDING-ROD
RIFLE-BIRD
RIFLE-SHOT
RIGHTABLE
RIGHT-BANK
RIGHT-DOWN
RIGHTEOUS
RIGHT-HAND
RIGHTLESS
RIGHTNESS
RIGHTWARD
RIGHT-WING
RIGIDNESS
RIGMAROLE
RIGWIDDIE
RIGWOODIE
RING-CANAL
RING-CROSS
RING-DANCE
RING-FENCE
RING-GAUGE
RINGINGLY
RINGLETED
RING-MONEY
RING-OUSEL
RING-OUZEL
RING-SHAKE
RINGSIDER
RING-SMALL
RING-SNAKE
RING-STAND
RIOTOUSLY

RIPIENIST
RIPPINGLY
RIPUARIAN
RISKINESS
RISK-MONEY
RITORNELL
RITUALISE
RITUALISM
RITUALIST
RIVALLESS
RIVALLING
RIVALSHIP
RIVER-BANK
RIVER-FLAT
RIVERHEAD
RIVER-JACK
RIVERLESS
RIVERLIKE
RIVER-SAND
RIVERSIDE
RIVER-TIDE
RIVER-WALL
RIVERWEED
RIVET-HEAD
RIVET-HOLE
RIVETTING
RIX-DOLLAR
ROAD-AGENT
ROADBLOCK
ROAD-BORNE
ROAD-CRAFT
ROADHOUSE
ROAD-MAKER
ROAD-METAL
ROAD-SENSE
ROADSTEAD
ROARINGLY
ROAST-BEEF
ROAST-MEAT
ROBBER-FLY
ROBE-MAKER
ROCAMBOLE
ROCK-BASIN
ROCK-BORER
ROCK-BOUND
ROCK-BRAKE
ROCKCRESS
ROCK-DRILL
ROCKETEER
ROCK-FLOUR
ROCK-GUANO
ROCKINESS
ROCK-PERCH
ROCK-PIPIT
ROCK-PLANT
ROCK-SHAFT
ROCK-SNAKE
ROCK-TRIPE
ROCKWATER
RODFISHER
ROGUESHIP
ROGUISHLY
ROISTERER
ROLL-ABOUT
ROMANCING
ROMANISER

ROME-PENNY
ROMEWARDS
ROMPINGLY
ROMPISHLY
ROOD-TOWER
ROOF-BOARD
ROOF-GUARD
ROOF-PLATE
ROOMINESS
ROOT-BOUND
ROOT-CAUSE
ROOT-EATER
ROOT-HOUSE
ROOT-PRUNE
ROOTSTOCK
ROPE-DANCE
ROPE-HOUSE
ROPE-MAKER
ROPE-SOLED
ROPE-TRICK
ROQUEFORT
RORSCHACH
ROSACEOUS
ROSA-SOLIS
ROSE-APPLE
ROSE-CROSS
ROSE-ELDER
ROSE-NOBLE
ROSE-TOPAZ
ROSE-WATER
ROSINANTE
ROSIN-WEED
ROSMARINE
ROSMINIAN
ROSTELLUM
ROSTRATED
ROTAPLANE
ROTATABLE
ROTOGRAPH
ROTOR-SHIP
ROTUNDATE
ROTUNDITY
ROUGHCAST
ROUGH-DRAW
ROUGH-HEWN
ROUGH-NECK
ROUGHNESS
ROUGH-SHOD
ROUMANIAN
ROUMANSCH
ROUNCEVAL
ROUND-ARCH
ROUNDELAY
ROUND-EYED
ROUND-FISH
ROUNDHAND
ROUNDHEAD
ROUNDNESS
ROUNDSMAN
ROUND-TRIP
ROUND-WORM
ROUSEMENT
ROUSINGLY
ROUSSETTE
ROUTE-STEP
ROUTINEER

ROUTINISM
ROUTINIST
ROUTOUSLY
ROWAN-TREE
ROWDINESS
ROWDOWDOW
ROWEL-HEAD
ROWELLING
ROWEL-SPUR
ROXBURGHE
ROYSTERER
ROZINANTE
RUBBERISE
RUBBISHLY
RUBELLITE
RUBIACEAE
RUBICELLE
RUBINEOUS
RUBRICATE
RUBRICIAN
RUCTATION
RUDBECKIA
RUDDINESS
RUDDLEMAN
RUE-LEAVED
RUFESCENT
RUFF-A-DUFF
RUFFIANLY
RUG-HEADED
RUINATION
RUINOUSLY
RULERSHIP
RUM-BUTTER
RUMINATOR
RUMMINESS
RUMP-STEAK
RUM-RUNNER
RUNCINATE
RUNECRAFT
RUNE-STAVE
RUNNINGLY
RURALNESS
RURITANIA
RUSH-GROWN
RUSHINESS
RUSHLIGHT
RUSSETING
RUSSOPHIL
RUSTICATE
RUSTICIAL
RUSTICISE
RUSTICITY
RUSTINESS
RUST-PROOF
RUSTY-BACK
RUTACEOUS
RUTHENIAN
RUTHENIUM
RUTHFULLY
RUTILATED
RYE-COFFEE
RYE-WHISKY

S
SABADILLA
SABBATINE

SABBATISE
SABBATISM
SABELLIAN
SABIANISM
SABRE-WING
SACCHARIC
SACCHARIN
SACCHARUM
SACCIFORM
SACHEMDOM
SACKCLOTH
SACRAMENT
SACRARIUM
SACRIFICE
SACRILEGE
SACRISTAN
SADDLEBAG
SAFETY-PIN
SAFFLOWER
SAFFRONED
SAFRANINE
SAGACIOUS
SAGAPENUM
SAGE-APPLE
SAGE-BRUSH
SAGE-GREEN
SAGENITIC
SAGITTARY
SAGITTATE
SAIL-BORNE
SAIL-BROAD
SAIL-CLOTH
SAIL-FLUKE
SAILOR-HAT
SAILORING
SAILOR-MAN
SAILPLANE
SAINTFOIN
SAINTHOOD
SAINTLIKE
SAINTLING
SAINTSHIP
SALACIOUS
SALANGANE
SALE-PRICE
SALERATUS
SALES-TALK
SALICETUM
SALICYLIC
SALIENTIA
SALIENTLY
SALIFYING
SALLEE-MAN
SALLOWISH
SALLYPORT
SALMON-FLY
SALMON-FRY
SALMONOID
SALOMONIC

SALOON-BAR
SALOON-CAR
SALOONIST
SALTATION
SALTATORY
SALT-GLAZE
SALT-HORSE
SALTINESS
SALTISHLY
SALT-MARSH
SALT-MONEY
SALTPETRE
SALT-RHEUM
SALT-SPOON
SALT-WATER
SALT-WORKS
SALUBRITY
SALVARSAN
SALVATION
SALVATORY
SAMARITAN
SAMOYEDIC
SANBENITO
SANCTUARY
SANDALLED
SANDARACH
SAND-BLAST
SAND-BLIND
SAND-BREAK
SAND-CRACK
SAND-DANCE
SAND-DEVIL
SAND-GLASS
SAND-GRAIN
SAND-GRASS
SANDINESS
SAND-MASON
SANDPAPER
SANDPIPER
SAND-PRIDE
SAND-SCREW
SAND-SNAKE
SAND-SPOUT
SANDSTONE
SAND-STORM
SAND-TABLE
SAND-YACHT
SANFORISE
SANG-FROID
SANHEDRIM
SANHEDRIN
SANITARIA
SANS-APPEL
SANTONICA
SAPAN-WOOD
SAPHEADED
SAPIDLESS
SAPIENTLY
SAPODILLA
SAPONARIA
SAPPHIRED
SAPPINESS
SAPRAEMIA
SAPRAEMIC
SARACENIC
SARBACANE

SARCASTIC
SARCOCARP
SARCODINA
SARCOLOGY
SARCOMATA
SARCOPTES
SARCOPTIC
SARDINIAN
SARDONIAN
SARMATIAN
SARMENTUM
SARTORIAL
SARTORIAN
SARTORIUS
SASH-FRAME
SASKATOON
SASSAFRAS
SASSANIAN
SASSARARA
SASSENACH
SASSOLITE
SATANICAL
SATEDNESS
SATELLITE
SATIATION
SATIN-BIRD
SATINETTA
SATINETTE
SATIN-SPAR
SATINWOOD
SATI-OUTAN
SATIRICAL
SATISFIED
SATISFIER
SATURABLE
SATURATED
SATURATOR
SATURNIAN
SATURNINE
SATURNISM
SATURNIST
SATYRICAL
SATYRIDAE
SATYRINAE
SAUCER-EYE
SAUCERFUL
SAUCINESS
SAUCISSON
SAUNTERER
SAUROPODA
SAUTERNES
SAVAGEDOM
SAVOURILY
SAXIFRAGA
SAXIFRAGE
SAXOPHONE
SAY-MASTER
'SBODIKINS
SCAFF-RAFF
SCAGLIOLA
SCALD-CROW
SCALD-FISH
SCALD-HEAD
SCALDINGS
SCALE-BEAM
SCALE-FERN

SCALE-FISH
SCALE-LEAF
SCALELESS
SCALELIKE
SCALE-MOSS
SCALE-WORK
SCALINESS
SCALLAWAG
SCALLOPED
SCALLYWAG
SCALPLESS
SCALP-LOCK
SCALY-BARK
SCAMBLING
SCAMP-WORK
SCANSORES
SCANTLING
SCANTNESS
SCAPEGOAT
SCAPELESS
SCAPEMENT
SCAPHOPOD
SCAPOLITE
SCAPULARY
SCARABOID
SCARECROW
SCARE-HEAD
SCARE-LINE
SCARF-RING
SCARFSKIN
SCARFWISE
SCARIFIED
SCARIFIER
SCARPETTI
SCARPETTO
SCARPINES
SCART-FREE
SCATHEFUL
SCATOLOGY
SCATTERED
SCATTERER
SCAUP-DUCK
SCAVENGER
SCAZONTIC
SCELERATE
SCENARISE
SCENARIST
SCENE-DOCK
SCENTLESS
SCEPTICAL
SCHEDULED
SCHEELITE
SCHEMATIC
SCHIAVONE
SCHILLING
SCHISTOSE
SCHISTOUS
SCHIZOPOD
SCHLEMIEL
SCHLEMIHL
SCHLIEREN
SCHMALTZY
SCHNAPPER
SCHNAUZER
SCHNORKEL
SCHNORRER

SCHOLARCH
SCHOLARLY
SCHOLIAST
SCHOOLBAG
SCHOOLBOY
SCHOOL-DAY
SCHOOLERY
SCHOOLING
SCHOOLMAN
SCIAENOID
SCIARIDAE
SCIATICAL
SCIENTIAL
SCIENTISM
SCIENTIST
SCINTILLA
SCIOSOPHY
SCIRRHOUS
SCISSORER
SCIURIDAE
SCLEREIDE
SCLERITIS
SCLEROSIS
SCLEROTAL
SCLEROTIA
SCLEROTIC
SCOLECITE
SCOLECOID
SCOLIOSIS
SCOLIOTIC
SCOLYTOID
SCOMBROID
SCONCHEON
SCORBUTIC
SCORCHING
SCORIFIER
SCORODITE
SCORPAENA
SCORPIOID
SCOTCHMAN
SCOTIFIED
SCOTISTIC
SCOTOMATA
SCOUNDREL
SCOUTHERY
SCRAGGILY
SCRAMBLER
SCRAP-BOOK
SCRAPE-GUT
SCRAP-HEAP
SCRAP-IRON
SCRAPPILY
SCRAPPING
SCRATCHER
SCRAWLING
SCREAMING
SCREECHER
SCREENING
SCREEVING
SCREWBALL
SCREW-BOLT
SCREW-DOWN
SCREW-NAIL
SCREW-PILE
SCREW-PINE
SCREW-WISE

SCRIBABLE
SCRIBBLER
SCRIMMAGE
SCRIMPILY
SCRIMSHAW
SCRIPPAGE
SCRIPTORY
SCRIPTURE
SCRIVENER
SCRODDLED •
SCROG-BUSH
SCROG-BUSS
SCROLLERY
SCROLL-SAW
SCROUNGER
SCRUBBING
SCRUB-BIRD
SCRUM-HALF
SCRUMMAGE
SCRUTABLE
SCRUTATOR
SCRUTOIRE
SCUDDALER
SCULPTURE
SCUMBLING
SCUMMINGS
SCUNCHEON
SCURRIOUR
SCUTCHEON
SCUTCHING
SCUTELLAR
SCUTELLUM
SCUTIFORM
SCYBALOUS
SCYPHOZOA
SCYTHEMAN
SEA-ANCHOR
SEA-BATHER
SEA-BEATEN
SEA-BOTTLE
SEA-BOTTOM
SEA-BREACH
SEA-BREEZE
SEA-CANARY
SEA-CHANGE
SEA-DRAGON
SEAFARING
SEA-FISHER
SEA-GINGER
SEA-GIRDLE
SEA-ISLAND
SEA-LAWYER
SEA-LENTIL
SEA-LETTER
SEAMINESS
SEAMY-SIDE
SEA-NETTLE
SEANNACHY
SEA-ORACHE
SEA-ORANGE
SEA-PARROT
SEA-RANGER
SEARCHING
SEA-ROBBER
SEA-ROCKET
SEA-ROVING

SEA-SALMON
SEA-SATYRE
SEA-SLEEVE
SEASONING
SEA-SORROW
SEA-SPIDER
SEA-SQUIRT
SEA-STRAND
SEA-TANGLE
SEAT-STICK
SEA-TURTLE
SEA-URCHIN
SEA-WALLED
SEAWARDLY
SEAWORTHY
SEBACEOUS
SE-BAPTIST
SECATEURS
SECERNENT
SECESSION
SECLUSION
SECLUSIVE
SECONDARY
SECOND-DAY
SECRETAGE
SECRETARY
SECRETION
SECRETIVE
SECRETORY
SECTARIAL
SECTARIAN
SECTILITY
SECTIONAL
SECTORIAL
SECULARLY
SECUNDINE
SECURABLE
SECURANCE
SECURITAN
SEDENTARY
SEDGE-BIRD
SEDGE-WREN
SEDITIOUS
SEDUCTION
SEDUCTIVE
SEED-CORAL
SEED-DRILL
SEED-FIELD
SEEDINESS
SEED-PEARL
SEED-PLANT
SEED-STALK
SEEMINGLY
SEEMLIEST
SEEMLIHED
SEGHOLATE
SEGMENTAL
SEGMENTED
SEGREGATE
SEIGNIORY
SEIGNORAL
SEINE-BOAT
SELACHIAN
SELDSHOWN
SELECTION
SELECTIVE

SELECT-MAN
SELENIOUS
SELENITIC
SELF-ABUSE
SELF-BEGOT
SELF-BORNE
SELF-DOUBT
SELF-DRIVE
SELF-FACED
SELFISHLY
SELF-MOVED
SELF-PIOUS
SELF-SLAIN
SELF-TRUST
SELF-WRONG
SELJUKIAN
SEMANTEME
SEMANTRON
SEMAPHORE
SEMBLABLE
SEMBLABLY
SEMBLANCE
SEMEIOTIC
SEMESTRAL
SEMI-ANGLE
SEMI-ARIAN
SEMI-BAJAN
SEMIBREVE
SEMICOLON
SEMIFINAL
SEMIFLUID
SEMIGRAND
SEMILATUS
SEMILUNAR
SEMI-METAL
SEMINALLY
SEMIOLOGY
SEMIOTICS
SEMIPLUME
SEMI-RIGID
SEMI-SAXON
SEMITONIC
SEMIVOWEL
SEMPITERN
SEMUNCIAL
SENESCENT
SENESCHAL
SENHORITA
SENIORITY
SENNACHIE
SENSATION
SENSELESS
SENSITISE
SENSITIVE
SENSORIAL
SENSORIUM
SENSUALLY
SENTENCER
SENTIENCE
SENTIENCY
SENTIMENT
SENTRY-BOX
SEPARABLE
SEPARABLY
SEPARATOR
SEPARATUM

SEPHARDIC
SEPHARDIM
SEPIOLITE
SEPTARIAN
SEPTARIUM
SEPTATION
SEPTEMBER
SEPTEMFID
SEPTEMVIR
SEPTENARY
SEPTENNIA
SEPTICITY
SEPTIFORM
SEPTIMOLE
SEPTUPLET
SEPULCHRE
SEPULTURE
SEQUACITY
SEQUESTER
SERAPHIMS
SERAPHINE
SERAPHINS
SERASKIER
SERBONIAN
SERENADER
SERGEANCY
SERIALISE
SERIALISM
SERIALIST
SERIALITY
SERIATELY
SERICEOUS
SERICITIC
SERIGRAPH
SERINETTE
SERIOUSLY
SERJEANCY
SERJEANTY
SERMONEER
SERMONISE
SERMONISH
SERPENTRY
SERPULITE
SERRANOID
SERRATION
SERRATURE
SERREFILE
SERRICORN
SERRULATE
SERVANTRY
SERVIETTE
SERVILELY
SERVILISM
SERVILITY
SERVITUDE
SESSIONAL
SESTERTIA
SETACEOUS
SETTER-OFF
SETTER-OUT
SETTLE-BED
SEVENFOLD
SEVENTEEN
SEVENTHLY
SEVENTIES
SEVERABLE

SEVERALLY
SEVERALTY
SEVERANCE
SEX-APPEAL
SEXENNIAL
SEX-KITTEN
SEX-LINKED
SEXTANTAL
SEXTONESS
SEXTUPLET
SEXUALISE
SEXUALISM
SEXUALIST
SEXUALITY
SEXVALENT
SFORZANDO
SGRAFFITI
SGRAFFITO
SHADELESS
SHADE-TREE
SHADINESS
SHADOWING
SHAFTLESS
SHAG-EARED
SHAKEABLE
SHAKE-DOWN
SHAKERISM
SHAKINESS
SHALE-MINE
SHALLOWLY
SHAMANISM
SHAMANIST
SHAMATEUR
SHAMBLING
SHAMBOLIC
SHAMEFAST
SHAMELESS
SHAMIANAH
SHAMPOOED
SHAMPOOER
SHANACHIE
SHANGHAI'D
SHANGRI-LA
SHANK-BONE
SHANTYMAN
SHAPEABLE
SHAPELESS
SHARE-CROP
SHARESMAN
SHARKSKIN
SHARPENER
SHARP-EYED
SHARPNESS
SHARP-SHOD
SHAVELING
SHAWLLESS
SHEAR-HULK
SHEARLING
SHEAT-FISH
SHEATHING
SHEBEENER
SHECHINAH
SHEEP-COTE
SHEEPFOLD
SHEEP-HOOK
SHEEP-LICE

SHEEP'S-BIT
SHEEP-SCAB
SHEEP'S-EYE
SHEEPSKIN
SHEEP-TICK
SHEEPWALK
SHEEP-WASH
SHEER-HULK
SHEET-IRON
SHEET-LEAD
SHELDDUCK
SHELDRAKE
SHELF-MARK
SHELFROOM
SHELLBACK
SHELLBARK
SHELLDUCK
SHELLFIRE
SHELLFISH
SHELL-HEAP
SHELL-HOLE
SHELL-LESS
SHELL-LIKE
SHELL-LIME
SHELL-MARL
SHELL-SAND
SHELLWORK
SHELTERED
SHELTERER
SHEMOZZLE
SHERIFIAN
SHEWBREAD
SHICKERED
SHIELD-BUG
SHIELD-MAY
SHIELDUCK
SHIFTLESS
SHILLELAH
SHIMOZZLE
SHINELESS
SHINGLING
SHININGLY
SHINTOISM
SHINTOIST
SHIPBOARD
SHIP-CANAL
SHIP-FEVER
SHIP-MONEY
SHIP-OWNER
SHIP-POUND
SHIPSHAPE
SHIPWRECK
SHIRE-MOOT
SHIRT-BAND
SHIRTLESS
SHIRT-STUD
SHIRT-TAIL
SHIVERING
SHLIMAZEL
SHOAL-MARK
SHOALNESS
SHOALWISE
SHOCK-HEAD
SHOEBLACK
SHOE-BRUSH
SHOEMAKER

SHOGUNATE
SHOOTABLE
SHOP-BOARD
SHOPFLOOR
SHOP-FRONT
SHOPWOMAN
SHORE-BOAT
SHORE-CRAB
SHORELESS
SHORELINE
SHORE-SIDE
SHORESMAN
SHOREWARD
SHORE-WEED
SHORTCAKE
SHORT-COAT
SHORTENER
SHORTFALL
SHORTGOWN
SHORTHAND
SHORT-HORN
SHORT-LIST
SHORTNESS
SHORT-SLIP
SHORT-STOP
SHORT-TERM
SHORT-WAVE
SHOT-PROOF
SHOT-TOWER
SHOULDEST
SHOVELFUL
SHOVEL-HAT
SHOVELLED
SHOVELLER
SHOWBREAD
SHOWERFUL
SHOWERING
SHOWINESS
SHOW-PLACE
SHREDDING
SHREDLESS
SHREW-MICE
SHRIEKING
SHRIEK-OWL
SHRILLING
SHRIMPING
SHRIMP-NET
SHRINKAGE
SHROFFAGE
SHROUDING
SHRUBBERY
SHRUBLESS
SHRUGGING
SHUFFLING
SHUTTERED
SIALOGRAM
SIALOLITH
SIBILANCE
SIBILANCY
SIBYLLINE
SIBYLLIST
SICCATIVE
SICILIANA
SICILIANO
SICK-BERTH
SICKENING

SICK-HOUSE
SICKISHLY
SICK-LEAVE
SICKLEMAN
SICK-NURSE
SICK-TIRED
SIDEBOARD
SIDE-BONES
SIDE-BURNS
SIDE-CHAIN
SIDE-ISSUE
SIDE-LIGHT
SIDERITIC
SIDEROSIS
SIDE-TABLE
SIDE-TRACK
SIDEWARDS
SIDE-WHEEL
SIEVE-TUBE
SIFTINGLY
SIGHINGLY
SIGHT-HOLE
SIGHTLESS
SIGHTSEER
SIGILLARY
SIGILLATE
SIGMATION
SIGMATISM
SIGMATRON
SIGMOIDAL
SIGNAL-BOX
SIGNALISE
SIGNALLED
SIGNALLER
SIGNALMAN
SIGNATORY
SIGNATURE
SIGNBOARD
SIGNEURIE
SIGNIFICS
SIGNIFIED
SIGNORIAL
SIGNORINA
SILICEOUS
SILICIOUS
SILICOSIS
SILICOTIC
SILIQUOSE
SILK-GLAND
SILK-GRASS
SILKINESS
SILLINESS
SILURIDAE
SILVER-FIR
SILVER-FOX
SILVERING
SILVERISE
SIMEONITE
SIMILARLY
SIMMENTAL
SIMONIOUS
SIMPATICO
SIMPERING
SIMPLETON
SIMPLICES
SIMULACRA

SIMULACRE
SIMULATOR
SINCERELY
SINCERITY
SIN-EATING
SINEWLESS
SINGINGLY
SINGLE-END
SINGLETON
SINGSPIEL
SINHALESE
SINISTRAL
SINK-A-PACE
SINLESSLY
SINNINGIA
SINOEKETE
SINOLOGUE
SINOPHILE
SINOPHILY
SINUATELY
SINUATION
SINUOSITY
SINUOUSLY
SINUSITIS
SIPHONAGE
SIPHONATE
SIPHUNCLE
SISAL-HEMP
SISSERARY
SISTERING
SISYPHEAN
SITIOLOGY
SITUATION
SITZKRIEG
SIVAISTIC
SIX-FOOTER
SIXTEENER
SIXTEENMO
SIXTEENTH
SIZARSHIP
SKATOLOGY
SKEDADDLE
SKEESICKS
SKETCHILY
SKEW-TABLE
SKEW-WHIFF
SKIAGRAPH
SKIAMACHY
SKIASCOPY
SKI-KITING
SKILFULLY
SKILL-LESS
SKIN-DIVER
SKINFLINT
SKIN-TIGHT
SKIRTLESS
SKI-SCHOOL
SKRIMMAGE
SKUNK-BIRD
SKY-COLOUR
SKY-DIVING
SKY-ROCKET
SKY-TROOPS
SLABBERER
SLAB-SIDED
SLABSTONE

SLACK-BAKE
SLACKNESS
SLACK-ROPE
SLAISTERY
SLAKELESS
SLAMMAKIN
SLANDERER
SLANGULAR
SLANTWAYS
SLANTWISE
SLAP-HAPPY
SLAPSTICK
SLATE-CLUB
SLATE-GRAY
SLATE-GREY
SLATINESS
SLAUGHTER
SLAVE-BORN
SLAVE-FORK
SLAVE-HUNT
SLAVERING
SLAVE-SHIP
SLAVISHLY
SLAVOCRAT
SLAVONIAN
SLAVONISE
SLAVOPHIL
SLEEKNESS
SLEEPLESS
SLEEVE-DOG
SLEEVE-NUT
SLEIGHING
SLENDERLY
SLICKNESS
SLIDE-REST
SLIDE-RULE
SLIDINGLY
SLIGHTISH
SLIMINESS
SLING-BACK
SLING-SHOT
SLINKSKIN
SLINKWEED
SLIP-BOARD
SLIP-COACH
SLIPPERED
SLIVOVICA
SLIVOVITZ
SLIVOWITZ
SLOETHORN
SLOGGORNE
SLOGHORNE
SLOP-BASIN
SLOP-BUILT
SLOPEWISE
SLOPINGLY
SLOP-POUCH
SLOTH-BEAR
SLOT-METER
SLOUCH-HAT
SLOUCHING
SLOVAKIAN
SLOVAKISH
SLOVENIAN
SLOWCOACH
SLOW-HOUND

SLOW-MATCH
SLOW-PACED
SLUGGABED
SLUGHORNE
SLUMBERER
SLUMBROUS
SLUNG-SHOT
SMALL-ARMS
SMALL-COAL
SMALL-DEBT
SMALL-HAND
SMALLNESS
SMALL-TALK
SMALL-TIME
SMARTNESS
SMART-WEED
SMATTERER
SMELL-LESS
SMELL-TRAP
SMIKE-HOLE
SMILELESS
SMILINGLY
SMOCK-RACE
SMOKE-BALL
SMOKE-BOMB
SMOKE-BUSH
SMOKE-JACK
SMOKELESS
SMOKE-ROOM
SMOKE-SAIL
SMOKE-TREE
SMOKINESS
SMOOTHING
SMOOTHISH
SMORZANDO
SMOTHERED
SMOTHERER
SMUG-FACED
SMUGGLING
SNAIL-FISH
SNAIL-LIKE
SNAIL-SLOW
SNAKEBIRD
SNAKEBITE
SNAKE-CULT
SNAKELIKE
SNAKEROOT
SNAKEWEED
SNAKEWISE
SNAKEWOOD
SNAKINESS
SNAPHANCE
SNAPPER-UP
SNARE-DRUM
SNATCHILY
SNEAK-RAID
SNECK-DRAW
SNEESHING
SNEEZE-BOX
SNIGGERER
SNIGGLING
SNIPE-FISH
SNIVELLED
SNIVELLER
SNORT-MAST
SNOW-BERRY

SNOW-BLIND
SNOW-BLINK
SNOW-BOUND
SNOW-BREAK
SNOW-BROTH
SNOWDRIFT
SNOWFIELD
SNOWFINCH
SNOWFLAKE
SNOWFLECK
SNOWFLICK
SNOW-GOOSE
SNOW-GUARD
SNOWINESS
SNOW-PLANT
SNOWSCAPE
SNOWSTORM
SNOW-WATER
SNOW-WHITE
SNUB-NOSED
SNUFF-DISH
SNUFFLING
SNUFF-MILL
SNUFF-MULL
SOAKINGLY
SOAPBERRY
SOAPINESS
SOAPSTONE
SOAPWORKS
SOAR-EAGLE
SOARINGLY
SOBBINGLY
SOBERNESS
SOBRIQUET
SOB-SISTER
SOCIALISE
SOCIALISM
SOCIALIST
SOCIALITE
SOCIALITY
SOCIATIVE
SOCIETARY
SOCIOGRAM
SOCIOLOGY
SOCIOPATH
SOCKETING
SOCRATISE
SODA-SCONE
SODA-WATER
SODOMITIC
SOFA-TABLE
SOFTENING
SOFT-GOODS
SOFT-GRASS
SOFT-NOSED
SOFT-PASTE
SOFT-PEDAL
SOFT-SHELL
SOGGINESS
SOI-DISANT
SOIL-BOUND
SOILINESS
SOJOURNER
SOKEMANRY
SOLACIOUS
SOLDERING

SOLDIERLY
SOLEMNESS
SOLEMNISE
SOLEMNITY
SOLENETTE
SOLFATARA
SOLFEGGIO
SOLFERINO
SOLIDNESS
SOLIFUGAE
SOLILOQUY
SOLIPSISM
SOLIPSIST
SOLITAIRE
SOLOMONIC
SOLUTREAN
SOLUTRIAN
SOLVATION
SOMASCOPE
SOMETHING
SOMETIMES
SOMEWHERE
SOMEWHILE
SOMMELIER
SOMNOLENT
SONGCRAFT
SONG-CYCLE
SONGFULLY
SONGSMITH
SONNETARY
SONNETEER
SONNETING
SONNETISE
SONNETIST
SONS-IN-LAW
SOOPSTAKE
SOOTERKIN
SOOTFLAKE
SOOTHFAST
SOOTHLICH
SOOTINESS
SOPHISTER
SOPHISTIC
SOPHISTRY
SOPHOMORE
SOPORIFIC
SOPPINESS
SOPRANINO
SOPRANIST
SORB-APPLE
SORBONIST
SORCERESS
SORCEROUS
SOREDIATE
SORE-EAGLE
SORICIDAE
SORRINESS
SORROWFUL
SORROWING
SORTATION
SORTILEGE
SORTILEGY
SORTITION
SOSTENUTO
SOTTISHLY
SOTTISIER

SOUARI-NUT
SOUBRETTE
SOUDANESE
SOUL-CURER
SOULFULLY
SOUND-BODY
SOUND-FILM
SOUND-HOLE
SOUNDLESS
SOUNDNESS
SOUND-POST
SOUND-WAVE
SOUP-PLATE
SOUPSPOON
SOUR-CROUT
SOUR-DOUGH
SOUR-GOURD
SOURISHLY
SOUSEWIFE
SOUTENEUR
SOUTHDOWN
SOUTH-EAST
SOUTHERLY
SOUTHLAND
SOUTHMOST
SOUTHROUN
SOUTHWARD
SOUTH-WEST
SOU'WESTER
SOVENANCE
SOVEREIGN
SOVIETISE
SOVIETISM
SOW-GELDER
SOYA-FLOUR
SPACE-BAND
SPACELESS
SPACESHIP
SPACE-SUIT
SPACE-TIME
SPADASSIN
SPADE-BONE
SPADE-FOOT
SPADESMAN
SPADEWORK
SPADILLIO
SPAGHETTI
SPAGYRIST
SPANAEMIA
SPANAEMIC
SPANGLING
SPARELESS
SPARENESS
SPARINGLY
SPARKLESS
SPARKLING
SPARK-PLUG
SPARSEDLY
SPARTANLY
SPARTERIE
SPASMATIC
SPASMODIC
SPATANGUS
SPATIALLY
SPATULATE
SPAULD-ILL

SPAWN-CAKE
SPEAKABLE
SPEAK-EASY
SPEAL-BONE
SPEARFISH
SPEARHEAD
SPEARMINT
SPEAR-SIDE
SPEAR-WOOD
SPEARWORT
SPECIALLY
SPECIALTY
SPECIFIED
SPECKLESS
SPECTACLE
SPECTATOR
SPECULATE
SPEECHFUL
SPEECHIFY
SPEED-BALL
SPEED-BOAT
SPEEDLESS
SPEEDSTER
SPEEDWELL
SPEERINGS
SPEIRINGS
SPELDRING
SPELLABLE
SPELLBIND
SPELLDOWN
SPELLIKIN
SPENDABLE
SPERMARIA
SPERMATIA
SPERMATIC
SPERMATID
SPERM-CELL
SPEWINESS
SPHACELUS
SPHAERITE
SPHAGNOUS
SPHENDONE
SPHENODON
SPHERICAL
SPHERULAR
SPHINCTER
SPHYGMOID
SPICE-BUSH
SPICE-CAKE
SPICILEGE
SPICINESS
SPICULATE
SPIDER-LEG
SPIDER-MAN
SPIDER-WEB
SPIGELIAN
SPIKE-FISH
SPIKE-NAIL
SPIKENARD
SPIKE-RUSH
SPIKINESS
SPILLIKIN
SPILOSITE
SPINDLING
SPIN-DRIER
SPINDRIFT

SPINELESS
SPINIFORM
SPININESS
SPINNAKER
SPINNERET
SPINOSITY
SPINOZISM
SPINOZIST
SPINULATE
SPINULOSE
SPINULOUS
SPIRACULA
SPIRALITY
SPIRASTER
SPIRATION
SPIRELESS
SPIREWISE
SPIRILLAR
SPIRILLUM
SPIRITFUL
SPIRIT-GUM
SPIRITING
SPIRITISM
SPIRITIST
SPIRITOSO
SPIRITOUS
SPIRITUAL
SPIRITUEL
SPIROGYRA
SPLASHILY
SPLASHING
SPLAY-FOOT
SPLEENFUL
SPLEENISH
SPLENDENT
SPLENDOUR
SPLENETIC
SPLENITIS
SPLEUCHAN
SPLINTERY
SPLITTING
SPLUTTERY
SPODUMENE
SPOIL-BARK
SPOIL-FIVE
SPOIL-HEAP
SPOILSMAN
SPOKESMAN
SPOKESMEN
SPOKEWISE
SPOLIATOR
SPONGE-BAG
SPONGEOUS
SPONGIOSE
SPONGIOUS
SPONSALIA
SPONSIBLE
SPOON-BAIT
SPOONBILL
SPOON-FEED
SPOON-FOOD
SPOON-HOOK
SPOON-MEAT
SPOONWAYS
SPOONWISE
SPORANGIA

SPORE-CASE
SPORIDESM
SPORIDIAL
SPORIDIUM
SPOROCARP
SPOROCYST
SPOROGENY
SPORTABLE
SPORTANCE
SPORTLESS
SPORTSMAN
SPORULATE
SPOT-CHECK
SPOT-LIGHT
SPOUT-HOLE
SPOUTLESS
SPRAGGING
SPRAICKLE
SPRAUCHLE
SPRAWLING
SPRECHERY
SPRECKLED
SPRIGGING
SPRIGHTLY
SPRINGALD
SPRING-BED
SPRINGBOK
SPRING-BOX
SPRING-GUN
SPRINGILY
SPRINGING
SPRINGLET
SPRINKLER
SPRINTING
SPRITEFUL
SPRITSAIL
SPROUTING
SPRUCE-FIR
SPULEBANE
SPULEBONE
SPUR-ROWEL
SPUR-ROYAL
SPUR-WHANG
SPUR-WHEEL
SPUTTERER
SQUABBISH
SQUABBLER
SQUAILING
SQUALIDLY
SQUALLING
SQUAMELLA
SQUAMOSAL
SQUARE-LEG
SQUARROSE
SQUASHILY
SQUATNESS
SQUATTING
SQUAWKING
SQUEAKERY
SQUEAKILY
SQUEAKING
SQUEALING
SQUEAMISH
SQUEEZING
SQUELCHER

SQUIBBING
SQUINANCY
SQUINT-EYE
SQUINTING
SQUIRALTY
SQUIRARCH
SQUIREAGE
SQUIREDOM
SQUIRTING
STABILISE
STABILITY
STABLE-BOY
STABLE-MAN
STACK-ROOM
STACKYARD
STADIA-ROD
STAFF-DUTY
STAFFROOM
STAFF-TREE
STAG-DANCE
STAGE-DOOR
STAGE-HAND
STAGE-NAME
STAGE-PLAY
STAGGERED
STAGGERER
STAGHOUND
STAGINESS
STAGIRITE
STAGNANCY
STAG-PARTY
STAGYRITE
STAHLHELM
STAIDNESS
STAINLESS
STAIRCASE
STAIRFOOT
STAIRHEAD
STAIR-WELL
STAIRWISE
STAIR-WORK
STALACTIC
STALEMATE
STALENESS
STALINISM
STALK-EYED
STALKLESS
STALL-FEED
STALWORTH
STAMINATE
STAMINEAL
STAMINODE
STAMINODY
STAMINOID
STAMMERER
STAMP-DUTY
STAMP-MILL
STAMP-NOTE
STANCHING
STANCHION
STANDER-BY
STAND-PIPE
STAPEDIAL
STAPEDIUS
STAPHYLEA
STAR-ANISE

STAR-APPLE
STARBOARD
STARCHILY
STAR-CROST
STAR-DRIFT
STARGAZER
STAR-GRASS
STARINGLY
STAR-JELLY
STARKNESS
STARLIGHT
STAR-NOSED
STAR-PROOF
STAR-SHELL
STARSHINE
STAR-STONE
STARTLING
STARTLISH
STAR-WHEEL
STASIDION
STATEHOOD
STATELESS
STATELILY
STATEMENT
STATEROOM
STATESMAN
STATEWIDE
STATIONAL
STATIONER
STATISTIC
STATOCYST
STATOLITH
STATUETTE
STATUTORY
STAUNCHLY
STAY-MAKER
STEADFAST
STEADIEST
STEADYING
STEAMBOAT
STEAM-COAL
STEAM-DOME
STEAM-PIPE
STEAM-PORT
STEAMSHIP
STEAM-TRAP
STEATITIC
STEATOSIS
STEEL-BLUE
STEEL-CLAD
STEEL-GRAY
STEEL-GREY
STEEL-TRAP
STEEL-WARE
STEEL-WOOL
STEELWORK
STEELYARD
STEENKIRK
STEEP-DOWN
STEEPNESS
STEERLING
STEERSMAN
STEGNOSIS
STEGNOTIC
STEGOMYIA
STEGOSAUR

STEINBOCK
STELLARIA
STELLATED
STELLULAR
STENOPAIC
STENOTYPE
STENOTYPY
STEPBAIRN
STEPCHILD
STEP-DANCE
STEP-FAULT
STEPSTONE
STERADIAN
STERCORAL
STERCULIA
STERILISE
STERILITY
STERNEBRA
STERN-FAST
STERNITIC
STERNMOST
STERNPORT
STERN-POST
STERNWARD
STEVEDORE
STEWARDRY
STEWARTRY
STICHERON
STICHIDIA
STIFFENER
STIFF-NECK
STIFFNESS
STIGMARIA
STIGMATIC
STILL-BORN
STILL-HEAD
STILL-HUNT
STILL-LIFE
STILLNESS
STILL-ROOM
STILT-BIRD
STILTEDLY
STIMULANT
STIMULATE
STINGAREE
STING-BULL
STING-FISH
STINGLESS
STINK-BALL
STINK-BIRD
STINK-BOMB
STINKHORN
STINK-TRAP
STINK-WOOD
STINTEDLY
STINTLESS
STIPITATE
STIPPLING
STIPULARY
STIPULATE
STIRABOUT
STITCHERY
STITCHING
STOCK-DOVE
STOCKFISH
STOCKINET

STOCKLESS
STOCK-LIST
STOCK-LOCK
STOCKPILE
STOCK-ROOM
STOCK-WHIP
STOCKWORK
STOCKYARD
STOICALLY
STOKEHOLD
STOKE-HOLE
STOLIDITY
STOMACHAL
STOMACHED
STOMACHER
STOMACHIC
STONE-CAST
STONE-CELL
STONE-CHAT
STONE-COAL
STONE-COLD
STONECROP
STONE-DEAD
STONE-DEAF
STONE-HARD
STONE-HAWK
STONELESS
STONE-LILY
STONE-MILL
STONE-PINE
STONESHOT
STONEWALL
STONEWARE
STONEWORK
STONEWORT
STONINESS
STOOLBALL
STOP-PRESS
STOP-WATCH
STORE-FARM
STOREROOM
STORE-SHIP
STORIATED
STORIETTE
STORM-BEAT
STORM-BELT
STORM-BIRD
STORM-COCK
STORM-CONE
STORM-DRUM
STORMLESS
STORM-SAIL
STORM-STAY
STORM-WIND
STORNELLI
STORNELLO
STORTHING
STORY-BOOK
STORYETTE
STOUTHRIE
STOUTNESS
STOVE-PIPE
STOWNLINS
STRAGGLER
STRAINING
STRAMAÇON

STRAMAZON
STRANGELY
STRANGLER
STRANGLES
STRANGURY
STRAP-GAME
STRAP-HANG
STRAPLESS
STRAPPADO
STRAPPING
STRAP-WORK
STRAPWORT
STRATAGEM
STRATEGIC
STRATONIC
STRAWLESS
STRAW-ROPE
STRAW-STEM
STRAW-WORM
STRAW-YARD
STRAYLING
STREAKILY
STREAKING
STREAM-ICE
STREAMING
STREAMLET
STREAM-TIN
STREETAGE
STREET-BOY
STREET-CAR
STREETFUL
STREETWAY
STRENUITY
STRENUOUS
STRESSFUL
STRETCHED
STRETCHER
STREWMENT
STRIATION
STRIATURE
STRICTISH
STRICTURE
STRIDENCE
STRIDENCY
STRIDLING
STRIFEFUL
STRIGGING
STRIKE-PAY
STRING-BAG
STRINGENT
STRINGILY
STRINGING
STRINGOPS
STRING-PEA
STRING-TIE
STRIP-LEAF
STRIPLING
STRIP-MINE
STRIPPING
STROBILAE
STROBILUS
STROKE-OAR
STROLLING
STROMATIC
STRONG-ARM
STRONG-BOX

STRONGEST
STRONGISH
STRONGYLE
STRONTIUM
STROPPING
STROSSERS
STROUDING
STRUCTURE
STRUGGLER
STRUMATIC
STRUMITIS
STRUMMING
STRUTTING
STRYCHNIA
STRYCHNIC
STUDENTRY
STUD-GROOM
STUD-HORSE
STUDIEDLY
STUFF-GOWN
STUMP-WORK
STUPEFIED
STUPEFIER
STUPIDITY
STUPOROUS
STURNIDAE
STUTTERER
STYLE-BOOK
STYLELESS
STYLIFORM
STYLISHLY
STYLISTIC
STYLOBATE
STYPTICAL
SUABILITY
SUASIVELY
SUBACTION
SUBAERIAL
SUBAGENCY
SUBAHDARY
SUBAHSHIP
SUBALPINE
SUBALTERN
SUBARCTIC
SUBASTRAL
SUBATOMIC
SUBCANTOR
SUBCAUDAL
SUBCOSTAL
SUBDEACON
SUBDIVIDE
SUBDOLOUS
SUBDUABLE
SUBDUEDLY
SUBEDITOR
SUBENTIRE
SUBFAMILY
SUBINCISE
SUBJACENT
SUBJECTED
SUBJUGATE
SUBLATION
SUBLESSEE
SUBLESSOR
SUBLETHAL
SUBLETTER

SUBLIMATE
SUBLIMELY
SUBLIMING
SUBLIMISE
SUBLIMITY
SUBLINEAR
SUBLUNARY
SUBLUNATE
SUBMARINE
SUBMENTAL
SUBMENTUM
SUBMERGED
SUBMERSED
SUBMICRON
SUBMISSLY
SUBMITTED
SUBMITTER
SUBNEURAL
SUBNIVEAL
SUBNIVEAN
SUBNORMAL
SUBOCTAVE
SUBOCULAR
SUBPOENA'D
SUBREGION
SUBROGATE
SUBSACRAL
SUBSCRIBE
SUBSCRIPT
SUBSECIVE
SUBSELLIA
SUBSIDISE
SUBSOILER
SUBSTANCE
SUBSTRACT
SUBSTRATA
SUBSTRATE
SUBSTRUCT
SUBSTYLAR
SUBSULTUS
SUBTENANT
SUBTILELY
SUBTILETY
SUBTILISE
SUBTILIST
SUBTILITY
SUBTROPIC
SUBUNGUAL
SUBURSINE
SUBVASSAL
SUBVERSAL
SUBVERTER
SUBWARDEN
SUCCEEDER
SUCCENTOR
SUCCESSOR
SUCCINATE
SUCCINITE
SUCCOTASH
SUCCOURER
SUCCUBINE
SUCCUBOUS
SUCCULENT
SUCCURSAL
SUCTIONAL
SUCTORIAL

SUDAMINAL
SUDORIFIC
SUFFERING
SUFFICING
SUFFOCATE
SUFFRAGAN
SUFFUSION
SUFIISTIC
SUGAR-ALLY
SUGAR-BEAN
SUGAR-BEET
SUGARCANE
SUGARLESS
SUGAR-LOAF
SUGAR-MILL
SUGAR-MITE
SUGAR-PALM
SUGAR-PINE
SUGAR-PLUM
SUGGESTER
SULCALISE
SULCATION
SULKINESS
SULPHATIC
SULPHONIC
SULPHURET
SULPHURIC
SULTANATE
SULTANESS
SUMMARILY
SUMMARISE
SUMMARIST
SUMMATION
SUMMATIVE
SUMMERING
SUMMERSET
SUMMING-UP
SUMPSIMUS
SUMPTUARY
SUMPTUOUS
SUNBATHER
SUNBEAMED
SUN-BEATEN
SUN-BONNET
SUN-BRIGHT
SUNBURNED
SUNDERING
SUNDOWNER
SUNFLOWER
SUNNINESS
SUNRISING
SUN-SPURGE
SUNSTROKE
SUNSTRUCK
SUNTANNED
SUPERABLE
SUPERABLY
SUPERBITY
SUPERCOOL
SUPERFINE
SUPERFLUX
SUPERFUSE
SUPERHEAT
SUPERHIVE
SUPERNOVA
SUPERPLUS

SUPERPOSE
SUPERSALT
SUPERSEDE
SUPERVENE
SUPERVISE
SUPINATOR
SUPPLIANT
SUPPLICAT
SUPPLYING
SUPPORTER
SUPPOSING
SUPPURATE
SUPREMACY
SUPREMELY
SUPREMITY
SURCHARGE
SURCINGLE
SURFACING
SURF-BOARD
SURF-CANOE
SURFEITED
SURFEITER
SURFICIAL
SURGELESS
SURGEONCY
SURLINESS
SURMASTER
SURMISING
SURMULLET
SURPLICED
SURPRISAL
SURPRISED
SURPRISER
SURQUEDRY
SURREINED
SURREJOIN
SURRENDER
SURRENDRY
SURROGATE
SURVIVING
SUSCEPTOR
SUSCITATE
SUSPECTED
SUSPENDED
SUSPENDER
SUSPENSOR
SUSPICION
SUSSARARA
SUSTAINED
SUSTAINER
SUSTINENT
SUSURRANT
SUTTEEISM
SUTURALLY
SWAG-BELLY
SWAGGERER
SWALLOWER
SWAN-GOOSE
SWANS-DOWN
SWARAJIST
SWART-BACK
SWARTNESS
SWASHWORK
SWEAR-WORD
SWEEPBACK
SWEET-CORN

SWEETENER
SWEET-FLAG
SWEET-GALE
SWEETMEAT
SWEETNESS
SWEETWOOD
SWEETWORT
SWEIRNESS
SWELTERED
SWEPT-BACK
SWIFT-FOOT
SWIFTNESS
SWIMMABLE
SWIMMERET
SWINDLING
SWINEFISH
SWINEHERD
SWINEHOOD
SWING-BACK
SWINGBOAT
SWING-DOOR
SWINGEING
SWINGLING
SWINGTREE
SWING-WING
SWINISHLY
SWITCHING
SWITCHMAN
SWIVEL-EYE
SWIVEL-GUN
SWORD-BEAN
SWORD-BELT
SWORD-BILL
SWORD-CANE
SWORDFISH
SWORD-HAND
SWORD-KNOT
SWORDLESS
SWORDLIKE
SWORDPLAY
SWORD-RACK
SWORDSMAN
SWORD-TAIL
SYBARITIC
SYCOPHANT
SYLLABARY
SYLLABICS
SYLLABISE
SYLLABISM
SYLLABLED
SYLLEPSES
SYLLEPSIS
SYLLEPTIC
SYLLOGISE
SYLLOGISM
SYLVANITE
SYLVIIDAE
SYLVIINAE
SYLVINITE
SYMBIOSIS
SYMBIOTIC
SYMBOLICS
SYMBOLISE
SYMBOLISM
SYMBOLIST
SYMBOLLED

SYMBOLOGY	TABESCENT	TAPE-GRASS	TEDIOSITY
SYMMETRAL	TABLATURE	TAPERNESS	TEDIOUSLY
SYMMETRIC	TABLE-BEER	TAPER-RING	TEE-SQUARE
SYMPHONIC	TABLE-BOOK	TAPERWISE	TEESWATER
SYMPHYSIS	TABLELAND	TAPPIT-HEN	TEGMENTAL
SYMPHYTIC	TABLE-LEAF	TARANTARA	TEGMENTUM
SYMPHYTUM	TABLE-MAID	TARANTASS	TEGULARLY
SYMPODIAL	TABLE-TALK	TARANTISM	TEGULATED
SYMPODIUM	TABLEWARE	TARANTULA	TEKNONYMY
SYMPOSIAC	TABLEWISE	TARAXACUM	TELAMONES
SYMPOSIAL	TABLE-WORK	TARBOGGIN	TELEGENIC
SYMPOSIUM	TABULARLY	TARDINESS	TELEGRAPH
SYMPTOSIS	TABULATOR	TARGETEER	TELEMETER
SYMPTOTIC	TACAMAHAC	TARGUMIST	TELEMETRY
SYNAGOGAL	TACHOGRAM	TARNATION	TELEOLOGY
SYNAGOGUE	TACHYLITE	TARNISHED	TELEOSAUR
SYNANGIUM	TACHYLYTE	TARNISHER	TELEOSTEI
SYNANTHIC	TACITNESS	TARPAULIN	TELEPATHY
SYNAPHEIA	TACKINESS	TARRAGONA	TELEPHEME
SYNAPTASE	TACTFULLY	TARRIANCE	TELEPHONE
SYNCHRONY	TACTICIAN	TARRINESS	TELEPHONY
SYNCHYSIS	TACTICITY	TARSALGIA	TELEPHOTO
SYNCLINAL	TACTILIST	TARTAREAN	TELESCOPE
SYNCOPATE	TACTILITY	TARTARIAN	TELESCOPY
SYNCOPTIC	TACTUALLY	TARTARISE	TELESTICH
SYNCRETIC	TAENIASIS	TARTUFIAN	TELEVISOR
SYNCYTIAL	TAHSILDAR	TARTUFISH	TELLINGLY
SYNCYTIUM	TAIL-BOARD	TARTUFISM	TELLURATE
SYNDACTYL	TAIL-ENDER	TASIMETER	TELLURIAN
SYNDICATE	TAIL-LIGHT	TASK-FORCE	TELLURIDE
SYNECTICS	TAILORESS	TASK-GROUP	TELLURITE
SYNEDRIAL	TAILORING	TASMANIAN	TELLURIUM
SYNEDRION	TAIL-PIECE	TASSELLED	TELLUROUS
SYNEDRIUM	TAINTLESS	TASTE-BULB	TELOPHASE
SYNERESIS	TAINT-WORM	TASTELESS	TEMPERATE
SYNERGISM	TAKE-LEAVE	TATTINESS	TEMPERING
SYNERGIST	TAKING-OFF	TAURIFORM	TEMPORARY
SYNGAMOUS	TALBOTYPE	TAUTOLOGY	TEMPORISE
SYNIZESIS	TALEGALLA	TAWNINESS	TEMPTABLE
SYNODICAL	TALKATIVE	TAXED-CART	TEMPTRESS
SYNOECETE	TALKING-TO	TAXIDERMY	TEMULENCE
SYNOECISE	TALLIABLE	TAXIMETER	TEMULENCY
SYNOECISM	TALLOW-DIP	TAXONOMER	TENACIOUS
SYNOICOUS	TALLOWISH	TAXONOMIC	TENACULUM
SYNONYMIC	TALLYSHOP	TEACHABLE	TENAILLON
SYNOVITIS	TALMUDIST	TEACHLESS	TENDERING
SYNTACTIC	TAMBOURIN	TEA-CUPFUL	TENDERISE
SYNTHESES	TAMPERING	TEA-GARDEN	TENDINOUS
SYNTHESIS	TAMPONADE	TEA-KETTLE	TENEBRIST
SYNTHETIC	TANAGRINE	TEARFULLY	TENEBRITY
SYNTONOUS	TANGERINE	TEAR-GLAND	TENEBROSE
SYPHILISE	TANGHININ	TEAR-SHEET	TENEBROUS
SYPHILOID	TANKA-BOAT	TEAR-SHELL	TENOR-CLEF
SYPHILOMA	TANK-WAGON	TEASELING	TENSENESS
SYRIACISM	TAN-LIQUOR	TEASELLED	TENSILITY
SYRIANISM	TAN-PICKLE	TEASELLER	TENTACLED
SYRINGEAL	TANTALATE	TEASINGLY	TENTACULA
SYRPHIDAE	TANTALEAN	TEA-TASTER	TENTATION
SYSTALTIC	TANTALIAN	TEA-THINGS	TENTATIVE
SYSTEMISE	TANTALISE	TECHNICAL	TENT-CLOTH
	TANTALISM	TECHNIQUE	TENT-MAKER
T	TANTALITE	TECTIFORM	TENTORIAL
	TANTARARA	TECTONICS	TENTORIUM
TABANIDAE	TAOISEACH	TECTORIAL	TEPHIGRAM
TABASHEER	TAP-CINDER	TECTRICES	TEPHRITIC
TABBYHOOD	TAP-DANCER	TEDDY-BEAR	TEPHROITE
TABELLION			

TEPIDNESS
TERATOGEN
TEREBINTH
TEREBRANT
TEREBRATE
TERENTIAN
TERMAGANT
TERMINATE
TERMINISM
TERMINIST
TERMITARY
TERNATELY
TERRACING
TERRAMARA
TERRAMARE
TERRARIUM
TERRENELY
TERRICOLE
TERRIFIED
TERRITORY
TERRORISE
TERRORISM
TERRORIST
TERSENESS
TERVALENT
TERZA-RIMA
TESSELLAE
TESSELLAR
TESSITURA
TESTAMENT
TESTATION
TESTATRIX
TESTIFIED
TESTIFIER
TESTIMONY
TESTINESS
TEST-MATCH
TEST-PAPER
TÊTE-À-TÊTE
TÊTE-BÊCHE
TETRADITE
TETRAGRAM
TETRALOGY
TETRAPODY
TETRARCHY
TETTEROUS
TEUTONISE
TEUTONISM
TEUTONIST
TEXTORIAL
TEXTUALLY
THALASSIC
THANATISM
THANATIST
THANATOID
THANEHOOD
THANESHIP
THANKLESS
THARGELIA
THATCHING
THEANDRIC
THEARCHIC
THEATRICS
THEFTBOOT
THEFTBOTE
THEFTUOUS

THEGITHER
THELEMITE
THELYTOKY
THENABOUT
THEOBROMA
THEOCRACY
THEOCRASY
THEOGONIC
THEOLOGER
THEOLOGIC
THEOLOGUE
THEOMACHY
THEOMANCY
THEOMANIA
THEOPATHY
THEOPHAGY
THEOPHANY
THEORBIST
THEORETIC
THEORIQUE
THEORISER
THEOSOPHY
THEOTOKOS
THERALITE
THERAPIST
THEREAWAY
THEREFORE
THEREFROM
THEREINTO
THERENESS
THEREUNTO
THEREUPON
THEREWITH
THERIACAL
THERMALLY
THERMICAL
THERMIDOR
THERMOTIC
THEROLOGY
THERSITIC
THESAURUS
THEURGIST
THICKENER
THICKETED
THICK-EYED
THICKHEAD
THICK-KNEE
THICK-LIPS
THICKNESS
THICKSKIN
THICK-SOWN
THIEF-LIKE
THIGH-BONE
THIN-BELLY
THIN-FACED
THINGHOOD
THINGNESS
THINGUMMY
THINKABLE
THINK-TANK
THIRD-HAND
THIRD-RATE
THIRDSMAN
THIRSTFUL
THIRSTILY
THIRTIETH

THIRTYISH
THOLOBATE
THOMISTIC
THORNBACK
THORN-BUSH
THORNLESS
THORN-TREE
THOROW-WAX
THOUGHTED
THOUGHTEN
THRALLDOM
THRASHING
THRASONIC
THREATFUL
THREE-CARD
THREE-DECK
THREEFOLD
THREE-FOOT
THREENESS
THREE-PAIR
THREE-PART
THREE-PILE
THREESOME
THRENETIC
THRENODIC
THRESHING
THRESHOLD
THRIFTIER
THRIFTILY
THRILLANT
THRILLING
THROATILY
THROBBING
THROBLESS
THROCHITE
THROMBOSE
THRONGFUL
THROTTLER
THROUGHLY
THROW-AWAY
THROW-BACK
THROW-DOWN
THROWSTER
THRUM-EYED
THRUMMING
THRUST-HOE
THRUSTING
THUMB-HOLE
THUMBKINS
THUMBLESS
THUMBLING
THUMB-MARK
THUMBNAIL
THUMB-RING
THUMB-TACK
THUNDERER
THUNDROUS
THWACKING
THWARTING
THYESTEAN
THYLACINE
THYRATRON
THYRISTOR
THYROXINE
THYSANURA
TICKER-DAY

TIDE-TABLE
TIDE-WATER
TIE-AND-DYE
TIE-DYEING
TIERCELET
TIERCERON
TIGER-LILY
TIGER-MOTH
TIGER'S-EYE
TIGER-TAIL
TIGER-WOLF
TIGER-WOOD
TIGHTENER
TIGHT-LACE
TIGHTNESS
TIGHT-ROPE
TILE-STONE
TILIACEAE
TIMBERING
TIMBER-MAN
TIME-LAPSE
TIME-LIMIT
TIMENOGUY
TIMEOUSLY
TIMEPIECE
TIME-TABLE
TIMIDNESS
TIMOCRACY
TIMORSOME
TIMPANIST
TIM-WHISKY
TINDER-BOX
TING-A-LING
TINGUAITE
TIN-OPENER
TINSELLED
TINT-BLOCK
TINTINESS
TIP-AND-RUN
TIP-CHEESE
TIPSINESS
TIPSTAFFS
TIPSTAVES
TIPSY-CAKE
TIP-TILTED
TIPTOEING
TIPULIDAE
TIREDNESS
TIRE-WOMAN
TIRRA-LYRA
TISIPHONE
TITHE-BARN
TITHE-FREE
TITILLATE
TITLE-DEED
TITLE-LEAF
TITLELESS
TITLE-PAGE
TITLE-POEM
TITLE-ROLE
TITRATION
TITTERING
TITTIVATE
TITTLEBAT
TITUBANCY
TITULARLY

T-JUNCTION	TORPITUDE	TRADUCIAN	TREMOLANT
TOAD-EATER	TORQUATED	TRADUCING	TREMOLITE
TOAD-GRASS	TORREFIED	TRAGEDIAN	TREMULANT
TOAD-STONE	TORRIDITY	TRAGELAPH	TREMULATE
TOADSTOOL	TORSIONAL	TRAGULINE	TREMULOUS
TOAST-RACK	TORTILITY	TRAINABLE	TRENCHANT
TOCCATINA	TORTRICES	TRAIN-BAND	TREPANNED
TOCHARIAN	TORTRICID	TRAIPSING	TREPANNER
TOCHARISH	TORTURING	TRAITORLY	TREPASSER
TODDY-PALM	TORTUROUS	TRAITRESS	TREPIDANT
TOD-LOWRIE	TORUFFLED	TRAMPLING	TRESSURED
TOILET-SET	TORULOSIS	TRAMPOLIN	TRIACTINE
TOKHARIAN	TOTALISER	TRANCEDLY	TRIAL-FIRE
TOKHARISH	TOTALLING	TRANSCEND	TRIALOGUE
TOLERABLE	TOTANINAE	TRANSENNA	TRIANDRIA
TOLERABLY	TOTTERING	TRANSFORM	TRIANGLED
TOLERANCE	TOUCHABLE	TRANSFUSE	TRIATOMIC
TOLERATOR	TOUCH-BACK	TRANSHUME	TRIBADISM
TOLLBOOTH	TOUCH-DOWN	TRANSIENT	TRIBALISM
TOLL-HOUSE	TOUCH-HOLE	TRANSLATE	TRIBELESS
TOL-LOLISH	TOUCHLESS	TRANSMOVE	TRIBESMAN
TOMBSTONE	TOUCH-LINE	TRANSMUTE	TRIBOLOGY
TOMENTOSE	TOUCH-TYPE	TRANSONIC	TRIBUNATE
TOMENTOUS	TOUCHWOOD	TRANSPIRE	TRIBUTARY
TOMMY-SHOP	TOUGHENER	TRANSPORT	TRICERION
TOMOGRAPH	TOUGHNESS	TRANSPOSE	TRICHOSIS
TONGA-BEAN	TOURISTIC	TRANSSHIP	TRICHROIC
TONGUELET	TOURNEDOS	TRANSUMPT	TRICHROME
TONKA-BEAN	TOURNEYER	TRANSVEST	TRICKLING
TONNISHLY	TOWELLING	TRAPESING	TRICKSOME
TONOMETER	TOWEL-RACK	TRAPEZIAL	TRICKSTER
TONSILLAR	TOWEL-RAIL	TRAPEZIUM	TRICLINIC
TONSORIAL	TOWERLESS	TRAPEZOID	TRICOLOUR
TOOLHOUSE	TOW-HEADED	TRAPPINGS	TRICROTIC
TOOTHACHE	TOWING-NET	TRAP-STAIR	TRICUSPID
TOOTHCOMB	TOWN-CLERK	TRAP-STICK	TRICYCLER
TOOTHLESS	TOWN-CRIER	TRASHTRIE	TRICYCLIC
TOOTHPICK	TOWNHOUSE	TRATTORIA	TRIDACTYL
TOOTHSOME	TOWNSCAPE	TRAUMATIC	TRIDENTAL
TOOTHWASH	TOWNSFOLK	TRAVAILED	TRIDENTED
TOOTHWORT	TOXICALLY	TRAVELLED	TRIDYMITE
TOP-BOOTED	TOXOPHILY	TRAVELLER	TRIENNIAL
TOP-DRAWER	TRABEATED	TRAVERSED	TRIERARCH
TOPECTOMY	TRABECULA	TRAVERSER	TRIETERIC
TOP-HAMPER	TRACEABLE	TRAVERTIN	TRIFACIAL
TOPIARIAN	TRACEABLY	TRAY-CLOTH	TRIFOCALS
TOPIARIST	TRACELESS	TREACHERY	TRIFOLIUM
TOPICALLY	TRACERIED	TREACHOUR	TRIFORIUM
TOPONYMAL	TRACHEARY	TREADLING	TRIFORMED
TOPONYMIC	TRACHEATA	TREADMILL	TRIGAMIST
TOPPINGLY	TRACHEATE	TREASURER	TRIGAMOUS
TOP-SAWYER	TRACHEIDE	TREATABLE	TRIGONOUS
TORBANITE	TRACHINUS	TREATMENT	TRIGYNIAN
TORCH-LILY	TRACHITIS	TREBUCHET	TRIGYNOUS
TORCH-RACE	TRACHYTIC	TREDRILLE	TRIHEDRAL
TORCH-SONG	TRACK-BOAT	TREE-ONION	TRIHYBRID
TOREUTICS	TRACKLESS	TREE-SHREW	TRIHYDRIC
TORMENTED	TRACKROAD	TREE-TRUNK	TRILINEAR
TORMENTIL	TRACTABLE	TREFOILED	TRILITHIC
TORMENTOR	TRACTATOR	TREGETOUR	TRILITHON
TORMENTUM	TRADELESS	TREILLAGE	TRILOBATE
TORMINOUS	TRADEMARK	TRELLISED	TRILOBITA
TORNADOES	TRADE-NAME	TREMATODA	TRILOBITE
TORPEDOER	TRADESMAN	TREMATODE	TRIMEROUS
TORPEDOES	TRADITION	TREMATOID	TRIMESTER
TORPIDITY	TRADITIVE	TREMBLING	TRIMETHYL

TRINKETER	TRUNK-WORK	TURRET-GUN	TYRANNISE
TRINKETRY	TRUSS-BEAM	TUSK-SHELL	TYRANNOUS
TRINOMIAL	TRUST-DEED	TUTIORISM	
TRIONYMAL	TRUSTIEST	TUTIORIST	**U**
TRIPE-SHOP	TRUSTLESS	TUTORSHIP	UDDERLESS
TRIPEWIFE	TRUTHLESS	TUTWORKER	UDOMETRIC
TRIPITAKA	TRUTHLIKE	TWADDLING	UFOLOGIST
TRIPTYQUE	TSAREVICH	TWALHOURS	UINTAHITE
TRIPUDIUM	TUBBINESS	TWA-LOFTED	UITLANDER
TRIQUETRA	TUBERCLED	TWALPENNY	UKRAINIAN
TRIRADIAL	TUBERCULE	TWANGLING	ULIGINOUS
TRISAGION	TUBE-SKIRT	TWATTLING	ULMACEOUS
TRISECTOR	TUBICOLAR	TWAY-BLADE	ULOTRICHY
TRITENESS	TUBULARIA	'TWEEN-DECK	ULTIMATUM
TRITHEISM	TUBULATED	TWELFTHLY	ULTRA-HIGH
TRITHEIST	TUFACEOUS	TWENTIETH	ULULATION
TRITICISM	TUGGINGLY	TWENTYISH	UMBELLATE
TRITURATE	TUILLETTE	TWICE-BORN	UMBELLULE
TRIUMPHAL	TUITIONAL	TWICE-LAID	UMBER-BIRD
TRIUMPHER	TULAREMIA	TWICE-TOLD	UMBILICAL
TRIUMVIRI	TULIP-ROOT	TWIDDLING	UMBILICUS
TRIUMVIRY	TULIP-TREE	TWIFORKED	UMBRATILE
TRIVALENT	TULIP-WOOD	TWIFORMED	UMPTEENTH
TRIVALVED	TUMBLE-BUG	TWIN-BIRTH	UNABASHED
TRIVIALLY	TUMBLE-CAR	TWININGLY	UNACCUSED
TRI-WEEKLY	TUMEFYING	TWINKLING	UNACTABLE
TROCHIDAE	TUMESCENT	TWIN-PLANE	UNADAPTED
TROCHILIC	TUMIDNESS	TWIN-SCREW	UNADMIRED
TROCHILUS	TUNEFULLY	TWISTABLE	UNADOPTED
TROCHLEAR	TUNGSTATE	TWITCHING	UNADORNED
TROLLOPEE	TUNGUSIAN	TWITTERER	UNADVISED
TROOP-SHIP	TUNICATED	TWO-BOTTLE	UNAIDABLE
TROPARION	TUNING-KEY	TWO-DECKER	UNALLAYED
TROPISTIC	TUNING-PEG	TWO-FISTED	UNALLOYED
TROPOLOGY	TUNING-PIN	TWO-FOOTED	UNALTERED
TROT-COSEY	TUNNELLED	TWO-FORKED	UNAMENDED
TROTHLESS	TUNNELLER	TWO-HANDED	UNAMERCED
TROTH-RING	TUNNEL-NET	TWO-HEADED	UNAMIABLE
TROUBLING	TUPAIIDAE	TWO-LEAFED	UNAMUSING
TROUBLOUS	TUPTOWING	TWO-LEAVED	UNANIMITY
TROUNCING	TURBIDITY	TWO-LEGGED	UNANIMOUS
TROUSERED	TURBINATE	TWO-LIPPED	UNANXIOUS
TROUSSEAU	TURBO-PROP	TWO-MASTED	UNAPPAREL
TROUT-FARM	TURBULENT	TWO-MASTER	UNAPPLIED
TROUTLESS	TURCOPHIL	TWO-PARTED	UNAPTNESS
TROUTLING	TURCOPOLE	TWO-ROOMED	UNASHAMED
TROWELLED	TURF-DRAIN	TWO-SEATER	UNASSAYED
TROWELLER	TURFINESS	TWO-STOREY	UNASSUMED
TRUBENISE	TURF-SPADE	TWOSTROKE	UNASSURED
TRUCELESS	TURGENTLY	TWO-TIMING	UNATTIRED
TRUCK-FARM	TURGIDITY	TWYFORKED	UNAVENGED
TRUCKLING	TURKEY-HEN	TWYFORMED	UNAVOIDED
TRUCULENT	TURMAGANT	TYCOONATE	UNBAFFLED
TRUEPENNY	TURNABOUT	TYCOONERY	UNBALANCE
TRUMP-CARD	TURNAGAIN	TYMPANIST	UNBAPTISE
TRUMPED-UP	TURNERIAN	TYPE-GENUS	UNBASEDLY
TRUMPETED	TURNIP-FLY	TYPE-METAL	UNBASHFUL
TRUMPETER	TURNIP-TOP	TYPEWRITE	UNBEARDED
TRUNCATED	TURN-PENNY	TYPHACEAE	UNBEARING
TRUNCHEON	TURN-ROUND	TYPHLITIS	UNBEGUILE
TRUNK-CALL	TURN-SCREW	TYPHOIDAL	UNBEKNOWN
TRUNK-FISH	TURNSTILE	TYPHONIAN	UNBELIEVE
TRUNK-HOSE	TURNSTONE	TYPICALLY	UNBELOVED
TRUNK-LINE	TURNTABLE	TYPIFYING	UNBENDING
TRUNK-MAIL	TURPITUDE	TYPOMANIA	UNBESPEAK
TRUNK-ROAD	TURQUOISE	TYRANNESS	UNBIASSED

UNBINDING
UNBLENDED
UNBLESSED
UNBLINDED
UNBLOODED
UNBLOTTED
UNBLUNTED
UNBOOKISH
UNBOSOMER
UNBOUNDED
UNBRAIDED
UNBRIDGED
UNBRIDLED
UNBRITISH
UNBRIZZED
UNBRUISED
UNBRUSHED
UNBUILT-ON
UNBURTHEN
UNCANDOUR
UNCANNILY
UNCANONIC
UNCAPABLE
UNCAREFUL
UNCEASING
UNCERTAIN
UNCESSANT
UNCHAINED
UNCHANGED
UNCHARGED
UNCHARITY
UNCHARMED
UNCHARNEL
UNCHARTED
UNCHECKED
UNCHEERED
UNCHRISOM
UNCINATED
UNCIVILLY
UNCLAIMED
UNCLASSED
UNCLEANED
UNCLEANLY
UNCLEARED
UNCLEARLY
UNCLESHIP
UNCLIPPED
UNCLOGGED
UNCLOTHED
UNCLOUDED
UNCOMBINE
UNCONCERN
UNCONFINE
UNCONFORM
UNCONGEAL
UNCORDIAL
UNCORRUPT
UNCOUNTED
UNCOUPLED
UNCOURTLY
UNCOUTHLY
UNCOVERED
UNCREATED
UNCROPPED
UNCROSSED
UNCROWNED

UNCRUDDED
UNCURABLE
UNCURDLED
UNCURIOUS
UNCURLING
UNCURRENT
UNCURTAIN
UNDAMAGED
UNDAUNTED
UNDAWNING
UNDAZZLED
UNDEBASED
UNDECAYED
UNDECEIVE
UNDECIDED
UNDECIMAL
UNDEFACED
UNDEFILED
UNDEFINED
UNDELAYED
UNDELIGHT
UNDELUDED
UNDERBEAR
UNDERBITE
UNDERBRED
UNDERBUSH
UNDERCAST
UNDERCLAD
UNDERCLAY
UNDERCOAT
UNDERCOOK
UNDERCOOL
UNDERDECK
UNDERDOER
UNDERDONE
UNDERDRAW
UNDERFEED
UNDERFELT
UNDERFIRE
UNDERFONG
UNDERFOOT
UNDERGIRD
UNDERGOWN
UNDERHAND
UNDERHUNG
UNDERKEEP
UNDERKING
UNDERLAID
UNDERLAIN
UNDERLINE
UNDERLING
UNDERMINE
UNDERMOST
UNDERNOTE
UNDERPAID
UNDERPASS
UNDERPEEP
UNDERPLAY
UNDERPLOT
UNDERPROP
UNDERRATE
UNDER-RIPE
UNDER-ROOF
UNDERSEAL
UNDERSELF
UNDERSELL

UNDERSHOT
UNDERSIDE
UNDERSIGN
UNDERSOIL
UNDERSONG
UNDERTAKE
UNDERTIME
UNDERTINT
UNDERTONE
UNDERTOOK
UNDERVEST
UNDERWEAR
UNDERWING
UNDERWOOD
UNDERWORK
UNDESERVE
UNDESIRED
UNDIGNIFY
UNDILUTED
UNDIVIDED
UNDOUBTED
UNDRAINED
UNDREADED
UNDREAMED
UNDRESSED
UNDRILLED
UNDROWNED
UNDULANCY
UNDULATED
UNDUTEOUS
UNDUTIFUL
UNDYINGLY
UNEARTHED
UNEARTHLY
UNEATABLE
UNEFFACED
UNELECTED
UNEMPTIED
UNENDOWED
UNENGAGED
UN-ENGLISH
UNENTERED
UNENVIOUS
UNENVYING
UNEQUABLE
UNEQUALLY
UNESSAYED
UNESSENCE
UNETHICAL
UNEXALTED
UNEXCITED
UNEXPIRED
UNEXPOSED
UNEXTINCT
UNFADABLE
UNFAILING
UNFEARFUL
UNFEARING
UNFEELING
UNFEIGNED
UNFIGURED
UNFITNESS
UNFITTING
UNFLEDGED
UNFLESHED
UNFLESHLY

UNFLOORED
UNFOCUSED
UNFOLDING
UNFORTUNE
UNFOUNDED
UNFRANKED
UNFRAUGHT
UNFREEMAN
UNFRETTED
UNFROCKED
UNFUELLED
UNFURNISH
UNGAINFUL
UNGALLANT
UNGARBLED
UNGENTEEL
UNGENUINE
UNGHOSTLY
UNGIRTHED
UNGLOSSED
UNGODLIKE
UNGODLILY
UNGRAVELY
UNGROOMED
UNGRUDGED
UNGUARDED
UNGUESSED
UNGUIFORM
UNHANDILY
UNHANDLED
UNHAPPILY
UNHARBOUR
UNHARMFUL
UNHARMING
UNHARNESS
UNHASTING
UNHATCHED
UNHATTING
UNHAUNTED
UNHEALTHY
UNHEARD-OF
UNHEARSED
UNHEEDFUL
UNHEEDILY
UNHEEDING
UNHELPFUL
UNHOPEFUL
UNHUMBLED
UNHURRIED
UNHURTFUL
UNICOLOUR
UNIFIABLE
UNIFORMED
UNIFORMLY
UNILLUMED
UNIMPEDED
UNIMPOSED
UNINCITED
UNINDEXED
UNINJURED
UNINSURED
UNINVITED
UNIONIDAE
UNIONISED
UNIPAROUS
UNIPLANAR

UNISERIAL	UNPERPLEX	UNROYALLY	UNSTUDIED
UNISEXUAL	UNPERVERT	UNRUFFLED	UNSTUFFED
UNISONANT	UNPIERCED	UNRUMPLED	UNSUBDUED
UNISONOUS	UNPILOTED	UNSADDLED	UNSUBJECT
UNITARIAN	UNPITIFUL	UNSAINTLY	UNSUCCESS
UNITIVELY	UNPITYING	UNSALABLE	UNSUED-FOR
UNIVALENT	UNPLAGUED	UNSALUTED	UNSUITING
UNIVERSAL	UNPLAINED	UNSATABLE	UNSULLIED
UNJEALOUS	UNPLAITED	UNSATIATE	UNSUSPECT
UNJOINTED	UNPLANKED	UNSAVOURY	UNSWADDLE
UNKINDLED	UNPLANNED	UNSAYABLE	UNTAINTED
UNKNELLED	UNPLANTED	UNSCANNED	UNTAMABLE
UNKNOWING	UNPLEASED	UNSCARRED	UNTAMABLY
UNLEARNED	UNPLEATED	UNSCATHED	UNTANGLED
UNLIGHTED	UNPLEDGED	UNSCENTED	UNTEMPTED
UNLIMITED	UNPLIABLE	UNSCOURED	UNTENABLE
UNLIVED-IN	UNPLIABLY	UNSCYTHED	UNTHANKED
UNLOADING	UNPLUCKED	UNSECULAR	UNTHRIFTY
UNLOCATED	UNPLUGGED	UNSECURED	UNTIMEOUS
UNLOGICAL	UNPLUMBED	UNSEDUCED	UNTIRABLE
UNLOSABLE	UNPOINTED	UNSEEABLE	UNTOILING
UNLOVABLE	UNPOLICED	UNSEEMING	UNTOUCHED
UNLUCKILY	UNPOLITIC	UNSELFISH	UNTRACKED
UNMAKABLE	UNPOPULAR	UNSETTLED	UNTRAINED
UNMANACLE	UNPOTABLE	UNSEVERED	UNTREATED
UNMANAGED	UNPRAISED	UNSHACKLE	UNTRESSED
UNMANLIKE	UNPRECISE	UNSHAPELY	UNTRIMMED
UNMANURED	UNPREDICT	UNSHEATHE	UNTRODDEN
UNMARRIED	UNPREPARE	UNSHRIVED	UNTRUSSED
UNMASKING	UNPRESSED	UNSHRIVEN	UNTRUSSER
UNMATCHED	UNPRINTED	UNSHUNNED	UNTUMBLED
UNMATURED	UNPROPPED	UNSHUTTER	UNTUNABLE
UNMEANING	UNPROVOKE	UNSICKLED	UNTUNABLY
UNMERITED	UNPURSUED	UNSIGHING	UNTUNEFUL
UNMINDFUL	UNQUALIFY	UNSIGHTED	UNTURNING
UNMINGLED	UNQUEENED	UNSIGHTLY	UNTUTORED
UNMIXEDLY	UNQUEENLY	UNSINEWED	UNTWISTED
UNMONEYED	UNQUELLED	UNSISTING	UNUSHERED
UNMOTIVED	UNQUIETLY	UNSIZABLE	UNUSUALLY
UNMOULDED	UNRAZORED	UNSKILFUL	UNUTTERED
UNMOUNTED	UNREACHED	UNSKILLED	UNVARYING
UNMOVABLE	UNREADILY	UNSKIMMED	UNVISITED
UNMOVABLY	UNREALISE	UNSKINNED	UNVOICING
UNMOVEDLY	UNREALISM	UNSLEPT-IN	UNWAKENED
UNMUSICAL	UNREALITY	UNSMILING	UNWARLIKE
UNMUZZLED	UNREBATED	UNSMITTEN	UNWASTING
UNNAMABLE	UNREBUKED	UNSNUFFED	UNWATCHED
UNNATURAL	UNREDREST	UNSOLACED	UNWATERED
UNNEEDFUL	UNREDUCED	UNSOLIDLY	UNWEARIED
UNNERVING	UNREFINED	UNSOUNDED	UNWEETING
UNNOTICED	UNREFUTED	UNSOUNDLY	UNWEIGHED
UNOBVIOUS	UNRELATED	UNSPARING	UNWELCOME
UNOFFERED	UNRELAXED	UNSPILLED	UNWHIPPED
UNOPPOSED	UNREMOVED	UNSPOILED	UNWILLING
UNORDERED	UNRENEWED	UNSPOTTED	UNWINDING
UNORDERLY	UNRESERVE	UNSQUARED	UNWINKING
UNPACKING	UNRESTFUL	UNSTAINED	UNWISHFUL
UNPAINFUL	UNRESTING	UNSTAMPED	UNWISHING
UNPAINTED	UNREVISED	UNSTAYING	UNWITTILY
UNPALSIED	UNREVOKED	UNSTIFLED	UNWITTING
UNPAPERED	UNRIDABLE	UNSTILLED	UNWOMANLY
UNPARTIAL	UNRIDDLER	UNSTINTED	UNWORKING
UNPAYABLE	UNRIPENED	UNSTOCKED	UNWORLDLY
UNPENNIED	UNRIPPING	UNSTOPPED	UNWORRIED
UNPEOPLED	UNROSINED	UNSTOPPER	UNWOUNDED
UNPERFECT	UNROUNDED	UNSTRIPED	UNWREAKED

UNWREATHE
UNWRINKLE
UNWRITING
UNWRITTEN
UNWROUGHT
UNZEALOUS
UPAITHRIC
UP-AND-DOWN
UPANISHAD
UPBOUNDEN
UPBRAIDER
UPBROUGHT
UPBURNING
UP-CHANNEL
UPCHEERED
UP-COUNTRY
UP-CURRENT
UP-DRAUGHT
UPFILLING
UPGROWING
UPGUSHING
UPHEAPING
UPHOLDING
UPHOLSTER
UPLANDISH
UPLIFTING
UPLIGHTED
UP-PERCHED
UPPERMOST
UP-PRICKED
UPPUTTING
UPRIGHTLY
UPROOTING
UPS-A-DAISY
UPSETTING
UPSITTING
UPSTARING
UPTHUNDER
UPTRILLED
UPTURNING
UPWROUGHT
URALITISE
URANINITE
URANISCUS
URANOLOGY
URCEOLATE
UREDINEAE
UREDINIAL
UREDINIUM
UREDINOUS
URICONIAN
URINATION
URINATIVE
URINOLOGY
URN-SHAPED
UROCHORDA
UROCHROME
URODELOUS
UROGRAPHY
UROPYGIAL
UROPYGIUM
URTICARIA
USELESSLY
USHERETTE
USHERSHIP
USUALNESS

USUCAPION
USURPEDLY
UTEROTOMY
UTRAQUISM
UTRAQUIST
UTRICULAR
UTRICULUS
UTTERABLE
UTTERANCE
UTTERLESS
UTTERMOST
UTTERNESS
UVAROVITE
UXORICIDE

V

VACCINATE
VACCINIAL
VACCINIUM
VACILLANT
VACILLATE
VACUATION
VACUOLATE
VACUOUSLY
VADE-MECUM
VAGARIOUS
VAGINATED
VAGINITIS
VAGUENESS
VAINGLORY
VAISHNAVA
VALDENSES
VALENTINE
VALIANTLY
VALIDNESS
VALKYRIUR
VALLECULA
VALUATION
VALUELESS
VALVASSOR
VALVELESS
VAMBRACED
VAMPIRISE
VAMPIRISM
VANDALISM
VANISHING
VANITY-BAG
VANITY-BOX
VANTBRACE
VANT-BRASS
VAPIDNESS
VAPORABLE
VAPORIFIC
VAPORISER
VAPOURING
VAPOURISH
VARANGIAN
VARANIDAE
VARIATION
VARIATIVE
VARICELLA
VARIEGATE
VARIETIES
VARIOLATE
VARIOLITE
VARIOLOID

VARIOLOUS
VARIOUSLY
VARISCITE
VARLETESS
VARNISHER
VARVELLED
VASECTOMY
VASOMOTOR
VASSALAGE
VASSALESS
VASTIDITY
VASTITUDE
VATICINAL
VECTORIAL
VEE-GUTTER
VEERINGLY
VEGETABLE
VEGETABLY
VEGETATED
VEHEMENCE
VEHEMENCY
VEHICULAR
VEILLEUSE
VEINSTONE
VEINSTUFF
VELARISED
VELDSKOEN
VELLICATE
VELODROME
VELOUTINE
VELVETEEN
VELVETING
VENATICAL
VENDITION
VENEERING
VENEFICAL
VENERABLE
VENERABLY
VENERATOR
VENEREOUS
VENGEABLE
VENGEABLY
VENGEANCE
VENGEMENT
VENIALITY
VENIREMAN
VENTIDUCT
VENTIFACT
VENTILATE
VENTOSITY
VENTRALLY
VENTRICLE
VENTURING
VENTUROUS
VERACIOUS
VERATRINE
VERBALISE
VERBALISM
VERBALIST
VERBALITY
VERBARIAN
VERBASCUM
VERBERATE
VERBICIDE
VERBOSELY
VERBOSITY

VERDANTLY
VERDIGRIS
VERDUROUS
VERGILIAN
VERIDICAL
VERIFYING
VERITABLE
VERITABLY
VERJUICED
VERMEILLE
VERMICIDE
VERMICULE
VERMIFORM
VERMIFUGE
VERMILION
VERMINATE
VERMINOUS
VERNALISE
VERNALITY
VERNATION
VERRUCOSE
VERRUCOUS
VERSATILE
VERSIFIED
VERSIFIER
VERSIFORM
VERSIONAL
VERSIONER
VERTEBRAE
VERTEBRAL
VERTICITY
VERTIPORT
VERVELLED
VESICULAR
VESTIBULE
VESTIGIAL
VESTIGIUM
VESTIMENT
VESTITURE
VESTRYMAN
VETCHLING
VETTURINI
VETTURINO
VEXATIOUS
VEXEDNESS
VEXILLARY
VIABILITY
VIATICALS
VIATORIAL
VIBRACULA
VIBRAHARP
VIBRATILE
VIBRATION
VIBRATIVE
VIBRATORY
VIBRISSAE
VICARIATE
VICARIOUS
VICARSHIP
VICENNIAL
VICE-QUEEN
VICE-REGAL
VICEREINE
VICIOSITY
VICIOUSLY
VICTIMISE

VICTORESS
VICTORIAN
VICTORINE
VIDELICET
VIDEOTAPE
VIEWINESS
VIEWPOINT
VIGESIMAL
VIGILANCE
VIGILANTE
VIGNETTER
VIKINGISM
VILIFYING
VILLAGERY
VILLANAGE
VILLANOUS
VILLENAGE
VILLIFORM
VILLOSITY
VIMINEOUS
VINACEOUS
VINDEMIAL
VINDICATE
VINE-STOCK
VINGT-ET-UN
VINTAGING
VIOLACEAE
VIOLATION
VIOLATIVE
VIOLENTLY
VIOLIN-BOW
VIOLINIST
VIPERIDAE
VIRAGOISH
VIRESCENT
VIRGILIAN
VIRGINIAN
VIRGINITY
VIRGINIUM
VIRTUALLY
VIRTUOSIC
VIRULENCE
VIRULENCY
VISAGISTE
VISCERATE
VISCIDITY
VISCOSITY
VISCOUNTY
VISIONARY
VISIONING
VISIONIST
VISITABLE
VISITATOR
VISITRESS
VISOR-MASK
VISTALESS
VISUALISE
VISUALIST
VISUALITY
VITALISER
VITASCOPE
VITECETUM
VITELLARY
VITELLINE
VITIATION
VITIOSITY

VITRIFIED
VITRIFORM
VITRIOLIC
VITRUVIAN
VIVACIOUS
VIVAMENTE
VIVANDIER
VIVERRINE
VIVIANITE
VIVIDNESS
VIZIERATE
VIZIERIAL
VIZIRSHIP
VOCABULAR
VOCALISER
VOCALNESS
VOICELESS
VOISINAGE
VOITURIER
VOLAGEOUS
VOL-AU-VENT
VOLCANIAN
VOLCANISE
VOLCANISM
VOLCANIST
VOLCANOES
VOLITIENT
VOLKSLIED
VOLKSRAAD
VOLTE-FACE
VOLTIGEUR
VOLTINISM
VOLTMETER
VOLUCRINE
VOLUMETER
VOLUMINAL
VOLUNTARY
VOLUNTEER
VOODOOISM
VOODOOIST
VORACIOUS
VORTICISM
VORTICIST
VORTICOSE
VOUCHSAFE
VOWELLESS
VOW-FELLOW
VOYEURISM
VRAICKING
VULCANIAN
VULCANISE
VULCANISM
VULCANIST
VULCANITE
VULGARIAN
VULGARISE
VULGARISM
VULGARITY
VULNERARY
VULNERATE
VULPICIDE
VULPINISM
VULPINITE
VULSELLAE
VULSELLUM
VULTURINE

VULTURISH
VULTURISM
VULTUROUS
VULVIFORM

W

WACKINESS
WADSETTER
WAFER-CAKE
WAGENBOOM
WAGER-BOAT
WAGES-FUND
WAGGISHLY
WAGHALTER
WAGNERIAN
WAGNERISM
WAGNERIST
WAGNERITE
WAGONETTE
WAGON-LOAD
WAGON-LOCK
WAGON-ROOF
WAGONS-LIT
WAHABIISM
WAHABIITE
WAILINGLY
WAISTBAND
WAISTBELT
WAISTBOAT
WAISTCOAT
WAIST-DEEP
WAIST-HIGH
WAISTLINE
WAITERAGE
WAITERING
WAITINGLY
WAKEFULLY
WAKE-ROBIN
WALACHIAN
WALDENSES
WALDFLUTE
WALDGRAVE
WALKABOUT
WALL-BOARD
WALL-CRESS
WALL-FRUIT
WALLOPING
WALLOWING
WALLPAPER
WALL-PLATE
WALL-SPACE
WALLYDRAG
WALPURGIS
WALTONIAN
WANCHANCY
WANDERING
WANG-TOOTH
WANTONISE
WAPENSHAW
WAPENTAKE
WAPINSHAW
WAPPER-JAW
WARBLE-FLY
WARDROBER
WAREHOUSE
WARFARING

WARLOCKRY
WARMONGER
WARNINGLY
WARRANTED
WARRANTEE
WARRANTER
WARRANTOR
WART-CRESS
WAR-WASTED
WASEGOOSE
WASH-BASIN
WASH-BOARD
WASH-CLOTH
WASHED-OUT
WASHERMAN
WASH-HOUSE
WASHINESS
WASHING-UP
WASH-STAND
WASPISHLY
WASP-STUNG
WASSAILER
WASSAILRY
WASSERMAN
WASTE-BOOK
WASTE-GATE
WASTENESS
WASTE-PIPE
WASTERFUL
WASTERIFE
WATCH-BILL
WATCH-CASE
WATCH-FIRE
WATCHWORD
WATER-BATH
WATER-BIRD
WATER-BUCK
WATER-BULL
WATER-BUTT
WATER-CART
WATER-CASK
WATER-CELL
WATER-COCK
WATER-COOL
WATER-CORE
WATER-CURE
WATER-DECK
WATER-DEER
WATER-DROP
WATERFALL
WATER-FERN
WATER-FLAG
WATER-FLEA
WATER-FLOW
WATERFOWL
WATER-GAGE
WATER-GALL
WATER-GATE
WATER-HEAD
WATER-HOLE
WATER-JUMP
WATER-LEAF
WATER-LENS
WATERLESS
WATER-LILY
WATER-LINE

...AIN	WELL-DOING	WHIP-ROUND	WIND-HOVER
...MARK	WELL-DRAIN	WHIP-SNAKE	WINDINESS
...R-MILL	WELL-FAMED	WHIP-STAFF	WINDINGLY
...TER-MOLE	WELL-FAURT	WHIPSTALL	WINDOW-BAR
...ATER-PIPE	WELL-FOUND	WHIP-STOCK	WINDOW-BOX
WATER-POET	WELL-GIVEN	WHIRL-BONE	WINDOW-TAX
WATER-POLO	WELL-HOUSE	WHIRLIGIG	WIND-SHAK'D
WATER-PORE	WELL-KNOWN	WHIRLPOOL	WINDSWEPT
WATER-PUMP	WELL-LINED	WHIRLWIND	WIND-SWIFT
WATER-RAIL	WELL-MEANT	WHISKERED	WIND-TIGHT
WATER-RATE	WELL-OILED	WHISPERER	WINDWARDS
WATER-RICE	WELL-SET-UP	WHISTLING	WINE-BERRY
WATER-SEAL	WELL-SMACK	WHITEBAIT	WINE-GLASS
WATERSHED	WELL-TIMED	WHITEBASS	WINE-PARTY
WATER-SHOT	WELSH-HARP	WHITEBEAM	WINE-PRESS
WATERSIDE	WELSH-HOOK	WHITE-BEAR	WINE-STONE
WATER-VINE	WELTERING	WHITEFISH	WINE-VAULT
WATER-VOLE	WERNERIAN	WHITEHALL	WING-SHELL
WATER-WAVE	WERNERITE	WHITE-HASS	WING-SNAIL
WATER-WEED	WEST-ABOUT	WHITE-HEAD	WINK-A-PEEP
WATER-WORK	WESTERING	WHITE-LADY	WINKINGLY
WATER-WORN	WESTERNER	WHITE-LIME	WINNINGLY
WATTMETER	WESTNORTH	WHITENESS	WINNOWING
WAVEFRONT	WESTWARDS	WHITENING	WINSOMELY
WAVEGUIDE	WHALE-BACK	WHITE-RENT	WINTER-BUD
WAVELLITE	WHALE-BOAT	WHITE-SALT	WINTERISE
WAVEMETER	WHALEBONE	WHITE-SEAM	WIRE-DRAWN
WAVESHAPE	WHALE-CALF	WHITEWASH	WIRE-GAUZE
WAX-FLOWER	WHALE-HEAD	WHITEWING	WIRE-GRASS
WAX-INSECT	WHALE-LINE	WHITEWOOD	WIRE-GUARD
WAXWORKER	WHATSOE'ER	WHITTAWER	WIRE-PHOTO
WAYFARING	WHEAT-BIRD	WHIZZ-BANG	WIRE-SEWED
WAY-WARDEN	WHEAT-CORN	WHOA-HO-HOA	WISECRACK
WAYWARDLY	WHEAT-MOTH	WHODUNNIT	WISHFULLY
WAYZGOOSE	WHEAT-WORM	WHOLE-MEAL	WISTFULLY
WEAK-KNEED	WHEEDLING	WHOLENESS	WITCHETTY
WEALTHILY	WHEELBASE	WHOLESALE	WITCH-KNOT
WEARILESS	WHEEL-LOCK	WHOLESOME	WITCH-MEAL
WEARINESS	WHEEL-RACE	WHORE'S-EGG	WITCH-WIFE
WEARISOME	WHEEL-SPIN	WHORISHLY	WITHDRAWN
WEASEL-CAT	WHEELWORK	WHOSOEVER	WITHERING
WEATHERED	WHENCEVER	WHUNSTANE	WITHERITE
WEATHERLY	WHEREFORE	WIDE-ANGLE	WITHHAULT
WEB-FOOTED	WHEREFROM	WIDE-AWAKE	WITHOUTEN
WEDGEWISE	WHEREINTO	WIDOW-BIRD	WITHSTAND
WEDNESDAY	WHERENESS	WIDOWHOOD	WITHSTOOD
WEED-ENDER	WHEREUNTO	WIDOW-WAIL	WITHYWIND
WEED-GROWN	WHEREUPON	WIELDABLE	WITLESSLY
WEEDICIDE	WHEREWITH	WIELDLESS	WIT-MONGER
WEEDINESS	WHERRYMAN	WILDERING	WITNESSER
WEEL-FAIRD	WHET-SLATE	WILD-GEESE	WITTICISM
WEEL-FAUR'D	WHETSTONE	WILD-GOOSE	WITTINESS
WEEPINGLY	WHEY-FACED	WILD-GRAPE	WITTINGLY
WEETINGLY	WHICHEVER	WILDGRAVE	WITWANTON
WEEVILLED	WHIFFLERY	WILD-HONEY	WOEBEGONE
WEHRMACHT	WHIFFLING	WILD-OLIVE	WOFULNESS
WEIGHABLE	WHILLYWHA	WILLEMITE	WOLF-HOUND
WEIGH-BANK	WHIMPERER	WILLESDEN	WOLFISHLY
WEIGHTILY	WHIMSICAL	WILLINGLY	WOLFSBANE
WEIGHTING	WHININESS	WILLOWISH	WOLF'S-CLAW
WEIRDNESS	WHININGLY	WINCOPIPE	WOLF'S-FOOT
WELFARISM	WHINNYING	WIND-BOUND	WOLF-TOOTH
WELLANEAR	WHINSTONE	WIND-BREAK	WOLVERENE
WELLBEING	WHIPCORDY	WIND-CHART	WOLVERINE
WELL-BORER	WHIP-GRAFT	WIND-CHEST	WOMAN-BODY
WELL-BUILT	WHIPPER-IN	WIND-GAUGE	WOMAN-BORN

WOMANHOOD
WOMANKIND
WOMAN-LIKE
WOMAN-POST
WOMENFOLK
WOMENKIND
WONDERFUL
WONDERING
WONDEROUS
WOODBLOCK
WOOD-BORER
WOODCHUCK
WOODCRAFT
WOOD-FIBRE
WOOD-FLOUR
WOOD-HONEY
WOOD-HORSE
WOOD-HOUSE
WOODINESS
WOOD-LOUSE
WOOD-NYMPH
WOOD-PAPER
WOOD-REEVE
WOOD-SCREW
WOOD-SHOCK
WOOD-SPITE
WOOD-STAMP
WOOD-STONE
WOOD-SUGAR
WOOD-WAXEN
WOOMERANG
WORCESTER
WORD-BOUND
WORDINESS
WORKFOLKS
WORKHOUSE
WORKMANLY
WORKPIECE
WORK-TABLE
WORKWOMAN
WORLDLING
WORLD-WIDE
WORM-EATEN
WORM-FENCE
WORM-FEVER
WORM-GRASS
WORM-HOLED
WORM-WHEEL
WORRIMENT
WORRISOME
WORTHLESS
WOUNDABLE
WOUNDLESS
WOUNDWORT
WRANGLING

WRATHLESS
WREAKLESS
WRENCHING
WRESTLING
WRIGGLING
WRING-BOLT
WRISTBAND
WRIST-DROP
WRIST-SHOT
WRITATIVE
WRITERESS
WRONG-DOER
WRONGNESS
WROUGHT-UP
WRY-NECKED
WULFENITE
WUTHERING
WYANDOTTE
WYCLIFITE
WYLIE-COAT

X

XANTHIPPE
XANTHOURA
XENARTHRA
XENOCRYST
XENOGRAFT
XENOMANIA
XENOMENIA
XENOPHOBE
XENOPHOBY
XEROCHASY
XERODERMA
XEROMORPH
XEROPHAGY
XEROPHILY
XEROPHYTE
XEROSTOMA
XIPHIIDAE
XIPHOIDAL
XIPHOSURA
X-PARTICLE
XYLOGRAPH
XYLOIDINE
XYLOMETER
XYLOPHAGA
XYLOPHAGE
XYLOPHONE
XYRIDALES

Y

YACHT-CLUB
YACHTSMAN
YAJURVEDA
YAKETY-YAK

YAKITY-YAK
YAMMERING
YANKEEDOM
YANKEEISM
YARDSTICK
YATTERING
YAWNINGLY
YELLOW-BOY
YELLOW-DOG
YELLOWISH
YESTERDAY
YESTEREVE
YGGDRASIL
YIDDISHER
YIELDABLE
YIRD-HOUSE
YO-HEAVE-HO
YOHIMBINE
YOKE-DEVIL
YOLK-STALK
YORKSHIRE
YOUNG-EYED
YOUNGLING
YOUNGNESS
YOUNGSTER
YOUNGTHLY
YOUTHHEAD
YOUTHHOOD
YOUTHSOME
YRAVISHED
YTTERBIUM

Z

ZAMBOORAK
ZAMINDARI
ZANTE-WOOD
ZANZIBARI
ZAPATEADO
ZAPODIDAE
ZAPOTILLA
ZEALOTISM
ZEALOUSLY
ZEBRA-WOOD
ZECHSTEIN
ZEITGEIST
ZELOTYPIA
ZEMINDARI
ZEMINDARY
ZERNEBOCK
ZESTFULLY
ZEUGLODON
ZEUGMATIC
ZIBELLINE
ZIGZAGGED
ZINC-BLOOM

ZINC-COLIC
ZINC-WHITE
ZINKENITE
ZIPHIIDAE
ZIRCONIUM
ZOECHROME
ZOETROPIC
ZOIATRICS
ZONURIDAE
ZOOBIOTIC
ZOOCYTIUM
ZOOGAMETE
ZOOGAMOUS
ZOOGENOUS
ZOOGLOEIC
ZOOGONOUS
ZOOGRAPHY
ZOOLATRIA
ZOOLITHIC
ZOOLOGIST
ZOOMANTIC
ZOOMETRIC
ZOOMORPHY
ZOONOMIST
ZOOPERIST
ZOOPHAGAN
ZOOPHILIA
ZOOPHOBIA
ZOOPHORIC
ZOOPHORUS
ZOOPHYTIC
ZOOPLASTY
ZOOSCOPIC
ZOOSPORIC
ZOOTECHNY
ZOOTHECIA
ZOOTHEISM
ZOOTOMIST
ZOOTROPHY
ZUCCHETTO
ZUMBOORUK
ZWANZIGER
ZWINGLIAN
ZYGAENINE
ZYGAENOID
ZYGANTRUM
ZYGOMATIC
ZYGOPHYTE
ZYGOSPERM
ZYGOSPORE
ZYMOGENIC
ZYMOLOGIC
ZYMOLYSIS
ZYMOMETER

A

ABBEY-LAIRD
ABBEY-PIECE

ABBREVIATE
ABDICATION

ABDOMINOUS
ABERDEVINE

ABERDONIAN
ABERRATION
ABHORRENCE
ABHORRENCY
ABIOGENIST
ABITURIENT
ABJECTNESS
ABJUNCTION
ABJURATION
ABLE-BODIED
ABNEGATION
ABNORMALLY
ABOMINABLE
ABOMINABLY
ABOMINATOR
ABORIGINAL
ABORIGINES
ABORTICIDE
ABORTIVELY
ABOVE-BOARD
ABOVE-NAMED
ABRAHAM-MAN
ABREACTION
ABRIDGMENT
ABROGATION
ABROGATIVE
ABRUPTNESS
ABSCISSION
ABSOLUTELY
ABSOLUTION
ABSOLUTISM
ABSOLUTIST
ABSOLUTORY
ABSOLVITOR
ABSORBABLE
ABSORBEDLY
ABSORBENCY
ABSORPTION
ABSORPTIVE
ABSTEMIOUS
ABSTENTION
ABSTERGENT
ABSTERSION
ABSTERSIVE
ABSTINENCE
ABSTINENCY
ABSTRACTED
ABSTRACTER
ABSTRACTLY
ABSTRACTOR
ABSTRUSELY
ABSURDNESS
ABUNDANTLY
ABYSSINIAN
ACADEMICAL
ACANACEOUS
ACAROPHILY
ACATALEPSY
ACCELERANT
ACCELERATE
ACCENTUATE
ACCEPTABLE
ACCEPTABLY
ACCEPTANCE
ACCEPTANCY
ACCESSIBLE

ACCESSIBLY
ACCIDENTAL
ACCIDENTED
ACCOMPLICE
ACCOMPLISH
ACCOMPTANT
ACCORDABLE
ACCORDANCE
ACCORDANCY
ACCOSTABLE
ACCOUCHEUR
ACCOUNTANT
ACCOUNTING
ACCOUTRING
ACCREDITED
ACCRESCENT
ACCUBATION
ACCUMULATE
ACCURATELY
ACCUSATION
ACCUSATIVE
ACCUSEMENT
ACCUSTOMED
ACEPHALOUS
ACERACEOUS
ACERVATION
ACETABULAR
ACETABULUM
ACHERONTIC
ACHIEVABLE
ACHITOPHEL
ACHROMATIC
ACHROMATIN
ACIDIFYING
ACIDIMETER
ACIDIMETRY
ACINACEOUS
ACOLOUTHIC
ACOLOUTHOS
ACORN-SHELL
ACOTYLEDON
ACOUSTICAL
ACQUAINTED
ACQUIRABLE
ACQUITMENT
ACQUITTING
ACRIFLAVIN
ACROAMATIC
ACROBATICS
ACROBATISM
ACROGENOUS
ACROMEGALY
ACRONYCHAL
ACROPHOBIA
ACROPHONIC
ACROTERIAL
ACROTERION
ACROTERIUM
ACTABILITY
ACTINOLITE
ACTIONABLE
ACTIVATION
ACTIVENESS
ACUMINATED
ADAMANTEAN
ADAMANTINE

ADAMITICAL
ADAPTATION
ADAPTATIVE
ADAPTIVELY
ADDER-STONE
ADDER'S-WORT
ADDITAMENT
ADDITIONAL
ADDITIVELY
ADDLE-PATED
ADELANTADO
ADENECTOMY
ADEQUATELY
ADEQUATIVE
ADHESIVELY
ADHIBITION
ADIAPHORON
ADJACENTLY
ADJECTIVAL
ADJUDGMENT
ADJUDICATE
ADJUNCTION
ADJUNCTIVE
ADJURATION
ADJURATORY
ADJUSTABLE
ADJUSTMENT
ADMINISTER
ADMIRATION
ADMIRATIVE
ADMIRINGLY
ADMISSIBLE
ADMITTABLE
ADMITTANCE
ADMITTEDLY
ADMONITION
ADMONITIVE
ADMONITORY
ADOLESCENT
ADROITNESS
ADSORPTION
ADULLAMITE
ADULTERANT
ADULTERATE
ADULTERESS
ADULTERINE
ADULTERISE
ADULTEROUS
ADVENTURER
ADVERSARIA
ADVERTENCE
ADVERTENCY
ADVERTISER
ADVICE-BOAT
ADVISATORY
ADVISEMENT
ADVOCATION
ADVOCATORY
AEDILESHIP
AEOLOTROPY
AERENCHYMA
AEROBATICS
AEROBIOSIS
AEROBIOTIC
AEROENGINE
AEROGRAMME

AEROGRAPHY
AEROLOGIST
AEROMETRIC
AERONAUTIC
AERONOMIST
AEROPHOBIA
AEROPHOBIC
AEROSTATIC
AEROTACTIC
AEROTROPIC
AERUGINOUS
AESTHETICS
AETHIOPIAN
AFFABILITY
AFFECTEDLY
AFFEERMENT
AFFETTUOSO
AFFILIABLE
AFFINITIVE
AFFIRMABLE
AFFIRMANCE
AFFLICTING
AFFLICTION
AFFLICTIVE
AFFLUENTLY
AFFRICATED
AFFRIGHTED
AFFRIGHTEN
AFFRONTING
AFFRONTIVE
AFICIONADO
AFRICANDER
AFRICANISE
AFRICANISM
AFRICANIST
AFRICANOID
AFRIKANDER
AFRORMOSIA
AFTERBIRTH
AFTERGRASS
AFTER-GUARD
AFTER-IMAGE
AFTER-LIGHT
AFTERPAINS
AFTERPIECE
AFTERSHAFT
AFTERTASTE
AFTERWARDS
AGGLUTININ
AGGRANDISE
AGGRESSION
AGGRESSIVE
AGITATEDLY
AGONISEDLY
AGONISTICS
AGROLOGIST
AGRONOMIAL
AGRONOMIST
AHITHOPHEL
AHORSEBACK
AHURAMAZDA
AIDE-DE-CAMP
AIR-BLADDER
AIR-COOLING
AIR-CUSHION
AIR-GRATING

AIR-HOSTESS
AIRMANSHIP
AIR-MARSHAL
AIR-OFFICER
AIR-TRAFFIC
AKOLOUTHOS
ALABANDINE
ALABANDITE
ALANG-ALANG
ALARM-CLOCK
ALARMINGLY
ALBESCENCE
ALBIGENSES
ALBUMENISE
ALBUMINATE
ALBUMINISE
ALBUMINOID
ALBUMINOUS
ALCHEMICAL
ALCOHOLISE
ALCOHOLISM
ALCYONARIA
ALDERMANIC
ALDERMANLY
ALDERMANRY
ALEXANDERS
ALGEBRAIST
ALGOLAGNIA
ALGOLOGIST
ALGONQUIAN
ALIENATION
ALIMENTARY
ALINEATION
ALISMACEAE
ALKALINITY
ALL-DREADED
ALLEGATION
ALLEGEANCE
ALLEGIANCE
ALLEGORISE
ALLEGORIST
ALLEGRETTO
ALLEVIATOR
ALL-FIREDLY
ALL-HALLOWS
ALLIACEOUS
ALLIGATION
ALLITERATE
ALLOCATION
ALLOCHIRIA
ALLOCUTION
ALLOGAMOUS
ALLOPATHIC
ALLOTROPIC
ALL-OVERISH
ALL-ROUNDER
ALLUREMENT
ALLURINGLY
ALLUSIVELY
ALLYCHOLLY
ALMACANTAR
ALMOND-EYED
ALMOND-TREE
ALMUCANTAR
ALONGSHORE
ALPENSTOCK

ALPHABETIC
ALPHAMERIC
ALPHONSINE
ALTAR-CLOTH
ALTARPIECE
ALTAR-RAILS
ALTAR-STONE
ALTAZIMUTH
ALTERATION
ALTERATIVE
ALTERNANCE
ALTERNATIM
ALTERNATOR
ALTISONANT
ALTITONANT
ALTOGETHER
ALTRUISTIC
AMALGAMATE
AMANUENSES
AMANUENSIS
AMARANTHUS
AMARANTINE
AMATEURISH
AMATEURISM
AMATORIOUS
AMAZEDNESS
AMAZON-LIKE
AMBAGITORY
AMBARVALIA
AMBASSADOR
AMBIDEXTER
AMBIVALENT
AMBLYOPSIS
AMBLYSTOMA
AMBULACRAL
AMBULACRUM
AMBULATION
AMBULATORY
AMBUSCADOS
AMBUSHMENT
AMELIORATE
AMENDATORY
AMERCEMENT
AMERCIABLE
AMETABOLIC
AMIABILITY
AMIDO-GROUP
AMINO-GROUP
AMMONIACAL
AMMONIACUM
AMMONIATED
AMMUNITION
AMOEBIFORM
AMPELOPSIS
AMPHIBIOUS
AMPHIBOLIC
AMPHIBRACH
AMPHICTYON
AMPHIMACER
AMPHIMIXIS
AMPHINEURA
AMPHISCIAN
AMPHITRYON
AMPHOTERIC
AMPLIATION
AMPLIATIVE

AMPLIFYING
AMPUSSY-AND
AMPUTATION
AMRITATTVA
AMYGDALOID
AMYLACEOUS
ANABAPTISE
ANABAPTISM
ANABAPTIST
ANACARDIUM
ANACLASTIC
ANACOLUTHA
ANACRUSTIC
ANADROMOUS
ANADYOMENE
ANAGLYPHIC
ANAGLYPTIC
ANAGOGICAL
ANALOGICAL
ANALPHABET
ANALYSABLE
ANALYTICAL
ANAMORPHIC
ANAPAESTIC
ANAPHYLAXY
ANAPLASTIC
ANAPTYCTIC
ANARCHICAL
ANARTHROUS
ANASTIGMAT
ANASTOMOSE
ANASTROPHE
ANATOMICAL
ANATROPOUS
ANCESTRESS
ANCHORETIC
ANCHOR-HOLD
ANCHORLESS
ANCHOR-RING
ANCHYLOSED
ANCHYLOSIS
ANCIPITOUS
ANDALUSIAN
ANDALUSITE
ANDROECIUM
ANDROGENIC
ANDROPHORE
ANECDOTAGE
ANECDOTIST
ANEMOGRAPH
ANEMOMETER
ANEMOMETRY
ANEMOPHILY
ANEURYSMAL
ANGARALAND
ANGELOLOGY
ANGEL-WATER
ANGIOSPERM
ANGLO-IRISH
ANGLOMANIA
ANGLOPHOBE
ANGLOPHONE
ANGLO-SAXON
ANGUIFAUNA
ANGUILLULA
ANGULARITY

ANGWANTIBO
ANHARMONIC
ANHELATION
ANIMADVERT
ANIMALCULA
ANIMALCULE
ANIMATEDLY
ANISOTROPY
ANNALISTIC
ANNEXATION
ANNIHILATE
ANNOTATION
ANNOYINGLY
ANNULARITY
ANNULATION
ANNUNCIATE
ANNUNTIATE
ANONACEOUS
ANOPHELINE
ANSCHAUUNG
ANSWERABLE
ANSWERABLY
ANSWERLESS
ANTAGONISE
ANTAGONISM
ANTAGONIST
ANTE-BELLUM
ANTECEDENT
ANTECESSOR
ANTECHAPEL
ANTE-NICENE
ANTEPENULT
ANTERIORLY
ANTHELICES
ANTHEMWISE
ANTHERIDIA
ANTHOMANIA
ANTHONOMUS
ANTHOPHORE
ANTHRACENE
ANTHRACITE
ANTHRACOID
ANTHROPOID
ANTIADITIS
ANTIBIOSIS
ANTIBIOTIC
ANTICHRIST
ANTICHTHON
ANTICIPANT
ANTICIPATE
ANTICIVISM
ANTICLIMAX
ANTICLINAL
ANTIFREEZE
ANTI-HEROIC
ANTILOGOUS
ANTILOPINE
ANTIMASQUE
ANTI-MATTER
ANTIMONATE
ANTIMONIAL
ANTIMONIDE
ANTIMONITE
ANTINOMIAN
ANTIOCHENE
ANTIOCHIAN

ANTIPATHIC
ANTIPHONAL
ANTIPHONER
ANTIPHONIC
ANTIPODEAN
ANTIPROTON
ANTIQUATED
ANTISEMITE
ANTISEPSIS
ANTISEPTIC
ANTISOCIAL
ANTITHEISM
ANTITHEIST
ANTITHESES
ANTITHESIS
ANTITHETIC
ANTITRAGUS
ANTLER-MOTH
ANYWHITHER
APAGOGICAL
APHAERESIS
APHIDICIDE
APHORISTIC
APHRODISIA
APICULTURE
APLACENTAL
APLANATISM
APOCARPOUS
APOCHROMAT
APOCRYPHAL
APOCRYPHON
APODEICTIC
APOLAUSTIC
APOLITICAL
APOLLONIAN
APOLOGETIC
APOMORPHIA
APOPEMPTIC
APOPHTHEGM
APOPLECTIC
APOSEMATIC
APOSPOROUS
APOSTATISE
APOSTOLATE
APOSTROPHE
APOTHECARY
APOTHECIAL
APOTHECIUM
APOTHEOSES
APOTHEOSIS
APOTROPAIC
APOTROPOUS
APPARELLED
APPARENTLY
APPARITION
APPEALABLE
APPEARANCE
APPEASABLE
APPENDICES
APPENDIXES
APPERCEIVE
APPETISING
APPETITION
APPETITIVE
APPLAUDING

APPLAUSIVE
APPLE-WOMAN
APPLICABLE
APPLICABLY
APPOINTIVE
APPOSITELY
APPOSITION
APPOSITIVE
APPRECIATE
APPRENTICE
APPROVABLE
APPROVANCE
APRICATION
APRON-STAGE
APTERYGOTA
AQUABATICS
AQUAFORTIS
AQUAMANALE
AQUAMANILE
AQUAMARINE
AQUAPLANER
ARABESQUED
ARACHNIDAN
ARAEOMETER
ARAEOMETRY
ARAEOSTYLE
ARALIACEAE
ARBALESTER
ARBALISTER
ARBITRABLE
ARBITRATOR
ARCHAICISM
ARCHAISTIC
ARCHBISHOP
ARCH-CHIMIC
ARCHDEACON
ARCHEGONIA
ARCHER-FISH
ARCHETYPAL
ARCH-FLAMEN
ARCHITRAVE
ARCHONSHIP
ARCH-PIRATE
ARCH-PRIEST
ARCTOGAEAN
ARCTOGAEIC
ARCUBALIST
ARC-WELDING
AREFACTION
ARENACEOUS
AREOGRAPHY
AREOLATION
AREOPAGITE
ARGONAUTIC
ARGUMENTUM
ARGUTENESS
ARGYRODITE
ARIMASPIAN
ARISTIPPUS
ARISTOCRAT
ARISTOLOGY
ARITHMETIC
ARLES-PENNY
ARMAGEDDON
ARMIGEROUS
ARMIPOTENT

ARMOUR-CLAD
ARMOURLESS
ARPEGGIATE
ARRAGONITE
ARRAIGNING
ARRESTABLE
ARRESTMENT
ARRIÈRE-BAN
ARROGANTLY
ARROGATION
ARROW-GRASS
ARTFULNESS
ARTHRALGIA
ARTHRALGIC
ARTHROMERE
ARTHROPODA
ARTHURIANA
ARTICULATA
ARTICULATE
ARTIFICIAL
ARTISTICAL
ARTOCARPUS
ARTY-CRAFTY
ARVICOLINE
ARYBALLOID
ARYTAENOID
ASAFOETIDA
ASARABACCA
ASBESTOSIS
ASCARIASIS
ASCENDABLE
ASCENDANCE
ASCENDANCY
ASCENDENCE
ASCENDENCY
ASCENDIBLE
ASCETICISM
ASCOMYCETE
ASCRIBABLE
ASCRIPTION
ASEPTICISE
ASEPTICISM
ASEXUALITY
ASHKENAZIM
ASHLAR-WORK
ASIATICISM
ASPARAGINE
ASPECTABLE
ASPHYXIANT
ASPHYXIATE
ASPIDISTRA
ASPIRATION
ASPIRATORY
ASPIRINGLY
ASSAFETIDA
ASSAILABLE
ASSAILMENT
ASSAY-PIECE
ASSEMBLAGE
ASSENTATOR
ASSENTIENT
ASSERTABLE
ASSESSABLE
ASSESSMENT
ASSEVERATE
ASSIBILATE

ASSIGNABLE
ASSIGNMENT
ASSIMILATE
ASSISTANCE
ASSOCIABLE
ASSOILMENT
ASSONANTAL
ASSORTMENT
ASSUMINGLY
ASSUMPTION
ASSUMPTIVE
ASSURGENCY
ASSYTHMENT
ASTARBOARD
ASTERIATED
ASTEROIDAL
ASTEROIDEA
ASTIGMATIC
ASTOMATOUS
ASTONISHED
ASTOUNDING
ASTRAGALUS
ASTRICTION
ASTRICTIVE
ASTRINGENT
ASTROLATRY
ASTROLOGER
ASTROLOGIC
ASTRONOMER
ASTRONOMIC
ASTUTENESS
ASYMMETRIC
ASYMPTOTIC
ASYNARTETE
ASYNTACTIC
ASYSTOLISM
ATELEIOSIS
ATHANASIAN
ATHERMANCY
ATMOLOGIST
ATMOSPHERE
ATRAMENTAL
ATTACHABLE
ATTACHMENT
ATTACKABLE
ATTAINABLE
ATTAINMENT
ATTAINTURE
ATTEMPERED
ATTENDANCE
ATTENDANCY
ATTENDMENT
ATTENUATED
ATTENUATOR
ATTESTABLE
ATTIREMENT
ATTORNMENT
ATTRACTANT
ATTRACTION
ATTRACTIVE
ATTUNEMENT
AUBERGISTE
AUCTIONARY
AUCTIONEER
AUDIBILITY
AUDIOMETER

AUDIOPHILE
AUDITORIUM
AUGER-SHELL
AUGUSTNESS
AUREOMYCIN
AURICULATE
AURIFEROUS
AUSCULTATE
AUSPICIOUS
AUSTENITIC
AUSTRALIAN
AUSTRALITE
AUSTRALORP
AUSTRINGER
AUTARCHIST
AUTARKICAL
AUTECOLOGY
AUTHORLESS
AUTHORSHIP
AUTOCHTHON
AUTOCRATIC
AUTODIDACT
AUTOEROTIC
AUTOGAMOUS
AUTOGENOUS
AUTOGRAPHY
AUTO-IMMUNE
AUTOMATION
AUTOMATISM
AUTOMATIST
AUTOMATONS
AUTOMOBILE
AUTOMOTIVE
AUTONOMICS
AUTONOMIST
AUTONOMOUS
AUTOPLASTY
AUTOPTICAL
AUTOSTRADA
AUTOTHEISM
AUTOTHEIST
AUTUMNALLY
AVAILINGLY
AVANT-GARDE
AVANTURINE
AVARICIOUS
AVENACEOUS
AVENGEMENT
AVENGERESS
AVENTURINE
AVERRHOISM
AVERRHOIST
AVERSENESS
AVICULARIA
AVICULIDAE
AVICULTURE
AVOUCHABLE
AWKWARDISH
AXINOMANCY
AXIOLOGIST
AXIOMATICS
AZEOTROPIC
AZOBENZENE

B

BABBLATIVE

BABBLEMENT
BABIROUSSA
BABY-FARMER
BABY-JUMPER
BABYLONIAN
BABYLONISH
BABY-RIBBON
BABY-SITTER
BACCHANALS
BACKBITING
BACK-BLOCKS
BACK-FRIEND
BACKGAMMON
BACK-GARDEN
BACKGROUND
BACKHANDED
BACKHANDER
BACK-NUMBER
BACKSHEESH
BACKSLIDER
BACKSPAULD
BACKSTAIRS
BACKSTITCH
BACKSTROKE
BACKVELDER
BACKWARDLY
BACTERIOID
BADDERLOCK
BAFFLINGLY
BAGASSOSIS
BAGGAGE-CAR
BAILIESHIP
BAIRN'S-PART
BAKING-SODA
BALBRIGGAN
BALBUTIENT
BALCONETTE
BALDERDASH
BALD-HEADED
BALLERINAS
BALLET-GIRL
BALL-FLOWER
BALLISTICS
BALLISTITE
BALLOONING
BALLOONIST
BALNEATION
BALNEOLOGY
BALUSTERED
BALUSTRADE
BANDERILLA
BANDMASTER
BAND-STRING
BANISHMENT
BANK-CHEQUE
BANKER-MARK
BANKRUPTCY
BANQUETEER
BANQUETING
BANTINGISM
BAPHOMETIC
BAPTISTERY
BARBED-WIRE
BARBELLATE
BARBITURIC
BARCAROLLE

BARDOLATRY
BAREBACKED
BAREFOOTED
BAREHEADED
BARELEGGED
BARGE-BOARD
BARK-BEETLE
BARKENTINE
BARLEY-BREE
BARLEY-BROO
BARLEYCORN
BARMECIDAL
BAROMETRIC
BARONETAGE
BARONETESS
BAR-PARLOUR
BARRACKING
BARRACOOTA
BARRACOUTA
BARRAMUNDA
BARRATROUS
BARREL-BULK
BARRELFULS
BARRENNESS
BARRENWORT
BARRING-OUT
BARROW-TRAM
BARTHOLMEW
BARTISANED
BARYSPHERE
BASEBALLER
BASE-MINDED
BASERUNNER
BASHAWSHIP
BASKETBALL
BASKETFULS
BASKET-HILT
BASKETWORK
BASSET-HORN
BASS-FIDDLE
BASSOONIST
BASTARD-BAR
BASTARDISE
BASTARDISM
BASTINADED
BATFOWLING
BATHING-BOX
BATHING-HUT
BATHOLITIC
BATHOMETER
BATHYLITIC
BATHYMETER
BATHYMETRY
BATHYSCAPH
BATHYSCOPE
BATOLOGIST
BATRACHIAN
BATTLEDOOR
BATTLEDORE
BATTLEMENT
BATTLESHIP
BAWDY-HOUSE
BEACH-LA-MAR
BEADLEHOOD
BEADLESHIP
BEADSWOMAN

BEAM-ENGINE
BEARD-GRASS
BEAR-GARDEN
BEARLEADER
BEATIFICAL
BEAUJOLAIS
BEAUTICIAN
BEAUTIFIER
BEAUTY-SPOT
BEAVER-TREE
BEAVER-WOOD
BECCAFICOS
BÊCHE-DE-MER
BECOMINGLY
BEDCHAMBER
BEDCLOTHES
BEDELLSHIP
BEDEVILLED
BEDLINGTON
BEDPRESSER
BEDRAGGLED
BED-SWERVER
BEECH-DROPS
BEEF-BREWIS
BEEF-WITTED
BEEKEEPING
BEER-BARREL
BEER-BOTTLE
BEER-ENGINE
BEER-GARDEN
BEESWINGED
BEETLE-EYED
BEETLE-HEAD
BEETMISTER
BEFOREHAND
BEFORETIME
BEHIND-DOOR
BEHIND-HAND
BEL-ACCOYLE
BELGRAVIAN
BELIEFLESS
BELIEVABLE
BELITTLING
BELLADONNA
BELLAMOURE
BELLARMINE
BELLETRIST
BELL-FLOWER
BELLHANGER
BELL-RINGER
BELL-SHAPED
BELL-SILLER
BELL-TURRET
BELL-WETHER
BELLY-DANCE
BELLY-LAUGH
BELONGINGS
BENEDICITE
BENEDICTUS
BENEFACTOR
BENEFICENT
BENEFICIAL
BENEFITING
BENEVOLENT
BENIGHTING
BENIGNANCY

BENTHAMISM
BENTHAMITE
BENUMBMENT
BENZEDRINE
BENZOCAINE
BENZPYRENE
BEQUEATHAL
BERGSONIAN
BERGSONISM
BERIBBONED
BERKELEIAN
BESCRIBBLE
BESEECHING
BESOM-RIDER
BESOTTEDLY
BESPRINKLE
BESTIALISE
BESTIALISM
BESTIALITY
BESTOWMENT
BESTRADDLE
BESTRAUGHT
BESTRIDDEN
BESTSELLER
BETELGEUSE
BETELGEUZE
BETTERMENT
BETTERMOST
BETTERNESS
BETULACEAE
BETWEENITY
BEWELTERED
BEWILDERED
BEWITCHERY
BEWITCHING
BIBLICALLY
BIBLIOLOGY
BIBLIOPEGY
BIBLIOPHIL
BIBLIOPOLE
BIBLIOPOLY
BICHROMATE
BIDENTATED
BIENNIALLY
BIFURCATED
BIGAMOUSLY
BIG-BELLIED
BIJOUTERIE
BILGE-WATER
BILINGUIST
BILIVERDIN
BILL-BROKER
BILLET-DOUX
BILLET-HEAD
BILLPOSTER
BILOCATION
BIMESTRIAL
BIMETALLIC
BINAURALLY
BIOCHEMIST
BIODYNAMIC
BIOECOLOGY
BIOGENESIS
BIOGENETIC
BIOGRAPHER
BIOGRAPHIC

BIOLOGICAL
BIOMETRICS
BIOMORPHIC
BIOPHYSICS
BIOPOIESIS
BIPARTISAN
BIPETALOUS
BIPINNARIA
BIQUINTILE
BIRD-CHERRY
BIRD-PEPPER
BIRD-SKIING
BIRD-SPIDER
BIRD-STRIKE
BIRD-WITTED
BIROSTRATE
BIRTHNIGHT
BIRTHPLACE
BIRTHRIGHT
BISHOP-BIRD
BISSEXTILE
BISULPHATE
BISULPHIDE
BITONALITY
BITTER-KING
BITTERLING
BITTERNESS
BITTER-ROOT
BITTER-SPAR
BITTERWOOD
BITUMINATE
BITUMINISE
BITUMINOUS
BIVALVULAR
BIVOUACKED
BIZARRERIE
BLACKAMOOR
BLACKBERRY
BLACKBOARD
BLACK-BULLY
BLACKFACED
BLACKGUARD
BLACKHEART
BLACKSHIRT
BLACKSMITH
BLACKTHORN
BLACKWATER
BLADDER-NUT
BLAMEFULLY
BLANCMANGE
BLANKETING
BLANQUETTE
BLASPHEMER
BLASTOCYST
BLASTODERM
BLASTOIDEA
BLASTOMERE
BLASTOPORE
BLEARINESS
BLEPHARISM
BLETHERING
BLIND-ALLEY
BLIND-DRUNK
BLIND-STORY
BLISSFULLY
BLISTER-FLY

BLISTERING
BLITHENESS
BLITHERING
BLITHESOME
BLIZZARDLY
BLOCK-CHAIN
BLOCKHOUSE
BLONDE-LACE
BLOOD-COUNT
BLOOD-DONOR
BLOOD-GROUP
BLOOD-HORSE
BLOODHOUND
BLOOD-MONEY
BLOOD-PLATE
BLOOD-ROYAL
BLOOD-SIZED
BLOODSTAIN
BLOODSTOCK
BLOODSTONE
BLOOD-WAGON
BLOODY-EYED
BLOODY-HAND
BLOOMSBURY
BLOSSOMING
BLOTTESQUE
BLUE-BONNET
BLUEBOTTLE
BLUEBREAST
BLUE-CHEESE
BLUEJACKET
BLUE-PENCIL
BLUETHROAT
BLUE-TONGUE
BLUEY-GREEN
BLUNDERING
BLUSHINGLY
BLUSTERING
BLUSTEROUS
BOARD-WAGES
BOASTFULLY
BOAT-RACING
BOBBIN-LACE
BOBBYSOXER
BODY-CAVITY
BODY-COLOUR
BOGTROTTER
BOILER-SUIT
BOISTEROUS
BOLLANDIST
BOLL-WEEVIL
BOLSHEVISE
BOLSHEVISM
BOLSHEVIST
BOLSTERING
BOMBARDIER
BOMB-VESSEL
BOMBYCIDAE
BONDHOLDER
BONDSWOMAN
BOND-TIMBER
BONESETTER
BONESHAKER
BONE-SPAVIN
BOOBY-PRIZE
BOOK-BINDER

BOOK-HOLDER
BOOK-HUNTER
BOOKKEEPER
BOOKMAKING
BOOK-MUSLIN
BOOKSELLER
BOONDOGGLE
BOOT-CLOSER
BOOTLEGGER
BOOTLESSLY
BOOTLICKER
BOOTMAKING
BORDERLAND
BORDERLESS
BORDERLINE
BORDRAGING
BOSWELLIAN
BOSWELLISE
BOSWELLISM
BOTHERSOME
BOTRYOIDAL
BOTTLE-FISH
BOTTLE-HEAD
BOTTLE-NECK
BOTTLE-NOSE
BOTTLE-TREE
BOTTOM-FISH
BOTTOM-LAND
BOUILLOTTE
BOUNTIHOOD
BOURBONISM
BOURBONIST
BOURIGNIAN
BOUSINGKEN
BOWDLERISE
BOWDLERISM
BOWERWOMAN
BOWERWOMEN
BOYISHNESS
BRACHIOPOD
BRACHYAXIS
BRACHYDOME
BRACHYLOGY
BRACHYURAL
BRADYSEISM
BRAGADISME
BRAGGINGLY
BRAHMANISM
BRAHMINISM
BRAINCHILD
BRAIN-CORAL
BRAIN-DRAIN
BRAIN-FEVER
BRAININESS
BRAINSTORM
BRAKE-BLOCK
BRAKEWHEEL
BRAMAH-LOCK
BRANCHIATE
BRANCHLESS
BRANCH-WORK
BRANDERING
BRANDY-BALL
BRANDY-SNAP
BRANT-GOOSE
BRASSINESS

BRATTICING
BRAWNINESS
BRAZEN-FACE
BRAZENNESS
BRAZIL-WOOD
BREADBERRY
BREAD-CRUMB
BREADFRUIT
BREADSTUFF
BREAKWATER
BREASTBONE
BREAST-DEEP
BREAST-HIGH
BREASTKNOT
BREASTRAIL
BREAST-WALL
BREASTWORK
BREATHLESS
BRECCIATED
BREECHLESS
BREEZELESS
BRENT-GOOSE
BRESSUMMER
BREVETTING
BRICK-EARTH
BRICKFIELD
BRICKLAYER
BRICKMAKER
BRIDEGROOM
BRIDE'S-CAKE
BRIDESMAID
BRIDGEHEAD
BRIDGELESS
BRIDGERAMA
BRIDLE-HAND
BRIDLE-PATH
BRIDLE-REIN
BRIDLE-ROAD
BRIGANDAGE
BRIGANDINE
BRIGANTINE
BRIGHTNESS
BRIGHTSOME
BRILLIANCE
BRILLIANCY
BRITISHISM
BROAD-ARROW
BROADCLOTH
BROAD-GAUGE
BROADPIECE
BROADSHEET
BROADSWORD
BROCATELLE
BROIDERING
BROKEN-DOWN
BROKENNESS
BROME-GRASS
BRONCHITIC
BRONCHITIS
BRONZEWING
BROODINESS
BROODINGLY
BROODPOUCH
BROOMSTAFF
BROOMSTICK
BROTHER-MAN

BROW-ANTLER
BROWNSHIRT
BROWNSTONE
BRUSHWHEEL
BRUSQUERIE
BRUTIFYING
BRYOLOGIST
BUBBLY-JOCK
BUCCINATOR
BUCEPHALUS
BUCHMANISM
BUCHMANITE
BUCK-BASKET
BUCKETFULS
BUCK-JUMPER
BUCK-RABBIT
BUDDHISTIC
BUDGERIGAR
BUFFALO-NUT
BUFF-JERKIN
BUFFLEHEAD
BUFFOONERY
BULK-BUYING
BULL-BEEVES
BULL-BEGGAR
BULLET-HEAD
BULLET-TREE
BULL-HEADED
BULLIONIST
BULL-NECKED
BULL-ROARER
BUM-BAILIFF
BUMBLE-FOOT
BUMPKINISH
BUNCH-GRASS
BUNCHINESS
BUNGLINGLY
BURDENSOME
BUREAUCRAT
BURGLARISE
BURNET-MOTH
BURNETTISE
BURNISHING
BURRAMUNDI
BURROSTOWN
BURROW-DUCK
BURSARSHIP
BUR-THISTLE
BUSHELLING
BUSH-HARROW
BUSHMASTER
BUSHRANGER
BUSH-SHRIKE
BUTCHERING
BUTLERSHIP
BUTTER-BAKE
BUTTER-BEAN
BUTTER-BIRD
BUTTER-BOAT
BUTTER-BUMP
BUTTER-DISH
BUTTERDOCK
BUTTER-FISH
BUTTER-MILK
BUTTER-TREE
BUTTER-WIFE

BUTTERWORT
BUTTERY-BAR
BUTTON-BALL
BUTTON-BUSH
BUTTONED-UP
BUTTON-HOLD
BUTTON-HOLE
BUTTON-HOOK
BUTTON-WOOD
BY-DRINKING
BY-ELECTION
BYSSACEOUS
BYSSINOSIS

C

CABALISTIC
CABBAGE-FLY
CACHINNATE
CACK-HANDED
CACODAEMON
CACOGENICS
CACOGRAPHY
CACOMISTLE
CACOPHONIC
CACOTROPHY
CACTACEOUS
CACUMINOUS
CADAVEROUS
CADDIS-CASE
CAESARSHIP
CAESPITOSE
CAFFEINISM
CA'ING-WHALE
CAJOLEMENT
CALAMANDER
CALAMITOUS
CALCAREOUS
CALCEIFORM
CALCEOLATE
CALCIFEROL
CALCINABLE
CALC-SINTER
CALCULABLE
CALCULATED
CALCULATOR
CALCULUSES
CALEDONIAN
CALEFACTOR
CALENDARER
CALESCENCE
CALF-GROUND
CALICO-BUSH
CALICO-TREE
CALICO-WOOD
CALIGINOUS
CALLIATURE
CALORIFIER
CALOTYPIST
CALUMNIATE
CALUMNIOUS
CALVE'S-FOOT
CALYCIFORM
CALYPTRATE
CAMBERWELL
CAMEL-CORPS
CAMELOPARD

CAMEO-SHELL
CAMERATION
CAMERLENGO
CAMERLINGO
CAMERONIAN
CAMOUFLAGE
CAMPAIGNER
CAMPANULAR
CAMPESTRAL
CAMPHORATE
CAMPTONITE
CAMSTEERIE
CANALICULI
CANARY-BIRD
CANARY-SEED
CANARY-WOOD
CANCELLATE
CANCELLING
CANCELLOUS
CANCER-BOOT
CANCIONERO
CANCRIFORM
CANCRIZANS
CANDELABRA
CANDELILLA
CANDESCENT
CANDIDNESS
CANDLE-BOMB
CANDLE-COAL
CANDLE-DOUP
CANDLE-FISH
CANDLE-TREE
CANDLEWICK
CANDLE-WOOD
CANDY-FLOSS
CANEPHORUS
CANESCENCE
CANKEREDLY
CANKER-WORM
CANNEL-COAL
CANNELLONI
CANNIBALLY
CANNONBALL
CANNON-GAME
CANNON-SHOT
CANONICALS
CANONICITY
CANONISTIC
CANOROUSLY
CANTATRICE
CANTERBURY
CANTILEVER
CANTILLATE
CANTONMENT
CANTUARIAN
CANVAS-BACK
CANVASWORK
CANZONETTA
CANZONETTE
CAOUTCHOUC
CAPABILITY
CAPACITATE
CAPERNAITE
CAPERNOITY
CAPER-SAUCE
CAPILLAIRE

CAPITALISE
CAPITALISM
CAPITALIST
CAPITATION
CAPITELLUM
CAPITOLIAN
CAPITOLINE
CAPITULANT
CAPITULARY
CAPITULATE
CAPNOMANCY
CAPPUCCINO
CAPREOLATE
CAPRICIOUS
CAPSIZABLE
CAPTIOUSLY
CARABINEER
CARABINIER
CARAMELISE
CARAPACIAL
CARAVANEER
CARAVANING
CARAVANNED
CARBUNCLED
CARCINOGEN
CARCINOSIS
CARD-CASTLE
CARDIALGIA
CARDINALLY
CARDIOGRAM
CARDIOLOGY
CARE-CRAZED
CARELESSLY
CARICACEAE
CARICATURA
CARICATURE
CARMAGNOLE
CARNALLITE
CARNASSIAL
CAROTENOID
CAROTINOID
CARPELLARY
CARPET-MOTH
CARPHOLOGY
CARPOPHORE
CARRAGHEEN
CARRIER-BAG
CARRYING-ON
CARTHAMINE
CARTHUSIAN
CARTOMANCY
CARTONNAGE
CARTOONIST
CARTOPHILY
CARTWRIGHT
CARUNCULAR
CARYATIDAL
CARYATIDES
CARYATIDIC
CASCARILLA
CASE-BOTTLE
CASE-HARDEN
CASEMENTED
CASE-WORKER
CASH-CREDIT
CASHEW-NUTS

CASHIERING
CASH-KEEPER
CASSEGRAIN
CASSIA-BARK
CASSIOPEIA
CASSOLETTE
CASSUMUNAR
CASTIGATOR
CASTING-NET
CASTRATION
CASUALNESS
CATABOLISM
CATACUMBAL
CATAFALQUE
CATALECTIC
CATALEPTIC
CATALOGUER
CATAMENIAL
CATAPHONIC
CATAPHRACT
CATAPULTIC
CATARRHINE
CATARRHOUS
CATASTASIS
CAT-BURGLAR
CATCH-BASIN
CATCH-DRAIN
CATCHPENNY
CAT-CRACKER
CATECHESIS
CATECHETIC
CATECHISER
CATECHUMEN
CATEGORIAL
CATEGORIES
CATEGORISE
CATEGORIST
CATENARIAN
CATENATION
CATHODE-RAY
CATHOLICON
CATHOLICOS
CATOPTRICS
CAT'S-CRADLE
CATTLE-GRID
CAULESCENT
CAULICULUS
CAULIFLORY
CAUSEWAYED
CAUSTICITY
CAUTIONARY
CAUTIOUSLY
CAVALIERLY
CAVALRYMAN
CAVICORNIA
CAVITATION
CECIDOMYIA
CECUTIENCY
CELEBRATED
CELEBRATOR
CELLAR-BOOK
CELLAR-FLAP
CELLOPHANE
CELLULATED
CELLULITIS
CELLULOSIC

CELTOMANIA
CENSORIOUS
CENSORSHIP
CENSURABLE
CENSURABLY
CENTAURIAN
CENTENNIAL
CENTESIMAL
CENTIGRADE
CENTILITRE
CENTILLION
CENTIMETER
CENTIMETRE
CENTRALISE
CENTRALISM
CENTRALITY
CENTRE-BACK
CENTRE-HALF
CENTRE-RAIL
CENTRICITY
CENTRIFUGE
CENTROSOME
CENTUMVIRI
CEPHALAGRA
CEPHALITIS
CEPHALOPOD
CEREBELLAR
CEREBELLUM
CEREBRITIS
CEREMONIAL
CERINTHIAN
CEROGRAPHY
CERTIFYING
CERTIORARI
CERUMINOUS
CESSIONARY
CESTOIDEAN
CESTRACION
CHAFFINGLY
CHAIN-CABLE
CHAIN-DRIVE
CHAIN-STORE
CHAIR-ORGAN
CHAIRWOMAN
CHAISE-CART
CHAISELESS
CHALCEDONY
CHALCIDIAN
CHALKBOARD
CHALKINESS
CHALKSTONE
CHALLENGER
CHALUMEAUX
CHALYBEATE
CHAMAELEON
CHAMAEROPS
CHAMBERING
CHAMBER-LYE
CHAMBERPOT
CHAMBERTIN
CHAMPIGNON
CHANCELESS
CHANCELLOR
CHANDELIER
CHANDLERLY
CHANGEABLE

CHANGEABLY
CHANGELESS
CHANGELING
CHANGEOVER
CHANK-SHELL
CHANNELLED
CHAPARAJOS
CHAPAREJOS
CHAPFALLEN
CHAPLAINCY
CHAPLAINRY
CHARABANCS
CHARACTERY
CHARADRIUS
CHARGEABLE
CHARGEABLY
CHARGE-HAND
CHARGELESS
CHARIOTEER
CHARITABLE
CHARITABLY
CHARITY-BOY
CHARLESTON
CHARMINGLY
CHAROLLAIS
CHAROPHYTA
CHARTHOUSE
CHARTREUSE
CHARTULARY
CHASMOGAMY
CHASSE-CAFÉ
CHASTENESS
CHÂTELAINE
CHATOYANCE
CHATTERBOX
CHATTERING
CHAUCERIAN
CHAUCERISM
CHAUDFROID
CHAUD-MELLÉ
CHAUFFEUSE
CHAULMUGRA
CHAUNTRESS
CHAUTAUQUA
CHAUVINISM
CHAUVINIST
CHEAPSKATE
CHECK-CLERK
CHECKLATON
CHECK-TAKER
CHEECHALKO
CHEEK-POUCH
CHEEK-TOOTH
CHEERFULLY
CHEERINESS
CHEESECAKE
CHEESE-MITE
CHEESINESS
CHEIROLOGY
CHEIRONOMY
CHELICERAE
CHEMIATRIC
CHEMICALLY
CHEMICKING
CHEMISETTE
CHEMONASTY

CHEMOTAXIS
CHEQUE-BOOK
CHERIMOYER
CHERRY-BEAN
CHERRY-COAL
CHERRY-PLUM
CHERSONESE
CHERUBICAL
CHERUBIMIC
CHESSBOARD
CHESSYLITE
CHEST-VOICE
CHEVESAILE
CHEVISANCE
CHEVROTAIN
CHEWING-GUM
CHICKENPOX
CHICKEN-RUN
CHIEF-BARON
CHIFF-CHAFF
CHIFFONIER
CHILDBIRTH
CHILDERMAS
CHILDISHLY
CHILD-STUDY
CHILIARCHY
CHILLINESS
CHIMERICAL
CHIMNEY-CAN
CHIMNEY-POT
CHIMNEY-TOP
CHIMPANZEE
CHINACHINA
CHINCHILLA
CHINQUAPIN
CHIONODOXA
CHIP-BASKET
CHIROGNOMY
CHIROGRAPH
CHIROMANCY
CHIRONOMER
CHIRONOMIC
CHIRONOMID
CHIRONOMUS
CHIROPTERA
CHIRURGEON
CHIRURGERY
CHISELLING
CHITARRONE
CHITTAGONG
CHITTERING
CHIVALROUS
CHLAMYDATE
CHLORALISM
CHLORIDATE
CHLORIDISE
CHLORINATE
CHLORINISE
CHLORODYNE
CHLOROFORM
CHLOROPHYL
CHLOROQUIN
CHOCKSTONE
CHOCK-TIGHT
CHOICENESS
CHOIR-ORGAN

CHOKE-BERRY
CHOLAGOGIC
CHOLAGOGUE
CHOLIAMBIC
CHONDRITIC
CHOPFALLEN
CHOPSTICKS
CHOREOLOGY
CHORIAMBIC
CHORUS-GIRL
CHOTA-HAZRI
CHREMATIST
CHRISTHOOD
CHRISTIANA
CHRISTLESS
CHRISTLIKE
CHRISTMASY
CHROMATICS
CHROMATYPE
CHROME-ALUM
CHROMIDIUM
CHROMOGRAM
CHROMOSOME
CHROMOTYPE
CHRONICLER
CHRONOGRAM
CHRONOLOGY
CHRONOTRON
CHRYSALIDS
CHRYSOLITE
CHRYSOPHAN
CHRYSOTILE
CHUBBINESS
CHUCKER-OUT
CHUCK-WAGON
CHUFFINESS
CHURCH-GOER
CHURCHLESS
CHURCH-RATE
CHURCH-TEXT
CHURCHWARD
CHURCHYARD
CHURLISHLY
CHURN-DRILL
CHURN-STAFF
CICATRICES
CICATRIXES
CICERONIAN
CICISBEISM
CILIOPHORA
CINCHONINE
CINCHONISE
CINCHONISM
CINCINNATE
CINDER-CONE
CINDERELLA
CINDER-PATH
CINE-CAMERA
CINERATION
CINNABARIC
CINNAMONIC
CINQUE-FOIL
CINQUE-PACE
CIRCASSIAN
CIRCENSIAN
CIRCUITEER

CIRCUITOUS
CIRCULABLE
CIRCULARLY
CIRCULATOR
CIRCUMCISE
CIRCUMDUCE
CIRCUMDUCT
CIRCUMFLEX
CIRCUMFUSE
CIRCUMMURE
CIRCUMPOSE
CIRCUMVENT
CIRRHIPEDE
CIRRHOPODA
CIRRIGRADE
CIRRIPEDIA
CISLEITHAN
CISMONTANE
CISPONTINE
CISTERCIAN
CITIZENESS
CITIZENISE
CITRONELLA
CLACK-VALVE
CLAIRCOLLE
CLAMMINESS
CLANGOROUS
CLANNISHLY
CLANSWOMAN
CLAPPERBOY
CLAPPERING
CLARABELLA
CLARENCEUX
CLARICHORD
CLARIFYING
CLASP-KNIFE
CLASSICISM
CLASSICIST
CLASSIFIED
CLASSIFIER
CLAVICHORD
CLAVICULAR
CLAW-HAMMER
CLAY-GROUND
CLAY-PIGEON
CLEANSABLE
CLEAR-STORY
CLEMENTINE
CLERESTORY
CLERGIABLE
CLERGYABLE
CLEROMANCY
CLEVERNESS
CLEW-GARNET
CLICK-CLACK
CLIENTSHIP
CLIMATICAL
CLINGSTONE
CLINICALLY
CLINKSTONE
CLINOMETER
CLINOMETRY
CLISH-CLASH
CLISTOGAMY
CLOACALINE
CLOCKMAKER

CLODHOPPER
CLOGGINESS
CLOISTERED
CLOISTERER
CLOISTRESS
CLOSE-STOOL
CLOSET-PLAY
CLOSTRIDIA
CLOTHES-PEG
CLOTHES-PIN
CLOTTINESS
CLOUDBERRY
CLOUD-BUILT
CLOUDBURST
CLOUDINESS
CLOVE-HITCH
CLOVERLEAF
CLOWNISHLY
CLUB-FOOTED
CLUB-HEADED
CLUBMASTER
CLUMSINESS
CLUSIACEAE
CLUSTER-CUP
CLUSTERING
CLYDESDALE
CLYPEIFORM
CNIDOBLAST
COACERVATE
COACH-HORSE
COACH-HOUSE
COACH-STAND
COACH-WHEEL
COACTIVITY
COADJACENT
COADJUTANT
COADJUTRIX
COAGULABLE
COAL-BUNKER
COAL-CELLAR
COAL-CUTTER
COALESCENT
COAL-HEAVER
COALMASTER
COAL-PORTER
COAPTATION
COARSENESS
COASTGUARD
COASTWARDS
COAT-ARMOUR
COAT-HANGER
COATI-MONDI
COATI-MUNDI
COAT-OF-ARMS
COBALT-BLUE
COBWEBBERY
COCCINEOUS
COCHLEARIA
COCHLEATED
COCK-A-BONDY
COCKALORUM
COCKATRICE
COCKCHAFER
COCKERNONY
COCKNEYDOM
COCKNEYISH

COCKNEYISM
COCK-PADDLE
COCK-PAIDLE
COCKSINESS
COCKTAILED
COCKYLEEKY
COCOA-BEANS
COCONUT-OIL
COCONUT-SHY
CODFISHERY
CODFISHING
CODLIN-MOTH
CODSWALLOP
COELACANTH
COELOMATIC
COENOBITIC
COEQUALITY
COERCIVELY
COETANEOUS
COETERNITY
COEXISTENT
COFFEE-BEAN
COFFEE-MILL
COFFEE-ROOM
COFFEE-TREE
COFFER-FISH
COFFIN-BONE
COFFIN-SHIP
COGITATION
COGITATIVE
COGNISABLE
COGNISABLY
COGNISANCE
COGNOMINAL
COHABITANT
COHERENTLY
COHESIVELY
COHIBITION
COHIBITIVE
COINCIDENT
COLATITUDE
COLBERTINE
COLCHICINE
COLD-CHISEL
COLEOPTERA
COLEORHIZA
COLLAR-BEAM
COLLAR-BONE
COLLARETTE
COLLAR-STUD
COLLAR-WORK
COLLATABLE
COLLATERAL
COLLEAGUED
COLLECTING
COLLECTION
COLLECTIVE
COLLEGIATE
COLLEMBOLA
COLLIMATOR
COLLIQUANT
COLLIQUATE
COLLOCUTOR
COLLOQUIAL
COLLOQUISE
COLLOQUIST

COLLOQUIUM
COLONNADED
COLORATION
COLORATURA
COLOSTROUS
COLOURABLE
COLOURABLY
COLOURLESS
COLPORTAGE
COLPORTEUR
COLTRALTOS
COLUBRIDAE
COLUMNATED
COMANCHERO
COMBATABLE
COMBURGESS
COMBUSTION
COMBUSTIVE
COME-AT-ABLE
COMÉDIENNE
COMEDIETTA
COME-HITHER
COMELINESS
COMESTIBLE
COMETOLOGY
COMEUPANCE
COMICALITY
COMITATIVE
COMMANDANT
COMMANDEER
COMMANDERY
COMMANDING
COMMEASURE
COMMENTARY
COMMERCIAL
COMMINGLED
COMMIPHORA
COMMISSARY
COMMISSION
COMMISSURE
COMMITMENT
COMMiTTING
COMMIXTION
COMMIXTURE
COMMODIOUS
COMMONABLE
COMMONALTY
COMMONNESS
COMMONWEAL
COMMUNALLY
COMMUNIQUE
COMMUTABLE
COMMUTATOR
COMPACTION
COMPACTURE
COMPANYING
COMPARABLE
COMPARABLY
COMPARATOR
COMPARISON
COMPASSING
COMPASSION
COMPASS-SAW
COMPATIBLE
COMPATIBLY
COMPATRIOT

COMPEARANT
COMPELLING
COMPENDIUM
COMPENSATE
COMPETENCE
COMPETENCY
COMPETITOR
COMPILATOR
COMPLACENT
COMPLAINER
COMPLANATE
COMPLECTED
COMPLEMENT
COMPLETELY
COMPLETION
COMPLETIVE
COMPLETORY
COMPLEXION
COMPLEXITY
COMPLIABLE
COMPLIANCE
COMPLIANCY
COMPLICACY
COMPLICANT
COMPLICATE
COMPLICITY
COMPLIMENT
COMPLOTTED
COMPLUVIUM
COMPONENCY
COMPOSEDLY
COMPOSITAE
COMPOSITOR
COMPOTATOR
COMPOUNDER
COMPRADORE
COMPREHEND
COMPRESSED
COMPRESSOR
COMPROMISE
COMPULSION
COMPULSIVE
COMPULSORY
COMPUTABLE
COMPUTATOR
COMSTOCKER
CONACREISM
CONCEITFUL
CONCENTRED
CONCENTRIC
CONCEPTION
CONCEPTIVE
CONCEPTUAL
CONCERNING
CONCERTINA
CONCERTINO
CONCESSION
CONCESSIVE
CONCETTISM
CONCETTIST
CONCHIFORM
CONCHOIDAL
CONCHOLOGY
CONCILIARY
CONCILIATE
CONCINNITY

CONCINNOUS
CONCIPIENT
CONCLAVIST
CONCLUDING
CONCLUSION
CONCLUSIVE
CONCLUSORY
CONCOCTION
CONCOCTIVE
CONCORDANT
CONCORDIAL
CONCRETELY
CONCRETION
CONCRETISM
CONCRETIST
CONCRETIVE
CONCURRENT
CONCURRING
CONCUSSION
CONCUSSIVE
CONDENSATE
CONDENSERY
CONDESCEND
CONDOLENCE
CONDUCIBLE
CONDUCTION
CONDUCTIVE
CONE-IN-CONE
CONFABULAR
CONFECTION
CONFERENCE
CONFERMENT
CONFERRING
CONFERVOID
CONFESSION
CONFIDANTE
CONFIDENCE
CONFIDENCY
CONFINABLE
CONFIRMING
CONFISCATE
CONFLATION
CONFLUENCE
CONFORMIST
CONFORMITY
CONFOUNDED
CONFUSEDLY
CONFUTABLE
CONGENERIC
CONGENETIC
CONGENITAL
CONGESTION
CONGESTIVE
CONGLOBATE
CONGREGATE
CONGRUENCE
CONGRUENCY
CONIFEROUS
CONJECTURE
CONJOINTLY
CONJUGALLY
CONJUGATAE
CONJUGATED
CONJUNCTLY
CONJURATOR
CONNASCENT

CONNATURAL
CONNECTION
CONNECTIVE
CONNIPTION
CONNIVANCE
CONNIVANCY
CONNIVENCE
CONNIVENCY
CONOIDICAL
CONQUERESS
CONQUERING
CONSCIENCE
CONSECRATE
CONSECTARY
CONSENSION
CONSENSUAL
CONSEQUENT
CONSERVANT
CONSIGNIFY
CONSILIENT
CONSIMILAR
CONSISTENT
CONSISTORY
CONSOCIATE
CONSOLABLE
CONSONANCE
CONSONANCY
CONSORTISM
CONSORTIUM
CONSPECTUS
CONSPIRACY
CONSPIRANT
CONSTANTAN
CONSTANTIA
CONSTANTLY
CONSTIPATE
CONSTITUTE
CONSTRAINT
CONSTRINGE
CONSUBSIST
CONSUETUDE
CONSULSHIP
CONSULTANT
CONSULTING
CONSULTIVE
CONSULTORY
CONSUMABLE
CONSUMEDLY
CONSUMMATE
CONTACTUAL
CONTADINAS
CONTAGIOUS
CONTEMNING
CONTENDENT
CONTENDING
CONTENTION
CONTESTANT
CONTESTING
CONTEXTUAL
CONTEXTURE
CONTIGUITY
CONTIGUOUS
CONTINENCE
CONTINENCY
CONTINGENT
CONTINUANT

CONTINUATE
CONTINUITY
CONTINUOUS
CONTORTION
CONTORTIVE
CONTRABAND
CONTRABASS
CONTRACTED
CONTRACTOR
CONTRADICT
CONTRAHENT
CONTRAPLEX
CONTRAPROP
CONTRARILY
CONTRAVENE
CONTRECOUP
CONTRIBUTE
CONTRIFIED
CONTRITELY
CONTRITION
CONTROLLED
CONTROLLER
CONTROVERT
CONVALESCE
CONVECTION
CONVECTIVE
CONVENABLE
CONVENANCE
CONVENIENT
CONVENTION
CONVENTUAL
CONVERGENT
CONVERGING
CONVERSANT
CONVERSELY
CONVERSION
CONVERTEND
CONVERTITE
CONVEXEDLY
CONVEXNESS
CONVEYABLE
CONVEYANCE
CONVICTION
CONVICTISM
CONVICTIVE
CONVINCING
CONVOLUTED
CONVULSANT
CONVULSION
CONVULSIVE
CONY-BURROW
COOL-HEADED
COOM-CEILED
CO-OPERATOR
CO-OPTATION
CO-OPTATIVE
CO-ORDINATE
COPARCENER
COPARTNERY
COPERNICAN
COPESETTIC
COPPERHEAD
COPPER-NOSE
COPPERSKIN
COPPERWORK
COPPER-WORM

CO-PRESENCE
COPROLALIA
COPROLITIC
COPULATION
COPULATIVE
COPULATORY
COPYHOLDER
COPYING-INK
COPYWRITER
COQUELICOT
COQUETTING
COQUETTISH
COQUIMBITE
CO-RADICATE
CORAL-BERRY
CORAL-SNAKE
CORBELLING
CORBICULAE
CORDIALISE
CORDIALITY
CORDIERITE
CORDILLERA
CORDWAINER
COREGONINE
CO-RELATION
CO-RELATIVE
CORIACEOUS
CORINTHIAN
CORK-CARPET
CORK-CUTTER
CORK-HEELED
CORKING-PIN
CORK-JACKET
CORMOPHYTE
CORN-BRANDY
CORNCOCKLE
CORN-CUTTER
CORN-DEALER
CORN-DODGER
CORNEL-TREE
CORNERWISE
CORN-FACTOR
CORNFLOWER
CORNHUSKER
CORNICULUM
CORN-KISTER
CORN-MAIDEN
CORNMILLER
CORN-POPPER
CORN-SPIRIT
CORNSTARCH
CORN-THRIPS
CORNUCOPIA
CORN-WEEVIL
CORN-WHISKY
COROMANDEL
CORONATION
CORPORALLY
CORPORATOR
CORPOREITY
CORPSE-GATE
CORPULENCE
CORPULENCY
CORPUSCULE
CORRECTION
CORRECTIVE

CORRECTORY
CORREGIDOR
CORREPTION
CORRESPOND
CORRIGENDA
CORRIGIBLE
CORROBOREE
CORRODIBLE
CORROSIBLE
CORRUGATED
CORRUGATOR
CORRUPTION
CORRUPTIVE
CORSETIÈRE
CORTICATED
CORYBANTES
CORYBANTIC
CORYDALINE
CORYPHAEUS
CO-SENTIENT
COSMETICAL
COSMICALLY
COSMOGONIC
COSMOLATRY
COSMOPOLIS
COSMORAMIC
COSTEANING
COSTEAN-PIT
COSTLINESS
COSTUS-ROOT
COTE-HARDIE
COTINGIDAE
COTTIERISM
COTTON-BOLL
COTTON-MILL
COTTON-SEED
COTTONTAIL
COTTON-TREE
COTTON-WEED
COTTON-WOOD
COTTON-WOOL
COTTON-WORM
COTYLIFORM
COUCH-GRASS
COUMARILIC
COUNCILLOR
COUNCILMAN
COUNSELLED
COUNSELLOR
COUNTERACT
COUNTRY-BOX
COUNTRYMAN
COUNT-WHEEL
COUPLEMENT
COURAGEFUL
COURAGEOUS
COURT-BARON
COURTCRAFT
COURT-DRESS
COURTESIED
COURT-GUIDE
COURT-HOUSE
COURTIERLY
COURT-SWORD
COUSCOUSOU
COUSINHOOD

COUSINSHIP
COUTURIÈRE
COVENANTED
COVENANTEE
COVENANTER
COVENANTOR
COVETINGLY
COVETOUSLY
COWARDSHIP
COWCATCHER
COW-CHERVIL
COWDIE-PINE
COWERINGLY
COW-PARSLEY
COW-PARSNIP
COWPUNCHER
COWRIE-PINE
COXCOMICAL
COYISHNESS
CRAB-STONES
CRACKAJACK
CRACKBRAIN
CRACK-TRYST
CRADLEWALK
CRAFT-GUILD
CRAFTINESS
CRAGGINESS
CRAIGFLUKE
CRAKE-BERRY
CRANESBILL
CRANIOLOGY
CRANIOTOMY
CRANKINESS
CRANKSHAFT
CRANK-SIDED
CRAPULENCE
CRASHPROOF
CRASSITUDE
CRAVENNESS
CREAM-FACED
CREAMINESS
CREAM-SLICE
CREATININE
CREATIONAL
CREATIVELY
CREATIVITY
CREATURELY
CREDENTIAL
CREDITABLE
CREDITABLY
CREEPINGLY
CREEPMOUSE
CRENELLATE
CRENULATED
CRÊPE-PAPER
CRÊPE-SOLED
CREPUSCULE
CRESCENTED
CRESCENTIC
CRETACEOUS
CRETINISED
CREWELLERY
CREWELWORK
CRIB-BITING
CRIBRATION
CRIBRIFORM

CRICKETING
CRIMINALLY
CRINGELING
CRINGINGLY
CRINOIDEAN
CRINOLETTE
CRINOLINED
CRIO-SPHINX
CRIPPLEDOM
CRISPATION
CRISPATURE
CRISS-CROSS
CRISTIFORM
CRITICALLY
CROCHETING
CROCODILIA
CROCODILUS
CROCOISITE
CROOK-KNEED
CROP-DUSTER
CROSS-ARMED
CROSSBENCH
CROSS-BIRTH
CROSSBONES
CROSSBOWER
CROSSBREED
CROSS-CHECK
CROSSLIGHT
CROSSPATCH
CROSSPIECE
CROSS-RATIO
CROSSROADS
CROSS-STAFF
CROSS-STONE
CROTALARIA
CROTALIDAE
CROTCHETED
CROUCH-WARE
CROUPINESS
CROW-FLOWER
CROWKEEPER
CROWN-AGENT
CROWN-GLASS
CROWN-GRAFT
CROWN-GREEN
CROWN-JEWEL
CROWN-PIECE
CROWN-WHEEL
CROWSHRIKE
CRUCIFERAE
CRUCIFYING
CRUET-STAND
CRUMB-BRUSH
CRUMB-CLOTH
CRUSHINGLY
CRUSTACEAN
CRUSTATION
CRUSTINESS
CRYOCONITE
CRYOGENICS
CRYOMETRIC
CRYOPHORUS
CRYOSCOPIC
CRYPTOGAMY
CRYPTOGRAM
CRYPTOLOGY

CTENOPHORA
CTENOPHORE
CUB-HUNTING
CUCKOLDISE
CUCKOO-PINT
CUCKOO-SPIT
CUCULLATED
CUCUMIFORM
CUCURBITAL
CUDGELLING
CUDGEL-PLAY
CUIRASSIER
CUL-DE-LAMPE
CULICIFORM
CULTIVABLE
CULTIVATOR
CULTRIFORM
CULTURABLE
CULVERTAGE
CUMBERLESS
CUMBERMENT
CUMBERSOME
CUMBROUSLY
CUMMERBUND
CUMULATION
CUMULATIVE
CUMULIFORM
CUNCTATION
CUNCTATIVE
CUNCTATORY
CUP-AND-BALL
CUP-AND-RING
CUPIDINOUS
CURABILITY
CURATESHIP
CURB-MARKET
CURB-TRADER
CURB-VENDOR
CURFEW-BELL
CURLED-PATE
CURMUDGEON
CURMURRING
CURRANT-BUN
CURRICULAR
CURRICULUM
CURSEDNESS
CURVACEOUS
CURVACIOUS
CURVETTING
CUSPIDATED
CUSSEDNESS
CUSTARD-PIE
CUSTOMABLE
CUSTOM-MADE
CUTTLE-BONE
CUTTLEFISH
CUTTY-STOOL
CYANOMETER
CYATHIFORM
CYBERNETIC
CYCLO-CROSS
CYCLOGRAPH
CYCLOIDIAN
CYCLOMETER
CYCLOPEDIA
CYCLOPEDIC

CYCLOSTOME
CYCLOSTYLE
CYLINDRITE
CYLINDROID
CYMOTRICHY
CYPERACEAE
CYPRINIDAE
CYSTOSCOPE
CYSTOSCOPY
CYTOCHROME
CYTOLOGIST
CZAREVITCH

D

DABBLINGLY
DAFFODILLY
DAGGLETAIL
DAGUERREAN
DAINTINESS
DAISY-CHAIN
DAMAGEABLE
DAMASCEENE
DAME-SCHOOL
DAMP-COURSE
DAMPING-OFF
DANCE-MUSIC
DANDY-BRUSH
DANDY-FEVER
DANDY-HORSE
DAPPERLING
DAPPLE-GREY
DASYURIDAE
DATAMATION
DATE-CODING
DAUGHTERLY
DAUPHINESS
DAY-BOARDER
DAY-RELEASE
DAY-SCHOLAR
DAY-WEARIED
DAZZLEMENT
DAZZLINGLY
DEACONHOOD
DEACONSHIP
DEACTIVATE
DEAD-FINISH
DEAD-GROUND
DEAD-LETTER
DEAD-LIGHTS
DEADLINESS
DEAD-NETTLE
DEAD-STROKE
DEAD-WEIGHT
DEAF-MUTISM
DEALBATION
DEARBOUGHT
DEASPIRATE
DEATH-ADDER
DEATH-AGONY
DEATH'S-HEAD
DEATH-THROE
DEATH-TOKEN
DEATH-WATCH
DEATH-WOUND
DEBASEMENT
DEBASINGLY

DEBATEABLE
DEBATINGLY
DEBAUCHERY
DEBENTURED
DEBILITATE
DEBONAIRLY
DEBONNAIRE
DEBOUCHURE
DECAGRAMME
DECAGYNIAN
DECAGYNOUS
DECAHEDRAL
DECAHEDRON
DECALOGIST
DECAMEROUS
DECAMPMENT
DECANDRIAN
DECANDROUS
DECAPITATE
DECAPODOUS
DECEIVABLE
DECEIVABLY
DECELERATE
DECEMBERLY
DECEMBRIST
DECEMVIRAL
DECENNOVAL
DECEPTIBLE
DECEPTIOUS
DECIGRAMME
DECIMALISE
DECIMALISM
DECIMALIST
DECIMATION
DECINORMAL
DECISIVELY
DECIVILISE
DECK-BRIDGE
DECKLE-EDGE
DECK-QUOITS
DECK-TENNIS
DECLAIMANT
DECLAIMING
DECLARABLE
DECLARATOR
DECLAREDLY
DECLENSION
DECLINABLE
DECLINATOR
DECOCTIBLE
DECOLLATED
DECOLORANT
DECOLORATE
DECOLORISE
DECOMPOUND
DECOMPRESS
DECORATION
DECORATIVE
DECOROUSLY
DECRASSIFY
DECREEABLE
DECRESCENT
DECUMBENCE
DECUMBENCY
DECURRENCY
DECUSSATED

DEDICATION
DEDICATORY
DEDUCEMENT
DEDUCTIBLE
DEEP-BROWED
DEEP-FREEZE
DEEP-SEATED
DEEP-SINKER
DEER-FOREST
DEFACEMENT
DEFACINGLY
DEFALCATOR
DEFAMATION
DEFAMATORY
DEFEASANCE
DEFEASIBLE
DEFECATION
DEFECTIBLE
DEFENDABLE
DEFENSIBLE
DEFENSIBLY
DEFICIENCE
DEFICIENCY
DEFILEMENT
DEFINEMENT
DEFINITELY
DEFINITION
DEFINITIVE
DEFINITUDE
DEFLAGRATE
DEFLECTION
DEFLECTIVE
DEFLOWERER
DEFOLIATED
DEFOLIATOR
DEFORCIANT
DEFORMEDLY
DEFRAYMENT
DEFUNCTION
DEFUNCTIVE
DEGENERACY
DEGENERATE
DEHISCENCE
DEHUMANISE
DEHUMIDIFY
DEINOCERAS
DEJECTEDLY
DELAMINATE
DELAYINGLY
DELECTABLE
DELECTABLY
DELEGATION
DELIBATION
DELIBERATE
DELICATELY
DELIGATION
DELIGHTFUL
DELINEABLE
DELINEATOR
DELINQUENT
DELIQUESCE
DELIRATION
DELPHINIUM
DELPHINOID
DELTIOLOGY
DELUSIONAL

DELUSIVELY
DEMAGOGISM
DEMANDABLE
DEMI-CANNON
DEMI-DITONE
DEMIREPDOM
DEMOBILISE
DEMOCRATIC
DEMOGORGON
DEMOGRAPHY
DEMOISELLE
DEMOLITION
DEMONETISE
DEMONIACAL
DEMONOLOGY
DEMORALISE
DEMOTICIST
DEMURENESS
DEMURRABLE
DENATURANT
DENDRIFORM
DENDROBIUM
DENDROLOGY
DENDROPHIS
DENEGATION
DENIGRATOR
DENIZATION
DENOMINATE
DENOTATION
DENOTATIVE
DENOTEMENT
DÉNOUEMENT
DENSIMETER
DENTIFRICE
DENUDATION
DENUNCIATE
DEODORISER
DEONTOLOGY
DEOPPILATE
DEOXIDISER
DEPARTMENT
DEPENDABLE
DEPENDENCE
DEPENDENCY
DEPILATION
DEPILATORY
DEPLORABLE
DEPLORABLY
DEPLOYMENT
DEPOLARISE
DEPOPULATE
DEPORTMENT
DEPOSITARY
DEPOSITION
DEPOSITIVE
DEPOSITORY
DEPRAVEDLY
DEPRECABLE
DEPRECATOR
DEPRECIATE
DEPREDATOR
DEPRESSANT
DEPRESSING
DEPRESSION
DEPRESSIVE
DEPRIVABLE

DEPURATION
DEPURATIVE
DEPURATORY
DEPUTATION
DERACINATE
DERAILLEUR
DERAILMENT
DERIDINGLY
DERISIVELY
DERIVATION
DERIVATIVE
DERMAPTERA
DERMATITIS
DERMATOGEN
DERMOPTERA
DEROGATELY
DEROGATION
DEROGATORY
DESALINATE
DESCENDANT
DESCENDENT
DESCENDING
DESCENSION
DESECRATER
DESECRATOR
DESERTLESS
DESERVEDLY
DÉSHABILLÉ
DESICCATOR
DESIDERATA
DESIDERATE
DESIDERIUM
DESIGNABLE
DESIGNATOR
DESIGNEDLY
DESIGNLESS
DESIGNMENT
DESIPIENCE
DESIRELESS
DESIROUSLY
DESISTANCE
DESISTENCE
DESOLATELY
DESOLATION
DESOLATORY
DESORPTION
DESPAIRFUL
DESPAIRING
DESPERADOS
DESPICABLE
DESPICABLY
DESPISABLE
DESPITEFUL
DESPITEOUS
DESPONDENT
DESPONDING
DESPOTICAL
DESQUAMATE
DESSIATINE
DESSYATINE
DESTROYING
DESTRUCTOR
DETACHABLE
DETACHEDLY
DETACHMENT
DETAINMENT

DETECTABLE
DETECTIBLE
DETERGENCE
DETERGENCY
DETESTABLE
DETESTABLY
DETHRONING
DETONATION
DETOXICANT
DETOXICATE
DETRACTING
DETRACTION
DETRACTIVE
DETRACTORY
DETRUNCATE
DEVALORISE
DEVANAGARI
DEVASTAVIT
DEVELOPING
DEVILISHLY
DEVITALISE
DEVOCALISE
DEVOLUTION
DEVOTIONAL
DEVOURMENT
DEVOUTNESS
DEWAR-FLASK
DEW-RETTING
DEXTERWISE
DEXTRALITY
DEXTROUSLY
DHARMSHALA
DIABETICAL
DIABOLICAL
DIACAUSTIC
DIACONICON
DIACOUSTIC
DIADELPHIA
DIAGNOSTIC
DIAGOMETER
DIAGONALLY
DIAGRAPHIC
DIALECTICS
DIALECTRIC
DIALLAGOID
DIALYSABLE
DIAPEDESIS
DIAPEDETIC
DIAPHANOUS
DIARRHOEAL
DIARRHOEIC
DIASKEUAST
DIASTALTIC
DIASTEMATA
DIATHERMAL
DIATHERMIC
DIATRIBIST
DIATROPISM
DIAZEUCTIC
DIBRANCHIA
DICE-PLAYER
DICHROITIC
DICHROMATE
DICHROMISM
DICKCISSEL
DICKENSIAN

DICTAPHONE
DICTATRESS
DICTIONARY
DICTOGRAPH
DICYNODONT
DIDACTICAL
DIDASCALIC
DIDELPHIAN
DIDELPHINE
DIDELPHOUS
DIDGERIDOO
DIDUNCULUS
DIDYNAMIAN
DIDYNAMOUS
DIE-SINKING
DIETETICAL
DIFFERENCE
DIFFERENCY
DIFFICULTY
DIFFIDENCE
DIFFORMITY
DIFFUSEDLY
DIFFUSIBLE
DIGESTEDLY
DIGESTIBLE
DIGGER-WASP
DIGITATELY
DIGITATION
DIGITIFORM
DIGITORIUM
DIGLADIATE
DIGNIFYING
DIGONEUTIC
DIGRESSION
DIGRESSIVE
DIJUDICATE
DIKA-BUTTER
DILACERATE
DILAPIDATE
DILATATION
DILATORILY
DILDO-GLASS
DILEMMATIC
DILETTANTE
DILETTANTI
DILIGENTLY
DILLY-DALLY
DILUCIDATE
DILUTENESS
DIMINISHED
DIMINUENDO
DIMINUTION
DIMINUTIVE
DIMORPHISM
DIMORPHOUS
DIMPLEMENT
DINANDERIE
DINING-HALL
DINING-ROOM
DINNER-GOWN
DINNER-HOUR
DINNERLESS
DINNER-PAIL
DINNER-TIME
DINOSAURIA
DIOPHYSITE

DIOPTRICAL
DIORTHOSIS
DIORTHOTIC
DIOTHELETE
DIOTHELISM
DIPETALOUS
DIPHTHERIA
DIPHTHERIC
DIPHYLETIC
DIPHYODONT
DIPLODOCUS
DIPLOMATIC
DIPSOMANIA
DIRECTNESS
DIRECTOIRE
DIRECTRESS
DIRT-EATING
DIRT-ROTTEN
DISABILITY
DISADVANCE
DISANIMATE
DISAPPAREL
DISAPPOINT
DISAPPROVE
DISARRANGE
DISASTROUS
DISAVAUNCE
DISBELIEVE
DISBURTHEN
DISCERNING
DISCHARGER
DISCIPLINE
DISCISSION
DISCLAIMER
DISCLOSURE
DISCOBOLUS
DISCOMFORT
DISCOMMEND
DISCOMMODE
DISCOMPOSE
DISCONCERT
DISCONNECT
DISCONSENT
DISCONTENT
DISCOPHILE
DISCOPHORA
DISCORDANT
DISCORDFUL
DISCOUNSEL
DISCOUNTER
DISCOURAGE
DISCOURSER
DISCOVERER
DISCREETLY
DISCREPANT
DISCRETELY
DISCRETION
DISCRETIVE
DISCULPATE
DISCURSION
DISCURSIST
DISCURSIVE
DISCURSORY
DISCUSSION
DISCUSSIVE
DISCUTIENT

DISDAINFUL
DISEASEFUL
DISEMBOGUE
DISEMBOSOM
DISEMBOWEL
DISEMBROIL
DISENCHAIN
DISENCHANT
DISENCLOSE
DISENDOWED
DISENGAGED
DISENNOBLE
DISENSLAVE
DISENTHRAL
DISENTITLE
DISENTRAIN
DISENTWINE
DISENVELOP
DISENVIRON
DISESPOUSE
DISFEATURE
DISFURNISH
DISGARNISH
DISGLORIFY
DISGRUNTLE
DISGUISING
DISGUSTFUL
DISGUSTING
DISHABILLE
DISHARMONY
DISHEARTEN
DISHERISON
DISHERITOR
DISHONESTY
DISIMAGINE
DISIMPROVE
DISINCLINE
DISINCLOSE
DISINHERIT
DISINTHRAL
DISINVOLVE
DISISTENCE
DISJECTION
DISJOINTED
DISJUNCTOR
DISK-FLORET
DISK-FLOWER
DISK-HARROW
DISK-JOCKEY
DISK-PLOUGH
DISLIKABLE
DISLIKEFUL
DISLOYALLY
DISLOYALTY
DISMALNESS
DISMISSION
DISMISSIVE
DISMISSORY
DISNATURED
DISORDERED
DISORDERLY
DISORGANIC
DISOWNMENT
DISPARAGER
DISPARATES
DISPASSION

DISPATCHER	DISTRACTED	DOMESTICAL	DREADFULLY
DISPELLING	DISTRAINER	DOMINANTLY	DREAMINESS
DISPENSARY	DISTRAINOR	DOMINATION	DREAMINGLY
DISPERSANT	DISTRAUGHT	DOMINATIVE	DREAMWHILE
DISPERSION	DISTRESSED	DONATISTIC	DREAM-WORLD
DISPERSIVE	DISTRIBUTE	DONKEY-PUMP	DREARIHEAD
DISPERSOID	DISTRINGAS	DONKEY-WORK	DREARIHOOD
DISPIRITED	DISTROPHIA	DONNYBROOK	DREARIMENT
DISPITEOUS	DISTROPHIC	DOOR-KEEPER	DREARINESS
DISPLEASED	DISTROUBLE	DOOR-TO-DOOR	DREARISOME
DISPLENISH	DISTURBANT	DOPPLERITE	DREGGINESS
DISPLOSION	DISULPHATE	DORSIFIXED	DREIKANTER
DISPONDAIC	DISULPHIDE	DORSIGRADE	DRESS-GOODS
DISPOSABLE	DISUTILITY	DOUBLE-BASS	DRESS-GUARD
DISPOSEDLY	DISWORSHIP	DOUBLE-CHIN	DRESSMAKER
DISPOSITOR	DISYLLABIC	DOUBLE-DYED	DRESS-SHIRT
DISPOSSESS	DISYLLABLE	DOUBLE-EYED	DRILL-PRESS
DISPRAISER	DITCH-WATER	DOUBLE-FLAT	DRINK-MONEY
DISPROFESS	DITHEISTIC	DOUBLE-GILD	DRIVELLING
DISPROVIDE	DITHELETIC	DOUBLE-HUNG	DRIVING-BOX
DISPUTABLE	DITHIONATE	DOUBLENESS	DROOPINGLY
DISPUTABLY	DITRIGLYPH	DOUBLE-TAKE	DROP-HAMMER
DISQUALIFY	DITROCHEAN	DOUBLE-TALK	DROP-LETTER
DISQUIETEN	DIURNALIST	DOUBTFULLY	DROSOMETER
DISQUIETLY	DIUTURNITY	DOUBTINGLY	DROSOPHILA
DISRESPECT	DIVAGATION	DOUGH-BAKED	DROSSINESS
DISRUPTION	DIVARICATE	DOUGH-FACED	DROWSINESS
DISRUPTIVE	DIVE-BOMBER	DOUGHINESS	DRUDGINGLY
DISSATISFY	DIVE-DAPPER	DOULOCRACY	DRUG-ADDICT
DISSECTING	DIVERGENCE	DOVE-COLOUR	DRUMBLEDOR
DISSECTION	DIVERGENCY	DOWEL-JOINT	DRUPACEOUS
DISSECTIVE	DIVERTIBLE	DOWER-HOUSE	DRY-CUPPING
DISSEMBLER	DIVESTIBLE	DOWN-AND-OUT	DRYSALTERY
DISSENSION	DIVESTMENT	DOWN-AT-HEEL	DUBITATION
DISSENTING	DIVINATION	DOWN-EASTER	DUBITATIVE
DISSERTATE	DIVINATORY	DOWNFALLEN	DUCK-BILLED
DISSERVICE	DIVINENESS	DOWNSTAIRS	DUCK-LEGGED
DISSEVERED	DIVINERESS	DOWNSTREAM	DUKKERIPEN
DISSHEATHE	DIVING-BELL	DOWNSTROKE	DULCILOQUY
DISSIDENCE	DIVISIONAL	DOWNWARDLY	DULL-BROWED
DISSILIENT	DOCETISTIC	DOXOGRAPHY	DULL-WITTED
DISSIMILAR	DOCHMIACAL	DRABBINESS	DUMBLEDORE
DISSIPABLE	DOCIBILITY	DRACONITES	DUMB-WAITER
DISSIPATED	DOCIMASTIC	DRACONTIUM	DUMFOUNDER
DISSOCIATE	DOCIMOLOGY	DRAFT-HORSE	DUMPY-LEVEL
DISSOLUBLE	DOCK-MASTER	DRAGON-FISH	DUNDERFUNK
DISSOLVENT	DOCTOR-FISH	DRAGONHEAD	DUNDERHEAD
DISSOLVING	DOCTORSHIP	DRAGONLIKE	DUNDERPATE
DISSONANCE	DOCUMENTAL	DRAGONNADE	DUNG-BEETLE
DISSONANCY	DOG-BISCUIT	DRAGON-ROOT	DUNG-HUNTER
DISSUASION	DOG-FANCIER	DRAGON-TREE	DUNIWASSAL
DISSUASIVE	DOGGEDNESS	DRAG-RACING	DUODECIMAL
DISSUASORY	DOGMATISER	DRAKESTONE	DUODENITIS
DISTENSILE	DOG-PARSLEY	DRAMATICAL	DUPABILITY
DISTENSION	DOG'S-FENNEL	DRAMATURGE	DUPLICATOR
DISTENSIVE	DOG'S-TONGUE	DRAMATURGY	DURABILITY
DISTENTION	DOLCEMENTE	DRAUGHT-BAR	DUST-JACKET
DISTICHOUS	DOLESOMELY	DRAUGHTMAN	DUTCHWOMAN
DISTILLAND	DOLICHOTIS	DRAUGHT-NET	DUTCHWOMEN
DISTILLATE	DOLICHURUS	DRAWBRIDGE	DUUMVIRATE
DISTILLERY	DOLLARLESS	DRAWCANSIR	DWARFISHLY
DISTILLING	DOLLARSHIP	DRAWING-PEN	DYER'S-BROOM
DISTINCTLY	DOLL'S-HOUSE	DRAWING-PIN	DYNAMISTIC
DISTINGUEE	DOLOMITISE	DRAWLINGLY	DYNAMITARD
DISTORTION	DOLOROUSLY	DRAWSTRING	DYNAMOGENY
DISTORTIVE	DOLPHIN-FLY	DRAY-PLOUGH	DYOPHYSITE

DYOTHELETE
DYOTHELISM
DYSCRASITE
DYSENTERIC
DYSGRAPHIA
DYSGRAPHIC
DYSPROSIUM
DYSTHYMIAC

E

EAGLE-STONE
EAR-BUSSING
EARD-HUNGER
EARD-HUNGRY
EAR-KISSING
EARLIERISE
EARTH-BOARD
EARTHBOUND
EARTH-HOUSE
EARTHINESS
EARTH-PLATE
EARTHQUAKE
EARTH-SHINE
EARTH-SMOKE
EARTH-TABLE
EAR-TRUMPET
EAR-WITNESS
EASSELGATE
EASSELWARD
EASTERLING
EASTERMOST
EASTERTIDE
EASTERTIME
EATANSWILL
EBIONITISM
ÉBOULEMENT
EBRACTEATE
EBULLIENCE
EBULLIENCY
EBULLITION
EBURNATION
ECARDINATE
ECCHYMOSED
ECCHYMOSIS
ECCHYMOTIC
ECCLESIAST
ECCOPROTIC
ECHINODERM
ECHINOIDEA
ECHOPRAXIA
ECHOPRAXIS
ECOLOGICAL
ECONOMICAL
ECONOMISER
ECPHONESIS
ECPHRACTIC
ECTHLIPSIS
ECTODERMAL
ECTODERMIC
ECTOGENOUS
ECTOMORPHY
ECTOPHYTIC
ECUMENICAL
ECZEMATOUS
EDACIOUSLY
EDAPHOLOGY

EDENTULOUS
EDIBLENESS
EDIFYINGLY
EDITORSHIP
EDULCORANT
EDULCORATE
EFFACEABLE
EFFACEMENT
EFFECTIBLE
EFFECTLESS
EFFECTUATE
EFFEMINACY
EFFEMINATE
EFFEMINISE
EFFERVESCE
EFFICACITY
EFFICIENCE
EFFICIENCY
EFFIGURATE
EFFLEURAGE
EFFLORESCE
EFFORTLESS
EFFRONTERY
EFFULGENCE
EFFUSIVELY
EGG-AND-DART
EGG-BINDING
EGG-CAPSULE
EGLANDULAR
EGOCENTRIC
EGURGITATE
EGYPTOLOGY
EIGENVALUE
EIGHTEENMO
EIGHTEENTH
EIGHTPENCE
EIGHTPENNY
EIGHTSCORE
EISTEDDFOD
ELABORATOR
ELASTICATE
ELASTICISE
ELASTICITY
ELATEDNESS
ELBOW-CHAIR
ELDERBERRY
ELECAMPANE
ELECTIVELY
ELECTIVITY
ELECTORATE
ELECTORESS
ELECTORIAL
ELECTRICAL
ELECTROMER
ELECTRONIC
ELEMENTARY
ELEUSINIAN
ELEVENTHLY
ELIMINABLE
ELIMINATOR
ELLIPTICAL
ELOIGNMENT
ELONGATION
ELOQUENTLY
ELUCIDATOR
ELUTRIATOR

ELYTRIFORM
EMACIATION
EMANCIPATE
EMANCIPIST
EMARGINATE
EMASCULATE
EMBALMMENT
EMBANKMENT
EMBARGOING
EMBARKMENT
EMBASEMENT
EMBASSADOR
EMBER-GOOSE
EMBITTERED
EMBITTERER
EMBLAZONER
EMBLAZONRY
EMBLEMATIC
EMBLEMENTS
EMBODIMENT
EMBOLDENER
EMBOLISMAL
EMBOLISMIC
EMBONPOINT
EMBOSSMENT
EMBOUCHURE
EMBOWELLED
EMBROIDERY
EMBROWNING
EMBRYOGENY
EMBRYOLOGY
EMBRYONATE
EMBRYOTOMY
EMBRYULCIA
EMENDATION
EMENDATORY
EMERGENTLY
EMERY-BOARD
EMERY-CLOTH
EMERY-PAPER
EMERY-WHEEL
EMETICALLY
EMIGRATION
EMIGRATORY
EMINENTIAL
EMISSIVITY
EMMENOLOGY
EMMENTALER
EMMETROPIA
EMMETROPIC
EMOLLITION
EMPANELLED
EMPARADISE
EMPATHETIC
EMPHATICAL
EMPHRACTIC
EMPIRICISM
EMPIRICIST
EMPLASTRON
EMPLASTRUM
EMPLOYABLE
EMPLOYMENT
EMPOISONED
EMPOVERISH
EMULATRESS
EMULSIFIER

ENAMELLING
ENAMELLIST
ENAMOURING
ENANTIOSIS
ENARRATION
ENCAMPMENT
ENCASEMENT
ENCASHMENT
ENCEPHALIC
ENCEPHALON
ENCHANTING
ENCINCTURE
ENCIRCLING
ENCLOISTER
ENCOURAGER
ENCRINITAL
ENCRINITIC
ENCROACHER
ENCYCLICAL
ENCYSTMENT
ENDANGERER
ENDEARMENT
ENDEMICITY
ENDERMATIC
ENDERMICAL
ENDOCRINAL
ENDOCRINIC
ENDOCRITIC
ENDODERMAL
ENDODERMIC
ENDODERMIS
ENDOGAMOUS
ENDOGENOUS
ENDOMORPHY
ENDOPHYTIC
ENDOPLEURA
ENDOPODITE
ENDORHIZAL
ENDORSABLE
ENDOSCOPIC
ENDOSMOSIS
ENDOSMOTIC
END-PRODUCT
END-STOPPED
ENDURINGLY
ENERGETICS
ENERVATING
ENERVATION
ENERVATIVE
ENFACEMENT
ENFESTERED
ENFOLDMENT
ENFORCEDLY
ENGAGEMENT
ENGAGINGLY
ENGARRISON
ENGENDRURE
ENGINE-ROOM
ENGLISHMAN
ENGOUEMENT
ENGROSSING
ENGULFMENT
ENHARMONIC
ENHYDRITIC
ENIGMATISE
ENIGMATIST

ENJAMBMENT
ENJOINMENT
ENLACEMENT
ENLARGEDLY
ENLEVEMENT
ENLISTMENT
ENNEAGONAL
ENNEANDRIA
ENNEASTYLE
ENORMOUSLY
ENRAGEMENT
ENRAPTURED
ENREGIMENT
ENREGISTER
ENRICHMENT
ENSANGUINE
ENSCHEDULE
ENSIGNSHIP
ENTAILMENT
ENTEROCELE
ENTEROLITH
ENTEROTOMY
ENTERPRISE
ENTHRALDOM
ENTHRALLED
ENTHRONISE
ENTHUSIASM
ENTHUSIAST
ENTICEABLE
ENTICEMENT
ENTICINGLY
ENTIRENESS
ENTOILMENT
ENTOMBMENT
ENTOMOLOGY
ENTOPHYTAL
ENTOPHYTIC
ENTRANCING
ENTRAPMENT
ENTREASURE
ENTREATING
ENTREATIVE
ENTREMESSE
ENUMERATOR
ENUNCIABLE
ENUNCIATOR
ENWRAPMENT
ENWRAPPING
ENZYMOLOGY
EOSINOPHIL
EPANAPHORA
EPAULEMENT
EPEIROGENY
EPENTHESIS
EPENTHETIC
EPEXEGESIS
EPEXEGETIC
EPHEMERIST
EPHEMEROUS
EPIBLASTIC
EPICANTHIC
EPICANTHUS
EPICENTRAL
EPICYCLOID
EPIDEICTIC
EPIDEMICAL

EPIDERMOID
EPIDIORITE
EPIDOTISED
EPIGASTRIC
EPIGENESIS
EPIGENETIC
EPIGLOTTIC
EPIGLOTTIS
EPIGRAPHER
EPIGRAPHIC
EPILOGUISE
EPIMELETIC
EPIPHONEMA
EPIPHYTISM
EPIPLASTRA
EPISCOPACY
EPISCOPANT
EPISCOPATE
EPISCOPISE
EPISEMATIC
EPISODICAL
EPISPASTIC
EPISTERNAL
EPISTERNUM
EPISTOLARY
EPISTOLISE
EPISTOLIST
EPISTROPHE
EPITAPHIAN
EPITAPHIST
EPITHELIAL
EPITHELIUM
EPITHEMATA
EPITHERMAL
EPITOMICAL
EPITOMISER
EPONYCHIUM
ÉPROUVETTE
EQUABILITY
EQUANIMITY
EQUANIMOUS
EQUATORIAL
EQUESTRIAN
EQUIPOTENT
EQUITATION
EQUIVALENT
EQUIVOCATE
ERADIATION
ERADICABLE
ERADICATED
ERADICATOR
ERECTILITY
EREMITICAL
ERETHISMIC
ERETHISTIC
EREWHONIAN
ERGATOGYNE
ERGODICITY
ERGONOMICS
ERGONOMIST
ERGOPHOBIA
ERGOSTEROL
ERICACEOUS
ERIOCAULON
ERIOPHORUM
EROTOGENIC

EROTOMANIA
ERRAND-GIRL
ERUBESCENT
ERUBESCITE
ERUCTATION
ERUPTIONAL
ERYSIPELAS
ERYTHRITIC
ESCALATION
ESCALLONIA
ESCALLOPED
ESCAPELESS
ESCAPEMENT
ESCAPOLOGY
ESCARPMENT
ESCHAROTIC
ESCHEATAGE
ESCRITOIRE
ESCUTCHEON
ESPADRILLE
ESPECIALLY
ESSAYISTIC
ESTANCIERO
ESTATESMAN
ESTIMATION
ESTIMATIVE
ESTRANGELO
ETERNALISE
ETERNALIST
ETHEOSTOMA
ETHEREALLY
ETHOLOGIST
ETHYLAMINE
ETIOLATION
EUBACTERIA
EUCALYPTOL
EUCALYPTUS
EUCHLORINE
EUDEMONISM
EUDEMONIST
EUDIOMETER
EUGLENALES
EUHARMONIC
EUHEMERISE
EUHEMERISM
EUHEMERIST
EULOGISTIC
EUPHONICAL
EUPHONIOUS
EUPHORBIUM
EUPHROSYNE
EUPHUISTIC
EURAFRICAN
EURHYTHMIC
EUROCLYDON
EUROMARKET
EUROVISION
EURYPTERID
EURYPTERUS
EUSTACHIAN
EUTHANASIA
EUTHYNEURA
EVACUATION
EVACUATIVE
EVALUATION
EVALUATIVE

EVANESCENT
EVANGELIAR
EVANGELISE
EVANGELISM
EVANGELIST
EVAPORABLE
EVAPORATOR
EVEN-HANDED
EVEN-MINDED
EVENTUALLY
EVER-LIVING
EVERYTHING
EVERYWHERE
EVIDENTIAL
EVIL-MINDED
EVIL-WORKER
EVINCEMENT
EVISCERATE
EVITERNITY
EVOLVEMENT
EXACERBATE
EXACTITUDE
EXAGGERATE
EXALTATION
EXAMINABLE
EXAMINATOR
EXASPERATE
EXCAVATION
EXCELLENCE
EXCELLENCY
EXCEPTIOUS
EXCERPTING
EXCERPTION
EXCITATION
EXCITATIVE
EXCITATORY
EXCITEMENT
EXCOGITATE
EXCREMENTA
EXCRESCENT
EXCRUCIATE
EXCURSUSES
EXCUSATORY
EXECRATION
EXECRATIVE
EXECRATORY
EXECUTABLE
EXECUTANCY
EXECUTRESS
EXEGETICAL
EXENTERATE
EXHALATION
EXHAUST-GAS
EXHAUSTION
EXHAUSTIVE
EXHEREDATE
EXHIBITION
EXHIBITIVE
EXHIBITORY
EXHILARANT
EXHILARATE
EXHUMATION
EXOPHAGOUS
EXOPODITIC
EXORBITANT
EXORBITATE

EXOSPHERIC
EXOSPOROUS
EXOTERICAL
EXOTHERMAL
EXOTHERMIC
EXPANSIBLE
EXPANSIBLY
EXPATIATOR
EXPATRIATE
EXPECTANCE
EXPECTANCY
EXPECTEDLY
EXPEDIENCE
EXPEDIENCY
EXPEDITATE
EXPEDITELY
EXPEDITION
EXPEDITIVE
EXPENDABLE
EXPERIENCE
EXPERIMENT
EXPERTNESS
EXPIRATION
EXPIRATORY
EXPLICABLE
EXPLICITLY
EXPLOITAGE
EXPORTABLE
EXPOSITION
EXPOSITIVE
EXPOSITORY
EXPRESSAGE
EXPRESSION
EXPRESSIVE
EXPRESSMAN
EXPRESSURE
EXPRESSWAY
EXPROBRATE
EXPUGNABLE
EXPUNCTION
EXPURGATOR
EXSANGUINE
EXSICCATOR
EXSUFFLATE
EXTEMPORAL
EXTENDABLE
EXTENDEDLY
EXTENDIBLE
EXTENSIBLE
EXTENUATOR
EXTERIORLY
EXTERNALLY
EXTINCTION
EXTINCTIVE
EXTINCTURE
EXTINGUISH
EXTIRPABLE
EXTIRPATOR
EXTRACTANT
EXTRACTION
EXTRACTIVE
EXTRADOTAL
EXTRA-MURAL
EXTRANEITY
EXTRANEOUS
EXTRA-SOLAR

EXTRICABLE
EXUBERANCE
EXUBERANCY
EXULCERATE
EXULTATION
EXULTINGLY
EXUVIATION
EYAS-MUSKET
EYELET-HOLE
EYE-SERVANT
EYE-SERVICE
EYE-SPOTTED
EYE-WITNESS

F

FABRICATOR
FABULOSITY
FABULOUSLY
FACE-POWDER
FACE-SAVING
FACILENESS
FACILITATE
FACILITIES
FACINOROUS
FACTIONARY
FACTIONIST
FACTIOUSLY
FACTITIOUS
FACTORSHIP
FACTUALITY
FADELESSLY
FAHRENHEIT
FAINT-HEART
FAIR-BODING
FAIRGROUND
FAIR-HAIRED
FAIR-HEADED
FAIR-LEADER
FAIR-MINDED
FAIR-SPOKEN
FAIRY-BEADS
FAIRY-CYCLE
FAIRY-MONEY
FAIRY-STONE
FAITHFULLY
FALCON-EYED
FALDISTORY
FALLACIOUS
FALLING-OFF
FALLOW-CHAT
FALLOWNESS
FALSE-FACED
FALSIDICAL
FALSIFYING
FAMILIARLY
FAMISHMENT
FAMOUSNESS
FANATICISE
FANATICISM
FANCIFULLY
FAN-CRICKET
FANTASTICO
FANTOCCINI
FARCICALLY
FAR-FETCHED
FARRANDINE

FAR-SIGHTED
FASCIATION
FASCICULAR
FASCICULUS
FASCINATOR
FASHIONIST
FASTENS-EVE
FAST-HANDED
FASTIDIOUS
FASTIGIATE
FATALISTIC
FAT-BRAINED
FATHERHOOD
FATHERLAND
FATHERLESS
FATHERSHIP
FATHOMABLE
FATHOMETER
FATHOMLESS
FATHOM-LINE
FATIGUABLE
FATISCENCE
FAULTINESS
FAVOURABLE
FAVOURABLY
FAVOURLESS
FAYING-FACE
FEARLESSLY
FEARNOUGHT
FEARSOMELY
FEATEOUSLY
FEATHER-BED
FEATHERING
FEBRIFUGAL
FEDERALISE
FEDERALISM
FEDERALIST
FEDERATION
FEDERATIVE
FEEBLENESS
FEED-HEATER
FELICITATE
FELICITOUS
FELLMONGER
FELLOW-HEIR
FELLOWSHIP
FELSPATHIC
FEMALENESS
FEMINALITY
FEMINILITY
FEMININELY
FEMININISM
FEMININITY
FEN-CRICKET
FENESTELLA
FENESTRATE
FER-DE-LANCE
FERMENTIVE
FERNTICKLE
FERNTICLED
FERRANDINE
FERROALLOY
FERRONIÈRE
FERROPRINT
FERRY-HOUSE
FERTILISER

FERVESCENT
FERVIDNESS
FESCENNINE
FESSEEWISE
FESSE-POINT
FESTOONERY
FETTERLESS
FETTERLOCK
FEUILLETON
FEVERISHLY
FIANCHETTO
FIBREBOARD
FIBREGLASS
FIBRILLARY
FIBRILLATE
FIBRILLOSE
FIBRILLOUS
FIBRINOGEN
FIBROSITIS
FICKLENESS
FICTIONIST
FICTITIOUS
FIDDLEHEAD
FIDDLEWOOD
FIDUCIALLY
FIELDBOOTS
FIELDMOUSE
FIELDPIECE
FIELDSTONE
FIELDWARDS
FIERCENESS
FIFTY-FIFTY
FIGURATION
FIGURATIVE
FIGUREHEAD
FILARIASIS
FILCHINGLY
FILE-CUTTER
FILE-LEADER
FILIBUSTER
FILICINEAE
FILICINEAN
FILTERABLE
FILTHINESS
FILTRATION
FIMBRIATED
FIMICOLOUS
FINE-SPOKEN
FINGER-BOWL
FINGERHOLD
FINGERHOLE
FINGERLESS
FINGERLING
FINGERMARK
FINGERNAIL
FINGERPOST
FINGER'S-END
FINICALITY
FINITENESS
FINNO-UGRIC
FIRE-BASKET
FIRE-BLIGHT
FIRE-BUCKET
FIRE-ENGINE
FIRE-ESCAPE
FIRE-MASTER

FIRE-OFFICE
FIRE-PLOUGH
FIRE-POLICY
FIRE-RAISER
FIRE-SCREEN
FIRE-SHOVEL
FIRE-WALKER
FIRE-WARDEN
FIRING-STEP
FIRST-CLASS
FIRST-FLOOR
FIRST-FRUIT
FIRST-NIGHT
FIRST-THING
FISH-CARVER
FISH-GUTTER
FISHING-ROD
FISH-KETTLE
FISH-LADDER
FISH-MANURE
FISHMONGER
FISH-TROWEL
FITFULNESS
FITTING-OUT
FIVEFINGER
FIVE-PARTED
FIVE-SQUARE
FIZZENLESS
FLABBINESS
FLABELLATE
FLACCIDITY
FLAG-BASKET
FLAGELLANT
FLAGELLATA
FLAGELLATE
FLAGGINESS
FLAGITIOUS
FLAGRANTLY
FLAG-WAVING
FLAKE-WHITE
FLAMBOYANT
FLAMINGANT
FLAMINGOES
FLAMINICAL
FLANCONADE
FLANNELLED
FLAPDOODLE
FLAPDRAGON
FLAPPERISH
FLASH-BOARD
FLASH-HOUSE
FLASHINESS
FLASHLIGHT
FLASH-POINT
FLAT-FOOTED
FLATTERING
FLATULENCE
FLATULENCY
FLAVESCENT
FLAVOURING
FLEA-BITTEN
FLEA-CIRCUS
FLEDGELING
FLEECELESS
FLEECEWOOL
FLEECHMENT

FLEERINGLY
FLEETINGLY
FLESH-BROTH
FLESH-BRUSH
FLESH-EATER
FLESHINESS
FLESH-WOUND
FLEUR-DE-LIS
FLEUR-DE-LYS
FLICK-KNIFE
FLIGHT-DECK
FLIGHTLESS
FLIMSINESS
FLINDERSIA
FLINT-GLASS
FLINT-HEART
FLINTINESS
FLIPPANTLY
FLIRTATION
FLIRTINGLY
FLOATATION
FLOAT-BOARD
FLOATINGLY
FLOAT-STONE
FLOCCULATE
FLOCCULENT
FLOCK-PAPER
FLOODLIGHT
FLOODWATER
FLOOR-CLOTH
FLOPPINESS
FLORENTINE
FLORESCENT
FLORIDEOUS
FLORIDNESS
FLORILEGIA
FLORISTICS
FLOSCULOUS
FLOURISHED
FLOUTINGLY
FLOWER-BELL
FLOWER-GIRL
FLOWER-HEAD
FLOWERLESS
FLOWER-SHOW
FLUENTNESS
FLUFFINESS
FLUGELHORN
FLUNKEYDOM
FLUNKEYISH
FLUNKEYISM
FLUORIDATE
FLUORIDISE
FLUORINATE
FLUOROTYPE
FLUTE-MOUTH
FLUVIALIST
FLUVIATILE
FLUXIONARY
FLUXIONIST
FLY-BY-NIGHT
FLY-CATCHER
FLY-FISHING
FLY-FLAPPER
FOEDERATUS
FOETICIDAL

FOISONLESS
FOLIACEOUS
FOLKLORIST
FOLK-MEMORY
FOLKSINESS
FOLK-SPEECH
FOLLICULAR
FONTANELLE
FONTICULUS
FONTINALIS
FOOL-BEGGED
FOOTBALLER
FOOTBRIDGE
FOOT-GUARDS
FOOT-LICKER
FOOT-RACING
FOOT-WARMER
FORAMINOUS
FORBEARANT
FORBEARING
FORBIDDING
FORCEDNESS
FORCEFULLY
FORCING-PIT
FORCIPATED
FORE-ADVISE
FORE-AND-AFT
FOREBODING
FORECASTED
FORECASTER
FORECASTLE
FORECHOSEN
FORECOURSE
FORE-DAMNED
FOREFATHER
FOREFINGER
FOREGATHER
FOREGROUND
FORE-HAMMER
FOREHANDED
FORENOTICE
FORE-ORDAIN
FORE-QUOTED
FORERUNNER
FORESEEING
FORESHADOW
FORESHEWED
FORESHOWED
FOREST-BORN
FOREST-BRED
FOREST-TREE
FORETAUGHT
FORETELLER
FORFEITURE
FORFEUCHEN
FORFOUGHEN
FORGETTERY
FORGETTING
FORGIVABLE
FORINSECAL
FORKEDNESS
FORKIT-TAIL
FORMIDABLE
FORMIDABLY
FORMLESSLY
FORNICATOR

FORSAKENLY
FORTEPIANO
FORTHGOING
FORTHRIGHT
FORTIFYING
FORTISSIMO
FORTUITISM
FORTUITIST
FORTUITOUS
FORTY-NINER
FORWARDING
FOSSICKING
FOSTERLING
FOUDROYANT
FOUL-SPOKEN
FOUNDATION
FOUNDEROUS
FOURCHETTE
FOUR-FIGURE
FOUR-FOOTED
FOUR-HANDED
FOURIERISM
FOUR-INCHED
FOUR-IN-HAND
FOUR-LEAFED
FOUR-LEAVED
FOUR-LEGGED
FOUR-LETTER
FOUR-O-CLOCK
FOUR-PARTED
FOUR-POSTER
FOURSCORTH
FOUR-SEATER
FOURSQUARE
FOUR-STROKE
FOURTEENER
FOURTEENTH
FOURTH-RATE
FOWLING-NET
FOWL-PLAGUE
FOX-HUNTING
FOX-TERRIER
FRACTIONAL
FRAGMENTAL
FRAGMENTED
FRAGRANTLY
FRAMBOESIA
FRAME-HOUSE
FRAME-MAKER
FRANCHISER
FRANCISCAN
FRANCOPHIL
FRANGIPANE
FRANGIPANI
FRANTIC-MAD
FRATERCULA
FRATERNISE
FRATERNITY
FRATRICIDE
FRAUDFULLY
FRAUDULENT
FRAUGHTAGE
FRAXINELLA
FREAKINESS
FREAKISHLY
FREE-AGENCY

FREEBOOTER
FREE-DIVING
FREEDWOMAN
FREEDWOMEN
FREE-FISHER
FREE-FOODER
FREE-FOOTED
FREE-FOR-ALL
FREE-HANDED
FREEHOLDER
FREE-LABOUR
FREELOADER
FREEMARTIN
FREE-MINDED
FREE-SCHOOL
FREE-SELECT
FREE-SOILER
FREE-SPOKEN
FREE-TRADER
FREE-VERSER
FREIGHTAGE
FREIGHT-CAR
FREMESCENT
FRENETICAL
FREQUENTER
FREQUENTLY
FRESH-BLOWN
FRESHERDOM
FRESHWATER
FRIABILITY
FRICANDEAU
FRICASSEED
FRIENDLESS
FRIENDLILY
FRIENDSHIP
FRIGHTENED
FRIGHTSOME
FRIGIDNESS
FRIGORIFIC
FRINGELESS
FRISKINESS
FRISKINGLY
FRITHSOKEN
FRITHSTOOL
FRITILLARY
FROEBELIAN
FROEBELISM
FROG-HOPPER
FROG'S-MOUTH
FROLICKING
FROLICSOME
FRONT-BENCH
FRONTWARDS
FROSTBOUND
FROSTINESS
FROST-SMOKE
FROTHINESS
FROWNINGLY
FRUITARIAN
FRUITERESS
FRUITFULLY
FRUIT-KNIFE
FRUSTRATED
FUDDY-DUDDY
FUGITATION
FUGITIVELY

FULFILLING
FULFILMENT
FULIGINOUS
FULL-BODIED
FULL-BOTTOM
FULL-COCKED
FULL-HANDED
FULL-LENGTH
FULL-SAILED
FULL-SUMMED
FULL-VOICED
FULL-WINGED
FULMINEOUS
FUMBLINGLY
FUMIGATION
FUMIGATORY
FUNCTIONAL
FUND-HOLDER
FUNGICIDAL
FUNICULATE
FURROW-WEED
FURUNCULAR
FUSIBILITY
FUSTANELLA
FUSTIANISE
FUSTIANIST
FUTURELESS
FUTURISTIC
FUTURITION
FUTUROLOGY

G

GABBLEMENT
GABBROITIC
GADOLINITE
GADOLINIUM
GADROONING
GAG-TOOTHED
GAINGIVING
GAINSAYING
GAINSTRIVE
GALIMATIAS
GALLERYITE
GALLEY-WEST
GALLEY-WORM
GALLIAMBIC
GALLOGLASS
GALLOMANIA
GALLOPHILE
GALLOPHOBE
GALLOWS-LEE
GALRAVITCH
GALVANISER
GAMBIT-PAWN
GAMBOLLING
GAME-DEALER
GAMEKEEPER
GAMETANGIA
GAMOTROPIC
GANDER-MOON
GANGLIATED
GANGLIFORM
GANGLIONIC
GANGRENOUS
GAP-TOOTHED
GARBAGEMAN

GARGANTUAN
GARISHNESS
GARLANDAGE
GARMENTURE
GARNET-ROCK
GARNIERITE
GARNISHING
GARROTTING
GAS-BRACKET
GASCONADER
GAS-FURNACE
GASHLINESS
GASOMETRIC
GASTEROPOD .
GASTRALGIA
GASTRALGIC
GASTROLOGY
GASTRONOME
GASTRONOMY
GASTROPODA
GASTROSOPH
GASTROTOMY
GAS-TURBINE
GATE-KEEPER
GATE-LEGGED
GATLING-GUN
GAUDY-GREEN
GAUDY-NIGHT '
GAUGE-GLASS
GAUGING-ROD
GAULTHERIA
GAUNTLETED
GELATINATE
GELATINISE
GELATINOUS
GELDER-ROSE
GEM-CUTTING
GEMINATION
GEMMACEOUS
GENERALISE
GENERALIST
GENERALITY
GENERATION
GENERATIVE
GENERATRIX
GENEROSITY
GENEROUSLY
GENESIACAL
GENETHLIAC
GENETICIST
GENEVANISM
GENEVRETTE
GENIALNESS
GENICULATE
GENITIVELY
GENSDARMES
GENTEELISH
GENTEELISM
GENTILESSE
GENTLEFOLK
GENTLEHOOD
GENTLENESS
GEOCENTRIC
GEOCHEMIST
GEODESICAL
GEODETICAL

GEODYNAMIC
GEOGNOSTIC
GEOGRAPHER
GEOGRAPHIC
GEOLOGICAL
GEOMEDICAL
GEOMETRISE
GEOMETRIST
GEOPHAGISM
GEOPHAGIST
GEOPHAGOUS
GEOPHILOUS
GEOPHYSICS
GEOPONICAL
GEOSTATICS
GEOTHERMAL
GEOTHERMIC
GEOTROPISM
GERIATRICS
GERIATRIST
GERMAN-BAND
GERUNDIVAL
GHASTFULLY
GHOST-STORY
GIBBERELLA
GIDDY-PACED
GIGGLESOME
GILBERTIAN
GILBERTINE
GILLRAVAGE
GILRAVAGER
GIMLET-EYED
GINGERSNAP
GINGIVITIS
GINGLIMOID
GINKGOALES
GIRLFRIEND
GLACIALIST
GLACIATION
GLACIOLOGY
GLAD-HANDER
GLADIATORY
GLADSOMELY
GLAGOLITIC
GLANCE-COAL
GLANCINGLY
GLANDIFORM
GLANDULOUS
GLASS-CLOTH
GLASS-COACH
GLASS-FACED
GLASSFULLS
GLASS-HOUSE
GLASSINESS
GLASS-PAPER
GLASS-SNAKE
GLASWEGIAN
GLAUBERITE
GLAUCONITE
GLEBE-HOUSE
GLEEMAIDEN
GLENDOVEER
GLIMMERING
GLISTERING
GLITTERAND
GLITTERING

GLOBULARLY
GLOMERULAR
GLOOMINESS
GLORIFYING
GLORIOUSLY
GLOSSARIAL
GLOSSARIST
GLOSSINESS
GLOSSOLOGY
GLOTTOLOGY
GLOVE-FIGHT
GLOVE-MONEY
GLUCOSURIA
GLUMACEOUS
GLUTTONISE
GLUTTONISH
GLUTTONOUS
GLYCOSURIA
GNAPHALIUM
GNASHINGLY
GNEISSITIC
GNOMONICAL
GNOSTICISM
GNOTOBIOTE
GOAL-KEEPER
GOAT-SALLOW
GOAT'S-BEARD
GOAT'S-THORN
GOATSUCKER
GOAT-WILLOW
GOBBELINES
GODFEARING
GOGGLE-EYED
GOLD-BEATER
GOLD-BEETLE
GOLD-DIGGER
GOLD-END-MAN
GOLDEN-SEAL
GOLDILOCKS
GOLD-THREAD
GOLD-WASHER
GOLF-COURSE
GOLIARDERY
GOLIATHISE
GOLOE-SHOES
GOLOPTIOUS
GOLUPTIOUS
GOMBEENMAN
GONIOMETER
GONIOMETRY
GONOCOCCAL
GONOCOCCUS
GONORRHOEA
GOODFATHER
GOOD-FELLOW
GOOD-HUMOUR
GOODLIHEAD
GOOD-LIKING
GOODLINESS
GOODLYHEAD
GOOD-MORROW
GOODMOTHER
GOOD-NATURE
GOODSISTER
GOODS-TRAIN
GOODY-GOODY

GOONEY-BIRD
GOOSEBERRY
GOOSE-FLESH
GOOSE-GRASS
GOOSE-QUILL
GOR-BELLIED
GORGEOUSLY
GORGONEION
GORGONZOLA
GORMANDISE
GORMANDISM
GOSPELLISE
GOURDINESS
GOVERNABLE
GOVERNANCE
GOVERNANTE
GOVERNESSY
GOVERNMENT
GRACEFULLY
GRACIOSITY
GRACIOUSLY
GRADIENTER
GRADUALISM
GRADUALIST
GRADUALITY
GRADUATION
GRAMICIDIN
GRAMINEOUS
GRAMMARIAN
GRAMMATIST
GRAMOPHONE
GRAMOPHONY
GRANADILLA
GRANDCHILD
GRAND-DUCAL
GRANDMAMMA
GRANDNIECE
GRANDSTAND
GRANDUNCLE
GRANGERISE
GRANGERISM
GRANOPHYRE
GRANT-IN-AID
GRANULARLY
GRANULITIC
GRAPEFRUIT
GRAPE-LOUSE
GRAPESTONE
GRAPHEMICS
GRAPHITISE
GRAPHITOID
GRAPHOLOGY
GRAPLEMENT
GRAPTOLITE
GRASPINGLY
GRASS-CLOTH
GRASS-GREEN
GRASS-GROWN
GRASSINESS
GRASS-ROOTS
GRASS-SNAKE
GRASS-WIDOW
GRASS-WRACK
GRATEFULLY
GRATIFYING
GRATILLITY

GRATUITOUS
GRAVELLING
GRAVEL-WALK
GRAVE-MAKER
GRAVEOLENT
GRAVESTONE
GRAVIMETER
GRAVIMETRY
GREASEWOOD
GREASINESS
GREAT-NIECE
GREAT-UNCLE
GRECO-ROMAN
GREEDINESS
GREENCLOTH
GREEN-DRAKE
GREENFINCH
GREENHEART
GREENHOUSE
GREENSHANK
GREENSTICK
GREENSTONE
GREENSTUFF
GREENSWARD
GREGARIOUS
GREISENISE
GRENADILLA
GRESSORIAL
GREY-COATED
GREY-HAIRED
GREY-HEADED
GREY-WETHER
GRIEVINGLY
GRIEVOUSLY
GRIFFINISH
GRIFFINISM
GRIMLOOKED
GRINDSTONE
GRISLINESS
GRITH-STOOL
GRITTINESS
GROBIANISM
GROCETERIA
GROGGINESS
GROTTO-WORK
GROUND-BAIT
GROUND-BASS
GROUND-DOVE
GROUNDEDLY
GROUND-HOLD
GROUNDLESS
GROUNDLING
GROUNDMASS
GROUNDPLAN
GROUNDPLOT
GROUND-RENT
GROUNDSELL
GROUNDSILL
GROUNDSMAN
GROUNDWORK
GROUND-ZERO
GROVELLING
GROWLINGLY
GRUDGINGLY
GRUMPINESS
GRUNTINGLY

GUARANTEED
GUARD-HOUSE
GUBERNATOR
GUESSINGLY
GUEST-HOUSE
GUEST-NIGHT
GUILEFULLY
GUILLOTINE
GUILTINESS
GUILTY-LIKE
GUINEA-CORN
GUINEA-FOWL
GUINEA-WORM
GUNFIGHTER
GUNRUNNING
GUNSLINGER
GUT-SCRAPER
GUTTIFERAE
GUTTURALLY
GYMNASIAST
GYMNOSOPHY
GYMNOSPERM
GYNANDRISM
GYNANDROUS
GYPSOPHILA
GYRATIONAL
GYRE-CARLIN
GYROCOPTER
GYROSCOPIC
GYROSTATIC

H

HABILATORY
HABILIMENT
HABILITATE
HABITATION
HABITAUNCE
HABIT-CLOTH
HABIT-MAKER
HABITUALLY
HACKBUTEER
HACKMATACK
HACKNEYMAN
HAEMANTHUS
HAEMATOSIS
HAEMATURIA
HAEMOCONIA
HAEMOLYSIS
HAEMOLYTIC
HAGIOCRACY
HAGIOLATER
HAGIOLATRY
HAGIOLOGIC
HAGIOSCOPE
HAIL-FELLOW
HAIR-PENCIL
HAIR-POWDER
HAIR-RAISER
HAIR-SPRING
HAIRSTREAK
HAIRSTROKE
HAIR-WAVING
HAKENKREUZ
HALBERDIER
HALF-A-CROWN
HALF-A-DOZEN

HALF-COCKED
HALF-DOLLAR
HALFE-HORSY
HALF-KIRTLE
HALF-LENGTH
HALF-NELSON
HALF-SISTER
HALF-VOLLEY
HALF-WITTED
HALF-YEARLY
HALIEUTICS
HALIOTIDAE
HALLELUIAH
HALLELUJAH
HALLOYSITE
HALOGENATE
HALOGENOUS
HALOPHYTIC
HAMBURGHER
HAMESUCKEN
HAMMER-BEAM
HAMMER-FISH
HAMMERHEAD
HAMMERLESS
HAMMERLOCK
HAMMER-POND
HAMSHACKLE
HAND-BARROW
HAND-BASKET
HAND-GALLOP
HANDICRAFT
HANDICUFFS
HAND-IN-HAND
HANDMAIDEN
HAND-ME-DOWN
HANDSCREEN
HANDSELLED
HANDSOMELY
HANDSPRING
HAND-WEEDED
HANDWORKED
HANDY-DANDY
HANKY-PANKY
HANOVERIAN
HANSARDISE
HANSELLING
HARANGUING
HARASSEDLY
HARASSMENT
HARBOURAGE
HARBOUR-BAR
HARD-BILLED
HARD-BITTEN
HARD-BOILED
HARD-EARNED
HARD-FISTED
HARD-FOUGHT
HARD-GOTTEN
HARD-HANDED
HARD-HEADED
HARD-PUSHED
HARD-RIDING
HARE-LIPPED
HARMAN-BECK
HARMLESSLY
HARMONICAL

HARMONICON
HARMONIOUS
HARMONISER
HARPOONEER
HARPOON-GUN
HARPY-EAGLE
HARQUEBUSE
HARQUEBUSS
HARTEBEEST
HARTIEHALE
HARUSPICAL
HARUSPICES
HARVEST-BUG
HARVEST-FLY
HARVESTMAN
HATEWORTHY
HAUNTINGLY
HAUSTELLUM
HAUSTORIUM
HAWK-BEAKED
HAWK-BILLED
HAWKSBEARD
HAWSER-LAID
HAZARDABLE
HEAD-BUMMER
HEAD-CHEESE
HEAD-HUGGER
HEAD-HUNTER
HEAD-LUGGED
HEADMASTER
HEADSQUARE
HEADSTREAM
HEADSTRONG
HEADWORKER
HEALTHLESS
HEALTHSOME
HEARING-AID
HEARSE-LIKE
HEART-BLOCK
HEART-BLOOD
HEARTBREAK
HEART-GRIEF
HEARTINESS
HEART-OUAKE
HEART'S-EASE
HEART-SPOON
HEART-THROB
HEARTWHOLE
HEATHENDOM
HEATHENISE
HEATHENISH
HEATHENISM
HEATH-POULT
HEATSTROKE
HEAVEN-BORN
HEAVEN-BRED
HEAVEN-SENT
HEAVENWARD
HEAVY-ARMED
HEAVY-LADEN
HEBDOMADAL
HEBDOMADAR
HEBETATION
HEBRAICISM
HEBRAISTIC
HECTOGRAPH

HECTOLITRE
HECTOMETRE
HECTORSHIP
HECTOSTERE
HEDONISTIC
HEEDLESSLY
HELIACALLY
HELIANTHUS
HELICOIDAL
HELICONIAN
HELICOPTER
HELIOGRAPH
HELIOLATER
HELIOLATRY
HELIOMETER
HELIOPHOBI
HELIOPHYTE
HELIOSCOPE
HELIOTAXIS
HELIOTROPE
HELIOTROPY
HELIOTYPIC
HELL-BENDER
HELMINTHIC
HELPLESSLY
HEMIANOPIA
HEMICHORDA
HEMICYCLIC
HEMIHEDRAL
HEMIHEDRON
HEMIPLEGIA
HEMIPLEGIC
HEMIPTERAL
HEMIPTERAN
HEMISPHERE
HEMITROPAL
HEMITROPIC
HEMP-NETTLE
HENCEFORTH
HENDECAGON
HEN-HARRIER
HEN-HEARTED
HENOTHEISM
HENOTHEIST
HENPECKERY
HEORTOLOGY
HEPATOLOGY
HEPTACHORD
HEPTAGONAL
HEPTAGYNIA
HEPTAMERON
HEPTAMETER
HEPTANDRIA
HEPTAPODIC
HEPTARCHIC
HEPTATEUCH
HEPTATONIC
HERACLEIAN
HERACLIDAN
HERALD-DUCK
HERALDSHIP
HERBARTIAN
HERB-BENNET
HERBICIDAL
HERB-ROBERT
HEREABOUTS

HEREDITARY
HERESIARCH
HERESY-HUNT
HERETICATE
HERETOFORE
HERIOTABLE
HERITRICES
HERITRIXES
HERMETICAL
HERMIT-CRAB
HERMITICAL
HERNIOTOMY
HEROICALLY
HEROICNESS
HEROI-COMIC
HERRENVOLK
HERRNHUTER
HESITATION
HESITATIVE
HESITATORY
HESPERIDES
HETEROCERA
HETEROCONT
HETERODONT
HETERODOXY
HETERODYNE
HETEROGAMY
HETEROGENY
HETEROGONY
HETEROKONT
HETEROLOGY
HETERONOMY
HETEROPODA
HETEROTAXY
HETMANSHIP
HEULANDITE
HEXACTINAL
HEXAEMERON
HEXAGYNIAN
HEXAGYNOUS
HEXAHEDRAL
HEXAHEDRON
HEXAMEROUS
HEXAMETRIC
HEXANDRIAN
HEXANDROUS
HEXAPLARIC
HEY-DE-GUISE
HEY-DE-GUYES
HIBERNACLE
HIDALGOISH
HIDALGOISM
HIDDENMOST
HIDDENNESS
HIERA-PICRA
HIERARCHAL
HIERARCHIC
HIEROCRACY
HIEROGLYPH
HIEROGRAPH
HIEROLATRY
HIEROLOGIC
HIEROMANCY
HIERONYMIC
HIEROPHANT
HIEROSCOPY

HIGH-BINDER	HOBBLINGLY	HONEY-MOUSE	HOW-DO-YOU-DO
HIGHERMOST	HOBBY-HORSE	HONEY-STALK	HOWLEGLASS
HIGH-FLYING	HOBJOBBING	HONEY-STONE	HOWSOMEVER
HIGH-HANDED	HOBNOBBING	HONEY-SWEET	HOYDENHOOD
HIGH-HEELED	HOCUS-POCUS	HONEY-WAGON	HUCKLE-BONE
HIGHJACKER	HODDEN-GREY	HONORARIUM	HUCKSTRESS
HIGH-KILTED	HODDY-DODDY	HONOURABLE	HUG-ME-TIGHT
HIGHLANDER	HODGEPODGE	HONOURABLY	HULLABALOO
HIGH-MINDED	HOEOMEROUS	HONOURLESS	HUMANENESS
HIGH-NECKED	HOG-CHOLERA	HONOURSMAN	HUMANISTIC
HIGH-OCTANE	HOGEN-MOGEN	HOODIECROW	HUMBLENESS
HIGH-PLACED	HOITY-TOITY	HOOKEDNESS	HUMBLINGLY
HIGH-PRICED	HOKEY-POKEY	HOOTANANNY	HUMBUGGERY
HIGH-RAISED	HOLING-PICK	HOOTENANNY	HUMBUGGING
HIGH-RANKER	HOLLANDISH	HOOTNANNIE	HUMDUDGEON
HIGH-REARED	HOLLOW-EYED	HOOTS-TOOTS	HUMGRUFFIN
HIGH-ROLLER	HOLLOWNESS	HOP-BITTERS	HUMIDIFIER
HIGH-SOULED	HOLLOW-WARE	HOPELESSLY	HUMILIATOR
HIGH-STRUNG	HOLOGRAPHY	HOPSACKING	HUMMING-TOP
HIGH-TASTED	HOLOHEDRAL	HOP-TREFOIL	HUMORALISM
HIGHWAYMAN	HOLOHEDRON	HORIZONTAL	HUMORALIST
HIGRY-PIGRY	HOLOPHOTAL	HORNBLENDE	HUMORESQUE
HILL-DIGGER	HOLOPHRASE	HORNED-POUT	HUMORISTIC
HIMYARITIC	HOLOPHYTIC	HORNFELSES	HUMOROUSLY
HINDERANCE	HOLOSTERIC	HORN-FOOTED	HUMOURLESS
HINDERLAND	HOLUS-BOLUS	HORN-RIMMED	HUMOURSOME
HINDERLANS	HOMALOIDAL	HOROGRAPHY	HUMPBACKED
HINDERLINS	HOMBURG-HAT	HOROLOGIST	HUNTING-BOX
HINDERMOST	HOME-BREWED	HOROLOGIUM	HUNTING-CAP
HINDUSTANI	HOME-COMING	HOROSCOPIC	HUNTING-COG
HINGE-BOUND	HOMELINESS	HORRENDOUS	HUPAITHRIC
HINGE-JOINT	HOMEOMERIC	HORRIDNESS	HURDLE-RACE
HINTERLAND	HOMEOMORPH	HORRIFYING	HURDY-GURDY
HIPPETY-HOP	HOMEOPATHY	HORSE-BREAD	HURL-BARROW
HIPPIATRIC	HOME-SIGNAL	HORSE-CLOTH	HURLY-BURLY
HIPPOCAMPI	HOME-THRUST	HORSE-COPER	HURRYINGLY
HIPPOCRENE	HOMILETICS	HORSE-FACED	HURTLESSLY
HIPPODROME	HOMOBLASTY	HORSEFLESH	HUSBANDAGE
HIPPOGRIFF	HOMOCERCAL	HORSE-GOWAN	HUSBANDMAN
HIPPOGRYPH	HOMOCHROMY	HORSELAUGH	HUSKING-BEE
HIPPOMANES	HOMOCYCLIC	HORSE-LEECH	HYALOMELAN
HIPPOPHAGY	HOMOEOMERY	HORSE-POWER	HYALOPHANE
HIPPURITIC	HOMOEOPATH	HORSESHOER	HYALOPLASM
HIRDY-GIRDY	HOMOGAMOUS	HORSE-TAMER	HYBRIDISER
HIRUDINEAN	HOMOGENISE	HORSE-THIEF	HYDRAGOGUE
HIRUDINOID	HOMOGENOUS	HORSE-WOMAN	HYDRAULICS
HIRUDINOUS	HOMOLOGATE	HOSPITABLE	HYDRAZIDES
HISTIOLOGY	HOMOLOGISE	HOSPITABLY	HYDRICALLY
HISTOBLAST	HOMOLOGOUS	HOSTELLING	HYDROCHORE
HISTOGENIC	HOMONYMOUS	HOT-BLOODED	HYDROLOGIC
HISTOLOGIC	HOMOOUSIAN	HOT-BRAINED	HYDROLYSIS
HISTOLYSIS	HOMOPHONIC	HOTCHPOTCH	HYDROLYTIC
HISTOLYTIC	HOMOPLASMY	HOT-COCKLES	HYDROMANCY
HISTORICAL	HOMOSEXUAL	HOT-LIVERED	HYDROMETER
HISTRIONIC	HOMOTAXIAL	HOT-MOUTHED	HYDROMETRY
HIT-AND-MISS	HOMOTHALLY	HOUNDS-FOOT	HYDROPATHY
HITCH-HIKER	HOMOTONOUS	HOUR-CIRCLE	HYDROPHANE
HITHERMOST	HOMOZYGOTE	HOUSE-AGENT	HYDROPHILY
HITHERSIDE	HOMOZYGOUS	HOUSECRAFT	HYDROPHONE
HITHERWARD	HOMUNCULAR	HOUSELLING	HYDROPHYTE
HITOPADESA	HOMUNCULUS	HOUSE-PARTY	HYDROPLANE
HITTY-MISSY	HONEY-CHILE	HOUSE-PROUD	HYDROPOLYP
HOAR-HEADED	HONEY-CROCK	HOUTS-TOUTS	HYDROSCOPE
HOARSENESS	HONEY-EATER	HOVERCRAFT	HYDROSOMAL
HOBBIANISM	HONEY-GUIDE	HOVERINGLY	HYDROSOMES
HOBBLE-BUSH	HONEYMONTH	HOVERTRAIN	HYDROTAXIS

HYDROTHECA
HYETOGRAPH
HYETOMETER
HYGROCHASY
HYGROGRAPH
HYGROMETER
HYGROMETRY
HYGROPHOBE
HYGROPHYTE
HYGROSCOPE
HYLOTHEISM
HYLOTHEIST
HYLOTOMOUS
HYLOZOICAL
HYMENEAEAL
HYMENEAEAN
HYOPLASTRA
HYOSCYAMUS
HYPABYSSAL
HYPAETHRAL
HYPAETHRON
HYPALGESIA
HYPALGESIC
HYPANTHIUM
HYPERACUTE
HYPERAEMIA
HYPERAEMIC
HYPERBARIC
HYPERBATIC
HYPERBATON
HYPERBOLIC
HYPERDULIA
HYPERGOLIC
HYPERSONIC
HYPHENATED
HYPNAGOGIC
HYPNOGENIC
HYPNOGOGIC
HYPNOIDISE
HYPNOTISER
HYPOCORISM
HYPOCRITIC
HYPODERMAL
HYPODERMIC
HYPODERMIS
HYPODORIAN
HYPOGAEOUS
HYPOGYNOUS
HYPOLYDIAN
HYPOPHYSIS
HYPOSTASIS
HYPOSTATIC
HYPOTACTIC
HYPOTENUSE
HYPOTHESES
HYPOTHESIS
HYPOTHETIC
HYPSOMETER
HYPSOMETRY
HYPSOPHYLL
HYRACOIDEA
HYSTERESIS
HYSTERETIC
HYSTERICAL
HYSTERICKY
HYSTERITIS

I

IAMBICALLY
IATROGENIC
ICE-BREAKER
ICE-HILLING
ICELAND-DOG
ICE-PEARLED
ICHTHYOSIS
ICHTHYOTIC
ICONOCLASM
ICONOCLAST
ICONOLATER
ICONOLATRY
ICONOMACHY
ICONOMATIC
ICONOMETER
ICONOMETRY
ICONOSCOPE
ICOSAHEDRA
ICOSANDRIA
IDEALISTIC
IDEATIONAL
IDENTIFIED
IDEOGRAPHY
IDEOLOGIST
IDIOPATHIC
IDLE-HEADED
IDOLATRESS
IDOLATRISE
IDOLATROUS
IDOLOCLAST
IGNES-FATUI
IGNIPOTENT
IGNOBILITY
IGNORANTLY
IGNORATION
ILANG-ILANG
ILL-ADVISED
ILLAQUEATE
ILLATIVELY
ILLAUDABLE
ILLAUDABLY
ILLECEBRUM
ILLEGALISE
ILLEGALITY
ILL-FEELING
ILLITERACY
ILLITERATE
ILL-LOOKING
ILL-NATURED
ILL-STARRED
ILLUMINANT
ILLUMINATE
ILLUMINATI
ILLUMINISM
ILLUSIVELY
ILLUSTRATE
IMAGINABLE
IMAGINABLY
IMBECILITY
IMBIBITION
IMBROCCATA
IMBRUEMENT
IMMACULACY
IMMACULATE

IMMANATION
IMMANENTAL
IMMATERIAL
IMMATURELY
IMMATURITY
IMMEASURED
IMMEMORIAL
IMMERITOUS
IMMINENTLY
IMMISCIBLE
IMMOBILISE
IMMOBILITY
IMMODERACY
IMMODERATE
IMMODESTLY
IMMOLATION
IMMORALISM
IMMORALIST
IMMORALITY
IMMORTALLY
IMMORTELLE
IMMOVEABLE
IMMUNOLOGY
IMMUREMENT
IMPAIRMENT
IMPALEMENT
IMPALPABLE
IMPALPABLY
IMPANATION
IMPARADISE
IMPARLANCE
IMPARTIBLE
IMPARTMENT
IMPASSABLE
IMPASSABLY
IMPASSIBLE
IMPATIENCE
IMPECCABLE
IMPECCANCY
IMPEDIMENT
IMPEDITIVE
IMPENDENCE
IMPENDENCY
IMPENITENT
IMPERATIVE
IMPERIALLY
IMPERILLED
IMPERSONAL
IMPERVIOUS
IMPICTURED
IMPISHNESS
IMPLACABLE
IMPLACABLY
IMPLEXUOUS
IMPLICITLY
IMPLORATOR
IMPOLITELY
IMPORTABLE
IMPORTANCE
IMPORTANCY
IMPORTLESS
IMPORTUNER
IMPOSINGLY
IMPOSITION
IMPOSSIBLE
IMPOSTHUME

IMPOSTUMED
IMPOUNDAGE
IMPOVERISH
IMPREGNANT
IMPREGNATE
IMPRESARIO
IMPRESSION
IMPRESSIVE
IMPRESSURE
IMPRIMATUR
IMPRINTING
IMPROBABLE
IMPROBABLY
IMPROPERLY
IMPROVABLE
IMPROVABLY
IMPROVIDED
IMPROVISER
IMPRUDENCE
IMPUDENTLY
IMPUDICITY
IMPUGNABLE
IMPUGNMENT
IMPUISSANT
IMPURENESS
IMPUTATION
IMPUTATIVE
INACCURACY
INACCURATE
INACTIVATE
INACTIVELY
INACTIVITY
INADAPTIVE
INADEQUACY
INADEQUATE
INANIMATED
INAPPETENT
INAPPOSITE
INAPTITUDE
INARTISTIC
INAUGURATE
INBREEDING
INBRINGING
INCANDESCE
INCANTATOR
INCAPACITY
INCASEMENT
INCAUTIOUS
INCEDINGLY
INCENDIARY
INCESTUOUS
INCHOATELY
INCHOATION
INCHOATIVE
INCIDENTAL
INCINERATE
INCIPIENCE
INCIPIENCY
INCISIFORM
INCISIVELY
INCISORIAL
INCITATION
INCITATIVE
INCITEMENT
INCITINGLY
INCIVILITY

INCLEMENCY
INCLINABLE
INCLUDIBLE
INCOGITANT
INCOHERENT
INCOHESION
INCOHESIVE
INCOMPARED
INCOMPLETE
INCOMPOSED
INCONSTANT
INCORONATE
INCORPORAL
INCRASSATE
INCREASING
INCREDIBLE
INCREDIBLY
INCRESCENT
INCUBATION
INCUBATIVE
INCUBATORY
INCULCATOR
INCULPABLE
INCULPABLY
INCUMBENCY
INCUNABULA
INCURRABLE
INCURVATED
INDAGATION
INDAGATIVE
INDAGATORY
INDEBTMENT
INDECENTLY
INDECISION
INDECISIVE
INDECOROUS
INDEFINITE
INDELICACY
INDELICATE
INDICATION
INDICATIVE
INDICATORY
INDICTABLE
INDICTMENT
INDIGENOUS
INDIGENTLY
INDIGESTED
INDIGNANCE
INDIGO-BLUE
INDIGOFERA
INDIRECTLY
INDISCREET
INDISCRETE
INDISPOSED
INDISTINCT
INDITEMENT
INDIVIDUAL
INDIVIDUUM
INDOCILITY
INDOLENTLY
INDONESIAN
INDUCEMENT
INDUCTANCE
INDULGENCE
INDULGENCY
INDUMENTUM

INDURATION
INDURATIVE
INDUSTRIAL
INDWELLING
INEBRITOUS
INEDUCABLE
INEFFICACY
INELEGANCE
INELEGANCY
INELIGIBLE
INELIGIBLY
INELOQUENT
INEPTITUDE
INEQUALITY
INEQUATION
INERASABLE
INERASABLY
INERASIBLE
INERASIBLY
INESCULENT
INEVITABLE
INEVITABLY
INEXISTENT
INEXORABLE
INEXORABLY
INEXPIABLE
INEXPIABLY
INEXPLICIT
INEXTENDED
INFALLIBLE
INFALLIBLY
INFAMONISE
INFAMOUSLY
INFARCTION
INFATUATED
INFEASIBLE
INFECTIOUS
INFEFTMENT
INFELICITY
INFERIORLY
INFERNALLY
INFERRABLE
INFERRIBLE
INFIBULATE
INFIDELITY
IN-FIGHTING
INFILTRATE
INFINITANT
INFINITARY
INFINITATE
INFINITELY
INFINITIVE
INFINITUDE
INFIRMNESS
INFLAMABLE
INFLATABLE
INFLECTION
INFLECTIVE
INFLEXIBLE
INFLEXIBLY
INFLICTION
INFLICTIVE
INFLUENZAL
INFORMALLY
INFRACTION
INFRAGIBLE

INFRAGRANT
INFRAHUMAN
INFRASONIC
INFREQUENT
INFUSORIAL
INFUSORIAN
INGEMINATE
INGENERATE
INGESTIBLE
INGLE-CHEEK
INGLORIOUS
INGRATEFUL
INGRATIATE
INGREDIENT
INGRESSION
INHABITANT
INHALATION
INHARMONIC
INHERENTLY
INHERITRIX
INHIBITION
INHIBITORY
INHUMANITY
INHUMATION
INIMICALLY
INIMITABLE
INIMITABLY
INIQUITOUS
INITIALISE
INITIALLED
INITIATION
INITIATIVE
INITIATORY
INJUDICIAL
INJUNCTION
INK-SLINGER
INNATENESS
INNOCENTLY
INNOMINATE
INNOVATION
INNUENDOES
INNUMERACY
INNUMERATE
INNUMEROUS
INNUTRIENT
INOBEDIENT
INOCULABLE
INOCULATOR
INOPERABLE
INORDINACY
INORDINATE
INOSCULATE
INQUIETUDE
INQUIRENDO
INQUISITOR
INSALIVATE
INSALUTARY
INSANENESS
INSANITARY
INSATIABLE
INSATIABLY
INSECURELY
INSECURITY
INSELBERGE
INSEMINATE
INSENSIBLE

INSENSIBLY
INSENSUOUS
INSENTIENT
INSESSORES
INSIGHTFUL
INSINUATOR
INSIPIDITY
INSIPIENCE
INSISTENCE
INSOBRIETY
INSOCIABLE
INSOLATION
INSOLENTLY
INSOLIDITY
INSOLVABLE
INSOLVENCY
INSOMNIOUS
INSOUCIANT
INSPANNING
INSPECTION
INSPECTIVE
INSPIRABLE
INSPIRATOR
INSPISSATE
INSTALLING
INSTALMENT
INSTANTIAL
INSTIGATOR
INSTILLING
INSTILMENT
INSTITUTOR
INSTRUCTOR
INSTRUMENT
INSUFFLATE
INSULARISM
INSULARITY
INSULATION
INSULTABLE
INSULTMENT
INSURANCER
INSURGENCE
INSURGENCY
INTACTNESS
INTANGIBLE
INTANGIBLY
INTEGRABLE
INTEGRALLY
INTEGRATOR
INTEGUMENT
INTENDANCY
INTENDEDLY
INTENDMENT
INTENERATE
INTENTNESS
INTERBREED
INTERCALAR
INTERCEDER
INTERCHAIN
INTERCLUDE
INTERCROSS
INTERESTED
INTERFERER
INTERFERON
INTERGRADE
INTERGROWN
INTERIORLY

INTERLACED
INTERLEAVE
INTERLOPER
INTERLUNAR
INTERMARRY
INTERMEZZI
INTERMEZZO
INTERNALLY
INTERNMENT
INTERNODAL
INTERPHASE
INTERPHONE
INTERPLANT
INTERPLEAD
INTERPOLAR
INTERPOSAL
INTERPOSER
INTERRAMAL
INTERREGAL
INTERREGES
INTERREGNA
INTERREIGN
INTERSPACE
INTERSTATE
INTERSTICE
INTERTIDAL
INTERTRIGO
INTERTWINE
INTERTWIST
INTERUNION
INTERURBAN
INTERVENER
INTERVENOR
INTERVITAL
INTERVOLVE
INTERWEAVE
INTERWOUND
INTERZONAL
INTESTINAL
INTIMATELY
INTIMATION
INTIMIDATE
INTINCTION
INTOLERANT
INTONATION
INTONINGLY
INTOXICANT
INTOXICATE
INTRAMURAL
INTRA-URBAN
INTREPIDLY
INTRIGANTE
INTRIGUANT
INTRIGUING
INTRODUCER
INTRORSELY
INTROSPECT
INTUBATION
INUNDATION
INURBANELY
INURBANITY
INVAGINATE
INVALIDATE
INVALIDING
INVALIDISH
INVALIDISM

INVALIDITY
INVALUABLE
INVALUABLY
INVARIABLE
INVARIABLY
INVARIANCE
INVENDIBLE
INVENTIBLE
INVENTRESS
INVERACITY
INVERTEDLY
INVESTMENT
INVETERACY
INVETERATE
INVIGILATE
INVIGORANT
INVIGORATE
INVINCIBLE
INVINCIBLY
INVIOLABLE
INVIOLABLY
INVIOLATED
INVITATION
INVITATORY
INVITEMENT
INVITINGLY
INVOCATION
INVOCATORY
INVOLUCRAL
INVOLUCRUM
INVOLUTION
INWARDNESS
IODOMETRIC
IONISATION
IONOSPHERE
IRACUNDITY
IREFULNESS
IRIDACEOUS
IRIDECTOMY
IRIDESCENT
IRIDOSMINE
IRISHWOMAN
IRON-GLANCE
IRON-HANDED
IRONICALLY
IRON-LIQUOR
IRON-MASTER
IRON-MINING
IRONMONGER
IRON-WITTED
IRON-WORDED
IRRADIANCE
IRRADIANCY
IRRADICATE
IRRATIONAL
IRREGULOUS
IRRELATION
IRRELATIVE
IRRELEVANT
IRRELIGION
IRREMEABLE
IRRENOWNED
IRRESOLUTE
IRREVERENT
IRRIGATION
IRRITATION

IRRITATIVE
ISABELLINE
ISCHURETIC
ISENTROPIC
ISHMAELITE
ISMAILITIC
ISOCHASMIC
ISOCHEIMAL
ISOCHEIMIC
ISOCHRONAL
ISODYNAMIC
ISOETACEAE
ISOGENETIC
ISOGLOSSAL
ISOGLOTTAL
ISOMETRICS
ISOMORPHIC
ISONIAZIDE
ISOPTEROUS
ISOSEISMAL
ISOSEISMIC
ISOSPOROUS
ISOTHERMAL
ISOTROPISM
ISOTROPOUS
ISRAELITIC
ITALIANATE
ITALIANISE
ITALIANISM
ITALIANIST
ITINERANCY
IVORY-BLACK
IVY-MANTLED

J

JACK-A-DANDY
JACKANAPES
JACK-PRIEST
JACK-RABBIT
JACK-RAFTER
JACOBINISE
JACOBINISM
JACOBITISM
JACULATION
JACULATORY
JAGGEDNESS
JAGUARONDI
JAGUARUNDI
JAMESONITE
JANITORIAL
JANIZARIAN
JANUS-FACED
JAPAN-EARTH
JAPANESERY
JAPANESQUE
JARDINIÈRE
JARGONELLE
JASPERWARE
JASPIDEOUS
JAUNTINESS
JAVELIN-MAN
JAW-BREAKER
JAW-TWISTER
JAYWALKING
JEHOVISTIC
JEISTIECOR

JEJUNENESS
JELLYGRAPH
JEOPARDISE
JEOPARDOUS
JERKED-MEAT
JERKINHEAD
JERRY-BUILT
JESUITICAL
JEW-BAITING
JEWEL-HOUSE
JEWISHNESS
JEW'S-MALLOW
JEW'S-MYRTLE
JIGGER-MAST
JIGGETY-JOG
JIMSON-WEED
JINGOISTIC
JINRICKSHA
JINRIKISHA
JOCKEYSHIP
JOCOSENESS
JOCULARITY
JOCUNDNESS
JOHNNY-CAKE
JOHNSONESE
JOHNSONIAN
JOHNSONISM
JOINT-STOCK
JOINT-STOOL
JOINTURESS
JOLTERHEAD
JOSTLEMENT
JOURNAL-BOX
JOURNALESE
JOURNALISE
JOURNALISM
JOURNALIST
JOURNEYING
JOURNEYMAN
JOVIALNESS
JOYFULNESS
JOYOUSNESS
JUBILANTLY
JUBILATION
JUDAICALLY
JUDICATION
JUDICATIVE
JUDICATORY
JUDICATURE
JUDICIALLY
JUGGERNAUT
JUGGLINGLY
JULY-FLOWER
JUMBLE-SALE
JUMBLINGLY
JUNCACEOUS
JUNK-BOTTLE
JUNK-DEALER
JURISTICAL
JURY-RIGGED
JURY-RUDDER
JUSTICIARY
JUSTIFYING
JUVENALIAN
JUVENILITY

K

KACK-HANDED
KAFFIR-BOOM
KAISERSHIP
KANTIANISM
KARMATHIAN
KARYOPLASM
KATABOLISM
KEEPERSHIP
KELTOMANIA
KEMPERY-MAN
KENNEL-COAL
KENNELLING
KENNEL-MAID
KENOTICIST
KENSINGTON
KENSPECKLE
KENTISH-MAN
KENTISH-RAG
KERATINISE
KERATINOUS
KERB-MARKET
KERB-TRADER
KERB-VENDOR
KERCHIEFED
KERSANTITE
KERSEYMERE
KERYGMATIC
KETTLEDRUM
KETTLE-PINS
KHEDIVIATE
KHIDMUTGAR
KHITMUTGAR
KIDNAPPING
KIDNEY-BEAN
KIESELGUHR
KILMARNOCK
KILOGRAMME
KIMBERLITE
KINCHIN-LAY
KINDLINESS
KIND-SPOKEN
KINEMATICS
KINESIPATH
KING-ARCHON
KING-AT-ARMS
KINGFISHER
KINGLIHOOD
KINGLINESS
KING-OF-ARMS
KING-SALMON
KING'S-CHAIR
KINGS-SPEAR
KIRN-DOLLIE
KITCHENDOM
KITCHEN-FEE
KITE-FLYING
KITTEN-MOTH
KITTLE-PINS
KLANGFARBE
KLENDUSITY
KNACKINESS
KNAGGINESS
KNAP-BOTTLE
KNAVE-BAIRN

KNEE-TIMBER
KNICK-KNACK
KNIFE-BOARD
KNIFE-MONEY
KNIGHTHOOD
KNIGHTLESS
KNOBBINESS
KNOBKERRIE
KNOCKABOUT
KNOCK-KNEED
KNOTTINESS
KNUCKLE-BOW
KOOKABURRA
KRIEGSPIEL
KUOMINTANG

L

LABORATORY
LABOURSOME
LACCOLITIC
LACE-PILLOW
LACERATION
LACERATIVE
LACERTILIA
LACHRYMARY
LACHRYMOSE
LACINIATED
LACKADAISY
LACK-LUSTRE
LACONICISM
LACQUERING
LACRIMATOR
LACRYMATOR
LACTESCENT
LACUSTRINE
LADY-CHAPEL
LADY-KILLER
LADY'S-SMOCK
LAEOTROPIC
LAGGEN-GIRD
LAKE-LAWYER
LAMARCKIAN
LAMARCKISM
LAMBDACISM
LAMBDOIDAL
LAMBREQUIN
LAMELLATED
LAMENTABLE
LAMENTABLY
LAMINARIAN
LAMINARISE
LAMINATION
LAMMAS-TIDE
LAMP-BURNER
LAMP-HOLDER
LAMPOONERY
LAMPOONIST
LANCEOLATE
LANDAMMANN
LAND-BREEZE
LAND-BRIDGE
LANDHOLDER
LAND-HUNGER
LANDING-NET
LAND-JOBBER
LAND-LOCKED

LAND-LOUPER
LANDLUBBER
LANDOWNING
LAND-PIRATE
LAND-SPRING
LANDSTHING
LAND-WAITER
LANGUISHED
LANGUISHER
LANGUOROUS
LANIFEROUS
LANIGEROUS
LANSQUENET
LANTERNIST
LANUGINOSE
LANUGINOUS
LANZKNECHT
LAPAROTOMY
LAPIDARIAN
LAPIDARIST
LAPIDATION
LAPIDIFIED
LAP-JOINTED
LAPLANDISH
LAPPER-MILK
LAPPET-HEAD
LARDACEOUS
LARK-HEELED
LARVICIDAL
LARYNGITIC
LARYNGITIS
LASCIVIOUS
LATERALITY
LATESCENCE
LATIFUNDIA
LATITATION
LATTER-BORN
LATTERMATH
LATTER-MINT
LATTERMOST
LAUGHINGLY
LAUNCEGAYE
LAUNDROMAT
LAUNDRY-MAN
LAURACEOUS
LAURDALITE
LAUREATION
LAURENTIAN
LAURUSTINE
LAURVIKITE
LAVALLIÈRE
LAVATORIAL
LAVISHMENT
LAVISHNESS
LAW-ABIDING
LAW-BREAKER
LAW-BURROWS
LAWFULNESS
LAWN-TENNIS
LAW-OFFICER
LAWRENCIUM
LEAD-ARMING
LEADENNESS
LEADERETTE
LEADERSHIP
LEAD-GLANCE

LEAD-PENCIL
LEAF-BRIDGE
LEAF-CUTTER
LEAF-HOPPER
LEAF-INSECT
LEAF-MOSAIC
LEAF-SHEATH
LEAN-WITTED
LEASTAWAYS
LEATHERING
LEBENSRAUM
LECTIONARY
LECTORSHIP
LEDERHOSEN
LEDGER-BAIT
LEDGER-LINE
LEECHCRAFT
LEFT-FOOTED
LEFT-HANDED
LEFT-HANDER
LEFTWARDLY
LEGATESHIP
LEGIBILITY
LEGISLATOR
LEGITIMACY
LEGITIMATE
LEGITIMISE
LEGITIMIST
LEG-PULLING
LEGUMINOUS
LEIBNIZIAN
LEIOTRICHY
LEISHMANIA
LEISURABLE
LEISURABLY
LEMNISCATE
LEMON-GRASS
LEMUROIDEA
LENGTHWAYS
LENGTHWISE
LENOCINIUM
LENTAMENTE
LENTICULAR
LENTIGINES
LEONTIASIS
LEOPARD-CAT
LEOPARDESS
LEPIDOLITE
LEPRECHAUN
LEPRECHAWN
LEPROSERIE
LEPTOSPIRA
LESBIANISM
LETHARGIED
LETHARGISE
LETTER-BOOK
LETTER-CARD
LETTER-CLIP
LETTER-FILE
LETTERHEAD
LETTERLESS
LETTER-WOOD
LEUCHAEMIA
LEUCOCYTIC
LEUCOPLAST
LEVER-WATCH

LEVIGATION
LEVIRATION
LEVITATION
LEXICOLOGY
LEXIGRAPHY
LEY-FARMING
LHERZOLITE
LIBERALISE
LIBERALISM
LIBERALIST
LIBERALITY
LIBERATION
LIBERATORY
LIBERTY-MAN
LIBIDINIST
LIBIDINOUS
LIBRETTIST
LICENSABLE
LICENTIATE
LICENTIOUS
LIEUTENANT
LIFE-ESTATE
LIFE-GIVING
LIFE-JACKET
LIFELESSLY
LIFE-MORTAR
LIFE-RENTER
LIFE-ROCKET
LIFE-SAVING
LIFE-SCHOOL
LIFE-TENANT
LIGAMENTAL
LIGHT-ARMED
LIGHTENING
LIGHTERAGE
LIGHTERMAN
LIGHT-FACED
LIGHT-HORSE
LIGHTHOUSE
LIGHTING-UP
LIGHT-O'-LOVE
LIGHT-ORGAN
LIGHTPROOF
LIGHT-TIGHT
LIGHT-TOWER
LIGNIFYING
LIGNOCAINE
LIKELIHOOD
LIKELINESS
LILIACEOUS
LIMACIFORM
LIMBER-NECK
LIMB-GIRDLE
LIMBURGITE
LIME-BURNER
LIMICOLOUS
LIMITARIAN
LIMITATION
LIMITATIVE
LIMITROPHE
LIMNAEIDAE
LINE-FISHER
LINE-SQUALL
LINGUIFORM
LINGUISTER
LINGUISTIC

LINGUISTRY
LINGULELLA
LINK-MOTION
LINSEED-OIL
LION-HUNTER
LIPIZZANER
LIPOCHROME
LIPOGRAPHY
LIPOMATOUS
LIPPIZANER
LIPPIZZANA
LIP-READING
LIP-SERVICE
LIQUEFYING
LIQUESCENT
LIQUIDATOR
LIQUIDNESS
LISSOMNESS
LISTENER-IN
LISTLESSLY
LITANY-DESK
LITERALISE
LITERALISM
LITERALIST
LITERALITY
LITERARILY
LITERATURE
LITEROSITY
LITHISTIDA
LITHOCLAST
LITHODOMUS
LITHOGLYPH
LITHOGRAPH
LITHOLATRY
LITHOLOGIC
LITHOMANCY
LITHOMARGE
LITHOPHANE
LITHOPHYSA
LITHOPHYSE
LITHOPHYTE
LITHOTOMIC
LITHOTRITE
LITHOTRITY
LITIGATION
LITTER-LOUT
LITTLE-EASE
LITTLENESS
LITURGICAL
LIVELIHEAD
LIVELIHOOD
LIVELINESS
LIVER-FLUKE
LIVER-GROWN
LIVE-WEIGHT
LIVING-ROOM
LOAN-OFFICE
LOATHINGLY
LOBE-FOOTED
LOBSTER-POT
LOBULATION
LOCK-KEEPER
LOCKSTITCH
LOCOMOBILE
LOCOMOTION
LOCOMOTIVE

LOCOMOTORY
LOCULAMENT
LOCUST-BEAN
LOCUSTIDAE
LOCUST-TREE
LOGANBERRY
LOGAN-STONE
LOGGERHEAD
LOGICALITY
LOGISTICAL
LOGOGRAPHY
LOGORRHOEA
LOG-ROLLING
LOLLARDISM
LOLL-SHRAUB
LONESOMELY
LONGAEVOUS
LONG-HAIRED
LONG-HEADED
LONG-LEGGED
LONGPRIMER
LONG-STAPLE
LONG-WINDED
LOOKING-FOR
LOOSE-COVER
LOQUACIOUS
LORDLINESS
LORDOLATRY
LORICATION
LOSS-LEADER
LOUD-LUNGED
LOUD-VOICED
LOUIS-SEIZE
LOUNDERING
LOUNGE-SUIT
LOUNGINGLY
LOUPING-ILL
LOUVERDOOR
LOUVRE-DOOR
LOVE-AFFAIR
LOVE-BROKER
LOVE-FAVOUR
LOVE-LETTER
LOVELIHEAD
LOVELINESS
LOVE-MAKING
LOVEMONGER
LOVE-POTION
LOVER'S-KNOT
LOVEWORTHY
LOVINGNESS
LOW-COUNTRY
LOWER-CLASS
LOWERINGLY
LOW-PITCHED
LOXODROMIC
LUBRICATOR
LUBRICIOUS
LUCIFERASE
LUCIFERIAN
LUCIFEROUS
LUCIFUGOUS
LUCKLESSLY
LUCKY-PIECE
LUCUBRATOR
LUCULENTLY

LUFFING-JIB
LUGGAGE-VAN
LUGUBRIOUS
LUKEWARMLY
LUKEWARMTH
LUMBANG-OIL
LUMBER-CAMP
LUMBER-JACK
LUMBER-MILL
LUMBER-ROOM
LUMBERSOME
LUMBER-YARD
LUMBRICOID
LUMINARISM
LUMINARIST
LUMINATION
LUMINOSITY
LUMINOUSLY
LUMPSUCKER
LUPERCALIA
LUSCIOUSLY
LUSITANIAN
LUST-DIETED
LUSTRATION
LUSTRELESS
LUSTROUSLY
LUTESTRING
LUXURIANCE
LUXURIANCY
LYCAENIDAE
LYCHNAPSIA
LYCOPODIUM
LYMPHOCYTE
LYOPHILISE
LYSENKOISM
LYSIGENOUS
LYTHRACEAE

M
MABINOGION
MACADAMISE
MACARONIES
MACCABAEAN
MACE-BEARER
MACERATION
MACHINATOR
MACHINE-GUN
MACHINEMAN
MACKINTOSH
MACONOCHIE
MACROBIOTA
MACROBIOTE
MACROPRISM
MACROSPORE
MACULATION
MACULATURE
MAD-BRAINED
MADDER-LAKE
MADELENIAN
MADONNAISH
MADREPORIC
MAFFICKING
MAGELLANIC
MAGISTRACY
MAGISTRAND
MAGISTRATE

MAGNETICAL	MANDINGOES	MARSHALLED	MEANDERING
MAGNETISER	MANDRAGORA	MARSHALLER	MEANINGFUL
MAGNIFICAL	MANDUCABLE	MARSHALSEA	MEASLINESS
MAGNIFICAT	MAN-ENTERED	MARSH-FEVER	MEASURABLE
MAGNIFYING	MANFULNESS	MARSHINESS	MEASURABLY
MAHOMMEDAN	MANGABEIRA	MARSHLOCKS	MEASUREDLY
MAIDENHAIR	MANGOSTEEN	MARTELLATO	MEAT-MARKET
MAIDENHEAD	MANIACALLY	MARTIALISM	MEATSCREEN
MAIDENHOOD	MANICHAEAN	MARTIALIST	MECHANICAL
MAIDENLIKE	MANICHEISM	MARTINGALE	MECONOPSIS
MAIDEN-MEEK	MANICURIST	MARVELLING	MEDDLESOME
MAIDENWEED	MANIFESTLY	MARVELLOUS	MEDIATRESS
MAIMEDNESS	MANIFOLDER	MARXIANISM	MEDICAMENT
MAIN-COURSE	MANIFOLDLY	MASHING-TUB	MEDICASTER
MAINLANDER	MANIPULATE	MASKED-BALL	MEDICATION
MAINLINING	MANNA-CROUP	MASQUERADE	MEDICATIVE
MAINPERNOR	MANNA-GRASS	MASSORETIC	MEDIEVALLY
MAINSPRING	MANNA-LARCH	MASS-PRIEST	MEDIOCRITY
MAINSTREAM	MANOEUVRER	MASTECTOMY	MEDITATION
MAINTAINER	MANOMETRIC	MASTER-CARD	MEDITATIVE
MAISONETTE	MANOR-HOUSE	MASTER-HAND	MEDUSIFORM
MAJESTICAL	MAN-QUELLER	MASTERHOOD	MEERSCHAUM
MAKE-BELIEF	MAN-SERVANT	MASTERLESS	MEGALITHIC
MAKE-WEIGHT	MAN-STEALER	MASTER-MIND	MEGALOSAUR
MALABAR-RAT	MANSUETUDE	MASTERSHIP	MEGANEWTON
MALACOLOGY	MANTELTREE	MASTER-WORK	MEGASCOPIC
MALADAPTED	MANUMITTED	MASTERWORT	MELACONITE
MALADDRESS	MANUSCRIPT	MASTICABLE	MELANAEMIA
MALAGUETTA	MANY-FOLDED	MASTICATOR	MELANCHOLY
MALAPERTLY	MANY-HEADED	MASTURBATE	MELANESIAN
MALAPROPOS	MANZANILLA	MATCHBOARD	MELANISTIC
MALAXATION	MAP-MOUNTER	MATCH-JOINT	MELANUTRIA
MALCONTENT	MAP-READING	MATCHMAKER	MELIACEOUS
MALEDICENT	MAQUILLAGE	MATCH-POINT	MELIC-GRASS
MALEFACTOR	MARASCHINO	MATELLASSE	MELICOTTON
MALEFICENT	MARATHONER	MATERIALLY	MELIORATOR
MALEFICIAL	MARCANTANT	MATERNALLY	MELISMATIC
MALEVOLENT	MARCESCENT	MATHEMATIC	MELLOWNESS
MALFEASANT	MARCGRAVIA	MATRIARCHY	MELOCOTOON
MALIGNANCE	MARCHANTIA	MATRICIDAL	MELOMANIAC
MALIGNANCY	MARCH-STONE	MATRICULAR	MELTING-POT
MALIGNMENT	MARCIONIST	MATRILOCAL	MEMBERSHIP
MALINGERER	MARCIONITE	MATROCLINY	MEMBRANOUS
MALLEATION	MARGARITIC	MATRONHOOD	MEMORANDUM
MALLEE-BIRD	MARGINALIA	MATRON-LIKE	MEMORATIVE
MALLEE-FOWL	MARGINALLY	MATRONSHIP	MENACINGLY
MALLEIFORM	MARGINATED	MATRONYMIC	MENDACIOUS
MALLOPHAGA	MARGRAVATE	MATTERLESS	MENDICANCY
MALODOROUS	MARGRAVINE	MATURATION	MENINGIOMA
MALPIGHIAN	MARGUERITE	MATURATIVE	MENINGITIS
MALPOSITON	MARIOLATER	MATURENESS	MENSTRUATE
MALTHUSIAN	MARIOLATRY	MAUDLINISM	MENSTRUOUS
MALVACEOUS	MARIONETTE	MAUNDERING	MENSURABLE
MAMILLATED	MARKER-BOMB	MAVOURNEEN	MEPHITICAL
MAMMOGENIC	MARKER-FLAG	MAXILLIPED	MERCANTILE
MAMMY-WAGON	MARKETABLE	MAXILLULAE	MERCAPTIDE
MANAGEABLE	MARKET-BELL	MAXIMALIST	MERCERISER
MANAGEABLY	MARKET-HALL	MAY-BLOSSOM	MERCHANTRY
MANAGEMENT	MARKET-TOWN	MAY-MORNING	MERCIFULLY
MANAGERESS	MARKING-INK	MAYOLOGIST	MERIDIONAL
MANAGERIAL	MARKING-NUT	MAYONNAISE	MERRYMAKER
MANCHESTER	MARKSWOMAN	MAZARINADE	MERRY-NIGHT
MANCHINEEL	MARMAROSIS	McCARTHYISM	MESENTERIC
MANCHURIAN	MARQUISATE	MEADOW-LARK	MESENTERON
MANDAMUSES	MARROW-BONE	MEAGRENESS	MESMERICAL
MANDIBULAR	MARROWLESS	MEAL-MONGER	MESMERISER

MESOLITHIC
MESOMERISM
MESOMORPHY
MESOPHYTIC
MESOSCAPHE
MESOTHORAX
MESSAGE-BOY
MESSIANISM
MESSIANIST
METABOLISE
METABOLISM
METABOLITE
METACARPAL
METACARPUS
METACENTRE
METAGALAXY
METALEPSIS
METALEPTIC
METALLURGY
METAMERISM
METAPHORIC
METAPHRASE
METAPHRAST
METAPHYSIC
METAPLASIA
METAPLASIS
METASTABLE
METASTASES
METASTASIS
METASTATIC
METATARSAL
METATARSUS
METATHERIA
METATHESES
METATHESIS
METATHETIC
METATHORAX
METAZOICAL
METEORITAL
METEORITIC
METHEDRINE
METHINKETH
METHODICAL
METHOMANIA
METHUSELAH
METICULOUS
METRICALLY
METROMANIA
METRONOMIC
METRONYMIC
METROPOLIS
METROSTYLE
METTLESOME
MEZZO-FORTE
MEZZOTINTO
MIAROLITIC
MIASMATOUS
MICA-SCHIST
MICHAELMAS
MICROBIOTA
MICROCLINE
MICROCOCCI
MICROFARAD
MICROFICHE
MICROGRAPH
MICROHENRY

MICROLITIC
MICROLOGIC
MICROMETER
MICROMETRY
MICROPHONE
MICROPHYTE
MICROPYLAR
MICROSCOPE
MICROSCOPY
MICROSEISM
MICROSPORE
MICROTOMIC
MIDDEN-COCK
MIDDLE-AGED
MIDDLEBROW
MIDDLEMOST
MIDSHIPMAN
MIGHTINESS
MIGNONETTE
MILD-SPOKEN
MILE-CASTLE
MILITANTLY
MILITARISE
MILITARISM
MILITARIST
MILITIAMAN
MILLEFIORI
MILLENNIAL
MILLENNIUM
MILLESIMAL
MILLET-SEED
MILLIONARY
MILLOCRACY
MILL-STREAM
MILLWRIGHT
MIMEOGRAPH
MIMOGRAPHY
MIMOSACEAE
MINAUDERIE
MINDEDNESS
MINDERERUS
MIND-HEALER
MINDLESSLY
MINERALISE
MINERALIST
MINERALOGY
MINESTRONE
MINE-WORKER
MINGLEMENT
MINGLINGLY
MINI-BUFFET
MINIMALIST
MINIMISING
MINI-ROCKET
MINISTRANT
MINISTRESS
MINSTRELSY
MINT-MASTER
MINUSCULAR
MINUTE-BELL
MINUTE-BOOK
MINUTE-DROP
MINUTE-HAND
MINUTE-JACK
MINUTENESS
MIRACULOUS

MIRRORWISE
MIRTHFULLY
MISADVISED
MISARRANGE
MISBEHAVED
MISBELIEVE
MISCELLANY
MISCHANTER
MISCHMETAL
MISCOMPUTE
MISCONCEIT
MISCONDUCT
MISCONTENT
MISCORRECT
MISCOUNSEL
MISCREANCE
MISCREATED
MISCREATOR
MISDEEMFUL
MISDEEMING
MISDRAWING
MISENTREAT
MISERICORD
MISFEATURE
MISFORTUNE
MISHGUGGLE
MISHNAYOTH
MISIMPROVE
MISJOINDER
MISLEADING
MISMANNERS
MISMEASURE
MISOBSERVE
MISOCAPNIC
MISOGAMIST
MISOGYNIST
MISOGYNOUS
MISOLOGIST
MISPRISION
MISREADING
MISSEEMING
MISSEL-BIRD
MISSEL-TREE
MISSIONARY
MISSIONISE
MISSPELLED
MISTAKABLE
MISTAKENLY
MIST-FLOWER
MISTHOUGHT
MISTRAYNED
MISTRESSLY
MISTRYSTED
MISVENTURE
MISWANDRED
MISWORDING
MISWORSHIP
MITHRIDATE
MITIGATION
MITIGATIVE
MITIGATORY
MITRE-JOINT
MITRE-SHELL
MITRE-WHEEL
MITTEN-CRAB
MIXED-MEDIA

MIXOLYDIAN
MIXTY-MAXTY
MIZZEN-MAST
MIZZEN-SAIL
MNEMONICAL
MOBOCRATIC
MOCK-HEROIC
MOCK-MODEST
MOCK-ORANGE
MOCK-PRIVET
MODALISTIC
MODERATELY
MODERATION
MODERATISM
MODERATRIX
MODERNISER
MODERNNESS
MODIFIABLE
MODISHNESS
MODULATION
MOHAMMEDAN
MOISTURISE
MOLENDINAR
MOLIMINOUS
MOLLIFYING
MOLLITIOUS
MOLLUSCOID
MOLLUSCOUS
MOLYBDENUM
MOLYBDOSIS
MONACTINAL
MONADIFORM
MONADOLOGY
MONANDROUS
MONARCHIAL
MONARCHIAN
MONARCHISE
MONARCHISM
MONARCHIST
MONASTICAL
MONAXONIDA
MONEY-BOUND
MONEY-MAKER
MONEY-ORDER
MONEY-TAKER
MONGRELISE
MONGRELISM
MONILIASIS
MONILIFORM
MONISTICAL
MONITORIAL
MONKEY-BOAT
MONKEY-GAFF
MONKEY-PUMP
MONKEY-RAIL
MONKEY-ROPE
MONKEY-SUIT
MONKEY-TAIL
MONOCARPIC
MONOCEROUS
MONOCHASIA
MONOCHROIC
MONOCHROME
MONOCHROMY
MONOCLINAL
MONOCLINIC

MONOCRATIC
MONOCULOUS
MONOCYCLIC
MONOECIOUS
MONOGAMIST
MONOGAMOUS
MONOGENISM
MONOGENIST
MONOGENOUS
MONOGRAPHY
MONOGYNIAN
MONOGYNOUS
MONOHYBRID
MONOHYDRIC
MONOLITHIC
MONOLOGISE
MONOLOGIST
MONOMACHIA
MONOMANIAC
MONOPHASIC
MONOPHOBIA
MONOPLEGIA
MONOPODIAL
MONOPODIUM
MONOPOLISE
MONOPOLIST
MONOPTERAL
MONOPTERON
MONOPTEROS
MONORCHISM
MONORHINAL
MONORHYMED
MONOSODIUM
MONOSTYLAR
MONOTHECAL
MONOTHEISM
MONOTHEIST
MONOTOCOUS
MONOTONOUS
MONOVALENT
MONOXYLOUS
MONSIGNORE
MONSIGNORI
MONSIGNORS
MONSTRANCE
MONTAGNARD
MONTBRETIA
MONTERO-CAP
MONTICULUS
MONUMENTAL
MOON-FLOWER
MOON-RAISED
MOONRAKING
MOONSHINER
MOONSTRIKE
MOONSTRUCK
MOPISHNESS
MORALISTIC
MORATORIUM
MORBIDEZZA
MORBIDNESS
MORBILLOUS
MORDACIOUS
MORGANATIC
MORIGERATE
MORIGEROUS

MORISONIAN
MOROSENESS
MORPHEMICS
MORPHINISM
MORPHOGENY
MORPHOLOGY
MORRIS-PIKE
MORRIS-TUBE
MORTIFYING
MOSAICALLY
MOSASAUROS
MOSQUITOES
MOSSBUNKER
MOSS-LITTER
MOTHER-CELL
MOTHER-CITY
MOTHERHOOD
MOTHERLAND
MOTHERLESS
MOTHER-SHIP
MOTHER-SPOT
MOTHERWORT
MOTH-FLOWER
MOTH-HUNTER
MOTIONLESS
MOTIVATION
MOTIVELESS
MOTOR-COACH
MOTOR-CYCLE
MOTOR-LORRY
MOUCHARABY
MOUDIEWART
MOUDIEWORT
MOULD-BOARD
MOULDINESS
MOUNTAINED
MOUNTEBANK
MOURNFULLY
MOURNINGLY
MOUSE-PIECE
MOUSE-SIGHT
MOUSSELINE
MOUSTACHED
MOUSTERIAN
MOUTH-ORGAN
MOUTHPIECE
MOVABILITY
MOVELESSLY
MOWDIEWART
MOWDIEWORT
MOZZARELLA
MUCEDINOUS
MUCIFEROUS
MUCK-MIDDEN
MUCK-RAKING
MUCORINEAE
MUCRONATED
MUDDLEHEAD
MUD-SKIPPER
MUD-SLINGER
MUD-VOLCANO
MUFFIN-BELL
MUHAMMADAN
MUHAMMEDAN
MULATTRESS
MULIEBRITY

MULISHNESS
MULLIGRUBS
MULTICYCLE
MULTIFACED
MULTILOBED
MULTILOQUY
MULTIMEDIA
MULTIPLANE
MULTIPLIED
MULTIPLIER
MULTIPOLAR
MULTISTAGE
MULTISTORY
MULTIVIOUS
MULTIVOCAL
MUMBLEMENT
MUMBLE-NEWS
MUMBLINGLY
MUMBO-JUMBO
MUMMIFYING
MUMMY-CLOTH
MUMMY-WHEAT
MUMPING-DAY
MUNIFICENT
MUNIFIENCE
MURAENIDAE
MUSCARDINE
MUSCOVITIC
MUSCULARLY
MUSHROOMER
MUSICALITY
MUSIC-DRAMA
MUSIC-FOLIO
MUSIC-HOUSE
MUSICIANER
MUSICIANLY
MUSICOLOGY
MUSIC-PAPER
MUSIC-SHELL
MUSIC-STAND
MUSIC-STOOL
MUSK-BEETLE
MUSKET-REST
MUSKET-SHOT
MUSK-MALLOW
MUSLIN-KALE
MUSQUETOON
MUSSEL-PLUM
MUSSULMANS
MUSTARD-GAS
MUSTARD-OIL
MUSTELIDAE
MUSTELINAE
MUSTER-BOOK
MUSTER-FILE
MUSTER-ROLL
MUTABILITY
MUTESSARIF
MUTILATION
MUTINOUSLY
MUTTON-BIRD
MUTTON-CHOP
MUTTON-FIST
MUTTON-HEAD
MUTTON-SUET
MYCETOLOGY

MYCETOZOAN
MYCOLOGIST
MYCOPLASMA
MYCORHIZAL
MYCORRHIZA
MYLONITISE
MYOBLASTIC
MYOCARDIUM
MYOGRAPHIC
MYOLOGICAL
MYRIADFOLD
MYRICACEAE
MYRINGITIS
MYRIOSCOPE
MYRTACEOUS
MYSOPHOBIA
MYSTAGOGIC
MYSTAGOGUE
MYSTAGOGUS
MYSTERIOUS
MYSTERY-MAN
MYSTICALLY
MYSTIFYING
MYTHICALLY
MYTHICISER
MYTHOLOGER
MYTHOLOGIC
MYTHOMANIA
MYTHOPOEIC
MYTILIFORM
MYXOMATOUS
MYXOMYCETE

N

NABATHAEAN
NACHSCHLAG
NAIADACEAE
NAIL-HEADED
NAMBY-PAMBY
NAMELESSLY
NAMEWORTHY
NANISATION
NANOSECOND
NAPHTHALIC
NAPKINRING
NAPOLEONIC
NARCISSISM
NARCISSIST
NARCOLEPSY
NARRATABLE
NARROWNESS
NASTURTIUM
NATALITIAL
NATATORIAL
NATATORIUM
NATHELESSE
NATIONALLY
NATIONHOOD
NATIONLESS
NATIVE-BORN
NATIVENESS
NATIVISTIC
NATTERJACK
NATURALISE
NATURALISM
NATURALIST

NATURE-CURE
NATURE-MYTH
NATURISTIC
NATUROPATH
NAUSEATING
NAUSEATIVE
NAUSEOUSLY
NAUTICALLY
NAUTILUSES
NAVIGATION
NAZARITISM
NEAPOLITAN
NEAR-BEGAUN
NEAR-LEGGED
NEAT-CATTLE
NEAT-HANDED
NEBULOSITY
NEBULOUSLY
NECESSAIRE
NECROLATER
NECROLATRY
NECROLOGIC
NECROMANCY
NECROPHILE
NECROPHILY
NECROPOLIS
NECROSCOPY
NECTAREOUS
NECTOCALYX
NEEDLE-BATH
NEEDLE-CASE
NEEDLECORD
NEEDLE-FISH
NEEDLESSLY
NEEDLEWORK
NE'ER-DO-WEEL
NE'ER-DO-WELL
NEGATIVELY
NEGATIVISM
NEGATIVITY
NEGATONIST
NEGLECTFUL
NEGLECTION
NEGLECTIVE
NEGLIGENCE
NEGLIGIBLE
NEGLIGIBLY
NEGOTIABLE
NEGOTIATOR
NEGROPHILE
NEGROPHOBE
NEMATOCYST
NEMATOIDEA
NEMERTINEA
NEOCLASSIC
NEO-KANTIAN
NEOLOGICAL
NEOPLASTIC
NEOTERICAL
NEPENTHEAN
NEPHOGRAPH
NEPHOLOGIC
NEPHOSCOPE
NEPHRALGIA
NEPHRIDIUM
NEPHROLOGY

NEPHROPEXY
NEPHROTOMY
NERO-ANTICO
NERVE-FIBRE
NESTING-BOX
NET-FISHERY
NET-FISHING
NETHERMORE
NETHERMOST
NETHERWARD
NETTLE-CELL
NETTLE-FISH
NETTLE-RASH
NETTLE-TREE
NEURILEMMA
NEUROLEMMA
NEUROLYSIS
NEUROPATHY
NEUROPLASM
NEUROPTERA
NEUROTOXIN
NEUTRALISE
NEUTRALISM
NEUTRALIST
NEUTRALITY
NEVER-NEVER
NEWFANGLED
NEW-FLEDGED
NEW-MARRIED
NEWSCASTER
NEWSDEALER
NEWSLETTER
NEWSMONGER
NEWSREADER
NEWSVENDOR
NEWSWORTHY
NEWSWRITER
NIBBLINGLY
NIBELUNGEN
NICKELLING
NICKNACKET
NICKUMPOOP
NICOTINISM
NICROSILAL
NIDAMENTAL
NIDAMENTUM
NIDDERLING
NIDICOLOUS
NIDIFICATE
NIDIFUGOUS
NIDULATION
NIFFY-NAFFY
NIGER-SEEDS
NIGGARDISE
NIGGERHEAD
NIGGERLING
NIGHT-CHAIR
NIGHT-CHURR
NIGHT-CLOUD
NIGHTDRESS
NIGHT-GLASS
NIGHT-HERON
NIGHT-HOUSE
NIGHT-LATCH
NIGHT-LIGHT
NIGHT-PALSY

NIGHTPIECE
NIGHT-RAVEN
NIGHT-RIDER
NIGHTSHADE
NIGHTSHIFT
NIGHTSHIRT
NIGHT-SIGHT
NIGHT-SPELL
NIGHT-STEED
NIGHT-STICK
NIGHT-STOOL
NIGHT-TAPER
NIGHT-WATCH
NIGRESCENT
NIGROMANCY
NIHILISTIC
NIMBLENESS
NINCOMPOOP
NINETEENTH
NIPPLEWORT
NITRIFYING
NITRO-GROUP
NITROMETER
NOBILITATE
NOBLEWOMAN
NODULATION
NOEMATICAL
NOETIANISM
NO-MAN'S-LAND
NOMINALISM
NOMINALIST
NOMINATELY
NOMINATION
NOMINATIVE
NOMOGRAPHY
NOMOLOGIST
NOMOTHETES
NOMOTHETIC
NON-ABILITY
NON-ALIGNED
NON-ARRIVAL
NONCHALANT
NON-CONTENT
NON-FERROUS
NON-FICTION
NON-GREMIAL
NON-JOINDER
NON-NATURAL
NON-PAYMENT
NON-PLAYING
NONPLUSSED
NON-SMOKING
NON-SOCIETY
NON-STARTER
NON-UTILITY
NON-VIOLENT
NOOGENESIS
NORBERTINE
NORTH-BOUND
NORTHERNER
NORTHWARDS
NOSOCOMIAL
NOSOGRAPHY
NOSOLOGIST
NOSOPHOBIA
NOSTOLOGIC

NOSTOMANIA
NOSTOPATHY
NOTABILITY
NOTARIALLY
NOTCH-BOARD
NOTE-SHAVER
NOTEWORTHY
NOTHINGISM
NOTICEABLE
NOTICEABLY
NOTIFIABLE
NOTIONALLY
NOTODONTID
NOTONECTAL
NOTORYCTES
NOURICE-FEE
NOURISHING
NOURRITURE
NOVACULITE
NOVELISTIC
NOVICEHOOD
NOVICESHIP
NUBIFEROUS
NUBIGENOUS
NUCIFEROUS
NUCIVOROUS
NUCLEATION
NUCLEOLATE
NUCLEONICS
NUDIBRANCH
NULLA-NULLA
NULLIFYING
NUMBERLESS
NUMERATION
NUMEROLOGY
NUMEROSITY
NUMEROUSLY
NUMISMATIC
NUMMULATED
NUMMULITIC
NUMSKULLED
NUNCIATURE
NUN'S-FIDDLE
NUPTIALITY
NURSE-CHILD
NURSEHOUND
NURSERYMAN
NUTATIONAL
NUTCRACKER
NUTRITIOUS
NYCTALOPES
NYCTALOPIA
NYCTALOPIC
NYCTINASTY
NYMPHOLEPT
NYSTAGMOID

O

OAK-LEATHER
OBDURATELY
OBDURATION
OBEDIENTLY
OBELISCOID
OBFUSCATED
OBITUARIST
OBJECT-BALL

OBJECTLESS
OBJECT-SOUL
OBJURATION
OBLATENESS
OBLIGATION
OBLIGATORY
OBLIGEMENT
OBLIGINGLY
OBLITERATE
OBNUBILATE
OBSEQUIOUS
OBSERVABLE
OBSERVABLY
OBSERVANCE
OBSERVANCY
OBSERVATOR
OBSIDIONAL
OBSOLETELY
OBSOLETION
OBSOLETISM
OBSTETRICS
OBSTRUCTER
OBSTRUCTOR
OBTAINABLE
OBTAINMENT
OBTRUNCATE
OBTURATION
OBTUSENESS
OCCASIONAL
OCCASIONER
OCCIDENTAL
OCCULTNESS
OCCUPATION
OCCUPATIVE
OCCURRENCE
OCEANARIUM
OCEAN-BASIN
OCEANOLOGY
OCELLATION
OCHLOCRACY
OCHRACEOUS
OCTAHEDRAL
OCTAHEDRON
OCTAMEROUS
OCTANDRIAN
OCTANDROUS
OCTANGULAR
OCTAPLOIDY
OCTODECIMO
OCTOGENARY
OCTOGYNOUS
OCTOHEDRON
OCTONARIAN
OCTOPLOIDY
OCTOPODOUS
ODD-LOOKING
ODIOUSNESS
ODONTALGIA
ODONTALGIC
ODONTOCETE
ODONTOGENY
ODONTOLITE
ODONTOLOGY
OECUMENISM
OEDEMATOSE
OEDEMATOUS

OENOLOGIST
OESOPHAGUS
OFFENDRESS
OFFICE-GIRL
OFFICIALLY
OFFICIALTY
OFFICIATOR
OFF-LICENCE
OFFPUTTING
OFTENTIMES
OIREACHTAS
OLDE-WORLDE
OLD-FOGYISH
OLD-MAIDISH
OLD-MAIDISM
OLEAGINOUS
OLEIFEROUS
OLEOGRAPHY
OLERACEOUS
OLFACTIBLE
OLIGARCHAL
OLIGARCHIC
OLIGOCLASE
OLIGOPSONY
OLIVACEOUS
OLIVE-SHELL
OMBROMETER
OMBROPHILE
OMBROPHOBE
OMMATIDIUM
OMNIFEROUS
OMNIGENOUS
OMNIPARITY
OMNIPAROUS
OMNIPOTENT
OMNISCIENT
OMNIVOROUS
OMOPHAGOUS
OMOPHORION
ONAGRACEAE
ONEIROLOGY
ONE-SIDEDLY
ONIRODYNIA
ONIROMANCY
ONIROSCOPY
ONOCENTAUR
ONOMASTICS
ONTOLOGIST
ONYCHOPAGY
ONYCHOPORA
ONYX-MARBLE
OOPHORITIS
OPALESCENT
OPAQUENESS
OPEN-HANDED
OPEN-HEARTH
OPEN-MINDED
OPEN-SESAME
OPEN-STITCH
OPERA-CLOAK
OPERA-GLASS
OPERA-HOUSE
OPERATIONS
OPERCULATE
OPERETTIST
OPHICLEIDE

OPHIOLATER
OPHIOLATRY
OPHIOLOGIC
OPHIOMORPH
OPHTHALMIA
OPHTHALMIC
OPINIONIST
OPISOMETER
OPIUM-EATER
OPOTHERAPY
OPPILATION
OPPILATIVE
OPPOSELESS
OPPOSITELY
OPPOSITION
OPPOSITIVE
OPPRESSION
OPPRESSIVE
OPPROBRIUM
OPPUGNANCY
OPSIOMETER
OPSOMANIAC
OPTATIVELY
OPTIMALISE
OPTIMISTIC
OPTIONALLY
OPTOLOGIST
ORACULARLY
ORANGE-LILY
ORANGE-PEEL
ORANGE-ROOT
ORANGE-TREE
ORANGE-WIFE
ORANGE-WOOD
ORATORICAL
ORCHARDING
ORCHARDIST
ORCHARD-MAN
ORCHESTICS
ORCHESTRAL
ORCHESTRIC
ORCHIDEOUS
ORDAINABLE
ORDAINMENT
ORDINARILY
ORDINATELY
ORDINATION
ORDONNANCE
ORDOVICIAN
OREOGRAPHY
OREOLOGIST
ORE-WROUGHT
ORGANICISM
ORGANICIST
ORGANISMAL
ORGANOGENY
ORGANOGRAM
ORGAN-POINT
ORIENTALLY
ORIENTATED
ORIENTATOR
ORIGINALLY
ORIGINATOR
ORNAMENTAL
ORNAMENTER
ORNATENESS

ORNITHOSIS
OROGENESIS
OROGENETIC
OROGRAPHIC
OROLOGICAL
OROTUNDITY
ORPHANHOOD
ORPHEOREON
ORTHOBORIC
ORTHOCAINE
ORTHOCERAS
ORTHOCLASE
ORTHODROMY
ORTHOEPIST
ORTHOGENIC
ORTHOGONAL
ORTHOGRAPH
ORTHOPAEDY
ORTHOPEDIA
ORTHOPEDIC
ORTHOPHYRE
ORTHOPNOEA
ORTHOPRISM
ORTHOPTERA
ORTHOPTICS
ORTHOPTIST
ORTHOTONIC
ORTHOTROPY
ORYCTOLOGY
OSCILLATOR
OSCITANTLY
OSCITATION
OSCULATION
OSCULATORY
OSMETERIUM
OSMIDROSIS
OSMIRIDIUM
OSSIFEROUS
OSSIVOROUS
OSTENSIBLE
OSTENSIBLY
OSTEOBLAST
OSTEOCLAST
OSTEOCOLLA
OSTEOGENIC
OSTEOLEPIS
OSTEOPATHY
OSTEOPHYTE
OSTRACEOUS
OSTRICH-EGG
OSTRICHISM
OTHERGATES
OTHERGUESS
OTHERWHERE
OTHERWHILE
OTHERWORLD
OTTER-BOARD
OTTER-HOUND
OTTER-SHREW
OTTER-TRAWL
OUGHTLINGS
OUTBALANCE
OUTBARGAIN
OUTBLUSTER
OUTBREATHE
OUTCLASSED

OUT-DWELLER
OUTFIELDER
OUTFITTING
OUTFLOWING
OUTGASSING
OUTGENERAL
OUTJETTING
OUTJUTTING
OUTLANDISH
OUTLODGING
OUTMEASURE
OUT-OF-DOORS
OUTPASSION
OUT-PATIENT
OUT-PENSION
OUTPOURING
OUTRAGEOUS
OUTSETTING
OUTSIDE-CAR
OUTSPECKLE
OUTSTRETCH
OUTSWEETEN
OUTSWINGER
OUTVILLAIN
OUTWITTING
OUTWROUGHT
OUVIRANDRA
OVARIOTOMY
OVERABOUND
OVERBIDDER
OVERBOLDLY
OVERBOUGHT
OVERBRIDGE
OVERBURDEN
OVERCANOPY
OVERCAUGHT
OVERCHARGE
OVERCOLOUR
OVERDARING
OVERDOSAGE
OVEREXCITE
OVEREXPOSE
OVERFLIGHT
OVERFLOWED
OVERFONDLY
OVERFREELY
OVERGLANCE
OVERGREEDY
OVERGROUND
OVERGROWTH
OVERHANDED
OVERINFORM
OVERINSURE
OVERLABOUR
OVERLANDER
OVERLAUNCH
OVERLAYING
OVERLEAVEN
OVERLOOKER
OVERMANTEL
OVERMASTER
OVERNICELY
OVEROFFICE
OVERPEOPLE
OVERPLACED
OVERPRAISE

OVERRASHLY
OVERRAUGHT
OVERRECKON
OVERREFINE
OVERRIDING
OVERRUNNER
OVERSHADOW
OVERSHOWER
OVERSLAUGH
OVERSPREAD
OVERSTRAIN
OVERSTRESS
OVERSTRIDE
OVERSTRIKE
OVERSTRONG
OVERSTRUCK
OVERSTRUNG
OVERSUBTLE
OVERSUPPLY
OVERTHRUST
OVERTHWART
OVERTIMELY
OVERTURNER
OVERWEIGHT
OVERWINTER
OVERWISELY
OVIPOSITOR
OWLISHNESS
OWLSPIEGEL
OX-ANTELOPE
OXIDISABLE
OXY-BROMIDE
OXYGENATOR
OYSTER-BANK
OYSTER-FARM
OYSTER-PARK
OYSTER-WIFE

P

PACESETTER
PACHYMETER
PACIFIABLE
PACIFICATE
PACIFICISM
PACIFICIST
PACK-ANIMAL
PACKET-BOAT
PACKET-NOTE
PACKET-SHIP
PACKING-BOX
PACK-SADDLE
PACKTHREAD
PADDING-KEN
PADDLE-BOAT
PADDLE-WOOD
PADDY-FIELD
PADDYMELON
PADDY-WHACK
PAEDAGOGIC
PAEDAGOGUE
PAEDERASTY
PAEDEUTICS
PAEDIATRIC
PAEDOPHILE
PAEDOTRIBE

PAEDOTRIBE
PAGINATION
PAGODA-TREE
PAIDEUTICS
PAIN-KILLER
PAINLESSLY
PAINSTAKER
PAINT-BRUSH
PAINTINESS
PALAEOGAEA
PALAEOGENE
PALAEOLITH
PALAEOTYPE
PALAEOZOIC
PALAESTRAL
PALAESTRIC
PALAGONITE
PALATALISE
PALATINATE
PALEACEOUS
PALFRENIER
PALIMPSEST
PALINDROME
PALISADOES
PALISANDER
PALLADIOUS
PALL-BEARER
PALLESCENT
PALLIAMENT
PALLIATION
PALLIATIVE
PALLIATORY
PALLIDNESS
PALMACEOUS
PALMATIFID
PALM-BRANCH
PALM-BUTTER
PALMER-WORM
PALM-GREASE
PALM-KERNEL
PALTRINESS
PALUDAMENT
PALUDINOUS
PALUSTRIAN
PALUSTRINE
PALYNOLOGY
PANAMANIAN
PANARITIUM
PANCRATIAN
PANCRATIST
PANCRATIUM
PANCREATIC
PANCREATIN
PANDECTIST
PANDEMONIC
PANDERMITE
PANDURATED
PANEGYRISE
PANEGYRIST
PANGENESIS
PANGENETIC
PANGLOSSIC
PANHANDLER
PANIC-GRASS
PANICULATE
PANISLAMIC

PANJANDRUM
PANNICULUS
PANOPHOBIA
PANOPTICON
PAN-SLAVISM
PAN-SLAVIST
PANSOPHISM
PANSOPHIST
PANSPERMIC
PANTHERESS
PANTHERINE
PANTHERISH
PANTOGRAPH
PANTOMIMIC
PANTON-SHOE
PANTOPHAGY
PANTOSCOPE
PANTRYMAID
PAPAVERINE
PAPAVEROUS
PAPER-BIRCH
PAPER-CIGAR
PAPER-CLOTH
PAPER-FACED
PAPER-GAUGE
PAPER-KNIFE
PAPER-MAKER
PAPER-RULER
PAPILLATED
PAPILLITIS
PAPISTICAL
PAPULATION
PAPYROLOGY
PARABEMATA
PARABIOSIS
PARABIOTIC
PARABLEPSY
PARABOLISE
PARABOLIST
PARABOLOID
PARADIDDLE
PARADISAIC
PARADISEAN
PARADISIAC
PARADISIAL
PARADISIAN
PARADOCTOR
PARADOXIST
PARADOXURE
PARAENESIS
PARAENETIC
PARAFFINIC
PARAGLIDER
PARAGLOSSA
PARAGNOSIS
PARAGONITE
PARALIPSIS
PARALLELED
PARALLELLY
PARALOGISE
PARALOGISM
PARAMECIUM
PARAMEDICO
PARAMETRAL
PARAMETRIC
PARAMNESIA

PARAMOUNCY	PARSONICAL	PEACH-STONE	PENETRANCY
PARANOIDAL	PARTIALISM	PEACH-WATER	PENETRATOR
PARANORMAL	PARTIALIST	PEACOCKERY	PEN-FEATHER
PARAPHASIA	PARTIALITY	PEACOCKISH	PENGUINERY
PARAPHASIC	PARTIALIZE	PEACOCKORE	PENICILLIN
PARAPHILIA	PARTICIPLE	PEARL-DIVER	PENINSULAR
PARAPHONIA	PARTICULAR	PEARLINESS	PENITENTLY
PARAPHONIC	PARTING-CUP	PEARL-SHELL	PENMANSHIP
PARAPHRASE	PARTURIENT	PEARL-STONE	PENNACEOUS
PARAPHRAST	PASIGRAPHY	PEARL-WHITE	PENNILLION
PARAPHYSES	PASQUILANT	PEARMONGER	PENNISETUM
PARAPHYSIS	PASQUINADE	PEAR-SWITCH	PENNY-A-LINE
PARAPINEAL	PASSAGEWAY	PEASE-BROSE	PENNY-BLACK
PARAPLEGIA	PASSAMEZZO	PEASE-STRAW	PENNY-CRESS
PARAPLEGIC	PASSIFLORA	PEASHOOTER	PENNYPIECE
PARAPODIAL	PASSIMETER	PEAT-CASTER	PENNYROYAL
PARAPODIUM	PASSIONARY	PEA-TRAINER	PENNY-STANE
PARARTHRIA	PASSIONATE	PEAT-REEKER	PENNY-STONE
PARASCENIA	PASSIONIST	PEBBLE-WARE	PENNYWORTH
PARASELENE	PASTEBOARD	PECCADILLO	PENOLOGIST
PARASITISM	PASTE-GRAIN	PECTINATED	PENONCELLE
PARASITOID	PASTEURIAN	PECTORALLY	PENSIONARY
PARASTICHY	PASTEURISE	PECULATION	PENTACHORD
PARATACTIC	PASTEURISM	PECULIARLY	PENTAGONAL
PARATHESIS	PASTICHEUR	PEDAGOGICS	PENTAGRAPH
PARATROOPS	PASTORALLY	PEDAGOGISM	PENTAGYNIA
PARBREAKED	PASTORSHIP	PEDAL-BOARD	PENTAMERON
PARCEL-BAWD	PASTRYCOOK	PEDAL-ORGAN	PENTAMETER
PARCEL-GILT	PASTURABLE	PEDAL-POINT	PENTANDRIA
PARCELLING	PASTY-FACED	PEDANTICAL	PENTAPLOID
PARCELWISE	PATAGONIAN	PEDESTRIAN	PENTAPODIC
PARCHMENTY	PATAVINITY	PEDICULATE	PENTAPOLIS
PARDONABLE	PATCHCOCKE	PEDICULATI	PENTASTICH
PARDONABLY	PATENTABLE	PEDICULOUS	PENTASTYLE
PARDONLESS	PATEREROES	PEDICURIST	PENTATEUCH
PARENCHYMA	PATERNALLY	PEDIMENTAL	PENTATHLON
PARENTALLY	PATHETICAL	PEDIMENTED	PENTATHLUM
PARENTERAL	PATHFINDER	PEDIPALPUS	PENTATOMIC
PARENTHOOD	PATHOGENIC	PEDOLOGIST	PENTATONIC
PARENTLESS	PATHOGNOMY	PEDUNCULAR	PENTELICAN
PARGETTING	PATHOLOGIC	PEEL-AND-EAT	PENTETERIC
PARI-MUTUEL	PATIBULARY	PEELGARLIC	PENTIMENTI
PARISCHANE	PATINATION	PEERLESSLY	PENTIMENTO
PARISIENNE	PATRIALISE	PEGMATITIC	PENTSTEMON
PARKKEEPER	PATRIALISM	PEG-TANKARD	PEPPER-CAKE
PARKLEAVES	PATRIARCHY	PEJORATION	PEPPERCORN
PARLIAMENT	PATRICIATE	PEJORATIVE	PEPPERMILL
PARLOUR-CAR	PATRICIDAL	PELECYPODA	PEPPERMINT
PARMACITIE	PATRILOCAL	PELLAGROUS	PEPPERWORT
PARNASSIAN	PATRIOTISM	PELLICULAR	PERCEIVING
PARNELLISM	PATRISTICS	PELLUCIDLY	PERCENTAGE
PARNELLITE	PATROLLING	PELMATOZOA	PERCENTILE
PARONOMASY	PATRONISER	PELTMONGER	PERCEPTION
PARONYCHIA	PATRONLESS	PELVIMETER	PERCEPTIVE
PARONYMOUS	PATRONYMIC	PELVIMETRY	PERCEPTUAL
PAROXYSMAL	PATTER-SONG	PEMPHIGOID	PERCHLORIC
PAROXYTONE	PAULIANIST	PEMPHIGOUS	PERCIPIENT
PARPEN-WALL	PAUSEFULLY	PENANNULAR	PERCOLATOR
PARQUETTED	PAWN-BROKER	PENCIL-CASE	PERCURRENT
PARRAMATTA	PAWNTICKET	PENCIL-LEAD	PERCURSORY
PARRICIDAL	PAY-STATION	PENCILLING	PERCUSSANT
PARROT-BEAK	PEACEFULLY	PENDENTIVE	PERCUSSION
PARROT-BILL	PEACEMAKER	PENELOPISE	PERCUSSIVE
PARROT-COAL	PEACE-PARTY	PENETRABLE	PERCUTIENT
PARROT-FISH	PEACH-BLOOM	PENETRABLY	PERDENDOSI
PARSON-BIRD	PEACHERINO	PENETRALIA	PERDURABLE

PERDURABLY
PERDURANCE
PEREMPTORY
PERFECTION
PERFECTIVE
PERFERVOUR
PERFICIENT
PERFIDIOUS
PERFOLIATE
PERFORABLE
PERFORATOR
PERFORATUS
PERFORMING
PERICLINAL
PERICULOUS
PERICYCLIC
PERIDERMAL
PERIDINIAN
PERIDINIUM
PERIDOTITE
PERIEGESIS
PERIGONIAL
PERIGONIUM
PERIGYNOUS
PERIHELION
PERILOUSLY
PERIMETRIC
PERINEURAL
PERIODICAL
PERIOSTEAL
PERIOSTEUM
PERIPETEIA
PERIPHERAL
PERIPHERIC
PERIPHRASE
PERIPTERAL
PERISCOPIC
PERISHABLE
PERISHABLY
PERISTOMAL
PERISTYLAR
PERITHECIA
PERITONEAL
PERITONEUM
PERIWIGGED
PERIWINKLE
PERJINKETY
PERJINKITY
PERJURIOUS
PERMAFROST
PERMANENCE
PERMANENCY
PERMEATION
PERMEATIVE
PERMISSION
PERMISSIVE
PERMITTING
PERMUTABLE
PERNICIOUS
PERNICKETY
PERORATION
PEROXIDISE
PERPETRATE
PERPETUATE
PERPETUITY
PERPLEXING

PERPLEXITY
PERQUISITE
PERRUQUIER
PERSECUTOR
PERSIANISE
PERSICARIA
PERSIFLAGE
PERSIFLEUR
PERSISTENT
PERSISTIVE
PERSONABLE
PERSONALIA
PERSONALLY
PERSONALTY
PERSONATED
PERSONATOR
PERSPIRATE
PERSTRINGE
PERSUASION
PERSUASIVE
PERSUASORY
PERTINENCE
PERTINENCY
PERTURBANT
PERTURBATE
PERVERSELY
PERVERSION
PERVERSITY
PERVERSIVE
PERVIOUSLY
PESTERMENT
PESTICIDAL
PESTILENCE
PETER-SEE-ME
PETIOLATED
PETITIONER
PETRARCHAL
PETRARCHAN
PETRIFYING
PÉTRISSAGE
PETROGLYPH
PETROLATUM
PETROLEOUS
PETROLLING
PETRONELLA
PETTEDNESS
PETTICHAPS
PETTYCHAPS
PETULANTLY
PEWTER-MILL
PHAELONION
PHAENOLOGY
PHAENOTYPE
PHAGEDAENA
PHAGEDENIC
PHAGOCYTIC
PHALANGEAL
PHALANGIST
PHALLICISM
PHALLOIDIN
PHANEROGAM
PHANTASIME
PHANTASMAL
PHANTASMIC
PHANTASTIC
PHANTASTRY

PHANTOMISH
PHARISAISM
PHARMACIST
PHARYNGEAL
PHEASANTRY
PHELLODERM
PHENACETIN
PHENOCRYST
PHENOGAMAE
PHENOGAMIC
PHENOMENAL
PHENOMENON
PHENOTYPIC
PHIALIFORM
PHILATELIC
PHILIPPIAN
PHILIPPINA
PHILIPPINE
PHILIPPISE
PHILISTEAN
PHILISTIAN
PHILISTINE
PHILLUMENY
PHILOLOGER
PHILOLOGIC
PHILOLOGUE
PHILOMATHY
PHILOPOENA
PHILOSOPHE
PHILOSOPHY
PHLEBOLITE
PHLEBOTOMY
PHLEGMASIA
PHLEGMATIC
PHLEGMONIC
PHLOGISTIC
PHLOGISTON
PHLOGOPITE
PHOCOMELIA
PHOENICIAN
PHOLIDOSIS
PHONEMATIC
PHONETICAL
PHONEYNESS
PHONOGRAPH
PHONOLITIC
PHONOMETER
PHONOPHORE
PHONOTYPIC
PHOSPHATIC
PHOSPHORET
PHOSPHORIC
PHOSPHORUS
PHOSPHURET
PHOTODIODE
PHOTOFLOOD
PHOTOGENIC
PHOTOGLYPH
PHOTOGRAPH
PHOTOLYSIS
PHOTOLYTIC
PHOTOMETER
PHOTONASTY
PHOTOPHILY
PHOTOPHOBE
PHOTOPHONE

PHOTOPHONY
PHOTOPHORE
PHOTOTAXIS
PHOTOTROPE
PHOTOTROPY
PHOTOTYPIC
PHRASE-BOOK
PHRASELESS
PHRENESIAC
PHRENOLOGY
PHTHISICAL
PHTHISICKY
PHYLACTERY
PHYLLOPODA
PHYLLOTAXY
PHYLLOXERA
PHYSICALLY
PHYSICKING
PHYSIOCRAT
PHYSIOLOGY
PHYTOGENIC
PHYTOLACCA
PIANISSIMO
PIANOFORTE
PIANO-ORGAN
PIANO-STOOL
PICARESQUE
PICAYUNISH
PICCADILLO
PICCADILLY
PICCALILLI
PICCANINNY
PICHICIAGO
PICKANINNY
PICK-CHEESE
PICKEDNESS
PICKET-DUTY
PICK-POCKET
PICNICKING
PICROTOXIN
PICTOGRAPH
PICTORICAL
PICTURE-HAT
PICTURE-ROD
PIECE-GOODS
PIE-COUNTER
PIED-À-TERRE
PIERCEABLE
PIERCINGLY
PIETRA-DURA
PIEZOMETER
PIGEON-HOLE
PIGEON-PAIR
PIGEON-POST
PIGEON-TOED
PIGEON-WING
PIGMENTARY
PIG-STICKER
PIKE-KEEPER
PILASTERED
PILE-DRIVER
PILEORHIZA
PILGARLICK
PILGRIMAGE
PILGRIMISE
PILIFEROUS

PILLAR-ROOT
PILLIONIST
PILLIWINKS
PILLORYING
PILLOW-BEER
PILLOW-BERE
PILLOWCASE
PILLOW-LACE
PILLOW-LAVA
PILLOWSLIP
PILOCARPUS
PILOT-CLOTH
PILOT-HOUSE
PILOT-LIGHT
PILOT-PLANT
PILOT-WHALE
PIMPINELLA
PINACOIDAL
PINAKOIDAL
PINAKOTHEK
PIN-BUTTOCK
PINCE-NEZED
PINCHINGLY
PINCHPENNY
PINCUSHION
PINE-BARREN
PINE-BEAUTY
PINE-BEETLE
PINE-CARPET
PINE-CHAFER
PINE-KERNEL
PINEMARTEN
PINE-NEEDLE
PIN-FEATHER
PINGUICULA
PINGUIDITY
PINGUITUDE
PINNATIFID
PINNIPEDIA
PINNULATED
PIPE-LAYING
PIPERACEAE
PIPERIDINE
PIPE-WRENCH
PIROUETTER
PISCIFAUNA
PISTILLARY
PISTILLATE
PISTILLODE
PISTOLLING
PISTOL-SHOT
PITCH-BLACK
PITCHERFUL
PITCHINESS
PITCHSTONE
PITCH-WHEEL
PITILESSLY
PIT-VILLAGE
PITYRIASIS
PIXILLATED
PLACIDNESS
PLAGIARISE
PLAGIARISM
PLAGIARIST
PLAGUESOME
PLAGUE-SORE

PLAGUE-SPOT
PLAIN-CHANT
PLAINTLESS
PLANCHETTE
PLANE-TABLE
PLANETARIA
PLANETICAL
PLANGENTLY
PLANIGRAPH
PLANIMETER
PLANIMETRY
PLANKTONIC
PLANOBLAST
PLANOMETER
PLANTATION
PLANT-HOUSE
PLANT-LOUSE
PLASMODESM
PLASMODIUM
PLASMOGAMY
PLASMOLYSE
PLASMOSOMA
PLASMOSOME
PLASTERING
PLASTICINE
PLASTICISE
PLASTICITY
PLASTIDULE
PLASTILINA
PLASTOGAMY
PLATEFLEET
PLATE-GLASS
PLATE-LAYER
PLATE-PROOF
PLATONICAL
PLATYPUSES
PLAUDITORY
PLAY-ACTING
PLAYFELLOW
PLAYGROUND
PLAYWRIGHT
PLAY-WRITER
PLEADINGLY
PLEASANTLY
PLEASANTRY
PLEASINGLY
PLEBISCITE
PLECOPTERA
PLENILUNAR
PLENISHING
PLENTITUDE
PLEOCHROIC
PLEONASTIC
PLEROMATIC
PLEROPHORY
PLESIOSAUR
PLEXIMETER
PLEXIMETRY
PLIABILITY
PLIANTNESS
PLIOHIPPUS
PLODDINGLY
PLOTTINGLY
PLOUGHABLE
PLOUGHGATE
PLOUGH-IRON

PLOUGHLAND
PLOUGH-TAIL
PLOUGH-TREE
PLOUGHWISE
PLUCKINESS
PLUMASSIER
PLUM-COLOUR
PLUME-GRASS
PLUMULARIA
PLUNDERAGE
PLUNDEROUS
PLUPERFECT
PLUTOCRACY
PLUTOLATRY
PNEUMATICS
POACHINESS
POCKET-BOOK
POCKET-COMB
POCKETFULS
POCKET-HOLE
POCKETLESS
POCKMANTIE
POCKMARKED
POCKPITTED
POCULIFORM
PODAGRICAL
PODIATRIST
PODOCARPUS
PODOSTEMON
POETASTERY
POETICALLY
POGONOTOMY
POIGNANTLY
POIKILITIC
POINSETTIA
POINT-BLANK
POISONABLE
POISON-FANG
POKE-BONNET
POKER-FACED
POKERISHLY
POLEMICIST
POLEMONIUM
POLIANTHES
POLICE-TRAP
POLICY-SHOP
POLISHABLE
POLISHINGS
POLISHMENT
POLITENESS
POLITICIAN
POLITICISE
POLL-DEGREE
POLLENOSIS
POLLEN-TUBE
POLL-PARROT
POLLUTEDLY
POLT-FOOTED
POLYACTINE
POLYANDRIA
POLYANTHUS
POLYATOMIC
POLYAXONIC
POLYCARPIC
POLYCHAETA
POLYCHAETE

POLYCHREST
POLYCHROIC
POLYCHROME
POLYCHROMY
POLYCLINIC
POLYCROTIC
POLYCYCLIC
POLYDACTYL
POLYDIPSIA
POLYGAMIST
POLYGAMOUS
POLYGENISM
POLYGENIST
POLYGENOUS
POLYGRAPHY
POLYGYNIAN
POLYGYNOUS
POLYHALITE
POLYHEDRAL
POLYHEDRIC
POLYHEDRON
POLYHISTOR
POLYHYBIRD
POLYHYDRIC
POLYHYMNIA
POLYMASTIA
POLYMASTIC
POLYMATHIC
POLYMERIDE
POLYMERISE
POLYMERISM
POLYMEROUS
POLYNESIAN
POLYNOMIAL
POLYONYMIC
POLYPHASIC
POLYPHEMIC
POLYPHEMUS
POLYPHONIC
POLYPLOIDY
POLYPODIUM
POLYSEMANT
POLYSTYLAR
POLYTHEISM
POLYTHEIST
POLYTOCOUS
POLYVALENT
POME-CITRON
POMERANIAN
POMIFEROUS
POMOLOGIST
POMPELMOUS
PONDERABLE
PONDERANCE
PONDERANCY
PONDERMENT
POND-MASTER
PONEROLOGY
PONTEDERIA
PONTEFRACT
PONTIFICAL
PONTIFICES
PONTONNIER
PONY-ENGINE
POOR'S-HOUSE
POP-CONCERT

POPLINETTE
POPSY-WOPSY
POPULARISE
POPULARITY
POPULATION
POPULOUSLY
PORIFEROUS
PORISMATIC
PORISTICAL
PORNOCRACY
POROSCOPIC
POROUSNESS
PORPENTINE
PORPHYRITE
PORPHYROUS
PORRACEOUS
PORRECTION
PORTAMENTO
PORTCULLIS
PORTENTOUS
PORTFOLIOS
PORTIONIST
PORTLINESS
PORTMANTLE
PORTMANTUA
PORTUGUESE
POSITIONAL
POSITIONED
POSITIVELY
POSITIVISM
POSITIVIST
POSITIVITY
POSSESSION
POSSESSIVE
POSSESSORY
POSTAL-CARD
POST-BELLUM
POSTCHAISE
POST-EXILIC
POSTHUMOUS
POSTILLATE
POSTILLION
POST-LETTER
POSTLIMINY
POSTMASTER
POST-MORTEM
POST-NICENE
POST-OFFICE
POST-PARTUM
POSTULATUM
POTAMOLOGY
POTATO-TRAP
POT-BELLIED
POT-BOILING
POTENTIARY
POTENTIATE
POTENTILLA
POT-HUNTING
POTTLE-DEEP
POT-VALIANT
POT-WABBLER
POT-WOBBLER
POUNCET-BOX
POURPARLER
POUSSE-CAFÉ
POWDER-DOWN

POWDER-HORN
POWDER-MILL
POWDER-PUFF
POWDER-ROOM
POWERFULLY
POWER-HOUSE
POWER-LATHE
POWER-PLANT
POWER-POINT
POWER-PRESS
POZZOLANIC
POZZUOLANA
PRACTICIAN
PRACTISANT
PRACTISING
PRAECOCIAL
PRAELUDIUM
PRAEMUNIRE
PRAEPOSTOR
PRAESIDIUM
PRAETORIAN
PRAETORIUM
PRAGMATISE
PRAGMATISM
PRAGMATIST
PRAIRIE-DOG
PRAIRIE-HEN
PRAISELESS
PRAISINGLY
PRANCINGLY
PRANKINGLY
PRATINCOLE
PRATTLEBOX
PRAYER-BEAD
PRAYER-BOOK
PRAYERLESS
PREACHMENT
PRE-ADAMITE
PREAPPOINT
PREARRANGE
PREBENDARY
PRECARIOUS
PRECAUTION
PRECEDENCE
PRECEDENCY
PRECENTRIX
PRECEPTIAL
PRECEPTIVE
PRECEPTORY
PRECESSION
PRECIOSITY
PRECIOUSLY
PRECIPICED
PRECIPITIN
PRECLUSION
PRECLUSIVE
PRECOCIOUS
PRECOMPOSE
PRECONCEIT
PRECONCERT
PRECONDEMN
PRECONSUME
PRECORDIAL
PRECURSIVE
PRECURSORY
PREDACEOUS

PREDACIOUS
PREDECEASE
PREDENTATE
PREDESTINE
PREDESTINY
PREDEVELOP
PREDICABLE
PREDICTION
PREDICTIVE
PREDISPOSE
PRE-EMINENT
PRE-EMPTION
PRE-EMPTIVE
PRE-EXILIAN
PREFECTURE
PREFERABLE
PREFERABLY
PREFERENCE
PREFERMENT
PREFERRING
PREFIXTURE
PREFRONTAL
PREFULGENT
PRE-GLACIAL
PREGNANTLY
PREHENSILE
PREHENSION
PREHENSIVE
PREHENSORY
PREHISTORY
PREJUDICED
PRELATICAL
PRELECTION
PRELINGUAL
PRELUDIOUS
PREMARITAL
PREMAXILLA
PREMONITOR
PREPARATOR
PREPAREDLY
PREPAYABLE
PREPAYMENT
PREPENSELY
PREPENSIVE
PREPOLLENT
PREPOSITOR
PREPOSSESS
PREPOTENCE
PREPOTENCY
PRERELEASE
PRESAGEFUL
PRESBYOPIA
PRESBYOPIC
PRESBYTERY
PRESCIENCE
PRESCRIBER
PRESENSION
PRESENT-DAY
PRESENTIAL
PRESENTIVE
PRESIDENCY
PRESIDIARY
PRESIGNIFY
PRESS-AGENT
PRESSED-DAY
PRESSINGLY

PRESS-MONEY
PRESS-PROOF
PRESSURISE
PRESTATION
PRESTERNUM
PRESUMABLE
PRESUMABLY
PRESUPPOSE
PRESURMISE
PRETENDANT
PRETENDENT
PRETENSION
PRETTINESS
PREVAILING
PREVALENCE
PREVALENCY
PREVENANCY
PREVENIENT
PREVENTION
PREVENTIVE
PREVIOUSLY
PRICK-EARED
PRICK-LOUSE
PRICKLY-ASH
PRIDEFULLY
PRIESTHOOD
PRIEST-KING
PRIEST-LIKE
PRIESTLING
PRIESTSHIP
PRIGGISHLY
PRIMATICAL
PRIMOGENIT
PRIMORDIAL
PRIMORDIUM
PRINCEHOOD
PRINCELIKE
PRINCELING
PRINCESSLY
PRINCIFIED
PRINCIPATE
PRINCIPIAL
PRINCIPIUM
PRINCIPLED
PRINT-WORKS
PRISMOIDAL
PRISON-BARS
PRISON-CROP
PRISON-DOOR
PRISONMENT
PRISON-SHIP
PRIVILEGED
PRIZE-COURT
PRIZE-FIGHT
PRIZE-MONEY
PROAIRESIS
PROCACIOUS
PROCEDURAL
PROCEEDING
PROCESSION
PROCIDENCE
PROCLAIMER
PROCLIVITY
PROCOELOUS
PROCREATOR
PROCRYPSIS

PROCRYPTIC
PROCTALGIA
PROCTORAGE
PROCTORAIL
PROCTORISE
PROCUMBENT
PROCURABLE
PROCURATOR
PRODIGALLY
PRODIGIOUS
PRODUCIBLE
PRODUCTILE
PRODUCTION
PRODUCTIVE
PROFESSING
PROFESSION
PROFFERING
PROFICIENT
PROFITABLE
PROFITABLY
PROFITLESS
PROFLIGACY
PROFLIGATE
PROFLUENCE
PROFOUNDLY
PROFULGENT
PROFUNDITY
PROGENITOR
PROGLOTTIS
PROGNATHIC
PROGNOSTIC
PROGRAMMED
PROHIBITER
PROHIBITOR
PROJECTILE
PROJECTING
PROJECTION
PROJECTIVE
PROJECTURE
PROLICIDAL
PROLIFICAL
PROLIXIOUS
PROLIXNESS
PROLOCUTOR
PROLOGUISE
PROLONGATE
PROMENADER
PROMETHEAN
PROMETHEUM
PROMETHIUM
PROMINENCE
PROMINENCY
PROMISEFUL
PROMISSIVE
PROMISSORY
PROMONTORY
PROMPT-BOOK
PROMPT-COPY
PROMPTNESS
PROMPT-NOTE
PROMPT-SIDE
PROMPTUARY
PROMULGATE
PRONOMINAL
PRONOUNCED
PRONOUNCER

PROOF-HOUSE
PROOF-SHEET
PROPAGABLE
PROPAGANDA
PROPAGATOR
PROPELLANT
PROPELLENT
PROPELLING
PROPELMENT
PROPENDENT
PROPENSELY
PROPENSION
PROPENSITY
PROPENSIVE
PROPERNESS
PROPERTIED
PROPHESIED
PROPHESIER
PROPHETESS
PROPHETISM
PROPITIATE
PROPITIOUS
PROPORTION
PROPOSABLE
PROPOUNDER
PROPRAETOR
PROPRIETOR
PROPROCTOR
PROPULSION
PROPULSIVE
PROPULSORY
PROPYLAEUM
PROSAICISM
PROSCENIUM
PROSCRIBER
PROSECUTOR
PROSEUCHAE
PROSILIENT
PROSODICAL
PROSPECTOR
PROSPECTUS
PROSPERITY
PROSPEROUS
PROSTATISM
PROSTHESIS
PROSTHETIC
PROSTITUTE
PROSTOMIAL
PROSTOMIUM
PROTANOPIC
PROTEACEAE
PROTECTING
PROTECTION
PROTECTIVE
PROTECTORY
PROTECTRIX
PROTEIFORM
PROTEINOUS
PROTENSION
PROTENSITY
PROTENSIVE
PROTEOLYSE
PROTERVITY
PROTESTANT
PROTHALLIA
PROTHALLUS

PROTOPHYTA
PROTOPHYTE
PROTOPLASM
PROTOPLAST
PROTOTYPAL
PROTRACTED
PROTRACTOR
PROTREPTIC
PROTRUSILE
PROTRUSION
PROTRUSIVE
PROUD-FLESH
PROVEDITOR
PROVENANCE
PROVERBIAL
PROVIDABLE
PROVIDENCE
PROVINCIAL
PROVITAMIN
PROVOCABLE
PROVOCATOR
PROVOKABLE
PROWLINGLY
PROXIMALLY
PRUDENTIAL
PRURIENTLY
PSALMODISE
PSALMODIST
PSALTERIAN
PSALTERIUM
PSAMMOPHIL
PSELLISMUS
PSEPHOLOGY
PSEUDIMAGO
PSEUDO-ACID
PSEUDOBULB
PSEUDOCARP
PSEUDOLOGY
PSILOCYBIN
PSITTACINE
PSOCOPTERA
PSYCHIATER
PSYCHIATRY
PSYCHOGONY
PSYCHOGRAM
PSYCHOLOGY
PSYCHOPATH
PSYCHOPOMP
PTERYGOTUS
PTERYLOSIS
PTOLEMAEAN
PTOLEMAIST
PUBERULENT
PUBERULOUS
PUBESCENCE
PUBLICNESS
PUDDING-BAG
PUDDING-PIE
PUERPERIUM
PUFF-PASTRY
PUGILISTIC
PUGNACIOUS
PUIR'S-HOOSE
PUIR'S-HOUSE
PUISSANTLY
PUISSAUNCE

PULMONARIA
PULP-CAVITY
PULP-ENGINE
PULSATANCE
PULSATILLA
PULSIMETER
PULSOMETER
PULTACEOUS
PULVERABLE
PULVERISER
PULVILISED
PULVINATED
PUMMELLING
PUMP-HANDLE
PUMPLE-NOSE
PUNCH-DRUNK
PUNCH-LADLE
PUNCTATION
PUNCTUALLY
PUNCTUATOR
PUNCTULATE
PUNDIGRION
PUNDONORES
PUNICACEAE
PUNISHABLE
PUNISHMENT
PUPIGEROUS
PUPILARITY
PUPIPAROUS
PUPPET-PLAY
PUPPET-SHOW
PURBECKIAN
PURBLINDLY
PURISTICAL
PURITANISE
PURITANISM
PURPLE-BORN
PURPLE-HUED
PURPOSEFUL
PURSE-PRIDE
PURSE-PROUD
PURSERSHIP
PURSE-SEINE
PURSUANTLY
PURSUINGLY
PURSUIVANT
PURULENTLY
PURVEYANCE
PUSEYISTIC
PUSH-BUTTON
PUSHSTROKE
PUT-AND-TAKE
PUTREFYING
PUTRESCENT
PUTRESCINE
PUTRIDNESS
PUTTY-FACED
PUTTY-KNIFE
PUZZLE-HEAD
PUZZLEMENT
PUZZLINGLY
PYCNOGONID
PYCNOMETER
PYCNOSPORE
PYCNOSTYLE
PYKNOMETER

PYRACANTHA
PYRAMIDION
PYRAMIDIST
PYRENOCARP
PYRETOLOGY
PYRIDOXINE
PYRO-ACETIC
PYROGALLIC
PYROGALLOL
PYROGRAPHY
PYROLACEAE
PYROLUSITE
PYROMANIAC
PYROMANTIC
PYROMERIDE
PYROMETRIC
PYROPHORIC
PYROPHORUS
PYROTECHNY
PYROXENITE
PYROXYLINE
PYRRHICIST
PYRRHONIAN
PYRRHONISM
PYRRHONIST
PYRRHOTINE
PYRRHOTITE
PYTHOGENIC

Q

QUADRANGLE
QUADRANTAL
QUADRANTES
QUADRATRIX
QUADRATURE
QUADRENNIA
QUADRICEPS
QUADRICONE
QUADRIFORM
QUADRILLER
QUADRIREME
QUADRIVIAL
QUADRIVIUM
QUADRUMANA
QUADRUMANE
QUADRUMVIR
QUADRUPLET
QUADRUPLEX
QUAESTUARY
QUAGGINESS
QUAINTNESS
QUAKER-BIRD
QUALIFYING
QUALMISHLY
QUANTIFIER
QUANTITIVE
QUARANTINE
QUARRELLED
QUARRELLER
QUARRENDER
QUARRIABLE
QUARTATION
QUARTERAGE
QUARTER-BOY
QUARTER-DAY
QUARTER-ILL

QUARTERING
QUARTEROON
QUARTZITIC
QUARTZ-MILL
QUARTZ-ROCK
QUATERNARY
QUATERNATE
QUATERNION
QUATERNITY
QUATORZAIN
QUATREFOIL
QUEASINESS
QUEEN-APPLE
QUEENCRAFT
QUENCHABLE
QUENCHLESS
QUERCITRON
QUERNSTONE
QUERSPRUNG
QUERYINGLY
QUESTIONER
QUICKENING
QUICK-FIRER
QUICK-GRASS
QUICK-HEDGE
QUICK-LUNCH
QUICKMATCH
QUICK-SANDY
QUICK-STICK
QUICKTHORN
QUICK-TRICK
QUICK-WATER
QUIESCENCE
QUIESCENCY
QUIETENING
QUIETISTIC
QUINAQUINA
QUINSY-WORT
QUINT-MAJOR
QUINT-MINOR
QUINTUPLET
QUIRINALIA
QUIRKINESS
QUIZ-MASTER
QUIZZINESS
QUOTATIOUS

R

RABBINICAL
RABBIT-FISH
RABBIT-HOLE
RABBLEMENT
RACCOON-DOG
RACECOURSE
RACE-HATRED
RACEMATION
RACHMANISM
RACKABONES
RACKET-TAIL
RACK-RENTER
RACONTEUSE
RADICALISE
RADICALISM
RADICALITY
RADICATION
RADICIFORM

RADICULOSE
RADIOGENIC
RADIOGRAPH
RADIOLARIA
RADIOMETER
RADIOPHONE
RADIOPHONY
RADIOSCOPY
RADULIFORM
RAFT-BRIDGE
RAFTER-BIRD
RAGAMUFFIN
RAGGED-LADY
RAGGEDNESS
RAGMATICAL
RAILROADER
RAIN-DOCTOR
RAIN-FOREST
RAIN-PLOVER
RAIN-SHADOW
RAISING-BEE
RAIYATWARI
RAJPRAMUKH
RAKISHNESS
RALLYINGLY
RAMBLINGLY
RAMPACIOUS
RAMPAGEOUS
RAMPALLIAN
RAMSHACKLE
RANCIDNESS
RANDLE-BALK
RANDLE-TREE
RANDOMWISE
RANGERSHIP
RANIVOROUS
RANK-RIDING
RANSHACKLE
RANSOMABLE
RANSOMLESS
RANUNCULUS
RANZELLAAR
RAPPORTEUR
RAREFIABLE
RASCAL-LIKE
RASCALLION
RATABILITY
RAT-CATCHER
RAT-HUNTING
RATIONALLY
RATION-BOOK
RATION-CARD
RATTLE-HEAD
RATTLE-PATE
RATTLE-TRAP
RAVENOUSLY
RAVENS-BONE
RAVENS-DUCK
RAVISHMENT
RAZOR-BLADE
RAZOR-SHELL
RAZOR-STROP
RAZZMATAZZ
REACCUSTOM
REACTIVATE
REACTIVELY

REACTIVITY
READERSHIP
READING-BOY
READOPTION
READY-MONEY
REAFFOREST
REAL-ESTATE
REALISABLE
REALLOCATE
REAMING-BIT
REAPPRAISE
REAP-SILVER
REAR-BOILED
REAR-DORTER
REARMAMENT
REASONABLE
REASONABLY
REASONLESS
REASSEMBLE
REASSEMBLY
REASSURING
REASTINESS
REBATEMENT
REBECCAISM
REBECCAITE
REBELLIOUS
REBUKINGLY
REBUTTABLE
RECALLABLE
RECALLMENT
RECAPTURER
RECEIVABLE
RECENTNESS
RECEPTACLE
RECEPTIBLE
RECHRISTEN
RECIDIVISM
RECIDIVIST
RECIPIENCE
RECIPIENCY
RECIPROCAL
RECITATION
RECITATIVE
RECITATIVO
RECKLESSLY
RECOGNISER
RECOLONISE
RECOMMENCE
RECOMPENSE
RECONCILER
RECONDENSE
RECONQUEST
RECONSIDER
RECORDABLE
RECOUPMENT
RECREANTLY
RECREATION
RECREATIVE
RECRUDESCE
RECRUITING
RECTANGLED
RECTIFYING
RECTORSHIP
RECTRICIAL
RECUMBENCE
RECUMBENCY

RECUPERATE
RECURELESS
RECURRENCE
RECURRENCY
RECUSATION
REDBLOODED
REDCURRANT
REDECORATE
REDEDICATE
REDEEMABLE
REDEEMLESS
REDELIVERY
REDEMPTION
REDEMPTIVE
REDEMPTORY
REDESCRIBE
REDEVELOPE
RED-FIGURED
REDISBURSE
REDISCOVER
REDISSOLVE
REDIVISION
RED-LATTICE
RED-MURRAIN
REDOLENTLY
REDOUNDING
REDRESSIVE
REDRUTHITE
RED-SANDERS
REDUNDANCE
REDUNDANCY
REED-THRUSH
RE-ELECTION
REELIGIBLE
RE-ENLISTER
RE-ENTERING
RE-ENTRANCE
RE-ENTRANCY
RE-ERECTION
REFERENDUM
REFERRIBLE
REFINEMENT
REFLECTING
REFLECTION
REFLECTIVE
REFLEXIBLE
REFORMABLE
REFRACTING
REFRACTION
REFRACTIVE
REFRACTORY
REFRACTURE
REFRESHFUL
REFRESHING
REFRINGENT
REFULGENCE
REFULGENCY
REFUNDMENT
REFUTATION
REGAINABLE
REGAINMENT
REGALEMENT
REGARDABLE
REGARDLESS
REGELATION
REGENERACY

REGENERATE
REGENT-BIRD
REGENTSHIP
REGIMENTAL
REGIONALLY
REGISTERED
REGISTRANT
REGISTRARY
REGRESSION
REGRESSIVE
REGRETTING
REGULARISE
REGULARITY
REGULATION
REGULATIVE
REGULATORY
REHANDLING
REHEARSING
REICHSBANK
REICHSLAND
REICHSMARK
REICHSRATH
REILLUMINE
REIM-KENNAR
REINCREASE
REINSPIRIT
REISSUABLE
REITERANCE
REITERATED
REJECTABLE
REJECTIBLE
REJOICEFUL
REJOINDURE
REJUVENATE
REJUVENISE
RELATIONAL
RELATIVELY
RELATIVISM
RELATIVIST
RELATIVITY
RELAXATION
RELAXATIVE
RELEASABLE
RELEGATION
RELENTLESS
RELENTMENT
RELEVANTLY
RELIEFLESS
RELIEVABLE
RELIGIONER
RELINQUISH
RELIQUAIRE
RELISHABLE
RELUCTANCE
RELUCTANCY
REMARKABLE
REMARKABLY
REMARRIAGE
REMEDIABLE
REMEDIALLY
REMEDILESS
REMEMBERER
REMIGATION
REMISSIBLE
REMISSNESS

REMITTANCE
REMONETISE
REMORSEFUL
REMOTENESS
REMUNERATE
RENASCENCE
RENCOUNTER
RENDERABLE
RENDEZVOUS
RENEGATION
RENOVATION
RENT-CHARGE
REORGANISE
REPAINTING
REPAIRABLE
REPAIR-SHOP
REPARATION
REPARATIVE
REPARATORY
REPATRIATE
REPEALABLE
REPEATABLE
REPEATEDLY
REPELLANCE
REPELLANCY
REPELLENCE
REPELLENCY
REPENTANCE
REPERTOIRE
RÉPÉTITEUR
REPETITION
REPETITIVE
REPINEMENT
REPININGLY
REPORTABLE
REPOSITION
REPOSITORY
REPOUSSAGE
REPRESSION
REPRESSIVE
REPROACHER
REPROBANCE
REPROBATOR
REPRODUCER
REPTILIOUS
REPUBLICAN
REPUDIABLE
REPUDIATOR
REPUGNANCE
REPUGNANCY
REPURCHASE
REPUTATION
REPUTATIVE
REPUTELESS
REQUIESCAT
REQUIRABLE
REQUISITOR
REQUITABLE
REQUITEFUL
REREDORTER
REREGISTER
RERE-SUPPER
RESCISSION
RESCISSORY
RESEARCHER
RESEDACEAE

RESEMBLANT
RESEMBLING
RESENTMENT
RESERVABLE
RESERVEDLY
RESHIPMENT
RESIDENTER
RESIGNEDLY
RESIGNMENT
RESILIENCE
RESILIENCY
RESINOUSLY
RESISTANCE
RESISTIBLE
RESISTIBLY
RESISTLESS
RESOLUTELY
RESOLUTION
RESOLUTIVE
RESOLVABLE
RESOLVEDLY
RESONANTLY
RESORCINOL
RESORPTION
RESORPTIVE
RESOUNDING
RESPECTANT
RESPECTFUL
RESPECTING
RESPECTIVE
RESPIRABLE
RESPIRATOR
RESPONDENT
RESPONSIVE
RESPONSORY
RESTAURANT
RESTCENTRE
REST-HARROW
RESTITUTOR
RESTLESSLY
RESTORABLE
RESTRAINED
RESTRAINER
RESTRICTED
RESULTLESS
RESUMPTION
RESUMPTIVE
RESUPINATE
RESURGENCE
RETAILMENT
RETAINABLE
RETAINMENT
RETALIATOR
RETARDMENT
RETICULARY
RETICULATE
RETINACULA
RETINALITE
RETIREMENT
RETIRINGLY
RETRACTILE
RETRACTION
RETRACTIVE
RETRANSFER
RETRANSMIT
RETRIBUTOR

RETRIEVING
RETROCHOIR
RETROGRADE
RETROGRESS
RETRORSELY
RETROSPECT
RETURNABLE
RETURNLESS
REUNIONISM
REUNIONIST
REVALIDATE
REVALORISE
REVANCHISM
REVANCHIST
REVEALABLE
REVEALMENT
REVELATION
REVELATIVE
REVELATORY
REVENGEFUL
REVERENCER
REVERENTLY
REVERSEDLY
REVERSIBLE
REVERTIBLE
REVESTIARY
REVIEWABLE
REVIEW-COPY
REVILEMENT
REVILINGLY
REVISIONAL
REVISITANT
REVITALISE
REVIVALISM
REVIVALIST
REVIVEMENT
REVIVIFIED
REVIVINGLY
REVOCATION
REVOCATORY
REVOKEMENT
REVOLUTION
REVOLVENCY
REWARDABLE
REWARDLESS
RHABDOLITH
RHAMNACEAE
RHAPSODISE
RHAPSODIST
RHEINBERRY
RHEOLOGIST
RHEOTROPIC
RHETORICAL
RHEUMATISE
RHEUMATISM
RHEUMATIZE
RHEUMATOID
RHINEBERRY
RHINEGRAVE
RHINESTONE
RHINOCEROS
RHINOLALIA
RHINOPHYMA
RHINOSCOPE
RHINOSCOPY
RHINOTHECA

RHIPIPTERA
RHIZOGENIC
RHIZOMORPH
RHIZOPHORA
RHIZOPHORE
RH-NEGATIVE
RHODOPHANE
RHODYMENIA
RHOEADALES
RHOMBOIDAL
RHOMBOIDES
RH-POSITIVE
RHYME-ROYAL
RHYNIACEAE
RHYTHMICAL
RHYTHMLESS
RIBBON-FISH
RIBBON-SEAL
RIBBON-WEED
RIBBON-WORM
RIBOFLAVIN
RIB-ROASTER
RICINOLEIC
RICKBARTON
RICK-BURNER
RICKETTSIA
RICK-LIFTER
RICOCHETED
RIDABILITY
RIDDLE-LIKE
RIDDLINGLY
RIDE-AND-TIE
RIDGE-PIECE
RIDICULOUS
RIDING-BOOT
RIDING-COAT
RIDING-CROP
RIDING-HOOD
RIDING-ROBE
RIDING-SUIT
RIDING-WHIP
RIEBECKITE
RIEMANNIAN
RIFLE-CORPS
RIFLE-GREEN
RIFLE-RANGE
RIGHT-ABOUT
RIGHT-DRAWN
RIGHTFULLY
RIGHT-LINED
RIGHT-OF-WAY
RIGHTWARDS
RIGHT-WHALE
RIGOROUSLY
RINDERPEST
RINGELMANN
RING-FINGER
RING-LEADER
RING-MASTER
RING-NECKED
RING-PLOVER
RING-POROUS
RING-TAILED
RIPIDOLITE
RIPPING-SAW
RIPPLE-MARK

RIPPLINGLY
RIP-ROARING
RIP-SNORTER
RISIBILITY
RITARDANDO
RITORNELLE
RITORNELLI
RITORNELLO
RITT-MASTER
RIVER-BASIN
RIVER-CRAFT
RIVER-DRIFT
RIVER-FRONT
RIVER-HORSE
RIVER-MOUTH
RIVERSCAPE
RIVER-WATER
ROAD-BRIDGE
ROAD-MAKING
ROAD-MENDER
ROAD-ROLLER
ROAD-RUNNER
ROADWORTHY
ROBBER-CRAB
ROBERDSMAN
ROBERTSMAN
ROBING-ROOM
ROBUSTIOUS
ROBUSTNESS
ROCKABILLY
ROCK-BADGER
ROCK-BOTTOM
ROCK-BUTTER
ROCK-GARDEN
ROCK-HOPPER
ROCK-LIZARD
ROCK-PIGEON
ROCK-RABBIT
ROCK-RIBBED
ROCK-SALMON
ROCK-TEMPLE
ROCK-TURBOT
ROCK-VIOLET
RODFISHING
ROGUE-MONEY
ROISTEROUS
ROLLCOLLAR
ROLLICKING
ROLLING-PIN
ROMANCICAL
ROMANESQUE
ROMANISTIC
ROMANTICAL
ROME-RUNNER
ROMPER-SUIT
RONDOLETTO
RÖNTGENISE
ROOD-SCREEN
ROOF-GARDEN
ROOM-FELLOW
ROOM-RIDDEN
ROOTEDNESS
ROOT-FALLEN
ROOT-RUBBER
ROOT-SHEATH
ROOT-SYSTEM

ROPE-DANCER
ROPE-LADDER
ROPE-MAKING
ROPE-STITCH
ROPE-WALKER
ROPING-DOWN
ROQUELAURE
ROSANILINE
ROSE-BEETLE
ROSE-CHAFER
ROSE-COLOUR
ROSE-COMBED
ROSE-ENGINE
ROSE-GARDEN
ROSE-LAUREL
ROSE-LIPPED
ROSE-MALLOW
ROSE-QUARTZ
ROSE-WINDOW
ROSIN-PLANT
ROSY-FOOTED
ROTATIONAL
RÔTISSERIE
ROTOR-PLANE
ROTTENNESS
ROTTWEILER
ROUGH-DRAFT
ROUGH-GRIND
ROUGH-HEWER
ROUGH-HOUND
ROUGH-HOUSE
ROUGH-RIDER
ROUGH-STUFF
ROUNDABOUT
ROUND-EARED
ROUND-FACED
ROUND-HOUSE
ROUND-MOUTH
ROUND-NOSED
ROUND-TABLE
ROUSEABOUT
ROUSTABOUT
ROUTE-MARCH
ROVE-BEETLE
ROWAN-BERRY
ROWDY-DOWDY
ROWING-BOAT
ROYSTEROUS
RUB-A-DUB-DUB
RUBBER-NECK
RUBBISHING
RUBBLE-WORK
RUBIACEOUS
RUBIGINOUS
RUBRICALLY
RUBRICATOR
RUBY-SILVER
RUBY-SPINEL
RUBY-THROAT
RUDDER-FISH
RUDDERLESS
RUDIMENTAL
RUE-BARGAIN
RUEFULNESS
RUFFIANISH
RUFFIANISM

RUGGEDNESS
RUMBLINGLY
RUM-BLOSSOM
RUMBULLION
RUMFUSTIAN
RUMINANTIA
RUMINANTLY
RUMINATION
RUMINATIVE
RUMPLE-BANE
RUM-RUNNING
RUNNER-BEAN
RUPESTRIAN
RUPICOLINE
RUPICOLOUS
RURITANIAN
RUSH-CANDLE
RUSH-HOLDER
RUSSEL-CORD
RUSSELLITE
RUSSIANISE
RUSSIANISM
RUSSIANIST
RUSSOPHILE
RUSSOPHOBE
RUST-FUNGUS
RUSTICALLY
RUSTIC-WARE
RUSTIC-WORK
RUSTLINGLY
RUTHERFORD
RUTHLESSLY

S
SABBATH-DAY
SABBATICAL
SABRETACHE
SABRE-TOOTH
SACCHARATE
SACCHARIDE
SACCHARIFY
SACCHARINE
SACCHAROID
SACCHAROSE
SACCULATED
SACERDOTAL
SACHEMSHIP
SACK-POSSET
SACREDNESS
SACRIFICER
SACROILIAC
SACROSANCT
SADDLEBACK
SADDLE-FAST
SADDLELESS
SADDLE-ROOF
SADDLE-ROOM
SADDLE-SICK
SADDLE-SORE
SADDLE-TREE
SADDUCAEAN
SAD-HEARTED
SAFETY-ARCH
SAFETY-BELT
SAFETY-CAGE
SAFETY-PLUG

SAFETY-REIN
SAFETY-STOP
SAGE-CHEESE
SAGE-GROUSE
SAGE-RABBIT
SAGINATION
SAGITTALLY
SAGITTARIA
SAIL-FLYING
SAILORLESS
SAILOR-LIKE
SALABILITY
SALAL-BERRY
SALAMANDER
SALES-CLERK
SALESWOMAN
SALICACEAE
SALICIONAL
SALICORNIA
SALICYLATE
SALIFEROUS
SALIFIABLE
SALIVATION
SALLENDERS
SALLOWNESS
SALMAGUNDI
SALMAGUNDY
SALMONELLA
SALMONIDAE
SALMON-LEAP
SALOON-DECK
SALPINGIAN
SALTARELLO
SALT-BUTTER
SALT-CELLAR
SALTIGRADE
SALT-SPRING
SALUBRIOUS
SALUTARILY
SALUTATION
SALUTATORY
SALVIFICAL
SAMARSKITE
SANATORIUM
SANCTIFIED
SANCTIFIER
SANCTIMONY
SANCTITUDE
SANDALWOOD
SANDBAGGED
SANDBAGGER
SAND-BINDER
SAND-BUNKER
SANDCASTLE
SAND-CHERRY
SAND-DOLLAR
SANDERLING
SANDGROPER
SAND-GROUSE
SAND-HOPPER
SAND-LAUNCE
SAND-LIZARD
SAND-MARTIN
SAND-SAUCER
SAND-SUCKER
SANGUINARY

SANGUINELY
SANGUINITY
SANHEDRIST
SANITARIAN
SANITARILY
SANITARIST
SANITARIUM
SANITATION
SAOUARI-NUT
SAPIENTIAL
SAPLING-CUP
SAPONIFIED
SAPOTACEAE
SAPPAN-WOOD
SAPPERMENT
SAPPHIRINE
SAPROGENIC
SAPROPELIC
SAPROPHYTE
SARACENISM
SARCOCOLLA
SARCOLEMMA
SARCOPHAGA
SARCOPHAGI
SARCOPHAGY
SARDONICAL
SARMENTOSE
SARMENTOUS
SARRACENIA
SASH-WINDOW
SATANOLOGY
SATCHELLED
SATELLITES
SATELLITIC
SATIN-PAPER
SATIN-STONE
SATISFYING
SATRAPICAL
SATURATION
SATURNALIA
SATYAGRAHA
SATYRESQUE
SATYRIASIS
SAUCE-ALONE
SAUCER-EYED
SAUCERFULS
SAUERKRAUT
SAUNTERING
SAUROPSIDA
SAUSSURITE
SAVAGENESS
SAVINGNESS
SAVOURLESS
SAW-TOOTHED
SAXICAVOUS
SAXICOLINE
SAXICOLOUS
'SBUDDIKINS
SCABBINESS
SCABRIDITY
SCAFFOLDER
SCAITHLESS
SCALD-BERRY
SCALE-BOARD
SCALE-STAIR
SCAMPISHLY

SCANDALISE
SCANDALLED
SCANDALOUS
SCANSORIAL
SCANTINESS
SCAPEGRACE
SCAPE-WHEEL
SCAPHOPODA
SCAPULATED
SCARABAEID
SCARABAEUS
SCARAMOUCH
SCARCEMENT
SCARCENESS
SCARF-JOINT
SCARIFYING
SCARLATINA
SCARLET-HAT
SCATHELESS
SCATHINGLY
SCATOPHAGY
SCATTER-GUN
SCATTERING
SCATTINESS
SCATURIENT
SCAVENGERY
SCAVENGING
SCENICALLY
SCENT-GLAND
SCENT-ORGAN
SCENT-SCALE
SCEPTICISE
SCEPTICISM
SCHALSTEIN
SCHEMATISE
SCHEMATISM
SCHEMATIST
SCHEMOZZLE
SCHERZANDO
SCHIPPERKE
SCHISMATIC
SCHISM-SHOP
SCHIZOCARP
SCHIZOGONY
SCHIZOIDAL
SCHIZOPODA
SCHLIMAZEL
SCHOLASTIC
SCHOOL-BELL
SCHOOL-BOOK
SCHOOL-BRED
SCHOOL-DAME
SCHOOLGIRL
SCHOOLMA'AM
SCHOOLMAID
SCHOOL-MATE
SCHOOL-MISS
SCHOOLROOM
SCHOOL-SHIP
SCHOOL-TERM
SCHOOL-TIDE
SCHOOL-TIME
SCHOOLWARD
SCHOOLWORK
SCHORL-ROCK
SCIAENIDAE

SCIENTIFIC
SCILLONIAN
SCIOLISTIC
SCISSOR-CUT
SCISSOR-LEG
SCLERIASIS
SCLERODERM
SCLEROTIUM
SCOFFINGLY
SCOLYTIDAE
SCOMBRESOX
SCOMBRIDAE
SCOOPED-OUT
SCOPELIDAE
SCORDATURA
SCORE-BOARD
SCORNFULLY
SCORPIONIC
SCORZONERA
SCOTCHNESS
SCOTIFYING
SCOTODINIA
SCOTSWOMAN
SCOTTICISE
SCOTTICISM
SCOTTIFIED
SCOUTCRAFT
SCOWDERING
SCOWLINGLY
SCRAGGLING
SCRAG-WHALE
SCRAMBLING
SCRAPE-GOOD
SCRAP-METAL
SCRATCHILY
SCRATCHING
SCRATCH-WIG
SCREECH-OWL
SCREENINGS
SCREEN-PLAY
SCREW-PLATE
SCREW-PRESS
SCRIBBLING
SCRIMMAGER
SCRIMPNESS
SCRIMSHANK
SCRIPTORIA
SCRIPTURAL
SCRITCH-OWL
SCRIVENING
SCROFULOUS
SCROG-APPLE
SCROLLWISE
SCROLLWORK
SCROUNGING
SCRUB-RIDER
SCRUMMAGER
SCRUPULOUS
SCRUTINEER
SCRUTINISE
SCRUTINOUS
SCULDUDDRY
SCULPTRESS
SCULPTURAL
SCULPTURED
SCURFINESS

SCURRILITY
SCURRILOUS
SCURVINESS
SCUTELLATE
SCUTTLEFUL
SDEIGNFULL
SDRUCCIOLA
SEA-ANEMONE
SEA-BATHING
SEA-BISCUIT
SEA-BLUBBER
SEA-BURDOCK
SEA-CAPTAIN
SEA-FEATHER
SEA-FISHING
SEA-GODDESS
SEA-LEOPARD
SEA-LETTUCE
SEAL-FISHER
SEALING-DAY
SEALING-WAX
SEAMANLIKE
SEAMANSHIP
SEA-MONSTER
SEAMSTRESS
SEANNACHIE
SEA-PASSAGE
SEA-POACHER
SEAQUARIUM
SEARCHABLE
SEARCHLESS
SEAREDNESS
SEA-SERPENT
SEA-SERVICE
SEA-SOLDIER
SEASONABLE
SEASONABLY
SEASONALLY
SEASONLESS
SEA-SURGEON
SEA-SWALLOW
SEA-UNICORN
SEA-WHISTLE
SEBIFEROUS
SEBORRHOEA
SECERNMENT
SECLUDEDLY
SECOND-BEST
SECOND-HAND
SECOND-MARK
SECOND-RATE
SECRETAIRE
SECRETNESS
SECTIONISE
SECULARISE
SECULARISM
SECULARIST
SECULARITY
SECUREMENT
SECURENESS
SECURIFORM
SEDAN-CHAIR
SEDATENESS
SEDUCEMENT
SEDUCINGLY
SEDUCTRESS

SEDULOUSLY
SEECATCHIE
SEED-OYSTER
SEED-POTATO
SEED-VESSEL
SEEMELESSE
SEEMLIHEAD
SEEMLINESS
SEERSUCKER
SEGMENTARY
SEGMENTATE
SEGREGABLE
SEGUIDILLA
SEIGNEURIE
SEIGNORAGE
SEISMICITY
SEISMOGRAM
SEISMOLOGY
SELBORNIAN
SELDOMNESS
SELECTNESS
SELENODONT
SELENOLOGY
SELEUCIDAE
SELEUCIDAN
SELF-ABUSER
SELF-ACTING
SELF-ACTION
SELF-BINDER
SELF-BOUNTY
SELF-BREATH
SELF-COCKER
SELF-COLOUR
SELF-DANGER
SELF-DECEIT
SELF-DENIAL
SELF-DRIVEN
SELF-ESTEEM
SELF-FEEDER
SELF-FILLER
SELF-GLAZED
SELF-KILLED
SELF-KILLER
SELF-LOVING
SELF-METTLE
SELF-MOTION
SELF-MURDER
SELF-OPENED
SELF-POISED
SELF-SEEKER
SELF-SEVERE
SELF-STYLED
SELF-TAUGHT
SELF-UNABLE
SELF-SLAYER
SELF-WILLED
SELTZOGENE
SEMBLATIVE
SEMEIOLOGY
SEMEIOTICS
SEMESTRIAL
SEMI-ANNUAL
SEMICHORUS
SEMICIRCLE
SEMICIRQUE
SEMI-DIVINE

SEMI-DOUBLE
SEMI-DRYING
SEMI-LIQUID
SEMILUCENT
SEMILUNATE
SEMINALITY
SEMINARIAL
SEMINARIAN
SEMINARIST
SEMINATION
SEMI-OPAQUE
SEMIQUAVER
SEMITERETE
SEMI-UNCIAL
SEMI-WEEKLY
SEMPSTRESS
SENATORIAL
SENESCENCE
SENSE-DATUM
SENSE-ORGAN
SENSITISED
SENSITISER
SENSUALISE
SENSUALISM
SENSUALIST
SENSUALITY
SENSUOUSLY
SENTENTIAL
SEPARATELY
SEPARATION
SEPARATISM
SEPARATIST
SEPARATIVE
SEPARATORY
SEPARATRIX
SEPTEMVIRI
SEPTEMVIRS
SEPTENNATE
SEPTENNIAL
SEPTENNIUM
SEPTICALLY
SEPTICIDAL
SEPTILLION
SEPTUAGINT
SEPULCHRAL
SEPULTURAL
SEQUACIOUS
SEQUENTIAL
SEQUIALTER
SERAPHICAL
SERBO-CROAT
SERENENESS
SERGEANTCY
SERIGRAPHY
SERIOCOMIC
SERJEANTCY
SERJEANTRY
SERMONETTE
SERMONICAL
SERMONISER
SEROLOGIST
SEROTINOUS
SERPENT-GOD
SERPENTINE
SERPENTISE
SERRADELLA

SERRADILLA
SERRANIDAE
SERRASALMO
SERRULATED
SERTULARIA
SERVANT-MAN
SERVICEMAN
SERVING-MAN
SERVITRESS
SERVO-MOTOR
SESTERTIUM
SETTERWORT
SETTLEMENT
SEVEN-A-SIDE
SEVENPENCE
SEVENPENNY
SEVEN-SCORE
SEVENTH-DAY
SEVENTIETH
SEVERENESS
SEWAGE-FARM
SEXAGENARY
SEXAGESIMA
SEXIVALENT
SEX-LIMITED
SEXLOCULAR
SEXPARTITE
SEXTILLION
SEXTONSHIP
SHABBINESS
SHADE-PLANT
SHADOWCAST
SHADOWLESS
SHADOW-MARK
SHADOW-PLAY
SHAFT-HORSE
SHAGGINESS
SHAG-HAIRED
SHAGREENED
SHALE-MINER
SHALLOWING
SHAMEFACED
SHAMEFULLY
SHAME-PROOF
SHANDRYDAN
SHANDYGAFF
SHANGHAIED
SHANGHAIER
SHARD-BORNE
SHARP-EDGED
SHARP-NOSED
SHAVE-GRASS
SHEABUTTER
SHEAR-STEEL
SHEAR-WATER
SHEATHFISH
SHEATHLESS
SHEBEENING
SHECKLATON
SHEEP-BITER
SHEEP-FACED
SHEEPISHLY
SHEEP-LOUSE
SHEEP-PLANT
SHEEP'S-FOOT
SHEEP-SHANK

SHEEP'S-HEAD
SHEEP-TRACK
SHEET-GLASS
SHEET-METAL
SHELLACKED
SHELLBOUND
SHELLDRAKE
SHELLINESS
SHELL-MONEY
SHELL-MOUND
SHELLPROOF
SHELLSHOCK
SHELLYCOAT
SHELTERING
SHENANIGAN
SHERARDISE
SHEREEFIAN
SHERIFFDOM
SHIBBOLETH
SHIELD-FERN
SHIELD-HAND
SHIELDLESS
SHIELDLING
SHIELD-MAID
SHIELDRAKE
SHIELDWALL
SHIFTINESS
SHILLELAGH
SHIMMERING
SHIN-BARKER
SHIP-BROKER
SHIP-HOLDER
SHIP-LETTER
SHIP-MASTER
SHIP-RIGGED
SHIPWRIGHT
SHIRE-HORSE
SHIRE-REEVE
SHIRT-FRILL
SHIRT-FRONT
SHIRTWAIST
SHLEMOZZLE
SHOAL-WATER
SHOCKINGLY
SHOCK-PROOF
SHODDINESS
SHOE-BUCKLE
SHOEMAKING
SHOESTRING
SHOPKEEPER
SHOP-LIFTER
SHOP-SOILED
SHOP-WALKER
SHOP-WINDOW
SHORE-GOING
SHORE-LEAVE
SHOREWARDS
SHORTBREAD
SHORT-COATS
SHORT-DATED
SHORTENING
SHORT-LIVED
SHORT-SWORD
SHOT-WINDOW
SHOULDERED
SHOUTINGLY

SHOVE-GROAT
SHOVELFULS
SHOVEL-HEAD
SHOVELLING
SHOWER-BATH
SHOWERLESS
SHOW-GROUND
SHREWDNESS
SHREWISHLY
SHREW-MOUSE
SHRIEVALTY
SHRILLNESS
SHRIMP-GIRL
SHRINKABLE
SHRITCH-OWL
SHRIVELLED
SHROUDLESS
SHROUD-LINE
SHROVETIDE
SHUDDERING
SHUFFLE-CAP
SHUTTERING
SIALAGOGIC
SIALAGOGUE
SIALOGOGUE
SIBILATION
SIBILATORY
SICILIENNE
SICKERNESS
SICK-FALLEN
SICKLE-BILL
SICKLE-CELL
SICKLINESS
SICK-LISTED
SICK-MAKING
SIDE-EFFECT
SIDE-GLANCE
SIDERATION
SIDEROLITE
SIDEROSTAT
SIDE-SADDLE
SIDE-STROKE
SIEGECRAFT
SIEGE-PIECE
SIEGE-TRAIN
SIEGE-WORKS
SIEVE-PLATE
SIGILLARIA
SIGNALLING
SIGNET-RING
SIGNIFYING
SIGN-MANUAL
SIGN-WRITER
SILENTIARY
SILENTNESS
SILHOUETTE
SILICIFIED
SILICULOSE
SILK-COTTON
SILK-GROWER
SILK-SCREEN
SILVER-BATH
SILVER-BELL
SILVER-FISH
SILVER-FOIL
SILVER-GILT

SILVER-LEAF
SILVERLING
SILVERSIDE
SILVERSKIN
SILVER-TREE
SILVERWEED
SIMILARITY
SIMILATIVE
SIMILITUDE
SIMMENTHAL
SIMNEL-CAKE
SIMONIACAL
SIMPLENESS
SIMPLICITY
SIMPLIFIED
SIMPLIFIER
SIMPLISTIC
SIMULACRUM
SIMULATION
SIMULATIVE
SIMULATORY
SINCIPITAL
SINECURISM
SINECURIST
SINFULNESS
SINGHALESE
SINGING-MAN
SINGLE-EYED
SINGLE-FOOT
SINGLENESS
SINGLETREE
SINGULARLY
SINISTERLY
SINISTROUS
SINKE-A-PACE
SINOLOGIST
SINUSOIDAL
SIPHONOGAM
SIPUNCULID
SISAL-GRASS
SISTERHOOD
SISTER-HOOK
SISTERLESS
SISTER-LIKE
SITOPHOBIA
SIX-SHOOTER
SKAITHLESS
SKENE-OCCLE
SKETCHABLE
SKETCH-BOOK
SKEW-BRIDGE
SKEW-CORBEL
SKI-BOBBING
SKI-JUMPING
SKIKJÖRING
SKIMMINGLY
SKIMPINGLY
SKIN-DIVING
SKINNINESS
SKIP-KENNEL
SKIPPINGLY
SKIRMISHER
SKI-RUNNING
SKITTISHLY
SKRIMSHANK
SKULKINGLY

SKUPSHTINA	SMALL-SWORD	SNUBBINGLY	SONGSTRESS
SKY-JUMPING	SMALL-TOOTH	SNUFF-BROWN	SONG-THRUSH
SKYLARKING	SMALL-WARES	SNUFFINESS	SONOROUSLY
SKY-PARLOUR	SMARAGDINE	SNUFF-PAPER	SOOTHINGLY
SKY-PLANTED	SMARAGDITE	SNUFF-SPOON	SOOTHSAYER
SKYSCRAPER	SMART-ALECK	SNUFF-TAKER	SOPHICALLY
SKY-WRITING	SMART-ALICK	SOAP-BOILER	SOPHOCLEAN
SLABBINESS	SMART-MONEY	SOAP-BUBBLE	SOPHOMORIC
SLACKENING	SMATTERING	SOBERSIDES	SOPS-IN-WINE
SLACK-WATER	SMEARINESS	SOCDOLAGER	SORBONICAL
SLAMMERKIN	SMELL-FEAST	SOCDOLIGER	SORBONNIST
SLANDEROUS	SMELLINESS	SOCDOLOGER	SORDAMENTE
SLANGINESS	SMICKERING	SOCIALNESS	SORDIDNESS
SLANGINGLY	SMIFLIGATE	SOCIOLOGIC	SORE-FALCON
SLANG-WHANG	SMITHCRAFT	SOCIOMETRY	SORE-HEADED
SLANTINGLY	SMOCK-FACED	SOCIOPATHY	SORICIDENT
SLATTERNLY	SMOCK-FROCK	SOCRATICAL	SORORIALLY
SLAUGHTERY	SMOKE-BLACK	SODDENNESS	SORORICIDE
SLAVE-GROWN	SMOKE-BOARD	SOFT-BILLED	SORROWLESS
SLAVE-OWNER	SMOKE-DRIED	SOFT-BODIED	SORTILEGER
SLAVE-TRADE	SMOKE-HOUSE	SOFT-BOILED	SOUBRIQUET
SLAVOCRACY	SMOKEPROOF	SOFT-FINNED	SOULLESSLY
SLAVOPHILE	SMOKE-STACK	SOFT-FOOTED	SOUND-BOARD
SLAVOPHOBE	SMOKETIGHT	SOFT-HEADED	SOUNDINGLY
SLEAZINESS	SMOOTH-BORE	SOFT-SAWDER	SOUNDPROOF
SLEEKSTONE	SMOOTHNESS	SOFT-SPOKEN	SOUND-SHIFT
SLEEPINESS	SMOOTH-SHOD	SOGDOLAGER	SOUND-TRACK
SLEEPY-HEAD	SMØRREBRØD	SOGDOLIGER	SOUP-MAIGRE
SLEETINESS	SMOTHER-FLY	SOGDOLOGER	SOUP-MEAGRE
SLEEVE-FISH	SMOTHERING	SOJOURNING	SOUP-TICKET
SLEEVE-HAND	SMUDGINESS	SOLACEMENT	SOUP-TUREEN
SLEEVELESS	SMUT-FUNGUS	SOLANACEAE	SOURCE-BOOK
SLEEVE-LINK	SMUTTINESS	SOLDIERING	SOURDELINE
SLEIGH-BELL	SNAFFLE-BIT	SOLECISTIC	SOUTERRAIN
SLICKSTONE	SNAIL-PACED	SOLEMNISER	SOUTH-BOUND
SLIDE-VALVE	SNAIL-SHELL	SOLEMNNESS	SOUTHERING
SLIGHTNESS	SNAIL-WHEEL	SOLENOIDAL	SOUTHERNER
SLING-FRUIT	SNAKE-DANCE	SOLFATARIC	SOUTHERNLY
SLINGSTONE	SNAKE-FENCE	SOLICITUDE	SOUTH-POLAR
SLIPPERILY	SNAKE'S-HEAD	SOLIDARISM	SOUTHSAYER
SLIPPINESS	SNAKESTONE	SOLIDARIST	SOUTHWARDS
SLIPSLOPPY	SNAPDRAGON	SOLIDARITY	SOVENAUNCE
SLIPSTREAM	SNAPHAUNCE	SOLIDIFIED	SOW-THISTLE
SLIP-STRING	SNAPHAUNCH	SOLID-STATE	SPACECRAFT
SLIT-POCKET	SNAPPINGLY	SOLIFIDIAN	SPACEWOMAN
SLIT-TRENCH	SNAPPISHLY	SOLIPEDOUS	SPACIOUSLY
SLOOP-OF-WAR	SNEAKINESS	SOLITARIAN	SPADE-BEARD
SLOPPINESS	SNEAKINGLY	SOLITARILY	SPADICEOUS
SLOP-SELLER	SNEAKISHLY	SOLIVAGANT	SPAGERICAL
SLOTHFULLY	SNEAK-THIEF	SOLOMONIAN	SPAGIRICAL
SLOVENLIKE	SNEERINGLY	SOLSTITIAL	SPAGYRICAL
SLOW-FOOTED	SNEEZEWEED	SOLUBILISE	SPALLATION
SLOW-GAITED	SNEEZEWOOD	SOLUBILITY	SPANCELLED
SLOW-MOTION	SNEEZEWORT	SOLUTIONAL	SPANIOLATE
SLOW-MOVING	SNICK-A-SNEE	SOMATOLOGY	SPANIOLISE
SLOW-WINGED	SNIFFINESS	SOMATOTYPE	SPANKINGLY
SLUBBERING	SNIFFINGLY	SOMBRENESS	SPARGANIUM
SLUGGISHLY	SNIGGERING	SOMBRERITE	SPARKISHLY
SLUICE-GATE	SNIVELLING	SOMEBODIES	SPARSENESS
SLUMBERFUL	SNOBOCRACY	SOMERSAULT	SPARTACIST
SLUMBERING	SNORTINGLY	SOMEWHENCE	SPASMODIST
SLUMBEROUS	SNOTTINESS	SOMNAMBULE	SPASTICITY
SLUTTISHLY	SNOW-CAPPED	SOMNILOQUY	SPATANGOID
SMALL-CRAFT	SNOWMOBILE	SOMNOLENCE	SPATCHCOCK
SMALL-HOURS	SNOW-PLOUGH	SOMNOLENCY	SPATHULATE
SMALL-PIPES	SNOW-WREATH	SONG-SCHOOL	SPATIALITY

SPAULD-BONE
SPAWN-BRICK
SPEAKINGLY
SPEAR-GRASS
SPEAR-POINT
SPEAR-SHAFT
SPECIALISE
SPECIALISM
SPECIALIST
SPECIALITY
SPECIATION
SPECIFICAL
SPECIFYING
SPECIOSITY
SPECIOUSLY
SPECTACLED
SPECTACLES
SPECTATRIX
SPECTRALLY
SPECTRE-BAT
SPECULATOR
SPEECHLESS
SPEEDFULLY
SPEEDINESS
SPEED-LIMIT
SPELLBOUND
SPELLINGLY
SPELL-STOPT
SPENCERIAN
SPENSERIAN
SPERMACETI
SPERMADUCT
SPERMARIUM
SPERMATIST
SPERMATIUM
SPERMIDUCT
SPERMOGONE
SPERM-WHALE
SPERRYLITE
SPHACELATE
SPHAERIDIA
SPHALERITE
SPHENISCUS
SPHENOGRAM
SPHENOIDAL
SPHERE-BORN
SPHERELESS
SPHERE-LIKE
SPHERICITY
SPHEROIDAL
SPHERULITE
SPHINGIDAE
SPHINX-MOTH
SPIDER-CRAB
SPIDER-LIKE
SPIDER-LINE
SPIDER-WORK
SPIDER-WORT
SPIFLICATE
SPIKE-GRASS
SPILLIKINS
SPINACEOUS
SPINDLE-OIL
SPINESCENT
SPINIGRADE
SPINNERULE

SPINSTERLY
SPINSTRESS
SPIRACULAR
SPIRACULUM
SPIRIT-BLUE
SPIRIT-DUCK
SPIRITEDLY
SPIRIT-LAMP
SPIRIT-LEAF
SPIRITLESS
SPIRITUOUS
SPIROGRAPH
SPIROMETER
SPIROMETRY
SPIROPHORE
SPISSITUDE
SPITCH-COCK
SPITEFULLY
SPLANCHNIC
SPLASHDOWN
SPLEENLESS
SPLEEN-WORT
SPLENDIDLY
SPLINT-BONE
SPLINT-COAL
SPLINTWOOD
SPLIT-LEVEL
SPLUTTERER
SPODOMANCY
SPOILSPORT
SPOKESHAVE
SPOLIATION
SPOLIATIVE
SPOLIATORY
SPONDYLOUS
SPONGE-BATH
SPONGE-CAKE
SPONGEWOOD
SPONGIFORM
SPONGINESS
SPONGOLOGY
SPONSIONAL
SPONSORIAL
SPOOKINESS
SPOONDRIFT
SPOONERISM
SPORADICAL
SPORANGIAL
SPORANGIUM
SPOROPHORE
SPOROPHYLL
SPOROPHYTE
SPOROZOITE
SPORTFULLY
SPORTINESS
SPORTINGLY
SPORTIVELY
SPORTSWEAR
SPORTWOMAN
SPOT-BARRED
SPOTLESSLY
SPOT-STROKE
SPOTTINESS
SPOUSELESS
SPREAD-OVER
SPREAGHERY

SPRIGHTFUL
SPRINGBUCK
SPRING-CART
SPRINGHAAS
SPRING-HALT
SPRING-HARE
SPRINGHEAD
SPRINGLESS
SPRINGLIKE
SPRING-LOCK
SPRING-TAIL
SPRINGTIDE
SPRINGTIME
SPRINGWOOD
SPRINGWORT
SPRINKLING
SPRUCE-BEER
SPRUCENESS
SPULEBLADE
SPUMESCENT
SPUR-HEELED
SPURIOSITY
SPURIOUSLY
SPUR-WINGED
SPUTTERING
SQUABASHER
SQUADRONAL
SQUADRONED
SQUALIDITY
SQUAMATION
SQUAMIFORM
SQUAMOSITY
SQUAMULOSE
SQUANDERED
SQUANDERER
SQUARE-FACE
SQUARE-HEAD
SQUARENESS
SQUARE-ROOT
SQUARE-SAIL
SQUARE-TOED
SQUARE-TOES
SQUAREWISE
SQUEEZABLE
SQUEEZE-BOX
SQUELCHING
SQUETEAGUE
SQUINT-EYED
SQUINT-EYES
SQUIRALITY
SQUIRARCHY
SQUIREARCH
SQUIREHOOD
SQUIRE-LIKE
SQUIRELING
SQUIRESHIP
STABBINGLY
STABILISER
STABLENESS
STABLE-ROOM
STADHOLDER
STAFF-CORPS
STAG-BEETLE
STAGECOACH
STAGECRAFT
STAGE-FEVER

STAGE-HORSE
STAGE-WAGON
STAGGERING
STAG-HEADED
STAGNANTLY
STAGNATION
STAIR-TOWER
STALACTITE
STALAGMITE
STALLENGER
STALLINGER
STALL-PLATE
STALWARTLY
STAMINEOUS
STAMMERING
STAMP-ALBUM
STAMP-PAPER
STANCHLESS
STANCHNESS
STANDERS-BY
STANDPOINT
STANDSTILL
STANNARIES
STANNOTYPE
STAPHYLINE
STAPHYLOMA
STAR-BRIGHT
STARCHEDLY
STARGAZING
STARK-NAKED
STARMONGER
STARR-GRASS
STARRINESS
STARRY-EYED
STAR-SHAPED
STARTINGLY
START-NAKED
STARVATION
STARVELING
STATE-AIDED
STATE-CABIN
STATECRAFT
STATE-HOUSE
STATE-PAPER
STATE-TRIAL
STATICALLY
STATIONARY
STATIONERY
STATOSCOPE
STATUESQUE
STATUTABLE
STATUTABLY
STATUTE-CAP
STATUTE-LAW
STAUROLITE
STAVESACRE
STAY-AT-HOME
STAY-TACKLE
STEADINESS
STEALINGLY
STEALTHILY
STEAM-CHEST
STEAM-CRANE
STEAM-GAUGE
STEAMINESS
STEAM-NAVVY

STEAM-POWER
STEAMTIGHT
STEAM-YACHT
STEATOCELE
STEELINESS
STEEL-PLATE
STEELWORKS
STEEPINESS
STEEPLE-HAT
STEERSMATE
STEGANOPOD
STELLATELY
STELLIFIED
STELLIFORM
STELLULATE
STEMMATOUS
STEMWINDER
STENCH-TRAP
STENCILLED
STENCILLER
STENOGRAPH
STENOPAEIC
STENOTYPER
STENTORIAN
STEP-DANCER
STEPFATHER
STEPHANITE
STEP-LADDER
STEPMOTHER
STEPPARENT
STEP-ROCKET
STEPSISTER
STERCORARY
STERCORATE
STEREOBATE
STEREOGRAM
STEREOPSIS
STEREOTOMY
STEREOTYPE
STEREOTYPY
STERIGMATA
STERILISER
STERNBOARD
STERN-CHASE
STERN-FRAME
STERNSHEET
STERNWARDS
STERNWORKS
STERTOROUS
STEWARDESS
STIBIALISM
STICHARION
STICHIDIUM
STICHOLOGY
STICKINESS
STICKY-BACK
STIFFENING
STIFF-RUMPT
STIFLE-BONE
STIFLINGLY
STIGMARIAN
STIGMATISE
STIGMATISM
STIGMATIST
STIGMATOSE
STILETTOED

STILLATORY
STILL-BIRTH
STILL-HOUSE
STILLICIDE
STILL-STAND
STILTINESS
STIMULABLE
STIMULANCY
STIMULATOR
STINGINESS
STINGINGLY
STINK-BRAND
STINKINGLY
STINKSTONE
STINTINGLY
STIPELLATE
STIPULATOR
STIRRINGLY
STIRRUP-CUP
STITCHWORT
STOCHASTIC
STOCKINESS
STOCKINGED
STOCKINGER
STOCK-RIDER
STOCKSTILL
STODGINESS
STOLENWISE
STOLIDNESS
STOMACHFUL
STOMACHOUS
STOMATITIS
STOMATOPOD
STOMODAEUM
STONE-BLIND
STONE-BORER
STONE-BRASH
STONE-BREAK
STONE-BROKE
STONE-CANAL
STONE-EATER
STONE-FRUIT
STONEHORSE
STONE-MASON
STONE-SNIPE
STONE-STILL
STONE-THROW
STONY-BROKE
STOOPINGLY
STOREHOUSE
STORIOLOGY
STORK'S-BILL
STORMBOUND
STORMFULLY
STORM-GLASS
STORMINESS
STORMPROOF
STORM-TRACK
STORM-WATER
STOUTHERIE
STOUTHRIEF
STOVE-PLANT
STRABISMAL
STRABISMIC
STRABISMUS
STRABOTOMY

STRACCHINO
STRADIVARI
STRAGGLING
STRAIGHTEN
STRAIGHTLY
STRAINEDLY
STRAITENED
STRAIT-LACE
STRAITNESS
STRAMONIUM
STRAP-HINGE
STRATEGICS
STRATEGIST
STRATHSPEY
STRATIFIED
STRATIFORM
STRATIOTES
STRATOCRAT
STRAVAIGER
STRAWBERRY
STRAWBOARD
STRAW-PLAIT
STREAMERED
STREAM-GOLD
STREAMLESS
STREAMLINE
STREAMLING
STREET-ARAB
STREET-DOOR
STREET-ROOM
STREET-WARD
STRELITZES
STRELITZIA
STRENGTHEN
STREPEROUS
STREPITANT
STREPITOSO
STREPITOUS
STRESSLESS
STRICTNESS
STRICTURED
STRIDELEGS
STRIDENTLY
STRIDEWAYS
STRIDULANT
STRIDULATE
STRIDULOUS
STRIFELESS
STRIGIFORM
STRIKER-OUT
STRIKINGLY
STRING-BAND
STRING-BEAN
STRINGENCY
STRINGENDO
STRINGHALT
STRINGLESS
STRINKLING
STRIPELESS
STRIPINESS
STRIPPINGS
STRIP-TEASE
STRIVINGLY
STROBILATE
STROBILINE
STROBILOID

STROKESMAN
STROMATOUS
STRONGHOLD
STRONG-KNIT
STRONG-ROOM
STROPHIOLE
STRUCTURAL
STRUCTURED
STRUGGLING
STRULDBRUG
STRUTHIOID
STRUTHIOUS
STRYCHNINE
STRYCHNISM
STUBBINESS
STUBBLE-FED
STUBBORNLY
STUDIOUSLY
STUFFINESS
STULTIFIED
STULTIFIER
STUMPINESS
STUNNINGLY
STUPEFYING
STUPENDOUS
STUPIDNESS
STUPRATION
STURDINESS
STUTTERING
STYLISTICS
STYLOGRAPH
STYLOPISED
STYPTICITY
SUAVEOLENT
SUBACIDITY
SUBANGULAR
SUBAQUATIC
SUBAQUEOUS
SUBARCUATE
SUBATOMICS
SUBCENTRAL
SUBCHANTER
SUBCLAVIAN
SUBCORDATE
SUBCULTURE
SUBDEANERY
SUBDIVIDER
SUBDUCTION
SUBDUEMENT
SUBFUSCOUS
SUBGENERIC
SUBGLACIAL
SUBGLOBOSE
SUBHEADING
SUBINTRANT
SUBJECTIFY
SUBJECTION
SUBJECTIVE
SUBJOINDER
SUBJUGATOR
SUBKINGDOM
SUBLETTING
SUBLIMABLE
SUBLIMATED
SUBLIMINAL
SUBLINGUAL

SUBMARINER
SUBMEDIANT
SUBMERSION
SUBMISSION
SUBMISSIVE
SUBMITTING
SUBMONTANE
SUBNASCENT
SUBNATURAL
SUBOCTUPLE
SUBORBITAL
SUBORDINAL
SUBPREFECT
SUBREPTION
SUBREPTIVE
SUBROUTINE
SUBSCRIBED
SUBSCRIBER
SUBSECTION
SUBSELLIUM
SUBSEQUENT
SUBSESSILE
SUBSHRUBBY
SUBSIDENCE
SUBSIDENCY
SUBSIDIARY
SUBSISTENT
SUBSOILING
SUBSPECIES
SUBSPINOUS
SUBSTATION
SUBSTELLAR
SUBSTERNAL
SUBSTITUTE
SUBSTRATAL
SUBSTRATUM
SUBSULTIVE
SUBSURFACE
SUBTANGENT
SUBTENANCY
SUBTERFUGE
SUBTERRENE
SUBTILNESS
SUBTLENESS
SUBTRACTOR
SUBTRAHEND
SUBTROPICS
SUBVARIETY
SUBVENTION
SUBVERSION
SUBVERSIVE
SUCCEEDING
SUCCESSFUL
SUCCESSION
SUCCESSIVE
SUCCINCTLY
SUCCUBUSES
SUCCULENCE
SUCCULENCY
SUCCURSALE
SUCCUSSION
SUCCUSSIVE
SUCKING-PIG
SUDATORIUM
SUDDENNESS
SUEABILITY

SUFFERABLE
SUFFERABLY
SUFFERANCE
SUFFICIENT
SUFFIGANCE
SUFFISANCE
SUFFRAGIST
SUGAR-APPLE
SUGAR-BAKER
SUGAR-CANDY
SUGAR-DADDY
SUGAR-GRASS
SUGAR-HOUSE
SUGARINESS
SUGAR-MAPLE
SUGAR-WRACK
SUGGESTION
SUGGESTIVE
SUICIDALLY
SULLENNESS
SULPHONATE
SULPHURATE
SULPHUROUS
SULTANSHIP
SULTRINESS
SUMMERLIKE
SUMMER-TIDE
SUMMERTIME
SUMMER-TREE
SUMMITLESS
SUMMONABLE
SUNBATHING
SUN-BITTERN
SUNDERANCE
SUNDERMENT
SUN-GLASSES
SUN-PARLOUR
SUN-PICTURE
SUNSETTING
SUN-WORSHIP
SUPERACUTE
SUPERALLOY
SUPERALTAR
SUPERATION
SUPERBNESS
SUPERCARGO
SUPER-DUPER
SUPEREXALT
SUPERHUMAN
SUPERIORLY
SUPERLUNAR
SUPERNALLY
SUPERORDER
SUPERPOSED
SUPERROYAL
SUPERSEDER
SUPERSONIC
SUPERSOUND
SUPER-STATE
SUPERTONIC
SUPERVISAL
SUPERVISOR
SUPINATION
SUPINENESS
SUPPERLESS
SUPPERTIME

SUPPLANTER
SUPPLEMENT
SUPPLENESS
SUPPLETIVE
SUPPLETORY
SUPPLIANCE
SUPPLICANT
SUPPLICATE
SUPPLYMENT
SUPPORTING
SUPPORTIVE
SUPPORTURE
SUPPOSABLE
SUPPOSABLY
SUPPOSEDLY
SUPPRESSED
SUPPRESSOR
SUPRALUNAR
SUPRARENAL
SURCHARGED
SURCHARGER
SURE-ENOUGH
SURE-FOOTED
SURETYSHIP
SURFACEMAN
SURFACTANT
SURF-BATHER
SURFEITING
SURF-RIDING
SURGICALLY
SURMISABLE
SURMOUNTED
SURMOUNTER
SURNOMINAL
SURPASSING
SURPLUSAGE
SURPRISING
SURREALISM
SURREALIST
SURROGATUM
SURVEYANCE
SURVIVANCE
SUSCEPTIVE
SUSCIPIENT
SUSPECTFUL
SUSPENSION
SUSPENSIVE
SUSPENSOID
SUSPENSORY
SUSPICIOUS
SUSPIRIOUS
SUSTAINING
SUSTENANCE
SUSTENTATE
SUSTENTION
SUSTENTIVE
SUTURATION
SUZERAINTY
SWADESHISM
SWAGGERING
SWAN-MAIDEN
SWAN-MUSSEL
SWAN-UPPING
SWARM-SPORE
SWEATHBAND
SWEATINESS

SWEAT-SHIRT
SWEEPINGLY
SWEEPSTAKE
SWEETBREAD
SWEET-BRIAR
SWEET-BRIER
SWEETENING
SWEETHEART
SWEETSTUFF
SWEET-WATER
SWELLINGLY
SWELTERING
SWERVELESS
SWIMMINGLY
SWINE-DRUNK
SWINE-FEVER
SWINESTONE
SWINGINGLY
SWINGLE-BAR
SWING-MUSIC
SWING-SHELF
SWING-STOCK
SWING-SWANG
SWING-WHEEL
SWITCHBACK
SWITCH-OVER
SWIVEL-HOOK
SWOONINGLY
SWORD-BLADE
SWORDCRAFT
SWORD-DANCE
SWORD-GRASS
SWORD-GUARD
SWORDPROOF
SWORD-STICK
SYBARITICA
SYBARITISH
SYBARITISM
SYCOPHANCY
SYLLABICAL
SYLLABUSES
SYLLOGISER
SYLPHIDINE
SYMBOLICAL
SYMBOLISER
SYMMETRIAN
SYMMETRISE
SYMPATHISE
SYMPETALAE
SYMPHILISM
SYMPHILOUS
SYMPHONION
SYMPHONIST
SYMPHYLOUS
SYMPHYSEAL
SYMPHYSIAL
SYNAERESIS
SYNALOEPHA
SYNANDRIUM
SYNANDROUS
SYNANTHOUS
SYNAXARION
SYNCARPOUS
SYNCHRONAL
SYNCHRONIC
SYNCLASTIC

SYNCOPATED
SYNCOPATOR
SYNCRETISE
SYNCRETISM
SYNCRETIST
SYNDERESIS
SYNDICATOR
SYNECDOCHE
SYNEIDESIS
SYNERGETIC
SYNGENESIA
SYNGENESIS
SYNGENETIC
SYNOECIOUS
SYNONYMIST
SYNONYMITY
SYNONYMOUS
SYNOPTICAL
SYNOSTOSIS
SYNTAGMATA
SYNTENOSIS
SYNTERESIS
SYNTHECTIC
SYNTHESISE
SYNTHESIST
SYNTHETISE
SYNTHETIST
SYNTHRONUS
SYPHILITIC
SYRINGITIS
SYSTEMATIC
SYSTEMLESS

T

TABERNACLE
TABESCENCE
TABLE-CLOTH
TABLE-COVER
TABLE-D'HÔTE
TABLE-KNIFE
TABLE-LINEN
TABLE-MONEY
TABLE-MUSIC
TABLESPOON
TABLE-SPORT
TABLE-WATER
TABULARISE
TABULATION
TABULATORY
TACHOGRAPH
TACHOMETER
TACHOMETRY
TACHYGRAPH
TACHYLYTIC
TACHYMETER
TACHYMETRY
TACHYPNOEA
TACITURNLY
TACTICALLY
TACTLESSLY
TACTUALITY
TAILOR-BIRD
TAILOR-MADE
TAKINGNESS
TALC-SCHIST
TALE-BEARER

TALENTLESS
TALE-TELLER
TALISMANIC
TALKY-TALKY
TALLOW-FACE
TALLOW-TREE
TALLY-TRADE
TALLYWOMAN
TALMUDICAL
TAMABILITY
TAMBOURINE
TANAGRIDAE
TANDEMWISE
TANGENTIAL
TANGLEFOOT
TANGLEMENT
TANGLESOME
TANGLINGLY
TANK-ENGINE
TANTALISER
TANTAMOUNT
TAP-DANCING
TAPE-RECORD
TAPERINGLY
TAPESTRIED
TAPOTEMENT
TAPPET-LOOM
TARADIDDLE
TARANTELLA
TARDIGRADA
TARDIGRADE
TAR-MACADAM
TARPAULING
TARSIA-WORK
TARTAREOUS
TARTUFFIAN
TARTUFFISH
TARTUFFISM
TASEOMETER
TASKMASTER
TASSEILING
TASTEFULLY
TATTIE-CLAW
TATTIE-SHAW
TATTLINGLY
TAUNTINGLY
TAUROMACHY
TAUTOLOGIC
TAUTOMERIC
TAUTOPHONY
TAWDRINESS
TAWDRY-LACE
TAXABILITY
TAXI-DANCER
TAXIDERMAL
TAXIDERMIC
TAXONOMIST
TEA-CLIPPER
TEA-DRINKER
TEA-MEETING
TEAM-SPIRIT
TEA-PLANTER
TEAR-BOTTLE
TEAR-JERKER
TEASELLING
TEA-SERVICE

TEA-TROLLEY
TECHNETIUM
TECHNICIAN
TECHNICIST
TECHNOCRAT
TECHNOLOGY
TECTRICIAL
TEDIOUSOME
TEENY-WEENY
TEETOTALLY
TEGUMENTAL
TEICHOPSIA
TEINOSCOPE
TELECAMERA
TELECASTER
TELEGRAPHY
TELEMETRIC
TELEOLOGIC
TELEOSTEAN
TELEOSTOME
TELEOSTOMI
TELEPATHIC
TELEPHONER
TELEPHONIC
TELESCOPIC
TELESCREEN
TELESMATIC
TELEVÉRITÉ
TELEVIEWER
TELEVISION
TELEVISUAL
TELEWRITER
TELLERSHIP
TELLING-OFF
TELPHERAGE
TELPHERMAN
TELPHERWAY
TEMEROUSLY
TEMPERABLE
TEMPERANCE
TEMPEREDLY
TEMPESTIVE
TEMPORALLY
TEMPORALTY
TEMPORISER
TEMPTATION
TEMPTINGLY
TEMULENTLY
TENABILITY
TENANTABLE
TENANTLESS
TENANTSHIP
TENDENTIAL
TENDERFEET
TENDERFOOT
TENDERLING
TENDERLOIN
TENDERNESS
TENDRILLAR
TENDRILLED
TENEBRIFIC
TENEBRIOUS
TENEMENTAL
TENNANTITE
TENNIS-BALL
TENNIS-SHOE

TEN-POINTER
TEN-POUNDER
TENSION-ROD
TENTACULAR
TENTACULUM
TENTERHOOK
TENT-STITCH
TEPIDARIUM
TERATOGENY
TERATOLOGY
TERATOMATA
TERMAGANCY
TERMINABLE
TERMINABLY
TERMINALIA
TERMINALLY
TERMINATOR
TERNEPLATE
TERRACOTTA
TERRA-FIRMA
TERRA-ROSSA
TERREPLEIN
TERRIFYING
TERRORISER
TERRORLESS
TERSANCTUS
TESCHENITE
TESSELLATE
TESTACEOUS
TEST-FLIGHT
TESTICULAR
TESTIFYING
TETCHINESS
TÊTE-DE-PONT
TETRACHORD
TETRACTINE
TETRAETHYL
TETRAGONAL
TETRAGYNIA
TETRAMERAL
TETRAMETER
TETRANDRIA
TETRAPLOID
TETRAPOLIS
TETRAPTOTE
TETRASEMIC
TETRASPORE
TETRASTICH
TETRASTYLE
TETRATHLON
TEXTUALIST
TEXTURALLY
THAILANDER
THALASSIAN
THALE-CRESS
THALICTRUM
THALLIFORM
THANATOSIS
THANKFULLY
THATCHLESS
THAUMASITE
THEATRICAL
THEISTICAL
THEMSELVES
THENABOUTS
THEOCRATIC

THEODICEAN
THEODOLITE
THEOGONIST
THEOLOGATE
THEOLOGIAN
THEOLOGISE
THEOLOGIST
THEOMANIAC
THEOMANTIC
THEOPHANIC
THEOPHOBIA
THEOPNEUST
THEOSOPHER
THEOSOPHIC
THEOTECHNY
THEREABOUT
THEREAFTER
THEREAMONG
THEREANENT
THEREUNDER
THERMIONIC
THERMISTOR
THERMOGRAM
THERMOLOGY
THERMOPHIL
THERMOPILE
THERMOSTAT
THERMOTICS
THETICALLY
THEURGICAL
THICKENING
THICK-GROWN
THICK-SKULL
THIEF-TAKER
THIEVISHLY
THILL-HORSE
THIMBLEFUL
THIMBLE-RIG
THINGINESS
THINGUMBOB
THINKINGLY
THIN-WALLED
THIOCYANIC
THIOPENTAL
THIRD-CLASS
THIRD-PARTY
THIRSTLESS
THIRTEENTH
THIRTYFOLD
THIXOTROPY
THORN-APPLE
THORN-DEVIL
THORN-HEDGE
THORNINESS
THOROUGHLY
THOUGHTFUL
THOUSANDTH
THREADBARE
THREAD-CELL
THREAD-LACE
THREADWORM
THREATENED
THREATENER
THREE-CLEFT
THREE-PARTS
THREEPENCE

THREEPENNY
THREE-PILED
THREE-POUND
THREESCORE
THREE-SIDED
THRENODIAL
THRENODIST
THRIFTIEST
THRIFTLESS
THRIVELESS
THRIVINGLY
THROAT-BAND
THROATFULL
THROATWORT
THROMBOSIS
THRONELESS
THRONE-ROOM
THROTTLING
THROUGHOUT
THROUGH-PUT
THROUGHWAY
THROWN-SILK
THROW-STICK
THRUPPENCE
THRUPPENNY
THUMBIKINS
THUMB-INDEX
THUMB-LATCH
THUMBPIECE
THUMBPRINT
THUMB-SCREW
THUMB-STALL
THUNDER-GOD
THUNDERING
THUNDEROUS
THWARTEDLY
THWARTSHIP
THWARTWAYS
THWARTWISE
THYRSOIDAL
TICKER-TAPE
TICKING-OFF
TICKLISHLY
TIDDLYWINK
TIDE-WAITER
TIDIVATION
TIGER-SHARK
TIGER-SNAKE
TIGHTISHLY
TIGHT-LACER
TILIACEOUS
TILLANDSIA
TILLER-ROPE
TILLY-FALLY
TILLY-VALLY
TILT-HAMMER
TIMBER-LINE
TIMBER-TOES
TIMBER-TREE
TIMBER-WOLF
TIMBER-YARD
TIMBROLOGY
TIME-KEEPER
TIME-KILLER
TIMELESSLY
TIMELINESS

TIME-SAVING
TIME-SERVER
TIME-SIGNAL
TIME-SPIRIT
TIME-SWITCH
TIME-THRUST
TIMOCRATIC
TIMOROUSLY
TIM-WHISKEY
TINCTORIAL
TINDER-LIKE
TINKLINGLY
TINSELLING
TINTOMETER
TIRAILLEUR
TIRELESSLY
TIRESOMELY
TIRING-ROOM
TIRLING-PIN
TIROCINIUM
TIRRA-LIRRA
TITANESQUE
TITHING-MAN
TITILLATOR
TITIVATION
TITLE-SHEET
TITUBATION
TITULARITY
TOAD-EATING
TOBOGGANER
TOCCATELLA
TOCHER-GOOD
TOCHERLESS
TOCOPHEROL
TODDY-LADLE
TODDY-STICK
TOFFEE-NOSE
TOGGLE-IRON
TOILETRIES
TOILET-ROLL
TOILET-SOAP
TOILINETTE
TOILSOMELY
TOKEN-MONEY
TOLERANTLY
TOLERATION
TOLLBRIDGE
TOMFOOLERY
TOMFOOLISH
TOMOGRAPHY
TONALITIVE
TONELESSLY
TONGUELESS
TONGUESTER
TONGUE-TIED
TONGUE-WORK
TONISHNESS
TONSILITIC
TONSILITIS
TOOTHBRUSH
TOOTHPASTE
TOOTH-SHELL
TOPAZOLITE
TOP-GALLANT
TOPHACEOUS
TOPICALITY

TOPI-WALLAH
TOP-KNOTTED
TOPOGRAPHY
TOPONYMICS
TOPPING-OUT
TOP-SOILING
TOPSYTURVY
TORBERNITE
TORCH-DANCE
TORCHLIGHT
TORCH-STAFF
TORMENTING
TORPEDOIST
TORPEDO-NET
TORPESCENT
TORPIDNESS
TORREFYING
TORRENT-BOW
TORRENTIAL
TORRIDNESS
TORTUOSITY
TORTUOUSLY
TOSSICATED
TOSTICATED
TOTEMISTIC
TOUCH-AND-GO
TOUCHINESS
TOUCHINGLY
TOUCH-JUDGE
TOUCH-ME-NOT
TOUCH-PAPER
TOUCH-PIECE
TOUCH-PLATE
TOUCHSTONE
TOUGHENING
TOURING-CAR
TOURMALINE
TOURNAMENT
TOURNIQUET
TOWARDNESS
TOWEL-GOURD
TOWEL-HORSE
TOWER-SHELL
TOWING-PATH
TOWN'S-BAIRN
TOWNSWOMAN
TOXICATION
TOXICOLOGY
TOXIPHOBIA
TOYISHNESS
TRABEATION
TRABECULAE
TRABECULAR
TRACE-HORSE
TRACHEARIA
TRACHEATED
TRACHEITIS
TRACHELATE
TRACHYTOID
TRACK-SCOUT
TRACTARIAN
TRACTIONAL
TRADE-FALNE
TRADESFOLK
TRADE-UNION
TRADUCTION

TRADUCTIVE
TRAFFICKED
TRAFFICKER
TRAGACANTH
TRAGICALLY
TRAGI-COMIC
TRAITORISM
TRAITOROUS
TRAJECTION
TRAJECTORY
TRAMMELLED
TRAMMELLER
TRAMMEL-NET
TRAMONTANA
TRAMONTANE
TRAMPOLINE
TRAMWAY-CAR
TRANQUILLY
TRANSACTOR
TRANSCRIBE
TRANSCRIPT
TRANSDUCER
TRANSEPTAL
TRANSFEREE
TRANSFEROR
TRANSFUSER
TRANSGRESS
TRANSIENCE
TRANSIENCY
TRANSISTOR
TRANSITION
TRANSITIVE
TRANSITORY
TRANSLATOR
TRANSLUCID
TRANSLUNAR
TRANSMUTER
TRANSPLANT
TRANSPOSAL
TRANSPOSER
TRANS-SHAPE
TRANS-SONIC
TRANSVALUE
TRANSVERSE
TRAP-LADDER
TRAPPINESS
TRASHINESS
TRAUMATISM
TRAVELATOR
TRAVELLING
TRAVELOGUE
TRAVERSING
TRAVERTINE
TRAVOLATOR
TREACHERER
TREAD-WHEEL
TREASONOUS
TREBLENESS
TRECENTIST
TREE-BURIAL
TREE-MALLOW
TREE-TOMATO
TREILLAGED
TREKSCHUIT
TREMENDOUS
TREMOLANDO

TREMOLITIC
TREMORLESS
TRENCHANCY
TRENCH-COAT
TRENCH-FEET
TREPANNING
TREY-ANTLER
TRIACONTER
TRIACTINAL
TRIANDRIAN
TRIANDROUS
TRIANGULAR
TRIAPSIDAL
TRIBOMETER
TRIBRACHIC
TRICHIASIS
TRICHINOUS
TRICHIURUS
TRICHOGYNE
TRICHOLOGY
TRICHOTOMY
TRICHROISM
TRICHROMAT
TRICHROMIC
TRICHTITIC
TRICKINESS
TRICKISHLY
TRICK-TRACK
TRICLINIUM
TRICOSTATE
TRICROTISM
TRICROTOUS
TRICUSPATE
TRICYCLING
TRICYCLIST
TRIDENTATE
TRIDENTINE
TRIERARCHY
TRIFARIOUS
TRIFLINGLY
TRIFOLIATE
TRIFURCATE
TRIGEMINAL
TRIGGERMAN
TRIGLYPHIC
TRIGRAMMIC
TRILATERAL
TRILINEATE
TRILINGUAL
TRILITERAL
TRILLIONTH
TRILOBATED
TRILOBITIC
TRILOCULAR
TRIMMINGLY
TRIMONTHLY
TRIMORPHIC
TRINACRIAN
TRINISCOPE
TRINKETING
TRIOECIOUS
TRIPARTITE
TRIPEWOMAN
TRIP-HAMMER
TRIPHYSITE
TRIPINNATE

TRIPLENESS
TRIPLICATE
TRIPLICITY
TRIPPERISH
TRIPPINGLY
TRIPTEROUS
TRIPTHTONG
TRIPUDIARY
TRIPUDIATE
TRIQUETRAL
TRIQUETRUM
TRIRADIATE
TRISECTION
TRISECTRIX
TRISKELION
TRISULCATE
TRITERNATE
TRITHIONIC
TRITICALLY
TRITICEOUS
TRITURATOR
TRIUMPHANT
TRIUMPHERY
TRIUMPHING
TRIUMVIRAL
TRIVALENCE
TRIVALENCY
TRIVIALISE
TRIVIALISM
TROCHANTER
TROCHISCUS
TROCHOIDAL
TROCHOTRON
TROCTOLITE
TROGLODYTE
TROGONIDAE
TROLLEY-BUS
TROLLEY-CAR
TROLLEY-MAN
TROLLOPEAN
TROLLOPIAN
TROLLOPING
TROLLOPISH
TROMBONIST
TROMOMETER
TROOP-HORSE
TROPAEOLUM
TROPHESIAL
TROPHOLOGY
TROPHONIAN
TROPICALLY
TROPIC-BIRD
TROPOLOGIC
TROPOPAUSE
TROPOPHYTE
TROTSKYISM
TROTSKYIST
TROTSKYITE
TROUBADOUR
TROUBLEDLY
TROU-DE-LOUP
TROU-MADAME
TROUSERING
TROUSER-LEG
TROUSSEAUX
TROUT-SPOON

TROUT-STONE
TROUVAILLE
TROWELLING
TRUANTSHIP
TRUCKLE-BED
TRUCULENCE
TRUCULENCY
TRUFFLE-DOG
TRUFFLE-PIG
TRUMPETING
TRUNCATELY
TRUNCATION
TRUNDLE-BED
TRUNK-MAKER
TRUNNIONED
TRUSTFULLY
TRUST-HOUSE
TRUSTINESS
TRUSTINGLY
TRUTHFULLY
TRUTH-VALUE
TRYPTOPHAN
TSAREVITCH
TUBERACEAE
TUBERCULAR
TUBERCULIN
TUBERCULUM
TUBERIFORM
TUBEROSITY
TUBICOLOUS
TUB-THUMBER
TUBULARIAN
TUBULARITY
TUBULATION
TUBULATURE
TUDORESQUE
TUFFACEOUS
TUFFAFFETY
TUFTAFFETY
TUFT-HUNTER
TUITIONARY
TULARAEMIA
TULIP-EARED
TUMBLE-CART
TUMBLE-DOWN
TUMBLE-DUNG
TUMBLERFUL
TUMBLE-WEED
TUMESCENCE
TUMULTUARY
TUMULTUATE
TUMULTUOUS
TUNBELLIED
TUNING-FORK
TUNNELLING
TURBIDNESS
TURBINATED
TURBULATOR
TURBULENCE
TURBULENCY
TURCOPHILE
TURCOPHOBE
TURGESCENT
TURGIDNESS
TURKEY-COCK
TURKEY-TROT

TURKO-TATAR	ULTRA-RAPID	UNBEATABLE	UNCREATING
TURNBROACH	ULTRASHORT	UNBEAVERED	UNCREDIBLE
TURNBUCKLE	ULTRASONIC	UNBECOMING	UNCRITICAL
TURNING-SAW	ULTRASOUND	UNBEDIMMED	UNCTUOSITY
TURNIP-FLEA	ULTRONEOUS	UNBEDINNED	UNCTUOUSLY
TURPENTINE	UMBELLATED	UNBEGOTTEN	UNCULTURED
TURPENTINY	UMBELLIFER	UNBEGUILED	UNCUMBERED
TURRET-SHIP	UMBILICATE	UNBEHOLDEN	UNCURBABLE
TURRITELLA	UMBONATION	UNBELIEVED	UNCUSTOMED
TURTLEBACK	UMBRACULUM	UNBELIEVER	UNDEBARRED
TURTLE-DOVE	UMBRAGEOUS	UNBENIGNLY	UNDECEIVED
TURTLE-SOUP	UMBRATICAL	UNBESOUGHT	UNDECIMOLE
TUSSER-SILK	UMBRELLAED	UNBESPOKEN	UNDECISIVE
TUTORIALLY	UMPIRESHIP	UNBESTOWED	UNDECLARED
TUTWORKMAN	UNABRIDGED	UNBETRAYED	UNDEFEATED
TUZZI-MUZZY	UNABSOLVED	UNBETTERED	UNDEFENDED
TWANGINGLY	UNACADEMIC	UNBEWAILED	UNDELAYING
TWEEDLEDEE	UNACCENTED	UNBIBLICAL	UNDEMANDED
TWEEDLEDUM	UNACTUATED	UNBIRTHDAY	UNDENIABLE
'TWEEN-DECKS	UNADJUSTED	UNBLAMABLE	UNDENIABLY
TWEET-TWEET	UNADMIRING	UNBLAMABLY	UNDEPLORED
TWELFTH-DAY	UNADMITTED	UNBLEACHED	UNDEPRAVED
TWELVEFOLD	UNAFFECTED	UNBLENCHED	UNDEPRIVED
TWELVE-NOTE	UNALLOTTED	UNBLINKING	UNDERACTOR
TWELVE-TONE	UNALTERING	UNBLISSFUL	UNDERAGENT
TWENTYFOLD	UNAMENABLE	UNBLOODIED	UNDERBELLY
TWENTY-FOUR	UN-AMERICAN	UNBLUSHING	UNDERBOARD
TWILIGHTED	UNAMUSABLE	UNBOASTFUL	UNDERBORNE
TWIN-SISTER	UNANALYSED	UNBONNETED	UNDERBOUGH
TWITTERING	UNANALYTIC	UNBORROWED	UNDERBRUSH
TWITTINGLY	UNANCHORED	UNBOTTOMED	UNDERBUILD
TWO-WHEELED	UNANIMATED	UNBRANCHED	UNDER-CLERK
TWO-WHEELER	UNANNEALED	UNBREACHED	UNDERCLIFF
TWO-YEAR-OLD	UNANSWERED	UNBREATHED	UNDERCOVER
TWYNATURED	UNAPPALLED	UNBREECHED	UNDER-CRAFT
TYBURN-TREE	UNAPPARENT	UNBRIBABLE	UNDERCREST
TYMPANITES	UNAPPEASED	UNBROKENLY	UNDERCROFT
TYMPANITIC	UNAPPRISED	UNBURDENED	UNDERDRAIN
TYMPANITIS	UNAPPROVED	UNBUTTERED	UNDERDRESS
TYPE-CUTTER	UNARGUABLE	UNBUTTONED	UNDERDRIVE
TYPE-HOLDER	UNARMOURED	UNCANDIDLY	UNDEREARTH
TYPESCRIPT	UNARRANGED	UNCANONISE	UNDERGLAZE
TYPE-SETTER	UNARTFULLY	UNCARED-FOR	UNDERGOING
TYPEWRITER	UNARTISTIC	UNCARPETED	UNDERGROVE
TYPHACEOUS	UNASCENDED	UNCENSORED	UNDERGROWN
TYPICALITY	UNASPIRING	UNCENSURED	UNDERJAWED
TYPOGRAPHY	UNASSAILED	UNCHANGING	UNDERLAYER
TYPOLOGIST	UNASSIGNED	UNCHARMING	UNDERLEASE
TYRANNIDAE	UNASSISTED	UNCHASTELY	UNDERLINEN
TYRANT-BIRD	UNASSUAGED	UNCHASTITY	UNDERLYING
TYROLIENNE	UNASSUMING	UNCHEERFUL	UNDERMINER
TYRRHENIAN	UNATONABLE	UNCHRISTEN	UNDERNEATH
	UNATTACHED	UNCLEANSED	UNDERNOTED
U	UNATTAINED	UNCLERICAL	UNDERNTIME
	UNATTENDED	UNCLOISTER	UNDER-POWER
UBIQUARIAN	UNATTESTED	UNCLUBABLE	UNDERPRIZE
UBIQUITARY	UNAVAILING	UNCOFFINED	UNDERPROOF
UBIQUITOUS	UNAVOWEDLY	UNCOLOURED	UNDERQUOTE
UGRO-FINNIC	UNAWAKENED	UNCOMMONLY	UNDERSCORE
UGSOMENESS	'UNBAILABLE	UNCOMMUTED	UNDERSCRUB
ULCERATION	UNBALANCED	UNCONFINED	UNDERSENSE
ULCERATIVE	UNBAPTISED	UNCONFUSED	UNDER-SEXED
ULCEROUSLY	UNBARBERED	UNCONJUGAL	UNDERSHIRT
ULSTERETTE	UNBATTERED	UNCONSOLED	UNDERSHOOT
ULTERIORLY	UNBEARABLE	UNCONSTANT	UNDERSHRUB
ULTIMATELY	UNBEARABLY	UNCONSUMED	UNDERSIZED
ULTRABASIC			

UNDERSKIRT
UNDERSLUNG
UNDERSTAND
UNDERSTATE
UNDERSTEER
UNDERSTOCK
UNDERSTOOD
UNDERSTUDY
UNDERTAKEN
UNDERTAKER
UNDERTIMED
UNDERTONED
UNDER-TRICK
UNDER-TUNIC
UNDERVALUE
UNDERVOICE
UNDERWATER
UNDERWORLD
UNDERWRITE
UNDESCRIED
UNDESERVED
UNDESERVER
UNDESIGNED
UNDESIRING
UNDESIROUS
UNDETECTED
UNDETERRED
UNDIGESTED
UNDIRECTED
UNDISMAYED
UNDISPOSED
UNDISPUTED
UNDIVERTED
UNDIVESTED
UNDIVORCED
UNDIVULGED
UNDOCTORED
UNDOMESTIC
UNDOUBTFUL
UNDOUBTING
UNDRAMATIC
UNDREADING
UNDREAMING
UNDRESSING
UNDROOPING
UNDULATELY
UNDULATING
UNDULATION
UNDULATORY
UNEASINESS
UNECLIPSED
UNECONOMIC
UNEDIFYING
UNEDUCABLE
UNEDUCATED
UNEFFECTED
UNEMBODIED
UNEMPHATIC
UNEMPLOYED
UNENCLOSED
UNENDEARED
UNENDINGLY
UNENRICHED
UNENSLAVED
UNENTAILED
UNENTITLED

UNENVIABLE
UNENVIABLY
UNEQUALLED
UNERRINGLY
UNESCORTED
UNEVENNESS
UNEVENTFUL
UNEXACTING
UNEXAMINED
UNEXAMPLED
UNEXCELLED
UNEXCITING
UNEXCLUDED
UNEXECUTED
UNEXPANDED
UNEXPECTED
UNEXPLORED
UNEXTENDED
UNFADINGLY
UNFAIRNESS
UNFAITHFUL
UNFALLIBLE
UNFAMILIAR
UNFASTENED
UNFATHERED
UNFATHERLY
UNFATHOMED
UNFEASIBLE
UNFEATURED
UNFEIGNING
UNFELLOWED
UNFEMININE
UNFETTERED
UNFILIALLY
UNFILLABLE
UNFILLETED
UNFILTERED
UNFINISHED
UNFLAGGING
UNFOCUSSED
UNFORCEDLY
UNFORCIBLE
UNFORDABLE
UNFORESEEN
UNFORESTED
UNFORETOLD
UNFORGIVEN
UNFORSAKEN
UNFORTUNED
UNFOSTERED
UNFOUGHTEN
UNFREQUENT
UNFRIENDED
UNFRIENDLY
UNFRIGHTED
UNFRUITFUL
UNFURROWED
UNGAINSAID
UNGARNERED
UNGARTERED
UNGATHERED
UNGENEROUS
UNGOVERNED
UNGRACEFUL
UNGRACIOUS
UNGRATEFUL

UNGROUNDED
UNGRUDGING
UNGUENTARY
UNHALLOWED
UNHAMPERED
UNHANDSOME
UNHARDENED
UNHAZARDED
UNHEALABLE
UNHEEDEDLY
UNHELMETED
UNHERALDED
UNHEROICAL
UNHISTORIC
UNHOLINESS
UNHOMELIKE
UNHONOURED
UNHOPED-FOR
UNHOUSELED
UNHOUZZLED
UNHUMANISE
UNHURRYING
UNHYGIENIC
UNIAXIALLY
UNICAMERAL
UNICENTRAL
UNICOSTATE
UNIDEALISM
UNIFLOROUS
UNIFORMITY
UNIGENITUS
UNILABIATE
UNILATERAL
UNILINGUAL
UNILITERAL
UNILOBULAR
UNILOCULAR
UNIMAGINED
UNIMMORTAL
UNIMPAIRED
UNIMPARTED
UNIMPLORED
UNIMPOSING
UNIMPROVED
UNINCLOSED
UNINDEARED
UNINFECTED
UNINFLAMED
UNINFLATED
UNINFORMED
UNINSPIRED
UNINTENDED
UNINUCLEAR
UNINVESTED
UNINVITING
UNINVOLVED
UNIPARTITE
UNIQUENESS
UNISERIATE
UNISONALLY
UNISONANCE
UNITEDNESS
UNIVALENCE
UNIVARIANT
UNIVARIATE
UNIVERSITY

UNIVOCALLY
UNIVOLTINE
UNJUSTNESS
UNKINDNESS
UNKINGLIKE
UNKNIGHTED
UNKNIGHTLY
UNKNOWABLE
UNLABELLED
UNLABOURED
UNLADYLIKE
UNLAMENTED
UNLAWFULLY
UNLEAVENED
UNLEISURED
UNLESSONED
UNLETTERED
UNLICENSED
UNLIKENESS
UNLIQUORED
UNLISTENED
UNLITERARY
UNLOVEABLE
UNLOVINGLY
UNMAIDENLY
UNMAILABLE
UNMANACLED
UNMANFULLY
UNMANNERED
UNMANNERLY
UNMASTERED
UNMATERIAL
UNMATERNAL
UNMEASURED
UNMECHANIC
UNMEETNESS
UNMELLOWED
UNMERCIFUL
UNMERITING
UNMETALLED
UNMETRICAL
UNMILITARY
UNMODIFIED
UNMOLESTED
UNMORALITY
UNMORTISED
UNMOTHERLY
UNMOVEABLE
UNMOVEABLY
UNMUZZLING
UNNOTICING
UNNUMBERED
UNNURTURED
UNOBEDIENT
UNOBSCURED
UNOBSERVED
UNOBTAINED
UNOCCUPIED
UNOFFENDED
UNOFFICIAL
UNORDAINED
UNORDINARY
UNORIGINAL
UNORTHODOX
UNOSSIFIED
UNOVERCOME

UNOXIDISED
UNPAMPERED
UNPANELLED
UNPARADISE
UNPARALLEL
UNPARDONED
UNPARENTAL
UNPARENTED
UNPASSABLE
UNPASTORAL
UNPASTURED
UNPATHETIC
UNPEACEFUL
UNPEERABLE
UNPEPPERED
UNPERFUMED
UNPERILOUS
UNPERISHED
UNPERJURED
UNPICKABLE
UNPILLARED
UNPILLOWED
UNPLAUSIVE
UNPLAYABLE
UNPLEASANT
UNPLEASING
UNPLOUGHED
UNPOETICAL
UNPOISONED
UNPOLICIED
UNPOLISHED
UNPOLITELY
UNPOLLUTED
UNPOPULOUS
UNPOSSIBLE
UNPOWDERED
UNPREGNANT
UNPREPARED
UNPRIESTLY
UNPRINCELY
UNPRISONED
UNPRIZABLE
UNPRODUCED
UNPROFANED
UNPROFITED
UNPROLIFIC
UNPROMISED
UNPROMPTED
UNPROPERLY
UNPROPOSED
UNPROVABLE
UNPROVIDED
UNPROVOKED
UNPUCKERED
UNPUNCTUAL
UNPUNISHED
UNPURIFIED
UNPURPOSED
UNPURVEYED
UNQUALITED
UNQUARRIED
UNQUENCHED
UNQUOTABLE
UNRANSOMED
UNRATIFIED
UNRAVELLED

UNRAVELLER
UNRAVISHED
UNREADABLE
UNREALISED
UNREASONED
UNRECALLED
UNRECEIVED
UNRECKONED
UNRECORDED
UNRECURING
UNREDEEMED
UNREFORMED
UNREGARDED
UNREJOICED
UNRELATIVE
UNRELIABLE
UNRELIEVED
UNRELISHED
UNREMARKED
UNREMEDIED
UNREMITTED
UNREPAIRED
UNREPEALED
UNREPEATED
UNREPELLED
UNREPENTED
UNREPINING
UNREPORTED
UNREPOSING
UNREPROVED
UNREQUIRED
UNREQUITED
UNRESENTED
UNRESERVED
UNRESISTED
UNRESOLVED
UNRESPITED
UNRESTORED
UNRETARDED
UNRETURNED
UNREVEALED
UNREVENGED
UNREVEREND
UNREVERENT
UNREVERSED
UNREVERTED
UNREWARDED
UNRIDEABLE
UNRIGHTFUL
UNRIPENESS
UNRIVALLED
UNROMANTIC
UNRUFFABLE
UNRULIMENT
UNRULINESS
UNSAFENESS
UNSALARIED
UNSALEABLE
UNSANCTIFY
UNSANITARY
UNSATIABLE
UNSATIATED
UNSCABBARD
UNSCALABLE
UNSCEPTRED
UNSCHOOLED

UNSCORCHED
UNSCRAMBLE
UNSCREENED
UNSCRIPTED
UNSCRUPLED
UNSEARCHED
UNSEASONED
UNSECONDED
UNSEIZABLE
UNSENSIBLE
UNSENSIBLY
UNSETTLING
UNSHACKLED
UNSHADOWED
UNSHAKABLE
UNSHAKABLY
UNSHAKENLY
UNSHEATHED
UNSHIELDED
UNSHIFTING
UNSHINGLED
UNSHOWERED
UNSHRUBBED
UNSINKABLE
UNSISTERED
UNSISTERLY
UNSIZEABLE
UNSLEEPING
UNSLIPPING
UNSMILED-ON
UNSMIRCHED
UNSMOOTHED
UNSOCIABLE
UNSOCIABLY
UNSOCIALLY
UNSOFTENED
UNSOLIDITY
UNSOLVABLE
UNSPEAKING
UNSPIRITED
UNSPORTING
UNSTANCHED
UNSTARCHED
UNSTEADILY
UNSTINTING
UNSTOOPING
UNSTRAINED
UNSTRAPPED
UNSTRESSED
UNSTRIATED
UNSTRINGED
UNSTRIPPED
UNSUBLIMED
UNSUITABLE
UNSUITABLY
UNSUMMERED
UNSUMMONED
UNSUPPLIED
UNSURMISED
UNSURVEYED
UNSWAYABLE
UNSWEARING
UNSWERVING
UNSYMMETRY
UNSYMPATHY
UNTAINTING

UNTALENTED
UNTALKED-OF
UNTAMEABLE
UNTAMEABLY
UNTANGIBLE
UNTASTEFUL
UNTEARABLE
UNTELLABLE
UNTEMPERED
UNTENANTED
UNTENDERED
UNTENDERLY
UNTETHERED
UNTHANKFUL
UNTHATCHED
UNTHINKING
UNTHREADED
UNTHRIFTLY
UNTIDINESS
UNTILLABLE
UNTIMBERED
UNTIRINGLY
UNTOCHERED
UNTORTURED
UNTOWARDLY
UNTRAMPLED
UNTRANQUIL
UNTREASURE
UNTRENCHED
UNTROUBLED
UNTRUENESS
UNTRUSSING
UNTRUSTFUL
UNTRUTHFUL
UNTUCKERED
UNTUNEABLE
UNTURNABLE
UNTWISTING
UNUPLIFTED
UNUSEFULLY
UNVALUABLE
UNVARIABLE
UNVENDIBLE
UNVERACITY
UNVERIFIED
UNVIOLATED
UNVIRTUOUS
UNVITIATED
UNWARENESS
UNWARINESS
UNWATCHFUL
UNWAVERING
UNWEAKENED
UNWEAPONED
UNWEARABLE
UNWEARYING
UNWEIGHING
UNWELCOMED
UNWELLNESS
UNWIELDILY
UNWIFELIKE
UNWINNOWED
UNWISENESS
UNWITHERED
UNWITHHELD
UNWONTEDLY

UNWORKABLE
UNWORTHILY
UNWRINKLED
UNYIELDING
UPBRAIDING
UPBRINGING
UPBUILDING
UPBUOYANCE
UPBURSTING
UPFLASHING
UPHILLWARD
UPHOLSTERY
UPPER-CLASS
UPPER-STOCK
UPPERWORKS
UPPISHNESS
UPRIGHT-MAN
UPROARIOUS
UPSIDE-DOWN
UPSTANDING
UPSURGENCE
UPWARDNESS
URAL-ALTAIC
URANOMETRY
URBANOLOGY
UREDINALES
UREDOSORUS
UREDOSPORE
UREDO-STAGE
URETERITIS
URETHRITIC
URETHRITIS
URINOMETER
URINOSCOPY
UROCHORDAL
UROGENITAL
UROGRAPHIC
UROPOIESIS
UROSTEGITE
UROSTHENIC
URTICACEAE
URTICARIAL
URTICATION
USEFULNESS
USQUEBAUGH
USTULATION
USUCAPIENT
USUCAPTION
USURIOUSLY
USURPATION
USURPATORY
USURPATURE
USURPINGLY
UTERECTOMY
UTILISABLE
UTILITY-MAN
UTOPIANISE
UTOPIANISM
UXORILOCAL
UXORIOUSLY

V

VACCINATOR
VACUOLATED
VACUUM-TUBE
VAGINISMUS

VALIDATION
VALLECULAR
VALOROUSLY
VALUE-ADDED
VALVULITIS
VAMPIRE-BAT
VANADINITE
VANISHMENT
VANITY-CASE
VANQUISHER
VAPORIFORM
VAPOROSITY
VAPOROUSLY
VAPOUR-BATH
VAPULATION
VARICELLAR
VARICOCELE
VARICOSITY
VARIEGATED
VARIEGATOR
VARIETALLY
VARIOLOTIC
VARIOMETER
VARNISHING
VASCULARLY
VATICANISM
VATICANIST
VATICINATE
VAUDEVILLE
VAUNTINGLY
VECTOGRAPH
VEGETARIAN
VEGETATING
VEGETATION
VEGETATIVE
VEHEMENTLY
VELDSCHOEN
VELITATION
VELOCIPEDE
VELUTINOUS
VELVET-CRAB
VELVET-DUCK
VELVET-LEAF
VELVET-PILE
VENATORIAL
VENEER-MOTH
VENEFICOUS
VENERATION
VENETIANED
VENGEFULLY
VENOMOUSLY
VENTILABLE
VENTILATOR
VENTRICOSE
VENTRICOUS
VENTRICULE
VENUS-SHELL
VERANDAHED
VERBENA-OIL
VERGE-BOARD
VERGERSHIP
VERIDICOUS
VERIFIABLE
VERMICELLI
VERMICIDAL
VERMICULAR

VERMIFUGAL
VERNACULAR
VERNISSAGE
VERSE-MAKER
VERSE-SMITH
VERSICULAR
VERSIFYING
VERSIONIST
VERTEBRATA
VERTEBRATE
VERTICALLY
VERTOSCOPE
VERULAMIAN
VESICATION
VESICATORY
VESICULATE
VESICULOSE
VESPER-BELL
VESPERTINE
VESPIARIES
VESTIBULAR
VESTIBULUM
VESTMENTED
VEST-POCKET
VESTRY-ROOM
VETERINARY
VEXINGNESS
VIBRACULUM
VIBRAPHONE
VIBROGRAPH
VIBROMETER
VICE-CONSUL
VICE-COUNTY
VICEGERENT
VICEREGENT
VICHYSSOIS
VICTIMISER
VICTORIANA
VICTORIOUS
VICTUALLED
VICTUALLER
VIDEOPHONE
VIETNAMESE
VIEW-FINDER
VIEW-HALLOO
VIEWLESSLY
VIGILANTLY
VIGNETTIST
VIGOROUSLY
VILLAINAGE
VILLAINESS
VILLAINOUS
VILLANELLE
VILLANOVAN
VILLEINAGE
VINCENTIAN
VINDEMIATE
VINDICABLE
VINDICATOR
VINDICTIVE
VINE-BRANCH
VINEGAR-EEL
VINEGAR-FLY
VINEGARISH
VINE-MILDEW
VINOLOGIST

VINYLIDENE
VIOLACEOUS
VIPERIFORM
VIPEROUSLY
VIRAGINIAN
VIRAGINOUS
VIREONIDAE
VIRESCENCE
VIRGINALLY
VIRGIN-BORN
VIRGIN-HOOD
VIROLOGIST
VIRTUALISM
VIRTUALIST
VIRTUALITY
VIRTUELESS
VIRTUOSITY
VIRTUOUSLY
VIRULENTLY
VISCACHERA
VISCOMETER
VISCOMETRY
VISCOUNTCY
VISIBILITY
VISIGOTHIC
VISIOGENIC
VISIONALLY
VISIONLESS
VISITATION
VISITATIVE
VISITORIAL
VISUALISER
VITALISING
VITALISTIC
VITALITIES
VITAMINISE
VITELLICLE
VITICOLOUS
VITIFEROUS
VITILIGATE
VITRAILLED
VITREOSITY
VITRESCENT
VITRIOLATE
VITRIOLISE
VITUPERATE
VIVANDIÈRE
VIVERRIDAE
VIVERRINAE
VIVIPARISM
VIVIPARITY
VIVIPAROUS
VIVISECTOR
VIZARD-MASK
VIZIERSHIP
VOCABULARY
VOCABULIST
VOCATIONAL
VOCIFERANT
VOCIFERATE
VOCIFEROUS
VOETGANGER
VOLAPÜKIST
VOLATILISE
VOLATILITY
VOLCANISED

VOLITATION
VOLITIONAL
VOLITORIAL
VOLLEY-BALL
VOLTAIREAN
VOLTAIRIAN
VOLTAIRISM
VOLTAMETER
VOLUBILITY
VOLUMETRIC
VOLUMINOUS
VOLUPTUARY
VOLUPTUOUS
VOLUTATION
VOMITORIUM
VORAGINOUS
VORTICALLY
VORTICELLA
VORTICULAR
VOUCHSAFED
VOYAGEABLE
VULCANALIA
VULNERABLE

W

WABBLINESS
WAFER-IRONS
WAFER-TONGS
WAFFLE-IRON
WAG-AT-THE-WA'
WAGE-FREEZE
WAGE-PACKET
WAGON-TRAIN
WAGON-VAULT
WAINSCOTED
WAINWRIGHT
WAISTCLOTH
WAIT-A-WHILE
WAITERHOOD
WALDENSIAN
WALK-AROUND
WALKY-TALKY
WALLACHIAN
WALLFLOWER
WALL-LIZARD
WALL-PEPPER
WALL-ROCKET
WAMBLINESS
WAMBLINGLY
WAMPUM-BELT
WAMPUMPEAG
WANCHANCIE
WANDERLUST
WANDER-YEAR
WANRESTFUL
WANTHRIVEN
WANTONNESS
WAPENSCHAW
WAPINSCHAW
WAPPENSHAW
WAPPER-EYED
WARBLINGLY
WARDENSHIP
WAR-GODDESS
WARMED-OVER
WARMING-PAN

WARRANDICE
WARRANTING
WARRANTISE
WARRIORESS
WAR-WEARIED
WASH-BOTTLE
WASHING-DAY
WASP-TONGUE
WASSAIL-CUP
WASSAILING
WASTEFULLY
WATCH-CLOCK
WATCHFULLY
WATCH-GLASS
WATCH-GUARD
WATCH-HOUSE
WATCH-LIGHT
WATCH-MAKER
WATCH-NIGHT
WATCH-PAPER
WATCH-TOWER
WATER-BLINK
WATER-BLOOM
WATER-BORNE
WATER-BOUND
WATER-BRASH
WATER-BREAK
WATER-BROSE
WATER-CHUTE
WATER-CLOCK
WATER-CRAFT
WATER-CRANE
WATER-CRESS
WATER-ELDER
WATER-FLOOD
WATER-FRAME
WATERFRONT
WATER-GAUGE
WATER-GLASS
WATER-GUARD
WATER-HORSE
WATERINESS
WATER-JOINT
WATER-LEMON
WATER-LEVEL
WATER-MELON
WATER-METER
WATER-MOTOR
WATER-MOUSE
WATER-MUSIC
WATER-NIXIE
WATER-NYMPH
WATER-OUZEL
WATER-PLANE
WATER-PLANT
WATER-PLATE
WATER-POWER
WATERPROOF
WATERQUAKE
WATER-SHOOT
WATERSMEET
WATER-SMOKE
WATER-SNAKE
WATER-SPOUT
WATER-TABLE
WATER-THIEF

WATERTIGHT
WATER-TOWER
WATER-TWIST
WATER-WAGON
WATER-WHEEL
WATER-WINGS
WATTEAUISH
WATTLEBARK
WATTLE-BIRD
WATTLE-WORK
WAVELENGTH
WAVE-MOTION
WAVERINGLY
WAYBAGGAGE
WAY-FREIGHT
WAY-STATION
WAY-TRAFFIC
WEAK-HANDED
WEAK-HEADED
WEAK-HINGED
WEAKLINESS
WEAK-MINDED
WEAPONLESS
WEAPONSHAW
WEARIFULLY
WEASEL-COOT
WEASEL-WORD
WEATHER-BOW
WEATHER-BOX
WEATHER-EYE
WEATHER-GAW
WEATHERING
WEATHERISE
WEATHER-MAP
WEAVER-BIRD
WEDDING-BED
WEDDING-DAY
WEEDKILLER
WEEK-ENDING
WEEPING-ASH
WEIGH-BOARD
WEIGH-HOUSE
WEIGHTLESS
WELL-BESEEN
WELL-BORING
WELL-EARNED
WELL-GOTTEN
WELL-GRACED
WELL-HEELED
WELL-JUDGED
WELL-LIKING
WELL-MARKED
WELL-MINDED
WELL-SINKER
WELL-SPOKEN
WELL-SPRING
WELL-THEWED
WELL-TO-LIVE
WELL-TURNED
WELL-WILLER
WELL-WISHED
WELL-WISHER
WELSH-ONION
WELTER-RACE
WENTLETRAP
WERTHERIAN

WERTHERISM
WERWOLFISH
WERWOLFISM
WESTERNISE
WESTERNISM
WESTWARDLY
WHALE-LOUSE
WHALE-SHARK
WHALING-GUN
WHARFINGER
WHATABOUTS
WHATSOEVER
WHEAT-BERRY
WHEAT-FIELD
WHEAT-MIDGE
WHEEL-CHAIR
WHEEL-HORSE
WHEEL-HOUSE
WHEEZINESS
WHENSOEVER
WHEREABOUT
WHERESOE'ER
WHEREUNDER
WHEREUNTIL
WHEWELLITE
WHIDAH-BIRD
WHIGGAMORE
WHIGGARCHY
WHIGGISHLY
WHILLYWHAW
WHIMPERING
WHIMSINESS
WHIP-HANDLE
WHIPPETING
WHIP-SOCKET
WHIP-STITCH
WHIP-TAILED
WHIRL-ABOUT
WHIRL-BLAST
WHIRLYBIRD
WHISKIFIED
WHISKY-JACK
WHISKY-JOHN
WHISPERING
WHIST-DRIVE
WHITE-BEARD
WHITE-BRASS
WHITE-FACED
WHITE-HAWSE
WHITE-HEART
WHITE-HORSE
WHITESMITH
WHITETHORN
WHITE-WATER
WHIT-MONDAY
WHITSUN-ALE
WHITSUNDAY
WHITTERICK
WHITY-BROWN
WHIZZINGLY
WHOLE-PLATE
WHOLESALER
WHOMSOEVER
WHOREHOUSE
WHORE'S-BIRD
WHYDAH-BIRD

WICKEDNESS
WICKERWORK
WICKET-GATE
WIDERSHINS
WIDESPREAD
WIELDINESS
WILD-CHERRY
WILDEBEEST
WILDERMENT
WILDERNESS
WILD-INDIGO
WILFULNESS
WILLOW-HERB
WILLOW-WEED
WILLOW-WREN
WILLY-NILLY
WINCEYETTE
WINCHESTER
WIND-BROKEN
WIND-DROPSY
WINDFALLEN
WIND-FLOWER
WINDJAMMER
WINDOW-BOLE
WINDOWLESS
WINDOW-PANE
WINDOW-SASH
WINDOW-SEAT
WINDOW-SILL
WINDSCREEN
WIND-SHAKEN
WINDSHIELD
WIND-SLEEVE
WIND-SUCKER
WIND-TUNNEL
WINE-BIBBER
WINE-CELLAR
WINE-COOLER
WINE-GROWER
WINE-TASTER
WINE-VAULTS
WING-FOOTED
WING-SHEATH
WING-SPREAD
WINTER-CLAD
WINTER-CROP
WINTER-TIDE
WINTRINESS
WIRE-BRIDGE
WIRE-DANCER
WIRED-GLASS
WIRE-HAIRED
WIRE-PULLER
WIRE-WALKER
WIREWORKER
WISHING-CAP
WISHY-WASHY
WITCH-ALDER
WITCHCRAFT
WITCH-HAZEL
WITCHINGLY
WIT-CRACKER
WITHDRAWAL
WITHDRAWER
WITHHOLDEN
WITHHOLDER

WITNESS-BOX
WIT-SNAPPER
WIZEN-FACED
WOBBLINESS
WOEFULNESS
WOEWEARIED
WOLFIANISM
WOLFRAMITE
WOLF'S-PEACH
WOLF-SPIDER
WOMAN-BUILT
WOMAN-CHILD
WOMANFULLY
WOMAN-GROWN
WOMAN-HATER
WOMANISHLY
WOMAN-TIRED
WOMENFOLKS
WONDERLAND
WONDERMENT
WONDER-WORK
WONDROUSLY
WONGA-WONGA
WONTEDNESS
WOOD-BORING
WOOD-CARVER
WOODCUTTER
WOODEN-HEAD
WOODENNESS
WOOD-GROUSE
WOODLANDER
WOODPECKER
WOOD-PIGEON
WOOD-SORREL
WOOD-SPIRIT
WOODTHRUSH
WOOL-CARDER
WOOL-COMBER
WOOL-DRIVER
WOOL-GROWER
WOOLLINESS
WOOLLY-BEAR
WOOLLY-HAND
WOOL-PACKER
WOOL-PICKER
WOOL-SHEARS
WOOLSORTER
WOOL-STAPLE
WOOL-WINDER
WORD-MEMORY
WORK-BASKET
WORK-FELLOW
WORKING-DAY
WORKMASTER
WORK-PEOPLE
WORLD-WEARY
WORM-EATING
WORM-POWDER
WORRYINGLY
WORSHIPFUL
WORSHIPPED
WORSHIPPER
WORTHINESS
WORTHWHILE
WRAP-RASCAL
WRATHFULLY

WRATHINESS
WREATHLESS
WRETCHEDLY
WRING-STAFF
WRIST-WATCH
WRITERSHIP
WRITHINGLY
WRITING-INK
WRITTEN-OFF
WRONG-DOING
WRONGFULLY
WRONGOUSLY
WRONG-TIMED
WRY-MOUTHED
WYCLIFFITE
WYKEHAMIST

X

XANTHOPSIA
XENARTHRAL
XENOGENOUS
XENOPHOBIA
XERODERMIA
XERODERMIC
XEROGRAPHY
XEROPHYTIC
XEROSTOMIA
XIPHOPAGIC
XIPHOPAGUS
XIPHOSURAN
XYLOCHROME
XYLOGENOUS
XYLOGRAPHY
XYLOPHAGAN
XYLOPHONIC
XYLOTOMOUS
XYRIDACEAE

Y

YACHT-BUILT
YACKETY-YAK
YAFFINGALE
YANKEEFIED
YARBOROUGH
YARD-MASTER
YEARNINGLY
YEASTINESS
YEAST-PLANT
YELLOWBACK
YELLOW-BIRD
YELLOW-EYED
YELLOW-FLAG
YELLOW-GIRL
YELLOWNESS
YELLOW-ROOT
YELLOW-SNOW
YELLOW-SOAP
YELLOW-SPOT
YELLOW-WASH
YELLOW-WEED
YELLOW-WOOD
YELLOW-WORT
YELLOW-YITE
YERD-HUNGER
YERD-HUNGRY
YESTEREVEN

YESTERMORN
YESTERYEAR
YGGDRASILL
YIELDINGLY
YIRD-HUNGER
YIRD-HUNGRY
YLANG-YLANG
YOKE-FELLOW
YOUNGBERRY
YOURSELVES
YOUTHFULLY
YPSILIFORM
YTHUNDERED
YUGOSLAVIC

Z

ZABAGLIONE
ZAPOROGIAN
ZEBRA-FINCH
ZEND-AVESTA
ZERO-VALENT
ZEUGLODONT
ZIGZAGGERY
ZIGZAGGING
ZINC-BLENDE
ZINCOGRAPH
ZINCOLYSIS
ZINC-WORKER
ZOANTHARIA
ZOANTHIDAE
ZOANTHROPY
ZOLLVEREIN
ZONE-TICKET
ZOOCHOROUS
ZOOCULTURE
ZOOGLOEOID
ZOOGRAPHER
ZOOGRAPHIC
ZOOLATROUS
ZOOLOGICAL
ZOOMORPHIC
ZOOPHAGOUS
ZOOPHILISM
ZOOPHILIST
ZOOPHILOUS
ZOOPHOBOUS
ZOOPHYTOID
ZOOPLASTIC
ZOOSPOROUS
ZOOTHAPSIS
ZOOTHECIAL
ZOOTHECIUM
ZOOTHERAPY
ZOOTOMICAL
ZOOTROPHIC
ZOOTSUITER
ZUMBOORUCK
ZWITTERION
ZYGAENIDAE
ZYGOBRANCH
ZYGODACTYL
ZYGOMORPHY
ZYGOMYCETE
ZYGOSPHENE
ZYMOLOGIST

A

ABACTINALLY
ABANDONEDLY
ABANDONMENT
ABBEY-LUBBER
ABBREVIATOR
ABDOMINALLY
ABECEDARIAN
ABHORRENTLY
ABIOGENESIS
ABIOGENETIC
ABLACTATION
ABLATITIOUS
ABLUTIONARY
ABNORMALISM
ABNORMALITY
ABOLISHABLE
ABOLISHMENT
ABOLITIONAL
ABOMINATION
ABORTIONIST
ABOUT-SLEDGE
ABOVE-GROUND
ABRACADABRA
ABRANCHIATE
ABRIDGEMENT
ABSCONDENCE
ABSENTEEISM
ABSORBINGLY
ABSTINENTLY
ABSTRACTION
ABSTRACTIVE
ABSTRICTION
ABUSIVENESS
ACADEMICIAN
ACADEMICISM
ACANTHACEAE
ACAROLOGIST
ACATALECTIC
ACATALEPTIC
ACAULESCENT
ACCELERANDO
ACCELERATOR
ACCENTUALLY
ACCEPTATION
ACCEPTIVITY
ACCESSORIAL
ACCESSORILY
ACCIPITRINE
ACCLAMATION
ACCLAMATORY
ACCLIMATION
ACCLIMATISE
ACCLIVITOUS
ACCOMMODATE
ACCOMPANIER
ACCOMPANIST
ACCOMPTABLE
ACCORDANTLY
ACCORDINGLY
ACCOUCHEUSE
ACCOUNTABLE
ACCOUNTABLY
ACCOUNTANCY
ACCOUNT-BOOK

ACCRESCENCE
ACCUMULATOR
ACCUSATIVAL
ACCUSTOMARY
ACHAENOCARP
ACHIEVEMENT
ACHROMATISE
ACHROMATISM
ACIDIFIABLE
ACINACIFORM
ACKNOWLEDGE
ACOLOUTHITE
ACOUSTICIAN
ACQUIESCENT
ACQUIREMENT
ACQUISITION
ACQUISITIVE
ACQUITTANCE
ACRE-BREADTH
ACRIFLAVINE
ACRIMONIOUS
ACROPETALLY
ACTINOMETER
ACTINOMYCES
ACTOTROPHIC
ACUMINATION
ACUPRESSURE
ACUPUNCTURE
ADDITITIOUS
ADDLE-HEADED
ADENOMATOUS
ADIAPHORISM
ADIAPHORIST
ADIAPHOROUS
ADIATHERMIC
ADJECTIVELY
ADJOURNMENT
ADJUDGEMENT
ADJUDICATOR
ADMINICULAR
ADMIRALSHIP
ADOLESCENCE
ADOPTIANISM
ADOPTIANIST
ADOPTIONISM
ADOPTIONIST
ADSCRIPTION
ADULTERATOR
ADUMBRATION
ADVANCEMENT
ADVENTURESS
ADVENTUROUS
ADVERBIALLY
ADVERSATIVE
ADVERSENESS
ADVERTENTLY
ADVERTISING
ADVISEDNESS
ADVISERSHIP
AENEOLITHIC
AEOLOTROPIC
AEROBICALLY
AEROBIOLOGY
AERODYNAMIC
AEROELASTIC
AEROLOGICAL

AERONAUTICS
AEROSTATICS
AEROSTATION
AEROTROPISM
AESCULAPIAN
AESTHETICAL
AESTIVATION
AFFECTATION
AFFECTINGLY
AFFECTIONAL
AFFECTIONED
AFFECTIVELY
AFFECTIVITY
AFFILIATION
AFFIRMATION
AFFIRMATIVE
AFFIRMATORY
AFFIRMINGLY
AFFORCEMENT
AFFRANCHISE
AFFRICATION
AFFRICATIVE
AFFRIGHTFUL
AFTERBURNER
AFTER-DINNER
AFTER-EFFECT
AFTERGROWTH
AFTERSUPPER
AGGLOMERATE
AGGLUTINANT
AGGLUTINATE
AGGRAVATING
AGGRAVATION
AGGREGATELY
AGGREGATION
AGGREGATIVE
AGNATICALLY
AGNOSTICISM
AGONISINGLY
AGONISTICAL
AGORAPHOBIA
AGRARIANISM
AGRICULTURE
AGROBIOLOGY
AGROLOGICAL
AGROSTOLOGY
AGUARDIENTE
AIDES-DE-CAMP
AIGUILLETTE
AILUROPHILE
AILUROPHOBE
AIMLESSNESS
AIR-CORRIDOR
AIRCRAFTMAN
AIR-MECHANIC
AIR-SICKNESS
AIR-TERMINAL
AIR-UMBRELLA
ALBIGENSIAN
ALBUGINEOUS
ALBUMINURIA
ALCYONARIAN
ALDER-LEAVED
ALDERMANITY
ALEMBICATED
ALEXANDRIAN

ALEXANDRINE
ALEXANDRITE
ALGEBRAICAL
ALGOLOGICAL
ALGORITHMIC
ALISMACEOUS
ALKALESCENT
ALKALIMETER
ALKALIMETRY
ALL-AMERICAN
ALL-CHEERING
ALLEGORICAL
ALLEGORISER
ALL-ELECTRIC
ALLELOMORPH
ALLEVIATION
ALLINEATION
ALLOCHEIRIA
ALLOPATHIST
ALLOPLASTIC
ALLOTROPISM
ALLOTROPOUS
ALL-POWERFUL
ALPHABETISE
ALTERCATION
ALTERCATIVE
ALTERNATELY
ALTERNATING
ALTERNATION
ALTERNATIVE
ALTITUDINAL
ALTO-RELIEVO
ALTO-RILIEVO
ALYCOMPAINE
AMARANTHINE
AMATEURSHIP
AMATIVENESS
AMATORIALLY
AMAZON-STONE
AMBIGUOUSLY
AMBITIOUSLY
AMBIVALENCE
AMBIVALENCY
AMBOINA-WOOD
AMBOYNA-WOOD
AMBROSIALLY
AMBUSCADOES
AMELANCHIER
AMENABILITY
AMENORRHOEA
AMENTACEOUS
AMERCIAMENT
AMERICANISE
AMERICANISM
AMERICANIST
AMETABOLISM
AMETABOLOUS
AMETHYSTINE
AMIABLENESS
AMICABILITY
AMINO-ACETIC
AMINOBUTENE
AMMOPHILOUS
AMONTILLADO
AMOROUSNESS
AMOUR-PROPRE

AMPHETAMINE
AMPHIBOLITE
AMPHIBOLOGY
AMPHIBOLOUS
AMPHICTYONY
AMPHIPODOUS
AMPHISBAENA
AMPLEXICAUL
AMPULLOSITY
AMUSIVENESS
ANACHRONISM
ANACHRONOUS
ANACOLUTHIA
ANACOLUTHON
ANACREONTIC
ANADIPLOSIS
ANAEROBIONT
ANAESTHESIA
ANAESTHESIS
ANAESTHETIC
ANAGNORISIS
ANALOGOUSLY
ANALPHABETE
ANAMORPHOUS
ANAPHYLAXIS
ANAPLEROSIS
ANAPLEROTIC
ANARCHISTIC
ANASTOMOSES
ANASTOMOSIS
ANASTOMOTIC
ANCESTORIAL
ANCHOR-STOCK
ANCHOVY-PEAR
ANCIENTNESS
ANDROGYNOUS
ANECDOTICAL
ANEMOMETRIC
ANENCEPHALY
ANFRACTUOUS
ANGELICALLY
ANGELOLATRY
ANGELOPHANY
ANGIOGRAPHY
ANGLICANISM
ANGLO-FRENCH
ANGLO-INDIAN
ANGLOMANIAC
ANGLO-NORMAN
ANGLOPHOBIA
ANGLOPHOBIC
ANGST-RIDDEN
ANIMALCULAR
ANIMALCULES
ANIMATINGLY
ANISOCERCAL
ANISOMEROUS
ANISOTROPIC
ANNABERGITE
ANNIHILATOR
ANNIVERSARY
ANNUNCIATOR
ANOMALISTIC
ANONYMOUSLY
ANTECEDENCE
ANTECHAMBER

ANTEMUNDANE
ANTENNIFORM
ANTENUPTIAL
ANTEORBITAL
ANTEPENDIUM
ANTERIORITY
ANTHERIDIUM
ANTHEROZOID
ANTHESTERIA
ANTHOCHLORE
ANTHOCYANIN
ANTHOLOGISE
ANTHOLOGIST
ANTHOMANIAC
ANTHRACITIC
ANTHRACOSIS
ANTHROPICAL
ANTIBILIOUS
ANTIBURGHER
ANTICATHODE
ANTICIPATOR
ANTICYCLONE
ANTI-FEDERAL
ANTIFOULING
ANTIHELICES
ANTI-HEROINE
ANTI-JACOBIN
ANTIMONIATE
ANTIMONIOUS
ANTINEUTRON
ANTINOMICAL
ANTIPATHIST
ANTIPHONARY
ANTIPHRASIS
ANTIPYRETIC
ANTIQUARIAN
ANTIQUATION
ANTIQUENESS
ANTIRRHINUM
ANTISEMITIC
ANTISPASTIC
ANTISTROPHE
ANTITHALIAN
ANTITYPICAL
ANTIVITAMIN
ANTONOMASIA
ANXIOUSNESS
APARTMENTAL
APATHETICAL
APHANIPTERA
APHRODISIAC
APHRODISIAN
APLANOSPORE
APOCALYPTIC
APOCOPATION
APOCYNACEAE
APODICTICAL
APODYTERIUM
APOGAMOUSLY
APOLITICISM
APOLLINARIS
APOLLONICON
APOLOGETICS
APOMORPHINE
APONEUROSIS
APONEUROTIC

APOPHYLLITE
APOSIOPESIS
APOSTATICAL
APOSTLESHIP
APOSTOLICAL
APOSTROPHIC
APOSTROPHUS
APOTHEOSISE
APPALLINGLY
APPARATCHIK
APPARATUSES
APPARELLING
APPARELMENT
APPEACHMENT
APPEALINGLY
APPEASEMENT
APPEASINGLY
APPELLATION
APPELLATIVE
APPERTINENT
APPLE-BLIGHT
APPLERINGIE
APPLE-SQUIRE
APPLICATION
APPLICATIVE
APPLICATORY
APPOINTMENT
APPORTENANT
APPRAISABLE
APPRECIABLE
APPRECIABLY
APPRECIATOR
APPROBATION
APPROBATIVE
APPROBATORY
APPROPINQUE
APPROPRIATE
APPROVINGLY
APPROXIMATE
APRON-STRING
AQUAFORTIST
AQUANAUTICS
AQUAPLANING
AQUARELLIST
ARACHNOIDAL
ARACHNOLOGY
ARAEOMETRIC
ARALIACEOUS
ARBITRAMENT
ARBITRARILY
ARBITRATION
ARBITRATRIX
ARBITREMENT
ARBORACEOUS
ARBORESCENT
ARCADIANISM
ARCHAEOLOGY
ARCHAICALLY
ARCHANGELIC
ARCHDIOCESE
ARCHDUCHESS
ARCHDUKEDOM
ARCHEGONIAL
ARCHEGONIUM
ARCHENTERON
ARCH-HERETIC

ARCHIMEDEAN
ARCHIPELAGO
ARCHITRAVED
ARCH-PRELATE
ARCH-TRAITOR
ARCH-VILLAIN
ARDUOUSNESS
ARENICOLOUS
AREOPAGITIC
AREOSYSTILE
ARGATHELIAN
ARGIE-BARGIE
ARGLE-BARGLE
ARISTOCRACY
ARMINIANISM
ARMOURED-CAR
ARMOUR-PLATE
ARQUEBUSADE
ARQUEBUSIER
ARRAIGNMENT
ARRANGEMENT
ARRESTATION
ARRHENOTOKY
ARROW-HEADED
ARROW-POISON
ARTERIALISE
ARTERIOTOMY
ARTHROPODAL
ARTHROSPORE
ARTICULABLE
ARTICULATED
ARTICULATOR
ARTILLERIST
ARTIODACTYL
ARTLESSNESS
ASBESTIFORM
ASCENTIONAL
ASCETICALLY
ASCITITIOUS
ASCLEPIADIC
ASCOMYCETES
ASHAMEDNESS
ASPERGATION
ASPERGILLUM
ASPERGILLUS
ASPERSORIUM
ASPHETERISE
ASPHETERISM
ASPHYXIATED
ASPHYXIATOR
ASPORTATION
ASSAFOETIDA
ASSASSINATE
ASSAY-MASTER
ASSEMBLANCE
ASSEMBLYMAN
ASSENTATION
ASSENTINGLY
ASSERTIVELY
ASSESSORIAL
ASSIDUOUSLY
ASSIGNATION
ASSIMILABLE
ASSOCIATION
ASSOCIATIVE
ASSUAGEMENT

ASSUBJUGATE
ASSUREDNESS
ASSYRIOLOGY
ASTHMATICAL
ASTIGMATISM
ASTONISHING
ASTOUNDMENT
ASTRAPHOBIA
ASTRINGENCY
ASTRONOMISE
ASTUCIOUSLY
ASYNARTETIC
ATHARVAVEDA
ATHEISTICAL
ATHERINIDAE
ATHERMANOUS
ATHLETICISM
ATMOSPHERIC
ATOMISATION
ATRABILIOUS
ATROCIOUSLY
ATTACHÉ-CASE
ATTAINTMENT
ATTEMPTABLE
ATTENTIVELY
ATTENUATION
ATTESTATION
ATTESTATIVE
ATTITUDINAL
ATTORNEYDOM
ATTORNEYISM
ATTRACTABLE
ATTRIBUTION
ATTRIBUTIVE
ATTUITIONAL
ATTUITIVELY
AUDACIOUSLY
AUDIBLENESS
AUDIOLOGIST
AUDIOMETRIC
AUDIO-TYPIST
AUDIO-VISUAL
AUDITORSHIP
AUGMENTABLE
AUGUSTINIAN
AULD-FARRANT
AURICULARLY
AURICULATED
AURIGNACIAN
AUSCULTATOR
AUSTERENESS
AUTARCHICAL
AUTECOLOGIC
AUTHENTICAL
AUTHORCRAFT
AUTOCEPHALY
AUTOCHTHONS
AUTOEROTISM
AUTOGRAPHIC
AUTOGRAVURE
AUTOMATICAL
AUTOMORPHIC
AUTONOMICAL
AUTOPHAGOUS
AUTOPHANOUS
AUTOPLASTIC

AUTOTROPHIC
AUXANOMETER
AVERRUNCATE
AVOIRDUPOIS
AWELESSNESS
AWESOMENESS
AWE-STRICKEN
AWKWARDNESS
AXEROPHTHOL
AXIOLOGICAL
AXIOMATICAL
AXONOMETRIC
AZOCOMPOUND
AZOTOBACTER

B

BABY-SITTING
BACCHANALIA
BACCIFEROUS
BACCIVOROUS
BACHELORDOM
BACHELORISM
BACILLACEAE
BACILLICIDE
BACILLIFORM
BACKBENCHER
BACK-BLOCKER
BACKBREAKER
BACK-COUNTRY
BACK-DRAUGHT
BACK-GANGING
BACKINGDOWN
BACKSCRATCH
BACKSLIDING
BACONIANISM
BACTERICIDE
BACTERIOSIS
BADDELEYITE
BAFFLE-PLATE
BAILLIESHIP
BALEFULNESS
BALLETOMANE
BALLOON-VINE
BALLOT-PAPER
BALM-CRICKET
BALMORALITY
BALTOSLAVIC
BANDY-LEGGED
BANEFULNESS
BANK-HOLIDAY
BANK-MANAGER
BANTERINGLY
BAPTISMALLY
BARBARESQUE
BARBAROUSLY
BARBASTELLE
BARBITURATE
BARCLAYCARD
BAREFACEDLY
BARGE-COUPLE
BARGE-MASTER
BARGE-STONES
BARLEY-BRAKE
BARLEY-BROTH
BARLEY-SUGAR
BARLEY-WATER

BARNSTORMER
BARON-BAILIE
BARONETICAL
BARQUENTINE
BARRAGE-FIRE
BARREL-HOUSE
BARREL-ORGAN
BARRIER-REEF
BAR-SINISTER
BARTHOLOMEW
BARYCENTRIC
BASHFULNESS
BASHI-BAZOUK
BASKET-CHAIR
BASKET-MAKER
BASSETHOUND
BASTARD-WING
BASTELHOUSE
BASTINADING
BASTINADOED
BATHING-SUIT
BATHOLITHIC
BATHOPHOBIA
BATHYLITHIC
BATHYMETRIC
BATHYSCAPHE
BATHYSPHERE
BATOLOGICAL
BATSMANSHIP
BATTLEDRESS
BATTLEFIELD
BATTLE-PIECE
BATTLEPLANE
BAUSON-FACED
BAY-WINDOWED
BEACHCOMBER
BEACH-MASTER
BEACH-RESCUE
BEAR-BAITING
BEARISHNESS
BEAR'S-BREECH
BEASTLINESS
BEAUMONTAGE
BEAUTEOUSLY
BEAUTIFULLY
BEAUTY-SLEEP
BEBLUBBERED
BEDEVILLING
BEDEVILMENT
BEDIZENMENT
BED-OF-HONOUR
BEECH-MARTEN
BEEF-BRAINED
BEFITTINGLY
BEGONIACEAE
BEGUILEMENT
BEGUILINGLY
BEHAVIOURAL
BELATEDNESS
BELIEVINGLY
BELLE-DE-NUIT
BELLETTRIST
BELL-FOUNDER
BELL-HEATHER
BELLICOSELY
BELLICOSITY

BELLIGERENT
BELLOWS-FISH
BELL-RINGING
BELLY-TIMBER
BELORUSSIAN
BELOWSTAIRS
BENCHERSHIP
BENEDICTINE
BENEDICTION
BENEDICTIVE
BENEDICTORY
BENEFACTION
BENEFACTORY
BENEFICENCE
BENEFICIARY
BENEFICIATE
BENEVOLENCE
BENIGHTMENT
BENIGNANTLY
BENTHOSCOPE
BENZYLIDINE
BEREAVEMENT
BERGSCHRUND
BERSAGLIERI
BERTHON-BOAT
BESEEMINGLY
BESIEGEMENT
BESIEGINGLY
BESPREADING
BESTRIDABLE
BETEL-PEPPER
BETROTHMENT
BETWEEN-MAID
BETWEENNESS
BETWEENTIME
BEVEL-WHEELS
BEWILDERING
BEWITCHMENT
BIAS-DRAWING
BIBLIOGICAL
BIBLIOLATER
BIBLIOLATRY
BIBLIOMANCY
BIBLIOMANIA
BIBLIOPEGIC
BIBLIOPHILE
BIBLIOPHILY
BIBLIOPOLIC
BIBLIOTHECA
BICARBONATE
BICENTENARY
BICORPORATE
BICUSPIDATE
BIFOLIOLATE
BIFURCATION
BILATERALLY
BILIOUSNESS
BILL-CHAMBER
BILLETS-DOUX
BILLIONAIRE
BILLSTICKER
BIMETALLISM
BIMETALLIST
BIMILLENARY
BINOCULARLY
BIOCHEMICAL

BIOCOENOSIS
BIOCOENOTIC
BIODYNAMICS
BIPARTITION
BIQUADRATIC
BIRD-BATTING
BIRD-CATCHER
BIRD-FANCIER
BIRD-NESTING
BISCUIT-ROOT
BISOCIATION
BISOCIATIVE
BITING-LOUSE
BITTER-APPLE
BITTER-CRESS
BITTER-EARTH
BITTERSWEET
BIVOUACKING
BLACK-AND-TAN
BLACK-A-VISED
BLACK-BEETLE
BLACKBIRDER
BLACK-BODING
BLACK-BROWED
BLACK-COATED
BLACKFELLOW
BLACKFISHER
BLACKGROUSE
BLACKHEADED
BLACKMAILER
BLACK-MARKET
BLADDER-WORM
BLADDERWORT
BLAMELESSLY
BLAMEWORTHY
BLARNEY-LAND
BLASPHEMOUS
BLASTOGENIC
BLEACH-FIELD
BLEMISHMENT
BLEPHARITIS
BLESSEDNESS
BLIGHTINGLY
BLINDFELLED
BLIZZARDOUS
BLOCKBUSTER
BLOCK-SYSTEM
BLOOD-BOUGHT
BLOOD-FLOWER
BLOOD-FROZEN
BLOOD-GUILTY
BLOODLETTER
BLOOD-SPAVIN
BLOODSPRENT
BLOODSTREAM
BLOODSUCKER
BLOOD-VESSEL
BLOODY-BONES
BLOODY-FACED
BLOODY-SWEAT
BLOTCHINESS
BLOTTING-PAD
BLUE-BLOODED
BLUNDERBUSS
BLUNT-WITTED
BLUSHLESSLY

BOARD-SCHOOL
BOAT-BUILDER
BODHISATTVA
BODY-BUILDER
BODY-POLITIC
BODY-SERVANT
BOG-ASPHODEL
BOGTROTTING
BOHEMIANISM
BOMBACACEAE
BOMBARDMENT
BOMBILATION
BOMBINATION
BONAPARTEAN
BONAPARTISM
BONAPARTIST
BONBONNIERE
BONDMANSHIP
BONDSERVANT
BOND-SERVICE
BOND-WASHING
BONE-BRECCIA
BONNE-BOUCHE
BONNET-LAIRD
BONNET-PIECE
BONNET-ROUGE
BOOK-ACCOUNT
BOOK-BINDING
BOOKING-HALL
BOOKISHNESS
BOOKKEEPING
BOOKSELLING
BOORISHNESS
BOOT-CATCHER
BOOTLEGGING
BOOTLICKING
BOOT-TOPPING
BORBORYGMIC
BORBORYGMUS
BOTANICALLY
BOTANOMANCY
BOTHERATION
BOTTLE-BRUSH
BOTTLE-CHART
BOTTLE-GLASS
BOTTLE-GOURD
BOTTLE-GREEN
BOTTLE-NOSED
BOTTLE-PARTY
BOTTOM-GLADE
BOTTOM-GRASS
BOULDER-CLAY
BOUNTEOUSLY
BOUNTIFULLY
BOUQUETIÈRE
BOURGEOISIE
BOURTREE-GUN
BOUTONNIÈRE
BOWDLERISER
BOWER-ANCHOR
BOWSTRINGED
BOW-WINDOWED
BOXING-GLOVE
BOX-JUNCTION
BOYSENBERRY
BRABBLEMENT

BRACHIATION
BRACHIOPODA
BRACHYPRISM
BRACHYUROUS
BRACTEOLATE
BRADYCARDIA
BRADYPEPTIC
BRAGGADOCIO
BRAGGARTISM
BRAHMANICAL
BRAHMINICAL
BRAINSICKLY
BRAINS-TRUST
BRAMAH-PRESS
BRAMBLE-BUSH
BRANCHIOPOD
BRANCH-PILOT
BRANFULNESS
BRANKURSINE
BRATTISHING
BRAZEN-FACED
BREAD-BASKET
BREADTHWAYS
BREADTHWISE
BREADWINNER
BREASTPLATE
BREAST-WHEEL
BREATHINESS
BRIBERY-OATH
BRICKLAYING
BRICKMAKING
BRICKSHAPED
BRIDEMAIDEN
BRIDGEBOARD
BRIDGE-DRIVE
BRIDGE-HOUSE
BRILLIANTLY
BRIMFULNESS
BRINE-SHRIMP
BRISSEL-COCK
BRISTLE-FERN
BRISTLE-TAIL
BRISTLE-WORM
BRISTLINESS
BRISTOL-MILK
BRITTLENESS
BRITTLE-STAR
BROACH-SPIRE
BROADCASTED
BROADCASTER
BROAD-MINDED
BROBDINGNAG
BROMIDROSIS
BROTHERHOOD
BROTHERLIKE
BRUCELLOSIS
BRUSH-TURKEY
BRUSQUENESS
BRUTISHNESS
BRYOLOGICAL
BUBBLE-SHELL
BUCCINATORY
BUCKET-WHEEL
BUCK-WASHING
BUFFALO-BIRD
BUFFALO-ROBE

BUFFER-STATE
BUFF-LEATHER
BULBIFEROUS
BULK-CARRIER
BULL-BAITING
BULLET-PROOF
BULLFIGHTER
BULLFRONTED
BULLISHNESS
BULL-MASTIFF
BULL-TERRIER
BUMBLE-PUPPY
BUMPTIOUSLY
BUNCH-BACKED
BUOYANTNESS
BUPRESTIDAE
BUREAUCRACY
BURGLARIOUS
BURGOMASTER
BURIAL-PLACE
BURLING-IRON
BUR-MARIGOLD
BURNISHMENT
BURN-THE-WIND
BURNT-SIENNA
BURROWSTOWN
BURSCHENISM
BURSERACEAE
BURSICULATE
BUSHELWOMAN
BUSHMANSHIP
BUSHWHACKER
BUSINESS-MAN
BUTCHER-BIRD
BUTTER-CLOTH
BUTTERFLIES
BUTTER-KNIFE
BUTTER-PAPER
BUTTER-PLATE
BUTTER-PRINT
BUTTER-WOMAN
BUTTOCK-MAIL
BUTT-WELDING
BYRONICALLY
BYZANTINISM

C

CAAING-WHALE
CABBAGE-MOTH
CABBAGE-PALM
CABBAGE-ROSE
CABBAGE-TREE
CABBAGE-WORM
CABBALISTIC
CABLE-LENGTH
CABLE-STITCH
CACHECTICAL
CACOGASTRIC
CACOGRAPHIC
CACOPHONOUS
CADDISHNESS
CAESALPINIA
CAFE-CONCERT
CALABAR-BEAN
CALCARIFORM
CALCEOLARIA

CALCICOLOUS
CALCIFEROUS
CALCIFUGOUS
CALCIGEROUS
CALCINATION
CALCULATING
CALCULATION
CALCULATIVE
CALEFACIENT
CALEFACTION
CALEFACTIVE
CALEFACTORY
CALENDARIST
CALENDERING
CALF-COUNTRY
CALIBRATION
CALIFORNIUM
CALISTHENIC
CALL-AT-LARGE
CALLIGRAMME
CALLIGRAPHY
CALLING-CRAB
CALLIPYGEAN
CALLIPYGOUS
CALLISTEMON
CALLITRICHE
CALLOUSNESS
CALORIMETER
CALORIMETRY
CALUMNIATOR
CALVINISTIC
CALYCANTHUS
CALYPTROGEN
CAMALDOLESE
CAMALDOLITE
CAMARADERIE
CAMEL-BACKED
CAMELEOPARD
CAMPANIFORM
CAMPANOLOGY
CAMPANULATE
CAMPBELLITE
CAMPESTRIAN
CAMP-MEETING
CANALICULAR
CANALICULUS
CANARIENSIS
CANARY-GRASS
CANCELLATED
CANCERATION
CANDELABRAS
CANDELABRUM
CANDESCENCE
CANDIDATURE
CANDLE-BERRY
CANDLE-LIGHT
CANDLE-POWER
CANDLE-STICK
CANDY-STRIPE
CANELLACEAE
CANISTERISE
CANNIBALISE
CANNIBALISM
CANNON-METAL
CANNON-PROOF
CANONICALLY

CANOPHILIST
CANTHARIDAL
CANTHARIDES
CANTHARIDIC
CANTING-COIN
CAPABLENESS
CAPACIOUSLY
CAPACITANCE
CAPARISONED
CAPERNAITIC
CAPERNOITED
CAPERNOITIE
CAPER-SPURGE
CAPILLARITY
CAPILLITIUM
CAPITULARLY
CAPPAH-BROWN
CAPPERNOITY
CAPRICCIOSO
CAPTAINSHIP
CAPTIVATING
CARAVANNING
CARAVANSARY
CARBOCYCLIC
CARBONALITE
CARBONARISM
CARBONATION
CARBONYLATE
CARBORUNDUM
CARBUNCULAR
CARBURATION
CARBURETION
CARBURETTED
CARBURETTER
CARBURETTOR
CARCINOLOGY
CARCINOMATA
CARDINALATE
CARDIOGRAPH
CARDOPHAGUS
CARD-SHARPER
CAREFULNESS
CARESSINGLY
CARILLONIST
CARLYLESQUE
CARMINATIVE
CARNATIONED
CARNIFICIAL
CARNIVOROUS
CAROLINGIAN
CAROUSINGLY
CARPET-SNAKE
CARPOGONIUM
CARPOSPORES
CARRAGEENIN
CARRIAGEWAY
CARRION-CROW
CARTOGRAPHY
CARUNCULATE
CARUNCULOUS
CARVEL-BUILT
CARYATIDEAN
CASH-ACCOUNT
CASHIERMENT
CASH-PAYMENT
CASH-RAILWAY

CASSIOPEIUM
CASSITERITE
CASTELLATED
CASTIGATION
CASTIGATORY
CASTING-VOTE
CASTLE-GUARD
CASUISTICAL
CATACAUSTIC
CATACHRESIS
CATACLASMIC
CATACLASTIC
CATACLYSMIC
CATADROMOUS
CATALLACTIC
CATALOGUISE
CATALYTICAL
CATAPHONICS
CATAPLECTIC
CATAPULTIER
CATASTROPHE
CATCH-PHRASE
CATCH-THE-TEN
CAT-CRACKING
CATECHETICS
CATECHISING
CATECHISMAL
CATECHISTIC
CATEGORICAL
CATERCORNER
CATER-COUSIN
CATERPILLAR
CATHARTICAL
CATHEDRATIC
CATHETERISM
CATHOLICISE
CATHOLICISM
CATHOLICITY
CAT'S-WHISKER
CAULICOLOUS
CAULICULATE
CAULIFLOWER
CAULIGENOUS
CAUSATIVELY
CAUSELESSLY
CAUSTICALLY
CAVALIERISH
CAVALIERISM
CAVE-DWELLER
CAVERNOUSLY
CAVERNULOUS
CAVILLATION
CAVO-RILIEVO
CEASELESSLY
CELEBRATION
CELESTIALLY
CELLIFEROUS
CEMENTATION
CEMENTATORY
CEMENT-STONE
CEMENT-WATER
CENESTHESIS
CENTENARIAN
CENTIGRAMME
CENTRE-BOARD
CENTRE-PIECE

CENTRICALLY
CENTRIFUGAL
CENTRIPETAL
CENTROBARIC
CENTURIATOR
CEPHALALGIA
CEPHALALGIC
CEPHALASPIS
CEPHALOPODA
CEPHALOTOMY
CERARGYRITE
CEREBELLOUS
CEREBRALISM
CEREBRALIST
CEREBRATION
CEREBRIFORM
CEREMONIOUS
CEROGRAPHIC
CEROPLASTIC
CERTIFIABLE
CERTIFIABLY
CERTIFICATE
CESAREVITCH
CESAREWITCH
CETEOSAURUS
CHAFF-CUTTER
CHAFF-ENGINE
CHAFING-DISH
CHAFING-GEAR
CHAIN-ARMOUR
CHAIN-BRIDGE
CHAIN-DRIVEN
CHAIN-HARROW
CHAIN-LETTER
CHAIN-PLATES
CHAIN-SMOKER
CHAIN-STITCH
CHALAZOGAMY
CHALCEDONIC
CHALCEDONYX
CHALLENGING
CHAMBERLAIN
CHAMBERMAID
CHAMELEONIC
CHAMPIONESS
CHANCE-COMER
CHANCELLERY
CHANCELLORY
CHANDLERING
CHANGEFULLY
CHANGE-HOUSE
CHANNELLING
CHANSONETTE
CHANSONNIER
CHANTARELLE
CHANTERELLE
CHANTICLEER
CHAOTICALLY
CHAPEAU-BRAS
CHAPERONAGE
CHARACINOID
CHARCUTERIE
CHARGE-HOUSE
CHARGE-SHEET
CHARISMATIC
CHARITY-GIRL

CHARLATANIC
CHARLATANRY
CHARMLESSLY
CHARS-À-BANCS
CHARTACEOUS
CHARTER-HAND
CHASMOGAMIC
CHASTENMENT
CHASTISABLE
CHAULMOOGRA
CHAUTAUQUAN
CHECK-ACTION
CHECK-STRING
CHEER-LEADER
CHEESECLOTH
CHEESE-PRESS
CHEESE-STRAW
CHEESE-WRING
CHEIROGNOMY
CHEIROMANCY
CHEIRONOMER
CHEIRONOMIC
CHEIROPTERA
CHELIFEROUS
CHEMOTACTIC
CHEMOTROPIC
CHEMURGICAL
CHENOPODIUM
CHEQUERWISE
CHEQUER-WORK
CHERISHMENT
CHERRY-STONE
CHEVAL-GLASS
CHIAROSCURO
CHIASTOLITE
CHICK-A-BIDDY
CHICKEN-FEED
CHICKEN-WIRE
CHIEFTAINCY
CHIEFTAINRY
CHILOGNATHA
CHIMNEY-NOOK
CHIMNEY-NUIK
CHINOISERIE
CHIP-CARVING
CHIPPENDALE
CHIRAGRICAL
CHIROGRAPHY
CHIROLOGIST
CHIROMANTIC
CHIROPODIST
CHIRURGICAL
CHISEL-TOOTH
CHITTERLING
CHITTY-FACED
CHLAMYDEOUS
CHLORIMETER
CHLORIMETRY
CHLOROMETER
CHLOROMETRY
CHLOROPHYLL
CHLOROPLAST
CHLOROPRENE
CHLOROQUINE
CHOCK-A-BLOCK
CHOICE-DRAWN

CHOIR-SCREEN
CHOIR-STALLS
CHOKE-CHERRY
CHOKING-COIL
CHOLESTERIC
CHOLESTERIN
CHOLESTEROL
CHONDROSTEI
CHORDOPHONE
CHOREGRAPHY
CHOREOGRAPH
CHOROGRAPHY
CHOROLOGIST
CHRISMATORY
CHRISTENDOM
CHRISTENING
CHRISTIANIA
CHRISTIANLY
CHRISTMASSY
CHRISTOLOGY
CHROME-STEEL
CHROMINANCE
CHROMOPLAST
CHROMOSCOPE
CHRONICALLY
CHRONOGRAPH
CHRONOLOGER
CHRONOLOGIC
CHRONOMETER
CHRONOMETRY
CHRONOSCOPE
CHRYSALIDES
CHRYSALISES
CHRYSAROBIN
CHRYSOBERYL
CHRYSOCOLLA
CHRYSOCRACY
CHRYSOPRASE
CHUCKLE-HEAD
CHURCH-BENCH
CHURCH-COURT
CHURCH-GOING
CHURCH-MOUSE
CHURCHWARDS
CHURCHWOMAN
CICATRICULA
CINCHONINIC
CINDER-TRACK
CINE-BIOLOGY
CINEMA-ORGAN
CINEMASCOPE
CINERITIOUS
CINNABARINE
CINQUECENTO
CIRCLE-RIDER
CIRCULARISE
CIRCULARITY
CIRCULATING
CIRCULATION
CIRCULATIVE
CIRCULATORY
CIRCUMCISER
CIRCUMFLECT
CIRCUMFUSED
CIRCUMPOLAR
CIRCUMSPECT

CIRCUMVOLVE
CIRRHIPEDIA
CISATLANTIC
CITHARISTIC
CITIZENSHIP
CITYSLICKER
CIVILISABLE
CIVIL-SUITED
CLAIM-JUMPER
CLAIRSCHACH
CLAIRVOYANT
CLAM-CHOWDER
CLAMOROUSLY
CLANDESTINE
CLANJAMFRAY
CLAPPERCLAW
CLARENCIEUX
CLASS-FELLOW
CLASSICALLY
CLASSIFYING
CLASS-LEADER
CLAVECINIST
CLAVICORNIA
CLAVIGEROUS
CLAY-BRAINED
CLEAN-LIMBED
CLEANLINESS
CLEAN-SHAVEN
CLEAR-HEADED
CLEARING-NUT
CLEISTOGAMY
CLERGYWOMAN
CLERICALISM
CLEVERALITY
CLICK-BEETLE
CLIFFHANGER
CLIMACTERIC
CLIMACTICAL
CLIMATOLOGY
CLINOCHLORE
CLINOMETRIC
CLODHOPPING
CLOG-ALMANAC
CLOISONNAGE
CLOSE-BANDED
CLOSE-BARRED
CLOSE-BODIED
CLOSED-CHAIN
CLOSE-FISTED
CLOSE-HANDED
CLOSE-HAULED
CLOSE-REEFED
CLOSET-DRAMA
CLOSTRIDIAL
CLOSTRIDIUM
CLOTHES-LINE
CLOTHES-MOTH
CLOTHES-POLE
CLOTHES-PROP
CLOUD-CASTLE
CLOUDLESSLY
CLOUD-TOPPED
CLOVER-GRASS
CLUSTER-PINE
CLYSTER-PIPE
COACH-OFFICE

COADJACENCY
COADJUTRESS
COADUNATION
COADUNATIVE
COAGULATION
COAGULATIVE
COAGULATORY
COALESCENCE
COALITIONAL
COALITIONER
COAL-SCUTTLE
COAL-TRIMMER
COAL-WHIPPER
COARCTATION
COAST-WAITER
COBBLESTONE
COCCIDIOSIS
COCHIN-CHINA
COCK-A-DOODLE
COCKALEEKIE
COCK-AND-BULL
COCK-CROWING
COCKLESHELL
COCK-SPARROW
COCOA-BUTTER
COCONSCIOUS
COCONUT-MILK
COCONUT-PALM
CODICILLARY
COEDUCATION
COEFFICIENT
COENENCHYMA
COENOBITISM
COERCIONIST
COESSENTIAL
COETERNALLY
COEXISTENCE
COEXTENSION
COEXTENSIVE
COFFEE-BERRY
COFFEE-HOUSE
COFFEE-STALL
COFFEE-TABLE
COGNITIVITY
COGNOMINATE
COGNOSCENTE
COGNOSCENTI
COGNOSCIBLE
COHORTATIVE
COINCIDENCE
COINCIDENCY
COINHERENCE
COINHERITOR
COINSURANCE
COLD-BLOODED
COLD-CASTING
COLD-FORGING
COLD-HEARTED
COLD-WELDING
COLD-WITHOUT
COLEOPTERAL
COLEORRHIZA
COLLABORATE
COLLAPSABLE
COLLAPSIBLE
COLLEAGUING

COLLECTABLE
COLLECTANEA
COLLECTEDLY
COLLECTIBLE
COLLEGIANER
COLLENCHYMA
COLLIGATION
COLLIGATIVE
COLLIMATION
COLLIQUABLE
COLLOCATION
COLLOCUTORY
COLLOQUIUMS
COLLUSIVELY
COLONELLING
COLONELSHIP
COLONIALISM
COLONIALIST
COLORIMETER
COLOURATION
COLOUR-BLIND
COLUBRIFORM
COLUMBARIUM
COLUMNARITY
COLUMNIATED
COMBINATION
COMBINATIVE
COMBINATORY
COMBUSTIBLE
COMBUSTIOUS
COMET-FINDER
COMEUPPANCE
COMFORTABLE
COMFORTABLY
COMFORTLESS
COMICALNESS
COMMANDMENT
COMMEMORATE
COMMENDABLE
COMMENDABLY
COMMENDATOR
COMMENSALLY
COMMENTATOR
COMMINATION
COMMINATIVE
COMMINATORY
COMMINUTION
COMMISERATE
COMMISSURAL
COMMONALITY
COMMONPLACE
COMMONSENSE
COMMON-SHORE
COMMOTIONAL
COMMUNALISM
COMMUNALIST
COMMUNICANT
COMMUNICATE
COMMUNISTIC
COMMUTATION
COMMUTATIVE
COMPACTEDLY
COMPACTNESS
COMPAGINATE
COMPANIABLE
COMPANIONED

COMPARATIVE
COMPARTMENT
COMPASSABLE
COMPASS-CARD
COMPEARANCE
COMPELLABLE
COMPENDIOUS
COMPENDIUMS
COMPENSATOR
COMPETENTLY
COMPETITION
COMPETITIVE
COMPILATION
COMPILATORY
COMPILEMENT
COMPLACENCE
COMPLACENCY
COMPLAINANT
COMPLAINING
COMPLAISANT
COMPLETABLE
COMPLEXNESS
COMPLIANTLY
COMPLICATED
COMPLOTTING
COMPONENTAL
COMPORTMENT
COMPOSITION
COMPOSITIVE
COMPOSSIBLE
COMPOST-HEAP
COMPOTATION
COMPOTATORY
COMPRESSION
COMPRESSIVE
COMPRESSURE
COMPRISABLE
COMPTOMETER
COMPTROLLER
COMPULSITOR
COMPUNCTION
COMPURGATOR
COMPUTATION
COMPUTATIVE
COMPUTERISE
COMRADESHIP
COMSTOCKERY
COMSTOCKISM
CONCATENATE
CONCEALABLE
CONCEALMENT
CONCEITEDLY
CONCEITLESS
CONCEIVABLE
CONCEIVABLY
CONCENTERED
CONCENTRATE
CONCENTRING
CONCEPTACLE
CONCEPTIOUS
CONCERNANCY
CONCERNEDLY
CONCERNMENT
CONCERTANTE
CONCERT-GOER
CONCESSIBLE

CONCILIABLE
CONCILIATOR
CONCIPIENCY
CONCISENESS
CONCOLORATE
CONCOLOROUS
CONCOMITANT
CONCORDANCE
CONCRESCENT
CONCUBINAGE
CONCUBINARY
CONCUBITANT
CONCURRENCE
CONCURRENCY
CONDEMNABLE
CONDENSABLE
CONDIGNNESS
CONDISCIPLE
CONDITIONAL
CONDITIONED
CONDITIONER
CONDOLATORY
CONDOLEMENT
CONDOMINIUM
CONDONATION
CONDOTTIERE
CONDOTTIERI
CONDUCEMENT
CONDUCTANCE
CONDUCTIBLE
CONDUCTRESS
CONDYLOMATA
CONFABULATE
CONFARREATE
CONFEDERACY
CONFEDERATE
CONFERRABLE
CONFESSEDLY
CONFIDENTLY
CONFIDINGLY
CONFIGURATE
CONFINELESS
CONFINEMENT
CONFIRMABLE
CONFIRMATOR
CONFISCABLE
CONFISCATOR
CONFLAGRANT
CONFLAGRATE
CONFLICTING
CONFLICTION
CONFLICTIVE
CONFLUENTLY
CONFORMABLE
CONFORMABLY
CONFUTATION
CONFUTATIVE
CONFUTEMENT
CONGEALABLE
CONGEALMENT
CONGELATION
CONGENEROUS
CONGENIALLY
CONGESTIBLE
CONGREGATED
CONGRESSMAN

CONGRUOUSLY
CONIROSTRAL
CONJECTURAL
CONJUGALITY
CONJUGATING
CONJUGATION
CONJUGATIVE
CONJUNCTION
CONJUNCTIVA
CONJUNCTIVE
CONJUNCTURE
CONJURATION
CONJUREMENT
CONNASCENCE
CONNASCENCY
CONNECTABLE
CONNECTEDLY
CONNECTIBLE
CONNOISSEUR
CONNOTATION
CONNOTATIVE
CONNUBIALLY
CONNUMERATE
CONQUERABLE
CONSANGUINE
CONSCIOUSLY
CONSECRATOR
CONSECUTION
CONSECUTIVE
CONSENTIENT
CONSEQUENCE
CONSERVABLE
CONSERVANCY
CONSERVATOR
CONSIDERATE
CONSIDERING
CONSIGNABLE
CONSIGNMENT
CONSILIENCE
CONSIMILITY
CONSISTENCE
CONSISTENCY
CONSOCIATED
CONSOLATION
CONSOLATORY
CONSOLATRIX
CONSOLEMENT
CONSOLIDATE
CONSONANTAL
CONSONANTLY
CONSPICUITY
CONSPICUOUS
CONSPIRATOR
CONSTELLATE
CONSTERNATE
CONSTIPATED
CONSTITUENT
CONSTRAINED
CONSTRICTED
CONSTRICTOR
CONSTRUABLE
CONSTRUCTER
CONSTRUCTOR
CONSTUPRATE
CONSUMMATOR
CONSUMPTION

CONSUMPTIVE
CONTAINABLE
CONTAINMENT
CONTAMINATE
CONTANGO-DAY
CONTEMPLANT
CONTEMPLATE
CONTENEMENT
CONTENTEDLY
CONTENTIOUS
CONTENTLESS
CONTENTMENT
CONTERMINAL
CONTESTABLE
CONTINENTAL
CONTINENTLY
CONTINGENCE
CONTINGENCY
CONTINUABLE
CONTINUALLY
CONTINUANCE
CONTINUATOR
CONTINUEDLY
CONTORNIATE
CONTRABASSO
CONTRACTILE
CONTRACTION
CONTRACTIVE
CONTRACTUAL
CONTRACTURE
CONTRA-DANCE
CONTRAPTION
CONTRARIETY
CONTRARIOUS
CONTRASTIVE
CONTRA-TENOR
CONTRAYERVA
CONTRETEMPS
CONTRIBUTOR
CONTRIVABLE
CONTRIVANCE
CONTROLLING
CONTROLMENT
CONTROVERSY
CONTUBERNAL
CONTUMACITY
CONURBATION
CONVALLARIA
CONVENIENCE
CONVENIENCY
CONVENTICLE
CONVERGENCE
CONVERGENCY
CONVERSABLE
CONVERSABLY
CONVERSANCE
CONVERSANCY
CONVERTIBLE
CONVERTIBLY
CONVEYANCER
CONVICINITY
CONVINCIBLE
CONVIVIALLY
CONVOCATION
CONVOLUTION
CONVOLVULUS

CONVULSIBLE
CONY-CATCHER
COOKERY-BOOK
COOK-GENERAL
COOKIE-SHINE
COOL-TANKARD
CO-OPERATING
CO-OPERATION
CO-OPERATIVE
CO-ORDINANCE
COPARCENARY
COPARCENERY
COPING-STONE
COPIOUSNESS
COPPER-BEECH
COPPER-FACED
COPPERPLATE
COPPERSMITH
COPPLE-CROWN
COPPLE-STONE
COPROLALIAC
COPROPHAGAN
COPROPHAGIC
COPROPHILIA
COPROSTEROL
CORAL-ISLAND
CORALLIFORM
CORALLOIDAL
CORBEL-TABLE
CORBICULATE
CORBIE-STEPS
CORDIALNESS
CORDWAINERY
CO-RIVALSHIP
CORK-CAMBIUM
CORMOPHYTIC
CORN-CRACKER
CORNER-STONE
CORNER-TEETH
CORNHUSKING
CORNICE-HOOK
CORNICE-POLE
CORNICE-RAIL
CORNICE-RING
CORNICULATE
CORNIFEROUS
CORNIGEROUS
CORNUCOPIAN
COROLLIFORM
CORONAGRAPH
CORONOGRAPH
CORPORALITY
CORPORATELY
CORPORATION
CORPORATIVE
CORPOREALLY
CORPULENTLY
CORPUSCULAR
CORRECTABLE
CORRECTIBLE
CORRECTNESS
CORRELATION
CORRELATIVE
CORRIGENDUM
CORROBORANT
CORROBORATE

CORRODENTIA
CORROSIVELY
CORRUGATION
CORRUPTIBLE
CORRUPTIBLY
CORRUPTNESS
CORUSCATION
CORYBANTISM
CO-SIGNATORY
COSMETICISE
COSMETICISM
COSMETOLOGY
COSMOCRATIC
COSMOGONIST
COSMOGRAPHY
COSMOLOGIST
COSMOPOLICY
COSMOPOLITE
COSMOSPHERE
COSMOTHEISM
COSMOTHETIC
COST-ACCOUNT
COSTIVENESS
COTONEASTER
COTTON-GRASS
COTTONMOUTH
COTTON-PLANT
COTTON-PRESS
COTTON-WASTE
COTYLOPHORA
COULOMMIERS
COUNSELLING
COUNTENANCE
COUNTER-BASE
COUNTER-BLOW
COUNTER-BOND
COUNTER-BUFF
COUNTER-CAST
COUNTERDRAW
COUNTERFEIT
COUNTERFOIL
COUNTER-FORT
COUNTER-GLOW
COUNTERMAND
COUNTERMARK
COUNTERMINE
COUNTER-MOVE
COUNTERMURE
COUNTER-PACE
COUNTERPANE
COUNTERPART
COUNTERPLEA
COUNTER-PLOT
COUNTER-ROLL
COUNTERSEAL
COUNTERSIGN
COUNTERSINK
COUNTER-TIME
COUNTER-TURN
COUNTERVAIL
COUNTER-VIEW
COUNTER-VOTE
COUNTER-WORK
COUNTING-OUT
COUNTRIFIED
COUNTRYFIED

COUNTRY-FOLK
COUNTRY-ROCK
COUNTRY-SEAT
COUNTRYSIDE
COUNTRYWIDE
COUPLING-BOX
COURTEOUSLY
COURTESYING
COURTIERISM
COURTLINESS
COXCOMBICAL
CRABBEDNESS
CRACKERJACK
CRACK-HALTER
CRACOVIENNE
CRAG-AND-TAIL
CRAGGEDNESS
CRAMBO-CLINK
CRANE-NECKED
CRANIOGNOMY
CRANIOMETER
CRANIOMETRY
CRANIOSCOPY
CRAPEHANGER
CRAPPIT-HEAD
CRAPPIT-HEID
CRAPULOSITY
CRASH-HELMET
CRATERELLUS
CRATERIFORM
CREAM-CHEESE
CREATIANISM
CREATIONISM
CREATIONIST
CREATORSHIP
CREDIBILITY
CREDULOUSLY
CRÉMAILLÈRE
CREMATORIAL
CREMATORIUM
CRENELLATED
CREOPHAGOUS
CREPEHANGER
CREPITATION
CREPITATIVE
CREPUSCULAR
CRESCENTADE
CRESTFALLEN
CRIMINALIST
CRIMINALITY
CRIMINATION
CRIMINATIVE
CRIMINATORY
CRIMINOLOGY
CRINIGEROUS
CRISPING-PIN
CRITHOMANCY
CRITICALITY
CRITICASTER
CROCIDOLITE
CROCODILIAN
CROCODILITE
CROOKBACKED
CROOKEDNESS
CROP-DUSTING
CROSSBANDED

CROSSBARRED
CROSSBEARER
CROSSBOWMAN
CROSS-COUSIN
CROSS-GARNET
CROSS-LEAVED
CROSS-LEGGED
CROSS-STITCH
CROSS-TINING
CROTCHETEER
CROWN-ANTLER
CROWN-LAWYER
CRUCIFEROUS
CRUCIFIXION
CRUCIGEROUS
CRUNCHINESS
CRUSTACEOUS
CRYOPHYSICS
CRYOSURGERY
CRYOTHERAPY
CRYPTOGAMIA
CRYPTOGAMIC
CRYPTOGRAPH
CRYPTOMERIA
CRYSTALLINE
CRYSTALLISE
CRYSTALLITE
CRYSTALLOID
CTENOPHORAN
CUBICALNESS
CUCKOO-CLOCK
CUDGEL-PROOF
CUIR-BOUILLI
CUIR-BOUILLY
CULMIFEROUS
CULMINATION
CULPABILITY
CULTIVATION
CULTURELESS
CULVERINEER
CUNCTATIOUS
CUNNILINGUS
CUNNINGNESS
CUPELLATION
CUPRIFEROUS
CUPRO-NICKEL
CUPULIFERAE
CURABLENESS
CURATORSHIP
CURIALISTIC
CURIOUSNESS
CURLING-POND
CURLY-GREENS
CURLY-HEADED
CURRANT-CAKE
CURRANT-LOAF
CURRANT-WINE
CURRENTNESS
CURRISHNESS
CURRY-POWDER
CURSORINESS
CURTAILMENT
CURTAIL-STEP
CURTAIN-FIRE
CURTAL-FRIAR
CURVILINEAR

CURVILINEAR
CUSHION-TIRE
CUSHION-TYRE
CUSTOMARILY
CUSTOM-BUILT
CUSTOM-HOUSE
CYATHEACEAE
CYBERNETICS
CYCADACEOUS
CYCLOPAEDIA
CYCLOPAEDIC
CYCLOSERINE
CYCLOTHYMIA
CYCLOTHYMIC
CYLINDRICAL
CYMOPHANOUS
CYNICALNESS
CYPERACEOUS
CYPRESS-KNEE
CYPRIPEDIUM
CYPRO-MINOAN
CYSTICERCUS
CYTOGENESIS
CYTOLOGICAL

D

DACTYLOGRAM
DACTYLOLOGY
DAISY-CUTTER
DAK-BUNGALOW
DAMASCENING
DAMASKSTEEL
DAME'S-VIOLET
DAMPISHNESS
DANCING-GIRL
DANDY-RIGGED
DANGEROUSLY
DARING-HARDY
DARK-LANTERN
DASIPODIDAE
DASTARDNESS
DAUNTLESSLY
DAY-LABOURER
DEAD-CLOTHES
DEAD-FREIGHT
DEAF-AND-DUMB
DEATH-DUTIES
DEATHLINESS
DEATH-MARKED
DEATH-RATTLE
DEATH-STROKE
DEBARCATION
DEBARKATION
DEBAUCHEDLY
DEBAUCHMENT
DEBOUCHMENT
DECAMERONIC
DECANTATION
DECARBONATE
DECARBONISE
DECARBURISE
DECEITFULLY
DECELERATOR
DECEMBERISH
DECEMVIRATE
DECEPTIVELY

DECEREBRATE
DECEREBRISE
DECKLE-EDGED
DECK-PASSAGE
DECLAMATION
DECLAMATORY
DECLARATION
DECLARATIVE
DECLARATORY
DECLINATION
DECLINATORY
DECLINATURE
DECLIVITOUS
DECOLLATION
DECOLOURISE
DECOMPOSITE
DECORTICATE
DECREPITATE
DECREPITUDE
DECRESCENDO
DECUMBENTLY
DECUMBITURE
DECURIONATE
DECURRENTLY
DECURSIVELY
DECUSSATELY
DECUSSATION
DEDUCTIVELY
DEEP-DRAWING
DEEP-MOUTHED
DEERSTALKER
DEFALCATION
DEFEASANCED
DEFECTIVELY
DEFENCELESS
DEFENSATIVE
DEFENSIVELY
DEFERENTIAL
DEFEUDALISE
DEFIANTNESS
DEFIBRINATE
DEFIBRINISE
DEFICIENTLY
DEFILIATION
DEFLAGRATOR
DEFLEXIONAL
DEFLORATION
DEFOLIATION
DEFORCEMENT
DEFORMATION
DEFRAUDMENT
DEGLUTINATE
DEGLUTITION
DEGLUTITIVE
DEGLUTITORY
DEGRADATION
DEGUSTATION
DEGUSTATORY
DEHORTATION
DEHORTATIVE
DEHORTATORY
DEHYDRATION
DEICTICALLY
DEIFICATION
DEISTICALLY
DELECTATION

DELETERIOUS
DELICIOUSLY
DELIGHTLESS
DELIGHTSOME
DELINEATION
DELINQUENCY
DELIRIOUSLY
DELITESCENT
DELIVERABLE
DELIVERANCE
DELIVERY-MAN
DELIVERY-VAN
DELLA-ROBBIA
DELPHINIDAE
DELUSIONIST
DEMAGNETISE
DEMAGOGICAL
DEMAGOGUERY
DEMAGOGUISM
DEMARCATION
DEMARKATION
DEMI-BASTION
DEMIGODDESS
DEMIGRATION
DEMOCRATISE
DEMOCRATIST
DEMOGRAPHER
DEMOGRAPHIC
DEMONIACISM
DEMONIANISM
DEMONOCRACY
DEMONOLATER
DEMONOLATRY
DEMONOLOGIC
DEMONOMANIA
DEMONSTRATE
DEMOSTHENIC
DEMOUNTABLE
DENDRACHATE
DENDRITICAL
DENDROGLYPH
DENDROLATRY
DENDROMETER
DENIGRATION
DENITRATION
DENIZENSHIP
DENOMINABLE
DENOMINATOR
DENTICULATE
DENTIGEROUS
DENUNCIATOR
DEOBSTRUENT
DEOXIDATION
DEOXYGENATE
DEOXYGENISE
DEOXYRIBOSE
DEPAUPERATE
DEPAUPERISE
DEPENDINGLY
DEPHLEGMATE
DEPLORATION
DEPLORINGLY
DEPLUMATION
DEPOPULATOR
DEPORTATION
DEPRAVATION

DEPRAVEMENT
DEPRAVINGLY
DEPRECATION
DEPRECATIVE
DEPRECATORY
DEPRECIATOR
DEPREDATION
DEPREDATORY
DEPRIVATION
DEPRIVATIVE
DEPRIVEMENT
DEPTH-CHARGE
DERACIALISE
DERANGEMENT
DERELICTION
DERMATOLOGY
DERMOGRAPHY
DESALINATOR
DESCENDABLE
DESCENDIBLE
DESCRIBABLE
DESCRIPTION
DESCRIPTIVE
DESECRATION
DESEGREGATE
DESENSITISE
DESERPIDINE
DESERVINGLY
DESEXUALISE
DESICCATION
DESICCATIVE
DESIDERATUM
DESIGNATION
DESILVERISE
DESPERADOES
DESPERATELY
DESPERATION
DESPOILMENT
DESPONDENCE
DESPONDENCY
DESPUMATION
DESTINATION
DESTITUTION
DESTRUCTION
DESTRUCTIVE
DESTUCTIBLE
DESULTORILY
DETECTIVIST
DETERIORATE
DETERIORISM
DETERIORITY
DETERMINACY
DETERMINANT
DETERMINATE
DETERMINISM
DETERMINIST
DETESTATION
DETRACTRESS
DETRAINMENT
DETRIMENTAL
DEUTEROGAMY
DEUTERONOMY
DEVALUATION
DEVASTATING
DEVASTATION
DEVELOPABLE

DEVELOPMENT
DEVIL-DODGER
DEVIOUSNESS
DEVOLVEMENT
DEVOTEDNESS
DEVOTIONIST
DEVOURINGLY
DEXIOTROPIC
DEXTEROUSLY
DIABOLOLOGY
DIACOUSTICS
DIACRITICAL
DIADELPHOUS
DIAGNOSTICS
DIALECTALLY
DIALECTICAL
DIALOGISTIC
DIAMAGNETIC
DIAMETRALLY
DIAMETRICAL
DIAMOND-DUST
DIAPHANEITY
DIAPHORESIS
DIAPHORETIC
DIAPHRAGMAL
DIAPOPHYSES
DIAPOPHYSIS
DIAPOSITIVE
DIARTHROSIS
DIASCORDIUM
DIASTEMATIC
DIASTROPHIC
DIATESSARON
DIATHERMACY
DIATHERMOUS
DICEPHALOUS
DICHOGAMOUS
DICHOTOMISE
DICHOTOMIST
DICHOTOMOUS
DICHROMATIC
DICHROSCOPE
DICOTYLEDON
DICTATORIAL
DIDACTICISM
DIDACTYLOUS
DIFFERENTIA
DIFFERENTLY
DIFFICULTLY
DIFFIDENTLY
DIFFRACTION
DIFFRACTIVE
DIFFUSENESS
DIFFUSIVELY
DIFFUSIVITY
DIGESTIVELY
DIGITIGRADE
DIGLADIATOR
DILAPIDATED
DILAPIDATOR
DILUVIALIST
DIMENSIONAL
DIMENSIONED
DIMIDIATION
DIMINISHING
DINING-TABLE

DINNER-DANCE
DINNER-TABLE
DINNER-WAGON
DINOTHERIUM
DIOPHANTINE
DIORISTICAL
DIOTHELETIC
DIPHTHEROID
DIPHTHONGAL
DIPHTHONGIC
DIPHYCERCAL
DIPHYSITISM
DIPLOMATISE
DIPLOMATIST
DIPROTODONT
DIPSACACEAE
DIPSOMANIAC
DIPTEROCARP
DIRECTIONAL
DIRECTIVITY
DIRECTORATE
DIRECTORIAL
DIRECTRICES
DIREFULNESS
DISABLEMENT
DISACCUSTOM
DISAFFECTED
DISAFFOREST
DISANNULLER
DISAPPROVAL
DISARMAMENT
DISASSEMBLE
DISASSEMBLY
DISAVENTURE
DISBANDMENT
DISBELIEVER
DISBOWELLED
DISCALCEATE
DISCARDMENT
DISCEPTATOR
DISCERNIBLE
DISCERNIBLY
DISCERNMENT
DISCERPTION
DISCERPTIVE
DISCIPLINAL
DISCIPLINER
DISCOGRAPHY
DISCOLOURED
DISCOMFITED
DISCOMYCETE
DISCONTINUE
DISCOPHORAN
DISCORDANCE
DISCORDANCY
DISCOTHEQUE
DISCOURSIVE
DISCOURTESY
DISCREPANCE
DISCREPANCY
DISCUSSABLE
DISCUSSIBLE
DISEMBITTER
DISEMBODIED
DISEMBURDEN
DISEMPLOYED

DISENCUMBER
DISENSHROUD
DISENTANGLE
DISENTHRALL
DISENTHRONE
DISENTRANCE
DISFAVOURER
DISGARRISON
DISGRACEFUL
DISGRACIOUS
DISGRUNTLED
DISGUISEDLY
DISGUSTEDLY
DISHARMONIC
DISHEVELLED
DISHONESTLY
DISHONORARY
DISHONOURER
DISILLUSION
DISILLUSIVE
DISIMPRISON
DISINCLINED
DISINFECTOR
DISINTEREST
DISJUNCTION
DISJUNCTIVE
DISJUNCTURE
DISLIKEABLE
DISLOCATION
DISLODGMENT
DISMASTMENT
DISMAYFULLY
DISMEMBERED
DISMUTATION
DISOBEDIENT
DISOBLIGING
DISORDINATE
DISORGANISE
DISPATCH-BOX
DISPATCHFUL
DISPENSABLE
DISPENSABLY
DISPENSATOR
DISPERSEDLY
DISPIRITING
DISPLEASANT
DISPLEASING
DISPLEASURE
DISPORTMENT
DISPOSINGLY
DISPOSITION
DISPOSITIVE
DISPROPERTY
DISPUTATION
DISPUTATIVE
DISQUIETFUL
DISQUIETING
DISQUIETIVE
DISQUIETOUS
DISQUIETUDE
DISREMEMBER
DISSECTIBLE
DISSEMBLING
DISSEMINATE
DISSEMINULE
DISSENTIENT

DISSENTIOUS
DISSEPIMENT
DISSERTATOR
DISSILIENCE
DISSIMILATE
DISSIMULATE
DISSIPATION
DISSIPATIVE
DISSOCIABLE
DISSOLUTELY
DISSOLUTION
DISSOLVABLE
DISSYMMETRY
DISTASTEFUL
DISTEMPERED
DISTENSIBLE
DISTILLABLE
DISTINCTION
DISTINCTIVE
DISTINCTURE
DISTINGUISH
DISTRACTION
DISTRACTIVE
DISTRESSFUL
DISTRESSING
DISTRIBUEND
DISTRIBUTER
DISTRIBUTOR
DISTRUSTFUL
DISTURBANCE
DISULPHURET
DISULPHURIC
DISUNIONIST
DISYLLABIFY
DISYLLABISM
DITHELETISM
DITHELITISM
DITHYRAMBIC
DITTOGRAPHY
DIVE-BOMBING
DIVELLICATE
DIVERGEMENT
DIVERGENTLY
DIVERGINGLY
DIVERSIFIED
DIVERTINGLY
DIVESTITURE
DIVING-BOARD
DIVING-DRESS
DIVINING-ROD
DIVISIONARY
DIVISIONISM
DIVORCEABLE
DIVORCEMENT
DIVULGATION
DOCH-AN-DORIS
DOCIBLENESS
DOCKISATION
DOCK-WARRANT
DOCTRINAIRE
DOCTRINALLY
DOCUMENTARY
DODECAGYNIA
DODECANDRIA
DODECAPHONY
DODECASTYLE

DOGBERRYDOM
DOGBERRYISM
DOGGISHNESS
DOGMATOLOGY
DOG'S-MERCURY
DOLABRIFORM
DOLEFULNESS
DOLLISHNESS
DOLTISHNESS
DOMESTICATE
DOMESTICITY
DOMICILIARY
DOMICILIATE
DOMINEERING
DOOR-KNOCKER
DORSIFEROUS
DOTING-PIECE
DOUBLE-AGENT
DOUBLE-CROSS
DOUBLE-DUTCH
DOUBLE-EAGLE
DOUBLE-EDGED
DOUBLE-ENDER
DOUBLE-ENTRY
DOUBLE-FACED
DOUBLE-LIVED
DOUBLE-MINED
DOUBLE-QUICK
DOUBLE-SHADE
DOUBLE-SHARP
DOUBLE-STOUT
DOUBLE-THINK
DOUBTLESSLY
DOUGHTINESS
DOUROUCOULI
DOVETAILING
DOWN-DRAUGHT
DOWN-HEARTED
DOWN-SETTING
DOWN-SITTING
DOWN-THE-LINE
DOWNTRODDEN
DOXOGRAPHER
DRACUNCULUS
DRAGGLE-TAIL
DRAGON'S-HEAD
DRAGOON-BIRD
DRAMATICISM
DRAMATURGIC
DRAM-DRINKER
DRAP-DE-BERRY
DRASTICALLY
DRAUGHTSMAN
DRAWING-ROOM
DREADLESSLY
DREADNAUGHT
DREADNOUGHT
DREAMLESSLY
DREDGING-BOX
DRESS-CIRCLE
DRESS-LENGTH
DRESS-REFORM
DRESS-SHIELD
DRIFT-ANCHOR
DRIFT-MINING
DRILL-BARROW

DRILL-HARROW
DRILL-MASTER
DRILL-PLOUGH
DRIPPING-PAN
DRIVING-BAND
DRIVING-GEAR
DROMOPHOBIA
DRONISHNESS
DROP-CURTAIN
DROP-FORGING
DROSERACEAE
DROUTHINESS
DRUCKENNESS
DRUNKENNESS
DUAL-CONTROL
DUAL-PURPOSE
DUBIOUSNESS
DUCKING-POND
DUKHOBORTSY
DULCIFLUOUS
DULL-BRAINED
DULL-SIGHTED
DUMBFOUNDER
DUMPISHNESS
DUNIEWASSAL
DUPLICATION
DUPLICATIVE
DUPLICATURE
DURABLENESS
DUSKISHNESS
DUSTY-MILLER
DUTEOUSNESS
DUTIFULNESS
DWINDLEMENT
DYER'S-ROCKET
DYNAMICALLY
DYNAMOGRAPH
DYNAMOMETER
DYNAMOMETRY
DYOTHELETIC
DYOTHELITIC
DYSFUNCTION
DYSHARMONIC
DYSLOGISTIC
DYSPATHETIC
DYSPEPTICAL

E

EAGLE-WINGED
EARNESTNESS
EAR-PIERCING
EARTH-CLOSET
EARTHENWARE
EARTH-HUNGER
EARTHLINESS
EARTH-PILLAR
EARTHQUAKED
EARTH-TREMOR
EAST-BY-NORTH
EAST-BY-SOUTH
EASTERNMOST
EATING-APPLE
EATING-HOUSE
ECBLASTESIS
ECCALEOBION
ECCENTRICAL

ECCLESIARCH
ECCRINOLOGY
ECHINODERMA
ECHO-SOUNDER
ECLECTICISM
ECONOMETRIC
ECTOBLASTIC
ECTOGENESIS
ECTOGENETIC
ECTOMORPHIC
ECTOPLASMIC
ECTOPLASTIC
ECUMENICISM
EDIFICATION
EDIFICATORY
EDITORIALLY
EDUCABILITY
EDUCATIONAL
EDULCORATOR
EFFECTIVELY
EFFECTUALLY
EFFICACIOUS
EFFICIENTLY
EFFULGENTLY
EGALITARIAN
EGLANDULOSE
EGOTISTICAL
EGREGIOUSLY
EIGHT-SQUARE
EINSTEINIUM
EJACULATION
EJACULATIVE
EJACULATORY
EJECTAMENTA
EJECTOR-SEAT
ELABORATELY
ELABORATION
ELABORATIVE
ELABORATORY
ELASTICALLY
ELASTICATED
ELASTICNESS
ELBOW-GREASE
ELDER-FLOWER
ELDERLINESS
ELECTIONEER
ELECTORSHIP
ELECTRICIAN
ELECTRICITY
ELECTRIFIED
ELECTROCUTE
ELECTROLIER
ELECTROLOGY
ELECTROLYSE
ELECTROLYTE
ELECTRONICS
ELECTROTINT
ELECTROTYPE
ELECTROTYPY
ELEMENTALLY
ELEPHANTINE
ELEPHANTOID
ELEUTHERIAN
ELICITATION
ELIGIBILITY
ELIMINATION

ELIMINATIVE
ELIMINATORY
ELIZABETHAN
ELLIPSOIDAL
ELLIPTICITY
ELSEWHITHER
ELUCIDATION
ELUCIDATIVE
ELUCIDATORY
ELUSORINESS
ELUTRIATION
EMANATIONAL
EMANCIPATOR
EMASCULATOR
EMBARCATION
EMBARKATION
EMBARRASSED
EMBELLISHER
EMBITTERING
EMBLEMATISE
EMBLEMATIST
EMBOÎTEMENT
EMBOWELLING
EMBOWELMENT
EMBOWERMENT
EMBRACEMENT
EMBRACINGLY
EMBROCATION
EMBROIDERER
EMBROILMENT
EMBRYOLOGIC
EMBRYONATED
EMERY-POWDER
EMMENAGOGIC
EMMENAGOGUE
EMMENTHALER
EMOLUMENTAL
EMOTIONABLE
EMOTIONALLY
EMOTIONLESS
EMPANELLING
EMPANELMENT
EMPERORSHIP
EMPHYTEUSIS
EMPHYTEUTIC
EMPIECEMENT
EMPIRICALLY
EMPIRICUTIC
EMPLACEMENT
EMPTY-HANDED
EMPTY-HEADED
EMPYREUMATA
EMULOUSNESS
EMULSIONISE
ENARTHROSIS
ENCAPSULATE
ENCARNALISE
ENCEPHALOID
ENCEPHALOUS
ENCHAINMENT
ENCHANTMENT
ENCHANTRESS
ENCHIRIDION
ENCHONDROMA
ENCOMIASTIC
ENCOURAGING

ENCRIMSONED
ENCRUSTMENT
ENCUMBRANCE
ENCYSTATION
ENDEARINGLY
ENDEMICALLY
ENDEMIOLOGY
ENDLESSNESS
ENDOCARDIAC
ENDOCARDIAL
ENDOCARDIUM
ENDOCHYLOUS
ENDOMETRIUM
ENDOMORPHIC
ENDOPHAGOUS
ENDOPLASMIC
ENDOPLASTIC
ENDORSEMENT
ENDOSPERMIC
ENDOTHERMIC
ENDOTROPHIC
ENERGETICAL
ENFEOFFMENT
ENFORCEABLE
ENFORCEMENT
ENFOULDERED
ENFRANCHISE
ENGINEERING
ENGORGEMENT
ENGRAFTMENT
ENGRAILMENT
ENGROSSMENT
ENHANCEMENT
ENIGMATICAL
ENJAMBEMENT
ENLARGEMENT
ENLIVENMENT
ENNEAHEDRAL
ENNEAHEDRON
ENNEANDRIAN
ENNEANDROUS
ENNOBLEMENT
ENQUIRATION
ENSANGUINED
ENSEPULCHRE
ENSLAVEMENT
ENTABLATURE
ENTERECTOMY
ENTEROSTOMY
ENTERPRISER
ENTERTAINER
ENTHRALLING
ENTHRALMENT
ENTOMOPHILY
ENTOPHYTOUS
ENTRAINMENT
ENTREATABLE
ENTREATMENT
ENTRUSTMENT
ENUCLEATION
ENUMERATION
ENUMERATIVE
ENUNCIATION
ENUNCIATIVE
ENUNCIATORY
ENVELOPMENT

ENVIOUSNESS
ENVIRONMENT
EOANTHROPUS
EPANALEPSIS
EPEIROGENIC
EPHEMERIDAE
EPHEMERIDES
EPICHEIREMA
EPIDIASCOPE
EPIGASTRIUM
EPIGENESIST
EPIGENETICS
EPIGRAPHIST
EPILEPTICAL
EPILOGISTIC
EPINEPHRINE
EPIPETALOUS
EPIPHYLLOUS
EPIPHYTICAL
EPIPLASTRAL
EPIPLASTRON
EPISCOPALLY
EPISEPALOUS
EPISTILBITE
EPISTOLICAL
EPITHALAMIA
EPITHALAMIC
EPITHELIOMA
EPITHYMETIC
EPITROCHOID
EPOCH-MAKING
EQUABLENESS
EQUIANGULAR
EQUIBALANCE
EQUIDISTANT
EQUILATERAL
EQUILIBRATE
EQUILIBRIST
EQUILIBRITY
EQUILIBRIUM
EQUINOCTIAL
EQUIPOLLENT
EQUISETALES
EQUISETINAE
EQUIVALENCE
EQUIVALENCY
EQUIVOCALLY
EQUIVOCATOR
ERADICATION
ERADICATIVE
ERASTIANISM
EREMACAUSIS
ERGATOCRACY
ERGATOMORPH
ERIODENDRON
ERIOPHOROUS
EROTOGENOUS
EROTOMANIAC
ERRATICALLY
ERRONEOUSLY
ERUBESCENCE
ERUBESCENCY
ERYTHEMATIC
ERYTHROCYTE
ESCHATOLOGY
ESCHEATABLE

ESCHEATMENT
ESCRITORIAL
ESEMPLASTIC
ESOTERICISM
ESPERANTIST
ESPIÉGLERIE
ESSENTIALLY
ESTABLISHED
ESTABLISHER
ESTRAMAZONE
ESTRANGHELO
ESTREPEMENT
ETHEREALISE
ETHEREALITY
ETHEROMANIA
ETHNOGRAPHY
ETHNOLOGIST
ETHOLOGICAL
ETRUSCOLOGY
ETYMOLOGISE
ETYMOLOGIST
EUBACTERIUM
EUCALYPTOLE
EUCHARISTIC
EUCHOLOGION
EUDAEMONISM
EUDAEMONIST
EUGENICALLY
EUPEPTICITY
EUPHEMISTIC
EURHYTHMICS
EURODOLLARS
EUROPEANISE
EURYPHARYNX
EURYPTERIDA
EURYPTEROID
EVAGINATION
EVANESCENCE
EVANGELIARY
EVANGELICAL
EVANISHMENT
EVAPORATION
EVAPORATIVE
EVASIVENESS
EVENING-STAR
EVENTRATION
EVENTUALISE
EVENTUALITY
EVERLASTING
EVERYWHENCE
EVIDENTIARY
EVIL-STARRED
EVITERNALLY
EVOLUTIONAL
EXAGGERATOR
EXALTEDNESS
EXAMINATION
EXANIMATION
EXANTHEMATA
EXASPERATOR
EXCEEDINGLY
EXCELLENTLY
EXCEPTIONAL
EXCESSIVELY
EXCLAMATION
EXCLAMATIVE

EXCLAMATORY
EXCLUSIVELY
EXCLUSIVISM
EXCOMMUNION
EXCORIATION
EXCORTICATE
EXCREMENTAL
EXCREMENTUM
EXCRESCENCE
EXCRESCENCY
EXCULPATION
EXCULPATORY
EXCURSIVELY
EXECUTIONER
EXECUTIVELY
EXECUTORIAL
EXECUTRICES
EXECUTRIXES
EXEMPLARILY
EXEMPLARITY
EXEMPLIFIED
EXERCISABLE
EXFOLIATION
EXFOLIATIVE
EXHAUSTIBLE
EXHAUSTLESS
EXHAUST-PIPE
EXHORTATION
EXHORTATIVE
EXHORTATORY
EXISTENTIAL
EXONERATION
EXONERATIVE
EXORBITANCE
EXORBITANCY
EXOSKELETAL
EXOSKELETON
EXOTERICISM
EXPANSIONAL
EXPANSIVELY
EXPANSIVITY
EXPATIATION
EXPATIATIVE
EXPATIATORY
EXPECTANTLY
EXPECTATION
EXPECTATIVE
EXPECTINGLY
EXPECTORANT
EXPECTORATE
EXPEDIENTLY
EXPEDITIOUS
EXPENDITURE
EXPENSIVELY
EXPERIENCED
EXPISCATION
EXPISCATORY
EXPLAINABLE
EXPLANATION
EXPLANATORY
EXPLICATION
EXPLICATIVE
EXPLICATORY
EXPLOITABLE
EXPLORATION
EXPLORATIVE

EXPLORATORY
EXPLOSIVELY
EXPONENTIAL
EXPORTATION
EXPOSEDNESS
EXPOSITRESS
EXPOSTULATE
EXPRESSIBLE
EXPRESSNESS
EXPROMISSOR
EXPROPRIATE
EXPUGNATION
EXPURGATION
EXPURGATORY
EXQUISITELY
EXSANGUINED
EXSICCATION
EXSICCATIVE
EXSTIPULATE
EXTEMPORARY
EXTEMPORISE
EXTENSIONAL
EXTENSIVELY
EXTENUATING
EXTENUATION
EXTENUATIVE
EXTENUATORY
EXTERIORISE
EXTERIORITY
EXTERMINATE
EXTERNALISE
EXTERNALISM
EXTERNALITY
EXTIRPATION
EXTIRPATORY
EXTORSIVELY
EXTORTIONER
EXTRACTABLE
EXTRACTIBLE
EXTRADITION
EXTRA-FLORAL
EXTRAPOLATE
EXTRAVAGANT
EXTRAVAGATE
EXTRAVASATE
EXTRICATION
EXTRINSICAL
EXUBERANTLY
EYEBROWLESS
EYE-CATCHING

F

FABRICATION
FABRICATIVE
FACE-LIFTING
FACETIOUSLY
FACINERIOUS
FACSIMILIST
FACT-FINDING
FACTORY-SHIP
FACTUALNESS
FACULTATIVE
FADDISHNESS
FAINÉANTISE
FAIR-DEALING
FAIR-SEEMING

FAIR-WEATHER
FAIRY-BUTTER
FAITH-HEALER
FAITHLESSLY
FAITHWORTHY
FALLALISHLY
FALLIBILITY
FALLOW-FINCH
FALSE-BEDDED
FALSIFIABLE
FALSTAFFIAN
FALTERINGLY
FAMILIARISE
FAMILIARITY
FANATICALLY
FANFARONADE
FANTASTICAL
FARAWAYNESS
FARCICALITY
FARDEL-BOUND
FARINACEOUS
FARM-OFFICES
FARRAGINOUS
FAR-REACHING
FARTHERMORE
FARTHERMOST
FARTHINGALE
FASCIA-BOARD
FASCICULATE
FASCINATING
FASCINATION
FASHIONABLE
FASHIONABLY
FASTERN'S-E'EN
FASTIGIATED
FATEFULNESS
FATHER-IN-LAW
FATIDICALLY
FATIGUE-DUTY
FATIGUINGLY
FATUOUSNESS
FAULT-FINDER
FAULTLESSLY
FAUXBOURDON
FAVOURITISM
FAWNINGNESS
FEARFULNESS
FEASIBILITY
FEATHER-EDGE
FEATHER-HEAD
FEATHER-PALM
FEATHER-PATE
FEATHER-STAR
FEATURELESS
FECUNDATION
FEHMGERICHT
FEIGNEDNESS
FELDSPATHIC
FELL-LURKING
FELONIOUSLY
FELSPATHOID
FENCE-LIZARD
FENDER-STOOL
FENESTRATED
FERMENTABLE
FERNITICKLE

FERNTICKLED
FERNYTICKLE
FEROCIOUSLY
FERRIFEROUS
FERRONICKEL
FERRONNIÈRE
FERRUGINOUS
FERULACEOUS
FESTINATELY
FESTINATION
FESTSCHRIFT
FETCH-CANDLE
FETICHISTIC
FETISHISTIC
FIANÇAILLES
FIBRILLATED
FIDDLE-DE-DEE
FIDDLESTICK
FIDGETINESS
FIELD-CORNET
FIELDWORKER
FIGURE-DANCE
FILAMENTARY
FILAMENTOUS
FILTER-PAPER
FIMBRIATION
FINANCIALLY
FINCH-BACKED
FINGER-BOARD
FINGER-GLASS
FINGER-GRASS
FINGERGUARD
FINGERPLATE
FINGERPRINT
FINGERSTALL
FINICALNESS
FINNO-UGRIAN
FIPPLE-FLUTE
FIRE-BALLOON
FIRE-BRIGADE
FIRE-CONTROL
FIRE-CRACKER
FIRE-FIGHTER
FIRE-FLAUGHT
FIRELIGHTER
FIRE-MARSHAL
FIRE-RAISING
FIRE-WALKING
FIRE-WATCHER
FIRE-WORSHIP
FIRMAMENTAL
FIRST-FOOTER
FIRST-FRUITS
FISH-BELLIED
FISH-FARMING
FISH-GUTTING
FISHING-FROG
FISH-PACKING
FISH-TORPEDO
FISSIONABLE
FISSIPARISM
FISSIPARITY
FISSIPAROUS
FITTING-SHOP
FIVEFINGERS
FLABBERGAST

FLACCIDNESS
FLAG-CAPTAIN
FLAGELLATED
FLAGELLATOR
FLAGITATION
FLAG-OFFICER
FLAG-WAGGING
FLAMBOYANCE
FLAMBOYANCY
FLAMBOYANTE
FLAMMULATED
FLANNELETTE
FLAP-MOUTHED
FLAPPERHOOD
FLATULENTLY
FLAUNTINGLY
FLAVOURLESS
FLAVOURSOME
FLAX-DRESSER
FLESH-COLOUR
FLESHLINESS
FLESH-MARKET
FLESH-MONGER
FLEURS-DE-LIS
FLEURS-DE-LYS
FLEXIBILITY
FLICKERTAIL
FLIGHTINESS
FLINCHINGLY
FLIRTATIOUS
FLOCCULENCE
FLOCK-MASTER
FLOOR-WALKER
FLORESCENCE
FLORIFEROUS
FLORILEGIUM
FLOURISHING
FLOWER-CLOCK
FLOWERINESS
FLOWER-STALK
FLOWINGNESS
FLUCTUATING
FLUCTUATION
FLUORESCEIN
FLUORESCENT
FLUOROSCOPE
FLUOROSCOPY
FLUSTERMENT
FLUSTRATION
FOLDING-DOOR
FOLLICULOSE
FOLLICULOUS
FOLLOW-BOARD
FOMENTATION
FONTARABIAN
FOOLISHNESS
FOOTBALLIST
FOOT-BREADTH
FOOTSLOGGER
FOOTSOLDIER
FOOTSTOOLED
FOPPISHNESS
FORAMINATED
FORAMINIFER
FORBEARANCE
FORBIDDANCE

FORBIDDENLY
FORCEBITTER
FORCING-PUMP
FORCIPATION
FORECLOSURE
FOREIGNNESS
FOREKNOWING
FOREMASTMAN
FOREPAYMENT
FOREREADING
FORE-RECITED
FORESHORTEN
FORESIGHTED
FORESIGNIFY
FORESPURRER
FORESTALLER
FORESTATION
FORETHINKER
FORETHOUGHT
FORETOPMAST
FOREVERMORE
FOREVOUCHED
FOREWARNING
FORFEITABLE
FORFICULATE
FORFOUGHTEN
FORGETFULLY
FORGET-ME-NOT
FORGETTABLE
FORGIVENESS
FORLORN-HOPE
FORLORNNESS
FORMICARIUM
FORMICATION
FORMULARISE
FORMULATION
FORNICATION
FORTHCOMING
FORTIFIABLE
FORTNIGHTLY
FORTUNATELY
FORTUNE-BOOK
FORTUNELESS
FORTUNE-TELL
FORWANDERED
FORWARDNESS
FOSTER-CHILD
FOSTER-NURSE
FOTHERGILLA
FOUL-MOUTHED
FOUNTAIN-PEN
FOUR-FLUSHER
FOUR-POUNDER
FOUR-WHEELED
FOUR-WHEELER
FRACTIONARY
FRACTIONATE
FRACTIONISE
FRACTIONLET
FRACTIOUSLY
FRAGMENTARY
FRANCOMANIA
FRANCOPHILE
FRANCOPHOBE
FRANCOPHONE
FRANC-TIREUR

FRANKFURTER
FRANKLINITE
FRANK-PLEDGE
FRANTICALLY
FRANTICNESS
FRATER-HOUSE
FRATERNALLY
FRATERNISER
FRATRICIDAL
FRAUDULENCE
FRAUDULENCY
FREE-AND-EASY
FREEBOOTERY
FREEBOOTING
FREE-HEARTED
FREEMASONIC
FREEMASONRY
FREE-THINKER
FREE-THOUGHT
FREE-TONGUED
FREIGHT-SHED
FREMESCENCE
FRENCHINESS
FRETFULNESS
FRIABLENESS
FRICANDEAUX
FRIGHTENING
FRIGHTFULLY
FRIGIDARIUM
FRIGORIFICO
FRINGILLINE
FRIVOLOUSLY
FRONDESCENT
FRONTLESSLY
FRONT-RANKER
FRONT-RUNNER
FROSTBITTEN
FROTH-BLOWER
FROTH-HOPPER
FROWARDNESS
FROWSTINESS
FRUCTUATION
FRUGIFEROUS
FRUGIVOROUS
FRUITLESSLY
FRUSTRATION
FULGURATION
FULL-ACORNED
FULL-BLOODED
FULL-CHARGED
FULLER'S-HERB
FULL-FLEDGED
FULL-FRAUGHT
FULL-HEARTED
FULLING-MILL
FULL-MOUTHED
FULMINATING
FULMINATION
FULMINATORY
FULSOMENESS
FUMARIACEAE
FUME-CHAMBER
FUNAMBULATE
FUNAMBULIST
FUNCTIONARY
FUNCTIONATE

FUNDAMENTAL
FURCIFEROUS
FURIOUSNESS
FURNISHINGS
FURNISHMENT
FURTHERANCE
FURTHERMORE
FURTHERMOST
FURTHERSOME
FURUNCULOUS
FUSHIONLESS
FUSILLATION
FUSING-POINT
FUSTIGATION
FUSTILARIAN
FUSTILIRIAN

G

GABERLUNZIE
GABLE-WINDOW
GAFF-TOPSAIL
GAIN-CONTROL
GAINFULNESS
GALLANTNESS
GALL-BLADDER
GALLEY-FOIST
GALLEY-PROOF
GALLEY-SLAVE
GALLIAMBICS
GALLIARDISE
GALLICANISM
GALLIMAUFRY
GALLOPHOBIA
GALLOVIDIAN
GALLOWEGIAN
GALLOWGLASS
GALLOWS-BIRD
GALLOWS-FOOT
GALLOWS-FREE
GALLOWSNESS
GALLOWS-RIPE
GALLOWS-TREE
GALLY-BAGGER
GALLY-BEGGAR
GAMBIT-PIECE
GAME-CHICKEN
GAMETANGIUM
GAMETOPHYTE
GAMING-HOUSE
GAMING-TABLE
GAMMERSTANG
GAMOGENESIS
GAMOTROPISM
GANDER-MONTH
GANGSTERISM
GARDEN-GLASS
GARDEN-HOUSE
GARGANTUISM
GARGANTUIST
GARLANDLESS
GARMENTLESS
GARNET-PAPER
GARNISHMENT
GARRULOUSLY
GARTER-SNAKE
GASEOUSNESS

GAS-FITTINGS
GASTEROPODA
GASTRECTOMY
GASTROLOGER
GASTROMANCY
GASTRONOMER
GASTRONOMIC
GASTROSOPHY
GASTROSTOMY
GATECRASHER
GAZING-STOCK
GEANTICLINE
GEGENSCHEIN
GEITONOGAMY
GELDERS-ROSE
GELSEMININE
GEMMIFEROUS
GEMMIPAROUS
GEMMOLOGIST
GEMMULATION
GENDARMERIE
GENEALOGISE
GENEALOGIST
GENERALSHIP
GENERICALLY
GENETICALLY
GENICULATED
GENITIVALLY
GENOUILLÈRE
GENTEELNESS
GENTIANELLA
GENTILITIAL
GENTILITIAN
GENTLEMANLY
GENTLEWOMAN
GENTLEWOMEN
GENUFLEXION
GENUINENESS
GEOCHEMICAL
GEODYNAMICS
GEOMAGNETIC
GEOMEDICINE
GEOMETRICAL
GEOMETRIDAE
GEOPHYSICAL
GEOPOLITICS
GEOSTROPHIC
GEOSYNCLINE
GEOTACTICAL
GEOTECTONIC
GERANIACEAE
GERMANESQUE
GERMANISTIC
GERMANOPHIL
GERMINATION
GERMINATIVE
GERONTOLOGY
GERONTOPHIL
GERRYMANDER
GESTATORIAL
GESTICULATE
GET-TOGETHER
GHASTLINESS
GHOSTLINESS
GHOST-WRITER
GIANT-POWDER

GIANT-STRIDE
GIBBERELLIC
GIBBERELLIN
GIBBOUSNESS
GIDDY-HEADED
GIGANTESQUE
GIGANTICIDE
GIGANTOLOGY
GILLRAVITCH
GILLYFLOWER
GIMCRACKERY
GINGERBREAD
GIRDLESTEAD
GIRLISHNESS
GLADFULNESS
GLADIOLUSES
GLADSTONIAN
GLAIKITNESS
GLARINGNESS
GLASS-BLOWER
GLASS-CUTTER
GLASS-GAZING
GLAUCESCENT
GLAUCONITIC
GLIMMER-GOWK
GLOBE-FLOWER
GLOBIGERINA
GLOBULARITY
GLOMERATION
GLOSSODYNIA
GLOSSOLALIA
GLOVE-SHIELD
GLUMIFEROUS
GLUMIFLORAE
GLUTINOUSLY
GLYPHOGRAPH
GLYPTOTHECA
GNATHONICAL
GNOMONOLOGY
GNOTOBIOSIS
GNOTOBIOTIC
GOATISHNESS
GODDAUGHTER
GODDESS-SHIP
GODFORSAKEN
GODLESSNESS
GOLD-BEATING
GOLD-DIGGING
GOLDENBERRY
GOLDSMITHRY
GOMEOPATHIC
GONFALONIER
GONIATITOID
GONIMOBLAST
GONIOMETRIC
GONORRHOEAL
GOODBROTHER
GOOD-EVENING
GOOD-LOOKING
GOOD-MORNING
GOODS-ENGINE
GOOSE-FLOWER
GOOSE-WINGED
GORMANDISER
GO-TO-MEETING
GOURMANDISE

GOUVERNANTE
GRACELESSLY
GRADATIONAL
GRADATIONED
GRADIOMETER
GRAECO-ROMAN
GRALLATORES
GRAMMALOGUE
GRAMMATICAL
GRAMOPHONIC
GRANDEESHIP
GRANDFATHER
GRANDIOSELY
GRANDIOSITY
GRANDMOTHER
GRANDNEPHEW
GRANDPARENT
GRANITIFORM
GRANIVOROUS
GRANOLITHIC
GRANOPHYRIC
GRANULATION
GRANULIFORM
GRAPHICALLY
GRAPHICNESS
GRAPTOLITIC
GRASS-CUTTER
GRASSHOPPER
GRATULATION
GRATULATORY
GRAVE-DIGGER
GRAVEL-BLIND
GRAVIMETRIC
GRAVING-DOCK
GRAVITATION
GRAVITATIVE
GREASE-HEELS
GREASE-PROOF
GREAT-NEPHEW
GREENBOTTLE
GREENGROCER
GREEN-KEEPER
GREENOCKITE
GREGARINIDA
GROATSWORTH
GROG-BLOSSOM
GROTESQUELY
GROTESQUERY
GROUCHINESS
GROUND-ROBIN
GROUNDSHEET
GROUND-SLOTH
GROUNDSPEED
GROUND-STATE
GROUND-WATER
GRUMBLINGLY
GRUMMETHOLE
GUANIFEROUS
GUARDEDNESS
GUBERNATION
GUELDER-ROSE
GUERRILLERO
GUESSTIMATE
GUILELESSLY
GUILTLESSLY
GUINEA-GRASS

GULL-CATCHER
GULLIBILITY
GULLY-HUNTER
GUMMIFEROUS
GURGITATION
GUTTA-PERCHA
GUTTER-BLOOD
GUTTERSNIPE
GUTTIFEROUS
GUTTURALISE
GYMNASIARCH
GYMNASTICAL
GYMNORHINAL
GYNAECOLOGY
GYNAECOMAST
GYNOSTEMIUM
GYROCOMPASS

H

HAAF-FISHING
HABERDASHER
HABILITATOR
HABITUATION
HACKING-COAT
HADROSAURUS
HAEMATOCELE
HAEMATOLOGY
HAEMOCYANIN
HAEMOGLOBIN
HAEMOPHILIA
HAEMOPTYSIS
HAEMORRHAGE
HAEMORRHOID
HAEMOSTATIC
HAGGADISTIC
HAGIOGRAPHA
HAGIOGRAPHY
HAGIOLOGIST
HAGIOSCOPIC
HAIR-BREADTH
HAIRDRESSER
HAIR-RAISING
HAIR-TRIGGER
HALE-MEASURE
HALF-AND-HALF
HALF-BAPTISE
HALF-BINDING
HALF-BLOODED
HALF-BROTHER
HALF-CHECKED
HALFENDEALE
HALF-HEARTED
HALF-HOLIDAY
HALF-LANDING
HALF-PENNIES
HALF-POUNDER
HALF-STARVED
HALL-BEDROOM
HALLEFLINTA
HALLUCINATE
HALOPHILOUS
HAMILTONIAN
HAMMER-BRACE
HAMMERCLOTH
HAMSTRINGED
HAND-BREADTH

HANDFASTING
HAND-FEEDING
HAND-GRENADE
HANDICAPPED
HANDICAPPER
HAND-KNITTED
HAND-PAINTED
HAND-PROMISE
HAND-RUNNING
HANDSELLING
HANDSHAKING
HAND-TO-MOUTH
HANDWRITING
HANDWROUGHT
HANGABILITY
HAPLESSNESS
HAPLOGRAPHY
HAPTOTROPIC
HARASSINGLY
HARBOUR-DUES
HARBOURLESS
HARD-AND-FAST
HARD-GRAINED
HARD-HEARTED
HARD-MOUTHED
HARD-PRESSED
HARD-VISAGED
HARDWAREMAN
HARD-WORKING
HARE-BRAINED
HARIOLATION
HARMFULNESS
HARMONIPHON
HARMONOGRAM
HARNESS-CASK
HARNESS-ROOM
HARPSICHORD
HARROWINGLY
HART'S-TONGUE
HARUM-SCARUM
HARUSPICATE
HARVEST-HOME
HARVEST-MITE
HARVEST-TICK
HASTY-WITTED
HATCHETTITE
HATEFULNESS
HATLESSNESS
HATTI-SHERIF
HAUGHTINESS
HAUSTELLATE
HAZARDOUSLY
HEADBOROUGH
HEAD-HUNTING
HEAD-STATION
HEALTHFULLY
HEALTHINESS
HEARSE-CLOTH
HEART-EASING
HEARTH-BRUSH
HEARTH-MONEY
HEARTH-PENNY
HEARTH-STONE
HEARTLESSLY
HEART'S-BLOOD
HEART-SHAPED

HEART-STRIKE
HEART-STRING
HEART-STRUCK
HEART-URCHIN
HEATHENESSE
HEAVENWARDS
HEAVY-HANDED
HEAVY-HEADED
HEAVYWEIGHT
HEBDOMADARY
HEBEPHRENIA
HEBEPHRENIC
HEBRAICALLY
HECTOGRAMME
HEDGE-HYSSOP
HEDGE-PARSON
HEDGE-PRIEST
HEDGE-SCHOOL
HEDGE-WRITER
HEDGING-BILL
HEEDFULNESS
HEGELIANISM
HEGEMONICAL
HEINOUSNESS
HELICOGRAPH
HELIOCHROME
HELIOCHROMY
HELIOGRAPHY
HELIOMETRIC
HELIOSCOPIC
HELISPHERIC
HELLEBORINE
HELLENISTIC
HELLGRAMITE
HELLISHNESS
HELMET-SHELL
HELMINTHOID
HELMINTHOUS
HELPFULNESS
HELVE-HAMMER
HEMERALOPIA
HEMIANOPSIA
HEMIANOPTIC
HEMIHEDRISM
HEMIMORPHIC
HEMIPTEROUS
HEMISPHERIC
HEMISTICAHL
HEMITROPOUS
HEPATECTOMY
HEPATOSCOPY
HEPPLEWHITE
HEPTAGYNOUS
HEPTAMEROUS
HEPTANDROUS
HEPTARCHIST
HERACLEIDAN
HERBIVOROUS
HERB-OF-GRACE
HERB-TRINITY
HERCOGAMOUS
HEREDITABLE
HEREINAFTER
HERESIOLOGY
HERETICALLY
HERMENEUTIC

HERO-WORSHIP
HERPETOLOGY
HERRING-BONE
HERRING-BUSS
HERRING-GULL
HERRING-POND
HERTOLOGIST
HESPERIDIUM
HESPERIIDAE
HETEROCERCY
HETEROCLITE
HETEROECISM
HETEROGRAFT
HETEROPTERA
HETEROSCIAN
HETEROSPORY
HETEROSTYLY
HETEROTAXIS
HETEROTROPH
HETEROTYPIC
HETEROUSIAN
HEXAGONALLY
HEXAMETRISE
HEXAMETRIST
HEXAPLARIAN
HEXASTICHAL
HEXATEUCHAL
HIBERNACULA
HIBERNATION
HIBERNICISE
HIBERNICISM
HIDE-AND-SEEK
HIDEOUSNESS
HIDING-PLACE
HIERARCHISM
HIEROCRATIC
HIEROGRAPHY
HIEROLOGIST
HIERONYMIAN
HIERONYMITE
HIERURGICAL
HIGH-BATTLED
HIGH-BLOODED
HIGHBROWISM
HIGH-FALUTIN
HIGH-FEEDING
HIGH-HEARTED
HIGHLANDMAN
HIGHLY-SEXED
HIGH-METTLED
HIGH-PITCHED
HIGH-POWERED
HIGH-RANKING
HIGH-ROLLING
HIGH-SIGHTED
HIGH-STEPPER
HIGHWROUGHT
HILARIOUSLY
HILL-PASTURE
HINDERLANDS
HINDERLINGS
HIPPIATRICS
HIPPIATRIST
HIPPOCAMPUS
HIPPOCRATIC
HIPPODAMIST

HIPPODAMOUS
HIPPODROMIC
HIPPOPOTAMI
HIRCOCERVUS
HIRSUTENESS
HISPANICISE
HISPANICISM
HISTOLOGIST
HISTORIATED
HISTORICISE
HISTORICISM
HISTORICIST
HISTORICITY
HISTORIETTE
HISTRIONICS
HISTRIONISM
HITHERWARDS
HOBBISTICAL
HOBBLEDEHOY
HOBGOBLINRY
HOGGISHNESS
HOG-SHOULDER
HOLOBLASTIC
HOLOGRAPHIC
HOLOHEDRISM
HOLOPHYTISM
HOLOTHURIAN
HOME-AND-AWAY
HOME-AND-HOME
HOME-CROFTER
HOME-DEFENCE
HOME-KEEPING
HOMEOMORPHY
HOMEOSTATIC
HOMESTEADER
HOME-STRETCH
HOMILETICAL
HOMOBLASTIC
HOMOCENTRIC
HOMOEOMERIC
HOMOEOMORPH
HOMOEOPATHY
HOMOGENEITY
HOMOGENEOUS
HOMOGENESIS
HOMOGENETIC
HOMOGENISER
HOMOIOUSIAN
HOMOLOGICAL
HOMOMORPHIC
HOMOPHONOUS
HOMOPLASTIC
HOMOPTEROUS
HOMOSPOROUS
HOMOTHALLIC
HOMOTHERMIC
HOMOZYGOSIS
HONEST-TO-GOD
HONEY-BADGER
HONEYCOMBED
HONEY-LOCUST
HONEYMOONER
HONEY-SUCKER
HONEYSUCKLE
HONEY-WAGGON
HONORIFICAL

HONOUR-POINT
HOOK-CLIMBER
HOOLIGANISM
HOPEFULNESS
HOPLOLOGIST
HOP-O'-MY-THUMB
HORN-MADNESS
HORNY-HANDED
HOROGRAPHER
HOROLOGICAL
HOROSCOPIST
HORRIPILANT
HORRIPILATE
HORRISONANT
HORRISONOUS
HORSE-COLLAR
HORSE-COUPER
HORSE-DEALER
HORSE-DOCTOR
HORSE-DRENCH
HORSE-LITTER
HORSERADISH
HORSE-RIDING
HOSPITALISE
HOSPITALITY
HOSPITALLER
HOSTESS-SHIP
HOSTILITIES
HOTEL-KEEPER
HOT-SPIRITED
HOT-TEMPERED
HOUNDS-BERRY
HOUND'S-TOOTH
HOUSE-ARREST
HOUSE-FACTOR
HOUSEFATHER
HOUSEHOLDER
HOUSEKEEPER
HOUSEMASTER
HOUSEMOTHER
HOUSEWIFELY
HOUSEWIFERY
HOVERBARROW
HOWSOMDEVER
HUCKLEBERRY
HUCKSTERAGE
HUCKSTERESS
HUDIBRASTIC
HUFFISHNESS
HUGEOUSNESS
HUMBUGGABLE
HUMECTATION
HUMGRUFFIAN
HUMILIATING
HUMILIATION
HUMILIATIVE
HUMILIATORY
HUMMING-BIRD
HUNCHBACKED
HUNDREDFOLD
HUNT-COUNTER
HUNTER'S-MOON
HUNTING-CROP
HUNTING-HORN
HUNTING-MASS
HUNTING-SEAT

HUNTING-SONG
HUNTING-TIDE
HUNTING-WHIP
HUNT-THE-GOWK
HURDLE-RACER
HURLEY-HOUSE
HURLY-HACKET
HURRIEDNESS
HURRY-SCURRY
HURRY-SKURRY
HURTFULNESS
HURTLEBERRY
HUSBANDLAND
HUSBANDLESS
HUSBANDLIKE
HYACINTHINE
HYALOMELANE
HYDNOCARPUS
HYDRA-HEADED
HYDRARGYRAL
HYDRARGYRUM
HYDROBROMIC
HYDROCARBON
HYDROCHARIS
HYDROCHORIC
HYDROCYANIC
HYDROGENATE
HYDROGENOUS
HYDROGRAPHY
HYDROLOGIST
HYDROMANTIC
HYDROMEDUSA
HYDROMETEOR
HYDROMETRIC
HYDROPATHIC
HYDROPHIDAE
HYDROPHILIC
HYDROPHOBIA
HYDROPHOBIC
HYDROPHYTIC
HYDROPHYTON
HYDROPONICS
HYDROSOMATA
HYDROSPHERE
HYDROSTATIC
HYDROTACTIC
HYDROTHORAX
HYDROTROPIC
HYETOGRAPHY
HYGROMETRIC
HYGROPHYTIC
HYGROSCOPIC
HYLOGENESIS
HYLOPATHISM
HYLOPATHIST
HYLOPHAGOUS
HYLOZOISTIC
HYMENOPTERA
HYMNOGRAPHY
HYMNOLOGIST
HYOPLASTRAL
HYOPLASTRON
HYOSCYAMINE
HYPALLACTIC
HYPERACUSIS
HYPERBOLISE

HYPERBOLISM
HYPERBOLOID
HYPERBOREAN
HYPERCHARGE
HYPERCRITIC
HYPERDACTYL
HYPERDORIAN
HYPEREMESIS
HYPEREMETIC
HYPERGAMOUS
HYPERINOSIS
HYPERINOTIC
HYPERLYDIAN
HYPERMARKET
HYPERPHAGIA
HYPERPLASIA
HYPERSONICS
HYPERSTHENE
HYPERTROPHY
HYPHENATION
HYPNOGENOUS
HYPNOPAEDIA
HYPNOPOMPIC
HYPNOTISTIC
HYPOAEOLIAN
HYPOBLASTIC
HYPOCORISMA
HYPOCYCLOID
HYPOGASTRIC
HYPOGLOSSAL
HYPOSTATISE
HYPOSTROPHE
HYPOTENSION
HYPOTHECARY
HYPOTHECATE
HYPOTHENUSE
HYPOTHERMIA
HYPOTHESISE
HYPOTHETISE
HYPOTYPOSIS
HYPSOMETRIC
HYPSOPHOBIA
HYSTERESIAL
HYSTEROIDAL
HYSTEROTOMY

I

ICHNOGRAPHY
ICHTHYOIDAL
ICHTHYOLITE
ICHTHYOLOGY
ICHTHYOPSID
ICHTHYORNIS
ICHTHYOSAUR
ICONOGRAPHY
ICONOLOGIST
ICONOSTASIS
ICOSAHEDRAL
ICOSAHEDRON
ICOSANDRIAN
ICOSANDROUS
ICTERITIOUS
IDENTICALLY
IDENTIFYING
IDEOGRAPHIC
IDEOLOGICAL

IDEOPRAXIST
IDIOGLOSSIA
IDIOGRAPHIC
IDIOMATICAL
IDIOMORPHIC
IDIOTICALLY
IGNIS-FATUUS
IGNOBLENESS
IGNOMINIOUS
IGNORAMUSES
IGNORANTINE
ILL-AFFECTED
ILLAQUEABLE
ILL-BREEDING
ILL-DISPOSED
ILL-FAVOURED
ILL-HUMOURED
ILLIBERALLY
ILLICITNESS
ILLIMITABLE
ILLIMITABLY
ILLIQUATION
ILL-MANNERED
ILLOGICALLY
ILL-TEMPERED
ILLUMINABLE
ILLUMINANCE
ILLUMINATOR
ILLUSIONISM
ILLUSIONIST
ILLUSTRATED
ILLUSTRATOR
ILLUSTRIOUS
ILL-WRESTING
IMAGINATION
IMAGINATIVE
IMBRICATION
IMITABILITY
IMITATIVELY
IMMANENTISM
IMMANENTIST
IMMARGINATE
IMMEDIATELY
IMMEDIATISM
IMMEDICABLE
IMMENSENESS
IMMIGRATION
IMMITIGABLE
IMMITIGABLY
IMMORTALISE
IMMORTALITY
IMMOVEABLES
IMPARKATION
IMPARTATION
IMPARTIALLY
IMPASSIONED
IMPASSIVELY
IMPASSIVITY
IMPASTATION
IMPATIENTLY
IMPEACHABLE
IMPEACHMENT
IMPECUNIOUS
IMPEDIMENTA
IMPENETRATE
IMPENITENCE

IMPENITENCY
IMPERCEABLE
IMPERFECTLY
IMPERFORATE
IMPERIALISE
IMPERIALISM
IMPERIALIST
IMPERIALITY
IMPERILMENT
IMPERIOUSLY
IMPERMANENT
IMPERMEABLE
IMPERMEABLY
IMPERSONATE
IMPERTINENT
IMPERVIABLE
IMPETIGINES
IMPETRATION
IMPETRATIVE
IMPETRATORY
IMPETUOSITY
IMPETUOUSLY
IMPIGNORATE
IMPINGEMENT
IMPLACENTAL
IMPLAUSIBLE
IMPLEMENTAL
IMPLICATION
IMPLICATIVE
IMPLORATION
IMPLORATORY
IMPLORINGLY
IMPOLITICAL
IMPOLITICLY
IMPONDEROUS
IMPORTANTLY
IMPORTATION
IMPORTUNACY
IMPORTUNATE
IMPORTUNELY
IMPORTUNING
IMPORTUNITY
IMPOSTHUMED
IMPOSTUMATE
IMPOUNDABLE
IMPOUNDMENT
IMPRACTICAL
IMPRECATION
IMPRECATORY
IMPRECISION
IMPREGNABLE
IMPREGNABLY
IMPRESSIBLE
IMPRESSMENT
IMPROBATION
IMPROBATIVE
IMPROBATORY
IMPROPRIATE
IMPROPRIETY
IMPROVEMENT
IMPROVIDENT
IMPROVINGLY
IMPROVISATE
IMPRUDENTLY
IMPUISSANCE
IMPULSIVELY

IMPULSIVITY
INADAPTABLE
INADVERTENT
INADVISABLE
INALIENABLE
INALIENABLY
INALTERABLE
INANIMATION
INAPPETENCE
INAPPETENCY
INATTENTION
INATTENTIVE
INAUGURATOR
INCALESCENT
INCANTATION
INCANTATORY
INCAPACIOUS
INCAPSULATE
INCARCERATE
INCARDINATE
INCARNADINE
INCARNATION
INCENDIVITY
INCENSE-BOAT
INCENSEMENT
INCERTITUDE
INCESSANTLY
INCINERATOR
INCIPIENTLY
INCLEMENTLY
INCLINATION
INCLINATORY
INCLUSIVELY
INCOERCIBLE
INCOGITABLE
INCOGITANCY
INCOGNISANT
INCOHERENCE
INCOHERENCY
INCOMMODITY
INCOMPETENT
INCOMPLETAE
INCOMPLIANT
INCOMPOSITE
INCONGRUENT
INCONGRUITY
INCONGRUOUS
INCONSCIENT
INCONSCIOUS
INCONSONANT
INCONSTANCY
INCONTINENT
INCORONATED
INCORPORALL
INCORPORATE
INCORPOREAL
INCORRECTLY
INCORRUPTLY
INCRASSATED
INCREASABLE
INCREASEFUL
INCREDULITY
INCREDULOUS
INCREMATION
INCREMENTAL
INCRIMINATE

INCULCATION
INCULCATIVE
INCULCATORY
INCULPATION
INCULPATORY
INCUMBENTLY
INCUNABULAR
INCUNABULUM
INCURIOSITY
INCURIOUSLY
INCURVATION
INCURVATURE
INDECIDUATE
INDECIDUOUS
INDEFINABLE
INDEFINABLY
INDEHISCENT
INDEMNIFIED
INDENTATION
INDEPENDENT
INDESIGNATE
INDEX-FINGER
INDEXTERITY
INDIA-RUBBER
INDIFFERENT
INDIGESTION
INDIGESTIVE
INDIGNANTLY
INDIGNATION
INDIRECTION
INDIVIDABLE
INDIVIDUATE
INDIVISIBLE
INDIVISIBLY
INDO-CHINESE
INDOMITABLE
INDOMITABLY
INDUBITABLE
INDUBITABLY
INDUCTILITY
INDUCTIONAL
INDUCTIVELY
INDUCTIVITY
INDULGENTLY
INDUPLICATE
INDUSTRIOUS
INEBRIATION
INEDIBILITY
INEFFECTIVE
INEFFECTUAL
INEFFICIENT
INELABORATE
INELEGANTLY
INELOQUENCE
INELUCTABLE
INENARRABLE
INEQUITABLE
INEQUITABLY
INESCAPABLE
INESSENTIAL
INESTIMABLE
INESTIMABLY
INEXACTNESS
INEXCITABLE
INEXCUSABLE
INEXCUSABLY

INEXECRABLE
INEXECUTION
INEXHAUSTED
INEXISTENCE
INEXPECTANT
INEXPEDIENT
INEXPENSIVE
INEXTENSION
INFANGTHIEF
INFANTICIDE
INFANTILISM
INFANTRYMAN
INFATUATION
INFECUNDITY
INFERENTIAL
INFERIORITY
INFERNALITY
INFERTILITY
INFESTATION
INFEUDATION
INFILTRATOR
INFINITIVAL
INFIRMARIAN
INFLAMMABLE
INFLAMMABLY
INFLATINGLY
INFLEXIONAL
INFLUENTIAL
INFORMALITY
INFORMATION
INFORMATIVE
INFORMATORY
INFRACOSTAL
INFREQUENCE
INFREQUENCY
INFRUCTUOUS
INGATHERING
INGENIOUSLY
INGENUOUSLY
INGRATITUDE
INGURGITATE
INHABITABLE
INHABITANCE
INHABITANCY
INHABITRESS
INHERITABLE
INHERITANCE
INHERITRESS
INITIALLING
INJUDICIOUS
INJURIOUSLY
INKHORN-MATE
INKING-TABLE
INNAVIGABLE
INNAVIGABLY
INNERVATION
INNOCUOUSLY
INNOMINABLE
INNOXIOUSLY
INNUMERABLE
INNUMERABLY
INNUTRITION
INOBEDIENCE
INOBSERVANT
INOBTRUSIVE
INOCULATION

INOCULATIVE
INOCULATORY
INODOROUSLY
INOFFENSIVE
INOFFICIOUS
INOPERATIVE
INOPPORTUNE
INORGANISED
INQUILINOUS
INQUINATION
INQUIRATION
INQUIRINGLY
INQUISITION
INQUISITIVE
INSALUBRITY
INSCRIBABLE
INSCRIPTION
INSCRIPTIVE
INSCRUTABLE
INSCRUTABLY
INSCULPTURE
INSECTARIUM
INSECTICIDE
INSECTIFORM
INSECTIFUGE
INSECTIVORA
INSECTIVORE
INSECTOLOGY
INSENSITIVE
INSEPARABLE
INSEPARABLY
INSESSORIAL
INSEVERABLE
INSIDIOUSLY
INSINCERELY
INSINCERITY
INSINUATING
INSINUATION
INSINUATIVE
INSINUATORY
INSIPIDNESS
INSISTENTLY
INSOUCIANCE
INSPECTRESS
INSPIRATION
INSPIRATIVE
INSPIRATORY
INSPIRINGLY
INSTABILITY
INSTALLMENT
INSTIGATION
INSTINCTIVE
INSTINCTUAL
INSTITORIAL
INSTITUTION
INSTITUTIST
INSTITUTIVE
INSTREAMING
INSTRUCTION
INSTRUCTIVE
INSUFFLATOR
INSULTINGLY
INSUPERABLE
INSUPERABLY
INTAGLIATED
INTEGRALITY

INTEGRATION
INTEGRATIVE
INTELLECTED
INTELLIGENT
INTEMPERANT
INTEMPERATE
INTENDIMENT
INTENSATIVE
INTENSENESS
INTENSIFIED
INTENSIFIER
INTENSITIVE
INTENSIVELY
INTENTIONAL
INTENTIONED
INTERACTION
INTERACTIVE
INTERALLIED
INTERBEDDED
INTERCALARY
INTERCALATE
INTERCEDENT
INTERCENSAL
INTERCEPTER
INTERCEPTOR
INTERCESSOR
INTERCHANGE
INTERCOSTAL
INTERCOURSE
INTERCRURAL
INTERDEALER
INTERDENTAL
INTERESTING
INTERFACIAL
INTERFLUENT
INTERFLUOUS
INTERFUSION
INTERGATORY
INTERGLOSSA
INTERGROWTH
INTERIORITY
INTERJACENT
INTERLEAVES
INTERLINEAR
INTERLINGUA
INTERLINING
INTERLUDIAL
INTERLUNARY
INTERMEDDLE
INTERMEDIAL
INTERMEDIUM
INTERMINATE
INTERMINGLE
INTERNALITY
INTERNECINE
INTERNECIVE
INTERNEURAL
INTERNODIAL
INTERNUNCIO
INTEROCULAR
INTEROSSEAL
INTERPOLATE
INTERPRETER
INTERRACIAL
INTERRADIAL
INTERRADIUS

INTERREGNUM
INTERROGANT
INTERROGATE
INTERRUPTED
INTERRUPTER
INTERRUPTOR
INTERSCRIBE
INTERSEPTAL
INTERSERTAL
INTERSEXUAL
INTERSPERSE
INTERSPINAL
INTERTANGLE
INTERTARSAL
INTERTRIBAL
INTERVALLIC
INTERVALLUM
INTERVENTOR
INTERVIEWEE
INTERVIEWER
INTOLERABLE
INTOLERABLY
INTOLERANCE
INTRACTABLE
INTRACTABLY
INTRATHECAL
INTRAVENOUS
INTRENCHANT
INTREPIDITY
INTRICATELY
INTRIGUANTE
INTRINSICAL
INTROMITTED
INTROMITTER
INTRUSIVELY
INTUITIONAL
INTUITIVELY
INTUITIVISM
INTUMESCENT
INTURBIDATE
INUSITATION
INUTTERABLE
INVALIDHOOD
INVALIDNESS
INVECTIVELY
INVENTIVELY
INVENTORIAL
INVESTIGATE
INVESTITIVE
INVESTITURE
INVIABILITY
INVIDIOUSLY
INVIGILATOR
INVIGORATOR
INVIOLATELY
INVOLUCRATE
INVOLUNTARY
INVOLVEMENT
ION-EXCHANGE
IONOSPHERIC
IPECACUANHA
IRIDESCENCE
IRIDISATION
IRKSOMENESS
IRON-FOUNDER
IRON-FOUNDRY

IRON-HEARTED
IRONMONGERY
IRRADIATION
IRRADIATIVE
IRRECEPTIVE
IRRECUSABLE
IRRECUSABLY
IRREDENTISM
IRREDENTIST
IRREDUCIBLE
IRREDUCIBLY
IRREDUCTION
IRREFLEXION
IRREFUTABLE
IRREFUTABLY
IRREGULARLY
IRRELEVANCE
IRRELEVANCY
IRRELIGIOUS
IRREMISSION
IRREMISSIVE
IRREMOVABLE
IRREMOVABLY
IRREPARABLE
IRREPARABLY
IRRESOLUBLE
IRRETENTION
IRRETENTIVE
IRREVERENCE
IRREVOCABLE
IRREVOCABLY
IRRUPTIVELY
ISAPOSTOLIC
ISOCHRONISM
ISOCHRONOUS
ISOELECTRIC
ISOGEOTHERM
ISOMETRICAL
ISOMORPHISM
ISOMORPHOUS
ISORHYTHMIC
ISRAELITISH
ISTIOPHORUS
ITACOLUMITE
ITHYPHALLIC
ITHYPHALLUS
ITINERANTLY

J

JABBERINGLY
JACK-PUDDING
JACOBINICAL
JACOBITICAL
JACOB'S-STAFF
JACQUEMINOT
JACTITATION
JAGGING-IRON
JANITORSHIP
JAUNTING-CAR
JEALOUSHOOD
JEALOUSNESS
JERRYMANDER
JIMPSON-WEED
JINRICKSHAW
JOCOSERIOUS
JOHN-A-DREAMS

JOHNSONIANA
JOINT-TENANT
JOURNEY-WORK
JOYLESSNESS
JUDAISATION
JUDGMENT-DAY
JUDICIOUSLY
JUMPING-BEAN
JUMPING-DEER
JUMPING-HARE
JUMPING-JACK
JUNGLE-GREEN
JURIDICALLY
JURY-PROCESS
JUSTICESHIP
JUSTICIABLE
JUSTIFIABLE
JUSTIFIABLY
JUVENESCENT

K
KAISAR-I-HIND
KANGAROO-RAT
KATABOTHRON
KATADROMOUS
KATAVOTHRON
KEELHAULING
KEEPING-ROOM
KENDAL-GREEN
KENTISH-FIRE
KERATOPHYRE
KIBBLE-CHAIN
KIDNEY-STONE
KIDNEY-VETCH
KIMERIDGIAN
KINCHIN-COVE
KINCHIN-MORT
KINDERSPIEL
KIND-HEARTED
KINDREDNESS
KINDREDSHIP
KINEMATICAL
KINESIATRIC
KINESIOLOGY
KINESIPATHY
KINETOGRAPH
KINETOSCOPE
KING-PENGUIN
KING'S-YELLOW
KING-VULTURE
KINNIKINICK
KIRK-SESSION
KISS-ME-QUICK
KITCHENETTE
KITCHEN-MAID
KITCHEN-SINK
KITE-BALLOON
KLEPTOMANIA
KNAVISHNESS
KNEE-TRIBUTE
KNICK-KNACKY
KNOCK-RATING
KNOWINGNESS
KNOW-NOTHING
KNUCKLE-BONE
KOMMERSBUCH

KRIEGSSPIEL
KULTURKAMPF
KULTURKREIS
KWASHIORKOR
KYMOGRAPHIC

L
LABEFACTION
LABIODENTAL
LABORIOUSLY
LABRADORITE
LABYRINTHAL
LABYRINTHIC
LACCOLITHIC
LACERTILIAN
LACHRYMATOR
LACINIATION
LACONICALLY
LACQUER-TREE
LACRIMATORY
LACRIMOSELY
LACRYMATORY
LACRYMOSELY
LACTESCENCE
LACTIFEROUS
LACTIFLUOUS
LACTOFLAVIN
LADY'S-FINGER
LADY'S-MANTLE
LADY-TRIFLES
LAKE-DWELLER
LAMELLICORN
LAMELLIFORM
LAMENTATION
LAMENTINGLY
LAMMERGEIER
LAMMERGEYER
LAMP-CHIMNEY
LAMPLIGHTER
LAMPROPHYRE
LANCASTRIAN
LANCEOLATED
LANCINATING
LANCINATION
LANDAULETTE
LAND-GRABBER
LANDGRAVINE
LANDHOLDING
LANDING-BEAM
LANDING-GEAR
LANDING-SHIP
LAND-JOBBING
LANDLORDISM
LAND-MEASURE
LANDSCAPIST
LANDSKNECHT
LAND-SPANIEL
LAND-STEWARD
LANGUESCENT
LANGUIDNESS
LANGUISHING
LANTHANIDES
LAPIDESCENT
LAPIDIFYING
LAPILLIFORM
LAPIS-LAZULI

LARCENOUSLY
LARGE-HANDED
LARGE-MINDED
LARRIKINISM
LARVIPAROUS
LARYNGISMUS
LARYNGOLOGY
LARYNGOTOMY
LASERPICIUM
LASTINGNESS
LATCH-STRING
LATERIGRADE
LATERITIOUS
LATIFUNDIUM
LATIROSTRAL
LATISEPTATE
LATITUDINAL
LATROCINIUM
LATTICE-LEAP
LATTICE-WORK
LAUGHING-GAS
LAUGHWORTHY
LAUNDERETTE
LAUNDRY-MAID
LAUREL-WATER
LAURUSTINUS
LAWLESSNESS
LAW-MERCHANT
LEACH-TROUGH
LEADER-CABLE
LEAF-CLIMBER
LEAF-CUSHION
LEAF-CUTTING
LEAGUER-LADY
LEAGUER-LASS
LEAPING-TIME
LEARNEDNESS
LEASEHOLDER
LEATHER-BACK
LEATHER-COAT
LEATHERETTE
LEATHER-HEAD
LEATHER-NECK
LEAVE-TAKING
LEAVING-SHOP
LECHEROUSLY
LECTURESHIP
LEESOME-LANE
LEGATISSIMO
LEG-BUSINESS
LEGERDEMAIN
LEGIBLENESS
LEGISLATION
LEGISLATIVE
LEGLESSNESS
LEG-OF-MUTTON
LEGUMINOSAE
LEIBNITZIAN
LEMON-YELLOW
LENGTHINESS
LENTIGINOSE
LENTIGINOUS
LEOPARD-WOOD
LEPIDOPTERA
LEPIDOSIREN
LEPIDOSTEUS

LEPROSARIUM
LEPTOCERCAL
LEPTODACTYL
LEPTORRHINE
LESEMAJESTY
LETHARGICAL
LETHIFEROUS
LETTER-BOARD
LETTERPRESS
LETTER-STAMP
LEUCORRHOEA
LEVEL-HEADED
LEVIRATICAL
LEVITICALLY
LEXIGRAPHIC
LEZE-LIBERTY
LEZEMAJESTY
LIBELLOUSLY
LIBERTARIAN
LIBERTICIDE
LIBERTINAGE
LIBERTINISM
LIBERTY-BOAT
LICHENOLOGY
LICKERISHLY
LICK-PLATTER
LICKSPITTLE
LIEUTENANCY
LIFE-ANNUITY
LIFE-HISTORY
LIFEMANSHIP
LIFE-PEERAGE
LIFE-PEERESS
LIFE-RENTRIX
LIGAMENTARY
LIGAMENTOUS
LIGHT-FOOTED
LIGHT-HANDED
LIGHT-HEADED
LIGHT-HEELED
LIGHTKEEPER
LIGHT-LEGGED
LIGHT-MINDED
LIGHTWEIGHT
LIGHT-WINGED
LIGNIVOROUS
LIGNUM-SCRUB
LIGNUM-SWAMP
LIGNUM-VITAE
LILLIPUTIAN
LILY-LIVERED
LIMITEDNESS
LIMITLESSLY
LIMNOLOGIST
LINE-FISHING
LINEN-DRAPER
LINEN-SCROLL
LINE-SHOOTER
LINGERINGLY
LINGUISTICS
LINSEED-CAKE
LINSEED-MEAL
LION-HEARTED
LIPOMATOSIS
LIPPIZZANER
LIP-ROUNDING

LIQUEFIABLE
LIQUESCENCE
LIQUESCENCY
LIQUIDAMBAR
LIQUIDATION
LISSOMENESS
LISTENERS-IN
LISTENING-IN
LITANY-STOOL
LITERALISER
LITERALNESS
LITERARYISM
LITERATURED
LITHOCHROMY
LITHODOMOUS
LITHOGENOUS
LITHOGRAPHY
LITHOLAPAXY
LITHOLOGIST
LITHOPHYSAE
LITHOPHYTIC
LITHOSPHERE
LITHOTOMIST
LITHOTOMOUS
LITHOTRIPSY
LITHOTRITIC
LITHOTRITOR
LITIGIOUSLY
LITTÉRATEUR
LITTLEWORTH
LIVABLE-WITH
LIVER-COLOUR
LIXIVIATION
LOAN-SOCIETY
LOATHEDNESS
LOATHLINESS
LOATHSOMELY
LOBBY-MEMBER
LOBELIACEAE
LOBLOLLY-BAY
LOBLOLLY-BOY
LOCHABER-AXE
LOCORESTIVE
LOCULICIDAL
LODGE-KEEPER
LOGANIACEAE
LOGARITHMIC
LOGGAN-STONE
LOGICALNESS
LOGODAEDALY
LOGOGRAPHER
LOGOGRAPHIC
LOGOMACHIST
LOITERINGLY
LOLIGINIDAE
LONGANIMITY
LONGANIMOUS
LONG-CLOTHES
LONGINQUITY
LONG-MEASURE
LONG-PLAYING
LONG-PURPLES
LONG-SIGHTED
LONG-TONGUED
LONG-VISAGED
LONG-WAISTED

LOOSE-BODIED
LOOSE-STRIFE
LOPHOBRANCH
LOTUS-EATERS
LOUD-MOUTHED
LOUDSPEAKER
LOUIS-QUINZE
LOUIS-TREIZE
LOUP-THE-DYKE
LOUTISHNESS
LOUVER-BOARD
LOUVRE-BOARD
LOVE-IN-A-MIST
LOW-PRESSURE
LOW-SPIRITED
LOXODROMICS
LUBRICATION
LUBRICATIVE
LUCKENGOWAN
LUCRATIVELY
LUCUBRATION
LUDICROUSLY
LUFFER-BOARD
LUKEWARMISH
LUMBAGINOUS
LUMBRICIDAE
LUMINESCENT
LUMPISHNESS
LUNCHEON-BAR
LUSKISHNESS
LUSTFULNESS
LUTHERANISM
LUXULIANITE
LUXULYANITE
LUXURIANTLY
LUXURIATION
LUXURIOUSLY
LYCANTHROPE
LYCANTHROPY
LYCHNOSCOPE
LYCOPODINAE
LYSIGENETIC

M

MACASSAR-OIL
MACERANDUBA
MACHAERODUS
MACHAIRODUS
MACHICOLATE
MACHINATION
MACHINE-MADE
MACHINE-SHOP
MACHINE-TOOL
MACHINE-WORK
MACKEREL-SKY
MACROBIOTIC
MACROCOSMIC
MACRODACTYL
MACROGAMETE
MACROSCOPIC
MADDENINGLY
MADEFACTION
MADEIRA-CAKE
MADONNA-LILY
MADONNAWISE
MADREPORITE

MADRIGALIAN
MADRIGALIST
MAGAZINE-GUN
MAGDALENIAN
MAGGOTORIUM
MAGISTERIAL
MAGISTERIUM
MAGISTRATIC
MAGLEMOSIAN
MAGNANIMITY
MAGNANIMOUS
MAGNESSTONE
MAGNETICIAN
MAGNIFIABLE
MAGNIFICENT
MAHABHARATA
MAID-SERVANT
MAIL-CARRIER
MAIL-CATCHER
MAILING-CARD
MAINTENANCE
MAINTOPMAST
MAINTOPSAIL
MAISONNETTE
MAISTERDOME
MAKE-BELIEVE
MALACCA-CANE
MALADAPTIVE
MALADJUSTED
MALADROITLY
MALAKATOONE
MALAPROPISM
MALARIOLOGY
MALEDICTION
MALEDICTORY
MALEFACTION
MALEFACTORY
MALEFICALLY
MALEFICENCE
MALEVOLENCE
MALFEASANCE
MALFUNCTION
MALICIOUSLY
MALIGNANTLY
MALLEE-SCRUB
MALPRACTICE
MALT-EXTRACT
MAMILLATION
MAMILLIFORM
MAMMALOGIST
MAMMIFEROUS
MAMMOGRAPHY
MAMMONISTIC
MAMMOTH-TREE
MANAGERSHIP
MANCIPATION
MANCIPATORY
MANDARINATE
MANDIBULATE
MANDUCATION
MANDUCATORY
MANICHAEISM
MANIPULABLE
MANIPULATOR
MAN-MILLINER
MANNA-GROATS

MANNA-LICHEN
MANNERISTIC
MANNIFEROUS
MANNISHNESS
MANSARD-ROOF
MANTELPIECE
MANTELSHELF
MANTUA-MAKER
MANUFACTORY
MANUFACTURE
MANUMISSION
MANUMITTING
MANY-TONGUED
MAP-MEASURER
MARANTACEAE
MARATHONIAN
MARBLE-EDGED
MARBLE-PAPER
MARCESCIBLE
MARCHIONESS
MARCONIGRAM
MARGINALISE
MARGRAVIATE
MARIVAUDAGE
MARKET-CROSS
MARKET-HOUSE
MARKET-PLACE
MARKET-PRICE
MARKET-VALUE
MARKET-WOMAN
MARLINSPIKE
MARQUESSATE
MARQUETERIE
MARQUISETTE
MARRIAGE-BED
MARSHALLING
MARSHALSHIP
MARSHLANDER
MARSHMALLOW
MARSUPIALIA
MARTINETISM
MARTYROLOGY
MASCULINELY
MASCULINISE
MASCULINITY
MASOCHISTIC
MASQUERADER
MASSIVENESS
MASS-MEETING
MASS-PRODUCE
MASTER-CLOCK
MASTERFULLY
MASTER-JOINT
MASTER-MASON
MASTERPIECE
MASTER-WHEEL
MASTICATION
MASTICATORY
MASTOIDITIS
MASTURBATOR
MATCHLESSLY
MATCHMAKING
MATERIALISE
MATERIALISM
MATERIALIST
MATERIALITY

MATHEMATICS
MATRIARCHAL
MATRICULATE
MATRILINEAL
MATRILINEAR
MATRIMONIAL
MATROCLINIC
MAWKISHNESS
MAXILLIPEDE
MAXIM-MONGER
MAY-MEETINGS
MEADOW-BROWN
MEADOW-GRASS
MEADOW-SWEET
MEANINGLESS
MEASURELESS
MEASUREMENT
MECHANICIAN
MECHANISTIC
MEDIAEVALLY
MEDIASTINAL
MEDIASTINUM
MEDIATENESS
MEDIATORIAL
MEDIATRICES
MEDICINABLE
MEDICINALLY
MEDICINE-MAN
MEDICO-LEGAL
MEDIEVALISM
MEDIEVALIST
MEDIUMISTIC
MEGALOMANIA
MEGALOPOLIS
MEGATHERIUM
MEKHITARIST
MELANCHOLIA
MELANCHOLIC
MELANOCHROI
MELANOPHORE
MELANTERITE
MELIORATION
MELIORATIVE
MELIPHAGOUS
MELLIFEROUS
MELLIFLUENT
MELLIFLUOUS
MELLIVOROUS
MELODIOUSLY
MELTINGNESS
MEMBRANEOUS
MEMORABILIA
MEMORIALISE
MEMORIALIST
MEN-CHILDREN
MENDELEVIUM
MENINGOCELE
MENISPERMUM
MEN-SERVANTS
MENSURATION
MENSURATIVE
MENTHOLATED
MENTIONABLE
MENTONNIÈRE
MEPROBAMATE
MERCENARILY

MERCHANDISE
MERCHANTMAN
MERCHANTMEN
MERCILESSLY
MERCURIALLY
MERITOCRACY
MERITORIOUS
MEROBLASTIC
MEROGENESIS
MEROGENETIC
MEROVINGIAN
MERRY-ANDREW
MERRYMAKING
MÉSALLIANCE
MESENTERIAL
MESOBLASTIC
MESOCEPHALY
MESOMORPHIC
MESSAGE-GIRL
MESSIAHSHIP
METACENTRIC
METACHROSIS
METAGENESIS
METAGENETIC
METALDEHYDE
METALLIDING
METALLOIDAL
METALLURGIC
METAL-WORKER
METAMORPHIC
METAPHORIST
METAPHRASIS
METAPHYSICS
METAPLASTIC
METAPSYCHIC
METASILICIC
METASOMATIC
METASTASISE
METEORITICS
METEOROGRAM
METEOROLITE
METEOROLOGY
METHODISTIC
METHODOLOGY
METHYLAMINE
METHYLATION
METONYMICAL
METOPOSCOPY
METRICATION
MICAWBERISH
MICAWBERISM
MICHURINISM
MICROAMPERE
MICROCEPHAL
MICROCOCCAL
MICROCOCCUS
MICROCOSMIC
MICROGAMETE
MICROGRAPHY
MICROGROOVE
MICROLITHIC
MICROLOGIST
MICROMETRIC
MICRONEEDLE
MICRONESIAN
MICROPHONIC

MICROPHYTIC
MICROSCOPIC
MICROSECOND
MICROTOMIST
MICTURITION
MIDDENSTEAD
MIDDLE-CLASS
MIDDLE-EARTH
MIDDLE-SIZED
MIDDLE-WORLD
MIDSHIPMITE
MILKING-TIME
MILK-KINSHIP
MILK-LIVERED
MILK-PUDDING
MILK-THISTLE
MILLEFLEURS
MILLENARIAN
MILLENARISM
MILLET-GRASS
MILLIAMPERE
MILLIONAIRE
MILLIONFOLD
MIMETICALLY
MIMOGRAPHER
MIND-BENDING
MIND-BLOWING
MINDFULNESS
MIND-HEALING
MIND-READING
MINE-CAPTAIN
MINERALISER
MINE-SWEEPER
MINE-THROWER
MINIATURISE
MINIATURIST
MINISTERIAL
MINISTERING
MINISTERIUM
MINNESINGER
MINUTE-GLASS
MINUTE-WATCH
MINUTEWHILE
MIRIFICALLY
MIRROR-IMAGE
MIRTHLESSLY
MISALLIANCE
MISANTHROPE
MISANTHROPY
MISBECOMING
MISBEGOTTEN
MISBELIEVER
MISBESTOWAL
MISCARRIAGE
MISCEGENATE
MISCEGENIST
MISCELLANEA
MISCHIEVOUS
MISCIBILITY
MISCONCEIVE
MISCONSTRUE
MISCREATION
MISCREATIVE
MISDEVOTION
MISDOUBTFUL
MISE-EN-SCÈNE

MISERICORDE
MISERLINESS
MISESTIMATE
MISFEASANCE
MISFEATURED
MISFORTUNED
MISGUIDANCE
MISGUIDEDLY
MISHALLOWED
MISINFORMER
MISINSTRUCT
MISJUDGMENT
MISMARRIAGE
MISONEISTIC
MISPERSUADE
MISPLEADING
MISRELATION
MISREMEMBER
MISSHEATHED
MISSISHNESS
MISSPELLING
MISTEMPERED
MISTREADING
MISTRUSTFUL
MITHRADATIC
MITHRAICISM
MITHRIDATIC
MITRAILLEUR
MIXOTROPHIC
MOCKING-BIRD
MOCK-MODESTY
MODERNISTIC
MOESO-GOTHIC
MOHAMMEDISM
MOHOROVICIC
MOISTURISER
MOLECATCHER
MOLE-CRICKET
MOLECULARLY
MOLENDINARY
MOLESTATION
MOLLYCODDLE
MOLYBDENITE
MOMENTARILY
MOMENTOUSLY
MONADELPHIA
MONARCHICAL
MONASTERIAL
MONASTICISM
MONCHIQUITE
MONEY-BROKER
MONEY-LENDER
MONEY-MAKING
MONEY-MARKET
MONEY-SPIDER
MONEY'S-WORTH
MONITORSHIP
MONKEY-BLOCK
MONKEY-BOARD
MONKEY-BREAD
MONKEY-GLAND
MONKEY-GRASS
MONKEY-SHINE
MONKEY-TRICK
MONKEY-WHEEL
MONOBLEPSIS

MONOCARDIAN
MONOCARPOUS
MONOCHASIAL
MONOCHASIUM
MONOCHROMAT
MONOCLINOUS
MONOCOTYLAE
MONOCULTURE
MONODELPHIA
MONODELPHIC
MONOGENESIS
MONOGENETIC
MONOGRAPHER
MONOGRAPHIC
MONOLATROUS
MONOLOGICAL
MONOLOGUISE
MONOLOGUIST
MONOMORPHIC
MONOMYARIAN
MONONUCLEAR
MONOPHAGOUS
MONOPHTHONG
MONOPHYSITE
MONOPOLISER
MONOTHECOUS
MONOTHELETE
MONOTHELISM
MONOTHELITE
MONOTREMATA
MONOZYGOTIC
MONSEIGNEUR
MONSTROSITY
MONSTROUSLY
MONTANISTIC
MONTGOLFIER
MONTICOLOUS
MONTICULATE
MONTICULOUS
MOON-GODDESS
MOONLIGHTER
MOON-MADNESS
MOOR-BUZZARD
MOORING-MAST
MORATORIUMS
MORAVIANISM
MORBIFEROUS
MORGENSTERN
MORIBUNDITY
MORINGACEAE
MORNING-GIFT
MORNING-GOWN
MORNING-LAND
MORNING-ROOM
MORNING-STAR
MORNING-TIDE
MORPHOLOGIC
MORRIS-DANCE
MORSING-HORN
MORTAR-BOARD
MORTICE-LOCK
MORTIFEROUS
MORTISE-LOCK
MOSSBLUITER
MOSS-CHEEPER
MOSS-TROOPER

MOTHERCRAFT
MOTHER-IN-LAW
MOTHER-NAKED
MOTHER-RIGHT
MOTHER'S-MARK
MOTHER-WATER
MOTOR-BANDIT
MOTOR-DRIVEN
MOTOR-LAUNCH
MOTTLE-FACED
MOULD-CANDLE
MOULD-FACING
MOUNTAIN-ASH
MOUNTAIN-CAT
MOUNTAIN-DEW
MOUNTAINEER
MOUNTAINOUS
MOUNTAIN-TEA
MOUNTAIN-TOP
MOUNTENANCE
MOUSE-COLOUR
MOUSTACHIAL
MOUTH-FRIEND
MOUTH-HONOUR
MOVABLENESS
MOXIBUSTION
MUDDY-HEADED
MUD-SLINGING
MUFFIN-FIGHT
MUFFIN-WORRY
MULBERRY-FIG
MULCIBERIAN
MULTANGULAR
MULTANIMOUS
MULTICOLOUR
MULTICUSPID
MULTIFIDOUS
MULTIJUGATE
MULTIJUGOUS
MULTILINEAL
MULTILINEAR
MULTILOBATE
MULTINOMIAL
MULTIPARITY
MULTIPAROUS
MULTIPLYING
MULTIPOTENT
MULTIRACIAL
MULTISERIAL
MULTISONANT
MULTISPIRAL
MULTISTOREY
MULTIVALENT
MUMPISHNESS
MUNICIPALLY
MUNIFICENCE
MUNITIONEER
MURDEROUSLY
MURMURATION
MURMURINGLY
MURMUROUSLY
MUSCATORIUM
MUSCHELKALK
MUSCLE-BOUND
MUSCOVY-DUCK
MUSCULARITY

MUSCULATION
MUSCULATURE
MUSEUM-PIECE
MUSICALNESS
MUSIC-HOLDER
MUSIC-MASTER
MUSIC-SELLER
MUSKET-PROOF
MUSK-THISTLE
MUSSEL-SCALP
MUSSEL-SCAUP
MUSSEL-SHELL
MUSSITATION
MUSSULWOMAN
MUSTACHIOED
MUSTARD-TREE
MUSTER-PARTY
MUTABLENESS
MUTATIONIST
MUTTERATION
MUTTERINGLY
MYCODOMATIA
MYCOLOGICAL
MYCOPHAGIST
MYCORRHIZAL
MYCOTROPHIC
MYOCARDITIS
MYOGRAPHIST
MYRMECOLOGY
MYRMIDONIAN
MYSTERY-PLAY
MYSTERY-SHIP
MYSTERY-TOUR
MYTHOGRAPHY
MYTHOLOGIAN
MYTHOLOGISE
MYTHOLOGIST
MYTHOMANIAC
MYTHOPOEIST
MYTHOPOETIC
MYXOMATOSIS
MYXOMYCETES
MYXOPHYCEAE

N

NAIL-VARNISH
NAME-CALLING
NAME-DROPPER
NANCY-PRETTY
NAPHTHALENE
NAPHTHALISE
NAPOLEONISM
NAPOLEONIST
NAPOLEONITE
NARCISSUSES
NARRATIVELY
NARROW-GAUGE
NASOFRONTAL
NATIONALISE
NATIONALISM
NATIONALIST
NATIONALITY
NATURAL-BORN
NATURALNESS
NATURE-STUDY
NATUROPATHY

NAUGHTINESS
NAUPLIIFORM
NAUTCH-GIRLS
NAVEL-ORANGE
NAVEL-STRING
NEANDERTHAL
NEAR-SIGHTED
NECESSARIAN
NECESSARILY
NECESSITATE
NECESSITIED
NECESSITOUS
NECKERCHIEF
NECK-HERRING
NECROBIOSIS
NECROLOGIST
NECROMANCER
NECROMANTIC
NECROPHILIA
NECROPHILIC
NECROPHOBIA
NECROPOLEIS
NECROSCOPIC
NECTAR-GUIDE
NEEDFULNESS
NEEDLECRAFT
NEEDLE-FURZE
NEEDLE-PAPER
NEEDLE-POINT
NEEDLEWOMAN
NEFARIOUSLY
NEGLECTABLE
NEGLIGEABLE
NEGLIGENTLY
NEGOTIATION
NEGOTIATRIX
NEGROPHOBIA
NEIGHBOURLY
NEMATOPHORE
NEO-CATHOLIC
NEOLOGISTIC
NEOPAGANISE
NEOPAGANISM
NEOPLATONIC
NEOTROPICAL
NEOVITALISM
NEOVITALIST
NEPHELINITE
NEPHOLOGIST
NEPHRECTOMY
NEPHRITICAL
NERVE-CENTRE
NERVE-ENDING
NERVOUSNESS
NERVURATION
NETHERLINGS
NETHERSTOCK
NETHERWARDS
NET-PRACTICE
NETTLE-CLOTH
NEUROLOGIST
NEUROPATHIC
NEUROTICISM
NEUROTROPIC
NEUTRALISER
NEVER-ENDING

NEVER-FADING
NEWSCASTING
NEWS-THEATRE
NICKEL-BLOOM
NICKEL-OCHRE
NICKELODEON
NICKEL-STEEL
NICKNACKORY
NICTITATION
NIERSTEINER
NIETZSCHEAN
NIGHT-ATTIRE
NIGHT-CELLAR
NIGHT-FARING
NIGHT-FLOWER
NIGHT-FLYING
NIGHT-HUNTER
NIGHTINGALE
NIGHTMARISH
NIGHT-PORTER
NIGHT-SCHOOL
NIGHT-SEASON
NIGHT-SHRIEK
NIGHT-WAKING
NIGHT-WALKER
NIGHTWORKER
NIGRESCENCE
NIKETHAMIDE
NINNY-HAMMER
NITRANILINE
NITROGENISE
NITROGENOUS
NITROSATION
NOBLE-MINDED
NOCTILUCENT
NOCTILUCOUS
NOCTIVAGANT
NOCTIVAGOUS
NOCTURNALLY
NOCUOUSNESS
NOISELESSLY
NOISOMENESS
NOMADICALLY
NOMENCLATOR
NOMINATIVAL
NOMOGRAPHER
NOMOLOGICAL
NONAGESIMAL
NONCHALANCE
NON-DELIVERY
NONDESCRIPT
NON-ELECTION
NON-ELECTIVE
NON-ELECTRIC
NONE-SPARING
NONETHELESS
NON-EXISTENT
NON-FEASANCE
NONILLIONTH
NON-ISSUABLE
NON-MARRYING
NON-METALLIC
NON-PARTISAN
NONPLUSSING
NON-PRIORITY
NON-PROVIDED

NON-RESIDENT
NONSENSICAL
NON-SEQUITUR
NON-SPECIFIC
NON-UNIONIST
NON-VIOLENCE
NOOK-SHOTTEN
NORTH-EASTER
NORTHERMOST
NORTHERNISE
NORTHERNISM
NORTHWARDLY
NORTH-WESTER
NOSE-NIPPERS
NOSOGRAPHER
NOSOGRAPHIC
NOSOLOGICAL
NOSTRADAMIC
NOSTRADAMUS
NOTABLENESS
NOTHING-GIFT
NOTHINGNESS
NOTHOFAGUST
NOTICE-BOARD
NOTIONALIST
NOTOCHORDAL
NOTORIOUSLY
NOTOTHERIUM
NOURISHABLE
NOURISHMENT
NOVATIANISM
NOVATIANIST
NOVELETTISH
NOVELETTIST
NOXIOUSNESS
NUBBING-COVE
NUCLEOLATED
NUDICAUDATE
NUDICAULOUS
NULLIFIDIAN
NULLIPARITY
NULLIPAROUS
NUMERICALLY
NUMISMATICS
NUMISMATIST
NUMMULATION
NUNCUPATION
NUNCUPATIVE
NUNCUPATORY
NUNNISHNESS
NUN'S-VEILING
NURSERYMAID
NURSE-TENDER
NUTRIMENTAL
NUTRITIONAL
NUTRITIVELY
NYCTINASTIC
NYCTITROPIC
NYCTOPHOBIA
NYMPHALIDAE
NYMPHOLEPSY
NYMPHOMANIA

O

OARSMANSHIP
OB-AND-SOLLER

OBEDIENTIAL
OBFUSCATION
OBJECT-GLASS
OBJECTIVATE
OBJECTIVELY
OBJECTIVISE
OBJECTIVISM
OBJECTIVIST
OBJECTIVITY
OBJURGATION
OBJURGATIVE
OBJURGATORY
OBLIQUATION
OBLIQUENESS
OBLIQUITOUS
OBLITERATED
OBLIVIOUSLY
OBMUTESCENT
OBNOXIOUSLY
OBSCENENESS
OBSCURATION
OBSCUREMENT
OBSCURENESS
OBSECRATION
OBSERVANTLY
OBSERVATION
OBSERVATIVE
OBSERVATORY
OBSERVINGLY
OBSESSIONAL
OBSIDIONARY
OBSIGNATION
OBSIGNATORY
OBSOLESCENT
OBSTETRICAL
OBSTINATELY
OBSTIPATION
OBSTRICTION
OBSTRUCTION
OBSTRUCTIVE
OBTEMPERATE
OBTESTATION
OBTRUSIVELY
OBUMBRATION
OBVIOUSNESS
OCCIPITALLY
OCCULTATION
OCEAN-STREAM
OCHLOCRATIC
OCHLOPHOBIA
OCTACHORDAL
OCTAGONALLY
OCTAHEDRITE
OCTAHEDRONS
OCTASTICHON
OCTAVE-FLUTE
OCTENNIALLY
OCTINGENARY
OCTONOCULAR
OCTUPLICATE
ODONTOBLAST
ODONTOGENIC
ODONTOGRAPH
ODONTOLOGIC
ODORIFEROUS
ODOROUSNESS

OD'S-BODIKINS
OD'S-PITIKINS
OECUMENICAL
ŒIL-DE-BŒUF
OENOLOGICAL
OENOPHILIST
OESOPHAGEAL
OESTROGENIC
OFF-COLOURED
OFFENCELESS
OFFENSIVELY
OFFHANDEDLY
OFFICE-BLOCK
OFFICIALDOM
OFFICIALESE
OFFICIALISM
OFFICIALITY
OFFICIOUSLY
OFF-SCOURING
OIL-PAINTING
OLD-MAIDHOOD
OLD-WOMANISH
OLFACTOLOGY
OLIGOCHAETA
OLIGOCHAETE
OLIGOCHROME
OLIGOMEROUS
OLIVINE-ROCK
OLLA-PODRIDA
OMINOUSNESS
OMMATOPHORE
OMNIFARIOUS
OMNIFORMITY
OMNIPATIENT
OMNIPOTENCE
OMNIPOTENCY
OMNIPRESENT
OMNISCIENCE
ONAGRACEOUS
ONEIRODYNIA
ONEIROMANCY
ONEIROSCOPY
ONEROUSNESS
ONIROCRITIC
ONOMASTICON
ONTOGENESIS
ONTOGENETIC
ONTOLOGICAL
ONYCHOMANCY
OPALESCENCE
OPEIDOSCOPE
OPEN-AND-SHUT
OPEN-CIRCUIT
OPEN-HEARTED
OPEN-MOUTHED
OPERA-DANCER
OPERA-SINGER
OPERATIONAL
OPERATIVELY
OPERCULATED
OPEROSENESS
OPHICALCITE
OPHIDIARIUM
OPHIOLOGIST
OPHIUROIDEA
OPHTHALMIST

OPINIONATED
OPIUM-SMOKER
OPPIGNERATE
OPPIGNORATE
OPPORTUNELY
OPPORTUNISM
OPPORTUNIST
OPPORTUNITY
OPPROBRIOUS
OPTOMETRIST
ORACULARITY
ORACULOUSLY
ORANGE-GRASS
ORANGE-STICK
ORANGE-TAWNY
ORANG-OUTANG
ORBICULARES
ORBICULARIS
ORBICULARLY
ORCHESTRATE
ORCHESTRINA
ORCHESTRION
ORCHIDACEAE
ORCHIDHOUSE
ORCHIDOLOGY
ORCHIECTOMY
ORDERLINESS
OREOGRAPHIC
OREOLOGICAL
ORGANICALLY
ORGANISABLE
ORGAN-SCREEN
ORIEL-WINDOW
ORIENTALISE
ORIENTALISM
ORIENTALIST
ORIENTALITY
ORIENTATION
ORIGENISTIC
ORIGINALITY
ORIGINATION
ORIGINATIVE
ORNAMENTIST
ORNITHOGAEA
ORNITHOLOGY
ORNITHOPTER
ORNITHOSAUR
ORTHOBORATE
ORTHOCENTRE
ORTHODONTIA
ORTHODONTIC
ORTHODROMIC
ORTHOEPICAL
ORTHOGENICS
ORTHOGRAPHY
ORTHOPAEDIC
ORTHOPEDICS
ORTHOPEDIST
ORTHOPHYRIC
ORTHOPRAXIS
ORTHOPTERAN
ORTHOSCOPIC
ORTHOSTATIC
ORTHOSTICHY
ORTHOTROPIC
OSCILLATING

OSCILLATION
OSCILLATIVE
OSCILLATORY
OSCILLOGRAM
OSMOTICALLY
OSMUNDACEAE
OSSIANESQUE
OSTENSIVELY
OSTENTATION
OSTEOCLASIS
OSTEODERMAL
OSTEODERMIC
OSTEOGENOUS
OSTEOGRAPHY
OSTEOLOGIST
OSTEOPATHIC
OSTEOPHYTIC
OSTEOPLASTY
OSTRACODERM
OSTREACEOUS
OSTREOPHAGE
OSTREOPHAGY
OSTRICH-FARM
OSTRICH-LIKE
OSTROGOTHIC
OTHERWHILES
OUT-AND-OUTER
OUTBREEDING
OUTBUILDING
OUTDISTANCE
OUT-OF-THE-WAY
OUT-PARAMOUR
OUTQUARTERS
OUTSTANDING
OUTWARDNESS
OVER-ANXIETY
OVER-ANXIOUS
OVERBALANCE
OVERBEARING
OVERBIDDING
OVERBRIMMED
OVERBURTHEN
OVERCAREFUL
OVERCASTING
OVERCOATING
OVERCORRECT
OVERDEVELOP
OVERDRAUGHT
OVERDROWSED
OVEREARNEST
OVERFLOWING
OVERFORWARD
OVERFRAUGHT
OVERFREEDOM
OVERFREIGHT
OVERFULNESS
OVERGRAINER
OVERHANDLED
OVERHASTILY
OVERINDULGE
OVERLEATHER
OVERMEASURE
OVERPAYMENT
OVERPICTURE
OVERPITCHED
OVERPRODUCE

OVERREACHED
OVERRUNNING
OVERSTRETCH
OVERSTUFFED
OVERTEDIOUS
OVERTHROWER
OVERTRADING
OVERVIOLENT
OVERWEATHER
OVERWEENING
OVERWRESTLE
OVERWROUGHT
OVIPAROUSLY
OVIPOSITION
OVULIFEROUS
OWNER-DRIVER
OXALIDACEAE
OXY-CHLORIDE
OXY-COMPOUND
OXY-FLUORIDE
OXYGENATION
OXY-HYDROGEN
OXYRHYNCHUS
OYSTER-FIELD
OYSTER-KNIFE
OYSTER-PATTY
OYSTER-PLANT
OYSTER-SHELL
OYSTER-TONGS
OYSTER-WENCH
OYSTER-WOMAN
OZONIFEROUS
OZONISATION
OZONOSPHERE

P

PACHYDACTYL
PACHYDERMAL
PACHYDERMIA
PACHYDERMIC
PACIFICALLY
PACIFICATOR
PACKING-CASE
PADDLE-BOARD
PADDLE-SHAFT
PADDLE-STAFF
PADDLE-WHEEL
PAD-ELEPHANT
PAEDERASTIC
PAEDIATRICS
PAEDIATRIST
PAEDODONTIC
PAEDOPHILIA
PAEDOPHILIC
PAEDOTROPHY
PAINFULNESS
PAINSTAKING
PAINT-BRIDGE
PAIRING-TIME
PALAEARCTIC
PALAEOTYPIC
PALE-HEARTED
PALESTINIAN
PALE-VISAGED
PALINDROMIC
PALINGENESY

PALLESCENCE
PALMATISECT
PALM-CABBAGE
PALMYRA-NUTS
PALMYRA-WOOD
PALPABILITY
PALPITATION
PALSGRAVINE
PAMPAS-GRASS
PAMPELMOOSE
PAMPELMOUSE
PAMPHLETEER
PAN-AMERICAN
PAN-ANGLICAN
PANATHENAEA
PANATHENAIC
PANCRATIAST
PANDANACEAE
PANDEMONIAC
PANDEMONIAN
PANDEMONIUM
PANDURIFORM
PANEGYRICAL
PANEGYRICON
PANGLOSSIAN
PANHELLENIC
PANIC-MONGER
PANIC-STRUCK
PANICULATED
PANISLAMISM
PANISLAMIST
PANJANDARUM
PANOMPHAEAN
PANPSYCHISM
PANPSYCHIST
PAN-SLAVONIC
PANSOPHICAL
PANSPERMISM
PANSPERMIST
PANTALETTED
PANTALETTES
PANTALOONED
PANTHEISTIC
PANTHEOLOGY
PANTISOCRAT
PANTOCRATOR
PANTOGRAPHY
PANTOMIMIST
PANTOPHOBIA
PANTOSCOPIC
PANTOTHENIC
PAPER-CREDIT
PAPER-CUTTER
PAPER-ENAMEL
PAPER-FEEDER
PAPER-FOLDER
PAPER-HANGER
PAPER-MAKING
PAPER-MUSLIN
PAPER-OFFICE
PAPER-SAILOR
PAPER-WEIGHT
PAPIER-MÂCHÉ
PAPILLIFORM
PAPILLULATE
PAPYRACEOUS

PARABAPTISM
PARABEMATIC
PARABLEPSIS
PARABLEPTIC
PARABOLANUS
PARABOLICAL
PARACELSIAN
PARACHUTIST
PARACROSTIC
PARADOXICAL
PARADOXIDES
PARAFFINOID
PARAFFIN-OIL
PARAFFIN-WAX
PARAGLIDING
PARAGLOSSAE
PARAGLOSSAL
PARAGRAPHER
PARAGRAPHIA
PARAGRAPHIC
PARALDEHYDE
PARALEIPSIS
PARALLACTIC
PARALLELING
PARALLELISE
PARALLELISM
PARALLELIST
PARAMAECIUM
PARAMASTOID
PARAMEDICAL
PARAMOECIUM
PARAMORPHIC
PARAMOUNTCY
PARAMOUNTLY
PARANEPHRIC
PARANEPHROS
PARANTHELIA
PARAPHILIAC
PARAPHRASER
PARAPHRAXIA
PARAPHRAXIS
PARAPLECTIC
PARAPSYCHIC
PARASCENIUM
PARASELENAE
PARASITICAL
PARASITOSIS
PARATHYROID
PARATROOPER
PARATYPHOID
PARCHEDNESS
PARENTHESES
PARENTHESIS
PARENTHETIC
PARHELIACAL
PARIPINNATE
PARISHIONER
PARK-OFFICER
PARLOUR-MAID
PAROCHIALLY
PARONOMASIA
PARONYCHIAL
PAROTIDITIS
PARPEN-STONE
PARSLEY-PERT
PARTIBILITY

PARTICIPANT
PARTICIPATE
PARTICIPIAL
PARTICOATED
PARTICULATE
PARTITIONER
PARTITIVELY
PARTNERSHIP
PART-PAYMENT
PART-SINGING
PARTURITION
PART-WRITING
PARTY-COATED
PARTY-SPIRIT
PARVANIMITY
PASCHAL-LAMB
PASIGRAPHIC
PASQUINADER
PASSACAGLIA
PASSAGE-BOAT
PASSIBILITY
PASSING-BELL
PASSING-NOTE
PASSIONLESS
PASSION-PLAY
PASSION-TIDE
PASSION-WEEK
PASSIVENESS
PASTEURISER
PASTORALISM
PASTORALIST
PASTOURELLE
PASTURE-LAND
PASTURELESS
PATAPHYSICS
PATCH-POCKET
PATELLIFORM
PATENT-RIGHT
PATENT-ROLLS
PATERNALISM
PATERNOSTER
PATHOGENOUS
PATHOGRAPHY
PATHOLOGIST
PATHOPHOBIA
PATRIARCHAL
PATRICIANLY
PATRILINEAL
PATRILINEAR
PATRIMONIAL
PATRISTICAL
PATROL-WAGON
PATRONISING
PATROONSHIP
PATTERN-SHOP
PAULINISTIC
PAUSELESSLY
PAVINGSTONE
PEACEMAKING
PEACE-MONGER
PEACE-PARTED
PEACH-BRANDY
PEACOCK-BLUE
PEACOCK-FISH
PEACOCK-LIKE
PEARL-BARLEY

PEARL-BUTTON
PEARL-FISHER
PEARL-MILLET
PEARL-MUSSEL
PEARL-OYSTER
PEARL-POWDER
PEAT-CASTING
PEBBLE-STONE
PECCABILITY
PECCADILLOS
PECTINATELY
PECTINATION
PECTISATION
PECULIARISE
PECULIARITY
PECUNIARILY
PEDAGOGICAL
PEDAGOGUERY
PEDAGOGUISH
PEDAGOGUISM
PEDAL-ACTION
PEDALIACEAE
PEDANTICISE
PEDANTICISM
PEDANTOCRAT
PEDDER-COFFE
PEDESTALLED
PEDETENTOUS
PEDICELLATE
PEDICULARIS
PEDICULATED
PEDICULOSIS
PEDIPALPIDA
PEDOLOGICAL
PEDUNCULATE
PEEP-THROUGH
PEEVISHNESS
PELAGIANISM
PELARGONIUM
PELICAN-FISH
PELLUCIDITY
PELOTHERAPY
PELTON-WHEEL
PENCIL-CEDAR
PENCIL-STONE
PENDANT-POST
PENDULOSITY
PENDULOUSLY
PENETRATING
PENETRATION
PENETRATIVE
PENICILLATE
PENICILLIUM
PENINSULATE
PENITENTIAL
PENNONCELLE
PENNY-A-LINER
PENNYWEIGHT
PENNYWINKLE
PENNY-WISDOM
PENOLOGICAL
PENSILENESS
PENSIONABLE
PENSIVENESS
PENTACRINUS
PENTACTINAL

PENTACYCLIC
PENTADACTYL
PENTAGYNIAN
PENTAGYNOUS
PENTAMERISM
PENTAMEROUS
PENTANDRIAN
PENTANDROUS
PENTANGULAR
PENTAPLOIDY
PENTATHLETE
PENTAVALENT
PENTAZOCINE
PENTECONTER
PENTECOSTAL
PENTHEMIMER
PENTLANDITE
PENULTIMATE
PENURIOUSLY
PEPPERCORNY
PEPPER-GRASS
PEPPERINESS
PEPTISATION
PERAMBULATE
PERCEIVABLE
PERCEIVABLY
PERCEPTIBLE
PERCEPTIBLY
PERCHLORATE
PERCIPIENCE
PERCIPIENCY
PERCOLATION
PERDUELLION
PERDURATION
PEREGRINATE
PEREGRINITY
PERENNATION
PERENNIALLY
PERFECTIBLE
PERFECTNESS
PERFORATION
PERFORATIVE
PERFORMABLE
PERFORMANCE
PERFUMELESS
PERFUNCTORY
PERICARDIAC
PERICARDIAL
PERICARDIAN
PERICARDIUM
PERICENTRAL
PERICENTRIC
PERICHYLOUS
PERICLITATE
PERICRANIAL
PERICRANIUM
PERIDESMIUM
PERIGASTRIC
PERIGENESIS
PERIGORDIAN
PERIHEPATIC
PERIMORPHIC
PERINEURIUM
PERIODICITY
PERIODONTAL
PERIODONTIA

PERIOSTITIC
PERIOSTITIS
PERIPATETIC
PERIPHRASES
PERIPHRASIS
PERISHINGLY
PERISPERMIC
PERISSOLOGY
PERISTALITH
PERISTALSIS
PERISTALTIC
PERISTERITE
PERISTOMIAL
PERITHECIAL
PERITHECIUM
PERITONAEAL
PERITONAEUM
PERITONITIC
PERITONITIS
PERIWIGGING
PERLUSTRATE
PERMANENTLY
PERMANGANIC
PERMISSIBLE
PERMISSIBLY
PERMITTANCE
PERMUTATION
PERPETRABLE
PERPETRATOR
PERPETUABLE
PERPETUALLY
PERPETUANCE
PERPETUATOR
PERPLEXEDLY
PERQUISITOR
PERSECUTION
PERSECUTIVE
PERSECUTORY
PERSEVERANT
PERSEVERATE
PERSEVERING
PERSISTENCE
PERSISTENCY
PERSONALISE
PERSONALISM
PERSONALIST
PERSONALITY
PERSONATING
PERSONATION
PERSONATIVE
PERSONIFIED
PERSONIFIER
PERSPECTIVE
PERSPICUITY
PERSPICUOUS
PERSPIRABLE
PERSUADABLE
PERSUASIBLE
PERSULPHATE
PERTINACITY
PERTINENTLY
PERTURBABLE
PERTURBANCE
PERTURBATOR
PERTURBEDLY
PERVASIVELY

PERVERTIBLE
PERVICACITY
PESSIMISTIC
PESTERINGLY
PESTIFEROUS
PESTILENTLY
PESTOLOGIST
PETALOMANIA
PETITIONARY
PETITIONING
PETITIONIST
PETRARCHIAN
PETRARCHISE
PETRARCHISM
PETRARCHIST
PETROGRAPHY
PETROLOGIST
PETTICOATED
PETTIFOGGER
PETTISHNESS
PHAENOGAMAE
PHAENOGAMIC
PHAENOMENON
PHAETHONTIC
PHAGEDAENIC
PHAGOCYTISM
PHAGOCYTOSE
PHALANSTERY
PHANTASIAST
PHANTASMATA
PHANTOMATIC
PHARISAICAL
PHARISEEISM
PHARYNGITIC
PHARYNGITIS
PHASMATIDAE
PHASMATODEA
PHENOGAMONS
PHENOLOGIST
PHENOMENISE
PHENOMENISM
PHENOMENIST
PHERECRATIC
PHILANDERER
PHILATELIST
PHILHELLENE
PHILLIPSITE
PHILOGYNIST
PHILOGYNOUS
PHILOLOGIAN
PHILOLOGIST
PHILOMATHIC
PHILOSOPHER
PHILOSOPHIC
PHLEGMONOID
PHLEGMONOUS
PHONEMICISE
PHONEMICIST
PHONETICIAN
PHONETICISE
PHONETICISM
PHONETICIST
PHONOGRAPHY
PHONOLOGIST
PHONOTYPIST
PHOSPHONIUM

PHOSPHORATE
PHOSPHORISE
PHOSPHORISM
PHOSPHORITE
PHOSPHOROUS
PHOTOACTIVE
PHOTOCHROMY
PHOTO-FINISH
PHOTOGLYPHY
PHOTOGRAPHY
PHOTONASTIC
PHOTOPERIOD
PHOTOPHILIC
PHOTOPHOBIA
PHOTOPHOBIC
PHOTOPHONIC
PHOTO-RELIEF
PHOTO-RESIST
PHOTOSPHERE
PHOTOTACTIC
PHOTOTROPIC
PHRASEMAKER
PHRASEOGRAM
PHRASEOLOGY
PHRENETICAL
PHRENOLOGIC
PHTHIRIASIS
PHYCOCYANIN
PHYCOLOGIST
PHYCOPHAEIN
PHYLACTERIC
PHYLLOCLADE
PHYLLOMANIA
PHYLLOTAXIS
PHYSICALITY
PHYSICIANCY
PHYSICIANER
PHYSIOCRACY
PHYSIOGNOMY
PHYSIOLATER
PHYSIOLATRY
PHYSIOLOGIC
PHYSIOLOGUS
PHYSITHEISM
PHYTOGRAPHY
PHYTOLOGIST
PHYTOPHAGIC
PHYTOSTEROL
PHYTOTOMIST
PIACULARITY
PIANO-PLAYER
PIANO-SCHOOL
PICK-AND-PICK
PICKELHAUBE
PICKET-FENCE
PICKET-GUARD
PICKWICKIAN
PICTOGRAPHY
PICTORIALLY
PICTURE-BOOK
PICTURE-CARD
PICTURE-CORD
PICTURE-GOER
PICTURE-PLAY
PICTURE-RAIL
PICTURESQUE

PICTURE-WIRE
PIETISTICAL
PIGEON-BERRY
PIGEON-FLIER
PIGEON-FLYER
PIGEON-HOUSE
PIGGISHNESS
PIGHEADEDLY
PIGNORATION
PIG-STICKING
PIG'S-WHISPER
PILFERINGLY
PILGARLICKY
PILGRIMAGER
PILLAR-SAINT
PILLION-SEAT
PILLOW-FIGHT
PILNIEWINKS
PILOCARPINE
PILOT-BURNER
PILOT-ENGINE
PILOT-JACKET
PINACOTHECA
PINCH-HITTER
PINKING-IRON
PINKISHNESS
PINNATISECT
PINNYWINKLE
PIPE-DREAMER
PIPE-LIGHTER
PIPERACEOUS
PIPE-STAPPLE
PIPE-STOPPLE
PIPISTRELLE
PIRATICALLY
PISCATORIAL
PISCICOLOUS
PISCIVOROUS
PISSASPHALT
PITCHBLENDE
PIT-DWELLING
PITEOUSNESS
PITIFULNESS
PIVOT-BRIDGE
PLACABILITY
PLACE-HUNTER
PLACE-MONGER
PLACENTALIA
PLACKET-HOLE
PLAGIOCLASE
PLAGIOSTOME
PLAGIOSTOMI
PLAICE-MOUTH
PLAIN-DEALER
PLAIN-SPOKEN
PLAINSTANES
PLAINSTONES
PLAINTIVELY
PLANETARIUM
PLANETOIDAL
PLANIMETRIC
PLANISPHERE
PLANOCONVEX
PLANOGAMETE
PLANTIGRADE
PLANULIFORM

PLASMATICAL
PLASMOLYSIS
PLASMOLYTIC
PLASTERWORK
PLASTICISER
PLATANACEAE
PLATE-ARMOUR
PLATE-BASKET
PLATE-POWDER
PLATERESQUE
PLATE-WARMER
PLATFORMING
PLATINOTYPE
PLATONICISM
PLATYRRHINE
PLAY-ACTRESS
PLAYER-PIANO
PLAYFULNESS
PLAYING-CARD
PLEASURABLE
PLEASURABLY
PLEASUREFUL
PLEBEIANISE
PLEBEIANISM
PLECTOPTERA
PLEIN-AIRIST
PLEIOMEROUS
PLEIOTROPIC
PLEISTOCENE
PLENIPOTENT
PLENTEOUSLY
PLENTIFULLY
PLEOCHROISM
PLEOMORPHIC
PLEROPHORIA
PLESSIMETER
PLESSIMETRY
PLETHORICAL
PLEURITICAL
PLEURODYNIA
PLEXIMETRIC
PLIABLENESS
PLOUGHSHARE
PLOUGH-STAFF
PLOUGH-STILT
PLUMBER-WORK
PLUM-BLOSSOM
PLUME-PLUCKT
PLUMIGEROUS
PLUM-PUDDING
PLUMULARIAN
PLURALISTIC
PLURISERIAL
PLUTOCRATIC
PLUTOLOGIST
PLUTONOMIST
PLUVIOMETER
PLYMOUTHISM
PLYMOUTHIST
PLYMOUTHITE
PNEUMATHODE
PNEUMATICAL
PNEUMONITIS
POCKET-GLASS
POCKET-KNIFE
POCKET-MONEY

POCKET-PIECE
POCKET-SIZED
POCK-PUDDING
POCOCURANTE
PODOPHYLLIN
PODOPHYLLUM
PODSNAPPERY
POENOLOGIST
POIKILOCYTE
POINT-DEVICE
POINT-DEVISE
POINTEDNESS
POINTILLISM
POINTILLIST
POINTLESSLY
POINT-SOURCE
POISON-GLAND
POISONOUSLY
POISON-SUMAC
POKING-STICK
POLARIMETER
POLARIMETRY
POLARISCOPE
POLEMICALLY
POLICE-COURT
POLICE-FORCE
POLICE-JUDGE
POLICE-STATE
POLICEWOMAN
POLITBUREAU
POLITICALLY
POLITICKING
POLLEN-GRAIN
POLLINATION
POLTERGEIST
POLTROONERY
POLYACTINAL
POLYANDROUS
POLYCARPOUS
POLYCHROISM
POLYCHROMIC
POLYCROTISM
POLYDACTYLY
POLYGENESIS
POLYGENETIC
POLYGLOTTAL
POLYGLOTTIC
POLYGONALLY
POLYGONATUM
POLYGRAPHIC
POLYHISTORY
POLYMASTISM
POLYMORPHIC
POLYONYMOUS
POLYPEPTIDE
POLYPHAGOUS
POLYPHEMIAN
POLYPHONIST
POLYSTYRENE
POLYTECHNIC
POLYTRICHUM
POLYZOARIAL
POLYZOARIUM
POMEGRANATE
POMFRET-CAKE
POMICULTURE,

POMOLOGICAL
POMPEIAN-RED
POMPELMOOSE
POMPELMOUSE
POMPOUSNESS
PONDERATION
PONDERINGLY
PONDEROSITY
PONDEROUSLY
PONTIFICALS
PONTIFICATE
POODLE-FAKER
POPPET-VALVE
POPULARISER
PORK-BUTCHER
PORNOGRAPHY
PORPHYRITIC
PORRIGINOUS
PORTABILITY
PORT-ADMIRAL
PORT-CHARGES
PORTER-HOUSE
PORTIONLESS
PORTLANDIAN
PORTMANTEAU
PORTRAITIST
PORTRAITURE
POSEIDONIAN
POSOLOGICAL
POSSIBILISM
POSSIBILIST
POSSIBILITY
POST-CAPTAIN
POSTERIORLY
POST-EXILIAN
POST-GLACIAL
POSTILLATOR
POST-NUPTIAL
POSTPONENCE
POSTSCENIUM
POSTULATION
POSTULATORY
POST-VILLAGE
POTAMOGETON
POTASH-WATER
POTASS-WATER
POTATO-APPLE
POTATO-BOGLE
POTATO-CHIPS
POTENTIALLY
POTING-STICK
POTTERINGLY
POT-VALOROUS
POT-WALLONER
POT-WALLOPER
POUND-KEEPER
POUND-MASTER
POUND-WEIGHT
POWDER-FLASK
POWER-DIVING
POWERLESSLY
PRACTICABLE
PRACTICABLY
PRACTICALLY
PRAECORDIAL
PRAETORSHIP

PRAGMATICAL
PRAGMATISER
PRAIRIE-WOLF
PRATTLEMENT
PRAYERFULLY
PRAYER-WHEEL
PREACHINESS
PREACQUAINT
PRE-ADAMICAL
PRE-ADAMITIC
PREADMONISH
PREAMBULARY
PREAMBULATE
PREANNOUNCE
PREAUDIENCE
PRE-CAMBRIAN
PRECAUTIOUS
PRECEDENTED
PRECEDENTLY
PRECENTRESS
PRECEPTRESS
PRECIPITANT
PRECIPITATE
PRECIPITOUS
PRECISENESS
PRECOGNOSCE
PRECONCEIVE
PRECONQUEST
PRECONTRACT
PREDATORILY
PREDECEASED
PREDECESSOR
PREDICAMENT
PREDICATION
PREDICATIVE
PREDICATORY
PREDICTABLE
PREDILECTED
PREDOMINANT
PREDOMINATE
PRE-ELECTION
PRE-EMINENCE
PRE-EMPTIBLE
PRE-EXISTENT
PREFATORIAL
PREFATORILY
PREFECTSHIP
PREFECTURAL
PREFERRABLE
PREFIGURATE
PREHENSIBLE
PREHISTORIC
PRE-IGNITION
PREJUDGMENT
PREJUDICANT
PREJUDICATE
PREJUDICIAL
PRELATESHIP
PRELIBATION
PRELIMINARY
PRELUSIVELY
PRELUSORILY
PREMATURELY
PREMATURITY
PREMEDITATE
PREMIERSHIP

PREMONITION
PREMONITIVE
PREMONITORY
PREMOVEMENT
PRENOMINATE
PREOCCUPANT
PREOCCUPATE
PREOCCUPIED
PREPARATION
PREPARATIVE
PREPARATORY
PREPOLLENCE
PREPOLLENCY
PREPOSITION
PREPOSITIVE
PREPUNCTUAL
PREROGATIVE
PRESAGEMENT
PRESANCTIFY
PRESBYTERAL
PRESCIENTLY
PRESCINDENT
PRESCISSION
PRESELECTOR
PRESENTABLE
PRESENTABLY
PRESENTIENT
PRESENTMENT
PRESENTNESS
PRESERVABLE
PRESS-BUTTON
PRESTIGIOUS
PRESTISSIMO
PRESTRESSED
PRESUMINGLY
PRESUMPTION
PRESUMPTIVE
PRETENDEDLY
PRETENTIOUS
PRETERHUMAN
PRETERITION
PRETERITIVE
PREVAILMENT
PREVALENTLY
PREVARICATE
PREVENIENCE
PREVENTABLE
PREVENTIBLE
PREVISIONAL
PRICELESSLY
PRICKLEBACK
PRICKLINESS
PRICKLY-HEAT
PRICKLY-PEAR
PRIESTCRAFT
PRIMARINESS
PRIMATESHIP
PRIMIGENIAL
PRIMING-IRON
PRIMING-WIRE
PRIMIPAROUS
PRIMITIVELY
PRIMITIVISM
PRIMULACEAE
PRINCIPALLY
PRINT-SELLER

PRISCIANIST
PRISMATICAL
PRISON-HOUSE
PRIVATENESS
PRIVATIVELY
PRIZE-WINNER
PROBABILISM
PROBABILIST
PROBABILITY
PROBATIONAL
PROBATIONER
PROBLEMATIC
PROBOSCIDEA
PROBOSCIDES
PROBOSCISES
PROCELLARIA
PROCEPHALIC
PROCEREBRAL
PROCEREBRUM
PROCHRONISM
PROCLAIMANT
PROCONSULAR
PROCREATION
PROCREATIVE
PROCRUSTEAN
PROCTODAEAL
PROCTODAEUM
PROCTORSHIP
PROCURATION
PROCURATORY
PROCUREMENT
PROCYONIDAE
PRODIGALISE
PRODIGALITY
PRODUCEMENT
PROFANATION
PROFANATORY
PROFANENESS
PROFESSEDLY
PROFICIENCE
PROFICIENCY
PROFITEROLE
PROFUSENESS
PROGENITRIX
PROGENITURE
PROGESTOGEN
PROGNATHISM
PROGNATHOUS
PROGRAMMING
PROGRESSION
PROGRESSISM
PROGRESSIST
PROGRESSIVE
PROHIBITION
PROHIBITIVE
PROHIBITORY
PROJECTMENT
PROLATENESS
PROLEGOMENA
PROLEPTICAL
PROLETARIAN
PROLETARIAT
PROLIFERATE
PROLIFEROUS
PROLIFICACY
PROLIFICITY

PROLOCUTION
PROLOCUTRIX
PROLONGABLE
PROMINENTLY
PROMISCUITY
PROMISCUOUS
PROMISELESS
PROMISINGLY
PROMPTITUDE
PROMULGATOR
PROMYCELIUM
PRONG-HORNED
PRONOUNCING
PROOF-CHARGE
PROOF-PULLER
PROOF-READER
PROOF-SPIRIT
PROPAGATION
PROPAGATIVE
PROPER-FALSE
PROPERTY-MAN
PROPHESYING
PROPHETHOOD
PROPHETICAL
PROPHETSHIP
PROPHYLAXIS
PROPINQUITY
PROPITIABLE
PROPITIATOR
PROPOSITION
PROPRIETARY
PROPRIETRIX
PROPYLAMINE
PROPYLITISE
PROROGATION
PROSAICALLY
PROSAICNESS
PROSECUTION
PROSECUTRIX
PROSELYTISE
PROSELYTISM
PROSENCHYMA
PROSE-WRITER
PROSILIENCY
PROSPECTING
PROSPECTION
PROSPECTIVE
PROSTATITIS
PROSTHETICS
PROSTITUTOR
PROSTRATION
PROTAGONIST
PROTANDROUS
PROTEACEOUS
PROTECTORAL
PROTECTRESS
PROTEOLYSIS
PROTEOLYTIC
PROTERANDRY
PROTEROGYNY
PROTEROZOIC
PROTHALLIAL
PROTHALLIUM
PROTHALLOID
PROTHORACIC
PROTOCOCCAL

PROTOCOCCUS
PROTOCOLISE
PROTOCOLIST
PROTOCOLLED
PROTOGYNOUS
PROTOMARTYR
PROTONOTARY
PROTOPHYTIC
PROTOTHERIA
PROTRACTILE
PROTRACTION
PROTRACTIVE
PROTRUDABLE
PROTRUSIBLE
PROTUBERANT
PROTUBERATE
PROUD-MINDED
PROVENIENCE
PROVIDENTLY
PROVISIONAL
PROVISORILY
PROVOCATION
PROVOCATIVE
PROVOCATORY
PROVOKEMENT
PROVOKINGLY
PROVOSTSHIP
PROXIMATELY
PROXY-WEDDED
PRUDISHNESS
PRUNING-BILL
PRUNING-HOOK
PRURIGINOUS
PRUSSIANISE
PRUSSIANISM
PSAMMOPHILE
PSAMMOPHYTE
PSEUDOCUBIC
PSEUDOGRAPH
PSEUDOMONAS
PSEUDOMORPH
PSEUDOPODIA
PSEUDOSCOPE
PSILOMELANE
PSILOPHYTON
PSILOTACEAE
PSITTACOSIS
PSYCHAGOGUE
PSYCHEDELIA
PSYCHEDELIC
PSYCHIATRIC
PSYCHICALLY
PSYCHODELIC
PSYCHODRAMA
PSYCHOGENIC
PSYCHOGRAPH
PSYCHOLOGIC
PSYCHOMETER
PSYCHOMETRY
PSYCHOMOTOR
PSYCHOPATHY
PTERICHTHYS
PTERIDOLOGY
PTERODACTYL
PTEROSAURIA
PTOCHOCRACY

PTYALAGOGIC
PTYALAGOGUE
PUBLICATION
PUBLISHABLE
PUDDING-PIPE
PUDDING-TIME
PUDIBUNDITY
PUERPERALLY
PUGILISTIAL
PULCHRITUDE
PULLET-SPERM
PULL-THROUGH
PULLULATION
PULMOBRANCH
PULVERATION
PULVERULENT
PUMICE-STONE
PUNCHINELLO
PUNCTILIOUS
PUNCTUALIST
PUNCTUALITY
PUNCTUATION
PUNCTUATIVE
PUNCTULATED
PUNICACEOUS
PUNT-FISHING
PUPILLARITY
PUPPET-VALVE
PUPPY-HEADED
PURCHASABLE
PURE-BLOODED
PURGATIVELY
PURGATORIAL
PURGATORIAN
PURIFICATOR
PURITANICAL
PURPORTEDLY
PURPORTLESS
PURPOSELESS
PURPOSE-LIKE
PURPRESTURE
PURSE-BEARER
PURSE-TAKING
PUSH-BICYCLE
PUSHFULNESS
PUSSYFOOTER
PUSSYWILLOW
PUSTULATION
PUTREFIABLE
PUTRESCÈNCE
PUTRESCIBLE
PUTTY-POWDER
PYCNOGONIDA
PYCNOGONOID
PYRAMIDALLY
PYRAMIDICAL
PYRARGYRITE
PYRITOHEDRA
PYROBALLOGY
PYROCLASTIC
PYROGENETIC
PYROGNOSTIC
PYROGRAVURE
PYROPHOROUS
PYROTECHNIC
PYTHAGOREAN

PYTHAGORISM

Q

QUACKSALVER
QUADRATICAL
QUADRENNIUM
QUADRIENNIA
QUADRILLION
QUADRUPEDAL
QUAESTORIAL
QUALIFIABLE
QUALIFIEDLY
QUALITATIVE
QUANDONG-NUT
QUANTOMETER
QUARRELLING
QUARRELLOUS
QUARREL-PANE
QUARRELSOME
QUARRINGTON
QUARRY-WATER
QUARTER-BRED
QUARTER-DECK
QUARTER-EVIL
QUARTER-JACK
QUARTER-NOTE
QUARTER-ROAD
QUARTER-SEAL
QUARTER-TONE
QUARTER-WIND
QUART-IODINE
QUAVERINGLY
QUEENLINESS
QUEEN-MOTHER
QUEEN-REGENT
QUEENSBERRY
QUEEN-STITCH
QUEEZ-MADDAM
QUERULOUSLY
QUESTIONARY
QUESTIONING
QUESTIONIST
QUIBBLINGLY
QUICK-CHANGE
QUICKEN-TREE
QUICK-FIRING
QUICK-FREEZE
QUICK-FROZEN
QUICKSILVER
QUICK-WITTED
QUIESCENTLY
QUILL-DRIVER
QUILTING-BEE
QUINCUNCIAL
QUINQUENNIA
QUINQUEREME
QUINSY-BERRY
QUINTILLION
QUITCH-GRASS
QUIVERINGLY
QUIZZICALLY
QUOTABILITY
QUOTEWORTHY

R

RABATTEMENT
RABBET-JOINT
RABBIT-HUTCH
RABBIT-PUNCH
RABELAISIAN
RACE-MEETING
RACE-SUICIDE
RACKET-COURT
RACKET-PRESS
RACK-RAILWAY
RADICALNESS
RADICELLOSE
RADIOACTIVE
RADIO-BEACON
RADIOCARBON
RADIOGRAPHY
RADIOLARIAN
RADIOLOGIST
RADIOMETRIC
RADIOPHONIC
RAFFISHNESS
RAGGED-ROBIN
RAIN-CHAMBER
RALLENTANDO
RALLYING-CRY
RAMGUNSHOCH
RANCOROUSLY
RANDLE-PERCH
RANGEFINDER
RAPACIOUSLY
RAPSCALLION
RAPTATORIAL
RAPTURELESS
RAPTUROUSLY
RAREFACTION
RAREFACTIVE
RASCALLIEST
RAT-CATCHING
RATEABILITY
RATE-CUTTING
RATIOCINATE
RATIONALISE
RATIONALISM
RATIONALIST
RATIONALITY
RATION-MONEY
RAT-KANGAROO
RATTLE-BRAIN
RATTLE-PATED
RATTLESNAKE
RAUCOUSNESS
RAVISHINGLY
REACH-ME-DOWN
REACTIONARY
REACTIONIST
READABILITY
READING-BOOK
READING-DESK
READING-LAMP
READING-ROOM
READMISSION
READY-MONIED
READY-TO-WEAR
READY-WITTED

REALIGNMENT
REALISATION
REALLOTMENT
REALPOLITIK
RE-AMENDMENT
REANIMATION
REAPING-HOOK
REAPPORTION
REAPPRAISAL
REAPPRAISER
REAR-ADMIRAL
REAR-ROASTED
REASCENSION
REASSERTION
REASSURANCE
REAWAKENING
REBARBATIVE
REBROADCAST
REBUKEFULLY
RECALCULATE
RECANTATION
RECEPTACULA
RECEPTIVITY
RECESSIONAL
RECESSIVELY
RECHABITISM
RECIPROCANT
RECIPROCATE
RECLAIMABLE
RECLAIMABLY
RECLAMATION
RECLINATION
RECLUSENESS
RECOGNITION
RECOGNITIVE
RECOGNITORY
RECOLLECTED
RECOMMENDER
RECOMMITTAL
RECONDITION
RECONNOITRE
RECONSTRUCT
RECORDATION
RECOUNTMENT
RECOVERABLE
RECREMENTAL
RECRUITMENT
RECTANGULAR
RECTIFIABLE
RECTILINEAL
RECTILINEAR
RECTIPETALY
RECTISERIAL
RECUMBENTLY
RECUPERABLE
RECUPERATOR
RECURRENTLY
REDACTORIAL
REDDING-COMB
REDDING-KAME
REDDISHNESS
REDELIVERER
REDETERMINE
REDISCOVERY
REDOUBTABLE
REDUCTIVELY

REDUNDANTLY
REDUPLICATE
REED-BUNTING
REED-DRAWING
REED-SPARROW
RE-EDUCATION
REED-WARBLER
REEF-BUILDER
RE-ELEVATION
RE-EMERGENCE
RE-ENACTMENT
RE-ENCOURAGE
RE-ENDOWMENT
RE-ESTABLISH
RE-EXISTENCE
RE-EXPANSION
REFECTIONER
REFECTORIAN
REFERENDARY
REFERENTIAL
REFINEDNESS
REFLECTANCE
REFLEXIVELY
REFOCILLATE
REFORMADOES
REFORMATION
REFORMATIVE
REFORMATORY
REFORMULATE
REFRACTABLE
REFRANGIBLE
REFRESHENER
REFRESHMENT
REFRIGERANT
REFRIGERATE
REFRINGENCY
REGARDFULLY
REGENERABLE
REGENERATOR
REGIONALISM
REGIONALIST
REGISTRABLE
REGREDIENCE
REGRETFULLY
REGRETTABLE
REGRETTABLY
REGURGITANT
REGURGITATE
REIFICATION
REINCARNATE
REINSERTION
REINSTATION
REINSURANCE
REINTEGRATE
REINTERMENT
REINTERPRET
REINTRODUCE
REITERATION
REITERATIVE
REJOICEMENT
REJOICINGLY
REJUVENATOR
REJUVENESCE
RELATEDNESS
RELATIONISM
RELATIONIST

RELEASEMENT
RELIABILITY
RELIC-MONGER
RELIGIONARY
RELIGIONISE
RELIGIONISM
RELIGIONIST
RELIGIOSITY
RELIGIOUSLY
RELUCTANTLY
RELUCTATION
REMEMBRANCE
REMIGRATION
REMINISCENT
REMITTENTLY
REMONSTRANT
REMONSTRATE
REMORSELESS
REMOVEDNESS
REMUNERABLE
REMUNERATOR
RENAISSANCE
RENEWEDNESS
REORIENTATE
REPARTITION
REPELLANTLY
REPELLENTLY
REPELLINGLY
REPENTANTLY
REPENTINGLY
REPETITIOUS
REPLACEABLE
REPLACEMENT
REPLENISHED
REPLENISHER
REPLETENESS
REPLEVIABLE
REPLICATION
REPORTINGLY
REPORTORIAL
REPOSEDNESS
REPOSEFULLY
REPOSSESION
REPREHENDER
REPRESENTER
REPRESSIBLE
REPRESSIBLY
REPROACHFUL
REPROBATION
REPROBATIVE
REPROBATORY
REPROVINGLY
REPUBLISHER
REPUDIATION
REPUDIATIVE
REPULSIVELY
REQUIREMENT
REQUISITION
REQUISITORY
REQUITELESS
REQUITEMENT
RESCUE-GRASS
RESEARCHFUL
RESEMBLANCE
RESENTFULLY
RESENTINGLY

RESERVATION
RESERVATORY
RESIDENTIAL
RESIGNATION
RESIPISCENT
RESISTINGLY
RESISTIVELY
RESISTIVITY
RESOURCEFUL
RESPECTABLE
RESPECTABLY
RESPECTLESS
RESPIRATION
RESPIRATORY
RESPLENDENT
RESPONDENCE
RESPONDENCY
RESPONSIBLE
RESPONSIBLY
RESPONSIONS
RESTATEMENT
RESTFULNESS
RESTITUTION
RESTITUTIVE
RESTITUTORY
RESTIVENESS
RESTORATION
RESTORATIVE
RESTRAINING
RESTRICTION
RESTRICTIVE
RESTRINGENT
RESULTATIVE
RESURRECTOR
RESUSCITANT
RESUSCITATE
RETALIATION
RETALIATIVE
RETALIATORY
RETARDATION
RETARDATIVE
RETARDATORY
RETENTIVELY
RETENTIVITY
RETICULARLY
RETICULATED
RETINACULAR
RETINACULUM
RETINISPORA
RETINOSCOPY
RETINOSPORA
RETIREDNESS
RETRACEABLE
RETRACTABLE
RETRANSLATE
RETRIBUTION
RETRIBUTIVE
RETRIBUTORY
RETRIEVABLE
RETRIEVABLY
RETROACTION
RETROACTIVE
RETROBULBAR
RETROCEDENT
RETROFLEXED
RETROROCKET

RETROUSSAGE
REVACCINATE
REVALUATION
REVENDICATE
REVENGELESS
REVENGEMENT
REVENGINGLY
REVERBERANT
REVERBERATE
REVERENTIAL
REVERSELESS
REVERSIONAL
REVERSIONER
REVINDICATE
REVISIONARY
REVISIONISM
REVISIONIST
REVIVESCENT
REVIVIFYING
REVIVISCENT
REVOLTINGLY
RHABDOMANCY
RHABDOMYOMA
RHABDOPHORA
RHAMNACEOUS
RHAMPHASTOS
RHAPSODICAL
RHEOTROPISM
RHETORICIAN
RHEUMATEESE
RHEUMATICAL
RHEUMATICKY
RHINOLOGIST
RHINOPLASTY
RHINORRHOEA
RHINOSCOPIC
RHIZANTHOUS
RHIZOCARPIC
RHIZOMATOUS
RHODIUM-WOOD
RHODODAPHNE
RHOMBOHEDRA
RHOPALOCERA
RHUMB-COURSE
RHYME-LETTER
RHYNCHOCOEL
RHYNCHODONT
RIBBON-GRASS
RIBESIACEAE
RIBONUCLEIC
RIB-ROASTING
RIB-VAULTING
RICE-BISCUIT
RICE-PUDDING
RICKETINESS
RICKETTSIAE
RICKETTSIAL
RICOCHETING
RICOCHETTED
RIDDLE-ME-REE
RIDING-CLOAK
RIDING-GLOVE
RIDING-HABIT
RIDING-HORSE
RIDING-LIGHT
RIDING-RHYME

RIDING-SKIRT
RIFACIMENTI
RIFACIMENTO
RIGGING-LOFT
RIGGING-TREE
RIGHT-ANGLED
RIGHTEOUSLY
RIGHT-HANDED
RIGHT-HANDER
RIGHT-MINDED
RIGHT-WINGER
RINFORZANDO
RING-CARRIER
RING-STOPPER
RING-STRAKED
RING-WINDING
RINTHEREOUT
RIOTOUSNESS
RIP-SNORTING
RITOURNELLE
RITUALISTIC
RIVAL-HATING
RIVERBOTTOM
RIVER-DRAGON
RIVER-DRIVER
RIVER-MUSSEL
RIVET-HEARTH
ROAD-HOGGISH
ROAD-MENDING
ROAD-SCRAPER
ROCK-BREAKER
ROCK-CRYSTAL
ROCKET-MOTOR
ROCKET-PLANE
ROCKET-RANGE
ROCK-FORMING
ROCKING-TOOL
ROCK-LEATHER
ROCK-SPARROW
RODENTICIDE
RODOMONTADE
ROGUISHNESS
ROLLER-SKATE
ROLLER-TOWEL
ROLLING-MILL
ROMANTICISE
ROMANTICISM
ROMANTICIST
ROMPISHNESS
ROOD-STEEPLE
ROOT-CLIMBER
ROOT-PRUNING
ROPE-MACHINE
ROSE-CAMPION
ROSE-CHEEKED
ROSE-DIAMOND
ROSEWOOD-OIL
ROSICRUCIAN
ROSY-BOSOMED
ROSY-CHEEKED
ROTARIANISM
ROTHER-BEAST
ROTOGRAVURE
ROTTENSTONE
ROUGE-ET-NOIR
ROUGH-COATED

ROUGH-FOOTED
ROUGH-LEGGED
ROUGH-SPOKEN
ROUGH-STRING
ROUND-ARCHED
ROUND-BACKED
ROUNDEDNESS
ROUND-HEADED
ROUND-LEAVED
ROUND-WINGED
ROUPING-WIFE
RUBBER-CORED
RUBBER-STAMP
RUBBING-POST
RUBBISH-HEAP
RUBBLE-STONE
RUBEFACIENT
RUBEFACTION
RUBICUNDITY
RUBRICATION
RÜDESHEIMER
RUDIMENTARY
RUFFIAN-LIKE
RUINOUSNESS
RULE-OF-THUMB
RUMBUSTICAL
RUMBUSTIOUS
RUMGUMPTION
RUMTI-IDDITY
RUNNING-GEAR
RUNNING-HAND
RUNNING-KNOT
RUNYONESQUE
RUPTUREWORT
RURIDECANAL
RUSH-BEARING
RUSSOPHOBIA
RUSTICATION

S

SABBATARIAN
SABBATHLESS
SABRE-RATTLE
SABURRATION
SACCHARATED
SACCULATION
SACRAMENTAL
SACRIFICIAL
SACRILEGIST
SACROCOSTAL
SAD-COLOURED
SADDLE-CLOTH
SADDLE-GIRTH
SADDLE-HORSE
SADDLE-NOSED
SADDUCEEISM
SAFE-BLOWING
SAFE-CONDUCT
SAFE-DEPOSIT
SAFE-KEEPING
SAFETY-CATCH
SAFETY-MATCH
SAFETY-VALVE
SAFFRON-CAKE
SAGACIOUSLY
SAGITTARIUS

SAILING-BOAT
SAILING-SHIP
SAILOR-MAKER
SAINTLINESS
SAINTPAULIA
SALABLENESS
SALACIOUSLY
SALEABILITY
SALICACEOUS
SALINOMETER
SALLAL-BERRY
SALLEE-ROVER
SALLOW-THORN
SALMON-BERRY
SALMON-COBLE
SALMON-SPEAR
SALMON-TROUT
SALOON-RIFLE
SALPINGITIC
SALPINGITIS
SALSUGINOUS
SALTATORIAL
SALTIERWISE
SALTIMBANCO
SALTISHNESS
SALVABILITY
SAMPLER-WORK
SANCHO-PEDRO
SANCTIFYING
SANCTUARISE
SANDEMANIAN
SANDERSWOOD
SAND-SKIPPER
SAND-THROWER
SANDWICH-MAN
SANG-DE-BOEUF
SANGUINARIA
SANGUINEOUS
SANGUISORBA
SANSCULOTTE
SANSEVIERIA
SANSKRITIST
SANTALACEAE
SAPINDACEAE
SAPLESSNESS
SAPONACEOUS
SAPONIFYING
SAPOTACEOUS
SAPROBIOTIC
SAPROGENOUS
SAPROLEGNIA
SAPROPELITE
SAPROPHYTIC
SAPUCAIA-NUT
SARCASTICAL
SARCENCHYME
SARCOCYSTIS
SARCOMATOUS
SARCOPHAGAL
SARCOPHAGUS
SARSEN-STONE
SARTORIALLY
SATANICALLY
SATANOPHANY
SATIABILITY
SATIN-FINISH

SATIN-STITCH
SATIRICALLY
SATISFIABLE
SATURNALIAN
SAUCE-CRAYON
SAUROPODOUS
SAUROPSIDAN
SAUSAGE-MEAT
SAUSAGE-ROLL
SAUSAGE-TREE
SAUSSURITIC
SAVABLENESS
SAVOIR-FAIRE
SAVOIR-VIVRE
SAVOURINESS
SAXOPHONIST
SCABBEDNESS
SCABERULOUS
SCAFFOLDAGE
SCAFFOLDING
SCALARIFORM
SCALE-ARMOUR
SCALE-INSECT
SCALPRIFORM
SCAMBLINGLY
SCANT-O'-GRACE
SCAPIGEROUS
SCARABAEIST
SCARABAEOID
SCAREMONGER
SCARLET-BEAN
SCATTEREDLY
SCATTERGOOD
SCATTERLING
SCENOGRAPHY
SCENT-BOTTLE
SCEPTICALLY
SCEPTRELESS
SCEUOPHYLAX
SCHECKLATON
SCHEMATICAL
SCHILLERISE
SCHISMATISE
SCHISM-HOUSE
SCHISTOSITY
SCHISTOSOMA
SCHISTOSOME
SCHIZANTHUS
SCHIZOGENIC
SCHIZOPHYTA
SCHIZOPODAL
SCHOLAR-LIKE
SCHOLARSHIP
SCHOLIASTIC
SCHOOL-BOARD
SCHOOL-CHILD
SCHOOLCRAFT
SCHOOLGOING
SCHOOLHOUSE
SCHOOL-POINT
SCHOOLWARDS
SCHOTTISCHE
SCHRECKLICH
SCHWÄRMEREI
SCIENTISTIC
SCIENTOLOGY

SCINTILLANT
SCINTILLATE
SCISSOR-BILL
SCISSOR-CASE
SCISSOR-TAIL
SCISSORWISE
SCITAMINEAE
SCLATE-STANE
SCLEROCAULY
SCLERODERMA
SCLEROMETER
SCLEROPHYLL
SCLEROTITIS
SCOLECIFORM
SCOLOPENDRA
SCOPOLAMINE
SCOPOPHILIA
SCOPOPHILIC
SCORBUTICAL
SCORCHINGLY
SCORIACEOUS
SCORING-CARD
SCORPION-FLY
SCORPIONIDA
SCOTCH-IRISH
SCOTCHWOMAN
SCOTTIFYING
SCOTTISHMAN
SCOUNDRELLY
SCOUTHERING
SCOUTMASTER
SCRAGGINESS
SCRAPE-PENNY
SCRAPPINESS
SCRATCH-BACK
SCRATCH-COAT
SCRATCHLESS
SCRATCH-WORK
SCRAWLINGLY
SCREAMINGLY
SCREECH-HAWK
SCREEN-WIPER
SCREW-DRIVER
SCREW-THREAD
SCREW-WRENCH
SCRIBACIOUS
SCRIMPINESS
SCRIMSHANDY
SCRIMSHONER
SCRIPTORIAL
SCRIPTORIUM
SCRIPTURISM
SCRIPTURIST
SCRIVE-BOARD
SCRUB-TURKEY
SCRUB-TYPHUS
SCRUFFINESS
SCRUMPTIOUS
SCRUTINISER
SCULDUDDERY
SCULPTURING
SCUPPERNONG
SCURVY-GRASS
SCUTTLE-BUTT
SCUTTLE-CASK
SCYPHISTOMA

SCYTHE-STONE
SDEIGNFULLY
SEA-COLEWORT
SEA-CRAWFISH
SEA-CRAYFISH
SEA-CUCUMBER
SEA-DOTTEREL
SEA-ELEPHANT
SEA-FURBELOW
SEA-HEDGEHOG
SEA-LAVENDER
SEAL-FISHING
SEA-LONGWORM
SEAL-ROOKERY
SEA-MILKWORT
SEAMING-LACE
SEAMSTRESSY
SEA-PURSLANE
SEARCHINGLY
SEARCHLIGHT
SEARCH-PARTY
SEARING-IRON
SEA-ROSEMARY
SEA-SCORPION
SEA-SCOUTING
SEASICKNESS
SEBORRHOEIC
SECONDARILY
SECOND-CLASS
SECOND-FLOOR
SECOND-RATER
SECONDS-HAND
SECOND-SIGHT
SECRETARIAL
SECRETARIAT
SECRETIONAL
SECRETIVELY
SECTIONALLY
SECTION-MARK
SEDENTARILY
SEDIGITATED
SEDIMENTARY
SEDITIONARY
SEDITIOUSLY
SEDUCTIVELY
SEEMINGNESS
SEGMENTALLY
SEGREGATION
SEGREGATIVE
SEIGNEURIAL
SEIGNIORAGE
SEIGNIORIAL
SEISMOGRAPH
SEISMOLOGIC
SEISMOMETER
SEISMOMETRY
SEISMONASTY
SEISMOSCOPE
SELAGINELLA
SELDOM-TIMES
SELECTIVELY
SELECTIVITY
SELECTORIAL
SELENOGRAPH
SELF-AFFAIRS
SELF-ASSUMED

SELF-ASSURED
SELF-BLINDED
SELF-CENTRED
SELF-CHARITY
SELF-CLOSING
SELF-COCKING
SELF-COMMAND
SELF-CONCEIT
SELF-CONTENT
SELF-CONTROL
SELF-COVERED
SELF-CULTURE
SELF-DEFENCE
SELF-DELIGHT
SELF-DENYING
SELF-DESPAIR
SELF-DEVOTED
SELF-DRAWING
SELF-ELECTED
SELF-EVIDENT
SELF-EXAMPLE
SELF-FEEDING
SELF-FEELING
SELF-FERTILE
SELF-FIGURED
SELF-HARMING
SELF-HEALING
SELF-IMPOSED
SELF-INVITED
SELFISHNESS
SELF-KNOWING
SELF-LIMITED
SELF-LOCKING
SELF-MASTERY
SELF-MISUSED
SELF-NEGLECT
SELF-OFFENCE
SELF-OPINION
SELF-PLANTED
SELF-SEEKING
SELF-SERVICE
SELF-STARTER
SELF-STERILE
SELF-SUBDUED
SELF-SUPPORT
SELF-TEMPTED
SELF-TORTURE
SELF-WINDING
SEMANTICIST
SEMASIOLOGY
SEMBLING-BOX
SEMI-ANNULAR
SEMICIRCLED
SEMI-DIURNAL
SEMI-ELLIPSE
SEMI-JUBILEE
SEMI-MONTHLY
SEMIPALMATE
SEMI-SKILLED
SEMI-TUBULAR
SEMPITERNAL
SEMPITERNUM
SENATE-HOUSE
SENATORSHIP
SENSATIONAL
SENSELESSLY

SENSIBILITY
SENSITIVELY
SENSITIVITY
SENSUALNESS
SENTENTIOUS
SENTIMENTAL
SEPIOSTAIRE
SEPTEMBRIST
SEPTENARIUS
SEPTENTRION
SEPTICAEMIA
SEPTIFEROUS
SEPTIFRAGAL
SEPULCHROUS
SEQUESTERED
SEQUESTRATE
SERENDIPITY
SERICULTURE
SERIGRAPHER
SERIGRAPHIC
SERIOUSNESS
SEROLOGICAL
SEROTHERAPY
SERPENTINIC
SERPENTLIKE
SERPENT-STAR
SERPIGINOUS
SERRATULATE
SERRULATION
SERTULARIAN
SERVANT-GIRL
SERVANT-LASS
SERVANTLESS
SERVANT-MAID
SERVANTSHIP
SERVICEABLE
SERVICEABLY
SERVICE-BOOK
SERVICE-FLAT
SERVICELESS
SERVICE-LINE
SERVICE-PIPE
SERVICE-ROOM
SERVICE-TREE
SERVICE-WIRE
SERVITORIAL
SESAME-GRASS
SESQUIOXIDE
SESQUIPEDAL
SESSILE-EYED
SESSIONALLY
SETTER-FORTH
SETTLEDNESS
SETTLING-DAY
SEVEN-LEAGUE
SEVENTEENTH
SEVERALFOLD
SEXAGESIMAL
SEXENNIALLY
SEXLESSNESS
SEX-REVERSAL
SEXTODECIMO
SHACKLE-BOLT
SHACKLE-BONE
SHAD-BELLIED
SHADOWINESS

SHAGGEDNESS
SHAKSPERIAN
SHALLOWNESS
SHAMANISTIC
SHAMELESSLY
SHAMEWORTHY
SHANGHAIING
SHAPELINESS
SHARD-BEETLE
SHAREHOLDER
SHARE-PUSHER
SHARP-GROUND
SHARP-TAILED
SHARP-WITTED
SHAVING-SOAP
SHAWNEEWOOD
SHEATH-KNIFE
SHEEP-BITING
SHEEP-FARMER
SHEEP-MASTER
SHEEP-SILVER
SHEET-ANCHOR
SHEET-COPPER
SHEET-RUBBER
SHELLACKING
SHELL-CRATER
SHELL-JACKET
SHELL-PARROT
SHELTERLESS
SHEPHERDESS
SHERIFFALTY
SHERIFFSHIP
SHERRIS-SACK
SHIFTLESSLY
SHIMMY-SHAKE
SHININGNESS
SHIN-PLASTER
SHINTY-STICK
SHIP-BISCUIT
SHIP-BREAKER
SHIPBUILDER
SHIP-CAPTAIN
SHIP-RAILWAY
SHIRT-BUTTON
SHIRT-SLEEVE
SHIVERINGLY
SHOCK-HEADED
SHOCK-TROOPS
SHOEING-HORN
SHOE-LATCHET
SHOE-LEATHER
SHOOTING-BOX
SHOPBREAKER
SHOPKEEPING
SHOP-LIFTING
SHOP-STEWARD
SHORTCHANGE
SHORTCOMING
SHORT-HANDED
SHORT-SPOKEN
SHORT-STAPLE
SHORT-WINDED
SHOULDERING
SHOVEL-BOARD
SHOWERINESS
SHOWER-PROOF

SHOW-JUMPING
SHOWMANSHIP
SHREW-STRUCK
SHRIEKINGLY
SHRINKINGLY
SHRINK-PROOF
SHRIVELLING
SHRUBBERIED
SHRUBBINESS
SHUDDERSOME
SHUFFLINGLY
SHUNAMITISM
SHUTTLECOCK
SHUTTLEWISE
SIALOGRAPHY
SIALORRHOEA
SICK-BENEFIT
SICK-CHAMBER
SICKENINGLY
SICKISHNESS
SICK-NURSING
SICK-SERVICE
SIDE-CUTTING
SIDEROPENIA
SIDE-WHISKER
SIEGE-BASKET
SIGHTLESSLY
SIGHTLINESS
SIGHT-PLAYER
SIGHT-READER
SIGHT-SCREEN
SIGHTSEEING
SIGHT-SINGER
SIGHTWORTHY
SIGILLARIAN
SIGILLATION
SIGMOIDALLY
SIGNIFIABLE
SIGNIFICANT
SIGNIFICATE
SIGN-PAINTER
SIGN-WRITING
SILK-THROWER
SILKWORM-GUT
SILLIMANITE
SILVER-GRAIN
SILVERINESS
SILVER-PAPER
SILVER-PLATE
SILVER-POINT
SILVERSMITH
SILVER-STICK
SILVER-WHITE
SILVESTRIAN
SIMNEL-BREAD
SIMPERINGLY
SIMPLICITER
SINCERENESS
SINGING-BIRD
SINGLE-ENTRY
SINGLE-PHASE
SINGLE-SOLED
SINGLE-STICK
SINGULARISE
SINGULARISM
SINGULARIST

SINGULARITY
SINISTERITY
SINISTRALLY
SINISTRORSE
SINKING-FUND
SINKING-RIPE
SINLESSNESS
SIN-OFFERING
SINOLOGICAL
SINOPHILISM
SINUOUSNESS
SINUPALLIAL
SIPHONOGAMY
SIPUNCULOID
SISTER-IN-LAW
SITIOPHOBIA
SITTING-ROOM
SITUATIONAL
SIVATHERIUM
SKATING-RINK
SKELETONISE
SKETCHINESS
SKILFULNESS
SKILLIGALEE
SKILLIGOLEE
SKIMMINGTON
SKIRMISHING
SKITTLE-BALL
SKULDUDDERY
SKULDUGGERY
SKY-ASPIRING
SKY-COLOURED
SLACK-HANDED
SLATE-PENCIL
SLATE-WRITER
SLAUGHTERER
SLAVE-DRIVER
SLAVE-HOLDER
SLAVE-LABOUR
SLAVE-OWNING
SLAVERINGLY
SLAVE-STATES
SLAVE-TRADER
SLAVISHNESS
SLAVONICISE
SLEDGE-CHAIR
SLEEK-HEADED
SLEEPING-BAG
SLEEPING-CAR
SLEEPLESSLY
SLEEP-WALKER
SLEEVE-BOARD
SLENDERNESS
SLEUTH-HOUND
SLICKENSIDE
SLIDING-KEEL
SLIDING-RULE
SLIGHTINGLY
SLIME-FUNGUS
SLING-BACKED
SLIPPER-WORT
SLOT-MACHINE
SLOW-SIGHTED
SLUGGARDISE
SLUMBERLAND
SLUMBERLESS

SLUMBERSOME
SLUMBROUSLY
SMALLHOLDER
SMALL-MINDED
SMALL-SCREEN
SMART-TICKET
SMILINGNESS
SMITHSONIAN
SMITHSONITE
SMOKE-HELMET
SMOKELESSLY
SMOKESCREEN
SMOOTH-FACED
SMOOTH-PACED
SMÖRGÅSBORD
SMOULDERING
SNAFFLE-REIN
SNAIL-FLOWER
SNAKISHNESS
SNAPSHOOTER
SNATCH-BLOCK
SNATCHINGLY
SNATCH-PURSE
SNATCH-THIEF
SNECK-DRAWER
SNICKERSNEE
SNOBBBISHLY
SNOBOGRAPHY
SNOTTY-NOSED
SNOW-BUNTING
SNOW-DROPPER
SNOW-GOGGLES
SNOW-LEOPARD
SNUFF-COLOUR
SNUFF-DIPPER
SNUFF-TAKING
SOAP-BOILING
SOBER-MINDED
SOBER-SUITED
SOCIABILITY
SOCIALISTIC
SOCIETARIAN
SOCINIANISE
SOCINIANISM
SOCIOLOGISM
SOCIOLOGIST
SOCIOMETRIC
SOCIOPATHIC
SOCKDOLAGER
SOCKDOLIGER
SOCKDOLOGER
SODOMITICAL
SOFT-HEARTED
SOFT-SHELLED
SOJOURNMENT
SOLANACEOUS
SOLDATESQUE
SOLDIER-CRAB
SOLDIERLIKE
SOLDIERSHIP
SOLID-HOOFED
SOLIDIFYING
SOLIFLUXION
SOLILOQUISE
SOLIPSISTIC
SOLMISATION

SOLUTIONIST
SOLVABILITY
SOMATICALLY
SOMATOGENIC
SOMATOLOGIC
SOMATOPLASM
SOMATOTONIA
SOMATOTONIC
SOMEWHITHER
SOMNAMBULAR
SOMNAMBULIC
SOMNICULOUS
SOMNIFEROUS
SOMNIVOLENT
SOMNOLENTLY
SONGFULNESS
SONG-SPARROW
SONOFABITCH
SOOTHFASTLY
SOOTHSAYING
SOPHISTICAL
SORBONNICAL
SOROPTIMIST
SORROWFULLY
SOTERIOLOGY
SOTTISHNESS
SOUL-FEARING
SOULFULNESS
SOUL-KILLING
SOUL-SLEEPER
SOUNDING-ROD
SOUNDLESSLY
SOUND-SHADOW
SOUP-KITCHEN
SOUTH-EASTER
SOUTHERMOST
SOUTHERNISE
SOUTHERNISM
SOUTHLANDER
SOUTHWARDLY
SOUTH-WESTER
SOVEREIGNLY
SOVEREIGNTY
SPACE-HEATER
SPACE-TRAVEL
SPADE-GUINEA
SPAGERICIST
SPAGIRICIST
SPAN-COUNTER
SPANG-COCKLE
SPANIEL-LIKE
SPARINGNESS
SPARKLESSLY
SPARKLINGLY
SPARROW-BILL
SPARROW-HAWK
SPASMATICAL
SPASMODICAL
SPASTICALLY
SPATHACEOUS
SPATTERDASH
SPATTER-DOCK
SPATTER-WORK
SPAWNING-BED
SPEAKERSHIP
SPECIALISER

SPECIFIABLE
SPECIFICATE
SPECIFICITY
SPECTACULAR
SPECTATRESS
SPECTRALITY
SPECTRE-CRAB
SPECTROGRAM
SPECTROLOGY
SPECULATION
SPECULATIST
SPECULATIVE
SPECULATORY
SPECULATRIX
SPEECHCRAFT
SPEECH-CRIER
SPEECHIFIER
SPEECH-MAKER
SPEEDOMETER
SPELAEOLOGY
SPELLBINDER
SPELLING-BEE
SPENDTHRIFT
SPERGULARIA
SPERMAPHYTA
SPERMAPHYTE
SPERMATHECA
SPERMATICAL
SPERMATOZOA
SPERM-CANDLE
SPERMOPHILE
SPERMOPHYTA
SPERMOPHYTE
SPESSARTITE
SPHACELATED
SPHAERIDIUM
SPHAGNACEAE
SPHAGNOLOGY
SPHERICALLY
SPHEROIDISE
SPHEROMETER
SPHERULITIC
SPHINCTERAL
SPHINCTERIC
SPHRAGISTIC
SPHYGMOGRAM
SPHYGMOLOGY
SPHYMOPHONE
SPIDER-WHEEL
SPIFFLICATE
SPILL-STREAM
SPINACH-BEET
SPINDLE-LEGS
SPINDLE-SIDE
SPINDLE-TREE
SPINELESSLY
SPINESCENCE
SPINIFEROUS
SPINIGEROUS
SPINNERETTE
SPINOZISTIC
SPINSTERDOM
SPINSTERIAL
SPINSTERIAN
SPINSTERISH
SPIRACULATE

SPIRILLOSIS
SPIRITISTIC
SPIRIT-LEVEL
SPIRITUALLY
SPIRITUALTY
SPIRITUELLE
SPIRIT-WORLD
SPIROCHAETA
SPIROCHAETE
SPIROMETRIC
SPLASH-BOARD
SPLASHPROOF
SPLAY-FOOTED
SPLEEN-STONE
SPLENDIDOUS
SPLENDOROUS
SPLENECTOMY
SPLENETICAL
SPLINTER-BAR
SPLIT-SECOND
SPLUTTERING
SPODOMANTIC
SPOKESWOMAN
SPONDULICKS
SPONDYLITIS
SPONGE-CLOTH
SPONSORSHIP
SPONTANEITY
SPONTANEOUS
SPORANGIOLE
SPOROCYSTIC
SPOROGENOUS
SPOROGONIUM
SPOROPHORIC
SPOROPHYTIC
SPORULATION
SPOTTEDNESS
SPREAD-EAGLE
SPREADINGLY
SPRIGHTLESS
SPRING-BOARD
SPRING-CLEAN
SPRING-HOUSE
SPRINGINESS
SPRING-WATER
SPRING-WHEAT
SPUD-BASHING
SPUMESCENCE
SPUR-GEARING
SPUR-LEATHER
SQUALIDNESS
SQUANDERING
SQUARE-BUILT
SQUARE-DANCE
SQUARSONAGE
SQUASHINESS
SQUATTINESS
SQUEAKINESS
SQUEAKINGLY
SQUEAMISHLY
SQUINTINGLY
SQUIRARCHAL
SQUIREARCHY
STACTOMETER
STADTHOLDER
STAFF-SYSTEM

STAGE-DRIVER
STAGE-EFFECT
STAGE-FLOWER
STAGE-FRIGHT
STAGE-MANAGE
STAGE-PLAYER
STAGE-STRUCK
STAGING-AREA
STAGING-BASE
STAGING-POST
STAHLHELMER
STAHLIANISM
STAINLESSLY
STAIR-CARPET
STAIR-TURRET
STALACTICAL
STALACTITAL
STALACTITED
STALACTITIC
STALAGMITIC
STALLING-KEN
STALL-MASTER
STALL-READER
STAMINODIUM
STAMP-OFFICE
STANCHIONED
STANDARDISE
STANDING-BED
STANDING-CUP
STAND-OFFISH
STAND-PATTER
STAPHYLITIS
STARCH-GRAIN
STARCHINESS
STARCH-PAPER
STAR-CROSSED
STAR-THISTLE
STARTLINGLY
STASIMORPHY
STATELINESS
STATE-MONGER
STATE-PRISON
STATESMANLY
STATESWOMAN
STATION-HAND
STATISTICAL
STATUTE-BOOK
STATUTORILY
STAUNCHNESS
STAUROLITIC
STAVE-CHURCH
STEADFASTLY
STEADY-GOING
STEAM-BOILER
STEAM-DIGGER
STEAM-DRIVEN
STEAM-ENGINE
STEAM-HAMMER
STEAM-JACKET
STEAM-LAUNCH
STEAM-PACKET
STEAM-PLOUGH
STEAM-ROLLER
STEAM-SHOVEL
STEAM-VESSEL
STEATOPYGIA

STEEL-HEADED
STEEL-PLATED
STEELWORKER
STEEPE-DOWNE
STEEPLE-BUSH
STEEPLE-FAIR
STEEPLEJACK
STEERAGE-WAY
STEGANOGRAM
STEGOSAURUS
STEINBERGER
STELLIFYING
STELLIONATE
STENCILLING
STENOCHROME
STENOCHROMY
STENOGRAPHY
STENOTYPIST
STENTMASTER
STEPBROTHER
STEP-DANCING
STEPHANOTIS
STEREOBATIC
STEREOGRAPH
STEREOMETER
STEREOMETRY
STEREOPHONY
STEREOPTICS
STEREOSCOPE
STEREOSCOPY
STEREOSONIC
STEREOTYPED
STEREOTYPER
STEREOTYPIC
STERN-CHASER
STERNOTRIBE
STERNSHEETS
STERNUTATOR
STETHOSCOPE
STETHOSCOPY
STEVENGRAPH
STEWARDSHIP
STICHOMETRY
STICK-INSECT
STICKLEBACK
STIFF-NECKED
STIFF-RUMPED
STIFLE-JOINT
STIGMATICAL
STILETTOING
STILL-HUNTER
STILTEDNESS
STILT-PLOVER
STILT-WALKER
STIMULATING
STIMULATION
STIMULATIVE
STINTEDNESS
STIPENDIARY
STIPENDIATE
STIPULATION
STIPULATORY
STIRRUP-BONE
STIRRUP-DRAM
STIRRUP-IRON
STIRRUP-PUMP

STITCHCRAFT
STOCKBROKER
STOCK-FARMER
STOCK-FEEDER
STOCK-HOLDER
STOCKINETTE
STOCKJOBBER
STOCK-MARKET
STOCKPILING
STOCK-SADDLE
STOCKTAKING
STOICALNESS
STOMACH-ACHE
STOMACHICAL
STOMACHLESS
STOMACH-PUMP
STOMATOLOGY
STOMATOPODA
STONE-BRUISE
STONE-COLOUR
STONE-CURLEW
STONE-CUTTER
STONE-FALCON
STONE-HAMMER
STONE-MARTEN
STONE-PLOVER
STONE'S-THROW
STONEWALLER
STOOL-PIGEON
STOPPING-OUT
STORE-CATTLE
STORE-FARMER
STOREKEEPER
STORM-BEATEN
STORM-CENTRE
STORM-PETREL
STORM-SIGNAL
STORM-STAYED
STORM-TOSSED
STORM-TROOPS
STORM-WINDOW
STORY-TELLER
STRABOMETER
STRADUARIUS
STRAIGHT-CUT
STRAIGHTISH
STRAIGHT-JET
STRAIGHT-OUT
STRAIGHTWAY
STRAIT-LACED
STRAIT-LACER
STRAMINEOUS
STRANGENESS
STRANGULATE
STRAP-HANGER
STRAP-SHAPED
STRATEGETIC
STRATEGICAL
STRATIFYING
STRATOCRACY
STRAW-COLOUR
STRAW-CUTTER
STREAKINESS
STREAMINESS
STREAMINGLY
STREAMLINED

STREETWARDS
STRENGTHFUL
STRENUOSITY
STRENUOUSLY
STRETCHLESS
STRIDULATOR
STRIKE-FAULT
STRING-BOARD
STRINGENTLY
STRINGINESS
STRING-PIECE
STRINGY-BARK
STROBOSCOPE
STRONG-POINT
STRONGYLOID
STRUTHIONES
STRUTTINGLY
STUBBLE-RAKE
STUDENTSHIP
STUDIEDNESS
STUFFING-BOX
STULTIFYING
STULTILOQUY
STUMBLINGLY
STUMP-ORATOR
STUMP-SPEECH
STUNTEDNESS
STUPENDIOUS
STYLIFEROUS
STYLISATION
STYLISHNESS
STYLOGRAPHY
STYLOPODIUM
STYRACACEAE
SUASIVENESS
SUBAERIALLY
SUBARRATION
SUBAUDITION
SUBAXILLARY
SUBCATEGORY
SUBCLINICAL
SUBCONTRACT
SUBCONTRARY
SUBCORTICAL
SUBCRITICAL
SUBDEACONRY
SUBDIACONAL
SUBDISTRICT
SUBDIVISION
SUBDIVISIVE
SUBDOMINANT
SUBDUEDNESS
SUBGLOBULAR
SUBINCISION
SUBINDICATE
SUBITANEOUS
SUBJECTSHIP
SUBJUGATION
SUBJUNCTIVE
SUBLIMATION
SUBLIMENESS
SUBLITTORAL
SUBLUXATION
SUBMARGINAL
SUBMERGENCE
SUBMERGIBLE

SUBMERSIBLE
SUBMISSIBLE
SUBMISSNESS
SUBMULTIPLE
SUBORDINARY
SUBORDINATE
SUBORNATION
SUBPANATION
SUBREGIONAL
SUBROGATION
SUBSCAPULAR
SUBSCRIBING
SUBSCRIPTON
SUBSENSIBLE
SUBSEQUENCE
SUBSERVIENT
SUBSISTENCE
SUBSPECIFIC
SUBSTANDARD
SUBSTANTIAL
SUBSTANTIVE
SUBSTITUENT
SUBSTITUTED
SUBSTRACTOR
SUBSUMPTION
SUBSUMPTIVE
SUBTACKSMAN
SUBTERHUMAN
SUBTILENESS
SUBTRACTION
SUBTRACTIVE
SUBTROPICAL
SUBUMBRELLA
SUBUNGULATA
SUBUNGULATE
SUBURBANISE
SUBURBANISM
SUBURBANITE
SUBURBANITY
SUBVERTICAL
SUBVITREOUS
SUCCEDANEUM
SUCCESSLESS
SUCCINCTORY
SUCCOURABLE
SUCCOURLESS
SUCCULENTLY
SUCH-AND-SUCH
SUCKING-FISH
SUFFICIENCE
SUFFICIENCY
SUFFOCATING
SUFFOCATION
SUFFOCATIVE
SUFFRAGETTE
SUFFUMIGATE
SUGAR-COATED
SUGGESTIBLE
SUITABILITY
SULPHURATOR
SULPHUREOUS
SULPHUR-ROOT
SULPHURWORT
SUMMARINESS
SUMMATIONAL
SUMMER-HOUSE

SUMMIT-LEVEL
SUMPTUOSITY
SUMPTUOUSLY
SUNLESSNESS
SUPERABOUND
SUPERCHARGE
SUPERCHERIE
SUPERDAINTY
SUPERFAMILY
SUPERFATTED
SUPERFETATE
SUPERFICIAL
SUPERFICIES
SUPERFLUITY
SUPERFLUOUS
SUPERFUSION
SUPERHEATER
SUPERIMPOSE
SUPERINDUCE
SUPERINTEND
SUPERIORESS
SUPERIORITY
SUPERJACENT
SUPERLATIVE
SUPERLUNARY
SUPERMARKET
SUPERNATANT
SUPERNATURE
SUPERNORMAL
SUPEROCTAVE
SUPERPRAISE
SUPERSCRIBE
SUPERSCRIPT
SUPERSEDEAS
SUPERSEDERE .
SUPERSEDURE
SUPERSTRUCT
SUPERSUBTLE
SUPERTANKER
SUPERVISION
SUPERVISORY
SUPERVOLUTE
SUPPLIANTLY
SUPPLICAVIT
SUPPORTABLE
SUPPORTABLY
SUPPORTANCE
SUPPORTLESS
SUPPORTMENT
SUPPORTRESS
SUPPOSITION
SUPPOSITIVE
SUPPOSITORY
SUPPRESSION
SUPPRESSIVE
SUPPURATION
SUPPURATIVE
SUPRACOSTAL
SUPREMATISM
SUPREMATIST
SUPREMENESS
SURADDITION
SURBASEMENT
SURFACE-MAIL
SURF-BATHING
SURGEON-FISH

SURGEONSHIP
SURMOUNTING
SURPASSABLE
SURPRISEDLY
SURREBUTTAL
SURREBUTTER
SURRENDEREE
SURRENDERER
SURRENDEROR
SURROGATION
SURROUNDING
SURTARBRAND
SURTURBRAND
SURVEILLANT
SUSCEPTIBLE
SUSCEPTIBLY
SUSCITATION
SUSPECTABLE
SUSPECTEDLY
SUSPECTLESS
SUSPENSEFUL
SUSPENSIBLE
SUSPIRATION
SUSTAINABLE
SUSTAINEDLY
SUSTAINMENT
SUSTENTATOR
SUSURRATION
SVARABHAKTI
SWAG-BELLIED
SWAGGER-CANE
SWAGGERCOAT
SWALLOW-DIVE
SWALLOW-HOLE
SWALLOW-TAIL
SWALLOW-WORT
SWAN-HOPPING
SWARTHINESS
SWEATER-GIRL
SWEEPSTAKES
SWEEP-WASHER
SWEET-CICELY
SWEET-POTATO
SWEET-WILLOW
SWELL-HEADED
SWIFT-FOOTED
SWIFT-WINGED
SWIM-BLADDER
SWINE'S-CRESS
SWING-BRIDGE
SWINGEINGLY
SWING-HANDLE
SWINGLE-HAND
SWINGLETREE
SWING-PLOUGH
SWINISHNESS
SWITCHBOARD
SWITCH-PLANT
SWORD-BEARER
SWORD-DOLLAR
SWORDPLAYER
SWORD-SHAPED
SYCOPHANTIC
SYCOPHANTRY
SYLLABARIUM
SYLLEPTICAL

SYLLOGISTIC
SYLVESTRIAN
SYMBOLISTIC
SYMBOLOLOGY
SYMMETRICAL
SYMPATHETIC
SYMPATHISER
SYMPETALOUS
SYMPHONIOUS
SYMPLIFYING
SYMPODIALLY
SYMPOSIARCH
SYMPTOMATIC
SYNAGOGICAL
SYNANTHESIS
SYNANTHETIC
SYNCHORESIS
SYNCHRONISE
SYNCHRONISM
SYNCHRONOUS
SYNCHROTRON
SYNCOPATION
SYNDESMOSIS
SYNDESMOTIC
SYNDICALISM
SYNDICALIST
SYNDICATION
SYNDYASMIAN
SYNECDOCHIC
SYNERGISTIC
SYNODICALLY
SYNOECIOSIS
SYNOECOLOGY
SYNONIMICAL
SYNONYMATIC
SYNONYMICON
SYNOPTISTIC
SYNTACTICAL
SYNTECTICAL
SYNTHETICAL
SYPHILOLOGY
SYRINGOTOMY
SYSSARCOSIS
SYSTEMATICS
SYSTEMATISE
SYSTEMATISM
SYSTEMATIST
SYSTEM-BUILT
SYSTEM-MAKER

T
TABEFACTION
TABERNACLED
TABLE-NAPKIN
TABLE-TENNIS
TABLE-TOPPED
TACHEOMETER
TACHEOMETRY
TACHYCARDIA
TACHYGRAPHY
TACITURNITY
TAIL-FEATHER
TAINTLESSLY
TALE-BEARING
TALIACOTIAN
TALKATIVELY

TALK-YOU-DOWN
TALLOW-CATCH
TALLOW-FACED
TALLY-SYSTEM
TALMUDISTIC
TAMEABILITY
TAN-COLOURED
TANGIBILITY
TANK-FARMING
TANTALISING
TANTALUS-CUP
TAP-DRESSING
TAPE-MACHINE
TAPE-MEASURE
TAPHEPHOBIA
TAPHOPHOBIA
TARATANTARA
TARDY-GAITED
TARGUMISTIC
TARNISHABLE
TARRADIDDLE
TARRY-BREEKS
TASSELL-GENT
TASTELESSLY
TATTERSALL'S
TATTIE-BOGLE
TAUROBOLIUM
TAUTOCHRONE
TAUTOLOGISE
TAUTOLOGISM
TAUTOLOGIST
TAUTOLOGOUS
TAUTOMERISM
TAUTOMETRIC
TAUTONYMOUS
TAX-GATHERER
TAXIDERMISE
TAXIDERMIST
TAXONOMICAL
TEA-CANISTER
TEACHERSHIP
TEA-EQUIPAGE
TEAR-FALLING
TEARFULNESS
TEAR-STAINED
TEASPOONFUL
TECHNICALLY
TECHNOCRACY
TECTIBRANCH
TEDIOUSNESS
TEETER-BOARD
TEETOTALISM
TEETOTALLER
TEGUMENTARY
TEKNONYMOUS
TELEARCHICS
TELECONTROL
TELEFERIQUE
TELEGRAMMIC
TELEGRAPHER
TELEGRAPHIC
TELEKINESIS
TELEKINETIC
TELEOLOGISM
TELEOLOGIST
TELEOSAURUS

TELEPATHISE
TELEPATHIST
TELEPHONIST
TELEPRINTER
TELESCOPIST
TELESCOPIUM
TELLURETTED
TELPHER-LINE
TEMERARIOUS
TEMPERAMENT
TEMPERATELY
TEMPERATIVE
TEMPERATURE
TEMPEST-TOST
TEMPESTUOUS
TEMPORALITY
TEMPORARILY
TEMPORISING
TEMPTATIOUS
TENABLENESS
TENACIOUSLY
TENANT-RIGHT
TENDENCIOUS
TENDENTIOUS
TENDER-DYING
TENEBROSITY
TENEMENTARY
TENNIS-COURT
TENNIS-MATCH
TENSIBILITY
TENTACULATE
TENTACULITE
TENTATIVELY
TENTERHOOKS
TENTIGINOUS
TENT-PEGGING
TEPHROMANCY
TERATOGENIC
TERATOLOGIC
TEREBRATION
TEREBRATULA
TERMAGANTLY
TERMINATION
TERMINATIVE
TERMINATORY
TERMINOLOGY
TERMITARIUM
TERPSICHORE
TERRAQUEOUS
TERREMOTIVE
TERRESTRIAL
TERRIBILITY
TERRICOLOUS
TERRIGENOUS
TERRITORIAL
TERRITORIED
TESSARAGLOT
TESSELLATED
TESTAMENTAL
TESTAMENTAR
TESTICULATE
TESTIFICATE
TESTIMONIAL
TETRACTINAL
TETRACYCLIC
TETRADACTYL

TETRADRACHM
TETRAGONOUS
TETRAGYNIAN
TETRAGYNOUS
TETRAHEDRAL
TETRAHEDRON
TETRAMERISM
TETRAMEROUS
TETRANDRIAN
TETRANDROUS
TETRAPLOIDY
TETRAPODOUS
TETRAPTERAN
TETRARCHATE
TETRASPORIC
TETRATHEISM
TETRAVALENT
TEUTONICISM
TEXTURELESS
THALIDOMIDE
THALLOPHYTA
THALLOPHYTE
THANATOLOGY
THANATOPSIS
THANKLESSLY
THANKSGIVER
THANKWORTHY
THARBOROUGH
THATCH-BOARD
THAUMATROPE
THAUMATURGE
THEANTHROPY
THEATRE-GOER
THEATRICALS
THEATRICISE
THEATRICISM
THEFTUOUSLY
THELYTOKOUS
THENCEFORTH
THEOBROMINE
THEOCRITEAN
THEOGONICAL
THEOLOGICAL
THEOLOGISER
THEOMACHIST
THEOMORPHIC
THEOPHAGOUS
THEOPHOBIST
THEOPNEUSTY
THEOREMATIC
THEORETICAL
THEOSOPHISE
THEOSOPHISM
THEOSOPHIST
THEOTECHNIC
THERAPEUTAE
THERAPEUTIC
THEREBESIDE
THERETOFORE
THEREWITHAL
THEREWITHIN
THERIOLATRY
THERIOMORPH
THERMICALLY
THERMIONICS
THERMODURIC

THERMOGENIC
THERMOGRAPH
THERMOLYSIS
THERMOLYTIC
THERMOMETER
THERMOMETRY
THERMONASTY
THERMOPHILE
THERMOSCOPE
THERMOTAXIS
THERMOTICAL
THEROMORPHA
THESMOTHETE
THICK-COMING
THICK-HEADED
THICK-LIPPED
THICK-RIBBED
THIMBLECASE
THINGLINESS
THINGUMAJIG
THIN-SKINNED
THIOCYANATE
THIOPENTONE
THIRD-STREAM
THIRSTINESS
THIRTY-TWOMO
THISTLE-DOWN
THITHERWARD
THIXOTROPIC
THOMISTICAL
THOROUGHWAX
THOUGHTLESS
THOUGHT-SICK
THOUGHT-WAVE
THRASONICAL
THREADINESS
THREAD-PAPER
THREATENING
THREE-BOTTLE
THREE-COLOUR
THREE-DECKER
THREE-HANDED
THREE-LEAFED
THREE-LEAVED
THREE-LEGGED
THREE-MASTED
THREE-MASTER
THREE-NOOKED
THREE-PARTED
THREE-SQUARE
THREE-SUITED
THRENETICAL
THRIFTINESS
THRILLINGLY
THROATINESS
THROAT-LATCH
THROAT-STRAP
THROBBINGLY
THROUGH-BOLT
THROUGHFARE
THROUGH-GAUN
THRUMMINGLY
THRUST-PLANE
THUMB-MARKED
THUNDERBOLT
THUNDER-CLAP

THUNDER-DART
THUNDERLESS
THUNDER-LIKE
THUNDER-PEAL
THURIFEROUS
THWARTINGLY
THWARTSHIPS
THYROIDITIS
THYROSTRACA
THYSANUROUS
TICHORRHINE
TICKET-PUNCH
TICKLE-BRAIN
TIGER-BEETLE
TIGER-FLOWER
TIGER-FOOTED
TIGHT-FISTED
TIGHT-LACING
TIGHT-LIPPED
TILLER-CHAIN
TIMBROMANIA
TIMBROPHILY
TIME-BARGAIN
TIME-EXPIRED
TIME-KILLING
TIME-PLEASER
TIME-SERVICE
TIME-SERVING
TIN-STREAMER
TIRE-VALIANT
TIRING-GLASS
TIRING-HOUSE
TIRING-WOMAN
TIRONENSIAN
TISSUE-PAPER
TITANOMACHY
TITHE-PAYING
TITIANESQUE
TITILLATION
TITTIVATION
TOAD-SPOTTED
TOAST-MASTER
TOBACCONIST
TOBACCO-PIPE
TOBOGGANING
TOBOGGANIST
TOFFEE-APPLE
TOFFEE-NOSED
TOFFISHNESS
TOGGLE-JOINT
TOILET-CLOTH
TOILET-COVER
TOILET-GLASS
TOILET-PAPER
TOILET-TABLE
TOLBUTAMIDE
TOM-AND-JERRY
TOMOGRAPHIC
TONNISHNESS
TONQUIN-BEAN
TONSILLITIC
TONSILLITIS
TONSILOTOMY
TOOTH-DRAWER
TOOTH-PICKER
TOOTH-POWDER

TOP-DRESSING
TOPLOFTICAL
TOPOGRAPHER
TOPOGRAPHIC
TOPONYMICAL
TOP-PRIORITY
TORCH-BEARER
TORCH-SINGER
TORCH-STAVES
TORMENTEDLY
TORPEDINOUS
TORPEDO-BOAT
TORPEDO-BOOM
TORPEDO-TUBE
TORPESCENCE
TORQUE-METER
TORRENTUOUS
TORRIDONIAN
TORSIBILITY
TORSIOGRAPH
TORTICOLLIS
TORTRICIDAE
TORTURINGLY
TOSTICATION
TOTALISATOR
TOTTERINGLY
TOUCH-TYPIST
TOUGH-MINDED
TOURBILLION
TOUS-LES-MOIS
TOWING-BITTS
TOWN-COUNCIL
TOWN-DWELLER
TOWN-MEETING
TOWNSCAPING
TOWNSPEOPLE
TOXICOMANIA
TOXIPHAGOUS
TOXIPHOBIAC
TOXOPHILITE
TRABECULATE
TRACELESSLY
TRACHEARIAN
TRACHEOTOMY
TRACHINIDAE
TRACKLESSLY
TRACK-WALKER
TRADE-FALLEN
TRADESWOMAN
TRADITIONAL
TRADITIONER
TRADUCEMENT
TRADUCINGLY
TRAFFICATOR
TRAFFICKING
TRAFFICLESS
TRAGEDIENNE
TRAGELAPHUS
TRAGI-COMEDY
TRAIN-BEARER
TRAITORHOOD
TRAITORSHIP
TRAMMELLING
TRANSACTION
TRANSALPINE
TRANSANDINE

TRANSCRIBER
TRANSDUCTOR
TRANSEPTATE
TRANSFER-DAY
TRANSFERRED
TRANSFERRER
TRANSFIGURE
TRANSFIXION
TRANSFORMED
TRANSFORMER
TRANSFUSION
TRANSFUSIVE
TRANSHIPPER
TRANSHUMANT
TRANSIENTLY
TRANSILIENT
TRANSIT-DUTY
TRANSLATION
TRANSLATORY
TRANSLOCATE
TRANSLUCENT
TRANSLUNARY
TRANSMARINE
TRANSMITTAL
TRANSMITTED
TRANSMITTER
TRANSPADANE
TRANSPARENT
TRANSPIERCE
TRANSPONDER
TRANSPORTAL
TRANSPORTED
TRANSPORTER
TRANSPOSING
TRANS-SEXUAL
TRANSURANIC
TRANSVERSAL
TRANSVESTIC
TRAPEZIFORM
TRAPEZOIDAL
TRAPPISTINE
TRAVAIL-PAIN
TRAVAIL-PANG
TRAVERSABLE
TREACHEROUS
TREACHETOUR
TREACLINESS
TREASONABLE
TREASONABLY
TREBLE-DATED
TREE-CREEPER
TREE-WORSHIP
TRELLIS-WORK
TREMBLEMENT
TREMBLINGLY
TREMULOUSLY
TRENCHANTLY
TRENCHER-CAP
TRENCHER-FED
TRENCHER-MAN
TRENCH-FEVER
TRENDLE-TAIL
TREND-SETTER
TREPANATION
TREPIDATION
TREPIDATORY

TRESTLE-WORK
TRIANGULATE
TRIBULATION
TRIBUNESHIP
TRIBUNITIAL
TRIBUNITIAN
TRIBUTARILY
TRICERATOPS
TRICHINELLA
TRICHINISED
TRICHINOSED
TRICHINOSIS
TRICHINOTIC
TRICHOMONAD
TRICHOMONAS
TRICHOPTERA
TRICHRONOUS
TRICKSINESS
TRICOLOURED
TRIDOMINIUM
TRIENNIALLY
TRIERARCHAL
TRIFURCATED
TRIMESTRIAL
TRIMORPHISM
TRIMORPHOUS
TRINDLE-TAIL
TRINITARIAN
TRIPERSONAL
TRIPETALOUS
TRIPE-VISAG'D
TRIPHIBIOUS
TRIPHTONGAL
TRIPHYLLOUS
TRIQUETROUS
TRISTICHOUS
TRISULPHINE
TRISYLLABIC
TRISYLLABLE
TRITAGONIST
TRITHEISTIC
TRITHIONATE
TRITURATION
TRIUMVIRATE
TRIVALVULAR
TRIVIALNESS
TROCHILIDAE
TROCHOMETER
TROGLODYTES
TROGLODYTIC
TROLL-MY-DAME
TROMOMETRIC
TROPHOTAXIS
TROPOPHYTIC
TROPOSPHERE
TROTH-PLIGHT
TROUBLESOME
TROUBLE-TOWN
TROUBLE-WORD
TROUBLOUSLY
TROUGH-FAULT
TROUGH-SHELL
TROUS-DE-LOUP
TROUSER-CLIP
TROUSER-SUIT
TROUT-BASKET

TROUT-STREAM
TRUCK-FARMER
TRUCULENTLY
TRUE-DEVOTED
TRUE-HEARTED
TRUE-SEEMING
TRUMPET-CALL
TRUMPET-FISH
TRUMPET-TONE
TRUMPET-TREE
TRUMPET-WOOD
TRUNCHEONED
TRUNCHEONER
TRUNDLE-TAIL
TRUNKSLEEVE
TRUST-BUSTER
TRUSTEESHIP
TRUST-ESTATE
TRUSTWORTHY
TRUTH-TELLER
TRYPANOCIDE
TRYPANOSOMA
TRYPANOSOME
TRYPTOPHANE
TRYSTING-DAY
TSESAREVICH
TUBERACEOUS
TUBERCULATE
TUBERCULISE
TUBERCULOMA
TUBERCULOSE
TUBERCULOUS
TUBIFLOROUS
TUB-THUMPING
TUCKING-MILL
TUFT-HUNTING
TUFTTAFFETA
TULIPOMANIA
TUMEFACTION
TUNABLENESS
TUNEFULNESS
TURBELLARIA
TURBINE-PUMP
TURBO-RAM-JET
TURBULENTLY
TURCOPOLIER
TURFING-IRON
TURGESCENCE
TURGESCENCY
TURNERESQUE
TURNPIKE-MAN
TURRET-CLOCK
TURTLE-SHELL
TURTLE-STONE
TUSSAC-GRASS
TUSSOCK-MOTH
TUTTI-FRUTTI
TWALPENNIES
TWANGLINGLY
TWEEZER-CASE
TWELFTH-CAKE
TWELFTH-TIDE
TWELVEMONTH
TWELVE-PENNY
TWIN-BROTHER
TWITCH-GRASS

TWITTERBONE
TWOFOLDNESS
TWOPENN'ORTH
TWO-STOREYED
TYMPANIFORM
TYPE-FOUNDER
TYPE-FOUNDRY
TYPE-SETTING
TYPE-SPECIES
TYPEWRITING
TYPEWRITTEN
TYPICALNESS
TYPOGRAPHER
TYPOGRAPHIA
TYPOGRAPHIC
TYPOLOGICAL
TYRANNICIDE
TYRANNOUSLY
TYROGLYPHID
TYROGLYPHUS
TYRONENSIAN

U

ULOTRICHOUS
ULTRAMARINE
ULTRA-MODERN
ULTRASONICS
ULTRAVIOLET
UMBELLATELY
UMBRACULATE
UMBRATILOUS
UMBRELLA-ANT
UMBRELLA-FIR
UMBRIFEROUS
UNABOLISHED
UNABROGATED
UNACCOUNTED
UNACCUSABLE
UNACCUSABLY
UNADAPTABLE
UNADDRESSED
UNADVISABLE
UNADVISABLY
UNADVISEDLY
UNAFFECTING
UNAGREEABLE
UNALIENABLE
UNALIENABLY
UNALLOWABLE
UNALTERABLE
UNALTERABLY
UNAMBIGUOUS
UNAMBITIOUS
UNAMENDABLE
UNAMUSINGLY
UNANIMOUSLY
UNANNOTATED
UNANNOUNCED
UNAPOSTOLIC
UNAPPOINTED
UNAPPROVING
UNASHAMEDLY
UNASPIRATED
UNASSERTIVE
UNASSISTING
UNATTAINTED

UNATTEMPTED
UNATTENDING
UNATTENTIVE
UNAUGMENTED
UNAUTHENTIC
UNAVAILABLE
UNAVAILABLY
UNAVERTABLE
UNAVOIDABLE
UNAVOIDABLY
UNAWAKENING
UNAWARENESS
UNBALLASTED
UNBARRICADE
UNBEAUTIFUL
UNBEFITTING
UNBEGINNING
UNBEKNOWNST
UNBELIEVING
UNBENDINGLY
UNBENEFICED
UNBENEFITED
UNBENIGHTED
UNBENIGNANT
UNBESEEMING
UNBIASSEDLY
UNBLAMEABLE
UNBLAMEABLY
UNBLEMISHED
UNBLENCHING
UNBLINDFOLD
UNBOUNDEDLY
UNBREAKABLE
UNBREATHING
UNBROTHERLY
UNBURNISHED
UNBURTHENED
UNCALLED-FOR
UNCANNINESS
UNCANONICAL
UNCANONISED
UNCEASINGLY
UNCERTAINLY
UNCERTAINTY
UNCERTIFIED
UNCHARTERED
UNCHASTENED
UNCHASTISED
UNCHECKABLE
UNCHILDLIKE
UNCHRISTIAN
UNCIVILISED
UNCLASSICAL
UNCLEANNESS
UNCLEARNESS
UNCLUBBABLE
UNCOLLECTED
UNCOMATABLE
UNCOMFORTED
UNCOMMENDED
UNCOMMITTED
UNCOMPACTED
UNCOMPANIED
UNCOMPELLED
UNCOMPLETED
UNCOMPLYING

UNCONCEALED
UNCONCEIVED
UNCONCERNED
UNCONCERTED
UNCONCOCTED
UNCONFESSED
UNCONFIRMED
UNCONGENIAL
UNCONNECTED
UNCONNIVING
UNCONQUERED
UNCONSCIOUS
UNCONTEMNED
UNCONTESTED
UNCONVERTED
UNCONVICTED
UNCONVINCED
UNCORRECTED
UNCORRUPTED
UNCOUNTABLE
UNCOURTEOUS
UNCOUTHNESS
UNCRUSHABLE
UNCUCKOLDED
UNCURTAILED
UNCURTAINED
UNDAUNTEDLY
UNDEBAUCHED
UNDECIDABLE
UNDECIDEDLY
UNDECLINING
UNDEFINABLE
UNDELEGATED
UNDELIGHTED
UNDELIVERED
UNDEPENDING
UNDEPRESSED
UNDERACTION
UNDERBEARER
UNDERBIDDER
UNDERBITTEN
UNDERBREATH
UNDERBRIDGE
UNDERCHARGE
UNDERCLOTHE
UNDERCOVERT
UNDER-DRIVEN
UNDERESPIAL
UNDERGROUND
UNDERGROWTH
UNDERHANDED
UNDERHONEST
UNDER-KEEPER
UNDERLETTER
UNDERLOOKER
UNDERMANNED
UNDERMASTED
UNDERMINING
UNDERPRAISE
UNDERSAWYER
UNDER-SCHOOL
UNDERSELLER
UNDERSHAPEN
UNDERSIGNED
UNDERSLEEVE
UNDERSTATED

UNDERSTRATA
UNDERTAKING
UNDERTENANT
UNDERTHIRST
UNDERVALUER
UNDERVIEWER
UNDERWEIGHT
UNDERWORKER
UNDERWRITER
UNDESCRIBED
UNDESERVING
UNDESIGNING
UNDESIRABLE
UNDESIRABLY
UNDESPOILED
UNDESTROYED
UNDEVELOPED
UNDEVIATING
UNDIGNIFIED
UNDISCERNED
UNDISCLOSED
UNDISCUSSED
UNDISGUISED
UNDISPENSED
UNDISSOLVED
UNDISTILLED
UNDISTORTED
UNDISTURBED
UNDIVERTING
UNDIVIDABLE
UNDIVIDEDLY
UNDOUBTABLE
UNDOUBTEDLY
UNDRAINABLE
UNDRINKABLE
UNDUTIFULLY
UNDYINGNESS
UNELABORATE
UNEMOTIONAL
UNEMOTIONED
UNENCHANTED
UNENDURABLE
UNENDURABLY
UN-ENGLISHED
UNENQUIRING
UNEQUITABLE
UNEQUIVOCAL
UNESCAPABLE
UNESSENTIAL
UNEVIDENCED
UNEXCAVATED
UNEXCITABLE
UNEXCLUSIVE
UNEXERCISED
UNEXHAUSTED
UNEXPECTANT
UNEXPENSIVE
UNEXPERIENT
UNEXPLAINED
UNEXPRESSED
UNFAILINGLY
UNFALTERING
UNFASHIONED
UNFEARFULLY
UNFEATHERED
UNFEELINGLY

UNFEIGNEDLY
UNFERMENTED
UNFEUDALISE
UNFILTRABLE
UNFINISHING
UNFITTINGLY
UNFIXEDNESS
UNFLAPPABLE
UNFLINCHING
UNFLUSTERED
UNFORBIDDEN
UNFOREKNOWN
UNFORFEITED
UNFORGIVING
UNFORGOTTEN
UNFORTIFIED
UNFORTUNATE
UNFOUNDEDLY
UNFRUCTUOUS
UNFULFILLED
UNFURNISHED
UNGALLANTLY
UNGARMENTED
UNGARNISHED
UNGAZED-UPON
UNGENITURED
UNGENTEELLY
UNGENTILITY
UNGETATABLE
UNGODLINESS
UNGRAMMATIC
UNGRATIFIED
UNGUARDEDLY
UNGUERDONED
UNGUICULATE
UNGULIGRADE
UNHABITABLE
UNHACKNEYED
UNHANDINESS
UNHANDSELED
UNHAPPINESS
UNHARBOURED
UNHARMFULLY
UNHARNESSED
UNHARVESTED
UNHAZARDOUS
UNHEALTHFUL
UNHEALTHILY
UNHEEDFULLY
UNHEEDINGLY
UNHIDEBOUND
UNHINGEMENT
UNHOPEFULLY
UNHURRIEDLY
UNHURTFULLY
UNHUSBANDED
UNICELLULAR
UNICOLORATE
UNICOLOROUS
UNICOLOURED
UNICORN-MOTH
UNIDIOMATIC
UNIFICATION
UNIFORMNESS
UNIGENITURE
UNILLUMINED

UNIMPEACHED
UNIMPEDEDLY
UNIMPORTANT
UNIMPRESSED
UNINFLECTED
UNINFORMING
UNINHABITED
UNINHIBITED
UNINITIATED
UNINQUIRING
UNINSCRIBED
UNINSPIRING
UNINUCLEATE
UNINVENTIVE
UNINVIDIOUS
UNIPERSONAL
UNIPOLARITY
UNISERIALLY
UNISEXUALLY
UNIVALVULAR
UNIVERSALLY
UNJAUNDICED
UNKNOWINGLY
UNKNOWNNESS
UNLABORIOUS
UNLABOURING
UNLEARNEDLY
UNLEISURELY
UNLIGHTENED
UNLIGHTSOME
UNLIMITEDLY
UNLIQUEFIED
UNLISTENING
UNLOOKED-FOR
UNLOVERLIKE
UNLUCKINESS
UNLUXURIANT
UNLUXURIOUS
UNMALICIOUS
UNMALLEABLE
UNMANLINESS
UNMARRIABLE
UNMASCULINE
UNMATCHABLE
UNMEANINGLY
UNMECHANISE
UNMEDITATED
UNMELODIOUS
UNMERCENARY
UNMERITABLE
UNMERITEDLY
UNMINDFULLY
UNMITIGABLE
UNMITIGABLY
UNMITIGATED
UNMODULATED
UNMOISTENED
UNMORALISED
UNMORTGAGED
UNMORTIFIED
UNMURMURING
UNMUSICALLY
UNMUTILATED
UNNATURALLY
UNNAVIGABLE
UNNAVIGATED

UNNECESSARY
UNNEEDFULLY
UNNOURISHED
UNOBNOXIOUS
UNOBSERVANT
UNOBSERVING
UNOBTRUSIVE
UNOFFENDING
UNOFFENSIVE
UNOFFICERED
UNOFFICIOUS
UNOPERATIVE
UNORGANISED
UNORIGINATE
UNORTHODOXY
UNPAINTABLE
UNPALATABLE
UNPALATABLY
UNPARAGONED
UNPARDONING
UNPASSIONED
UNPATHWAYED
UNPATRIOTIC
UNPATTERNED
UNPEACEABLE
UNPEDIGREED
UNPENSIONED
UNPERCEIVED
UNPERFECTLY
UNPERFORMED
UNPERISHING
UNPERPLEXED
UNPERSUADED
UNPERTURBED
UNPERVERTED
UNPITIFULLY
UNPITYINGLY
UNPLASTERED
UNPLAUSIBLE
UNPLAUSIBLY
UNPOLARISED
UNPOLITICAL
UNPOPULARLY
UNPORTIONED
UNPOSSESSED
UNPRACTICAL
UNPRACTISED
UNPREACHING
UNPREFERRED
UNPRESUMING
UNPREVENTED
UNPRINTABLE
UNPROFESSED
UNPROFITING
UNPROJECTED
UNPROMISING
UNPROPHETIC
UNPROTECTED
UNPROTESTED
UNPROVIDENT
UNPROVOKING
UNPUBLISHED
UNPURCHASED
UNQUALIFIED
UNQUALITIED
UNQUANTISED

UNQUEENLIKE
UNQUICKENED
UNQUIETNESS
UNRAVELLING
UNRAVELMENT
UNREACHABLE
UNREADINESS
UNREALISTIC
UNREASONING
UNRECALLING
UNRECEIPTED
UNRECEPTIVE
UNRECLAIMED
UNRECOUNTED
UNRECOVERED
UNRECTIFIED
UNREDRESSED
UNREDUCIBLE
UNREFLECTED
UNREFRACTED
UNREFRESHED
UNREGARDING
UNREGULATED
UNREHEARSED
UNREJOICING
UNRELENTING
UNRELIGIOUS
UNRELUCTANT
UNREMAINING
UNREMITTENT
UNREMITTING
UNREMOVABLE
UNREPENTANT
UNREPENTING
UNREPOSEFUL
UNREPRIEVED
UNREPROVING
UNREPUGNANT
UNREQUISITE
UNRESCINDED
UNRESENTFUL
UNRESENTING
UNRESISTING
UNRESPECTED
UNRESTINGLY
UNRESTRAINT
UNRETENTIVE
UNRETURNING
UNREVEALING
UNREWARDING
UNRIGHTEOUS
UNROMANISED
UNSANDALLED
UNSATIATING
UNSATIRICAL
UNSATISFIED
UNSATURATED
UNSAVOURILY
UNSCHOLARLY
UNSCISSORED
UNSCRATCHED
UNSEAWORTHY
UNSECTARIAN
UNSEGMENTED
UNSELFISHLY
UNSENSITIVE

UNSENTENCED
UNSEPARABLE
UNSETTLEDLY
UNSHAKEABLE
UNSHAKEABLY
UNSHARPENED
UNSHELTERED
UNSHRINKING
UNSHUNNABLE
UNSIGHED-FOR
UNSKILFULLY
UNSLUMBROUS
UNSMILINGLY
UNSOCIALISM
UNSOCIALITY
UNSOFTENING
UNSOLDIERLY
UNSOLICITED
UNSOUNDABLE
UNSOUNDNESS
UNSPARINGLY
UNSPEAKABLE
UNSPEAKABLY
UNSPECIFIED
UNSPIRITUAL
UNSPRINKLED
UNSTAIDNESS
UNSTAINABLE
UNSTEADFAST
UNSUBDUABLE
UNSUBJECTED
UNSUBMERGED
UNSUCCEEDED
UNSUCCOURED
UNSUPPORTED
UNSURPASSED
UNSUSPECTED
UNSUSPENDED
UNSUSPICION
UNSUSTAINED
UNSWALLOWED
UNSWEETENED
UNSYLLABLED
UNTAINTEDLY
UNTAMEDNESS
UNTARNISHED
UNTEACHABLE
UNTECHNICAL
UNTEMPERING
UNTERRIFIED
UNTHICKENED
UNTHINKABLE
UNTHOUGHT-OF
UNTIMEOUSLY
UNTINCTURED
UNTORMENTED
UNTOUCHABLE
UNTRACEABLE
UNTRACTABLE
UNTRAVELLED
UNTRAVERSED
UNTREATABLE
UNTREMBLING
UNTREMULOUS
UNTUNEFULLY
UNUSUALNESS

UNUTTERABLE
UNUTTERABLY
UNVARNISHED
UNVENERABLE
UNVERACIOUS
UNVISITABLE
UNVITRIFIED
UNVOCALISED
UNVULGARISE
UNWANDERING
UNWARRANTED
UNWEARIABLE
UNWEARIABLY
UNWEARIEDLY
UNWEATHERED
UNWEDGEABLE
UNWEETINGLY
UNWELCOMELY
UNWHOLESOME
UNWILLINGLY
UNWINKINGLY
UNWISHED-FOR
UNWITHERING
UNWITHSTOOD
UNWITNESSED
UNWITTINGLY
UNWOUNDABLE
UP-AND-COMING
UPCAST-SHAFT
UPHOLSTERER
UPHOLSTRESS
UPLIFTINGLY
UPPING-BLOCK
UPPING-STOCK
UPPING-STONE
UPRIGHTNESS
URANOGRAPHY
URANOPLASTY
URANOSCOPUS
URCHIN-SHOWS
URINIFEROUS
URINIPAROUS
UROCHORDATE
URTICACEOUS
URTICARIOUS
USELESSNESS
USUCAPTIBLE
UTILISATION
UTILITARIAN
UTOPIANISER
UTRICULARIA

V

VACATIONIST
VACCINATION
VACCINATORY
VACILLATING
VACILLATION
VACILLATORY
VACUOLATION
VACUOUSNESS
VACUUM-BRAKE
VACUUM-CLEAN
VACUUM-FLASK
VAGABONDAGE
VAGABONDISE

VAGABONDISH
VAGABONDISM
VAIVODESHIP
VALEDICTION
VALEDICTORY
VALENTINIAN
VALLECULATE
VALLISNERIA
VALUATIONAL
VANISHINGLY
VANTAGELESS
VAPORIMETER
VAPORISABLE
VAPOURINGLY
VARIABILITY
VARIATIONAL
VARICELLOID
VARICELLOUS
VARIEGATION
VARIOLATION
VARIOUSNESS
VARNISH-TREE
VARSOVIENNE
VASCULARISE
VASCULARITY
VASCULIFORM
VASODILATOR
VASOPRESSIN
VASOPRESSOR
VATICINATOR
VECTORSCOPE
VEDETTE-BOAT
VEHMGERICHT
VELLICATION
VELOCIPEDER
VELVETINESS
VELVET-PAPER
VENATICALLY
VENDÉMIAIRE
VENDIBILITY
VENDITATION
VENEFICIOUS
VENEREOLOGY
VENESECTION
VENTILATION
VENTILATIVE
VENTRICULAR
VENTRICULUS
VENTRILOQUY
VENTURESOME
VENTURINGLY
VENTUROUSLY
VERACIOUSLY
VERBENACEAE
VERBERATION
VERBIGERATE
VERBOSENESS
VERD-ANTIQUE
VERDE-ANTICO
VERDURELESS
VERIDICALLY
VERISIMILAR
VERMICULATE
VERMICULITE
VERMICULOUS
VERMINATION

VERMIVOROUS
VERRUCIFORM
VERSABILITY
VERSATILELY
VERSATILITY
VERSE-MAKING
VERSE-MONGER
VERSLIBRIST
VERTEBRALLY
VERTEBRATED
VERTICALITY
VERTIGINOUS
VESICULATED
VESPERTINAL
VESTIMENTAL
VESTRY-CLERK
VESUVIANITE
VEXATIOUSLY
VEXILLATION
VIBRATILITY
VIBRATIONAL
VICAR-CHORAL
VICAR-FORANE
VICARIOUSLY
VICE-ADMIRAL
VICEGERENCY
VICE-MARSHAL
VICEROYALTY
VICEROYSHIP
VICHYSSOISE
VICIOUSNESS
VICISSITUDE
VICTORYLESS
VICTUALLAGE
VICTUALLESS
VICTUALLING
VILLANOUSLY
VILLICATION
VINAIGRETTE
VINCIBILITY
VINDICATION
VINDICATIVE
VINDICATORY
VINE-DISEASE
VINE-DRESSER
VINE-FRETTER
VINICULTURE
VIOLONCELLO
VIRIDESCENT
VIRILESCENT
VIRTUE-PROOF
VISCOMETRIC
VISCOUNTESS
VISCOUSNESS
VISIBLENESS
VISITING-DAY
VITICULTURE
VITRAILLIST
VITRESCENCE
VITRESCIBLE
VITRIFIABLE
VITUPERABLE
VITUPERATOR
VIVACIOUSLY
VIVACISSIMO
VIVISECTION

VIVISECTIVE
VOCIFERANCE
VOCIFERATOR
VOIVODESHIP
VOLCANICITY
VOLCANOLOGY
VOLITIONARY
VOLUBLENESS
VOLUMOMETER
VOLUNTARILY
VOLUNTARISM
VOLUNTATIVE
VOMERONASAL
VOODOOISTIC
VOORTREKKER
VORACIOUSLY
VORTIGINOUS
VOUCHSAFING
VULCANICITY
VULCANOLOGY
VULNERATION

W
WAGE-EARNING
WAGGISHNESS
WAGNERESQUE
WAGON-WRIGHT
WAINSCOTING
WAINSCOTTED
WAIST-ANCHOR
WAITING-LIST
WAITING-MAID
WAITING-ROOM
WAIVODESHIP
WAKEFULNESS
WALDGRAVINE
WALKING-BEAM
WALKING-CANE
WALKING-FISH
WALKING-LADY
WALKING-LEAF
WALKING-PART
WALKING-TOAD
WALKING-TWIG
WALL-MUSTARD
WALNUT-JUICE
WANDERINGLY
WANDERJAHRE
WANT-CATCHER
WAPPENSCHAW
WAPPER-JAWED
WAREHOUSING
WARLIKENESS
WARM-B-LOODED
WARM-HEARTED
WARRANTABLE
WARRANTABLY
WASHERWOMAN
WASH-GILDING
WASHING-BLUE
WASHING-SODA
WASH-LEATHER
WASPISHNESS
WASP-TONGUED
WASP-WAISTED
WASSAIL-BOUT

WASSAIL-BOWL
WASTE-BASKET
WASTEL-BREAD
WASTERFULLY
WATCH-MAKING
WATCH-POCKET
WATCH-SPRING
WATER-BAILIE
WATER-BARREL
WATER-BEARER
WATER-BEETLE
WATER-BOTTLE
WATER-BOUGET
WATER-CANNON
WATER-CEMENT
WATER-CLOSET
WATER-COLOUR
WATER-COOLED
WATER-COOLER
WATERCOURSE
WATER-DOCTOR
WATERED-DOWN
WATER-ENGINE
WATER-FINDER
WATER-HAMMER
WATERING-CAN
WATERING-CAP
WATERING-POT
WATER-JACKET
WATERLOGGED
WATER-MEADOW
WATER-MONKEY
WATER-PEPPER
WATER-PISTOL
WATER-PURPIE
WATER-SKIING
WATER-SOUCHY
WATER-SPIDER
WATER-SPLASH
WATER-SPRING
WATER-SPRITE
WATER-SUPPLY
WATER-TUNNEL
WATER-VIOLET
WAX-CHANDLER
WAX-PAINTING
WAYWARDNESS
WEAK-HEARTED
WEAK-SIGHTED
WEALTHINESS
WEAPON-SALVE
WEAPONSCHAW
WEARISOMELY
WEASAND-PIPE
WEASEL-FACED
WEATHERCOCK
WEATHER-FEND
WEATHER-GAGE
WEATHER-GALL
WEATHER-HELM
WEATHERMOST
WEATHER-ROLL
WEATHER-SHIP
WEATHER-SIDE
WEATHER-SIGN
WEATHER-WISE

WEB-FINGERED
WEDDING-CAKE
WEDDING-RING
WEDGE-HEELED
WEDGE-SHAPED
WEDGE-TAILED
WEEDING-FORK
WEEDING-HOOK
WEEPING-RIPE
WEEPING-ROCK
WEEPING-TREE
WEIGH-BRIDGE
WEIGHTINESS
WEISMANNISM
WELCOMENESS
WELDABILITY
WELL-ADVISED
WELL-BEHAVED
WELL-BELOVED
WELL-COUPLED
WELL-DERIVED
WELL-DESIRED
WELL-ENTERED
WELL-FOUNDED
WELLINGTONS
WELL-JUDGING
WELL-LOOKING
WELL-MEANING
WELL-ORDERED
WELL-ROUNDED
WELL-SINKING
WELL-THUMBED
WELL-WISHING
WELSH-RABBIT
WELWITSCHIA
WENSLEYDALE
WEREWOLFISH
WEREWOLFISM
WESLEYANISM
WEST-BY-NORTH
WEST-BY-SOUTH
WESTERNMOST
WESTMINSTER
WESTPHALIAN
WHALE-FISHER
WHALING-PORT
WHAT-D'YE-CALL
WHATSOMEVER
WHEAT-MILDEW
WHEEDLESOME
WHEEL-ANIMAL
WHEELBARROW
WHEEL-CUTTER
WHEEL-PLOUGH
WHEEL-WINDOW
WHEELWRIGHT
WHENCEFORTH
WHEREABOUTS
WHERESOEVER
WHEREWITHAL
WHEYISHNESS
WHICHSOEVER
WHICKET-DOOR
WHIFFLETREE
WHIGMALEERY
WHIMSICALLY

WHIPPING-BOY
WHIPPING-TOP
WHIPPLETREE
WHISKERANDO
WHISKEYFIED
WHISKY-LIVER
WHISTLE-FISH
WHISTLE-STOP
WHISTLINGLY
WHIST-PLAYER
WHITE-BILLED
WHITE-BONNET
WHITE-BOTTLE
WHITEBOYISM
WHITECHAPEL
WHITE-COLLAR
WHITE-EYELID
WHITE-FOOTED
WHITE-HANDED
WHITE-HEADED
WHITE-RUMPED
WHITETHROAT
WHITEWASHER
WHITE-WINGED
WHITHERWARD
WHITING-POUT
WHITING-TIME
WHITISHNESS
WHITLEATHER
WHITLOW-WORT
WHITSUNTIDE
WHITSUNWEEK
WHOLE-FOOTED
WHOLE-HOGGER
WHOLE-HOOFED
WHOLE-LENGTH
WHOLESOMELY
WHOLE-SOULED
WHOLE-STITCH
WHOREMASTER
WHOREMONGER
WHORISHNESS
WHOSESOEVER
WIDDERSHINS
WIDE-CHAPPED
WIDE-WATERED
WIDOWERHOOD
WIDOW'S-BENCH
WILD-FOWLING
WILLINGNESS
WILL-WORSHIP
WINDCHEATER
WIND-FURNACE
WINDLESTRAE
WINDLESTRAW
WINDOW-BARNE
WINDOW-BLIND
WINDOW-FRAME
WINDOW-GLASS
WINDSOR-SOAP
WINE-BIBBING
WINE-BISCUIT
WINE-GROWING
WINE-MEASURE
WING-AND-WING
WING-LOADING

WINNINGNESS
WINNING-POST
WINSOMENESS
WINTER-APPLE
WINTER-BERRY
WINTER-BLOOM
WINTER-CRESS
WINTERGREEN
WINTER'S-BARK
WINTER-WHEAT
WIRE-DANCING
WIRE-DRAWING
WIRE-NETTING
WIRE-PULLING
WIREWORKING
WISDOM-TOOTH
WISE-HEARTED
WISHFULNESS
WISHING-BONE
WISHING-TREE
WISHING-WELL
WISHTONWISH
WISTFULNESS
WITCH-DOCTOR
WITCHES-MEAT
WITCH-FINDER
WITCH-RIDDEN
WITENAGEMOT
WITHERINGLY
WITHERSHINS
WITHER-WRUNG
WITHOUT-DOOR
WITHSTANDER
WITLESSNESS
WOBBLE-BOARD
WOLF-WHISTLE
WOMANLINESS
WOMAN-VESTED
WONDERFULLY
WONDERINGLY
WOOD-ALCOHOL

WOOD-ANEMONE
WOOD-CARVING
WOODCUTTING
WOOD-FRETTER
WOOD-NAPHTHA
WOOD-SWALLOW
WOOD-VINEGAR
WOOD-WARBLER
WOODY-TONGUE
WOOL-BEARING
WOOL-CARDING
WOOL-COMBING
WOOL-GROWING
WOOLLEN-MILL
WOOL-STAPLER
WORDISHNESS
WORD-PAINTER
WORD-PERFECT
WORD-PICTURE
WORKABILITY
WORKING-BEAM
WORKING-EDGE
WORKING-FACE
WORKMANLIKE
WORKMANSHIP
WORLDLINESS
WORLDLY-WISE
WORM-GEARING
WORSHIPABLE
WORSHIPLESS
WORSHIPPING
WORSTED-WORK
WORTHLESSLY
WRANGLESOME
WRECK-MASTER
WRINGING-WET
WRING-STAVES
WRITING-BOOK
WRITING-CASE
WRITING-DESK
WRONG-HEADED

WRONG-MINDED
WROUGHT-IRON

X

XANTHOCHROI
XANTHOPHYLL
XANTHOXYLUM
X-CHROMOSOME
XENODOCHIUM
XENOGENESIS
XENOGENETIC
XENOGLOSSIA
XENOMORPHIC
XENOPLASTIC
XERANTHEMUM
XEROMORPHIC
XEROPHILOUS
XEROTRIPSIS
XIPHOPAGOUS
XYLOCARPOUS
XYLOGRAPHER
XYLOGRAPHIC
XYLOPHAGOUS
XYLOPHILOUS
XYLOPHONIST
XYRIDACEOUS

Y

YACKETY-YACK
YATTERINGLY
Y-CHROMOSOME
YEARD-HUNGER
YEARD-HUNGRY
YEAST-POWDER
YELLOW-AMMER
YELLOW-EARTH
YELLOW-FEVER
YELLOW-METAL
YESTERNIGHT
YINCE-ERRAND
YTTRIFEROUS

YTTROCERITE
YUGOSLAVIAN

Z

ZANTHOXYLUM
ZEALOUSNESS
ZEOLITIFORM
ZERO-GRAZING
ZESTFULNESS
ZINCIFEROUS
ZINCOGRAPHY
ZINKIFEROUS
ZIP-FASTENER
ZOANTHARIAN
ZOANTHROPIC
ZONOTRICHIA
ZOOCHEMICAL
ZOODENDRIUM
ZOOGONIDIUM
ZOOGRAFTING
ZOOGRAPHIST
ZOOMAGNETIC
ZOOMORPHISM
ZOOPHYTICAL
ZOOPLANKTON
ZOOSPERMIUM
ZOOTECHNICS
ZOOTHEISTIC
ZOROASTRIAN
ZYGOCARDIAC
ZYGOMORPHIC
ZYGOMYCETES
ZYGOPHYLLUM
ZYGOPLEURAL
ZYMOLOGICAL
ZYMOSIMETER
ZYMOTECHNIC
ZYMOTICALLY

A

ABBEY-COUNTER
ABBREVIATION
ABBREVIATORY
ABBREVIATURE
ABOLITIONARY
ABOLITIONISM
ABOLITIONIST
ABORIGINALLY
ABORTIVENESS
ABSENT-MINDED
ABSINTHIATED
ABSOLUTENESS
ABSORPTIVITY
ABSQUATULATE

ABSTEMIOUSLY
ABSTRACTEDLY
ABSTRACTNESS
ABSTRUSENESS
ACADEMICALLY
ACANTHACEOUS
ACARIDOMATIA
ACARODOMATIA
ACCELERATION
ACCELERATIVE
ACCELERATORY
ACCENTUALITY
ACCENTUATION
ACCIACCATURA
ACCIDENTALLY
ACCOMMODABLE

ACCOMMODATOR
ACCOMPANYIST
ACCOMPLISHED
ACCOMPLISHER
ACCORDIONIST
ACCOUCHEMENT
ACCOUTREMENT
ACCUMULATION
ACCUMULATIVE
ACCURATENESS
ACCUSATORIAL
ACETALDEHYDE
ACHLAMYDEOUS
ACOUSTICALLY
ACQUAINTANCE
ACQUIESCENCE

ACRE'S-BREADTH
ACROAMATICAL
ACRONYCHALLY
ACROPHONETIC
ACTION-TAKING
ADAPTABILITY
ADAPTIVENESS
ADDER'S-TONGUE
ADDICTEDNESS
ADDITIONALLY
ADDLE-BRAINED
ADEQUATENESS
ADHESIVENESS
ADJECTIVALLY
ADJUDICATION
ADJUNCTIVELY
ADMINICULATE
ADMINISTRANT
ADMINISTRATE
ADMONISHMENT
ADORABLENESS
ADSCITITIOUS
ADULTERATION
ADULTEROUSLY
ADVANTAGEOUS
ADVENTITIOUS
ADVERBIALISE
ADVISABILITY
AECIDIOSPORE
AERODYNAMICS
AEROEMBOLISM
AERONAUTICAL
AERONEUROSIS
AEROPLANKTON
AEROSIDERITE
AESTHESIOGEN
AESTHETICIAN
AESTHETICISE
AESTHETICISM
AESTHETICIST
AETHRIOSCOPE
AETIOLOGICAL
AFFECTEDNESS
AFFECTIONATE
AFFLUENTNESS
AFFORESTABLE
AFFRIGHTEDLY
AFFRIGHTENED
AFFRIGHTMENT
AFFRONTINGLY
AFORETHOUGHT
AFRO-AMERICAN
AFTERBURNING
AFTERTHOUGHT
AGALMATOLITE
AGAMOGENESIS
AGGLOMERATED
AGGLUTINABLE
AGGLUTINOGEN
AGGRESSIVELY
AGREEABILITY
AGRIBUSINESS
AGRICULTURAL
AILOUROPHILE
AILOUROPHOBE
AILUROPHILIA

AILUROPHOBIA
AIR-AMBULANCE
AIR-COMMODORE
AIR-CONDITION
AIRCRAFTSMAN
ALDER-LIEFEST
ALDERMANLIKE
ALDERMANSHIP
ALEXIPHARMIC
ALHAMBRESQUE
ALIENABILITY
ALIMENTATION
ALIMENTATIVE
ALKALESCENCE
ALKALESCENCY
ALLITERATION
ALLITERATIVE
ALL-ROUNDNESS
ALLUSIVENESS
ALPHABETICAL
ALPHAMERICAL
ALPHANUMERIC
ALSTROEMERIA
ALTALTISSIMO
ALTERABILITY
ALTITUDINOUS
AMALGAMATION
AMALGAMATIVE
AMARANTACEAE
AMATEURISHLY
AMBASSADRESS
AMBIDEXTROUS
AMBITIONLESS
AMELIORATION
AMELIORATIVE
AMENABLENESS
AMENTIFEROUS
AMICABLENESS
AMISSIBILITY
AMITOTICALLY
AMORTISATION
AMPELOGRAPHY
AMPHIBRACHIC
AMPHICTYONIC
AMPHIGASTRIA
AMPHISBAENIC
AMPHISTOMOUS
AMPHITHEATRE
AMPHITROPOUS
AMYGDALOIDAL
ANABAPTISTIC
ANACATHARSIS
ANACATHARTIC
ANAEROBIOSIS
ANAEROBIOTIC
ANAESTHETISE
ANAESTHETIST
ANAGOGICALLY
ANAGRAMMATIC
ANALOGICALLY
ANALPHABETIC
ANALYTICALLY
ANAMORPHOSIS
ANAPAESTICAL
ANAPHYLACTIC
ANARCHICALLY

ANARTHROUSLY
ANASTIGMATIC
ANATHEMATISE
ANATOMICALLY
ANCHORETICAL
ANEMOGRAPHIC
ANEMOPHILOUS
ANENCEPHALIA
ANENCEPHALIC
ANGELICA-TREE
ANGIOCARPOUS
ANGIOSPERMAE
ANGIOSPERMAL
ANGIOSTOMOUS
ANGLOPHOBIAC
ANGUILLIFORM
ANIMADVERTER
ANIMALCULIST
ANNIHILATION
ANNIHILATIVE
ANNOUNCEMENT
ANNUNCIATION
ANNUNCIATIVE
ANOTHERGUESS
ANTAGONISTIC
ANTARTHRITIC
ANTASTHMATIC
ANTECEDENTLY
ANTEDILUVIAL
ANTEDILUVIAN
ANTEMERIDIAN
ANTEPRANDIAL
ANTHELMINTIC
ANTHEROZOOID
ANTHOCARPOUS
ANTHOPHILOUS
ANTHOXANTHIN
ANTHROPOGENY
ANTHROPOGONY
ANTHROPOIDAL
ANTHROPOLOGY
ANTHROPOTOMY
ANTI-AIRCRAFT
ANTIBACCHIUS
ANTIBARBARUS
ANTICATHOLIC
ANTICHTHONES
ANTICIPATION
ANTICIPATIVE
ANTICIPATORY
ANTICLERICAL
ANTICYCLONIC
ANTIFRICTION
ANTI-GALLICAN
ANTIGROPELOS
ANTILEGOMENA
ANTIMACASSAR
ANTIMALARIAL
ANTIMETABOLE
ANTIMNEMONIC
ANTI-NATIONAL
ANTINEUTRINO
ANTIPARALLEL
ANTIPARTICLE
ANTIPATHETIC
ANTIPERIODIC

ANTIPETALOUS
ANTIPHONICAL
ANTIPHRASTIC
ANTIPRURITIC
ANTIRACHITIC
ANTISEMITISM
ANTISEPALOUS
ANTISOCIALLY
ANTISTROPHIC
ANTISTROPHON
ANTITHEISTIC
ANTITHETICAL
ANTITHROMBIN
ANTONINIANUS
APAGOGICALLY
APERIODICITY
APICULTURIST
APLANOGAMETE
APOCHROMATIC
APOCYNACEOUS
APODEICTICAL
APOGEOTROPIC
APOLITICALLY
APOLLINARIAN
APOLOGETICAL
APOPLECTICAL
APOSTOLICISM
APOSTOLICITY
APOSTROPHISE
APOTHEGMATIC
APPARENTNESS
APPARITIONAL
APPENDECTOMY
APPENDICITIS
APPENDICULAR
APPERCEPTION
APPERCEPTIVE
APPERCIPIENT
APPERTAINING
APPETISEMENT
APPETISINGLY
APPLAUDINGLY
APPLAUSIVELY
APPLE-BLOSSOM
APPOGGIATURA
APPOSITENESS
APPOSITIONAL
APPRAISEMENT
APPRECIATION
APPRECIATIVE
APPRECIATORY
APPREHENSION
APPREHENSIVE
APPROACHABLE
APPROACH-SHOT
APPROPRIATOR
APPURTENANCE
APRON-STRINGS
ARAEOSYSTYLE
ARBORESCENCE
ARBORISATION
ARCHDEACONRY
ARCHEGONIATE
ARCHILOCHIAN
ARCHIPELAGIC
ARCHITECTURE

ARFVEDSONITE
ARGILLACEOUS
ARISTOCRATIC
ARISTOLOCHIA
ARISTOPHANIC
ARISTOTELEAN
ARISTOTELIAN
ARISTOTELISM
ARITHMETICAL
ARITHMOMETER
ARMOUR-BEARER
ARMOUR-PLATED
ARTICULATELY
ARTICULATION
ARTICULATORY
ARTIFICIALLY
ARTILLERY-MAN
ARTIODACTYLA
ARTISTICALLY
ASCENSION-DAY
ASCLEPIADEAN
ASPARAGINASE
ASPHYXIATION
ASPIRINGNESS
ASSASSINATOR
ASSENTANEOUS
ASSESSORSHIP
ASSEVERATING
ASSEVERATION
ASSIBILATION
ASSIMILATION
ASSIMILATIVE
ASSORTEDNESS
ASSUEFACTION
ASTONISHMENT
ASTOUNDINGLY
ASTRINGENTLY
ASTROGEOLOGY
ASTROLOGICAL
ASTRONAUTICS
ASTRONOMICAL
ASTROPHYSICS
ASYMMETRICAL
ASYMPTOTICAL
ASYNCHRONISM
ASYNCHRONOUS
ATHEOLOGICAL
ATHEROMATOUS
ATHLETICALLY
ATMOSPHERICS
ATTITUDINISE
ATTORNEYSHIP
ATTRACTINGLY
ATTRACTIVELY
AUGMENTATION
AUGMENTATIVE
AUSCULTATION
AUSCULTATORY
AUSPICIOUSLY
AUSTRALASIAN
AUSTRONESIAN
AUTHENTICATE
AUTHENTICITY
AUTHOCHTHONY
AUTHORISABLE
AUTOCATALYSE

AUTOCHTHONES
AUTODIDACTIC
AUTO-IMMUNITY
AUTOMOBILISM
AUTOMOBILIST
AUTOMORPHISM
AUTOPTICALLY
AVAILABILITY
AVANT-GARDISM
AVANT-GARDIST
AVARICIOUSLY
AVERRUNCATOR
AVITAMINOSIS
AVOWABLENESS
AWE-INSPIRING
AYE-REMAINING

B

BABINGTONITE
BABY-SNATCHER
BACCALAUREAN
BACCHANALIAN
BACHELOR-GIRL
BACHELORHOOD
BACHELORSHIP
BACKBONELESS
BACKBREAKING
BACKSTARTING
BACKSWORDMAN
BACKWARDNESS
BACKWOODSMAN
BACKWOUNDING
BACTERICIDAL
BACTERIOLOGY
BACTERIOSTAT
BADGER-LEGGED
BAGGAGE-TRAIN
BAKING-POWDER
BALAAM-BASKET
BALAAMITICAL
BALANCE-SHEET
BALANCE-WHEEL
BALLADMONGER
BALLANWRASSE
BALL-BEARINGS
BALLET-DANCER
BALLET-MASTER
BALLETOMANIA
BALNEOLOGIST
BANDERILLERO
BANDERSNATCH
BANTAM-WEIGHT
BARBER-MONGER
BARE-BREACHED
BARMY-BRAINED
BAROMETRICAL
BARON-OFFICER
BARRATROUSLY
BARRIER-CREAM
BARRISTERIAL
BASELESSNESS
BASE-SPIRITED
BASIDIOSPORE
BASKET-MAKING
BASSO-RELIEVO
BASSO-RILIEVO

BASTARD-TITLE
BASTINADOING
BATE-BREEDING
BATHING-DRESS
BATHYPELAGIC
BATTERING-RAM
BATTLEMENTED
BATTOLOGICAL
BEACHCOMBING
BEARABLENESS
BEATIFICALLY
BEAUMONTAGUE
BECOMINGNESS
BEDAZZLEMENT
BED-OF-JUSTICE
BEETLE-BROWED
BEETLE-HEADED
BEGGARLINESS
BEHAVIOURISM
BEHAVIOURIST
BELITTLEMENT
BELL-BOTTOMED
BELLETRISTIC
BELLIGERENCE
BELLIGERENCY
BELLY-LANDING
BENCH-WARRANT
BEND-SINISTER
BENEFACTRESS
BENEFICENTLY
BENEFICIALLY
BENEVOLENTLY
BENIGHTENING
BENJAMIN-TREE
BENUMBEDNESS
BENZALDEHYDE
BEQUEATHABLE
BEQUEATHMENT
BERTHOLLETIA
BERTILLONAGE
BESEECHINGLY
BESOTTEDNESS
BESPECTACLED
BETWEEN-DECKS
BEWILDERMENT
BEWITCHINGLY
BIBBLE-BABBLE
BIBLIOGRAPHY
BIBLIOLOGIST
BIBLIOMANIAC
BIBLIOPEGIST
BIBLIOPHOBIA
BIBLIOPOLIST
BICENTENNIAL
BIGNONIACEAE
BILATERALISM
BILHARZIASIS
BILHARZIOSIS
BILINGUALISM
BILLIARD-BALL
BILLINGSGATE
BIMILLENNIUM
BIOCHEMISTRY
BIOFLAVONOID
BIOGEOGRAPHY
BIOGRAPHICAL

BIOLOGICALLY
BIOMECHANICS
BIOMETRICIAN
BIOSYNTHESIS
BIOSYNTHETIC
BIRD-CATCHING
BIRDING-PIECE
BIRD'S-NESTING
BIREFRINGENT
BIRTHDAY-BOOK
BIRTHDAY-SUIT
BLABBERMOUTH
BLACK-AND-BLUE
BLACKBALLING
BLACKBIRDING
BLACKCURRANT
BLACK-FISHING
BLACKGUARDLY
BLACK-HEARTED
BLACKPUDDING
BLACK-QUARTER
BLACK-VISAGED
BLADDER-WRACK
BLAMABLENESS
BLAMEFULNESS
BLANC-DE-CHINE
BLANDISHMENT
BLAST-FURNACE
BLASTOSPHERE
BLASTULATION
BLATHERSKITE
BLENNORRHOEA
BLETHERATION
BLETHERSKATE
BLISSFULNESS
BLISTER-STEEL
BLITHESOMELY
BLOCKBUSTING
BLOOD-BROTHER
BLOODLETTING
BLOOD-PUDDING
BLOODSTAINED
BLOODSUCKING
BLOODTHIRSTY
BLOODY-MINDED
BLOW-MOULDING
BLUESTOCKING
BLUNDERINGLY
BLUSTERINGLY
BOARDING-PIKE
BOARD-MEASURE
BOASTFULNESS
BOBBY-DAZZLER
BODY-SNATCHER
BOILING-POINT
BOISTEROUSLY
BOLTING-HUTCH
BOMBACACEOUS
BOMB-DISPOSAL
BONNET-MONKEY
BONNY-CLABBER
BOOGIE-WOOGIE
BOOKING-CLERK
BOOK-LEARNING
BOOK-SCORPION
BOOTLESSNESS

BORAGINACEAE
BOROUGH-REEVE
BOTTLE-HOLDER
BOTTLE-SLIDER
BOTTLE-WASHER
BOTTOM-SAWYER
BOUGAINVILIA
BOULEVARDIER
BOUND-BAILIFF
BOW-COMPASSES
BOWLING-ALLEY
BOWLING-GREEN
BRACHYCEPHAL
BRACHYDACTYL
BRACHYGRAPHY
BRACKISHNESS
BRAINWASHING
BRAMBLE-BERRY
BRAMBLE-FINCH
BRANCHIOPODA
BRANDING-IRON
BRANDY-BOTTLE
BRANDY-PAWNEE
BRASS-BOUNDER
BRASSFOUNDER
BREAD-CHIPPER
BREAKFAST-SET
BREAK-PROMISE
BREAKTHROUGH
BREAST-GIRDLE
BREASTPLOUGH
BREASTSTROKE
BREASTSUMMER
BREATHALYSER
BREATHALYZER
BREATHLESSLY
BREATHTAKING
BREECHES-BUOY
BREECHLOADER
BREVIPENNATE
BRICKFIELDER
BRICK-NOGGING
BRIDE-CHAMBER
BRIGADE-MAJOR
BRILLIANTINE
BRIMFULLNESS
BRINKMANSHIP
BRISTOL-BOARD
BRISTOL-BRICK
BROADCASTING
BROKEN-BACKED
BROKEN-WINDED
BROMELIACEAE
BRONCO-BUSTER
BRONTOSAURUS
BRONZE-PIGEON
BROTHER-IN-LAW
BUCCANEERING
BUCCANEERISH
BUCKLE-BEGGAR
BUFFALO-BERRY
BUFFALO-GRASS
BULLET-HEADED
BULLFIGHTING
BULL-OF-THE-BOG
BUNKO-STEERER

BUNSEN-BURNER
BURIAL-GROUND
BURNET-LEAVED
BURNING-GLASS
BURNING-HOUSE
BURNING-POINT
BURNT-ALMONDS
BURROWING-OWL
BURSERACEOUS
BURYING-PLACE
BUSHWHACKING
BUSINESS-LIKE
BUSINESS-WISE
BUTTER-COOLER
BUTTERFLY-BOW
BUTTERFLY-NUT
BUTTER-MUSLIN
BUTTER-SCOTCH
BUTTERY-HATCH
BUTTRESS-ROOT
BUTTY-COLLIER
BUTYRACEOUS
BUZZARDCLOCK
BYELORUSSIAN

C

CABALISTICAL
CABBAGE-WHITE
CABIN-CRUISER
CABINET-MAKER
CABLE-RAILWAY
CABLE'S-LENGTH
CABLE-TRAMWAY
CACHINNATION
CACHINNATORY
CACOPHONICAL
CACOPHONIOUS
CAFÉ-CHANTANT
CAIN-COLOURED
CALABASH-TREE
CALAMITOUSLY
CALCEAMENTUM
CALENDAR-LINE
CALICO-FLOWER
CALIGINOSITY
CALISTHENICS
CALLIGRAPHER
CALLIGRAPHIC
CALLISTHENIC
CALORESCENCE
CALUMNIATION
CALUMNIATORY
CALUMNIOUSLY
CALYCANTHEMY
CALYCIFLORAE
CALYCOIDEOUS
CAMIKNICKERS
CAMPANULARIA
CAMP-FOLLOWER
CAMPODEIFORM
CAMP-PREACHER
CAMP-SHEDDING
CAMP-SHEETING
CANALICULATE
CANALISATION
CANCELLATION

CANDLE-HOLDER
CANDLE-WASTER
CANE-BOTTOMED
CANISTER-SHOT
CANKEREDNESS
CANNON-FODDER
CANONISATION
CANOROUSNESS
CANTABRIGIAN
CANTANKEROUS
CANTHARIDIAN
CANTHARIDINE
CANTILLATION
CANTILLATORY
CANTING-WHEEL
CANVAS-LENGTH
CAPE-COLOURED
CAPERCAILLIE
CAPERCAILZIE
CAPILLACEOUS
CAPITALISTIC
CAPITULATION
CAPITULATORY
CAPPAGH-BROWN
CAPRICIOUSLY
CAPTIOUSNESS
CARAVANSARAI
CARAVANSERAI
CARBOHYDRATE
CARBONACEOUS
CARBON-DATING
CARCINOGENIC
CARDINAL-BIRD
CARDINALSHIP
CARDIOGRAPHY
CARDIOLOGIST
CARELESSNESS
CARICATURIST
CARLOVINGIAN
CARNAL-MINDED
CARPENTER-BEE
CARPETBAGGER
CARPET-KNIGHT
CARPETMONGER
CARPOPHAGOUS
CARRAGHEENIN
CARRIAGEABLE
CARRIAGE-FREE
CARRIAGE-PAID
CARRIWITCHET
CARTE-BLANCHE
CARTOGRAPHER
CARTOGRAPHIC
CARTOLOGICAL
CARTON-PIERRE
CARTOPHILIST
CARVING-KNIFE
CASHEW-APPLES
CASH-REGISTER
CATACHRESTIC
CATACOUSTICS
CATADIOPTRIC
CATALLACTICS
CATAMOUNTAIN
CATAPHORESIS
CATAPHRACTIC

CATAPHYLLARY
CATAPHYSICAL
CATASTROPHIC
CATECHETICAL
CATEGORIALLY
CATERWAULING
CATHETOMETER
CATHODOGRAPH
CATILINARIAN
CATTLE-LIFTER
CATTLE-PLAGUE
CAULKING-IRON
CAUSATIONISM
CAUSATIONIST
CAUTIOUSNESS
CEDRELACEOUS
CELIBATARIAN
CEMENT-COPPER
CEMENTITIOUS
CENSORIOUSLY
CENTESIMALLY
CENTILLIONTH
CENTROCLINAL
CENTROSPHERE
CENTUMVIRATE
CENTUPLICATE
CENTURIATION
CERAMOGRAPHY
CEREBROTONIA
CEREMONIALLY
CEROGRAPHIST
CEROPLASTICS
CERTIFICATED
CHAIN-GEARING
CHAIRMANSHIP
CHAISE-LONGUE
CHALAZOGAMIC
CHALCOGRAPHY
CHALCOLITHIC
CHALCOPYRITE
CHAMPIONSHIP
CHANCE-MEDLEY
CHANNEL-STANE
CHANNEL-STONE
CHAPELMASTER
CHAPLAINSHIP
CHAPTER-HOUSE
CHARACINIDAE
CHARACTERISE
CHARACTERISM
CHARADRIIDAE
CHARLATANISM
CHARNEL-HOUSE
CHARTER-CHEST
CHARTERHOUSE
CHARTER-MAYOR
CHARTERPARTY
CHARTOGRAPHY
CHASSÉ-CROISÉ
CHASTISEMENT
CHAUVINISTIC
CHECKER-BERRY
CHECKER-BOARD
CHECKINGROOM
CHECK-WEIGHER
CHEERFULNESS

CHEERISHNESS
CHEESEBURGER
CHEESE-CUTTER
CHEESE-HOPPER
CHEESEMONGER
CHEESE-PARING
CHEESE-RENNET
CHEESE-TASTER
CHEIROGRAPHY
CHEIROLOGIST
CHEIROMANTIC
CHEMOTHERAPY
CHEMOTROPISM
CHERRY-BOUNCE
CHERRY-LAUREL
CHERRY-PEPPER
CHERUBICALLY
CHESTERFIELD
CHICK-A-DIDDLE
CHIEF-JUSTICE
CHIEFTAINESS
CHILDBEARING
CHILDCROWING
CHILDISHNESS
CHILIAHEDRON
CHIMERICALLY
CHIMNEY-BOARD
CHIMNEY-PIECE
CHIMNEY-SHAFT
CHIMNEY-STACK
CHIMNEY-STALK
CHIMNEY-SWEEP
CHIQUICHIQUI
CHIROGRAPHER
CHIRONOMIDAE
CHIROPRACTIC
CHIROPRACTOR
CHIROPTEROUS
CHIRURGEONLY
CHIVALROUSLY
CHLORIMETRIC
CHLORINATION
CHLOROFORMER
CHLOROMETRIC
CHOCOLATE-BOX
CHONDRIOSOME
CHORDOPHONIC
CHOREOGRAPHY
CHOREOLOGIST
CHORIPETALAE
CHORIZONTIST
CHOROGRAPHIC
CHOROLOGICAL
CHREMATISTIC
CHRESTOMATHY
CHRISOM-CLOTH
CHRISTIANISE
CHRISTIANISM
CHRISTIANITY
CHRISTLINESS
CHRISTOLATRY
CHRISTOPHANY
CHRIST'S-THORN
CHROMATICISM
CHROMATICITY
CHROMATOGRAM

CHROMATOPSIA
CHROME-SPINEL
CHROME-YELLOW
CHROMOSPHERE
CHRONOGRAPHY
CHRONOLOGIST
CHRONOMETRIC
CHRYSOPHANIC
CHUCKIE-STANE
CHUCKIE-STONE
CHURCHIANITY
CHURCH-PARADE
CHURCH-WARDEN
CHURLISHNESS
CICHORACEOUS
CICINDELIDAE
CINEMATHÈQUE
CINNAMON-BEAR
CIRCASSIENNE
CIRCLE-RIDING
CIRCUITOUSLY
CIRCUIT-RIDER
CIRCUMCENTRE
CIRCUMCISION
CIRCUMFLUENT
CIRCUMFLUOUS
CIRCUMFUSILE
CIRCUMFUSION
CIRCUMGYRATE
CIRCUMJACENT
CIRCUMLOCUTE
CIRCUMNUTATE
CIRCUMSCRIBE
CIRCUMSTANCE
CIRROCUMULUS
CIRROSTRATUS
CIVILISATION
CLAIRAUDIENT
CLAIR-OBSCURE
CLAIRVOYANCE
CLAMJAMPHRIE
CLANGOROUSLY
CLANNISHNESS
CLAPTRAPPERY
CLARE-OBSCURE
CLARINETTIST
CLASSICALITY
CLASSIFIABLE
CLATTERINGLY
CLAUDICATION
CLAUSTRATION
CLAVICEMBALO
CLEAR-OBSCURE
CLEAR-SIGHTED
CLEISTOGAMIC
CLICHE-RIDDEN
CLIFFHANGING
CLINCHER-WORK
CLINKER-BLOCK
CLINKER-BUILT
CLIQUISHNESS
CLOSE-GRAINED
CLOSE-TONGUED
CLOTHES-BRUSH
CLOTHES-HORSE
CLOTHES-PRESS

CLOUD-CHAMBER
CLOUD-KISSING
CLOVEN-FOOTED
CLOVEN-HOOFED
CLOWNISHNESS
COACERVATION
COACHBUILDER
COALITIONIST
COAL-TITMOUSE
COCCIDIOSTAT
COCKFIGHTING
COCKIELEEKIE
COCK-THROWING
CODIFICATION
COELENTERATA
COELENTERATE
COENOBITICAL
COERCIVENESS
COHABITATION
COHESIBILITY
COHESIVENESS
COINCIDENTAL
COINCIDENTLY
COLD-MOULDING
COLD-SHOULDER
COLEOPTERIST
COLEOPTEROUS
COLLABORATOR
COLLATERALLY
COLLECTIVELY
COLLECTIVISE
COLLECTIVISM
COLLECTIVIST
COLLECTORATE
COLLEGIALISM
COLLEGIALITY
COLLIQUATION
COLLIQUATIVE
COLLISION-MAT
COLLOQUIALLY
COLLUCTATION
COLLYWOBBLES
COLOGNE-EARTH
COLONISATION
COLOQUINTIDA
COLOSSUS-WISE
COLOSTRATION
COLUMNIATION
COMBINATIONS
COMBRETACEAE
COME-BY-CHANCE
COMETOGRAPHY
COMMANDINGLY
COMMEMORABLE
COMMEMORATOR
COMMENCEMENT
COMMENDATION
COMMENDATORY
COMMENSALISM
COMMENSURATE
COMMENTATION
COMMERCIALLY
COMMISERABLE
COMMISERATOR
COMMISSARIAL
COMMISSARIAT

COMMISSIONED
COMMISSIONER
COMMODIOUSLY
COMMON-RIDING
COMMONWEALTH
COMMUNICABLE
COMMUNICABLY
COMMUNICATOR
COMPANIONATE
COMPANION-WAY
COMPASS-PLANE
COMPASS-PLANT
COMPATRIOTIC
COMPELLATION
COMPELLATIVE
COMPENSATION
COMPENSATORY
COMPLACENTLY
COMPLAISANCE
COMPLANATION
COMPLEMENTAL
COMPLETENESS
COMPLEXIONAL
COMPLEXIONED
COMPLICATION
COMPLICATIVE
COMPLIMENTAL
COMPLIMENTER
COMPOSEDNESS
COMPRESSIBLE
COMPULSATIVE
COMPULSATORY
COMPULSIVELY
COMPULSORILY
COMPUNCTIOUS
COMPURGATION
COMPURGATORY
CONCENTERING
CONCENTRATOR
CONCENTRICAL
CONCERT-GRAND
CONCHIFEROUS
CONCHOLOGIST
CONCILIATION
CONCILIATIVE
CONCILIATORY
CONCLAMATION
CONCLUSIVELY
CONCOMITANCE
CONCOMITANCY
CONCORDANTLY
CONCORPORATE
CONCREMATION
CONCRESCENCE
CONCRETENESS
CONCUBITANCY
CONCUPISCENT
CONCURRENTLY
CONDEMNATION
CONDEMNATORY
CONDENSATION
CONDITIONATE
CONDITIONING
CONDUCTIVITY
CONDUPLICATE
CONFABULATOR

CONFECTIONER
CONFERENTIAL
CONFESSIONAL
CONFESSORESS
CONFIDENTIAL
CONFIRMATION
CONFIRMATIVE
CONFIRMATORY
CONFISCATION
CONFISCATORY
CONFORMATION
CONFOUNDEDLY
CONFRONTMENT
CONFUCIANISM
CONFUCIANIST
CONFUSEDNESS
CONGENERICAL
CONGENIALITY
CONGENITALLY
CONGLOBATION
CONGLOBULATE
CONGLOMERATE
CONGLUTINANT
CONGLUTINATE
CONGRATULANT
CONGRATULATE
CONGREGATION
CONIDIOPHORE
CONIDIOSPORE
CONJUNCTIVAL
CONNATURALLY
CONNECTIVELY
CONNING-TOWER
CONNUBIALITY
CONQUERINGLY
CONQUISTADOR
CONSCIONABLE
CONSCIONABLY
CONSCRIPTION
CONSECRATION
CONSECRATORY
CONSENSUALLY
CONSENTIENCE
CONSENTINGLY
CONSEQUENTLY
CONSERVATION
CONSERVATISM
CONSERVATIVE
CONSERVATORY
CONSERVATRIX
CONSIDERABLE
CONSIDERABLY
CONSIGNATION
CONSIGNATORY
CONSISTENTLY
CONSISTORIAL
CONSISTORIAN
CONSOCIATION
CONSOLE-TABLE
CONSOLIDATED
CONSOLIDATOR
CONSPECTUITY
CONSPIRATION
CONSPIRINGLY
CONSTABULARY
CONSTIPATION

CONSTITUENCY
CONSTITUTION
CONSTITUTIVE
CONSTRICTION
CONSTRICTIVE
CONSTRINGENT
CONSTRUCTION
CONSTRUCTIVE
CONSTRUCTURE
CONSULTATION
CONSULTATIVE
CONSULTATORY
CONSUMMATELY
CONSUMMATION
CONSUMMATIVE
CONSUMMATORY
CONTABESCENT
CONTAGIONIST
CONTAGIOUSLY
CONTAINERISE
CONTAMINABLE
CONTEMPLABLE
CONTEMPLATOR
CONTEMPORARY
CONTEMPORISE
CONTEMPTIBLE
CONTEMPTIBLY
CONTEMPTUOUS
CONTERMINANT
CONTERMINATE
CONTERMINOUS
CONTESTATION
CONTESTINGLY
CONTEXTUALLY
CONTIGNATION
CONTIGUOUSLY
CONTINGENTLY
CONTINUATION
CONTINUATIVE
CONTINUOUSLY
CONTORTIONAL
CONTRACTABLE
CONTRACTEDLY
CONTRACTIBLE
CONTRADICTOR
CONTRANATANT
CONTRAPPOSTO
CONTRAPUNTAL
CONTRARINESS
CONTRARIWISE
CONTRIBUTION
CONTRIBUTIVE
CONTRIBUTORY
CONTRITENESS
CONTRITURATE
CONTRIVEMENT
CONTROLLABLE
CONTUMACIOUS
CONTUMELIOUS
CONVALESCENT
CONVECTIONAL
CONVENIENTLY
CONVENTICLER
CONVENTIONAL
CONVENTIONER
CONVERSATION

CONVEYANCING
CONVEYOR-BELT
CONVINCEMENT
CONVINCINGLY
CONVIVIALIST
CONVIVIALITY
CONVULSIONAL
CONVULSIVELY
COOKING-APPLE
COOKING-RANGE
CO-ORDINATELY
CO-ORDINATION
CO-ORDINATIVE
CO-POLYMERISE
COPPER-GLANCE
COPPER-NICKEL
COPROPHAGIST
COPROPHAGOUS
COPROPHILOUS
COPYING-PRESS
COQUETTISHLY
CORALLACEOUS
CORDAITACEAE
CO-RESPONDENT
CORK-LINOLEUM
CORN-CHANDLER
CORN-EXCHANGE
CORNING-HOUSE
CORN-MARIGOLD
CORN-MERCHANT
CORN-SHUCKING
COROLLACEOUS
CORPORALSHIP
CORPOREALISE
CORPOREALISM
CORPOREALIST
CORPOREALITY
CORPSE-CANDLE
CORRECTIONAL
CORRECTIONER
CORRECTITUDE
CORROBORABLE
CORROBORATOR
COSCINOMANCY
COSMETICALLY
COSMOGONICAL
COSMOGRAPHER
COSMOGRAPHIC
COSMOLOGICAL
COSMONAUTICS
COSMOPLASTIC
COSMOPOLITAN
COSMOPOLITIC
COSTERMONGER
COTTONOCRACY
COTYLEDONARY
COTYLEDONOUS
COUGH-LOZENGE
COUGH-MIXTURE
COUNCIL-BOARD
COUNCIL-HOUSE
COUNCILMANIC
COUNSELLABLE
COUNTENANCER
COUNTERAGENT
COUNTER-BLAST

COUNTER-BRACE
COUNTER-CHARM
COUNTERCHECK
COUNTER-CLAIM
COUNTER-DRAIN
COUNTER-FLORY
COUNTER-FORCE
COUNTER-GAUGE
COUNTER-GUARD
COUNTERLIGHT
COUNTERMARCH
COUNTER-PALED
COUNTERPLEAD
COUNTERPOINT
COUNTERPOISE
COUNTERPROOF
COUNTER-ROUND
COUNTERSCARP
COUNTER-SENSE
COUNTERSHAFT
COUNTER-STAND
COUNTER-TALLY
COUNTER-TENOR
COUNTER-WEIGH
COUNTER-WHEEL
COUNTING-ROOM
COUNTRY-DANCE
COUNTRY-HOUSE
COUNTRYWOMAN
COURAGEOUSLY
COURT-DRESSER
COURTIERLIKE
COURT-MARTIAL
COURT-PLASTER
COUSIN-GERMAN
COVETIVENESS
COVETOUSNESS
COWARDLINESS
CRACKBRAINED
CRADLE-SCYTHE
CRAFT-BROTHER
CRAFTMANSHIP
CRAFTSMASTER
CRAMBO-JINGLE
CRANIOLOGIST
CRASH-LANDING
CRASSAMENTUM
CRASSULACEAE
CREATIVENESS
CREATURESHIP
CREDIBLENESS
CREEPY-CRAWLY
CREMATIONIST
CRENELLATION
CRÊPE-DE-CHINE
CREPUSCULOUS
CRIMPING-IRON
CRISPING-IRON
CRITICALNESS
CRITICISABLE
CROSS-AND-PILE
CROSSBANDING
CROSS-BEDDING
CROSSBENCHER
CROSS-BUTTOCK
CROSS-COUNTRY

CROSSCUTTING
CROSS-EXAMINE
CROSSGRAINED
CROSSING-OVER
CROSS-LATERAL
CROSS-LIGHTED
CROSS-PURPOSE
CROSS-SECTION
CRUEL-HEARTED
CRUSH-BARRIER
CRYPTOGAMIAN
CRYPTOGAMIST
CRYPTOGAMOUS
CRYPTOGRAPHY
CRYPTOLOGIST
CRYPTONYMOUS
CRYSTAL-CLEAR
CRYSTAL-GAZER
CRYSTALLITIS
CUCKING-STOOL
CUCKOLD-MAKER
CUCKOO-FLOWER
CUCUMBER-TREE
CUISSE-MADAME
CULPABLENESS
CULTIVATABLE
CULVERTAILED
CUMBER-GROUND
CUMBROUSNESS
CUMULATIVELY
CUMULOCIRRUS
CUMULONIMBUS
CUPBOARD-LOVE
CUPPING-GLASS
CUPRAMMONIUM
CUPULIFEROUS
CURB-CRAWLING
CURB-MERCHANT
CURIETHERAPY
CURLIEWURLIE
CURLING-IRONS
CURLING-STONE
CURLING-TONGS
CURMUDGEONLY
CURRANT-BREAD
CURRANT-JELLY
CURVICAUDATE
CURVICOSTATE
CURVIFOLIATE
CURVIROSTRAL
CUSHION-PLANT
CUSTARD-APPLE
CUSTOM-SHRUNK
CUTINISATION
CYANOPHYCEAE
CYCLOPROPANE
CYCLOSTOMATA
CYCLOSTOMOUS
CYLINDER-HEAD
CYLINDER-SEAL
CYLINDRICITY
CYLINDRIFORM
CYMOTRICHOUS
CYNOCEPHALUS
CYPRESS-SWAMP
CYTOGENETICS

CZECHOSLOVAK

D

DACTYLIOLOGY
DAMNABLENESS
DANTOPHILIST
DARLINGTONIA
DASYPHYLLOUS
DAUGHTERLING
DAY-BLINDNESS
DEACTIVATION
DEAD-AND-ALIVE
DEAMBULATORY
DEARTICULATE
DEASPIRATION
DEATH-DEALING
DEATH-WARRANT
DEBILITATION
DEBONAIRNESS
DECALESCENCE
DECAPITATION
DECASYLLABIC
DECASYLLABLE
DECELERATION
DECENTRALISE
DECIPHERABLE
DECIPHERMENT
DECISIVENESS
DECITIZENISE
DECLINOMETER
DECOLORATION
DECOMPOSABLE
DECOMPRESSOR
DECONGESTANT
DECONGESTIVE
DECONSECRATE
DECOROUSNESS
DECREASINGLY
DECREPITNESS
DECRUSTATION
DEDICATORIAL
DEDUCIBILITY
DEERSTALKING
DEFAMATORILY
DEFECTIONIST
DEFINITENESS
DEFINITIVELY
DEFLAGRATION
DEFLATIONARY
DEFLATIONIST
DEFLECTIONAL
DEFORCIATION
DEFORMEDNESS
DEFRAUDATION
DEGENERATELY
DEGENERATING
DEGENERATION
DEGENERATIVE
DEINOTHERIUM
DEJECTEDNESS
DELAMINATION
DELIBERATELY
DELIBERATION
DELIBERATIVE
DELICATENESS
DELICATESSEN

DELIGHTFULLY
DELIMITATION
DELINQUENTLY
DELIQUESCENT
DELITESCENCE
DELIVERY-PIPE
DELIVERY-TUBE
DELLA-CRUSCAN
DELTIOLOGIST
DELUSIVENESS
DEMI-CULVERIN
DEMI-DISTANCE
DEMI-MONDAINE
DEMOCRATICAL
DEMONIACALLY
DEMONOLOGIST
DEMONSTRABLE
DEMONSTRABLY
DEMONSTRATOR
DEMORALISING
DENATURALISE
DENDROLOGIST
DENOMINATION
DENOMINATIVE
DENOTATIVELY
DENOUNCEMENT
DENTICULATED
DENTILINGUAL
DENTIROSTRAL
DENUNCIATION
DENUNCIATORY
DEONTOLOGIST
DEOPPILATION
DEOPPILATIVE
DEPARTMENTAL
DEPHLEGMATOR
DEPOPULATION
DEPOSITATION
DEPRAVEDNESS
DEPRECIATION
DEPRECIATIVE
DEPRECIATORY
DEPRESSINGLY
DERISIVENESS
DERIVATIONAL
DERIVATIVELY
DERMATOPHYTE
DEROGATORILY
DESALINATION
DESCENSIONAL
DESIDERATION
DESIDERATIVE
DESIRABILITY
DESIROUSNESS
DESOLATENESS
DESPAIRINGLY
DESPISEDNESS
DESPITEFULLY
DESPOLIATION
DESPONDENTLY
DESPONDINGLY
DESPOTICALLY
DESPOTOCRACY
DESQUAMATION
DESQUAMATIVE
DESQUAMATORY

DESSERTSPOON
DESULPHURATE
DESULPHURISE
DETACHEDNESS
DETECTOPHONE
DETERMINABLE
DETERMINABLY
DETERMINEDLY
DETHRONEMENT
DETOXICATION
DETRACTINGLY
DETRUNCATION
DETUMESCENCE
DEUCH-AN-DORIS
DEUTERONOMIC
DEUTEROSCOPY
DEVIATIONISM
DEVIATIONIST
DEVIL-IN-A-BUSH
DEVIL-MAY-CARE
DEVIL-WORSHIP
DEVOTIONALLY
DEXTROCARDIA
DEXTROGYRATE
DEXTROUSNESS
DIABOLICALLY
DIAGEOTROPIC
DIAGRAMMATIC
DIALECTICIAN
DIALECTICISM
DIALECTOLOGY
DIAMAGNETISM
DIAMOND-DRILL
DIAMOND-FIELD
DIAMOND-HITCH
DIAMOND-WHEEL
DIAPHANOUSLY
DIAPOPHYSIAL
DIASTROPHISM
DIATHERMANCY
DIATOMACEOUS
DIATONICALLY
DIBRANCHIATA
DIBRANCHIATE
DICARPELLARY
DICHROMATISM
DICHROOSCOPE
DICHROSCOPIC
DICTATORSHIP
DIDACTICALLY
DIDELPHYIDAE
DIETETICALLY
DIETHYLAMINE
DIFFAREATION
DIFFERENTIAE
DIFFERENTIAL
DIFFRANGIBLE
DIFFUSEDNESS
DIGLADIATION
DIGRESSIONAL
DIGRESSIVELY
DIJUDICATION
DILACERATION
DILAPIDATION
DILATABILITY
DILATORINESS

DILETTANTISH
DILETTANTISM
DILUCIDATION
DIMINISHABLE
DIMINISHMENT
DIMINUTIVELY
DINGLE-DANGLE
DINNER-JACKET
DIPHTHERITIC
DIPHTHERITIS
DIPHTHONGISE
DIPLOGENESIS
DIPLOMATICAL
DIPRIONIDIAN
DIRECTORSHIP
DISACCHARIDE
DISACCORDANT
DISADVANTAGE
DISADVENTURE
DISAFFECTION
DISAGREEABLE
DISAGREEABLY
DISAGREEMENT
DISALLOWABLE
DISALLOWANCE
DISANNULLING
DISANNULMENT
DISAPPOINTED
DISASSOCIATE
DISASTROUSLY
DISAUTHORISE
DISAVENTROUS
DISBOWELLING
DISBURSEMENT
DISCEPTATION
DISCERPTIBLE
DISCIPLESHIP
DISCIPLINANT
DISCIPLINARY
DISCLAMATION
DISCOGRAPHER
DISCOMEDUSAE
DISCOMEDUSAN
DISCOMFITING
DISCOMFITURE
DISCOMMODITY
DISCOMMUNITY
DISCOMPOSURE
DISCOMYCETES
DISCONNECTED
DISCONNEXION
DISCONSOLATE
DISCONTENTED
DISCOPHOROUS
DISCORDANTLY
DISCORPORATE
DISCOUNTABLE
DISCOURAGING
DISCOURTEOUS
DISCOVERABLE
DISCOVERTURE
DISCREETNESS
DISCRETENESS
DISCRETIONAL
DISCRETIVELY
DISCRIMINANT

DISCRIMINATE
DISCURSIVELY
DISDAINFULLY
DISEASEDNESS
DISEMBARRASS
DISEMBELLISH
DISEMBRANGLE
DISENCHANTER
DISENDOWMENT
DISESTABLISH
DISFRANCHISE
DISGORGEMENT
DISGRADATION
DISGREGATION
DISGUISELESS
DISGUISEMENT
DISGUSTFULLY
DISGUSTINGLY
DISHARMONISE
DISHEARTENED
DISHEVELLING
DISHEVELMENT
DISINCENTIVE
DISINFECTANT
DISINFECTION
DISINFLATION
DISINGENUITY
DISINGENUOUS
DISINHERISON
DISINTEGRATE
DISINTERMENT
DISINTRICATE
DISJOINTEDLY
DISLOCATEDLY
DISLODGEMENT
DISMAYEDNESS
DISOBEDIENCE
DISORIENTATE
DISPATCH-BOAT
DISPAUPERISE
DISPENSATION
DISPENSATIVE
DISPENSATORY
DISPERSONATE
DISPIRITEDLY
DISPIRITMENT
DISPITEOUSLY
DISPLACEABLE
DISPLACEMENT
DISPLEASEDLY
DISPOSSESSED
DISPOSSESSOR
DISPRIVACIED
DISPRIVILEGE
DISPROPRIATE
DISPUTATIOUS
DISQUIETNESS
DISQUISITION
DISQUISITIVE
DISQUISITORY
DISREGARDFUL
DISRELISHING
DISREPUTABLE
DISREPUTABLY
DISSATISFIED
DISSEMBLANCE

DISSEMINATED
DISSEMINATOR
DISSENTERISH
DISSENTERISM
DISSENTINGLY
DISSERTATION
DISSERTATIVE
DISSEVERANCE
DISSEVERMENT
DISSIMILARLY
DISSIMULATOR
DISSOCIALISE
DISSOCIALITY
DISSOCIATION
DISSOCIATIVE
DISSUASIVELY
DISSYMMETRIC
DISTANCELESS
DISTEMPERATE
DISTILLATION
DISTILLATORY
DISTINCTNESS
DISTRACTEDLY
DISTRAINABLE
DISTRAINMENT
DISTRIBUTARY
DISTRIBUTION
DISTRIBUTIVE
DISTRUSTLESS
DISTURBATIVE
DITHEISTICAL
DITHELETICAL
DITHYRAMBIST
DITRIGLYPHIC
DIVARICATION
DIVERSIFYING
DIVERSIONARY
DIVERSIONIST
DIVERTICULAR
DIVERTICULUM
DIVERTIMENTO
DIVINATORIAL
DIVISIBILITY
DIVISIVENESS
DOATING-PIECE
DOCH-AN-DORACH
DOCK-LABOURER
DOCTRINARIAN
DODECAGYNIAN
DODECAGYNOUS
DODECAHEDRAL
DODECAHEDRON
DODECANDROUS
DODECAPHONIC
DOGMATICALLY
DOGTOOTH-SPAR
DO-IT-YOURSELF
DOLLAROCRACY
DOLORIFEROUS
DOLOROUSNESS
DOMESDAY-BOOK
DOMESTICALLY
DOMESTICATED
DOMESTICATOR
DONATISTICAL
DONKEY-ENGINE

DO-NOTHINGISM
DOOMSDAY-BOOK
DOPPEL-GANGER
DORMER-WINDOW
DORMITORY-CAR
DORSIFLEXION
DORSIVENTRAL
DOUBLE-ACTING
DOUBLE-BANKED
DOUBLE-BITING
DOUBLE-CHARGE
DOUBLE-DAGGER
DOUBLE-DEALER
DOUBLE-DECKED
DOUBLE-DECKER
DOUBLE-FORMED
DOUBLE-GLAZED
DOUBLE-HANDED
DOUBLE-HEADED
DOUBLE-LOCKED
DOUBLE-MANNED
DOUBLE-STOREY
DOUBTFULNESS
DOUGH-KNEADED
DOWN-AND-OUTER
DOWNWARDNESS
DRACONTIASIS
DRAGON'S-BLOOD
DRAINAGE-TUBE
DRAMATICALLY
DRAMATISABLE
DRAMATURGIST
DRAUGHTBOARD
DRAUGHT-HOOKS
DRAUGHT-HORSE
DRAUGHT-HOUSE
DRAUGHTINESS
DRAWING-BOARD
DRAWING-FRAME
DRAWING-KNIFE
DRAWING-PAPER
DRAWING-TABLE
DRAWLINGNESS
DREADFULNESS
DRESSING-CASE
DRESSING-DOWN
DRESSING-GOWN
DRESSING-ROOM
DRESSING-SACK
DRINKING-BOUT
DRINKING-HORN
DRIVING-SHAFT
DRIVING-WHEEL
DRONGO-CUCKOO
DRONGO-SHRIKE
DROPPED-SCONE
DROPPING-WELL
DROSERACEOUS
DROUGHTINESS
DUBITATIVELY
DUCKING-STOOL
DUNDERHEADED
DUNNIEWASSAL
DUODECENNIAL
DUODENECTOMY
DURALUMINIUM

DWARFISHNESS
DYNAMOMETRIC
DYOTHELETISM
DYSAESTHESIA
DYSAESTHETIC
DYSMENORRHEA
DYSTELEOLOGY

E

EAGLE-SIGHTED
EARNEST-MONEY
EARNEST-PENNY
EARTH-CREATED
EARTHQUAKING
EASTINDIAMAN
EAVESDROPPER
EBRACTEOLATE
EBULLIOSCOPE
EBULLIOSCOPY
ECCENTRICITY
ECCLESIASTES
ECCLESIASTIC
ECCLESIOLOGY
ECHINOCACTUS
ECHINOCOCCUS
ECHO-SOUNDING
ECLECTICALLY
ECOLOGICALLY
ECONOMETRICS
ECONOMICALLY
ECSTATICALLY
ECTOPARASITE
ECTYPOGRAPHY
EDACIOUSNESS
EDUCATIONIST
EDULCORATION
EDULCORATIVE
EFFECTUALITY
EFFECTUATION
EFFEMINATELY
EFFERVESCENT
EFFIGURATION
EFFLORESCENT
EFFUSIOMETER
EFFUSIVENESS
EGG-APPARATUS
EGYPTOLOGIST
EIGHTEEN-HOLE
EIGHTEENTHLY
ELASMOBRANCH
ELECTRICALLY
ELECTRIFYING
ELECTROGRAPH
ELECTROLYSIS
ELECTROLYTIC
ELECTROMERIC
ELECTROMETER
ELECTROMETRY
ELECTROMOTOR
ELECTRON-VOLT
ELECTROPLATE
ELECTROPOLAR
ELECTROSCOPE
ELECTROTONIC
ELECTROTONUS
ELECTROTYPER

ELECTROTYPIC
ELEEMOSYNARY
ELEMENTALISM
ELEUTHERARCH
ELLIPSOGRAPH
ELLIPTICALLY
ELOCUTIONARY
ELOCUTIONIST
ELUCUBRATION
ELYTRIGEROUS
EMANCIPATION
EMARGINATION
EMASCULATION
EMASCULATORY
EMBARQUEMENT
EMBATTLEMENT
EMBEZZLEMENT
EMBITTERMENT
EMBLAZONMENT
EMBLEMATICAL
EMBRANCHMENT
EMBRYOLOGIST
EMIGRATIONAL
EMOLLESCENCE
EMOLUMENTARY
EMOTIONALISM
EMPHATICALLY
EMPOISONMENT
EMPYREUMATIC
ENANTIOMORPH
ENANTIOPATHY
ENANTIOSTYLY
ENANTIOTROPY
ENARTHRODIAL
ENCEPHALITIC
ENCEPHALITIS
ENCHANTINGLY
ENCHEIRIDION
ENCIRCLEMENT
ENCLITICALLY
ENCROACHMENT
ENCRUSTATION
ENCUMBERMENT
ENCUMBRANCER
ENCYCLOPÆDIA
ENDAMAGEMENT
ENDANGERMENT
ENDOCARDITIS
ENDOMETRITIS
ENDOPARASITE
ENDOPHYLLOUS
ENDOSKELETAL
ENDOSKELETON
ENDOSMOMETER
ENFEEBLEMENT
ENGAGINGNESS
ENGINE-DRIVER
ENGINE-FITTER
ENGRAFTATION
ENHARMONICAL
ENHYPOSTASIA
ENHYPOSTATIC
ENLARGEDNESS
ENORMOUSNESS
ENSWATHEMENT
ENTANGLEMENT

ENTEROMORPHA
ENTEROPNEUST
ENTEROPTOSIS
ENTERPRISING
ENTERTAINING
ENTHRONEMENT
ENTHUSIASTIC
ENTOMOLOGISE
ENTOMOLOGIST
ENTOMOSTRACA
ENTOPLASTRAL
ENTOPLASTRON
ENTRANCEMENT
ENTREATINGLY
ENTRENCHMENT
ENTREPRENEUR
ENVIABLENESS
ENVISAGEMENT
ENZYMOLOGIST
EPACRIDACEAE
EPANORTHOSIS
EPENCEPHALIC
EPENCEPHALON
EPEXEGETICAL
EPHEMERALITY
EPHEMERIDIAN
EPICUREANISM
EPICYCLOIDAL
EPIDEICTICAL
EPIDEMICALLY
EPIDEMIOLOGY
EPIGRAMMATIC
EPIPHENOMENA
EPIRRHEMATIC
EPISCOPALIAN
EPISODICALLY
EPISTEMOLOGY
EPISTOLARIAN
EPISTOLATORY
EPITHALAMION
EPITHALAMIUM
EPOCH-MARKING
EQUALISATION
EQUALITARIAN
EQUANIMOUSLY
EQUATORIALLY
EQUESTRIENNE
EQUIDISTANCE
EQUILIBRATOR
EQUIMULTIPLE
EQUIPOLLENCE
EQUIPOLLENCY
EQUIPROBABLE
EQUISETACEAE
EQUISETIFORM
EQUIVALENTLY
EQUIVOCATION
EQUIVOCATORY
ERUPTIVENESS
ERYTHEMATOUS
ERYTHROMYCIN
ESCAPOLOGIST
ESCHATOLOGIC
ESCUTCHEONED
ESOTERICALLY
ESPAGNOLETTE

ESSENTIALITY
ESTRANGEMENT
ETEPIMELETIC
ETERNITY-RING
ETHEOSTOMINE
ETHERISATION
ETHEROMANIAC
ETHNOCENTRIC
ETHNOGRAPHER
ETHNOGRAPHIC
ETHNOLOGICAL
ETYMOLOGICAL
ETYMOLOGICON
ETYMOLOGICUM
EUCALYPTUSES
EUGLENOIDINA
EUHEMERISTIC
EUNUCHOIDISM
EUPHONIOUSLY
EURO-AMERICAN
EVANESCENTLY
EVANGELICISM
EVANGELISTIC
EVAPORIMETER
EVAPOROGRAPH
EVENING-DRESS
EVERYDAYNESS
EVERYWHITHER
EVIDENTIALLY
EVIL-FAVOURED
EVIL-SPEAKING
EVISCERATION
EVOLUTIONARY
EVOLUTIONISM
EVOLUTIONIST
EXACERBATION
EXAGGERATION
EXAGGERATIVE
EXAGGERATORY
EXALBUMINOUS
EXANTHEMATIC
EXASPERATING
EXASPERATION
EXASPERATIVE
EXCHANGEABLE
EXCITABILITY
EXCLUSIONISM
EXCLUSIONIST
EXCOGITATION
EXCRUCIATING
EXCRUCIATION
EXCURSIONISE
EXCURSIONIST
EXECRATIVELY
EXECUTORSHIP
EXEGETICALLY
EXEMPLIFYING
EXENTERATION
EXERCISE-BOOK
EXERCITATION
EXHAUST-STEAM
EXHEREDATION
EXHIBITIONER
EXHILARATING
EXHILARATION
EXHILARATIVE

EXHILARATORY
EXIGUOUSNESS
EXOPHTHALMIA
EXOPHTHALMIC
EXOPHTHALMOS
EXOPHTHALMUS
EXORBITANTLY
EXOSPHERICAL
EXOTERICALLY
EXPANSIONARY
EXPANSIONISM
EXPANSIONIST
EXPATRIATION
EXPEDIENTIAL
EXPEDITATION
EXPERIENTIAL
EXPERIMENTAL
EXPERIMENTED
EXPERIMENTER
EXPLANTATION
EXPLICITNESS
EXPLOITATION
EXPOSTULATOR
EXPRESSIONAL
EXPRESSIVELY
EXPROBRATION
EXPROBRATIVE
EXPROBRATORY
EXPROMISSION
EXSANGUINITY
EXSANGUINOUS
EX-SERVICEMAN
EXSUFFLATION
EXSUFFLICATE
EXTENSIONIST
EXTENSOMETER
EXTERMINABLE
EXTERMINATOR
EXTINGUISHER
EXTORTIONARY
EXTORTIONATE
EXTRADITABLE
EXTRA-LIMITAL
EXTRA-MARITAL
EXTRA-MUNDANE
EXTRANEOUSLY
EXTRA-REGULAR
EXTRA-SENSORY
EXTRA-SPECIAL
EXTRA-UTERINE
EXTRAVAGANCE
EXTRAVAGANCY
EXTRAVAGANZA
EXTRAVERSION
EXTROVERSION
EXULCERATION

F
FABULOUSNESS
FACILITATION
FACTIONALISM
FACTIONALIST
FACTIOUSNESS
FACTITIOUSLY
FAINT-HEARTED
FAINTISHNESS

FAIRNITICKLE
FAIRNYTICKLE
FAITHFULNESS
FAITH-HEALING
FALCON-GENTIL
FALCON-GENTLE
FALLACIOUSLY
FALSE-HEARTED
FANCIFULNESS
FANTASTICATE
FANTASTICISM
FARADISATION
FARM-LABOURER
FARTHINGLAND
FARTHINGLESS
FASCICULATED
FASHION-PLATE
FASHIOUSNESS
FAST-AND-LOOSE
FASTIDIOUSLY
FATHER-FIGURE
FATHER-LASHER
FATHERLINESS
FATHERS-IN-LAW
FATIGUE-DRESS
FATIGUE-PARTY
FAULT-FINDING
FAVOUREDNESS
FEARLESSNESS
FEASIBLENESS
FEATHER-BRAIN
FEATHER-GRASS
FEATHERINESS
FEBRIFACIENT
FEBRONIANISM
FEEBLE-MINDED
FEEING-MARKET
FEHMGERICHTE
FELDSPATHOID
FELICITATION
FELICITOUSLY
FELLOW-MEMBER
FEMININENESS
FENESTRATION
FENNEL-FLOWER
FENT-MERCHANT
FERMENTATION
FERMENTATIVE
FERRICYANIDE
FERROCYANIDE
FERRUGINEOUS
FESTOON-BLIND
FEVERISHNESS
FIBRILLATION
FIBRINOLYSIN
FICTIONALISE
FICTITIOUSLY
FIDDLEFADDLE
FIDDLESTICKS
FIDDLE-STRING
FIELD-SPANIEL
FIENDISHNESS
FIGURABILITY
FIGURATIVELY
FIGURE-CASTER
FILIBUSTERER

FILTER-PASSER
FILTRABILITY
FINANCIALIST
FINGER-AND-TOE
FIRE-FIGHTING
FIREPROOFING
FIRE-WATCHING
FIRST-NIGHTER
FISH-HATCHERY
FISH-SALESMAN
FISSICOSTATE
FISSILINGUAL
FISSIROSTRAL
FLABELLATION
FLABELLIFORM
FLAGELLATION
FLAGELLATORY
FLAGELLIFORM
FLAGITIOUSLY
FLAMBOYANTLY
FLAME-THROWER
FLAMMABILITY
FLAMMIFEROUS
FLAMMULATION
FLANNELGRAPH
FLATTERINGLY
FLESH-POTTERY
FLEXIBLENESS
FLICKERINGLY
FLINT-HEARTED
FLINT-KNAPPER
FLIPPANTNESS
FLITTER-MOUSE
FLOCCULATION
FLOODLIGHTED
FLORICULTURE
FLOWER-DELICE
FLOWER-DE-LUCE
FLOWER-GARDEN
FLUIDISATION
FLUORESCENCE
FLUORIDATION
FLUORINATION
FLUOROCARBON
FOLK-MEDICINE
FOLLICULATED
FOOLISH-WITTY
FOOT-AND-MOUTH
FOOTPLATEMEN
FOOTSLOGGING
FORAMINIFERA
FORBEARINGLY
FORBIDDINGLY
FORCIBLENESS
FORCING-HOUSE
FORE-ADMONISH
FORE-AND-AFTER
FOREBODEMENT
FOREBODINGLY
FORECARRIAGE
FOREGONENESS
FOREIGN-BUILT
FOREJUDGMENT
FORESEEINGLY
FORESIGHTFUL
FORESTALLING

FORESTALMENT
FORETOKENING
FORGETTINGLY
FORMALDEHYDE
FORMLESSNESS
FORNICATRESS
FORSAKENNESS
FORSET-SELLER
FORSWORNNESS
FORTH-PUTTING
FORTUITOUSLY
FOSSET-SELLER
FOSTER-FATHER
FOSTER-MOTHER
FOSTER-PARENT
FOSTER-SISTER
FOUNDATIONER
FOUNTAIN-HEAD
FOUNTAINLESS
FOURFOLDNESS
FOURTEENTHLY
FOWLING-PIECE
FRACTIONATOR
FRAGRANTNESS
FRAME-BREAKER
FRANCO-GERMAN
FRANGIBILITY
FRANKALMOIGN
FRANKENSTEIN
FRANKINCENSE
FRAUDULENTLY
FREAKISHNESS
FREE-SELECTOR
FREE-SWIMMING
FREE-THINKING
FREE-WHEELING
FREEZE-DRYING
FREEZING-DOWN
FREIGHT-LINER
FREIGHT-TRAIN
FRENETICALLY
FREQUENTNESS
FRESHMANSHIP
FRICASSEEING
FRICTIONLESS
FRIENDLINESS
FRINGILLIDAE
FROLICSOMELY
FRONDESCENCE
FRONDIFEROUS
FRONT-BENCHER
FRONTIERSMAN
FRONTISPIECE
FRUCTIFEROUS
FRUCTIVOROUS
FRUITFULNESS
FRUIT-MACHINE
FRUMENTATION
FUGIE-WARRANT
FUGITIVENESS
FULIGINOSITY
FULIGINOUSLY
FULL-BOTTOMED
FULL-THROATED
FUME-CUPBOARD
FUNAMBULATOR

FUNCTIONALLY
FUNCTIONLESS
FURFURACEOUS
FUSTILLIRIAN
FUTILITARIAN
FUTTOCK-PLATE
FUTUROLOGIST

G

GAINLESSNESS
GALACTAGOGUE
GALACTOMETER
GALLIGASKINS
GALLINACEOUS
GALLOWS-MAKER
GALVANOMETER
GALVANOMETRY
GALVANOSCOPE
GAMBLING-HELL
GAMESMANSHIP
GAMESOMENESS
GAMOPETALOUS
GAMOPHYLLOUS
GAMOSEPALOUS
GANDER-MOONER
GANG-THERE-OUT
GAOL-DELIVERY
GARRET-MASTER
GARTER-STITCH
GAS-CONDENSER
GAS-DISCHARGE
GASIFICATION
GASOMETRICAL
GASTROCNEMII
GASTRONOMIST
GASTROPODOUS
GASTROSOPHER
GASTRULATION
GATHERING-CRY
GAZETTEERISH
GEANTICLINAL
GELATINATION
GEM-ENGRAVING
GENEALOGICAL
GENEROUSNESS
GENETHLIACAL
GENETHLIACON
GENICULATION
GENTIANACEAE
GENTILITIOUS
GENUFLECTION
GEOCENTRICAL
GEOCHEMISTRY
GEODYNAMICAL
GEOGNOSTICAL
GEOGRAPHICAL
GEOLOGICALLY
GEOMAGNETISM
GEOMETRICIAN
GEOPHYSICIST
GEOSYNCLINAL
GEOTECTONICS
GERIATRICIAN
GERMANICALLY
GERMANOPHILE
GERMANOPHOBE

GERONTOCRACY
GERONTOPHILE
GESNERIACEAE
GESTICULATOR
GIANT'S-KETTLE
GIANT'S-STRIDE
GIBBLE-GABBLE
GIBRALTARIAN
GIGANTICALLY
GIGANTOMACHY
GINGIVECTOMY
GLACIOLOGIST
GLADIATORIAL
GLADIATORIAN
GLADSOMENESS
GLANDIFEROUS
GLASS-BLOWING
GLASS-CUTTING
GLASSY-HEADED
GLAUCESCENCE
GLAUCOMATOUS
GLIMMERINGLY
GLITTERINGLY
GLOBE-THISTLE
GLOBE-TROTTER
GLOCKENSPIEL
GLORIOUSNESS
GLOSSOGRAPHY
GLOSSOLOGIST
GLUTTONOUSLY
GLYPHOGRAPHY
GLYPTOGRAPHY
GNOMONICALLY
GNOTOBIOLOGY
GNOTOBIOTICS
GOAT-ANTELOPE
GOBBLEDEGOOK
GOBBLEDYGOOK
GODFORGOTTEN
GONADOTROPIC
GONADOTROPIN
GONDWANALAND
GOOD-BREEDING
GOOD-HUMOURED
GOOD-TEMPERED
GOOSE-PIMPLES
GORGEOUSNESS
GORMANDISING
GOVERNMENTAL
GOVERNORSHIP
GRACEFULNESS
GRACIOUSNESS
GRALLATORIAL
GRAMINACEOUS
GRAMMATICISE
GRAMMATICISM
GRAM-MOLECULE
GRAM-NEGATIVE
GRAMOPHONIST
GRAM-POSITIVE
GRANDISONIAN
GRANODIORITE
GRAPESEED-OIL
GRAPPLE-PLANT
GRASPINGNESS
GRATEFULNESS

GRATIFYINGLY
GRATUITOUSLY
GRAVE-CLOTHES
GRAVEL-VOICED
GREASE-MONKEY
GREAT-BELLIED
GREAT-HEARTED
GREENISHNESS
GREGARIANISM
GREGARIOUSLY
GRIEVOUSNESS
GRISEOFULVIN
GROLIERESQUE
GROSSULARITE
GROUND-BEETLE
GROUND-CHERRY
GROUND-CUCKOO
GROUND-FEEDER
GROUNDLESSLY
GROUND-PIGEON
GROUP-CAPTAIN
GROWING-PAINS
GROWING-POINT
GRUESOMENESS
GUARANTEEING
GUARDIANSHIP
GUEST-CHAMBER
GUILD-BROTHER
GUILEFULNESS
GYMNOSOPHIST
GYNAECOCRACY
GYNAECOMASTY
GYNODIOECISM
GYROMAGNETIC

H

HABEAS-CORPUS
HABERDASHERY
HABILITATION
HABITABILITY
HABIT-FORMING
HAEMATEMESIS
HAEMATOBLAST
HAEMATOLYSIS
HAEMATOXYLIN
HAEMATOXYLON
HAEMOPHILIAC
HAEMORRHAGIC
HAGIOGRAPHER
HAGIOGRAPHIC
HAGIOLOGICAL
HAIRDRESSING
HAIR-RESTORER
HAIR'S-BREADTH
HAIR-SPLITTER
HALF-MOURNING
HALF-SEAS-OVER
HALF-TIMBERED
HALLAN-SHAKER
HALLUCINOGEN
HALLUCINOSIS
HAMARTHRITIS
HAMARTIOLOGY
HAMMER-HEADED
HANDKERCHIEF
HAND'S-BREADTH

H12

HANDSOMENESS
HAPPENSTANCE
HAPPY-GO-LUCKY
HAPTOTROPISM
HARBOUR-LIGHT
HARD-FAVOURED
HARD-FEATURED
HARLEQUINADE
HARMLESSNESS
HARMONICALLY
HARMONICHORD
HARMONIOUSLY
HARMONIPHONE
HARMONIUMIST
HARMONOGRAPH
HARMONOMETER
HARNESS-MAKER
HARVEST-FEAST
HARVEST-FIELD
HARVEST-GOOSE
HARVEST-LOUSE
HARVEST-MOUSE
HATCHET-FACED
HATELESSNESS
HAUSSMANNISE
HEADMISTRESS
HEADQUARTERS
HEADSHRINKER
HEARTBREAKER
HEARTBURNING
HEART-FAILURE
HEART-RENDING
HEART-SERVICE
HEART-TO-HEART
HEART-WARMING
HEAT-APOPLEXY
HEATER-SHIELD
HEATHENISHLY
HEATHER-BLEAT
HEAVEN-FALLEN
HEAVEN-GIFTED
HEAVENLINESS
HEAVY-HEARTED
HEBDOMADALLY
HEBDOMADARER
HEBEPHRENIAC
HEBETUDINOUS
HECTOGRAPHIC
HEDGE-CREEPER
HEDGE-MUSTARD
HEDGE-PARSLEY
HEDGE-SPARROW
HEDGE-WARBLER
HEEBY-JEEBIES
HEIR-APPARENT
HEIR-BY-CUSTOM
HELIANTHEMUM
HELIOCENTRIC
HELIOCHROMIC
HELIOGRAPHER
HELIOGRAPHIC
HELIOGRAVURE
HELIOLATROUS
HELIOPHILOUS
HELIOTHERAPY
HELIOTROPISM

HELLGRAMMITE
HELPLESSNESS
HEMEROCALLIS
HEMICHORDATA
HEMIMORPHISM
HEMIMORPHITE
HEMIPARASITE
HEMISPHEROID
HEMP-AGRIMONY
HENCEFORWARD
HENDECAGONAL
HENOTHEISTIC
HEPATICOLOGY
HEPATISATION
HEPATOLOGIST
HEPHTHEMIMER
HERALDICALLY
HERD-INSTINCT
HEREDITAMENT
HEREDITARILY
HEREINBEFORE
HERESY-HUNTER
HERITABILITY
HERMENEUTICS
HERMENEUTIST
HERMETICALLY
HEROICALNESS
HEROI-COMICAL
HERPETOLOGIC
HERSIOGRAPHY
HESITATINGLY
HETERAUXESIS
HETEROBLASTY
HETEROCERCAL
HETEROCHRONY
HETEROCLITIC
HETEROCONTAE
HETEROCYCLIC
HETERODACTYL
HETEROECIOUS
HETEROGONOUS
HETEROKONTAN
HETEROLOGOUS
HETEROMEROUS
HETEROMORPHY
HETERONOMOUS
HETEROOUSIAN
HETEROPHYLLY
HETEROPLASIA
HETEROPLASTY
HETEROSEXUAL
HETEROSOMATA
HETEROSTYLED
HETEROTACTIC
HETEROTHALLY
HETEROTROPHY
HETEROZYGOTE
HETEROZYGOUS
HEXADACTYLIC
HIBERNACULUM
HIBERNIANISM
HIBERNICALLY
HIERARCHICAL
HIEROGLYPHIC
HIEROGRAMMAT
HIEROGRAPHER

HIEROGRAPHIC
HIEROPHANTIC
HIGGLE-HAGGLE
HIGH-COLOURED
HIGH-FALUTING
HIGH-FIDELITY
HIGHLY-STRUNG
HIGH-PRESSURE
HIGH-PRIESTLY
HIGH-REACHING
HIGH-SEASONED
HIGH-SOUNDING
HIGH-SPIRITED
HIGH-STEPPING
HIGHTY-TIGHTY
HIGH-VELOCITY
HILDEBRANDIC
HINDFOREMOST
HINDOOSTANEE
HINDQUARTERS
HIP-HIP-HURRAH
HIPPOCENTAUR
HIPPOCRATISE
HIPPOCRATISM
HIPPOCREPIAN
HIPPOPHAGIST
HIPPOPHAGOUS
HIPPOPOTAMIC
HIPPOPOTAMUS
HIRE-PURCHASE
HISPANICALLY
HISPANIOLISE
HISTIOPHORUS
HISTOGENESIS
HISTOGENETIC
HISTOLOGICAL
HISTORICALLY
HISTORIOLOGY
HISTRIONICAL
HOBBESIANISM
HOBGOBLINISM
HOBSON-JOBSON
HODGE-PUDDING
HOG-CONSTABLE
HOLIDAY-MAKER
HOLLOW-GROUND
HOME-CROFTING
HOMELESSNESS
HOMEOMORPHIC
HOMEOPATHIST
HOMEOTHERMAL
HOMEOTHERMIC
HOME-PRODUCED
HOMESICKNESS
HOMOCHROMOUS
HOMOEOMEROUS
HOMOEOMORPHY
HOMOEOPATHIC
HOMOEOSTATIC
HOMOIOMEROUS
HOMOLOGATION
HOMOLOGUMENA
HOMOMORPHISM
HOMOMORPHOUS
HOMONYMOUSLY
HOMOTHALLISM

HOMOTHERMOUS
HONEY-BUZZARD
HONEY-MOUTHED
HONEY-TONGUED
HOODMAN-BLIND
HOOD-MOULDING
HOOPING-COUGH
HOPELESSNESS
HORIZONTALLY
HOROMETRICAL
HORRIBLENESS
HORROR-STRUCK
HORSE-BREAKER
HORSE-COURSER
HORSE-KNACKER
HORSEMANSHIP
HORSESHOEING
HORSE-TRADING
HORSE-TRAINER
HORTICULTURE
HOSPITAL-SHIP
HOUND'S-TONGUE
HOUSE-BREAKER
HOUSEKEEPING
HOUSE-STEWARD
HOUSE-SURGEON
HOUSE-TO-HOUSE
HOUSE-TRAINED
HOUSE-WARMING
HOUSEY-HOUSEY
HUBBLE-BUBBLE
HUCKLE-BACKED
HUDIBRASTICS
HUGGER-MUGGER
HUMANISATION
HUMANITARIAN
HUMIFICATION
HUMOROUSNESS
HUMPTY-DUMPTY
HUNDRED-GATED
HUNGER-BITTEN
HUNGER-STRIKE
HUNTING-FIELD
HUNTING-KNIFE
HUNTING-LODGE
HUNTING-SWORD
HUNTSMANSHIP
HURDLE-RACING
HURTLESSNESS
HYBRIDISABLE
HYDATIDIFORM
HYDRARGYRISM
HYDRAULICKED
HYDROCHLORIC
HYDRODYNAMIC
HYDROFLUORIC
HYDROGRAPHER
HYDROGRAPHIC
HYDROLOGICAL
HYDROMEDUSAE
HYDROMEDUSAN
HYDROPATHIST
HYDROPHANOUS
HYDROPHILITE
HYDROPHILOUS
HYDROPHOBOUS

HYDROPHYTOUS
HYDROQUINONE
HYDROSTATICS
HYDROTHERAPY
HYDROTHERMAL
HYDROTROPISM
HYDROZINCITE
HYETOGRAPHIC
HYGIENICALLY
HYGROCHASTIC
HYGROGRAPHIC
HYGROPHILOUS
HYMNOGRAPHER
HYPERACIDITY
HYPERALGESIA
HYPERALGESIC
HYPERBOLICAL
HYPERDACTYLY
HYPERICACEAE
HYPERIDROSIS
HYPERPLASTIC
HYPERPYRETIC
HYPERPYREXIA
HYPERSARCOMA
HYPERSENSUAL
HYPERSTHENIA
HYPERSTHENIC
HYPERTENSION
HYPERTROPHIC
HYPNOGENESIS
HYPNOGENETIC
HYPNOTHERAPY
HYPNOTICALLY
HYPNOTISABLE
HYPOCHLORITE
HYPOCHONDRIA
HYPOCORISTIC
HYPOCRITICAL
HYPOGASTRIUM
HYPOGLYCEMIA
HYPOGNATHISM
HYPOGNATHOUS
HYPOPHRYGIAN
HYPOPLASTRON
HYPOSTATICAL
HYPOSULPHATE
HYPOSULPHITE
HYPOTHALAMIC
HYPOTHALAMUS
HYPOTHECATOR
HYPOTHETICAL
HYPOTROCHOID
HYSTERECTOMY
HYSTERICALLY
HYSTEROMANIA

I

IAMBOGRAPHER
IATROCHEMIST
ICHNEUMON-FLY
ICHNOGRAPHIC
ICHTHYOCOLLA
ICHTHYOLATRY
ICHTHYOLITIC
ICHTHYOPHAGY
ICHTHYOPSIDA

ICONOCLASTIC
ICONOMACHIST
ICONOPHILISM
ICONOPHILIST
IDEALISATION
IDEATIONALLY
IDENTIFIABLE
IDIORHYTHMIC
IDIOSYNCRASY
IDIOTHERMOUS
IDOLATROUSLY
IGNITABILITY
IGNITIBILITY
ILLAQUEATION
ILL-BESEEMING
ILLEGIBILITY
ILLEGITIMACY
ILLEGITIMATE
ILLIBERALISE
ILLIBERALITY
ILLIMITATION
ILLITERATELY
ILL-NATUREDLY
ILL-TREATMENT
ILLUMINATION
ILLUMINATIVE
ILLUSIVENESS
ILLUSTRATION
ILLUSTRATIVE
ILLUSTRATORY
IMAGE-BREAKER
IMAGE-WORSHIP
IMMACULATELY
IMMATERIALLY
IMMATURENESS
IMMEASURABLE
IMMEASURABLY
IMMEMORIALLY
IMMENSURABLE
IMMERSIONISM
IMMERSIONIST
IMMETHODICAL
IMMODERATELY
IMMODERATION
IMMOVABILITY
IMMUNISATION
IMMUNOLOGIST
IMMUTABILITY
IMPARTIALITY
IMPASSIONATE
IMPEDIMENTAL
IMPENETRABLE
IMPENETRABLY
IMPENITENTLY
IMPERATIVELY
IMPERATORIAL
IMPERCEPTIVE
IMPERFECTION
IMPERFORABLE
IMPERFORATED
IMPERISHABLE
IMPERISHABLY
IMPERMANENCE
IMPERMANENCY
IMPERSISTENT
IMPERSONALLY

IMPERSONATOR
IMPERTINENCE
IMPERTINENCY
IMPERVIOUSLY
IMPETIGINOUS
IMPIERCEABLE
IMPLANTATION
IMPLICITNESS
IMPOLITENESS
IMPONDERABLE
IMPOSINGNESS
IMPOSTHUMATE
IMPREGNATION
IMPRESSIVELY
IMPRISONMENT
IMPROPRIATOR
IMPROVIDENCE
IMPROVISATOR
IMPUTABILITY
IMPUTATIVELY
INABSTINENCE
INACCESSIBLE
INACCESSIBLY
INACCURATELY
INACTIVATION
INADAPTATION
INADEQUATELY
INADMISSIBLE
INADMISSIBLY
INADVERTENCE
INADVERTENCY
INAPPEASABLE
INAPPLICABLE
INAPPOSITELY
INARTICULACY
INARTICULATE
INARTIFICIAL
INARTISTICAL
INAUDIBILITY
INAUGURATION
INAUGURATORY
INAUSPICIOUS
INCALCULABLE
INCALCULABLY
INCALESCENCE
INCANDESCENT
INCAPABILITY
INCAPACITATE
INCATENATION
INCAUTIOUSLY
INCENDIARISM
INCESTUOUSLY
INCIDENTALLY
INCINERATION
INCISIVENESS
INCIVILITIES
INCLINOMETER
INCOAGULABLE
INCOGITATIVE
INCOGNISABLE
INCOGNISANCE
INCOHERENTLY
INCOMMODIOUS
INCOMMUTABLE
INCOMMUTABLY
INCOMPARABLE

INCOMPARABLY
INCOMPATIBLE
INCOMPATIBLY
INCOMPETENCE
INCOMPETENCY
INCOMPLETELY
INCOMPLETION
INCOMPLIANCE
INCOMPUTABLE
INCONCINNITY
INCONCINNOUS
INCONCLUSION
INCONCLUSIVE
INCONSEQUENT
INCONSISTENT
INCONSOLABLE
INCONSOLABLY
INCONSONANCE
INCONSTANTLY
INCONSUMABLE
INCONSUMABLY
INCONTIGUOUS
INCONTINENCE
INCONTINENCY
INCONVENIENT
INCONVERSANT
INCOORDINATE
INCORONATION
INCORPORATOR
INCORPOREITY
INCORRIGIBLE
INCORRIGIBLY
INCORRODIBLE
INCORROSIBLE
INCORRUPTION
INCORRUPTIVE
INCRASSATION
INCRASSATIVE
INCREASINGLY
INCRUSTATION
INCUNABULIST
INCURABILITY
INDEBTEDNESS
INDECISIVELY
INDECLINABLE
INDECLINABLY
INDECOROUSLY
INDEFEASIBLE
INDEFEASIBLY
INDEFECTIBLE
INDEFENSIBLE
INDEFENSIBLY
INDEFINITELY
INDEHISCENCE
INDELIBILITY
INDELICATELY
INDEMNIFYING
INDEPENDENCE
INDEPENDENCY
INDETECTABLE
INDETECTIBLE
INDETERMINED
INDICATIVELY
INDIFFERENCE
INDIFFERENCY
INDIGENOUSLY

INDIGESTIBLE
INDIGESTIBLY
INDIRECTNESS
INDISCIPLINE
INDISCREETLY
INDISCRETELY
INDISCRETION
INDISPUTABLE
INDISPUTABLY
INDISSOLUBLE
INDISSOLUBLY
INDISTINCTLY
INDIVERTIBLE
INDIVIDUALLY
INDOCTRINATE
INDO-EUROPEAN
INDO-GERMANIC
INDUSTRIALLY
INEFFACEABLE
INEFFACEABLY
INEFFICIENCY
INELASTICITY
INERADICABLE
INERADICABLY
INESCUTCHEON
INEXACTITUDE
INEXECUTABLE
INEXHAUSTIVE
INEXPANSIBLE
INEXPECTANCY
INEXPEDIENCE
INEXPEDIENCY
INEXPERIENCE
INEXPERTNESS
INEXPLICABLE
INEXPLICABLY
INEXPRESSIVE
INEXPUGNABLE
INEXPUGNABLY
INEXTENSIBLE
INEXTRICABLE
INEXTRICABLY
INFANTICIDAL
INFECTIOUSLY
INFELICITOUS
INFIBULATION
INFILTRATION
INFINITENESS
INFINITIVELY
INFLAMMATION
INFLAMMATORY
INFLATIONARY
INFLATIONISM
INFLATIONIST
INFLECTIONAL
INFORMIDABLE
INFRAORBITAL
INFREQUENTLY
INFRINGEMENT
INFUNDIBULAR
INGEMINATION
INGLORIOUSLY
INGRATIATING
INHABITATION
INHALATORIUM
INHARMONICAL

INHARMONIOUS
INHOSPITABLE
INHOSPITABLY
INIMICITIOUS
INIQUITOUSLY
INJUDICIALLY
INKING-ROLLER
INNUTRITIOUS
INOBEDIENTLY
INOBSERVABLE
INOBSERVANCE
INOCCUPATION
INOPERCULATE
INORDINATELY
INORDINATION
INOSCULATION
INQUISITRESS
INSALIVATION
INSALUBRIOUS
INSECT-POWDER
INSEMINATION
INSOLUBILISE
INSOLUBILITY
INSOMNOLENCE
INSPECTINGLY
INSPECTIONAL
INSPECTORATE
INSPECTORIAL
INSPISSATION
INSTALLATION
INSTAURATION
INSTEP-RAISER
INSTILLATION
INSTRUCTIBLE
INSTRUCTRESS
INSTRUMENTAL
INSTRUMENTED
INSUBJECTION
INSUFFERABLE
INSUFFERABLY
INSUFFICIENT
INSUFFLATION
INSURRECTION
INSUSCEPTIVE
INTELLECTION
INTELLECTIVE
INTELLECTUAL
INTELLIGENCE
INTELLIGIBLE
INTELLIGIBLY
INTEMPERANCE
INTEMPESTIVE
INTENERATION
INTENSIFYING
INTERBEDDING
INTERCEPTION
INTERCEPTIVE
INTERCESSION
INTERCESSORY
INTERCHANGER
INTERCHAPTER
INTERCIPIENT
INTERCLUSION
INTERCOLLINE
INTERCOMMUNE
INTERCONNECT

INTERCROPPED
INTERCURRENT
INTERDICTION
INTERDICTIVE
INTERDICTORY
INTERDIGITAL
INTERESTEDLY
INTERFEMORAL
INTERFERENCE
INTERFLUENCE
INTERFOLIATE
INTERFRETTED
INTERFRONTAL
INTERGLACIAL
INTERJACENCY
INTERJECTION
INTERLOBULAR
INTERLOCUTOR
INTERMAXILLA
INTERMEDDLER
INTERMEDIACY
INTERMEDIARY
INTERMEDIATE
INTERMINABLE
INTERMINABLY
INTERMISSION
INTERMISSIVE
INTERMITTENT
INTERMIXTURE
INTERMUNDANE
INTERNUNCIAL
INTEROCEANIC
INTERORBITAL
INTEROSSEOUS
INTERPELLATE
INTERPLEADER
INTERPLEURAL
INTERPOLABLE
INTERPOLATOR
INTERPRETATE
INTERPRETESS
INTERROGABLE
INTERROGATOR
INTERRUPTION
INTERRUPTIVE
INTERSCIENCE
INTERSECTION
INTERSERVICE
INTERSPATIAL
INTERSPERSAL
INTERSPINOUS
INTERSTELLAR
INTERSTITIAL
INTERTEXTURE
INTERTISSUED
INTERTRAFFIC
INTERTWINING
INTERVENIENT
INTERVENTION
INTERVOCALIC
INTERWREATHE
INTERWROUGHT
INTIMIDATION
INTIMIDATORY
INTOLERANTLY
INTOLERATION

INTOXICATING
INTOXICATION
INTRACARDIAC
INTRAMUNDANE
INTRANSIGENT
INTRANSITIVE
INTRA-UTERINE
INTRIGUINGLY
INTRINSICATE
INTRODUCIBLE
INTRODUCTION
INTRODUCTIVE
INTRODUCTORY
INTROJECTION
INTROMISSION
INTROMISSIVE
INTROMITTENT
INTROMITTING
INTROVERSION
INTROVERSIVE
INTROVERTIVE
INTRUSIONIST
INTUITIONISM
INTUITIONIST
INTUMESCENCE
INTUSSUSCEPT
INVAGINATION
INVALIDATION
INVEIGLEMENT
INVERTEBRATA
INVERTEBRATE
INVESTIGABLE
INVESTIGATOR
INVETERATELY
INVIGILATION
INVIGORATION
INVISIBILITY
INVITINGNESS
INVOLUTIONAL
INVULNERABLE
INVULNERABLY
INVULTUATION
IONOPHORESIS
IRACUNDULOUS
IRASCIBILITY
IRONING-BOARD
IRRATIONALLY
IRREALISABLE
IRREBUTTABLE
IRRECIPROCAL
IRRECONCILED
IRREDEEMABLE
IRREDEEMABLY
IRREFLECTION
IRREFLECTIVE
IRREFORMABLE
IRREFRAGABLE
IRREFRAGABLY
IRREGULARITY
IRRELATIVELY
IRRELEVANTLY
IRREMEDIABLE
IRREMEDIABLY
IRREMISSIBLE
IRREPAIRABLE
IRREPEALABLE

IRREPEALABLY
IRREPROVABLE
IRREPROVABLY
IRRESISTANCE
IRRESISTIBLE
IRRESISTIBLY
IRRESOLUTELY
IRRESOLUTION
IRRESOLVABLE
IRRESPECTIVE
IRRESPIRABLE
IRRESPONSIVE
IRREVERENTLY
IRREVERSIBLE
IRREVERSIBLY
IRRITABILITY
ISHMAELITISH
ISOBILATERAL
ISOCHEIMENAL
ISOCHROMATIC
ISOCHRONALLY
ISODIAMETRIC
ISODIMORPHIC
ISOLATIONISM
ISOLATIONIST
ISOPERIMETER
ISOPERIMETRY
ISOSTEMONOUS
ISOTHERMALLY

J

JACK-A-LANTERN
JACK-IN-OFFICE
JACK-IN-THE-BOX
JACK-O'-LANTERN
JACOB'S-LADDER
JACQUARD-LOOM
JAIL-DELIVERY
JEFFERSONIAN
JENNY-SPINNER
JEOPARDOUSLY
JERRY-BUILDER
JESTING-STOCK
JESUITICALLY
JET-PROPELLED
JINGLE-JANGLE
JOINTING-RULE
JOINT-TENANCY
JOURNALISTIC
JOURNEY-BATED
JUDGMENT-DEBT
JUDGMENT-HALL
JUDGMENT-SEAT
JUMPING-MOUSE
JURISCONSULT
JURISDICTION
JURISDICTIVE
JURISPRUDENT
JURISTICALLY
JUSTIFICATOR
JUVENESCENCE
JUVENILENESS

K

KAKISTOCRACY
KALEIDOPHONE

KALEIDOSCOPE
KARYOKINESIS
KATZENJAMMER
KEEKING-GLASS
KERATOGENOUS
KERATOPLASTY
KERAUNOGRAPH
KERB-CRAWLING
KERB-MERCHANT
KETTLEHOLDER
KICKIE-WICKIE
KICKING-STRAP
KICKSY-WICKSY
KIDNEY-POTATO
KILFUD-YOKING
KILL-COURTESY
KILOWATT-HOUR
KINAESTHESIA
KINAESTHESIS
KINAESTHETIC
KINDERGARTEN
KINESIPATHIC
KING'S-CUSHION
KIRSCHWASSER
KISSING-CRUST
KITCHEN-KNAVE
KITCHEN-RANGE
KITCHEN-STUFF
KITCHEN-WENCH
KLEPTOMANIAC
KLIPSPRINGER
KNEE-BREECHES
KNEE-CROOKING
KNICK-KNACKET
KNIFE-AND-FORK
KNIFE-GRINDER
KNIGHT-ERRANT
KNIGHTLINESS
KNOCKING-SHOP
KNOWABLENESS
KNUCKLE-JOINT
KRAMERIACEAE
KURCHATOVIUM

L

LABANOTATION
LABOUR-SAVING
LABYRINTHIAN
LABYRINTHINE
LACHRYMATORY
LACHRYMOSELY
LADY'S-CUSHION
LADY'S-FINGERS
LADY'S-SLIPPER
LADY'S-THISTLE
LAISSER-ALLER
LAISSER-FAIRE
LAISSEZ-ALLER
LAISSEZ-FAIRE
LAKE-DWELLING
LAMB'S-LETTUCE
LAMPADEDROMY
LAMPADOMANCY
LAMPROPHYRIC
LANCASTERIAN
LANCEOLATELY

LAND-GRABBING
LANDGRAVIATE
LANDING-CRAFT
LANDING-FIELD
LANDING-PLACE
LANDING-SPEED
LANDING-STAGE
LANDING-STRIP
LANDLUBBERLY
LAND-SURVEYOR
LAND-YACHTING
LANGUAGELESS
LANGUISHMENT
LANTERN-JAWED
LAODICEANISM
LAPIDESCENCE
LAPIDICOLOUS
LAPPERED-MILK
LARGE-HEARTED
LARKING-GLASS
LARYNGOPHONY
LARYNGOSCOPE
LARYNGOSCOPY
LASCIVIOUSLY
LATERISATION
LATH-SPLITTER
LATICIFEROUS
LATIROSTRATE
LATITUDINOUS
LAUDABLENESS
LAUNCHING-PAD
LAUREATESHIP
LAW-STATIONER
LAXATIVENESS
LEAPING-HOUSE
LEASING-MAKER
LEATHER-CLOTH
LEATHER-KNIFE
LEDGER-TACKLE
LEFT-HANDEDLY
LEGACY-HUNTER
LEGALISATION
LEGISLATRESS
LEGITIMATELY
LEGITIMATION
LEGLISLATURE
LEIOTRICHOUS
LENTICELLATE
LENTICULARLY
LEOPARD'S-BANE
LEPIDOMELANE
LESE-HUMANITY
LETTER-WEIGHT
LETTER-WRITER
LEUCOCYTOSIS
LEVELLING-ROD
LEVOROTATORY
LEXICOGRAPHY
LEXICOLOGIST
LIBERALISTIC
LIBIDINOSITY
LIBIDINOUSLY
LICENTIOUSLY
LICK-TRENCHER
LIEUTENANTRY
LIFE-AND-DEATH

LIFE-INTEREST
LIFELESSNESS
LIGHT-HEARTED
LIGHTNING-BUG
LIGHTNING-ROD
LIGNIPERDOUS
LIGULIFLORAE
LIGULIFLORAL
LILLIBULLERO
LILLIBURLERO
LIMNOLOGICAL
LIMNOPHILOUS
LINCOLN-GREEN
LINE-ENGRAVER
LINGUISTICAL
LIQUEFACIENT
LIQUEFACTION
LIQUEUR-GLASS
LIRIODENDRON
LISTLESSNESS
LITERARINESS
LITHOGRAPHER
LITHOGRAPHIC
LITHOLATROUS
LITHOLOGICAL
LITHOPHAGOUS
LITHOPHILOUS
LITHOSPERMUM
LITHOTOMICAL
LITHOTRIPTIC
LITHOTRIPTOR
LITHOTRITISE
LITHOTRITIST
LITTLE-ENDIAN
LITURGICALLY
LITURGIOLOGY
LIVE-FEATHERS
LIVERPUDLIAN
LIVERY-STABLE
LOATHFULNESS
LOBLOLLY-TREE
LOCALISATION
LOCK-HOSPITAL
LOCOMOTIVITY
LOCUM-TENENCY
LODGING-HOUSE
LOGGERHEADED
LOGGING-STONE
LOGODAEDALUS
LONESOMENESS
LONG-BREATHED
LONG-DISTANCE
LONG-DIVISION
LONG-DRAWN-OUT
LONGICAUDATE
LONGIPENNATE
LONGITUDINAL
LONGSHOREMAN
LONG-STANDING
LOOKING-GLASS
LOQUACIOUSLY
LORD-SUPERIOR
LORRY-HOPPING
LOSS-ADJUSTER
LOUNGE-LIZARD
LOUVER-WINDOW

LOUVRE-WINDOW
LOVELORNNESS
LOW-CHURCHISM
LOW-CHURCHMAN
LOWER-BRACKET
LOW-FREQUENCY
LOW-THOUGHTED
LOW-WATERMARK
LOXODROMICAL
LUCIFER-MÁTCH
LUCKLESSNESS
LUGUBRIOUSLY
LUKEWARMNESS
LUMBER-JACKET
LUMBRICIFORM
LUMINESCENCE
LUMINIFEROUS
LUMINOUSNESS
LUNCHEON-MEAT
LURKING-PLACE
LUSCIOUSNESS
LUST-BREATHED
LUXULLIANITE
LYCANTHROPIC
LYCOPODIALES
LYCOPODINEAE
LYMANTRIIDAE
LYMPHANGITIS

M

MACABERESQUE
MACHAIRODONT
MACHICOLATED
MACHINE-RULER
MACHTPOLITIK
MACMILLANITE
MACROBIOTICS
MACROCEPHALY
MACRODACTYLY
MACROPTEROUS
MADEMOISELLE
MAGISTRATURE
MAGNETICALLY
MAGNETISABLE
MAGNETOGRAPH
MAGNETOMETER
MAGNIFICALLY
MAGNIFICENCE
MAGNILOQUENT
MAGNOLIACEAE
MAIDENLINESS
MAIL-CARRIAGE
MAINTAINABLE
MAJESTICALLY
MAJESTICNESS
MAJOR-GENERAL
MAKE-AND-BREAK
MALACOLOGIST
MALACOSTRACA
MALAPERTNESS
MALCONTENTED
MALEVOLENTLY
MALFORMATION
MALLEABILITY
MALLOPHAGOUS
MALNUTRITION

MALTREATMENT
MALVERSATION
MAMMALOGICAL
MAMMEE-SAPOTA
MAN-ABOUT-TOWN
MANDIBULATED
MANGEL-WURZEL
MANICHEANISM
MANIFESTABLE
MANIFESTIBLE
MANIFESTNESS
MANIFOLDNESS
MANIPULATION
MANIPULATIVE
MANIPULATORY
MANNERLINESS
MANOEUVRABLE
MAN-OF-WAR'S-MAN
MANOMETRICAL
MANSION-HOUSE
MANSLAUGHTER
MANUFACTURAL
MANUFACTURER
MANY-COLOURED
MARATTIACEAE
MARBLE-CUTTER
MARBLED-WHITE
MARCATISSIMO
MARCH-TREASON
MARCIONITISM
MARCOBRUNNER
MARCONIGRAPH
MARIOLATROUS
MARKER-BEACON
MARKET-GARDEN
MARKET-SQUARE
MARLINESPIKE
MARRIAGEABLE
MARRIAGE-BONE
MARRIAGE-RING
MARROW-SQUASH
MARSEILLAISE
MARSH-HARRIER
MARSILEACEAE
MARVELLOUSLY
MASSARANDUBA
MASSERANDUBA
MASS-PRODUCED
MASTER-AT-ARMS
MASTERLINESS
MASTERSTROKE
MASTER-SWITCH
MASTIGOPHORA
MASTURBATION
MATERIALNESS
MATHEMATICAL
MATRIARCHATE
MATROCLINOUS
MATTER-OF-FACT
MEALY-MOUTHED
MEAN-SPIRITED
MEASURING-ROD
MEAT-OFFERING
MEAT-SALESMAN
MECHANICALLY
MECHITHARIST

MEDIAEVALISM
MEDIAEVALIST
MEDIATORSHIP
MEDICAMENTAL
MEDICINE-BALL
MEDITATIVELY
MEETING-HOUSE
MEGALOMANIAC
MELANCHOLIAC
MELANOCHROIC
MELLIFLUENCE
MELODRAMATIC
MELTING-POINT
MENDACIOUSLY
MENSTRUATION
MERCANTILISM
MERCANTILIST
MERCHANTABLE
MERCHANTLIKE
MERCIFULNESS
MERCURIALISE
MERCURIALISM
MERCURIALIST
MERETRICIOUS
MERIDIONALLY
MERISTEMATIC
MERRY-GO-ROUND
MERRY-THOUGHT
MESOCEPHALIC
MESOTHORACIC
MESSEIGNEURS
METACHRONISM
METAGNATHOUS
METALANGUAGE
METALEPTICAL
METALLICALLY
METALLOPHONE
METALLURGIST
METAL-WORKING
METAMORPHISM
METAMORPHIST
METAMORPHOSE
METAPHORICAL
METAPHRASTIC
METAPHYSICAL
METAPSYCHICS
METASILICATE
METASOMATISM
METATHETICAL
METATHORACIC
METEORICALLY
METEOROGRAPH
METEOROLOGIC
METHODICALLY
METICULOUSLY
METOPOSCOPIC
METROPOLISES
METROPOLITAN
MEZZO-RILIEVO
MEZZO-SOPRANO
MICROBALANCE
MICROBIOLOGY
MICROCAPSULE
MICROCEPHALY
MICROCIRCUIT
MICROCLIMATE

MICROCOPYING
MICROGRANITE
MICROGRAPHER
MICROGRAPHIC
MICROLOGICAL
MICROPHYSICS
MICROPIPETTE
MICROPTEROUS
MICROSCOPIST
MICROSEISMIC
MICROTOMICAL
MIDDLEWEIGHT
MID-VICTORIAN
MIGRATIONIST
MILITARISTIC
MILK-AND-WATER
MILKING-STOOL
MILK-PORRIDGE
MILLER'S-THUMB
MILLESIMALLY
MILL-MOUNTAIN
MILL-SIXPENCE
MINDLESSNESS
MINERALOGISE
MINERALOGIST
MINGLE-MANGLE
MINIFICATION
MINIMISATION
MINI-MOTORWAY
MINISTRATION
MINISTRATIVE
MIRACULOUSLY
MIRROR-WRITER
MIRTHFULNESS
MISADVENTURE
MISADVISEDLY
MISALLOTMENT
MISANTHROPIC
MISANTHROPOS
MISAPPREHEND
MISBEHAVIOUR
MISBELIEVING
MISCALCULATE
MISCEGENATOR
MISCELLANIST
MISCHALLENGE
MISCHANCEFUL
MISCONSTRUCT
MISCONTENTED
MISDEMEANANT
MISDEMEANOUR
MISDIRECTION
MISEDUCATION
MISFEATURING
MISFORMATION
MISINFORMANT
MISINTERPRET
MISJUDGEMENT
MISKNOWLEDGE
MISLEADINGLY
MISMATCHMENT
MISPLACEMENT
MISPRONOUNCE
MISPUNCTUATE
MISQUOTATION
MISRECKONING

MISREPRESENT
MISSEL-THRUSH
MISSIONARISE
MISSTATEMENT
MISSUMMATION
MISTAKENNESS
MISTRANSLATE
MISTREATMENT
MISTRESSLESS
MISTRESS-SHIP
MISTRUSTLESS
MISVENTUROUS
MITHRIDATISM
MITOCHONDRIA
MITRAILLEUSE
MIXOBARBARIC
MIXTER-MAXTER
MIXTIE-MAXTIE
MIZZEN-COURSE
MNEMOTECHNIC
MOBILISATION
MOCK-HEROICAL
MODERATENESS
MODIFICATION
MODIFICATIVE
MODIFICATORY
MOISTURELESS
MOLECULARITY
MOLLUSCICIDE
MOLLUSCOIDEA
MOMENTANEOUS
MONADELPHOUS
MONARCHISTIC
MONASTICALLY
MONETISATION
MONEY-CHANGER
MONEY-GRUBBER
MONEY-LENDING
MONEY-SPINNER
MONITORIALLY
MONKEY-ENGINE
MONKEY-FLOWER
MONKEY-HAMMER
MONKEY-JACKET
MONKEY-PUZZLE
MONKEY-WRENCH
MONOCHROMASY
MONOCHROMATE
MONOCHROMIST
MONO-COMPOUND
MONODELPHIAN
MONODELPHOUS
MONODRAMATIC
MONOFILAMENT
MONOGENISTIC
MONOGRAPHIST
MONOMANIACAL
MONOMETALLIC
MONOMORPHOUS
MONOPETALOUS
MONOPHYLETIC
MONOPHYODONT
MONOPHYSITIC
MONOPODIALLY
MONOPOLISTIC
MONOSEPALOUS

MONOSTICHOUS
MONOSTROPHIC
MONOSYLLABIC
MONOSYLLABLE
MONOTHALAMIC
MONOTHEISTIC
MONOTHELETIC
MONOTONOUSLY
MONTESSORIAN
MONTICELLITE
MONUMENTALLY
MOONLIGHTING
MOONSTRICKEN
MORALISATION
MORALITY-PLAY
MORBILLIFORM
MORDACIOUSLY
MORIGERATION
MORNING-DRESS
MORNING-GLORY
MORNING-WATCH
MORPHALLAXIS
MORPHOGRAPHY
MORPHOLOGIST
MORPHOTROPIC
MORRIS-DANCER
MOSCHIFEROUS
MOSS-TROOPING
MOTHER-CHURCH
MOTHER-FIGURE
MOTHERLINESS
MOTHER-LIQUOR
MOTHERS-IN-LAW
MOTHER-TONGUE
MOTIVATIONAL
MOTLEY-MINDED
MOTOR-BICYCLE
MOTOR-CYCLING
MOTOR-CYCLIST
MOTORISATION
MOTOR-TRACTOR
MOUND-BUILDER
MOUNTAIN-BLUE
MOUNTAIN-CORK
MOUNTAIN-FLAX
MOUNTAIN-HARE
MOUNTAIN-HIGH
MOUNTAIN-LION
MOUNTAIN-MEAL
MOUNTAIN-SIDE
MOUNTAIN-SOAP
MOUNTAIN-WOOD
MOUNTENAUNCE
MOURNFULNESS
MOURNING-DOVE
MOURNING-RING
MOUSE-BUTTOCK
MOUSQUETAIRE
MOUSTACHE-CUP
MOUTH-BREEDER
MOUTH-FILLING
MOVEABLENESS
MOVELESSNESS
MUCILAGINOUS
MUCOPURULENT
MUDDLEHEADED

MUDDY-METTLED
MUGGLETONIAN
MULLIGATAWNY
MULTICAULINE
MULTICENTRAL
MULTICIPITAL
MULTICOSTATE
MULTIDENTATE
MULTIFARIOUS
MULTIFLOROUS
MULTIFOLIATE
MULTIFORMITY
MULTILATERAL
MULTILINGUAL
MULTILOBULAR
MULTILOCULAR
MULTILOQUENT
MULTILOQUOUS
MULTINUCLEAR
MULTIPARTITE
MULTIPLIABLE
MULTIPLICAND
MULTIPLICATE
MULTIPLICITY
MULTIPRESENT
MULTIPURPOSE
MULTISCIENCE
MULTISEPTATE
MULTISERIATE
MULTISULCATE
MULTIVALENCE
MULTIVALENCY
MULTIVARIATE
MULTIVARIOUS
MULTIVERSITY
MULTIVOLTINE
MULTUNGULATE
MUNICIPALISE
MUNICIPALISM
MUNICIPALITY
MUNIFICENTLY
MUNITIONETTE
MUSICIANSHIP
MUSICOLOGIST
MUSIC-TEACHER
MUSTER-MASTER
MUTESSARIFAT
MUTINOUSNESS
MUTTON-CUTLET
MUTTON-HEADED
MUZZLE-LOADER
MYCODOMATIUM
MYCOPLASMATA
MYOGRAPHICAL
MYRINGOSCOPE
MYRMECOLOGIC
MYRMECOPHAGA
MYRMECOPHILY
MYSTERIOUSLY
MYSTICALNESS
MYTHOGENESIS
MYTHOGRAPHER
MYTHOLOGICAL
MYTHOLOGISER

N

NAIL-HEAD-SPAR
NAIL-SCISSORS
NAMBY-PAMBIES
NAME-DROPPING
NAMELESSNESS
NANOPLANKTON
NAPLES-YELLOW
NARCOTHERAPY
NARCOTICALLY
NARROW-MINDED
NASALISATION
NASOLACRYMAL
NATURALISTIC
NATUROPATHIC
NAUSEOUSNESS
NAVIGABILITY
NAVIGATIONAL
NEBULISATION
NEBULOUSNESS
NECK-MOULDING
NECROGRAPHER
NECROLOGICAL
NECROPHAGOUS
NECROPHILIAC
NECROPHILISM
NECROPHILOUS
NECROPHOROUS
NECROPOLISES
NECTOCALYCES
NEEDLESSNESS
NEGATIVENESS
NEGLECTFULLY
NEGLECTINGLY
NEGOTIATRESS
NEGROPHILISM
NEGROPHILIST
NEIGHBOURING
NEMATOMORPHA
NEO-CHRISTIAN
NEOCLASSICAL
NEO-DARWINIAN
NEO-DARWINISM
NEO-DARWINIST
NEO-HELLENISM
NEOLOGICALLY
NEONOMIANISM
NEOPLATONISM
NEOPLATONIST
NEOTERICALLY
NEPENTHACEAE
NEPHELOMETER
NEPHOLOGICAL
NEPHROLOGIST
NEPHROPTOSIS
NERVE-RACKING
NESTING-PLACE
NESTORIANISM
NETHERLANDER
NEURASTHENIA
NEURASTHENIC
NEUROANATOMY
NEUROBIOLOGY
NEUROLOGICAL
NEUROPATHIST

NEUROPTERIST
NEUROPTEROUS
NEUROSURGEON
NEUROSURGERY
NEURYPNOLOGY
NEVER-FAILING
NEVERTHELESS
NEVERTHEMORE
NEWFANGLEDLY
NEW-FASHIONED
NEWFOUNDLAND
NEWSPAPERDOM
NEWSPAPERISM
NEWSPAPERMAN
NICKEL-SILVER
NICOTANAMIDE
NIDDLE-NODDLE
NIDIFICATION
NIGHT-BRAWLER
NIGHT-CLOTHES
NIGHT-CRAWLER
NIGHT-FISHERY
NIGHT-TERRORS
NIMBLE-FOOTED
NIMBLE-WITTED
NIMINY-PIMINY
NINETEENTHLY
NIPPLE-SHIELD
NITROANILINE
NITROBENZENE
NITROSO-GROUP
NITROTOLUENE
NOBILITATION
NOCTAMBULISM
NOCTAMBULIST
NOCTILUCENCE
NOEMATICALLY
NOMADISATION
NOMENCLATIVE
NOMENCLATURE
NOMINALISTIC
NOMINATIVELY
NON-ADMISSION
NONAGENARIAN
NON-ALCOHOLIC
NON-ALIGNMENT
NON-ATTENTION
NONCHALANTLY
NON-CHRISTIAN
NON-COMBATANT
NON-COMMITTAL
NON-COMMUNION
NON-COMPLYING
NON-CONDUCTOR
NON-EFFECTIVE
NON-EFFICIENT
NONE-SO-PRETTY
NON-ESSENTIAL
NON-EUCLIDEAN
NON-EXISTENCE
NON-FLAMMABLE
NON-INTRUSION
NON-NUCLEATED
NON-OBJECTIVE
NON-RESIDENCE
NON-RESISTANT

NON-RESISTING
NORADRENALIN
NORMAN-FRENCH
NORTH-COUNTRY
NORTH-EASTERN
NORTHERNMOST
NORTH-SEEKING
NORTHUMBRIAN
NORTH-WESTERN
NOSE-BLEEDING
NOSE-PAINTING
NOSTOLOGICAL
NOTHINGARIAN
NOTIFICATION
NOTODONTIDAE
NOTONECTIDAE
NOVELISATION
NUBBING-CHEAT
NUGATORINESS
NUMERABILITY
NUMEROUSNESS
NUMINOUSNESS
NURSERY-RHYME
NURSE-TENDING
NUTRITIOUSLY
NYCHTHEMERAL
NYCHTHEMERON
NYCTITROPISM
NYMPHAEACEAE
NYMPHOLEPTIC
NYMPHOMANIAC

O

OATH-BREAKING
OBCOMPRESSED
OBDURATENESS
OBEDIENTIARY
OBJECT-FINDER
OBJECT-LESSON
OBLANCEOLATE
OBLIGATORILY
OBLIGINGNESS
OBLITERATION
OBLITERATIVE
OBLIVISCENCE
OBMUTESCENCE
OBNUBILATION
OBREPTITIOUS
OBSCURANTISM
OBSCURANTIST
OBSEQUIOUSLY
OBSERVANTINE
OBSESSIONIST
OBSOLESCENCE
OBSOLETENESS
OBSTETRICIAN
OBSTREPERATE
OBSTREPEROUS
OBTUSE-ANGLED
OCCASIONALLY
OCCIDENTALLY
OCCUPATIONAL
OCEANOGRAPHY
OCHROLEUCOUS
OCTASTICHOUS
OCTASTROPHIC

OCTOGENARIAN
OCTOPETALOUS
OCTOSEPALOUS
OCTOSTICHOUS
OCTOSYLLABIC
OCTOSYLLABLE
ODD-COME-SHORT
ODONTOGRAPHY
ODONTOLOGIST
ODONTOMATOUS
ODONTOPHORAL
ODONTOPHORAN
OECUMENICISM
ŒILS-DE-BŒUF
OFFICE-BEARER
OFFICE-HOLDER
OFFICE-HUNTER
OFFICE-SEEKER
OFF-RECKONING
OLD-FASHIONED
OLIGARCHICAL
OMBROPHILOUS
OMBROPHOBOUS
OMNIPOTENTLY
OMNIPRESENCE
OMNISCIENTLY
OMPHALOMANCY
ONCORHYNCHUS
ONE-AND-THIRTY
ONEIROCRITIC
ONE-SIDEDNESS
ONE-UPMANSHIP
ONIROSCOPIST
ONOMATOPOEIA
ONOMATOPOEIC
OOPHORECTOMY
OPERATICALLY
OPHIOGLOSSUM
OPHIOLATROUS
OPHIOLOGICAL
OPHIOMORPHIC
OPHIOPHAGOUS
OPHIOPHILIST
OPHTHALMITIS
OPINIONATELY
OPINIONATIVE
OPISTHODOMOS
OPISTHOGRAPH
OPISTHOTONIC
OPISTHOTONOS
OPPOSABILITY
OPPOSITENESS
OPPOSITIONAL
OPPRESSIVELY
OPTIMISATION
ORACULARNESS
ORANGE-FLOWER
ORATORICALLY
ORCHARD-GRASS
ORCHARD-HOUSE
ORCHESTRATOR
ORCHIDACEOUS
ORCHIDECTOMY
ORCHIDOMANIA
ORCHILLA-WEED
OREOPITHECUS

ORGAN-BUILDER
ORGAN-GALLERY
ORGAN-GRINDER
ORGANISATION
ORGANOGRAPHY
ORGANOLEPTIC
ORICHALCEOUS
ORIENTEERING
ORNAMENTALLY
ORNITHOGALUM
ORNITHOMANCY
ORNITHOMORPH
ORNITHOPHILY
ORNITHOSCOPY
OROGRAPHICAL
OROROTUNDITY
ORPHAN-ASYLUM
ORTHOBORACIC
ORTHOCOUSINS
ORTHODONTICS
ORTHODONTIST
ORTHODROMICS
ORTHOGENESIS
ORTHOGENETIC
ORTHOGNATHIC
ORTHOGONALLY
ORTHOGRAPHER
ORTHOGRAPHIC
ORTHOPAEDICS
ORTHOPAEDIST
ORTHOPEDICAL
ORTHOPTERIST
ORTHOPTEROID
ORTHOPTEROUS
ORTHORHOMBIC
ORTHOSILICIC
ORTHOTONESIS
ORTHOTROPISM
ORTHOTROPOUS
OSCILLOGRAPH
OSCILLOSCOPE
OSSIFICATION
OSTENTATIOUS
OSTEODERMOUS
OSTEOGENESIS
OSTEOGENETIC
OSTEOLOGICAL
OSTEOMALACIA
OSTEOPATHIST
OSTEOPLASTIC
OSTEOPOROSIS
OTHERWORLDLY
OTOSCLEROSIS
OTTER-HUNTING
OUGHLY-HEADED
OURANG-OUTANG
OUTFANGTHIEF
OUTLANDISHLY
OUTMANOEUVRE
OUT-PENSIONER
OUTRAGEOUSLY
OUTSPREADING
OUTWARD-BOUND
OVARIOTOMIST
OVERCANOPIED
OVERESTIMATE

OVEREXERTION
OVEREXPOSURE
OVERFINENESS
OVERFLOURISH
OVERFONDNESS
OVERFULLNESS
OVERKINDNESS
OVERLORDSHIP
OVERMULTIPLY
OVERNICENESS
OVERPERSUADE
OVERPOPULATE
OVERPOWERING
OVERPRAISING
OVERPRESSURE
OVERRASHNESS
OVERRIPENESS
OVERSCUTCHED
OVERSIMPLIFY
OVERSTRAINED
OVERSUBTLETY
OVERWEIGHTED
OVERWHELMING
OXY-ACETYLENE

P

PACHYCARPOUS
PACHYDACIOUS
PACHYDERMATA
PACHYDERMOUS
PACIFICATION
PACIFICATORY
PACKING-PAPER
PACKING-PRESS
PACKING-SHEET
PADDOCK-STOOL
PAEDOBAPTISM
PAEDOBAPTIST
PAEDODONTICS
PAEDOGENESIS
PAEDOGENETIC
PAEDOPHILIAC
PAINLESSNESS
PALAEOBOTANY
PALAEOGRAPHY
PALAEOLITHIC
PALAESTRICAL
PALATABILITY
PALETTE-KNIFE
PALIFICATION
PALINDROMIST
PALINGENESIA
PALINGENESIS
PALLADIANISM
PALPABLENESS
PALUDAMENTUM
PALUDICOLOUS
PAMPEREDNESS
PANAESTHESIA
PANARTHRITIS
PANATHENAEAN
PANCHATANTRA
PANCHROMATIC
PANCREATITIS
PANDAEMONIUM
PANDANACEOUS

PAN-GERMANISM
PANHELLENION
PANHELLENISM
PANHELLENIST
PANHELLENIUM
PANICULATELY
PANIFICATION
PANPHARMACON
PANSEXUALISM
PANSEXUALIST
PANSPERMATIC
PANTALOONERY
PANTECHNICON
PANTISOCRACY
PANTOGRAPHER
PANTOGRAPHIC
PANTOMIMICAL
PANTOPHAGIST
PANTOPHAGOUS
PAPAVERACEAE
PAPER-MARBLER
PAPER-STAINER
PAPER-WASHING
PAPILIONIDAE
PAPISTICALLY
PAPYROLOGIST
PARABOLOIDAL
PARACENTESIS
PARACHRONISM
PARA-COMPOUND
PARACYANOGEN
PARADE-GROUND
PARADIGMATIC
PARADISAICAL
PARADISE-FISH
PARADISEIDAE
PARADISIACAL
PARADOXIDIAN
PARADOXOLOGY
PARADOXURINE
PARAENETICAL
PARAESTHESIA
PARAGLOSSATE
PARAGNATHISM
PARAGNATHOUS
PARAGRAPHIST
PARALIPOMENA
PARALLELWISE
PARAMAGNETIC
PARAMETRICAL
PARAMILITARY
PARAMORPHISM
PARANTHELION
PARAPHIMOSIS
PARAPHRASTIC
PARAPOPHYSES
PARAPOPHYSIS
PARAPSYCHISM
PARAQUADRATE
PARASITICIDE
PARASITOLOGY
PARASPHENOID
PARASYNTHETA
PARATACTICAL
PARCHMENTISE
PARENTERALLY

PARENTHESISE
PARISYLLABIC
PARKING-PLACE
PARKINSONISM
PAROCCIPITAL
PAROCHIALISE
PAROCHIALISM
PAROCHIALITY
PAROEMIOLOGY
PARONOMASTIC
PARROT-WRASSE
PARSIMONIOUS
PARSLEY-PIERT
PARTICIPABLE
PARTICIPATOR
PARTICULARLY
PARTISANSHIP
PARTITIONIST
PARTY-CAPITAL
PARTY-VERDICT
PASQUE-FLOWER
PASSABLENESS
PASSAGE-MONEY
PASSEMEASURE
PASSE-PARTOUT
PASSIBLENESS
PASSIONATELY
PASSION-FRUIT
PASSION-MUSIC
PASSY-MEASURE
PATHETICALLY
PATHOGENESIS
PATHOGENETIC
PATHOLOGICAL
PATIENCE-DOCK
PATRIARCHATE
PATRIARCHISM
PATRILINEAGE
PATRIPASSIAN
PATRISTICISM
PATTERN-MAKER
PATTERN-WHEEL
PAVILION-ROOF
PAY-AS-YOU-EARN
PEACE-BREAKER
PEACEFULNESS
PEACE-OFFICER
PEACE-WARRANT
PEACH-BLOSSOM
PEACH-YELLOWS
PEACOCK-STONE
PEARL-ESSENCE
PEARL-FISHERY
PEARL-FISHING
PEARL-SHELLER
PEARL-TAPIOCA
PEASE-BANNOCK
PEASE-BLOSSOM
PEASE-PUDDING
PEBBLE-POWDER
PECCADILLOES
PECKSNIFFIAN
PECTINACEOUS
PECTORILOQUY
PEDAL-CLAVIER
PEDANTICALLY

PEDANTOCRACY
PEDICELLARIA
PEDICULATION
PEDUNCULATED
PEERLESSNESS
PEJORATIVELY
PELICAN'S-FOOT
PELLUCIDNESS
PENALISATION
PENANG-LAWYER
PENCIL-SKETCH
PEN-FEATHERED
PENITENTIARY
PENNY-WEDDING
PENNY-WHISTLE
PENTACRINOID
PENTADACTYLE
PENTADACTYLY
PENTAGONALLY
PENTAPOLITAN
PENTATEUCHAL
PEPPER-CASTER
PEPPER-CASTOR
PERADVENTURE
PERAMBULATOR
PERCEPTIONAL
PERCEPTIVITY
PERCUSSIONAL
PERCUSSIVELY
PERCUTANEOUS
PEREGRINATOR
PEREMPTORILY
PERFECTATION
PERFECTIVELY
PERFERVIDITY
PERFIDIOUSLY
PERGAMENEOUS
PERICARDITIS
PERICHAETIAL
PERICHAETIUM
PERILOUSNESS
PERIMORPHOUS
PERINEURITIS
PERIODICALLY
PERIODONTICS
PERIOSTRACUM
PERIPHERICAL
PERIPHRASTIC
PERISPOMENON
PERISTERONIC
PERISTOMATIC
PERISTREPHIC
PERIWIG-PATED
PERMANGANATE
PERMEABILITY
PERMISSIVELY
PERMITTIVITY
PERNICIOUSLY
PERNOCTATION
PEROXIDATION
PERPETRATION
PERPETUALISM
PERPETUALIST
PERPETUALITY
PERPETUATION
PERPLEXINGLY

PERQUISITION
PERSEVERANCE
PERSEVERATOR
PERSISTENTLY
PERSISTINGLY
PERSONIFYING
PERSPICACITY
PERSPIRATION
PERSPIRATORY
PERSUASIVELY
PERSULPHURIC
PERTINACIOUS
PERTURBATION
PERTURBATIVE
PERTURBATORY
PERVERSENESS
PERVICACIOUS
PERVIOUSNESS
PESTALOZZIAN
PESTILENTIAL
PESTOLOGICAL
PETRIFACTION
PETRIFACTIVE
PETROGLYPHIC
PETROGRAPHER
PETROGRAPHIC
PETROLOGICAL
PETTIFOGGERY
PETTIFOGGING
PHAENOGAMOUS
PHAEOMELANIN
PHAEOPHYCEAE
PHAGOCYTICAL
PHAGOCYTOSIS
PHANEROGAMAE
PHANEROGAMIA
PHANEROGAMIC
PHANTASMALLY
PHANTASMICAL
PHARMACEUTIC
PHARMACOLOGY
PHARYNGOTOMY
PHEASANT'S-EYE
PHENOLOGICAL
PHENOMENALLY
PHENOTYPICAL
PHENYLALANIN
PHILANTHROPE
PHILANTHROPY
PHILHARMONIC
PHILHELLENIC
PHILISTINISE
PHILISTINISM
PHILLUMENIST
PHILODENDRON
PHILOLOGICAL
PHILOSOPHESS
PHILOSOPHISE
PHILOSOPHISM
PHILOSOPHIST
PHLEBOTOMISE
PHLEBOTOMIST
PHLEGMAGOGIC
PHLEGMAGOGUE
PHONASTHENIA
PHONEMICALLY

PHONETICALLY
PHONOCAMPTIC
PHONOGRAPHER
PHONOGRAPHIC
PHONOLOGICAL
PHONOTYPICAL
PHOSPHATURIA
PHOSPHORESCE
PHOTOCHROMIC
PHOTOCOPYING
PHOTO-ETCHING
PHOTO-FISSION
PHOTOGEOLOGY
PHOTOGLYPHIC
PHOTOGRAPHER
PHOTOGRAPHIC
PHOTOGRAVURE
PHOTOKINESIS
PHOTOMONTAGE
PHOTOPHILOUS
PHOTO-PROCESS
PHOTOSETTING
PHOTOSPHERIC
PHOTOTHERAPY
PHOTOTROPISM
PHRASEMONGER
PHRASEOGRAPH
PHRASEOLOGIC
PHREATOPHYTE
PHRENOLOGISE
PHRENOLOGIST
PHRONTISTERY
PHYCOLOGICAL
PHYCOMYCETES
PHYCOXANTHIN
PHYLLOTACTIC
PHYLOGENESIS
PHYLOGENETIC
PHYSIOCRATIC
PHYSIOGNOMIC
PHYSIOGRAPHY
PHYSIOLOGIST
PHYTOBENTHOS
PHYTOGENESIS
PHYTOGENETIC
PHYTOGRAPHER
PHYTOGRAPHIC
PHYTOLOGICAL
PHYTONADIONE
PHYTOPHAGOUS
PICKEREL-WEED
PICROCARMINE
PICTOGRAPHIC
PICTORICALLY
PICTURE-FRAME
PICTURE-HOUSE
PICTURE-PHONE
PIERCINGNESS
PIGEON-FLYING
PIGEON'S-BLOOD
PIGMENTATION
PILE-DWELLING
PILLION-RIDER
PILOT-BALLOON
PINCHCOMMONS
PIN-FEATHERED

PINNIEWINKLE
PISCICULTURE
PITCH-AND-TOSS
PITCHER-PLANT
PITIABLENESS
PITILESSNESS
PITTER-PATTER
PLACABLENESS
PLACENTATION
PLACENTIFORM
PLAGIOTROPIC
PLAIN-CLOTHES
PLAIN-DEALING
PLAIN-HEARTED
PLANETESIMAL
PLANET-STRUCK
PLANISPHERIC
PLANOCONCAVE
PLANOCONICAL
PLASTERBOARD
PLASTERINESS
PLASTERSTONE
PLATANACEOUS
PLATE-LEATHER
PLATONICALLY
PLATT-DEUTSCH
PLAUSIBILITY
PLAYING-FIELD
PLEASANTNESS
PLEASANTRIES
PLEASINGNESS
PLEASURE-BOAT
PLEASURELESS
PLEASURE-TRIP
PLEBISCITARY
PLECOPTEROUS
PLECTOGNATHI
PLEIOCHASIUM
PLEIOTROPISM
PLENIPOTENCE
PLENIPOTENCY
PLEOMORPHISM
PLEOMORPHOUS
PLEONASTICAL
PLESSIMETRIC
PLEURISY-ROOT
PLEURONECTES
PLOUGH-JOGGER
PLOUGHWRIGHT
PLUMBAGINOUS
PLUMBER-BLOCK
PLUMBIFEROUS
PLUMMER-BLOCK
PLUM-PORRIDGE
PLUMULACEOUS
PLURILITERAL
PLURILOCULAR
PLURISERIATE
PLUVIOMETRIC
PNEUMATICITY
PNEUMATOLOGY
POCKET-GOPHER
POCKET-PISTOL
POENOLOGICAL
POETASTERING
POINTILLISME

POINTILLISTE
POINT-TO-POINT
POISON-SUMACH
POLARIMETRIC
POLARISATION
POLICE-MANURE
POLICE-OFFICE
POLICY-HOLDER
POLITICASTER
POLLEN-BASKET
POLLING-BOOTH
POLLUTEDNESS
POLONISATION
POLYADELPHIA
POLYANTHUSES
POLYEMBRYONY
POLYETHYLENE
POLYGALACEAE
POLYGLOTTOUS
POLYGONACEAE
POLYHISTORIC
POLYISOPRENE
POLYMORPHISM
POLYMORPHOUS
POLYPETALOUS
POLYPHYLETIC
POLYPHYLLOUS
POLYSEPALOUS
POLYSILOXANE
POLYSYLLABIC
POLYSYLLABLE
POLYSYNDETON
POLYTHEISTIC
POLYTONALITY
POLYURETHANE
POMPHOLYGOUS
PONTIFICALLY
PONY-CARRIAGE
PONY-TREKKING
POOR-SPIRITED
POPULOUSNESS
PORCELAINISE
PORCELAINOUS
PORCELLANISE
PORCELLANITE
PORCELLANOUS
PORISMATICAL
PORNOGRAPHER
PORNOGRAPHIC
PORTE-COCHERE
PORTENTOUSLY
PORTMANTEAUS
PORTMANTEAUX
PORTRAIT-BUST
POSITIVENESS
POSITIVISTIC
POSSESSIONED
POSSESSIVELY
POSTAGE-STAMP
POST-DILUVIAL
POST-DILUVIAN
POST-DOCTORAL
POSTERIORITY
POSTGRADUATE
POSTHUMOUSLY
POSTILLATION

POSTLIMINARY
POSTLIMINOUS
POST-MERIDIAN
POSTMISTRESS
POSTPONEMENT
POSTPOSITION
POSTPOSITIVE
POST-PRANDIAL
POST-TERTIARY
POSTURE-MAKER
POTAMOLOGIST
POTATO-FINGER
POTATO-SPIRIT
POT-COMPANION
POTENTIALITY
POTICHOMANIA
POTTLE-BODIED
POT-WALLOPING
POUND-FOOLISH
POWDER-CLOSET
POWDERING-TUB
POWDER-MONKEY
POWERFULNESS
POWER-STATION
PRACTICALISM
PRACTICALIST
PRACTICALITY
PRACTITIONER
PRAISEWORTHY
PRALLTRILLER
PRASEODYMIUM
PRAXINOSCOPE
PRAYERLESSLY
PRAYER-MONGER
PREACHERSHIP
PREASSURANCE
PRECANCEROUS
PRECARIOUSLY
PRECAUTIONAL
PRECEDENTIAL
PRECEPTORIAL
PRECESSIONAL
PRECHRISTIAN
PRECIOUSNESS
PRECIPITABLE
PRECIPITANCE
PRECIPITANCY
PRECIPITATOR
PRECISIANISM
PRECISIANIST
PRECISIONIST
PRECLASSICAL
PRECLUSIVELY
PRECOCIOUSLY
PRECOGNITION
PRECOGNITIVE
PRECONDITION
PRECONSCIOUS
PREDESIGNATE
PREDESTINATE
PREDETERMINE
PREDIGESTION
PREDILECTION
PREDISPOSING
PREDOMINANCE
PREDOMINANCY

PRE-DRAVIDIAN
PRE-EMINENTLY
PRE-ESTABLISH
PRE-EXISTENCE
PREFABRICATE
PREFECTORIAL
PREFERENTIAL
PREFLORATION
PREFOLIATION
PREFORMATION
PREFORMATIVE
PREGUSTATION
PREHENSILITY
PREHENSORIAL
PREHISTORIAN
PREJUDGEMENT
PRELATICALLY
PREMAXILLARY
PREMONSTRANT
PRENTICESHIP
PREOCCUPANCY
PREORDINANCE
PREPAREDNESS
PREPONDERANT
PREPONDERATE
PREPOSSESSED
PREPOSTEROUS
PREREQUISITE
PREROGATIVED
PRESBYTERATE
PRESBYTERIAL
PRESBYTERIAN
PRESCRIPTION
PRESCRIPTIVE
PRESELECTION
PRESENTATION
PRESENTATIVE
PRESENTIALLY
PRESENTIMENT
PRESERVATION
PRESERVATIVE
PRESERVATORY
PRESIDENTESS
PRESIDENTIAL
PRESS-CUTTING
PRESS-GALLERY
PRESSURE-COOK
PRESSURE-SUIT
PRESTIGIATOR
PRESTRICTION
PRESUMPTUOUS
PRETENCELESS
PRETENDINGLY
PRETERMITTED
PRETTY-PRETTY
PRETTY-SPOKEN
PREVAILINGLY
PREVARICATOR
PREVENTATIVE
PREVENTIVELY
PREVIOUSNESS
PRICE-CURRENT
PRICE-CUTTING
PRICE-RIGGING
PRIDEFULNESS
PRIESTLINESS

PRIEST-RIDDEN
PRIGGISHNESS
PRIMIGRAVIDA
PRIMOGENITAL
PRIMOGENITOR
PRIMORDIALLY
PRIMULACEOUS
PRINCE-BISHOP
PRINCELINESS
PRINCIPALITY
PRIVATEERING
PRIZE-FIGHTER
PRO-AND-CONNED
PROBATIONARY
PROBOSCIDEAN
PROBOULEUTIC
PROCATHEDRAL
PROCELLARIAN
PROCESS-BLOCK
PROCESSIONAL
PROCESSIONER
PROCLAMATION
PROCLAMATORY
PROCONSULATE
PROCTORIALLY
PRODIGIOSITY
PRODIGIOUSLY
PRODITORIOUS
PRODUCTIONAL
PRODUCTIVELY
PRODUCTIVITY
PROFESSIONAL
PROFESSORATE
PROFESSORESS
PROFESSORIAL
PROFICIENTLY
PROFITEERING
PROFITLESSLY
PROFLIGATELY
PROFOUNDNESS
PROGENITRESS
PROGESTERONE
PROGLOTTIDES
PROGRAMMATIC
PROGYMNASIUM
PROJECTIONAL
PROJECTIVITY
PROLEGOMENON
PROLETARIATE
PROLIFICALLY
PROLIFICNESS
PROLONGATION
PROMISSORILY
PROMULGATION
PROMUSCIDATE
PRONOMINALLY
PRONOUNCEDLY
PROOF-CORRECT
PROOF-READING
PROPAEDEUTIC
PROPAGANDISE
PROPAGANDISM
PROPAGANDIST
PROPENSENESS
PROPERTY-ROOM
PROPHYLACTIC

PROPITIATION
PROPITIATIVE
PROPITIATORY
PROPITIOUSLY
PROPORTIONAL
PROPORTIONED
PROPRIETRESS
PROPUGNATION
PROSCRIPTION
PROSCRIPTIVE
PROSECTORIAL
PROSECUTABLE
PROSELYTISER
PROSODICALLY
PROSOPOPOEIA
PROSPECTUSES
PROSPEROUSLY
PROSTITUTION
PROSYLLOGISM
PROTACTINIUM
PROTECTINGLY
PROTECTIVELY
PROTECTORATE
PROTECTORIAL
PROTESTATION
PROTESTINGLY
PROTHALAMION
PROTHONOTARY
PROTISTOLOGY
PROTOCOLLING
PROTO-HISTORY
PROTOPLASMIC
PROTOPLASTIC
PROTOTYPICAL
PROTOZOOLOGY
PROTRACTEDLY
PROTREPTICAL
PROTRUSIVELY
PROTUBERANCE
PROUD-HEARTED
PROVERBIALLY
PROVIDENTIAL
PROVINCIALLY
PROVISIONARY
PRUDENTIALLY
PRUNING-KNIFE
PRUSSIANISER
PSAMMOPHYTIC
PSEPHOLOGIST
PSEUDOCYESIS
PSEUDO-GOTHIC
PSEUDOGRAPHY
PSEUDOMARTYR
PSEUDONYMITY
PSEUDONYMOUS
PSEUDOPODIUM
PSILANTHROPY
PSYCHIATRIST
PSYCHOACTIVE
PSYCHOGRAPHY
PSYCHOLOGISM
PSYCHOLOGIST
PSYCHOMETRIC
PSYCHOPATHIC
PSYCHOTROPIC
PSYCHROMETER

PSYCHROMETRY
PTERIDOMANIA
PTERIDOPHYTA
PTERIDOPHYTE
PTERIDOSPERM
PTERODACTYLE
PTEROSAURIAN
PUBLIC-SCHOOL
PUDDING-FACED
PUDDING-STONE
PUGNACIOUSLY
PULVERISABLE
PULVERULENCE
PULVILLIFORM
PUMPERNICKEL
PUNCTULATION
PUNCTURATION
PUPILABILITY
PURBLINDNESS
PURIFICATION
PURIFICATIVE
PURIFICATORY
PURPOSEFULLY
PURSE-STRINGS
PUSEYISTICAL
PUTREFACIENT
PUTREFACTION
PUTREFACTIVE
PUTTING-CLEEK
PUTTING-GREEN
PUTTING-STONE
PUZZLE-HEADED
PUZZLE-MONKEY
PYJAMA-JACKET
PYRITHIAMINE
PYRITIFEROUS
PYRITOHEDRAL
PYRITOHEDRON
PYRO-ELECTRIC
PYROLIGNEOUS
PYROMANIACAL
PYROMETRICAL
PYROMORPHITE
PYROPHYLLITE
PYROTARTARIC
PYROTARTRATE
PYROTECHNICS
PYROTECHNIST

Q

QUACKSALVING
QUADRAGESIMA
QUADRANGULAR
QUADRIENNIAL
QUADRIENNIUM
QUADRIPLEGIA
QUADRIPLEGIC
QUADRIVALENT
QUADRUMANOUS
QUAESTIONARY
QUAESTORSHIP
QUAKER-BUTTON
QUAKER-COLOUR
QUAKING-GRASS
QUALIFICATOR
QUALMISHNESS

QUANTITATIVE
QUANTIVALENT
QUAQUAVERSAL
QUARRYMASTER
QUARTER-BLOOD
QUARTER-BOUND
QUARTER-GUARD
QUARTER-HORSE
QUARTERN-LOAF
QUARTER-PLATE
QUARTER-ROUND
QUARTER-STAFF
QUARTZ-SCHIST
QUATERNIONED
QUATTROCENTO
QUEEN-CONSORT
QUEEN-DOWAGER
QUEEN-REGNANT
QUENCHLESSLY
QUERIMONIOUS
QUESTIONABLE
QUESTIONABLY
QUESTIONLESS
QUESTION-MARK
QUICK-SCENTED
QUICK-SELLING
QUICK-SIGHTED
QUICKSILVERY
QUIDDITATIVE
QUILL-DRIVING
QUILL-FEATHER
QUINQUENNIAD
QUINQUENNIAL
QUINQUENNIUM
QUINTESSENCE
QUIXOTICALLY
QUIZZICALITY
QUOTABLENESS

R

RABBETING-SAW
RABBINICALLY
RABBIT-SUCKER
RABBIT-WARREN
RACCOON-BERRY
RACEMISATION
RACKETEERING
RACKET-GROUND
RACKET-TAILED
RADICICOLOUS
RADICIVOROUS
RADIOBIOLOGY
RADIO-COMPASS
RADIO-ELEMENT
RADIOGRAPHIC
RADIO-ISOTOPE
RADIOLOGICAL
RADIOPHONICS
RADIOTHERAPY
RADIO-THORIUM
RAGGLE-TAGGLE
RAIL-SPLITTER
RAINBOW-TROUT
RAMBUNCTIOUS
RAMIFICATION
RANUNCULUSES

RATCHET-WHEEL
RATIFICATION
RATTLE-HEADED
RAVENOUSNESS
RAZZLEDAZZLE
REABSORPTION
REACTIVATION
REACTIVENESS
READABLENESS
READJUSTMENT
READMITTANCE
READY-MONEYED
REALLOCATION
RE-ANNEXATION
REAPPEARANCE
REASSEMBLAGE
REASSESSMENT
REASSIGNMENT
REASSUMPTION
REASSURINGLY
REBELLIOUSLY
RECALCITRANT
RECALCITRATE
RECALESCENCE
RECAPITULATE
RECEIVING-SET
RECEPTACULAR
RECEPTACULUM
RECEPTIONIST
RECIPROCALLY
RECIPROCATOR
RECITING-NOTE
RECKLESSNESS
RECOGNISABLE
RECOGNISABLY
RECOGNISANCE
RECOLLECTION
RECOLLECTIVE
RECOMFORTURE
RECOMMISSION
RECOMMITMENT
RECONCILABLE
RECONCILABLY
RECONNOITRER
RECONSECRATE
RECONSITUENT
RECONSTITUTE
RECONVERSION
RECONVEYANCE
RECORDERSHIP
RECREATIONAL
RECRIMINANTE
RECRIMINATOR
RECRUDESCENT
RECTIROSTRAL
RECUPERATION
RECUPERATIVE
RECUPERATORY
REDEMPTIONER
REDEMPTORIST
REDEPLOYMENT
REDINTEGRATE
REDISCOVERER
REDISTRIBUTE
REDOUBLEMENT
REDUCIBILITY

REDUCTIONISM
REDUCTIONIST
REED-PHEASANT
RE-EMBODIMENT
RE-ENGAGEMENT
RE-ENLISTMENT
REFLATIONARY
REFLECTINGLY
REFLECTIVELY
REFLECTIVITY
REFOUNDATION
REFRACTIVITY
REFRACTORILY
REFRESHFULLY
REFRESHINGLY
REFRIGERATOR
REGARDLESSLY
REGENERATION
REGENERATIVE
REGENERATORY
REGISTRATION
REGRESSIVELY
REGRESSIVITY
REHABILITATE
REIMPOSITION
REINSPECTION
REINSTALMENT
REINVESTMENT
REINVIGORATE
REITERATEDLY
REJUVENATION
RELATIONALLY
RELATIONLESS
RELATIONSHIP
RELATIVENESS
RELATIVISTIC
RELATIVITIST
RELENTLESSLY
RELIABLENESS
RELIGIONLESS
REMAINDER-MAN
REMBRANDTISH
REMBRANDTISM
REMEDILESSLY
REMEMBERABLE
REMEMBERABLY
REMEMBRANCER
REMINISCENCE
REMONSTRANCE
REMONSTRATOR
REMORSEFULLY
REMOVABILITY
REMUNERATION
REMUNERATIVE
REMUNERATORY
RENOUNCEMENT
RENUNCIATION
RENUNCIATIVE
RENUNCIATORY
REOCCUPATION
REORDINATION
REPARABILITY
REPATRIATION
REPERCUSSION
REPERCUSSIVE
REPETITIONAL

REPETITIVELY
REPLANTATION
REPLEVISABLE
REPREHENSION
REPREHENSIVE
REPRESENTANT
REPRESSIVELY
REPROACHABLE
REPROACHLESS
REPRODUCIBLE
REPRODUCTION
REPRODUCTIVE
REPUTATIVELY
RESERVEDNESS
RESETTLEMENT
RESIDENTIARY
RESIDENTSHIP
RESIGNEDNESS
RESINIFEROUS
RESIPISCENCE
RESIPISCENCY
RESISTLESSLY
RESOLUTENESS
RESOLUTIONER
RESOLVEDNESS
RESONANCE-BOX
RESOUNDINGLY
RESOURCELESS
RESPECTFULLY
RESPECTIVELY
RESPLENDENCE
RESPLENDENCY
RESPONDENTIA
RESPONSELESS
RESPONSIVELY
RESPONSORIAL
RESTAURATEUR
RESTINGPLACE
RESTINGSPORE
RESTINGSTAGE
RESTLESSNESS
RESTRAINABLE
RESTRAINEDLY
RESTRICTEDLY
RESUMPTIVELY
RESUPINATION
RESURRECTION
RESURRECTIVE
RESUSCITABLE
RESUSCITATOR
RETAINERSHIP
RETICULATELY
RETICULATION
RETIRINGNESS
RETRACTATION
RETRACTILITY
RETRACTIVELY
RETRENCHMENT
RETRIEVEMENT
RETROCESSION
RETROCESSIVE
RETROFLECTED
RETROFLEXION
RETROMINGENT
RETROPULSION
RETROPULSIVE

REUNIONISTIC
REVELATIONAL
REVENGEFULLY
REVERBERATOR
REVERSIONARY
REVICTUALLED
REVISITATION
REVIVABILITY
REVIVALISTIC
REVIVESCENCE
REVIVESCENCY
REVIVISCENCE
REVIVISCENCY
REVOCABILITY
REVOLUTIONAL
REVOLUTIONER
REVULSIONARY
RHABDOSPHERE
RHAMPHOTHECA
RHESUS-FACTOR
RHETORICALLY
RHEUMATISMAL
RHEUMATOLOGY
RHINEGRAVINE
RHINOCERICAL
RHINOCEROSES
RHINOCEROTIC
RHINOLOGICAL
RHINOPLASTIC
RHINORRHAGIA
RHINORRHOEAL
RHIPIDOPTERA
RHIZOCARPOUS
RHIZOCEPHALA
RHIZOGENETIC
RHIZOPHAGOUS
RHIZOPHILOUS
RHODODENDRON
RHODOMONTADE
RHODOPHYCEAE
RHOMBOHEDRAL
RHOMBOHEDRON
RHOPALOCERAL
RHUMB-SAILING
RHYNCHONELLA
RHYNCHOPHORA
RHYTHMICALLY
RHYTHMOMETER
RHYTHMOPOEIA
RIBBLE-RABBLE
RIBONUCLEASE
RICOCHETTING
RIDICULOUSLY
RIDING-MASTER
RIDING-SCHOOL
RIFLE-GRENADE
RIFLEMAN-BIRD
RIGHT-AND-LEFT
RIGHTFULNESS
RIGOROUSNESS
RING-ARMATURE
RING-COMPOUND
RING-DOTTEREL
RING-DROPPING
RING-STREAKED
RIPPLE-MARKED

RISORGIMENTO
RIVER-TERRACE
ROAD-SURVEYOR
ROASTING-JACK
ROBUSTIOUSLY
ROCHELLE-SALT
ROCKING-CHAIR
ROCKING-HORSE
ROCKING-STONE
ROCK-SCORPION
RODOMONTADER
ROEBUCK-BERRY
ROLLER-SKATER
ROLLER-SKATES
ROLLING-STOCK
ROMANISATION
ROMANTICALLY
RÖNTGENOGRAM
RÖNTGENOLOGY
ROOMING-HOUSE
ROOT-PARASITE
ROOT-PRESSURE
ROOT-TUBERCLE
ROPE-DRILLING
ROSE-COLOURED
ROSMINIANISM
ROSY-COLOURED
ROSY-FINGERED
ROTOR-STATION
ROUGH-GRAINED
ROUGH-PERFECT
ROUGH-WROUGHT
ROUNDABOUTLY
ROUND-MOUTHED
ROUTE-PROVING
RUBBING-STONE
RUBY-COLOURED
RUBY-THROATED
RUMBLE-TUMBLE
RUMINATINGLY
RUMINATIVELY
RUMPTI-IDDITY
RUNNING-BOARD
RURALISATION
RUSH-BOTTOMED
RUSHY-FRINGED
RUSSOPHILISM
RUSSOPHILIST
RUSSOPHOBIST
RUST-COLOURED
RUTHLESSNESS

S

SABELLIANISM
SABRE-RATTLER
SACCHARINITY
SACCHAROIDAL
SACERDOTALLY
SACK-DOUDLING
SACRAMENTARY
SACRILEGIOUS
SADDLEBACKED
SADDLE-HACKLE
SADDLE-PILLAR

SADDLE-SHAPED
SADDLE-SPRING
SAFE-BREAKING
SAFEGUARDING
SAGE-THRASHER
SALAMANDRIAN
SALAMANDRINE
SALAMANDROID
SALEABLENESS
SALESMANSHIP
SALIFICATION
SALLOW-KITTEN
SALMON-COLOUR
SALMON-FISHER
SALMON-LADDER
SALMON-TACKLE
SALOON-KEEPER
SALOON-PISTOL
SALSOLACEOUS
SALTATORIOUS
SALTPETREMAN
SALUBRIOUSLY
SALUTARINESS
SALUTATIONAL
SALUTATORIAN
SALUTATORILY
SALUTIFEROUS
SALVATIONISM
SALVATIONIST
SALVER-SHAPED
SALVIFICALLY
SALVINIACEAE
SAMARITANISM
SANCTIFIEDLY
SAND-BLASTING
SAND-YACHTING
SANGUIFEROUS
SANGUINARILY
SANGUINENESS
SANGUINOLENT
SANGUIVOROUS
SANSCULOTTIC
SANTALACEOUS
SAPINDACEOUS
SAPONIFIABLE
SAPPHIRE-WING
SAPROPHAGOUS
SAPROPHYTISM
SARCOPHAGOUS
SARDONICALLY
SARRUSOPHONE
SARSAPARILLA
SATISFACTION
SATISFACTORY
SATISFYINGLY
SAUCEPAN-FISH
SAUNTERINGLY
SAUROGNATHAE
SCABBARD-FISH
SCABBARDLESS
SCABROUSNESS
SCALLOP-SHELL
SCALPING-TUFT
SCAMPISHNESS
SCANDALOUSLY
SCANDINAVIAN

SCANNING-DISK
SCAPEGALLOWS
SCAPULIMANCY
SCARABAEIDAE
SCARE-HEADING
SCARIFICATOR
SCATOLOGICAL
SCATOPHAGOUS
SCATTER-BRAIN
SCATTERINGLY
SCATTERMOUCH
SCAVENGERING
SCENE-PAINTER
SCENE-SHIFTER
SCENOGRAPHIC
SCHILLER-SPAR
SCHINDYLESIS
SCHINDYLETIC
SCHISMATICAL
SCHIZAEACEAE
SCHIZOGENOUS
SCHIZOGONOUS
SCHIZOMYCETE
SCHIZOPHRENE
SCHIZOPODOUS
SCHIZOTHYMIA
SCHNEIDERIAN
SCHOLASTICAL
SCHOOLBOYISH
SCHOOL-DIVINE
SCHOOL-DOCTOR
SCHOOLFELLOW
SCHOOL-FRIEND
SCHOOL-LEAVER
SCHOOLMASTER
SCHOOL-TAUGHT
SCHORLACEOUS
SCIENTIFICAL
SCINTILLATOR
SCISSIPARITY
SCISSOR-BLADE
SCISSOR-TOOTH
SCITAMINEOUS
SCIUROPTERUS
SCLERENCHYMA
SCLERODERMIA
SCLERODERMIC
SCLEROPHYLLY
SCOLOPACEOUS
SCOLOPACIDAE
SCOPOPHILIAC
SCOPTOPHILIA
SCORING-BOARD
SCORNFULNESS
SCORPAENIDAE
SCORPION-FISH
SCORPIONIDEA
SCOTTISHNESS
SCOUNDRELDOM
SCOUNDRELISM
SCOURING-RUSH
SCRAGGEDNESS
SCRAMBLINGLY
SCRAPER-BOARD
SCRATCH-BRUSH
SCRATCHINESS

SCRATCHINGLY
SCREEN-WRITER
SCREW-STEAMER
SCRIBBLEMENT
SCRIBBLINGLY
SCRIMSHANDER
SCRIPTURALLY
SCRIPT-WRITER
SCROBICULATE
SCROPHULARIA
SCRUPULOSITY
SCRUPULOUSLY
SCRUTINISING
SCRUTINOUSLY
SCULLERY-MAID
SCULLING-BOAT
SCULPTURALLY
SCURRILOUSLY
SCUTELLATION
SEA-BUCKTHORN
SEA-BUTTERFLY
SEAL-CYLINDER
SEA-PORCUPINE
SEASIDE-GRAPE
SEASONING-TUB
SECESSIONISM
SECESSIONIST
SECLUSIONIST
SECRETARIATE
SECTARIANISE
SECTARIANISM
SECTIONALISM
SECULARISTIC
SEDGE-WARBLER
SEDULOUSNESS
SEGMENTATION
SEIGNIORALTY
SEIGNIORSHIP
SEINE-FISHING
SEISMOGRAPHY
SEISMOLOGIST
SEISMOMETRIC
SEISMONASTIC
SEISMOSCOPIC
SELENOGRAPHY
SELENOLOGIST
SELF-ABSORBED
SELF-ACTIVITY
SELF-AFFECTED
SELF-APPLAUSE
SELF-BALANCED
SELF-BEGOTTEN
SELF-COLOURED
SELF-CONSUMED
SELF-CONTEMPT
SELF-DECEIVED
SELF-DECEIVER
SELF-DELUSION
SELF-DEPRAVED
SELF-DEVOTION
SELF-DIRECTED
SELF-DIRECTOR
SELF-DISLIKED
SELF-DISTRUST
SELF-EDUCATED
SELF-EFFACING

SELF-ELECTION
SELF-ELECTIVE
SELF-EMPLOYED
SELF-ENDEARED
SELF-EVIDENCE
SELF-EXCITING
SELF-EXISTENT
SELF-GLORIOUS
SELF-GRACIOUS
SELF-IDENTITY
SELF-INDEARED
SELF-INTEREST
SELF-INVOLVED
SELFLESSNESS
SELF-LIGHTING
SELF-LUMINOUS
SELF-MURDERER
SELF-PLEASING
SELF-PORTRAIT
SELF-THINKING
SELF-VIOLENCE
SELLING-PRICE
SEMANTICALLY
SEMI-ANNUALLY
SEMI-ARIANISM
SEMI-ATTACHED
SEMICIRCULAR
SEMICOMATOSE
SEMICYLINDER
SEMIDEPONENT
SEMI-DETACHED
SEMI-DIAMETER
SEMIFINALIST
SEMIGLOBULAR
SEMI-IMBECILE
SEMINIFEROUS
SEMI-OFFICIAL
SEMIPARASITE
SEMI-PELAGIAN
SEMIPELLUCID
SEMI-PRECIOUS
SEMITISATION
SEMITROPICAL
SEMIWATER-GAS
SEMPITERNITY
SENATORIALLY
SENSATIONISM
SENSATIONIST
SENSIBLENESS
SENSITOMETER
SENSUALISTIC
SENSUOUSNESS
SENTENTIALLY
SEPARABILITY
SEPARATENESS
SEPTEMBERISH
SEPTEMBRISER
SEPTEMVIRATE
SEPTENNIALLY
SEPTILATERAL
SEPTUAGENARY
SEPTUAGESIMA
SEPTUAGINTAL
SEQUENTIALLY
SEQUESTRATOR
SERAPHICALLY

SERASKIERATE
SERGEANT-FISH
SERGEANTSHIP
SERIOCOMICAL
SERJEANTSHIP
SERPENT-EATER
SERPENTIFORM
SERPENTINELY
SERPENTINING
SERPENTINISE
SERPENTINOUS
SERPENT-STONE
SERUM-THERAPY
SERVICE-BERRY
SERVICE-COURT
SERVITORSHIP
SERVO-CONTROL
SESQUIALTERA
SESQUITERTIA
SESSION-CLERK
SESSION-HOUSE
SEVENTY-EIGHT
SEXAGENARIAN
SEXCENTENARY
SEXTON-BEETLE
SHADOW-BOXING
SHADOW-FIGURE
SHADOW-FLIGHT
SHAKSPERIANA
SHAMEFACEDLY
SHAMEFULNESS
SHARE-CAPITAL
SHARE-CROPPER
SHARP-LOOKING
SHARP-POINTED
SHARPSHOOTER
SHARP-SIGHTED
SHARP-TOOTHED
SHARP-VISAGED
SHATTER-BRAIN
SHATTER-PROOF
SHAVING-BRUSH
SHAVING-STICK
SHAWL-PATTERN
SHEALING-HILL
SHEATH-WINGED
SHEELING-HILL
SHEEPISHNESS
SHEEP-SCORING
SHEEP-SHEARER
SHEEP-STEALER
SHELLSHOCKED
SHEPHERDLESS
SHEPHERDLING
SHERIFF-CLERK
SHERIFF-COURT
SHERIFF'S-POST
SHIELD-BEARER
SHIELD-MAIDEN
SHIELD-SHAPED
SHIELING-HILL
SHILLINGLESS
SHILLY-SHALLY
SHIPBUILDING
SHIP-CHANDLER
SHIRTWAISTER

SHOCKINGNESS
SHOEING-SMITH
SHOOTING-IRON
SHOOTING-STAR
SHOPBREAKING
SHORTCHANGER
SHORT-CIRCUIT
SHORT-CLOTHES
SHORT-SIGHTED
SHOULDER-BELT
SHOULDER-BONE
SHOULDER-HIGH
SHOULDER-KNOT
SHOULDER-MARK
SHOULDER-NOTE
SHOULDER-SLIP
SHOW-BUSINESS
SHREWISHNESS
SHRILL-GORGED
SHRILL-VOICED
SHRIVING-TIME
SHUDDERINGLY
SHUFFLE-BOARD
SICK-HEADACHE
SICKLE-CELLED
SICKLE-SHAPED
SIGHT-PLAYING
SIGHT-READING
SIGHT-SINGING
SIGNIFICANCE
SIGNIFICANCY
SIGNIFICATOR
SILICICOLOUS
SILICIFEROUS
SILVER-BEATER
SILVER-FOOTED
SILVER-GLANCE
SILVER-PLATED
SILVER-VOICED
SILVICULTURE
SIMARUBACEAE
SIMMENTHALER
SIMONIACALLY
SIMPLE-MINDED
SIMULTANEITY
SIMULTANEOUS
SINANTHROPUS
SINGABLENESS
SINGING-HINNY
SINGLE-ACTING
SINGLE-DECKER
SINGLE-HANDED
SINGLE-MINDED
SINGLE-SEATER
SINGLE-WICKET
SINISTERWISE
SINISTRALITY
SINISTRORSAL
SINISTROUSLY
SINUPALLIATE
SINUSOIDALLY
SIPHONAPTERA
SIPHONOPHORA
SIPHONOSTELE
SIPUNCULACEA
SIR-REVERENCE

SISTERLINESS
SIVAPITHECUS
SKIPPING-ROPE
SKIRT-DANCING
SKITTISHNESS
SKITTLE-ALLEY
SKRIMSHANKER
SKUNK-CABBAGE
SKUTTERUDITE
SKY-TINCTURED
SLANDEROUSLY
SLANG-WHANGER
SLANTINGWAYS
SLATE-WRITING
SLAUGHTERMAN
SLAUGHTEROUS
SLAVE-HOLDING
SLAVE-TRAFFIC
SLEDGE-HAMMER
SLEEPING-PILL
SLEEP-WALKING
SLEEVE-BUTTON
SLICKENSIDED
SLINK-BUTCHER
SLIP-CARRIAGE
SLIPPERINESS
SLOCKDOLAGER
SLOP-CLOTHING
SLOTHFULNESS
SLOUCH-HATTED
SLOVENLINESS
SLUBBERINGLY
SLUGGISHNESS
SLUMBERINGLY
SLUMBEROUSLY
SLUTTISHNESS
SMALL-CLOTHES
SMALLHOLDING
SMASH-AND-GRAB
SMATTERINGLY
SMITHEREEENS
SMOOTH-BROWED
SMOOTH-COATED
SMOOTH-LEAVED
SMOOTH-SPOKEN
SMOTHERINESS
SMOTHERINGLY
SNACK-COUNTER
SNAFFLING-LAY
SNAKE-CHARMER
SNAPPISHNESS
SNAPSHOOTING
SNARLING-IRON
SNARLING-TOOL
SNEAKISHNESS
SNECK-DRAWING
SNEESHIN-MULL
SNIGGERINGLY
SNIPPETINESS
SNOBBISHNESS
SNOBOGRAPHER
SNOWDROP-TREE
SNOW-IN-SUMMER
SNUBBING-POST
SNUFF-DIPPING
SOBER-BLOODED

SOBOLIFEROUS
SOCIABLENESS
SOCIOLOGICAL
SOCRATICALLY
SODA-FOUNTAIN
SODDEN-WITTED
SOLARISATION
SOLECISTICAL
SOLENOIDALLY
SOLIDIFIABLE
SOLIFLUCTION
SOLITARINESS
SOLITUDINOUS
SOLOMON'S-SEAL
SOMATOPLEURE
SOMNAMBULANT
SOMNAMBULARY
SOMNAMBULATE
SOMNAMBULISM
SOMNAMBULIST
SOMNILOQUISE
SOMNILOQUISM
SOMNILOQUIST
SOMNOLESCENT
SONNETEERING
SONOROUSNESS
SOPHISTICATE
SOPORIFEROUS
SORBEFACIENT
SOUGHING-TILE
SOULLESSNESS
SOUL-STIRRING
SOUNDING-LEAD
SOUNDING-LINE
SOUTHCOTTIAN
SOUTH-COUNTRY
SOUTH-EASTERN
SOUTHERNMOST
SOUTHERNWOOD
SOUTH-SEEKING
SOUTH-WESTERN
SPACE-HEATING
SPACE-LATTICE
SPACE-STATION
SPACIOUSNESS
SPAN-FARTHING
SPARKING-PLUG
SPARROW-GRASS
SPATANGOIDEA
SPEAKING-TUBE
SPEAR-RUNNING
SPEAR-THISTLE
SPEAR-THROWER
SPECIALISTIC
SPECIFICALLY
SPECIOUSNESS
SPECKLEDNESS
SPECKTIONEER
SPECTATORIAL
SPECTRE-LEMUR
SPECTROGRAPH
SPECTROMETIC
SPECTROMETRY
SPECTROSCOPE
SPECTROSCOPY
SPEECHLESSLY

SPEECH-MAKING
SPEED-BOATING
SPEISS-COBALT
SPELLING-BOOK
SPERMAPHYTIC
SPERMATHECAL
SPERMATOCELE
SPERMATOCYTE
SPERMATOGENY
SPERMATOZOID
SPERMATOZOON
SPERMOGONIUM
SPERMOPHYTIC
SPHACELATION
SPHERICALITY
SPHINCTERIAL
SPHRAGISTICS
SPHYGMOGRAPH
SPHYGMOMETER
SPHYGMOSCOPE
SPIDER-LEGGED
SPIDER-MONKEY
SPIDER-STITCH
SPIEGELEISEN
SPIFLICATION
SPILLING-LINE
SPINDLE-SHELL
SPINDLE-WHORL
SPINE-CHILLER
SPINNING-MILL
SPINSTERHOOD
SPINSTERSHIP
SPINULESCENT
SPIRE-STEEPLE
SPIRITEDNESS
SPIRITLESSLY
SPIRIT-RAPPER
SPIRITUALISE
SPIRITUALISM
SPIRITUALIST
SPIRITUALITY
SPIRITUOSITY
SPITEFULNESS
SPITTLE-HOUSE
SPLAY-MOUTHED
SPLENDIDIOUS
SPLENDIDNESS
SPLENISATION
SPLENOMEGALY
SPLINT-ARMOUR
SPLINTER-BONE
SPONGE-FINGER
SPONGE-FISHER
SPONGE-RUBBER
SPONGICOLOUS
SPONGOLOGIST
SPORADICALLY
SPORANGIOLUM
SPOROGENESIS
SPOROPHOROUS
SPORTABILITY
SPORTFULNESS
SPORTIVENESS
SPOTLESSNESS
SPRAT-WEATHER
SPRIGHTFULLY

SPRING-BEAUTY
SPRING-BEETLE
SPRING-BLADED
SPRING-HEADED
SPRING-HEELED
SPRING-KEEPER
SPRING-LOADED
SPURGE-LAUREL
SPURIOUSNESS
SPURTLE-BLADE
SPUTTERINGLY
SQUARE-RIGGED
SQUATTOCRACY
SQUIREARCHAL
SQUIRREL-CAGE
SQUIRREL-TAIL
STABILISATOR
STABLISHMENT
STAFF-COLLEGE
STAFF-OFFICER
STAFF-SURGEON
STAGE-MANAGER
STAGE-WHISPER
STAGGERINGLY
STAGHORN-FERN
STAHLHELMIST
STAKHANOVITE
STALACTIFORM
STALWARTNESS
STAMMERINGLY
STAMPING-MILL
STANDARDISER
STANDARD-WING
STANDING-BOWL
STANDING-ROOM
STAND-PATTISM
STANNIFEROUS
STAR-BLASTING
STARCHEDNESS
STAR-SPANGLED
STARTING-HOLE
STARTING-POST
STATION-HOUSE
STATION-WAGON
STATISTICIAN
STATUESQUELY
STAYING-POWER
STEALTHINESS
STEAM-TURBINE
STEAM-WHISTLE
STEATOMATOUS
STEATOPYGOUS
STEEPLECHASE
STEEPLE-CROWN
STEEPLE-HOUSE
STEERING-GEAR
STEGANOGRAPH
STEGANOPODES
STEGOCARPOUS
STEGOPHILIST
STEGOSAURIAN
STELLENBOSCH
STELLIFEROUS
STENCIL-PLATE
STENOGRAPHER
STENOGRAPHIC

STENTORPHONE
STEPDAUGHTER
STEPMOTHERLY
STERCORANISM
STERCORANIST
STEREOCHROME
STEREOCHROMY
STEREOGRAPHY
STEREOISOMER
STEREOMETRIC
STEREOPHONIC
STEREOPTICON
STEREOSCOPIC
STEREOTYPING
STERNUTATION
STERNUTATIVE
STERNUTATORY
STERN-WHEELER
STERTOROUSLY
STETHOSCOPIC
STICHOMETRIC
STICHOMYTHIA
STICHOMYTHIC
STICKLER-LIKE
STIFF-HEARTED
STILBOESTROL
STILL-HUNTING
STILL-PEERING
STILL-PIECING
STIPULACEOUS
STIRRUP-STRAP
STOCK-AND-HORN
STOCK-BREEDER
STOCKBROKING
STOCKINGETTE
STOCKING-FOOT
STOCKINGLESS
STOCKING-SOLE
STOCK-IN-TRADE
STOCKISHNESS
STOCKJOBBERY
STOCKJOBBING
STOCK-RAISING
STOMATODAEUM
STONE-BOILING
STONE-BRAMBLE
STONE-BREAKER
STONE-CHATTER
STONE-CUTTING
STONE-DRESSER
STONEWALLING
STONY-HEARTED
STOOP-GALLANT
STORIOLOGIST
STORMFULNESS
STORM-LANTERN
STORM-SHUTTER
STORM-TROOPER
STORM-WARNING
STORMY-PETREL
STORY-TELLING
STOUT-HEARTED
STRABISMICAL
STRADDLE-BACK
STRADIVARIUS
STRAGGLINGLY

STRAIGHTAWAY
STRAIGHT-EDGE
STRAIGHTENER
STRAIGHTNESS
STRAIGHTWAYS
STRAIT-JACKET
STRAIT-LACING
STRANGLEHOLD
STRANGLEMENT
STRANGLE-WEED
STRANGULATED
STRATIGRAPHY
STRATOCRATIC
STRATOSPHERE
STRAW-BREADTH
STREAM-ANCHOR
STREET-KEEPER
STREET-RAKING
STREET-WALKER
STRENGTHENER
STRENGTHLESS
STREPITATION
STREPSIPTERA
STREPTOCOCCI
STREPTOMYCIN
STREPTONEURA
STRIDELEGGED
STRIDULATION
STRIDULATORY
STRIGIFORMES
STRIKINGNESS
STRING-COURSE
STROBILATION
STROBILIFORM
STROBOSCOPIC
STRONG-MINDED
STRONGYLOSIS
STRONTIANITE
STROPHANTHIN
STROPHANTHUS
STROPHIOLATE
STRUCTURALLY
STRUGGLINGLY
STRYCHNINISM
STUBBLE-FIELD
STUBBLE-GOOSE
STUBBORNNESS
STUDDING-SAIL
STUDIOUSNESS
STUMP-ORATORY
STUPEFACIENT
STUPEFACTION
STUPEFACTIVE
STUPENDOUSLY
STUTTERINGLY
STYLOGRAPHIC
SUBACIDULOUS
SUBALTERNANT
SUBALTERNATE
SUBALTERNITY
SUBAPOSTOLIC
SUBARACHNOID
SUBARCUATION
SUBARRHATION
SUBCELESTIAL
SUBCOMMITTEE

SUBCONSCIOUS
SUBCONTINENT
SUBCUTANEOUS
SUBDIACONATE
SUBDIVISIBLE
SUBDUPLICATE
SUBEDITORIAL
SUBERISATION
SUBFEUDATION
SUBFEUDATORY
SUBHASTATION
SUBINFEUDATE
SUBINSPECTOR
SUBINTRODUCE
SUBJECTIVELY
SUBJECTIVISE
SUBJECTIVISM
SUBJECTIVIST
SUBJECTIVITY
SUBLAPSARIAN
SUBLIBRARIAN
SUBLINEATION
SUBMAXILLARY
SUBMERGEMENT
SUBMISSIVELY
SUBNORMALITY
SUBOCCIPITAL
SUBOPERCULAR
SUBOPERCULUM
SUBORDINANCY
SUBREFERENCE
SUBSCRIBABLE
SUBSCRIPTIVE
SUBSEQUENTLY
SUBSERVIENCE
SUBSERVIENCY
SUBSIDIARILY
SUBSTANTIALS
SUBSTANTIATE
SUBSTANTIVAL
SUBSTITUTION
SUBSTITUTIVE
SUBSTRACTION
SUBSTRUCTION
SUBSTRUCTURE
SUBSULTORILY
SUBTEMPERATE
SUBTERJACENT
SUBTERRANEAN
SUBTHRESHOLD
SUBTREASURER
SUBUMBRELLAR
SUBVERTEBRAL
SUCCEDANEOUS
SUCCESSANTLY
SUCCESSFULLY
SUCCESSIONAL
SUCCESSIVELY
SUCCINCTNESS
SUCCUSSATION
SUDORIFEROUS
SUDORIPAROUS
SUFFICIENTLY
SUFFRUTICOSE
SUGAR-REFINER
SUGGESTIVELY

SUITABLENESS
SULPHONAMIDE
SULPHURATION
SULPHURETTED
SUMPHISHNESS
SUN-AND-PLANET
SUN-EXPELLING
SUNSHINE-ROOF
SUPERANNUATE
SUPERCARGOES
SUPERCHARGER
SUPERCILIARY
SUPERCILIOUS
SUPEREMINENT
SUPEREROGANT
SUPEREROGATE
SUPERFRONTAL
SUPERHIGHWAY
SUPERHUMANLY
SUPERHUMERAL
SUPERIMPOSED
SUPERIORSHIP
SUPERMUNDANE
SUPERNACULAR
SUPERNACULUM
SUPERNATURAL
SUPERORDINAL
SUPERORGANIC
SUPERPOSABLE
SUPERREALISM
SUPERREALIST
SUPERSEDENCE
SUPERSENSORY
SUPERSENSUAL
SUPERSESSION
SUPERSTITION
SUPERSTRATUM
SUPERSUBTILE
SUPERVENIENT
SUPERVENTION
SUPPLEMENTAL
SUPPLEMENTER
SUPPLICATING
SUPPLICATION
SUPPLICATORY
SUPPOSITIOUS
SUPPRESSEDLY
SUPPRESSIBLE
SUPRACILIARY
SUPRAMUNDANE
SUPRA-ORBITAL
SURE-FOOTEDLY
SURFACE-CRAFT
SURFACE-TO-AIR
SURFACE-WATER
SURF-BOARDING
SURFING-BOARD
SURMOUNTABLE
SURPASSINGLY
SURPRISINGLY
SURREALISTIC
SURREJOINDER
SURVEILLANCE
SURVEYORSHIP
SURVIVORSHIP
SUSCEPTIVITY

SUSPENSIVELY
SUSPENSORIAL
SUSPENSORIUM
SUSPICIOUSLY
SUSTENTATION
SUSTENTATIVE
SWAGGERINGLY
SWAGGER-STICK
SWAINISHNESS
SWASHBUCKLER
SWEEPINGNESS
SWEET-AND-SOUR
SWEETISHNESS
SWEET-SCENTED
SWEET-TOOTHED
SWEET-WILLIAM
SWELL-MOBSMAN
SWIMMING-BATH
SWIMMING-BELL
SWIMMINGNESS
SWIMMING-POND
SWIMMING-POOL
SWINE-KEEPING
SWINGING-BOOM
SWINGING-POST
SWIZZLE-STICK
SWORD-BAYONET
SWORD-BREAKER
SYCOPHANTISE
SYCOPHANTISH
SYLLABICALLY
SYLVICULTURE
SYMBOLICALLY
SYMBOLOLATRY
SYMPTOMATISE
SYNADELPHITE
SYNAESTHESIA
SYNAESTHETIC
SYNANTHEROUS
SYNARTHROSIS
SYNCHRONICAL
SYNCHRONISER
SYNCLINORIUM
SYNCRETISTIC
SYNDACTYLISM
SYNDACTYLOUS
SYNDETICALLY
SYNECDOCHISM
SYNGENESIOUS
SYNGNATHIDAE
SYNONYMOUSLY
SYNOPTICALLY
SYNTAGMATITE
SYNTHETICISM
SYSTEMATICAL
SYSTEMATISER
SYSTEM-MONGER

T

TABERNACULAR
TABLE-MANNERS
TABLE-TURNING
TACHYGRAPHER
TACHYGRAPHIC
TACTLESSNESS
TAGLIACOTIAN

TALISMANICAL
TALKEE-TALKEE
TALKING-POINT
TALLOW-CANDLE
TAMARICACEAE
TAMELESSNESS
TANGENTIALLY
TANGIBLENESS
TANTALUM-LAMP
TAPE-RECORDER
TAPPET-MOTION
TAPSALTEERIE
TARDENOISIAN
TASKMISTRESS
TASSEL-GENTLE
TASTEFULNESS
TAUTOLOGICAL
TAX-COLLECTOR
TAXING-MASTER
TEACHABILITY
TECHNICALITY
TECHNICOLOUR
TECHNOLOGIST
TECTONICALLY
TEEING-GROUND
TEETER-TOTTER
TELAESTHESIA
TELAUTOGRAPH
TELEASTHETIC
TELEGRAPHESE
TELEGRAPHIST
TELEOLOGICAL
TELEOSAURIAN
TELEOSTOMOUS
TELEPROMPTER
TELERGICALLY
TELESCOPICAL
TELESMATICAL
TELEUTOSPORE
TELEVISIONAL
TEMPERALITIE
TEMPORANEOUS
TEMPTABILITY
TEMPTINGNESS
TENANT-AT-WILL
TENANT-FARMER
TENDER-HEFTED
TENNIS-PLAYER
TENNIS-RACKET
TENUIROSTRAL
TERATOLOGIST
TERATOMATOUS
TERCEL-GENTLE
TERCEL-JERKIN
TERCENTENARY
TEREBINTHINE
TERGIVERSATE
TERRIBLENESS
TERRIFICALLY
TESSELLATION
TESTAMENTARY
TESTICULATED
TESTIFICATOR
TESTOSTERONE
TESTUDINEOUS
TETANISATION

TETRACHORDAL
TETRACHOTOMY
TETRADACTYLY
TETRADYNAMIA
TETRAHEDRITE
TETRAMORPHIC
TETRAPOLITAN
TETRAPTEROUS
TETRASPOROUS
TETRASTICHAL
TETRASTICHIC
THANKFULNESS
THANKSGIVING
THANK-YOU-MA'AM
THAUMATOGENY
THAUMATURGIC
THAUMATURGUS
THEANTHROPIC
THEATRICALLY
THEATROMANIA
THEATROPHONE
THEMATICALLY
THEOCRATICAL
THEOLOGASTER
THEOMORPHISM
THEOPASCHITE
THEOPATHETIC
THEOPHYLLINE
THEOREMATIST
THEORETICIAN
THEOSOPHICAL
THERAPEUTICS
THERAPEUTIST
THEREAGAINST
THEREINAFTER
THERETHROUGH
THERIODONTIA
THERIOMORPHA
THERMIDORIAN
THERMOCOUPLE
THERMOGRAPHY
THERMOLABILE
THERMOMETRIC
THERMOPHILIC
THERMOSCOPIC
THERMOSTABLE
THERMOSTATIC
THERMOTACTIC
THERMOTROPIC
THESMOPHORIA
THICK-AND-THIN
THICK-SIGHTED
THICK-SKINNED
THICK-SKULLED
THIEF-CATCHER
THIEVISHNESS
THIGMOTROPIC
THIOBACILLUS
THIRDBOROUGH
THIRTEENTHLY
THITHERWARDS
THOROUGH-BASS
THOROUGHBRED
THOROUGHFARE
THOROUGHNESS
THOUGHTFULLY

THOUSANDFOLD
THOUSANDLEGS
THOUSANDYEAR
THREE-CENTRED
THREE-HA'PORTH
THREE-MONTHLY
THREE-POUNDER
THREE-PRICKER
THREE-QUARTER
THRIFTLESSLY
THRIVINGNESS
THROSTLE-COCK
THROTTLE-PIPE
THROUGH-GOING
THROUGH-OTHER
THROUGH-STANE
THROUGH-STONE
THROUGH-TRAIN
THUNDER-CLOUD
THUNDER-DRIVE
THUNDERINGLY
THUNDEROUSLY
THUNDER-PLUMP
THUNDER-STONE
THUNDER-STORM
THYSANOPTERA
TICKET-PORTER
TICKET-WRITER
TICKLISHNESS
TILLEY-VALLEY
TIMBROLOGIST
TIME-BEWASTED
TIME-EXPOSURE
TIME-HONOURED
TIMELESSNESS
TIMELY-PARTED
TIMOCRATICAL
TIMOROUSNESS
TIMOTHY-GRASS
TIN-STREAMING
TINTINNABULA
TIRELESSNESS
TIRESOMENESS
TIRLIE-WIRLIE
TITANIFEROUS
TITANOSAURUS
TITHE-PROCTOR
TITTLE-TATTLE
TOASTING-FORK
TOASTING-IRON
TOBACCO-HEART
TOBACCO-PLANT
TOBACCO-POUCH
TOGETHERNESS
TOGGLESWITCH
TOILSOMENESS
TOLERABILITY
TOLL-GATHERER
TONELESSNESS
TONGUE-TACKED
TONSILLOTOMY
TOOTH-DRAWING
TOPLOFTINESS
TOPSIDE-TURVY
TOPSYTURVILY
TORCH-THISTLE

TORMENTINGLY
TORPEDINIDAE
TORREFACTION
TORRENTIALLY
TORRICELLIAN
TORTUOUSNESS
TOTALISATION
TOTALITARIAN
TOUCHINGNESS
TOWARDLINESS
TOWN-PLANNING
TOXICOLOGIST
TOXICOPHOBIA
TRABECULATED
TRACEABILITY
TRACHEOSCOPY
TRACHEOSTOMY
TRACHYPTERUS
TRACING-PAPER
TRACTABILITY
TRACTORATION
TRADESCANTIA
TRADESPEOPLE
TRADITIONARY
TRADITIONIST
TRADUCIANISM
TRADUCIANIST
TRAGELAPHINE
TRAGICALNESS
TRAGI-COMICAL
TRAINING-SHIP
TRAITOROUSLY
TRALATICIOUS
TRALATITIOUS
TRAMPOLINIST
TRANQUILLISE
TRANQUILLITY
TRANSCENDENT
TRANSDUCTION
TRANSFERABLE
TRANSFER-BOOK
TRANSFERENCE
TRANSFERRING
TRANSFORMING
TRANSFORMISM
TRANSFORMIST
TRANSFUSIBLE
TRANSGRESSOR
TRANSHIPPING
TRANSHUMANCE
TRANSILIENCY
TRANSITIONAL
TRANSITIVELY
TRANSITORILY
TRANSIT-TRADE
TRANSLATABLE
TRANSLEITHAN
TRANSLUCENCE
TRANSLUCENCY
TRANSMIGRANT
TRANSMIGRATE
TRANSMISSION
TRANSMISSIVE
TRANSMITTING
TRANSMOGRIFY
TRANSMUTABLE

TRANSMUTABLY
TRANSOCEANIC
TRANSPARENCE
TRANSPARENCY
TRANSPICIOUS
TRANSPIRABLE
TRANSPLANTER
TRANSPONTINE
TRANSPORTING
TRANSPORTIVE
TRANSPOSABLE
TRANSSHIPPER
TRANSUDATION
TRANSUDATORY
TRANSUMPTION
TRANSUMPTIVE
TRANSURANIUM
TRANSVERSELY
TRANSVERSION
TRANSVESTISM
TRANSVESTITE
TRAVEL-SOILED
TREASURE-CITY
TREE-KANGAROO
TREMENDOUSLY
TRENCH-MORTAR
TRENCH-PLOUGH
TREND-SETTING
TRESTLE-TABLE
TRIADELPHOUS
TRIANGULARLY
TRIBUTE-MONEY
TRICEPHALOUS
TRICHINIASIS
TRICHIURIDAE
TRICHOLOGIST
TRICHOPHYTON
TRICHOTOMISE
TRICHOTOMOUS
TRICHROMATIC
TRICKISHNESS
TRICKSTERING
TRICORPORATE
TRIDACTYLOUS
TRIFLINGNESS
TRIFURCATION
TRIGGER-HAPPY
TRIGONOMETER
TRIGONOMETRY
TRIGRAMMATIC
TRIMETHYLENE
TRINOMIALISM
TRINOMIALIST
TRIPARTITION
TRIPLE-HEADED
TRIPLE-TURNED
TRIPLICATION
TRIPUDIATION
TRISMEGISTUS
TRITICALNESS
TRITUBERCULY
TRIUMPHANTLY
TROCHANTERIC
TROCHEAMETER
TROGLODYTISM
TROLLEY-TABLE

TROLLEY-WHEEL
TROLLING-BAIT
TROLL-MY-DAMES
TROOP-CARRIER
TROPHALLAXIS
TROPHOBIOSIS
TROPHOBIOTIC
TROPHOTACTIC
TROPHOTROPIC
TROPOLOGICAL
TROPOSPHERIC
TROUBLE-HOUSE
TROUBLEMAKER
TROUBLE-MIRTH
TROUBLE-STATE
TRUCE-BREAKER
TRUE-LOVE-KNOT
TRUMPET-MAJOR
TRUMPET-SHELL
TRUSTFULNESS
TRUTHFULNESS
TRUTH-TELLING
TRYPAFLAVINE
TRYPANOCIDAL
TRYSTING-TREE
TSESAREVITCH
TUBERCULATED
TUBERCULOSED
TUBERCULOSIS
TUBERIFEROUS
TUBULIFLORAE
TUBULIFLORAL
TUMBLER-DRIER
TUMULTUATION
TUMULTUOUSLY
TUNING-HAMMER
TURACOVERDIN
TURBELLARIAN
TURBINACIOUS
TURCOPHILISM
TURNING-LATHE
TURNING-POINT
TURNPIKE-ROAD
TURRICULATED
TURTLE-NECKED
TUSSOCK-GRASS
TU-WHIT-TU-WHOO
TWELFTH-NIGHT
TWENTY-FOUR-MO
TWITTERBONED
TWITTERINGLY
TWO-SIDEDNESS
TYBURN-TICKET
TYBURN-TIPPET
TYPE-CYLINDER
TYPE-FOUNDING
TYPIFICATION
TYPOGRAPHIST
TYRANNICALLY
TYRANNICIDAL

U

UBIQUITARIAN
UBIQUITOUSLY
UGLIFICATION
UINTATHERIUM

ULCEROUSNESS
ULOTRICHALES
ULTRAMONTANE
ULTRAMUNDANE
ULTRASENSUAL
ULTRONEOUSLY
UMBELLIFERAE
UMBRAGEOUSLY
UMBRELLA-BIRD
UMBRELLA-TREE
UNACCEPTABLE
UNACCEPTANCE
UNACCREDITED
UNACCUSTOMED
UNACHIEVABLE
UNACQUAINTED
UNADMONISHED
UNADULTERATE
UNAFFECTEDLY
UNAMIABILITY
UNANALYSABLE
UNANALYTICAL
UNANSWERABLE
UNANSWERABLY
UNAPPARELLED
UNAPPEALABLE
UNAPPEASABLE
UNAPPETISING
UNAPPLAUSIVE
UNAPPROACHED
UNARTICULATE
UNARTIFICIAL
UNARTISTLIKE
UNASCENDABLE
UNASCENDIBLE
UNASPIRINGLY
UNASSAILABLE
UNASSIGNABLE
UNASSISTEDLY
UNASSOCIATED
UNASSUAGABLE
UNASSUMINGLY
UNATTAINABLE
UNATTAINABLY
UNATTRACTIVE
UNAUSPICIOUS
UNAUTHORISED
UNBECOMINGLY
UNBEFRIENDED
UNBELIEVABLE
UNBELIEVABLY
UNBENEFICIAL
UNBETTERABLE
UNBIASEDNESS
UNBLINKINGLY
UNBLUSHINGLY
UNBREACHABLE
UNBREATHABLE
UNBREATHED-ON
UNBROKENNESS
UNCALCULATED
UNCANDIDNESS
UNCAPSIZABLE
UNCATALOGUED
UNCELEBRATED
UNCENSORIOUS

UNCHALLENGED
UNCHANGEABLE
UNCHANGEABLY
UNCHANGINGLY
UNCHARITABLE
UNCHARITABLY
UNCHASTENESS
UNCHEERFULLY
UNCHIVALROUS
UNCHRISTENED
UNCHRONICLED
UNCLASSIFIED
UNCLOISTERED
UNCOMEATABLE
UNCOMELINESS
UNCOMMERCIAL
UNCOMMONNESS
UNCOMPOSABLE
UNCOMPOUNDED
UNCONCEALING
UNCONCERNING
UNCONCLUSIVE
UNCONFINABLE
UNCONFINEDLY
UNCONFORMING
UNCONFORMITY
UNCONFUSEDLY
UNCONSECRATE
UNCONSENTING
UNCONSIDERED
UNCONSTRAINT
UNCONTROLLED
UNCONVERSANT
UNCONVINCING
UNCOQUETTISH
UNCOUNSELLED
UNCOVENANTED
UNCREDITABLE
UNCRITICALLY
UNCTUOUSNESS
UNCULTIVABLE
UNCULTIVATED
UNDECEIVABLE
UNDECOMPOSED
UNDELECTABLE
UNDELIBERATE
UNDELIGHTFUL
UNDEMOCRATIC
UNDEPENDABLE
UNDERBEARING
UNDERBUILDER
UNDERCLOTHED
UNDERCLOTHES
UNDERCURRENT
UNDERDEVELOP
UNDERDRESSED
UNDERGARMENT
UNDER-HANGMAN
UNDERKINGDOM
UNDERLETTING
UNDERPASSION
UNDERPAYMENT
UNDERPEOPLED
UNDERPINNING
UNDERRUNNING
UNDERSEALING

UNDER-SHERIFF
UNDERSKINKER
UNDER-STAFFED
UNDERSTANDED
UNDERSTANDER
UNDERSTRATUM
UNDERTAKABLE
UNDERTENANCY
UNDER-TURNKEY
UNDERWORKMAN
UNDERWRITING
UNDERWROUGHT
UNDESERVEDLY
UNDESIGNEDLY
UNDESPAIRING
UNDETERMINED
UNDIMINISHED
UNDISCERNING
UNDISCHARGED
UNDISCIPLINE
UNDISCORDANT
UNDISCORDING
UNDISCOVERED
UNDISMANTLED
UNDISORDERED
UNDISPATCHED
UNDISPUTEDLY
UNDISSEMBLED
UNDISSOLVING
UNDISTRACTED
UNDISTURBING
UNDIVESTEDLY
UNDOUBTINGLY
UNDULATINGLY
UNECONOMICAL
UNELABORATED
UNEMBITTERED
UNEMPLOYABLE
UNEMPLOYMENT
UNENCUMBERED
UNENDANGERED
UNENDINGNESS
UNENTHRALLED
UNERRINGNESS
UNEVENTFULLY
UNEXPECTEDLY
UNEXPRESSIVE
UNEXPUGNABLE
UNEXPURGATED
UNEXTENUATED
UNFADINGNESS
UNFAITHFULLY
UNFAMILIARLY
UNFASTIDIOUS
UNFATHOMABLE
UNFATHOMABLY
UNFAVOURABLE
UNFAVOURABLY
UNFERTILISED
UNFILTERABLE
UNFITTEDNESS
UNFLAGGINGLY
UNFLATTERING
UNFOREBODING
UNFORESEEING
UNFOREWARNED

UNFORMALISED
UNFORMIDABLE
UNFOSSILISED
UNFRANCHISED
UNFREQUENTED
UNFREQUENTLY
UNFRIENDSHIP
UNFRIGHTENED
UNFRUITFULLY
UNGAINLINESS
UNGENEROUSLY
UNGENTLENESS
UNGOVERNABLE
UNGOVERNABLY
UNGRACEFULLY
UNGRACIOUSLY
UNGRATEFULLY
UNGROUNDEDLY
UNGRUDGINGLY
UNGUENTARIUM
UNGUICULATED
UNHABITUATED
UNHANDSOMELY
UNHARMONIOUS
UNHEROICALLY
UNHESITATING
UNHISTORICAL
UNHOSPITABLE
UNICORN-SHELL
UNICORN-WHALE
UNIDEALISTIC
UNIDENTIFIED
UNIFOLIOLATE
UNILATERALLY
UNIMAGINABLE
UNIMAGINABLY
UNIMPORTANCE
UNIMPORTUNED
UNIMPRESSIVE
UNIMPRISONED
UNIMPUGNABLE
UNINCUMBERED
UNINFLUENCED
UNINSTRUCTED
UNINTEGRATED
UNINTERESTED
UNINTRODUCED
UNISERIATELY
UNISEXUALITY
UNITARIANISM
UNIVERSALISE
UNIVERSALISM
UNIVERSALIST
UNIVERSALITY
UNKINDLINESS
UNLAWFULNESS
UNLIBIDINOUS
UNLIKELIHOOD
UNLIKELINESS
UNLIQUIDATED
UNLISTENED-TO
UNLIVELINESS
UNLOVELINESS
UNLOVINGNESS
UNMANAGEABLE
UNMANAGEABLY

UNMARKETABLE
UNMEASURABLE
UNMEASURABLY
UNMECHANICAL
UNMECHANISED
UNMERCIFULLY
UNMETHODICAL
UNMETHODISED
UNMIRACULOUS
UNMISTAKABLE
UNMISTAKABLY
UNMODERNISED
UNMODIFIABLE
UNMORALISING
UNMUNITIONED
UNNATURALISE
UNNOTICEABLE
UNNOURISHING
UNOBSERVABLE
UNOBSERVANCE
UNOBSERVEDLY
UNOBSTRUCTED
UNOBTAINABLE
UNOFFICIALLY
UNOPPRESSIVE
UNORIGINATED
UNORNAMENTAL
UNORNAMENTED
UNOVERTHROWN
UNPARALLELED
UNPARDONABLE
UNPARDONABLY
UNPASSIONATE
UNPATRONISED
UNPAVILIONED
UNPEACEFULLY
UNPERFECTION
UNPERFORATED
UNPERFORMING
UNPERISHABLE
UNPERSECUTED
UNPERSUASIVE
UNPLEASANTLY
UNPLEASANTRY
UNPLEASINGLY
UNPOETICALLY
UNPOLISHABLE
UNPOLITENESS
UNPOPULARITY
UNPOSSESSING
UNPREJUDICED
UNPRELATICAL
UNPREPAREDLY
UNPRESCRIBED
UNPRETENDING
UNPRETTINESS
UNPREVAILING
UNPRINCIPLED
UNPRIVILEGED
UNPROCLAIMED
UNPROCURABLE
UNPRODUCTIVE
UNPROFITABLE
UNPROFITABLY
UNPROHIBITED
UNPRONOUNCED

UNPROPERTIED
UNPROPITIOUS
UNPROSPEROUS
UNPROTESTING
UNPROVIDEDLY
UNPROVOKEDLY
UNPUNCTUATED
UNPUNISHABLE
UNPUNISHABLY
UNQUANTIFIED
UNQUENCHABLE
UNQUENCHABLY
UNQUESTIONED
UNREASONABLE
UNREASONABLY
UNRECALLABLE
UNRECOGNISED
UNRECONCILED
UNREDEEMABLE
UNREFLECTING
UNREFORMABLE
UNREFRESHING
UNREGENERACY
UNREGENERATE
UNREGISTERED
UNRELIEVABLE
UNRELIEVEDLY
UNREMARKABLE
UNREMEMBERED
UNREMITTEDLY
UNREMORSEFUL
UNREPAIRABLE
UNREPEALABLE
UNREPEATABLE
UNREPENTANCE
UNREPININGLY
UNREPORTABLE
UNREPROACHED
UNREPROVABLE
UNREPULSABLE
UNREQUITEDLY
UNRESERVEDLY
UNRESISTIBLE
UNRESOLVABLE
UNRESPECTIVE
UNRESPONSIVE
UNRESTRAINED
UNRESTRICTED
UNRETURNABLE
UNREVEALABLE
UNREVENGEFUL
UNREWARDEDLY
UNRHYTHMICAL
UNRIDDLEABLE
UNRIGHTFULLY
UNROMANTICAL
UNSAILORLIKE
UNSALABILITY
UNSANCTIFIED
UNSANCTIONED
UNSATISFYING
UNSCIENTIFIC
UNSCOTTIFIED
UNSCRIPTURAL
UNSCRUPULOUS
UNSCULPTURED

UNSEARCHABLE
UNSEARCHABLY
UNSEASONABLE
UNSEASONABLY
UNSEEMLINESS
UNSEGREGATED
UNSEMINARIED
UNSENSITISED
UNSENSUALISE
UNSEPULCHRED
UNSETTLEMENT
UNSHADOWABLE
UNSHRINKABLE
UNSLUMBERING
UNSOCIALISED
UNSOLICITOUS
UNSPECTACLED
UNSTABLENESS
UNSTANCHABLE
UNSTATUTABLE
UNSTATUTABLY
UNSTEADINESS
UNSTERILISED
UNSTIMULATED
UNSTOCKINGED
UNSTRATIFIED
UNSTRUCTURED
UNSUBLIMATED
UNSUBMISSIVE
UNSUBMITTING
UNSUBSCRIBED
UNSUBSIDISED
UNSUCCESSFUL
UNSUCCESSIVE
UNSUFFERABLE
UNSUFFICIENT
UNSUPPOSABLE
UNSUPPRESSED
UNSUSPECTING
UNSUSPICIOUS
UNSUSTAINING
UNSWERVINGLY
UNSYSTEMATIC
UNTENABILITY
UNTENANTABLE
UNTERMINATED
UNTERRIFYING
UNTHANKFULLY
UNTHINKINGLY
UNTHOUGHTFUL
UNTHREATENED
UNTIMELINESS
UNTOWARDNESS
UNTRAMMELLED
UNTRANSLATED
UNTRANSMUTED
UNTREMENDOUS
UNTRUSTINESS
UNTRUTHFULLY
UNTUMULTUOUS
UNUSEFULNESS
UNVACCINATED
UNVANQUISHED
UNVARIEGATED
UNVENTILATED
UNVERIFIABLE

UNVIRTUOUSLY
UNVOYAGEABLE
UNVULNERABLE
UNWATCHFULLY
UNWAVERINGLY
UNWEARYINGLY
UNWIELDINESS
UNWITHHOLDEN
UNWONTEDNESS
UNWORSHIPFUL
UNWORSHIPPED
UNWORTHINESS
UNYIELDINGLY
UPROARIOUSLY
URBANISATION
URBANOLOGIST
URINOGENITAL
USTILAGINEAE
USTILAGINOUS
USUFRUCTUARY
USURIOUSNESS
UXORIOUSNESS

V

VACATIONLESS
VACCINIACEAE
VACCINOIDEAE
VACUUM-PACKED
VAGINICOLINE
VAGINICOLOUS
VAINGLORIOUS
VALENCIENNES
VALETUDINARY
VALORISATION
VALUABLENESS
VANQUISHABLE
VANQUISHMENT
VANTAGE-POINT
VAPORISATION
VAPOROUSNESS
VARIABLENESS
VARIATIONIST
VARICOLOURED
VASE-PAINTING
VASODILATORY
VATICINATION
VAUDEVILLIST
VAUNT-COURIER
VEGETATIVELY
VEHMGERICHTE
VELLOZIACEAE
VELOCIPEDEAN
VELOCIPEDIAN
VELOCIPEDIST
VELVET-GUARDS
VELVET-SCOTER
VENDIBLENESS
VENEPUNCTURE
VENGEFULNESS
VENIPUNCTURE
VENOMOUSNESS
VENTRIPOTENT
VERBENACEOUS
VERIDICALITY
VERIFICATION
VERIFICATORY

VERISIMILITY
VERISIMILOUS
VERMICULATED
VERMIN-KILLER
VERNACULARLY
VERSIFICATOR
VERTEBRATION
VERTICALNESS
VERTICILLATE
VESICULATION
VESTIMENTARY
VETERINARIAN
VIBRAPHONIST
VIBRATIUNCLE
VICAR-GENERAL
VICE-CHAIRMAN
VICE-GOVERNOR
VICTORIANISM
VICTORIOUSLY
VIGOROUSNESS
VILIFICATION
VILLAINOUSLY
VINDICATRESS
VINDICTIVELY
VINEGAR-PLANT
VINEGARRETTE
VIOLIN-STRING
VIRGIN'S-BOWER
VIRIDESCENCE
VIRILESCENCE
VIRTUOSOSHIP
VIRTUOUSNESS
VISCEROTONIA
VISCEROTONIC
VISCOSIMETER
VISCOSIMETRY
VISCOUNTSHIP
VISITATIONAL
VISITATORIAL
VISITING-BOOK
VISITING-CARD
VITALISATION
VITATIVENESS
VITREOUSNESS
VITRIFACTION
VITRIFACTURE
VITRIOLATION
VITRO-DI-TRINA
VITUPERATION
VITUPERATIVE
VITUPERATORY
VIVIFICATION
VIVIPAROUSLY
VOCABULARIAN
VOCABULARIED
VOCALISATION
VOCATIONALLY
VOCICULTURAL
VOCIFERATION
VOCIFEROSITY
VOCIFEROUSLY
VOICEFULNESS
VOIDING-LOBBY
VOLATILENESS
VOLCANICALLY
VOLGA-BALTAIC

VOLITATIONAL
VOLITIONALLY
VOLITIONLESS
VOLUMETRICAL
VOLUMINOSITY
VOLUMINOUSLY
VOLUNTARYISM
VOLUNTARYIST
VOLUPTUOSITY
VOLUPTUOUSLY
VOMITURITION
VULCANISABLE
VULVO-UTERINE

W

WAG-AT-THE-WALL
WAG-BY-THE-WALL
WAGNERIANISM
WAINSCOTTING
WAISTCOATEER
WAISTCOATING
WAITING-WOMAN
WALKIE-TALKIE
WALKING-STAFF
WALKING-STICK
WALKING-STRAW
WALL-PAINTING
WALLYDRAIGLE
WAREHOUSEMAN
WARMONGERING
WASHING-BOARD
WASHING-HOUSE
WASHINGTONIA
WASTEFULNESS
WATCH-CRYSTAL
WATCHFULNESS
WATCH-OFFICER
WATER-BAILIFF
WATER-BALLAST
WATER-BATTERY
WATER-BELLOWS
WATER-BISCUIT
WATER-BOATMAN
WATER-BUFFALO
WATER-COOLING
WATER-CULTURE
WATER-DIVINER
WATER-DRINKER
WATER-FLOWERS
WATER-FLOWING
WATER-GILDING
WATER-HEMLOCK
WATERING-CALL
WATERISHNESS
WATERMANSHIP
WATER-MEASURE
WATER-MILFOIL
WATER-PARSNIP
WATER-PARTING
WATER-SOLDIER
WATER-SPANIEL
WATER-STRIDER
WATER-TURBINE
WATER-WAGTAIL
WAVE-OFFERING
WAVERINGNESS

WAY-PASSENGER
WEAK-SPIRITED
WEAL-BALANCED
WEANING-BRASH
WEATHER-BOARD
WEATHER-BOUND
WEATHER-CLOTH
WEATHER-GAUGE
WEATHER-GLASS
WEATHER-GLEAM
WEATHER-HOUSE
WEATHER-PROOF
WEATHER-STAIN
WEATHER-STRIP
WEDDING-CARDS
WEDDING-DOWER
WEDDING-DRESS
WEDDING-MARCH
WEEDING-TONGS
WEEPING-BIRCH
WEEPING-CROSS
WELL-BALANCED
WELL-BECOMING
WELL-BREATHED
WELL-DIRECTED
WELL-DISPOSED
WELL-DRESSING
WELL-EDUCATED
WELL-FAVOURED
WELL-GROUNDED
WELL-INFORMED
WELLINGTONIA
WELL-MANNERED
WELL-PLEASING
WELL-PLIGHTED
WELL-TEMPERED
WELL-TIMBERED
WELTER-STAKES
WELTER-WEIGHT
WHALE-FISHERY
WHALE-FISHING
WHAT'S-HER-NAME
WHAT'S-HIS-NAME
WHAT'S-ITS-NAME
WHENCESOEVER
WHEREAGAINST
WHERETHROUGH
WHIGGISHNESS
WHIGMALEERIE
WHIMPERINGLY
WHIMSICALITY
WHIP-AND-DERRY
WHIP-GRAFTING
WHIPPING-POST
WHIP-POOR-WILL
WHIP-SCORPION
WHISKY-FRISKY
WHISPERINGLY
WHISPEROUSLY
WHISTLE-DRUNK
WHITE-BEARDED
WHITE-BELLIED
WHITE-CRESTED
WHITE-CROWNED

WHITE-FRONTED
WHITE-HERRING
WHITE-LIVERED
WHITE-PUDDING
WHITHERWARDS
WHITLOW-GRASS
WHOLE-HEARTED
WHOLE-SKINNED
WHOOPING-SWAN
WHORTLEBERRY
WICKET-KEEPER
WIDE-SPECTRUM
WIGGLE-WAGGLE
WILD-WILLIAMS
WILLIEWAUGHT
WILL-O'-THE-WISP
WILLOW-GROUSE
WIND-CHANGING
WINDING-SHEET
WINDING-STAIR
WINDOW-SCREEN
WINDSOR-CHAIR
WINE-COLOURED
WINE-GLASSFUL
WINE-MERCHANT
WING-SHOOTING
WINNOWING-FAN
WINTER-BARLEY
WINTER-BEATEN
WINTER-BOURNE
WINTER-CHERRY
WINTER-CLOVER
WINTER-GARDEN
WINTER-GROUND
WINTER-WEIGHT
WIRE-STITCHED
WIRE-STRINGED
WISECRACKING
WISHING-STONE
WITCHES-BROOM
WITHDRAWMENT
WITHEREDNESS
WITHHOLDMENT
WOLLASTONITE
WOMANISHNESS
WOMAN-QUELLER
WONDER-MONGER
WONDER-STRUCK
WONDER-WORKER
WONDROUSNESS
WOODBURYTYPE
WOOD-ENGRAVER
WOODEN-HEADED
WOODEN-TONGUE
WOOD-HYACINTH
WOODLESSNESS
WOOD-OFFERING
WOOLLY-HAIRED
WOOLLY-HEADED
WORD-BUILDING
WORD-PAINTING
WORKABLENESS
WORKING-CLASS
WORKING-HOUSE
WORKING-MODEL

WORKMISTRESS
WORLD-WEARIED
WORSHIPFULLY
WOULFE-BOTTLE
WRANGLERSHIP
WRATHFULNESS
WRETCHEDNESS
WRITER'S-CRAMP
WRITING-PAPER
WRITING-TABLE
WRONGFULNESS

X

XANTHOCHROIA
XANTHOCHROIC
XANTHOCHROID
XANTHOMATOUS
XANTHOPTERIN
XERODERMATIC
XEROMORPHOUS
XIPHISTERNUM
XIPHOPHYLLUS
XYLOBALSAMUM

Y

YANKEE-DOODLE
YELLOW-BACKED
YELLOW-BILLED
YELLOW-FOOTED
YELLOW-HAMMER
YELLOW-HEADED
YELLOW-HORNED
YELLOW-LEGGED
YELLOW-NECKED
YELLOW-RATTLE
YELLOW-RINGED
YELLOW-RUMPED
YELLOW-YOWLEY
YIELDINGNESS
YOUTHFULNESS

Z

ZALAMBDODONT
ZANTEDESCHIA
ZARATHUSTRIC
ZENITH-SECTOR
ZEUGLODONTIA
ZINCOGRAPHER
ZINCOGRAPHIC
ZOOCHEMISTRY
ZOOGEOGRAPHY
ZOOGRAPHICAL
ZOOLOGICALLY
ZOOMAGNETISM
ZOOPATHOLOGY
ZOOPHYTOLOGY
ZOOSPERMATIC
ZOOTOMICALLY
ZYGAPOPHYSES
ZYGAPOPHYSIS
ZYGODACTYLIC
ZYGOMORPHISM
ZYGOMORPHOUS
ZYGOMYCETOUS
ZYMOTECHNICS

A

ABORIGINALISM
ABORIGINALITY
ABORTIFACIENT
ABSORBABILITY
ABSTRACTIONAL
ACADEMICALISM
ACARIDOMATIUM
ACARODOMATIUM
ACCELEROMETER
ACCEPTABILITY
ACCEPTILATION
ACCESSIBILITY
ACCIDENTALISM
ACCIDENTALITY
ACCIDENT-PRONE
ACCLIMATATION
ACCOMMODATING
ACCOMMODATION
ACCOMMODATIVE
ACCOMPANIMENT
ACCREDITATION
ACCULTURATION
ACETIFICATION
ACIDIFICATION
ACOTYLEDONOUS
ACQUIESCENTLY
ACQUIESCINGLY
ACQUIRABILITY
ACRIMONIOUSLY
ACRYLONITRILE
ACTINOMORPHIC
ACTINOMYCOSIS
ACTINOTHERAPY
ACTUALISATION
ADENOIDECTOMY
ADIABATICALLY
ADMEASUREMENT
ADMINISTRABLE
ADMINISTRATOR
ADMIRABLENESS
ADMISSIBILITY
ADVANTAGEABLE
ADVENTURESOME
ADVENTUROUSLY
ADVERTISEMENT
ADVISABLENESS
AERODYNAMICAL
AEROLITHOLOGY
AESTHETICALLY
AFFENPINSCHER
AFFIRMATIVELY
AFFORESTATION
AFFREIGHTMENT
AGGLOMERATION
AGGLOMERATIVE
AGGLUTINATION
AGGLUTINATIVE
AGGRAVATINGLY
AGONISTICALLY
AGREEABLENESS
AGRICULTURIST
AGROBIOLOGIST
AGROSTOLOGIST
AILOUROPHILIA

AILOUROPHOBIA
AIR-COMPRESSOR
AIRWORTHINESS
ALCOHOLOMETER
ALCOHOLOMETRY
ALLEGORICALLY
ALLELOMORPHIC
ALL-HALLOWMASS
ALL-HALLOWTIDE
ALLOWABLENESS
ALMOND-BLOSSOM
ALONGSHOREMAN
ALPHABETARIAN
ALPHABETIFORM
ALTERNATIVELY
ALUMINIFEROUS
AMARANTACEOUS
AMARANTHACEAE
AMBASSADORIAL
AMBIDEXTERITY
AMBIDEXTEROUS
AMBIGUOUSNESS
AMBITIOUSNESS
AMPHIGASTRIUM
AMPHITHEATRAL
AMPLIFICATION
AMYGDALACEOUS
ANACARDIACEAE
ANACHRONISTIC
ANACHRONOUSLY
ANAEROBICALLY
ANAGRAMMATISE
ANAGRAMMATISM
ANAGRAMMATIST
ANALOGOUSNESS
ANAPHRODISIAC
ANASTIGMATISM
ANATHEMATICAL
ANDRODIOECISM
ANFRACTUOSITY
ANGIOSPERMOUS
ANGLO-AMERICAN
ANGLO-CATHOLIC
ANGLO-SAXONDOM
ANIMADVERSION
ANIMALISATION
ANIMAL-WORSHIP
ANISOPHYLLOUS
ANNEXATIONIST
ANOMALISTICAL
ANSWERABILITY
ANTENNIFEROUS
ANTHELMINTHIC
ANTHOPHYLLITE
ANTHROPOLATRY
ANTHROPOMETRY
ANTHROPOMORPH
ANTHROPOPATHY
ANTHROPOPHAGI
ANTHROPOPHAGY
ANTHROPOSOPHY
ANTICHRISTIAN
ANTICLIMACTIC
ANTICLINORIUM
ANTICOAGULANT
ANTIGROPELOES

ANTIHISTAMINE
ANTILOGARITHM
ANTINEPHRITIC
ANTINOMIANISM
ANTIOCHIANISM
ANTI-PERSONNEL
ANTIQUITARIAN
ANTISCORBUTIC
ANTISEPTICISE
ANTISEPTICISM
ANTISOCIALISM
ANTISOCIALIST
ANTISOCIALITY
ANTISPASMODIC
ANYTHINGARIAN
APATHETICALLY
APHANIPTEROUS
APHELIOTROPIC
APOCALYPTICAL
APOCATASTASIS
APOCHROMATISM
APODICTICALLY
APOGEOTROPISM
APOPHLEGMATIC
APOTHEGMATISE
APOTHEGMATIST
APPEALINGNESS
APPELLATIONAL
APPELLATIVELY
APPENDICULATE
APPERTAINANCE
APPERTAINMENT
APPLICABILITY
APPORTIONMENT
APPREHENSIBLE
APPROPINQUATE
APPROPINQUITY
APPROPRIATELY
APPROPRIATION
APPROPRIATIVE
APPROXIMATELY
APPROXIMATION
APPROXIMATIVE
AQUA-MIRABILIS
AQUIFOLIACEAE
ARACHNOLOGIST
ARAEOMETRICAL
ARBITRARINESS
ARBORICULTURE
ARCHAEOLOGIST
ARCHAEOPTERYX
ARCHBISHOPRIC
ARCHEGONIATAE
ARCHIDIACONAL
ARCHIMANDRITE
ARCHITECTONIC
ARCHITECTURAL
ARGENTIFEROUS
ARGUMENTATION
ARGUMENTATIVE
ARISTOCRATISM
ARITHMETICIAN
ARMOURED-TRAIN
ARSENO-PYRITES
ARTIFICIALISE
ARTIFICIALITY

ARUNDINACEOUS
ASCENSIONTIDE
ASCERTAINABLE
ASCERTAINMENT
ASSASSINATION
ASSENTIVENESS
ASSERTIVENESS
ASSIDUOUSNESS
ASSOCIABILITY
ASSOCIATESHIP
ASSOCIATIVITY
ASSUMPTIONIST
ASSYRIOLOGIST
ASTHENOSPHERE
ASTHMATICALLY
ASTONISHINGLY
ASTRAPOPHOBIA
ASTROPHYSICAL
ATHEISTICALLY
ATHEMATICALLY
ATLANTOSAURUS
ATMOSPHERICAL
ATOMISTICALLY
ATROCIOUSNESS
ATTAINABILITY
ATTENTIVENESS
ATTITUDINISER
ATTRIBUTIVELY
ATTTRIBUTABLE
AUDACIOUSNESS
AUDIO-ENGINEER
AUDIO-LOCATION
AUSTRALIANISM
AUSTROASIATIC
AUTECOLOGICAL
AUTHENTICALLY
AUTHENTICATOR
AUTHORISATION
AUTHORITARIAN
AUTHORITATIVE
AUTOBIOGRAPHY
AUTOCATALYSIS
AUTOCATALYTIC
AUTOCEPHALOUS
AUTOCHTHONISM
AUTOCHTHONOUS
AUTODIGESTION
AUTOEROTICISM
AUTOMATICALLY
AUTOSCHEDIASM
AUTOSCHEDIAZE
AVAILABLENESS
AVANT-GARDISTE
AVERRUNCATION
AVICULARIIDAE
AXIOMATICALLY

B

BACCALAUREATE
BACK-FORMATION
BACK-PEDALLING
BACK-SCRATCHER
BACKWARDATION
BACTERIOLYSIN
BACTERIOLYSIS

BACTERIOLYTIC
BACTERIOPHAGE
BADGER-BAITING
BADGER-DRAWING
BAGGAGE-ANIMAL
BALANOGLOSSUS
BALKANISATION
BALLAST-HEAVER
BALL-CARTRIDGE
BALNEOTHERAPY
BALSAMIFEROUS
BALSAMINACEAE
BALTOSLAVONIC
BAMBOOZLEMENT
BARBARISATION
BARBAROUSNESS
BARBER-SURGEON
BAREFACEDNESS
BARGAIN-HUNTER
BARNACLE-GOOSE
BARREL-VAULTED
BARRISTERSHIP
BATHYMETRICAL
BATON-SINISTER
BATTLE-CRUISER
BATTLE-SCARRED
BEATIFICATION
BEAUTEOUSNESS
BEETLE-CRUSHER
BEGGING-LETTER
BEGINNINGLESS
BELEAGUERMENT
BELLES-LETTRES
BENEDICTIONAL
BENEFICENTIAL
BERBERIDACEAE
BERKELEIANISM
BERNICLE-GOOSE
BESEEMINGNESS
BESPOTTEDNESS
BETWEENWHILES
BEWILDERINGLY
BIBLIOGRAPHER
BIBLIOGRAPHIC
BIBLIOLATRIST
BIBLIOLATROUS
BIBLIOPHAGIST
BIBLIOPHILISM
BIBLIOPHILIST
BIBLIOPOLICAL
BIBLIOTHECARY
BIDDING-PRAYER
BILDUNGSROMAN
BILLIARD-CLOTH
BILLIARD-TABLE
BIODEGRADABLE
BIOGEOGRAPHER
BIREFRINGENCE
BIRMINGHAMISE
BLACK-AND-WHITE
BLACKGUARDISM
BLADDER-CHERRY
BLANKET-STITCH
BLANKETY-BLANK
BLASPHEMOUSLY

BLASTOGENESIS
BLEEDING-HEART
BLINDMAN'S-BUFF
BLISTER-BEETLE
BLOOD-BOLTERED
BLOOD-CURDLING
BLOODLESSNESS
BLOOD-RELATION
BLOOMSBURYITE
BLOTTING-PAPER
BOARDING-HOUSE
BOATSWAIN-BIRD
BOMBASTICALLY
BONE-TURQUOISE
BONHEUR-DU-JOUR
BOOK-CANVASSER
BOOKING-OFFICE
BOROUGH-MONGER
BOTTLE-COASTER
BOUILLABAISSE
BOULTING-HUTCH
BOUNDARY-LAYER
BOUNDARY-RIDER
BOUNDLESSNESS
BOUNTEOUSNESS
BOUNTIFULNESS
BOUSTROPHEDON
BOWLING-CREASE
BOWSTRING-HEMP
BRACHYCEPHALY
BRACHYDACTYLY
BRACHYPTEROUS
BRAINSICKNESS
BRANCH-OFFICER
BRASSFOUNDING
BRATTICE-CLOTH
BREAKABLENESS
BREATHING-TIME
BREECHLOADING
BRIDGE-OF-BOATS
BRILLIANTNESS
BROAD-SPECTRUM
BROKEN-HEARTED
BROMELIACEOUS
BROTHER-GERMAN
BROTHERLINESS
BRUTALISATION
BUBBLE-CHAMBER
BUILDING-BLOCK
BUILDING-BOARD
BULLOCK'S-HEART
BUMPTIOUSNESS
BUREAUCRATIST
BURGLARIOUSLY
BURNING-MIRROR
BURNT-OFFERING
BURSERACEOUS
BURYING-BEETLE
BURYING-GROUND
BUTCHER'S-BROOM
BUTTER-BISCUIT
BUTTER-FINGERS
BUTTERFLY-FISH
BUTTERFLY-WEED
BUTTON-THROUGH

C

CABBALISTICAL
CABINET-MAKING
CABLE-MOULDING
CAESAROPAPISM
CALCIFICATION
CALIATURE-WOOD
CALICO-PRINTER
CALLIGRAPHIST
CALLISTHENICS
CALVINISTICAL
CAMPANOLOGIST
CAMPANULACEAE
CAMPEACHY-WOOD
CAMPHORACEOUS
CAMP-SHEATHING
CANALICULATED
CANARY-CREEPER
CANDIDATESHIP
CANDLE-DIPPING
CANDLE-LIGHTER
CANDLE-SNUFFER
CANNIBALISTIC
CANVAS-CLIMBER
CAPACIOUSNESS
CAPELLMEISTER
CAPERCAILLZIE
CAPPARIDACEAE
CAPRIFICATION
CARBONIFEROUS
CARBONISATION
CARBONYLATION
CARBURISATION
CARCINOLOGIST
CARCINOMATOUS
CARD-CATALOGUE
CARDIOGRAPHER
CARNIVOROUSLY
CARPET-BEATING
CARPET-BEDDING
CARPET-BOMBING
CARPET-SLIPPER
CARPET-SWEEPER
CARRIAGE-DRIVE
CARRIER-PIGEON
CARRION-FLOWER
CARTE-DE-VISITE
CARTILAGINOUS
CARTRIDGE-BELT
CARYOCARACEAE
CASE-HARDENING
CASEMENT-CLOTH
CASSEGRAINIAN
CASTING-WEIGHT
CASUALISATION
CASUARINACEAE
CATASTROPHISM
CATASTROPHIST
CATECHISTICAL
CATECHUMENATE
CATECHUMENISM
CATEGOREMATIC
CATEGORICALLY
CATERCORNERED
CATHODOGRAPHY

CAT-O'-NINE-TAILS
CATTLE-LIFTING
CAUSELESSNESS
CAUTERISATION
CAYENNE-PEPPER
CELLULIFEROUS
CENTRE-FORWARD
CENTRICALNESS
CENTRIFUGALLY
CENTRIFUGENCE
CEPHALOCHORDA
CEPHALOTHORAX
CERCOPITHECUS
CEREBROSPINAL
CEREMONIALISM
CEREMONIOUSLY
CEROGRAPHICAL
CERTIFICATION
CERTIFICATORY
CHAIN-MOULDING
CHALCOGRAPHER
CHALLENGEABLE
CHALLENGINGLY
CHAMBER-FELLOW
CHAMELEONLIKE
CHANGEABILITY
CHANGEFULNESS
CHANGING-PIECE
CHARACTERLESS
CHARITY-SCHOOL
CHARLATANICAL
CHARTER-MEMBER
CHATEAUBRIAND
CHEIROGRAPHER
CHEIROPTEROUS
CHEIROTHERIUM
CHEMORECEPTOR
CHEST-REGISTER
CHEVAL-DE-FRISE
CHICKEN-HAZARD
CHIEFTAINSHIP
CHIMNEY-CORNER
CHINKERINCHEE
CHIROGRAPHIST
CHIROMANTICAL
CHLAMYDOSPORE
CHLORARGYRITE
CHLOROCRUORIN
CHLOROFORMIST
CHLOROMYCETIN
CHLOROPHYCEAE
CHOLECYSTITIS
CHOPPING-BLOCK
CHOPPING-BOARD
CHOPPING-KNIFE
CHOREOGRAPHER
CHOREOGRAPHIC
CHOREPISCOPAL
CHREMATISTICS
CHRESTOMATHIC
CHRISTIANLIKE
CHRISTIANNESS
CHRISTMAS-TIDE
CHRISTMAS-TIME
CHRISTMAS-TREE
CHRISTOLOGIST

CHROMATOPHORE
CHROME-LEATHER
CHROME-PLATING
CHROME-TANNING
CHRONOGRAPHER
CHRONOLOGICAL
CHRYSANTHEMUM
CHRYSOPHILITE
CHUCK-FARTHING
CHURCH-OFFICER
CHURCH-SERVICE
CHYMIFICATION
CICATRISATION
CICERONIANISM
CIGARETTE-CARD
CINCHONACEOUS
CINEMATOGRAPH
CINE-PROJECTOR
CINNAMON-STONE
CINQUE-SPOTTED
CIRCUMAMBAGES
CIRCUMAMBIENT
CIRCUMDUCTION
CIRCUMDUCTORY
CIRCUMFERENCE
CIRCUMFLEXION
CIRCUMFLUENCE
CIRCUMJACENCY
CIRCUMSCRIBER
CIRCUMSPECTLY
CIRCUMVALLATE
CIRCUMVENTION
CIRCUMVENTIVE
CITRONELLA-OIL
CLAIRAUDIENCE
CLAMOROUSNESS
CLANDESTINELY
CLAPPERBOARDS
CLAPPERCLAWER
CLARIFICATION
CLASSICALNESS
CLAY-IRONSTONE
CLEAN-TIMBERED
CLEARING-HOUSE
CLEAR-STARCHER
CLEAVABLENESS
CLEISTOGAMOUS
CLIMACTERICAL
CLIMACTICALLY
CLIMATOGRAPHY
CLIMATOLOGIST
CLINCHER-BUILT
CLINODIAGONAL
CLINOPINACOID
CLINOPINAKOID
CLISHMACLAVER
CLOAK-AND-SWORD
CLOISTER-GARTH
CLOTHES-BASKET
CLOTHES-SCREEN
COACHBUILDING
COACHWHIP-BIRD
COADJUTORSHIP
COAGULABILITY
COARSE-GRAINED
COASTGUARDMAN

COBALTIFEROUS
COBELLIGERENT
COCAINISATION
COCHLEARIFORM
COCKLE-BRAINED
COCK-OF-THE-ROCK
COCK-THRAPPLED
COCK-THROPPLED
COCONUT-BUTTER
COEDUCATIONAL
COENAESTHESIS
COFFEE-DISEASE
COGNOMINATION
COINHERITANCE
COLD-BLOODEDLY
COLLABORATION
COLLEAGUESHIP
COLLECTEDNESS
COLLECTING-BOX
COLLECTORSHIP
COLLIESHANGIE
COLLOQUIALISM
COLLOQUIALIST
COMBATIVENESS
COMBINATORIAL
COMMANDERSHIP
COMMEASURABLE
COMMELINACEAE
COMMEMORATION
COMMEMORATIVE
COMMEMORATORY
COMMENSURABLE
COMMENSURABLY
COMMERCIALESE
COMMERCIALISE
COMMERCIALISM
COMMERCIALIST
COMMERCIALITY
COMMISERATION
COMMISERATIVE
COMMITTEESHIP
COMMUNICATION
COMMUNICATIVE
COMMUNICATORY
COMMUNITARIAN
COMMUTABILITY
COMMUTATIVELY
COMPACTEDNESS
COMPAGINATION
COMPANIONABLE
COMPANIONABLY
COMPANIONHOOD
COMPANIONLESS
COMPANIONSHIP
COMPARATIVELY
COMPASSIONATE
COMPASS-SIGNAL
COMPASS-TIMBER
COMPASS-WINDOW
COMPATIBILITY
COMPATRIOTISM
COMPENDIOUSLY
COMPLAININGLY
COMPLAISANTLY
COMPLEMENTARY
COMPLEXEDNESS

COMPLIMENTARY
COMPOSITENESS
COMPOSITIONAL
COMPREHENSION
COMPREHENSIVE
COMPRESSIONAL
COMPROVINCIAL
COMPULSIONIST
COMPUTATIONAL
CONCATENATION
CONCAVO-CONVEX
CONCEITEDNESS
CONCENTRATION
CONCENTRATIVE
CONCENTRICITY
CONCEPTIONIST
CONCEPTUALISM
CONCEPTUALIST
CONCERNEDNESS
CONCESSIONARY
CONCESSIONIST
CONCHOLOGICAL
CONCOMITANTLY
CONCRETIONARY
CONCUPISCENCE
CONCUPISCIBLE
CONCYCLICALLY
CONDESCENDING
CONDESCENSION
CONDITIONALLY
CONDUCTORSHIP
CONDYLOMATOUS
CONFABULATION
CONFABULATORY
CONFARREATION
CONFECTIONARY
CONFECTIONERY
CONFEDERATION
CONFEDERATIVE
CONFESSIONARY
CONFESSORSHIP
CONFIDINGNESS
CONFIGURATION
CONFLAGRATION
CONFOUNDINGLY
CONFRATERNITY
CONFRONTATION
CONGLOMERATIC
CONGLUTINATOR
CONGRATULABLE
CONGRATULATOR
CONGRESSIONAL
CONGRESSWOMAN
CONGREVE-MATCH
CONGRUOUSNESS
CONJECTURABLE
CONJECTURALLY
CONJUGATIONAL
CONJUNCTIONAL
CONJUNCTIVELY
CONNATURALISE
CONNATURALITY
CONNECTING-ROD
CONNUMERATION
CONQUISTADORS
CONSANGUINITY

CONSCIENTIOUS
CONSCIOUSNESS
CONSECTANEOUS
CONSECUTIVELY
CONSENESCENCE
CONSENESCENCY
CONSENTANEITY
CONSENTANEOUS
CONSEQUENTIAL
CONSERVATOIRE
CONSIDERATELY
CONSIDERATION
CONSIDERATIVE
CONSIDERINGLY
CONSIMILARITY
CONSIMILITUDE
CONSOLIDATION
CONSOLIDATIVE
CONSPICUOUSLY
CONSPIRATRESS
CONSPURCATION
CONSTABLESHIP
CONSTABLEWICK
CONSTANTINIAN
CONSTELLATION
CONSTELLATORY
CONSTERNATION
CONSTRAINABLE
CONSTRAINEDLY
CONSTRINGENCY
CONSTRUCTABLE
CONSTRUCTIBLE
CONSTUPRATION
CONSUMPTIVELY
CONSUMPTIVITY
CONTABESCENCE
CONTAMINATION
CONTAMINATIVE
CONTEMPLATION
CONTEMPLATIST
CONTEMPLATIVE
CONTENTEDNESS
CONTENTIOUSLY
CONTINUEDNESS
CONTORTIONATE
CONTORTIONIST
CONTRABANDISM
CONTRABANDIST
CONTRABASSOON
CONTRACEPTION
CONTRACEPTIVE
CONTRACTILITY
CONTRADICTION
CONTRADICTIVE
CONTRADICTORY
CONTRAFAGOTTO
CONTRAPUNTIST
CONTRARIOUSLY
CONTRATERRENE
CONTRAVENTION
CONTRIBUTABLE
CONTRISTATION
CONTROVERSIAL
CONTROVERTIST
CONVALESCENCE
CONVALESCENCY

CONVENTIONARY
CONVENTIONIST
CONVERSAZIONE
CONVERSAZIONI
CONVERTIPLANE
CONVEXO-CONVEX
CONVOCATIONAL
CONVULSIONARY
CONVULSIONIST
COOK-HOUSEMAID
COPARTNERSHIP
COPPER-CAPTAIN
COPPER-PYRITES
COPPLE-CROWNED
COPYING-PENCIL
CORALLIFEROUS
CORALLIGENOUS
CO-RELIGIONIST
CORIANDER-SEED
CORINTHIANISE
CORNELIAN-TREE
CORNET-À-PISTON
CORNIFICATION
COROLLIFLORAE
COROLLIFLORAL
CORPORATENESS
CORRELATIVELY
CORRELATIVITY
CORRESPONDENT
CORRESPONDING
CORRESPONSIVE
CORRIDOR-TRAIN
CORRIGIBILITY
CORROBORATION
CORROBORATIVE
CORROBORATORY
CORROSIBILITY
CORROSIVENESS
CORRUPTIONIST
COSMOPOLITICS
COSMOPOLITISM
COSMOTHETICAL
COSTARDMONGER
COST-EFFECTIVE
COTTON-SPINNER
COTTON-THISTLE
COUNSEL-KEEPER
COUNTERACTION
COUNTERACTIVE
COUNTER-ATTACK
COUNTER-CASTER
COUNTER-CHANGE
COUNTERCHARGE
COUNTERFEITER
COUNTERFEITLY
COUNTER-FLEURY
COUNTER-JUMPER
COUNTER-MOTION
COUNTER-PAROLE
COUNTER-POISON
COUNTER-SIGNAL
COUNTERSTROKE
COUNTER-WEIGHT
COUNTING-HOUSE
COURSING-JOINT
COURT-CUPBOARD

COURTEOUSNESS
COURTS-MARTIAL
COXCOMBICALLY
CRACKER-BARREL
CRAFTSMANSHIP
CRANBERRY-TREE
CRANIOLOGICAL
CRANIOSCOPIST
CREAM-COLOURED
CREDULOUSNESS
CREOSOTE-PLANT
CRIBBAGE-BOARD
CRIMINOLOGIST
CRIMINOUSNESS
CRINICULTURAL
CRISS-CROSS-ROW
CROSSBREEDING
CROSS-CROSSLET
CROSS-DIVISION
CROSS-GARTERED
CROSS-HATCHING
CROSS-QUARTERS
CROSS-QUESTION
CROSS-SPRINGER
CROSS-VAULTING
CROWN-IMPERIAL
CRUISER-WEIGHT
CRYPTOGRAPHER
CRYPTOGRAPHIC
CRYPTOLOGICAL
CRYSTAL-GAZING
CUCKOO-SPITTLE
CUCURBITACEAE
CUPBOARD-FAITH
CURTAIN-RAISER
CUSTARD-COFFIN
CUSTOMARINESS
CYATHOPHYLLUM
CYCLANTHACEAE
CYCLOSPERMOUS
CYLINDER-BLOCK
CYLINDRACEOUS
CYTODIAGNOSIS

D

DACTYLIOMANCY
DACTYLOGRAPHY
DADDY-LONG-LEGS
DAGUERREOTYPE
DAGUERREOTYPY
DAMNIFICATION
DANCING-MASTER
DANGEROUSNESS
DARNING-NEEDLE
DASTARDLINESS
DAUGHTER-IN-LAW
DAUNTLESSNESS
DEAD-COLOURING
DEAD-RECKONING
DEATHLESSNESS
DEBAUCHEDNESS
DECEITFULNESS
DECEPTIBILITY
DECEPTIVENESS
DECEREBRATION
DECIDUOUSNESS

DECK-PASSENGER
DECLAMATORILY
DECLARATIVELY
DECLARATORILY
DECOMPOSITION
DECOMPRESSION
DECONTAMINATE
DECORTICATION
DECREPITATION
DEFEASIBILITY
DEFECTIBILITY
DEFECTIVENESS
DEFENCELESSLY
DEFENSIBILITY
DEFERENTIALLY
DEFERVESCENCE
DEFERVESCENCY
DEFIBRINATION
DEFICIENTNESS
DEFORESTATION
DEIPNOSOPHIST
DELETERIOUSLY
DELICIOUSNESS
DELIQUESCENCE
DELIRIFACIENT
DELIRIOUSNESS
DEMATERIALISE
DEMONOLOGICAL
DEMONSTRATION
DEMONSTRATIVE
DEMONSTRATORY
DENATIONALISE
DENDROCALAMUS
DENDROLOGICAL
DENTICULATION
DEOCH-AN-DORUIS
DEODORISATION
DEONTOLOGICAL
DEPERSONALISE
DEPHLEGMATION
DEPRECATINGLY
DERELIGIONISE
DERIVATIONIST
DERMATOGRAPHY
DERMATOLOGIST
DESCRIPTIVELY
DESEGREGATION
DESIRABLENESS
DESOBLIGEANTE
DESPERATENESS
DESPICABILITY
DESTRUCTIONAL
DESTRUCTIVELY
DESTRUCTIVIST
DESTRUCTIVITY
DESULTORINESS
DETERIORATION
DETERIORATIVE
DETERMINATELY
DETERMINATION
DETERMINATIVE
DETERMINISTIC
DEUTEROGAMIST
DEUTERONOMIST
DEUTEROSCOPIC
DEVASTATINGLY

DEVELOPMENTAL
DEVOLUTIONARY
DEVOLUTIONIST
DEVOTIONALIST
DEXTEROUSNESS
DEXTROCARDIAC
DIACATHOLICON
DIAGEOTROPISM
DIAGNOSTICIAN
DIALECTICALLY
DIALOGISTICAL
DIALYPETALOUS
DIAMETRICALLY
DIAMOND-BEETLE
DIAMOND-POWDER
DIAPHANOMETER
DIAPHOTOTROPY
DIAPHRAGMATIC
DIATHERMANOUS
DICHLAMYDEOUS
DICHOTOMOUSLY
DICHROOSCOPIC
DICOTYLEDONES
DICTATORIALLY
DIESELISATION
DIFFERENTIATE
DIFFUSIBILITY
DIFFUSION-TUBE
DIFFUSIVENESS
DIGESTIBILITY
DIGNIFICATION
DILETTANTEISM
DIMENSIONLESS
DIMETHYLAMINE
DIMINISHINGLY
DINNER-SERVICE
DIORISTICALLY
DIOSCOREACEAE
DIOTHELETICAL
DIPHTHONGALLY
DIPLEIDOSCOPE
DIPLOMATOLOGY
DIPPING-NEEDLE
DIPROTODONTIA
DIPTEROCARPUS
DISAFFECTEDLY
DISAFFIRMANCE
DISAGREEABLES
DISAPPEARANCE
DISAPPOINTING
DISARTICULATE
DISASSIMILATE
DISCAPACITATE
DISCEPTATIOUS
DISCHARGE-TUBE
DISCIPLINABLE
DISCOLORATION
DISCOMMISSION
DISCOMMODIOUS
DISCOMYCETOUS
DISCONCERTION
DISCONFORMITY
DISCONNECTION
DISCONTENTFUL
DISCONTENTING
DISCONTINUITY

DISCONTINUOUS
DISCREDITABLE
DISCREDITABLY
DISCRETIONARY
DISCRIMINATOR
DISEMBARKMENT
DISEMBODIMENT
DISENGAGEMENT
DISESTIMATION
DISFELLOWSHIP
DISFIGURATION
DISFIGUREMENT
DISGOSPELLING
DISGRACEFULLY
DISGUISEDNESS
DISHABILITATE
DISHARMONIOUS
DISHEARTENING
DISHONOURABLE
DISHONOURABLY
DISILLUMINATE
DISILLUSIONED
DISINTEGRABLE
DISINTEGRATOR
DISINTERESTED
DISINVIGORATE
DISJUNCTIVELY
DISMEMBERMENT
DISNATURALISE
DISOBEDIENTLY
DISOBLIGATION
DISOBLIGATORY
DISOBLIGEMENT
DISOBLIGINGLY
DISORDINATELY
DISPARAGEMENT
DISPARAGINGLY
DISPARATENESS
DISPASSIONATE
DISPATCH-RIDER
DISPERSEDNESS
DISPLANTATION
DISPLEASINGLY
DISPOSITIONAL
DISPOSITIONED
DISPOSITIVELY
DISPRAISINGLY
DISPROPORTION
DISPURVEYANCE
DISREPUTATION
DISRESPECTFUL
DISSEMBLINGLY
DISSEMINATION
DISSEMINATIVE
DISSEPIMENTAL
DISSEVERATION
DISSIMILARITY
DISSIMILATION
DISSIMILITUDE
DISSIMULATION
DISSOLUBILITY
DISSOLUTENESS
DISTANT-SIGNAL
DISTASTEFULLY
DISTINCTIVELY
DISTINGUISHED

DISTINGUISHER
DISTRESSFULLY
DISTRESSINGLY
DISTRIBUTABLE
DISTRUSTFULLY
DIVERSIFIABLE
DIVERTIBILITY
DIVERTICULATE
DIVERTISEMENT
DOCTRINAIRISM
DOCUMENTATION
DODECAPHONIST
DOG-PERIWINKLE
DOG'S-TAIL-GRASS
DOLICHOCEPHAL
DOLICHOSAURIA
DOLICHOSAURUS
DOMESTICATION
DOMICILIATION
DO-NOTHINGNESS
DOUBLE-COCONUT
DOUBLE-CONCAVE
DOUBLE-CROSSER
DOUBLE-DEALING
DOUBLE-FOUNTED
DOUBLE-GLAZING
DOUBLE-GLOSTER
DOUBLE-HEARTED
DOUBLE-JOINTED
DOUBLE-NATURED
DOUBLE-SHOTTED
DOUBLE-SHUFFLE
DOUBLE-TONGUED
DOWNCAST-SHAFT
DOWNRIGHTNESS
DRAFTSMANSHIP
DRAGGLE-TAILED
DRAINAGE-BASIN
DRAMATISATION
DRAUGHT-ANIMAL
DRAUGHT-ENGINE
DRAUGHT-SCREEN
DRAWING-MASTER
DRAWING-PENCIL
DREADLESSNESS
DREAMLESSNESS
DRESS-IMPROVER
DRESSING-TABLE
DRILLING-LATHE
DRILL-SERGEANT
DRINKABLENESS
DRINK-OFFERING
DULCIFICATION
DUNDERHEADISM
DWELLING-HOUSE
DWELLING-PLACE
DYED-IN-THE-WOOL
DYNAMOGENESIS
DYOTHELETICAL
DYSMENORRHEAL
DYSMENORRHOEA
DYSPEPTICALLY

E

EAGLE-FLIGHTED
EARTHLY-MINDED

EARTH-MOVEMENT
EAST-NORTH-EAST
EAST-SOUTH-EAST
EAVESDROPPING
EBULLIOSCOPIC
ECCENTRICALLY
ECCLESIOLATRY
ECHINODERMATA
ECONOMISATION
ECUMENICALISM
EDUCATIONALLY
EFFECTIVENESS
EFFERVESCENCE
EFFERVESCENCY
EFFERVESCIBLE
EFFICACIOUSLY
EFFLORESCENCE
EGOCENTRICITY
EGOTISTICALLY
EGREGIOUSNESS
EGYPTOLOGICAL
EIGHTEEN-PENCE
EIGHTEEN-PENNY
ELABORATENESS
ELECTIONEERER
ELECTRIFIABLE
ELECTRISATION
ELECTROCEMENT
ELECTROCHEMIC
ELECTROCUTION
ELECTROGRAPHY
ELECTROMAGNET
ELECTROMERISM
ELECTROMETRIC
ELECTROMOTIVE
ELECTROPHORUS
ELECTROSCOPIC
ELECTROSTATIC
ELECTROTHERMY
ELECTROTYPIST
ELECTROVALENT
ELEPHANTIASIS
ELEPHANT'S-EARS
ELEPHANT'S-FOOT
EMBARRASSMENT
EMBELLISHMENT
EMBRACINGNESS
EMBRANGLEMENT
EMBRYOLOGICAL
EMERALD-COPPER
EMIGRATIONIST
EMPHYSEMATOUS
EMPYREUMATISE
ENANTIOMORPHY
ENANTIOTROPIC
ENATIOMORPHIC
ENCAPSULATION
ENCEPHALARTOS
ENCEPHALOCELE
ENCEPHALOGRAM
ENCEPHALOTOMY
ENCOMIASTICAL
ENCOMPASSMENT
ENCOURAGEMENT
ENCOURAGINGLY
ENCROACHINGLY

ENCYCLOPAEDIA
ENCYCLOPAEDIC
ENDEARINGNESS
ENDOCRINOLOGY
ENDOSMOMETRIC
ENDURABLENESS
ENERGETICALLY
ENGINE-TURNING
ENHYPOSTATISE
ENIGMATICALLY
ENJOYABLENESS
ENLIGHTENMENT
ENTEROPNEUSTA
ENTERTAINMENT
ENTOMOLOGICAL
ENTOMOPHAGOUS
ENTOMOPHILOUS
ENTOMOSTRACAN
ENVIRONMENTAL
EPANADIPLOSIS
EPEIROGENESIS
EPEIROGENETIC
EPHEMEROPTERA
EPIDOTISATION
EPIGENETICIST
EPIGRAMMATISE
EPIGRAMMATIST
EPINASTICALLY
EPIPHENOMENON
EPITRACHELION
EQUESTRIANISM
EQUIDIFFERENT
EQUIDISTANTLY
EQUILIBRATION
EQUINOCTIALLY
EQUIPONDERANT
EQUIPONDERATE
EQUIPOTENTIAL
EQUISETACEOUS
EQUITABLENESS
EQUIVOCALNESS
ERGATOMORPHIC
ERIOCAULACEAE
ERRONEOUSNESS
ERYSIPELATOUS
ESCHATOLOGIST
ESCHSCHOLTZIA
ESSENTIALNESS
ESTABLISHMENT
ESTRANGEDNESS
ETHANOLAMINES
ETHNOCENTRISM
ETRUSCOLOGIST
EUBACTERIALES
EUCHARISTICAL
EUPHORBIACEAE
EUSPORANGIATE
EVANGELIARION
EVANGELIARIUM
EVANGELICALLY
EVANGELISTARY
EVEN-CHRISTIAN
EVERLASTINGLY
EVOCATIVENESS
EXANTHEMATOUS
EXCEPTIONABLE

EXCEPTIONABLY
EXCEPTIONALLY
EXCESSIVENESS
EXCITABLENESS
EXCLUSIVENESS
EXCOMMUNICATE
EXCORTICATION
EXCRESCENTIAL
EXCURSIVENESS
EXCUSABLENESS
EXEMPLARINESS
EXEMPLIFIABLE
EXHIBITIONISM
EXHIBITIONIST
EXOTHERMICITY
EXPANSIBILITY
EXPANSIVENESS
EXPECTORATION
EXPECTORATIVE
EXPEDITIONARY
EXPEDITIOUSLY
EXPENSIVENESS
EXPERIMENTIST
EXPLANATORILY
EXPLOSIVENESS
EXPONENTIALLY
EXPOSTULATION
EXPOSTULATIVE
EXPOSTULATORY
EXPRESSIONISM
EXPRESSIONIST
EXPROPRIATION
EXPURGATORIAL
EXQUISITENESS
EXSANGUINEOUS
EXTEMPORARILY
EXTENSIBILITY
EXTENSIONALLY
EXTENSIVENESS
EXTENUATINGLY
EXTERMINATION
EXTERMINATIVE
EXTERMINATORY
EXTERRITORIAL
EXTRA-AXILLARY
EXTRA-CELLULAR
EXTRA-GALACTIC
EXTRA-JUDICIAL
EXTRA-LIMITARY
EXTRA-METRICAL
EXTRAORDINARY
EXTRA-PHYSICAL
EXTRAPOLATION
EXTRA-TROPICAL
EXTRAVAGANTLY
EXTRAVASATION
EXTRA-VASCULAR
EXTRINSICALLY

F

FACETIOUSNESS
FACULTATIVELY
FAIR-AND-SQUARE
FAITHLESSNESS
FALSIFICATION
FANTASTICALLY

FATIGABLENESS
FAULTLESSNESS
FEATHER-BONNET
FEATHER-DUSTER
FEATHER-STITCH
FEATHER-WEIGHT
FEEDING-BOTTLE
FELLOW-CITIZEN
FELLOW-FEELING
FELLOW-SERVANT
FELONIOUSNESS
FENCING-MASTER
FERMENTITIOUS
FEROCIOUSNESS
FERRICYANOGEN
FERROCHROMIUM
FERROCONCRETE
FERROCYANOGEN
FERROMAGNETIC
FERROSOFERRIC
FERTILISATION
FEUDALISATION
FEUILLETONISM
FEUILLETONIST
FIBROVASCULAR
FICTIONALISED
FIDDLEFADDLER
FIFTH-MONARCHY
FIGURE-CASTING
FIGURE-WEAVING
FILIBUSTERING
FILIBUSTERISM
FILIBUSTEROUS
FILIPENDULOUS
FILTERABILITY
FINDON-HADDOCK
FINGER-BREADTH
FINGER-POINTER
FINNAN-HADDOCK
FIRE-INSURANCE
FIRE-RESISTING
FIRST-BEGOTTEN
FIRST-OFFENDER
FISHING-TACKLE
FISSIPAROUSLY
FLAGELLANTISM
FLAME-COLOURED
FLIGHT-FEATHER
FLINT-KNAPPING
FLOCCILLATION
FLOODLIGHTING
FLORICULTURAL
FLOURISHINGLY
FLOUTINGSTOCK
FLOWER-SERVICE
FLUVIOGLACIAL
FOLK-ETYMOLOGY
FOLLOW-THROUGH
FOOLHARDINESS
FOOT-LAND-RAKER
FOOT-PASSENGER
FORAMINIFERAL
FOREFEELINGLY
FOREKNOWINGLY
FOREKNOWLEDGE
FOREMENTIONED

FORESHADOWING
FORESIGHTLESS
FORGETFULNESS
FORGOTTENNESS
FORMIDABILITY
FORMULARISTIC
FORTIFICATION
FORTISSISSIMO
FORTITUDINOUS
FORTUNATENESS
FORTUNE-HUNTER
FORTUNE-TELLER
FOSSILIFEROUS
FOSSILISATION
FOSTER-BROTHER
FOUNDATION-NET
FOUNDER-MEMBER
FRACTIONALISE
FRACTIONALISM
FRACTIONALIST
FRACTIONATION
FRACTIOUSNESS
FRAGMENTARILY
FRAGMENTATION
FRANCHISEMENT
FRANCO-RUSSIAN
FRANKENIACEAE
FRANK-TENEMENT
FREE-SELECTION
FREEZING-POINT
FREQUENTATION
FREQUENTATIVE
FRIGHTENINGLY
FRIGHTFULNESS
FRINGILLIFORM
FRIVOLOUSNESS
FRUITLESSNESS
FRUMENTACEOUS
FRUMENTARIOUS
FUGACIOUSNESS
FULL-FASHIONED
FUNAMBULATION
FUNAMBULATORY
FUNCTIONALISM
FUNCTIONALIST
FUNDAMENTALLY
FURACIOUSNESS
FUTURE-PERFECT
FUTUROLOGICAL

G

GAIDHEALTACHD
GALACTORRHOEA
GALACTOSAEMIA
GALEOPITHECUS
GALVANISATION
GALVANOPLASTY
GAMBLING-HOUSE
GAMETOGENESIS
GARLIC-MUSTARD
GARNETIFEROUS
GARNISHEEMENT
GARRULOUSNESS
GASTEROPODOUS
GASTROCNEMIUS
GASTROENTERIC

GASTROLOGICAL
GATHERING-COAL
GATHERING-PEAT
GAUNTLET-GUARD
GEITONOGAMOUS
GENERALISABLE
GENERALISSIMO
GENERATIONISM
GENETHLIALOGY
GENITO-URINARY
GENTLE-HEARTED
GENTLEMANHOOD
GENTLEMANLIKE
GENTLEMANSHIP
GENTLEWOMANLY
GEOCENTRICISM
GEOCHEMICALLY
GEOCHRONOLOGY
GEOMETRICALLY
GEOMORPHOLOGY
GEOSTATIONARY
GEOTROPICALLY
GERMANISATION
GERONTOPHILIA
GERUND-GRINDER
GESTICULATION
GESTICULATORY
GILLIE-WETFOOT
GLACIOLOGICAL
GLADIATORSHIP
GLAMORISATION
GLASS-GRINDING
GLASS-PAINTING
GLOBE-TROTTING
GLORIFICATION
GLOSSOGRAPHER
GLOSSOLOGICAL
GLYPHOGRAPHIC
GLYPTOGRAPHIC
GO-AS-YOU-PLEASE
GOLDEN-CRESTED
GOLDEN-WEDDING
GOLIATH-BEETLE
GONADOTROPHIC
GONADOTROPHIN
GONIOMETRICAL
GOOD-KING-HENRY
GOOD-NATUREDLY
GRACELESSNESS
GRAMINIVOROUS
GRAMMATICALLY
GRANDDAUGHTER
GRANDFATHERLY
GRANDILOQUENT
GRANDILOQUOUS
GRANDMOTHERLY
GRANITISATION
GRANULIFEROUS
GRAPPLING-IRON
GRATICULATION
GRATIFICATION
GRAVIMETRICAL
GRAVITATIONAL
GREAT-GRANDSON
GRIEF-STRICKEN
GROIN-CENTRING

GROTESQUENESS
GROUND-ANGLING
GROUND-CONTROL
GROUND-OFFICER
GROUSE-DISEASE
GRUMBLETONIAN
GUBERNATORIAL
GUILELESSNESS
GUILTLESSNESS
GUMPLE-FOISTED
GYMNASTICALLY
GYMNOSPERMOUS
GYNAECOCRATIC
GYNAECOLOGIST
GYNAECOMASTIA
GYNANDROMORPH
GYNODIOECIOUS
GYNOMONOECISM
GYROMAGNETISM

H

HABITABLENESS
HACKING-JACKET
HAEMATOLOGIST
HAEMORRHOIDAL
HAGIOGRAPHIST
HAIR-SPLITTING
HALF-HEARTEDLY
HALF-SOVEREIGN
HALLUCINATION
HALLUCINATIVE
HALLUCINATORY
HAMMERKLAVIER
HAPHAZARDNESS
HARBOUR-MASTER
HARD-HEARTEDLY
HARE-AND-HOUNDS
HARMONISATION
HARUSPICATION
HARVEST-SPIDER
HAZARDOUSNESS
HEALTHFULNESS
HEARTBREAKING
HEARTLESSNESS
HEART-SICKNESS
HEART-STIRRING
HEART-STRICKEN
HEATH-ROBINSON
HEAVEN-KISSING
HEAVE-OFFERING
HEAVE-SHOULDER
HEDGE-ACCENTOR
HEDGE-MARRIAGE
HEEBIE-JEEBIES
HEIR-PORTIONER
HELISPHERICAL
HELLENISTICAL
HELMINTHIASIS
HELMINTHOLOGY
HELTER-SKELTER
HEMEROBAPTIST
HEMIPARASITIC
HEMISPHERICAL
HEPTASYLLABIC
HERESIOLOGIST
HERMAPHRODITE

HERMENEUTICAL
HERPETOLOGIST
HETEROBLASTIC
HETEROCARPOUS
HETEROCHRONIC
HETEROCLITOUS
HETEROGENEITY
HETEROGENEOUS
HETEROGENESIS
HETEROGENETIC
HETEROMORPHIC
HETEROPLASTIC
HETEROPTEROUS
HETEROSPOROUS
HETEROSTROPHY
HETEROSTYLISM
HETEROSTYLOUS
HETEROTHALLIC
HETEROTHERMAL
HETEROTROPHIC
HEURISTICALLY
HEXACTINELLID
HEXADACTYLOUS
HEXOBARBITONE
HIBERNISATION
HIDE-AND-GO-SEEK
HIEROGLYPHIST
HIEROGRAMMATE
HIGH-CHURCHISM
HIGH-CHURCHMAN
HIGH-EXPLOSIVE
HIGH-STOMACHED
HIGH-WATERMARK
HILDEBRANDISM
HIPPOPOTAMIAN
HISTIOPHOROID
HOBBY-HORSICAL
HOLE-AND-CORNER
HOLLOW-HEARTED
HOLOMETABOLIC
HOLOTHUROIDEA
HOMEOMORPHISM
HOMEÖMORPHOUS
HOMEOTELEUTON
HOMEOTHERMOUS
HOMEWARD-BOUND
HOMOEOMORPHIC
HOMOEOPATHIST
HOMOEOTHERMAL
HOMOEOTHERMIC
HOMOGENETICAL
HOMOIOTHERMAL
HOMOIOTHERMIC
HOMOLOGOUMENA
HOMOMORPHOSIS
HOMOSEXUALIST
HOMOSEXUALITY
HONEYCOMB-MOTH
HONORIFICALLY
HORIZONTALITY
HORRIPILATION
HORSE-AND-BUGGY
HORSE-CHESTNUT
HORSE-SICKNESS
HORTICULTURAL
HOUND-TRAILING

HOUSE-BREAKING
HOUSEWIFESHIP
HOUSEWIFESKEP
HUBRISTICALLY
HUMBLE-MOUTHED
HUNDREDWEIGHT
HUNGER-MARCHER
HUNGER-STRIKER
HUNTINGDONIAN
HUNTING-GROUND
HURRICANE-DECK
HURRICANE-LAMP
HUTCHINSONIAN
HYBRIDISATION
HYDRAULICALLY
HYDRAULICKING
HYDRO-AIRPLANE
HYDROCEPHALIC
HYDROCEPHALUS
HYDROCHLORIDE
HYDROCRACKING
HYDRODYNAMICS
HYDROELECTRIC
HYDROGENATION
HYDROKINETICS
HYDROMEDUSOID
HYDROMETRICAL
HYDROPATHICAL
HYDROSOMATOUS
HYDROSTATICAL
HYDROSULPHIDE
HYDROSULPHITE
HYDROXYLAMINE
HYGROMETRICAL
HYGROSCOPICAL
HYMENOMYCETES
HYMENOPTEROUS
HYPERCALCEMIA
HYPERCRITICAL
HYPERGLYCEMIA
HYPERHIDROSIS
HYPERMETRICAL
HYPERMETROPIA
HYPERMETROPIC
HYPERPHRYGIAN
HYPERPHYSICAL
HYPERSARCOSIS
HYPERSTHENITE
HYPERTROPHIED
HYPERTROPHOUS
HYPHENISATION
HYPNOANALYSIS
HYPNOTISATION
HYPOCHONDRIAC
HYPOCHONDRIUM
HYPOCYCLOIDAL
HYPOGLYCAEMIA
HYPOPHOSPHITE
HYPOSULPHURIC
HYPOTHECATION
HYPSOPHYLLARY
HYSTERANTHOUS

I

IATROCHEMICAL
ICHTHYOGRAPHY

ICHTHYOLOGIST
ICHTHYOPSIDAN
ICHTHYOSAURIA
ICHTHYOSAURUS
ICONOMATICISM
IDENTICALNESS
IDEOGRAPHICAL
IDIOMATICALLY
IDIORRHYTHMIC
IDIOSYNCRATIC
IGNOMINIOUSLY
ILLECEBRACEAE
ILLEGIBLENESS
ILL-FAVOUREDLY
ILLOGICALNESS
ILLUSTRIOUSLY
IMITATIVENESS
IMMARCESCIBLE
IMMARCESSIBLE
IMMATERIALISE
IMMATERIALISM
IMMATERIALIST
IMMATERIALITY
IMMEDIATENESS
IMMISCIBILITY
IMMOVABLENESS
IMMUTABLENESS
IMPALPABILITY
IMPARIPINNATE
IMPARTIALNESS
IMPARTIBILITY
IMPASSABILITY
IMPASSIBILITY
IMPASSIVENESS
IMPECCABILITY
IMPECUNIOSITY
IMPENETRATION
IMPERCEPTIBLE
IMPERCEPTIBLY
IMPERFECTIBLE
IMPERFECTNESS
IMPERFORATION
IMPERIALISTIC
IMPERIOUSNESS
IMPERSEVERANT
IMPERSONALISE
IMPERSONALITY
IMPERSONATION
IMPERTINENTLY
IMPERTURBABLE
IMPERTURBABLY
IMPETUOUSNESS
IMPIGNORATION
IMPLACABILITY
IMPLICATIVELY
IMPOLITICALLY
IMPONDERABLES
IMPORTUNATELY
IMPOSSIBILISM
IMPOSSIBILIST
IMPOSSIBILITY
IMPOSTUMATION
IMPRACTICABLE
IMPRACTICABLY
IMPRESSIONISM
IMPRESSIONIST

IMPROBABILITY
IMPROPRIATION
IMPROVABILITY
IMPROVIDENTLY
IMPROVISATION
IMPROVISATORY
IMPROVISATRIX
IMPULSIVENESS
IMPUTABLENESS
INADVERTENTLY
INANIMATENESS
INAPPRECIABLE
INAPPROPRIATE
INATTENTIVELY
INAUDIBLENESS
INCANDESCENCE
INCARCERATION
INCENSE-BURNER
INCLINATIONAL
INCLINATORIUM
INCOGNOSCIBLE
INCOMBUSTIBLE
INCOMBUSTIBLY
INCOMMISCIBLE
INCOMMUNICADO
INCOMPETENTLY
INCOMPOSSIBLE
INCONCEIVABLE
INCONCEIVABLY
INCONDENSABLE
INCONGRUOUSLY
INCONSCIENTLY
INCONSECUTIVE
INCONSEQUENCE
INCONSIDERATE
INCONSISTENCE
INCONSISTENCY
INCONSONANTLY
INCONSPICUOUS
INCONTESTABLE
INCONTESTABLY
INCONTINENTLY
INCONVENIENCE
INCONVENIENCY
INCONVERSABLE
INCONVERTIBLE
INCONVERTIBLY
INCONVINCIBLE
INCORPORATING
INCORPORATION
INCORPORATIVE
INCORPOREALLY
INCORRECTNESS
INCORRUPTIBLE
INCORRUPTIBLY
INCORRUPTNESS
INCREDIBILITY
INCREDULOUSLY
INCRIMINATORY
INCURABLENESS
INCURIOUSNESS
INDEFATIGABLE
INDEFATIGABLY
INDELIBLENESS
INDEPENDENTLY
INDESCRIBABLE

INDESCRIBABLY
INDETERMINACY
INDETERMINATE
INDETERMINISM
INDETERMINIST
INDEX-LEARNING
INDIFFERENTLY
INDISCERNIBLE
INDISCERNIBLY
INDISPENSABLE
INDISPENSABLY
INDISPOSITION
INDISSOCIABLE
INDISSOLVABLE
INDISSUADABLE
INDISSUADABLY
INDISTINCTION
INDISTINCTIVE
INDIVIDUALISE
INDIVIDUALISM
INDIVIDUALIST
INDIVIDUALITY
INDIVIDUATION
INDOCTRINATOR
INDUPLICATION
INDUSTRIALISE
INDUSTRIALISM
INDUSTRIALIST
INDUSTRIOUSLY
INEDUCABILITY
INEFFABLENESS
INEFFECTIVELY
INEFFECTUALLY
INEFFICACIOUS
INEFFICIENTLY
INELABORATELY
INELIGIBILITY
INEVITABILITY
INEXHAUSTIBLE
INEXHAUSTIBLY
INEXORABILITY
INEXPEDIENTLY
INEXPENSIVELY
INEXPERIENCED
INEXPRESSIBLE
INEXPRESSIBLY
INFALLIBILISM
INFALLIBILIST
INFALLIBILITY
INFEASIBILITY
INFECTIVENESS
INFERENTIALLY
INFINITESIMAL
INFLEXIBILITY
INFLEXIONLESS
INFLORESCENCE
INFLUENTIALLY
INFRUCTUOUSLY
INFUNDIBULATE
INGENIOUSNESS
INGENUOUSNESS
INGURGITATION
INHOSPITALITY
INIMITABILITY
INJUDICIOUSLY
INJURIOUSNESS

INNOCUOUSNESS
INNOVATIONIST
INNOXIOUSNESS
INOBSERVATION
INOBTRUSIVELY
INOCULABILITY
INODOROUSNESS
INOFFENSIVELY
INOPPORTUNELY
INOPPORTUNIST
INOPPORTUNITY
INORGANICALLY
INQUISITIONAL
INQUISITIVELY
INQUISITORIAL
INSATIABILITY
INSCRIPTIONAL
INSECTIVOROUS
INSECTOLOGIST
INSENSATENESS
INSENSIBILITY
INSIDIOUSNESS
INSIGNIFICANT
INSINUATINGLY
INSOCIABILITY
INSOLUBLENESS
INSPECTORSHIP
INSPIRATIONAL
INSTANTANEITY
INSTANTANEOUS
INSTINCTIVELY
INSTINCTIVITY
INSTITUTIONAL
INSTRUCTIONAL
INSTRUCTIVELY
INSUBORDINATE
INSUBSTANTIAL
INSUFFICIENCE
INSUFFICIENCY
INSUPPORTABLE
INSUPPORTABLY
INSUPPRESSIVE
INSUSCEPTIBLE
INTANGIBILITY
INTEGUMENTARY
INTELLIGENCER
INTELLIGENTLY
INTEMPERATELY
INTENSIVENESS
INTENTIONALLY
INTERBREEDING
INTERCALATION
INTERCALATIVE
INTERCELLULAR
INTERCOLONIAL
INTERCOLUMNAR
INTERCROPPING
INTERCURRENCE
INTERDENTALLY
INTERDIGITATE
INTERESTINGLY
INTERFERINGLY
INTERGALACTIC
INTERJACULATE
INTERJECTURAL
INTERLACEMENT

INTERLOCATION
INTERLOCUTION
INTERLOCUTORY
INTERLOCUTRIX
INTERLUNATION
INTERMARRIAGE
INTERMEDIATOR
INTERMITTENCE
INTERMITTENCY
INTERNATIONAL
INTEROSCULANT
INTEROSCULATE
INTERPARIETAL
INTERPETIOLAR
INTERPILASTER
INTERPOLATION
INTERPOLATIVE
INTERPOSITION
INTERPRETABLE
INTERPRETRESS
INTERPUNCTION
INTERRADIALLY
INTERRELATION
INTERROGATION
INTERROGATIVE
INTERROGATORY
INTERRUPTEDLY
INTERSCAPULAR
INTERSIDEREAL
INTERSPECIFIC
INTERSPERSION
INTERSTELLARY
INTERSTRATIFY
INTERTROPICAL
INTRA-ARTERIAL
INTRACAPSULAR
INTRACELLULAR
INTRAMUSCULAR
INTRANSIGENCE
INTRANSIGENCY
INTRAPARIETAL
INTRAPETIOLAR
INTRATROPICAL
INTRICATENESS
INTRINSICALLY
INTROSPECTION
INTROSPECTIVE
INTROVERSIBLE
INTRUSIVENESS
INVARIABILITY
INVENDIBILITY
INVENTIVENESS
INVENTORIALLY
INVESTIGATION
INVESTIGATIVE
INVESTIGATORY
INVIDIOUSNESS
INVINCIBILITY
INVIOLABILITY
INVIOLATENESS
INVISIBLENESS
INVOLUCELLATE
INVOLUNTARILY
IONTOPHORESIS
IONTOPHORETIC
IRRATIONALISE

IRRATIONALISM
IRRATIONALIST
IRRATIONALITY
IRRECIPROCITY
IRRECLAIMABLE
IRRECLAIMABLY
IRRECOGNITION
IRRECOVERABLE
IRRECOVERABLY
IRREDEEMABLES
IRREFRANGIBLE
IRRELIGIOUSLY
IRREPLACEABLE
IRREPRESSIBLE
IRREPRESSIBLY
IRRESPONSIBLE
IRRESPONSIBLY
IRRETRIEVABLE
IRRETRIEVABLY
IRREVERENTIAL
IRRITABLENESS
ISMATICALNESS
ISOBAROMETRIC
ISOCHRONOUSLY
ISODIMORPHISM
ISODIMORPHOUS
ISOGEOTHERMAL
ISOMERISATION
ISOMETRICALLY
ISOSTATICALLY
ITALICISATION

J

JACK-CROSSTREE
JAMESTOWN-WEED
JENNY-LONG-LEGS
JERRY-BUILDING
JET-PROPULSION
JIGGERY-POKERY
JOHNSONIANISM
JOLLIFICATION
JOURNEY-WEIGHT
JUDAISTICALLY
JUDAS-COLOURED
JUDGE-ADVOCATE
JUDICIOUSNESS
JURISPRUDENCE
JUSTIFICATION
JUSTIFICATIVE
JUSTIFICATORY
JUXTAPOSITION

K

KALEIDOSCOPIC
KANGAROO-APPLE
KANGAROO-GRASS
KANGAROO-THORN
KAPELLMEISTER
KETTLEDRUMMER
KEYHOLE-LIMPET
KIDDERMINSTER
KINDERGÄRTNER
KINDLY-NATURED
KINEMATOGRAPH
KINESIOLOGIST
KINESIPATHIST

KINESITHERAPY
KISSING-COMFIT
KISS-IN-THE-RING
KITCHEN-GARDEN
KITCHEN-MIDDEN
KITTLY-BENDERS
KLETTERSCHUHE
KNICKERBOCKER
KNICK-KNACKERY
KNIGHT-MARSHAL
KNIGHTS-ERRANT
KNIGHT-SERVICE
KNOWLEDGEABLE
KNUCKLEDUSTER

L

LABEFACTATION
LABORIOUSNESS
LABYRINTHICAL
LABYRINTHITIS
LACKADAISICAL
LADY-IN-WAITING
LAEVOROTATION
LAEVOROTATORY
LAISSEZ-PASSER
LAMARCKIANISM
LAMELLIBRANCH
LAMELLICORNES
LAMPADEPHORIA
LANCE-CORPORAL
LANDING-GROUND
LAND-MEASURING
LANDOWNERSHIP
LAND-SURVEYING
LANGUISHINGLY
LARYNGOLOGIST
LARYNGOSCOPIC
LASIOCAMPIDAE
LATIN-AMERICAN
LATTICE-BRIDGE
LATTICE-GIRDER
LAUGHABLENESS
LAUGHING-STOCK
LAUNCHING-WAYS
LAVENDER-WATER
LAWN-SPRINKLER
LEAD-POISONING
LEASING-MAKING
LEATHER-JACKET
LEATHER-LUNGED
LEATHER-WINGED
LECHEROUSNESS
LECTISTERNIUM
LECYTHIDACEAE
LEFT-HANDINESS
LEGISLATIVELY
LEGISLATORIAL
LEIBNIZIANISM
LEISHMANIASIS
LEISHMANIOSIS
LEMON-COLOURED
LEPIDODENDRON
LEPIDOPTERIST
LEPIDOPTEROUS
LEPIDOSTROBUS
LEPTOCEPHALIC

LEPTOCEPHALUS
LEPTOSPIROSIS
LETHARGICALLY
LETTER-CARRIER
LETTER-FOUNDER
LETTER-PERFECT
LETTERS-PATENT
LEUCITOHEDRON
LEUCO-COMPOUND
LEVEL-CROSSING
LEXICOGRAPHER
LEXICOGRAPHIC
LEXIGRAPHICAL
LIBERATIONISM
LIBERATIONIST
LIBRARIANSHIP
LICHENOLOGIST
LICKERISHNESS
LIFE-ASSURANCE
LIFE-INSURANCE
LIFE-PRESERVER
LIFE-RENDERING
LIFTING-BRIDGE
LIGHT-FINGERED
LIGHT-HORSEMAN
LIGHTHOUSEMAN
LIGHT-INFANTRY
LIGHTNING-TUBE
LIGHTSOMENESS
LIGHT-SPIRITED
LIGNIFICATION
LIMITLESSNESS
LINE-ENGRAVING
LINE-FISHERMAN
LINSEY-WOOLSEY
LIPOGRAMMATIC
LISSOTRICHOUS
LISTENING-POST
LITHESOMENESS
LITHONTRIPTIC
LITHONTRIPTOR
LITHOTRIPTIST
LITIGIOUSNESS
LIVER-COLOURED
LIVERY-COMPANY
LIVERY-SERVANT
LOATHSOMENESS
LOGARITHMICAL
LOGOGRAPHICAL
LONG-DESCENDED
LONG-SUFFERING
LOUIS-QUATORZE
LOZENGE-SHAPED
LUDICROUSNESS
LUXURIOUSNESS
LYCANTHROPIST
LYCOPODIACEAE

M

MACHIAVELLIAN
MACHIAVELLISM
MACHICOLATION
MACHINE-GUNNER
MACKEREL-GUIDE
MACKEREL-MIDGE
MACKEREL-SHARK

MACROCEPHALIC
MACRODACTYLIC
MACRODIAGONAL
MACROMOLECULE
MACROPINAKOID
MAGAZINE-RIFLE
MAGINOT-MINDED
MAGISTERIALLY
MAGISTRATICAL
MAGNANIMOUSLY
MAGNETISATION
MAGNETOMOTIVE
MAGNETO-OPTICS
MAGNETOSPHERE
MAGNIFICATION
MAGNIFICENTLY
MAGNILOQUENCE
MAGNOLIACEOUS
MAIDEN-TONGUED
MAIDEN-WIDOWED
MALACOLOGICAL
MALACOPHILOUS
MALACOSTRACAN
MALADAPTATION
MALADJUSTMENT
MALADROITNESS
MALARIOLOGIST
MALICIOUSNESS
MALLEABLENESS
MALLEMAROKING
MALPIGHIACEAE
MALTHUSIANISM
MAMMALIFEROUS
MANAGEABILITY
MANGANIFEROUS
MANGOLD-WURZEL
MANICHAEANISM
MANIFESTATION
MANIFESTATIVE
MANIFOLD-PAPER
MANIPULATABLE
MANUFACTURING
MANY-SIDEDNESS
MARBLE-HEARTED
MARKETABILITY
MARRIAGE-LINES
MARSH-MARIGOLD
MARSH-SAMPHIRE
MARSIPOBRANCH
MARTYROLOGIST
MASCULINENESS
MASHIE-NIBLICK
MASTER-BUILDER
MASTERFULNESS
MASTER-MARINER
MASTERPASSION
MASTIGOPHORIC
MATCHBOARDING
MATCHLESSNESS
MATERFAMILIAS
MATERIALISTIC
MATHEMATICIAN
MATRICULATION
MATRILINEALLY
MATRIMONIALLY
MEADOW-SAFFRON

MEALS-ON-WHEELS
MEASURING-TAPE
MEASURING-WORM
MECHANISATION
MEDIATISATION
MEDIATORIALLY
MEDICAMENTARY
MEDICINE-CHEST
MEDITERRANEAN
MEGACEPHALOUS
MEGALOSAURIAN
MEGASPORANGIA
MEISTERSINGER
MELANCHOLIOUS
MELANOCHROOUS
MELASTOMACEAE
MELLIFICATION
MELLIFLUENTLY
MELLIFLUOUSLY
MELODIOUSNESS
MELODRAMATIST
MEMBRANACEOUS
MENSURABILITY
MERCERISATION
MERCHANDISING
MERCILESSNESS
MERIDIONALITY
MERITORIOUSLY
MERMAID'S-GLOVE
MERMAID'S-PURSE
MESATICEPHALY
MESENCEPHALIC
MESENCEPHALON
MESMERISATION
MESOCEPHALISM
MESOCEPHALOUS
MESSENGER-WIRE
MESSERSCHMITT
METAGRABOLISE
METAGROBOLISE
METALLIFEROUS
METALLISATION
METALLOGRAPHY
METALLURGICAL
METAMORPHOSES
METAMORPHOSIS
METAPHOSPHATE
METAPHYSICIAN
METAPSYCHICAL
METASTABILITY
METEMPIRICISM
METEMPIRICIST
METEOROLOGIST
METHODISTICAL
METONYMICALLY
METOPOSCOPIST
METRIFICATION
MICROANALYSIS
MICROCEPHALIC
MICROCOSMICAL
MICRODETECTOR
MICROFELSITIC
MICROGRANITIC
MICROMETRICAL
MICRONUTRIENT
MICRO-ORGANISM

MICROPHYLLOUS
MICROSCOPICAL
MICROTONALITY
MIDDLE-BRACKET
MIGHT-HAVE-BEEN
MILK-CHOCOLATE
MILK-DENTITION
MILLEFEUILLES
MILLENNIALIST
MILLENNIANISM
MILLENNIARISM
MILLIONAIRESS
MILLSTONE-GRIT
MINERALOGICAL
MINISTERIALLY
MINI-SUBMARINE
MIRACLE-MONGER
MIRROR-WRITING
MIRTHLESSNESS
MISADVENTURED
MISADVENTURER
MISADVERTENCE
MISANTHROPIST
MISAPPRECIATE
MISCEGENATION
MISCELLANEOUS
MISCHIEF-MAKER
MISCHIEVOUSLY
MISCOMPREHEND
MISCONCEPTION
MISCONJECTURE
MISCORRECTION
MISEMPLOYMENT
MISERABLENESS
MISGOVERNMENT
MISMANAGEMENT
MISOBSERVANCE
MISPERSUASION
MISPROPORTION
MISSHAPENNESS
MISTRUSTFULLY
MISTRUSTINGLY
MISUNDERSTAND
MISUNDERSTOOD
MNEMOTECHNICS
MNEMOTECHNIST
MOCKING-THRUSH
MODERATORSHIP
MODERNISATION
MOHAMMEDANISE
MOHAMMEDANISM
MOLLIFICATION
MOLLUSCICIDAL
MOMENTARINESS
MOMENTOUSNESS
MONARCHIANISM
MONOCHROMATIC
MONOCOTYLEDON
MONODACTYLOUS
MONOGRAMMATIC
MONOGRAPHICAL
MONOMETALLISM
MONOMETALLIST
MONONUCLEOSIS
MONOPHTHONGAL
MONOPHYSITISM

MONOSTROPHICS
MONOSYLLABISM
MONOSYMMETRIC
MONOTELEPHONE
MONOTHALAMOUS
MONOTHELETISM
MONOTHELITISM
MONOTREMATOUS
MONSTROUSNESS
MORISONIANISM
MORNING-PRAYER
MORPHINOMANIA
MORPHOGENESIS
MORPHOGENETIC
MORPHOGRAPHER
MORPHOLOGICAL
MORPHOPHONEME
MORTAL-STARING
MORTIFICATION
MOTHER-COUNTRY
MOTHER-OF-PEARL
MOTION-PICTURE
MOTOR-TRACTION
MOULDING-BOARD
MOUNTAIN-CHAIN
MOUNTAIN-SHEEP
MOUNTAINS-HIGH
MOUNTEBANKERY
MOUNTEBANKING
MOUNTEBANKISM
MOUNTING-BLOCK
MOURNING-BRIDE
MOURNING-CLOAK
MOURNING-COACH
MOURNING-PIECE
MOURNING-STUFF
MOUSECOLOURED
MOUTH-BREATHER
MOWING-MACHINE
MULBERRY-FACED
MULTICAMERATE
MULTICAPITATE
MULTICELLULAR
MULTICOLOURED
MULTIDIGITATE
MULTIFILAMENT
MULTILOBULATE
MULTILOCULATE
MULTILOQUENCE
MULTINUCLEATE
MULTIPLICABLE
MULTIPLICATOR
MULTIPRESENCE
MULTIRAMIFIED
MULTITUDINARY
MULTITUDINOUS
MUMMIFICATION
MUNDIFICATION
MUNDIFICATIVE
MUSCLE-READING
MUSIC-MISTRESS
MUSICOLOGICAL
MUTTON-DUMMIES
MUTTON-THUMPER
MUTUALISATION
MUZZLE-LOADING

MYRISTICACEAE
MYRMECOLOGIST
MYSTERY-MONGER
MYSTIFICATION

N

NAMBY-PAMBICAL
NAMBY-PAMBYISH
NAMBY-PAMBYISM
NAPHTHYLAMINE
NARCOANALYSIS
NARCOHYPNOSIS
NATIONALISTIC
NATURE-WORSHIP
NAVIGABLENESS
NEANDERTHALER
NECESSARINESS
NECESSITARIAN
NECESSITATION
NECESSITOUSLY
NECROMANTICAL
NECROSCOPICAL
NECTARIFEROUS
NEEDLE-POINTED
NEFARIOUSNESS
NEGLECTEDNESS
NEGLIGIBILITY
NEGOTIABILITY
NEIGHBOURHOOD
NEMATHELMINTH
NEOCLASSICISM
NEOCLASSICIST
NEOGRAMMARIAN
NEO-KANTIANISM
NEO-LAMARCKIAN
NEOLOGISTICAL
NEO-MELANESIAN
NEOPLASTICISM
NEPHELOMETRIC
NERVELESSNESS
NETHERLANDISH
NETTING-NEEDLE
NEURASTHENIAC
NEUROPATHICAL
NEUROVASCULAR
NEWFANGLENESS
NICKELIFEROUS
NICKEL-PLATING
NICKNACKATORY
NIGGARDLINESS
NIGHT-TRIPPING
NIGHT-WANDERER
NIGHT-WARBLING
NIGHT-WATCHMAN
NITRIFICATION
NITROBACTERIA
NITRO-COMPOUND
NOCTIVAGATION
NOISELESSNESS
NOLI-ME-TANGERE
NOMENCLATURAL
NOMINATIVALLY
NON-ACCEPTANCE
NON-AGGRESSION
NON-APPEARANCE
NON-ATTENDANCE

NON-COGNISABLE
NON-COLLEGIATE
NON-COMPLIANCE
NON-COMPOUNDER
NON-CONDUCTING
NONCONFORMING
NONCONFORMIST
NONCONFORMITY
NON-FORFEITING
NON-FULFILMENT
NON-OBSERVANCE
NON-PRODUCTION
NON-PROFICIENT
NON-REGARDANCE
NON-RESISTANCE
NONSENSICALLY
NON-SPECIALIST
NORMALISATION
NORTH-EASTERLY
NORTH-EASTWARD
NORTHERLINESS
NORTH-WESTERLY
NORTH-WESTWARD
NOSTALGICALLY
NOTORIOUSNESS
NUCLEO-PROTEIN
NULLIFICATION
NUMISMATOLOGY
NURSING-FATHER
NYCTAGINACEAE

O

OBJECTIONABLE
OBJECTIONABLY
OBJECTIVATION
OBJECTIVENESS
OBJECTIVISTIC
OBLIVIOUSNESS
OBNOXIOUSNESS
OBSERVATIONAL
OBSTINATENESS
OBSTRUCTIVELY
OBTRUSIVENESS
OBTUSE-ANGULAR
OCCASIONALISM
OCCASIONALIST
OCCASIONALITY
OCCIDENTALISE
OCCIDENTALISM
OCCIDENTALIST
OCEANOGRAPHER
OCEANOGRAPHIC
OCHLOCRATICAL
OCTOCENTENARY
ODONTOGLOSSUM
ODONTOLOGICAL
ODONTOPHOROUS
ODONTORNITHES
ODORIFEROUSLY
OFFENSIVENESS
OFFHANDEDNESS
OFFICIOUSNESS
OLD-CLOTHESMAN
OLEOMARGARINE
OLFACTOLOGIST
OMNICOMPETENT

OMOPLATOSCOPY
ONEIROSCOPIST
ONIROCRITICAL
ONOMATOPOESIS
ONOMATOPOETIC
ONTOGENICALLY
ONTOLOGICALLY
ONYCHOPHAGIST
OPERATIVENESS
OPHIOMORPHOUS
OPHTHALMOLOGY
OPISTHOBRANCH
OPISTHOGRAPHY
OPPIGNORATION
OPPORTUNENESS
OPPOSITIONIST
OPPROBRIOUSLY
ORACULOUSNESS
ORANGE-BLOSSOM
ORCHESOGRAPHY
ORCHESTRALIST
ORCHESTRATION
ORCHIDOLOGIST
ORCHIDOMANIAC
OREOGRAPHICAL
ORGANOGENESIS
ORGANOTHERAPY
ORNAMENTATION
ORNITHICHNITE
ORNITHOLOGIST
ORNITHOMANTIC
OROBANCHACEAE
ORTHO-COMPOUND
ORTHODIAGONAL
ORTHOGNATHISM
ORTHOGNATHOUS
ORTHOGRAPHIST
ORTHOPAEDICAL
ORTHOPINAKOID
ORTHOSILICATE
ORTHOSTICHOUS
OSTENSIBILITY
OSTEOMYELITIS
OSTODERMATOUS
OSTREICULTURE
OSTREOPHAGOUS
OTHERWORLDISH
OTTER-TRAWLING
OUTRECUIDANCE
OUT-SETTLEMENT
OUTSPOKENNESS
OUTSTANDINGLY
OVERABOUNDING
OVERABUNDANCE
OVER-ANXIOUSLY
OVERBEARINGLY
OVER-CONFIDENT
OVERCREDULITY
OVERCREDULOUS
OVEREXCITABLE
OVER-EXQUISITE
OVERFLOWINGLY
OVERHASTINESS
OVERINDULGENT
OVERINSURANCE
OVERMULTITUDE

OVERSTATEMENT
OVERSUBSCRIBE
OVERVALUATION
OVOVIVIPAROUS
OWNER-OCCUPIED
OWNER-OCCUPIER
OYSTER-CATCHER
OYSTER-FISHERY

P

PACKING-NEEDLE
PADDLE-STEAMER
PAEDIATRICIAN
PAEDOMORPHISM
PALAEOCRYSTIC
PALAEOGRAPHER
PALAEOGRAPHIC
PALAEONTOLOGY
PALAEOTHERIUM
PALAEOZOOLOGY
PALATABLENESS
PALINDROMICAL
PALINGENESIST
PALLETISATION
PALMIFICATION
PALPABLE-GROSS
PANAESTHETISM
PANCHROMATISM
PANDEMONIACAL
PANDICULATION
PANEGYRICALLY
PANGRAMMATIST
PANHARMONICON
PANIC-STRICKEN
PANOPHTHALMIA
PANPSYCHISTIC
PANSPERMATISM
PANSPERMATIST
PANTAGRUELIAN
PANTAGRUELION
PANTAGRUELISM
PANTAGRUELIST
PANTHEISTICAL
PANTHEOLOGIST
PANTISOCRATIC
PAPAPRELATIST
PAPAVERACEOUS
PAPER-FASTENER
PAPER-HANGINGS
PAPER-MULBERRY
PAPILIONACEAE
PAPILLIFEROUS
PAPILLOMATOUS
PARABOLICALLY
PARADOXICALLY
PARAFFIN-SCALE
PARAGRAPHICAL
PARALEIPOMENA
PARALIPOMENON
PARALLACTICAL
PARALLELISTIC
PARALLELOGRAM
PARAMAGNETISM
PARAPHERNALIA
PARAPOPHYSIAL
PARAPSYCHICAL

PARAPSYCHOSIS
PARASITICALLY
PARASYNTHESIS
PARASYNTHETIC
PARASYNTHETON
PARENCEPHALON
PARENTHETICAL
PARLIAMENTARY
PARLIAMENTING
PARLIAMENT-MAN
PARNASSIANISM
PARROT-DISEASE
PARTHENOCARPY
PARTICIPANTLY
PARTICIPATION
PARTICIPATIVE
PARTICIPIALLY
PARTI-COLOURED
PARTICULARISE
PARTICULARISM
PARTICULARIST
PARTICULARITY
PARTITIONMENT
PARTITION-WALL
PARTRIDGE-WOOD
PARTY-COLOURED
PARTY-POLITICS
PARTY-SPIRITED
PASCHAL-CANDLE
PASCHAL-FLOWER
PASIGRAPHICAL
PASSEMENTERIE
PASSERIFORMES
PASSION-FLOWER
PASSION-SUNDAY
PATENT-LEATHER
PATERFAMILIAS
PATHOGNOMONIC
PATRIMONIALLY
PATRIOTICALLY
PATRONISINGLY
PAUPERISATION
PEACEABLENESS
PEACELESSNESS
PEACE-OFFERING
PEACH-COLOURED
PEACOCK-COPPER
PEACOCK-FLOWER
PEACOCK-THRONE
PEARL-SHELLING
PEASE-PORRIDGE
PEDAGOGICALLY
PEDANTOCRATIC
PEDESTRIANISE
PEDESTRIANISM
PEDICELLARIAE
PEIRASTICALLY
PELICAN-FLOWER
PELOPONNESIAN
PENCIL-COMPASS
PENDRAGONSHIP
PENDULOUSNESS
PENETRABILITY
PENETRATINGLY
PENETRATIVELY
PENICILLIFORM

PENINSULARITY
PENITENTIALLY
PENNILESSNESS
PENNY-FARTHING
PENTADACTYLIC
PENTADELPHOUS
PENTASTICHOUS
PENTASYLLABIC
PENTHEMIMERAL
PENURIOUSNESS
PEPPER-AND-SALT
PEPTONISATION
PERAMBULATION
PERAMBULATORY
PERCUSSION-CAP
PERDITIONABLE
PERDURABILITY
PEREGRINATION
PERENNIBRANCH
PERFECTIONATE
PERFECTIONISM
PERFECTIONIST
PERFERVIDNESS
PERFUNCTORILY
PERICHONDRIUM
PERIGASTRITIS
PERIHEPATITIS
PERIODICALIST
PERIODISATION
PERIPATETICAL
PERISHABILITY
PERISSODACTYL
PERITYPHLITIS
PERLUSTRATION
PERMUTABILITY
PERPENDICULAR
PERPLEXEDNESS
PERSCRUTATION
PERSEVERATION
PERSEVERINGLY
PERSPECTIVELY
PERSPICACIOUS
PERSPICUOUSLY
PERVASIVENESS
PESSIMISTICAL
PESTIFEROUSLY
PETRIFICATION
PETROCHEMICAL
PETROLIFEROUS
PHAENOLOGICAL
PHALANSTERIAN
PHALANSTERISM
PHALANSTERIST
PHANEROGAMOUS
PHANTASMALIAN
PHANTASMALITY
PHARISAICALLY
PHARMACEUTICS
PHARMACEUTIST
PHARMACOPOEIA
PHARYNGOSCOPE
PHARYNGOSCOPY
PHASE-CONTRAST
PHELLOGENETIC
PHELLOPLASTIC
PHENOMENALISE

PHENOMENALISM
PHENOMENALIST
PHENOMENALITY
PHENOMENOLOGY
PHENYLALANINE
PHERECRATAEAN
PHILADELPHIAN
PHILANTHROPIC
PHILHELLENISM
PHILHELLENIST
PHILOMATHICAL
PHILOSOPHICAL
PHILOSOPHISER
PHLEGETHONTIC
PHLOGISTICATE
PHONAUTOGRAPH
PHONOCAMPTICS
PHONOGRAPHIST
PHOSPHORETTED
PHOSPHORYLASE
PHOSPHURETTED
PHOTOCHEMICAL
PHOTOCHROMICS
PHOTOCHROMISM
PHOTOELECTRIC
PHOTOELECTRON
PHOTO-EMISSION
PHOTOGRAPHIST
PHOTOPERIODIC
PHOTOPHORESIS
PHOTO-RECEPTOR
PHRASEOLOGIST
PHREATOPHYTIC
PHRENETICALLY
PHRENOLOGICAL
PHTHALOCYANIN
PHYCOERYTHRIN
PHYLACTERICAL
PHYLLOPHAGOUS
PHYLLOQUINONE
PHYSHARMONICA
PHYSICIANSHIP
PHYSIOGNOMIST
PHYSIOGRAPHER
PHYSIOGRAPHIC
PHYSIOLOGICAL
PHYSIOTHERAPY
PHYSITHEISTIC
PHYTOPLANKTON
PICKLE-HERRING
PICTURE-PALACE
PICTURESQUELY
PICTURE-WINDOW
PIEZOELECTRIC
PIEZOMAGNETIC
PIGEON-HEARTED
PIGEON-LIVERED
PIGHEADEDNESS
PILGRIM-BOTTLE
PINEAPPLE-WEED
PINKING-SHEARS
PISCICULTURAL
PITCH-FARTHING
PLAGIOSTOMATA
PLAGIOSTOMOUS
PLAGIOTROPISM

PLAGIOTROPOUS
PLAIN-SPEAKING
PLAINTIVENESS
PLANIMETRICAL
PLANTAIN-EATER
PLANTIE-CRUIVE
PLATE-PRINTING
PLATINIFEROUS
PLATITUDINISE
PLATITUDINOUS
PLATYCEPHALIC
PLAUSIBLENESS
PLEASURE-HOUSE
PLEBIFICATION
PLECTOGNATHIC
PLENITUDINOUS
PLENTEOUSNESS
PLENTIFULNESS
PLESIOSAURIAN
PLETHORICALLY
PLOTTING-PAPER
PLUMBISOLVENT
PLUMBOSOLVENT
PLURALISATION
PLURIPRESENCE
PNEUMATICALLY
PNEUMATOLYSIS
PNEUMATOLYTIC
PNEUMATOMETER
PNEUMATOPHORE
PNEUMOGASTRIC
PNEUMONECTOMY
POCKET-BOROUGH
POCKET-PICKING
POCOCURANTISM
POCOCURANTIST
PODOPHTHALMUS
PODOSTEMACEAE
POIKILOTHERMY
POINTING-STOCK
POINTLESSNESS
POISONOUSNESS
POLEMONIACEAE
POLICE-OFFICER
POLICE-STATION
POLIOMYELITIS
POLLICITATION
POLLINIFEROUS
POLYADELPHOUS
POLYCARBONATE
POLYCHROMATIC
POLYCYTHAEMIA
POLYDACTYLISM
POLYDACTYLOUS
POLYEMBRYONIC
POLYGALACEOUS
POLYGONACEOUS
POLYHISTORIAN
POLYNOMIALISM
POLYPHLOISBIC
POLYPODIACEAE
POLYPROPYLENE
POLYPROTODONT
POLYSYLLABISM
POLYSYNTHESIS
POLYSYNTHETIC

POLYTECHNICAL
POLYTHALAMOUS
POMPIER-LADDER
PONDERABILITY
PONDEROUSNESS
PONTIFICALITY
PONTOON-BRIDGE
POPPING-CREASE
PORCELAIN-CLAY
PORCELAINEOUS
PORCELLANEOUS
PORCUPINE-WOOD
PORRIDGE-STICK
PORTULACACEAE
POSSESSIONARY
POSSESSIONATE
POSSESSORSHIP
POST-COMMUNION
POST-EXISTENCE
POSTLIMINIARY
POSTULATIONAL
POSTURE-MASTER
POTAMOLOGICAL
POTATO-DISEASE
POTENTIOMETER
POWDERING-GOWN
POWDERING-ROOM
POWERLESSNESS
POWER-POLITICS
PRACTICALNESS
PRAGMATICALLY
PRAIRIE-OYSTER
PRAIRIE-TURNIP
PRAYERFULNESS
PRAYER-MEETING
PRE-ADAMITICAL
PREADAPTATION
PREADMONITION
PREAMBULATORY
PRECAUTIONARY
PRECENTORSHIP
PRECIPITANTLY
PRECIPITATELY
PRECIPITATION
PRECIPITATIVE
PRECIPITOUSLY
PRECONCEPTION
PRECONISATION
PREDATORINESS
PREDEFINITION
PREDESTINATOR
PREDICABILITY
PREDICAMENTAL
PREDICATIVELY
PREDOMINANTLY
PREDOMINATION
PRE-ENGAGEMENT
PREFABRICATED
PREFABRICATOR
PREFATORIALLY
PREFERABILITY
PREFIGURATION
PREFIGURATIVE
PREFIGUREMENT
PREHISTORICAL
PREJUDICATION

PREJUDICATIVE
PREJUDICIALLY
PRELIMINARIES
PRELIMINARILY
PREMANDIBULAR
PREMATURENESS
PREMEDITATION
PREMEDITATIVE
PREMILLENNIAL
PREMONITORILY
PREOCCUPATION
PREORDAINMENT
PREORDINATION
PREPARATIVELY
PREPARATORILY
PREPONDERANCE
PREPONDERANCY
PREPOSITIONAL
PREPOSSESSING
PREPOSSESSION
PRE-RAPHAELISM
PRE-RAPHAELITE
PREROGATIVELY
PRESBYTERSHIP
PRESCIENTIFIC
PRESCRIPTIBLE
PRESENTIALITY
PRESIDENTSHIP
PRESS-FASTENER
PRESSURE-CABIN
PRESUMPTIVELY
PRETENDERSHIP
PRETENTIOUSLY
PRETERITENESS
PRETERMISSION
PRETERMITTING
PRETERNATURAL
PRETERPERFECT
PREVARICATION
PRICELESSNESS
PRICES-CURRENT
PRICK-ME-DAINTY
PRICK-THE-LOUSE
PRIMIGRAVIDAE
PRIMING-POWDER
PRIMITIVENESS
PRIMOGENITARY
PRIMOGENITIVE
PRIMOGENITRIX
PRIMOGENITURE
PRIMORDIALISM
PRIMORDIALITY
PRINCE-CONSORT
PRINCESS-ROYAL
PRINCIPALNESS
PRINCIPALSHIP
PRINTING-HOUSE
PRINTING-PRESS
PRISMATICALLY
PRISON-BREAKER
PRISONERS'-BASE
PRIVATEERSMAN
PRIZE-FIGHTING
PRO-AND-CONNING
PROBABILITIES
PROBE-SCISSORS

PROBLEMATICAL
PROCESSIONARY
PROCESSIONING
PROCESS-SERVER
PROCONSULSHIP
PROCRASTINATE
PROCURATORIAL
PRODUCIBILITY
PROFECTITIOUS
PROFESSORIATE
PROFESSORSHIP
PROFITABILITY
PROFIT-SHARING
PROGENITORIAL
PROGNOSTICATE
PROGRESSIONAL
PROGRESSIVELY
PROHIBITIVELY
PROJECTIONIST
PROLEGOMENARY
PROLEGOMENOUS
PROLEPTICALLY
PROLIFERATION
PROLIFERATIVE
PROLIFEROUSLY
PROLIFICATION
PROMISCUOUSLY
PROMISE-BREACH
PRONOUNCEABLE
PRONOUNCEMENT
PRONUNCIATION
PROPAROXYTONE
PROPHETICALLY
PROPORTIONATE
PROPORTIONING
PROPOSITIONAL
PROPRAETORIAL
PROPRAETORIAN
PROPRIETORIAL
PROPRIOCEPTOR
PROSAICALNESS
PROSECTORSHIP
PROSECUTRICES
PROSECUTRIXES
PROSPECT-GLASS
PROSPECTIVELY
PROSTHODONTIA
PROTECTIONISM
PROTECTIONIST
PROTECTORLESS
PROTECTORSHIP
PROTERANDROUS
PROTEROGYNOUS
PROTESTANTISE
PROTESTANTISM
PROTOACTINIUM
PROTOCOCCALES
PROTO-HISTORIC
PROTONOTARIAL
PROTONOTARIAT
PROTOSPATAIRE
PROTUBERANTLY
PROTUBERATION
PROVERBIALISE
PROVERBIALISM
PROVERBIALIST

PROVINCIALISE
PROVINCIALISM
PROVINCIALITY
PROVISIONALLY
PROVOCATIVELY
PRUDENTIALISM
PRUDENTIALIST
PRUDENTIALITY
PRUNING-SHEARS
PSAMMOPHILOUS
PSEUDO-ARCHAIC
PSILANTHROPIC
PSILOPHYTALES
PSI-PHENOMENON
PSYCHASTHENIA
PSYCHIATRICAL
PSYCHOANALYSE
PSYCHOANALYST
PSYCHODYNAMIC
PSYCHOGENESIS
PSYCHOGENETIC
PSYCHOGRAPHIC
PSYCHOKINESIS
PSYCHOLOGICAL
PSYCHOMETRICS
PSYCHOPATHIST
PSYCHOPHYSICS
PSYCHOSOMATIC
PSYCHOSURGERY
PSYCHOTHERAPY
PSYCHROMETRIC
PTERIDOLOGIST
PTERYLOGRAPHY
PUCCINIACEOUS
PUDDING-HEADED
PUDDING-SLEEVE
PULSELESSNESS
PULVERISATION
PUNCTILIOUSLY
PUNISHABILITY
PURITANICALLY
PURPLE-IN-GRAIN
PURPOSELESSLY
PURPOSIVENESS
PURSE-SNATCHER
PUSILLANIMITY
PUSILLANIMOUS
PUSS-GENTLEMAN
PUTTY-COLOURED
PYCNIDIOSPORE
PYCNOCONIDIUM
PYRAMIDICALLY
PYRENOMYCETES
PYRETOTHERAPY
PYRHELIOMETER
PYRIMETHAMINE
PYROPHOSPHATE
PYROSULPHURIC
PYROTECHNICAL

Q

QUADRAGESIMAL
QUADRENNIALLY
QUADRICIPITAL
QUADRIFARIOUS
QUADRIFOLIATE

QUADRIGEMINAL
QUADRILATERAL
QUADRILITERAL
QUADRILLIONTH
QUADRILOCULAR
QUADRINGENARY
QUADRINOMINAL
QUADRIPARTITE
QUADRISECTION
QUADRIVALENCE
QUADRUMVIRATE
QUADRUPLICITY
QUADRUPLICATE
QUALIFICATION
QUALIFICATIVE
QUALIFICATORY
QUALITATIVELY
QUANTIVALENCE
QUARRELSOMELY
QUARTER-DECKER
QUARTER-GUNNER
QUARTERMASTER
QUARTODECIMAN
QUARTZ-CRYSTAL
QUARTZ-HALOGEN
QUARTZIFEROUS
QUATCH-BUTTOCK
QUATERNIONIST
QUATREFEUILLE
QUEENSLAND-NUT
QUERULOUSNESS
QUESTIONINGLY
QUESTIONNAIRE
QUICK-ANSWERED
QUICK-SCENTING
QUICKSILVERED
QUICK-TEMPERED
QUILTING-FRAME
QUINCENTENARY
QUINCUNCIALLY
QUINGENTENARY
QUINQUAGESIMA
QUINQUEVALENT
QUINTILLIONTH
QUINTUPLICATE
QUIZZINGGLASS
QUOTATION-MARK

R
RADIALISATION
RADIO-ACTINIUM
RADIOACTIVITY
RADIOLOCATION
RADIOTELEGRAM
RAFFLESIACEAE
RAG-AND-BONE-MAN
RAILWAY-STITCH
RAINBOW-CHASER
RAINBOW-TINTED
RALLYING-POINT
RANUNCULACEAE
RANZ-DES-VACHES
RAPACIOUSNESS
RAPPROCHEMENT
RASPBERRY-BUSH
RATIOCINATION

RATIOCINATIVE
RATIOCINATORY
RATIONALISTIC
RATTLE-BRAINED
REACTIONARISM
REACTIONARIST
REAFFIRMATION
REALISTICALLY
REAPPLICATION
REAPPOINTMENT
REARRANGEMENT
REBECCA-EUREKA
RECALCITRANCE
RECEIVABILITY
RECEIVING-ROOM
RECEIVING-SHIP
RECEPTIBILITY
RECEPTION-ROOM
RECEPTIVENESS
RECESSIVENESS
RECIPROCALITY
RECIPROCATION
RECIPROCATIVE
RECITATIONIST
RECOLLECTEDLY
RECOMBINATION
RECOMFORTLESS
RECOMMENDABLE
RECOMMENDABLY
RECOMPOSITION
RECONCILEMENT
RECONSOLIDATE
RECONSTRUCTOR
RECRIMINATION
RECRIMINATIVE
RECRIMINATORY
RECRUDESCENCE
RECRUDESCENCY
RECRYSTALLISE
RECTANGULARLY
RECTIFICATION
RECTILINEARLY
RECTIPETALITY
REDDING-STRAIK
REDEEMABILITY
REDELIVERANCE
REDEMPTIONIST
REDEVELOPMENT
REDISSOLUTION
REDUCIBLENESS
REDUPLICATION
REDUPLICATIVE
RE-EDIFICATION
REEFING-JACKET
RE-ELIGIBILITY
RE-EMBARKATION
RE-ENFORCEMENT
RE-EXAMINATION
RE-EXPORTATION
REFASHIONMENT
REFERENCE-MARK
REFERENTIALLY
REFLEXIBILITY
REFOCILLATION
REFORMABILITY
REFRACTOMETER

REFRIGERATION
REFRIGERATIVE
REFRIGERATORY
REGARDFULNESS
REGIMENTATION
REGISTER-PLATE
REGISTRARSHIP
REGURGITATION
REIMBURSEMENT
REINCARNATION
REINFORCEMENT
REINSTATEMENT
REINTEGRATION
REINTERROGATE
REJUVENESCENT
RELIGIOUSNESS
REMEASUREMENT
REMINISCENTLY
REMISSIBILITY
REMITTANCE-MAN
REMONSTRANTLY
REMONSTRATION
REMONSTRATIVE
REMONSTRATORY
REMORSELESSLY
RENT-COLLECTOR
REORIENTATION
REPETITIONARY
REPETITIOUSLY
REPLENISHMENT
REPREHENSIBLE
REPREHENSIBLY
REPRESENTABLE
REPRESENTAMEN
REPRESENTMENT
REPROACHFULLY
REPTILIFEROUS
REPUBLICANISE
REPUBLICANISM
REPUBLICATION
REPULSIVENESS
REQUISITENESS
RESISTANCE-BOX
RESISTIBILITY
RESOLVABILITY
RESPLENDENTLY
RESTAURANT-CAR
RESTORATIVELY
RESTRICTIVELY
RESUSCITATION
RESUSCITATIVE
RETENTIVENESS
RETINOSCOPIST
RETRANSLATION
RETROACTIVELY
RETROACTIVITY
RETROGRESSION
RETROGRESSIVE
RETROMINGENCY
RETROSPECTION
RETROSPECTIVE
REVACCINATION
REVELATIONIST
REVENDICATION
REVENUE-CUTTER
REVERBERATION

REVERBERATIVE
REVERBERATORY
REVERENTIALLY
REVERSIBILITY
REVERSIONALLY
REVICTUALLING
REVINDICATION
REVOCABLENESS
REVOLUTIONARY
REVOLUTIONISE
REVOLUTIONISM
REVOLUTIONIST
RHABDOMANTIST
RHADAMANTHINE
RHAETOROMANIC
RHAPSODICALLY
RHEUMATICALLY
RHINOSCLEROMA
RHODOCHROSITE
RHOMBPORPHYRY
RHOPALOCEROUS
RHYPAROGRAPHY
RICKETTSIALES
RIDING-CLOTHES
RIGHTEOUSNESS
RIGHT-THINKING
RITUALISATION
ROAD-METALLING
ROBE-DE-CHAMBRE
ROE-BLACKBERRY
ROGUE-ELEPHANT
ROLLER-BANDAGE
ROLLER-COASTER
ROLLER-SKATING
ROLL-ON-ROLL-OFF
ROMANO-BRITISH
ROMANTICALITY
RÖNTGENOSCOPY
ROOT-AND-BRANCH
ROUGH-AND-READY
RUDIMENTARILY
RUMEL-GUMPTION
RUMLE-GUMPTION
RUSSIFICATION
RUST-RESISTANT
RUSTY-COLOURED

S

SABBATH-BREACH
SABLE-COLOURED
SABRE-RATTLING
SACCHARIMETER
SACCHARIMETRY
SACCHAROMETER
SACCHAROMYCES
SACERDOTALISE
SACERDOTALISM
SACERDOTALIST
SACRAMENTALLY
SACRIFICIALLY
SACROSANCTITY
SADDLE-BLANKET
SADDLE-FEATHER
SADO-MASOCHISM
SADO-MASOCHIST
SAGACIOUSNESS

SAILING-MASTER
SAINT-SIMONIAN
SAINT-SIMONISM
SAINT-SIMONIST
SALACIOUSNESS
SALE-CATALOGUE
SALMON-DISEASE
SALMONELLOSIS
SALMON-FISHERY
SALMON-FISHING
SALMON-LEISTER
SALPINGECTOMY
SALVINIACEOUS
SANCTIFYINGLY
SANCTIMONIOUS
SANDWICH-BOARD
SANDY-LAVEROCK
SANITARIANISM
SANITATIONIST
SANSCULOTTISM
SANSCULOTTIST
SANTANOPHOBIA
SARACEN'S-STONE
SARCASTICALLY
SARCOPHAGUSES
SARMENTACEOUS
SATANICALNESS
SATIN-SHEETING
SATIRICALNESS
SAUROGNATHOUS
SAUROPTERYGIA
SAUSSURITISED
SAVANNA-FOREST
SAVANNA-WATTLE
SAXIFRAGACEAE
SCALENOHEDRON
SCALING-LADDER
SCALPELLIFORM
SCALPING-KNIFE
SCAMBLING-DAYS
SCANDAL-BEARER
SCANDALMONGER
SCAPHOCEPHALY
SCAPULIMANTIC
SCARIFICATION
SCARLET-RUNNER
SCATHEFULNESS
SCENARISATION
SCHADENFREUDE
SCHEMATICALLY
SCHIZOCARPOUS
SCHIZOGENESIS
SCHIZOGENETIC
SCHIZOMYCETES
SCHIZOPHRENIA
SCHIZOPHRENIC
SCHOLARLINESS
SCHOLASTICISM
SCHOOLGIRLISH
SCHOOL-LEAVING
SCHOOL-TEACHER
SCHOOL-TRAINED
SCHUTZSTAFFEL
SCHWENKFELDER
SCINTILLATION
SCLEROCAULOUS

SCLERODERMITE
SCLERODERMOUS
SCLEROPROTEIN
SCOLECIFORMIA
SCOLOPENDRINE
SCOLOPENDRIUM
SCORCHINGNESS
SCORIFICATION
SCORPION-GRASS
SCOTIFICATION
SCOURING-STICK
SCRAP-MERCHANT
SCREECH-MARTIN
SCREECH-THRUSH
SCRIPTURALISM
SCRIPTURALIST
SCRIVENERSHIP
SCRUMPTIOUSLY
SCULPTURESQUE
SCYPHOMEDUSAE
SEA-GOOSEBERRY
SEAL-ENGRAVING
SEARCHINGNESS
SEARCH-WARRANT
SEA-SHOULDRING
SEA-WATER-GREEN
SEAWORTHINESS
SECONDARINESS
SECRETARY-BIRD
SECRETARYSHIP
SECRETIVENESS
SECTION-CUTTER
SEDENTARINESS
SEDIMENTATION
SEDITIOUSNESS
SEDUCTIVENESS
SEEK-NO-FURTHER
SEEMING-SIMPLE
SEINE-SHOOTING
SEISMOGRAPHER
SEISMOGRAPHIC
SEISMOLOGICAL
SELENOGRAPHER
SELENOGRAPHIC
SELENOLOGICAL
SELF-ABASEMENT
SELF-ADMISSION
SELF-APPOINTED
SELF-APPROVING
SELF-ASSERTING
SELF-ASSERTION
SELF-ASSERTIVE
SELF-ASSURANCE
SELF-COLLECTED
SELF-COMMUNION
SELF-CONCEITED
SELF-CONDEMNED
SELF-CONFIDENT
SELF-CONFIDING
SELF-CONJUGATE
SELF-CONSCIOUS
SELF-CONSUMING
SELF-CONTAINED
SELF-CONVICTED
SELF-CRITICISM
SELF-DECEITFUL

SELF-DECEPTION
SELF-DEFEATING
SELF-DENYINGLY
SELF-DIRECTING
SELF-DIRECTION
SELF-DISPRAISE
SELF-ENJOYMENT
SELF-EXISTENCE
SELF-FERTILITY
SELF-FORGETFUL
SELF-GOVERNING
SELF-IMPORTANT
SELF-INDUCTION
SELF-INDULGENT
SELF-INFECTION
SELF-INFLICTED
SELF-INSURANCE
SELF-KNOWLEDGE
SELF-MURDERING
SELF-OPINIONED
SELF-POLLUTION
SELF-SATISFIED
SELF-SHIELDING
SELF-SLAUGHTER
SELF-STERILITY
SELF-SUFFICING
SELF-SUPPORTED
SELF-SURRENDER
SELF-SURVIVING
SELF-SUSTAINED
SELF-TORMENTOR
SEMI-AUTOMATIC
SEMI-BARBARIAN
SEMI-BARBARISM
SEMICARBAZIDE
SEMICONDUCTOR
SEMICONSCIOUS
SEMILOGARITHM
SEMIMENSTRUAL
SEMI-OVIPAROUS
SEMIPALMATION
SEMIPARASITIC
SEMIPERIMETER
SEMIPERMEABLE
SEMIPORCELAIN
SEMI-SAGITTATE
SEMNOPITHECUS
SEMPSTRESSING
SENESCHALSHIP
SENSATIONALLY
SENSELESSNESS
SENSITISATION
SENSITIVENESS
SENTENTIOUSLY
SENTIMENTALLY
SEPARABLENESS
SEPARATIONIST
SEPTENTRIONAL
SEPTENTRIONES
SEQUENTIALITY
SEQUESTRATION
SERBO-CROATIAN
SERGEANT-MAJOR
SERIALISATION
SERICICULTURE
SERICULTURIST

SERJEANT-AT-LAW
SEROLOGICALLY
SERPENT-LIZARD
SERVING-MALLET
SESQUIPLICATE
SESSIONS-HOUSE
SEVENTEENTHLY
SEWING-MACHINE
SEXAGESIMALLY
SEX-CHROMOSOME
SEX-INTERGRADE
SHABBY-GENTEEL
SHADOWCASTING
SHAKESPEAREAN
SHAKESPEARIAN
SHAMEFASTNESS
SHAMELESSNESS
SHAMMY-LEATHER
SHAPELESSNESS
SHARPSHOOTING
SHEEP-SHEARING
SHEEP-STEALING
SHELL-ORNAMENT
SHELL-PARAKEET
SHERIFF-DEPUTE
SHERRY-COBBLER
SHIFTLESSNESS
SHINGLE-ROOFED
SHIP-CARPENTER
SHIP-CHANDLERY
SHIP-OF-THE-LINE
SHOCK-ABSORBER
SHOOTING-BOARD
SHOOTING-BRAKE
SHOOTING-LODGE
SHOOTING-RANGE
SHOOTING-STICK
SHOP-ASSISTANT
SHORT-DIVISION
SHORT-TEMPERED
SHOULDER-BLADE
SHOULDER-JOINT
SHOULDER-STRAP
SHRILL-TONGUED
SICK-FEATHERED
SICKLE-FEATHER
SICK-THOUGHTED
SIDE-SPLITTING
SIGHTLESSNESS
SIGNATURE-TUNE
SIGNIFICANTLY
SIGNIFICATION
SIGNIFICATIVE
SIGNIFICATORY
SILK-THROWSTER
SILVER-MOUNTED
SILVER-SHAFTED
SILVER-TONGUED
SIMPLE-HEARTED
SIMPLIFICATOR
SINGING-MASTER
SINGLE-CHAMBER
SINGLE-HEARTED
SIPUNCULOIDEA
SKELETOGENOUS
SKETCHABILITY

SKIRL-IN-THE-PAN
SKIRTING-BOARD
SKITTLE-GROUND
SKULKING-PLACE
SLATE-COLOURED
SLEEP-LEARNING
SLEEPLESSNESS
SLEIGHT-OF-HAND
SMALL-AND-EARLY
SMELLING-SALTS
SMELTING-HOUSE
SMELTING-WORKS
SMOKE-CONSUMER
SMOKELESSNESS
SMOOTH-CHINNED
SMOOTH-DITTIED
SMOOTH-TONGUED
SNAFFLE-BRIDLE
SNIFTING-VALVE
SNOW-BLINDNESS
SNUFF-COLOURED
SOCIALISATION
SOCIOLOGISTIC
SOCK-SUSPENDER
SODOMITICALLY
SOLDERING-BOLT
SOLDERING-IRON
SOLDIERLINESS
SOLEMNISATION
SOLIDUNGULATE
SOLIDUNGULOUS
SOLIFIDIANISM
SOMATOLOGICAL
SOMNAMBULANCE
SOMNAMBULATOR
SOMNILOQUENCE
SOOTHFASTNESS
SOPHISTICALLY
SOPHISTICATED
SOPHISTICATOR
SORROWFULNESS
SOUL-SEARCHING
SOUND-BOARDING
SOUNDING-BOARD
SOUNDPROOFING
SOUTH-EASTERLY
SOUTH-EASTWARD
SOUTHERLINESS
SOUTH-WESTERLY
SOUTH-WESTWARD
SOVIETOLOGIST
SOWING-MACHINE
SPACE-PLATFORM
SPADICIFLORAL
SPARGANIACEAE
SPASMODICALLY
SPEAKING-VOICE
SPECIES-MONGER
SPECIFICATION
SPECTACULARLY
SPECTATORSHIP
SPECTRE-INSECT
SPECTRE-SHRIMP
SPECTROGRAPHY
SPECTROSCOPIC
SPECULATIVELY

SPEECHFULNESS
SPEECH-READING
SPELAEOLOGIST
SPENCERIANISM
SPERMATOBLAST
SPERMATOGENIC
SPERMATOPHORE
SPERMATOPHYTA
SPERMATOPHYTE
SPERMATOTHECA
SPHAGNICOLOUS
SPHAGNOLOGIST
SPHERICALNESS
SPHERISTERION
SPHEROIDICITY
SPHYGMOGRAPHY
SPIFFLICATION
SPIKE-LAVENDER
SPINDLE-LEGGED
SPINDLE-SHANKS
SPINDLE-SHAPED
SPINE-CHILLING
SPINELESSNESS
SPINNING-HOUSE
SPINNING-JENNY
SPINNING-WHEEL
SPINULIFEROUS
SPIRITOUSNESS
SPIRIT-RAPPING
SPIRITUALISER
SPIRITUALNESS
SPIRIT-VARNISH
SPLANCHNOCELE
SPLENDIFEROUS
SPLENETICALLY
SPLINTER-PROOF
SPLUTTERINGLY
SPONGE-FISHING
SPONGING-HOUSE
SPONTANEOUSLY
SPORTSMANLIKE
SPORTSMANSHIP
SPRIGHTLINESS
SPRING-BALANCE
SPRING-CLEANER
SPROCKET-WHEEL
SPUNGING-HOUSE
SQUANDERINGLY
SQUANDERMANIA
SQUARE-BASHING
SQUARE-DANCING
SQUARE-MEASURE
SQUARE-PIERCED
SQUEAMISHNESS
SQUEEZABILITY
SQUINANCY-WORT
SQUIRREL-SHREW
STABILISATION
STACCATISSIMO
STAFF-NOTATION
STAFF-SERGEANT
STAGECOACHING
STAGECOACHMAN
STAINLESSNESS
STALACTITICAL
STALACTITIOUS

STALAGMITICAL
STALAGMOMETER
STALAGMOMETRY
STALKING-HORSE
STAMINIFEROUS
STANDING-PLACE
STANDING-STONE
STAPHYLEACEAE
STAPHYLINDIAE
STAR-CATALOGUE
STARTING-POINT
STARTING-PRICE
STATELESSNESS
STATE-RELIGION
STATES-GENERAL
STATESMANLIKE
STATESMANSHIP
STATION-MASTER
STATISTICALLY
STATUTE-LABOUR
STEADFASTNESS
STEAM-CARRIAGE
STEAM-GOVERNOR
STEEPLECHASER
STEERING-WHEEL
STEGANOGRAPHY
STEGANOPODOUS
STEGOCEPHALIA
STENOGRAPHIST
STEPPING-STONE
STERCORACEOUS
STERCORARIOUS
STERCULIACEAE
STEREOGRAPHIC
STEREOSCOPIST
STERILISATION
STERN-FOREMOST
STETHOSCOPIST
STICKING-PLACE
STICKING-POINT
STICK-IN-THE-MUD
STIGMATICALLY
STILL-PIERCING
STILL-ROOM-MAID
STIRPICULTURE
STOCK-BREEDING
STOCKING-FRAME
STOICHIOMETRY
STOLONIFEROUS
STONE-COLOURED
STOPPING-PLACE
STORMING-PARTY
STRAIGHTFORTH
STRAIGHT-PIGHT
STRAINING-BEAM
STRANGULATION
STRATEGETICAL
STRATEGICALLY
STRATIGRAPHER
STRATIGRAPHIC
STRATOCRUISER
STRATOCUMULUS
STRATOSPHERIC
STRAW-COLOURED
STREET-ORDERLY
STREET-RAILWAY

STREET-SWEEPER
STREET-WALKING
STRENGTHENING
STRENUOUSNESS
STREPTOCOCCAL
STREPTOCOCCIC
STREPTOCOCCUS
STRETCHER-BOND
STRIKE-BREAKER
STRINGENTNESS
STRING-PULLING
STROBILACEOUS
STROMBULIFORM
STROPHIOLATED
STRUCTURALISM
STRUCTURELESS
STULTILOQUENT
STYLISTICALLY
SUBAPPEARANCE
SUBCLAVICULAR
SUBCONTIGUOUS
SUBCONTINUOUS
SUBCONTRACTOR
SUBDEACONSHIP
SUBDIVISIONAL
SUBEDITORSHIP
SUBINDICATION
SUBINDICATIVE
SUBIRRIGATION
SUBJECT-MATTER
SUBJECT-OBJECT
SUBJUNCTIVELY
SUBLANCEOLATE
SUBLIEUTENANT
SUBMACHINE-GUN
SUBORDINATELY
SUBORDINATION
SUBORDINATIVE
SUBPREFECTURE
SUBREPTITIOUS
SUBSEQUENTIAL
SUBSERVIENTLY
SUBSISTENTIAL
SUBSTANTIALLY
SUBSTANTIVELY
SUBSTANTIVISE
SUBSTANTIVITY
SUBSTRUCTURAL
SUBTERNATURAL
SUBTERRANEOUS
SUBTILE-WITTED
SUBTILISATION
SUBTRIANGULAR
SUBTRIPLICATE
SUBURBICARIAN
SUBVERSIONARY
SUCCESSIONIST
SUCCESSLESSLY
SUCCESSORSHIP
SUCCINCTORIUM
SUCKING-BOTTLE
SUFFICINGNESS
SUFFOCATINGLY
SUFFRAGANSHIP
SUFFUMIGATION
SUGAR-REFINERY

SUGAR-REFINING
SUGGESTIONISE
SUGGESTIONISM
SUGGESTIONIST
SULPHUR-BOTTOM
SULPHUREOUSLY
SULPHUR-YELLOW
SUMMER-SEEMING
SUMPTUOUSNESS
SUN-ANIMALCULE
SUN-WORSHIPPER
SUOVETAURILIA
SUPERABUNDANT
SUPERADDITION
SUPERANNUATED
SUPERCALENDER
SUPERCRITICAL
SUPERDOMINANT
SUPEREMINENCE
SUPERFETATION
SUPERFICIALLY
SUPERFINENESS
SUPERFLUIDITY
SUPERFLUOUSLY
SUPERHUMANISE
SUPERHUMANITY
SUPERLATIVELY
SUPERNATIONAL
SUPERNUMERARY
SUPERORDINARY
SUPERORDINATE
SUPERPHYSICAL
SUPERPOSITION
SUPERSATURATE
SUPERSENSIBLE
SUPERSENSIBLY
SUPERSTITIOUS
SUPERVENIENCE
SUPPLANTATION
SUPPLEMENTARY
SUPPOSITIONAL
SUPRA-AXILLARY
SUPRANATIONAL
SUPRASENSIBLE
SUPRATEMPORAL
SURCHARGEMENT
SURFACE-VESSEL
SURREPTITIOUS
SURROGATESHIP
SUSPECTEDNESS
SUSPENDER-BELT
SUSPERCOLLATE
SUSPICIONLESS
SUSTENTACULAR
SUSTENTACULUM
SWADDLING-BAND
SWALLOW-TAILED
SWEDENBORGIAN
SWEET-SAVOURED
SWEET-TEMPERED
SWELLED-HEADED
SWINE'S-SUCCORY
SWINGEBUCKLER
SWINGING-BLOCK
SWORDSMANSHIP
SYCOPHANTICAL

SYLLABICATION
SYLLEPTICALLY
SYLLOGISATION
SYLLOGISTICAL
SYMBIOTICALLY
SYMBOLISATION
SYMBOLISTICAL
SYMBOLOGRAPHY
SYMMETRICALLY
SYMPATHECTOMY
SYMPATHETICAL
SYMPHYSEOTOMY
SYMPHYSIOTOMY
SYMPIESOMETER
SYMPTOMATICAL
SYNALLAGMATIC
SYNAPOSEMATIC
SYNARTHRODIAL
SYNCHONDROSIS
SYNCHRONISTIC
SYNCHRONOLOGY
SYNCHRONOUSLY
SYNDICALISTIC
SYNECDOCHICAL
SYNECPHONESIS
SYNTACTICALLY
SYNTHETICALLY
SYPHILISATION
SYPHILOLOGIST
SYPHILOPHOBIA
SYROPHOENICIA
SYSTEMATICIAN
SYSTEMATOLOGY
SYSTEMISATION

T

TABLE-SKITTLES
TABLESPOONFUL
TACHISTOSCOPE
TACHOMETRICAL
TACHYGRAPHIST
TACHYMETRICAL
TALKATIVENESS
TANGENTIALITY
TANTALISATION
TANTALISINGLY
TAPE-RECORDING
TARRY-FINGERED
TASTELESSNESS
TATTIE-LIFTING
TAUROMORPHOUS
TAUTOCHRONISM
TAUTOCHRONOUS
TAUTOMETRICAL
TAUTOPHONICAL
TAXONOMICALLY
TEACHABLENESS
TEA-PLANTATION
TECHNICALNESS
TECHNOLOGICAL
TELAUTOGRAPHY
TELEGRAMMATIC
TELEGRAPH-POLE
TELEGRAPH-WIRE
TELERECORDING
TELESCOPIFORM

TELEVISIONARY
TEMERARIOUSLY
TEMPERAMENTAL
TEMPERATENESS
TEMPEST-BEATEN
TEMPEST-TOSSED
TEMPESTUOUSLY
TEMPORARINESS
TEMPORISATION
TEMPORISINGLY
TEMPTABLENESS
TENACIOUSNESS
TENANT-IN-CHIEF
TENDENTIOUSLY
TENDER-HEARTED
TENEBRIONIDAE
TENPENNY-PIECE
TENT-PREACHING
TERATOLOGICAL
TERCENTENNIAL
TERGIVERSATOR
TERMINABILITY
TERMINATIONAL
TERMINATIVELY
TERPSICHOREAN
TERRA-JAPONICA
TERRESTRIALLY
TERRITORIALLY
TERRORISATION
TESTICARDINES
TESTIFICATION
TESTIFICATORY
TETARTOHEDRAL
TETRABRANCHIA
TETRADYNAMOUS
TETRASTICHOUS
TETRASYLLABIC
TETRASYLLABLE
TEUTONISATION
THALAMIFLORAE
THALAMIFLORAL
THALASSOCRACY
THALATTOCRACY
THANATOGRAPHY
THANATOPHOBIA
THANKLESSNESS
THANK-OFFERING
THANKWORTHILY
THAUMATOLATRY
THAUMATURGICS
THAUMATURGISM
THAUMATURGIST
THEANTHROPISM
THEANTHROPIST
THEATRICALISE
THEATRICALISM
THEATRICALITY
THENCEFORWARD
THEOLOGICALLY
THEOPASCHITIC
THEOREMATICAL
THEORETICALLY
THEREINBEFORE
THERIOMORPHIC
THERMOBALANCE
THERMOCHEMIST

THERMODYNAMIC
THERMOGENESIS
THERMOGENETIC
THERMONUCLEAR
THERMOPHILOUS
THERMOPLASTIC
THERMOSETTING
THERMOTROPISM
THICK-PLEACHED
THIGMOTROPISM
THIMBLE-RIGGER
THING-IN-ITSELF
THOROUGHBRACE
THOROUGH-GOING
THOROUGH-PACED
THOUGHTLESSLY
THOUGHT-READER
THOUSANDPOUND
THRASHINGMILL
THRASONICALLY
THREATENINGLY
THREE-CORNERED
THREE-FARTHING
THREEFOLDNESS
THREEPENN'ORTH
THREE-PER-CENTS
THREMMATOLOGY
THRESHER-SHARK
THRESHER-WHALE
THRESHING-MILL
THRILLINGNESS
THROTTLE-LEVER
THROTTLE-VALVE
THROUGH-TICKET
THROWING-STICK
THROWING-TABLE
THUNDER-BEARER
THUNDER-DARTER
THUNDER-MASTER
THUNDER-SHOWER
THUNDER-STRIKE
THUNDER-STROKE
THUNDER-STRUCK
THURIFICATION
THYMELAEACEAE
TIC-DOULOUREUX
TICKET-OF-LEAVE
TICKET-WRITING
TICKLY-BENDERS
TIDDLEDYWINKS
TIMBROPHILIST
TIME-BEGUILING
TIME-BETTERING
TIME-CONSUMING
TIME-SIGNATURE
TINTINNABULAR
TINTINNABULUM
TIPPLING-HOUSE
TITANOTHERIUM
TITHE-GATHERER
TITTLE-TATTLER
TOAD-IN-THE-HOLE
TOBACCANALIAN
TOILET-SERVICE
TOLERATIONIST
TONGUE-DOUBTIE

TONGUE-IN-CHEEK
TONGUE-TWISTER
TONSILLECTOMY
TOOTHACHE-TREE
TOOTH-ORNAMENT
TOOTHSOMENESS
TOPOGRAPHICAL
TOPSIDE-TURVEY
TOPSYTURVYDOM
TORRENTIALITY
TORTOISE-PLANT
TORTOISE-SHELL
TOUCHABLENESS
TOXICOLOGICAL
TOXICOPHAGOUS
TOXOPLASMOSIS
TRACEABLENESS
TRACKLESSNESS
TRACTABLENESS
TRACTARIANISM
TRADESMANLIKE
TRADE-UNIONISM
TRADE-UNIONIST
TRADITIONALLY
TRAFFIC-LIGHTS
TRAM-CONDUCTOR
TRANQUILLISER
TRANSATLANTIC
TRANSCENDENCE
TRANSCENDENCY
TRANSCRIPTION
TRANSCRIPTIVE
TRANSFER-PAPER
TRANSFERRABLE
TRANSFERRIBLE
TRANSFORMABLE
TRANSFUSIVELY
TRANSGRESSION
TRANSGRESSIVE
TRANSIENTNESS
TRANSISTHMIAN
TRANSISTORISE
TRANSIT-CIRCLE
TRANSITIONARY
TRANSLATIONAL
TRANSLITERATE
TRANSLOCATION
TRANSLUCENTLY
TRANSLUCIDITY
TRANSMIGRATOR
TRANSMISSIBLE
TRANSMITTABLE
TRANSMUTATION
TRANSMUTATIVE
TRANSPARENTLY
TRANSPIRATION
TRANSPIRATORY
TRANSPLANTING
TRANSPORTABLE
TRANSPORTANCE
TRANSPORTEDLY
TRANSPORT-SHIP
TRANSPOSITION
TRANSPOSITIVE
TRANSSHIPPING
TRANSVERSALLY

TRAPEZOHEDRON
TRAUMATICALLY
TRAUMATONASTY
TRAVELLER'S-JOY
TRAVEL-STAINED
TRAVEL-TAINTED
TREACHEROUSLY
TREASURE-CHEST
TREASURE-HOUSE
TREASURERSHIP
TREMULOUSNESS
TRESTLE-BRIDGE
TRIANGULARITY
TRIANGULATELY
TRIANGULATION
TRIBUNITICIAL
TRIBUNITICIAN
TRIBUTARINESS
TRICARPELLARY
TRICHOLOGICAL
TRICHOPTERIST
TRICHOPTEROUS
TRICHROMATISM
TRIETHYLAMINE
TRIGONOMETRIC
TRILITERALISM
TRIPLE-CROWNED
TRIQUETROUSLY
TRISACCHARIDE
TRISYLLABICAL
TRITHEISTICAL
TRITUBERCULAR
TROGLODYTICAL
TROLLING-SPOON
TROPAEOLACEAE
TROPHALLACTIC
TROPHOTROPISM
TROTH-PLIGHTED
TROUBLESOMELY
TROUBLOUSNESS
TROUSER-BUTTON
TROUSER-POCKET
TROUT-COLOURED
TRUE-DISPOSING
TRUMPET-FLOWER
TRUMPET-SHAPED
TRUNK-BREECHES
TRUSTLESSNESS
TRUSTWORTHILY
TRUTHLESSNESS
TRYSTING-PLACE
TRYSTING-STILE
TUBERCULATION
TUMBLER-SWITCH
TURKEY-BUZZARD
TURNIP-LANTERN
TURQUOISE-BLUE
TWIDDLING-LINE
TWOPENCEWORTH
TWOPENNYWORTH
TYPOGRAPHICAL

U

ULTRA-TROPICAL
ULTRA-VIRTUOUS

UMBELLIFEROUS
UMBRACULIFORM
UMBRELLA-STAND
UNABBREVIATED
UNACCOMPANIED
UNACCOUNTABLE
UNACCOUNTABLY
UNADULTERATED
UNADVENTUROUS
UNADVISEDNESS
UNAMBIGUOUSLY
UNAMBITIOUSLY
UN-AMERICANISE
UNAMIABLENESS
UNAPOSTOLICAL
UNAPPRECIATED
UNAPPREHENDED
UNAPPROPRIATE
UNAPPROVINGLY
UNARTICULATED
UNASCERTAINED
UNASSIMILABLE
UNASSIMILATED
UNBELIEVINGLY
UNBENDINGNESS
UNBESEEMINGLY
UNBIASSEDNESS
UNBLESSEDNESS
UNBOUNDEDNESS
UNBRIDLEDNESS
UNBROTHERLIKE
UNCALCULATING
UNCEREMONIOUS
UNCERTAINNESS
UNCHASTISABLE
UNCHRISTIANLY
UNCIRCUMCISED
UNCLEANLINESS
UNCLOUDEDNESS
UNCOMFORTABLE
UNCOMFORTABLY
UNCOMMENDABLE
UNCOMMENDABLY
UNCOMPANIONED
UNCOMPENSATED
UNCOMPLAINING
UNCOMPLAISANT
UNCOMPLICATED
UNCONCEALABLE
UNCONCEIVABLY
UNCONCERNEDLY
UNCONCERNMENT
UNCONDITIONAL
UNCONDITIONED
UNCONFORMABLE
UNCONFORMABLY
UNCONJECTURED
UNCONJUNCTIVE
UNCONQUERABLE
UNCONQUERABLY
UNCONSCIOUSLY
UNCONSECRATED
UNCONSIDERING
UNCONSTRAINED
UNCONTENTIOUS
UNCONTESTABLE

UNCONVERSABLE
UNCONVERTIBLE
UNCOOPERATIVE
UNCOORDINATED
UNCOURTLINESS
UNCREATEDNESS
UNDAUNTEDNESS
UNDEPRECIATED
UNDERCARRIAGE
UNDERCLOTHING
UNDERESTIMATE
UNDEREXPOSURE
UNDERGRADUATE
UNDERHANDEDLY
UNDERNICENESS
UNDER-SHEPHERD
UNDERSTANDING
UNDERSTRAPPER
UNDESCENDABLE
UNDESCENDIBLE
UNDESCRIBABLE
UNDESERVINGLY
UNDETERMINATE
UNDEVIATINGLY
UNDIFFERENCED
UNDISCERNEDLY
UNDISCERNIBLE
UNDISCERNIBLY
UNDISCIPLINED
UNDISCOMFITED
UNDISCOURAGED
UNDISCUSSABLE
UNDISCUSSIBLE
UNDISGUISABLE
UNDISGUISEDLY
UNDISHONOURED
UNDISTEMPERED
UNDISTINCTIVE
UNDISTRACTING
UNDISTRIBUTED
UNDISTURBEDLY
UNDIVERSIFIED
UNDIVIDEDNESS
UNDOMESTICATE
UNDULATIONIST
UNDUTIFULNESS
UNEARTHLINESS
UNEATABLENESS
UNELECTRIFIED
UNEMBARRASSED
UNEMOTIONALLY
UNENLIGHTENED
UNENTERTAINED
UNEQUIVOCALLY
UNESTABLISHED
UNEVANGELICAL
UNEXAGGERATED
UNEXCEPTIONAL
UNEXCLUSIVELY
UNEXEMPLIFIED
UNEXPENSIVELY
UNEXPERIENCED
UNEXPLAINABLE
UNEXPRESSIBLE
UNFALTERINGLY
UNFAMILIARITY

UNFASHIONABLE
UNFASHIONABLY
UNFEELINGNESS
UNFEIGNEDNESS
UNFLINCHINGLY
UNFORESEEABLE
UNFORESKINNED
UNFORGETTABLE
UNFORGETTABLY
UNFORGIVEABLE
UNFORGIVENESS
UNFORTUNATELY
UNGAINSAYABLE
UNGENTLEMANLY
UNGENUINENESS
UNGRAMMATICAL
UNGUARDEDNESS
UNHEALTHFULLY
UNHEALTHINESS
UNHURTFULNESS
UNICAMERALISM
UNICAMERALIST
UNILATERALITY
UNILLUMINATED
UNILLUSTRATED
UNIMAGINATIVE
UNIMPASSIONED
UNIMPEACHABLE
UNIMPREGNATED
UNIMPRESSIBLE
UNINAUGURATED
UNINFLAMMABLE
UNINFLUENTIAL
UNINHABITABLE
UNINQUISITIVE
UNINSTRUCTIVE
UNINTELLIGENT
UNINTENTIONAL
UNINTERESTING
UNINTERMITTED
UNINTERRUPTED
UNJUSTIFIABLE
UNJUSTIFIABLY
UNKNOWINGNESS
UNLEARNEDNESS
UNLIMITEDNESS
UNMACADAMISED
UNMEANINGNESS
UNMEDICINABLE
UNMENTIONABLE
UNMINDFULNESS
UNMINISTERIAL
UNMISTRUSTFUL
UNMITIGATEDLY
UNMURMURINGLY
UNNATURALISED
UNNATURALNESS
UNNECESSARILY
UNNEIGHBOURED
UNNEIGHBOURLY
UNOBSTRUCTIVE
UNOBTRUSIVELY
UNORIGINALITY
UNPERCEIVABLE
UNPERCEIVABLY
UNPERCEIVEDLY

UNPERFECTNESS
UNPERPETRATED
UNPERSUADABLE
UNPHILOSOPHIC
UNPITIFULNESS
UNPLEASURABLE
UNPLEASURABLY
UNPOLARISABLE
UNPRACTICABLE
UNPRACTICALLY
UNPRECEDENTED
UNPREDICTABLE
UNPREOCCUPIED
UNPRESENTABLE
UNPRETENTIOUS
UNPREVENTABLE
UNPROGRESSIVE
UNPROMISINGLY
UNPROPHETICAL
UNPROVIDED-FOR
UNPROVISIONED
UNPROVOCATIVE
UNPUNCTUALITY
UNPURCHASABLE
UNQUALIFIEDLY
UNQUESTIONING
UNREASONINGLY
UNRECLAIMABLE
UNRECLAIMABLY
UNRECOGNISING
UNRECOLLECTED
UNRECOMMENDED
UNRECOMPENSED
UNRECOVERABLE
UNRECOVERABLY
UNRELENTINGLY
UNRELIABILITY
UNREMEMBERING
UNREMITTENTLY
UNREMITTINGLY
UNREMORSELESS
UNREPENTINGLY
UNREPLACEABLE
UNREPLENISHED
UNREPRESENTED
UNREPRIEVABLE
UNREPROACHFUL
UNREPROACHING
UNRESISTINGLY
UNRESTFULNESS
UNRESTINGNESS
UNRETURNINGLY
UNRIGHTEOUSLY
UNSAINTLINESS
UNSALEABILITY
UNSATISFIABLE
UNSAVOURINESS
UNSCAVENGERED
UNSCHOLARLIKE
UNSCRUTINISED
UNSELFISHNESS
UNSENSATIONAL
UNSENTIMENTAL
UNSERVICEABLE
UNSETTLEDNESS
UNSHRINKINGLY

UNSIGHTLINESS
UNSKILFULNESS
UNSMOTHERABLE
UNSOCIABILITY
UNSOLDIERLIKE
UNSPARINGNESS
UNSPECIALISED
UNSPECULATIVE
UNSPIRITUALLY
UNSPOTTEDNESS
UNSTEADFASTLY
UNSTERCORATED
UNSTIGMATISED
UNSUBSTANTIAL
UNSUITABILITY
UNSUPERFLUOUS
UNSUPPORTABLE
UNSUPPORTEDLY
UNSURPASSABLE
UNSURPASSABLY
UNSUSCEPTIBLE
UNSUSPECTEDLY
UNSUSTAINABLE
UNSYMMETRICAL
UNSYMMETRISED
UNSYMPATHETIC
UNTAINTEDNESS
UNTAMABLENESS
UNTENABLENESS
UNTERRESTRIAL
UNTHEOLOGICAL
UNTHRIFTINESS
UNTRANSFORMED
UNTRANSMITTED
UNTRANSPARENT
UNTRAVERSABLE
UNTREMBLINGLY
UNTRESPASSING
UNTRUSTWORTHY
UNTUNABLENESS
UNTUNEFULNESS
UNVITRIFIABLE
UNWARRANTABLE
UNWARRANTABLY
UNWARRANTEDLY
UNWELCOMENESS
UNWHOLESOMELY
UNWILLINGNESS
UNWITHDRAWING
UNWITHHOLDING
UNWITTINGNESS
UNWOMANLINESS
UNWORKMANLIKE
UNWORLDLINESS
UPPPER-BRACKET
UPRIGHTEOUSLY
UP-TO-THE-MINUTE
UP-TO-THE-MOMENT
URALITISATION
URCHIN-SNOUTED
USTILAGINALES
USTILAGINEOUS
UTTERABLENESS

V

VACILLATINGLY
VACUOLISATION
VACUUM-CLEANER
VALEDICTORIAN
VALERIANACEAE
VANSITTARTISM
VANTAGE-GROUND
VAPOURISHNESS
VARNISHING-DAY
VAULTING-HORSE
VAULTING-HOUSE
VEGETARIANISM
VELT-MARESCHAL
VELVET-FIDDLER
VENERABLENESS
VENEREOLOGIST
VENTRILOQUIAL
VENTRILOQUISE
VENTRILOQUISM
VENTRILOQUIST
VENTRILOQUOUS
VENTURESOMELY
VENTUROUSNESS
VERBALISATION
VERBIGERATION
VERIFIABILITY
VERISIMILARLY
VERMICULATION
VERNACULARISE
VERNACULARISM
VERNACULARIST
VERNACULARITY
VERNALISATION
VERSATILENESS
VERSICOLOURED
VERSIFICATION
VERTICILLATED
VERTIGINOUSLY
VEXATIOUSNESS
VIBRACULARIUM
VIBRATIONLESS
VICARIOUSNESS
VICE-ADMIRALTY
VICE-CONSULATE
VICE-PRESIDENT
VICE-PRINCIPAL
VICTIMISATION
VILLEGGIATURA
VINDICABILITY
VINDICATORILY
VINICULTURIST
VIOL-DE-GAMBOYS
VIOLONCELLIST
VISCEROPTOSIS
VISCOMETRICAL
VISCOSIMETRIC
VISIONARINESS
VISUALISATION
VITELLIGENOUS
VITICULTURIST
VITRIFICATION
VIVACIOUSNESS
VIVISECTIONAL
VIVISECTORIUM

VIVISEPULTURE
VOCATIONALISM
VOICELESSNESS
VOLATILISABLE
VOLCANISATION
VOLTA-ELECTRIC
VOLTAIREANISM
VOLTAIRIANISM
VOLUMENOMETER
VOLUNTARINESS
VOLUNTARISTIC
VORACIOUSNESS
VOTE-SPLITTING
VOUCHSAFEMENT
VRAISEMBLANCE
VULCANISATION
VULCANOLOGIST
VULGARISATION
VULNERABILITY

W

WAITING-VASSAL
WALKING-ORDERS
WALKING-PAPERS
WALKING-TICKET
WAMBLE-CROPPED
WASHHAND-BASIN
WASHHAND-STAND
WASHING-BOTTLE
WASHING-POWDER
WASPISH-HEADED
WASTERFULNESS
WATER-BREATHER
WATER-CARRIAGE
WATER-CHESTNUT
WATER-DROPWORT
WATER-HYACINTH
WATERING-HOUSE
WATERING-PLACE
WATER-MOCASSIN
WATER-PLANTAIN
WATERPROOFING
WATER-SAPPHIRE
WATER-SOFTENER
WATER-SPRINKLE
WATER-STANDING
WATER-VASCULAR
WAYFARING-TREE
WEAPONSHAWING
WEARISOMENESS
WEATHER-ANCHOR
WEATHER-BEATEN
WEATHER-BITTEN
WEATHER-DRIVEN
WEATHER-HEADED

WEATHEROMETER
WEATHER-REPORT
WEATHER-SYMBOL
WEDDING-FAVOUR
WEDDING-FINGER
WEEPING-SPRING
WEEPING-WILLOW
WELL-APPOINTED
WELL-BESEEMING
WELL-CONDUCTED
WELL-REGULATED
WELL-RESPECTED
WELL-THOUGHT-OF
WELL-WARRANTED
WELL-WORKED-OUT
WHALING-MASTER
WHAT-D'YE-CALL-EM
WHAT-D'YE-CALL-IT
WHEEL-CARRIAGE
WHEREINSOEVER
WHIMSICALNESS
WHIPPING-CHEER
WHIRLING-TABLE
WHISKERANDOED
WHISTLED-DRUNK
WHISTLING-SHOP
WHITE-BREASTED
WHITE-FAVOURED
WHITHERSOEVER
WHOLE-COLOURED
WHOLESOMENESS
WHOOPING-COUGH
WHOREMASTERLY
WIDE-AWAKENESS
WIDE-STRETCHED
WIDOW'S-CHAMBER
WILLOW-WARBLER
WILLS-O'-THE-WISP
WINDING-ENGINE
WINDING-STRIPS
WINDOW-CURTAIN
WING-COMMANDER
WINKLE-PICKERS
WINTER-ACONITE
WITCHES-BUTTER
WOMAN-SUFFRAGE
WOMEN-CHILDREN
WONDERFULNESS
WONDER-WORKING
WONDER-WOUNDED
WOODCOCK'S-HEAD
WOOD-ENGRAVING
WOOD-GERMANDER
WOOD-SANDPIPER
WOOL-GATHERING

WOOLLEN-DRAPER
WORD-BLINDNESS
WORD-SPLITTING
WORDSWORTHIAN
WORLDLY-MINDED
WORTHLESSNESS
WRAPPING-PAPER
WRISTLET-WATCH
WRITING-MASTER
WRITING-SCHOOL
WRONG-HEADEDLY

X

XANTHOCHROISM
XANTHOCHROMIA
XANTHOCHROOUS
XANTHOPTERINE
XERODERMATOUS
XEROPHTHALMIA
XIPHIPLASTRAL
XIPHIPLASTRON
XYLOGRAPHICAL

Y

YACHTSMANSHIP
YELLOW-BELLIED
YELLOW-BUNTING
YELLOW-COVERED
YELLOW-CROWNED
YELLOW-FRONTED
YELLOWISHNESS
YELLOW-SPOTTED
YELLOW-YORLING
YESTEREVENING
YESTERMORNING
YIELDABLENESS

Z

ZARATHUSTRIAN
ZARATHUSTRISM
ZEBRA-PARAKEET
ZINCIFICATION
ZINGIBERACEAE
ZINJANTHROPUS
ZINKIFICATION
ZOOGEOGRAPHER
ZOOGEOGRAPHIC
ZOOPSYCHOLOGY
ZOOSPORANGIUM
ZYGAPOPHYSEAL
ZYGAPOPHYSIAL
ZYGODACTYLISM
ZYGODACTYLOUS
ZYMOTECHNICAL

A

ABOMINABLENESS
ABOVE-MENTIONED

ABSENT-MINDEDLY
ABSORPTIOMETER

ABSORPTIVENESS
ABSTEMIOUSNESS
ABSTRACTEDNESS
ABSTRACTIONIST
ACANTHOCEPHALA
ACCEPTABLENESS
ACCOMPLISHABLE
ACCOMPLISHMENT
ACCOUNTABILITY
ACCOUNTANTSHIP
ACCUSTOMEDNESS
ACHONDROPLASIA
ACHROMATICALLY
ACKNOWLEDGMENT
ADMINISTRATION
ADMINISTRATIVE
ADMINISTRATRIX
ADVANTAGEOUSLY
ADVENTITIOUSLY
AERENCHYMATOUS
AEROBIOLOGICAL
AEROBIOTICALLY
AERODYNAMICIST
AEROELASTICIAN
AEROHYDROPLANE
AESTHESIOGENIC
AFFECTIONATELY
AFOREMENTIONED
AFRICANISATION
AGGRANDISEMENT
AGGRESSIVENESS
AGROBIOLOGICAL
AGROSTOLOGICAL
AIRCRAFTSWOMAN
AIR-VICE-MARSHAL
ALBIGENSIANISM
ALCOHOLISATION
ALDER-BUCKTHORN
ALEXIPHARMAKON
ALIMENTIVENESS
ALLEGORISATION
ALLELOMORPHISM
ALLOIOSTROPHOS
ALL-OVERISHNESS
ALPHABETICALLY
ALPHANUMERICAL
ALTITUDINARIAN
ALTRUISTICALLY
AMARANTHACEOUS
AMARYLLIDACEAE
AMATEURISHNESS
AMBASSADORSHIP
AMPHIBOLOGICAL
ANACARDIACEOUS
ANAGRAMMATICAL
ANDROCEPHALOUS
ANDRODIOECIOUS
ANDROMEDOTOXIN
ANDROMONOECISM
ANGIOSTOMATOUS
ANGLO-ISRAELITE
ANGUSTIFOLIATE
ANISODACTYLOUS
ANTAGONISATION
ANTAPHRODISIAC
ANTEDILUVIALLY

ANTHROPOGRAPHY
ANTHROPOLOGIST
ANTHROPOMETRIC
ANTHROPOPATHIC
ANTHROPOPHUISM
ANTICIPATIVELY
ANTICIPATORILY
ANTICONVULSANT
ANTIFEDERALISM
ANTIFEDERALIST
ANTI-JACOBINISM
ANTILYMPHOCYTE
ANTIMETATHESIS
ANTIMONARCHIST
ANTIODONTALGIC
ANTIPATHETICAL
ANTIPERISTASIS
ANTIPHLOGISTIC
ANTIPHONICALLY
ANTIPHRASTICAL
ANTIQUARIANISM
ANTISCRIPTURAL
ANTISEPTICALLY
ANTITHETICALLY
APHELIOTROPISM
APHORISTICALLY
APODEICTICALLY
APOLOGETICALLY
APOPHTHEGMATIC
APOPLECTICALLY
APOTHEGMATICAL
APPENDICECTOMY
APPENDICULARIA
APPRENTICEHOOD
APPRENTICEMENT
APPRENTICESHIP
APPROACH-STROKE
AQUIFOLIACEOUS
ARACHNOLOGICAL
ARBORICULTURAL
ARCHAEOLOGICAL
ARCHAEORNITHES
ARCHGENETHLIAC
ARCHIEPISCOPAL
ARCTOSTAPHYLOS
ARISTOCRATICAL
ARITHMETICALLY
ARRONDISSEMENT
ARTICULATENESS
ARTIFICIALNESS
ARTILLERY-PLANT
ASCLEPIADACEAE
ASPARAGUS-STONE
ASSEVERATINGLY
ASTROGEOLOGIST
ASTROLOGICALLY
ASTROPHYSICIST
ASYMMETRICALLY
ASYMPTOTICALLY
ATTAINABLENESS
ATTEMPTABILITY
ATTITUDINARIAN
ATTRACTIVENESS
AUDIO-FREQUENCY
AUDIOMETRICIAN
AUGUSTINIANISM

AUSPICIOUSNESS
AUTHENTICATION
AUTOBIOGRAPHER
AUTOBIOGRAPHIC
AUTOCRATICALLY
AUTO-INTOXICANT
AUTORADIOGRAPH
AUTO-SUGGESTION
AUTOTYPOGRAPHY
AVARICIOUSNESS

B

BACK-SCRATCHING
BACTERIOLOGIST
BACTERIOSTASIS
BACTERIOSTATIC
BALLET-MISTRESS
BALUCHITHERIUM
BANQUETING-HALL
BARGAIN-COUNTER
BAROMETRICALLY
BARRAGE-BALLOON
BASHI-BAZOUKERY
BASIDIOMYCETES
BASTARDISATION
BATHING-COSTUME
BATHING-MACHINE
BATHYGRAPHICAL
BEAR-ANIMALCULE
BEAUTIFICATION
BED-SITTING-ROOM
BELLETRISTICAL
BENEFICIALNESS
BERBERIDACEOUS
BESEECHINGNESS
BIBLIOMANIACAL
BILL-DISCOUNTER
BILLIARD-MARKER
BIODEGRADATION
BIOELECTRICITY
BIOENGINEERING
BIOGRAPHICALLY
BIOSYSTEMATICS
BIRD-OF-PARADISE
BITUMINISATION
BLACK-MARKETEER
BLADDER-CAMPION
BLANK-CARTRIDGE
BLETHERANSKATE
BLISTERED-STEEL
BLISTER-PLASTER
BLITHESOMENESS
BLOCKADE-RUNNER
BLOOD-BESPOTTED
BLOOD-CONSUMING
BLOOD-POISONING
BLOOD-SACRIFICE
BOA-CONSTRICTOR
BOARDING-SCHOOL
BOISTEROUSNESS
BOOK-MINDEDNESS
BOROUGH-ENGLISH
BOUGAINVILLAEA
BOULEVERSEMENT
BOWDLERISATION
BRACHYCEPHALIC

BRACHYDACTYLIC
BRACHYDIAGONAL
BRACHYPINAKOID
BREAD-AND-BUTTER
BREAKFAST-TABLE
BREATHING-SPACE
BREATHING-WHILE
BREATHLESSNESS
BREMSSTRAHLUNG
BRISTOL-DIAMOND
BROBDINGNAGIAN
BRONCHIECTASIS
BRONCHO-DILATOR
BULL-HEADEDNESS
BURLING-MACHINE
BURSCHENSCHAFT
BUTTER-FINGERED
BUTTERFLY-SCREW

C
CABBAGE-LETTUCE
CABINET-EDITION
CABINET-PUDDING
CADAVEROUSNESS
CAIRNGORM-STONE
CALAMITOUSNESS
CALLIGRAPHICAL
CALORIFICATION
CALYCANTHACEAE
CAMELOPARDALIS
CAMPANOLOGICAL
CAMPANULACEOUS
CAMPYLOTROPOUS
CANNONBALL-TREE
CANTANKEROUSLY
CAPITALISATION
CAPPARIDACEOUS
CAPRICIOUSNESS
CAPRIFOLIACEAE
CAPTAIN-GENERAL
CARCINOGENESIS
CARCINOLOGICAL
CARCINOMATOSIS
CARDINAL-FLOWER
CARDIOVASCULAR
CARTOGRAPHICAL
CARTRIDGE-PAPER
CASEMENT-WINDOW
CASTANOSPERMUM
CASTLE-BUILDING
CASTRAMETATION
CATACHRESTICAL
CATADIOPTRICAL
CATECHETICALLY
CATECHUMENICAL
CATECHUMENSHIP
CATHERINE-WHEEL
CATHODOGRAPHER
CENSORIOUSNESS
CENSURABLENESS
CENTENARIANISM
CENTIMETRE-GRAM
CENTRALISATION
CENTRIFUGALISE
CENTRIFUGATION
CENTRIPETALISM

CENTUPLICATION
CHAETODONTIDAE
CHAIN-LIGHTNING
CHALCOGRAPHIST
CHAMBER-COUNSEL
CHANCELLORSHIP
CHANGEABLENESS
CHARACTERISTIC
CHARGEABLENESS
CHARITABLENESS
CHARLEY-PITCHER
CHEIROGRAPHIST
CHEIROMANTICAL
CHEMORECEPTION
CHEMORECEPTIVE
CHENOPODIACEAE
CHEST-PROTECTOR
CHEVAUX-DE-FRISE
CHICKEN-HEARTED
CHIMNEY-SWALLOW
CHIMNEY-SWEEPER
CHINCHERINCHEE
CHITTAGONG-WOOD
CHIVALROUSNESS
CHLORITE-SCHIST
CHLORITISATION
CHLORPROMAZINE
CHOLECYSTOTOMY
CHOLELITHIASIS
CHONDROCRANIUM
CHONDROGENESIS
CHOROGRAPHICAL
CHRIST-CROSS-ROW
CHRISTOLOGICAL
CHROMATOGRAPHY
CHROMATOSPHERE
CHRONOMETRICAL
CIGARETTE-PAPER
CINCHONISATION
CINEMATOGRAPHY
CIRCUIT-BREAKER
CIRCUITOUSNESS
CIRCUMAMBIENCE
CIRCUMAMBIENCY
CIRCUMAMBULATE
CIRCUMBENDIBUS
CIRCUMFERENTOR
CIRCUMFORANEAN
CIRCUMGYRATION
CIRCUMGYRATORY
CIRCUMLITTORAL
CIRCUMLOCUTION
CIRCUMLOCUTORY
CIRCUMNAVIGATE
CIRCUMNUTATION
CIRCUMNUTATORY
CIRCUMPOSITION
CIRCUMSCISSILE
CIRCUMSPECTION
CIRCUMSPECTIVE
CIRCUMSTANTIAL
CIRCUMVOLUTION
CLASS-CONSCIOUS
CLASSIFICATION
CLASSIFICATORY
CLAUSTROPHOBIA

CLAUSTROPHOBIC
CLAVICYTHERIUM
CLAW-HAMMER-COAT
CLEAR-STARCHING
CLIMATOLOGICAL
CLITTER-CLATTER
CLOAK-AND-DAGGER
COASTGUARDSMAN
COCK-A-DOODLE-DOO
COCONUT-MATTING
COELANAGLYPHIC
COESSENTIALITY
COLLIQUESCENCE
COLONEL-IN-CHIEF
COLOUR-SERGEANT
COMBUSTIBILITY
COMMANDANTSHIP
COMMENSURATELY
COMMENSURATION
COMMENTATORIAL
COMMISSARYSHIP
COMMISSIONAIRE
COMMODIOUSNESS
COMMON-OR-GARDEN
COMMONSENSICAL
COMPANION-HATCH
COMPARABLENESS
COMPASSIONABLE
COMPATIBLENESS
COMPENSATIONAL
COMPLEXIONLESS
COMPOSING-STICK
COMPOSSIBILITY
COMPREHENSIBLE
COMPREHENSIBLY
COMPUNCTIOUSLY
COMPURGATORIAL
CONCAVO-CONCAVE
CONCEIVABILITY
CONCENTRICALLY
CONCESSIONAIRE
CONCLUSIVENESS
CONDENSABILITY
CONDESCENDENCE
CONDITIONALITY
CONDUCTIBILITY
CONFIDENTIALLY
CONFORMABILITY
CONGLOMERATION
CONGLUTINATION
CONGLUTINATIVE
CONGRATULATION
CONGRATULATORY
CONGREGATIONAL
CONJUNCTIVITIS
CONNATURALNESS
CONQUISTADORES
CONSANGUINEOUS
CONSCRIPTIONAL
CONSERVATIONAL
CONSERVATORIUM
CONSOCIATIONAL
CONSPIRATORIAL
CONSTITUTIONAL
CONSTRUABILITY
CONSTRUCTIONAL

CONSTRUCTIVELY
CONSTRUCTIVISM
CONSUBSTANTIAL
CONSUETUDINARY
CONSULTING-ROOM
CONTAGIOUSNESS
CONTEMPERATION
CONTEMPERATURE
CONTEMPORANEAN
CONTEMPTUOUSLY
CONTESSERATION
CONTIGUOUSNESS
CONTINENTALISM
CONTINENTALIST
CONTINUOUSNESS
CONTRACTEDNESS
CONTRADICTABLE
CONTRADICTIOUS
CONTRAINDICANT
CONTRAINDICATE
CONTRAPOSITION
CONTRAPOSITIVE
CONTRAROTATING
CONTROLLERSHIP
CONTROVERTIBLE
CONTROVERTIBLY
CONTUMACIOUSLY
CONTUMELIOUSLY
CONVENTIONALLY
CONVERSATIONAL
CONVERSAZIONES
CONVERTIBILITY
CONVEXO-CONCAVE
CONVOCATIONIST
CONVOLVULACEAE
CONVULSIVENESS
CO-ORDINATENESS
COPPER-BOTTOMED
COPPER-FASTENED
COQUETTISHNESS
CORNET-À-PISTONS
COROLLIFLOROUS
CORPUSCULARIAN
CORPUSCULARITY
CORRESPONDENCE
CORRESPONDENCY
CORRUPTIBILITY
CORTICOSTEROID
COSMOGRAPHICAL
COSMOPOLITICAL
COST-ACCOUNTANT
COST-ACCOUNTING
COUNCIL-CHAMBER
COUNSEL-KEEPING
COUNSELLORSHIP
COUNTERBALANCE
COUNTER-BATTERY
COUNTER-CHANGED
COUNTER-CURRENT
COUNTER-MEASURE
COUNTER-OPENING
COUNTER-PASSANT
COUNTER-SALIENT
COUNTER-SKIPPER
COUNTER-SUBJECT
COUNTER-WROUGHT

COUNTRY-DANCING
COURAGEOUSNESS
COXCOMBICALITY
CREDITABLENESS
CRINKUM-CRANKUM
CROSSOPTERYGII
CROSS-REFERENCE
CROUCHED-FRIARS
CRUTCHED-FRIARS
CRYPTAESTHESIA
CRYPTAESTHETIC
CRYPTOGRAPHIST
CRYSTALLISABLE
CRYSTALLOMANCY
CUCURBITACEOUS
CURRENT-BEDDING
CURVILINEARITY
CYANOCOBALAMIN
CYCLANTHACEOUS

D

DACTYLIOGRAPHY
DAFFADOWNDILLY
DAUGHTERLINESS
DAUGHTERS-IN-LAW
DAVENPORT-TRICK
DAYLIGHT-SAVING
DAZZLE-PAINTING
DEATH-PRACTISED
DECEIVABLENESS
DECHRISTIANISE
DECIMALISATION
DECOLORISATION
DECOMPOUNDABLE
DECONSECRATION
DECORATIVENESS
DEFEASIBLENESS
DEFENESTRATION
DEFINITIVENESS
DEFLAGRABILITY
DEGENERATENESS
DELECTABLENESS
DELIBERATENESS
DELIBERATIVELY
DELIGHTFULNESS
DEMI-SEMIQUAVER
DEMOBILISATION
DEMOCRATICALLY
DEMORALISATION
DENITRIFICATOR
DENOMINATIONAL
DENOMINATIVELY
DEPARTMENTALLY
DEPLORABLENESS
DEPOLARISATION
DEPOSIT-RECEIPT
DERMATOLOGICAL
DEROGATORINESS
DESPICABLENESS
DESPITEFULNESS
DESPOTICALNESS
DESSERT-SERVICE
DESTRUCTIONIST
DESULPHURATION
DETESTABLENESS
DETOXIFICATION

DEUTERONOMICAL
DEVALORISATION
DEVIL-ON-THE-NECK
DEVITALISATION
DEXTROROTATION
DEXTROROTATORY
DIAHELIOTROPIC
DIALECTOLOGIST
DIAMANTIFEROUS
DIAMONDIFEROUS
DIAMOND-JUBILEE
DIAMOND-WEDDING
DIAPHANOUSNESS
DIAPHOTOTROPIC
DIATHERMANEITY
DICOTYLEDONOUS
DIESEL-ELECTRIC
DIFFERENTIALLY
DIFFERENTIATOR
DIFFRACTOMETER
DIMINUTIVENESS
DINITROBENZENE
DINOFLAGELLATE
DIOSCOREACEOUS
DIPLOMATICALLY
DIPLOSTEMONOUS
DIPTEROCARPOUS
DISACCOMMODATE
DISACKNOWLEDGE
DISADVENTUROUS
DISAFFIRMATION
DISAPPOINTMENT
DISAPPROBATION
DISAPPROBATIVE
DISAPPROBATORY
DISAPPROPRIATE
DISAPPROVINGLY
DISARRANGEMENT
DISASSOCIATION
DISCEPTATORIAL
DISCERPIBILITY
DISCIPLINARIAN
DISCIPLINARIUM
DISCOLOURATION
DISCOMBOBERATE
DISCOMBOBULATE
DISCOMFORTABLE
DISCOMMENDABLE
DISCONCERTMENT
DISCONFORMABLE
DISCONNECTEDLY
DISCONSOLATELY
DISCONSOLATION
DISCONTENTEDLY
DISCONTENTMENT
DISCONTINUANCE
DISCOUNT-BROKER
DISCOUNTENANCE
DISCOURAGEMENT
DISCOURAGINGLY
DISCOURTEOUSLY
DISCRETIONALLY
DISCRIMINATELY
DISCRIMINATING
DISCRIMINATION
DISCRIMINATIVE

DISCRIMINATORY
DISCURSIVENESS
DISDAINFULNESS
DISEMBARKATION
DISEMBOGUEMENT
DISEMBOWELMENT
DISENCHANTMENT
DISENCHANTRESS
DISENCUMBRANCE
DISENFRANCHISE
DISENGAGEDNESS
DISENTHRALMENT
DISENTRAINMENT
DISFURNISHMENT
DISGUSTFULNESS
DISGUSTINGNESS
DISILLUSIONARY
DISILLUSIONISE
DISIMPASSIONED
DISINCARCERATE
DISINCLINATION
DISINCORPORATE
DISINFESTATION
DISINFORMATION
DISINGENUOUSLY
DISINHERITANCE
DISINTEGRATION
DISINTEGRATIVE
DISINVESTITURE
DISJOINTEDNESS
DISORDERLINESS
DISORIENTATION
DISPENSABILITY
DISPENSATIVELY
DISPENSATORILY
DISPIRITEDNESS
DISPITEOUSNESS
DISPLEASEDNESS
DISPLENISHMENT
DISPUTABLENESS
DISPUTATIOUSLY
DISQUISITIONAL
DISREGARDFULLY
DISRESPECTABLE
DISSERTATIONAL
DISSERVICEABLE
DISSOCIABILITY
DISSOLUBLENESS
DISSOLUTIONISM
DISSOLUTIONIST
DISSOLVABILITY
DISSYMMETRICAL
DISTEMPERATURE
DISTENSIBILITY
DISTINGUISHING
DISTRACTEDNESS
DISTRIBUTIONAL
DISTRIBUTIVELY
DIVERTICULATED
DIVERTISSEMENT
DIVIDING-ENGINE
DODECASYLLABIC
DODECASYLLABLE
DOG'S-TOOTH-GRASS
DOGTOOTH-VIOLET
DOLICHOCEPHALY

DOLOMITISATION
DOUBLE-BREASTED
DOUBLE-FLOWERED
DOUBLE-STOPPING
DRAGON-STANDARD
DRESSING-JACKET
DRESS-REHEARSAL
DRILL-HUSBANDRY
DURCHKOMPONIRT
DURCHMUSTERUNG
DYER'S-GREENWEED
DYNAMO-ELECTRIC
DYNAMOMETRICAL
DYSMENORRHOEAL
DYSTELEOLOGIST

E

EARLY-VICTORIAN
EBURNIFICATION
ECCLESIASTICAL
ECCLESIASTICUS
ECCLESIOLOGIST
ECONOMETRICIAN
EDRIOPHTHALMIC
EDUCATIONALIST
EFFEMINATENESS
EGALITARIANISM
EIGEN-FREQUENCY
ELASMOBRANCHII
ELECTIONEERING
ELECTROBIOLOGY
ELECTROCHEMIST
ELECTROCULTURE
ELECTROGILDING
ELECTRONICALLY
ELECTROPLATING
ELECTROSTATICS
ELECTROTHERAPY
ELECTROTHERMAL
ELECTROTHERMIC
ELECTROVALENCY
ELECTROWINNING
ELIZABETHANISM
EMBELLISHINGLY
EMBLEMATICALLY
EMPHATICALNESS
EMPYREUMATICAL
EMULSIFICATION
ENANTIOSTYLOUS
ENCEPHALOGRAPH
ENCYCLOPAEDIAN
ENCYCLOPAEDISM
ENCYCLOPAEDIST
ENDORADIOSONDE
ENDOSMOTICALLY
ENGAGEMENT-RING
ENHARMONICALLY
ENIGMATOGRAPHY
ENTEROCENTESIS
ENTERPRISINGLY
ENTERTAININGLY
ENTHRONISATION
ENTHUSIASTICAL
ENTHYMEMATICAL
ENTOMOSTRACOUS
EPEXEGETICALLY

EPIDEMIOLOGIST
EPIGRAMMATICAL
EPISTEMOLOGIST
EPISTOLOGRAPHY
EQUIANGULARITY
EQUIPONDERANCE
ERYTHROPOIESIS
ESCHATOLOGICAL
ESTERIFICATION
ETHERIFICATION
ETHNOLOGICALLY
ETYMOLOGICALLY
EULOGISTICALLY
EUPHORBIACEOUS
EUPHUISTICALLY
EUTROPHICATION
EVANGELICALISM
EVANGELISATION
EXACERBESCENCE
EXCLAUSTRATION
EXCOMMUNICABLE
EXCREMENTITIAL
EXCRUCIATINGLY
EXHILARATINGLY
EXISTENTIALISM
EXISTENTIALIST
EXPERIENCELESS
EXPERIMENTALLY
EXPRESSIONLESS
EXPRESSIVENESS
EXTEMPORANEITY
EXTEMPORANEOUS
EXTENSIONALITY
EXTINGUISHABLE
EXTINGUISHMENT
EXTRA-CONDENSED
EXTRAFORANEOUS
EXTRA-PAROCHIAL
EXTRINSICALITY

F

FACINOROUSNESS
FACTITIOUSNESS
FAINT-HEARTEDLY
FAIRY-GODMOTHER
FALLACIOUSNESS
FALSIFIABILITY
FARTHINGSWORTH
FASHION-MONGING
FASTIDIOUSNESS
FATHERLESSNESS
FATIGUABLENESS
FAVOURABLENESS
FELLOW-COMMONER
FELLOW-CREATURE
FELLOW-TOWNSMAN
FERMENTABILITY
FERMENTESCIBLE
FERROMAGNESIAN
FERROMANGANESE
FERROPRUSSIATE
FIBROCARTILAGE
FIDDLEFADDLING
FIGURATIVENESS
FINGER-ALPHABET
FINGERPRINTING

FINGER'S-BREADTH
FIRE-WORSHIPPER
FLAGELLIFEROUS
FLAGITIOUSNESS
FLAG-LIEUTENANT
FLAMBOYANT-TREE
FLAT-FOOTEDNESS
FLIGHT-RECORDER
FLORICULTURIST
FLOWERY-KIRTLED
FOLDING-MACHINE
FOLLOW-MY-LEADER
FOOD-CONTROLLER
FORAMINIFEROUS
FORBIDDINGNESS
FORE-ORDINATION
FORESHORTENING
FORETHOUGHTFUL
FORISFAMILIATE
FORMIDABLENESS
FORTUITOUSNESS
FORTUNE-TELLING
FORWARD-LOOKING
FOSTER-DAUGHTER
FOUNDATION-STOP
FRATERNISATION
FREE-SPOKENNESS
FRIENDLESSNESS
FRINGILLACEOUS
FROLICSOMENESS
FRUCTIFICATION
FUNDAMENTALISM
FUNDAMENTALIST
FUNDAMENTALITY
FURFURALDEHYDE
FUTTOCK-SHROUDS

G

GALACTOPHOROUS
GALACTOPOIETIC
GALEOPITHECINE
GALEOPITHECOID
GALVANOPLASTIC
GASTEROMYCETES
GELATINISATION
GENEALOGICALLY
GENERALISATION
GENERAL-PURPOSE
GENETHLIACALLY
GENETHLIALOGIC
GENTLEMAN-CADET
GEOCENTRICALLY
GEOGNOSTICALLY
GEOGRAPHICALLY
GEOTHERMOMETER
GLANDULIFEROUS
GLOVE-STRETCHER
GNATHOBDELLIDA
GOLD-OF-PLEASURE
GOOD-FELLOWSHIP
GOOD-FOR-NOTHING
GOOD-HUMOUREDLY
GOOSEBERRY-BUSH
GOOSEBERRY-FOOL
GOOSEBERRY-MOTH
GOOSEBERRY-WINE

GRACE-AND-FAVOUR
GRAM-EQUIVALENT
GRAMMATICASTER
GRANDILOQUENCE
GREGARIOUSNESS
GREISENISATION
GREYWACKESLATE
GROUNDLESSNESS
GROUND-SQUIRREL
GUTTER-MERCHANT
GYNAECOLOGICAL
GYNANDROMORPHY
GYNOMONOECIOUS
GYROSTABILISER

H

HAEMATOGENESIS
HAGIOGRAPHICAL
HALF-A-SOVEREIGN
HALF-PENNYWORTH
HALLUCINOGENIC
HALORAGIDACEAE
HAMAMELIDACEAE
HANDICRAFTSMAN
HANDKERCHIEVES
HAPLOSTEMONOUS
HARMONIOUSNESS
HEALTHLESSNESS
HEART-HEAVINESS
HEART-SEARCHING
HEATHENISHNESS
HEATHER-BLEATER
HEATHER-BLUITER
HEATHER-BLUTTER
HEATHER-MIXTURE
HEAVEN-DIRECTED
HEAVENLY-MINDED
HEAVIER-THAN-AIR
HEBETUDINOSITY
HEBRAISTICALLY
HELIOSCIOPHYTE
HELMINTHOLOGIC
HEMISPHEROIDAL
HEN-AND-CHICKENS
HEPATICOLOGIST
HEPHTHEMIMERAL
HEREDITABILITY
HEREDITARINESS
HERESIOGRAPHER
HERMAPHRODITIC
HERPETOLOGICAL
HERRING-FISHERY
HETEROCHROMOUS
HETEROCHRONISM
HETEROCHRONOUS
HETEROMORPHISM
HETEROMORPHOUS
HETEROPHYLLOUS
HETEROSOMATOUS
HETEROSTROPHIC
HETEROTHALLISM
HEXACTINELLIDA
HICKERY-PICKERY
HIERARCHICALLY
HIEROGLYPHICAL
HIEROGRAMMATIC

HIEROGRAPHICAL
HIEROSOLYMITAN
HIGH-HANDEDNESS
HIGHLY-SEASONED
HIGH-MINDEDNESS
HIGH-PRIESTHOOD
HIGH-PRINCIPLED
HIPPETY-HOPPETY
HIPPOPOTAMUSES
HISTOCHEMISTRY
HISTOPATHOLOGY
HISTORIOGRAPHY
HISTRIONICALLY
HISTRIONISCISM
HOBBLEDEHOYDOM
HOBBLEDEHOYISH
HOBBLEDEHOYISM
HOLIER-THAN-THOU
HOLOMETABOLISM
HOMOEOMORPHISM
HOMOEOMORPHOUS
HOMOEOTELEUTON
HOMOEOTHERMLIC
HOMOEOTHERMOUS
HOMOGENISATION
HOMOIOTHERMOUS
HONOURABLENESS
HORROR-STRICKEN
HORSE-GODMOTHER
HORTICULTURIST
HOSPITABLENESS
HOUSE-PHYSICIAN
HUCKLEBERRYING
HUMIDIFICATION
HUMOURSOMENESS
HUNDRED-PER-CENT
HUNT-THE-SLIPPER
HYDRO-AEROPLANE
HYDROCEPHALOUS
HYDROCORALLINE
HYDRODYNAMICAL
HYDROEXTRACTOR
HYDROGRAPHICAL
HYDROMECHANICS
HYDRONEPHROSIS
HYDRONEPHROTIC
HYDROPTERIDEAE
HYDROSULPHURIC
HYETOGRAPHICAL
HYGROGRAPHICAL
HYGROSCOPICITY
HYPERACUTENESS
HYPERAESTHESIA
HYPERAESTHESIC
HYPERAESTHETIC
HYPERBATICALLY
HYPERBOLICALLY
HYPERCALCAEMIA
HYPERCATALEXIS
HYPERCRITICISE
HYPERCRITICISM
HYPERGLYCAEMIA
HYPERSENSITISE
HYPERSENSITIVE
HYPERTROPHICAL
HYPOCHONDRIASM

HYPOCHONDRIAST
HYPOCORISTICAL
HYPOCRITICALLY
HYPODERMICALLY
HYPOMIXOLYDIAN
HYPOSTATICALLY
HYPOSULPHUROUS
HYPOTHETICALLY

I

IATROCHEMISTRY
ICHNOGRAPHICAL
ICHTHYOLATROUS
ICHTHYOLOGICAL
ICHTHYOPHAGIST
ICHTHYOPHAGOUS
ICHTHYOSAURIAN
IDEALISTICALLY
IDENTIFICATION
IDIOPATHICALLY
ILL-CONDITIONED
ILLEGITIMATELY
ILLEGITIMATION
ILLITERATENESS
ILL-NATUREDNESS
ILLUSTRATIONAL
ILLUSTRATIVELY
IMAGINABLENESS
IMMACULATENESS
IMMETHODICALLY
IMMOBILISATION
IMMODERATENESS
IMPARISYLLABIC
IMPASSABLENESS
IMPASSIBLENESS
IMPERMEABILITY
IMPERTURBATION
IMPERVIABILITY
IMPERVIOUSNESS
IMPLACABLENESS
IMPLAUSIBILITY
IMPLEMENTATION
IMPONDERABILIA
IMPOSTHUMATION
IMPOVERISHMENT
IMPRACTICALITY
IMPREGNABILITY
IMPRESSIBILITY
IMPRESSIONABLE
IMPRESSIVENESS
IMPROVABLENESS
INADEQUATENESS
INADVISABILITY
INALIENABILITY
INALTERABILITY
INAPPOSITENESS
INAPPRECIATION
INAPPRECIATIVE
INAPPREHENSION
INAPPREHENSIVE
INAPPROACHABLE
INAPPROACHABLY
INARTICULATELY
INARTICULATION
INARTIFICIALLY
INARTISTICALLY

INAUSPICIOUSLY
INCAPACITATION
INCAUTIOUSNESS
INCESTUOUSNESS
INCIDENTALNESS
INCLINABLENESS
INCOGITABILITY
INCOMMENSURATE
INCOMMODIOUSLY
INCOMMUNICABLE
INCOMMUNICABLY
INCOMPLETENESS
INCOMPRESSIBLE
INCONCLUSIVELY
INCONSCIONABLE
INCONSEQUENTLY
INCONSIDERABLE
INCONSIDERABLY
INCONSISTENTLY
INCONTIGUOUSLY
INCONTROLLABLE
INCONTROLLABLY
INCONVENIENTLY
INCOORDINATION
INCORPOREALISM
INCORPOREALITY
INCREDIBLENESS
INDECIPHERABLE
INDECISIVENESS
INDECOMPOSABLE
INDECOROUSNESS
INDEFINITENESS
INDEMONSTRABLE
INDESTRUCTIBLE
INDESTRUCTIBLY
INDETERMINABLE
INDETERMINABLY
INDIFFERENTISM
INDIFFERENTIST
INDISCERPTIBLE
INDISCOVERABLE
INDISCREETNESS
INDISCRETENESS
INDISCRIMINATE
INDISPOSEDNESS
INDISTINCTNESS
INDIVISIBILITY
INDOCTRINATION
INDUBITABILITY
INEFFECTUALITY
INEVITABLENESS
INEXCUSABILITY
INEXORABLENESS
INEXPIABLENESS
INEXPRESSIBLES
INFECTIOUSNESS
INFLAMMABILITY
INFLECTIONLESS
INFLEXIBLENESS
INFRALAPSARIAN
INFRAMAXILLARY
INFRANGIBILITY
INFRASTRUCTURE
INGLORIOUSNESS
INHABITIVENESS
INHARMONIOUSLY

INIMITABLENESS
INNUMERABILITY
INORDINATENESS
INORGANISATION
INQUISITURIENT
INSATIABLENESS
INSCRUTABILITY
INSENSIBLENESS
INSEPARABILITY
INSIGNIFICANCE
INSIGNIFICANCY
INSPIRATIONISM
INSPIRATIONIST
INSTITUTIONARY
INSTRUMENTALLY
INSUFFICIENTLY
INSUPERABILITY
INSUPPRESSIBLE
INSURMOUNTABLE
INSURMOUNTABLY
INSURRECTIONAL
INTANGIBLENESS
INTEGRATIONIST
INTELLECTUALLY
INTELLIGENTIAL
INTELLIGENTSIA
INTELLIGENTZIA
INTEMPESTIVITY
INTERACTIONISM
INTERACTIONIST
INTERAMBULACRA
INTERCESSIONAL
INTERCESSORIAL
INTERCOMMUNION
INTERCOMMUNITY
INTERCONNEXION
INTERDEPENDENT
INTERESTEDNESS
INTERFERENTIAL
INTERFEROMETER
INTERFEROMETRY
INTERGRADATION
INTERJECTIONAL
INTERLINEATION
INTERLOCUTRESS
INTERLOCUTRICE
INTERMAXILLARY
INTERMEDIATELY
INTERMEDIATION
INTERMEDIATORY
INTERMIGRATION
INTERMITTENTLY
INTERMITTINGLY
INTERMOLECULAR
INTERNATIONALE
INTERPELLATION
INTERPENETRATE
INTERPLANETARY
INTERPRETATION
INTERPRETATIVE
INTERPUNCTUATE
INTERRUPTIVELY
INTERSECTIONAL
INTERSEXUALITY
INTERSPATIALLY
INTERTWINEMENT

INTERTWININGLY
INTOLERABILITY
INTRA-ABDOMINAL
INTRACTABILITY
INTRAMERCURIAL
INTRAMOLECULAR
INTRANSITIVELY
INTRANSMUTABLE
INTRINSICALITY
INTRODUCTORILY
INTUITIONALISM
INTUITIONALIST
INTUSSUSCEPTED
INVARIABLENESS
INVETERATENESS
INVINCIBLENESS
INVIOLABLENESS
IRRECOGNISABLE
IRRECONCILABLE
IRRECONCILABLY
IRREDUCIBILITY
IRREMOVABILITY
IRREPARABILITY
IRREPROACHABLE
IRREPROACHABLY
IRREPRODUCIBLE
IRRESOLUTENESS
IRRESPECTIVELY
IRRESTRAINABLE
IRRESUSCITABLE
IRRESUSCITABLY
IRREVOCABILITY
ISODIAMETRICAL
IVORY-PORCELAIN

J

JACK-BY-THE-HEDGE
JACK-IN-THE-GREEN
JOHANNISBERGER
JOUKERY-PAWKERY
JURISDICTIONAL

K

KERATINISATION
KINDERGARTENER
KINETHEODOLITE
KISSING-STRINGS
KNAPPING-HAMMER
KNEADING-TROUGH
KNIGHT-BACHELOR
KNIGHT-BANNERET
KNIGHT-ERRANTRY
KNITTING-NEEDLE
KNOTENSCHIEFER
KNOW-NOTHINGISM
KUPFERSCHIEFER

L

LABYRINTHODONT
LAMELLIROSTRAL
LAPIDIFICATION
LARYNGOLOGICAL
LARYNGOSCOPIST
LASCIVIOUSNESS
LATITUDINARIAN
LAVENDER-COTTON

LEADEN-STEPPING
LEADING-STRINGS
LEATHER-MOUTHED
LEFT-HANDEDNESS
LEGISLATORSHIP
LEGITIMATENESS
LEIBNITZIANISM
LEPIDODENDROID
LEPTODACTYLOUS
LEUCOCYTHAEMIA
LEUCOCYTOLYSIS
LEUCOCYTOPENIA
LEVELLING-STAFF
LEXICOGRAPHIST
LIBERALISATION
LIBERTARIANISM
LIBIDINOUSNESS
LICENTIOUSNESS
LIEUTENANTSHIP
LIGHTER-THAN-AIR
LIGHT-HEARTEDLY
LINGUISTICALLY
LIPOGRAMMATISM
LIPOGRAMMATIST
LITHOCHROMATIC
LITHOGRAPHICAL
LITHONTHRYPTIC
LITHONTRIPTIST
LITURGIOLOGIST
LONG-HEADEDNESS
LONGITUDINALLY
LONGS-AND-SHORTS
LONG-WINDEDNESS
LOQUACIOUSNESS
LOUPING-ON-STANE
LOVE-IN-IDLENESS
LOVING-KINDNESS
LUGGAGE-CARRIER
LUMBERSOMENESS
LUNCHEON-BASKET
LYOPHILISATION

M

MACADAMISATION
MACKEREL-BREEZE
MACROCEPHALOUS
MACRODACTYLOUS
MAGNILOQUENTLY
MAIDENHAIR-TREE
MAINTENANCE-MAN
MAJESTICALNESS
MAJOR-GENERALCY
MALACOPTERYGII
MALACOSTRACOUS
MALAPPROPRIATE
MALCONTENTEDLY
MALFUNCTIONING
MALODOROUSNESS
MANAGEABLENESS
MANIFOLD-WRITER
MARBLE-BREASTED
MARBLE-CONSTANT
MARCGRAVIACEAE
MARCHANTIACEAE
MARKETABLENESS
MARKET-GARDENER

MARRIAGE-BROKER
MARRIAGE-FAVOUR
MARTYROLOGICAL
MARVELLOUSNESS
MASS-PRODUCTION
MASTIGOPHOROUS
MATHEMATICALLY
MATRIARCHALISM
MEASURABLENESS
MEDDLESOMENESS
MEDICAMENTALLY
MEDICINE-BOTTLE
MEDITATIVENESS
MEGASPORANGIUM
MEGASPOROPHYLL
MENISPERMACEAE
MEPHISTOPHELES
MEPHISTOPHELIC
MEPHISTOPHILIS
MEPHOSTOPHILUS
MERETRICIOUSLY
MESATICEPHALIC
MESDEMOISELLES
METALLOGRAPHER
METALLOGRAPHIC
METAPHORICALLY
METAPHOSPHORIC
METAPHYSICALLY
METEMPSYCHOSES
METEMPSYCHOSIS
METEOROLOGICAL
METICULOUSNESS
METOPOSCOPICAL
METROPOLITICAL
METTLESOMENESS
MICROCEPHALOUS
MICROCHEMISTRY
MICROCOMPONENT
MICRODETECTION
MICROLOGICALLY
MICROMETEORITE
MICROMINIATURE
MICROPEGMATITE
MICROSEISMICAL
MICROSPORANGIA
MICROSTRUCTURE
MILITARISATION
MILKING-MACHINE
MILKING-PARLOUR
MILLENARIANISM
MINERALISATION
MINISTERIALIST
MIRACULOUSNESS
MISACCEPTATION
MISADVENTUROUS
MISADVISEDNESS
MISANTHROPICAL
MISAPPLICATION
MISAPPROPRIATE
MISARRANGEMENT
MISCALCULATION
MISCELLANARIAN
MISCHIEF-MAKING
MISCOMPUTATION
MISCONTENTMENT
MISIMPROVEMENT

MISINFORMATION
MISINSTRUCTION
MISINTERPRETER
MISMEASUREMENT
MISOGYNISTICAL
MISPUNCTUATION
MISTRANSLATION
MOCCASIN-FLOWER
MOCK-HEROICALLY
MOHOROVICICIAN
MONEY-SCRIVENER
MONOCARPELLARY
MONOCHLAMYDEAE
MONOCHROMATISM
MONOPHTHONGISE
MONOPLACOPHORA
MONOPRIONIDIAN
MONOSACCHARIDE
MONOTHEISTICAL
MONOTHELETICAL
MONOTONOUSNESS
MORGANATICALLY
MORPHINOMANIAC
MORPHOPHONEMIC
MOSQUITO-WEIGHT
MOTIVELESSNESS
MOUNTAIN-BEAVER
MOUNTAINEERING
MOUNTAIN-LAUREL
MOUNTAIN-MARROW
MOUNTAIN-TALLOW
MOURNING-BORDER
MUCOVISCIDOSIS
MUDDLEHEADEDLY
MULTARTICULATE
MULTICUSPIDATE
MULTIFARIOUSLY
MULTIFOLIOLATE
MULTINUCLEATED
MULTIPLICATION
MULTIPLICATIVE
MULTIRACIALISM
MUNITION-WORKER
MURDERING-PIECE
MUSHROOM-ANCHOR
MUSTARD-PLASTER
MUZZLE-VELOCITY
MYLONITISATION
MYRMECOLOGICAL
MYRMECOPHAGOUS
MYRMECOPHILOUS
MYSTERIOUSNESS
MYTHOLOGICALLY

N

NAMBY-PAMBINESS
NARCOCATHARSIS
NARCOSYNTHESIS
NATURALISATION
NATURE-PRINTING
NEANDERTHALOID
NECESSARIANISM
NECK-SWEETBREAD
NECTAREOUSNESS
NEGLECTFULNESS
NEOCOLONIALISM

NEOPYTHAGOREAN
NEUROANATOMIST
NEUROHYPNOLOGY
NEUROPATHOLOGY
NEUROPTEROIDEA
NEUTRALISATION
NEVER-NEVER-LAND
NEWFANGLEDNESS
NEWSWORTHINESS
NIETZSCHEANISM
NIGHT-BLINDNESS
NIGHT-FLOWERING
NIGHT-FOSSICKER
NIGHT-FOUNDERED
NIGHT-WANDERING
NIMBLE-FINGERED
NITROCELLULOSE
NITROGLYCERINE
NOCTAMBULATION
NOMENCLATORIAL
NON-COMMUNICANT
NON-COMPEARANCE
NON-CONCURRENCE
NON-CONTENTIOUS
NON-COOPERATION
NON-ELECTROLYTE
NON-INVOLVEMENT
NON-OPERATIONAL
NON-PERFORMANCE
NONSENSICALITY
NORTH-EASTWARDS
NORTH-NORTH-EAST
NORTH-NORTH-WEST
NORTH-WESTWARDS
NOTEWORTHINESS
NUCLEAR-POWERED
NUDIBRANCHIATA
NUTRITIOUSNESS

O

OBLIGATORINESS
OBSEQUIOUSNESS
OBSERVABLENESS
OBSTREPEROUSLY
OBSTRUCTIONIST
OCEAN-GREYHOUND
OCTINGENTENARY
ODD-COME-SHORTLY
OECUMENICALISM
OLD-GENTLEMANLY
OLEAGINOUSNESS
OLIGOCYTHAEMIA
OMNIBENEVOLENT
OMNICOMPETENCE
OMNIUM-GATHERUM
ONEIROCRITICAL
ONIROCRITICISM
ONOMATOPOIESIS
OPEN-HANDEDNESS
OPEN-MINDEDNESS
OPHTHALMOMETER
OPHTHALMOMETRY
OPHTHALMOSCOPE
OPHTHALMOSCOPY
OPINIONATIVELY
OPISTHOCOELIAN

OPISTHOCOELOUS
OPISTHOGLOSSAL
OPISTHOGRAPHIC
OPPRESSIVENESS
OPTIMALISATION
OPTIMISTICALLY
ORANGE-COLOURED
ORANGE-SQUEEZER
ORGAN-HARMONIUM
ORGANISABILITY
ORGANISATIONAL
ORGANOMETALLIC
ORNITHODELPHIA
ORNITHODELPHIC
ORNITHOLOGICAL
ORNITHOMORPHIC
ORNITHOPHILOUS
OROBANCHACEOUS
ORTHOCHROMATIC
ORTHOGRAPHICAL
ORTHOPHOSPHATE
ORTHOPTEROLOGY
OSTENTATIOUSLY
OSTEO-ARTHRITIS
OSTEOGLOSSIDAE
OSTRICH-FEATHER
OTTRELITE-SLATE
OUTLANDISHNESS
OUTRAGEOUSNESS
OUTWARD-SAINTED
OVERBURDENSOME
OVERCAPITALISE
OVERCOMPENSATE
OVER-CONFIDENCE
OVERCORRECTION
OVERDETERMINED
OVERESTIMATION
OVERINDULGENCE
OVERPOPULATION
OVERPOWERINGLY
OVERPRODUCTION
OVERREFINEMENT
OVERSCRUPULOUS
OVERSPECIALISE
OVERWHELMINGLY
OXY-HAEMOGLOBIN

P

PACHYDERMATOUS
PAINTER-STAINER
PALAEANTHROPIC
PALAEANTHROPUS
PALAEETHNOLOGY
PALAEGEOGRAPHY
PALAEOBOTANIST
PALAEOGRAPHIST
PALAEOPEDOLOGY
PALAGONITE-TUFF
PALINGENETICAL
PALMATIPARTITE
PAMPHLETEERING
PAN-AMERICANISM
PANTOGRAPHICAL
PANTOMIMICALLY
PANTOPRAGMATIC
PAPILIONACEOUS

PARADIGMATICAL
PARAGRAMMATIST
PARALEI-POMENON
PARALLELEPIPED
PARALLELOPIPED
PARALLEL-VEINED
PARAPHRASTICAL
PARAPSYCHOLOGY
PARAROSANILINE
PARASITOLOGIST
PARATACTICALLY
PARDONABLENESS
PARENCHYMATOUS
PARLIAMENT-CAKE
PARLIAMENT-HEEL
PARLOUR-BOARDER
PAROEMIOGRAPHY
PARONOMASTICAL
PARSIMONIOUSLY
PARTHENOCARPIC
PARTICULARNESS
PARTRIDGE-BERRY
PASSIFLORACEAE
PASSIONATENESS
PASTEURISATION
PATHOLOGICALLY
PATRESFAMILIAS
PATRIALISATION
PATRIARCHALISM
PENETRABLENESS
PENNATULACEOUS
PENNY-A-LINERISM
PENNY-IN-THE-SLOT
PENNYSTONE-CAST
PENTADACTYLISM
PENTADACTYLOUS
PEPPERMINT-DROP
PERCEPTIBILITY
PERCEPTIVENESS
PERCUSSION-FUSE
PERCUSSION-LOCK
PERCUTANEOUSLY
PEREMPTORINESS
PERFECTIBILIAN
PERFECTIBILISM
PERFECTIBILIST
PERFECTIBILITY
PERFIDIOUSNESS
PERIODONTOLOGY
PERIOPHTHALMUS
PERIPATETICISM
PERIPHRASTICAL
PERISHABLENESS
PERISSODACTYLA
PERMISSIBILITY
PERMISSIVENESS
PERNICIOUSNESS
PERNICKETINESS
PERSONABLENESS
PERSON-TO-PERSON
PERSUASIBILITY
PERSUASIVENESS
PERTINACIOUSLY
PERTURBATIONAL
PESTILENTIALLY
PETRARCHIANISM

PETRARCHIANIST
PETROGRAPHICAL
PETROLOGICALLY
PETTICOAT-TAILS
PHANTASMAGORIA
PHANTASMAGORIC
PHARMACEUTICAL
PHARMACOLOGIST
PHARMACOPOEIAL
PHARMACOPOEIAN
PHARMACOPOLIST
PHELLOPLASTICS
PHENOBARBITONE
PHENYLBUTAZONE
PHILANTHROPIST
PHILOLOGICALLY
PHILOSOPHASTER
PHILOSOPHERESS
PHILOSOPHISTIC
PHLEGMATICALLY
PHONEMATICALLY
PHOSPHOR-BRONZE
PHOSPHORESCENT
PHOTOCHEMISTRY
PHOTO-ENGRAVING
PHOTOGRAMMETRY
PHOTOGRAPHICAL
PHOTOPERIODISM
PHOTOSENSITISE
PHOTOSENSITIVE
PHOTOSYNTHESIS
PHOTOSYNTHETIC
PHOTOTELEGRAPH
PHRASEOLOGICAL
PHTHALOCYANINE
PHYLLOTACTICAL
PHYSIOGNOMICAL
PHYTOGENETICAL
PHYTOGEOGRAPHY
PHYTOLACCACEAE
PHYTOPATHOLOGY
PIANO-ACCORDION
PICTURE-GALLERY
PICTURE-WRITING
PIEZOCHEMISTRY
PIEZOMAGNETISM
PIGEON-BREASTED
PINCER-MOVEMENT
PINNATIPARTITE
PISCICULTURIST
PLAGUE-STRICKEN
PLANE-POLARISED
PLANET-STRICKEN
PLANING-MACHINE
PLANTAGINACEAE
PLANT-FORMATION
PLATYCEPHALOUS
PLEASURE-GIVING
PLEASURE-GROUND
PLEASURE-SEEKER
PLECTOGNATHOUS
PLENIPOTENTIAL
PLEONASTICALLY
PLEURAPOPHYSES
PLEURAPOPHYSIS
PLEURONECTIDAE

PLUMBAGINACEAE
PLUTODEMOCRACY
PLUVIOMETRICAL
PNEUMATOLOGIST
PNEUMOCONIOSIS
PNEUMOKONIOSIS
POIKILOTHERMAL
POIKILOTHERMIC
POLEMONIACEOUS
POLISHING-PASTE
POLISHING-SLATE
POLYEMBRYONATE
POLYMERISATION
POLYPLACOPHORA
POLYSACCHARIDE
POLYSYLLABICAL
POLYSYNTHETISM
POLYTHEISTICAL
PONTEDERIACEAE
PONTEFRACT-CAKE
POPULARISATION
PORCUPINE-GRASS
PORPHYROGENITE
PORTENTOUSNESS
POSSESSIVENESS
POSTMASTERSHIP
POST-MILLENNIAL
POSTPOSITIONAL
POSTPOSITIVELY
POTASSIUM-ARGON
POWDER-MAGAZINE
PRACTICABILITY
PRAERAPHAELITE
PRAGMATICALITY
PRAIRIE-CHICKEN
PRAISEWORTHILY
PRAYERLESSNESS
PREACHING-CROSS
PREACHING-FRIAR
PREACHING-HOUSE
PREARRANGEMENT
PRECARIOUSNESS
PRECOCIOUSNESS
PRECONCERTEDLY
PREDESIGNATION
PREDESIGNATORY
PREDESTINARIAN
PREDESTINATION
PREDESTINATIVE
PREDETERMINATE
PREDETERMINISM
PREDEVELOPMENT
PREDICTABILITY
PREDISPOSITION
PREFABRICATION
PREFERENTIALLY
PREMEDITATEDLY
PREMILLENARIAN
PREPONDERANTLY
PREPOSTEROUSLY
PRE-REFORMATION
PRESBYTERIALLY
PRESCRIPTIVELY
PRESENTABILITY
PRESENTATIONAL
PRESENTIMENTAL

PRESENTIVENESS
PRESERVABILITY
PRESSURE-HELMET
PRESUMPTUOUSLY
PRESUPPOSITION
PRETTIFICATION
PREVENTABILITY
PREVENTIVENESS
PRIBBLE-PRABBLE
PRICK-THE-GARTER
PRINCE-IMPERIAL
PRINTING-OFFICE
PRISON-BREAKING
PRITTLE-PRATTLE
PROBABILIORISM
PROBABILIORIST
PROCELEUSMATIC
PROCRASTINATOR
PROCRYPTICALLY
PROCURATORSHIP
PRODIGIOUSNESS
PRODUCTIBILITY
PRODUCTIVENESS
PROFESSIONALLY
PROFESSORIALLY
PROFITABLENESS
PROGENITORSHIP
PROGNOSTICATOR
PROGRESSIONARY
PROGRESSIONISM
PROGRESSIONIST
PROHIBITIONARY
PROHIBITIONISM
PROHIBITIONIST
PROLETARIANISM
PROLOCUTORSHIP
PROMISE-BREAKER
PROMISE-CRAMMED
PROMISE-KEEPING
PRONUNCIAMENTO
PROPAEDEUTICAL
PROPELLER-SHAFT
PROPERTY-MASTER
PROPITIATORILY
PROPITIOUSNESS
PROPORTIONABLE
PROPORTIONABLY
PROPORTIONALLY
PROPORTIONLESS
PROPORTIONMENT
PROPRIETORSHIP
PROPRIOCEPTIVE
PROSCRIPTIVELY
PROSENCEPHALIC
PROSENCEPHALON
PROSPEROUSNESS
PROTECTIVENESS
PROTEVANGELIUM
PROTHONOTARIAL
PROTHONOTARIAT
PROTISTOLOGIST
PROTOSPATHAIRE
PROTOTRACHEATA
PROTOZOOLOGIST
PROTRUSIVENESS
PROUD-STOMACHED

PROVIDENTIALLY
PROVINCIAL-ROSE
PROVOST-MARSHAL
PRUSSIFICATION
PSEPHOANALYSIS
PSEUDAESTHESIA
PSEUDEPIGRAPHA
PSEUDEPIGRAPHY
PSEUDO-ARCHAISM
PSEUDOMEMBRANE
PSEUDONYMOUSLY
PSEUDOSOLUTION
PSEUDOSYMMETRY
PSILANTHROPISM
PSILANTHROPIST
PSYCHOANALYSIS
PSYCHOANALYTIC
PSYCHOCHEMICAL
PSYCHODYNAMICS
PSYCHOMETRICAL
PSYCHONEUROSIS
PSYCHONEUROTIC
PSYCHOPHYSICAL
PSYCHOSOMATICS
PTERIDOPHILIST
PTERYLOGRAPHIC
PUBLIC-SPIRITED
PUGILISTICALLY
PUGNACIOUSNESS
PURPLE-COLOURED
PURPOSEFULNESS
PURSE-SNATCHING
PYJAMA-TROUSERS
PYRENOMYCETOUS
PYRHELIOMETRIC
PYROPHOSPHORIC
PYROPHOTOGRAPH
PYTHAGOREANISM

Q

QUADRAGENARIAN
QUADRANGULARLY
QUADRIENNIALLY
QUADRIGEMINATE
QUADRIGEMINOUS
QUADRISYLLABIC
QUADRISYLLABLE
QUANTIFICATION
QUANTITATIVELY
QUAQUAVERSALLY
QUARTER-GALLERY
QUARTZ-PORPHYRY
QUATTROCENTISM
QUATTROCENTIST
QUERIMONIOUSLY
QUESTION-MASTER
QUICKSILVERING
QUICKSILVERISH
QUILTING-COTTON
QUINQUAGESIMAL
QUINQUECOSTATE
QUINQUEFARIOUS
QUINQUEFOLIATE
QUINQUENNIALLY
QUINQUEVALENCE
QUINTESSENTIAL

QUIZZIFICATION

R

RABBETING-PLANE
RABBIT-SQUIRREL
RABELAISIANISM
RADIOASTRONOMY
RADIOAUTOGRAPH
RADIOCHEMISTRY
RADIOSENSITISE
RADIOSENSITIVE
RADIO-STRONTIUM
RADIOTELEGRAPH
RADIOTELEPHONE
RADIOTELEPHONY
RADIO-TELESCOPE
RAMBUNCTIOUSLY
RAMPAGEOUSNESS
RANUNCULACEOUS
REAPING-MACHINE
REAPPRAISEMENT
REAR-VIEW-MIRROR
REASONABLENESS
REBELLIOUSNESS
RECALCITRATION
RECAPITULATION
RECAPITULATIVE
RECAPITULATORY
RECEIVABLENESS
RECEIVING-HOUSE
RECEIVING-ORDER
RECEPTION-ORDER
RECITATION-ROOM
RECOLONISATION
RECOMMENCEMENT
RECOMMENDATION
RECOMMENDATORY
RECONCILIATION
RECONCILIATORY
RECONDENSATION
RECONNAISSANCE
RECONSECRATION
RECONSTITUTION
RECONSTRUCTION
RECONSTRUCTIVE
RECOVERABILITY
RECTANGULARITY
RECTILINEARITY
RECURVIROSTRAL
REDINTEGRATION
REDISTILLATION
REDISTRIBUTION
REED-INSTRUMENT
REFLECTIONLESS
REFLECTIVENESS
REFORMATIONIST
REFRACTORINESS
REFRANGIBILITY
REGARDLESSNESS
REGENERATIVELY
REGRESSIVENESS
REGULARISATION
REHABILITATION
REINTRODUCTION
REINVIGORATION
REJUVENESCENCE

RELENTLESSNESS
RELINQUISHMENT
REMARKABLENESS
REMBRANDTESQUE
REMEDILESSNESS
REMINISCENTIAL
REMONETISATION
REMORSEFULNESS
REORGANISATION
REPETITIVENESS
REPREHENSIVELY
REPRESENTATION
REPRESENTATIVE
REPRODUCTIVELY
REPRODUCTIVITY
REPUDIATIONIST
REQUISITIONARY
REQUISITIONIST
RESINIFICATION
RESISTANCE-COIL
RESISTLESSNESS
RESPECTABILITY
RESPECTFULNESS
RESPONSIBILITY
RESPONSIVENESS
RESTITUTIONISM
RESTITUTIONIST
RESTORABLENESS
RESTORATIONISM
RESTORATIONIST
RESTRAINEDNESS
RESTRICTIONIST
RESULTLESSNESS
RESURRECTIONAL
RETALIATIONIST
RETRANSMISSION
RETROCOGNITION
RETROGRADATION
RETROOPERATIVE
REVALORISATION
REVENGEFULNESS
REVIVIFICATION
REWARDABLENESS
RHEUMATOLOGIST
RHINENCEPHALIC
RHINENCEPHALON
RHINOCEROS-BIRD
RHINOCEROTIDAE
RHIZOPHORACEAE
RHOMBENPORPHYR
RHYNCHOPHOROUS
RHYPAROGRAPHER
RHYPAROGRAPHIC
RIBBON-BUILDING
RICE-POLISHINGS
RICKETTSIACEAE
RIDICULOUSNESS
RIDING-BREECHES
RIDING-INTEREST
ROAD-WORTHINESS
ROBIN-REDBREAST
ROBUSTIOUSNESS
ROCHELLE-POWDER
RÖNTGENOGRAPHY
ROSICRUCIANISM
ROSTROCARINATE

ROUGH-AND-TUMBLE
ROUNDABOUTEDLY
ROUNDABOUTNESS
RUBBER-SOLUTION
RUMBLE-GUMPTION
RUMMEL-GUMPTION
RUMMLE-GUMPTION
RUNNING-BANQUET
RUSSIANISATION
RUSSO-BYZANTINE

S

SABBATARIANISM
SABBATH-BREAKER
SACCHARIFEROUS
SACRAMENTALISM
SACRAMENTALIST
SACRAMENTARIAN
SACRAMENT-HOUSE
SACRILEGIOUSLY
SALAMANDER-LIKE
SALMON-COLOURED
SALOON-CARRIAGE
SALTPETRE-PAPER
SALUBRIOUSNESS
SANCTIFICATION
SANGUIFICATION
SANGUINARINESS
SANGUINIVOROUS
SANSCULOTTERIE
SAPONIFICATION
SAPPHIRE-QUARTZ
SARRACENIACEAE
SATISFACTORILY
SAUROPTERYGIAN
SAUSAGE-BASSOON
SAVANNA-SPARROW
SAXIFRAGACEOUS
SCALE-STAIRCASE
SCANDALISATION
SCANDALMONGING
SCANDALOUSNESS
SCAPHOCEPHALIC
SCAPHOCEPHALUS
SCAREMONGERING
SCATTER-BRAINED
SCEUOPHYLACIUM
SCHEMATISATION
SCHISMATICALLY
SCHIZOGNATHOUS
SCHOLASTICALLY
SCHOOL-DIVINITY
SCHOOLMASTERLY
SCHOOLMISTRESS
SCHOOL-TEACHING
SCHOONER-RIGGED
SCHWENKFELDIAN
SCIENTIFICALLY
SCINTILLOSCOPE
SCINTOLLOMETER
SCLEROPHYLLOUS
SCOMBRESOCIDAE
SCORPION-SPIDER
SCOTTIFICATION
SCREW-PROPELLER
SCRIBBLING-BOOK

SCRUBBING-BOARD
SCRUBBING-BRUSH
SCRUPULOUSNESS
SCRUTINISINGLY
SCURRILOUSNESS
SEA-GILLIFLOWER
SEASONABLENESS
SECULARISATION
SEGREGATIONIST
SEISMOMETRICAL
SELF-ABNEGATION
SELF-ABSORPTION
SELF-ACCUSATION
SELF-ACCUSATORY
SELF-ADVERTISER
SELF-AFFRIGHTED
SELF-ASSUMPTION
SELF-COMPARISON
SELF-COMPLACENT
SELF-CONDEMNING
SELF-CONFIDENCE
SELF-CONSEQUENT
SELF-CONSISTENT
SELF-CONTROLLED
SELF-CONVICTION
SELF-DETERMINED
SELF-DISCIPLINE
SELF-DISPLEASED
SELF-EFFACEMENT
SELF-EMPLOYMENT
SELF-EXPRESSION
SELF-GOVERNMENT
SELF-HETERODYNE
SELF-IMMOLATION
SELF-IMPORTANCE
SELF-INDUCTANCE
SELF-INDULGENCE
SELF-INTERESTED
SELF-NEGLECTING
SELF-SATISFYING
SELF-SUFFICIENT
SELF-SUGGESTION
SELF-SUPPORTING
SELF-SUSTAINING
SELF-SUSTENANCE
SELF-TORMENTING
SELF-TORTURABLE
SEMAPHORICALLY
SEMICARBAZONES
SEMI-CENTENNIAL
SEMICIRCULARLY
SEMI-ELLIPTICAL
SEMI-OCCASIONAL
SEMI-OFFICIALLY
SEMPSTRESS-SHIP
SENSATIONALISM
SENSATIONALIST
SENSUALISATION
SENTIMENTALISE
SENTIMENTALISM
SENTIMENTALIST
SENTIMENTALITY
SEPTUAGENARIAN
SEQUACIOUSNESS
SERGEANT-AT-ARMS
SERICITISATION

S14

SERJEANT-AT-ARMS
SERPENT-GODDESS
SERPENTINE-ROCK
SERPENTININGLY
SERPENT-WORSHIP
SERRATIROSTRAL
SERVICEABILITY
SERVO-MECHANISM
SESQUIPEDALIAN
SESQUIPEDALITY
SESQUISULPHIDE
SHAKESPEARIANA
SHAMEFACEDNESS
SHATTER-BRAINED
SHAWLWAISTCOAT
SHEEP-WHISTLING
SHEET-LIGHTNING
SHELF-CATALOGUE
SHELL-LIMESTONE
SHERIFF-OFFICER
SHIFTING-BOARDS
SHILLINGSWORTH
SHILLY-SHALLIER
SHIP'S-CARPENTER
SHOOTING-JACKET
SHORT-SIGHTEDLY
SHOULDER-GIRDLE
SHOULDER-HEIGHT
SHOVE-HALFPENNY
SHRILL-SHRIKING
SIEGE-ARTILLERY
SIGILLARIACEAE
SILICIFICATION
SILVER-SHEDDING
SIMPLIFICATION
SIMPLIFICATIVE
SIMULTANEOUSLY
SINGING-GALLERY
SINGLE-BREASTED
SINISTRORSALLY
SKELETON-SHRIMP
SKIMBLE-SKAMBLE
SKUNK-BLACKBIRD
SLANDEROUSNESS
SLANTENDICULAR
SLANTINDICULAR
SLATTERNLINESS
SLAUGHTER-HOUSE
SLAUGHTEROUSLY
SLEEPY-SICKNESS
SLUG-FOOT-SECOND
SMELLING-BOTTLE
SMOKING-CONCERT
SNAPPING-TURTLE
SNIPPER-SNAPPER
SNIP-SNAP-SNORUM
SNOW-SPECTACLES
SOLECISTICALLY
SOLICITOUSNESS
SOLIDIFICATION
SOLITAIRE-BOARD
SOLITUDINARIAN
SOLUBILISATION
SOMNAMBULATION
SOMNAMBULISTIC
SONNET-SEQUENCE

SOPHISTICATION
SOPORIFEROUSLY
SOTERIOLOGICAL
SOUL-CONFIRMING
SOUTH-EASTWARDS
SOUTH-SOUTH-EAST
SOUTH-SOUTH-WEST
SOUTH-WESTWARDS
SOVIETOLOGICAL
SPACE-TRAVELLER
SPADE-HUSBANDRY
SPARROW-BLASTED
SPATIOTEMPORAL
SPAWNING-GROUND
SPECIALISATION
SPECTACULARITY
SPECTROGRAPHIC
SPECTROLOGICAL
SPECTROSCOPIST
SPEECHLESSNESS
SPEECH-TRAINING
SPELAEOLOGICAL
SPERMATOGENOUS
SPERMATOGONIUM
SPERMATOPHYTIC
SPERMATORRHOEA
SPHAEROCRYSTAL
SPHYGMOGRAPHIC
SPINDLE-SHANKED
SPINTHARISCOPE
SPIRITLESSNESS
SPIRIT-STIRRING
SPIRITUALISTIC
SPIRITUOUSNESS
SPIROCHAETOSIS
SPORANGIOPHORE
SPORANGIOSPORE
SPREAD-EAGLEISM
SPRIGHTFULNESS
SPRING-CARRIAGE
SPRING-CLEANING
SPRING-LIGAMENT
SPRING-MATTRESS
SQUADRON-LEADER
SQUIRREL-MONKEY
STAGE-DIRECTION
STALACTITIFORM
STAMP-COLLECTOR
STAMPING-GROUND
STANDARD-BEARER
STANDING-GROUND
STAPHYLOCOCCUS
STAPHYLORRAPHY
STARCH-HYACINTH
STAR-OF-THE-EARTH
STAR-OF-THE-NIGHT
STATIONARINESS
STATION-MANAGER
STATUESQUENESS
STEEL-ENGRAVING
STEEPLECHASING
STEEPLE-CROWNED
STEGANOGRAPHER
STEGANOGRAPHIC
STEGOCEPHALIAN
STEGOCEPHALOUS

STENOGRAPHICAL
STENTOROPHONIC
STEREOISOMERIC
STEREOMETRICAL
STEREOSCOPICAL
STERTOROUSNESS
STETHOSCOPICAL
STICHOMETRICAL
STIGMATIFEROUS
STIGMATISATION
STILETTO-HEELED
STIRRUP-LEATHER
STOICHEIOMETRY
STOMACHFULNESS
STOMATOGASTRIC
STOOPE-GALLAUNT
STOUT-HEARTEDLY
STRABISMOMETER
STRADDLE-LEGGED
STRAND-SCOURING
STRATIFICATION
STRATIGRAPHIST
STRAWBERRY-LEAF
STRAWBERRY-MARK
STRAWBERRY-TREE
STREET-RAILROAD
STREPSIPTEROUS
STRETCHING-BOND
STRETCHING-IRON
STRIKE-BREAKING
STROBILISATION
STULTIFICATION
STULTILOQUENCE
STUMBLING-BLOCK
STUMBLING-STONE
STUPENDOUSNESS
STURMABTEILUNG
SUBALTERNATION
SUBARBORESCENT
SUBCONSCIOUSLY
SUBCONTINENTAL
SUBCONTRARIETY
SUBCUTANEOUSLY
SUBGENERICALLY
SUBINFEUDATION
SUBINFEUDATORY
SUBINSINUATION
SUBJECT-HEADING
SUBJECTIVENESS
SUBJECTIVISTIC
SUBMERGIBILITY
SUBMERSIBILITY
SUBMISSIVENESS
SUBSTANTIALISE
SUBSTANTIALISM
SUBSTANTIALITY
SUBSTANTIATION
SUBSTANTIVALLY
SUBSTITUTIONAL
SUBTERPOSITION
SUBTERRESTRIAL
SUBTERSENSUOUS
SUCCESSFULNESS
SUCCESSIONALLY
SUCCESSIONLESS
SUCCESSIVENESS

SUCCULENT-HOUSE
SUFFERABLENESS
SUGGESTIBILITY
SUGGESTIVENESS
SULPHANILAMIDE
SULPHAPYRIDINE
SULPHATHIAZOLE
SUPERABUNDANCE
SUPERANNUATION
SUPERCARGOSHIP
SUPERCELESTIAL
SUPERCILIOUSLY
SUPERCONDUCTOR
SUPERELEVATION
SUPEREMINENTLY
SUPEREROGATIVE
SUPEREROGATORY
SUPERESSENTIAL
SUPEREXCELLENT
SUPERFICIALISE
SUPERFICIALITY
SUPERFOETATION
SUPERINCUMBENT
SUPERINDUCTION
SUPERINTENDENT
SUPERNATURALLY
SUPEROVULATION
SUPERPHOSPHATE
SUPERSCRIPTION
SUPERSENSITIVE
SUPERSTRUCTION
SUPERSTRUCTIVE
SUPERSTRUCTURE
SUPERVISORSHIP
SUPPLEMENTALLY
SUPPLICATINGLY
SUPPOSITIONARY
SUPPOSITITIOUS
SUPRALAPSARIAN
SURE-FOOTEDNESS
SURPASSINGNESS
SURPRISINGNESS
SUSCEPTIBILITY
SUSPENSIBILITY
SUSPICIOUSNESS
SWADDLING-CLOTH
SWATHING-CLOUTS
SWEET-AND-TWENTY
SWINDGE-BUCKLER
SWINGLING-STOCK
SWOOPSTAKE-LIKE
SWORD-SWALLOWER
SYCOPHANTISHLY
SYMBOLICALNESS
SYMMETRISATION
SYMMETROPHOBIA
SYMPTOMATOLOGY
SYNAPOSEMATISM
SYNCHRONICALLY
SYNONYMOUSNESS
SYROPHOENICIAN
SYSTEMATICALLY

T

TABERNACLEWORK
TABULARISATION

TACHEOMETRICAL
TACHISTOSCOPIC
TACHYGRAPHICAL
TALKING-MACHINE
TALLOW-CHANDLER
TARIFF-REFORMER
TATTERDEMALION
TAUTOLOGICALLY
TELANGIECTASIS
TELANGIECTATIC
TELAUTOGRAPHIC
TELEGRAPH-BOARD
TELEGRAPH-CABLE
TELEGRAPH-PLANT
TELEOLOGICALLY
TELEPATHICALLY
TELEPHONICALLY
TELEPHOTOGRAPH
TELESCOPICALLY
TELESMATICALLY
TELETYPEWRITER
TEMPERAMENTFUL
TERGIVERSATION
TERMINABLENESS
TERMINOLOGICAL
TERRITORIALISE
TERRITORIALISM
TERRITORIALIST
TERRITORIALITY
TERROR-STRICKEN
TESTAMENTARILY
TESTIMONIALISE
TETRACHOTOMOUS
TETRADACTYLOUS
TETRAGRAMMATON
THALASSOGRAPHY
THAUMATOGRAPHY
THAUMATURGICAL
THEATRICALNESS
THEOCRATICALLY
THEOPASCHITISM
THEOSOPHICALLY
THERIANTHROPIC
THERIOMORPHISM
THERIOMORPHOUS
THERMOCHEMICAL
THERMODYNAMICS
THERMO-ELECTRIC
THERMOMETRICAL
THIMBLE-RIGGING
THIRD-PROGRAMME
THOUGHTFULNESS
THOUGHT-PROCESS
THOUGHT-READING
THRASHINGFLOOR
THREADBARENESS
THREE-FARTHINGS
THREE-HALFPENCE
THREE-HALFPENNY
THRESHING-FLOOR
THRIFTLESSNESS
THROMBOPLASTIN
THROUGH-GANGING
THROUGH-TRAFFIC
THYMELAEACEOUS
THYROTOXICOSIS

THYSANOPTEROUS
TIDE-WAITERSHIP
TINTINNABULANT
TINTINNABULARY
TINTINNABULATE
TINTINNABULOUS
TITTLE-TATTLING
TOBACCO-STOPPER
TOPSYTURVINESS
TORSION-BALANCE
TOWN-COUNCILLOR
TRACHYPTERIDAE
TRACTION-ENGINE
TRADITIONALISM
TRADITIONALIST
TRADITIONALITY
TRADITIONARILY
TRAFFIC-MANAGER
TRAFFIC-RETURNS
TRAFFIC-SIGNALS
TRAGI-COMICALLY
TRAITOROUSNESS
TRANSCENDENTAL
TRANSCENDENTLY
TRANSFER-TICKET
TRANSFORMATION
TRANSFORMATIVE
TRANSFORMISTIC
TRANSFUSIONIST
TRANSITIONALLY
TRANSITIVENESS
TRANSITORINESS
TRANSLITERATOR
TRANSMIGRATION
TRANSMIGRATIVE
TRANSMIGRATORY
TRANSMISSIONAL
TRANSMISSIVITY
TRANSMOGRIFIED
TRANSPLANTABLE
TRANSPORTATION
TRANSPORTINGLY
TRANSPORT-RIDER
TRANS-SEXUALISM
TRANSVALUATION
TRANSVERSALITY
TRANSVESTITISM
TRAVELLER'S-TREE
TREACLE-MUSTARD
TREE-WORSHIPPER
TREMENDOUSNESS
TRENCHER-FRIEND
TRENCHER-KNIGHT
TRICHINISATION
TRICHOBACTERIA
TRICHOMONIASIS
TRICHOPHYTOSIS
TRICHOTOMOUSLY
TRICONSONANTAL
TRICONSONANTIC
TRIDIMENSIONAL
TRIMETHYLAMINE
TRINITARIANISM
TRINITROPHENOL
TRINITROTOLUOL
TRINKUM-TRANKUM

TRIPERSONALISM
TRIPERSONALIST
TRIPERSONALITY
TRIPHENYLAMINE
TRISOCTAHEDRON
TRITUBERCULATE
TRITUBERCULISM
TRIVIALISATION
TROCHELMINTHES
TROPHONEUROSIS
TROPOLOGICALLY
TROUBLESHOOTER
TRUE-LOVER'S-KNOT
TRUMPET-TONGUED
TUMULTUOUSNESS
TURBINE-STEAMER
TURF-ACCOUNTANT
TURPENTINE-TREE
TURQUOISE-GREEN
TWO-DIMENSIONAL
TWO-FOR-HIS-HEELS
TYRANNICALNESS

U

ULTIMOGENITURE
ULTRACREPIDATE
ULTRAMICROTOME
ULTRAMONTANISM
ULTRAMONTANIST
ULTRA-NEPTUNIAN
ULTRASTRUCTURE
ULTRONEOUSNESS
UMBRAGEOUSNESS
UNACCOMMODATED
UNACCOMPLISHED
UNACKNOWLEDGED
UNACQUAINTANCE
UNAFFECTEDNESS
UNAPPRECIATIVE
UNAPPREHENSIVE
UNAPPROACHABLE
UNAPPROACHABLY
UNAPPROPRIATED
UNARTIFICIALLY
UNASPIRINGNESS
UNASSUMINGNESS
UNATTRACTIVELY
UNAUTHENTICITY
UNAVOIDABILITY
UNBEARABLENESS
UNBECOMINGNESS
UNBLAMABLENESS
UNBUSINESSLIKE
UNCERTIFICATED
UNCHEERFULNESS
UNCHRISTIANISE
UNCIRCUMCISION
UNCOMMUNICABLE
UNCOMMUNICATED
UNCOMPREHENDED
UNCOMPROMISING
UNCONCEIVEABLE
UNCONCILIATORY
UNCONFEDERATED
UNCONGENIALITY
UNCONSCIONABLE

UNCONSCIONABLY
UNCONSOLIDATED
UNCONTAMINATED
UNCONTEMPLATED
UNCONTRADICTED
UNCONTROLLABLE
UNCONTROLLABLY
UNCONTROLLEDLY
UNCONTROVERTED
UNCONVENTIONAL
UNCORROBORATED
UNCRYSTALLISED
UNDECIPHERABLE
UNDECOMPOSABLE
UNDEMONSTRABLE
UNDENIABLENESS
UNDERCLERKSHIP
UNDERDEVELOPED
UNDERGRADUETTE
UNDERMENTIONED
UNDERNOURISHED
UNDER-SECRETARY
UNDERSTANDABLE
UNDERSTATEMENT
UNDERSTRAPPING
UNDERVALUATION
UNDESERVEDNESS
UNDESIGNEDNESS
UNDESIRABILITY
UNDESPAIRINGLY
UNDETERMINABLE
UNDIMINISHABLE
UNDISCOVERABLE
UNDISCOVERABLY
UNDISTRACTEDLY
UNDOMESTICATED
UNENTERPRISING
UNENTERTAINING
UNEXPECTEDNESS
UNEXTINGUISHED
UNFAITHFULNESS
UNFLAPPABILITY
UNFLATTERINGLY
UNFOREKNOWABLE
UNFRIENDEDNESS
UNFRIENDLINESS
UNFRUITFULNESS
UNGRACEFULNESS
UNGRACIOUSNESS
UNGRATEFULNESS
UNGROUNDEDNESS
UNHANDSOMENESS
UNHESITATINGLY
UNIDIRECTIONAL
UNIFORMITARIAN
UNILLUMINATING
UNINCORPORATED
UNINTELLECTUAL
UNINTELLIGIBLE
UNINTELLIGIBLY
UNINTERMITTING
UNINTOXICATING
UNIVERSALISTIC
UNIVERSITARIAN
UNKNIGHTLINESS
UNKNOWABLENESS

UNMALLEABILITY
UNMANNERLINESS
UNMANUFACTURED
UNMARRIAGEABLE
UNMATERIALISED
UNMATHEMATICAL
UNMATRICULATED
UNMENTIONABLES
UNMERCHANTABLE
UNMERCIFULNESS
UNMETAPHORICAL
UNMETAPHYSICAL
UNOSTENTATIOUS
UNPASSABLENESS
UNPLEASANTNESS
UNPOETICALNESS
UNPRACTICALITY
UNPRAISEWORTHY
UNPREMEDITABLE
UNPREMEDITATED
UNPREPAREDNESS
UNPREPOSSESSED
UNPRESUMPTUOUS
UNPRETENDINGLY
UNPRODUCTIVELY
UNPRODUCTIVITY
UNPROFESSIONAL
UNPROPITIOUSLY
UNPROPORTIONED
UNPROSPEROUSLY
UNPURCHASEABLE
UNQUESTIONABLE
UNQUESTIONABLY
UNREADABLENESS
UNRECOGNISABLE
UNRECOGNISABLY
UNRECONCILABLE
UNRECONCILABLY
UNREFLECTINGLY
UNRELIABLENESS
UNREMORSEFULLY
UNREMUNERATIVE
UNREPRODUCIBLE
UNRESERVEDNESS
UNRESOLVEDNESS
UNRESPONSIVELY
UNRESTRAINABLE
UNRESTRAINEDLY
UNRESTRICTEDLY
UNRHYTHMICALLY
UNRIGHTFULNESS
UNROMANTICALLY
UNSATISFACTION
UNSATISFACTORY
UNSCRIPTURALLY
UNSCRUPULOUSLY
UNSECTARIANISM
UNSISTERLINESS
UNSOCIABLENESS
UNSOPHISTICATE
UNSPIRITUALISE
UNSPLINTERABLE
UNSTRENGTHENED
UNSUCCESSFULLY
UNSUITABLENESS
UNSURMOUNTABLE

UNSUSPECTINGLY
UNSUSPICIOUSLY
UNSYMPATHISING
UNSYSTEMATICAL
UNSYSTEMATISED
UNTAMEABLENESS
UNTHANKFULNESS
UNTHINKABILITY
UNTHINKINGNESS
UNTHOUGHTFULLY
UNTOWARDLINESS
UNTRANSFERABLE
UNTRANSLATABLE
UNTRANSLATABLY
UNTRANSMUTABLE
UNTRUTHFULNESS
UNVANQUISHABLE
UNWATCHFULNESS
UNYIELDINGNESS
UPROARIOUSNESS
USTILAGINACEAE
UTEROGESTATION
UTILITARIANISE
UTILITARIANISM

V

VAINGLORIOUSLY
VALENTINIANISM
VALERIANACEOUS
VALETUDINARIAN
VASODILATATION
VASODILATATORY
VEGETATIVENESS
VERISIMILITUDE
VERSE-MONGERING
VERTICILLASTER
VIBROFLOTATION
VICAR-APOSTOLIC
VICE-CHANCELLOR
VICE-CONSULSHIP
VICE-PRESIDENCY
VICTORIOUSNESS
VIGESIMO-QUARTO

VINDICTIVENESS
VITALISTICALLY
VITILITIGATION
VITRESCIBILITY
VITRIOLISATION
VITUPERATIVELY
VIVIPAROUSNESS
VIVISECTIONIST
VOCIFEROUSNESS
VOLATILISATION
VOLCANOLOGICAL
VOLUMETRICALLY
VOLUMINOUSNESS
VOLUPTUOUSNESS
VULCANOLOGICAL
VULNERABLENESS

W

WARRANT-OFFICER
WASHING-MACHINE
WATCH-COMMITTEE
WATER-BAROMETER
WATER-BREATHING
WATER-COLOURIST
WATERING-TROUGH
WATER-PRIVILEGE
WATER-REPELLENT
WATERTIGHTNESS
WEAK-MINDEDNESS
WEAPONSCHAWING
WEARING-APPAREL
WEATHER-PROPHET
WEATHER-STATION
WEDDING-GARMENT
WEEDING-FORCEPS
WEIGHTLESSNESS
WELL-ACQUAINTED
WELL-THOUGHT-OUT
WESTERNISATION
WHIPPER-SNAPPER
WHISPERING-DOME
WHITTIE-WHATTIE
WHOLE-HEARTEDLY

WIDOW-BEWITCHED
WILHELMSTRASSE
WILLING-HEARTED
WIND-INSTRUMENT
WINDOW-DRESSING
WINDOW-SHOPPING
WINTER-QUARTERS
WITCHES-THIMBLE
WITHERING-FLOOR
WONDER-STRICKEN
WOOD-NIGHTSHADE
WOOLLEN-DRAPERY
WORCESTER-BERRY
WORCESTER-SAUCE
WORKING-DRAWING
WORSHIPFULNESS
WREATH-FILAMENT

X

XANTHOMELANOUS
XIPHIHUMERALIS
XYLOPYROGRAPHY
XYLOTYPOGRAPHY

Y

YELLOW-BREASTED
YELLOW-CENTAURY
YELLOW-YOLDRING
YTTROCOLUMBITE
YTTROTANTALITE

Z

ZEBRA-PARRAKEET
ZENITH-DISTANCE
ZINCKIFICATION
ZINCOGRAPHICAL
ZINGIBERACEOUS
ZINZIBERACEOUS
ZOOPHYTOLOGIST
ZOROASTRIANISM
ZYGOBRANCHIATA
ZYGOBRANCHIATE
ZYGOPHYLLACEAE

A

ABIOGENETICALLY
ACCLIMATISATION
ACCOUNTABLENESS
ACHONDROPLASTIC
ACKNOWLEDGEABLE
ACKNOWLEDGEABLY
ACKNOWLEDGEMENT
ACQUISITIVENESS
ADJUTANT-GENERAL
ADVENTUROUSNESS
AFFRANCHISEMENT
AGRICULTURALIST

AIR-CHIEF-MARSHAL
AIR-CONDITIONING
AIRCRAFT-CARRIER
ALL-CHANGING-WORD
ALLOTRIOMORPHIC
AMARYLLIDACEOUS
AMBULANCE-CHASER
AMPHITHEATRICAL
ANACREONTICALLY
ANAESTHESIOLOGY
ANAESTHETICALLY
ANCESTOR-WORSHIP
ANDROMONOECIOUS
ANGUSTIROSTRATE

ANKYLOSTOMIASIS
ANNIHILATIONISM
ANNUNCIATION-DAY
ANTEPENULTIMATE
ANTHROPOBIOLOGY
ANTHROPOCENTRIC
ANTHROPOGENESIS
ANTHROPOLOGICAL
ANTHROPOMORPHIC
ANTHROPOPATHISM
ANTHROPOPHAGITE
ANTHROPOPHAGOUS
ANTHROPOPSYCHIC
ANTHROPOSOPHIST

ANTICHRISTIANLY
ANTICLERICALISM
ANTI-GALLICANISM
ANTIMONARCHICAL
ANTIPERISTALTIC
ANTITRINITARIAN
ANTIVIVISECTION
APOCALYPTICALLY
APOLLINARIANISM
APOPHTHEGMATISE
APOPHTHEGMATIST
APPROACHABILITY
APPROPINQUATION
APPROPRIATENESS
ARBORICULTURIST
ARCHICHLAMYDEAE
ARCHIEPISCOPACY
ARCHIEPISCOPATE
ARCHITECTONICAL
ARGUMENTATIVELY
ARISTOTELIANISM
ARMOURED-CRUISER
ASCLEPIADACEOUS
ATHEROSCLEROSIS
ATMOSPHERICALLY
ATTORNEY-GENERAL
AUTHORITATIVELY
AUTOGRAPHICALLY
AUTOMORPHICALLY
AUTORADIOGRAPHY
AUTOSCHEDIASTIC

B

BACCHANALIANISM
BACTERIOLOGICAL
BANQUETING-HOUSE
BARGAIN-BASEMENT
BARTHOLOMEW-TIDE
BEFORE-MENTIONED
BIBLIOGRAPHICAL
BIOASTRONAUTICS
BIOGEOCHEMISTRY
BIOGEOGRAPHICAL
BIOLUMINESCENCE
BLOOD-AND-THUNDER
BLOOD-GUILTINESS
BOMB-CALORIMETER
BONING-TELESCOPE
BRACHISTOCHRONE
BRACHYCEPHALOUS
BRACHYDACTYLOUS
BUBBLE-AND-SQUEAK
BUTTERFLY-FLOWER
BUTTERFLY-ORCHIS

C

CABINET-MINISTER
CAESALPINIACEAE
CALLITRICHACEAE
CANISTERISATION
CANVAS-STRETCHER
CAPERNAITICALLY
CAPRIFOLIACEOUS
CARNIVOROUSNESS
CARPOMETACARPUS
CARRIAGE-FORWARD

CARYOPHYLLACEAE
CASEMENT-CURTAIN
CATALLACTICALLY
CATCH-AS-CATCH-CAN
CATEGORICALNESS
CEREBROVASCULAR
CEREMONIOUSNESS
CHAMBER-HANGINGS
CHAMBERLAINSHIP
CHARGE-D'AFFAIRES
CHEMOPSYCHIATRY
CHENOPODIACEOUS
CHLORAMPHENICOL
CHOLECYSTECTOMY
CHOLECYSTOSTOMY
CHONDRIFICATION
CHONDROPTERYGII
CHRESTOMATHICAL
CHRISTADELPHIAN
CHRISTY-MINSTREL
CHROMATOGRAPHIC
CHROMOXYLOGRAPH
CHRONOLOGICALLY
CIGARETTE-HOLDER
CINDERELLA-DANCE
CINEMATOGRAPHER
CINEMATOGRAPHIC
CINEMICROGRAPHY
CIRCUMAMBAGIOUS
CIRCUMFERENTIAL
CIRCUMFORANEOUS
CIRCUMINCESSION
CIRCUMINSESSION
CIRCUMNAVIGABLE
CIRCUMNAVIGATOR
CIRCUMSCRIBABLE
CIRCUMSCRIPTION
CIRCUMSCRIPTIVE
CIRCUMSPECTNESS
CIRCUMSTANTIALS
CIRCUMSTANTIATE
CIRCUMVALLATION
CITRONELLA-GRASS
CLEARING-STATION
CLOUD-COMPELLING
CLOUD-CUCKOO-LAND
CLOUD-CUCKOO-TOWN
COCKNEYFICATION
COCONSCIOUSNESS
COINSTANTANEITY
COINSTANTANEOUS
COLD-BLOODEDNESS
COLLENCHYMATOUS
COMBUSTIBLENESS
COMFORTLESSNESS
COMMENDABLENESS
COMMISSION-AGENT
COMMUNALISATION
COMMUNICABILITY
COMMUNICATIVELY
COMPANION-LADDER
COMPASSIONATELY
COMPENDIOUSNESS
COMPLEMENTARITY
COMPOTATIONSHIP
COMPREHENSIVELY

COMPRESSIBILITY
COMPUTERISATION
CONCEIVABLENESS
CONCEPTUALISTIC
CONDESCENDINGLY
CONFESSIONALISM
CONFESSIONALIST
CONGEALABLENESS
CONJUNCTIONALLY
CONJUNCTIVENESS
CONNOISSEURSHIP
CONQUERABLENESS
CONSCIENCE-PROOF
CONSCIENTIOUSLY
CONSCRIPTIONIST
CONSECRATEDNESS
CONSECUTIVENESS
CONSENTANEOUSLY
CONSEQUENTIALLY
CONSERVATIONIST
CONSERVATORSHIP
CONSIDERATENESS
CONSIDERATIVELY
CONSOLATION-RACE
CONSPICUOUSNESS
CONSTITUTIONIST
CONSTRUCTIONISM
CONSUBSTANTIATE
CONSUMPTIVENESS
CONTEMPLATIVELY
CONTEMPORANEITY
CONTEMPORANEOUS
CONTEMPTIBILITY
CONTENTIOUSNESS
CONTINUATION-DAY
CONTRACTABILITY
CONTRACTIBILITY
CONTRADICTIVELY
CONTRADICTORILY
CONTRAVALLATION
CONTROVERSIALLY
CONVENTIONALISE
CONVENTIONALISM
CONVENTIONALIST
CONVENTIONALITY
CONVERSATIONISM
CONVERSATIONIST
CORPORIFICATION
CORRELATIVENESS
CORRESPONDENTLY
CORRESPONDINGLY
CORRUPTIBLENESS
CO-SIGNIFICATIVE
COSMOPOLITANISM
COUNTERACTIVELY
COUNTER-APPROACH
COUNTER-EVIDENCE
COUNTERFEISANCE
COUNTER-FLOWERED
COUNTER-IRRITANT
COUNTERMANDABLE
COUNTER-MOVEMENT
COUNTER-PRESSURE
COUNTER-SECURITY
COUNTERVAILABLE
CREASE-RESISTANT

CREASE-RESISTING
CRIMPING-MACHINE
CROOK-SHOULDERED
CROSSING-SWEEPER
CROSS-LATERALITY
CROSSOPTERYGIAN
CRYPTOCHRISTIAN
CRYPTOCOMMUNIST
CRYSTALLISATION
CRYSTALLOGRAPHY

D

DECALCIFICATION
DECARBONISATION
DECARBURISATION
DECOLOURISATION
DECONTAMINATION
DEFENCELESSNESS
DEGENERATIONIST
DELETERIOUSNESS
DEMAGNETISATION
DEMOCRATIFIABLE
DEMONSTRABILITY
DEMONSTRATIVELY
DENITRIFICATION
DEPARTMENTALISE
DEPARTMENTALISM
DEPHLOGISTICATE
DERMATOGLYPHICS
DESCRIPTIVENESS
DESILVERISATION
DESSERTSPOONFUL
DESTRUCTIBILITY
DESTRUCTIVENESS
DETERMINABILITY
DEVELOPMENTALLY
DEVIL-WORSHIPPER
DEVITRIFICATION
DIAHELIOTROPISM
DIAMAGNETICALLY
DIAPHRAGMATITIS
DIESELHYDRAULIC
DIFFERENTIATION
DIFFRANGIBILITY
DIMETHYLANILINE
DIRECTION-FINDER
DISADVANTAGEOUS
DISAFFECTEDNESS
DISAFFECTIONATE
DISAFFORESTMENT
DISAGREEABILITY
DISARTICULATION
DISASSIMILATIVE
DISCOMMENDATION
DISCOMMODIOUSLY
DISCONTINUATION
DISCONTINUOUSLY
DISCRETIONARILY
DISENTANGLEMENT
DISENTRANCEMENT
DISGRACEFULNESS
DISHABILITATION
DISHARMONIOUSLY
DISILLUSIONMENT
DISIMPRISONMENT
DISINFLATIONARY

DISINTERESTEDLY
DISOBLIGINGNESS
DISORGANISATION
DISPASSIONATELY
DISPENSABLENESS
DISPLEASINGNESS
DISPROPORTIONAL
DISQUISITIONARY
DISREPUTABILITY
DISRESPECTFULLY
DISSATISFACTION
DISSATISFACTORY
DISSOLVABLENESS
DISTASTEFULNESS
DISTINCTIVENESS
DISTINGUISHABLE
DISTINGUISHABLY
DISTINGUISHMENT
DISTRESSFULNESS
DISTRUSTFULNESS
DITHYRAMBICALLY
DIVERSIFICATION
DIVIDEND-WARRANT
DOCTRINARIANISM
DOLICHOCEPHALIC
DORSIBRANCHIATE
DORSIVENTRALITY
DOUBLE-BARRELLED
DOUBLE-FACEDNESS
DRAWN-THREADWORK
DRESSING-STATION
DRILLING-MACHINE
DURCHKOMPONIERT
DYER'S-YELLOWWEED
DYSLOGISTICALLY
DYSMENORRHEALIC
DYSTELEOLOGICAL

E

EBULLIOSCOPICAL
ECCLESIOLOGICAL
ECHINODERMATOUS
ÉCLAIRCISSEMENT
EDRIOPHTHALMIAN
EDRIOPHTHALMOUS
EFFICACIOUSNESS
ELECTRIFICATION
ELECTROANALYSIS
ELECTROCHEMICAL
ELECTRODYNAMICS
ELECTROKINETICS
ELECTROMAGNETIC
ELECTROMETRICAL
ELECTROMYOGRAPH
ELECTRONEGATIVE
ELECTROPHORESIS
ELECTROPHORETIC
ELECTROPOSITIVE
ELECTROTECHNICS
ELECTROTHERMICS
ELEUTHERODACTYL
EMANCIPATIONIST
ENANTIOMORPHISM
ENANTIOMORPHOUS
ENCEPHALOGRAPHY
ENCOMIASTICALLY

ENCYCLOPAEDICAL
ENFRANCHISEMENT
ENTOMOLOGICALLY
ENTREPRENEURIAL
EPISCOPALIANISM
EPISTEMOLOGICAL
EPITHELIOMATOUS
EQUALITARIANISM
EQUIPROBABILITY
ERGATANDROMORPH
ERIOCAULONACEAE
ETHEREALISATION
ETHNOMUSICOLOGY
EUPHEMISTICALLY
EVANGELICALNESS
EVANGELISTARION
EVENING-PRIMROSE
EVERLASTINGNESS
EXCHANGEABILITY
EXCOMMUNICATION
EXCOMMUNICATORY
EXCREMENTITIOUS
EXEMPLIFICATION
EXHIBITIONISTIC
EXPEDITIOUSNESS
EXPERIENTIALISM
EXPERIENTIALIST
EXPERIMENTALISE
EXPERIMENTALISM
EXPERIMENTALIST
EXPERIMENTATION
EXPERIMENTATIVE
EXTEMPORARINESS
EXTEMPORISATION
EXTERNALISATION
EXTRA-CURRICULAR
EXTRA-ILLUSTRATE
EXTRA-JUDICIALLY
EXTRAORDINARIES
EXTRAORDINARILY
EXTRA-PROVINCIAL

F

FAITHWORTHINESS
FANTASTICALNESS
FASHIONABLENESS
FEATHER-BOARDING
FELLOW-TRAVELLER
FERROMOLYBDENUM
FIELD-SEQUENTIAL
FIFTH-MONARCHISM
FIFTH-MONARCHIST
FLAMBOYANTE-TREE
FLIBBERTIGIBBET
FORMULARISATION
FOUL-MOUTHEDNESS
FOUNDATION-STONE
FRAGMENTARINESS
FRANKING-MACHINE
FREE-HEARTEDNESS
FREEZING-MIXTURE
FRENCHIFICATION

G

GASTROENTERITIS
GATHERING-GROUND

GENTLEMAN-AT-ARMS
GENTLEMANLINESS
GEOCHRONOLOGIST
GEOMORPHOLOGIST
GILLIE-WHITEFOOT
GLEICHSCHALTUNG
GLOSSOGRAPHICAL
GNOTOBIOLOGICAL
GOOD-CONDITIONED
GOOSEBERRY-STONE
GOVERNOR-GENERAL
GRAMOPHONICALLY
GRANDILOQUENTLY
GRANITIFICATION
GRANULITISATION
GREAT-GRANDCHILD
GREENERY-YALLERY
GYNANDROMORPHIC

H

HACKNEY-CARRIAGE
HACKNEY-COACHMAN
HALF-HEARTEDNESS
HALF-WELLINGTONS
HARD-AND-FASTNESS
HARD-HEARTEDNESS
HARVEST-FESTIVAL
HEIR-PRESUMPTIVE
HELIOTROPICALLY
HELLENISTICALLY
HELMINTHOLOGIST
HEMICRYSTALLINE
HENDECASYLLABIC
HENDECASYLLABLE
HEPATICOLOGICAL
HERB-CHRISTOPHER
HERMAPHRODITISM
HERMENEUTICALLY
HETEROCERCALITY
HETERODACTYLOUS
HETEROGENEOUSLY
HETEROSEXUALITY
HIEROGRAMMATIST
HIGH-GRAVEL-BLIND
HISTORIOGRAPHER
HISTORIOGRAPHIC
HOBBLEDEHOYHOOD
HOLOCRYSTALLINE
HOMEOPATHICALLY
HOMOCHLAMYDEOUS
HOMOGENEOUSNESS
HOMOIOTHERMLOUS
HOSPITALISATION
HUMANITARIANISM
HYDROCORALLINAE
HYDRODYNAMICIST
HYDROPATHICALLY
HYDROSTATICALLY
HYETOMETROGRAPH
HYPERADRENALISM
HYPERCATALECTIC
HYPERCRITICALLY
HYPERTHYROIDISM
HYPNOTISABILITY
HYPOCHONDRIACAL
HYPOCHONDRIASIS

HYPOPHOSPHOROUS

I

ICHTHYODORULITE
ICHTHYODORYLITE
ICHTHYOPTERYGIA
IDEOGRAPHICALLY
IDIOSYNCRATICAL
ILL-FAVOUREDNESS
ILLIMITABLENESS
ILLUSTRIOUSNESS
IMAGINATIVENESS
IMMENSURABILITY
IMMORTALISATION
IMMUNOCHEMISTRY
IMPENETRABILITY
IMPERISHABILITY
IMPERMEABLENESS
IMPERVIABLENESS
IMPONDERABILITY
IMPORTUNATENESS
IMPRACTICALNESS
IMPRESCRIPTIBLE
IMPRESSIONISTIC
IMPROVISATORIAL
INACCESSIBILITY
INADMISSIBILITY
INADVISABLENESS
INAPPLICABILITY
INAPPREHENSIBLE
INAPPROPRIATELY
INATTENTIVENESS
INCALCULABILITY
INCAPACIOUSNESS
INCOMMENSURABLE
INCOMMENSURABLY
INCOMMUNICATIVE
INCOMMUTABILITY
INCOMPARABILITY
INCOMPATIBILITY
INCOMPREHENSION
INCOMPREHENSIVE
INCONGRUOUSNESS
INCONSEQUENTIAL
INCONSIDERATELY
INCONSIDERATION
INCONSPICUOUSLY
INCORRIGIBILITY
INCREDULOUSNESS
INDEFEASIBILITY
INDEFENSIBILITY
INDEMNIFICATION
INDETERMINATELY
INDETERMINATION
INDIGESTIBILITY
INDISCIPLINABLE
INDISSOLUBILITY
INDISTINCTIVELY
INDISTRIBUTABLE
INDIVIDUALISTIC
INDIVISIBLENESS
INDUBITABLENESS
INEFFECTUALNESS
INEFFICACIOUSLY
INEXCUSABLENESS
INEXPENSIVENESS

INEXPLICABILITY
INEXTENSIBILITY
INFINITESIMALLY
INFLAMMABLENESS
INFRANGIBLENESS
INFUNDIBULIFORM
INJUDICIOUSNESS
INNUMERABLENESS
INOBTRUSIVENESS
INOFFENSIVENESS
INQUISITIVENESS
INQUISITORIALLY
INSCRUTABLENESS
INSEPARABLENESS
INSIGNIFICANTLY
INSIGNIFICATIVE
INSTANTANEOUSLY
INSTRUCTIVENESS
INSTRUMENTALISM
INSTRUMENTALIST
INSTRUMENTALITY
INSTRUMENTATION
INSUBORDINATION
INSURRECTIONARY
INSURRECTIONIST
INTELLECTUALISE
INTELLECTUALISM
INTELLECTUALIST
INTELLECTUALITY
INTELLIGIBILITY
INTEMPERATENESS
INTENSIFICATION
INTERAMBULACRAL
INTERAMBULACRUM
INTERCHANGEABLE
INTERCHANGEABLY
INTERCHANGEMENT
INTERCLAVICULAR
INTERCOLLEGIATE
INTERCOLONIALLY
INTERCONNECTION
INTERDEPENDENCE
INTERDIGITATION
INTERESTINGNESS
INTERFASCICULAR
INTERFEROMETRIC
INTERJACULATORY
INTERJECTIONARY
INTERNATIONALLY
INTEROSCULATION
INTERPRETERSHIP
INTERPROVINCIAL
INTERROGATIVELY
INTERSCHOLASTIC
INTERSTRATIFIED
INTERTANGLEMENT
INTERTENTACULAR
INTERTWISTINGLY
INTERVENTIONISM
INTERVENTIONIST
INTOLERABLENESS
INTRACTABLENESS
INTRANSIGENTISM
INTRANSIGENTIST
INTRANSMISSIBLE
INTRINSICALNESS

INTROSUSCEPTION
INTUSSUSCEPTION
INTUSSUSCEPTIVE
INVOLUNTARINESS
INVULNERABILITY
IRRATIONALISTIC
IRRECONCILEMENT
IRREDEEMABILITY
IRREDUCIBLENESS
IRREDUCTIBILITY
IRREFRAGABILITY
IRRELIGIOUSNESS
IRREMOVABLENESS
IRREPARABLENESS
IRREPREHENSIBLE
IRREPREHENSIBLY
IRRESISTIBILITY
IRRESOLVABILITY
IRREVERSIBILITY
IRREVOCABLENESS
ISOPERIMETRICAL

J

JACK-IN-THE-PULPIT
JACK-OF-ALL-TRADES
JERRY-COME-TUMBLE
JOHNNY-HEAD-IN-AIR
JUNGERMANNIALES
JURISPRUDENTIAL
JUSTIFIABLENESS

K

KATATHERMOMETER
KIND-HEARTEDNESS
KNICK-KNACKATORY
KNITTING-MACHINE

L

LANDING-CARRIAGE
LANDSCAPE-MARBLE
LAUGHING-JACKASS
LEXICOGRAPHICAL
LIGHT-HEADEDNESS
LIGHT-MINDEDNESS
LISSENCEPHALOUS
LITHOCHROMATICS
LOB-LIE-BY-THE-FIRE
LOGARITHMICALLY
LOGOGRAPHICALLY
LONG-SIGHTEDNESS
LOPHOBRANCHIATE
LOW-SPIRITEDNESS

M

MACROSCOPICALLY
MACROSPORANGIUM
MAGISTERIALNESS
MAGNETO-ELECTRIC
MALACOPTERYGIAN
MALASSIMILATION
MALCONFORMATION
MALDISTRIBUTION
MALPRACTITIONER
MALPRESENTATION
MANIC-DEPRESSIVE
MANNERISTICALLY

MANOEUVRABILITY
MARGARITIFEROUS
MARKET-GARDENING
MARRIAGE-LICENCE
MARRIAGE-PORTION
MARSH-CINQUEFOIL
MARSIPOBRANCHII
MATERIALISATION
MATERIALISTICAL
MEADOW-SAXIFRAGE
MECHANISTICALLY
MEDICINE-DROPPER
MEGACHEIROPTERA
MEPHISTOPHELEAN
MEPHISTOPHELIAN
MERITORIOUSNESS
MEROBLASTICALLY
MESATICEPHALOUS
MESSENGER-AT-ARMS
METALINGUISTICS
METAMATHEMATICS
METHODISTICALLY
METROPOLITANATE
MICHAELMAS-DAISY
MICROANALYTICAL
MICRODISSECTION
MICROMICROCURIE
MICROMICROFARAD
MICROMILLIMETRE
MICROPEGMATITIC
MICROPHOTOGRAPH
MICROSCOPICALLY
MICROSPORANGIUM
MICROSPOROPHYLL
MIDDLE-OF-THE-ROAD
MIDDLE-STITCHING
MINERALOGICALLY
MINIATURISATION
MISAPPRECIATION
MISAPPRECIATIVE
MISAPPREHENSION
MISAPPREHENSIVE
MISBECOMINGNESS
MISCELLANEOUSLY
MISCHIEVOUSNESS
MISCONSTRUCTION
MISINTELLIGENCE
MISPROPORTIONED
MISTRUSTFULNESS
MOLE-ELECTRONICS
MONARCHIANISTIC
MONOCHLAMYDEOUS
MONOCOTYLEDONES
MONOSYMMETRICAL
MORNING-SICKNESS
MORPHOPHONEMICS
MORTIFEROUSNESS
MOUNTAIN-BRAMBLE
MOUNTAIN-LEATHER
MOUNTAIN-RAILWAY
MULTIARTICULATE
MULTINUCLEOLATE
MULTITUDINOUSLY
MYRISTICIVOROUS

N

NATIONALISATION
NATURE-KNOWLEDGE
NEAR-SIGHTEDNESS
NECESSITOUSNESS
NECROMANTICALLY
NEIGHBOURLINESS
NEMATHELMINTHES
NEMATHELMINTHIC
NEO-CHRISTIANITY
NEPHELINE-BASALT
NEUROPSYCHIATRY
NEW-COMMONWEALTH
NITRO-DERIVATIVE
NOBLE-MINDEDNESS
NON-COMMISSIONED
NON-CONTRIBUTORY
NON-INTERVENTION
NON-INTRUSIONIST
NON-PROFESSIONAL
NON-PROFIT-MAKING
NONSENSICALNESS
NORTH-COUNTRYMAN
NORTH-EASTWARDLY
NORTH-WESTWARDLY
NOTHINGARIANISM
NOTWITHSTANDING
NUMISMATOLOGIST

O

OBJECTIFICATION
OBSERVATIONALLY
OCHLOCRATICALLY
ODONTOSTOMATOUS
ODORIFEROUSNESS
OMNIBENEVOLENCE
OMNIDIRECTIONAL
ONEIROCRITICISM
ONTOGENETICALLY
ONYCHOCRYPTOSIS
OPEN-HEARTEDNESS
OPHIOGLOSSACEAE
OPHTHALMOLOGIST
OPHTHALMOPLEGIA
OPHTHALMOSCOPIC
OPISTHOBRANCHIA
OPISTHOGNATHOUS
OPPROBRIOUSNESS
ORNITHODELPHIAN
ORNITHODELPHOUS
ORNITHORHYNCHUS
ORTHOPHOSPHORIC
ORTHOPSYCHIATRY
OSTREICULTURIST
OVERBEARINGNESS
OVERDEVELOPMENT
OVERFORWARDNESS
OWNER-OCCUPATION

P

PALAEOBOTANICAL
PALAEOGEOGRAPHY
PALAEOGRAPHICAL
PALAEOLIMNOLOGY
PALAEOMAGNETISM

PALAEONTOLOGIST
PALAEOPHYTOLOGY
PALAEOZOOLOGIST
PANOPHTHALMITIS
PAN-PRESBYTERIAN
PANTECHNICON-VAN
PANTOPRAGMATICS
PARADOXICALNESS
PARAGRAPHICALLY
PARAHELIOTROPIC
PARASITICALNESS
PARASYMPATHETIC
PARENTHETICALLY
PARLIAMENTARIAN
PARLIAMENTARILY
PARLIAMENTARISM
PARLIAMENT-HINGE
PARLIAMENT-HOUSE
PAROEMIOGRAPHER
PARTHENOGENESIS
PARTHENOGENETIC
PARTICULARISTIC
PARTY-GOVERNMENT
PASSENGER-PIGEON
PATRIPASSIANISM
PAULO-POST-FUTURE
PEACOCK-PHEASANT
PEASECOD-BELLIED
PEASECOD-CUIRASS
PEDAGOGUISHNESS
PENCIL-SHARPENER
PENETRATIVENESS
PERFUNCTORINESS
PERGAMENTACEOUS
PERISSODACTYLIC
PERISSOSYLLABIC
PERISTALTICALLY
PERPENDICULARLY
PERSONALISATION
PERSONIFICATION
PERSPICACIOUSLY
PERSPICUOUSNESS
PESSIMISTICALLY
PHANTASMAGORIAL
PHARISAICALNESS
PHASE-DIFFERENCE
PHENAKISTOSCOPE
PHENOLPHTHALEIN
PHENOMENALISTIC
PHENYLKETONURIA
PHILANTHROPICAL
PHILOSOPHICALLY
PHONAUTOGRAPHIC
PHONEMICISATION
PHOSPHORESCENCE
PHOSPHORYLATION
PHOTOCONDUCTING
PHOTOCONDUCTIVE
PHOTOLITHOGRAPH
PHOTOMECHANICAL
PHOTOMICROGRAPH
PHOTOSENSITISER
PHOTOTELEGRAPHY
PHOTOXYLOGRAPHY
PHOTOZINCOGRAPH
PHRENOLOGICALLY

PHYSIOGRAPHICAL
PHYSIOLOGICALLY
PHYSIOTHERAPIST
PHYTOGEOGRAPHER
PHYTOGEOGRAPHIC
PICTURE-MOULDING
PICTURE-RESTORER
PICTURESQUENESS
PILLOW-STRUCTURE
PITHECANTHROPUS
PLAGIOSTOMATOUS
PLANTAGINACEOUS
PLATITUDINARIAN
PLATYHELMINTHES
PLEASURABLENESS
PLEASURE-SEEKING
PLENIPOTENTIARY
PLEURO-PNEUMONIA
PLUMBAGINACEOUS
PNEUMATOLOGICAL
POLICE-CONSTABLE
POLICE-INSPECTOR
POLISHING-POWDER
POLYCHLOROPRENE
POLYPHLOESBOEAN
POLYPROTODONTIA
POLYSYLLABICISM
POLYSYNTHETICAL
PORCELAIN-CEMENT
PORTMANTEAU-WORD
PORTRAIT-GALLERY
PORTRAIT-PAINTER
POST-MILLENARIAN
POSTULATIONALLY
POVERTY-STRICKEN
POWDERING-CLOSET
PRACTICABLENESS
PRAGMATICALNESS
PRAIRIE-SCHOONER
PREACQUAINTANCE
PRECIPITABILITY
PRECIPITOUSNESS
PREDETERMINABLE
PREDICTABLENESS
PREFERENTIALISM
PREFERENTIALIST
PREFORMATIONISM
PREFORMATIONIST
PREHISTORICALLY
PREPOSITIONALLY
PREPOSSESSINGLY
PRE-RAPHAELISTIC
PRE-RAPHAELITISH
PRE-RAPHAELITISM
PRESBYTERIANISE
PRESBYTERIANISM
PRESENCE-CHAMBER
PRESENTATIONISM
PRESENTATIONIST
PRESTIDIGITATOR
PRETENTIOUSNESS
PRETERNATURALLY
PRINTING-MACHINE
PROBATIONERSHIP
PROBLEMATICALLY
PROCESSIONALIST

PROCRASTINATING
PROCRASTINATION
PROCRASTINATIVE
PROCRASTINATORY
PROCREATIVENESS
PROFESSIONALISE
PROFESSIONALISM
PROGNOSTICATION
PROGNOSTICATIVE
PROGRESSIVENESS
PROHIBITIVENESS
PROOF-CORRECTING
PROOF-CORRECTION
PROPERISPOMENON
PROPORTIONALITY
PROPORTIONATELY
PROPRIETORIALLY
PROPYLITISATION
PROSENCHYMATOUS
PROSPECTIVENESS
PROTOSPATHARIUS
PROTOZOOLOGICAL
PROVOCATIVENESS
PROVOST-SERGEANT
PSEUDEPIGRAPHIC
PSEUDOHEXAGONAL
PSYCHOCHEMISTRY
PSYCHOGENETICAL
PSYCHOGRAPHICAL
PSYCHOMETRICIAN
PSYCHOPATHOLOGY
PSYCHOPHYSICIST
PSYCHOSOMIMETIC
PSYCHOTHERAPIST
PSYCHOTOMIMETIC
PSYCHROMETRICAL
PTEROYLGLUTAMIC
PULCHRITUDINOUS
PULMOBRANCHIATE
PUNCTILIOUSNESS
PURPOSELESSNESS
PUSILLANIMOUSLY
PYRO-ELECTRICITY
PYROPHOTOGRAPHY
PYROTECHNICALLY

Q

QUADRIPARTITION
QUADRUPLICATION
QUARRELSOMENESS
QUARTERMISTRESS
QUARTER-SESSIONS
QUASIHISTORICAL
QUATERCENTENARY
QUESTION-BEGGING
QUICK-CONCEIVING
QUICK-WITTEDNESS
QUINQUAGENARIAN
QUINTUPLICATION

R

RADIOGONIOMETER
RADIOGRAMOPHONE
RADIOTELEGRAPHY
RAILWAY-CARRIAGE
RAILWAY-CROSSING

RAINBOW-COLOURED
RATIONALISATION
REAFFORESTATION
REAPPORTIONMENT
RECEIVER-GENERAL
RECEIVING-OFFICE
RECOLLECTEDNESS
RECONCILABILITY
RECONSIDERATION
RECONSOLIDATION
RECONVALESCENCE
RECOVERABLENESS
RECREMENTITIOUS
REDETERMINATION
REESTABLISHMENT
REFORTIFICATION
REFRESHMENT-ROOM
REINTERROGATION
REMONSTRATINGLY
REMORSELESSNESS
RENT-RESTRICTION
REPETITIOUSNESS
REPROACHFULNESS
RESOURCEFULNESS
RESPECTABLENESS
RESURRECTIONARY
RESURRECTIONISE
RESURRECTIONISM
RESURRECTIONIST
RESURRECTION-MAN
RESURRECTION-PIE
RETRIEVABLENESS
RETROGRESSIONAL
RETROGRESSIVELY
RETROSPECTIVELY
RHAMPHORHYNCHUS
RHEUMATOLOGICAL
RHOMBENCEPHALON
RHOMBENPORPHYRY
RHYNCHOBDELLIDA
RHYNCHOCEPHALIA
RIDING-COMMITTEE
RIGHT-HANDEDNESS
RIGHT-MINDEDNESS
RITUALISTICALLY
ROMANTICISATION
RÖNTGENOTHERAPY
ROUNDABOUTATION
ROUNDABOUTILITY
ROUND-SHOULDERED
RUDIMENTARINESS

S
SABBATH-BREAKING
SADDLER-CORPORAL
SADDLER-SERGEANT
SADO-MASOCHISTIC
SALOON-PASSENGER
SANCTIMONIOUSLY
SANDWORT-SPURREY
SARCENCHYMATOUS
SCAPHOCEPHALOUS
SCHILLERISATION
SCHISTOSOMIASIS
SCHIZOPHRENETIC

SCHOOL-INSPECTOR
SCHOOLMASTERING
SCHOOLMASTERISH
SCHRECKLICHKEIT
SCLERODERMATOUS
SCOLOPENDRIFORM
SCRIBACIOUSNESS
SCRIBBLING-PAPER
SCRIPTURE-READER
SEAPLANE-CARRIER
SECOND-ADVENTIST
SECOND-IN-COMMAND
SECONDS-PENDULUM
SECUNDOGENITURE
SEEMING-VIRTUOUS
SEISMOGRAPHICAL
SELAGINELLACEAE
SELENOGRAPHICAL
SELF-ABANDONMENT
SELF-AFFIRMATION
SELF-CAPACITANCE
SELF-COMPLACENCE
SELF-CONFIDENTLY
SELF-CONSEQUENCE
SELF-CONSIDERING
SELF-CONSISTENCY
SELF-CONSTITUTED
SELF-DESTRUCTION
SELF-DESTRUCTIVE
SELF-DETERMINING
SELF-EXAMINATION
SELF-EXPLANATORY
SELF-EXPLICATION
SELF-FORGETFULLY
SELF-HUMILIATION
SELF-OPINIONATED
SELF-POLLINATION
SELF-PORTRAITURE
SELF-SLAUGHTERED
SELF-SOVEREIGNTY
SELF-SUBSTANTIAL
SELF-SUFFICIENCY
SELF-SUSTAINMENT
SEMI-DOCUMENTARY
SEMI-INDEPENDENT
SEMI-PELAGIANISM
SEMITRANSPARENT
SENSATION-MONGER
SENSE-PERCEPTION
SENTENTIOUSNESS
SEPTENTRIONALLY
SERGEANT-DRUMMER
SERICICULTURIST
SERVICEABLENESS
SEVENTEEN-HUNDER
SHADOW-PANTOMIME
SHOOTING-GALLERY
SHOULDER-CLAPPER
SHOULDER-SHOTTEN
SHOULDER-SLIPPED
SHRINK-RESISTANT
SIGNIFICATIVELY
SINGLE-HEARTEDLY
SINGULARISATION
SLANTINGDICULAR
SLAVE-TRAFFICKER

SLEEPING-DRAUGHT
SLEEPING-PARTNER
SLOTTING-MACHINE
SMELTING-FURNACE
SOBER-MINDEDNESS
SOCIALISTICALLY
SOFTLY-SPRIGHTED
SOUTH-EASTWARDLY
SOUTH-WESTWARDLY
SPACE-TRAVELLING
SPEAKING-TRUMPET
SPECTROSCOPICAL
SPECULATIVENESS
SPEECHIFICATION
SPERMATOBLASTIC
SPERMATOGENESIS
SPERMATOGENETIC
SPHAEROSIDERITE
SPHENISCIFORMES
SPHEROIDISATION
SPONTANEOUSNESS
SPREAD-EAGLEWISE
STALACTITICALLY
STALAGMITICALLY
STAMPING-MACHINE
STANDARDISATION
STANDING-RIGGING
STAND-OFFISHNESS
STAPLING-MACHINE
STAR-OF-BETHLEHEM
STEAM-NAVIGATION
STEGANOGRAPHIST
STEREOCHEMISTRY
STEREOGRAPHICAL
STEREOISOMERISM
STICKING-PLASTER
STIFF-NECKEDNESS
STILPNOSIDERITE
STRAIGHTFORWARD
STRAIT-WAISTCOAT
STRATIGRAPHICAL
STRAWBERRY-SHRUB
STRETCHER-BEARER
STRETCHING-FRAME
STROMBULIFEROUS
SUBINTELLECTION
SUBINTELLIGENCE
SUBINTELLIGITUR
SUBLAPSARIANISM
SUBORDINATENESS
SUBSPECIFICALLY
SUBSTANTIALNESS
SUBSTANTIVENESS
SUBSTITUTIONARY
SUBSTRATOSPHERE
SUBTERRANEOUSLY
SUBURBANISATION
SUCCESSLESSNESS
SULPHUR-BACTERIA
SULPHUREOUSNESS
SUPERABUNDANTLY
SUPERCALENDERED
SUPERCONDUCTING
SUPERCONDUCTIVE
SUPEREROGATIION
SUPEREXALTATION

SUPEREXCELLENCE
SUPERFICIALNESS
SUPERFLUOUSNESS
SUPERHETERODYNE
SUPERIMPOSITION
SUPERINCUMBENCE
SUPERINDUCEMENT
SUPERINTENDENCE
SUPERINTENDENCY
SUPERLATIVENESS
SUPERNATURALISE
SUPERNATURALISM
SUPERNATURALIST
SUPERORDINATION
SUPERSATURATION
SUPERSTITIOUSLY
SUPERSTRUCTURAL
SUPLHAGUANIDINE
SUPPLEMENTARILY
SUPPLEMENTATION
SUPPORTABLENESS
SUPPOSITIONALLY
SURREPTITIOUSLY
SUSCEPTIBLENESS
SWATHING-CLOTHES
SWORD-AND-BUCKLER
SYCOPHANTICALLY
SYLLABIFICATION
SYLLOGISTICALLY
SYMMETRICALNESS
SYMPATHETICALLY
SYMPTOMATICALLY
SYNARTHRODIALLY
SYNCHRONISATION
SYNCHRONOUSNESS
SYNECDOCHICALLY
SYSTEMATISATION

T

TARSOMETATARSAL
TARSOMETATARSUS
TECHNOLOGICALLY
TECTIBRANCHIATA
TECTIBRANCHIATE
TELEGRAPHICALLY
TELEPHOTOGRAPHY
TEMPERAMENTALLY
TEMPESTUOUSNESS
TENDENTIOUSNESS
TENDER-HEARTEDLY
TENTACULIFEROUS
TESTAMENT-DATIVE
TETRABRANCHIATA
TETRABRANCHIATE
TETRACTINELLIDA
TETRASPORANGIUM
TETRASYLLABICAL
THALASSOGRAPHER
THALASSOGRAPHIC
THANATOGNOMONIC
THANKWORTHINESS
THEOREMATICALLY
THEOSOPHISTICAL
THERAPEUTICALLY
THERIANTHROPISM
THERIOMORPHOSIS

THERMOCHEMISTRY
THIN-SKINNEDNESS
THOUGHTLESSNESS
THREEPENCEWORTH
THREEPENNYWORTH
TICKET-COLLECTOR
TOPOGRAPHICALLY
TORQUE-CONVERTER
TOTALITARIANISM
TRAINING-COLLEGE
TRANSCRIPTIONAL
TRANSCRIPTIVELY
TRANSFERRIBILTY
TRANSFIGURATION
TRANSFIGUREMENT
TRANSGRESSIONAL
TRANSGRESSIVELY
TRANSILLUMINATE
TRANSLITERATION
TRANSMOGRIFYING
TRANSMUTABILITY
TRANSPARENTNESS
TRANSPLANTATION
TRANSPORTEDNESS
TRANSPOSITIONAL
TREACHEROUSNESS
TREASONABLENESS
TRIGONOMETRICAL
TRINITROBENZENE
TRINITROTOLUENE
TRISYLLABICALLY
TROUBLESOMENESS
TRUE-HEARTEDNESS
TRUSTWORTHINESS
TRYPANOSOMIASIS
TUBERCULISATION
TWO-PAIR-OF-STAIRS
TYPOGRAPHICALLY

U

ULTRACENTRIFUGE
ULTRAMICROSCOPE
ULTRAMICROSCOPY
ULTRA-PROTESTANT
UNACCOMMODATING
UNADVISABLENESS
UNALTERABLENESS
UNAPOSTOLICALLY
UNAPPREHENSIBLE
UNASCERTAINABLE
UNAUTHENTICATED
UNAUTHORITATIVE
UNAVAILABLENESS
UNAVOIDABLENESS
UNBLAMEABLENESS
UNCANONICALNESS
UNCEREMONIOUSLY
UNCHALLENGEABLE
UNCHALLENGEABLY
UNCHANGEABILITY
UNCHRISTIANLIKE
UNCIRCUMSCRIBED
UNCOMMUNICATIVE
UNCOMPANIONABLE
UNCOMPASSIONATE
UNCOMPLAININGLY

UNCOMPLAISANTLY
UNCOMPLIMENTARY
UNCOMPREHENDING
UNCOMPREHENSIVE
UNCONCERNEDNESS
UNCONDITIONALLY
UNCONSCIENTIOUS
UNCONSCIOUSNESS
UNCONSENTANEOUS
UNCONSTRAINABLE
UNCONSTRAINEDLY
UNCOOPERATIVELY
UNDEMONSTRATIVE
UNDER-EMPLOYMENT
UNDERHANDEDNESS
UNDER-PRIVILEGED
UNDER-PRODUCTION
UNDERSTANDINGLY
UNDER-THE-COUNTER
UNDESIRABLENESS
UNDETERMINATION
UNDISCIPLINABLE
UNDISTINGUISHED
UNEXCEPTIONABLE
UNEXCEPTIONABLY
UNEXCEPTIONALLY
UNFORGIVINGNESS
UNFORTUNATENESS
UNFOSSILIFEROUS
UNGENTLEMANLIKE
UNGRAMMATICALLY
UNHEALTHFULNESS
UNINTENTIONALLY
UNINTERESTINGLY
UNINTERMITTEDLY
UNINTERPRETABLE
UNINTERRUPTEDLY
UNNECESSARINESS
UNOBJECTIONABLE
UNOBJECTIONABLY
UNOBTRUSIVENESS
UNPARLIAMENTARY
UNPATRIOTICALLY
UNPEACEABLENESS
UNPHILOSOPHICAL
UNPRACTISEDNESS
UNPRECEDENTEDLY
UNPREMEDITATION
UNPREPOSSESSING
UNPROGRESSIVELY
UNPRONOUNCEABLE
UNPROPORTIONATE
UNPROTECTEDNESS
UNPROTESTANTISE
UNQUALIFIEDNESS
UNRECOMMENDABLE
UNRECONCILIABLE
UNRECONSTRUCTED
UNRELENTINGNESS
UNREMITTINGNESS
UNRIGHTEOUSNESS
UNSATISFIEDNESS
UNSEAWORTHINESS
UNSELFCONSCIOUS
UNSOPHISTICATED
UNSPORTSMANLIKE

UNSTATESMANLIKE
UNSTEADFASTNESS
UNSUBSTANTIATED
UNSUSPECTEDNESS
UNSYMMETRICALLY
UNTEACHABLENESS
UNTRACTABLENESS
UNTRANSMIGRATED
UNTRANSMISSIBLE
UNTRUSTWORTHILY
UNVERIFIABILITY
UNWHOLESOMENESS

V

VASOCONSTRICTOR
VEHICLE-ACTUATED
VENTRILOQUIALLY
VENTRILOQUISTIC
VENTURESOMENESS
VERTIGINOUSNESS

VICE-CHAMBERLAIN
VICISSITUDINOUS
VICTUALLING-BILL
VICTUALLING-SHIP
VICTUALLING-YARD
VINDICATIVENESS
VISCOSIMETRICAL

W

WALL-GILLYFLOWER
WARM-HEARTEDNESS
WARRANTABLENESS
WATER-EQUIVALENT
WEATHER-BOARDING
WEATHER-FORECAST
WEATHER-NOTATION
WEIGHING-MACHINE
WELL-ACCOMPLISHT
WELL-CONDITIONED
WELL-INTENTIONED

WHEEL-ANIMALCULE
WHIRLING-DERVISH
WHIRLING-MACHINE
WINDOW-GARDENING
WITHDRAWING-ROOM
WONDER-MONGERING
WOODY-NIGHTSHADE
WORLD-WITHOUT-END
WRINGING-MACHINE
WRONG-HEADEDNESS

X

XERORADIOGRAPHY
XYLOTYPOGRAPHIC

Z

ZOOGEOGRAPHICAL
ZOOPHYTOLOGICAL

A

ABSENT-MINDEDNESS
ACANTHOPTERYGIAN
ACQUAINTANCESHIP
ADVANTAGEOUSNESS
AFFECTIONATENESS
ANAEROBIOTICALLY
ANAGRAMMATICALLY
ANATHEMATISATION
ANCHYLOSTOMIASIS
ANGLO-CATHOLICISM
ANIMAL-WORSHIPPER
ANNUNCIATION-LILY
ANTAGONISTICALLY
ANTHROPOMORPHISE
ANTHROPOMORPHISM
ANTHROPOMORPHIST
ANTHROPOMORPHITE
ANTHROPOMORPHOUS
ANTHROPOPITHECUS
ANTHROPOPSYCHISM
ANTICHRISTIANISM
ANTIPHRASTICALLY
ANTISTROPHICALLY
ANYTHINGARIANISM
APOGEOTROPICALLY
APOPHTHEGMATICAL
APOTHEGMATICALLY
APPREHENSIBILITY
APPREHENSIVENESS
ARCHAEOLOGICALLY
ARISTOCRATICALLY
ARISTOLOCHIACEAE
ARTERIOSCLEROSIS
ARTERIOSCLEROTIC
AUSTRALOPITHECUS

AUTHORITARIANISM
AUTOBIOGRAPHICAL
AUTO-IMMUNISATION
AUTO-INTOXICATION

B

BACHELOR'S-BUTTONS
BLOODTHIRSTINESS
BLOOD-TRANSFUSION
BLOODY-MINDEDNESS
BOTTLE-SHOULDERED
BRIGADIER-GENERAL
BUREAUCRATICALLY

C

CABBAGE-BUTTERFLY
CADUCIBRANCHIATE
CANTANKEROUSNESS
CARYOPHYLLACEOUS
CATACHRESTICALLY
CATECHUMENICALLY
CENTIMETRE-GRAMME
CHARACTERISATION
CHARACTERISTICAL
CHEMOPSYCHIATRIC
CHEMORECEPTIVITY
CHROMOLITHOGRAPH
CHROMOTYPOGRAPHY
CHROMOXYLOGRAPHY
CHRYSELEPHANTINE
CIGARETTE-LIGHTER
CINEMATOGRAPHIST
CIRCUMAMBULATION
CIRCUMDENUDATION
CIRCUMNAVIGATION
CIRCUMSTANTIALLY
CLEAR-SIGHTEDNESS

CLIMATOGRAPHICAL
CLOSET-STRATEGIST
CLOVE-GILLYFLOWER
CLOW-GILLIEFLOWER
COLLABORATIONIST
COMMANDER-IN-CHIEF
COMMENSURABILITY
COMMENSURATENESS
COMMISSIONERSHIP
COMMONWEALTHSMAN
COMMUNICABLENESS
COMPARTMENTALISE
COMPRESSIBLENESS
CONSCIONABLENESS
CONSERVATIVENESS
CONSIDERABLENESS
CONSIGNIFICATION
CONSIGNIFICATIVE
CONSOLATION-MATCH
CONSOLATION-PRIZE
CONSTITUTIONALLY
CONSTRUCTIVENESS
CONSUBSTANTIALLY
CONTAINERISATION
CONTEMPORARINESS
CONTEMPTIBLENESS
CONTEMPTUOUSNESS
CONTRADICTIOUSLY
CONTRAINDICATION
CONTRAINDICATIVE
CONTROVERSIALIST
CONTUMACIOUSNESS
CONTUMELIOUSNESS
CO-POLYMERISATION
COPYING-INK-PENCIL
CORRIDOR-CARRIAGE
COUNTERCLOCKWISE

COUNTER-ESPIONAGE
COUNTER-INFLUENCE
COUNTER-OFFENSIVE
COUNTER-SIGNATURE
COUNTER-STATEMENT
CROSS-EXAMINATION
CROSSGRAINEDNESS
CROSS-POLLINATION
CRYSTALLOGENETIC
CRYSTALLOGRAPHER

D

DEADLY-NIGHTSHADE
DECENTRALISATION
DEHUMIDIFICATION
DEMONSTRABLENESS
DENNROCHRONOLOGY
DEOXYRIBONUCLEIC
DESTRUCTIBLENESS
DETERIORATIONIST
DETERMINABLENESS
DEUTEROCANONICAL
DEVIL-ON-TWO-STICKS
DIAGEOTROPICALLY
DIAGRAMMATICALLY
DIPTEROCARPACEAE
DISACCOMMODATION
DISADVANTAGEABLE
DISAFFORESTATION
DISAGREEABLENESS
DISCONSOLATENESS
DISCONTENTEDNESS
DISCOURTEOUSNESS
DISCRIMINATINGLY
DISCRIMINATIVELY
DISEMBARRASSMENT
DISESTABLISHMENT
DISFRANCHISEMENT
DISINCARCERATION
DISINCORPORATION
DISINDIVIDUALISE
DISINGENUOUSNESS
DISPROPORTIONATE
DISPUTATIOUSNESS
DISQUALIFICATION
DISREPUTABLENESS
DOLICHOCEPHALISM
DOLICHOCEPHALOUS
DOUBLE-MINDEDNESS
DRINKING-FOUNTAIN
DYNAMO-ELECTRICAL
DYSMENORRHOEALIC

E

ECCLESIASTICALLY
ELECTROBIOLOGIST
ELECTROCHEMISTRY
ELECTROHYDRAULIC
ELECTROLYTICALLY
ELECTROMAGNETISM
ELECTROMECHANICS
ELECTROMYOGRAPHY
ENTHUSIASTICALLY
ENTREPRENEURSHIP
EPIGRAMMATICALLY
EPIPHENOMENALISM

EPIPHENOMENALIST
EUHEMERISTICALLY
EVIL-FAVOUREDNESS
EXTEMPORANEOUSLY
EXTERRITORIALITY
EXTRA-TERRESTRIAL
EXTRA-TERRITORIAL

F

FAINT-HEARTEDNESS
FASHION-MONGERING
FELLOW-COUNTRYMAN
FERMENTATIVENESS
FIRE-EXTINGUISHER
FLIGHT-LIEUTENANT
FORISFAMILIATION
FOUNDATION-MUSLIN

G

GASTROENTEROLOGY
GASTROINTESTINAL
GENETHLIALOGICAL
GEOCHRONOLOGICAL
GEOMORPHOLOGICAL
GIGA-ELECTRON-VOLT
GLAUCONITISATION
GOVERNORS-GENERAL
GRASS-OF-PARNASSUS
GREAT-GRANDFATHER
GREAT-GRANDMOTHER
GROWTH-ORIENTATED
GYNANDROMORPHISM
GYNANDROMORPHOUS

H

HANDICRAFTSWOMAN
HARD-FAVOUREDNESS
HARD-FEATUREDNESS
HAUSSMANNISATION
HELIOCENTRICALLY
HELIOGRAPHICALLY
HELMINTHOLOGICAL
HERB-OF-REPENTANCE
HERMAPHRODITICAL
HERPETOLOGICALLY
HETEROCHRONISTIC
HIEROGLYPHICALLY
HIEROGRAMMATICAL
HIGGLEDY-PIGGLEDY
HIPPOCASTANACEAE
HISTOGENETICALLY
HISTOPATHOLOGIST
HOMOEOPATHICALLY
HONEST-TO-GOODNESS
HUCKLE-SHOULDERED
HUNDREDPERCENTER
HYDROCHARITACEAE
HYDROELECTRICITY
HYDROFERRICYANIC
HYDROFERROCYANIC
HYDROGRAPHICALLY
HYDROMETEOROLOGY
HYDROTHERAPEUTIC
HYMENOPHYLLACEAE
HYPERSENSITIVITY
HYPERVITAMINOSIS

HYPNOANAESTHESIA
HYPOCHONDRIACISM
HYPOCORISTICALLY
HYPOCOTYLEDONARY
HYPOCOTYLEDONARY
HYSTERON-PROTERON

I

ICHNOGRAPHICALLY
ICOSITETRAHEDRON
IMMEASURABLENESS
IMPERCEPTIBILITY
IMPERFECTIBILITY
IMPERISHABLENESS
IMPERTURBABILITY
IMPONDERABLENESS
IMPRACTICABILITY
INACCESSIBLENESS
INARTICULATENESS
INAUSPICIOUSNESS
INCALCULABLENESS
INCENSE-BREATHING
INCOGNOSCIBILITY
INCOMBUSTIBILITY
INCOMMENSURATELY
INCOMMODIOUSNESS
INCOMMUTABLENESS
INCOMPARABLENESS
INCOMPATIBLENESS
INCOMPOSSIBILITY
INCOMPREHENSIBLE
INCOMPREHENSIBLY
INCONCEIVABILITY
INCONCLUSIVENESS
INCONSOLABLENESS
INCONTESTABILITY
INCONTIGUOUSNESS
INCONTROVERTIBLE
INCONTROVERTIBLY
INCONVERTIBILITY
INCORRIGIBLENESS
INCORRUPTIBILITY
INDESCRIBABILITY
INDICATOR-DIAGRAM
INDISCRIMINATELY
INDISCRIMINATING
INDISCRIMINATION
INDISCRIMINATIVE
INDISPENSABILITY
INDISPUTABLENESS
INDISSOLUBLENESS
INEXHAUSTIBILITY
INEXPLICABLENESS
INEXPRESSIVENESS
INEXTINGUISHABLE
INEXTINGUISHABLY
INHARMONIOUSNESS
INHOSPITABLENESS
INSTITUTIONALISE
INSTITUTIONALISM
INSTITUTIONALIST
INSUBSTANTIALITY
INSUSCEPTIBILITY
INTELLIGIBLENESS
INTERCOMMUNICATE
INTERCONTINENTAL

INTERCONVERTIBLE
INTERJECTIONALLY
INTERMINABLENESS
INTERNATIONALISE
INTERNATIONALISM
INTERNATIONALIST
INTERPENETRATION
INTERPENETRATIVE
INTERPRETATIVELY
INTERPUNCTUATION
INTERTERRITORIAL
INTRATERRITORIAL
INTROSPECTIONIST
INVULNERABLENESS
IRREDEEMABLENESS
IRREFRAGABLENESS
IRREMEDIABLENESS
IRREMISSIBLENESS
IRREPROVABLENESS
IRRESISTIBLENESS
IRRESOLVABLENESS
IRRESPONSIBILITY
IRRESPONSIVENESS
IRREVERSIBLENESS

J

JEW'S-FRANKINCENSE
JOHNNY-COME-LATELY

K

KITCHEN-FURNITURE
KNIGHTHOOD-ERRANT
KULTURGESCHICHTE

L

LANDSCAPE-PAINTER
LENTIBULARIACEAE
LEPIDODENDRACEAE
LEPTOSPORANGIATE
LIGHT-HEARTEDNESS
LIGHT-HEAVYWEIGHT
LIGHTHOUSEKEEPER
LINE-OF-BATTLESHIP
LITHOGRAPHICALLY
LOVE-LIES-BLEEDING
LUSITANO-AMERICAN

M

MACHIAVELLIANISM
MAGNETOSTRICTION
MAJOR-GENERALSHIP
MALAPPROPRIATION
MALCONTENTEDNESS
MARRIAGEABLENESS
MARRIAGE-CONTRACT
MEALY-MOUTHEDNESS
MEAN-SPIRITEDNESS
MERETRICIOUSNESS
MESEMBRIANTHEMUM
MESEMBRYANTHEMUM
MICROCHEIROPTERA
MICROCLIMATOLOGY
MICROCOSMOGRAPHY
MICROCRYSTALLINE
MICROELECTRONICS
MICROLEPIDOPTERA

MICROMETEOROLOGY
MICROMINIATURISE
MICROPHOTOGRAPHY
MICROSEISMOGRAPH
MICROSEISMOMETER
MICROSEISMOMETRY
MISANTHROPICALLY
MISAPPROPRIATION
MISCEGENATIONIST
MISCOMPREHENSION
MISPRONUNCIATION
MISSIONARY-BISHOP
MISUNDERSTANDING
MONOCOTYLEDONOUS
MOTHER-OF-MILLIONS
MOUNTAIN-SICKNESS
MOUSSELINE-DE-SOIE
MUCILAGINOUSNESS
MUDDLEHEADEDNESS
MULTIDENTICULATE
MULTIDIMENSIONAL
MULTIFARIOUSNESS
MULTIMILLIONAIRE
MULTIPLEPOINDING
MULTITUBERCULATE
MUNICIPALISATION

N

NARROW-MINDEDNESS
NECESSITARIANISM
NEIGHBOUR-STAINED
NEO-IMPRESSIONISM
NEO-MALTHUSIANISM
NIPPERTY-TIPPERTY
NON-PROLIFERATION
NURSERY-GOVERNESS

O

OBDIPLOSTEMONOUS
OBSTREPEROUSNESS
OLD-FASHIONEDNESS
OPHTHALMOLOGICAL
OPINIONATIVENESS
ORNITHOLOGICALLY
ORTHOGRAPHICALLY
ORTHOPTEROLOGIST
OSTENTATIOUSNESS
OTHERWORLDLINESS
OVERCOMPENSATION
OVERCOMPENSATORY
OVEREXCITABILITY
OVERSUBSCRIPTION

P

PALAEICHTHYOLOGY
PALAEONTOLOGICAL
PALAEOZOOLOGICAL
PALINGENETICALLY
PARADIGMATICALLY
PARAHELIOTROPISM
PARALLELEPIPEDON
PARALLELOGRAMMIC
PARALLELOPIPEDON
PARANITROANILINE
PARAPHRASTICALLY
PARAPSYCHOLOGIST

PARSIMONIOUSNESS
PEACOCK-BUTTERFLY
PERCUSSION-BULLET
PERCUSSION-HAMMER
PERCUSSION-POWDER
PERIPHRASTICALLY
PERISSODACTYLATE
PERISSODACTYLOUS
PERPENDICULARITY
PERTINACIOUSNESS
PERVICACIOUSNESS
PETROGRAPHICALLY
PHALANSTERIANISM
PHANTASMAGORICAL
PHANTASMOGENETIC
PHARMACEUTICALLY
PHENOMENOLOGICAL
PHILOPROGENITIVE
PHILOSOPHISTICAL
PHONOGRAPHICALLY
PHOTOCOMPOSITION
PHOTOELECTRICITY
PHOTOELECTRONICS
PHOTOGRAPHICALLY
PHOTOLITHOGRAPHY
PHOTOMICROGRAPHY
PHOTO-SENSITIVITY
PHOTOTHERAPEUTIC
PHOTOZINCOGRAPHY
PHRASEOLOGICALLY
PHYLOGENETICALLY
PHYSIOGNOMICALLY
PHYTOPATHOLOGIST
PICTOGRAPHICALLY
PIEZOELECTRICITY
PLAGIOTROPICALLY
PLAIN-HEARTEDNESS
PLANT-ASSOCIATION
PNEUMONOKONIOSIS
POLICE-MAGISTRATE
POLITICO-ECONOMIC
POLYCOTYLEDONOUS
POLYSYLLABICALLY
POLYSYNTHETICISM
POLYTHEISTICALLY
POOR-SPIRITEDNESS
PORNOGRAPHICALLY
PORPHYROGENITISM
PORPHYROGENITURE
PORTERHOUSE-STEAK
PORTRAIT-PAINTING
POSTPOSITIONALLY
POTAMOGETONACEAE
POWDER-METALLURGY
PRAISEWORTHINESS
PRECONCERTEDNESS
PRECONSCIOUSNESS
PREDETERMINATION
PREDISPOSITIONAL
PREMILLENNIALISM
PREMILLENNIALIST
PREPONDERATINGLY
PREPOSTEROUSNESS
PRESCRIPTIBILITY
PRESCRIPTIVENESS
PRESIGNIFICATION

PRESTIDIGITATION
PRESUMPTUOUSNESS
PRETERITE-PRESENT
PRETERITO-PRESENT
PRETERNATURALISM
PRETERPLUPERFECT
PRETTY-PRETTINESS
PROCURATOR-FISCAL
PROFIT-ORIENTATED
PROSLAMBANOMENOS
PROSPECTIVE-GLASS
PSEUDOCLASSICISM
PSYCHOANALYTICAL
PSYCHOPANNYCHISM
PSYCHOPANNYCHIST
PSYCHOPHYSIOLOGY
PTERYLOGRAPHICAL
PUBLIC-SPIRITEDLY
PUZZLE-HEADEDNESS
PYROPHOTOGRAPHIC

Q

QUADRICENTENNIAL
QUEEN-OF-THE-MEADOW
QUESTIONABLENESS
QUICK-SIGHTEDNESS

R

RAMBUNCTIOUSNESS
RECONCILABLENESS
RECONSTRUCTIONAL
RECRUITING-GROUND
REGISTRAR-GENERAL
REINCARNATIONISM
REINCARNATIONIST
REINTERPRETATION
REMUNERATIVENESS
REPRESENTATIONAL
REPRESENTATIVELY
REPRODUCTIVENESS
RESIDENTIARYSHIP
RHINOCEROS-BEETLE
RHINOPHARYNGITIS
ROBIN-RUN-THE-HEDGE

S

SACRILEGIOUSNESS
SAINT-SIMONIANISM
SATISFACTORINESS
SAUSAGE-POISONING
SCANDALMONGERING
SCENOGRAPHICALLY
SCHISMATICALNESS
SCHOOL-FRIENDSHIP
SCHOOLMASTERSHIP
SCISSORS-AND-PASTE
SCLERENCHYMATOUS
SCROPHULARIACEAE
SECOND-LIEUTENANT
SELF-CONDEMNATION
SELF-IMPREGNATION
SELF-INCOMPATIBLE
SELF-OPINIONATIVE
SELF-SATISFACTION
SELF-SUSTENTATION
SEMICONDUCTIVITY

SEMI-DOMESTICATED
SEMI-OCCASIONALLY
SEMITRANSPARENCY
SENSATIONALISTIC
SERPENTINISATION
SERVICE-RESERVOIR
SESQUICENTENNIAL
SEX-DETERMINATION
SHERIFF-PRINCIPAL
SHIPPING-ARTICLES
SHORT-SIGHTEDNESS
SHOULDER-OF-MUTTON
SHRINK-RESISTANCE
SIDE-SADDLE-FLOWER
SIMPLE-MINDEDNESS
SIMULTANEOUSNESS
SINGLE-MINDEDNESS
SLEEPING-CARRIAGE
SLEEPING-SICKNESS
SLUBBERDEGULLION
SOLICITOR-GENERAL
SOPORIFEROUSNESS
SPECTROGRAPHICAL
SPECTROHELIOGRAM
SPECTROLOGICALLY
SPHAEROCOBALTITE
SPHYGMOMANOMETER
SPIRITUALISATION
SQUARE-SHOULDERED
STENOGRAPHICALLY
STEREOMETRICALLY
STEREOPHONICALLY
STEREOSCOPICALLY
STETHOSCOPICALLY
STICHOMETRICALLY
STOCK-GILLYFLOWER
STOUT-HEARTEDNESS
STRAWBERRY-TOMATO
STRETCHING-COURSE
STRONG-MINDEDNESS
STYLOGRAPHICALLY
SUBCONSCIOUSNESS
SUBINSPECTORSHIP
SUBJECT-CATALOGUE
SUBORDINATIONISM
SUBSTITUTIONALLY
SUNSHINE-RECORDER
SUPERCILIOUSNESS
SUPERDREADNOUGHT
SUPERNATIONALISM
SUPERNATURALNESS
SUPERSERVICEABLE
SUPERSUBSTANTIAL
SUPERTERRESTRIAL
SUPPOSITITIOUSLY
SURFACE-TO-SURFACE
SURREALISTICALLY
SUSPENSION-BRIDGE
SWADDLING-CLOTHES
SWATHLING-CLOTHES
SWEDENBORGIANISM
SWOTHLING-CLOTHES
SYNCATEGOREMATIC
SYNCHROCYCLOTRON

T

TELEPHOTOGRAPHIC
TERMINOLOGICALLY
TERNSTROEMIACEAE
THEOPHILANTHROPY
THERMOMETRICALLY
THERMOMETROGRAPH
THERMOSCOPICALLY
THERMOSTATICALLY
THOUGHT-EXECUTING
THRASHING-MACHINE
THREE-DIMENSIONAL
THRESHING-MACHINE
TINTINNABULATION
TRANQUILLISATION
TRANQUILLISINGLY
TRANSCENDENTALLY
TRANSCENDENTNESS
TRANSCONTINENTAL
TRANSFERRABILITY
TRANSFORMATIONAL
TRANSMISSIBILITY
TRANSMUTABLENESS
TRANSMUTATIONIST
TRANSPORTABILITY
TRANSUBSTANTIATE
TRENTE-ET-QUARANTE
TRICHLORETHYLENE
TRIGGER-HAPPINESS
TROUSER-STRETCHER
TYRANT-FLYCATCHER

U

ULTRACREPIDARIAN
ULTRA-FASHIONABLE
ULTRAMICROSCOPIC
UNACCEPTABLENESS
UNACCOMPLISHMENT
UNACCOUNTABILITY
UNACCUSTOMEDNESS
UNACQUAINTEDNESS
UNANSWERABLENESS
UNATTAINABLENESS
UNATTRACTIVENESS
UNCHANGEABLENESS
UNCHARITABLENESS
UNCOMPROMISINGLY
UNCONDITIONALITY
UNCONFORMABILITY
UNCONSTITUTIONAL
UNCONTROVERTIBLE
UNCRYSTALLISABLE
UNDENOMINATIONAL
UNDEPENDABLENESS
UNDERCOUNTENANCE
UNDERDEVELOPMENT
UNDERNOURISHMENT
UNDIFFERENTIATED
UNDISCRIMINATING
UNDISTINGUISHING
UNDISTRACTEDNESS
UNEXTINGUISHABLE
UNEXTINGUISHABLY
UNFATHOMABLENESS
UNFAVOURABLENESS

UNFREQUENTEDNESS
UNGOVERNABLENESS
UNIMAGINABLENESS
UNIMPRESSIONABLE
UNINTENTIONALITY
UNINTERMITTINGLY
UNIVERSALISATION
UNMANAGEABLENESS
UNMODIFIABLENESS
UNOSTENTATIOUSLY
UNPARDONABLENESS
UNPREDICTABILITY
UNPREMEDITATEDLY
UNPRODUCTIVENESS
UNPROFESSIONALLY
UNPROFITABLENESS
UNPROPITIOUSNESS
UNPROPORTIONABLE
UNPROPORTIONABLY
UNPROSPEROUSNESS
UNREASONABLENESS
UNRESPONSIVENESS
UNSATISFACTORILY

UNSATISFYINGNESS
UNSCIENTIFICALLY
UNSCRUPULOUSNESS
UNSEARCHABLENESS
UNSEASONABLENESS
UNSOPHISTICATION
UNSUBSTANTIALISE
UNSUBSTANTIALITY
UNSUBSTANTIATION
UNSUCCESSFULNESS
UNSUSPECTINGNESS
UNSUSPICIOUSNESS
UNSYSTEMATICALLY
UNTHOUGHTFULNESS

V

VAINGLORIOUSNESS
VASOCONSTRICTION
VASOCONSTRICTORY
VELOCIPEDESTRIAN
VENTRICULOGRAPHY
VICE-CHAIRMANSHIP
VICE-PRESIDENTIAL

VOLTA-ELECTRICITY

W

WALKING-GENTLEMAN
WASTEPAPER-BASKET
WATER-THERMOMETER
WEATHER-SATELLITE
WEDDING-BREAKFAST
WELL-PROPORTIONED
WHITE-HONEYSUCKLE
WHITE-PRECIPITATE
WILLOWING-MACHINE
WINNOWING-MACHINE
WISDOM-LITERATURE
WOODEN-HEADEDNESS

Y

YELLOW-SHOULDERED

Z

ZARATHUSTRIANISM

A

ACCOMMODATIVENESS
ACCORDION-PLEATING
ADMINISTRATORSHIP
AMBASSADOR-AT-LARGE
AMPHITHEATRICALLY
ANACHRONISTICALLY
ANAESTHESIOLOGIST
ANGELS-ON-HORSEBACK
ANTHROPOGEOGRAPHY
ANTHROPOLOGICALLY
ANTHROPOMORPHITIC
ANTHROPOMORPHOSIS
ANTHROPOPHAGINIAN
ANTICLIMACTICALLY
APPROPRIATIVENESS
ARCHITECTONICALLY
ARGUMENTATIVENESS
AUSTRALOPITHECINE
AUTHORITATIVENESS

B

BATHYOROGRAPHICAL
BEGGAR-MY-NEIGHBOUR

C

CABINET-PHOTOGRAPH
CALLIPER-COMPASSES
CHAMBER-COUNSELLOR
CHARACTERLESSNESS
CHEMOTHERAPEUTICS
CHIROPTEROPHILOUS
CHROMOLITHOGRAPHY

CINEMATOGRAPHICAL
CIRCUMLOCUTIONIST
CIRCUMSTANTIALITY
CO-INSTANTANEOUSLY
COLONEL-COMMANDANT
COMMENSURABLENESS
COMMUNICATIVENESS
COMPANIONABLENESS
COMPASSIONATENESS
COMPREHENSIBILITY
COMPREHENSIVENESS
CONCENTRATIVENESS
CONGREGATIONALISM
CONGREGATIONALIST
CONSCIENCE-SMITTEN
CONSCIENTIOUSNESS
CONSENTANEOUSNESS
CONSTITUTIONALISE
CONSTITUTIONALISM
CONSTITUTIONALIST
CONSTITUTIONALITY
CONSUBSTANTIALISM
CONSUBSTANTIALIST
CONSUBSTANTIALITY
CONSUBSTANTIATION
CONTEMPLATIVENESS
CONTEMPORANEOUSLY
CONTRADICTORINESS
CONTRADISTINCTION
CONTRADISTINCTIVE
CONTRADISTINGUISH
CONVERSATIONALIST
COUNTER-ATTRACTION
COUNTER-ATTRACTIVE

COUNTER-IRRITATION
COUNTER-PRODUCTIVE
COUNTER-REVOLUTION
CRYPTOCRYSTALLINE

D

DEFLAGRATING-SPOON
DEMONSTRATIVENESS
DENATIONALISATION
DENOMINATIONALISM
DIPTEROCARPACEOUS
DISADVANTAGEOUSLY
DISHONOURABLENESS
DISINTERESTEDNESS
DISPROPORTIONABLE
DISPROPORTIONABLY
DISPROPORTIONALLY
DISRESPECTFULNESS
DISYLLABIFICATION

E

EARTHLY-MINDEDNESS
ELECTROCARDIOGRAM
ELECTROCONVULSIVE
ELECTRODEPOSITION
ELECTROEXTRACTION
ELECTROMECHANICAL
ELECTROMETALLURGY
ELECTROPHYSIOLOGY
ETHNOMUSICOLOGIST
EXTRA-ILLUSTRATION
EXTRAORDINARINESS
EXTRA-PROFESSIONAL

F
FOURTH-DIMENSIONAL

G
GENTLEMAN-COMMONER
GENTLEWOMANLINESS

H
HAIL-FELLOW-WELL-MET
HEDGE-SCHOOLMASTER
HEMIPARASITICALLY
HETEROCHLAMYDEOUS
HETEROGENEOUSNESS
HIGGLEDY-PIGGELEDY
HISTORIOGRAPHICAL
HYDROTHERAPEUTICS
HYMENOPHYLLACEOUS

I
IMMUNOSUPPRESSIVE
IMPERCEPTIBLENESS
IMPRACTICABLENESS
IMPRESSIONABILITY
INAPPROPRIATENESS
INCOMBUSTIBLENESS
INCOMMUNICABILITY
INCOMMUNICATIVELY
INCOMPRESSIBILITY
INCONCEIVABLENESS
INCONSECUTIVENESS
INCONSEQUENTIALLY
INCONSIDERATENESS
INCONSPICUOUSNESS
INCORRUPTIBLENESS
INDEFATIGABLENESS
INDEMONSTRABILITY
INDESTRUCTIBILITY
INDETERMINATENESS
INDISCERPTIBILITY
INDISPENSABLENESS
INDISTINCTIVENESS
INDISTINGUISHABLE
INDISTINGUISHABLY
INDIVIDUALISATION
INDUSTRIALISATION
INFRALAPSARIANISM
INSTANTANEOUSNESS
INSUPPORTABLENESS
INSURMOUNTABILITY
INTERCOLUMNIATION
INTERCOMMUNICABLE
INTERDEPARTMENTAL
INTERFENESTRATION
INTERRAMIFICATION
INTERRELATIONSHIP
INTRANSMUTABILITY
IRRECLAIMABLENESS
IRRECONCILABILITY
IRRECOVERABLENESS
IRRETRIEVABLENESS

J
JACK-GO-TO-BED-AT-NOON
JOHN-GO-TO-BED-AT-NOON

L
LAMELLIBRANCHIATA
LAMELLIBRANCHIATE
LANDSCAPE-PAINTING
LATITUDINARIANISM
LIEUTENANT-COLONEL
LIEUTENANT-GENERAL
LIGHTNING-ARRESTER

M
MAGNETO-ELECTRICAL
MALADMINISTRATION
MARSIPOBRANCHIATE
MATERIALISTICALLY
MEDICO-CHIRURGICAL
MICROMANIPULATION
MICROPHOTOGRAPHER
MICROPHOTOGRAPHIC
MISAPPREHENSIVELY
MISCELLANEOUSNESS
MISINTERPRETATION
MISREPRESENTATION
MOUSSELINE-DE-LAINE
MULTITUBERCULATED
MULTITUDINOUSNESS

N
NEOPYTHAGOREANISM

O
OPHTHALMOSCOPICAL

P
PALAEOCLIMATOLOGY
PARAPSYCHOLOGICAL
PARTICULARISATION
PECTINIBRANCHIATE
PEDESTRIANISATION
PENNILLION-SINGING
PEPPER-GINGERBREAD
PERENNIBRANCHIATE
PETTICOAT-BREECHES
PHILANTHROPICALLY
PHOTOCONDUCTIVITY
PHOTOLITHOGRAPHER
PHOTOLITHOGRAPHIC
PHOTOMECHANICALLY
PHOTOMICROGRAPHER
PHOTOMICROGRAPHIC
PHOTOTHERAPEUTICS
PHYSIOTHERAPEUTIC
PHYTOPATHOLOGICAL
POLUPHLOISBOIOTIC
POLYSYNTHETICALLY
POST-IMPRESSIONISM
POST-IMPRESSIONIST
POSTMASTER-GENERAL
POST-MILLENNIALISM
PREDESTINARIANISM
PREMILLENARIANISM
PREMONSTRATENSIAN
PRE-RAPHAELITISTIC
PRESANCTIFICATION
PRESSURE-WAISTCOAT
PRETERNATURALNESS

PRIMOGENITURESHIP
PROPORTIONATENESS
PSEUDEPIGRAPHICAL
PSYCHOPATHOLOGIST
PSYCHOPROPHYLAXIS

Q
QUEEN-OF-THE-MEADOWS

R
RADIOTHERAPEUTICS
RATIONALISTICALLY
RECONSTRUCTIONARY
RECONSTRUCTIONIST
RECRYSTALLISATION
REPRESENTATIONISM
REPRESENTATIONIST
RESISTANCE-WELDING
RESURRECTION-PLANT
RIBBON-DEVELOPMENT

S
SACRAMENTARIANISM
SANCTIMONIOUSNESS
SCHIZOPHRENETICAL
SCROPHULARIACEOUS
SELF-ADVERTISEMENT
SELF-CONCEITEDNESS
SELF-CONCENTRATION
SELF-CONSCIOUSNESS
SELF-CONTRADICTION
SELF-CONTRADICTORY
SELF-DETERMINATION
SELF-DISPARAGEMENT
SELF-DRAMATISATION
SELF-FERTILISATION
SESQUIPEDALIANISM
SHERIFF-SUBSTITUTE
SPECTROHELIOGRAPH
SPECTROPHOTOMETER
SPECTROSCOPICALLY
STEREOFLUOROSCOPE
STRAIGHTFORWARDLY
STRATIGRAPHICALLY
SUBINTELLIGENTIAL
SUGGESTIONISATION
SUPERCONDUCTIVITY
SUPERNATURALISTIC
SUPERSTITIOUSNESS
SUPRALAPSARIANISM
SYNCHRONISTICALLY

T
TELECOMMUNICATION
TENDER-HEARTEDNESS
THEATRE-IN-THE-ROUND
THEOPHILANTHROPIC
THERMO-ELECTRICITY
THREE-PAIR-OF-STAIRS
TOUCH-ME-NOTISHNESS
TRANSCENDENTALISE
TRANSCENDENTALISM
TRANSCENDENTALIST
TRANSILLUMINATION
TRANSISTORISATION
TRANSIT-INSTRUMENT

TRANSIT-THEODOLITE
TRANSMIGRATIONISM
TRANSMIGRATIONIST
TRANSUBSTANTIATOR
TRIAKISOCTAHEDRON
TRIGONOMETRICALLY
TRIPLICATE-TERNATE
TRISKAIDEKAPHOBIA
TWO-DIMENSIONALITY
TWOPENNY-HALFPENNY

U

ULTRA-CONSERVATISM
ULTRA-CONSERVATIVE
UNACCOUNTABLENESS
UNCEREMONIOUSNESS
UNCOMFORTABLENESS
UNCONCEIVABLENESS

UNCONFORMABLENESS
UNCONDITIONALNESS
UNCONFORMABLENESS
UNCONSCIENTIOUSLY
UNCONVENTIONALITY
UNDERGRADUATESHIP
UNDETERMINATENESS
UNDISTINGUISHABLE
UNDISTINGUISHABLY
UNFASHIONABLENESS
UNGENTLEMANLINESS
UNIFORMITARIANISM
UNIMAGINATIVENESS
UNINTELLIGIBILITY
UNMENTIONABLENESS
UNNEIGHBOURLINESS
UNPERSUADABLENESS
UNPHILOSOPHICALLY

UNPRETENTIOUSNESS
UNPREVENTABLENESS
UNPROGRESSIVENESS
UNPROPORTIONATELY
UNSELFCONSCIOUSLY
UNSYMPATHETICALLY
UNTRANSLATABILITY
UNTRUSTWORTHINESS

V

VALETUDINARIANISM
VERNACULARISATION
VICTUALLING-OFFICE

W

WELL-APPOINTEDNESS
WHISPERING-GALLERY
WORLDLY-MINDEDNESS

A

ANTHROPOMORPHITISM
ANTHROPOPATHICALLY
ANTITRINITARIANISM
ANTIVACCINATIONISM
ANTIVACCINATIONIST
ANTIVIVISECTIONISM
ANTIVIVISECTIONIST
APOPHTHEGMATICALLY
AUSTRALOPITHECINAE

B

BIOBIBLIOGRAPHICAL

C

CHARACTERISTICALLY
CHEIROPTEROPHILOUS
COMMISSION-MERCHANT
COMPREHENSIBLENESS
CONSTANTINOPOLITAN
COUNTER-REFORMATION
CROSS-FERTILISATION

D

DISCOMMENDABLENESS
DISENFRANCHISEMENT
DISPROPORTIONATELY

E

ELECTROCARDIOGRAPH
ELECTRODYNAMOMETER
ESTABLISHMENTARIAN
EXTEMPORANEOUSNESS

F

FLIPPERTY-FLOPPERTY
FORETOP-GALLANT-MAST

G

GASTROENTEROLOGIST

H

HEAVENLY-MINDEDNESS
HELTER-SKELTERINESS
HYPERSENSITIVENESS

I

IMPRESCRIPTIBILITY
INCOMMENSURABILITY
INCOMMENSURATENESS
INCOMMUNICABLENESS
INCOMPRESSIBLENESS
INCONSIDERABLENESS
INDESTRUCTIBLENESS
INDETERMINABLENESS
INTERCHANGEABILITY
INTERCOMMUNICATION
IRRECONCILABLENESS
IRREPROACHABLENESS

L

LANDSCAPE-GARDENING
LEERIE-LICHT-THE-LAMP
LIEUTENANT-GOVERNOR
LIGHTNING-CONDUCTOR

M

MAGNETO-ELECTRICITY
MAINTOP-GALLANT-MAST
MARRIAGE-SETTLEMENT
MICROENCAPSULATION

O

OVERCAPITALISATION
OVERMULTIPLICATION
OVERSCRUPULOUSNESS

OVERSIMPLIFICATION
OVERSPECIALISATION

P

PARA-AMINO-SALICYLIC
PARALLELOGRAMMATIC
PARALLELOGRAMMICAL
PERMO-CARBONIFEROUS
PERPETUAL-MOTIONIST
PESTILENCE-STRICKEN
PHYSIOTHERAPEUTICS
POCKET-HANDKERCHIEF
PROPORTIONABLENESS
PSEUDO-CHRISTIANITY
PSYCHOTHERAPEUTICS
PTERYLOGRAPHICALLY

Q

QUINTESSENTIALISE

R

RADIO-COMMUNICATION
REPRESENTATIVENESS
ROBIN-RUN-IN-THE-HEDGE

S

SELF-CONGRATULATION
SEMIDEMISEMIQUAVER
SHERIFFS-SUBSTITUTE
SUBJECTIVISTICALLY
SUPERINTENDENTSHIP
SUPERSENSITIVENESS
SUPPOSITITIOUSNESS

T

TETRAKISHEXAHEDRON
THEOPHILANTHROPISM
THEOPHILANTHROPIST

T-V **18**

THERMOLUMINESCENCE
TOPSYTURVIFICATION
TRANSMOGRIFICATION
TRANSUBSTANTIATION

U

UNAPPREHENSIVENESS
UNAPPROACHABLENESS

UNCOMPROMISINGNESS
UNCONSCIONABLENESS
UNCONSTITUTIONALLY
UNCONTROLLABLENESS
UNDERCONSCIOUSNESS
UNDER-SECRETARYSHIP
UNMARRIAGEABLENESS
UNOSTENTATIOUSNESS

UNPREMEDITATEDNESS
UNRECONCILABLENESS
UNSATISFACTORINESS
UNTRANSLATABLENESS

V

VICE-CHANCELLORSHIP

A-W **19**

A

ANTHROPOPSYCHICALLY

B

BACTERIOCHLOROPHYLL

C

CO-INSTANTANEOUSNESS
CONTACT-METAMORPHISM
CONTEMPORANEOUSNESS
COUNTER-INTELLIGENCE

D

DISADVANTAGEOUSNESS
DISSATISFACTORINESS
DOUBLE-DECOMPOSITION

E

ELECTROCARDIOGRAPHY
ELECTROLUMINESCENCE
ELECTROMETALLURGIST
ELECTROTHERAPEUTICS
EXHIBITIONISTICALLY
EXTRA-TERRITORIALITY

G

GERONTOTHERAPEUTICS
GOVERNOR-GENERALSHIP

H

HISTORIOGRAPHICALLY

I

IMPRESSIONISTICALLY
INCOMMENSURABLENESS
INCOMMUNICATIVENESS
INCOMPREHENSIBILITY
INCOMPREHENSIVENESS
INCONTROVERTIBILITY
INTERCHANGEABLENESS
INTERDENOMINATIONAL
INTERDEPARTMENTALLY
INTERSTRATIFICATION
IRREPREHENSIBLENESS

L

LIEUTENANTCOLONELCY
LIEUTENANT-COMMANDER

M

MAGNETO-HYDRODYNAMIC
MISAPPREHENSIVENESS
MOUNTAIN-EVERLASTING

N

NON-REPRESENTATIONAL

O

OPHTHALMOSCOPICALLY
OTORHINOLARYNGOLOGY

P

PHONAUTOGRAPHICALLY

PRETERITO-PRESENTIAL
PROCRASTINATIVENESS

R

RECIPROCATING-ENGINE

S

SCHIZOPHRENETICALLY
SPIRITUAL-MINDEDNESS
STRAIGHTFORWARDNESS

T

THOUGHT-TRANSFERENCE
THREE-DIMENSIONALITY
THREE-HALFPENNYWORTH
THUNDER-AND-LIGHTNING

U

ULTRAMICROCHEMISTRY
UNCOMMUNICATIVENESS
UNCONSCIENTIOUSNESS
UNCONSTITUTIONALITY
UNDEMONSTRATIVENESS
UNDENOMINATIONALISM
UNEXCEPTIONABLENESS
UNSELFCONSCIOUSNESS
UNSOPHISTICATEDNESS

W

WORCESTERSHIRE-SAUCE

A-I **20**

A

ADRENOCORTICOTROPHIC
ADRENOCORTICOTROPHIN

C

CHICKWEED-WINTERGREEN
COMPARTMENTALISATION

CONSUBSTANTIATIONIST

D

DISPROPORTIONATENESS

E

ELECTROENCEPHALOGRAM
ELECTROMETALLURGICAL

H

HUNDREDS-AND-THOUSANDS

I

INCOMPREHENSIBLENESS

M
MAGNETO-HYDRODYNAMICS
MAIDENHAIR-SPLEENWORT
MICROMINIATURISATION

N
NIEVIE-NIEVIE-NICKNACK

P
PARALLELOGRAMMATICAL
PHANTASMOGENETICALLY
PHILOPROGENITIVENESS

Q
QUARTERMASTER-GENERAL

S
SUNDAY-GO-TO-THE-MEETING
SYNCATEGOREMATICALLY

T
TESTAMENT-TESTAMENTAR

D-Z over **20**

D
DISPROPORTIONABLENESS

E
ELECTROENCEPHALOGRAPH

G
GOOSEBERRY-CATERPILLAR
GREAT-GREAT-GRANDFATHER

I
INDISTINGUISHABLENESS

L
LIEUTENANTGENERALSHIP

P
POLUPHLOISBOIOTATOTIC

Q
QUARTERMASTER-SERGEANT

R
RAWHEAD-AND-BLOODY-BONES

T
TRANSUBSTANTIATIONIST

U
UNDISTINGUISHABLENESS

E
ELECTROENCEPHALOGRAPHY

H
HONORIFICABILITUDINITY

L
LIEUTENANTGOVERNORSHIP

P
POLYTETRAFLUORETHYLENE

L
LIEUTENANTCOMMANDERSHIP

P
POLYTETRAFLUOROETHYLENE

T
TRANSUBSTANTIATIONALIST

F
FLOCCINAUCINIHILIPILIFICATION

D
DICHLORODIPHENYLTRICHLOROETHANE

P
PNEUMONOULTRAMICROSCOPICSILICOVOLCANOCONIOSIS